2011 | WORLD DEVELOPMENT INDICATORS

Photo credits: Front cover, Curt Carnemark/World Bank; page xxiv, Curt Carnemark/World Bank; page 30, Trevor
Samson/World Bank; page 122, Curt Carnemark/World Bank; page 188, Curt Carnemark/World Bank; page 262,
Ray Witlin/World Bank; page 318, Curt Carnemark/World Bank.

If you have questions or comments about this product, please contact:

Development Data Group
The World Bank
1818 H Street NW, Room MC2-812, Washington, D.C. 20433 USA
Hotline: 800 590 1906 or 202 473 7824; fax 202 522 1498
Email: data@worldbank.org
Web site: www.worldbank.org or data.worldbank.org

ISBN 978-0-8213-8709-2

ECO-AUDIT
Environmental Benefits Statement
The World Bank is committed to preserving endangered forests and natural resources. The Office of the Publisher
has chosen to print World Development Indicators 2011 on recycled paper with 50 percent post-consumer fiber in
accordance with the recommended standards for paper usage set by the Green Press Initiative, a nonprofit program
supporting publishers in using fiber that is not sourced from endangered forests. For more information, visit www.
greenpressinitiative.org.

Saved:
91 trees
29 million Btu of total energy
8,609 pounds of net greenhouse gases
41,465 gallons of waste water
2,518 pounds of solid waste

2011 | WORLD DEVELOPMENT INDICATORS

 THE WORLD BANK

PREFACE

World Development Indicators 2011, the 15th edition in its current format, aims to provide relevant, high-quality, internationally comparable statistics about development and the quality of people's lives around the globe. This latest printed volume is one of a group of products; others include an online dataset, accessible at http://data.worldbank.org; the popular *Little Data Book* series; and *DataFinder*, a data query and charting application for mobile devices.

Fifteen years ago, *World Development Indicators* was overhauled and redesigned, organizing the data to present an integrated view of development, with the goal of putting these data in the hands of policymakers, development specialists, students, and the public in a way that makes the data easy to use. Although there have been small changes, the format has stood the test of time, and this edition employs the same sections as the first one: world view, people, environment, economy, states and markets, and global links.

Technical innovation and the rise of connected computing devices have gradually changed the way users obtain and consume the data in the *World Development Indicators* database. Last year saw a more abrupt change: the decision in April 2010 to make the dataset freely available resulted in a large, immediate increase in the use of the on-line resources. Perhaps more important has been the shift in how the data are used. Software developers are now free to use the data in applications they develop—and they are doing just that. We applaud and encourage all efforts to use the World Bank's databases in creative ways to solve the world's most pressing development challenges.

This edition of *World Development Indicators* focuses on the impact of the decision to make data freely available under an open license and with better online tools. To help those who wish to use and reuse the data in these new ways, the section introductions discuss key issues in measuring the economic and social phenomena described in the tables and charts and introduce new sources of data.

World Development Indicators is possible only through the excellent collaboration of many partners who provide the data that form part of this collection, and we thank them all: the United Nations family, the International Monetary Fund, the World Trade Organization, the Organisation for Economic Co-operation and Development, the statistical offices of more than 200 economies, and countless others who make this unique product possible. As always, we welcome your ideas for making the data in *World Development Indicators* useful and relevant for improving the lives of people around the world.

Shaida Badiee
Director
Development Economics Data Group

ACKNOWLEDGMENTS

This book was prepared by a team led by Soong Sup Lee under the management of Neil Fantom and comprising Awatif Abuzeid, Mehdi Akhlaghi, Azita Amjadi, Uranbileg Batjargal, Maja Bresslauer, David Cieslikowski, Mahyar Eshragh-Tabary, Shota Hatakeyama, Masako Hiraga, Bala Bhaskar Naidu Kalimili, Buyant Khaltarkhuu, Elysee Kiti, Alison Kwong, Ibrahim Levent, Johan Mistiaen, Sulekha Patel, William Prince, Premi Rathan Raj, Evis Rucaj, Eric Swanson, Jomo Tariku, and Estela Zamora, working closely with other teams in the Development Economics Vice Presidency's Development Data Group. *World Development Indicators* electronic products were prepared by a team led by Reza Farivari, consisting of Ramvel Chandrasekaran, Ying Chi, Jean-Pierre Djomalieu, Ramgopal Erabelly, Shelley Fu, Gytis Kanchas, Ugendran Makhachkala, Vilas Mandlekar, Nacer Megherbi, Parastoo Oloumi, Malarvizhi Veerappan, and Vera Wen. The work was carried out under the direction of Shaida Badiee. Valuable advice was provided by Shahrokh Fardoust.

The choice of indicators and text content was shaped through close consultation with and substantial contributions from staff in the World Bank's four thematic networks—Sustainable Development, Human Development, Poverty Reduction and Economic Management, and Financial and Private Sector Development—and staff of the International Finance Corporation and the Multilateral Investment Guarantee Agency. Most important, the team received substantial help, guidance, and data from external partners. For individual acknowledgments of contributions to the book's content, please see *Credits*. For a listing of our key partners, see *Partners*.

Communications Development Incorporated (CDI) provided editorial services, led by Meta de Coquereaumont, Bruce Ross-Larson, and Christopher Trott. Jomo Tariku designed the cover, Deborah Arroyo and Elaine Wilson typeset the book, and Katrina Van Duyn provided proofreading. Azita Amjadi and Alison Kwong oversaw the production process. Staff from External Affairs Office of the Publisher oversaw printing and dissemination of the book.

TABLE OF CONTENTS

FRONT

1. WORLD VIEW

2. PEOPLE

3. ENVIRONMENT

TABLE OF CONTENTS

 ## 4. ECONOMY

 ## 5. STATES AND MARKETS

6. GLOBAL LINKS

BACK

PARTNERS

Defining, gathering, and disseminating international statistics is a collective effort of many people and organizations. The indicators presented in *World Development Indicators* are the fruit of decades of work at many levels, from the field workers who administer censuses and household surveys to the committees and working parties of the national and international statistical agencies that develop the nomenclature, classifications, and standards fundamental to an international statistical system. Nongovernmental organizations and the private sector have also made important contributions, both in gathering primary data and in organizing and publishing their results. And academic researchers have played a crucial role in developing statistical methods and carrying on a continuing dialogue about the quality and interpretation of statistical indicators. All these contributors have a strong belief that available, accurate data will improve the quality of public and private decisionmaking.

The organizations listed here have made *World Development Indicators* possible by sharing their data and their expertise with us. More important, their collaboration contributes to the World Bank's efforts, and to those of many others, to improve the quality of life of the world's people. We acknowledge our debt and gratitude to all who have helped to build a base of comprehensive, quantitative information about the world and its people.

For easy reference, Web addresses are included for each listed organization. The addresses shown were active on March 1, 2011. Information about the World Bank is also provided.

International and government agencies

Carbon Dioxide Information Analysis Center

The Carbon Dioxide Information Analysis Center (CDIAC) is the primary global climate change data and information analysis center of the U.S. Department of Energy. The CDIAC's scope includes anything that would potentially be of value to those concerned with the greenhouse effect and global climate change, including concentrations of carbon dioxide and other radiatively active gases in the atmosphere, the role of the terrestrial biosphere and the oceans in the biogeochemical cycles of greenhouse gases, emissions of carbon dioxide to the atmosphere, long-term climate trends, the effects of elevated carbon dioxide on vegetation, and the vulnerability of coastal areas to rising sea levels.

For more information, see http://cdiac.esd.ornl.gov/.

Deutsche Gesellschaft für Internationale Zusammenarbeit

The Deutsche Gesellschaft für Internationale Zusammenarbeit (GIZ) GmbH is a German government-owned corporation for international cooperation with worldwide operations. GIZ's aim is to positively shape political, economic, ecological, and social development in partner countries, thereby improving people's living conditions and prospects.

For more information, see www.giz.de/.

giz

Food and Agriculture Organization

The Food and Agriculture Organization, a specialized agency of the United Nations, was founded in October 1945 with a mandate to raise nutrition levels and living standards, to increase agricultural productivity, and to better the condition of rural populations. The organization provides direct development assistance; collects, analyzes, and disseminates information; offers policy and planning advice to governments; and serves as an international forum for debate on food and agricultural issues.

For more information, see www.fao.org/.

Internal Displacement Monitoring Centre

The Internal Displacement Monitoring Centre was established in 1998 by the Norwegian Refugee Council and is the leading international body monitoring conflict-induced internal displacement worldwide. The center contributes to improving national and international capacities to protect and assist the millions of people around the globe who have been displaced within their own country as a result of conflicts or human rights violations.

For more information, see www.internal-displacement.org/.

International Civil Aviation Organization

The International Civil Aviation Organization (ICAO), a specialized agency of the United Nations, is responsible for establishing international standards and recommended practices and procedures for the technical, economic, and legal aspects of international civil aviation operations. ICAO's strategic objectives include enhancing global aviation safety and security and the efficiency of aviation operations, minimizing the adverse effect of global civil aviation on the environment, maintaining the continuity of aviation operations, and strengthening laws governing international civil aviation.

For more information, see www.icao.int/.

International Energy Agency

The International Energy Agency (IEA) was founded in 1973/74 with a mandate to facilitate cooperation among the IEA member countries to increase energy efficiency, promoting use of clean energy and technology, and diversify their energy sources while protecting the environment. IEA publishes annual and quarterly statistical publications covering both OECD and non-OECD countries' statistics on oil, gas, coal, electricity and renewable sources of energy, energy supply and consumption, and energy prices and taxes. IEA also contributes in analysis of all aspects of sustainable development globally and provides policy recommendations.

For more information, see www.iea.org/.

International Labour Organization

The International Labour Organization (ILO), a specialized agency of the United Nations, seeks the promotion of social justice and internationally recognized human and labor rights. ILO helps advance the creation of decent jobs and the kinds of economic and working conditions that give working people and business people

PARTNERS

a stake in lasting peace, prosperity, and progress. As part of its mandate, the ILO maintains an extensive statistical publication program.

For more information, see www.ilo.org/.

International Monetary Fund

The International Monetary Fund (IMF) is an international organization of 187 member countries established to promote international monetary cooperation, a stable system of exchange rates, and the balanced expansion of international trade and to foster economic growth and high levels of employment. The IMF reviews national, regional, and global economic and financial developments; provides policy advice to member countries; and serves as a forum where they can discuss the national, regional, and global consequences of their policies.

The IMF also makes financing temporarily available to member countries to help them address balance of payments problems. Among the IMF's core missions are the collection and dissemination of high-quality macroeconomic and financial statistics as an essential prerequisite for formulating appropriate policies. The IMF provides technical assistance and training to member countries in areas of its core expertise, including the development of economic and financial data in accordance with international standards.

For more information, see www.imf.org/.

International Telecommunication Union

The International Telecommunication Union (ITU) is the leading UN agency for information and communication technologies. ITU's mission is to enable the growth and sustained development of telecommunications and information networks and to facilitate universal access so that people everywhere can participate in, and benefit from, the emerging information society and global economy. A key priority lies in bridging the so-called Digital Divide by building information and communication infrastructure, promoting adequate capacity building, and developing confidence in the use of cyberspace through enhanced online security. ITU also concentrates on strengthening emergency communications for disaster prevention and mitigation.

For more information, see www.itu.int/.

National Science Foundation

The National Science Foundation (NSF) is an independent U.S. government agency whose mission is to promote the progress of science; to advance the national health, prosperity, and welfare; and to secure the national defense. NSF's goals—discovery, learning, research infrastructure, and stewardship—provide an integrated strategy to advance the frontiers of knowledge, cultivate a world-class, broadly inclusive science and engineering workforce, expand the scientific literacy of all citizens, build the nation's research capability through investments in advanced instrumentation and facilities, and support excellence in science and engineering research and education through a capable and responsive organization.

For more information, see www.nsf.gov/.

Organisation for Economic Co-operation and Development

The Organisation for Economic Co-operation and Development (OECD) includes 34 member countries sharing a commitment to democratic government and the market economy to support sustainable economic growth, boost employment, raise living standards, maintain financial stability, assist other countries' economic development, and contribute to growth in world trade. With active relationships with some 100 other countries, it has a global reach. It is best known for its publications and statistics, which cover economic and social issues from macroeconomics to trade, education, development, and science and innovation.

The Development Assistance Committee (DAC, www.oecd.org/dac/) is one of the principal bodies through which the OECD deals with issues related to cooperation with developing countries. The DAC is a key forum of major bilateral donors, who work together to increase the effectiveness of their common efforts to support sustainable development. The DAC concentrates on two key areas: the contribution of international development to the capacity of developing countries to participate in the global economy and the capacity of people to overcome poverty and participate fully in their societies.

For more information, see www.oecd.org/.

Stockholm International Peace Research Institute

The Stockholm International Peace Research Institute (SIPRI) conducts research on questions of conflict and cooperation of importance for international peace and security, with the aim of contributing to an understanding of the conditions for peaceful solutions to international conflicts and for a stable peace. SIPRI's main publication, *SIPRI Yearbook,* is an authoritive and independent source on armaments and arms control and other conflict and security issues.

For more information, see www.sipri.org/.

Understanding Children's Work

As part of broader efforts to develop effective and long-term solutions to child labor, the International Labour Organization, the United Nations Children's Fund (UNICEF), and the World Bank initiated the joint interagency research program "Understanding Children's Work and Its Impact" in December 2000. The Understanding Children's Work (UCW) project was located at UNICEF's Innocenti Research Centre in Florence, Italy, until June 2004, when it moved to the Centre for International Studies on Economic Growth in Rome.

The UCW project addresses the crucial need for more and better data on child labor. UCW's online database contains data by country on child labor and the status of children.

For more information, see www.ucw-project.org/.

United Nations

The United Nations currently has 192 member states. The purposes of the United Nations, as set forth in its charter, are to maintain international peace and security; to develop friendly relations among nations; to cooperate in solving international economic, social, cultural, and humanitarian problems and in promoting respect for human rights and fundamental freedoms; and to be a center for harmonizing the actions of nations in attaining these ends.

For more information, see www.un.org/.

PARTNERS

United Nations Centre for Human Settlements, Global Urban Observatory

The Urban Indicators Programme of the United Nations Human Settlements Programme was established to address the urgent global need to improve the urban knowledge base by helping countries and cities design, collect, and apply policy-oriented indicators related to development at the city level.

With the Urban Indicators and Best Practices programs, the Global Urban Observatory is establishing a worldwide information, assessment, and capacity-building network to help governments, local authorities, the private sector, and nongovernmental and other civil society organizations.

For more information, see www.unhabitat.org/.

United Nations Children's Fund

The United Nations Children's Fund (UNICEF) works with other UN bodies and with governments and nongovernmental organizations to improve children's lives in more than 190 countries through various programs in education and health. UNICEF focuses primarily on five areas: child survival and development, basic education and gender equality (including girls' education), child protection, HIV/AIDS, and policy advocacy and partnerships.

For more information, see www.unicef.org/.

United Nations Conference on Trade and Development

The United Nations Conference on Trade and Development (UNCTAD) is the principal organ of the United Nations General Assembly in the field of trade and development. Its mandate is to accelerate economic growth and development, particularly in developing countries. UNCTAD discharges its mandate through policy analysis; intergovernmental deliberations, consensus building, and negotiation; monitoring, implementation, and follow-up; and technical cooperation.

For more information, see www.unctad.org/.

United Nations Department of Peacekeeping Operations

The United Nations Department of Peacekeeping Operations contributes to the most important function of the United Nations—maintaining international peace and security. The department helps countries torn by conflict to create the conditions for lasting peace. The first peacekeeping mission was established in 1948 and has evolved to meet the demands of different conflicts and a changing political landscape. Today's peacekeepers undertake a wide variety of complex tasks, from helping build sustainable institutions of governance, to monitoring human rights, to assisting in security sector reform, to disarmaming, demobilizing, and reintegrating former combatants.

For more information, see www.un.org/en/peacekeeping/.

United Nations Educational, Scientific, and Cultural Organization, Institute for Statistics

The United Nations Educational, Scientific, and Cultural Organization (UNESCO) is a specialized agency of the United Nations that promotes international cooperation among member states and associate members in education, science, culture, and communications. The UNESCO Institute for Statistics is the organization's

statistical branch, established in July 1999 to meet the growing needs of UNESCO member states and the international community for a wider range of policy-relevant, timely, and reliable statistics on these topics.

For more information, see www.uis.unesco.org/.

United Nations Environment Programme

The mandate of the United Nations Environment Programme is to provide leadership and encourage partnership in caring for the environment by inspiring, informing, and enabling nations and people to improve their quality of life without compromising that of future generations.

For more information, see www.unep.org/.

United Nations Industrial Development Organization

The United Nations Industrial Development Organization was established to act as the central coordinating body for industrial activities and to promote industrial development and cooperation at the global, regional, national, and sectoral levels. Its mandate is to help develop scientific and technological plans and programs for industrialization in the public, cooperative, and private sectors.

For more information, see www.unido.org/.

United Nations Office on Drugs and Crime

The United Nations Office on Drugs and Crime was established in 1977 and is a global leader in the fight against illicit drugs and international crime. The office assists member states in their struggle against illicit drugs, crime, and terrorism by helping build capacity, conducting research and analytical work, and assisting in the ratification and implementation of relevant international treaties and domestic legislation related to drugs, crime, and terrorism.

For more information, see www.unodc.org/.

The UN Refugee Agency

The UN Refugee Agency (UNHCR) is mandated to lead and coordinate international action to protect refugees and resolve refugee problems worldwide. Its primary purpose is to safeguard the rights and well-being of refugees. UNHCR also collects and disseminates statistics on refugees.

For more information, see www.unhcr.org/.

Upsalla Conflict Data Program

The Upsalla Conflict Data Program has collected information on armed violence since 1946 and is one of the most accurate and well used data sources on global armed conflicts. Its definition of armed conflict is becoming a standard in how conflicts are systematically defined and studied. In addition to data collection on armed violence, its researchers conduct theoretically and empirically based analyses of the causes, escalation, spread, prevention, and resolution of armed conflict.

For more information, see www.pcr.uu.se/research/UCDP/.

PARTNERS

World Bank

The World Bank is a vital source of financial and technical assistance for developing countries. The World Bank is made up of two unique development institutions owned by 187 member countries—the International Bank for Reconstruction and Development (IBRD) and the International Development Association (IDA). These institutions play different but collaborative roles to advance the vision of an inclusive and sustainable globalization. The IBRD focuses on middle-income and creditworthy poor countries, while IDA focuses on the poorest countries. Together they provide low-interest loans, interest-free credits, and grants to developing countries for a wide array of purposes, including investments in education, health, public administration, infrastructure, financial and private sector development, agriculture, and environmental and natural resource management. The World Bank's work focuses on achieving the Millennium Development Goals by working with partners to alleviate poverty.

For more information, see http://data.worldbank.org/.

World Health Organization

The objective of the World Health Organization (WHO), a specialized agency of the United Nations, is the attainment by all people of the highest possible level of health. It is responsible for providing leadership on global health matters, shaping the health research agenda, setting norms and standards, articulating evidence-based policy options, providing technical support to countries, and monitoring and assessing health trends.

For more information, see www.who.int/.

World Intellectual Property Organization

The World Intellectual Property Organization (WIPO) is a specialized agency of the United Nations dedicated to developing a balanced and accessible international intellectual property (IP) system, which rewards creativity, stimulates innovation, and contributes to economic development while safeguarding the public interest. WIPO carries out a wide variety of tasks related to the protection of IP rights. These include developing international IP laws and standards, delivering global IP protection services, encouraging the use of IP for economic development, promoting better understanding of IP, and providing a forum for debate.

For more information, see www.wipo.int/.

World Tourism Organization

The World Tourism Organization is an intergovernmental body entrusted by the United Nations with promoting and developing tourism. It serves as a global forum for tourism policy issues and a source of tourism know-how.

For more information, see www.unwto.org/.

World Trade Organization

The World Trade Organization (WTO) is the only international organization dealing with the global rules of trade between nations. Its main function is to ensure that trade flows as smoothly, predictably, and freely as possible. It does this by administering trade agreements, acting as a forum for trade negotiations, settling trade disputes, reviewing national trade policies, assisting developing countries in trade policy issues—through technical assistance and training programs—and cooperating with other international organizations. At the heart of the system—known as the multilateral trading system—are the WTO's agreements, negotiated and signed by a large majority of the world's trading nations and ratified by their parliaments.

For more information, see www.wto.org/.

Private and nongovernmental organizations

Containerisation International

Containerisation International Yearbook is one of the most authoritative reference books on the container industry. The information can be accessed on the Containerisation International Web site, which also provides a comprehensive online daily business news and information service for the container industry.

For more information, see www.ci-online.co.uk/.

DHL

DHL provides shipping and customized transportation solutions for customers in more than 220 countries and territories. It offers expertise in express, air, and ocean freight; overland transport; contract logistics solutions; and international mail services.

For more information, see www.dhl.com/.

International Institute for Strategic Studies

The International Institute for Strategic Studies (IISS) provides information and analysis on strategic trends and facilitates contacts between government leaders, business people, and analysts that could lead to better public policy in international security and international relations. The IISS is a primary source of accurate, objective information on international strategic issues.

For more information, see www.iiss.org/.

International Road Federation

The International Road Federation (IRF) is a nongovernmental, not-for-profit organization whose mission is to encourage and promote development and maintenance of better, safer, and more sustainable roads and road networks. Working together with its members and associates, the IRF promotes social and economic benefits that flow from well planned and environmentally sound road transport networks. It helps put in place technological solutions and management practices that provide maximum economic and social returns from national road investments. The IRF works in all aspects of road policy and development worldwide with governments and financial institutions, members, and the community of road professionals.

For more information, see www.irfnet.org/.

PARTNERS

Netcraft

Netcraft provides Internet security services such as antifraud and antiphishing services, application testing, code reviews, and automated penetration testing. Netcraft also provides research data and analysis on many aspects of the Internet and is a respected authority on the market share of web servers, operating systems, hosting providers, Internet service providers, encrypted transactions, electronic commerce, scripting languages, and content technologies on the Internet.

   For more information, see http://news.netcraft.com/.

PricewaterhouseCoopers

PricewaterhouseCoopers provides industry-focused services in the fields of assurance, tax, human resources, transactions, performance improvement, and crisis management services to help address client and stakeholder issues.

   For more information, see www.pwc.com/.

Standard & Poor's

Standard & Poor's is the world's foremost provider of independent credit ratings, indexes, risk evaluation, investment research, and data. S&P's *Global Stock Markets Factbook* draws on data from S&P's Emerging Markets Database (EMDB) and other sources covering data on more than 100 markets with comprehensive market profiles for 82 countries. Drawing a sample of stocks in each EMDB market, Standard & Poor's calculates indexes to serve as benchmarks that are consistent across national boundaries.

   For more information, see www.standardandpoors.com/.

World Conservation Monitoring Centre

The World Conservation Monitoring Centre provides information on the conservation and sustainable use of the world's living resources and helps others to develop information systems of their own. It works in close collaboration with a wide range of people and organizations to increase access to the information needed for wise management of the world's living resources.

   For more information, see www.unep-wcmc.org/.

World Economic Forum

The World Economic Forum (WEF) is an independent international organization committed to improving the state of the world by engaging leaders in partnerships to shape global, regional, and industry agendas. Economic research at the WEF—led by the Global Competitiveness Programme—focuses on identifying the impediments to growth so that strategies to achieve sustainable economic progress, reduce poverty, and increase prosperity can be developed. The WEF's competitiveness reports range from global coverage, such as *Global Competitiveness Report,* to regional and topical coverage, such as *Africa Competitiveness Report, The Lisbon Review,* and *Global Information Technology Report.*

For more information, see www.weforum.org/.

World Resources Institute

The World Resources Institute is an independent center for policy research and technical assistance on global environmental and development issues. The institute provides—and helps other institutions provide—objective information and practical proposals for policy and institutional change that will foster environmentally sound, socially equitable development. The institute's current areas of work include trade, forests, energy, economics, technology, biodiversity, human health, climate change, sustainable agriculture, resource and environmental information, and national strategies for environmental and resource management.

For more information, see www.wri.org/.

USERS GUIDE

Tables

The tables are numbered by section and display the identifying icon of the section. Countries and economies are listed alphabetically (except for Hong Kong SAR, China, which appears after China). Data are shown for 155 economies with populations of more than 1 million, as well as for Taiwan, China, in selected tables. Table 1.6 presents selected indicators for 58 other economies—small economies with populations between 30,000 and 1 million and smaller economies if they are members of the International Bank for Reconstruction and Development (IBRD) or, as it is commonly known, the World Bank. Data for these economies are included on the *World Development Indicators* CD-ROM and the World Bank's Open Data website at data.worldbank.org/.

The term *country*, used interchangeably with *economy*, does not imply political independence, but refers to any territory for which authorities report separate social or economic statistics. When available, aggregate measures for income and regional groups appear at the end of each table.

Indicators are shown for the most recent year or period for which data are available and, in most tables, for an earlier year or period (usually 1990 or 1995 in this edition). Time-series data for all 213 economies are available on the *World Development Indicators* CD-ROM and at data.worldbank.org/.

Known deviations from standard definitions or breaks in comparability over time or across countries are either footnoted in the tables or noted in *About the data*. When available data are deemed to be too weak to provide reliable measures of levels and trends or do not adequately adhere to international standards, the data are not shown.

Aggregate measures for income groups

The aggregate measures for income groups include 213 economies (the economies listed in the main tables plus those in table 1.6) whenever data are available. To maintain consistency in the aggregate measures over time and between tables, missing data are imputed where possible. The aggregates are totals (designated by a *t* if the aggregates include gap-filled estimates for missing data and by an *s*, for simple totals, where they do not), median values (*m*), weighted averages (*w*), or simple averages (*u*). Gap filling of amounts not allocated to countries may result in discrepancies between subgroup aggregates and overall totals. For further discussion of aggregation methods, see *Statistical methods*.

Aggregate measures for regions

The aggregate measures for regions include only low- and middle-income economies including economies with populations of less than 1 million listed in table 1.6.

The country composition of regions is based on the World Bank's analytical regions and may differ from common geographic usage. For regional classifications, see the map on the inside back cover and the list on the back cover flap. For further discussion of aggregation methods, see *Statistical methods*.

Statistics

Data are shown for economies as they were constituted in 2009, and historical data are revised to reflect current political arrangements. Exceptions are noted throughout the tables.

Additional information about the data is provided in *Primary data documentation*. That section summarizes national and international efforts to improve basic data collection and gives country-level information on primary sources, census years, fiscal years, statistical methods and concepts used, and other background information. *Statistical methods* provides technical information on some of the general calculations and formulas used throughout the book.

Data consistency, reliability, and comparability

Considerable effort has been made to standardize the data, but full comparability cannot be assured, and care must be taken in interpreting the indicators. Many factors affect data availability, comparability, and reliability: statistical systems in many developing economies are still weak; statistical methods, coverage, practices, and definitions differ widely; and cross-country and intertemporal comparisons involve complex technical and conceptual problems that cannot be resolved unequivocally. Data coverage may not be complete because of special circumstances affecting the collection and reporting of data, such as problems stemming from conflicts.

For these reasons, although data are drawn from sources thought to be the most authoritative, they should be construed only as indicating trends and characterizing major differences among economies rather than as offering precise quantitative measures of those differences. Discrepancies in data presented in different editions of *World Development Indicators* reflect updates by countries as well as revisions to historical series and changes in methodology. Thus readers are advised not to compare data series between editions of *World Development Indicators* or between different World Bank publications. Consistent time-series data for 1960–2009 are available on the *World Development Indicators* CD-ROM and at data.worldbank.org/.

Except where otherwise noted, growth rates are in real terms. (See *Statistical methods* for information on the methods used to calculate growth rates.) Data for some economic indicators for some economies are presented in fiscal years rather than calendar years; see *Primary data documentation*. All dollar figures are current U.S. dollars unless otherwise stated. The methods used for converting national currencies are described in *Statistical methods*.

Country notes

- Unless otherwise noted, data for China do not include data for Hong Kong SAR, China; Macao SAR, China; or Taiwan, China.

- Data for Indonesia include Timor-Leste through 1999 unless otherwise noted.

- Montenegro declared independence from Serbia and Montenegro on June 3, 2006. Where available, data for each country are shown separately. However, for the Serbia listing, some indicators continue to include data for Montenegro through 2005; these data are footnoted in the tables. Moreover, data from 1999 onward for Serbia for most indicators exclude data for Kosovo, 1999 being the year when Kosovo became a territory under international administration pursuant to UN Security Council Resolution 1244 (1999); any exceptions are noted. Kosovo became a World Bank member on June 29, 2009; available data are shown separately for Kosovo in the main tables.

- Netherlands Antilles ceased to exist on October 10, 2010. Curaçao and St. Maarten became countries within the Kingdom of the Netherlands. Bonaire, St. Eustatius, and Saba became special municipalities of the Netherlands.

Classification of economies

For operational and analytical purposes the World Bank's main criterion for classifying economies is gross national income (GNI) per capita (calculated by the *World Bank Atlas* method). Every economy is classified as low income, middle income (subdivided into lower middle and upper middle), or high income. For income classifications see the map on the inside front cover and the list on the front cover flap. Low- and middle-income economies are sometimes referred to as developing economies. The term is used for convenience; it is not intended to imply that all economies in the group are experiencing similar development or that other economies have reached a preferred or final stage of development. Note that classification by income does not necessarily reflect development status. Because GNI per capita changes over time, the country composition of income groups may change from one edition of *World Development Indicators* to the next. Once the classification is fixed for an edition, based on GNI per capita in the most recent year for which data are available (2009 in this edition), all historical data presented are based on the same country grouping.

Low-income economies are those with a GNI per capita of $995 or less in 2009. Middle-income economies are those with a GNI per capita of more than $995 but less than $12,196. Lower middle-income and upper middle-income economies are separated at a GNI per capita of $3,945. High-income economies are those with a GNI per capita of $12,196 or more. The 17 participating member countries of the Euro area are presented as a subgroup under high-income economies. Estonia joined the Euro area on January 1, 2011.

Symbols

..

means that data are not available or that aggregates cannot be calculated because of missing data in the years shown.

0 or 0.0

means zero or small enough that the number would round to zero at the displayed number of decimal places.

/

in dates, as in 2003/04, means that the period of time, usually 12 months, straddles two calendar years and refers to a crop year, a survey year, or a fiscal year.

$

means current U.S. dollars unless otherwise noted.

>

means more than.

<

means less than.

Data presentation conventions

- A blank means not applicable or, for an aggregate, not analytically meaningful.
- A billion is 1,000 million.
- A trillion is 1,000 billion.
- Figures in italics refer to years or periods other than those specified or to growth rates calculated for less than the full period specified.
- Data for years that are more than three years from the range shown are footnoted.

The cutoff date for data is February 1, 2011.

WORLD
VIEW

"Our aim is for open data, open knowledge, and open solutions."
—Robert Zoellick, Georgetown University, September 2010

World Development Indicators provides a comprehensive selection of national and international data that focus attention on critical development issues, facilitate research, encourage debate and analysis of policy options, and monitor progress toward development goals. Organized around six themes—world view, people, environment, economy, states and markets, and global links—the book contains more than 800 indicators for 155 economies with a population of 1 million people or more, together with relevant aggregates. The online database includes more than 1,100 indicators for 213 economies, with many time series extending back to 1960.

In 2010, to improve the impact of the indicators and to provide a platform for others to use the data to solve pressing development challenges, the World Development Indicators database and many other public databases maintained by the World Bank were made available as open data: free of charge, in accessible nonproprietary formats on the World Wide Web. This year, the first part of the introduction to the *World View* section provides an overview of the initiative, the impact of moving to an open data platform, a brief survey of the global open data movement, and an examination of its relevance to development. The second part reviews progress toward the Millennium Development Goals—whose target date of 2015 is now just four years away.

The World Bank Open Data Initiative
The Open Data Initiative is a new strategy for reaching data users and a major change in the Bank's business model for data, which had previously been a subscription-based model for licensing data access and use, using a network of university libraries, development agencies, and private firms, and free access provided through the World Bank's Public Information Centers and depository libraries. At the time of the open data announcement there were around 140,000 regular users of the subscription database annually—a substantial number for a highly specialized data product. But providing free and easier access to the databases has had an immediate and lasting impact on data use. Since April 2010 the new data website—http://data.worldbank.

org—has recorded well over 20 million page views. And at the time of printing this edition of *World Development Indicators,* it provides data to more than 100,000 unique visitors each week, three times as many as before (figure 1a).

Making the World Development Indicators and other databases free was only the first step in creating an open data environment. Open data should mean that users can access and search public datasets at no cost, combine data from different sources, add data and select data records to include or exclude in derived works, change the format or structure of the data, and give away or sell any products they create. For the World Bank, this required designing new user interfaces and developing new search tools to more easily find and report the data. It also required a new license defining the terms of

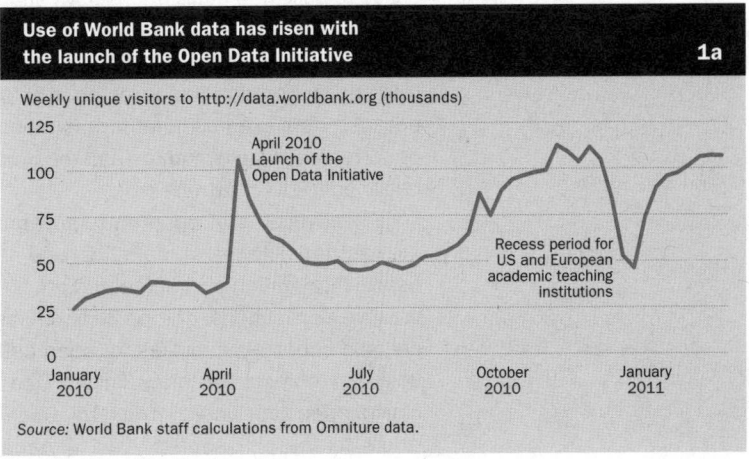

Use of World Bank data has risen with the launch of the Open Data Initiative   1a

Weekly unique visitors to http://data.worldbank.org (thousands)

April 2010
Launch of the
Open Data Initiative

Recess period for
US and European
academic teaching
institutions

Source: World Bank staff calculations from Omniture data.

use for data (box 1b). And it required new thinking to promote the use and reuse of data. To reach out to new audiences and communities of data users, the World Bank organized a global "Apps for Development" competition—one of the first of its kind—inviting developers to create new applications for desktop computers or mobile devices using World Bank datasets, including *World Development Indicators* data.

Open data and open government

Advocates of greater transparency in public agencies—the open government movement—have been among the most vocal proponents of open data. Likewise, those seeking databases to build new applications have supported freedom of information laws and unrestricted access to data created by public agencies. Opening public databases empowers people because data are essential for monitoring the performance of governments and the impact of public policies on citizens.

For advocates of open data, governments are vast repositories of statistical and nonstatistical information with unrealized potential for creative applications. The political, philosophical, and economic impulses for open data and open government are often linked. One advocate of open data writes, "The term 'Open Data' refers to the philosophical and methodological approach to the democratization of data

enabling citizens to access and create value through the reuse of public sector information" (Rahemtulla 2011).

The Sunlight Foundation, a U.S.-based civil society organization, describes its goals as "improving access to government information by making it available online, indeed redefining 'public' information as meaning 'online,' and . . . creating new tools and websites to enable individuals and communities to better access that information and put it to use. . . . We want to catalyze greater government transparency by engaging individual citizens and communities—technologists, policy wonks, open government advocates, and ordinary citizens—demanding policies that will enable all of us to hold government accountable" (http://sunlightfoundation.com/about/).

Digital information and communication technologies permitting dissemination of large amounts of data at little or no cost have strengthened the argument for providing free access to public sector information. Pollock (2010) estimates the direct benefit to the U.K. public of providing free access to public sector information that was previously sold to be £1.6–£6 billion, 4–15 times the forgone sales revenues of £400 million. Additional indirect benefits come from new products and services using open datasets or complementary products and services and from reducing the transaction costs to data users and reusers.

Open data and open government initiatives have progressed farther in rich countries than in developing ones. This may reflect a lack of political will or popular demand, but it often reflects a lack of technical capacity and resources to make data available in accessible formats. A study commissioned by the Transparency and Accountability Initiative (Hogge 2010) identified three drivers behind the success of the U.K. and U.S. data.gov initiatives:

- Civil society, particularly a small and motivated group of "civic hackers" responsible for developing grassroots political engagement websites.
- An engaged and well resourced "middle layer" of skilled government bureaucrats.
- A top-level mandate, motivated by an outside force (in the United Kingdom) or a refreshed political administration hungry for change (in the United States).

Statistical offices exemplify the "middle layer" of a government bureaucracy, uniquely skilled in collecting and organizing large data-sets. But even they may lack the motivation or resources to make their products freely available to the public unless they enjoy full support from the top.

In developing countries aid donors can act as fourth driver by providing technical assistance and funding for open data projects and by modeling transparency in their own practices. The International Aid Transparency Initiative—the World Bank is a founding member—aims to create a global repository of information on aid flows, starting from the commitment of funding from donors and continuing through its disbursement to recipient countries, the allocation of aid money in national budgets, the procurement of goods and services, and the measurement of results.

To fulfill the initiative's goal of providing a complete accounting of aid to the citizens of donor and developing countries will require cooperation among donors and recipients. Terminology and coding systems must be standardized and agreements reached on everything from the timing of reports to the mechanisms for posting and accessing the datasets. In many cases donor governments and international agencies will have to change their rules on access to information to provide full transparency to their aid programs (box 1c). For more information on the initiative, see www.aidtransparency.net.

Mapping for results—making data not just accessible but useful

The new Access to Information Policy and the Open Data Initiative provide much greater access to the World Bank Group's knowledge resources than before. But accessible information is not the same as usable information. Project documents contain a wealth of data about planned activities—for instance, on their location. But it may be difficult for many interested parties, such as project beneficiaries, citizen groups, and civil society organizations, to extract and visualize relevant data from long texts or tables.

To help solve this problem, the World Bank, on a pilot basis, has started to provide geolocation codes along with data and information about the projects that it supports. The objective is to improve aid effectiveness through enhanced transparency and accountability of project activities. Location information makes

---

Access to information at the World Bank **1c**

Opening the World Bank's databases is part of a broader effort to introduce greater transparency in the World Bank's operations, and a new policy on information disclosure went into effect on July 1, 2010. Besides formalizing the Open Data Initiative, the Access to Information Policy (www.worldbank.org/wbaccess) establishes the principle that the World Bank will disclose any information in its possession that is not on a specific list of exceptions. In the past, only documents selected for disclosure were available to the public. The new policy reverses the process and presumes that most information is disclosable. Exceptions include personal information and staff records, internal deliberations and administrative matters, and information received in confidence from clients and third parties. Some documents with restricted access are subject to a declassification schedule, ensuring that they will become available to the public in due course. A process for requesting documents has also been established that allows users to search for documents by country and topic in seven languages.

---

the data become "local" and much more accessible and relevant to project stakeholders. The data are open and available directly to software developers though an application programming interface and through an interactive web-based application called Mapping for Results (http://maps.worldbank.org).

In keeping with the philosophy of the Open Data Initiative, the Mapping for Results application uses the dataset of geo-located project activities and combines the data with subnational human and social development indicators, such as child mortality rates, poverty incidence, malnutrition, and population measures. But even more value may lie in what other researchers and software developers might do with the data, combining them with their own data or with data from other sources, performing their own analysis, or providing applications that help citizens and beneficiaries connect directly with the project during implementation, through feedback or other mechanisms.

Countdown to the Millennium Development Goals in 2015

There are four years to the target date for the Millennium Development Goals (MDGs). The MDGs have focused the world's attention on the living conditions of billions of people who live in poor and developing countries and on the need to improve the quality, frequency, and timeliness of the statistics used to track their progress. Progress toward the MDGs has been marked by slow changes in outcome indicators and by improvements in data availability.

World Development Indicators has monitored global and regional trends in poverty reduction, education, health, and the environment since 1997. After the UN Millennium Summit in 2000, *World Development Indicators* began closely tracking the progress of countries

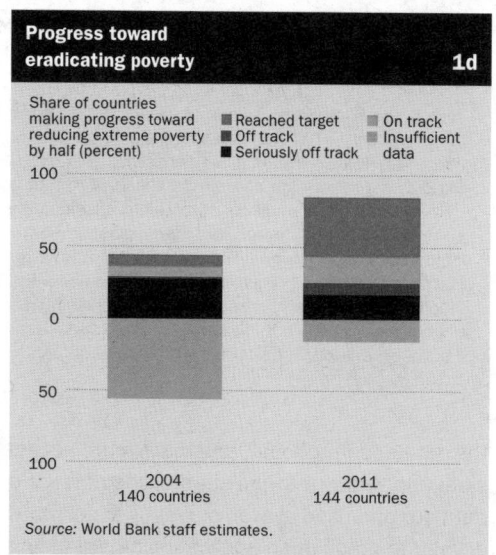

Progress toward eradicating poverty 1d

Share of countries making progress toward reducing extreme poverty by half (percent)

■ Reached target ■ On track
■ Off track ■ Insufficient
■ Seriously off track data

2004
140 countries

2011
144 countries

Source: World Bank staff estimates.

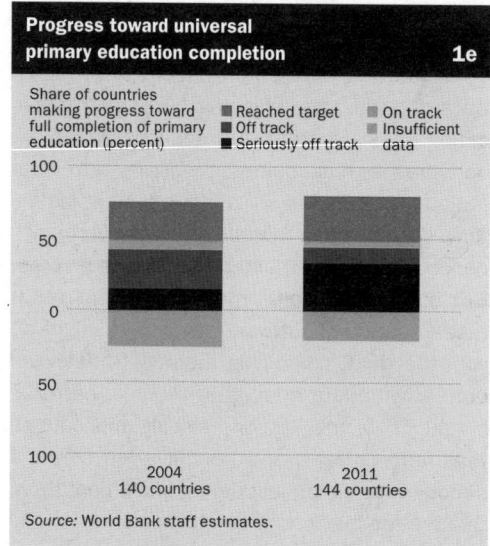

Progress toward universal primary education completion 1e

Share of countries making progress toward full completion of primary education (percent)

■ Reached target ■ On track
■ Off track ■ Insufficient
■ Seriously off track data

2004
140 countries

2011
144 countries

Source: World Bank staff estimates.

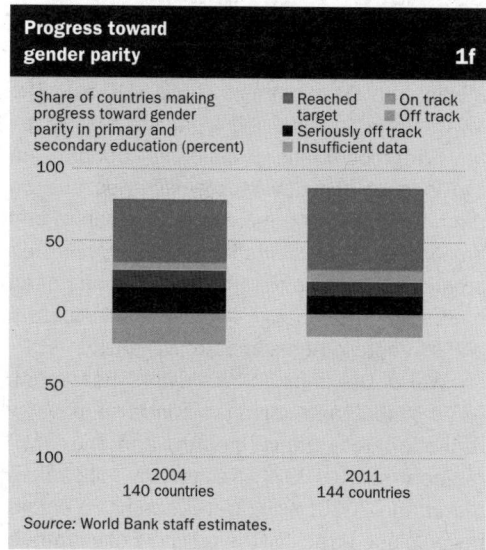

Progress toward gender parity 1f

Share of countries making progress toward gender parity in primary and secondary education (percent)

■ Reached target ■ On track
■ Off track
■ Seriously off track
■ Insufficient data

2004
140 countries

2011
144 countries

Source: World Bank staff estimates.

against the targets selected for the MDGs. The MDGs highlight important outcomes, but the focus on this limited set of indicators should not obscure the fact that development is a complex process whose course is determined in part by geographic location, historical circumstances, institutional capacity, and uncontrollable events such as weather and natural disasters. Success or failure, while not arbitrary or entirely accidental, still has a large component of chance.

This review employs the same assessment method that *World Development Indicators* has used since 2004 to track progress of countries toward the time-bound and quantified targets of the MDGs. Countries are "on track" if their past progress equals or exceeds the rate of change necessary to reach an MDG target. A few countries have already reached their targets. They are counted as having achieved the goal, although some may slip back. Countries making less than necessary progress are "off track," or "seriously off track" if their past rate progress would not allow them to reach the target even in another 25 years. The remaining countries do not have sufficient data to evaluate their progress—in some cases because there are no data for the benchmark period of 1990–99 and in others because more recent data are missing. But the situation is improving: starting from the earliest *World Development Indicators* progress assessments in 2004 (based on data for 1990–2002), the number of countries with insufficient data has fallen, enhancing our picture of progress toward the MDGs.

For more information on the work of the World Bank and its partners to achieve the MDGs, see www.worldbank.org/mdgs, which includes a link to the World Bank's MDG eAtlas.

Goal 1. Eradicate extreme poverty and hunger
The number of people living on less than $1.25 a day fell from 1.8 billion in 1990 to 1.4 billion in 2005. New global and regional estimates, to become available later in 2011, are likely to show a continuation of past trends, although the financial crisis of 2008 and the recent surge in food prices will have slowed progress in some countries. Because household income and expenditure surveys are expensive and time consuming, they are not conducted frequently and there are often difficulties in making reliable comparisons over time or across countries.

For 140 developing countries, figure 1d compares the progress assessments in 2005 and in 2011, based on available data. Forty-three countries are on track or have reached the target of cutting the extreme poverty rate in half, twice as many as in 2005. They include China, Brazil, and the Russian Federation. India, with more than 400 million people living in poverty lags behind, but with faster economic growth may well reach the 2015 target.

Goal 2. Achieve universal primary education

The goal of providing universal primary education has proved surprisingly hard to achieve. Completion rates measure the proportion of children enrolled in the final year of primary education after adjusting for repetition. In 2011, 49 countries had achieved or were on track to achieve 100 percent primary completion rates, only three more than in 2004, and the number of countries seriously off track has increased, especially in Sub-Saharan Africa (figure 1e). There are more and better data, but the goal remains elusive.

Goal 3. Promote gender equality

Gender equality and empowering women foster progress toward all the Millennium Development Goals. Equality of educational opportunities, measured by the ratio of girls' to boys' enrollments in primary and secondary education, is a starting point. Since the 2004 assessment, the number of countries on track to reach the target has increased steadily, driven by rising enrollments of girls, and the number of countries without sufficient data to measure progress has dropped (figure 1f).

Goal 4. Reduce child mortality

Of 144 countries with data in February 2011, 11 had achieved a two-thirds reduction in their under-five child mortality rate, and another 25 were on track to do so (figure 1g). This is remarkable progress since 2004, but more than 100 countries remain off track, and only a few of them are likely to reach the MDG target by 2015. Measuring child mortality is the product of a successful collaboration of international statisticians. By bringing together the most reliable data from multiple sources and applying appropriate estimation methods, consistent time series comparable across countries are available for monitoring this important indicator. More information about data sources

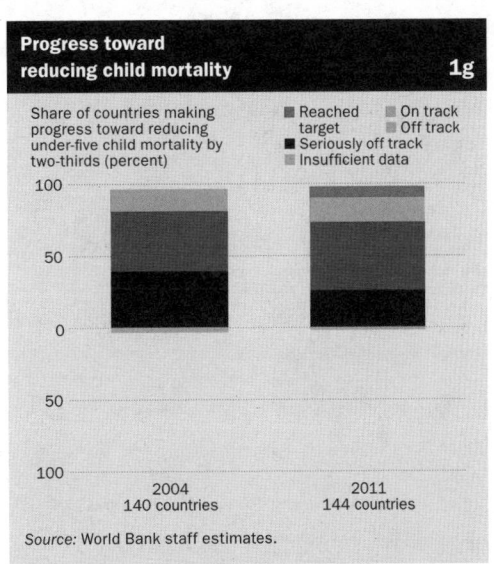

Progress toward reducing child mortality 1g

Share of countries making progress toward reducing under-five child mortality by two-thirds (percent)

■ Reached target   □ On track
■ Seriously off track   □ Off track
■ Insufficient data

2004
140 countries

2011
144 countries

Source: World Bank staff estimates.

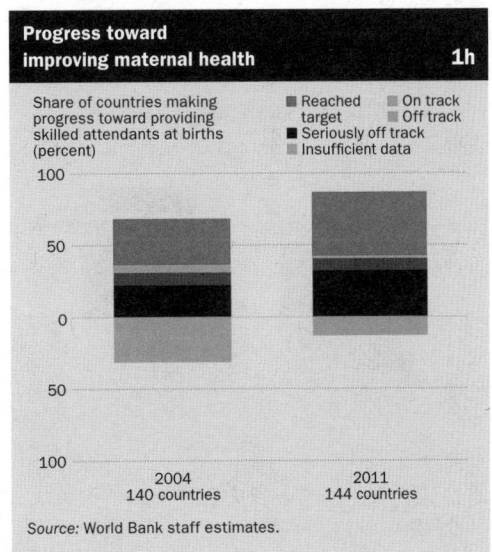

Progress toward improving maternal health 1h

Share of countries making progress toward providing skilled attendants at births (percent)

■ Reached target   □ On track
■ Seriously off track   □ Off track
■ Insufficient data

2004
140 countries

2011
144 countries

Source: World Bank staff estimates.

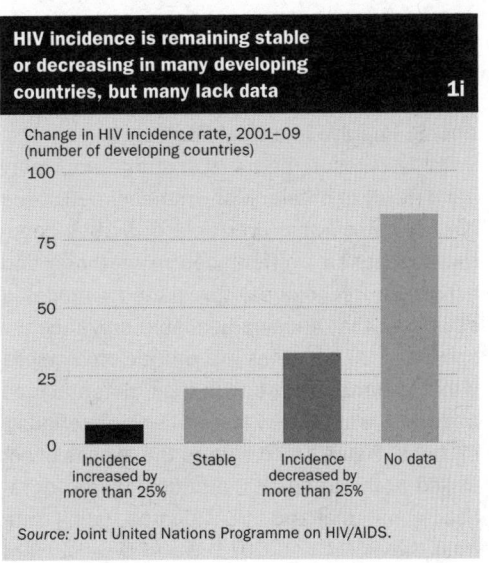

HIV incidence is remaining stable or decreasing in many developing countries, but many lack data 1i

Change in HIV incidence rate, 2001–09 (number of developing countries)

Incidence increased by more than 25%   Stable   Incidence decreased by more than 25%   No data

Source: Joint United Nations Programme on HIV/AIDS.

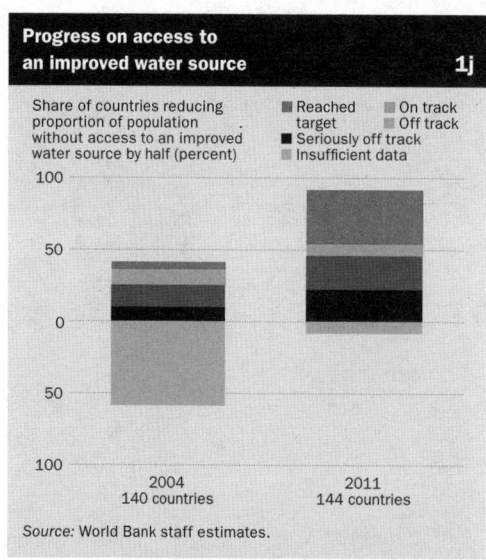

Progress on access to an improved water source 1j

Share of countries reducing proportion of population without access to an improved water source by half (percent)

Legend: ■ Reached target ■ On track ■ Off track ■ Seriously off track ■ Insufficient data

2004
140 countries

2011
144 countries

Source: World Bank staff estimates.

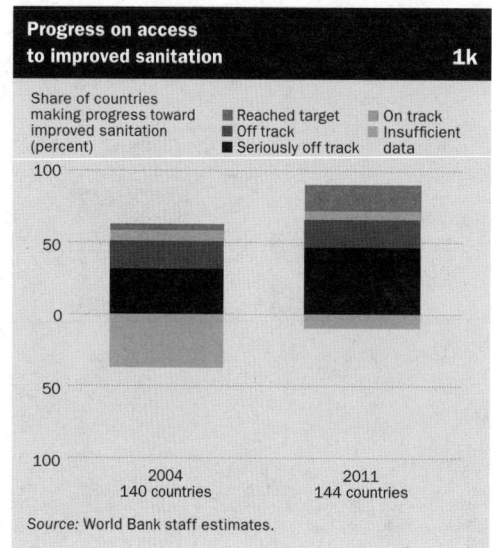

Progress on access to improved sanitation 1k

Share of countries making progress toward improved sanitation (percent)

Legend: ■ Reached target ■ Off track ■ Seriously off track ■ On track ■ Insufficient data

2004
140 countries

2011
144 countries

Source: World Bank staff estimates.

and estimation methods is available at www.childmortality.org.

Goal 5. Improve maternal health

Reliable measurements of maternal mortality are difficult to obtain. Many national estimates are not comparable over time or across countries because of differences in methods and estimation techniques. Consistently modeled estimates that became available only recently show that 30 countries are on track to achieve a three-quarter reduction in their maternal mortality ratio and that 94 are off track or seriously off track. Figure 1h compares the availability of skilled birth attendants, a critical factor for reducing maternal and infant deaths, using data from the 2004 and 2011 *World Development*

Indicators. While the number of countries seriously off track has increased, the number without adequate data has decreased, and the number providing skilled attendants at birth has risen 35 percent.

Goal 6. Combat HIV/AIDS, malaria, and other diseases

When the MDGs were formulated, the HIV/AIDS epidemic was spreading rapidly, engulfing many poor countries in Southern Africa. Data on the extent of the epidemic were derived from sentinel sites and limited reporting through health systems. The goal refers to halting and reversing the spread of HIV/AIDS. Under the circumstances it was impossible to set time-bound quantified targets. Now the statistical record is beginning to improve. UNAIDS, in its 2010 *Report on the Global AIDS Epidemic,* estimates that the annual number of new HIV infections has fallen 21 percent since its peak in 1997 (figure 1i). But reliable estimates of incidence are available for only 60 developing countries and do not include Brazil, China, and the Russian Federation.

Goal 7. Ensure environmental sustainability

Reversing environmental losses and ensuring a sustainable flow of services from the Earth's resources have many dimensions: preserving forests, protecting plant and animal species, reducing carbon emissions, and limiting and adapting to the effects of climate change. Improving the built environment is also important. The MDGs set targets for reducing the proportion of people without access to safe water and sanitation by half. The ability to measure progress toward both targets has improved significantly since 2004, and almost half the developing countries with sufficient data are on track to meet the water target (figure 1j). Progress in providing access to sanitation has been slower: almost half the countries are seriously off track (figure 1k).

Goal 8. Develop a global partnership for development

Partnership between high-income and developing economies, fundamental to achieving the MDGs, rests on four pillars: reducing external debt of developing countries, increasing their access to markets in OECD countries, realizing the benefits of new technologies and essential drugs, and providing financing for development programs in the poorest countries. Following the adoption of the MDGs, the International Conference on Financing for Development in 2002 urged developed countries "to make concrete efforts toward the target of 0.7 percent of gross national income [GNI] as official development assistance to developing countries."

Since then many countries have increased their official development assistance, but few have reached the target of 0.7 percent (figure 1l). In 2009, five countries provided more than 0.7 percent of their GNI as aid, but their share of total aid was only 15 percent. The largest share of total aid was provided by 10 donors that gave 0.3–0.7 percent of their GNI. The largest single donor, the United States, provided 0.21 percent of its GNI as official development assistance.

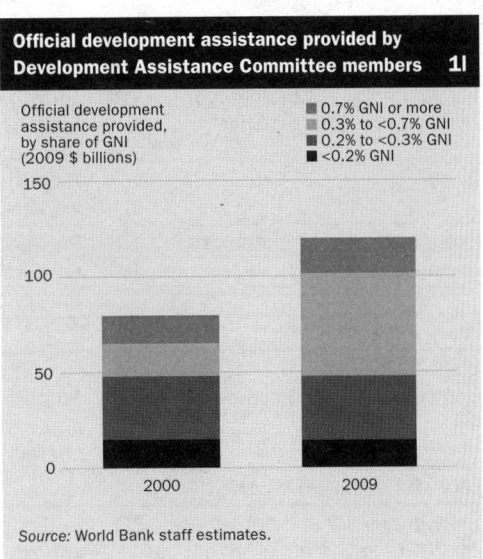

Official development assistance provided by Development Assistance Committee members 1l

Official development assistance provided, by share of GNI (2009 $ billions)

- 0.7% GNI or more
- 0.3% to <0.7% GNI
- 0.2% to <0.3% GNI
- <0.2% GNI

Source: World Bank staff estimates.

Millennium Development Goals

Goals and targets from the Millennium Declaration	Indicators for monitoring progress

Goal 1   Eradicate extreme poverty and hunger

Target 1.A Halve, between 1990 and 2015, the proportion of people whose income is less than $1 a day	1.1 Proportion of population below $1 purchasing power parity (PPP) a day[1] 1.2 Poverty gap ratio [incidence × depth of poverty] 1.3 Share of poorest quintile in national consumption
Target 1.B Achieve full and productive employment and decent work for all, including women and young people	1.4 Growth rate of GDP per person employed 1.5 Employment to population ratio 1.6 Proportion of employed people living below $1 (PPP) a day 1.7 Proportion of own-account and contributing family workers in total employment
Target 1.C Halve, between 1990 and 2015, the proportion of people who suffer from hunger	1.8 Prevalence of underweight children under five years of age 1.9 Proportion of population below minimum level of dietary energy consumption

Goal 2   Achieve universal primary education

Target 2.A Ensure that by 2015 children everywhere, boys and girls alike, will be able to complete a full course of primary schooling	2.1 Net enrollment ratio in primary education 2.2 Proportion of pupils starting grade 1 who reach last grade of primary education 2.3 Literacy rate of 15- to 24-year-olds, women and men

Goal 3   Promote gender equality and empower women

Target 3.A Eliminate gender disparity in primary and secondary education, preferably by 2005, and in all levels of education no later than 2015	3.1 Ratios of girls to boys in primary, secondary, and tertiary education 3.2 Share of women in wage employment in the nonagricultural sector 3.3 Proportion of seats held by women in national parliament

Goal 4   Reduce child mortality

Target 4.A Reduce by two-thirds, between 1990 and 2015, the under-five mortality rate	4.1 Under-five mortality rate 4.2 Infant mortality rate 4.3 Proportion of one-year-old children immunized against measles

Goal 5   Improve maternal health

Target 5.A Reduce by three-quarters, between 1990 and 2015, the maternal mortality ratio	5.1 Maternal mortality ratio 5.2 Proportion of births attended by skilled health personnel
Target 5.B Achieve by 2015 universal access to reproductive health	5.3 Contraceptive prevalence rate 5.4 Adolescent birth rate 5.5 Antenatal care coverage (at least one visit and at least four visits) 5.6 Unmet need for family planning

Goal 6   Combat HIV/AIDS, malaria, and other diseases

Target 6.A Have halted by 2015 and begun to reverse the spread of HIV/AIDS	6.1 HIV prevalence among population ages 15–24 years 6.2 Condom use at last high-risk sex 6.3 Proportion of population ages 15–24 years with comprehensive, correct knowledge of HIV/AIDS 6.4 Ratio of school attendance of orphans to school attendance of nonorphans ages 10–14 years
Target 6.B Achieve by 2010 universal access to treatment for HIV/AIDS for all those who need it	6.5 Proportion of population with advanced HIV infection with access to antiretroviral drugs
Target 6.C Have halted by 2015 and begun to reverse the incidence of malaria and other major diseases	6.6 Incidence and death rates associated with malaria 6.7 Proportion of children under age five sleeping under insecticide-treated bednets 6.8 Proportion of children under age five with fever who are treated with appropriate antimalarial drugs 6.9 Incidence, prevalence, and death rates associated with tuberculosis 6.10 Proportion of tuberculosis cases detected and cured under directly observed treatment short course

The Millennium Development Goals and targets come from the Millennium Declaration, signed by 189 countries, including 147 heads of state and government, in September 2000 (www.un.org/millennium/declaration/ares552e.htm) as updated by the 60th UN General Assembly in September 2005. The revised Millennium Development Goal (MDG) monitoring framework shown here, including new targets and indicators, was presented to the 62nd General Assembly, with new numbering as recommended by the Inter-agency and Expert Group on MDG Indicators at its 12th meeting on 14 November 2007. The goals and targets are interrelated and should be seen as a whole. They represent a partnership between the developed countries and the developing countries "to create an environment—at the national and global levels alike—which is conducive to development and the elimination of poverty." All indicators should be disaggregated by sex and urban-rural location as far as possible.

Goals and targets from the Millennium Declaration

Indicators for monitoring progress

Goal 7	**Ensure environmental sustainability**

Target 7.A Integrate the principles of sustainable development into country policies and programs and reverse the loss of environmental resources

7.1 Proportion of land area covered by forest
7.2 Carbon dioxide emissions, total, per capita and per $1 GDP (PPP)
7.3 Consumption of ozone-depleting substances

Target 7.B Reduce biodiversity loss, achieving, by 2010, a significant reduction in the rate of loss

7.4 Proportion of fish stocks within safe biological limits
7.5 Proportion of total water resources used
7.6 Proportion of terrestrial and marine areas protected
7.7 Proportion of species threatened with extinction

Target 7.C Halve by 2015 the proportion of people without sustainable access to safe drinking water and basic sanitation

7.8 Proportion of population using an improved drinking water source
7.9 Proportion of population using an improved sanitation facility

Target 7.D Achieve by 2020 a significant improvement in the lives of at least 100 million slum dwellers

7.10 Proportion of urban population living in slums[2]

Goal 8	**Develop a global partnership for development**

Target 8.A Develop further an open, rule-based, predictable, nondiscriminatory trading and financial system

(Includes a commitment to good governance, development, and poverty reduction—both nationally and internationally.)

Target 8.B Address the special needs of the least developed countries

(Includes tariff and quota-free access for the least developed countries' exports; enhanced program of debt relief for heavily indebted poor countries (HIPC) and cancellation of official bilateral debt; and more generous ODA for countries committed to poverty reduction.)

Target 8.C Address the special needs of landlocked developing countries and small island developing states (through the Programme of Action for the Sustainable Development of Small Island Developing States and the outcome of the 22nd special session of the General Assembly)

Some of the indicators listed below are monitored separately for the least developed countries (LDCs), Africa, landlocked developing countries, and small island developing states.

Official development assistance (ODA)
8.1 Net ODA, total and to the least developed countries, as percentage of OECD/DAC donors' gross national income
8.2 Proportion of total bilateral, sector-allocable ODA of OECD/DAC donors to basic social services (basic education, primary health care, nutrition, safe water, and sanitation)
8.3 Proportion of bilateral official development assistance of OECD/DAC donors that is untied
8.4 ODA received in landlocked developing countries as a proportion of their gross national incomes
8.5 ODA received in small island developing states as a proportion of their gross national incomes

Market access
8.6 Proportion of total developed country imports (by value and excluding arms) from developing countries and least developed countries, admitted free of duty
8.7 Average tariffs imposed by developed countries on agricultural products and textiles and clothing from developing countries
8.8 Agricultural support estimate for OECD countries as a percentage of their GDP
8.9 Proportion of ODA provided to help build trade capacity

Target 8.D Deal comprehensively with the debt problems of developing countries through national and international measures in order to make debt sustainable in the long term

Debt sustainability
8.10 Total number of countries that have reached their HIPC decision points and number that have reached their HIPC completion points (cumulative)
8.11 Debt relief committed under HIPC Initiative and Multilateral Debt Relief Initiative (MDRI)
8.12 Debt service as a percentage of exports of goods and services

Target 8.E In cooperation with pharmaceutical companies, provide access to affordable essential drugs in developing countries

8.13 Proportion of population with access to affordable essential drugs on a sustainable basis

Target 8.F In cooperation with the private sector, make available the benefits of new technologies, especially information and communications

8.14 Telephone lines per 100 population
8.15 Cellular subscribers per 100 population
8.16 Internet users per 100 population

---

1. Where available, indicators based on national poverty lines should be used for monitoring country poverty trends.

2. The proportion of people living in slums is measured by a proxy, represented by the urban population living in households with at least one of these characteristics: lack of access to improved water supply, lack of access to improved sanitation, overcrowding (3 or more persons per room), and dwellings made of nondurable material.

	Population	Surface area	Population density	Gross national income, Atlas method		Gross national income per capita, Atlas method		Purchasing power parity gross national income			Gross domestic product	
	millions	thousand sq. km	people per sq. km	$ billions	Rank	$	Rank	$ billions	Per capita $	Rank	% growth	Per capita % growth
	2009	2009	2009	2009	2009	2009	2009	2009	2009	2009	2008–09	2008–09
Afghanistan	30	652	46	9.1	125	310	207	25.1ª	860ª	201	40.8	37.1
Albania	3	29	115	12.6	114	4,000	116	27.3	8,640	106	2.5	2.1
Algeria	35	2,382	15	154.2	49	4,420	112	283.2ª	8,110ª	110	2.1	0.6
Angola	18	1,247	15	69.4	63	3,750	123	96.1	5,190	131	0.7	−1.9
Argentina	40	2,780	15	304.1	29	7,550	85	567.5	14,090	76	0.9	−0.1
Armenia	3	30	108	9.5	124	3,100	131	16.7	5,410	128	−14.4	−14.6
Australia	22	7,741	3	957.5	15	43,770	23	842.3	38,510	24	1.3	−0.8
Austria	8	84	101	388.5	25	46,450	17	321.3	38,410	25	−3.9	−4.2
Azerbaijan	9	87	106	42.5	76	4,840	106	79.2	9,020	101	9.3	8.0
Bangladesh	162	144	1,246	93.5	57	580	189	250.6	1,550	181	5.7	4.3
Belarus	10	208	48	53.7	68	5,560	100	123.1	12,740	88	1.4	1.6
Belgium	11	31	356	488.4	19	45,270	20	395.0	36,610	32	−2.8	−3.5
Benin	9	113	81	6.7	138	750	182	13.5	1,510	183	3.8	0.6
Bolivia	10	1,099	9	16.1	105	1,630	155	41.9	4,250	146	3.4	1.6
Bosnia and Herzegovina	4	51	74	17.7	103	4,700	107	33.0	8,770	105	−2.9	−2.7
Botswana	2	582	3	12.2	117	6,260	92	25.0	12,840	87	−3.7	−5.1
Brazil	194	8,515	23	1,564.2	8	8,070	83	1,968.0	10,160	98	−0.6	−1.5
Bulgaria	8	111	70	46.0	73	6,060	95	100.6	13,260	84	−4.9	−4.5
Burkina Faso	16	274	58	8.0	133	510	190	18.4	1,170	193	3.5	0.1
Burundi	8	28	323	1.2	186	150	213	3.3	390	211	3.5	0.6
Cambodia	15	181	84	9.7	123	650	185	27.0	1,820	176	−1.9	−3.5
Cameroon	20	475	41	23.2	93	1,190	162	42.8	2,190	169	2.0	−0.3
Canada	34	9,985	4	1,416.4	10	41,980	28	1,257.7	37,280	29	−2.5	−3.7
Central African Republic	4	623	7	2.0	177	450	195	3.3	750	207	2.4	0.5
Chad	11	1,284	9	6.7	139	600	187	13.0	1,160	194	−1.6	−4.2
Chile	17	756	23	160.7	48	9,470	75	227.7	13,420	81	−1.5	−2.5
China	1,331	9,600	143	4,856.2	3	3,650	125	9,170.1	6,890	119	9.1	8.5
Hong Kong SAR, China	7	1	6,721	221.1	37	31,570	40	311.9	44,540	18	−2.8	−3.1
Colombia	46	1,142	41	227.8	36	4,990	103	392.5	8,600	107	0.8	−0.6
Congo, Dem. Rep.	66	2,345	29	10.6	121	160	211	19.6	300	212	2.7	0.0
Congo, Rep.	4	342	11	7.7	135	2,080	147	11.2	3,040	157	7.6	5.6
Costa Rica	5	51	90	28.7	86	6,260	92	50.0ª	10,930ª	95	−1.5	−2.8
Côte d'Ivoire	21	322	66	22.5	95	1,070	168	34.5	1,640	179	3.6	1.2
Croatia	4	57	79	61.0	66	13,770	65	85.1	19,200	65	−5.8	−5.8
Cuba	11	110	105	62.2	65	5,550	98	..	..		4.3	4.3
Czech Republic	10	79	136	181.6	43	17,310	57	251.1	23,940	59	−4.2	−4.8
Denmark	6	43	130	326.5	28	59,060	9	214.4	38,780	23	−4.9	−5.5
Dominican Republic	10	49	209	45.9	74	4,550	110	81.9ª	8,110ª	110	3.5	2.0
Ecuador	14	256	55	54.1	67	3,970ᵇ	118	110.4	8,100	112	0.4	−0.7
Egypt, Arab Rep.	83	1,001	83	172.1	45	2,070	148	471.2	5,680	126	4.6	2.8
El Salvador	6	21	297	20.8	100	3,370	127	39.6ª	6,420ª	121	−3.5	−4.0
Eritrea	5	118	50	1.6	180	320	207	2.9ª	580ª	210	3.6	0.6
Estonia	1	45	32	18.9	102	14,060	63	25.6	19,120	66	−14.1	−14.1
Ethiopia	83	1,104	83	27.2	89	330	206	77.3	930	200	8.7	5.9
Finland	5	338	18	245.3	33	45,940	19	188.3	35,280	34	−8.0	−8.4
France	63ᶜ	549ᶜ	114ᶜ	2,750.9	5	42,620	25	2,191.2	33,950	36	−2.6	−3.2
Gabon	1	268	6	10.9	120	7,370	86	18.4	12,450	89	−1.0	−2.7
Gambia, The	2	11	171	0.7	196	440	196	2.3	1,330	186	4.6	1.8
Georgia	4	70	61	11.1ᵈ	118	2,530ᵈ	140	20.6ᵈ	4,700ᵈ	137	−3.9ᵈ	−4.0ᵈ
Germany	82	357	235	3,476.1	4	42,450	26	3,017.3	36,850	31	−4.7	−4.5
Ghana	24	239	105	28.4	87	1,190ᵉ	162	36.6	1,530	182	4.7	2.5
Greece	11	132	88	327.7	27	29,040	42	325.0	28,800	46	−2.0	−2.4
Guatemala	14	109	131	37.2	81	2,650	138	64.1ª	4,570ª	139	0.6	−1.9
Guinea	10	246	41	3.8	162	370	202	9.5	940	199	−0.3	−2.6
Guinea-Bissau	2	36	57	0.8	194	510	190	1.7	1,060	196	3.0	0.7
Haiti	10	28	364	..		..ᶠ		..	..		2.9	1.3
Honduras	7	112	67	13.5	111	1,800	153	27.7ª	3,710ª	148	−1.9	−3.8

Size of the economy

	Population	Surface area	Population density	Gross national income, *Atlas* method		Gross national income per capita, *Atlas* method		Purchasing power parity gross national income			Gross domestic product	
	millions	thousand sq. km	people per sq. km	$ billions	Rank	$	Rank	$ billions	Per capita $	Rank	% growth	Per capita % growth
	2009	**2009**	**2009**	**2009**	**2009**	**2009**	**2009**	**2009**	**2009**	**2009**	**2008–09**	**2008–09**
Hungary	10	93	112	130.1	51	12,980	66	191.3	19,090	67	−6.3	−6.2
India	1,155	3,287	389	1,405.7	11	1,220	160	3,786.3	3,280	154	9.1	7.7
Indonesia	230	1,905	127	471.0	20	2,050	149	855.0	3,720	147	4.5	3.4
Iran, Islamic Rep.	73	1,745	45	330.6	26	4,530	111	836.5	11,470	94	1.8	0.5
Iraq	31	438	72	69.7	62	2,210	146	105.0	3,330	151	4.2	1.6
Ireland	4	70	65	197.1	39	44,280	22	147.0	33,040	38	−7.1	−7.6
Israel	7	22	344	192.0	40	25,790	46	201.0	27,010	52	0.8	−1.0
Italy	60	301	205	2,114.5	7	35,110	35	1,919.2	31,870	41	−5.0	−5.7
Jamaica	3	11	249	12.4	116	4,590	109	19.5[a]	7,230[a]	117	−3.0	−3.5
Japan	128	378	350	4,857.2	2	38,080	32	4,265.3	33,440	37	−5.2	−5.1
Jordan	6	89	67	23.7	92	3,980[b]	117	34.1	5,730	125	2.3	−0.1
Kazakhstan	16	2,725	6	110.0	55	6,920	89	164.0	10,320	97	1.2	−0.2
Kenya	40	580	70	30.3	84	760	181	62.5	1,570	180	2.6	−0.1
Korea, Dem. Rep.	24	121	199	..		..[f]		..	..		..	..
Korea, Rep.	49	100	503	966.6	13	19,830	54	1,328.0	27,240	51	0.2	−0.1
Kosovo	2	11	166	5.9	143	3,240	129	..	..		4.0	3.4
Kuwait	3	18	157	*117.0*	50	*43,930*	10	*143.5*	*53,890*	6	4.4	1.9
Kyrgyz Republic	5	200	28	4.6	153	870	179	11.7	2,200	167	2.3	1.5
Lao PDR	6	237	27	5.6	146	880	178	13.9	2,200	167	6.4	4.5
Latvia	2	65	36	27.9	88	12,390	68	39.7	17,610	71	−18.0	−17.6
Lebanon	4	10	413	34.1	82	8,060	84	56.6	13,400	82	9.0	8.2
Lesotho	2	30	68	2.0	175	980[b]	175	3.7	1,800	178	0.9	0.0
Liberia	4	111	41	0.7	197	160	211	1.2	290	213	4.6	0.3
Libya	6	1,760	4	77.2	61	12,020	71	105.3[a]	16,400[a]	74	2.1	0.1
Lithuania	3	65	53	38.1	80	11,410	72	57.8	17,310	72	−15.0	−14.6
Macedonia, FYR	2	26	81	9.0	128	4,400	113	22.2	10,880	96	−0.7	−0.8
Madagascar	20	587	34	8.5	131	430	200	19.5	990	197	−3.7	−6.2
Malawi	15	118	162	4.4	156	290	210	11.9	780	206	7.6	4.7
Malaysia	27	331	84	201.8	38	7,350	87	376.6	13,710	78	−1.7	−3.3
Mali	13	1,240	11	8.9	129	680	184	15.4	1,190	189	4.3	1.9
Mauritania	3	1,031	3	3.3	166	990	174	6.4	1,940	173	−1.1	−3.3
Mauritius	1	2	628	9.2	127	7,250	88	16.9	13,270	83	2.1	1.6
Mexico	107	1,964	55	962.1	14	8,960	78	1,506.3	14,020	77	−6.5	−7.5
Moldova	4	34	110	5.6[g]	145	1,560[g]	157	10.7[g]	3,010[g]	158	−6.5[g]	−6.4[g]
Mongolia	3	1,564	2	4.4	157	1,630	155	8.9	3,330	151	−1.6	−2.7
Morocco	32	447	72	89.9[h]	58	2,770[h]	136	143.1[h]	4,400[h]	143	4.9[h]	3.6[h]
Mozambique	23	799	29	10.0	122	440	196	20.1	880	201	6.3	4.0
Myanmar	50	677	77	..		..[f]		..	..		..	..
Namibia	2	824	3	9.3	126	4,270	114	13.8	6,350	122	−0.8	−2.7
Nepal	29	147	205	13.0	113	440	196	34.7	1,180	191	4.7	2.8
Netherlands	17	42	490	801.1	16	48,460	15	657.0	39,740	22	−4.0	−4.5
New Zealand	4	268	16	124.3	53	28,810	43	120.0	27,790	48	−0.4	−1.5
Nicaragua	6	130	48	5.7	144	1,000	171	14.6[a]	2,540[a]	163	−5.6	−6.9
Niger	15	1,267	12	5.2	148	340	204	10.3	680	209	1.0	−2.9
Nigeria	155	924	170	184.7	42	1,190	162	321.0	2,070	170	5.6	3.2
Norway	5	324	16	408.5	24	84,640	3	267.5	55,420	8	−1.6	−2.8
Oman	3	310	9	*49.8*	69	*17,890*	56	*68.3*	*24,530*	54	*12.8*	*10.4*
Pakistan	170	796	220	169.8	46	1,000	171	454.7	2,680	162	3.6	1.4
Panama	3	75	46	22.7	94	6,570	91	42.1[a]	12,180[a]	91	2.4	0.8
Papua New Guinea	7	463	15	7.9	134	1,180	165	15.2[a]	2,260[a]	166	4.5	2.1
Paraguay	6	407	16	14.3	108	2,250	145	28.1	4,430	142	−3.8	−5.5
Peru	29	1,285	23	122.4	54	4,200	115	236.7	8,120	109	0.9	−0.3
Philippines	92	300	308	164.6	47	1,790	154	325.6	3,540	149	1.1	−0.7
Poland	38	313	125	467.6	21	12,260	69	697.9	18,290	69	1.7	1.6
Portugal	11	92	116	232.9	35	21,910	51	256.1	24,080	57	−2.6	−2.7
Puerto Rico	4	9	447	..		..[i]		..	..		..	..
Qatar	1	12	122	..		..[i]		..	..		8.6	−1.3

1.1 Size of the economy

	Population	Surface area	Population density	Gross national income, *Atlas* method		Gross national income per capita, *Atlas* method		Purchasing power parity gross national income			Gross domestic product	
	millions	thousand sq. km	people per sq. km	$ billions	Rank	$	Rank	$ billions	Per capita $	Rank	% growth	Per capita % growth
	2009	2009	2009	2009	2009	2009	2009	2009	2009	2009	2008–09	2008–09
Romania	21	238	93	178.9	44	8,330	81	312.4	14,540	75	−8.5	−8.4
Russian Federation	142	17,098	9	1,324.4	12	9,340	76	2,599.4	18,330	68	−7.9	−7.8
Rwanda	10	26	405	4.9	150	490	193	11.3	1,130	195	4.1	1.2
Saudi Arabia	25	2,000ʲ	13	436.9	23	17,210	58	609.8	24,020	58	0.6	−1.7
Senegal	13	197	65	13.1	112	1,040	170	22.7	1,810	177	2.2	−0.4
Serbia	7	88	83	43.9	75	6,000	96	85.6	11,700	93	−3.0	−2.6
Sierra Leone	6	72	80	1.9	178	340	204	4.5	790	205	4.0	1.5
Singapore	5	1	7,125	185.7	41	37,220	33	248.3	49,780	11	−1.3	−4.2
Slovak Republic	5	49	113	87.4	60	16,130	60	119.8	22,110	63	−6.2	−6.4
Slovenia	2	20	101	48.1	72	23,520	49	54.1	26,470	53	−7.8	−8.8
Somalia	9	638	15	..	..ᶠ			..	..		..	..
South Africa	49	1,219	41	284.3	31	5,760	97	495.6	10,050	99	−1.8	−2.8
Spain	46	505	92	1,476.2	9	32,120	39	1,447.2	31,490	43	−3.6	−4.5
Sri Lanka	20	66	324	40.4	77	1,990	151	95.8	4,720	136	3.5	2.8
Sudan	42	2,506	18	51.5	70	1,220	160	84.1	1,990	171	4.5	2.2
Swaziland	1	17	69	2.9	167	2,470	143	5.7	4,790	134	1.2	−0.3
Sweden	9	450	23	454.4	22	48,840	14	353.9	38,050	28	−5.1	−6.0
Switzerland	8	41	193	505.8	18	65,430	8	364.1	47,100	14	−1.9	−3.0
Syrian Arab Republic	21	185	115	50.9	71	2,410	144	97.3	4,620	138	4.0	1.5
Tajikistan	7	143	50	4.8	151	700	183	13.5	1,950	172	3.4	1.7
Tanzania	44	947	49	21.4ᵏ	97	500ᵏ	192	57.9ᵏ	1,360ᵏ	184	6.0ᵏ	3.0ᵏ
Thailand	68	513	133	254.7	32	3,760	122	517.5	7,640	115	−2.2	−2.8
Timor-Leste	1	15	76	2.7	169	2,460	141	5.2ᵃ	4,730ᵃ	133	1.9	−1.3
Togo	7	57	122	2.9	168	440	196	5.6	850	203	2.5	0.0
Trinidad and Tobago	1	5	261	22.4	96	16,700	59	33.4ᵃ	24,970ᵃ	55	−3.0	−3.4
Tunisia	10	164	67	38.9	78	3,720	124	81.4	7,810	113	3.1	2.1
Turkey	75	784	97	652.4	17	8,720	79	1,009.8	13,500	80	−4.7	−5.8
Turkmenistan	5	488	11	17.5	104	3,420	126	35.7ᵃ	6,980ᵃ	118	8.0	6.6
Uganda	33	241	166	15.2	106	460	194	39.0	1,190	189	7.1	3.6
Ukraine	46	604	79	128.9	52	2,800	135	284.4	6,180	123	−15.1	−14.6
United Arab Emirates	5	84	55	..	..ⁱ			..	..		−0.7	−3.2
United Kingdom	62	244	256	2,558.1	6	41,370	29	2,217.4	35,860	33	−4.9	−5.6
United States	307	9,832	34	14,233.5	1	46,360	18	14,011.0	45,640	16	−2.6	−3.5
Uruguay	3	176	19	30.2	85	9,010	77	43.1	12,900	86	2.9	2.5
Uzbekistan	28	447	65	30.6	83	1,100	167	80.9ᵃ	2,910ᵃ	159	8.1	6.3
Venezuela, RB	28	912	32	286.4	30	10,090	74	346.9	12,220	90	−3.3	−4.8
Vietnam	87	331	281	87.7	59	1,000ᵇ	171	243.6	2,790	161	5.3	4.0
West Bank and Gaza	4	6	672	..	..ˡ			..	..		..	..
Yemen, Rep.	24	528	45	25.0	90	1,060	169	55.0	2,330	165	3.8	0.8
Zambia	13	753	17	12.5	115	960	176	16.5	1,280	187	6.4	3.8
Zimbabwe	13	391	32	4.6	154	360	203	..	..		5.7	5.2
World	**6,775 s**	**134,123 s**	**52 w**	**59,162.8 t**		**8,732 w**		**71,774.4 t**	**10,594 w**		**−1.9 w**	**−3.0 w**
Low income	846	17,838	49	431.0		509		1,032.5	1,220		4.6	2.4
Middle income	4,813	80,558	61	16,346.7		3,397		30,653.8	6,370		2.6	1.5
Lower middle income	3,811	31,898	124	8,845.9		2,321		18,229.1	4,784		7.1	5.9
Upper middle income	1,002	48,659	21	7,515.1		7,502		12,461.9	12,440		−2.6	−3.4
Low & middle income	5,659	98,396	59	16,792.6		2,968		31,684.3	5,599		2.7	1.4
East Asia & Pacific	1,944	16,302	123	6,148.6		3,163		11,712.8	6,026		7.4	6.6
Europe & Central Asia	404	23,549	18	2,745.8		6,793		5,097.0	12,609		−5.8	−6.1
Latin America & Carib.	572	20,394	28	4,011.3		7,007		5,888.7	10,286		−1.9	−3.0
Middle East & N. Africa	331	8,778	38	1,190.2		3,597		2,617.6	7,911		3.4	1.6
South Asia	1,568	5,131	329	1,735.4		1,107		4,658.7	2,972		8.1	6.5
Sub-Saharan Africa	840	24,242	36	944.3		1,125		1,722.2	2,051		1.7	−0.7
High income	1,117	35,727	33	42,417.7		37,990		40,433.9	36,213		−3.3	−3.9
Euro area	327	2,583	128	12,723.2		38,872		11,127.6	33,997		−4.1	−4.5

a. Based on regression; others are extrapolated from the 2005 International Comparison Program benchmark estimates. b. Included in the aggregates for lower middle-income economies based on earlier data. c. Excludes the French overseas departments of French Guiana, Guadeloupe, Martinique, and Réunion. d. Excludes Abkhazia and South Ossetia. e. Included in the aggregates for low-income economies based on earlier data. f. Estimated to be low income ($995 or less). g. Excludes Transnistria. h. Includes Former Spanish Sahara. i. Estimated to be high income ($12,196 or more). j. Provisional estimate. k. Covers mainland Tanzania only. l. Estimated to be lower middle income ($996–$3,945).

Size of the economy | 1.1

Population, land area, income, and output are basic measures of the size of an economy. They also provide a broad indication of actual and potential resources. Population, land area, income (as measured by gross national income, GNI), and output (as measured by gross domestic product, GDP) are therefore used throughout *World Development Indicators* to normalize other indicators.

Population estimates are generally based on extrapolations from the most recent national census. For further discussion of the measurement of population and population growth, see *About the data* for table 2.1.

The surface area of an economy includes inland bodies of water and some coastal waterways. Surface area thus differs from land area, which excludes bodies of water, and from gross area, which may include offshore territorial waters. Land area is particularly important for understanding an economy's agricultural capacity and the environmental effects of human activity. (For measures of land area and data on rural population density, land use, and agricultural productivity, see tables 3.1–3.3.) Innovations in satellite mapping and computer databases have resulted in more precise measurements of land and water areas.

GNI measures total domestic and foreign value added claimed by residents. GNI comprises GDP plus net receipts of primary income (compensation of employees and property income) from nonresident sources. The World Bank uses GNI per capita in U.S. dollars to classify countries for analytical purposes and to determine borrowing eligibility. For definitions of the income groups in *World Development Indicators,* see *Users guide.* For discussion of the usefulness of national income and output as measures of productivity or welfare, see *About the data* for tables 4.1 and 4.2.

When calculating GNI in U.S. dollars from GNI reported in national currencies, the World Bank follows the *World Bank Atlas* conversion method, using a three-year average of exchange rates to smooth the effects of transitory fluctuations in exchange rates. (For further discussion of the *World Bank Atlas* method, see *Statistical methods*.)

Because exchange rates do not always reflect differences in price levels between countries, the table also converts GNI and GNI per capita estimates into international dollars using purchasing power parity (PPP) rates. PPP rates provide a standard measure allowing comparison of real levels of expenditure between countries, just as conventional price indexes allow comparison of real values over time.

PPP rates are calculated by simultaneously comparing the prices of similar goods and services among a large number of countries. In the most recent round of price surveys conducted by the International Comparison Program (ICP), 146 countries and territories participated in the data collection, including China for the first time, India for the first time since 1985, and almost all African countries. The PPP conversion factors presented in the table come from three sources. For 45 high- and upper middle-income countries conversion factors are provided by Eurostat and the Organisation for Economic Co-operation and Development (OECD), with PPP estimates for 34 European countries incorporating new price data collected since 2005. For the remaining 2005 ICP countries the PPP estimates are extrapolated from the 2005 ICP benchmark results, which account for relative price changes between each economy and the United States. For countries that did not participate in the 2005 ICP round, the PPP estimates are imputed using a statistical model.

More information on the results of the 2005 ICP is available at www.worldbank.org/data/icp.

All 213 economies shown in *World Development Indicators* are ranked by size, including those that appear in table 1.6. The ranks are shown only in table 1.1. No rank is shown for economies for which numerical estimates of GNI per capita are not published. Economies with missing data are included in the ranking at their approximate level, so that the relative order of other economies remains consistent.

- **Population** is based on the de facto definition of population, which counts all residents regardless of legal status or citizenship—except for refugees not permanently settled in the country of asylum, who are generally considered part of the population of their country of origin. The values shown are midyear estimates. See also table 2.1. • **Surface area** is a country's total area, including areas under inland bodies of water and some coastal waterways. • **Population density** is midyear population divided by land area in square kilometers. • **Gross national income (GNI)** is the sum of value added by all resident producers plus any product taxes (less subsidies) not included in the valuation of output plus net receipts of primary income (compensation of employees and property income) from abroad. Data are in current U.S. dollars converted using the *World Bank Atlas* method (see *Statistical methods*). • **GNI per capita** is GNI divided by midyear population. GNI per capita in U.S. dollars is converted using the *World Bank Atlas* method. • **Purchasing power parity (PPP) GNI** is GNI converted to international dollars using PPP rates. An international dollar has the same purchasing power over GNI that a U.S. dollar has in the United States. • **Gross domestic product (GDP)** is the sum of value added by all resident producers plus any product taxes (less subsidies) not included in the valuation of output. Growth is calculated from constant price GDP data in local currency. • **GDP per capita** is GDP divided by midyear population.

Population estimates are prepared by World Bank staff from a variety of sources (see *Data sources* for table 2.1). Data on surface and land area are from the Food and Agriculture Organization (see *Data sources* for table 3.1). GNI, GNI per capita, GDP growth, and GDP per capita growth are estimated by World Bank staff based on national accounts data collected by World Bank staff during economic missions or reported by national statistical offices to other international organizations such as the OECD. PPP conversion factors are estimates by Eurostat/OECD and by World Bank staff based on data collected by the ICP.

1.2 Millennium Development Goals: eradicating poverty and saving lives

	Eradicate extreme poverty and hunger					Achieve universal primary education		Promote gender equality		Reduce child mortality	
	Share of poorest quintile in national consumption or income %	Vulnerable employment Unpaid family workers and own-account workers % of total employment		Prevalence of malnutrition Underweight % of children under age 5		Primary completion rate %		Ratio of girls to boys enrollments in primary and secondary education %		Under-five mortality rate per 1,000	
	1995–2009a,b	1990	2008	1990	2004–09a	1991	2009c	1991	2009c	1990	2009
Afghanistan	9.0	..	..	..	32.9	28	..	54	62	250	199
Albania	8.1	..	..	..	6.6	..	90	96	100	51	15
Algeria	6.9	..	..	9.2	3.7	80	91	83	..	61	32
Angola	2.0d	..	..	..	..	33	..	..	..	258	161
Argentina	4.1d	..	20e	..	2.3	..	102	..	105	28	14
Armenia	8.8	..	..	..	4.2	..	98	..	103	56	22
Australia	..	10	9	..	..	..	..	100	97	9	5
Austria	8.6	..	9	..	..	..	99	95	97	9	4
Azerbaijan	8.0	..	53	..	8.4	95	92	100	102	98	34
Bangladesh	9.4	..	..	61.5	41.3	41	61	75	108	148	52
Belarus	9.2	..	..	..	1.3	94	96	..	101	24	12
Belgium	8.5	16	10	..	..	79	86	101	98	10	5
Benin	6.9	..	..	..	20.2	22	62	..	..	184	118
Bolivia	2.8	40e	..	9.7	4.5	71	99	..	99	122	51
Bosnia and Herzegovina	6.7	..	..	..	1.6	..	..	..	102	23	14
Botswana	..	..	..	..	..	90	95	109	100	60	57
Brazil	3.3	29e	27	..	2.2	93	..	..	103	56	21
Bulgaria	5.0	..	9	..	1.6	90	90	99	97	18	10
Burkina Faso	7.0	..	..	29.6	26.0	20	43	..	86	201	166
Burundi	9.0	..	..	..	30.2	46	52	82	93	189	166
Cambodia	6.6	..	..	..	28.8	..	83	..	90	117	88
Cameroon	5.6	..	..	18.0	16.6	53	73	83	86	148	154
Canada	7.2	..	10e	..	..	..	..	99	..	8	6
Central African Republic	5.2	..	..	..	..	28	38	61	69	175	171
Chad	6.3	94	..	..	33.9	18	33	41	64	201	209
Chile	8.6	..	25	..	0.5	..	95	100	99	22	9
China	5.7	..	..	12.6	4.5	107	..	86	105	46	19
Hong Kong SAR, China	5.3	6	7e	..	..	102	93	..	102	..	..
Colombia	2.5	28e	41	8.8	5.1	73	115	108	105	35	19
Congo, Dem. Rep.	5.5	..	..	..	28.2	48	56	70	77	199	199
Congo, Rep.	5.0	..	..	21.1	11.8	54	74	89	..	104	128
Costa Rica	4.2	25	20	2.5	..	79	96	101	102	18	11
Côte d'Ivoire	5.6	..	..	..	16.7	42	46	..	..	152	119
Croatia	8.1	..	22f	..	1.0	..	100	103	102	13	5
Cuba	..	..	..	..	..	99	98	106	99	14	6
Czech Republic	10.2	7	13	0.9	..	92	95	98	101	12	4
Denmark	8.3	7	5	..	..	98	101	101	102	9	4
Dominican Republic	4.4	39	42	8.4	3.4	..	90	..	97	62	32
Ecuador	4.2	36e	34e	..	6.2	..	103	100	103	53	24
Egypt, Arab Rep.	9.0	28e	25	10.5	6.8	..	95	81	..	90	21
El Salvador	4.3	35	36	11.1	..	65	89	101	98	62	17
Eritrea	..	..	..	36.9	..	..	48	82	77	150	55
Estonia	6.8	2e	6e	..	..	..	100	103	101	17	6
Ethiopia	9.3	..	52e	..	34.6	23	55	68	88	210	104
Finland	9.6	..	9	..	..	97	98	109	102	7	3
France	7.2	11	6	..	..	106	..	102	100	9	4
Gabon	6.1	48	..	..	..	62	..	96	..	93	69
Gambia, The	4.8	..	..	..	15.8	45	79	65	102	153	103
Georgia	5.3	..	62	..	2.3	..	107	98	96	47	29
Germany	8.5	..	7	..	1.1	100	104	99	98	9	4
Ghana	5.2	..	..	24.1	14.3	64	83	78	95	120	69
Greece	6.7	40e	27	..	..	99	101	99	97	11	3
Guatemala	3.4	..	..	27.8	..	..	80	87	94	76	40
Guinea	6.4	..	..	..	20.8	17	62	45	77	231	142
Guinea-Bissau	7.2	..	..	..	17.4	..	..	55	..	240	193
Haiti	2.5	..	..	23.7	18.9	27	..	..	..	152	87
Honduras	2.0	49e	..	15.8	8.6	64	90	104	107	55	30

Millennium Development Goals: eradicating poverty and saving lives **1.2**

	Eradicate extreme poverty and hunger					Achieve universal primary education		Promote gender equality		Reduce child mortality	
	Share of poorest quintile in national consumption or income %	Vulnerable employment Unpaid family workers and own-account workers % of total employment		Prevalence of malnutrition Underweight % of children under age 5		Primary completion rate %		Ratio of girls to boys enrollments in primary and secondary education %		Under-five mortality rate per 1,000	
	1995–2009[a,b]	1990	2008	1990	2004–09[a]	1991	2009[c]	1991	2009[c]	1990	2009
Hungary	8.4	7[e]	7	2.3	..	82	95	100	98	17	6
India	8.1	..	..	59.5	43.5	..	95	73	92	118	66
Indonesia	7.6	..	63	31.0	17.5[g]	93	109	93	98	86	39
Iran, Islamic Rep.	6.4	..	43	..	..	88	101	85	97	73	31
Iraq	..	..	..	10.4	7.1	58	64	79	81	53	44
Ireland	7.4	20	12	..	..	103	99	104	103	9	4
Israel	5.7	..	7	..	..	..	99	105	101	11	4
Italy	6.5	27	19	..	..	98	104	100	99	10	4
Jamaica	5.2	42	35	4.0	2.2	94	89	103	100	33	31
Japan	..	19	11	..	..	102	101	101	100	6	3
Jordan	7.2	..	..	4.8	1.9	101	100	101	102	39	25
Kazakhstan	8.7	..	..	..	4.9	..	106	..	99	60	29
Kenya	4.7	..	..	20.1	16.4	..	..	..	95	99	84
Korea, Dem. Rep.	..	..	..	..	20.6	..	..	..	..	45	33
Korea, Rep.	7.9	..	25	..	..	99	99	99	97	9	5
Kosovo	..	..	..	..	..	..	..	..	..	..	..
Kuwait	..	..	..	..	1.7	57	93	100	101	17	10
Kyrgyz Republic	8.8	..	47	..	2.7	..	94	102	101	75	37
Lao PDR	7.6	..	..	39.8	31.6	41	75	77	87	157	59
Latvia	6.8	..	7	..	..	..	95	101	100	16	8
Lebanon	..	..	..	..	4.2	..	85	101	104	40	12
Lesotho	3.0	38	..	13.8	16.6	59	70	124	107	93	84
Liberia	6.4	..	..	..	20.4	..	58	..	..	247	112
Libya	..	..	..	..	5.6	..	..	..	..	36	19
Lithuania	6.6	..	9	..	..	..	92	96	100	15	6
Macedonia, FYR	5.4	..	22	..	1.8	98	92	99	98	36	11
Madagascar	6.2	84	..	35.5	36.8	36	79	96	97	167	58
Malawi	7.0	..	..	24.4	15.5	31	59	82	100	218	110
Malaysia	4.5	29	22	22.1	..	91	97	101	103	18	6
Mali	6.5	..	..	29.0	27.9	..	59	58	78	250	191
Mauritania	6.2	..	..	43.3	16.7	33	64	71	103	129	117
Mauritius	..	12	17	..	..	115	89	102	101	24	17
Mexico	3.9	26	30	13.9	3.4	88	104	97	102	45	17
Moldova	6.8	..	32	..	3.2	..	93	105	101	37	17
Mongolia	7.1	..	..	10.8	5.3	..	93	109	103	101	29
Morocco	6.5	..	51	8.1	9.9	48	80	70	88	89	38
Mozambique	5.2	..	..	28.8	..	26	57	71	88	232	142
Myanmar	..	..	..	28.8	..	..	99	95	100	118	71
Namibia	..	..	..	21.5	17.5	74	87	106	104	73	48
Nepal	6.1	..	..	..	38.8	51	..	59	..	142	48
Netherlands	7.6	8	9	..	..	..	..	97	98	8	4
New Zealand	6.4	13	12	..	..	..	..	100	103	11	6
Nicaragua	3.8	..	45	9.6	4.3	42	75	119	102	68	26
Niger	8.3	..	..	41.0	39.9	17	40	53	75	305	160
Nigeria	5.1	..	..	35.1	26.7	..	79	77	85	212	138
Norway	9.6	..	6	..	..	100	98	102	99	9	3
Oman	..	..	..	21.4	..	74	80	89	97	48	12
Pakistan	9.0	..	62	39.0	..	..	61	48	82	130	87
Panama	3.6	34	28	..	..	86	102	99	101	31	23
Papua New Guinea	4.5	..	..	..	18.1	46	..	80	..	91	68
Paraguay	3.8	23[e]	47	2.8	..	68	94	98	100	42	23
Peru	3.9	36[e]	40[e]	8.8	5.4	..	101	96	99	78	21
Philippines	5.6	..	45[e]	29.8	..	88	94	99	102	59	33
Poland	7.6	28[e]	19	..	..	96	96	101	99	17	7
Portugal	5.8	25[e]	19	..	..	..	..	103	100	15	4
Puerto Rico	..	..	..	..	..	..	..	..	102	..	..
Qatar	3.9	..	..	..	..	71	108	98	120	19	11

	Eradicate extreme poverty and hunger					Achieve universal primary education		Promote gender equality		Reduce child mortality	
	Share of poorest quintile in national consumption or income %	Vulnerable employment Unpaid family workers and own-account workers % of total employment		Prevalence of malnutrition Underweight % of children under age 5		Primary completion rate %		Ratio of girls to boys enrollments in primary and secondary education %		Under-five mortality rate per 1,000	
	1995–2009a,b	1990	2008	1990	2004–09a	1991	2009c	1991	2009c	1990	2009
Romania	8.1	27e	31	5.0	..	96	96	99	99	32	12
Russian Federation	6.0	1	6	..	..	..	95	105	98	27	12
Rwanda	4.2	..	..	24.3	18.0	50	54	95	100	171	111
Saudi Arabia	..	..	..	..	5.3	..	93	..	91	43	21
Senegal	6.2	83	..	19.0	14.5	39	57	69	95	151	93
Serbia	9.1	..	23	..	1.8	..	96	..	101	29	7
Sierra Leone	6.1	..	..	25.4	21.3	..	88	64	84	285	192
Singapore	5.0	8	10	..	..	..	..	..	..	8	3
Slovak Republic	8.8	..	11	..	..	95	96	102	100	15	7
Slovenia	8.2	12e	11	..	..	95	96	103	99	10	3
Somalia	..	..	..	..	32.8	..	..	..	53	180	180
South Africa	3.1	..	3	..	..	76	93	104	99	62	62
Spain	7.0	22e	12	..	..	104	100	104	103	9	4
Sri Lanka	6.9	..	41e	29.3	21.6	101	97	102	..	28	15
Sudan	..	..	..	31.8	31.7	..	57	78	89	124	108
Swaziland	4.5	..	..	..	6.1	61	72	..	92	92	73
Sweden	9.1	..	7	..	..	96	94	102	99	7	3
Switzerland	7.6	9	10	..	..	53	94	97	97	8	4
Syrian Arab Republic	7.7	..	..	11.5	10.0	89	112	85	97	36	16
Tajikistan	9.3	..	..	..	14.9	..	98	..	91	117	61
Tanzania	6.8	..	88e	25.1	16.7	55	102	97	96	162	108
Thailand	3.9	70	53	16.3	7.0	..	..	99	103	32	14
Timor-Leste	9.0	..	..	..	..	..	80	..	..	184	56
Togo	5.4	..	..	21.2	22.3	35	61	59	75	150	98
Trinidad and Tobago	..	22	..	4.7	..	102	93	101	101	34	35
Tunisia	5.9	..	..	8.5	3.3	74	93	86	103	50	21
Turkey	5.7	..	35	8.7	3.5	90	93	81	93	84	20
Turkmenistan	6.0	..	..	..	..	..	..	..	..	99	45
Uganda	5.8	..	..	19.7	16.4	..	72	77	99	184	128
Ukraine	9.4	..	..	..	..	92	95	102	99	21	15
United Arab Emirates	..	..	..	..	..	103	99	104	100	17	7
United Kingdom	6.1	10	11	..	..	..	..	102	101	10	6
United States	5.4	..	..	..	1.3	..	95	100	100	11	8
Uruguay	5.6	..	25e	6.5	6.0	94	106	..	104	24	13
Uzbekistan	7.1	..	..	..	4.4	..	92	..	99	74	36
Venezuela, RB	4.9	..	30	6.7	3.7	81	95	105	102	32	18
Vietnam	7.3	..	..	40.7	20.2	..	..	..	..	55	24
West Bank and Gaza	..	..	36	..	2.2	..	82	..	104	43	30
Yemen, Rep.	7.2	..	..	29.6	..	..	61	..	..	125	66
Zambia	3.6	65	..	21.2	14.9	..	87	..	96	179	141
Zimbabwe	4.6	..	..	8.0	14.0	97	..	92	97	81	90
World	.. w	.. w	.. w	.. w	21.3 w	79 w	88 w	87 w	96 w	92 w	61 w
Low income	..	..	..	..	27.7	44	63	80	91	171	118
Middle income	..	..	..	31.7	20.8	83	92	85	97	85	51
Lower middle income	..	..	..	33.5	24.0	82	90	81	95	93	57
Upper middle income	..	..	26	..	..	88	100	98	101	51	22
Low & middle income	..	..	..	32.5	22.4	78	87	84	96	100	66
East Asia & Pacific	..	..	..	18.0	8.8	101	99	89	102	55	26
Europe & Central Asia	..	..	19	..	..	92	96	98	97	52	21
Latin America & Carib.	..	..	30	..	3.8	84	101	99	102	52	23
Middle East & N. Africa	..	..	37	..	6.8	..	95	80	96	76	33
South Asia	..	..	..	57.2	42.5	62	79	69	91	125	71
Sub-Saharan Africa	..	..	..	..	24.7	51	64	82	88	181	130
High income	..	..	12	..	..	..	98	100	99	12	7
Euro area	..	..	11	..	..	101	..	..	..	9	4

a. Data are for the most recent year available. b. See table 2.9 for survey year and whether share is based on income or consumption expenditure. c. Provisional data. d. Covers urban areas only. e. Limited coverage. f. Data are for 2009. g. Data are for 2010.

About the data

Tables 1.2–1.4 present indicators for 17 of the 21 targets specified by the Millennium Development Goals. Each of the eight goals includes one or more targets, and each target has several associated indicators for monitoring progress toward the target. Most of the targets are set as a value of a specific indicator to be attained by a certain date. In some cases the target value is set relative to a level in 1990. In others it is set at an absolute level. Some of the targets for goals 7 and 8 have not yet been quantified.

The indicators in this table relate to goals 1–4. Goal 1 has three targets between 1990 and 2015: to halve the proportion of people whose income is less than $1.25 a day, to achieve full and productive employment and decent work for all, and to halve the proportion of people who suffer from hunger. Estimates of poverty rates are in tables 2.7 and 2.8. The indicator shown here, the share of the poorest quintile in national consumption or income, is a distributional measure. Countries with more unequal distributions of consumption (or income) have a higher rate of poverty for a given average income. Vulnerable employment measures the portion of the labor force that receives the lowest wages and least security in employment. No single indicator captures the concept of suffering from hunger. Child malnutrition is a symptom of inadequate food supply, lack of essential nutrients, illnesses that deplete these nutrients, and undernourished mothers who give birth to underweight children.

Progress toward universal primary education is measured by the primary completion rate. Because many school systems do not record school completion on a consistent basis, it is estimated from the gross enrollment rate in the final grade of primary education, adjusted for repetition. Official enrollments sometimes differ significantly from attendance, and even school systems with high average enrollment ratios may have poor completion rates.

Eliminating gender disparities in education would help increase the status and capabilities of women. The ratio of female to male enrollments in primary and secondary education provides an imperfect measure of the relative accessibility of schooling for girls.

The targets for reducing under-five mortality rates are among the most challenging. Under-five mortality rates are harmonized estimates produced by a weighted least squares regression model and are available at regular intervals for most countries.

Most of the 60 indicators relating to the Millennium Development Goals can be found in *World Development Indicators*. Table 1.2a shows where to find the indicators for the first four goals. For more information about data collection methods and limitations, see *About the data* for the tables listed there. For information about the indicators for goals 5–8, see *About the data* for tables 1.3 and 1.4.

Definitions

• **Share of poorest quintile in national consumption or income** is the share of the poorest 20 percent of the population in consumption or, in some cases, income. • **Vulnerable employment** is the sum of unpaid family workers and own-account workers as a percentage of total employment. • **Prevalence of malnutrition** is the percentage of children under age 5 whose weight for age is more than two standard deviations below the median for the international reference population ages 0–59 months. The data are based on the new international child growth standards for infants and young children, called the Child Growth Standards, released in 2006 by the World Health Organization. • **Primary completion rate** is the percentage of students completing the last year of primary education. It is calculated as the total number of students in the last grade of primary education, minus the number of repeaters in that grade, divided by the total number of children of official graduation age. • **Ratio of girls to boys enrollments in primary and secondary education** is the ratio of the female to male gross-enrollment rate in primary and secondary education. • **Under-five mortality rate** is the probability that a newborn baby will die before reaching age five, if subject to current age-specific mortality rates. The probability is expressed as a rate per 1,000.

Location of indicators for Millennium Development Goals 1–4	1.2a
Goal 1. Eradicate extreme poverty and hunger	**Table**
1.1 Proportion of population below $1.25 a day	2.8
1.2 Poverty gap ratio	2.7, 2.8
1.3 Share of poorest quintile in national consumption	1.2, 2.9
1.4 Growth rate of GDP per person employed	2.4
1.5 Employment to population ratio	2.4
1.6 Proportion of employed people living below $1 per day	—
1.7 Proportion of own-account and unpaid family workers in total employment	1.2, 2.4
1.8 Prevalence of underweight in children under age five	1.2, 2.20
1.9 Proportion of population below minimum level of dietary energy consumption	2.20
Goal 2. Achieve universal primary education	
2.1 Net enrollment ratio in primary education	2.12
2.2 Proportion of pupils starting grade 1 who reach last grade of primary	2.13
2.3 Literacy rate of 15- to 24-year-olds	2.14
Goal 3. Promote gender equality and empower women	
3.1 Ratio of girls to boys in primary, secondary, and tertiary education	1.2, 2.12*
3.2 Share of women in wage employment in the nonagricultural sector	1.5, 2.3*
3.3 Proportion of seats held by women in national parliament	1.5
Goal 4. Reduce child mortality	
4.1 Under-five mortality rate	1.2, 2.22
4.2 Infant mortality rate	2.22
4.3 Proportion of one-year-old children immunized against measles	2.18

— No data are available in the World Development Indicators database. * Table shows information on related indicators.

Data sources

The indicators here and throughout this book have been compiled by World Bank staff from primary and secondary sources. Efforts have been made to harmonize the data series used to compile this table with those published on the United Nations Millennium Development Goals Web site (www.un.org/millenniumgoals), but some differences in timing, sources, and definitions remain. For more information see the data sources for the indicators listed in table 1.2a.

1.3 Millennium Development Goals: protecting our common environment

	Improve maternal health			Combat HIV/AIDS and other diseases		Ensure environmental sustainability					Develop a global partnership for development
	Maternal mortality ratio Modeled estimate per 100,000 live births	Contraceptive prevalence rate % of married women ages 15–49		HIV prevalence % of population ages 15–49	Incidence of tuberculosis per 100,000 people	Carbon dioxide emissions per capita metric tons		Proportion of species threatened with extinction %	Access to improved sanitation facilities % of population		Internet users per 100 people[a]
	2008	**1990**	**2004–09[b]**	**2009**	**2009**	**1990**	**2007**	**2008**	**1990**	**2008**	**2009**
Afghanistan	1,400	..	15	..	189	0.1	0.0	0.7	..	37	3.4
Albania	31	..	69	..	15	2.3	1.4	1.5	..	98	41.2
Algeria	120	47	61	0.1	59	3.1	4.1	2.1	88	95	13.5
Angola	610	..	..	2.0	298	0.4	1.4	1.4	25	57	3.3
Argentina	70	..	78	0.5	28	3.5	4.6	1.9	90	90	30.4
Armenia	29	..	53	0.1	73	1.1	1.6	0.9	..	90	6.8
Australia	8	..	..	0.1	6	17.2	17.7	4.7	100	100	72.0
Austria	5	..	..	0.3	11	7.9	8.3	1.9	100	100	73.5
Azerbaijan	38	..	51	0.1	110	6.0	3.7	0.8	..	45	42.0
Bangladesh	340	40	53	<0.1	225	0.1	0.3	1.9	39	53	0.4
Belarus	15	..	73	0.3	39	9.6	6.9	0.7	..	93	45.9
Belgium	5	78	75	0.2	9	10.8	9.7	1.3	100	100	75.2
Benin	410	..	17	1.2	93	0.1	0.5	1.5	5	12	2.2
Bolivia	180	30	61	0.2	140	0.8	1.4	0.8	19	25	11.2
Bosnia and Herzegovina	9	..	36	..	50	1.2	7.7	13.1	..	95	37.7
Botswana	190	33	53	24.8	694	1.6	2.6	0.5	36	60	6.2
Brazil	58	59	81	..	45	1.4	1.9	1.3	69	80	39.2
Bulgaria	13	..	..	0.1	41	8.8	6.8	1.1	99	100	44.8
Burkina Faso	560	..	17	1.2	215	0.1	0.1	1.0	6	11	1.1
Burundi	970	..	9	3.3	348	0.1	0.0	1.5	44	46	0.8
Cambodia	290	..	40	0.5	442	0.0	0.3	29.8	9	29	0.5
Cameroon	600	16	29	5.3	182	0.1	0.3	5.4	47	47	3.8
Canada	12	..	..	0.2	5	16.2	16.9	1.8	100	100	77.7
Central African Republic	850	..	19	4.7	327	0.1	0.1	0.6	11	34	0.5
Chad	1,200	..	3	3.4	283	0.0	0.0	1.0	6	9	1.7
Chile	26	56	58	0.4	11	2.6	4.3	2.4	84	96	34.0
China	38	85	85	0.1[c]	96	2.2	5.0	2.4	41	55	28.8
Hong Kong SAR, China	..	86	..	..	82	4.8	5.8	13.2	..	..	61.4
Colombia	85	66	78	0.5	35	1.7	1.4	1.2	68	74	45.5
Congo, Dem. Rep.	670	8	21	..	372	0.1	0.0	2.5	9	23	0.6
Congo, Rep.	580	..	44	3.4	382	0.5	0.4	1.0	..	30	6.7
Costa Rica	44	..	80	0.3	10	1.0	1.8	1.9	93	95	34.5
Côte d'Ivoire	470	..	13	3.4	399	0.5	0.3	3.9	20	23	4.6
Croatia	14	..	..	<0.1	25	3.8	5.6	1.8	..	99	50.4
Cuba	53	..	78	0.1	6	3.1	2.4	4.2	80	91	14.3
Czech Republic	8	78	..	<0.1	9	13.5	12.1	1.5	100	98	63.7
Denmark	5	78	..	0.2	7	9.8	9.1	1.6	100	100	85.9
Dominican Republic	100	56	73	0.9	70	1.3	2.1	2.1	73	83	26.8
Ecuador	140	53	73	0.4	68	1.6	2.2	10.4	69	92	15.1
Egypt, Arab Rep.	82	47	60	<0.1	19	1.3	2.3	4.1	72	94	20.0
El Salvador	110	47	73	0.8	30	0.5	1.1	1.8	75	87	14.4
Eritrea	280	..	..	0.8	99	..	0.1	15.0	9	14	4.9
Estonia	12	..	..	1.2	30	16.3	15.2	0.6	..	95	72.3
Ethiopia	470	4	15	..	359	0.1	0.1	1.3	4	12	0.5
Finland	8	77	..	0.1	9	10.2	12.1	1.3	100	100	83.9
France	8	81	71	0.4	6	7.0	6.0	2.5	100	100	71.3
Gabon	260	..	..	5.2	501	6.6	1.4	2.1	..	33	6.7
Gambia, The	400	12	..	2.0	269	0.2	0.2	2.2	..	67	7.6
Georgia	48	..	47	0.1	107	2.9	1.4	1.0	96	95	30.5
Germany	7	75	..	0.1	5	12.0	9.6	2.2	100	100	79.5
Ghana	350	13	24	1.8	201	0.3	0.4	3.7	7	13	5.4
Greece	2	..	..	0.1	5	7.2	8.8	2.1	97	98	44.1
Guatemala	110	..	54	0.8	62	0.6	1.0	2.4	65	81	16.3
Guinea	680	..	9	1.3	318	0.2	0.1	2.2	9	19	0.9
Guinea-Bissau	1,000	..	10	2.5	229	0.2	0.2	2.4	..	21	2.3
Haiti	300	10	32	1.9	238	0.1	0.2	2.3	26	17	10.0
Honduras	110	47	65	0.8	58	0.5	1.2	3.5	44	71	9.8

	Improve maternal health			Combat HIV/AIDS and other diseases		Ensure environmental sustainability					Develop a global partnership for development
	Maternal mortality ratio Modeled estimate per 100,000 live births	Contraceptive prevalence rate % of married women ages 15–49		HIV prevalence % of population ages 15–49	Incidence of tuberculosis per 100,000 people	Carbon dioxide emissions per capita metric tons		Proportion of species threatened with extinction %	Access to improved sanitation facilities % of population		Internet users per 100 people[a]
	2008	**1990**	**2004–09[b]**	**2009**	**2009**	**1990**	**2007**	**2008**	**1990**	**2008**	**2009**
Hungary	13	..	..	<0.1	16	6.1	5.6	1.8	100	100	61.6
India	230	43	54	0.3	168	0.8	1.4	3.3	18	31	5.3
Indonesia	240	50	57	0.2	189	0.8	1.8	3.4	33	52	8.7
Iran, Islamic Rep.	30	49	79	0.2	19	4.2	7.0	1.0	83	..	38.3
Iraq	75	14	50	..	64	2.8	3.3	11.0	..	73	1.0
Ireland	3	60	89	0.2	9	8.6	10.2	1.8	99	99	68.4
Israel	7	68	..	0.2	5	7.2	9.3	4.3	100	100	49.7
Italy	5	..	..	0.3	6	7.5	7.7	2.2	..	..	48.5
Jamaica	89	55	..	1.7	7	3.3	5.2	7.7	83	83	58.6
Japan	6	58	54	<0.1	21	9.3	9.8	4.9	100	100	77.7
Jordan	59	40	59	..	6	3.3	3.8	3.4	..	98	29.3
Kazakhstan	45	..	51	0.1	163	15.9	14.7	1.1	96	97	33.4
Kenya	530	27	46	6.3	305	0.2	0.3	3.9	26	31	10.0
Korea, Dem. Rep.	250	62	..	..	345	12.1	3.0	1.3	..	..	0.0
Korea, Rep.	18	79	80	<0.1	90	5.6	10.4	1.7	100	100	80.9
Kosovo	..	..	..	..	..	..	..	..	..	..	..
Kuwait	9	..	..	..	35	19.2	32.3	6.3	100	100	39.4
Kyrgyz Republic	81	..	48	0.3	159	2.4	1.2	0.8	..	93	41.2
Lao PDR	580	..	38	0.2	89	0.1	0.3	1.2	..	53	4.7
Latvia	20	..	..	0.7	45	5.1	3.4	1.4	..	78	66.7
Lebanon	26	..	58	0.1	15	3.1	3.2	1.2	..	..	23.7
Lesotho	530	23	47	23.6	634	..	..	0.6	32	29	3.7.
Liberia	990	..	11	1.5	288	0.2	0.2	3.8	11	17	0.5
Libya	64	..	..	..	40	9.2	9.3	1.6	97	97	5.5
Lithuania	13	..	..	0.1	71	6.0	4.5	0.9	..	..	58.8
Macedonia, FYR	9	..	14	..	23	5.6	5.5	0.9	..	89	51.8
Madagascar	440	17	40	0.2	261	0.1	0.1	6.4	8	11	1.6
Malawi	510	13	41	11.0	304	0.1	0.1	3.3	42	56	4.7
Malaysia	31	50	..	0.5	83	3.1	7.3	6.9	84	96	57.6
Mali	830	..	8	1.0	324	0.0	0.0	1.0	26	36	1.9
Mauritania	550	3	9	0.7	330	1.3	0.6	2.9	16	26	2.3
Mauritius	36	75	..	1.0	22	1.4	3.1	24.3	91	91	22.7
Mexico	85	..	73	0.3	17	4.3	4.5	3.2	66	85	26.5
Moldova	32	..	68	0.4	178	4.8	1.3	1.3	..	79	35.9
Mongolia	65	..	55	<0.1	224	4.5	4.0	1.1	..	50	13.1
Morocco	110	42	63	0.1	92	0.9	1.5	1.9	53	69	32.2
Mozambique	550	..	16	11.5	409	0.1	0.1	2.9	11	17	2.7
Myanmar	240	17	41	0.6	404	0.1	0.3	2.7	..	81	0.2
Namibia	180	29	55	13.1	727	0.0	1.5	2.1	25	33	5.9
Nepal	380	23	48	0.4	163	0.0	0.1	1.1	11	31	2.1
Netherlands	9	76	69	0.2	8	11.0	10.6	1.3	100	100	90.0
New Zealand	14	..	..	0.1	8	6.9	7.7	5.1	..	..	83.4
Nicaragua	100	..	72	0.2	44	0.6	0.8	1.3	43	52	3.5
Niger	820	4	11	0.8	181	0.1	0.1	1.0	5	9	0.8
Nigeria	840	6	15	3.6	295	0.5	0.6	4.3	37	32	28.4
Norway	7	74	88	0.1	6	7.4	9.1	1.5	100	100	91.8
Oman	20	9	..	0.1	13	5.6	13.7	4.2	85	..	43.5
Pakistan	260	15	30	0.1	231	0.6	1.0	1.7	28	45	12.0
Panama	71	..	..	0.9	48	1.3	2.2	2.9	58	69	27.8
Papua New Guinea	250	..	32	0.9	250	0.5	0.5	3.6	47	45	1.9
Paraguay	95	48	79	0.3	47	0.5	0.7	0.5	37	70	15.8
Peru	98	59	73	0.4	113	1.0	1.5	2.8	54	68	27.7
Philippines	94	36	51	<0.1	280	0.7	0.8	6.6	58	76	6.5
Poland	6	49	..	0.1	24	9.1	8.3	1.2	..	90	58.8
Portugal	7	..	67	0.6	30	4.5	5.5	2.8	92	100	48.6
Puerto Rico	18	..	..	..	2	..	..	3.6	..	..	25.2
Qatar	8	..	..	0.1	49	25.2	55.4	..	100	100	28.3

	Improve maternal health			Combat HIV/AIDS and other diseases		Ensure environmental sustainability					Develop a global partnership for development
	Maternal mortality ratio Modeled estimate per 100,000 live births	Contraceptive prevalence rate % of married women ages 15–49		HIV prevalence % of population ages 15–49	Incidence of tuberculosis per 100,000 people	Carbon dioxide emissions per capita metric tons		Proportion of species threatened with extinction %	Access to improved sanitation facilities % of population		Internet users per 100 people[a]
	2008	**1990**	**2004–09[b]**	**2009**	**2009**	**1990**	**2007**	**2008**	**1990**	**2008**	**2009**
Romania	27	..	70	0.1	125	6.8	4.4	1.6	71	72	36.2
Russian Federation	39	*34*	80	1.0	106	13.9	10.8	1.3	87	87	42.1
Rwanda	540	*21*	36	2.9	376	0.1	0.1	1.6	23	54	4.5
Saudi Arabia	24	..	24	..	18	13.2	16.6	3.8	..	..	38.6
Senegal	410	..	12	0.9	282	0.4	0.5	2.2	38	51	7.4
Serbia	8	..	41	0.1	21	..	..	..	..	92	56.1
Sierra Leone	970	..	8	1.6	644	0.1	0.2	3.2	..	13	0.3
Singapore	9	*65*	..	0.1	36	15.4	11.8	9.7	99	100	73.3
Slovak Republic	6	*74*	..	<0.1	9	8.6	6.8	1.1	100	100	75.0
Slovenia	18	..	..	<0.1	12	6.2	7.5	2.1	100	100	63.6
Somalia	1,200	*1*	15	0.7	285	0.0	0.1	3.2	..	23	1.2
South Africa	410	*57*	..	17.8	971	9.5	9.0	1.6	69	77	9.0
Spain	6	..	66	0.4	17	5.9	8.0	3.8	100	100	61.2
Sri Lanka	39	..	68	<0.1	66	0.2	0.6	14.0	70	91	8.7
Sudan	750	*9*	8	1.1	119	0.2	0.3	2.4	34	34	9.9
Swaziland	420	*20*	51	25.9	1,257	0.5	0.9	0.8	..	55	7.6
Sweden	5	..	..	0.1	6	6.0	5.4	1.4	100	100	90.3
Switzerland	10	..	..	0.4	5	6.4	5.0	1.4	100	100	70.9
Syrian Arab Republic	46	..	58	..	21	2.9	3.5	2.0	83	96	18.7
Tajikistan	64	..	37	0.2	202	3.9	1.1	0.8	..	94	10.1
Tanzania	790	*10*	26	5.6	183	0.1	0.1	5.1	24	24	1.5
Thailand	48	..	77	1.3	137	1.7	4.1	3.4	80	96	25.8
Timor-Leste	370	..	22[d]	..	498	..	0.2	..	..	50	
Togo	350	*34*	17	3.2	446	0.2	0.2	1.2	13	12	5.4
Trinidad and Tobago	55	..	43	1.5	23	13.9	27.9	1.7	93	92	36.2
Tunisia	60	*50*	60	<0.1	24	1.6	2.3	2.1	74	85	33.5
Turkey	23	*63*	73	<0.1	29	2.7	4.0	1.4	84	90	35.3
Turkmenistan	77	..	48	..	67	7.2	9.2	10.7	98	98	1.6
Uganda	430	*5*	24	6.5	293	0.0	0.1	2.5	39	48	9.8
Ukraine	26	..	67	1.1	101	*11.7*	6.8	1.1	95	95	33.3
United Arab Emirates	10	..	..	..	4	29.3	31.0	14.1	97	97	82.2
United Kingdom	12	..	..	0.2	12	10.0	8.8	2.8	100	100	83.2
United States	24	*71*	..	0.6	4	19.5	19.3	5.7	100	100	78.1
Uruguay	27	..	78	0.5	22	1.3	1.9	2.6	94	100	55.5
Uzbekistan	30	..	65	0.1	128	5.3	4.3	1.0	84	100	16.9
Venezuela, RB	68	..	..	..	33	6.2	6.0	1.1	82	..	31.2
Vietnam	56	*53*	80	0.4	200	0.3	1.3	3.5	35	75	27.5
West Bank and Gaza	..	..	50		19	..	0.6	..	..	89	8.8
Yemen, Rep.	210	*10*	28		54	0.8	1.0	12.6	18	52	1.8
Zambia	470	*15*	41	13.5	433	0.3	0.2	0.7	46	49	6.3
Zimbabwe	790	*43*	65	14.3	742	1.5	0.8	0.9	43	44	11.4
World	**260 w**	**57 w**	**61 w[b]**	**0.8 w**	**137 w**	**4.3[e] w**	**4.6[e] w**		**52 w**	**61 w**	**27.1 w**
Low income	580	23	33	2.7	294	0.7	0.3		23	35	2.7
Middle income	200	58	66	0.6	138	2.6	3.3		45	57	20.9
Lower middle income	230	60	63	0.4	147	1.6	2.8		37	50	17.2
Upper middle income	82	52	75	1.4	101	6.1	5.3		78	84	34.6
Low & middle income	290	54	61	0.9	161	2.4	2.9		43	54	18.1
East Asia & Pacific	89	75	77	0.2	136	1.9	4.0		42	59	24.1
Europe & Central Asia	32	..	69	0.6	89	10.7	7.2		87	89	36.4
Latin America & Carib.	86	..	75	0.5	45	2.3	2.7		69	79	31.5
Middle East & N. Africa	88	42	62	0.1	39	2.5	3.7		73	84	21.5
South Asia	290	40	51	0.3	180	0.7	1.2		22	36	5.5
Sub-Saharan Africa	650	15	21	5.4	342	0.9	0.8		27	31	8.8
High income	15	70	..	0.3	14	11.9	12.5		100	99	72.3
Euro area	7	..	..	0.3	9	8.6	8.2		100	100	67.3

a. Data are from the International Telecommunication Union's (ITU) World Telecommunication Development Report database. Please cite ITU for third-party use of these data. b. Data are for the most recent year available. c. Includes Hong Kong SAR, China. d. Data are for 2010. e. Includes emissions not allocated to specific countries.

The Millennium Development Goals address concerns common to all economies. Diseases and environmental degradation do not respect national boundaries. Epidemic diseases, wherever they occur, pose a threat to people everywhere. And environmental damage in one location may affect the well-being of plants, animals, and humans far away. The indicators in the table relate to goals 5, 6, and 7 and the targets of goal 8 that address access to new technologies. For the other targets of goal 8, see table 1.4.

The target of achieving universal access to reproductive health has been added to goal 5 to address the importance of family planning and health services in improving maternal health and preventing maternal death. Women with multiple pregnancies are more likely to die in childbirth. Access to contraception is an important way to limit and space births.

Measuring disease prevalence or incidence can be difficult. Most developing economies lack reporting systems for monitoring diseases. Estimates are often derived from survey data and report data from sentinel sites, extrapolated to the general population. Tracking diseases such as HIV/AIDS, which has a long latency between contraction of the virus and the appearance of symptoms, or malaria, which has periods of dormancy, can be particularly difficult. The table shows the estimated prevalence of HIV among adults ages 15–49. Prevalence among older populations can be affected by life-prolonging treatment. The incidence of tuberculosis is based on case notifications and estimates of cases detected in the population.

Carbon dioxide emissions are the primary source of greenhouse gases, which contribute to global warming, threatening human and natural habitats. In recognition of the vulnerability of animal and plant species, a new target of reducing biodiversity loss has been added to goal 7.

Access to reliable supplies of safe drinking water and sanitary disposal of excreta are two of the most important means of improving human health and protecting the environment. Improved sanitation facilities prevent human, animal, and insect contact with excreta.

Internet use includes narrowband and broadband Internet. Narrowband is often limited to basic applications; broadband is essential to promote e-business, e-learning, e-government, and e-health.

• **Maternal mortality ratio** is the number of women who die from pregnancy-related causes during pregnancy and childbirth, per 100,000 live births. Data are from various years and adjusted to a common 2008 base year. The values are modeled estimates (see *About the data* for table 2.19). • **Contraceptive prevalence rate** is the percentage of women ages 15–49 married or in union who are practicing, or whose sexual partners are practicing, any form of contraception. • **HIV prevalence** is the percentage of people ages 15–49 who are infected with HIV. • **Incidence of tuberculosis** is the estimated number of new tuberculosis cases (pulmonary, smear positive, and extrapulmonary). • **Carbon dioxide emissions** are those stemming from the burning of fossil fuels and the manufacture of cement. They include emissions produced during consumption of solid, liquid, and gas fuels and gas flaring (see table 3.8). • **Proportion of species threatened with extinction** is the total number of threatened mammal (excluding whales and porpoises), bird, and higher native, vascular plant species as a percentage of the total number of known species of the same categories. • **Access to improved sanitation facilities** is the percentage of the population with at least adequate access to excreta disposal facilities (private or shared, but not public) that can effectively prevent human, animal, and insect contact with excreta (facilities do not have to include treatment to render sewage outflows innocuous). Improved facilities range from simple but protected pit latrines to flush toilets with a sewerage connection. To be effective, facilities must be correctly constructed and properly maintained. • **Internet users** are people with access to the worldwide network.

Location of indicators for Millennium Development Goals 5–7	1.3a
Goal 5. Improve maternal health	**Table**
5.1 Maternal mortality ratio	1.3, 2.19
5.2 Proportion of births attended by skilled health personnel	2.19
5.3 Contraceptive prevalence rate	1.3, 2.19
5.4 Adolescent fertility rate	2.19
5.5 Antenatal care coverage	1.5, 2.19
5.6 Unmet need for family planning	2.19
Goal 6. Combat HIV/AIDS, malaria, and other diseases	
6.1 HIV prevalence among pregnant women ages 15–24	1.3*, 2.21*
6.2 Condom use at last high-risk sex	2.21*
6.3 Proportion of population ages 15–24 with comprehensive, correct knowledge of HIV/AIDS	—
6.4 Ratio of school attendance of orphans to school attendance of nonorphans ages 10–14	—
6.5 Proportion of population with advanced HIV infection with access to antiretroviral drugs	—
6.6 Incidence and death rates associated with malaria	—
6.7 Proportion of children under age 5 sleeping under insecticide-treated bednets	2.18
6.8 Proportion of children under age 5 with fever who are treated with appropriate antimalarial drugs	2.18
6.9 Incidence, prevalence, and death rates associated with tuberculosis	1.3, 2.21
6.10 Proportion of tuberculosis cases detected and cured under directly observed treatment short course	2.18
Goal 7. Ensure environmental sustainability	
7.1 Proportion of land area covered by forest	3.1
7.2 Carbon dioxide emissions, total, per capita and per $1 purchasing power parity GDP	3.8
7.3 Consumption of ozone-depleting substances	3.9*
7.4 Proportion of fish stocks within safe biological limits	—
7.5 Proportion of total water resources used	3.5
7.6 Proportion of terrestrial and marine areas protected	—
7.7 Proportion of species threatened with extinction	1.3
7.8 Proportion of population using an improved drinking water source	1.3, 2.18, 3.5
7.9 Proportion of population using an improved sanitation facility	1.3, 2.18, 3.11
Proportion of urban population living in slums	—

— No data are available in the World Development Indicators database. * Table shows information on related indicators.

1.4 Millennium Development Goals: overcoming obstacles

	Official development assistance (ODA) by donor		Least developed countries' access to high-income markets								Support to agriculture
	Net disbursements % of donor GNI	For basic social services[a] % of total sector-allocable ODA commitments	Goods (excluding arms) admitted free of tariffs % of exports from least developed countries		Agricultural products		Average tariff on exports of least developed countries % Textiles		Clothing		% of GDP
	2009	2009	2002	2008	2002	2008	2002	2008	2002	2008	2009[b]
Australia	0.29	14.5	95.9	100.0	0.2	0.0	5.1	0.0	19.7	0.0	0.15
Canada	0.30	25.5	67.2	100.0	0.3	0.1	5.7	0.2	17.9	1.7	0.75
European Union			97.0	98.7	1.8	0.9	0.1	0.1	1.2	1.2	0.84
Austria	0.30	6.3									
Belgium	0.55	12.7									
Denmark	0.88	21.3									
Finland	0.54	5.8									
France	0.46	8.8									
Germany	0.35	8.7									
Greece	0.19	11.2									
Ireland	0.54	32.1									
Italy	0.16	12.9									
Luxembourg	1.04	35.4									
Netherlands	0.82	11.9									
Portugal	0.23	3.6									
Spain	0.46	24.2									
Sweden	1.12	10.8									
United Kingdom	0.52	21.4									
Japan	0.18	18.6	33.2	99.6	4.8	1.4	2.8	2.6	0.1	0.1	1.11
Korea, Rep.[c]	0.10	6.7	14.6	57.7	26.1	28.5	11.4	4.0	12.5	3.7	2.44
New Zealand[c]	0.28	27.7	98.0	98.2	3.1	0.0	0.3	0.0	0.3	0.0	0.20
Norway	1.06	21.9	97.9	99.9	3.8	18.0	3.1	0.0	1.3	1.0	1.07
Switzerland	0.45	9.5	93.4	100.0	5.1	0.1	0.0	0.0	0.0	0.0	1.37
United States	0.21	31.7	61.7	83.8	6.3	5.8	6.6	5.7	12.5	11.3	0.87

	HIPC decision point[d]	HIPC completion point[d]	HIPC Initiative assistance end-2009 net present value $ millions	MDRI assistance end-2009 net present value $ millions		HIPC decision point[d]	HIPC completion point[d]	HIPC Initiative assistance end-2009 net present value $ millions	MDRI assistance end-2009 net present value $ millions
Afghanistan	Jul. 2007	Jan. 2010	654	20	Haiti	Nov. 2006	Jun. 2009	164	665
Benin	Jul. 2000	Mar. 2003	385	754	Honduras	Jul. 2000	Apr. 2005	816	1,893
Bolivia[e]	Feb. 2000	Jun. 2001	1,949	1,953	Liberia	Mar. 2008	Jun. 2010	2,958	243
Burkina Faso[e,f]	Jul. 2000	Apr. 2002	812	764	Madagascar	Dec. 2000	Oct. 2004	1,228	1,598
Burundi	Aug. 2005	Jan. 2009	1,009	58	Malawi[f]	Dec. 2000	Aug. 2006	1,379	898
Cameroon	Oct. 2000	Apr. 2006	1,861	646	Mali[e]	Sep. 2000	Mar. 2003	792	1,308
Central African Republic	Sep. 2007	Jun. 2009	675	435	Mauritania	Feb. 2000	Jun. 2002	913	558
Chad	May 2001	Floating	241	..	Mozambique[e]	Apr. 2000	Sep. 2001	3,147	1,322
Comoros	Jun. 2010	Floating	151	..	Nicaragua	Dec. 2000	Jan. 2004	4,861	1,191
Congo, Dem. Rep.	Jul. 2003	Jul. 2010	9,493	515	Niger[f]	Dec. 2000	Apr. 2004	947	651
Congo, Rep.	Mar. 2006	Jan. 2010	1,906	120	Rwanda[f]	Dec. 2000	Apr. 2005	956	283
Côte d'Ivoire	Mar. 2009	Floating	3,245	..	São Tomé & Principe[f]	Dec. 2000	Mar. 2007	172	34
Ethiopia[f]	Nov. 2001	Apr. 2004	2,735	1,862	Senegal	Jun. 2000	Apr. 2004	717	1,661
Gambia, The	Dec. 2000	Dec. 2007	98	232	Sierra Leone	Mar. 2002	Dec. 2006	919	465
Ghana	Feb. 2002	Jul. 2004	3,091	2,570	Tanzania	Apr. 2000	Nov. 2001	2,977	2,517
Guinea	Dec. 2000	Floating	801	..	Togo	Nov. 2008	Dec. 2010	305	463
Guinea-Bissau	Dec. 2000	Dec. 2010	746	77	Uganda[e]	Feb. 2000	May 2000	1,509	2,245
Guyana[e]	Nov. 2000	Dec. 2003	897	493	Zambia	Dec. 2000	Apr. 2005	3,672	1,962

a. Includes primary education, basic life skills for youth, adult and early childhood education, basic health care, basic health infrastructure, basic nutrition, infectious disease control, health education, health personnel development, population policy and administrative management, reproductive health care, family planning, sexually transmitted disease control including HIV/AIDS, personnel development for population and reproductive health, basic drinking water supply and basic sanitation, and multisector aid for basic social services.
b. Provisional data. c. Calculated by World Bank staff using the World Integrated Trade Solution based on the United Nations Conference on Trade and Development's Trade Analysis and Information Systems database. d. Refers to the Enhanced HIPC Initiative. e. Also reached completion point under the original HIPC Initiative. The assistance includes original debt relief. f. Assistance includes topping up at completion point.

About the data

Achieving the Millennium Development Goals requires an open, rule-based global economy in which all countries, rich and poor, participate. Many poor countries, lacking the resources to finance development, burdened by unsustainable debt, and unable to compete globally, need assistance from rich countries. For goal 8—develop a global partnership for development—many indicators therefore monitor the actions of members of the Organisation for Economic Co-operation and Development's (OECD) Development Assistance Committee (DAC).

Official development assistance (ODA) has risen in recent years as a share of donor countries' gross national income (GNI), but the poorest economies need additional assistance to achieve the Millennium Development Goals. In 2009 total net ODA from OECD DAC members rose 0.7 percent in real terms to $119.6 billion, representing 0.31 percent of DAC members' combined gross national income.

One important action that high-income economies can take is to reduce barriers to exports from low- and middle-income economies. The European Union has begun to eliminate tariffs on exports of "everything but arms" from least developed countries, and the United States offers special concessions to Sub-Saharan African exports. However, these programs still have many restrictions.

Average tariffs in the table reflect high-income OECD member tariff schedules for exports of countries designated least developed countries by the United Nations. Although average tariffs have been falling, averages may disguise high tariffs on specific goods (see table 6.8 for each country's share of tariff lines with "international peaks"). The averages in the table include ad valorem duties and equivalents.

Subsidies to agricultural producers and exporters in OECD countries are another barrier to developing economies' exports. Agricultural subsidies in OECD economies are estimated at $384 billion in 2009.

The Debt Initiative for Heavily Indebted Poor Countries (HIPCs), an important step in placing debt relief within the framework of poverty reduction, is the first comprehensive approach to reducing the external debt of the world's poorest, most heavily indebted countries. A 1999 review led to an enhancement of the framework. In 2005, to further reduce the debt of HIPCs and provide resources for meeting the Millennium Development Goals, the Multilateral Debt Relief Initiative (MDRI), proposed by the Group of Eight countries, was launched.

Under the MDRI four multilateral institutions—the International Development Association (IDA), International Monetary Fund (IMF), African Development Fund (AfDF), and Inter-American Development Bank (IDB)—provide 100 percent debt relief on eligible debts due to them from countries having completed the HIPC Initiative process. Data in the table refer to status as of March 2011 and might not show countries that have since reached the decision or completion point. Debt relief under the HIPC Initiative has reduced future debt payments by $59 billion (in end-2009 net present value terms) for 36 countries that have reached the decision point. And 32 countries that have reached the completion point have received additional assistance of $30 billion (in end-2009 net present value terms) under the MDRI.

Definitions

• **Official development assistance (ODA) net disbursements** are grants and loans (net of repayments of principal) that meet the DAC definition of ODA and are made to countries on the DAC list of recipients. • **ODA for basic social services** is aid commitments by DAC donors for basic education, primary health care, nutrition, population policies and programs, reproductive health, and water and sanitation services. • **Goods admitted free of tariffs** are exports of goods (excluding arms) from least developed countries admitted without tariff. • **Average tariff** is the unweighted average of the effectively applied rates for all products subject to tariffs. • **Agricultural products** are plant and animal products, including tree crops but excluding timber and fish products. • **Textiles** and **clothing** are natural and synthetic fibers and fabrics and articles of clothing made from them. • **Support to agriculture** is the value of gross transfers from taxpayers and consumers arising from policy measures, net of associated budgetary receipts, regardless of their objectives and impacts on farm production and income or consumption of farm products. • **HIPC decision point** is the date when a heavily indebted poor country with an established track record of good performance under adjustment programs supported by the IMF and the World Bank commits to additional reforms and a poverty reduction strategy and starts receiving debt relief. • **HIPC completion point** is the date when a country successfully completes the key structural reforms agreed on at the decision point, including implementing a poverty reduction strategy. The country then receives full debt relief under the HIPC Initiative without further policy conditions. • **HIPC Initiative assistance** is the debt relief committed as of the decision point (assuming full participation of creditors). Topping-up assistance and assistance provided under the original HIPC Initiative were committed in net present value terms as of the decision point and are converted to end-2009 terms. • **MDRI assistance** is 100 percent debt relief on eligible debt from IDA, IMF, AfDF, and IDB, delivered in full to countries having reached the HIPC completion point.

Data sources

Data on ODA are from the OECD. Data on goods admitted free of tariffs and average tariffs are from the World Trade Organization, in collaboration with the United Nations Conference on Trade and Development and the International Trade Centre. These data are available at www.mdg-trade. org. Data on subsidies to agriculture are from the OECD's *Producer and Consumer Support Estimates, OECD Database 1986–2009*. Data on the HIPC Initiative and MDRI are from the World Bank's Economic Policy and Debt Department.

Location of indicators for Millennium Development Goal 8 | **1.4a**

Goal 8. Develop a global partnership for development	Table
8.1 Net ODA as a percentage of DAC donors' gross national income	1.4, 6.14
8.2 Proportion of ODA for basic social services	1.4
8.3 Proportion of ODA that is untied	6.15b
8.4 Proportion of ODA received in landlocked countries as a percentage of GNI	—
8.5 Proportion of ODA received in small island developing states as a percentage of GNI	—
8.6 Proportion of total developed country imports (by value, excluding arms) from least developed countries admitted free of duty	1.4
8.7 Average tariffs imposed by developed countries on agricultural products and textiles and clothing from least developed countries	1.4, 6.8*
8.8 Agricultural support estimate for OECD countries as a percentage of GDP	1.4
8.9 Proportion of ODA provided to help build trade capacity	—
8.10 Number of countries reaching HIPC decision and completion points	1.4
8.11 Debt relief committed under new HIPC initiative	1.4
8.12 Debt services as a percentage of exports of goods and services	6.11*
8.13 Proportion of population with access to affordable, essential drugs on a sustainable basis	—
8.14 Telephone lines per 100 people	1.3*, 5.11
8.15 Cellular subscribers per 100 people	1.3*, 5.11
8.16 Internet users per 100 people	5.12

— No data are available in the World Development Indicators database. * Table shows information on related indicators.

Women in development

	Female population	Life expectancy at birth		Pregnant women receiving prenatal care	Teenage mothers	Women in wage employment in nonagricultural sector	Unpaid family workers		Female part-time employment	Ratio of female to male wages in manufacturing	Women in parliaments	
		years				% of nonagricultural wage employment	Male % of male employment	Female % of female employment		%		
	% of total	Male	Female	%	% of women ages 15–19				% of total		% of total seats	
	2009	**2009**	**2009**	**2004–09ᵃ**	**2004–09ᵃ**	**2008**	**2008**	**2008**	**2004–09ᵃ**	**2004–09ᵃ**	**1990**	**2010**
Afghanistan	48.2	44	44	36	..	..	..	..	..	..	4	28
Albania	50.6	74	80	97	..	..	..	..	..	..	29	16
Algeria	49.5	71	74	89	..	13	..	..	..	..	2	8
Angola	50.7	46	50	80	29	..	..	..	..	..	15	39
Argentina	51.0	72	79	99	..	45	0.7ᵇ	1.6ᵇ	61ᵇ	..	6	39
Armenia	53.4	71	77	93	5	45	..	..	..	..	36	9
Australia	50.3	79	84	..	..	47	0.2	0.4	71ᵇ	90	6	25
Austria	51.2	77	83	..	..	47	2.0	2.7	81	..	12	28
Azerbaijan	51.1	68	73	77	6	44	0.0	0.0	..	..	..	11
Bangladesh	49.4	66	68	51	33	..	..	..	..	..	10	19
Belarus	53.5	65	76	99	..	56	..	..	..	..	..	35
Belgium	51.0	78	84	..	..	47	0.4	2.2	81	86	9	39
Benin	49.5	61	63	84	21	..	..	..	..	..	3	11
Bolivia	50.1	64	68	86	..	38	..	..	..	..	9	25
Bosnia and Herzegovina	51.9	73	78	99	..	36	2.0	8.9	..	..	..	19
Botswana	50.0	55	55	94	..	43	..	..	..	66	5	8
Brazil	50.8	69	76	97	..	42	4.6	8.1	..	..	5	9
Bulgaria	51.7	70	77	..	..	51	0.6	1.5	54	69	21	21
Burkina Faso	50.1	52	55	85	..	..	..	..	..	..	..	15
Burundi	51.0	49	52	92	..	..	..	..	..	..	..	32
Cambodia	51.1	60	63	83ᵇ	8	..	..	..	..	..	..	21
Cameroon	50.0	51	52	82	28	..	..	..	..	..	14	14
Canada	50.5	79	84	..	..	50	0.1	0.2	68ᵇ	..	13	22
Central African Republic	50.9	46	49	69	..	..	..	..	..	..	4	10
Chad	50.3	48	50	39	37	..	..	..	..	..	..	5
Chile	50.5	76	82	..	..	36	0.9	2.8	56	..	..	14
China	48.1ᶜ	72ᶜ	75ᶜ	91	..	..	..	..	..	..	21	21
Hong Kong SAR, China	52.6	80	86	..	..	49	0.1ᵇ	1.1ᵇ	..	59	..	..
Colombia	50.8	70	77	94	21	48	3.2	6.1	..	60	5	8
Congo, Dem. Rep.	50.4	46	49	85	24	..	..	..	..	..	5	8
Congo, Rep.	50.1	53	55	86	27	..	..	..	..	..	14	7
Costa Rica	49.2	77	82	90	..	42	1.3	2.8	..	70	11	39
Côte d'Ivoire	49.1	57	59	85	..	..	..	..	..	..	6	9
Croatia	51.8	73	80	100ᵇ	4	45ᵈ	0.9ᵈ	3.9ᵈ	59	77	..	24
Cuba	49.9	77	81	100	..	43	..	..	..	..	34	43
Czech Republic	50.9	74	80	..	..	46	0.3	1.0	69	..	..	22
Denmark	50.4	77	81	..	..	49	0.3	0.5	62	87	31	38
Dominican Republic	49.8	70	76	99	21	39	2.9	3.4	..	..	8	21
Ecuador	49.9	72	78	84	19	39	4.4ᵇ	11.1ᵇ	..	..	5	32
Egypt, Arab Rep.	49.7	69	72	74	10	19	8.6	32.6	..	76	4	2
El Salvador	52.8	67	76	94	..	48	8.8	9.9	..	85	12	19
Eritrea	50.8	58	62	..	..	..	..	..	..	..	..	22
Estonia	53.9	70	80	..	..	52	0.0ᵇ	0.0ᵇ	68	..	..	23
Ethiopia	50.3	54	57	28	17	47	7.8ᵇ	12.7ᵇ	56ᵇ	..	..	28
Finland	51.0	77	83	..	..	51	0.6	0.4	64	84	32	40
France	51.4	78	85	..	..	49	0.3	0.9	80	82	7	19
Gabon	50.0	60	62	..	..	..	..	..	..	..	13	15
Gambia, The	50.4	55	58	98	..	..	..	..	..	..	8	8
Georgia	53.0	68	75	94	10	46	..	..	56	61	..	7
Germany	51.0	77	83	..	..	47	0.4	1.5	80	74	..	33
Ghana	49.3	56	58	90	13	..	..	..	..	..	..	8
Greece	50.4	78	83	..	..	42	3.4	9.8	68	..	7	17
Guatemala	51.3	67	74	..	..	43	..	..	..	..	7	12
Guinea	49.5	56	60	88	32	..	..	..	..	..	..	19
Guinea-Bissau	50.5	47	50	78	..	..	..	..	..	..	20	10
Haiti	50.6	60	63	85	14	..	..	..	..	..	..	4
Honduras	50.0	70	75	92	22	34	..	..	..	..	10	18

Women in development

1.5

	Female population	Life expectancy at birth		Pregnant women receiving prenatal care	Teenage mothers	Women in wage employment in nonagricultural sector	Unpaid family workers		Female part-time employment	Ratio of female to male wages in manufacturing	Women in parliaments	
		years				% of nonagricultural wage employment	Male % of male employment	Female % of female employment			% of total seats	
	% of total	Male	Female	%	% of women ages 15–19				% of total	%		
	2009	2009	2009	2004–09[a]	2004–09[a]	2008	2008	2008	2004–09[a]	2004–09[a]	1990	2010
Hungary	52.5	70	78	..	..	48	0.3	0.5	65	77	21	9
India	48.3	63	66	75	16	..	..	..	..	..	5	11
Indonesia	50.1	69	73	93	9	32	7.8	33.6	..	..	12	18
Iran, Islamic Rep.	49.2	70	73	98	..	..	5.4	32.7	..	..	2	3
Iraq	49.4	65	72	84	..	12	..	..	..	..	11	25
Ireland	49.9	77	82	..	..	49	0.6	0.8	77	..	8	14
Israel	50.4	80	84	..	..	49	0.1	0.4	73	..	7	18
Italy	51.4	79	84	..	..	44	1.2	2.5	78	..	13	21
Jamaica	51.1	69	75	91	..	48	0.5	2.2	..	..	5	13
Japan	51.3	80	86	..	..	42	1.1	7.3	70	60	1	11
Jordan	48.7	71	75	99	4	16	..	..	..	61	0	6
Kazakhstan	52.4	64	74	100	7	50	..	..	..	70	..	18
Kenya	50.0	54	55	92	..	..	..	..	..	..	1	10
Korea, Dem. Rep.	50.6	65	70	..	..	..	..	..	..	..	21	16
Korea, Rep.	50.5	77	84	..	..	42	1.2	12.7	59	57	2	15
Kosovo	..	68	72	..	..	..	..	..	..	..	..	8
Kuwait	40.5	76	80	..	..	..	..	..	..	..	..	8
Kyrgyz Republic	50.7	62	72	97	..	51	8.8	19.3	..	..	..	26
Lao PDR	50.1	64	67	35	17	..	26.4	64.2	..	..	6	25
Latvia	53.9	68	78	..	..	53	1.4	1.2	59	77	..	22
Lebanon	51.0	70	74	96	..	..	..	..	..	..	0	3
Lesotho	52.8	45	46	92	20	..	..	..	..	..	..	24
Liberia	50.3	57	60	79	38	..	..	..	..	..	..	13
Libya	48.3	72	77	..	..	..	..	..	..	..	..	8
Lithuania	53.2	68	79	..	..	53	1.0	2.0	60	71	..	19
Macedonia, FYR	50.1	72	77	94	..	42	7.0	14.9	47	..	..	33
Madagascar	50.2	59	62	86	34	..	..	..	..	..	7	8
Malawi	50.3	53	55	92	34	..	..	..	..	..	10	21
Malaysia	49.2	72	77	79	..	39	2.7	8.8	..	..	5	10
Mali	50.6	48	50	70	36	..	..	..	..	..	..	10
Mauritania	49.3	55	59	75	..	..	..	..	..	..	..	22
Mauritius	50.4	69	76	..	..	37	0.9	4.7	44	..	7	19
Mexico	50.8	73	78	94	..	39	4.9	10.0	65	70	12	26
Moldova	52.5	65	72	98	6	54	1.3	3.4	..	..	..	24
Mongolia	50.5	64	70	100	..	51	..	..	..	77	25	4
Morocco	50.9	69	74	68	7	21	16.5	51.8	..	..	0	11
Mozambique	51.4	47	49	89	..	..	..	..	..	..	16	39
Myanmar	51.2	60	64	80	..	..	..	..	..	89	..	..
Namibia	50.7	61	62	95	15	..	0.9	1.1	..	..	7	24
Nepal	50.3	66	68	44	19	..	..	..	..	..	6	33
Netherlands	50.4	79	83	..	..	48	0.2	0.8	75	82	21	41
New Zealand	50.6	78	82	..	..	48	0.8	1.5	72[b]	82	14	34
Nicaragua	50.5	70	77	90	25	38	12.2	9.1	..	..	15	21
Niger	49.9	51	53	46	39	36	..	..	..	..	5	12
Nigeria	49.9	48	49	58	23	..	..	..	..	..	..	7
Norway	50.3	79	83	..	..	49	0.2	0.4	71	89	36	40
Oman	43.6	75	78	..	..	22	..	..	..	..	..	0
Pakistan	48.5	67	67	61	9	13	18.6	61.9	..	..	10	22
Panama	49.6	73	79	..	..	42	2.3	4.0	47	95	8	9
Papua New Guinea	49.2	59	64	79	..	..	..	..	..	..	0	1
Paraguay	49.5	70	74	96	13	40	10.8	8.9	..	..	6	13
Peru	49.9	71	76	94	26	38	4.7[b]	9.9[b]	..	..	6	28
Philippines	49.6	70	74	91	10	42	9.0[b]	18.0[b]	..	91	9	21
Poland	51.8	72	80	..	..	47	2.7	5.9	68	..	14	20
Portugal	51.6	76	82	..	..	48	0.7	1.2	68	69	8	27
Puerto Rico	52.0	75	83	..	..	42	0.0	0.0	..	..	..	..
Qatar	24.6	75	77	..	..	13	..	..	..	142	..	0

	Female population	Life expectancy at birth		Pregnant women receiving prenatal care	Teenage mothers	Women in wage employment in nonagricultural sector	Unpaid family workers		Female part-time employment	Ratio of female to male wages in manufacturing	Women in parliaments	
			years			% of nonagricultural wage employment	Male % of male employment	Female % of female employment			% of total seats	
	% of total 2009	Male 2009	Female 2009	% 2004–09[a]	% of women ages 15–19 2004–09[a]	2008	2008	2008	% of total 2004–09[a]	% 2004–09[a]	1990	2010
Romania	51.4	70	77	94	..	46	6.0	18.9	49	74	34	11
Russian Federation	53.8	63	75	..	..	51	0.1	0.1	62	..	..	14
Rwanda	51.6	49	52	96	4	..	..	..	..	..	17	56
Saudi Arabia	44.8	73	74	..	..	15	..	..	..	..	..	0
Senegal	50.4	54	57	94	18	..	..	..	..	..	13	23
Serbia	50.5	71	76	98	..	44	3.1	11.9	..	..	..	22
Sierra Leone	51.3	47	49	87	34	..	..	..	..	..	..	13
Singapore	49.8	79	84	..	..	46	0.4[b]	1.3[b]	..	65	5	23
Slovak Republic	51.5	71	79	..	..	48	0.1	0.2	59	..	..	15
Slovenia	51.2	76	82	..	..	47	3.2	5.4	57	..	..	14
Somalia	50.4	49	52	26	..	..	..	..	..	..	4	7
South Africa	50.7	50	53	..	..	44	0.3	0.6	..	..	3	45
Spain	50.7	79	85	..	..	45	0.8	1.4	79	..	15	37
Sri Lanka	50.8	71	78	99	..	31	4.4[b]	21.7[b]	..	93	5	5
Sudan	49.6	57	60	64	..	..	..	..	..	..	..	26
Swaziland	51.1	47	46	85	23	..	..	..	..	..	4	14
Sweden	50.4	79	83	..	..	50	0.2	0.3	64	90	38	45
Switzerland	51.2	80	84	..	..	48	1.7[b]	3.2[b]	81	77	14	29
Syrian Arab Republic	49.5	73	76	84	..	16	..	..	..	..	9	12
Tajikistan	50.6	64	70	80	..	37	..	..	..	..	..	19
Tanzania	50.1	56	57	76	26	31	9.7	13.0	..	..	..	31
Thailand	50.8	66	72	98	..	45	14.0	29.9	..	..	3	13
Timor-Leste	49.1	61	63	..	..	..	..	..	..	..	..	29
Togo	50.5	61	65	84	..	..	..	..	..	..	5	11
Trinidad and Tobago	51.4	66	73	96	..	..	..	..	..	..	17	29
Tunisia	49.7	73	77	96	..	..	..	..	..	..	4	28
Turkey	49.8	70	75	95	..	22	5.3	37.7	58	..	1	9
Turkmenistan	50.7	61	69	99	..	..	..	..	..	..	26	17
Uganda	49.9	53	54	94	25	..	..	..	..	..	12	32
Ukraine	53.9	64	75	99	4	55	0.4	0.3	..	71	..	8
United Arab Emirates	32.7	77	79	..	..	20	..	..	..	..	0	23
United Kingdom	50.9	78	82	..	..	52	0.2	0.5	76	80	6	22
United States	50.7	76	81	..	..	48	0.1	0.1	67[b]	..	7	17
Uruguay	51.7	73	80	96	..	46	0.9[b]	3.0[b]	59[b]	..	6	15
Uzbekistan	50.3	65	71	99	..	39	..	..	..	..	..	22
Venezuela, RB	49.8	71	77	..	..	42	0.6	1.6	..	..	10	19
Vietnam	50.6	73	77	91	..	..	..	..	..	..	18	26
West Bank and Gaza	49.1	72	75	99	..	18	6.6	31.5	..	53	..	..
Yemen, Rep.	49.4	62	65	47	..	6	..	..	..	..	4	0
Zambia	50.1	46	47	94	28	..	..	..	..	..	7	14
Zimbabwe	51.7	45	46	93	21	..	..	..	..	..	11	15
World	**49.6 w**	**67 w**	**71 w**	**82 w**		**.. w**	**.. w**	**.. w**	**.. w**	**71 m**	**13 w**	**19 w**
Low income	50.1	56	59	67		..	..	..	..	89	..	19
Middle income	49.3	67	71	85		..	..	..	..	71	13	18
Lower middle income	48.8	66	70	83		..	..	..	..	85	13	17
Upper middle income	50.9	69	75	95		43	3.3	7.2	..	70	12	19
Low & middle income	49.4	65	69	82		..	..	..	..	71	13	18
East Asia & Pacific	48.8	71	74	91		..	..	..	..	91	17	19
Europe & Central Asia	52.2	66	75	..		48	1.9	5.3	..	71	..	15
Latin America & Carib.	50.6	71	77	95		41	4.0	7.5	..	70	12	24
Middle East & N. Africa	49.6	69	73	83		..	..	..	..	53	4	9
South Asia	48.5	63	66	70		..	..	..	..	93	6	19
Sub-Saharan Africa	50.2	51	54	71		..	..	..	..	66	..	20
High income	50.6	77	83	..		46	0.6	2.4	71	71	12	23
Euro area	51.1	78	83	..		47	0.8	1.8	78	73	12	26

a. Data are for the most recent year available. b. Limited coverage. c. Includes Taiwan, China. d. Data are for 2009.

About the data

Despite much progress in recent decades, gender inequalities remain pervasive in many dimensions of life—worldwide. But while disparities exist throughout the world, they are most prevalent in developing countries. Gender inequalities in the allocation of such resources as education, health care, nutrition, and political voice matter because of the strong association with well-being, productivity, and economic growth. These patterns of inequality begin at an early age, with boys routinely receiving a larger share of education and health spending than do girls, for example.

Because of biological differences girls are expected to experience lower infant and child mortality rates and to have a longer life expectancy than boys. This biological advantage may be overshadowed, however, by gender inequalities in nutrition and medical interventions and by inadequate care during pregnancy and delivery, so that female rates of illness and death sometimes exceed male rates. These gender bias can be seen in the child mortality rates (table 2.22) or life expectancy by gender. Female child mortality rates that are as high as or higher than male child mortality rates may indicate discrimination against girls.

Having a child during the teenage years limits girls' opportunities for better education, jobs, and income. Pregnancy is more likely to be unintended during the teenage years, and births are more likely to be premature and are associated with greater risks of complications during delivery and of death. In many countries maternal mortality (tables 1.3 and 2.19) is a leading cause of death among women of reproductive age, although most of them are preventable.

Women in wage employment in nonagricultural sector shows the extent that women have access to paid employment, which will affect their integration into the monetary economy. It also indicates the degree that labour markets are open to women in industry and services sectors which affects not only equal employment opportunity for women, but also economic efficiency through flexibility of the labor market and the economy's capacity to adapt to changes over time. In many developing countries, non-agricultural wage employment represents only a small portion of total employment. As a result the contribution of women to the national economy is underestimated and therefore misrepresented. The indicator is difficult to interpret, unless additional information is available on the share of women in total employment, which would allow an assessment to be made of whether women are under- or over-represented

in non-agricultural wage employment. The indicator does not reveal any differences in the quality of the different types of non-agricultural wage employment, regarding earnings, conditions of work, or the legal and social protection, which they offer. The indicator cannot reflect whether women are able to reap the economic benefits of such employment, either. Finally it should be noted that the female employment of any kind tends to be underreported in all kinds of surveys. In addition, the employment share of the agricultural sector, for both men and women, is severely underreported.

Women's wage work is important for economic growth and the well-being of families. But women often face such obstacles as restricted access to credit markets, capital, land, training, and education, time constraints due to their traditional family responsibilities, and labor market bias and discrimination. These obstacles force women to limit their full participation in paid economic activities, and to be less productive and to receive lower wages. More women than men are found in unpaid family employment and part time employment. The gender wage gap in manufacturing remains an unfortunate reality of almost all countries of the world, even though the gap may not be attributed entirely to discrimination.

Women are vastly underrepresented in decision-making positions in government, although there is some evidence of recent improvement. Gender parity in parliamentary representation is still far from being realized. In 2010 women accounted for 19 percent of parliamentarians worldwide, compared with 9 percent in 1987. Without representation at this level, it is difficult for women to influence policy.

For information on other aspects of gender, see tables 1.2 (Millennium Development Goals: eradicating poverty and saving lives), 1.3 (Millennium Development Goals: protecting our common environment), 2.3 (Employment by economic activity), 2.4 (Decent work and productive employment), 2.5 (Unemployment), 2.6 (Children at work), 2.10 (Assessing vulnerability and security), 2.13 (Education efficiency), 2.14 (Education completion and outcomes), 2.15 (Education gaps by income and gender), 2.19 (Reproductive health), 2.21 (Health risk factors and future challenges), and 2.22 (Mortality).

Definitions

• **Female population** is the percentage of the population that is female. • **Life expectancy at birth** is the number of years a newborn infant would live if prevailing patterns of mortality at the time of its birth were to stay the same throughout its life. • **Pregnant women receiving prenatal care** are the percentage of women attended at least once during pregnancy by skilled health personnel for reasons related to pregnancy. • **Teenage mothers** are the percentage of women ages 15–19 who already have children or are currently pregnant. • **Women in wage employment in nonagricultural sector** are female wage employees in the nonagricultural sector as a percentage of total nonagricultural wage employment. • **Unpaid family workers** are those who work without pay in a market-oriented establishment or activity operated by a related person living in the same household. • **Part-time employment, female** is a female share of total part-time workers. Part-time worker is an employed person whose normal hours of work are less than those of comparable full-time workers. Definition of part-time varies across countries. • **Ratio of female to male wages in manufacturing** is a ratio of women's wage to men's in manufacturing. • **Women in parliaments** are the percentage of parliamentary seats in a single or lower chamber held by women.

Data sources

Data on female population are from the United Nations Population Division's *World Population Prospects: The 2008 Revision*, and data on life expectancy for more than half the countries in the table (most of them developing countries) are from its *World Population Prospects: The 2008 Revision*, with additional data from census reports, other statistical publications from national statistical offices, Eurostat's *Demographic Statistics*, the Secretariat of the Pacific Community's Statistics and Demography Programme, and the U.S. Bureau of the Census International Data Base. Data on pregnant women receiving prenatal care are from UNICEF's *The State of the World's Children 2010* based on household surveys including Demographic and Health Surveys by Macro International and Multiple Indicator Cluster Surveys by UNICEF. Data on teenage mothers are from Demographic and Health Surveys by Macro International. Data on labor force, employment and wage are from the International Labour Organization's *Key Indicators of the Labour Market*, 6th edition. Data on women in parliaments are from the Inter-Parliamentary Union.

	Population	Surface area	Population density	Gross national income				Gross domestic product		Life expectancy at birth	Adult literacy rate	Carbon dioxide emissions
				Atlas method		Purchasing power parity						
	thousands	thousand sq. km	people per sq. km	$ millions	Per capita $	$ millions	Per capita $	% growth	Per capita % growth	years	% ages 15 and older	thousand metric tons
	2009	**2009**	**2009**	**2009**	**2009**	**2009**	**2009**	**2008–09**	**2008–09**	**2009**	**2005–09[a]**	**2007**
American Samoa	67	0.2	336	..	..[b]	..	..	..	..	..	..	..
Andorra	85	0.5	181	3,447	41,130	..	..	3.6	1.6	..	..	539
Antigua and Barbuda	88	0.4	199	1,062	12,130	1,548[c]	17,670[c]	–8.5	–9.5	..	99	436
Aruba	107	0.2	592	..	..[d]	..	..	..	..	75	98	2,396
Bahamas, The	342	13.9	34	7,136	21,390	..	..	2.8	1.5	74	..	2,147
Bahrain	791	0.8	1,041	19,712	25,420	26,130	33,690	6.3	4.1	76	91	22,446
Barbados	256	0.4	595	..	..[d]	..	..	..	..	77	..	1,345
Belize	333	23.0	15	1,205	3,740	1,929[c]	5,990[c]	0.0	–3.4	77	..	425
Bermuda	64	0.1	1,288	..	..[d]	..	..	–8.1	–8.4	79	..	513
Bhutan	697	38.4	18	1,405	2,020	3,692	5,290	7.4	5.8	67	53	579
Brunei Darussalam	400	5.8	76	..	..[d]	19,706	51,200	0.6	–1.3	78	95	7,599
Cape Verde	506	4.0	125	1,520	3,010	1,783	3,530	2.8	1.4	71	84	308
Cayman Islands	55	0.3	229	..	..[d]	..	..	..	..	..	99	539
Channel Islands	150	0.2	789	10,242	68,610	..	..	5.9	5.7	79	..	..
Comoros	659	1.9	354	531	810	779	1,180	1.8	–0.6	66	74	121
Cyprus	871	9.3	94	24,400[e]	30,480[e]	24,250[e]	30,290[e]	–1.0[e]	–1.9[e]	80	98	8,193
Djibouti	864	23.2	37	1,106	1,280	2,140	2,480	5.0	3.2	56	..	487
Dominica	74	0.8	98	360	4,900	623[c]	8,460[c]	–0.8	–1.3	..	..	121
Equatorial Guinea	676	28.1	24	8,398	12,420	13,069	19,330	–5.4	–7.8	51	93	4,793
Faeroe Islands	49	1.4	35	..	..[d]	..	..	..	..	80	..	696
Fiji	849	18.3	46	3,259	3,840[f]	3,850	4,530	–3.0	–3.6	69	..	1,458
French Polynesia	269	4.0	74	..	..[d]	..	..	..	..	75	..	806
Gibraltar	31	0.0	3,105	..	..[d]	..	..	..	..	..	..	407
Greenland	56	410.5	0[g]	1,467	26,160	..	..	–5.4	–5.0	68	..	520
Grenada	104	0.3	306	580	5,580	802[c]	7,710[c]	–6.8	–7.1	75	..	242
Guam	178	0.5	329	..	..[d]	..	..	..	..	76	..	..
Guyana	762	215.0	4	2,026	2,660	2,491[c]	3,270[c]	3.3	3.4	68	..	1,506
Iceland	319	103.0	3	13,858	43,430	10,478	32,840	–6.5	–7.0	81	..	2,338
Isle of Man	80	0.6	141	3,972	49,310	..	..	7.5	7.4	..	..	..

About the data

The table shows data for economies with populations between 30,000 and 1 million and for smaller economies if they are members of the World Bank. Where data on gross national income (GNI) per capita are not available, the estimated range is given. For more information on the calculation of GNI and purchasing power parity (PPP) conversion factors, see *About the data* for table 1.1. Additional data for the economies in the table are available on the *World Development Indicators* CD-ROM or in *WDI Online*.

Definitions

• **Population** is based on the de facto definition of population, which counts all residents regardless of legal status or citizenship—except for refugees not permanently settled in the country of asylum, who are generally considered part of the population of their country of origin. The values shown are midyear estimates. For more information, see *About the data* for table 2.1. • **Surface area** is a country's total area, including areas under inland bodies of water and some coastal waterways. • **Population density** is midyear population divided by land area in square kilometers. • **Gross national income (GNI), Atlas method,** is the sum of value added by all resident producers plus any product taxes (less subsidies) not included in the valuation of output plus net receipts of primary income (compensation of employees and property income) from abroad. Data are in current U.S. dollars converted using the *World Bank Atlas* method (see *Statistical methods*). • **Purchasing power parity (PPP) GNI** is GNI converted to international dollars using PPP rates. An international dollar has the same purchasing power over GNI that a U.S. dollar has in the United States. • **GNI per capita** is GNI divided by midyear population. • **Gross domestic product (GDP)** is the sum of value added by all resident producers plus any product taxes (less subsidies) not included in the valuation of output. Growth is calculated from constant price GDP data in local

Key indicators for other economies

	Population	Surface area	Population density	Gross national income				Gross domestic product		Life expectancy at birth	Adult literacy rate	Carbon dioxide emissions
				Atlas method		Purchasing power parity						
					Per capita		Per capita		Per capita		% ages 15 and older	thousand metric tons
	thousands	thousand sq. km	people per sq. km	$ millions	$	$ millions	$	% growth	% growth	years	and older	metric tons
	2009	2009	2009	2009	2009	2009	2009	2008–09	2008–09	2009	2005–09ᵃ	2007
Kiribati	98	0.8	121	180	1,830	324ᶜ	3,310ᶜ	–0.7	–2.2	..	..	33
Liechtenstein	36	0.2	224	4,906	136,630	..	..	–1.2	–1.9	83	..	..
Luxembourg	498	2.6	192	38,188	76,710	29,669	59,590	–4.1	–5.8	80	..	10,834
Macao SAR, China	538	0.0	19,213	21,275	39,550	30,874	57,390	1.3	–0.9	81	93	1,554
Maldives	309	0.3	1,031	1,229	3,970ʰ	1,625	5,250	–3.0	–4.4	72	98	898
Malta	415	0.3	1,297	7,621	18,360	9,616	23,170	–2.1	–2.8	80	92	2,722
Marshall Islands	61	0.2	339	186	3,060	..	..	0.0	–2.2	..	..	99
Mayotte	197	0.4	531	..	..ᵇ	..	..	..	..	76	..	..
Micronesia, Fed. Sts.	111	0.7	158	277	2,500	359ᶜ	3,240ᶜ	–1.5	–1.8	69	..	62
Monaco	33	0.0	16,406	6,483	197,590	..	..	–2.6	–2.9	..	..	..
Montenegro	624	13.8	46	4,149	6,650	8,183	13,110	–5.7	–6.0	74	..	..
Netherlands Antilles	198	0.8	248	..	..ᵈ	..	..	..	..	76	96	6,232
New Caledonia	250	18.6	14	..	..ᵈ	..	..	..	..	77	96	2,847
Northern Mariana Islands	87	0.5	189	..	..ᵈ	..	..	..	..	..	..	..
Palau	20	0.5	44	127	6,220	..	..	–2.1	–2.7	..	..	213
Samoa	179	2.8	63	508	2,840	763ᶜ	4,270ᶜ	–5.5	–5.5	72	99	161
San Marino	31	0.1	524	1,572	50,670	..	..	1.9	0.4	83	..	..
Sao Tome and Principe	163	1.0	170	185	1,130	301	1,850	4.0	2.4	66	88	128
Seychelles	88	0.5	191	746	8,480	1,477ᶜ	16,790ᶜ	–7.6	–8.7	74	92	623
Solomon Islands	523	28.9	19	477	910	974ᶜ	1,860ᶜ	–2.2	–4.5	67	..	198
St. Kitts and Nevis	50	0.3	191	503	10,150	676ᶜ	13,640ᶜ	–8.0	–8.8	..	..	249
St. Lucia	172	0.6	282	894	5,190	1,525ᶜ	8,860ᶜ	–3.8	–4.9	..	..	381
St. Vincent and the Grenadines	109	0.4	280	560	5,130	964ᶜ	8,830ᶜ	–2.8	–2.8	72	..	202
Suriname	520	163.8	3	2,454	4,760	3,469ᶜ	6,730ᶜ	5.1	4.2	69	95	2,437
Tonga	104	0.8	144	339	3,260	475ᶜ	4,570ᶜ	–0.4	–0.8	72	99	176
Turks and Caicos Islands	33	1.0	35	..	..ᵈ	..	..	..	..	..	..	158
Tuvalu	..	0.0	..	..	..ⁱ	..	..	..	..	..	..	..
Vanuatu	240	12.2	20	627	2,620	1,028ᶜ	4,290ᶜ	4.0	1.4	71	81	103
Virgin Islands (U.S.)	110	0.4	314	..	..ᵈ	..	..	..	..	79	..	..

a. Data are for the most recent year available. b. Estimated to be upper middle income ($3,946–$12,195). c. Based on regression; others are extrapolated from the 2005 International Comparison Program benchmark estimates. d. Estimated to be high income ($12,196 or more). e. Data are for the area controlled by the government of the Republic of Cyprus. f. Included in the aggregates for upper middle-income economies based on earlier data. g. Less than 0.5. h. Included in the aggregates for lower middle-income economies based on earlier data. i. Estimated to be lower middle income ($996–$3,945).

currency. • **GDP per capita** is GDP divided by midyear population. • **Life expectancy at birth** is the number of years a newborn infant would live if prevailing patterns of mortality at the time of its birth were to stay the same throughout its life. • **Adult literacy rate** is the percentage of adults ages 15 and older who can, with understanding, read and write a short, simple statement about their everyday life. • **Carbon dioxide emissions** are those stemming from the burning of fossil fuels and the manufacture of cement. They include carbon dioxide produced during consumption of solid, liquid, and gas fuels and gas flaring.

PEOPLE

Sustainable development is about improving the quality of peoples' lives and expanding their abilities to shape their futures. This generally calls for higher per capita incomes, but also for human capital development through improvements in health and education. Although developing countries have made large investments in human capital, good health and basic education remain elusive to many. This limits people's ability to take advantage of employment opportunities and work their way out of poverty.

The tables in this section review the achievements countries have made in improving the welfare of their people. They show the levels of poverty prevalent in countries, the distribution of income, and the prevalence of child labour—which while it reduces household poverty, is always at the expense of children's education and future human capital. The section also looks at investments in health and education and their impact on the worst aspects of nonincome poverty by reducing hunger and malnutrition, lowering mortality rates, and improving education outcomes.

This year's national and international poverty estimates were prepared by the World Bank's Global Poverty Working Group, recently established by the Poverty Board. The results of their work are evident in tables 2.7–2.9. The baseline database, with estimates for 231 data points (country and year combinations) covering 104 countries, was updated to include estimates for 577 data points covering 115 countries. Because of space restrictions in the printed edition, this report cannot include estimates for all countries. Thus, it includes only countries for which estimates are available since 2000. But the full range of these poverty estimates can be accessed through the Bank's Open Data Initiative (data.worldbank.org), and the entire database of $1.25 and $2 a day purchasing power parity poverty rate and poverty gap estimates will also be available through PovcalNet.

In addition, several new indicators have been added to existing tables. Data on children's learning assessment, from the Programme for International Student Assessment, have been added to table 2.14, and the lifetime risk of maternal death has been added to table 2.19. The new maternal mortality ratio, estimated by the Inter-Agency group, is now available in a consistent time series for the first time, and data for 1990 and the most recent year are presented in table 2.19. The entire time series can be accessed through data.worldbank.org; regional and income group aggregates for maternal mortality ratios are in figures 2a and 2b.

The next sections look at civil registration, highlighting the problems countries face in planning for

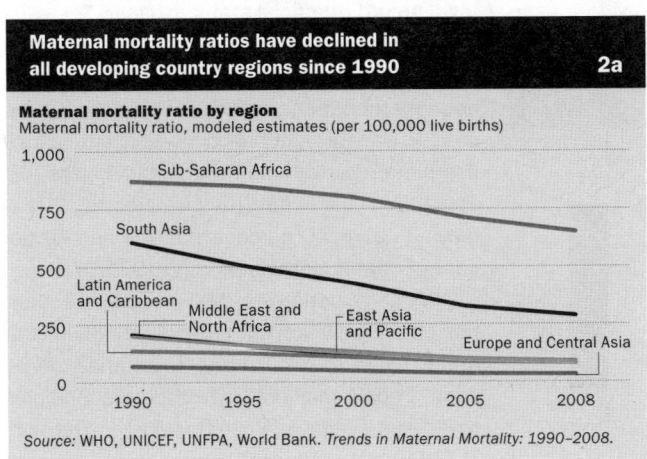

Maternal mortality ratios have declined in all developing country regions since 1990   **2a**

Maternal mortality ratio by region
Maternal mortality ratio, modeled estimates (per 100,000 live births)

Source: WHO, UNICEF, UNFPA, World Bank. *Trends in Maternal Mortality: 1990–2008.*

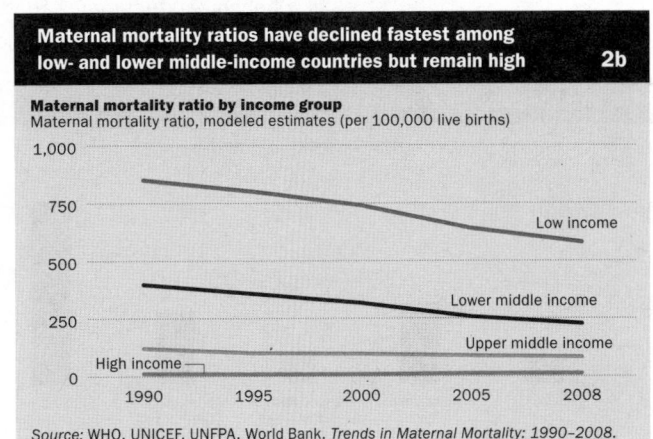

Maternal mortality ratios have declined fastest among low- and lower middle-income countries but remain high   **2b**

Maternal mortality ratio by income group
Maternal mortality ratio, modeled estimates (per 100,000 live births)

Source: WHO, UNICEF, UNFPA, World Bank. *Trends in Maternal Mortality: 1990–2008.*

the welfare of their people. Countries need to know, at a minimum, how many people are born and die each year. In most developing countries this is not easy. The discussion highlights the obstacles countries must surmount in recording births and deaths and the interim measures they have adopted, and it indicates the way forward for countries and their development partners.

Civil registration, the missing pillar

In 2009 the births of 50 million children went unrecorded. They entered the world with no proof of age, citizenship, or parentage. That same year 40 million people died unnoted except by family or friends. There are no records of where they died, when they died, and more importantly how they died.

In most high-income countries these vital events (births and deaths) are recorded by civil registration systems, which also record marriages, adoptions, and divorces. But in many developing countries registration systems are incomplete or absent. In South Asia only 1 percent of the population is covered by complete vital registration records (at least 90 percent coverage for births and deaths), and in Sub-Saharan Africa only 2 percent (UN, *Population and Vital Statistics Report, 2011*). Lacking effective registration systems, countries must rely on infrequent and expensive censuses and surveys to estimate the vital statistics needed to support the core functions of government and to plan for the future.

A state-of-the-art statistical system has three pillars: censuses and surveys, administrative records, and civil registration, each with an important and complementary role. Censuses give benchmark estimates that provide a base for and a check on vital statistics, and surveys provide detailed characteristics of the population recorded by censuses and civil registration systems. Administrative records from health and education systems add further information to manage those services and—combined with census, survey, and vital statistics—are used to plan for future needs.

Civil registration has two functions: administrative—providing legal documentation that protects identities, citizenship, property, and other economic, social, and human rights—and statistical—providing regular, frequent, and timely information on the dynamics of population growth, size, and distribution and on records of births and deaths by age, sex, and cause at the national and subnational levels. Vital statistics from civil registration systems are essential for planning basic social services and infrastructure development and for understanding and monitoring health status and health issues in the country.

A complete civil registration system has three strengths: it costs less than conducting a census or survey, data are based on a record of events rather than recall, and information can be made available at low cost. In a well functioning civil registration system a family member or caretaker reports births and deaths at the registration office in the local area and receives appropriate legal documentation. Medical certification of death from a health care provider identifies the cause of death.

To be considered complete, civil registration systems must collect information on at least 90 percent of vital events. Systems in most developing country regions fall well short of that standard. So today, most people in Africa and South Asia are born and die without a trace in any legal record or official statistic (figure 2c), causing a vicious cycle. These are the regions where most premature deaths occur and where the need for robust information for planning is most critical. Roughly half the countries claim to have complete registration of births and deaths (UN, *Population and Vital Statistics Report, 2011*), leaving nearly 40 percent of births and 70 percent of deaths unregistered (WHO 2007).

In many countries vital events are unreported or only partially reported for certain areas, ages, or populations for a variety of reasons. People may not know their responsibility to register events or where to register. They may choose not to register because of the distance to the registration offices or for cultural reasons.

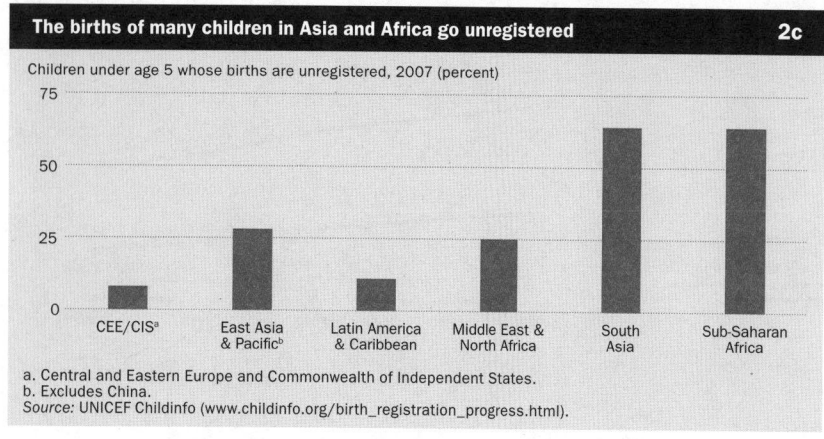

The births of many children in Asia and Africa go unregistered　　**2c**

Children under age 5 whose births are unregistered, 2007 (percent)

a. Central and Eastern Europe and Commonwealth of Independent States.
b. Excludes China.
Source: UNICEF Childinfo (www.childinfo.org/birth_registration_progress.html).

Or they cannot afford the registration costs. Data from Nigeria show that most unregistered births are found among the rural poor, for whom a significant barrier may be the distance to the nearest registration facility, and among poorly educated mothers (figures 2d–2f).

Where many infants die young, parents may be reluctant to go through the formalities of registration until they have some confidence in the child's survival or need a birth certificate for administrative purposes. In many cultures, especially in Western Africa, a child's death before age 2 is generally not registered. In Burkina Faso, for example, there are different words to express or describe death. The word for infant death among the Mossi is *lebame,* which translates literally to "s/he went back," which is different from *kiime,* which is used for a teenager or adult who has died (private conversation). Reporting is lower for deaths than for births because people perceive death as a private, sad event and because there are fewer incentives associated with registering a death, especially where formal inheritance is rare.

Such recording lapses have consequences for data quality. Even where there is complete registration, births and deaths may be recorded as need arises, rather than when they occur, reducing the timeliness and relevance of data. Not all administrative levels have the same capacity to maintain registers, resulting in omissions that may be difficult to quantify and therefore rectify, since underregistration cannot be assumed to be uniform across the population.

Correct information on cause of death is critical for guiding policies and priorities for the health system. Routine data from civil registration in the United Kingdom helped identify the causal association between smoking and lung cancer in the 1950s. But even when deaths are recorded, age or cause of death may be misreported or miscoded. Correct reporting of cause of death is particularly difficult in developing countries, where many deaths occur at home without medical care or certification. In Myanmar only 10 percent of deaths occur in the hospital (Mahar 2010). More than two-thirds of people live in countries where cause of death statistics are partially reported and therefore of limited use or where deaths are not reported at all (table 2g; Mahapatra and others 2007).

Because of the lack of reliable vital statistics from civil registration systems, the long-term social, economic, and demographic impact of major diseases in developing countries can be estimated using only models or intuition and educated guesses rather than facts (Cooper and others 1998). Without data on the cause of death, verbal autopsy (an interview with caregivers or family members after a death to establish probable cause of death) can be used. In Tanzania several districts implemented sentinel demographic surveillance systems that provided routine monitoring of vital events and data for cause of death derived from a validated set of core verbal autopsy procedures. District councils used this information

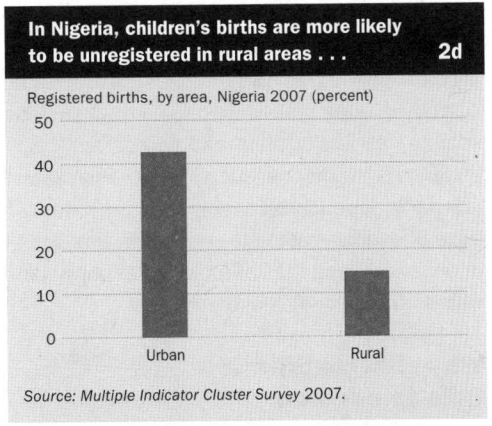

In Nigeria, children's births are more likely to be unregistered in rural areas . . . 2d

Registered births, by area, Nigeria 2007 (percent)

Source: *Multiple Indicator Cluster Survey 2007.*

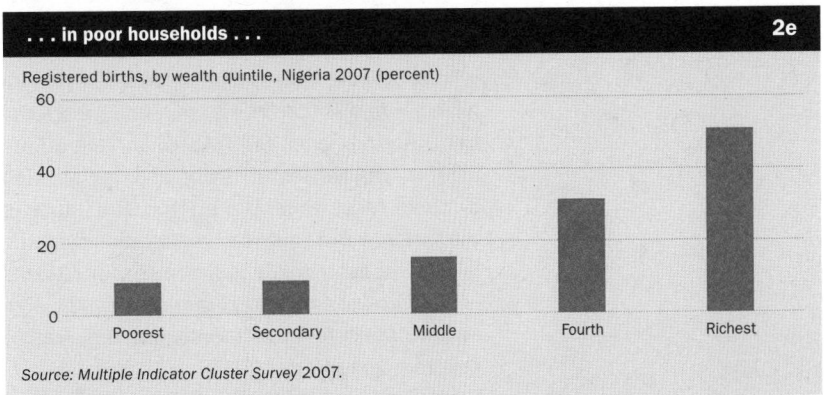

. . . in poor households . . . 2e

Registered births, by wealth quintile, Nigeria 2007 (percent)

Source: *Multiple Indicator Cluster Survey 2007.*

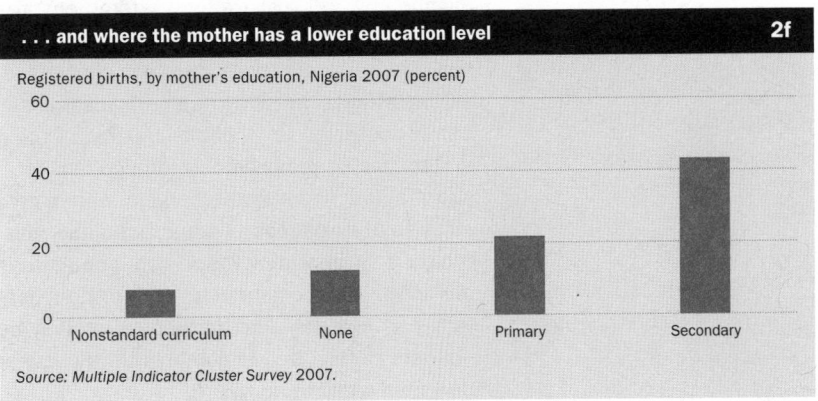

. . . and where the mother has a lower education level 2f

Registered births, by mother's education, Nigeria 2007 (percent)

Source: *Multiple Indicator Cluster Survey 2007.*

Most people live in countries with low-quality cause of death statistics 2g

Classification of countries based on the quality of cause of death statistics reported to the World Health Organization, 2007

Quality	Number of countries	Percent of global population
High	31	13
Medium	50	15
Low	26	7
Limited use	17	41
No report	68	24
Total	**192**	**100**

Source: Mahapatra and others 2007.

to identify disease burdens, set priorities, and allocate resources (Setel 2007). But verbal autopsy is often limited to small areas, such as sample vital registration and demographic surveillance systems, because it is expensive, and accuracy depends on family members' knowledge of events leading to the death, the skill of interviewers, and the competence of physicians who do the diagnosis and coding.

Why civil registration fails to develop

Good civil registration systems require long-term political commitment, a supportive legal framework, allocation of roles and responsibilities among stakeholders, mobilization of financial and human resources, and most critically, the trust of citizens (AbouZahr and others 2007). Although establishing civil registration systems takes time, there is no substitute in the long run. But when civil registration systems lack a sponsor or key stakeholder, or citizens lack incentives to participate, and when high initial costs deter investments, civil registration fails to take root.

No single blueprint for establishing and maintaining civil registration systems ensures the availability of timely and sound vital statistics. Each country faces different challenges, and strategies must be tailored accordingly. Some obstacles to a viable civil registration system can be removed only through long-term social and economic development. These generally relate to geography and population distribution, with widely dispersed populations requiring transportation to registration centers. And a largely illiterate population may be unaware of the need to comply with the law or be unmotivated to do so.

Other obstacles relate to the need for human and physical infrastructure to set up and maintain a civil registration system. While technical assistance and development grants can finance fixed costs and provide initial staff training, countries need to finance recurring costs to run a civil registration system efficiently. Because many developing countries have enormous economic and social development needs, this would claim low priority. A first and inexpensive step is adequate legislation. But while most countries have legislation requiring registration of vital events, many have not established organizational arrangements to direct, coordinate, and supervise the operation.

Interim approaches

Because of the time and expense of building complete civil registration systems, many countries have adopted alternative approaches to measure and monitor vital events and related sociodemographic information. But as dependence on these measures (often intended as interim) grows, national authorities have fewer incentives to invest in complete civil registration systems (figure 2h; Setel and others 2007).

These alternative approaches—notably censuses, demographic household surveys, sample registration systems with verbal autopsies, demographic surveillance sites, and facility-based information—effectively fill data gaps with up-to-date information in many developing countries. Figure 2i illustrates the high underreporting of deaths in the civil registration system in the Philippines, based on calculations by the Inter-agency Group for Child Mortality Estimation, using surveys and other sources of mortality data.

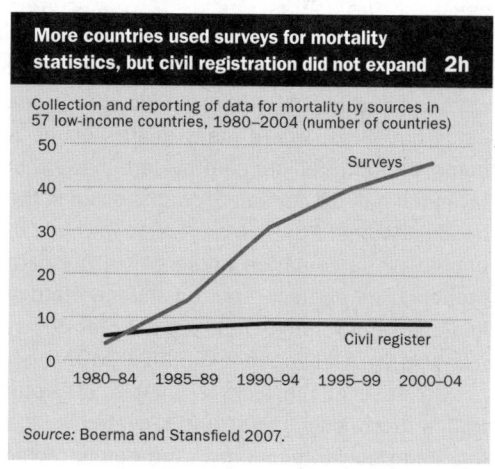

More countries used surveys for mortality statistics, but civil registration did not expand 2h

Collection and reporting of data for mortality by sources in 57 low-income countries, 1980–2004 (number of countries)

Source: Boerma and Stansfield 2007.

These interim approaches also produce supplemental information that is not collected through civil registration, such as socioeconomic information, risk factors, and health status. But these approaches are not a complete or permanent solution. Censuses and surveys are expensive, and developing countries often require international technical and financial assistance. They must be repeated regularly to yield useful data. And they must be supplemented or adjusted to produce satisfactory estimates. Burkina Faso, which has partial coverage of civil registration (birth registration coverage is 60 percent), has conducted four censuses (1975, 1985, 1996, 2006), five Demographic and Health Surveys (1991, 1993, 1998, 2003, 2010), two Multiple Indicator Cluster Surveys (1996, 2006), and a migration and urbanization survey (1993).

How to build a good civil registration system

Over the years, international and development agencies have tried to identify the strengths and weaknesses of national civil registration systems and assess the quality of the data they produce. In 2001 the United Nations updated the *Principles and Recommendations for a Vital Statistics System,* first published in 1973, to offer best practice guidelines for establishing a civil registration system and producing timely, complete, and accurate statistics. Regional initiatives by the United Nations include the 1994 African Workshop on Strategies for Accelerating the Improvement of Civil Registration and Vital Statistics Systems. In 2005 the World Health Organization (WHO) established the Health Metrics Network, which recommends an integrated approach for developing health information systems, including civil registration. Some 85 countries have used the network's Framework and Standards for Country Health Information Systems, which

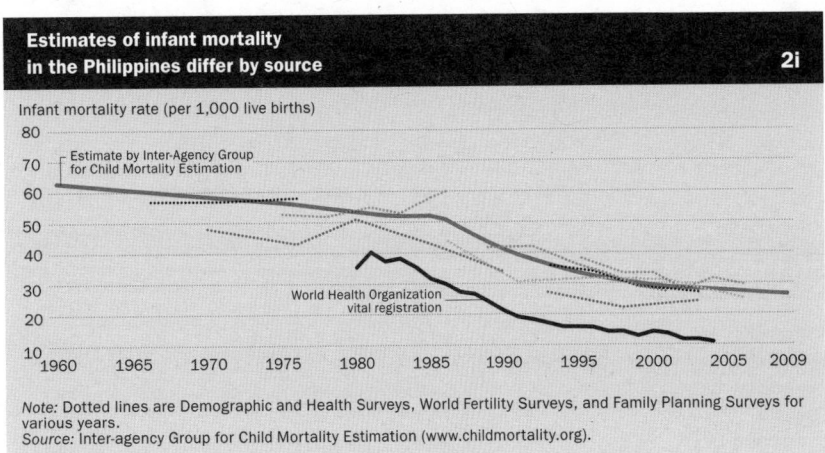

Estimates of infant mortality in the Philippines differ by source 2i

Infant mortality rate (per 1,000 live births)

Note: Dotted lines are Demographic and Health Surveys, World Fertility Surveys, and Family Planning Surveys for various years.
Source: Inter-agency Group for Child Mortality Estimation (www.childmortality.org).

aims to ensure consistency and comparability of statistics across countries and over time. Used correctly, these principles and guidelines improve data quality, as in Chile and Tanzania (Setel and others 2007), but in reality few countries have pursued or attained most recommendations.

The WHO's *International Classification of Diseases and Related Health Problems* has improved the comparability of cause of death data. Still, there are substantial differences in interpretation and application of these codes. In 2007 only 31 of 192 WHO member countries (13 percent of the world's population) reported reliable cause-of-death statistics to the WHO, most of them high-income countries (WHO 2007).

International support

The international community can continue its strong supportive rule by setting standards and guidelines for collecting and validating systems and data, publicizing the importance of civil registration, and providing comprehensive and integrated technical and financial assistance. Since no single UN agency has a clear mandate for guidance and technical support for civil registration, good coordination is key.

	Population			Average annual population growth		Population age composition			Dependency ratio		Crude death rate	Crude birth rate
					%	% Ages 0–14	Ages 15–64	Ages 65+	% of working-age population Young	Old	per 1,000 people	per 1,000 people
	millions 1990	2009	2015	1990–2009	2009–15	2009	2009	2009	2009	2009	2009	2009
Afghanistan	18.6	29.8	35.0	2.5	2.7	46	52	2	89	4	19	46
Albania	3.3	3.2	3.3	−0.2	0.5	24	67	10	35	14	6	15
Algeria	25.3	34.9	38.1	1.7	1.4	27	68	5	40	7	5	21
Angola	10.7	18.5	21.7	2.9	2.6	45	53	2	86	5	16	42
Argentina	32.5	40.3	42.4	1.1	0.9	25	64	11	39	16	8	17
Armenia	3.5	3.1	3.1	−0.7	0.2	20	68	11	30	16	9	15
Australia	17.1	21.9	23.4	1.3	1.2	19	67	14	28	20	6	14
Austria	7.7	8.4	8.4	0.4	0.1	15	68	17	22	26	9	9
Azerbaijan	7.2	8.8	9.4	1.1	1.1	24	69	7	35	10	6	17
Bangladesh	115.6	162.2	176.3	1.8	1.4	31	65	4	49	6	6	21
Belarus	10.2	9.7	9.4	−0.3	−0.4	15	72	14	21	19	14	12
Belgium	10.0	10.8	11.0	0.4	0.3	17	66	17	25	26	10	12
Benin	4.8	8.9	10.6	3.3	2.9	43	54	3	80	6	9	39
Bolivia	6.7	9.9	10.8	2.1	1.6	36	59	5	61	8	7	27
Bosnia and Herzegovina	4.3	3.8	3.7	−0.7	−0.2	15	71	14	22	20	10	9
Botswana	1.4	1.9	2.1	1.9	1.3	33	63	4	53	6	12	24
Brazil	149.6	193.7	202.4	1.4	0.7	26	67	7	39	10	6	16
Bulgaria	8.7	7.6	7.3	−0.7	−0.6	13	69	17	19	25	14	11
Burkina Faso	8.8	15.8	19.0	3.1	3.1	46	52	2	90	4	13	47
Burundi	5.7	8.3	9.4	2.0	2.1	38	59	3	65	5	14	34
Cambodia	9.7	14.8	16.4	2.2	1.7	33	63	3	53	6	8	25
Cameroon	12.2	19.5	22.2	2.5	2.1	41	56	4	74	6	14	36
Canada	27.8	33.7	35.7	1.0	0.9	17	70	14	24	20	7	11
Central African Republic	2.9	4.4	4.9	2.2	1.8	41	55	4	73	7	17	35
Chad	6.1	11.2	13.1	3.2	2.6	46	51	3	89	6	16	45
Chile	13.2	17.0	17.9	1.3	0.9	23	68	9	33	13	5	15
China	1,135.2	1,331.5	1,377.7	0.8	0.6	20[a]	72[a]	8[a]	28[a]	11[a]	7	12
Hong Kong SAR, China	5.7	7.0	7.3	1.1	0.8	12	75	13	16	17	6	12
Colombia	33.2	45.7	49.3	1.7	1.3	29	65	5	45	8	6	20
Congo, Dem. Rep.	37.0	66.0	77.4	3.0	2.6	47	51	3	92	5	17	44
Congo, Rep.	2.4	3.7	4.2	2.2	2.3	40	56	4	73	7	13	34
Costa Rica	3.1	4.6	4.9	2.1	1.3	26	68	6	38	9	4	16
Côte d'Ivoire	12.6	21.1	24.2	2.7	2.3	41	55	4	73	7	11	34
Croatia	4.8	4.4	4.4	−0.4	−0.2	15	68	17	22	25	12	10
Cuba	10.6	11.2	11.2	0.3	0.0	18	70	12	25	17	7	10
Czech Republic	10.4	10.5	10.6	0.1	0.2	14	71	15	20	21	10	11
Denmark	5.1	5.5	5.6	0.4	0.2	18	65	16	28	25	10	11
Dominican Republic	7.4	10.1	10.8	1.7	1.1	31	63	6	50	10	6	22
Ecuador	10.3	13.6	14.6	1.5	1.1	31	62	7	50	10	5	20
Egypt, Arab Rep.	57.8	83.0	91.7	1.9	1.7	32	63	5	51	7	6	24
El Salvador	5.3	6.2	6.4	0.8	0.6	32	61	7	53	12	7	20
Eritrea	3.2	5.1	6.0	2.5	2.8	42	56	2	74	4	8	36
Estonia	1.6	1.3	1.3	−0.8	−0.1	15	68	17	22	25	12	12
Ethiopia	48.3	82.8	96.2	2.8	2.5	44	53	3	82	6	12	38
Finland	5.0	5.3	5.4	0.4	0.3	17	67	17	25	25	9	11
France[b]	56.7	62.6	63.9	0.5	0.3	18	65	17	28	26	9	13
Gabon	0.9	1.5	1.6	2.4	1.8	36	60	4	61	7	10	27
Gambia, The	0.9	1.7	2.0	3.4	2.5	42	55	3	77	5	11	36
Georgia	5.5	4.3	4.1	−1.3	−0.7	17	69	14	24	21	12	12
Germany	79.4	81.9	80.6	0.2	−0.3	14	66	20	20	31	10	8
Ghana	15.0	23.8	26.6	2.4	1.8	38	58	4	66	6	11	32
Greece	10.2	11.3	11.4	0.6	0.2	14	68	18	21	27	10	11
Guatemala	8.9	14.0	16.2	2.4	2.4	42	54	4	78	8	6	32
Guinea	6.1	10.1	11.8	2.6	2.7	43	54	3	79	6	11	39
Guinea-Bissau	1.0	1.6	1.8	2.4	2.3	43	54	3	79	6	17	41
Haiti	7.1	10.0	10.7	1.8	1.1	36	59	4	61	7	9	27
Honduras	4.9	7.5	8.4	2.2	1.9	37	58	4	64	7	5	27

	Population			Average annual population growth		Population age composition			Dependency ratio		Crude death rate	Crude birth rate
							%		% of working-age population		per 1,000 people	per 1,000 people
		millions			%	Ages 0–14	Ages 15–64	Ages 65+	Young	Old		
	1990	2009	2015	1990–2009	2009–15	2009	2009	2009	2009	2009	2009	2009
Hungary	10.4	10.0	9.9	−0.2	−0.2	15	69	16	22	24	13	10
India	849.5	1,155.3	1,246.9	1.6	1.3	31	64	5	49	8	7	22
Indonesia	177.4	230.0	247.5	1.4	1.2	27	67	6	40	9	6	18
Iran, Islamic Rep.	54.4	72.9	78.6	1.5	1.2	24	71	5	34	7	6	19
Iraq	18.9	31.5	36.3	2.7	2.4	41	56	3	74	6	6	31
Ireland	3.5	4.5	4.8	1.3	1.1	21	68	11	30	16	7	17
Israel	4.7	7.4	8.2	2.5	1.6	28	62	10	45	16	5	22
Italy	56.7	60.2	60.8	0.3	0.1	14	66	20	22	31	10	10
Jamaica	2.4	2.7	2.8	0.6	0.4	29	63	8	47	12	7	16
Japan	123.5	127.6	125.3	0.2	−0.3	13	65	22	21	34	9	9
Jordan	3.2	6.0	6.8	3.3	2.2	34	62	4	56	6	4	25
Kazakhstan	16.3	15.9	16.9	−0.2	1.0	24	69	7	34	10	9	22
Kenya	23.4	39.8	46.4	2.8	2.6	43	55	3	78	5	11	38
Korea, Dem. Rep.	20.1	23.9	24.4	0.9	0.3	22	69	10	32	14	10	14
Korea, Rep.	42.9	48.7	49.3	0.7	0.2	17	73	11	23	15	5	10
Kosovo	1.9	1.8	1.9	−0.2	0.6	..	..	..	..	..	7	19
Kuwait	2.1	2.8	3.2	1.4	2.1	23	74	2	31	3	2	17
Kyrgyz Republic	4.4	5.3	5.7	1.0	1.3	29	65	5	45	8	7	25
Lao PDR	4.2	6.3	7.0	2.1	1.8	38	59	4	64	6	7	27
Latvia	2.7	2.3	2.2	−0.9	−0.5	14	69	17	20	25	13	10
Lebanon	3.0	4.2	4.4	1.8	0.8	25	67	7	38	11	7	16
Lesotho	1.6	2.1	2.2	1.3	0.8	39	56	5	69	8	17	29
Liberia	2.2	4.0	4.8	3.2	3.2	43	54	3	79	6	10	38
Libya	4.4	6.4	7.2	2.0	1.8	30	66	4	46	6	4	23
Lithuania	3.7	3.3	3.2	−0.5	−0.7	15	69	16	22	23	13	11
Macedonia, FYR	1.9	2.0	2.0	0.4	0.0	18	70	12	26	17	9	11
Madagascar	11.3	19.6	22.8	2.9	2.5	43	54	3	79	6	9	35
Malawi	9.5	15.3	18.0	2.5	2.7	46	51	3	91	6	12	40
Malaysia	18.1	27.5	30.0	2.2	1.5	29	66	5	45	7	5	20
Mali	8.7	13.0	15.4	2.1	2.8	44	54	2	83	4	15	42
Mauritania	2.0	3.3	3.7	2.7	2.1	39	58	3	68	5	10	33
Mauritius	1.1	1.3	1.3	1.0	0.4	23	70	7	32	10	7	12
Mexico	83.2	107.4	113.1	1.3	0.9	28	65	6	44	10	5	18
Moldova	4.4	3.6	3.5	−1.0	−0.7	17	72	11	23	15	13	12
Mongolia	2.2	2.7	2.9	1.0	1.1	26	70	4	37	6	7	19
Morocco	24.8	32.0	34.3	1.3	1.2	28	66	5	43	8	6	20
Mozambique	13.5	22.9	25.9	2.8	2.1	44	53	3	83	6	16	38
Myanmar	40.8	50.0	53.0	1.1	1.0	27	68	5	40	8	10	20
Namibia	1.4	2.2	2.4	2.2	1.7	37	60	4	62	6	8	27
Nepal	19.1	29.3	32.5	2.3	1.7	37	59	4	62	7	6	25
Netherlands	15.0	16.5	16.8	0.5	0.3	18	67	15	26	22	8	11
New Zealand	3.4	4.3	4.6	1.2	1.0	20	67	13	31	19	7	15
Nicaragua	4.1	5.7	6.3	1.7	1.4	35	60	5	58	7	5	24
Niger	7.9	15.3	19.1	3.5	3.7	50	48	2	104	4	15	53
Nigeria	97.3	154.7	178.7	2.4	2.4	43	54	3	78	6	16	39
Norway	4.2	4.8	5.1	0.7	0.8	19	66	15	29	22	9	13
Oman	1.8	2.8	3.2	2.3	1.9	31	66	3	48	5	3	22
Pakistan	108.0	169.7	193.5	2.4	2.2	37	59	4	63	7	7	30
Panama	2.4	3.5	3.8	1.9	1.5	29	64	7	46	10	5	20
Papua New Guinea	4.1	6.7	7.7	2.6	2.2	40	58	2	69	4	8	31
Paraguay	4.2	6.3	7.0	2.1	1.6	34	61	5	56	8	6	24
Peru	21.8	29.2	31.2	1.5	1.1	30	64	6	48	9	5	21
Philippines	62.4	92.0	102.7	2.0	1.8	34	62	4	55	7	5	24
Poland	38.1	38.1	38.0	0.0	−0.1	15	72	13	21	19	10	11
Portugal	9.9	10.6	10.7	0.4	0.0	15	67	18	23	26	10	9
Puerto Rico	3.5	4.0	4.0	0.6	0.3	20	66	14	31	21	8	12
Qatar	0.5	1.4	1.6	5.8[c]	2.4	16	83	1	19	1	2	12

	Population (millions)			Average annual population growth (%)		Population age composition (%)			Dependency ratio (% of working-age population)		Crude death rate (per 1,000 people)	Crude birth rate (per 1,000 people)
	1990	2009	2015	1990–2009	2009–15	Ages 0–14 2009	Ages 15–64 2009	Ages 65+ 2009	Young 2009	Old 2009	2009	2009
Romania	23.2	21.5	21.0	−0.4	−0.4	15	70	15	22	21	12	10
Russian Federation	148.3	141.9	139.0	−0.2	−0.3	15	72	13	21	18	14	12
Rwanda	7.2	10.0	11.7	1.8	2.7	42	55	2	77	5	14	41
Saudi Arabia	16.3	25.4	28.6	2.3	2.0	32	65	3	50	5	4	24
Senegal	7.5	12.5	14.5	2.7	2.4	44	54	2	81	4	11	38
Serbia	7.6	7.3	7.2	−0.2	−0.3	18[d]	68[d]	14[d]	26[d]	21[d]	14	10
Sierra Leone	4.1	5.7	6.6	1.8	2.3	43	55	2	79	3	15	40
Singapore	3.0	5.0	5.4	2.6	1.2	16	74	10	22	13	4	10
Slovak Republic	5.3	5.4	5.4	0.1	0.1	15	73	12	21	17	10	11
Slovenia	2.0	2.0	2.1	0.1	0.3	14	70	16	20	23	9	11
Somalia	6.6	9.1	10.7	1.7	2.7	45	52	3	86	5	16	44
South Africa	35.2	49.3	51.1	1.8	0.6	31	65	4	47	7	15	22
Spain	38.8	46.0	47.9	0.9	0.7	15	68	17	22	25	8	11
Sri Lanka	17.1	20.3	21.2	0.9	0.7	24	68	7	36	11	5	19
Sudan	27.1	42.3	47.7	2.3	2.0	39	57	4	68	6	10	31
Swaziland	0.9	1.2	1.3	1.7	1.4	39	57	3	69	6	15	30
Sweden	8.6	9.3	9.6	0.4	0.5	17	65	18	25	28	10	12
Switzerland	6.7	7.7	7.9	0.7	0.4	15	68	17	23	25	8	10
Syrian Arab Republic	12.7	21.1	24.1	2.7	2.2	35	62	3	57	5	3	27
Tajikistan	5.3	7.0	7.8	1.4	1.8	37	59	4	62	6	6	28
Tanzania	25.5	43.7	52.1	2.8	2.9	45	52	3	86	6	11	41
Thailand	56.7	67.8	69.9	0.9	0.5	22	71	8	31	11	9	14
Timor-Leste	0.7	1.1	1.4	2.2	3.3	45	52	3	86	6	8	40
Togo	3.9	6.6	7.6	2.7	2.3	40	57	4	71	6	8	32
Trinidad and Tobago	1.2	1.3	1.4	0.5	0.3	21	73	7	28	9	8	15
Tunisia	8.2	10.4	11.1	1.3	1.1	23	70	7	33	10	6	18
Turkey	56.1	74.8	79.9	1.5	1.1	27	67	6	40	9	6	18
Turkmenistan	3.7	5.1	5.5	1.7	1.2	29	66	4	45	6	8	22
Uganda	17.7	32.7	39.7	3.2	3.2	49	49	3	101	5	12	46
Ukraine	51.9	46.0	44.4	−0.6	−0.6	14	70	16	20	22	15	11
United Arab Emirates	1.9	4.6	5.2	4.7	2.0	19	80	1	24	1	2	14
United Kingdom	57.2	61.8	63.8	0.4	0.5	17	66	16	26	25	9	13
United States	249.6	307.0	323.5	1.1	0.9	20	67	13	30	19	8	14
Uruguay	3.1	3.3	3.4	0.4	0.2	23	63	14	36	22	9	15
Uzbekistan	20.5	27.8	30.2	1.6	1.4	29	66	4	44	7	5	22
Venezuela, RB	19.8	28.4	31.0	1.9	1.5	30	65	5	46	8	5	21
Vietnam	66.2	87.3	92.8	1.5	1.0	26	68	6	38	9	5	17
West Bank and Gaza	2.0	4.0	4.8	3.8	2.8	45	52	3	86	6	3	35
Yemen, Rep.	12.3	23.6	27.8	3.4	2.7	44	54	2	81	4	7	36
Zambia	7.9	12.9	15.0	2.6	2.4	46	51	3	91	6	17	42
Zimbabwe	10.5	12.5	14.0	0.9	1.9	40	56	4	71	7	15	30
World	**5,278.9 s**	**6,775.2 s**	**7,241.9 s**	**1.3 w**	**1.1 w**	**27 w**	**65 w**	**8 w**	**42 w**	**12 w**	**8 w**	**20 w**
Low income	547.3	846.1	962.6	2.3	2.1	39	57	4	69	6	11	34
Middle income	3,751.3	4,812.5	5,131.2	1.3	1.1	27	66	6	41	10	8	19
Lower middle income	2,930.9	3,810.8	4,084.9	1.4	1.2	28	66	6	42	9	8	20
Upper middle income	820.3	1,001.7	1,046.3	1.1	0.7	25	68	8	36	11	8	17
Low & middle income	4,298.6	5,658.7	6,093.8	1.4	1.2	29	65	6	45	9	8	21
East Asia & Pacific	1,599.6	1,943.8	2,035.8	1.0	0.8	23	70	7	32	11	7	14
Europe & Central Asia	392.4	404.2	409.0	0.2	0.2	19	70	11	28	16	11	15
Latin America & Carib.	435.6	572.5	606.9	1.4	1.0	28	65	7	43	10	6	18
Middle East & N. Africa	227.4	330.9	366.1	2.0	1.7	31	64	4	48	7	6	24
South Asia	1,128.7	1,567.7	1,706.5	1.7	1.4	32	63	5	51	7	7	24
Sub-Saharan Africa	514.9	839.6	969.5	2.6	2.4	43	54	3	78	6	14	38
High income	980.4	1,116.6	1,148.0	0.7	0.5	17	67	15	26	23	8	12
Euro area	301.6	327.3	332.3	0.4	0.3	15	66	18	23	27	9	10

a. Includes Taiwan, China. b. Excludes the French overseas departments of French Guiana, Guadeloupe, Martinique, and Réunion. c. Increase is due to a surge in the number of migrants since 2004. d. Includes Kosovo.

About the data

Population estimates are usually based on national population censuses. Estimates for the years before and after the census are interpolations or extrapolations based on demographic models. Errors and undercounting occur even in high income countries; in developing countries errors may be substantial because of limits in the transport, communications, and other resources required to conduct and analyze a full census.

The quality and reliability of official demographic data are also affected by public trust in the government, government commitment to full and accurate enumeration, confidentiality and protection against misuse of census data, and census agencies' independence from political influence. Moreover, comparability of population indicators is limited by differences in the concepts, definitions, collection procedures, and estimation methods used by national statistical agencies and other organizations that collect the data.

Of the 155 economies in the table and the 55 economies in table 1.6, 180 (about 86 percent) conducted a census during the 2000 census round (1995–2004). As of January 2011, 119 countries have completed a census for the 2010 census round (2005–14). The currentness of a census and the availability of complementary data from surveys or registration systems are objective ways to judge demographic data quality. Some European countries' registration systems offer complete information on population in the absence of a census. See table 2.17 and Primary data documentation for the most recent census or survey year and for the completeness of registration.

Current population estimates for developing countries that lack recent census data and pre- and post-census estimates for countries with census data are provided by the United Nations Population Division and other agencies. The cohort component method—a standard method for estimating and projecting population— requires fertility, mortality, and net migration data, often collected from sample surveys, which can be small or limited in coverage. Population estimates are from demographic modeling and so are susceptible to biases and errors from shortcomings in the model and in the data. Because the five-year age group is the cohort unit and five-year period data are used, interpolations to obtain annual data or single age structure may not reflect actual events or age composition.

The growth rate of the total population conceals age-group differences in growth rates. In many developing countries the once rapidly growing under-15 population is shrinking. Previously high fertility rates and declining mortality rates are now reflected in the larger share of the working-age population.

Dependency ratios capture variations in the proportions of children, elderly people, and working-age people in the population that imply the dependency burden that the working-age population bears in relation to children and the elderly. But dependency ratios show only the age composition of a population, not economic dependency. Some children and elderly people are part of the labor force, and many working-age people are not.

Vital rates are based on data from birth and death registration systems, censuses, and sample surveys by national statistical offices and other organizations, or on demographic analysis. Data for 2009 for most high-income countries are provisional estimates based on vital registers. The estimates for many countries are projections based on extrapolations of levels and trends from earlier years or interpolations of population estimates and projections from the United Nations Population Division.

Vital registers are the preferred source for these data, but in many developing countries systems for registering births and deaths are absent or incomplete because of deficiencies in the coverage of events or geographic areas. Many developing countries carry out special household surveys that ask respondents about recent births and deaths. Estimates derived in this way are subject to sampling errors and recall errors.

The United Nations Statistics Division monitors the completeness of vital registration systems. Progress has been made over the past 60 years in some countries. But many countries still have deficiencies in civil registration systems. For example, only 60 percent of countries and areas register at least 90 percent of births, and only 47 percent register at least 90 percent of deaths. Some of the most populous developing countries—Bangladesh, Brazil, India, Indonesia, Nigeria, Pakistan—lack complete vital registration systems.

International migration is the only other factor besides birth and death rates that directly determines a country's population growth. From 1990 to 2005 the number of migrants in high-income countries rose 40 million. About 195 million people (3 percent of the world population) live outside their home country. Estimating migration is difficult. At any time many people are located outside their home country as tourists, workers, or refugees or for other reasons. Standards for the duration and purpose of international moves that qualify as migration vary, and estimates require information on flows into and out of countries that is difficult to collect.

Definitions

• **Population** is based on the de facto definition of population, which counts all residents regardless of legal status or citizenship—except for refugees not permanently settled in the country of asylum, who are generally considered part of the population of their country of origin. The values shown are midyear estimates for 1990 and 2009 and projections for 2015. • **Average annual population growth** is the exponential change for the period indicated. See Statistical methods for more information. • **Population age composition** is the percentage of the total population that is in specific age groups. • **Dependency ratio** is the ratio of dependents—people younger than 15 or older than 64—to the working age population—those ages 15–64. • **Crude death rate and crude birth rate** are the number of deaths and the number of live births occurring during the year, per 1,000 people, estimated at midyear. Subtracting the crude death rate from the crude birth rate provides the rate of natural increase, which is equal to the population growth rate in the absence of migration.

Data sources

The World Bank's population estimates are compiled and produced by its Development Data Group in consultation with its Human Development Network, operational staff, and country offices. The United Nations Population Division's *World Population Prospects: The 2008 Revision* is a source of the demographic data for more than half the countries, most of them developing countries, and the source of data on age composition and dependency ratios for all countries. Other important sources are census reports and other statistical publications from national statistical offices; household surveys conducted by national agencies, Macro International, and the U.S. Centers for Disease Control and Prevention; Eurostat's Demographic Statistics; Secretariat of the Pacific Community, Statistics and Demography Programme; and U.S. Bureau of the Census, International Data Base.

	Labor force participation rate				Labor force				
	% ages 15 and older				**Total millions**		**Ages 15 and older average annual % growth**	**Female % of labor force**	
	Male		Female						
	1990	**2009**	**1990**	**2009**	**1990**	**2009**	**1990–2009**	**1990**	**2009**
Afghanistan	84	85	32	33	5.9	9.6	2.5	26.2	26.6
Albania	74	70	51	49	1.4	1.4	0.2	39.9	42.5
Algeria	75	80	23	37	7.0	14.8	3.9	23.4	31.6
Angola	90	88	74	75	4.6	8.3	3.1	46.3	46.9
Argentina	78	78	43	52	13.5	19.6	1.9	36.9	41.6
Armenia	78	75	61	60	1.7	1.6	−0.2	46.3	49.6
Australia	76	72	52	58	8.5	11.5	1.6	41.3	45.4
Austria	70	68	43	53	3.5	4.3	1.0	40.9	45.5
Azerbaijan	74	67	59	60	3.1	4.2	1.5	46.8	49.5
Bangladesh	89	83	61	59	49.5	78.6	2.4	39.9	41.2
Belarus	75	67	60	55	5.3	5.0	−0.3	48.9	49.5
Belgium	61	61	36	47	3.9	4.8	1.0	39.0	44.9
Benin	89	78	57	67	1.9	3.7	3.5	41.1	46.2
Bolivia	82	82	59	62	2.8	4.5	2.6	43.1	43.8
Bosnia and Herzegovina	67	68	53	55	2.0	1.9	0.0	45.2	47.1
Botswana	82	81	64	72	0.5	1.0	3.2	45.5	47.4
Brazil	85	82	45	60	62.6	101.5	2.5	35.1	43.7
Bulgaria	63	61	55	48	4.1	3.6	−0.7	47.9	46.1
Burkina Faso	91	91	77	78	3.9	7.1	3.2	48.0	47.1
Burundi	90	88	91	91	2.8	4.6	2.6	52.5	52.6
Cambodia	84	86	78	74	4.3	7.8	3.1	52.8	48.3
Cameroon	83	81	48	54	4.4	7.7	3.0	37.5	40.1
Canada	76	73	58	63	14.7	19.1	1.4	44.1	47.0
Central African Republic	87	87	69	72	1.3	2.1	2.5	45.6	46.5
Chad	81	78	65	63	2.4	4.3	3.1	45.6	45.2
Chile	77	73	32	42	5.0	7.5	2.1	30.5	37.2
China	85	80	73	67	643.9	783.2	1.0	44.8	44.6
Hong Kong SAR, China	80	69	47	52	2.9	3.7	1.4	36.3	46.3
Colombia	78	78	29	41	11.2	19.0	2.8	28.2	35.8
Congo, Dem. Rep.	85	86	53	57	13.4	24.9	3.3	39.9	40.6
Congo, Rep.	84	83	59	63	1.0	1.6	2.6	42.1	43.6
Costa Rica	84	80	33	45	1.2	2.1	3.2	27.4	35.5
Côte d'Ivoire	88	82	43	51	4.7	8.4	3.1	30.1	36.9
Croatia	69	60	47	46	2.2	2.0	−0.4	42.7	45.8
Cuba	73	67	36	41	4.4	5.0	0.6	33.0	38.1
Czech Republic	71	68	52	49	4.9	5.2	0.3	44.4	43.2
Denmark	75	71	62	60	2.9	3.0	0.1	46.1	46.9
Dominican Republic	85	80	43	51	2.9	4.5	2.3	33.2	38.8
Ecuador	78	78	33	47	3.5	5.9	2.7	29.5	38.0
Egypt, Arab Rep.	74	75	27	22	16.8	27.4	2.6	26.6	23.0
El Salvador	83	77	41	46	1.9	2.5	1.4	35.2	41.9
Eritrea	84	83	55	63	1.2	2.2	3.2	41.4	44.5
Estonia	77	69	63	55	0.8	0.7	−1.0	49.5	49.1
Ethiopia	91	90	72	81	21.5	40.0	3.3	45.1	47.9
Finland	72	65	59	57	2.6	2.7	0.2	47.1	48.1
France	65	62	46	51	25.0	28.7	0.7	43.3	46.8
Gabon	83	81	63	70	0.4	0.7	3.1	44.2	46.7
Gambia, The	86	85	71	71	0.4	0.8	3.4	46.2	46.2
Georgia	78	74	60	55	2.8	2.3	−1.2	46.9	46.8
Germany	73	67	45	53	38.8	42.3	0.5	40.7	45.6
Ghana	73	75	70	74	6.0	11.0	3.2	48.9	49.1
Greece	67	65	36	43	4.2	5.2	1.1	36.2	40.5
Guatemala	88	88	39	48	3.1	5.5	3.0	31.0	37.9
Guinea	90	89	79	79	2.9	4.8	2.7	46.8	46.9
Guinea-Bissau	81	84	59	60	0.4	0.7	2.4	43.0	42.4
Haiti	81	83	57	58	2.8	4.5	2.5	43.0	42.3
Honduras	88	80	41	40	1.7	2.8	2.6	32.3	33.9

	Labor force participation rate					Labor force			
	% ages 15 and older				Total millions		Ages 15 and older average annual % growth	Female % of labor force	
	Male		Female						
	1990	**2009**	**1990**	**2009**	**1990**	**2009**	**1990–2009**	**1990**	**2009**
Hungary	65	59	46	43	4.5	4.3	−0.3	44.5	45.1
India	84	81	34	33	317.8	457.5	1.9	27.1	27.6
Indonesia	81	86	50	52	74.9	115.6	2.3	38.4	38.1
Iran, Islamic Rep.	80	73	22	32	15.5	29.2	3.3	20.1	29.8
Iraq	73	69	11	14	4.3	7.7	3.0	13.1	16.7
Ireland	71	73	35	54	1.3	2.2	2.7	33.9	43.0
Israel	64	63	42	52	1.7	3.1	3.1	40.6	46.5
Italy	66	61	35	38	23.7	25.4	0.4	36.5	40.5
Jamaica	80	74	65	56	1.1	1.2	0.5	46.6	44.9
Japan	77	72	50	48	63.9	65.8	0.2	40.7	41.6
Jordan	71	74	15	23	0.7	1.9	5.0	16.2	23.0
Kazakhstan	78	76	62	66	7.8	8.6	0.5	47.0	49.8
Kenya	90	88	75	76	9.8	18.7	3.4	46.0	46.7
Korea, Dem. Rep.	80	78	55	55	10.0	12.4	1.1	42.6	42.7
Korea, Rep.	73	72	47	50	19.2	24.7	1.3	39.7	41.9
Kosovo	..	..	..	..	..	..	..	..	..
Kuwait	82	83	36	45	0.9	1.5	2.8	22.4	25.0
Kyrgyz Republic	74	79	58	55	1.8	2.5	1.7	46.1	42.3
Lao PDR	83	79	80	78	1.9	3.1	2.5	49.8	50.4
Latvia	77	70	63	54	1.4	1.2	−1.0	49.6	48.3
Lebanon	72	72	20	22	0.9	1.5	2.8	23.3	25.0
Lesotho	83	78	68	71	0.7	0.9	1.9	51.7	52.4
Liberia	78	76	65	67	0.8	1.6	3.4	46.7	47.6
Libya	75	79	15	25	1.2	2.4	3.7	14.8	22.5
Lithuania	74	62	59	50	1.9	1.6	−1.0	48.1	48.7
Macedonia, FYR	68	65	46	43	0.8	0.9	0.6	40.7	40.1
Madagascar	89	89	83	84	5.4	9.7	3.1	48.4	49.2
Malawi	80	79	76	75	3.9	6.3	2.5	50.7	49.8
Malaysia	80	79	43	44	7.0	12.0	2.8	34.5	35.4
Mali	68	67	37	38	2.5	3.8	2.2	36.1	37.3
Mauritania	82	81	53	59	0.7	1.4	3.3	39.8	42.0
Mauritius	81	75	38	41	0.4	0.6	1.3	32.1	36.1
Mexico	84	81	34	43	29.9	47.2	2.4	30.0	36.2
Moldova	74	53	61	47	2.1	1.5	−1.8	48.7	49.9
Mongolia	77	78	63	68	0.9	1.4	2.5	45.6	47.4
Morocco	81	80	25	26	7.8	12.0	2.2	23.7	25.8
Mozambique	88	87	85	85	6.3	11.0	3.0	53.2	52.0
Myanmar	89	85	71	63	20.7	27.0	1.4	45.3	44.2
Namibia	64	63	48	52	0.4	0.8	3.0	44.9	46.5
Nepal	85	80	52	63	7.5	13.3	3.0	38.0	45.4
Netherlands	70	73	43	60	6.9	9.0	1.4	38.8	45.7
New Zealand	74	76	54	62	1.7	2.4	1.7	43.0	46.1
Nicaragua	85	78	39	47	1.4	2.3	2.8	32.3	38.7
Niger	91	88	27	39	2.3	4.8	3.8	24.7	31.6
Nigeria	76	73	36	39	29.4	50.0	2.8	33.0	35.1
Norway	73	71	57	63	2.2	2.6	0.9	44.7	47.7
Oman	80	77	19	25	0.6	1.1	3.4	13.7	18.8
Pakistan	85	85	14	22	31.0	58.1	3.3	12.7	19.4
Panama	79	81	39	48	0.9	1.6	2.8	32.4	37.4
Papua New Guinea	74	74	71	72	1.8	3.0	2.8	46.9	48.9
Paraguay	87	87	47	57	1.7	3.0	3.1	34.9	39.4
Peru	75	76	49	58	8.3	13.6	2.6	39.7	43.6
Philippines	83	79	48	49	24.1	38.8	2.5	36.5	38.6
Poland	72	62	55	46	18.1	17.4	−0.2	45.4	45.0
Portugal	73	69	49	56	4.7	5.6	0.9	42.4	46.9
Puerto Rico	61	58	31	36	1.2	1.5	1.2	35.8	40.8
Qatar	94	93	40	50	0.3	1.0	6.9	13.5	11.9

	Labor force participation rate				Labor force				
	% ages 15 and older				Total millions		Ages 15 and older average annual % growth	Female % of labor force	
	Male		Female						
	1990	2009	1990	2009	1990	2009	1990–2009	1990	2009
Romania	73	60	60	45	11.8	9.5	–1.1	46.3	45.0
Russian Federation	76	69	60	58	76.8	75.9	–0.1	48.6	50.1
Rwanda	89	85	87	87	3.2	5.0	2.3	52.1	52.8
Saudi Arabia	80	74	15	17	5.0	8.6	2.8	11.5	14.9
Senegal	90	89	62	65	3.0	5.4	3.0	40.8	43.3
Serbia	..	..	..	..	..	..	..	..	..
Sierra Leone	68	68	66	65	1.6	2.1	1.6	50.9	51.4
Singapore	79	76	51	54	1.6	2.7	2.9	39.1	41.5
Slovak Republic	72	69	59	51	2.6	2.7	0.3	46.8	44.7
Slovenia	59	65	47	53	0.8	1.0	1.2	46.8	46.2
Somalia	84	85	58	57	2.6	3.5	1.6	41.8	40.9
South Africa	62	63	36	47	10.4	18.8	3.1	37.5	43.7
Spain	67	69	34	49	15.6	22.9	2.0	34.8	42.8
Sri Lanka	79	75	37	34	6.8	8.3	1.1	31.8	32.4
Sudan	79	74	27	31	8.0	13.5	2.7	26.0	29.5
Swaziland	81	75	45	53	0.3	0.5	2.7	41.2	43.4
Sweden	72	69	63	61	4.7	5.0	0.3	47.7	47.4
Switzerland	81	74	57	61	3.8	4.4	0.7	42.9	46.8
Syrian Arab Republic	81	80	18	21	3.3	6.9	4.0	18.3	20.9
Tajikistan	80	78	59	57	2.1	2.9	1.8	43.3	43.9
Tanzania	91	91	87	86	12.3	21.4	2.9	49.8	49.4
Thailand	87	81	75	66	32.1	38.7	1.0	47.0	46.1
Timor-Leste	82	83	58	59	0.3	0.4	1.8	40.4	40.9
Togo	87	86	56	64	1.5	3.0	3.5	40.1	43.5
Trinidad and Tobago	76	78	39	55	0.5	0.7	2.3	35.0	43.3
Tunisia	76	71	21	26	2.4	3.8	2.4	21.6	26.7
Turkey	81	70	34	24	20.7	25.6	1.1	29.7	25.7
Turkmenistan	72	74	58	62	1.4	2.4	2.9	46.1	47.1
Uganda	91	91	81	78	7.9	14.1	3.0	47.7	46.5
Ukraine	71	65	56	52	25.5	23.0	–0.5	49.2	49.0
United Arab Emirates	92	92	25	42	1.0	2.9	5.8	9.8	15.7
United Kingdom	74	70	52	55	29.0	31.8	0.5	43.2	45.7
United States	76	72	57	58	129.2	159.0	1.1	44.4	46.0
Uruguay	76	76	48	54	1.4	1.7	0.9	40.8	44.1
Uzbekistan	68	71	53	58	7.3	12.7	2.9	45.5	45.9
Venezuela, RB	81	80	36	52	7.2	13.1	3.2	30.5	39.3
Vietnam	82	76	74	68	31.1	46.6	2.1	50.7	48.6
West Bank and Gaza	66	68	11	17	0.4	1.0	4.4	13.8	19.0
Yemen, Rep.	74	74	16	20	2.6	6.2	4.5	18.0	21.1
Zambia	79	79	61	60	3.0	4.8	2.5	44.3	43.4
Zimbabwe	80	74	67	60	4.1	5.0	1.0	46.3	47.5
World	**81 w**	**78 w**	**52 w**	**52 w**	**2,342.6 t**	**3,175.8 t**	**1.6 w**	**39.4 w**	**40.1 w**
Low income	86	84	65	66	232.9	384.5	2.6	43.8	44.6
Middle income	82	79	52	50	1,646.7	2,244.8	1.6	38.1	38.4
Lower middle income	83	80	54	50	1,317.1	1,786.5	1.6	38.2	37.7
Upper middle income	78	75	45	48	329.6	458.2	1.7	37.6	40.8
Low & middle income	83	80	53	52	1,879.5	2,629.2	1.8	38.8	39.3
East Asia & Pacific	84	80	69	64	853.5	1,090.7	1.3	44.2	43.9
Europe & Central Asia	75	69	56	50	180.3	187.2	0.2	45.8	45.5
Latin America & Carib.	82	80	40	52	169.1	269.3	2.4	33.8	40.5
Middle East & N. Africa	77	75	22	26	63.3	115.2	3.2	22.0	25.7
South Asia	85	82	35	35	418.8	625.9	2.1	27.8	29.0
Sub-Saharan Africa	82	81	57	61	194.6	341.0	3.0	42.0	43.6
High income	73	70	49	52	463.0	546.6	0.9	41.6	43.9
Euro area	69	65	42	49	135.2	158.5	0.8	39.8	44.4

The labor force is the supply of labor available for producing goods and services in an economy. It includes people who are currently employed and people who are unemployed but seeking work as well as first-time job-seekers. Not everyone who works is included, however. Unpaid workers, family workers, and students are often omitted, and some countries do not count members of the armed forces. Labor force size tends to vary during the year as seasonal workers enter and leave.

Data on the labor force are compiled by the International Labour Organization (ILO) from labor force surveys, censuses, establishment censuses and surveys, and administrative records such as employment exchange registers and unemployment insurance schemes. For some countries a combination of these sources is used. Labor force surveys are the most comprehensive source for internationally comparable labor force data. They can cover all noninstitutionalized civilians, all branches and sectors of the economy, and all categories of workers, including people holding multiple jobs. By contrast, labor force data from population censuses are often based on a limited number of questions on the economic characteristics of individuals, with little scope to probe. The resulting data often differ from labor force survey data and vary considerably by country, depending on the census scope and coverage. Establishment censuses and surveys provide data only on the employed population, not unemployed workers, workers in small establishments, or workers in the informal sector (ILO, *Key Indicators of the Labour Market 2001–2002*).

The reference period of a census or survey is another important source of differences: in some countries data refer to people's status on the day of the census or survey or during a specific period before the inquiry date, while in others data are recorded without reference to any period. In developing countries, where the household is often the basic unit of production and all members contribute to output, but some at low intensity or irregularly, the estimated labor force may be much smaller than the numbers actually working.

Differing definitions of employment age also affect comparability. For most countries the working age is 15 and older, but in some countries children younger than 15 work full- or part-time and are included in the estimates. Similarly, some countries have an upper age limit. As a result, calculations may systematically over- or underestimate actual rates. For further information on source, reference period, or definition, consult the original source.

The labor force participation rates in the table are from the ILO's Key Indicators of the Labour Market, 6th edition, database. These harmonized estimates use strict data selection criteria and enhanced methods to ensure comparability across countries and over time, including collection and tabulation methodologies and methods applied to such country-specific factors as military service requirements.

Estimates are based mainly on labor force surveys, with other sources (population censuses and nationally reported estimates) used only when no survey data are available.

The labor force estimates in the table were calculated by applying labor force participation rates from the ILO database to World Bank population estimates to create a series consistent with these population estimates. This procedure sometimes results in labor force estimates that differ slightly from those in the ILO's Yearbook of Labour Statistics and its database Key Indicators of the Labour Market.

Estimates of women in the labor force and employment are generally lower than those of men and are not comparable internationally, reflecting that demographic, social, legal, and cultural trends and norms determine whether women's activities are regarded as economic. In many countries many women work on farms or in other family enterprises without pay, and others work in or near their homes, mixing work and family activities during the day.

• **Labor force participation rate** is the proportion of the population ages 15 and older that engages actively in the labor market, either by working or looking for work during a reference period. • **Total labor force** is people ages 15 and older who engage actively in the labor market, either by working or looking for work during a reference period. It includes both the employed and the unemployed. • **Average annual percentage growth of the labor force** is calculated using the exponential endpoint method (see *Statistical methods* for more information). • **Female labor force as a percentage of the labor force** shows the extent to which women are active in the labor force.

Data on labor force participation rates are from the ILO's Key Indicators of the Labour Market, 6th edition, database. Labor force numbers were calculated by World Bank staff, applying labor force participation rates from the ILO database to population estimates.

	Agriculture				Industry				Services			
	Male % of male employment		Female % of female employment		Male % of male employment		Female % of female employment		Male % of male employment		Female % of female employment	
	1990–92[a]	2005–08[a]	1990–92[a]	2005–08[a]	1990–92[a]	2005–08[a]	1990–92[a]	2005–08[a]	1990–92[a]	2005–08[a]	1990–92[a]	2005–08[a]
Afghanistan	..	..	..	..	..	..	..	..	..	..	..	..
Albania	..	..	..	..	..	..	..	..	..	..	..	..
Algeria	..	..	..	..	..	..	..	..	..	..	..	..
Angola	..	..	..	..	..	..	..	..	..	..	..	..
Argentina	0[b,c]	1[c]	0[b,c]	0[b,c]	40[c]	33[c]	18[c]	11[c]	59[c]	66[c]	81[c]	89[c]
Armenia	..	46	..	46	..	21	..	10	..	33	..	45
Australia	6	4	4	2	32	31	12	9	61	64	84	89
Austria	6	6	8	6	47	37	20	12	46	57	72	82
Azerbaijan	..	40	..	38	..	17	..	9	..	44	..	53
Bangladesh	54	42	85	68	16	15	9	13	25	43	2	19
Belarus	..	15	..	9	..	33	..	24	..	37	..	64
Belgium	3	2	2	1	41	36	16	11	56	61	81	88
Benin	..	..	..	..	..	..	..	..	..	..	..	..
Bolivia	..	..	..	..	..	..	..	..	..	..	..	..
Bosnia and Herzegovina	..	..	..	..	..	..	..	..	..	..	..	..
Botswana	..	35	..	24	..	19	..	11	..	46	..	65
Brazil	31[c]	23	25[c]	15	27[c]	28	10[c]	13	43[c]	50	65[c]	72
Bulgaria	..	9	..	6	..	42	..	29	..	49	..	65
Burkina Faso	..	..	..	..	..	..	..	..	..	..	..	..
Burundi	..	..	..	..	..	..	..	..	..	..	..	..
Cambodia	..	..	..	..	..	..	..	..	..	..	..	..
Cameroon	..	..	..	..	..	..	..	..	..	..	..	..
Canada	6[c]	3[c]	2[c]	2[c]	31[c]	32[c]	11[c]	11[c]	64[c]	65[c]	87[c]	88[c]
Central African Republic	..	..	..	..	..	..	..	..	..	..	..	..
Chad	..	..	..	..	..	..	..	..	..	..	..	..
Chile	24	16	6	6	32	31	15	11	45	53	79	84
China	..	..	..	..	..	..	..	..	..	..	..	..
Hong Kong SAR, China	1[c]	0[b,c]	0[b,c]	0[b,c]	37[c]	21[c]	27[c]	6[c]	63[c]	78[c]	73[c]	94[c]
Colombia	..	27	..	6	..	22	..	16	..	51	..	78
Congo, Dem. Rep.	..	..	..	..	..	..	..	..	..	..	..	..
Congo, Rep.	..	..	..	..	..	..	..	..	..	..	..	..
Costa Rica	32	18	5	5	27	28	25	13	41	54	69	82
Côte d'Ivoire	..	..	..	..	..	..	..	..	..	..	..	..
Croatia	..	13[d]	..	15[d]	..	39[d]	..	15[d]	..	48[d]	..	69[d]
Cuba	..	25	..	9	..	22	..	12	..	54	..	79
Czech Republic	..	4	..	2	..	51	..	27	..	45	..	71
Denmark	7	4	3	1	37	32	16	12	56	64	82	86
Dominican Republic	26	21	3	2	23	26	21	14	52	53	76	84
Ecuador	10[c]	11[c]	2[c]	4[c]	29[c]	28[c]	17[c]	13[c]	62[c]	61[c]	81[c]	83[c]
Egypt, Arab Rep.	35	28	52	43	25	26	10	6	41	46	37	51
El Salvador	48	29	15	5	23	26	23	19	29	45	63	76
Eritrea	..	..	..	..	..	..	..	..	..	..	..	..
Estonia	23	5	13	2	42	48	30	23	36	46	57	75
Ethiopia	..	9[c,d]	..	10[c,d]	..	25[c,d]	..	20[c,d]	..	76[c,d]	..	64[c,d]
Finland	11	6	6	3	38	39	15	11	51	54	78	86
France	7	4	5	2	39	34	17	11	54	61	78	86
Gabon	..	..	..	..	..	..	..	..	..	..	..	..
Gambia, The	..	..	..	..	..	..	..	..	..	..	..	..
Georgia	..	51	..	57	..	17	..	4	..	33	..	39
Germany	4	3	4	2	50	41	24	16	46	56	73	83
Ghana	66	..	59	..	10	..	10	..	23	..	32	..
Greece	20	11	26	12	29	30	17	9	51	59	57	79
Guatemala	..	44	..	16	..	24	..	21	..	32	..	63
Guinea	..	..	..	..	..	..	..	..	..	..	..	..
Guinea-Bissau	..	..	..	..	..	..	..	..	..	..	..	..
Haiti	76	..	50	..	9	..	9	..	13	..	38	..
Honduras	53[c]	51[c]	6[c]	13[c]	18[c]	20[c]	25[c]	23[c]	29[c]	29[c]	69[c]	63[c]

Employment by economic activity

	Agriculture				Industry				Services			
	Male % of male employment		Female % of female employment		Male % of male employment		Female % of female employment		Male % of male employment		Female % of female employment	
	1990–92[a]	2005–08[a]	1990–92[a]	2005–08[a]	1990–92[a]	2005–08[a]	1990–92[a]	2005–08[a]	1990–92[a]	2005–08[a]	1990–92[a]	2005–08[a]
Hungary	19	6	13	2	43	42	29	21	38	52	58	77
India	..	..	..	..	..	..	..	..	..	..	..	..
Indonesia	54	41	57	41	15	21	13	15	31	38	31	44
Iran, Islamic Rep.	..	21	..	33	..	33	..	29	..	47	..	38
Iraq	..	..	..	..	..	..	..	..	..	..	..	..
Ireland	19	9	3	2	33	38	18	10	48	53	78	88
Israel	5	3	2	1	38	32	15	11	57	65	83	88
Italy	8	5	9	3	41	39	23	16	52	57	68	81
Jamaica	36	26	16	8	25	27	12	5	39	47	72	87
Japan	6	4	7	4	40	35	27	17	54	59	65	77
Jordan	..	..	..	..	..	..	..	..	..	..	..	..
Kazakhstan	..	..	..	..	..	..	..	..	..	..	..	..
Kenya	..	..	..	..	..	..	..	..	..	..	..	..
Korea, Dem. Rep.	..	..	..	..	..	..	..	..	..	..	..	..
Korea, Rep.	14	7	18	8	40	33	28	16	46	60	54	76
Kosovo	..	..	..	..	..	..	..	..	..	..	..	..
Kuwait	..	..	..	..	..	..	..	..	..	..	..	..
Kyrgyz Republic	..	37	..	35	..	26	..	11	..	37	..	54
Lao PDR	..	..	..	..	..	..	..	..	..	..	..	..
Latvia	..	10	..	6	..	40	..	17	..	49	..	77
Lebanon	..	..	..	..	..	..	..	..	..	..	..	..
Lesotho	..	..	..	..	..	..	..	..	..	..	..	..
Liberia	..	..	..	..	..	..	..	..	..	..	..	..
Libya	..	..	..	..	..	..	..	..	..	..	..	..
Lithuania	..	10	..	6	..	41	..	19	..	49	..	75
Macedonia, FYR	..	19	..	17	..	33	..	29	..	48	..	54
Madagascar	..	82	..	83	..	5	..	2	..	13	..	16
Malawi	..	..	..	..	..	..	..	..	..	..	..	..
Malaysia	23	18	20	10	31	32	32	23	46	51	48	67
Mali	..	..	..	..	..	..	..	..	..	..	..	..
Mauritania	..	..	..	..	..	..	..	..	..	..	..	..
Mauritius	15	10	13	8	36	36	48	26	48	54	39	66
Mexico	34	19	11	4	25	31	19	18	41	50	70	77
Moldova	..	36	..	30	..	25	..	12	..	39	..	58
Mongolia	..	41	..	35	..	21	..	15	..	39	..	50
Morocco	..	35	..	60	..	24	..	15	..	41	..	25
Mozambique	..	..	..	..	..	..	..	..	..	..	..	..
Myanmar	..	..	..	..	..	..	..	..	..	..	..	..
Namibia	45	23	52	8	21	24	8	9	34	24	40	63
Nepal	75	..	91	..	4	..	1	..	20	..	8	..
Netherlands	5	3	2	2	33	27	10	8	60	63	81	85
New Zealand	13[c]	9	8[c]	5	31[c]	32	13[c]	10	56[c]	58	79[c]	85
Nicaragua	..	42	..	8	..	20	..	18	..	38	..	73
Niger	..	..	..	..	..	..	..	..	..	..	..	..
Nigeria	..	..	..	..	..	..	..	..	..	..	..	..
Norway	7	4	3	1	34	33	10	8	58	63	86	90
Oman	..	..	..	..	..	..	..	..	..	..	..	..
Pakistan	45	36	69	72	20	23	15	13	35	41	16	15
Panama	35	21	3	3	20	25	11	10	45	54	85	87
Papua New Guinea	..	..	..	..	..	..	..	..	..	..	..	..
Paraguay	..	33	..	24	..	24	..	9	..	43	..	68
Peru	1[c]	12[c]	0[b,c]	6[c]	30[c]	41[c]	13[c]	43[c]	69[c]	46[c]	87[c]	51[c]
Philippines	53[c]	42[d]	32[c]	23[d]	17[c]	18[d]	14[c]	10[d]	29[c]	41[d]	55[c]	68[d]
Poland	..	15[c]	..	14[c]	..	41[c]	..	18[c]	..	44[c]	..	68[c]
Portugal	10	11	13	12	39	40	24	17	51	49	63	71
Puerto Rico	5	2	0[b]	0[b]	27	26	19	10	67	72	80	89
Qatar	..	4	..	0	..	48	..	4	..	48	..	96

	Agriculture				Industry				Services			
	Male % of male employment		Female % of female employment		Male % of male employment		Female % of female employment		Male % of male employment		Female % of female employment	
	1990–92[a]	2005–08[a]	1990–92[a]	2005–08[a]	1990–92[a]	2005–08[a]	1990–92[a]	2005–08[a]	1990–92[a]	2005–08[a]	1990–92[a]	2005–08[a]
Romania	29	27	38	30	44	38	30	24	28	35	33	46
Russian Federation	..	11	..	7	..	38	..	20	..	51	..	73
Rwanda	..	..	..	..	..	..	..	..	..	..	..	..
Saudi Arabia	..	5[d]	..	0[b,d]	..	23[d]	..	2[d]	..	72[d]	..	98[d]
Senegal	..	34	..	33	..	20	..	5	..	33	..	42
Serbia	..	22	..	20	..	37	..	20	..	42	..	61
Sierra Leone	..	..	..	..	..	..	..	..	..	..	..	..
Singapore	1	2	0[b]	1	36	26	32	18	63	72	68	82
Slovak Republic	..	6	..	2	..	52	..	24	..	43	..	74
Slovenia	..	10[c]	..	10[c]	..	44[c]	..	23[c]	..	45[c]	..	65[c]
Somalia	..	..	..	..	..	..	..	..	..	..	..	..
South Africa	..	5[d]	..	3[d]	..	31[d]	..	13[d]	..	57[d]	..	79[d]
Spain	11	6	8	3	41	40	17	11	49	55	75	86
Sri Lanka	..	28[c]	..	37[c]	..	26[c]	..	27[c]	..	41[c]	..	34[c]
Sudan	..	..	..	..	..	..	..	..	..	..	..	..
Swaziland	..	..	..	..	..	..	..	..	..	..	..	..
Sweden	5[c]	3[c]	2[c]	1[c]	40[c]	33[c]	12[c]	9[c]	55[c]	64[c]	86[c]	90[c]
Switzerland	5	5	4	3	39	34	15	12	57	62	81	86
Syrian Arab Republic	23	..	54	..	28	..	8	..	49	..	38	..
Tajikistan	..	..	..	..	..	..	..	..	..	..	..	..
Tanzania	..	71	..	78	..	7	..	3	..	22	..	19
Thailand	59	43	62	40	17	22	13	19	24	35	25	41
Timor-Leste	..	..	..	..	..	..	..	..	..	..	..	..
Togo	..	..	..	..	..	..	..	..	..	..	..	..
Trinidad and Tobago	15	6	6	2	34	41	14	16	51	52	80	82
Tunisia	..	..	..	..	..	..	..	..	..	..	..	..
Turkey	33	18[d]	72	42[d]	26	21[d]	11	15[d]	41	53[d]	17	43[d]
Turkmenistan	..	..	..	..	..	..	..	..	..	..	..	..
Uganda	..	..	..	..	..	..	..	..	..	..	..	..
Ukraine	..	..	..	..	..	..	..	..	..	..	..	..
United Arab Emirates	..	6	..	0[b]	..	45	..	6	..	49	..	92
United Kingdom	3	2	1	1	41	32	16	9	55	66	82	90
United States	4	2	1	1	34	30	14	9	62	68	85	90
Uruguay	..	16[c]	..	5[c]	..	29[c]	..	13[c]	..	56[c]	..	83[c]
Uzbekistan	..	..	..	..	..	..	..	..	..	..	..	..
Venezuela, RB	17	13	2	2	32	30	16	12	52	56	82	86
Vietnam	..	..	..	..	..	..	..	..	..	..	..	..
West Bank and Gaza	..	11	..	36	..	27	..	10	..	61	..	53
Yemen, Rep.	44	..	83	..	14	..	2	..	38	..	13	..
Zambia	47	..	56	..	15	..	3	..	22	..	18	..
Zimbabwe	..	..	..	..	..	..	..	..	..	..	..	..
World	.. w	.. w	.. w	. w.	.. w	.. w	.. w	.. w	.. w	.. w	.. w	.. w
Low income	..	..	..	..	..	..	..	..	..	..	..	..
Middle income	..	..	..	..	..	..	..	..	..	..	..	..
Lower middle income	..	..	..	..	..	..	..	..	..	..	..	..
Upper middle income	..	17	..	12	..	32	..	20	..	50	..	68
Low & middle income	..	..	..	..	..	..	..	..	..	..	..	..
East Asia & Pacific	..	..	..	..	..	..	..	..	..	..	..	..
Europe & Central Asia	..	18	..	18	..	34	..	20	..	48	..	63
Latin America & Carib.	..	20	..	9	..	29	..	16	..	51	..	75
Middle East & N. Africa	..	..	..	..	..	..	..	..	..	..	..	..
South Asia	..	..	..	..	..	..	..	..	..	..	..	..
Sub-Saharan Africa	..	..	..	..	..	..	..	..	..	..	..	..
High income	6	4	5	3	38	34	19	13	55	61	76	84
Euro area	7	5	6	3	42	38	20	13	50	57	73	83

Note: Data across sectors may not sum to 100 percent because of workers not classified by sector.
a. Data are for the most recent year available. b. Less than 0.5. c. Limited coverage. d. Data are for 2009.

Employment by economic activity | 2.3

The International Labour Organization (ILO) classifies economic activity using the International Standard Industrial Classification (ISIC) of All Economic Activities, revision 2 (1968) and revision 3 (1990). Because this classification is based on where work is performed (industry) rather than type of work performed (occupation), all of an enterprise's employees are classified under the same industry, regardless of their trade or occupation. The categories should sum to 100 percent. Where they do not, the differences are due to workers who cannot be classified by economic activity.

Data on employment are drawn from labor force surveys, household surveys, official estimates, censuses and administrative records of social insurance schemes, and establishment surveys when no other information is available. The concept of employment generally refers to people above a certain age who worked, or who held a job, during a reference period. Employment data include both full-time and part-time workers.

There are many differences in how countries define and measure employment status, particularly members of the armed forces, self-employed workers, and unpaid family workers. Where members of the armed forces are included, they are allocated to the service sector, causing that sector to be somewhat overstated relative to the service sector in economies where they are excluded. Where data are obtained from establishment surveys, data cover only employees; thus self-employed and unpaid family workers are excluded. In such cases the employment share of the agricultural sector is severely underreported. Caution should be also used where the data refer only to urban areas, which record little or no agricultural work. Moreover, the age group and area covered could differ by country or change over time within a country. For detailed information on breaks in series, consult the original source.

Countries also take different approaches to the treatment of unemployed people. In most countries unemployed people with previous job experience are classified according to their last job. But in some countries the unemployed and people seeking their first job are not classifiable by economic activity. Because of these differences, the size and distribution of employment by economic activity may not be fully comparable across countries.

The ILO reports data by major divisions of the ISIC revision 2 or revision 3. In the table the reported divisions or categories are aggregated into three broad groups: agriculture, industry, and services.

Such broad classification may obscure fundamental shifts within countries' industrial patterns. A slight majority of countries report economic activity according to the ISIC revision 2 instead of revision 3. The use of one classification or the other should not have a significant impact on the information for the three broad sectors presented in the table.

The distribution of economic wealth in the world remains strongly correlated with employment by economic activity. The wealthier economies are those with the largest share of total employment in services, whereas the poorer economies are largely agriculture based.

The distribution of economic activity by gender reveals some clear patterns. Men still make up the majority of people employed in all three sectors, but the gender gap is biggest in industry. Employment in agriculture is also male-dominated, although not as much as industry. Segregating one sex in a narrow range of occupations significantly reduces economic efficiency by reducing labor market flexibility and thus the economy's ability to adapt to change. This segregation is particularly harmful for women, who have a much narrower range of labor market choices and lower levels of pay than men. But it is also detrimental to men when job losses are concentrated in industries dominated by men and job growth is centered in service occupations, where women have better chances, as has been the recent experience in many countries.

There are several explanations for the rising importance of service jobs for women. Many service jobs—such as nursing and social and clerical work—are considered "feminine" because of a perceived similarity to women's traditional roles. Women often do not receive the training needed to take advantage of changing employment opportunities. And the greater availability of part-time work in service industries may lure more women, although it is unclear whether this is a cause or an effect.

- **Agriculture** corresponds to division 1 (ISIC revision 2) or tabulation categories A and B (ISIC revision 3) and includes hunting, forestry, and fishing.
- **Industry** corresponds to divisions 2–5 (ISIC revision 2) or tabulation categories C–F (ISIC revision 3) and includes mining and quarrying (including oil production), manufacturing, construction, and public utilities (electricity, gas, and water). • **Services** correspond to divisions 6–9 (ISIC revision 2) or tabulation categories G–P (ISIC revision 3) and include wholesale and retail trade and restaurants and hotels; transport, storage, and communications; financing, insurance, real estate, and business services; and community, social, and personal services.

Data sources

Data on employment are from the ILO's Key Indicators of the Labour Market, 6th edition, database.

	Employment to population ratio				Gross enrollment ratio, secondary		Vulnerable employment				Labor productivity	
	Total % ages 15 and older		Youth % ages 15–24				Unpaid family workers and own-account workers				GDP per person employed % growth	
							Male % of male employment		Female % of female employment			
	1991	2008	1991	2008	1991	2009[a]	1990	2008	1990	2008	1990–92	2005–08
Afghanistan	54	55	45	47	16	44	..	..	..	..	..	..
Albania	49	46	37	36	89	72	..	..	..	..	–17.5	6.1
Algeria	39	49	25	31	60	..	..	..	..	..	–4.0	–0.7
Angola	77	76	71	69	12	..	..	..	..	..	–5.0	14.6
Argentina	53	57	42	36	74	85	..	22[b]	..	17[b]	9.0	3.7
Armenia	38	38	24	25	..	93	..	..	..	..	–24.8	12.2
Australia	56	59	58	64	132	149	12	11	9	7	3.3	0.7
Austria	52	55	61	53	102	100	..	9	..	9	0.7	0.4
Azerbaijan	57	60	38	39	88	99	..	41	..	66	–12.6	21.4
Bangladesh	74	68	66	56	18	42	..	..	..	..	1.9	4.0
Belarus	58	52	40	35	93	95	..	..	..	..	–4.0	8.7
Belgium	44	47	31	27	101	108	17	11	15	9	1.6	0.7
Benin	70	72	64	59	..	..	..	..	..	..	..	..
Bolivia	61	71	48	49	..	81	32[b]	..	50[b]	..	2.6	1.8
Bosnia and Herzegovina	42	42	17	18	..	91	..	..	..	..	–14.8	1.6
Botswana	47	46	34	27	49	82	..	..	..	..	..	..
Brazil	56	64	54	53	..	101	29[b]	30	30[b]	24	–0.3	3.2
Bulgaria	45	46	27	27	98	89	..	10	..	8	3.1	3.0
Burkina Faso	82	82	77	74	7	20	..	..	..	..	1.3	1.3
Burundi	85	84	74	73	5	21	..	..	..	..	..	..
Cambodia	77	75	66	68	25	40	..	..	..	..	4.0	6.5
Cameroon	59	59	37	33	26	41	..	..	..	..	–6.7	1.0
Canada	58	61	57	61	101	..	..	12[b]	..	9[b]	0.8	0.2
Central African Republic	73	73	59	58	12	14	..	..	..	..	..	..
Chad	67	70	51	50	6	24	..	..	..	..	..	..
Chile	51	50	34	24	97	90	..	25	..	24	6.6	0.2
China	75	71	71	55	41	78	..	..	..	..	6.8	10.6
Hong Kong SAR, China	62	57	54	38	..	82	..	10[b]	..	4[b]	5.3	3.0
Colombia	52	62	38	43	53	95	30[b]	41	26[b]	41	–0.7	4.8
Congo, Dem. Rep.	68	67	60	62	21	37	..	..	..	..	–12.9	2.9
Congo, Rep.	66	65	49	46	46	..	..	..	..	..	..	..
Costa Rica	56	57	48	43	45	96	26	20	21	20	2.4	1.9
Côte d'Ivoire	63	60	52	45	..	..	..	..	..	..	–3.6	–0.7
Croatia	50	46	27	29	83	90	..	23[c]	..	20[c]	–7.7	2.8
Cuba	52	54	40	32	94	90	..	..	..	..	..	..
Czech Republic	58	54	48	29	91	95	..	15	..	9	–5.2	3.4
Denmark	59	60	65	61	109	119	7	7	6	3	2.5	–0.7
Dominican Republic	44	53	28	34	..	77	42	49	30	30	0.7	5.4
Ecuador	52	61	39	40	55	81	33[b]	29[b]	41[b]	41[b]	–0.1	0.5
Egypt, Arab Rep.	43	43	22	23	69	..	..	20	..	44	2.1	4.4
El Salvador	59	54	42	39	38	64	..	29	..	44	..	..
Eritrea	66	66	60	54	11	32	..	..	..	..	..	..
Estonia	61	55	43	29	100	99	2[b]	8[b]	3[b]	4[b]	–9.4	2.4
Ethiopia	71	81	64	74	14	34	..	48[b]	..	56[b]	–8.4	7.4
Finland	57	55	45	44	116	110	..	11	..	7	1.4	1.5
France	47	48	28	29	100	113	11	7	10	5	1.4	0.6
Gabon	58	58	37	33	40	..	..	..	..	..	..	..
Gambia, The	73	72	59	55	19	51	..	..	..	..	..	..
Georgia	57	54	28	22	95	108	..	..	..	..	–25.3	10.1
Germany	54	52	58	44	98	102	..	7	..	6	3.7	0.9
Ghana	68	65	40	40	35	57	..	..	..	..	2.8	3.7
Greece	44	48	31	28	94	102	..	27	..	27	2.4	2.4
Guatemala	55	62	50	52	23	57	..	..	..	..	1.0	1.4
Guinea	82	81	75	73	11	37	..	..	..	..	..	..
Guinea-Bissau	66	67	57	63	5	..	..	..	..	..	..	..
Haiti	56	55	37	47	..	..	..	..	..	..	..	..
Honduras	59	56	49	43	33	65	48[b]	..	50[b]	..	..	..

Decent work and productive employment

	Employment to population ratio				Gross enrollment ratio, secondary		Vulnerable employment				Labor productivity	
							Unpaid family workers and own-account workers				GDP per person employed	
	Total % ages 15 and older		Youth % ages 15–24		% of relevant age group		Male % of male employment		Female % of female employment		% growth	
	1991	2008	1991	2008	1991	2009ᵃ	1990	2008	1990	2008	1990–92	2005–08
Hungary	48	45	37	20	86	97	8ᵇ	8	7ᵇ	6	0.3	2.0
India	58	56	46	40	46	60	..	..	..	..	1.0	5.9
Indonesia	63	62	46	41	46	79	..	60	..	68	6.2	3.8
Iran, Islamic Rep.	46	49	33	36	53	83	..	40	..	56	6.5	1.8
Iraq	37	37	27	23	40	51	..	..	..	..	–33.6	1.9
Ireland	44	58	38	44	100	115	25	17	9	5	2.4	0.7
Israel	45	50	25	27	92	90	..	9	..	5	0.0	1.3
Italy	43	44	30	25	79	101	29	21	24	15	0.6	–0.3
Jamaica	61	56	40	29	70	91	46	38	37	31	0.7	–2.2
Japan	61	54	43	40	97	101	15	10	26	12	0.7	1.2
Jordan	36	38	25	20	82	88	..	..	..	..	–5.5	2.5
Kazakhstan	63	64	46	42	98	99	..	..	..	..	–15.1	4.8
Kenya	73	73	62	59	..	59	..	..	..	..	–3.9	2.5
Korea, Dem. Rep.	62	64	46	39	..	..	..	..	..	..	..	..
Korea, Rep.	59	58	36	28	91	97	..	23	..	28	5.0	3.1
Kosovo	..	..	..	..	..	..	..	..	..	..	..	..
Kuwait	62	65	29	30	53	90	..	..	..	..	–0.2	3.2
Kyrgyz Republic	58	58	41	40	100	84	..	47	..	47	–13.1	4.3
Lao PDR	80	78	74	64	21	44	..	..	..	..	..	..
Latvia	58	55	43	35	92	98	..	8	..	6	–19.6	2.9
Lebanon	44	46	31	29	61	82	..	..	..	..	..	..
Lesotho	48	54	40	40	24	45	..	..	..	..	..	..
Liberia	66	66	57	57	..	..	..	..	..	..	..	..
Libya	45	49	28	27	..	..	..	..	..	..	..	..
Lithuania	54	50	36	18	92	99	..	11	..	8	–13.9	5.2
Macedonia, FYR	37	35	17	13	76	84	..	24	..	20	–5.6	1.2
Madagascar	79	83	65	71	19	32	..	..	..	..	–5.9	2.2
Malawi	72	72	48	49	17	30	..	..	..	..	–1.9	5.6
Malaysia	60	61	47	45	57	69	31	23	25	21	6.0	3.1
Mali	49	47	40	35	7	38	..	..	..	..	0.4	1.9
Mauritania	67	47	54	23	13	24	..	..	..	..	..	..
Mauritius	56	54	45	37	55	87	13	18	7	15	..	..
Mexico	57	57	50	42	54	90	29	28	15	32	1.0	1.0
Moldova	58	45	39	17	90	88	..	35	..	30	–22.0	6.9
Mongolia	50	52	39	35	82	92	..	..	..	..	..	..
Morocco	46	46	40	35	36	56	..	46	..	65	–1.7	2.8
Mozambique	80	78	67	66	7	23	..	..	..	..	–3.0	5.5
Myanmar	74	74	62	53	23	53	..	..	..	..	2.0	5.8
Namibia	45	43	24	14	43	66	..	..	..	..	..	..
Nepal	60	62	52	46	34	..	..	..	..	..	..	..
Netherlands	51	59	55	67	120	121	7	10	10	8	0.4	1.0
New Zealand	55	63	55	56	92	119	15	14	10	10	0.5	–0.3
Nicaragua	57	58	46	48	43	68	..	45	..	46	..	..
Niger	59	60	50	52	7	12	..	..	..	..	–5.7	2.3
Nigeria	53	52	29	24	24	30	..	..	..	..	–2.9	3.3
Norway	58	62	49	56	103	112	..	8	..	3	3.9	–1.1
Oman	53	51	30	29	45	91	..	..	..	..	0.2	3.7
Pakistan	48	52	38	44	23	33	..	58	..	75	6.5	2.5
Panama	50	59	33	40	62	73	44	30	19	24	..	..
Papua New Guinea	70	70	57	54	12	..	..	..	..	..	..	..
Paraguay	61	73	51	58	31	67	17ᵇ	45	31ᵇ	50	..	..
Peru	53	69	34	53	67	89	30ᵇ	33ᵇ	46ᵇ	47ᵇ	–0.8	0.2
Philippines	59	60	42	39	70	82	..	44ᵇ	..	47ᵇ	–3.3	3.9
Poland	53	48	31	27	87	100	..	20	..	18	2.8	1.9
Portugal	58	56	53	35	66	104	22	18	30	19	2.2	0.9
Puerto Rico	37	41	21	29	..	84	..	..	..	..	..	..
Qatar	73	77	35	47	84	85	..	..	..	..	0.1	13.3

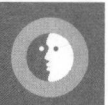

	Employment to population ratio				Gross enrollment ratio, secondary		Vulnerable employment				Labor productivity	
								Unpaid family workers and own-account workers				
	Total % ages 15 and older		Youth % ages 15–24		% of relevant age group		Male % of male employment		Female % of female employment		GDP per person employed % growth	
	1991	2008	1991	2008	1991	2009[a]	1990	2008	1990	2008	1990–92	2005–08
Romania	56	48	42	24	92	92	21	31	33	32	–9.3	6.5
Russian Federation	57	57	34	33	93	85	1	6	1	6	–7.9	6.4
Rwanda	87	80	79	64	18	27	..	..	..	..	..	..
Saudi Arabia	50	48	26	13	..	97	..	..	..	..	4.9	0.7
Senegal	67	66	60	55	15	30	77	..	91	..	–1.0	0.9
Serbia	49[d]	44[d]	28[d]	21[d]	..	91	..	25	..	20	..	..
Sierra Leone	64	65	38	42	16	35	..	..	..	..	..	..
Singapore	64	62	56	38	..	..	10	12	6	7	1.5	–1.8
Slovak Republic	55	53	43	30	88	92	..	14	..	6	–0.8	6.1
Slovenia	55	54	38	32	89	97	..	12	..	10	–2.3	3.0
Somalia	66	67	59	58	..	8	..	..	..	..	..	..
South Africa	39	41	19	15	69	94	..	2	..	3	–4.5	3.7
Spain	41	49	36	37	105	120	20[b]	13	24[b]	10	2.4	0.7
Sri Lanka	51	55	31	36	72	..	..	39[b]	..	44[b]	5.5	9.3
Sudan	46	47	29	23	20	38	..	..	..	..	–1.3	7.5
Swaziland	54	50	34	26	49	53	..	..	..	..	..	..
Sweden	62	58	59	45	90	103	..	9	..	4	1.9	0.6
Switzerland	65	61	69	63	98	96	8	10	11	11	–0.6	1.0
Syrian Arab Republic	47	45	38	32	48	75	..	..	..	..	6.5	0.3
Tajikistan	54	55	36	38	102	84	..	..	..	..	–20.4	6.3
Tanzania	87	78	79	70	5	27	..	82[b]	..	93[b]	–2.4	4.5
Thailand	77	72	70	46	31	76	67	51	74	56	6.8	2.7
Timor-Leste	64	67	51	58	..	51	..	..	..	..	..	..
Togo	66	65	58	53	20	41	..	..	..	..	..	..
Trinidad and Tobago	45	61	33	46	82	89	22	..	21	..	–3.5	5.4
Tunisia	41	41	29	22	45	92	..	..	..	..	2.6	2.7
Turkey	53	42	48	31	48	82	..	30	..	49	1.0	2.6
Turkmenistan	56	58	35	34	..	..	..	..	..	..	–13.0	7.9
Uganda	82	83	73	75	10	27	..	..	..	..	–1.1	6.1
Ukraine	57	54	37	34	94	94	..	..	..	..	–7.9	5.9
United Arab Emirates	71	76	43	46	68	95	..	..	..	..	–3.9	0.7
United Kingdom	56	56	66	56	87	99	13	14	6	7	2.0	2.2
United States	59	59	56	51	92	94	..	..	..	..	1.7	1.4
Uruguay	53	56	42	39	84	88	..	26[b]	..	24[b]	5.2	4.9
Uzbekistan	54	58	36	39	99	104	..	..	..	..	–7.8	5.9
Venezuela, RB	51	61	35	40	56	82	..	28	..	33	4.5	4.3
Vietnam	75	69	75	51	35	..	..	..	..	..	4.6	5.6
West Bank and Gaza	30	30	19	15	..	87	..	34	..	44	..	..
Yemen, Rep.	38	39	23	22	..	..	..	..	..	..	0.9	–0.8
Zambia	57	61	40	46	21	49	56	..	81	..	–2.5	3.9
Zimbabwe	70	65	48	50	49	..	..	..	..	..	–4.7	–7.7
World	**62 w**	**60 w**	**52 w**	**45 w**	**50 w**	**67 w**	**.. w**	**.. w**	**.. w**	**.. w**	**0.7 w**	**3.1 w**
Low income	71	70	60	58	26	38	..	..	..	..	–3.2	4.4
Middle income	63	61	52	42	47	68	..	..	..	..	1.3	6.2
Lower middle income	65	62	55	44	42	63	..	..	..	..	3.2	7.4
Upper middle income	53	56	41	38	67	88	..	26	..	26	–2.3	3.6
Low & middle income	63	62	53	45	44	63	..	..	..	..	1.1	6.1
East Asia & Pacific	73	69	67	51	41	74	..	..	..	..	6.5	8.7
Europe & Central Asia	55	53	38	33	85	89	..	19	..	19	–9.1	5.8
Latin America & Carib.	55	61	46	45	57	89	..	30	..	30	1.8	2.6
Middle East & N. Africa	43	45	29	29	54	73	..	33	..	52	1.4	2.2
South Asia	59	57	48	42	37	52	..	..	..	..	3.1	5.5
Sub-Saharan Africa	64	64	50	49	22	34	..	..	..	..	–5.3	4.1
High income	55	55	47	43	91	100	..	13	..	11	2.3	1.2
Euro area	48	50	41	37	..	..	..	12	..	9	2.4	0.7

a. Provisional data. b. Limited coverage. c. Data are for 2009. d. Includes Montenegro.

Decent work and productive employment | 2.4

Four targets were added to the UN Millennium Declaration at the 2005 World Summit High-Level Plenary Meeting of the 60th Session of the UN General Assembly. One was full and productive employment and decent work for all, which is seen as the main route for people to escape poverty. The four indicators for this target have an economic focus, and three of them are presented in the table.

The employment to population ratio indicates how efficiently an economy provides jobs for people who want to work. A high ratio means that a large proportion of the population is employed. But a lower employment to population ratio can be seen as a positive sign, especially for young people, if it is caused by an increase in their education. This indicator has a gender bias because women who do not consider their work employment or who are not perceived as working tend to be undercounted. This bias has different effects across countries and reflects demographic, social, legal, and cultural trends and norms.

Comparability of employment ratios across countries is also affected by variations in definitions of employment and population (see *About the data* for table 2.3). The biggest difference results from the age range used to define labor force activity. The population base for employment ratios can also vary (see table 2.1). Most countries use the resident, noninstitutionalized population of working age living in private households, which excludes members of the armed forces and individuals residing in mental, penal, or other types of institutions. But some countries include members of the armed forces in the population base of their employment ratio while excluding them from employment data (International Labour Organization, *Key Indicators of the Labour Market*, 6th edition).

The proportion of unpaid family workers and own-account workers in total employment is derived from information on status in employment. Each status group faces different economic risks, and unpaid family workers and own-account workers are the most vulnerable—and therefore the most likely to fall into poverty. They are the least likely to have formal work arrangements, are the least likely to have social protection and safety nets to guard against economic shocks, and often are incapable of generating sufficient savings to offset these shocks. A high proportion of unpaid family workers in a country indicates weak development, little job growth, and often a large rural economy.

Data on employment by status are drawn from labor force surveys and household surveys, supplemented by official estimates and censuses for a small group of countries. The labor force survey is the most comprehensive source for internationally comparable employment, but there are still some limitations for comparing data across countries and over time even within a country. Information from labor force surveys is not always consistent in what is included in employment. For example, information provided by the Organisation for Economic Co-operation and Development relates only to civilian employment, which can result in an underestimation of "employees" and "workers not classified by status," especially in countries with large armed forces. While the categories of unpaid family workers and self-employed workers, which include own-account workers, would not be affected, their relative shares would be. Geographic coverage is another factor that can limit cross-country comparisons. The employment by status data for many Latin American countries covers urban areas only. Similarly, in some countries in Sub-Saharan Africa, where limited information is available anyway, the members of producer cooperatives are usually excluded from the self-employed category. For detailed information on definitions and coverage, consult the original source.

Labor productivity is used to assess a country's economic ability to create and sustain decent employment opportunities with fair and equitable remuneration. Productivity increases obtained through investment, trade, technological progress, or changes in work organization can increase social protection and reduce poverty, which in turn reduce vulnerable employment and working poverty. Productivity increases do not guarantee these improvements, but without them—and the economic growth they bring—improvements are highly unlikely. For comparability of individual sectors labor productivity is estimated according to national accounts conventions. However, there are still significant limitations on the availability of reliable data. Information on consistent series of output in both national currencies and purchasing power parity dollars is not easily available, especially in developing countries, because the definition, coverage, and methodology are not always consistent across countries. For example, countries employ different methodologies for estimating the missing values for the nonmarket service sectors and use different definitions of the informal sector.

• **Employment to population ratio** is the proportion of a country's population that is employed. People ages 15 and older are generally considered the working-age population. People ages 15–24 are generally considered the youth population. • **Gross enrollment ratio, secondary,** is the ratio of total enrollment in secondary education, regardless of age, to the population of the age group that officially corresponds to secondary education. • **Vulnerable employment** is unpaid family workers and own-account workers as a percentage of total employment. • **Labor productivity** is the growth rate of gross domestic product (GDP) divided by the number of people engaged in the production of goods and services.

Data on employment to population ratio, vulnerable employment, and labor productivity are from the ILO's Key Indicators of the Labour Market, 6th edition, database. Data on gross enrollment ratios are from the United Nations Educational, Scientific, and Cultural Organization Institute for Statistics.

	Unemployment						Long-term unemployment			Unemployment by educational attainment		
	Total % of total labor force		Male % of male labor force		Female % of female labor force		% of total unemployment			% of total unemployment		
							Total	Male	Female	Primary	Secondary	Tertiary
	1990–92[a]	2006–09[a]	1990–92[a]	2006–09[a]	1990–92[a]	2006–09[a]	2006–09[a]	2006–09[a]	2006–09[a]	2006–09[a]	2006–09[a]	2006–09[a]
Afghanistan	..	..	..	..	..	..	..	..	..	..	..	..
Albania	..	12.7	..	..	..	..	..	..	..	..	..	..
Algeria	23.0	11.3	24.2	11.0	20.3	10.1	..	..	..	..	..	..
Angola	..	..	..	..	..	..	..	..	..	..	..	..
Argentina	6.7[b]	8.6[b]	6.4[b]	7.8[b]	7.0[b]	9.8[b]	..	..	..	48.1[b]	36.7[b]	15.3[b]
Armenia	..	28.6[b]	..	21.9[b]	..	35.0[b]	..	..	..	5.2	83.0	11.9
Australia	10.8	5.6[b]	11.4	5.7[b]	10.0	5.4[b]	14.7[b]	15.0[b]	14.4[b]	48.0	34.1	17.9
Austria	3.6	4.8	3.5	5.0	3.8	4.5	20.3	19.7	21.0	37.9[b]	52.1[b]	10.0[b]
Azerbaijan	..	6.1	..	7.1	..	4.9	..	..	..	6.3	78.9	14.9
Bangladesh	1.9	..	2.0	..	1.9	..	..	..	..	..	..	..
Belarus	..	..	..	..	..	..	..	..	..	10.8	38.6	50.6
Belgium	6.7	7.9	4.8	7.7	9.5	8.1	44.2	43.5	45.0	42.1	38.2	19.7
Benin	1.5	..	2.2	..	0.6	..	..	..	..	..	..	..
Bolivia	5.5[b]	5.2[b]	5.5[b]	4.5[b]	5.6[b]	6.0[b]	..	..	..	..	..	..
Bosnia and Herzegovina	17.6	23.9	15.5	21.8	21.6	27.1	..	..	..	95.7	..	4.0
Botswana	13.8	17.6[b]	11.7	15.3[b]	17.2	19.9[b]	..	..	..	..	..	..
Brazil	6.4[b]	8.3	5.4[b]	6.1	7.9[b]	11.0	..	..	..	51.6	33.6	3.6
Bulgaria	..	6.8	..	7.0	..	6.6	43.3	40.7	46.4	41.8	49.7	8.6
Burkina Faso	..	..	..	..	..	..	..	..	..	..	..	..
Burundi	0.5	..	0.7	..	0.3	..	..	..	..	..	..	..
Cambodia	..	..	..	..	..	..	..	..	..	..	..	..
Cameroon	..	2.9	..	2.5	..	3.3	..	..	..	..	..	..
Canada	11.2[b]	8.3[b]	12.0[b]	9.4[b]	10.2[b]	7.0[b]	7.8[b]	8.1[b]	7.4[b]	27.7[b]	41.1[b]	31.2[b]
Central African Republic	..	..	..	..	..	..	..	..	..	..	..	..
Chad	..	..	..	..	..	..	..	..	..	..	..	..
Chile	4.4	9.7	3.9	9.1	5.3	10.7	..	..	..	17.8	58.5	23.5
China	2.3[b]	4.3	..	..	..	..	..	..	..	..	..	..
Hong Kong SAR, China	2.0[b]	5.2[b]	2.0[b]	6.0[b]	1.9[b]	4.3[b]	..	..	..	40.8[b]	41.4[b]	16.6[b]
Colombia	9.5[b]	12.0	6.8[b]	9.3	13.0[b]	15.8	..	..	..	76.6	..	20.6
Congo, Dem. Rep.	..	..	..	..	..	..	..	..	..	..	..	..
Congo, Rep.	..	..	..	..	..	..	..	..	..	..	..	..
Costa Rica	4.1	4.9	3.5	4.1	5.4	6.2	..	..	..	65.2	27.3	6.4
Côte d'Ivoire	6.7	..	..	..	..	..	..	..	..	..	..	..
Croatia	11.1	9.1	11.1	8.0	11.2	10.2	56.2	50.8	61.0	16.0	70.4	11.6
Cuba	..	1.6	..	1.4	..	2.0	..	..	..	43.0	52.4	4.6
Czech Republic	2.3	6.7	2.4	5.8	2.1	7.7	31.2	29.0	33.4	26.8	68.8	4.3
Denmark	9.0	6.0	8.3	6.5	9.9	5.4	9.1	8.9	9.4	35.9	35.1	23.0
Dominican Republic	20.7	14.2	12.0	8.5	35.2	22.8	..	..	..	35.0	44.5	16.4
Ecuador	8.9[b]	6.5	6.0[b]	5.2	13.2[b]	8.4	..	..	..	74.0[b]	..	23.6[b]
Egypt, Arab Rep.	..	9.4	..	5.2	..	22.9	..	..	..	..	..	..
El Salvador	7.9[b]	5.9	8.4[b]	7.5	7.2[b]	3.6	..	..	..	..	..	..
Eritrea	..	..	..	..	..	..	..	..	..	..	..	..
Estonia	3.7[b]	13.7	3.9[b]	17.0	3.5[b]	10.8	27.4	26.8	28.4	23.1[b]	57.8[b]	16.6[b]
Ethiopia	1.3	20.5[b]	1.1	12.1[b]	1.6	29.9[b]	..	..	..	..	..	..
Finland	11.6	8.2	13.3	8.9	9.6	7.5	16.6	18.2	14.7	35.5	45.9	18.6
France	10.2	9.1	8.1	8.9	12.8	9.3	35.4	35.6	35.3	39.9	39.6	19.9
Gabon	..	..	..	..	..	..	..	..	..	..	..	..
Gambia, The	..	..	..	..	..	..	..	..	..	..	..	..
Georgia	..	16.5	..	16.8	..	16.1	..	..	..	5.1[b]	52.5[b]	42.3[b]
Germany	6.6	7.7	5.3	8.1	8.4	7.3	45.5	44.4	47.0	33.1	56.3	10.6
Ghana	4.7	..	3.7	..	5.5	..	..	..	..	..	..	..
Greece	7.8	9.5	4.9	6.9	12.9	13.1	40.8	34.4	45.6	29.3[b]	48.4[b]	21.8[b]
Guatemala	..	1.8	..	1.5	..	2.4	..	..	..	..	..	..
Guinea	..	..	..	..	..	..	..	..	..	..	..	..
Guinea-Bissau	..	..	..	..	..	..	..	..	..	..	..	..
Haiti	12.7	..	11.9	..	13.8	..	..	..	..	..	..	..
Honduras	3.2[b]	2.9[b]	3.3[b]	2.9[b]	3.0[b]	2.9[b]	..	..	..	..	..	..

	Unemployment						Long-term unemployment			Unemployment by educational attainment		
	Total % of total labor force		Male % of male labor force		Female % of female labor force		% of total unemployment			% of total unemployment		
	1990–92[a]	2006–09[a]	1990–92[a]	2006–09[a]	1990–92[a]	2006–09[a]	Total 2006–09[a]	Male 2006–09[a]	Female 2006–09[a]	Primary 2006–09[a]	Secondary 2006–09[a]	Tertiary 2006–09[a]
Hungary	9.9	10.0	11.0	10.3	8.7	9.7	42.6	42.4	42.8	33.1[b]	58.7[b]	8.1[b]
India	..	..	..	..	..	..	..	..	..	..	..	..
Indonesia	2.8	7.9	2.7	7.5	3.0	8.5	..	..	..	44.4	40.7	9.6
Iran, Islamic Rep.	11.1	10.5	9.5	9.1	24.4	16.8	..	..	..	..	..	..
Iraq	..	17.5	..	16.2	..	22.5	..	..	..	..	..	..
Ireland	15.0	11.7	14.9	14.7	15.2	8.0	29.0	32.1	21.7	39.8	37.2	18.2
Israel	11.2	7.6	9.2	7.6	13.9	7.6	28.6	32.3	25.0	12.2	12.8	72.5
Italy	9.3	7.8	6.7	6.8	13.9	9.3	44.4	42.0	46.9	46.5	40.6	11.3
Jamaica	15.4	11.4	9.4	8.5	22.2	14.8	..	..	..	9.7	4.3	8.4
Japan	2.2	5.0	2.1	5.3	2.2	4.7	28.5	34.8	18.8	67.2	..	32.8
Jordan	..	12.9	..	10.3	..	24.1	..	..	..	..	..	..
Kazakhstan	..	6.6	..	5.6	..	7.5	..	..	..	..	..	..
Kenya	..	..	..	..	..	..	..	..	..	..	..	..
Korea, Dem. Rep.	..	..	..	..	..	..	..	..	..	..	..	..
Korea, Rep.	2.5[b]	3.6[b]	2.8[b]	4.1[b]	2.1[b]	3.0[b]	0.5	0.6	0.3	15.2	49.7	35.2
Kosovo	..	45.4	..	40.7	..	56.4	81.7	82.8	79.8	64.0	46.0	15.0
Kuwait	..	..	..	..	..	..	..	..	..	19.4	41.4	9.6
Kyrgyz Republic	..	8.2	..	7.3	..	9.4	..	..	..	13.3	77.1	9.6
Lao PDR	..	..	..	..	..	..	..	..	..	..	..	..
Latvia	..	17.1	..	20.4	..	14.0	26.7	27.1	26.0	24.3[b]	59.9[b]	14.6[b]
Lebanon	..	9.0	..	8.6	..	10.1	..	..	..	..	..	..
Lesotho	..	..	..	..	..	..	..	..	..	..	..	..
Liberia	..	5.6	..	6.8	..	4.2	..	..	..	..	..	..
Libya	..	..	..	..	..	..	..	..	..	..	..	..
Lithuania	..	13.7	..	17.1	..	10.4	23.2	21.0	26.8	14.2[b]	70.4[b]	15.4[b]
Macedonia, FYR	..	32.2	..	31.7	..	33.0	81.6	82.2	80.6	..	..	..
Madagascar	..	..	..	..	..	..	..	..	..	..	..	..
Malawi	..	..	..	..	..	..	..	..	..	..	..	..
Malaysia	3.7	3.7	..	3.2	..	3.7	..	..	..	13.3	61.6	25.1
Mali	..	..	..	..	..	..	..	..	..	..	..	..
Mauritania	..	..	..	..	..	..	..	..	..	..	..	..
Mauritius	3.3	7.3	3.2	4.4	3.6	12.3	..	..	..	44.2	48.5	6.4
Mexico	3.1	5.2	2.7	5.4	4.0	4.8	1.9	1.8	2.1	50.7	24.5	22.9
Moldova	..	6.4	..	7.8	..	4.9	..	..	..	..	..	..
Mongolia	..	..	..	..	..	..	..	..	..	..	..	..
Morocco	16.0[b]	10.0	13.0[b]	9.8	25.3[b]	10.5	..	..	..	..	..	..
Mozambique	..	..	..	..	..	..	..	..	..	..	..	..
Myanmar	6.0	..	4.7	..	8.8	..	..	..	..	..	..	..
Namibia	19.0	37.6	20.0	32.5	19.0	43.0	..	..	..	..	..	..
Nepal	..	..	..	..	..	..	..	..	..	..	..	..
Netherlands	5.6	3.4	4.0	3.4	7.8	3.5	24.8	23.7	26.1	41.3	39.7	17.0
New Zealand	10.6[b]	6.1[b]	11.4[b]	6.1[b]	9.7[b]	6.1[b]	6.3[b]	6.3[b]	6.4[b]	30.6	38.8	26.9
Nicaragua	14.4	5.0	11.3	4.9	19.5	5.1	..	..	..	72.8	2.1	18.0
Niger	..	..	..	..	..	..	..	..	..	..	..	..
Nigeria	..	..	..	..	..	..	..	..	..	..	..	..
Norway	5.9	3.2	6.6	3.6	5.1	2.6	7.7	7.5	8.0	25.4	49.2	20.6
Oman	..	..	..	..	..	..	..	..	..	..	..	..
Pakistan	5.2	5.0	3.8	4.0	14.0	8.7	..	..	..	14.3	11.4	26.0
Panama	14.7	5.9	10.8	4.6	22.3	7.9	..	..	..	36.0	39.6	24.0
Papua New Guinea	7.7	..	9.0	..	5.9	..	..	..	..	..	..	..
Paraguay	5.0[b]	5.6	6.0[b]	4.4	3.7[b]	7.5	..	..	..	49.9	38.0	9.9
Peru	9.4[b]	6.8[b]	7.5[b]	5.4[b]	12.5[b]	8.3[b]	..	..	..	30.0[b]	31.9[b]	37.6[b]
Philippines	8.6[b]	7.5	7.9[b]	7.5	9.9[b]	7.4	..	..	..	13.8	45.2	41.1
Poland	13.3	8.2	12.2	7.8	14.7	8.7	25.2	23.3	27.3	16.4[b]	73.2[b]	10.4[b]
Portugal	4.1[b]	9.5	3.5[b]	8.9	5.0[b]	10.1	44.2	40.8	47.5	68.1[b]	15.4[b]	13.2[b]
Puerto Rico	16.9	13.4	19.1	14.9	13.3	11.6	..	..	..	..	..	..
Qatar	..	0.5	..	0.2	..	2.6	..	..	..	..	..	..

| | Unemployment | | | | | | Long-term unemployment | | | Unemployment by educational attainment | | |
| | Total % of total labor force | | Male % of male labor force | | Female % of female labor force | | % of total unemployment | | | % of total unemployment | | |
	1990–92[a]	2006–09[a]	1990–92[a]	2006–09[a]	1990–92[a]	2006–09[a]	Total 2006–09[a]	Male 2006–09[a]	Female 2006–09[a]	Primary 2006–09[a]	Secondary 2006–09[a]	Tertiary 2006–09[a]
Romania	..	6.9	..	7.7	..	5.8	31.6	32.2	30.6	25.8	66.3	6.1
Russian Federation	5.2	8.2	5.2	8.4	5.2	7.9	35.7	33.3	38.4	13.7	54.2	32.1
Rwanda	0.3	..	0.6	..	0.2	..	..	..	..	..	..	..
Saudi Arabia	..	5.4	..	3.5	..	15.9	..	..	..	7.5	48.6	43.6
Senegal	..	10.0	..	7.9	..	13.6	..	..	..	40.2	6.9	2.5
Serbia	..	16.6	..	15.3	..	18.4	71.1	70.1	72.1	20.3	68.4	11.2
Sierra Leone	..	..	..	..	..	..	..	..	..	..	..	..
Singapore	2.7[b]	5.9	2.7[b]	5.4	2.6[b]	6.5	..	..	..	31.0	25.6	43.2
Slovak Republic	..	12.1	..	11.4	..	12.9	50.9	47.8	54.4	29.2	65.3	5.3
Slovenia	7.1	5.9	8.1	5.9	6.0	5.8	30.1	28.3	32.1	25.0[b]	60.4[b]	12.5[b]
Somalia	..	..	..	..	..	..	..	..	..	..	..	..
South Africa	..	23.8	..	22.0	..	25.9	14.4	..	..	36.2	56.3	4.5
Spain	18.1	18.0	13.9	17.7	25.8	18.4	30.2	26.9	34.4	54.8[b]	23.6[b]	20.4[b]
Sri Lanka	14.2[b]	7.6	..	7.2	..	8.1	..	..	..	45.4[b]	22.0[b]	32.6[b]
Sudan	..	..	..	..	..	..	..	..	..	..	..	..
Swaziland	..	..	..	..	..	..	..	..	..	..	..	..
Sweden	5.7	8.3	6.7	8.6	4.6	8.0	12.8	13.1	12.4	32.2[b]	46.0[b]	17.1[b]
Switzerland	2.8	4.1	2.3	3.7	3.5	4.5	30.0	26.4	33.6	28.8	53.2	17.9
Syrian Arab Republic	6.8	8.4	5.2	5.2	14.0	25.7	..	..	..	..	..	..
Tajikistan	..	..	..	..	..	..	..	..	..	66.5	28.8	4.6
Tanzania	3.6[b]	4.3	2.8[b]	2.8	4.3[b]	5.8	..	..	..	..	..	..
Thailand	1.4	1.2	1.3	1.2	1.5	1.1	..	..	..	40.5	45.5	0.1
Timor-Leste	..	..	..	..	..	..	..	..	..	..	..	..
Togo	..	..	..	..	..	..	..	..	..	..	..	..
Trinidad and Tobago	19.6	5.3	17.0	3.5	23.9	6.2	..	..	..	..	..	..
Tunisia	..	14.2	..	..	..	..	..	..	..	..	..	..
Turkey	8.5	14.0	8.8	13.9	7.8	14.3	25.3	22.6	32.2	52.3	28.2	12.7
Turkmenistan	..	..	..	..	..	..	..	..	..	..	..	..
Uganda	1.0	..	1.3	..	0.6	..	..	..	..	..	..	..
Ukraine	..	8.8	..	6.6	..	6.1	..	..	..	8.5	52.2	39.3
United Arab Emirates	..	4.0	..	2.0	..	12.0	..	..	..	..	..	..
United Kingdom	9.7	7.7	11.5	8.8	7.3	6.4	24.6	26.5	21.5	37.3	47.7	14.3
United States	7.5[b]	9.3[b]	7.9[b]	10.3[b]	7.0[b]	8.1[b]	16.3[b]	16.4[b]	16.1[b]	18.7	35.5	45.7
Uruguay	9.0[b]	7.3	6.8[b]	5.3	11.8[b]	9.7	..	..	..	59.1[b]	27.0[b]	13.8[b]
Uzbekistan	..	..	..	..	..	..	..	..	..	..	..	..
Venezuela, RB	7.7	7.6	8.2	7.2	6.8	8.1	..	..	..	..	..	..
Vietnam	..	2.4	..	..	..	..	..	..	..	..	..	..
West Bank and Gaza	..	24.5	..	17.7	..	38.6	..	..	..	54.3	14.2	23.5
Yemen, Rep.	..	15.0	..	11.5	..	40.9	..	..	..	..	..	..
Zambia	18.9	..	16.3	..	22.4	..	..	..	..	..	..	..
Zimbabwe	..	..	..	..	..	..	..	..	..	..	..	..
World	.. w	.. w	.. w	.. w	.. w	.. w	.. w	.. w	.. w	.. w	.. w	.. w
Low income	..	..	..	..	..	..	..	..	..	..	..	..
Middle income	..	..	..	..	..	..	..	..	..	..	..	..
Lower middle income	..	..	..	..	..	..	..	..	..	..	..	..
Upper middle income	6.7	9.1	6.4	8.5	7.4	10.3	..	..	..	43.4	40.9	14.3
Low & middle income	..	..	..	..	..	..	..	..	..	..	..	..
East Asia & Pacific	2.5	4.6	..	..	..	..	..	..	..	..	..	..
Europe & Central Asia	..	9.2	..	9.9	..	8.6	..	..	..	26.7	50.2	24.1
Latin America & Carib.	6.6	7.9	5.4	6.6	8.4	9.8	..	..	..	50.8	34.9	12.3
Middle East & N. Africa	..	10.6	..	8.9	..	16.7	..	..	..	..	..	..
South Asia	..	..	..	..	..	..	..	..	..	..	..	..
Sub-Saharan Africa	..	..	..	..	..	..	..	..	..	..	..	..
High income	7.5	8.1	7.1	8.4	8.0	7.7	24.8	25.3	23.8	33.9	43.7	25.7
Euro area	9.1	9.4	7.2	9.2	11.9	9.6	38.2	36.7	39.8	41.3	43.0	14.9

a. Data are for the most recent year available. b. Limited coverage.

About the data

Unemployment and total employment are the broadest indicators of economic activity as reflected by the labor market. The International Labour Organization (ILO) defines the unemployed as members of the economically active population who are without work but available for and seeking work, including people who have lost their jobs or who have voluntarily left work. Some unemployment is unavoidable. At any time some workers are temporarily unemployed—between jobs as employers look for the right workers and workers search for better jobs. Such unemployment, often called frictional unemployment, results from the normal operation of labor markets.

Changes in unemployment over time may reflect changes in the demand for and supply of labor; they may also reflect changes in reporting practices. Paradoxically, low unemployment rates can disguise substantial poverty in a country, while high unemployment rates can occur in countries with a high level of economic development and low rates of poverty. In countries without unemployment or welfare benefits people eke out a living in vulnerable employment. In countries with well developed safety nets workers can afford to wait for suitable or desirable jobs. But high and sustained unemployment indicates serious inefficiencies in resource allocation.

The ILO definition of unemployment notwithstanding, reference periods, the criteria for people considered to be seeking work, and the treatment of people temporarily laid off or seeking work for the first time vary across countries. In many developing countries it is especially difficult to measure employment and unemployment in agriculture. The timing of a survey, for example, can maximize the effects of seasonal unemployment in agriculture. And informal sector employment is difficult to quantify where informal activities are not tracked.

Data on unemployment are drawn from labor force sample surveys and general household sample surveys, censuses, and official estimates, which are generally based on information from different sources and can be combined in many ways. Administrative records, such as social insurance statistics and employment office statistics, are not included in the table because of their limitations in coverage. Labor force surveys generally yield the most comprehensive data because they include groups not covered in other unemployment statistics, particularly people seeking work for the first time. These surveys generally use a definition of unemployment that follows the international recommendations more closely than that used by other sources and therefore generate statistics that are more comparable internationally. But the age group, geographic coverage, and collection methods could differ by country or change over time within a country. For detailed information, consult the original source.

Women tend to be excluded from the unemployment count for various reasons. Women suffer more from discrimination and from structural, social, and cultural barriers that impede them from seeking work. Also, women are often responsible for the care of children and the elderly and for household affairs. They may not be available for work during the short reference period, as they need to make arrangements before starting work. Furthermore, women are considered to be employed when they are working part-time or in temporary jobs, despite the instability of these jobs or their active search for more secure employment.

Long-term unemployment is measured by the length of time that an unemployed person has been without work and looking for a job. The data in the table are from labor force surveys. The underlying assumption is that shorter periods of joblessness are of less concern, especially when the unemployed are covered by unemployment benefits or similar forms of support. The length of time that a person has been unemployed is difficult to measure, because the ability to recall that time diminishes as the period of joblessness extends. Women's long-term unemployment is likely to be lower in countries where women constitute a large share of the unpaid family workforce.

Unemployment by level of educational attainment provides insights into the relation between the educational attainment of workers and unemployment and may be used to draw inferences about changes in employment demand. Information on educational attainment is the best available indicator of skill levels of the labor force. Besides the limitations to comparability raised for measuring unemployment, the different ways of classifying the education level may also cause inconsistency. Education level is supposed to be classified according to International Standard Classification of Education 1997 (ISCED97). For more information on ISCED97, see *About the data* for table 2.11.

Definitions

• **Unemployment** is the share of the labor force without work but available for and seeking employment. Definitions of labor force and unemployment may differ by country (see *About the data*). • **Long-term unemployment** is the number of people with continuous periods of unemployment extending for a year or longer, expressed as a percentage of the total unemployed. • **Unemployment by educational attainment** is the unemployed by level of educational attainment as a percentage of the total unemployment. The levels of educational attainment accord with the ISCED97 of the United Nations Educational, Scientific, and Cultural Organization.

Data sources

Data on unemployment are from the ILO's Key Indicators of the Labour Market, 6th edition, database.

2.6 | Children at work

	Survey year	Children in employment					Employment by economic activity[a]			Status in employment[a]		
		% of children ages 7–14			% of children ages 7–14 in employment		% of children ages 7–14 in employment			% of children ages 7–14 in employment		
		Total	Male	Female	Work only	Study and work	Agriculture	Manufacturing	Services	Self-employed	Wage	Unpaid family
Afghanistan		..	..	..	..	..	..	..	..	..	..	..
Albania	2005	25.0	18.8	22.0	6.7	93.3	..	..	..	..	1.4	94.5
Algeria		..	..	..	..	..	..	..	..	..	..	..
Angola[b]	2001	30.1	30.0	30.1	26.6	73.4	..	..	..	..	6.2	80.1
Argentina	2004	12.9	15.7	9.8	4.8	95.2	..	..	..	34.2	8.1	56.2
Armenia		..	..	..	..	..	..	..	..	..	..	..
Australia		..	..	..	..	..	..	..	..	..	..	..
Austria		..	..	..	..	..	..	..	..	..	..	..
Azerbaijan	2005	5.2	5.8	4.5	6.3	93.7	91.7	0.7	7.4	4.1	3.8	92.1
Bangladesh	2006	16.2	25.7	6.4	37.8	62.2	..	..	..	-	17.0	77.8
Belarus	2005	11.7	12.1	11.2	0.0	100.0	..	..	..	..	9.2	78.8
Belgium		..	..	..	..	..	..	..	..	..	..	..
Benin	2006	74.4	72.8	76.1	36.1	63.9	..	..	..	..	..	..
Bolivia	2008	32.1	33.0	31.1	5.2	94.8	73.2	6.1	19.2	0.9	9.2	89.9
Bosnia and Herzegovina	2006	10.6	11.7	9.5	0.1	99.9	..	..	..	..	1.6	92.1
Botswana		..	..	..	..	..	..	..	..	..	..	..
Brazil	2008	5.2	6.9	3.5	4.8	95.2	54..7	7.6	34.6	5.5	24.7	69.8[c]
Bulgaria		..	..	..	..	..	..	..	..	..	..	..
Burkina Faso	2006	42.1	49.0	34.5	67.7	32.3	70.9	1.4	24.9	1.9	2.2	95.8
Burundi	2005	11.7	12.5	11.0	38.9	61.1	..	..	..	..	25.9	68.6
Cambodia[d]	2003/04	48.9	49.6	48.1	13.8	86.2	82.3	4.2	12.9	6.0	4.1	89.4
Cameroon	2007	43.4	43.5	43.4	21.9	78.1	88.5	3.1	8.2	2.5	9.5	87.6
Canada		..	..	..	..	..	..	..	..	..	..	..
Central African Republic	2000	67.0	66.5	67.6	54.9	45.1	..	..	..	..	2.0	56.4
Chad	2004	60.4	64.4	56.2	49.1	50.9	..	..	..	..	1.8	77.2
Chile	2003	4.1	5.1	3.1	3.2	96.8	24.1	6.9	66.9	..	..	..
China		..	..	..	..	..	..	..	..	..	..	..
Hong Kong SAR, China		..	..	..	..	..	..	..	..	..	..	..
Colombia	2007	3.9	5.3	2.3	24.8	75.2	41.2	10.8	46.1	22.7	29.1	45.6
Congo, Dem. Rep.[d]	2000	39.8	39.9	39.8	35.7	64.3	..	..	..	..	6.6	76.7
Congo, Rep	2005	30.1	29.9	30.2	9.9	90.1	..	..	..	..	4.2	84.5
Costa Rica[d]	2004	5.7	8.1	3.5	44.6	55.4	40.3	9.5	49.0	15.8	57.7	26.6
Côte d'Ivoire	2006	45.7	47.7	43.6	46.8	53.2	..	..	..	..	2.4	88.0
Croatia		..	..	..	..	..	..	..	..	..	..	..
Cuba		..	..	..	..	..	..	..	..	..	..	..
Czech Republic		..	..	..	..	..	..	..	..	..	..	..
Denmark		..	..	..	..	..	..	..	..	..	..	..
Dominican Republic[d]	2005	5.8	9.0	2.7	6.2	93.8	18.5	9.8	57.5	23.8	19.5	56.2[e]
Ecuador	2006	14.3	16.9	11.6	21.0	79.0	69.3	6.3	22.8	3.6	15.2	81.2
Egypt, Arab Rep.	2005	7.9	11.5	4.3	21.0	79.0	..	..	..	..	11.4	87.4
El Salvador	2007	7.1	10.1	3.8	24.9	75.1	50.1	13.3	35.2	2.2	23.6	74.2
Eritrea		..	..	..	..	..	..	..	..	..	..	..
Estonia		..	..	..	..	..	..	..	..	..	..	..
Ethiopia	2005	56.0	64.3	47.1	69.4	30.6	94.6	1.5	3.7	1.7	2.4	95.8
Finland		..	..	..	..	..	..	..	..	..	..	..
France		..	..	..	..	..	..	..	..	..	..	..
Gabon		..	..	..	..	..	..	..	..	..	..	..
Gambia, The	2005	43.5	33.9	52.3	32.1	67.9	..	..	..	..	1.1	87.3
Georgia	2006	31.8	33.6	29.9	1.0	99.0	..	..	..	..	4.3	77.0
Germany		..	..	..	..	..	..	..	..	..	..	..
Ghana	2006	48.9	49.9	48.0	18.7	81.3	..	..	..	..	6.1	76.2
Greece		..	..	..	..	..	..	..	..	..	..	..
Guatemala	2006	18.2	24.5	11.7	28.4	71.6	63.7	9.7	24.7	2.0	18.8	79.2
Guinea	1994	48.3	47.2	49.5	98.6	1.4	..	..	..	..	..	..
Guinea-Bissau	2006	50.5	52.8	48.1	36.4	63.6	..	..	..	..	4.0	87.7
Haiti	2005	33.4	37.3	29.6	17.7	82.3	..	..	..	..	1.8	79.4
Honduras	2007	8.7	13.3	4.1	45.1	54.9	61.6	10.4	25.1	3.5	23.0	73.5

Children at work

PEOPLE **2.6**

	Survey year	Children in employment					Employment by economic activity[a]			Status in employment[a]		
		% of children ages 7–14			% of children ages 7–14 in employment		% of children ages 7–14 in employment			% of children ages 7–14 in employment		
		Total	Male	Female	Work only	Study and work	Agriculture	Manufacturing	Services	Self-employed	Wage	Unpaid family
Hungary	..	..	..	..	..	..	..	..	..	..	..	..
India	2004/05	4.2	4.2	4.2	84.9	15.2	69.4	16.0	12.4	7.1	6.8	59.3
Indonesia	2000	8.9	8.8	9.1	24.9	75.1	..	..	..	..	17.8	75.8[e]
Iran, Islamic Rep.	..	..	..	..	..	..	..	..	..	..	..	..
Iraq	2006	14.7	17.9	11.3	32.4	67.6	..	..	..	..	7.0	85.3
Ireland	..	..	..	..	..	..	..	..	..	..	..	..
Israel	..	..	..	..	..	..	..	..	..	..	..	..
Italy	..	..	..	..	..	..	..	..	..	..	..	..
Jamaica	2005	9.8	11.3	8.3	2.5	97.5	..	..	..	..	16.3	74.9
Japan	..	..	..	..	..	..	..	..	..	..	..	..
Jordan	..	..	..	..	..	..	..	..	..	..	..	..
Kazakhstan	2006	3.6	4.4	2.8	1.6	98.4	..	..	..	-	4.0	75.0
Kenya	2000	37.7	40.1	35.2	14.1	85.9	..	..	..	..	..	..
Korea, Dem. Rep.	..	..	..	..	..	..	..	..	..	..	..	..
Korea, Rep.	..	..	..	..	..	..	..	..	..	..	..	..
Kosovo	..	..	..	..	..	..	..	..	..	..	..	..
Kuwait	..	..	..	..	..	..	..	..	..	..	..	..
Kyrgyz Republic	2006	5.2	5.8	4.6	7.9	92.1	..	..	..	-	3.7	81.9
Lao PDR	..	..	..	..	..	..	..	..	..	..	..	..
Latvia	..	..	..	..	..	..	..	..	..	..	..	..
Lebanon	..	..	..	..	..	..	..	..	..	..	..	..
Lesotho	2002	2.6	4.0	1.3	74.4	25.6	58.0	0.0	10.4	3.7	36.6	59.7[c]
Liberia	2007	37.4	37.8	37.1	45.0	55.0	..	..	..	..	1.7	79.3
Libya	..	..	..	..	..	..	..	..	..	..	..	..
Lithuania	..	..	..	..	..	..	..	..	..	..	..	..
Macedonia, FYR	2005	11.8	14.8	8.6	2.8	97.2	..	..	..	..	3.9	89.5
Madagascar	2007	26.0	27.7	24.2	40.9	59.1	87.6	2.9	8.2	0.1	10.0	89.9
Malawi	2006	40.3	41.3	39.4	10.5	89.5	..	..	..	..	6.7	75.5
Malaysia	..	..	..	..	..	..	..	..	..	..	..	..
Mali	2006	49.5	55.0	44.1	59.5	40.5	..	..	..	..	1.6	80.4
Mauritania	..	..	..	..	..	..	..	..	..	..	..	..
Mauritius	..	..	..	..	..	..	..	..	..	..	..	..
Mexico[f]	2009	12.2	16.5	7.6	22.6	77.4	38.2	11.7	47.0	2.7	34.3	63.1
Moldova	2000	33.5	34.1	32.8	3.8	96.2	..	..	..	..	2.9	82.0
Mongolia	2006/07	10.1	11.4	8.6	16.4	83.6	91.3	0.3	6.3	5.1	0.1	94.7
Morocco	1998/99	13.2	13.5	12.8	93.2	6.8	60.6	8.3	10.1	2.1	10.0	81.7
Mozambique[d]	1996	1.8	1.9	1.7	100.0	0.0	..	..	..	..	..	..
Myanmar	..	..	..	..	..	..	..	..	..	..	..	..
Namibia	1999	15.4	16.2	14.7	9.5	90.5	91.5	0.4	8.0	0.1	4.5	95.0
Nepal	1999	47.2	42.2	52.4	35.6	64.4	87.0	1.4	11.1	4.2	3.3	92.4
Netherlands	..	..	..	..	..	..	..	..	..	..	..	..
New Zealand	..	..	..	..	..	..	..	..	..	..	..	..
Nicaragua	2005	10.1	16.2	3.9	30.8	69.2	70.5	9.7	19.3	1.2	13.8	85.0[c]
Niger	2006	47.1	49.2	45.0	66.5	33.5	..	..	..	4.8	74.5	..
Nigeria	..	..	..	..	..	..	..	..	..	..	..	..
Norway	..	..	..	..	..	..	..	..	..	..	..	..
Oman	..	..	..	..	..	..	..	..	..	..	..	..
Pakistan	..	..	..	..	..	..	..	..	..	..	..	..
Panama	2008	8.9	12.1	5.4	14.6	85.4	73.3	2.9	22.9	12.6	11.3	76.1[c]
Papua New Guinea	..	..	..	..	..	..	..	..	..	..	..	..
Paraguay[c]	2005	15.3	22.6	7.7	24.2	75.7	60.8	6.2	32.1	9.3	24.8	65.8
Peru	2007	42.2	44.8	39.5	4.0	96.0	62.6	5.0	31.1	3.8	7.6	88.6
Philippines	2001	13.3	16.3	10.0	14.8	85.2	64.3	4.1	30.6	4.1	22.8	73.1
Poland	..	..	..	..	..	..	..	..	..	..	..	..
Portugal	2001	3.6	4.6	2.6	3.6	96.4	48.5	11.2	33.3	..	..	..
Puerto Rico	..	..	..	..	..	..	..	..	..	..	..	..
Qatar	..	..	..	..	..	..	..	..	..	..	..	..

2011 World Development Indicators **57**

	Survey year	Children in employment					Employment by economic activity[a]			Status in employment[a]		
		% of children ages 7–14			% of children ages 7–14 in employment		% of children ages 7–14 in employment			% of children ages 7–14 in employment		
		Total	Male	Female	Work only	Study and work	Agriculture	Manufacturing	Services	Self-employed	Wage	Unpaid family
Romania	2000	1.4	1.7	1.1	20.7	79.3	97.1	0.0	2.3	4.5	..	92.9[e]
Russian Federation		..	..	..	..	..	..	..	..	..	..	..
Rwanda	2008	7.5	8.0	7.0	18.5	81.5	85.5	0.7	10.5	14.8	12.8	72.3
Saudi Arabia		..	..	..	..	..	..	..	..	..	..	..
Senegal	2005	18.5	24.4	12.6	61.9	38.1	79.1	5.0	14.0	6.3	4.4	84.1
Serbia	2005	6.9	7.2	6.6	2.1	97.9	..	..	..	..	5.2	89.4
Sierra Leone	2007	14.9	14.9	14.9	57.7	42.3	83.8	0.8	13.4	9.7	0.9	87.8
Singapore		..	..	..	..	..	..	..	..	..	..	..
Slovak Republic		..	..	..	..	..	..	..	..	..	..	..
Slovenia		..	..	..	..	..	..	..	..	..	..	..
Somalia	2006	43.5	45.5	41.5	53.5	46.5	..	..	..	..	1.6	94.8
South Africa	1999	27.7	29.0	26.4	5.1	94.9	..	..	..	7.1	7.1	85.8
Spain		..	..	..	..	..	..	..	..	..	..	..
Sri Lanka	1999	17.0	20.4	13.4	5.4	94.6	71.2	13.1	15.0	2.9	8.3	88.0
Sudan[g]	2000	19.1	21.5	16.8	55.9	44.1	..	..	..	..	7.3	81.3
Swaziland	2000	11.2	11.4	10.9	14.0	86.0	..	..	..	..	10.4	85.9
Sweden		..	..	..	..	..	..	..	..	..	..	..
Switzerland		..	..	..	..	..	..	..	..	..	..	..
Syrian Arab Republic	2006	6.6	8.8	4.3	34.6	65.4	..	..	..	..	21.5	68.8
Tajikistan	2005	8.9	8.7	9.1	9.0	91.0	..	..	..	..	24.2	71.3
Tanzania[h]	2005/06	31.1	35.0	27.1	28.2	71.8	85.3	0.7	14.0	56.3	0.9	42.8[e]
Thailand	2005	15.1	15.7	14.4	4.2	95.8	..	..	..	..	13.5	80.0
Timor-Leste		..	..	..	..	..	..	..	..	..	..	..
Togo	2006	38.7	39.8	37.4	29.8	70.2	82.9	1.3	15.1	5.0	1.6	93.4
Trinidad and Tobago	2000	3.9	5.2	2.8	12.8	87.2	..	..	..	..	29.8	64.9
Tunisia		..	..	..	..	..	..	..	..	..	..	..
Turkey[i]	2006	2.6	3.3	1.8	38.8	61.2	57.1	14.3	27.1	2.1	34.1	63.8
Turkmenistan		..	..	..	..	..	..	..	..	..	..	..
Uganda	2005/06	38.2	39.8	36.5	7.7	92.3	95.5	1.4	3.0	1.4	1.5	97.1
Ukraine	2005	17.3	18.0	16.6	0.1	99.9	..	..	..	..	3.1	79.3
United Arab Emirates		..	..	..	..	..	..	..	..	..	..	..
United Kingdom		..	..	..	..	..	..	..	..	..	..	..
United States		..	..	..	..	..	..	..	..	..	..	..
Uruguay		..	..	..	..	..	..	..	..	..	..	..
Uzbekistan	2005	5.1	5.3	4.9	1.0	99.0	..	..	..	..	3.8	78.6
Venezuela, RB[d]	2006	5.1	6.9	3.3	19.8	80.2	32.3	7.2	55.7	31.6	33.1	35.3
Vietnam	2006	21.3	21.0	21.6	11.9	88.1	..	..	..	..	5.9	91.2
West Bank and Gaza		..	..	..	..	..	..	..	..	..	..	..
Yemen, Rep.	2006	18.3	20.7	15.9	30.9	69.1	..	..	..	..	6.1	86.1
Zambia	2008	34.4	35.4	33.3	18.6	81.4	91.9	0.7	7.0	2.9	3.9	93.1
Zimbabwe	1999	14.3	15.3	13.3	12.0	88.0	..	..	..	..	3.4	28.4	68.2

a. Shares may not sum to 100 percent because of a residual category not included in the table. b. Covers only Angola-secured territory. c. Refers to unpaid workers, regardless of whether they are family workers. d. Covers children ages 10–14. e. Refers to family workers, regardless of whether they are paid. f. Covers children ages 12–14. g. Northern Sudan only. h. Refers mainly to work on own shamba. i. Estimates are for children ages 6–14.

Children at work | 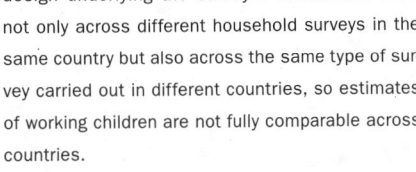 2.6

The data in the table refer to children's work in the sense of "economic activity"—that is, children in employment, a broader concept than child labor (see ILO 2009a for details on this distinction).

In line with the definition of economic activity adopted by the 13th International Conference of Labour Statisticians, the threshold for classifying a person as employed is to have been engaged at least one hour in any activity during the reference period relating to the production of goods and services set by the 1993 UN System of National Accounts. Children seeking work are thus excluded. Economic activity covers all market production and certain non-market production, including production of goods for own use. It excludes unpaid household services (commonly called "household chores")—that is, the production of domestic and personal services by household members for own-household consumption.

Data are from household surveys conducted by the International Labor Organization (ILO), the United Nations Children's Fund (UNICEF), the World Bank, and national statistical offices. The surveys yield data on education, employment, health, expenditure, and consumption indicators related to children's work.

Household survey data generally include information on work type—for example, whether a child is working for payment in cash or in kind or is involved in unpaid work, working for someone who is not a member of the household, or involved in any type of family work (on the farm or in a business). Country surveys define the ages for child labor as 5–17. The data in the table have been recalculated to present statistics for children ages 7–14.

Although efforts are made to harmonize the definition of employment and the questions on employment in survey questionnaires, significant differences remain in the survey instruments that collect data on children in employment and in the sampling design underlying the surveys. Differences exist not only across different household surveys in the same country but also across the same type of survey carried out in different countries, so estimates of working children are not fully comparable across countries.

The table aggregates the distribution of children in employment by the industrial categories of the International Standard Industrial Classification (ISIC): agriculture, manufacturing, and services. A residual category—which includes mining and quarrying; electricity, gas, and water; construction; extraterritorial organization; and other inadequately defined activities—is not presented. Both ISIC revision 2 and revision 3 are used, depending on the country's codification for describing economic activity. This does not affect the definition of the groups in the table.

The table also aggregates the distribution of children in employment by status in employment, based on the International Classification of Status in Employment (1993), which shows the distribution in employment by three major categories: selfemployed workers, wage workers (also known as employees), and unpaid family workers. A residual category—which includes those not classifiable by status—is not presented.

In most countries more boys are involved in employment or the gender difference is small. However, girls are often more present in hidden or under-reported forms of employment such as domestic service, and in almost all societies girls bear greater responsibility for household chores in their own homes, work that lies outside the System of National Accounts production boundary and is thus not considered in estimates of children's employment.

• **Survey year** is the year in which the underlying data were collected. • **Children in employment** are children involved in any economic activity for at least one hour in the reference week of the survey. • **Work only** refers to children who are employed and not attending school. • **Study and work** refer to children attending school in combination with employment. • **Employment by economic activity** is the distribution of children in employment by the major industrial categories (ISIC revision 2 or revision 3). • **Agriculture** corresponds to division 1 (ISIC revision 2) or categories A and B (ISIC revision 3) and includes agriculture and hunting, forestry and logging, and fishing. • **Manufacturing** corresponds to division 3 (ISIC revision 2) or category D (ISIC revision 3). • **Services** correspond to divisions 6–9 (ISIC revision 2) or categories G–P (ISIC revision 3) and include wholesale and retail trade, hotels and restaurants, transport, financial intermediation, real estate, public administration, education, health and social work, other community services, and private household activity. • **Self-employed workers** are people whose remuneration depends directly on the profits derived from the goods and services they produce, with or without other employees, and include employers, own-account workers, and members of producers cooperatives. • **Wage workers** (also known as employees) are people who hold explicit (written or oral) or implicit employment contracts that provide basic remuneration that does not depend directly on the revenue of the unit for which they work. • **Unpaid family workers** are people who work without pay in a market-oriented establishment operated by a related person living in the same household.

Data on children at work are estimates produced by the Understanding Children's Work project based on household survey data sets made available by the ILO's International Programme on the Elimination of Child Labour under its Statistical Monitoring Programme on Child Labour, UNICEF under its Multiple Indicator Cluster Survey program, the World Bank under its Living Standards Measurement Study program, and national statistical offices. Information on how the data were collected and some indication of their reliability can be found at www.ilo.org/public/english/standards/ipec/simpoc/, www.childinfo.org, and www.worldbank.org/lsms. Detailed country statistics can be found at www.ucw-project.org.

The largest sector for child labor remains agriculture, and the majority of children work as unpaid family members   2.6a

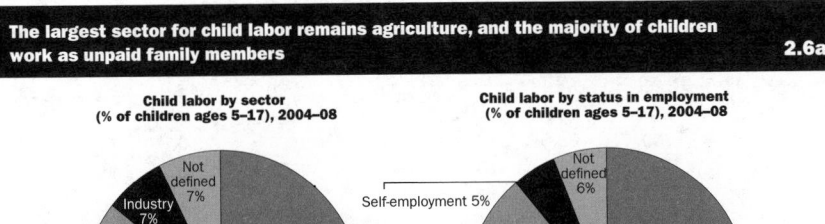

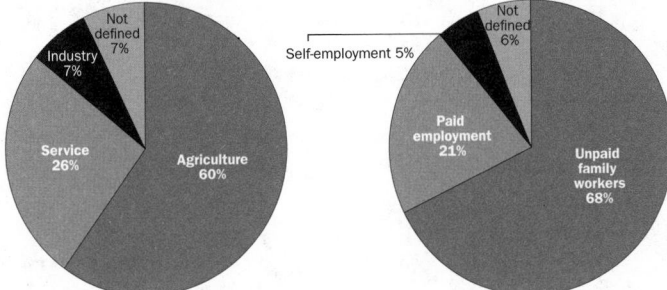

Child labor by sector
(% of children ages 5–17), 2004–08

Not defined 7%
Industry 7%
Service 26%
Agriculture 60%

Child labor by status in employment
(% of children ages 5–17), 2004–08

Not defined 6%
Self-employment 5%
Paid employment 21%
Unpaid family workers 68%

Source: Accelerating Action Against Child Labour, ILO, Geneva 2010.

	Population below national poverty line[a]							Poverty gap at national poverty line[a]			
	Survey year[b]	Rural %	Urban %	National %	Survey year[b]	Rural %	Urban %	National %	Survey year[b]	Rural %	Urban %	National %
Afghanistan[c]		..		..	2008[d]	37.5	29.0	36.0	2008[d]	8.3	6.2	7.9
Albania[c]	2005	24.2	11.2	18.5	2008	14:6	10.1	12.4	2008	2.6	1.9	2.3
Angola		..			2000[d]	..	62.3	..		..	..	..
Argentina	2008[e]	..	15.3	..	2009[e]	..	13.2			..	..	..
Armenia[c]	2008	22.9	23.8	23.5	2009	25.5	26.9	26.5	2009	..	..	4.9
Azerbaijan[c]	2001	42.5	55.7	49.6	2008	18.5	14.8	15.8	2008	..	..	2.0
Bangladesh	2000	52.3	35.2	48.9	2005	43.8	28.4	40.0	2005	9.8	6.5	9.0
Belarus	2008	..	..	6.1	2009	..	..	5.4		..	..	..
Benin		..	..	..	2003[d]	46.0	29.0	39.0	2003[d]	14.0	8.0	12.0
Bhutan					2007[d]	30.9	1.7	23.2	2007[d]	8.1	0.4	6.1
Bolivia	2006[e]	76.5	50.3	59.9	2007[e]	77.3	50.9	60.1		..	..	..
Bosnia and Herzegovina[c]	2004	22.0	11.3	17.7	2007	17.8	8.2	14.0		..	..	..
Botswana	1993	40.4	24.7	32.9	2003	44.8	19.4	30.6	2003	18.4	6.5	11.7
Brazil	2008[e]			22.6	2009[e]			21.4				
Bulgaria[c]	1997			36.0	2001			12.8	2001			4.2
Burkina Faso		..	..	..	2003[d]	52.4	19.2	46.4	2003[d]	17.6	5.1	15.3
Burundi					2006[d]	68.9	34.0	66.9	2006[d]	24.2	10.3	23.4
Cambodia[c]	2004	37.8	17.6	34.7	2007	34.5	11.8	30.1	2007	8.3	2.8	7.2
Cameroon					2007[d]	55.0	12.2	39.9	2007[d]	17.5	2.8	12.3
Cape Verde		..	..	..	2007[d]	44.3	13.2	26.6	2007[d]	14.3	3.3	8.1
Central African Republic		..	..	..	2008[d]	69.4	49.6	62.0	2008[d]	35.0	29.8	33.1
Chad		..		..	2003[d]	58.6	24.6	55.0	2003[d]	23.3	7.4	21.6
Chile	2006[e]	12.3	13.9	13.7	2009[e]	12.9	15.5	15.1		..	..	..
China	2004[e]	2.8	..	..	2005[e]	2.5	..	..		..	..	..
Colombia	2008[e]	65.2	39.8	46.0	2009[e]	64.3	39.6	45.5		..	..	..
Comoros		..	..	..	2004[d]	48.7	34.5	44.8	2004[d]	17.8	12.1	16.3
Congo, Dem. Rep.		..	..	..	2005	75.7	61.5	71.3	2005	34.9	26.2	32.2
Congo, Rep.		..		..	2005	57.7	..	50.1	2005	20.6	..	18.9
Costa Rica	2008[e]	22.2	19.5	20.7	2009[e]	..	..	21.7		..	..	..
Croatia	2002	..	..	11.2	2004	..	..	11.1	2004	..	..	2.6
Côte d'Ivoire[c]	2002	45.8	32.3	40.2	2008	54.2	29.4	42.7	2008	20.3	9.5	15.3
Dominican Republic	2005[e]	60.2	49.9	53.5	2006[e]	57.1	45.3	49.4		..	..	..
Ecuador	2008[e]	59.7	22.6	35.1	2009[e]	57.5	25.0	36.0		..	..	..
Egypt, Arab Rep.	2005	26.8	10.1	19.6	2008	30.0	10.6	22.0		..	..	..
El Salvador	2007[e,f]	43.8	29.8	34.6	2008[e,f]	49.0	35.7	40.0		..	..	..
Ethiopia	1999	45.4	36.9	44.2	2004	39.3	35.1	38.9	2004	8.5	7.7	8.3
Fiji	2003	40.0	28.0	35.0	2009	43.3	18.6	31.0	2009	14.8	5.4	10.1
Gabon		..	..	..	2005	44.6	29.8	32.7	2005	16.0	8.5	10.0
Gambia, The[c]		..	..	..	2003[d]	67.8	39.6	58.0	2003[d]	30.5	14.8	25.1
Georgia[c]		..	..	..	2007	29.7	18.3	23.6	2007	9.2	5.3	7.2
Ghana	1998	49.6	19.4	39.5	2006	39.2	10.8	28.5	2006	13.5	3.1	9.6
Guatemala	2000[e]	74.5	27.1	56.2	2006[e]	70.5	30.0	51.0		..	..	..
Guinea		..	..	..	2007[d]	63.0	30.5	53.0	2007[d]	22.0	7.7	17.6
Guinea-Bissau		..	..	..	2002	69.1	51.6	64.7	2002	27.8	16.9	25.0
Haiti		..	..	..	2001[e]	88.0	45.0	77.0		..	..	..
Honduras	2008[e,f]	64.1	55.0	59.6	2009[e,f]	64.4	52.8	58.8		..	..	..
India	1994	37.3	32.4	36.0	2005	28.3	25.7	27.5		..	..	..
Indonesia	2009	17.4	10.7	14.2	2010	16.6	9.9	13.3	2010	2.8	1.6	2.2
Iraq		..	..	..	2007	39.3	16.1	22.9	2007	9.0	2.7	4.5
Jamaica	2006[e]	..	..	14.3	2007[e]	..	..	9.9		..	..	..
Jordan	2002	18.7	12.9	14.2	2006	19.0	12.0	13.0	2006	..	..	2.8
Kazakhstan[c]	2001	23.2	13.0	17.6	2002	21.7	10.2	15.4	2002	4.5	2.0	3.1
Kenya		..	..	..	2005[d]	49.1	33.7	45.9	2005[d]	17.5	11.4	16.3
Kosovo[c]	2005	37.2	30.3	34.8	2006	49.2	37.4	45.0	2006	14.3	11.3	13.3
Kyrgyz Republic[c]	2003	57.5	35.7	49.9	2005	50.8	29.8	43.1	2005	12.0	7.0	10.0
Lao PDR[c]	2003	..	..	33.5	2008	31.7	17.4	27.6		..	..	..
Latvia[c]	2002	11.6	..	7.5	2004	12.7	..	5.9	2004	..	..	1.2

Poverty rates at national poverty lines

	Population below national poverty line[a]							Poverty gap at national poverty line[a]			
	Survey year[b]	Rural %	Urban %	National %	Survey year[b]	Rural %	Urban %	National %	Survey year[b]	Rural %	Urban %	National %
Lesotho[c]	1994	68.9	36.7	66.6	2003	60.5	41.5	56.6	..	..	..	..
Liberia[c]					2007	67.7	55.1	63.8	2007	26.3	20.2	24.4
Macedonia, FYR[c]	2005	21.2	19.8	20.4	2006	21.3	17.7	19.0	2006	7.7	6.9	7.2
Madagascar	2004	77.3	53.7	72.1	2005	73.5	52.0	68.7	2005	28.9	19.3	26.8
Malawi	1998	58.1	18.5	54.1	2004	55.9	25.4	52.4	2004	19.2	7.1	17.8
Malaysia[c]	2007	7.1	2.0	3.6	2009	8.2	1.7	3.8	2009	1.8	0.3	0.8
Mali	..	..	..		2006[d]	57.6	25.5	47.4	2006[d]	..	..	16.7
Mauritania		..	..	..	2000[d]	61.2	25.4	46.3	2000[d]	24.1	6.3	17.0
Mexico	2006[e]	54.7	35.6	42.6	2008[e]	60.8	39.8	47.4	..	..	..	..
Moldova[c]	2004	..	..	26.5	2005	..	..	29.0	..	..	..	..
Mongolia		..	..	..	2008[d]	46.6	26.9	35.2	2008[d]	13.4	7.7	10.1
Montenegro	2007	12.0	5.5	8.0	2008	8.9	2.4	4.9	2008	1.4	0.6	0.9
Morocco		..	..	..	2001	25.1	7.6	15.3	..	..	..	..
Mozambique	2002	55.3	51.5	54.1	2008	56.9	49.6	54.7	2008	22.2	19.1	21.2
Namibia		..	..	..	2003[d]	49.0	17.0	38.0	2003[d]	16.0	6.0	13.0
Nepal	1996	43.3	21.6	41.8	2004	34.6	9.6	30.9	2004	8.5	2.2	7.5
Nicaragua	2001[e]	67.8	30.1	45.8	2005[e]	67.9	29.1	46.2	..	..	..	..
Niger		..	..	..	2007[d]	63.9	36.7	59.5	2007[d]	21.2	11.3	19.6
Nigeria		..	..	..	2004[d]	63.8	43.1	54.7	2004[d]	26.6	16.2	22.8
Pakistan	2005	28.1	14.9	23.9	2006	27.0	13.1	22.3	..	..	..	..
Panama	2003	62.7	20.0	36.8	2008	59.8	17.7	32.7	..	..	..	..
Paraguay	2008[e]	48.8	30.2	37.9	2009[e]	49.8	24.7	35.1	..	..	..	..
Peru	2008	59.8	23.5	36.2	2009	60.3	21.1	34.8	..	..	..	..
Philippines	2006	..	..	26.4	2009	..	..	26.5	2009	..	..	2.7
Poland[c]	2001	..	..	15.6	2002	..	..	16.6	..	..	..	..
Romania[c]	2005	23.5	8.1	15.1	2006	22.3	6.8	13.8	2006	5.3	1.4	3.2
Russian Federation[c]	2005	22.7	8.1	11.9	2006	21.2	7.4	11.1	2006	5.5	1.7	2.7
Rwanda		..	..	..	2006[d]	64.2	23.2	58.5	2006[d]	26.0	8.0	24.0
São Tomé and Príncipe		..	..	..	2001	64.9	45.0	53.8	2001	24.7	14.9	19.2
Senegal[c]		..	..	..	2005[d]	61.9	35.1	50.8	2005[d]	21.5	9.3	16.4
Serbia[c]	2006	13.9	5.2	9.0	2007	9.8	4.3	6.6	2007	2.0	0.8	1.3
Sierra Leone		..	..	..	2003[d]	78.5	47.0	66.4	2003[d]	34.6	16.3	27.5
South Africa	2000	..	..	38.0	2005	..	..	23.0	2005	..	..	7.0
Sri Lanka	2002	24.7	7.9	22.7	2007	15.7	6.7	15.2	2007	3.2	1.3	3.1
Swaziland		..	..	..	2001[d]	75.0	49.0	69.2	2001[d]	37.0	20.0	32.9
Tajikistan[c]	2007	54.4	49.3	53.1	2009	49.2	41.8	47.2	..	..	..	..
Tanzania	2000	38.6	23.1	35.6	2007	37.4	21.8	33.4	2007	11.0	6.5	9.9
Thailand	2008	11.5	3.0	9.0	2009	10.4	3.0	8.1	..	..	..	..
Timor-Leste	2001	..	..	39.7	2007	..	..	49.9	..	..	..	..
Togo					2006	74.3	36.8	61.7	2006	29.3	10.3	22.9
Turkey	2008	34.6	9.4	17.1	2009	38.7	8.9	18.1	..	..	..	..
Uganda	2005	34.2	13.7	31.1	2009	27.2	9.1	24.5	2009	7.6	1.8	6.8
Ukraine[c]	2004	18.1	12.0	14.0	2005	11.3	6.3	7.9	2005	2.3	1.1	1.5
Uruguay	2007[e]	29.4	25.5	26.0	2008[e]	22.2	20.3	20.5	..	..	..	..
Venezuela, RB	2008[e]	..	..	32.6	2009[e]	..	..	29.0	..	..	..	..
Vietnam	2006	20.4	3.9	16.0	2008	18.7	3.3	14.5	2008	4.6	0.5	3.5
West Bank and Gaza	2007	..	..	31.2	2009	..	..	21.9	2009	..	..	4.9
Yemen, Rep.	1998	42.5	32.3	40.1	2005	40.1	20.7	34.8	2005	10.6	4.5	8.9
Zambia	2004	77.3	29.1	58.4	2006	76.8	26.7	59.3	2006	38.8	9.4	28.5
Zimbabwe		..	..	..	2003[d]	..	..	72.0	..	..	..	..

a. Based on per capita consumption estimated from household survey data, unless otherwise noted. b. Refers to the year in which the underlying household survey data were collected; in cases for which the data collection period bridged two calender years, the year in which most of the data were collected is reported. c. World Bank estimates. d. Estimates based on survey data from earlier year(s) are available, but are not comparable with the most recent year reported here; these are available online at http://data.worldbank.org. e. Based on income per capita estimated from household survey data. f. Measured as a share of households.

About the data

Estimates of poverty rates and gaps at national poverty lines are useful for comparing poverty across time within but not across countries. Table 2.8 shows poverty indicators at international poverty lines that allow for comparisons across countries.

For countries with an active poverty monitoring program, the World Bank—in collaboration with national institutions, other development agencies, and civil society—periodically prepares poverty assessments and other analytical reports to assess the extent and causes of poverty. These reports review levels and changes in poverty indicators over time and across regions within countries, assess the impact of growth and public policy on poverty and inequality, review the adequacy of monitoring and evaluation, and contain detailed technical overviews of the underlying household survey data and poverty measurement methods used. The reports are a key source of comprehensive information on poverty indicators at national poverty lines and generally feed into country-owned processes to reduce poverty, build in-country capacity, and support joint work.

An increasing number of countries have their own national programs to monitor and disseminate official poverty estimates at national poverty lines along with well documented household survey data sources and estimation methodology. Estimates from national poverty monitoring programs and the underlying methods used are periodically reviewed by the World Bank and included in the table.

The complete online database of poverty estimates at national poverty lines (available at http://data. worldbank.org) is regularly updated and may contain more recent data or revisions not incorporated in the table. It is maintained by the Global Poverty Working Group, a team of poverty experts from the Poverty Reduction and Equity Network, the Development Research Group, and the Development Data Group, which recently updated the database to cover 115 countries and more than 575 sets of poverty estimates at national poverty lines for 1974–2010.

Data quality

Poverty estimates at national poverty lines are computed from household survey data collected from nationally representative samples of households. These data must contain sufficiently detailed information to compute a comprehensive estimate of total household income or consumption (including consumption or income from own production), from which it is possible to construct a correctly weighted distribution of per capita consumption or income.

As with any indicator measured from household surveys, data quality issues can affect the precision of poverty estimates and their comparability over time. These include selective survey nonresponse, seasonality effects, differences in the number of income or consumption items in the questionnaire, and the time period over which respondents are asked to recall their expenditures.

National poverty lines

National poverty lines are the benchmark for estimating poverty indicators that are consistent with the country's specific economic and social circumstances. National poverty lines reflect local perceptions of the level and composition of consumption or income needed to be nonpoor. The perceived boundary between poor and nonpoor typically rises with the average income of a country and thus does not provide a uniform measure for comparing poverty rates across countries. While poverty rates at national poverty lines should not be used for comparing poverty rates across countries, they are appropriate for guiding and monitoring the results of country-specific national poverty reduction strategies.

Almost all national poverty lines are anchored to the cost of a food bundle—based on the prevailing national diet of the poor—that provides adequate nutrition for good health and normal activity, plus an allowance for nonfood spending. National poverty lines must be adjusted for inflation between survey years to remain constant in real terms and thus allow for meaningful comparisons of poverty over time. Because diets and consumption baskets change over time, countries periodically recalculate the poverty line based on new survey data. In such cases the new poverty lines should be deflated to obtain comparable poverty estimates from earlier years. The table reports indicators based on the two most recent years for which survey data is available. Countries for which the most recent indicators reported are not comparable to those based on survey data from an earlier year are footnoted in the table.

Definitions

• **Survey year** is the year in which the underlying household survey data were collected; when the data collection period bridged two calendar years, the year in which most of the data were collected is reported.
• **Population below national poverty line** is the percentage of the rural, urban, and national population living below the corresponding rural, urban, national poverty line, based on consumption estimated from household survey data, unless otherwise noted.
• **Poverty gap at national poverty line** is the mean shortfall from the rural, urban, or national poverty line (counting the nonpoor as having zero shortfall) as a percentage of the corresponding rural, urban, or national poverty line, based on consumption estimated from household survey data, unless otherwise noted. This measure reflects the depth of poverty as well as its incidence.

Data sources

Poverty rates at national poverty lines are compiled by the Global Poverty Working Group, based on data from World Bank's country poverty assessments and analytical reports as well as country Poverty Reduction Strategies and official poverty estimates. Further documentation of the data, measurement methods and tools, and research, as well as poverty assessments and analytical reports, are available at http://data.worldbank. org, www.worldbank.org/poverty, and http://econ. worldbank.org.

Poverty rates at international poverty lines

	International poverty line in local currency		Population below International poverty line[a]									
	$1.25 a day 2005	$2 a day 2005	Survey year[b]	Population below $1.25 a day %	Poverty gap at $1.25 a day %	Population below $2 a day %	Poverty gap at $2 a day %	Survey year[b]	Population below $1.25 a day %	Poverty gap at $1.25 a day %	Population below $2 a day %	Poverty gap at $2 a day %
Albania	75.5	120.8	2005	<2	<0.5	7.9	1.5	2008	<2	<0.5	4.3	0.9
Algeria	48.4[c]	77.5[c]	1988	6.6	1.8	23.8	6.6	1995	6.8	1.4	23.6	6.5
Angola	88.1	141.0	..	..	..	..	..	2000[d]	54.3	29.9	70.2	42.4
Argentina	1.7	2.7	2006[d,e]	2.8	0.6	8.0	2.4	2009[d,e]	<2	<0.5	<2	<0.5
Armenia	245.2	392.4	2003	10.6	1.9	43.5	11.3	2008	<2	<0.5	12.4	2.3
Azerbaijan	2,170.9	3,473.5	2005	<2	<0.5	<2	<0.5	2008	<2	<0.5	7.8	1.5
Bangladesh	31.9	51.0	2000[f]	57.8	17.3	85.4	38.8	2005[f]	49.6	13.1	81.3	33.8
Belarus	949.5	1,519.2	2005	<2	<0.5	<2	<0.5	2008	<2	<0.5	<2	<0.5
Belize	1.8[c]	2.9[c]	1995	14.0	5.4	23.6	10.5	1999[e]	12.1	4.7	23.9	9.7
Benin	344.0	550.4	..	..	..	..	..	2003	47.3	15.7	75.3	33.5
Bhutan	23.1	36.9	..	..	..	..	..	2003	26.2	7.0	49.5	18.8
Bolivia	3.2	5.1	2005[e]	19.6	9.7	30.4	15.5	2007[e]	14.0	5.8	24.7	10.9
Bosnia and Herzegovina	1.1	1.7	2004	<2	<0.5	<2	<0.5	2007	<2	<0.5	<2	<0.5
Botswana	4.2	6.8	1986	35.6	13.8	54.7	25.8	1994	31.2	11.0	49.4	22.3
Brazil	2.0	3.1	2008[e]	4.3	1.4	10.4	3.6	2009[e]	3.8	1.1	9.9	3.2
Bulgaria	0.9	1.5	2003	<2	<0.5	2.4	0.9	2007	<2	<0.5	7.3	1.5
Burkina Faso	303.0	484.8	1998	70.0	30.2	87.6	49.1	2003	56.5	20.3	81.2	39.3
Burundi	558.8	894.1	1998	86.4	47.3	95.4	64.1	2006	81.3	36.4	93.5	56.1
Cambodia	2,019.1	3,230.6	2004	40.2	11.3	68.2	28.0	2007	28.3	6.1	56.5	20.2
Cameroon	368.1	589.0	2001	32.8	10.2	57.7	23.7	2007	9.6	1.2	30.8	8.4
Cape Verde	97.7	156.3	..	..	..	..	..	2001	20.6	5.9	40.3	14.9
Central African Republic	384.3	614.9	1993	82.8	57.0	90.8	68.4	2003	62.4	28.3	81.9	45.3
Chad	409.5	655.1	..	..	..	..	..	2003	61.9	25.6	83.3	43.9
Chile	484.2	774.7	2006[e]	<2	<0.5	2.4	<0.5	2009[e]	<2	<0.5	<2	<0.5
China	5.1[g]	8.2[g]	2002[h]	28.4	8.7	51.1	20.6	2005[h]	15.9	4.0	36.3	12.2
Colombia	1,489.7	2,383.5	2003[e]	15.4	6.1	26.3	10.9	2006[e]	16.0	5.7	27.9	11.9
Comoros	368.0	588.8	..	..	..	..	..	2004	46.1	20.8	65.0	34.2
Congo, Dem. Rep.	395.3	632.5	..	..	..	..	..	2006	59.2	25.3	79.6	42.4
Congo, Rep.	469.5	751.1	..	..	..	..	..	2005	54.1	22.8	74.4	38.8
Costa Rica	348.7[c]	557.9[c]	2005[e]	2.4	<0.5	8.6	2.3	2009[e]	<2	<0.5	4.8	0.9
Croatia	5.6	8.9	2005	<2	<0.5	<2	<0.5	2008	<2	<0.5	<2	<0.5
Czech Republic	19.0	30.4	1993[e]	<2	<0.5	<2	<0.5	1996[e]	<2	<0.5	<2	<0.5
Côte d'Ivoire	407.3	651.6	2002	23.3	6.8	46.8	17.6	2008	23.8	7.5	46.0	17.9
Djibouti	134.8	215.6	1996	4.8	1.6	15.1	4.5	2002	18.8	5.3	41.2	14.6
Dominican Republic	25.5[c]	40.8[c]	2006[e]	4.0	0.7	13.5	3.7	2007[e]	4.3	0.9	13.6	3.9
Ecuador	0.6	1.0	2007[e]	4.7	1.2	12.8	4.0	2009[e]	5.1	1.6	13.4	4.4
Egypt, Arab Rep.	2.5	4.0	2000	<2	<0.5	19.4	3.5	2005	<2	<0.5	18.5	3.5
El Salvador	6.0[c]	9.6[c]	2005[e]	11.0	4.8	20.5	8.9	2008[e]	5.1	1.1	15.2	4.5
Estonia	11.0	17.7	2003	<2	<0.5	2.7	0.9	2004	<2	<0.5	<2	<0.5
Ethiopia	3.4	5.5	2000	55.6	16.2	86.4	37.9	2005	39.0	9.6	77.6	28.9
Gabon	554.7	887.5	..	..	..	..	..	2005	4.8	0.9	19.6	5.0
Gambia, The	12.9	20.7	1998	66.7	34.7	82.0	50.0	2003	34.3	12.1	56.7	24.9
Georgia	1.0	1.6	2005	13.4	4.4	30.4	10.9	2008	14.7	4.6	32.6	11.8
Ghana	5,594.8	8,951.6	1998	39.1	14.4	63.3	28.5	2006	30.0	10.5	53.6	22.3
Guatemala	5.7[c]	9.1[c]	2002[e]	16.9	6.5	29.8	12.9	2006[e]	12.7	3.8	25.7	9.6
Guinea	1,849.5	2,959.1	2003	70.1	32.2	87.2	50.3	2007	43.8	15.2	70.0	31.3
Guinea-Bissau	355.3	568.6	1993	52.1	20.6	75.7	37.4	2002	48.8	16.5	77.9	34.8
Guyana	131.5[c]	210.3[c]	1993[e]	5.8	2.6	15.0	5.4	1998[e]	7.7	3.9	16.8	6.9
Haiti	24.2[c]	38.7[c]	..	..	..	..	..	2001[e]	54.9	28.2	72.2	41.8
Honduras	12.1[c]	19.3[c]	2006[e]	18.2	8.2	29.7	14.2	2007[e]	23.2	11.3	35.6	18.1
Hungary	171.9	275.0	2004	<2	<0.5	<2	<0.5	2007	<2	<0.5	<2	<0.5
India	19.5[i]	31.2[i]	1994[h]	49.4	14.4	81.7	35.3	2005[h]	41.6	10.8	75.6	30.4
Indonesia	5,241.0[i]	8,385.7[i]	2005[h]	21.4	4.6	53.8	17.3	2009[h]	18.7	3.6	50.7	15.5
Iraq	799.8	1,279.7	..	..	..	..	..	2007	4.0	0.6	25.3	5.6
Jamaica	54.2[c]	86.7[c]	2002	<2	<0.5	8.7	1.6	2004	<2	<0.5	5.9	0.9
Jordan	0.6	1.0	2003	<2	<0.5	11.0	2.1	2006	<2	<0.5	3.5	0.6
Kazakhstan	81.2	129.9	2003	3.1	<0.5	17.2	3.9	2007	<2	<0.5	<2	<0.5

	International poverty line in local currency			Population below international poverty line[a]								
	$1.25 a day 2005	$2 a day 2005	Survey year[b]	Population below $1.25 a day %	Poverty gap at $1.25 a day %	Population below $2 a day %	Poverty gap at $2 a day %	Survey year[b]	Population below $1.25 a day %	Poverty gap at $1.25 a day %	Population below $2 a day %	Poverty gap at $2 a day %
Kenya	40.9	65.4	1997	19.6	4.6	42.7	14.7	2005	19.7	6.1	39.9	15.1
Kyrgyz Republic	16.2	26.0	2004	21.8	4.4	51.9	16.8	2007	<2	<0.5	29.4	5.5
Lao PDR	4,677.0	7,483.2	2002	44.0	12.1	76.9	31.1	2008	33.9	9.0	66.0	24.8
Latvia	0.4	0.7	2004	<2	<0.5	<2	<0.5	2008	<2	<0.5	<2	<0.5
Lesotho	4.3	6.9	1995	47.6	26.7	61.1	37.3	2003	43.4	20.8	62.3	33.1
Liberia	0.6	1.0		..	..	..	..	2007	83.7	40.8	94.8	59.5
Lithuania	2.1	3.3	2004	<2	<0.5	<2	<0.5	2008	<2	<0.5	<2	<0.5
Macedonia, FYR	29.5	47.2	2003	<2	<0.5	3.2	0.7	2008	<2	<0.5	4.3	0.7
Madagascar	945.5	1,512.8	2001	76.3	41.4	88.8	57.2	2005	67.8	26.5	89.6	46.9
Malawi	71.2	113.8	1998	83.1	46.0	93.5	62.3	2004	73.9	32.3	90.5	51.8
Malaysia	2.6	4.2	2004[e]	<2	<0.5	7.8	1.4	2009[e]	<2	<0.5	2.3	<0.5
Maldives	12.2	19.5		..	..	..	..	2004	<2	<0.5	12.2	2.5
Mali	362.1	579.4	2001	61.2	25.8	82.0	43.6	2006	51.4	18.8	77.1	36.5
Mauritania	157.1	251.3	1996	23.4	7.1	48.3	17.8	2000	21.2	5.7	44.1	15.9
Mexico	9.6	15.3	2006	<2	<0.5	4.8	1.0	2008	<2	<0.5	8.6	2.0
Micronesia, Fed. Sts.	0.8[c]	1.3[c]		..	..	..	..	2000	31.1	16.3	44.7	24.5
Moldova	6.0	9.7	2004	8.1	1.7	29.0	7.9	2008	<2	<0.5	12.5	2.6
Mongolia	653.1	1,045.0		..	..	..	..	2002	15.5	3.6	38.9	12.3
Montenegro	0.6	1.0		..	..	..	..	2008	<2	<0.5	<2	<0.5
Morocco	6.9	11.0	2001	6.3	0.9	24.3	6.3	2007	2.5	0.5	14.0	3.2
Mozambique	14,532.1	23,251.4	2003	74.7	35.4	90.0	53.6	2008	60.0	25.2	81.6	42.9
Namibia	6.3	10.1		..	..	..	..	1993[e]	49.1	24.6	62.2	36.5
Nepal	33.1	52.9	1996	68.4	26.7	88.1	46.8	2004	55.1	19.7	77.6	37.8
Nicaragua	9.1[c]	14.6[c]	2001[e]	19.4	6.7	37.5	14.5	2005[e]	15.8	5.2	31.9	12.3
Niger	334.2	534.7	2005	65.9	28.1	85.6	46.7	2007	43.1	11.9	75.9	30.6
Nigeria	98.2	157.2	1996	68.5	32.1	86.4	49.7	2004	64.4	29.6	83.9	46.9
Pakistan	25.9	41.4	2005	22.6	4.4	60.3	18.7	2006	22.6	4.1	61.0	18.8
Panama	0.8[c]	1.2[c]	2006[e]	9.5	3.1	17.9	7.1	2009[e]	2.4	<0.5	9.5	2.4
Papua New Guinea	2.1[c]	3.4[c]		..	..	..	..	1996	35.8	12.3	57.4	25.5
Paraguay	2,659.7	4,255.6	2007[e]	6.5	2.7	14.2	5.5	2008[e]	5.1	1.5	13.2	4.3
Peru	2.1	3.3	2006[e]	7.9	1.9	18.5	6.0	2009[e]	5.9	1.4	14.7	4.7
Philippines	30.2	48.4	2003	22.0	5.5	43.8	16.0	2006	22.6	5.5	45.0	16.4
Poland	2.7	4.3	2005	<2	<0.5	<2	<0.5	2008	<2	<0.5	<2	<0.5
Romania	2.1	3.4	2005	<2	<0.5	3.4	0.9	2008	<2	<0.5	<2	0.5
Russian Federation	16.7	26.8	2005	<2	<0.5	<2	<0.5	2008	<2	<0.5	<2	<0.5
Rwanda	295.9	473.5	2000	76.6	38.2	90.3	55.7	2005	76.8	40.9	89.6	57.2
São Tomé and Príncipe	7,953.9	12,726.3		..	..	..	..	2001	28.6	8.2	57.3	21.6
Senegal	372.6	596.5	2001	44.2	14.3	71.3	31.2	2005	33.5	10.8	60.4	24.7
Serbia	42.9	68.6		..	..	..	..	2008	<2	<0.5	<2	<0.5
Seychelles	5.6[c]	9.0[c]	2000	<2	<0.5	<2	<0.5	2007	<2	<0.5	<2	<0.5
Sierra Leone	1,745.3	2,792.4	1990	62.8	44.8	75.0	54.0	2003	53.4	20.3	76.1	37.5
Slovak Republic	23.5	37.7	1992[e]	<2	<0.5	<2	<0.5	1996[e]	<2	<0.5	<2	<0.5
Slovenia	198.2	317.2	2002	<2	<0.5	<2	<0.5	2004	<2	<0.5	<2	<0.5
South Africa	5.7	9.1	1995	21.4	5.2	39.9	15.0	2000	26.2	8.2	42.9	18.3
Sri Lanka	50.0	80.1	2002	14.0	2.6	39.7	11.9	2007	7.0	1.0	29.1	7.4
St. Lucia	2.4[c]	3.8[c]		..	..	..	..	1995[e]	20.9	7.2	40.6	15.5
Suriname	2.3[c]	3.7[c]		..	..	..	..	1999[e]	15.5	5.9	27.2	11.7
Swaziland	4.7	7.5	1995	78.6	47.7	89.3	61.7	2001	62.9	29.4	81.0	45.8
Syrian Arab Republic	30.8	49.3		..	..	..	..	2004	<2	<0.5	16.9	3.3
Tajikistan	1.2	1.9	2003	36.3	10.3	68.8	26.7	2004	21.5	5.1	50.9	16.8
Tanzania	603.1	964.9	2000	88.5	46.8	96.6	64.4	2007	67.9	28.1	87.9	47.5
Thailand	21.8	34.9	2004	<2	<0.5	11.5	2.0	2009	12.8	2.4	26.5	8.3
Timor-Leste	0.6[c]	1.0[c]	2001	52.9	19.1	77.5	37.1	2007	37.4	8.9	72.8	27.0
Togo	352.8	564.5		..	..	..	..	2006	38.7	11.4	69.3	27.9
Trinidad and Tobago	5.8[c]	9.2[c]	1988[e]	<2	<0.5	8.6	1.9	1992[e]	4.2	1.1	13.5	3.9
Tunisia	0.9	1.4	1995	6.5	1.3	20.4	5.8	2000	2.6	<0.5	12.8	3.0

	International poverty line in local currency			Population below International poverty line[a]									
	$1.25 a day 2005	$2 a day 2005	Survey year[b]	Population below $1.25 a day %	Poverty gap at $1.25 a day %	Population below $2 a day %	Poverty gap at $2 a day %	Survey year[b]	Population below $1.25 a day %	Poverty gap at $1.25 a day %	Population below $2 a day %	Poverty gap at $2 a day %
Turkmenistan	5,961.1[c]	9,537.7[c]	1993[e]	63.5	25.8	85.7	44.9	1998	24.8	7.0	49.7	18.4
Uganda	930.8	1,489.2	2005	51.5	19.1	75.6	36.4	2009	37.7	12.1	64.5	27.2
Ukraine	2.1	3.4	2005	<2	<0.5	<2	<0.5	2008	<2	<0.5	<2	<0.5
Uruguay	19.1	30.6	2006[e]	<2	<0.5	4.2	0.6	2009[e]	<2	<0.5	<2	<0.5
Uzbekistan	470.1[c]	752.1[c]	2002	42.3	12.4	75.6	30.6	2003	46.3	15.0	76.7	33.2
Venezuela, RB	1,563.9	2,502.2	2005[e]	10.0	4.5	19.8	8.4	2006[e]	3.5	1.1	10.2	3.2
Vietnam	7,399.9	11,839.8	2006	21.5	4.6	48.4	16.2	2008	13.1	2.3	38.4	10.8
Yemen, Rep.	113.8	182.1	1998	12.9	3.0	36.4	11.1	2005	17.5	4.2	46.6	14.8
Zambia	3,537.9	5,660.7	2003	64.6	27.1	85.2	45.8	2004	64.3	32.8	81.5	48.3

a. Based on nominal per capita consumption averages and distributions estimated from household survey data, unless otherwise noted. b. Refers to the year in which the underlying household survey data were collected; in cases for which the data collection period bridged two calender years, the year in which most of the data were collected is reported. c. Based on purchasing power parity (PPP) dollars imputed using regression. d. Urban areas only. e. Based on per capita income averages and distribution data estimated from household survey data. f. Adjusted by spatial consumer price index data. g. PPP conversion factor based on urban prices. h. Population-weighted average of urban and rural estimates. i. Based on benchmark national PPP estimate rescaled to account for cost-of-living differences in urban and rural areas.

Regional poverty estimates and progress toward the Millennium Development Goals

Global poverty measured at the $1.25 a day poverty line has been decreasing since the 1980s. The share of population living on less than $1.25 a day fell 10 percentage points, to 42 percent, in 1990 and then fell nearly 17 percentage points between 1990 and 2005. The number of people living in extreme poverty fell from 1.9 billion in 1981 to 1.8 billion in 1990 to about 1.4 billion in 2005 (figure 2.8a). This substantial reduction in extreme poverty over the past quarter century, however, disguises large regional differences.

The greatest reduction in poverty occurred in East Asia and Pacific, where the poverty rate declined from 78 percent in 1981 to 17 percent in 2005 and the number of people living on less than $1.25 a day dropped more than 750 million (figure 2.8b). Much of this decline was in China, where poverty fell from 84 percent to 16 percent, leaving 620 million fewer people in poverty.

Over the same period the poverty rate in South Asia fell from 59 percent to 40 percent (table 2.8c). In contrast, the poverty rate fell only slightly in Sub-Saharan Africa—from less than 54 percent in 1981 to more than 58 percent in 1999 then down to 51 percent in 2005. But the number of people living below the poverty line has nearly doubled. Only East Asia and Pacific is consistently on track to meet the Millennium Development Goal target of reducing 1990 poverty rates by half by 2015. A slight acceleration over historical growth rates could lift Latin America and the Caribbean and South Asia to the target. However, the recent slowdown in the global economy may leave these regions and many countries short of the target.

Most of the people who have escaped extreme poverty remain very poor by the standards of middle-income economies. The median poverty line for developing countries in 2005 was $2.00 a day. The poverty rate for all developing countries measured at this line fell from nearly 70 percent in 1981 to 47 percent in 2005, but the number of people living on less than $2.00 a day has remained nearly constant at 2.5 billion. The largest decrease, both in number and proportion, occurred in East Asia and Pacific, led by China. Elsewhere, the number of people living on less than $2.00 a day increased, and the number of people living between $1.25 and $2.00 a day nearly doubled, to 1.2 billion.

Once household survey data collected after 2005 in large countries—such as China and India, as well as some countries in Sub-Saharan Africa and the Middle East and North Africa—become available, the World Bank's Development Research Group will update regional poverty estimates at international poverty lines; see http://iresearch.worldbank.org/povcalnet/.

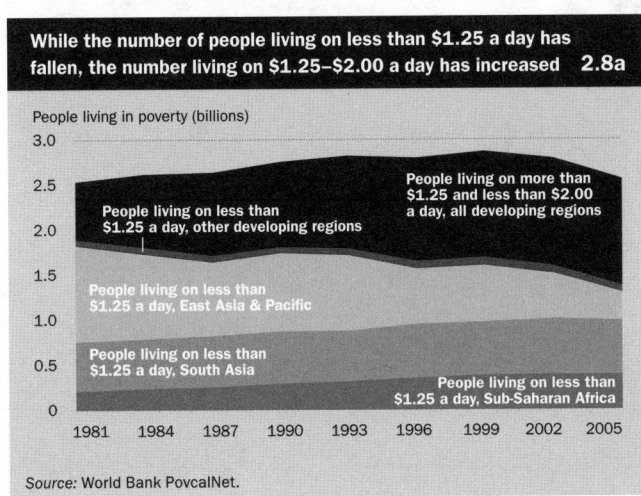

While the number of people living on less than $1.25 a day has fallen, the number living on $1.25–$2.00 a day has increased 2.8a

People living in poverty (billions)

People living on more than $1.25 and less than $2.00 a day, all developing regions
People living on less than $1.25 a day, other developing regions
People living on less than $1.25 a day, East Asia & Pacific
People living on less than $1.25 a day, South Asia
People living on less than $1.25 a day, Sub-Saharan Africa

Source: World Bank PovcalNet.

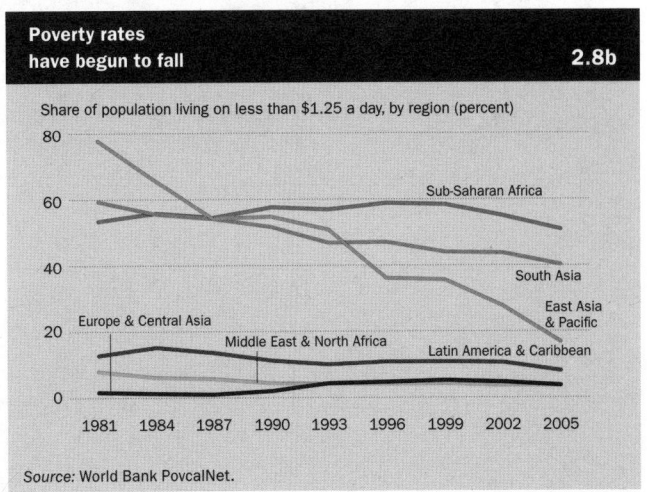

Poverty rates have begun to fall 2.8b

Share of population living on less than $1.25 a day, by region (percent)

Sub-Saharan Africa
South Asia
East Asia & Pacific
Europe & Central Asia
Middle East & North Africa
Latin America & Caribbean

Source: World Bank PovcalNet.

Regional poverty estimates									2.8c
Region or country	1981	1984	1987	1990	1993	1996	1999	2002	2005
People living on less than 2005 PPP $1.25 a day (millions)									
East Asia & Pacific	1,072	947	822	873	845	622	635	507	316
China	835	720	586	683	633	443	447	363	208
Europe & Central Asia	7	6	5	9	20	22	24	22	17
Latin America & Caribbean	47	59	57	50	47	53	55	57	45
Middle East & North Africa	14	12	12	10	10	11	12	10	11
South Asia	548	548	569	579	559	594	589	616	596
India	420	416	428	436	444	442	447	460	456
Sub-Saharan Africa	211	242	258	297	317	356	383	390	388
Total	1,900	1,814	1,723	1,818	1,799	1,658	1,698	1,601	1,374
Share of people living on less than 2005 PPP $1.25 a day (percent)									
East Asia & Pacific	77.7	65.5	54.2	54.7	50.8	36.0	35.5	27.6	16.8
China	84.0	69.4	54.0	60.2	53.7	36.4	35.6	28.4	15.9
Europe & Central Asia	1.7	1.3	1.1	2.0	4.3	4.6	5.1	4.6	3.7
Latin America & Caribbean	12.9	15.3	13.7	11.3	10.1	10.9	10.9	10.7	8.2
Middle East & North Africa	7.9	6.1	5.7	4.3	4.1	4.1	4.2	3.6	3.6
South Asia	59.4	55.6	54.2	51.7	46.9	47.1	44.1	43.8	40.3
India	59.8	55.5	53.6	51.3	49.4	46.6	44.8	43.9	41.6
Sub-Saharan Africa	53.4	55.8	54.5	57.6	56.9	58.8	58.4	55.0	50.9
Total	51.9	46.7	41.9	41.7	39.2	34.5	33.7	30.5	25.2
People living on less than 2005 PPP $2.00 a day (millions)									
East Asia & Pacific	1,278	1,280	1,238	1,274	1,262	1,108	1,105	954	729
China	972	963	907	961	926	792	770	655	474
Europe & Central Asia	35	28	25	32	49	56	68	57	42
Latin America & Caribbean	90	110	103	96	96	107	111	114	94
Middle East & North Africa	46	44	47	44	48	52	52	51	51
South Asia	799	836	881	926	950	1,009	1,031	1,084	1,092
India	609	635	669	702	735	757	783	813	828
Sub-Saharan Africa	294	328	351	393	423	471	509	536	556
Total	2,542	2,625	2,646	2,765	2,828	2,803	2,875	2,795	2,564
Share of people living on less than 2005 PPP $2.00 a day (percent)									
East Asia & Pacific	92.6	88.5	81.6	79.8	75.8	64.1	61.8	51.9	38.7
China	97.8	92.9	83.7	84.6	78.6	65.1	61.4	51.2	36.3
Europe & Central Asia	8.3	6.5	5.6	6.9	10.3	11.9	14.3	12.0	8.9
Latin America & Caribbean	24.6	28.1	24.9	21.9	20.7	22.0	21.8	21.6	17.1
Middle East & North Africa	26.7	23.1	22.7	19.7	19.8	20.2	19.0	17.6	16.9
South Asia	86.5	84.8	83.9	82.7	79.7	79.9	77.2	77.1	73.9
India	86.6	84.8	83.8	82.6	81.7	79.8	78.4	77.6	75.6
Sub-Saharan Africa	73.8	75.5	74.0	76.1	75.9	77.9	77.6	75.6	72.9
Total	69.4	67.7	64.3	63.4	61.6	58.3	57.1	53.3	47.0

Source: World Bank PovcalNet.

Poverty rates at international poverty lines

The World Bank produced its first global poverty estimates for developing countries for *World Development Report 1990: Poverty* using household survey data for 22 countries (Ravallion, Datt, and van de Walle 1991). Since then there has been considerable expansion in the number of countries that field household income and expenditure surveys. The World Bank's poverty monitoring database now includes more than 600 surveys representing 115 developing countries. More than 1.2 million randomly sampled households were interviewed in these surveys, representing 96 percent of the population of developing countries.

Data availability

The number of data sets within two years of any given year rose dramatically, from 13 between 1978 and 1982 to 158 between 2001 and 2006. Data coverage is improving in all regions, but the Middle East and North Africa and Sub-Saharan Africa continue to lag. A complete database of estimates, maintained by a team in the World Bank's Development Research Group, is updated annually as new survey data become available, and a major reassessment of progress against poverty is made about every three years. The most recent estimates and a complete overview of data availability by year and country are available at http://iresearch.worldbank.org/povcalnet/.

Data quality

Besides the frequency and timeliness of survey data, other data quality issues arise in measuring household living standards. The surveys ask detailed questions on sources of income and how it was spent, which must be carefully recorded by trained personnel. Income is generally more difficult to measure accurately, and consumption comes closer to the notion of living standards. And income can vary over time even if living standards do not. But consumption data are not always available: the latest estimates reported here use consumption for about two-thirds of countries.

However, even similar surveys may not be strictly comparable because of differences in timing or in the quality and training of enumerators. Comparisons of countries at different levels of development also pose a potential problem because of differences in the relative importance of the consumption of nonmarket goods. The local market value of all consumption in kind (including own production, particularly important in underdeveloped rural economies) should be included in total consumption expenditure, but may not be. Most survey data now include valuations for consumption or income from own production, but valuation methods vary.

The statistics reported here are based on consumption data or, when unavailable, on income surveys. Analysis of some 20 countries for which income and consumption expenditure data were both available from the same surveys found income to yield a higher mean than consumption but also higher inequality. When poverty measures based on consumption and income were compared, the two effects roughly cancelled each other out: there was no significant statistical difference.

International poverty lines

International comparisons of poverty estimates entail both conceptual and practical problems. Countries have different definitions of poverty, and consistent comparisons across countries can be difficult. Local poverty lines tend to have higher purchasing power in rich countries, where more generous standards are used, than in poor countries.

Poverty measures based on an international poverty line attempt to hold the real value of the poverty line constant across countries, as is done when making comparisons over time. Since *World Development Report 1990* the World Bank has aimed to apply a common standard in measuring extreme poverty, anchored to what poverty means in the world's poorest countries. The welfare of people living in different countries can be measured on a common scale by adjusting for differences in the purchasing power of currencies. The commonly used $1 a day standard, measured in 1985 international prices and adjusted to local currency using purchasing power parities (PPPs), was chosen for *World Development Report 1990* because it was typical of the poverty lines in low-income countries at the time.

Early editions of *World Development Indicators* used PPPs from the Penn World Tables to convert values in local currency to equivalent purchasing power measured in U.S dollars. Later editions used 1993 consumption PPP estimates produced by the World Bank. International poverty lines were recently revised using the new data on PPPs compiled in the 2005 round of the International Comparison Program, along with data from an expanded set of household income and expenditure surveys. The new extreme poverty line is set at $1.25 a day in 2005 PPP terms, which represents the mean of the poverty lines found in the poorest 15 countries ranked by per capita consumption. The new poverty line maintains the same standard for extreme poverty— the poverty line typical of the poorest countries in the world—but updates it using the latest information on the cost of living in developing countries.

PPP exchange rates are used to estimate global poverty, because they take into account the local prices of goods and services not traded internationally. But PPP rates were designed for comparing aggregates from national accounts, not for making international poverty comparisons. As a result, there is no certainty that an international poverty line measures the same degree of need or deprivation across countries. So-called poverty PPPs, designed to compare the consumption of the poorest people in the world, might provide a better basis for comparison of poverty across countries. Work on these measures is ongoing.

• **International poverty line in local currency** is the international poverty lines of $1.25 and $2.00 a day in 2005 prices, converted to local currency using the PPP conversion factors estimated by the International Comparison Program. • **Survey year** is the year in which the underlying household survey data were collected; when the data collection period bridged two calendar years, the year in which most of the data were collected is reported. • **Population below $1.25 a day and population below $2 a day** are the percentages of the population living on less than $1.25 a day and $2.00 a day at 2005 international prices based on nominal per capita consumption averages and distributions estimated from household survey data, unless otherwise noted. As a result of revisions in PPP exchange rates, poverty rates for individual countries cannot be compared with poverty rates reported in earlier editions. • **Poverty gap** is the mean shortfall from the poverty line (counting the nonpoor as having zero shortfall), expressed as a percentage of the poverty line. This measure reflects the depth of poverty as well as its incidence.

Data sources

The poverty measures are prepared by the World Bank's Development Research Group. The international poverty lines are based on nationally representative primary household surveys conducted by national statistical offices or by private agencies under the supervision of government or international agencies and obtained from government statistical offices and World Bank Group country departments. The World Bank Group has prepared an annual review of its poverty work since 1993. For details on data sources and methods used to derive the World Bank's latest estimates, further discussion of the results, and related publications, see http://iresearch.worldbank.org/ povcalnet/ and Shaohua Chen and Martin Ravallion's *"The Developing World Is Poorer Than We Thought, but No Less Successful in the Fight against Poverty"* (2008).

	Survey year	Gini index	Percentage share of income or consumption[a]						
			Lowest 10%	Lowest 20%	Second 20%	Third 20%	Fourth 20%	Highest 20%	Highest 10%
Afghanistan	2008[b]	29.4	3.8	9.0	13.1	16.9	22.3	38.7	24.0
Albania	2008[b]	34.5	3.5	8.1	12.1	15.9	20.9	43.0	29.0
Algeria	1995[b]	35.3	2.8	6.9	11.5	16.3	22.8	42.4	26.9
Angola[c]	2000[b]	58.6	0.6	2.0	5.7	10.8	19.7	61.9	44.7
Argentina[c]	2009[d]	45.8	1.5	4.1	8.9	14.3	22.2	50.5	33.6
Armenia	2008[b]	30.9	3.7	8.8	12.8	16.7	21.9	39.8	25.4
Australia	1994[d]	35.2	2.0	5.9	12.0	17.2	23.6	41.3	25.4
Austria	2000[d]	29.1	3.3	8.6	13.3	17.4	22.9	37.8	23.0
Azerbaijan	2008[b]	33.7	3.4	8.0	12.1	16.2	21.7	42.1	27.4
Bangladesh	2005[b]	31.0	4.3	9.4	12.6	16.1	21.1	40.8	26.6
Belarus	2008[b]	27.2	3.8	9.2	13.8	17.8	22.9	36.4	21.9
Belgium	2000[d]	33.0	3.4	8.5	13.0	16.3	20.8	41.4	28.1
Belize	1999[d]	54.4	1.2	3.4	7.2	11.9	19.1	58.5	43.5
Benin	2003[b]	38.6	2.9	6.9	10.9	15.1	21.2	45.9	31.0
Bolivia	2007[d]	57.3	1.0	2.8	6.4	11.1	18.8	61.0	45.4
Bosnia and Herzegovina	2007[b]	36.2	2.7	6.7	11.3	16.1	22.7	43.2	27.3
Botswana	1994[b]	61.0	1.3	3.1	5.8	9.6	16.4	65.0	51.2
Brazil	2009[d]	53.9	1.2	3.3	7.2	11.9	19.5	58.1	42.5
Bulgaria	2007[b]	45.3	2.0	5.0	9.1	13.9	21.0	51.0	35.2
Burkina Faso	2003[b]	39.6	3.0	7.0	10.6	14.7	20.6	47.1	32.4
Burundi	2006[b]	33.3	4.1	9.0	11.9	15.4	21.0	42.8	28.0
Cambodia	2007[b]	44.4	3.0	6.6	9.4	13.1	19.2	51.7	37.3
Cameroon	2001[b]	44.6	2.4	5.6	9.3	13.7	20.5	50.9	35.5
Canada	2000[d]	32.6	2.6	7.2	12.7	17.2	23.0	39.9	24.8
Central African Republic	2003[b]	43.6	2.1	5.2	9.4	14.3	21.7	49.4	33.0
Chad	2003[b]	39.8	2.6	6.3	10.4	15.0	21.8	46.6	30.8
Chile	2009[d]	22.6	3.1	8.6	15.5	20.2	24.7	30.9	16.5
China	2005[d]	41.5	2.4	5.7	9.8	14.7	22.0	47.8	31.4
Hong Kong SAR, China	1996[d]	43.4	2.0	5.3	9.4	13.9	20.7	50.7	34.9
Colombia	2006[d]	58.5	0.9	2.5	6.0	10.7	18.7	62.1	46.2
Congo, Dem. Rep.	2006[b]	44.4	2.3	5.5	9.2	13.8	20.9	50.6	34.7
Congo, Rep.	2005[b]	47.3	2.1	5.0	8.4	13.0	20.5	53.1	37.1
Costa Rica	2009[d]	50.3	1.7	4.2	7.8	12.5	20.1	55.4	39.4
Côte d'Ivoire	2008[b]	41.5	2.2	5.6	10.1	14.9	21.8	47.6	31.8
Croatia	2008[b]	33.7	3.3	8.1	12.2	16.2	21.6	42.0	27.5
Cuba	..	..	..	..					
Czech Republic	1996[d]	25.8	4.3	10.2	14.3	17.5	21.7	36.2	22.7
Denmark	1997[d]	24.7	2.6	8.3	14.7	18.2	22.9	35.8	21.3
Dominican Republic	2007[d]	48.4	1.7	4.4	8.4	13.1	20.5	53.6	37.8
Ecuador	2009[d]	49.0	1.6	4.2	8.3	13.2	20.4	53.9	38.3
Egypt, Arab Rep.	2005[b]	32.1	3.9	9.0	12.6	16.1	20.9	41.5	27.6
El Salvador	2007[d]	46.9	1.6	4.3	9.0	13.9	20.9	51.9	36.3
Eritrea	..	..	..	..	..	..	..	..	..
Estonia	2004[b]	36.0	2.7	6.8	11.6	16.2	22.5	43.0	27.7
Ethiopia	2005[b]	29.8	4.1	9.3	13.2	16.8	21.4	39.4	25.6
Finland	2000[d]	26.9	4.0	9.6	14.1	17.5	22.1	36.7	22.6
France	1995[d]	32.7	2.8	7.2	12.6	17.2	22.8	40.2	25.1
Gabon	2005[b]	41.5	2.5	6.1	10.1	14.6	21.2	47.9	32.7
Gambia, The	2003[b]	47.3	2.0	4.8	8.6	13.2	20.6	52.8	36.9
Georgia	2008[b]	41.3	2.0	5.3	10.3	15.2	22.1	47.2	31.3
Germany	2000[d]	28.3	3.2	8.5	13.7	17.8	23.1	36.9	22.1
Ghana	2006[b]	42.8	1.9	5.2	9.8	14.8	21.9	48.3	32.5
Greece	2000[d]	34.3	2.5	6.7	11.9	16.8	23.0	41.5	26.0
Guatemala	2006[d]	53.7	1.3	3.4	7.2	12.0	19.5	57.8	42.4
Guinea	2007[b]	39.4	2.7	6.4	10.5	15.1	21.9	46.2	30.3
Guinea-Bissau	2002[b]	35.5	2.9	7.2	11.6	16.0	22.1	43.0	28.0
Haiti	2001[d]	59.5	0.9	2.5	5.9	10.5	18.1	63.0	47.8
Honduras	2007[d]	57.7	0.6	2.0	6.0	11.3	20.0	60.8	43.8

Distribution of income or consumption

	Survey year[b]	Gini index	Percentage share of income or consumption[a]						
			Lowest 10%	Lowest 20%	Second 20%	Third 20%	Fourth 20%	Highest 20%	Highest 10%
Hungary	2007[b]	31.2	3.5	8.4	12.9	16.9	22.0	39.9	25.4
India	2005[b]	36.8	3.6	8.1	11.3	14.9	20.4	45.3	31.1
Indonesia	2009[b]	36.8	3.3	7.6	11.3	15.1	21.1	44.9	29.9
Iran, Islamic Rep.	2005[b]	38.3	2.6	6.4	10.9	15.6	22.2	45.0	29.6
Iraq		..	..	..	..	..	..	..	..
Ireland	2000[d]	34.3	2.9	7.4	12.3	16.3	21.9	42.0	27.2
Israel	2001[d]	39.2	2.1	5.7	10.5	15.9	23.0	44.9	28.8
Italy	2000[d]	36.0	2.3	6.5	12.0	16.8	22.8	42.0	26.8
Jamaica	2004[b]	45.5	2.1	5.2	9.0	13.8	20.9	51.2	35.6
Japan	1993[d]	24.9	4.8	10.6	14.2	17.6	22.0	35.7	21.7
Jordan	2006[b]	37.7	3.0	7.2	11.1	15.2	21.1	45.4	30.7
Kazakhstan	2007[b]	30.9	3.8	8.7	12.8	16.7	22.0	39.9	25.2
Kenya	2005[b]	47.7	1.8	4.7	8.8	13.3	20.3	53.0	37.8
Korea, Dem. Rep.		..	..	..	..	..	..	..	..
Korea, Rep.	1998[d]	31.6	2.9	7.9	13.6	18.0	23.1	37.5	22.5
Kosovo		..	..	..	..	..	..	..	..
Kuwait		..	..	..	..	..	..	..	..
Kyrgyz Republic	2007[b]	33.4	4.1	8.8	11.8	15.5	21.2	42.8	27.9
Lao PDR	2008[b]	36.7	3.3	7.6	11.3	15.3	20.9	44.8	30.3
Latvia	2008[b]	35.7	2.7	6.8	11.7	16.3	22.4	42.9	27.6
Lebanon		..	..	..	..	..	..	..	..
Lesotho	2003[b]	52.5	1.0	3.0	7.2	12.5	21.0	56.4	39.4
Liberia	2007[b]	52.6	2.4	6.4	11.4	15.7	21.6	45.0	30.1
Libya		..	..	..	..	..	..	..	..
Lithuania	2008[b]	37.6	2.6	6.6	11.1	15.7	22.1	44.4	29.1
Macedonia, FYR	2008[b]	44.2	2.2	5.4	9.3	14.0	21.0	50.3	34.5
Madagascar	2005[b]	47.2	2.6	6.2	9.6	13.1	17.7	53.5	41.5
Malawi	2004[b]	39.0	2.9	7.0	10.8	14.9	20.9	46.4	31.7
Malaysia	2009[d]	46.2	1.8	4.5	8.7	13.7	21.6	51.5	34.7
Maldives	2004[b]	37.4	2.7	6.5	10.9	15.7	22.7	44.2	28.0
Mali	2006[b]	39.0	2.7	6.5	10.7	15.2	21.6	46.0	30.5
Mauritania	2000[b]	39.0	2.5	6.2	10.5	15.4	22.3	45.7	29.6
Mauritius		..	..	..	..	..	..	..	..
Mexico	2008[d]	51.7	1.5	3.9	7.9	12.5	19.4	56.2	41.4
Micronesia	2000[b]	61.1	0.4	1.6	5.2	10.2	19.1	64.0	47.1
Moldova	2008[b]	38.0	2.9	6.8	10.9	15.4	21.7	45.3	29.8
Mongolia	2008[b]	36.5	3.0	7.1	11.2	15.6	22.1	44.0	28.4
Montenegro	2008[b]	30.0	3.6	8.5	13.1	17.2	22.4	38.8	24.1
Morocco	2007[b]	40.9	2.7	6.5	10.5	14.5	20.6	47.9	33.2
Mozambique	2008[b]	45.6	1.9	5.2	9.5	13.7	20.1	51.5	36.7
Myanmar		..	..	..	..	..	..	..	..
Namibia	1993[d]	74.3	0.6	1.5	2.8	5.5	12.0	78.3	65.0
Nepal	2004[b]	47.3	2.7	6.1	8.9	12.5	18.4	54.2	40.4
Netherlands	1999[d]	30.9	2.5	7.6	13.2	17.2	23.3	38.7	22.9
New Zealand	1997[d]	36.2	2.2	6.4	11.4	15.8	22.6	43.8	27.8
Nicaragua	2005[d]	52.3	1.4	3.8	7.7	12.3	19.4	56.9	41.8
Niger	2007[b]	34.0	3.7	8.3	12.0	15.8	21.1	42.8	28.5
Nigeria	2004[b]	42.9	2.0	5.1	9.7	14.7	21.9	48.6	32.4
Norway	2000[d]	25.8	3.9	9.6	14.0	17.2	22.0	37.2	23.4
Oman		..	..	..	..	..	..	..	..
Pakistan	2006[b]	32.7	4.0	9.0	12.4	15.8	20.7	42.1	28.3
Panama	2009[d]	52.3	1.3	3.6	7.4	12.2	20.1	56.8	40.6
Papua New Guinea	1996[b]	50.9	1.9	4.5	7.7	12.1	19.3	56.4	40.9
Paraguay	2008[d]	52.0	1.4	3.8	7.7	12.4	19.7	56.5	41.0
Peru	2009[d]	48.0	1.4	3.9	8.4	13.6	21.5	52.6	35.9
Philippines	2006[b]	44.0	2.4	5.6	9.1	13.7	21.2	50.4	33.9
Poland	2008[b]	34.2	3.2	7.6	12.0	16.3	22.0	42.2	27.2

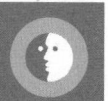

	Survey year	Gini index	Percentage share of income or consumption[a]						
			Lowest 10%	Lowest 20%	Second 20%	Third 20%	Fourth 20%	Highest 20%	Highest 10%
Portugal	1997[d]	38.5	2.0	5.8	11.0	15.5	21.9	45.9	29.8
Puerto Rico	..	..	..	..	..	..	..	..	..
Qatar	2007[b]	41.1	1.3	3.9	..	..	..	52.0	35.9
Romania	2008[b]	31.2	3.3	8.1	12.8	17.1	22.7	39.3	24.5
Russian Federation	2008[b]	42.3	2.6	6.0	9.8	14.3	20.9	48.9	33.5
Rwanda	2005[b]	53.1	1.7	4.2	7.7	11.7	18.2	58.2	44.0
São Tomé & Príncipe	2000[b]	50.8	2.2	5.2	8.5	12.2	17.7	56.4	43.6
Saudi Arabia	..	..	..	..	..	..	..	..	..
Senegal	2005[b]	39.2	2.5	6.2	10.6	15.3	22.0	45.9	30.1
Serbia	2008[b]	28.2	3.9	9.1	13.5	17.5	22.5	37.4	22.8
Seychelles	2007[b]	19.0	4.7	10.8	15.7	19.9	24.2	29.4	15.4
Sierra Leone	2003[b]	42.5	2.6	6.1	9.7	14.0	20.9	49.3	33.6
Singapore	1998[d]	42.5	1.9	5.0	9.4	14.6	22.0	49.0	32.8
Slovak Republic	1996[d]	25.8	3.1	8.8	14.9	18.6	22.9	34.8	20.8
Slovenia	2004[b]	31.2	3.4	8.2	12.8	17.0	22.6	39.4	24.6
Somalia	..	..	..	..	..	..	..	..	..
South Africa	2000[b]	57.8	1.3	3.1	5.6	9.9	18.8	62.7	44.9
Spain	2000[d]	34.7	2.6	7.0	12.1	16.4	22.5	42.0	26.6
Sri Lanka	2007[b]	40.3	3.1	6.9	10.4	14.4	20.5	47.8	32.9
Sudan	..	..	..	..	..	..	..	..	..
Swaziland	2001[b]	50.7	1.8	4.5	8.0	12.3	19.4	55.9	40.8
Sweden	2000[d]	25.0	3.6	9.1	14.0	17.6	22.7	36.6	22.2
Switzerland	2000[d]	33.7	2.9	7.6	12.2	16.3	22.6	41.3	25.9
Syrian Arab Republic	2004[b]	35.8	3.4	7.7	11.4	15.5	21.4	43.9	28.9
Tajikistan	2007[b]	29.4	4.0	9.3	13.4	16.7	21.5	39.0	25.2
Tanzania	2007[b]	37.6	2.8	6.8	11.1	15.6	21.7	44.8	29.6
Thailand	2009[b]	53.6	1.6	3.9	7.0	11.4	19.2	58.6	42.6
Timor-Leste	2007[b]	31.9	4.0	9.0	12.5	16.1	21.2	41.3	27.0
Togo	2006[b]	34.4	2.0	5.4	10.3	15.2	22.0	47.1	31.3
Trinidad and Tobago	1992[d]	40.3	2.1	5.5	10.3	15.5	22.7	45.9	29.9
Tunisia	2000[b]	40.8	2.4	5.9	10.2	14.9	21.8	47.2	31.6
Turkey	2008[b]	39.7	2.1	5.7	10.8	15.6	22.1	45.8	30.3
Turkmenistan	1998[b]	40.8	2.5	6.0	10.2	14.9	21.7	47.2	31.8
Uganda	2009[b]	44.3	2.4	5.8	9.6	13.8	20.0	50.7	36.1
Ukraine	2008[b]	27.5	4.1	9.4	13.6	17.5	22.5	37.1	22.6
United Arab Emirates	..	..	..	..	..	..	..	..	..
United Kingdom	1999[d]	36.0	2.1	6.1	11.4	16.0	22.5	44.0	28.5
United States	2000[d]	40.8	1.9	5.4	10.7	15.7	22.4	45.8	29.9
Uruguay	2009[d]	42.4	2.3	5.6	9.8	14.5	21.4	48.6	32.9
Uzbekistan	2003[b]	36.7	2.9	7.1	11.5	15.7	21.5	44.2	29.5
Venezuela, RB	2006[d]	43.5	1.9	4.9	9.6	14.7	21.8	49.0	33.0
Vietnam	2008[b]	37.6	3.2	7.3	10.9	15.1	21.3	45.4	30.2
West Bank and Gaza	..	..	..	..	..	..	..	..	..
Yemen, Rep.	2005[b]	37.7	2.9	7.2	11.3	15.3	21.0	45.3	30.8
Zambia	2004[b]	50.7	1.3	3.6	7.8	12.8	20.6	55.2	38.9
Zimbabwe	1995[b]	50.1	1.8	4.6	8.1	12.2	19.3	55.7	40.3

a. Percentage shares by quintile may not sum to 100 percent because of rounding. b. Refers to expenditure shares by percentiles of population, ranked by per capita expenditure.
c. Covers urban areas only. d. Refers to income shares by percentiles of population, ranked by per capita income.

Distribution of income or consumption | 2.9

Inequality in the distribution of income is reflected in the percentage shares of income or consumption accruing to portions of the population ranked by income or consumption levels. The portions ranked lowest by personal income receive the smallest shares of total income. The Gini index provides a convenient summary measure of the degree of inequality. Data on the distribution of income or consumption come from nationally representative household surveys. Where the original data from the household survey were available, they have been used to directly calculate the income or consumption shares by quintile. Otherwise, shares have been estimated from the best available grouped data.

The distribution data have been adjusted for household size, providing a more consistent measure of per capita income or consumption. No adjustment has been made for spatial differences in cost of living within countries, because the data needed for such calculations are generally unavailable. For further details on the estimation method for low- and middle-income economies, see Ravallion and Chen (1996).

Because the underlying household surveys differ in method and type of data collected, the distribution data are not strictly comparable across countries. These problems are diminishing as survey methods improve and become more standardized, but achieving strict comparability is still impossible (see *About the data* for tables 2.7 and 2.8).

Two sources of non-comparability should be noted in particular. First, the surveys can differ in many respects, including whether they use income or consumption expenditure as the living standard indicator. The distribution of income is typically more unequal than the distribution of consumption. In addition, the definitions of income used differ more often among surveys. Consumption is usually a much better welfare indicator, particularly in developing countries. Second, households differ in size (number of members) and in the extent of income sharing among members. And individuals differ in age and consumption needs. Differences among countries in these respects may bias comparisons of distribution.

World Bank staff have made an effort to ensure that the data are as comparable as possible. Wherever possible, consumption has been used rather than income. Income distribution and Gini indexes for high-income economies are calculated directly from the Luxembourg Income Study database, using an estimation method consistent with that applied for developing countries.

• **Survey year** is the year in which the underlying data were collected. • **Gini index** measures the extent to which the distribution of income (or consumption expenditure) among individuals or households within an economy deviates from a perfectly equal distribution. A Lorenz curve plots the cumulative percentages of total income received against the cumulative number of recipients, starting with the poorest individual. The Gini index measures the area between the Lorenz curve and a hypothetical line of absolute equality, expressed as a percentage of the maximum area under the line. Thus a Gini index of 0 represents perfect equality, while an index of 100 implies perfect inequality. • **Percentage share of income or consumption** is the share of total income or consumption that accrues to subgroups of population indicated by deciles or quintiles.

Data on distribution are compiled by the World Bank's Development Research Group using primary household survey data obtained from government statistical agencies and World Bank country departments. Data for high-income economies are from the Luxembourg Income Study database.

	Youth unemployment		Female-headed households	Pension contributors			Public expenditure on pensions			
	Male % of male labor force ages 15–24 **2006–09[a]**	Female % of female labor force ages 15–24 **2006–09[a]**	% of total **2006–09[a]**	Year	% of labor force	% of working-age population	Year	% of GDP	Year	Average pension % of average wage
Afghanistan	..	..	..	2005	..	2.2	2005	0.5		..
Albania	..	..	..	2007	51.1	34.7	2009	6.1		..
Algeria	..	..	..	2002	36.7	22.1	2002	3.2		..
Angola	..	..	25		..	..		..		..
Argentina	19[b]	25[b]	34	2008	41.9	31.3	2007	8.0	2000	43.8
Armenia	47[b]	69[b]	..	2008	39.2	23.9	2008	4.3	2007	20.3
Australia	13[b]	10[b]	..	2005	92.6	69.6	2005	3.5		..
Austria	10	9	..	2005	96.4	68.7	2005	12.6		..
Azerbaijan	19	10	25	2007	35.4	24.7	2007	3.8	2006	24.3
Bangladesh	..	..	13	2004	2.8	2.1	2006	0.3		..
Belarus	..	..	..	2008	93.5	66.8	2008	10.2	2002	41.6
Belgium	21	22	..	2005	94.2	61.6	2005	9.0		..
Benin	..	..	23		..	..	2006	1.5		..
Bolivia	..	..	..	2008	11.4	8.9	2000	4.5		..
Bosnia and Herzegovina	45	52	..	2009	70.2	28.7	2009	9.4		..
Botswana	..	..	..	2006	9.0	7.3		..		..
Brazil	14	23	..	2008	53.8	41.7	2004	12.6		..
Bulgaria	18	14	..	2008	72.7	49.6	2007	9.8	2004	42.9
Burkina Faso	..	..	..	2004	1.2	1.0		..		..
Burundi	..	..	..		..	..		..		..
Cambodia	..	..	..		..	..		..		..
Cameroon	..	..	..		..	..	2001	0.8		..
Canada	18[b]	12[b]	..	2007	66.9	53.6	2005	4.1		..
Central African Republic	..	..	..	2004	1.5	1.3	2004	0.8		..
Chad	..	..	..		..	..		..		..
Chile	21	24	..	2008	53.8	36.2	2001	2.9	2006	53.5
China	..	..	..	2007	19.3	15.9		..		..
Hong Kong SAR, China	15[b]	10[b]	..	2008	..	55.6		..		..
Colombia	18	30	19	2008	31.3	20.0	2008	3.0		..
Congo, Dem. Rep.	..	..	21		..	..		..		..
Congo, Rep.	..	..	..		..	..	2004	0.9		..
Costa Rica	10	13	..	2004	55.3	37.6	2006	2.4		..
Côte d'Ivoire	..	..	..		..	..		..		..
Croatia	19	27	24	2010	82.9	52.6	2009	10.3	2005	32.4
Cuba	3	4	46		..	..		..		..
Czech Republic	17	17	..	2007	84.5	67.3	2007	8.5	2005	40.7
Denmark	12	10	..	2007	94.4	86.9	2005	5.4		..
Dominican Republic	21	45	35	2008	21.0	15.2	2000	0.8		..
Ecuador	12[b]	18[b]	..	2004	31.6	21.1	2002	2.5		..
Egypt, Arab Rep.	17	48	..	2009	57.0	31.0	2004	4.1		..
El Salvador	13	8	..	2008	23.9	16.2	2006	1.9		..
Eritrea	..	..	..		..	..	2001	0.3		..
Estonia	32	21	..	2004	95.2	68.6	2007	10.9	2007	35.4
Ethiopia	20[b]	29[b]	..		..	..	2006	0.3		..
Finland	22	19	..	2005	88.7	67.2	2005	8.4		..
France	23	22	..	2005	89.9	61.4	2005	12.4		..
Gabon	..	..	..		..	..		..		..
Gambia, The	..	..	..	2006	2.7	2.2		..		..
Georgia	32[b]	41	..	2004	29.9	22.7	2004	3.0	2003	13.0
Germany	12	10	..	2005	88.2	65.5	2005	11.4		..
Ghana	..	..	34	2004	9.1	7.1	2002	1.3		..
Greece	19	34	..	2005	85.2	58.5	2005	11.5		..
Guatemala	..	..	..	2008	20.3	14.7	2005	1.0		..
Guinea	..	..	..	1993	1.5	1.8		..		..
Guinea-Bissau	..	..	..	2004	1.9	1.5	2005	2.1		..
Haiti	..	..	44		..	..		..		..
Honduras	..	..	26	2008	18.7	12.6		..		..

	Youth unemployment		Female-headed households	Pension contributors			Public expenditure on pensions			
	Male % of male labor force ages 15–24 **2006–09**[a]	Female % of female labor force ages 15–24 **2006–09**[a]	% of total **2006–09**[a]	Year	% of labor force	% of working-age population	Year	% of GDP	Year	Average pension % of average wage
Hungary	28	24	..	2008	92.0	56.7	2008	10.5	2005	39.8
India	..	..	14	2006	10.3	6.4	2007	2.2		..
Indonesia	22	23	13	2008	11.7	8.7		..		..
Iran, Islamic Rep.	20	34	..	2001	35.1	20.0	2000	1.1		..
Iraq	..	..	11	2009	16.8	15.2	2009	3.9		..
Ireland	31	17	..	2005	88.0	63.9	2005	3.4		..
Israel	16	14	..		..	..		..		..
Italy	23	29	..	2005	92.4	58.4	2005	14.0		..
Jamaica	22	33	..	2004	17.4	12.6		..		..
Japan	10	8	..	2005	95.3	75.0	2005	8.7		..
Jordan	23	46	10	2006	38.4	19.9	2001	2.2		..
Kazakhstan	7	8	..	2004	34.4	26.5	2009	3.2	2003	24.9
Kenya	..	..	..	2006	7.5	6.5	2003	1.1		..
Korea, Dem. Rep.	..	..	..		..	..		..		..
Korea, Rep.	12[b]	9[b]	..	2005	49.5	34.3	2005	1.6		..
Kosovo	..	..	..		..	..	2007	2.7[c]		..
Kuwait	..	..	..		..	..		..		..
Kyrgyz Republic	14	16	25	2006	42.2	28.9	2010	2.7	2003	27.5
Lao PDR	..	..	..		..	..		..		..
Latvia	38	28	..	2003	92.4	66.5	2009	8.5	2005	33.1
Lebanon	22	22	..	2003	33.1	19.9	2003	2.1		..
Lesotho	..	..	..	2005	5.7	3.6		..		..
Liberia	6[b]	4[b]	31		..	..		..		..
Libya	..	..	..	2004	65.5	38.1	2001	2.1		..
Lithuania	35	22	..	2007	99.3	68.7	2009	8.9	2005	30.9
Macedonia, FYR	53	59	8	2008	47.9	30.4	2008	9.4	2006	55.0
Madagascar	..	..	..		..	..		..		..
Malawi	..	..	..		..	..		..		..
Malaysia	10	12	..	2008	49.0	32.5		..		..
Mali	..	..	12		..	..		..		..
Mauritania	..	..	..		..	..		..		..
Mauritius	18	26	..	2000	51.4	33.6		..		..
Mexico	10	11	..	2008	30.3	20.6	2005	1.3		..
Moldova	16	15	..	2009	58.7	32.1	2009	9.1	2003	20.9
Mongolia	..	..	29	2005	27.9	21.3	2007	6.5[d]		..
Morocco	23	19	..	2007	23.8	13.6	2003	1.9		..
Mozambique	..	..	..		..	..		..		..
Myanmar	..	..	..		..	..		..		..
Namibia	..	..	44		..	..		..		..
Nepal	..	..	23	2008	3.4	2.6	2006	0.2		..
Netherlands	7	6	..	2005	90.7	70.7	2005	5.0[e]		..
New Zealand	16[b]	17[b]	..	2003	92.7	72.3	2005	4.4[e]		..
Nicaragua	8	10	..	2008	21.7	14.6		..		..
Niger	..	..	19	2006	1.9	1.2	2006	0.7		..
Nigeria	..	..	..	2004	1.9	1.1		..		..
Norway	10	8	..	2005	93.2	75.2	2005	4.8[e]		..
Oman	..	..	..		..	..		..		..
Pakistan	7	10	10	2008	3.9	2.2	2004	0.5		..
Panama	12	21	..		..	..		..		..
Papua New Guinea	..	..	..		..	..		..		..
Paraguay	9	17	..	2004	11.6	9.1	2001	1.2		..
Peru	13[b]	16[b]	22	2008	19.1	13.9	2000	2.6		..
Philippines	16	19	19	2007	25.0	17.0		..		..
Poland	20	21	..	2005	83.8	54.7	2009	10.0	2007	47.1
Portugal	19	22	..	2005	92.0	71.6	2005	10.2[e]		..
Puerto Rico	29[b]	22[b]	..		..	..		..		..
Qatar	1	7	..		..	..		..		..

	Youth unemployment		Female-headed households	Pension contributors			Public expenditure on pensions			
	Male % of male labor force ages 15–24 2006–09[a]	Female % of female labor force ages 15–24 2006–09[a]	% of total 2006–09[a]	Year	% of labor force	% of working-age population	Year	% of GDP	Year	Average pension % of average wage
Romania	21	20	..	2007	54.8	36.4	2009	8.3	2005	41.5
Russian Federation	18	19	..	2007	67.0	50.0	2007	4.7	2003	29.2
Rwanda	..	..	..	2004	4.6	4.1	..	..	..	..
Saudi Arabia	24	46	..	..	..	..	..	..	..	..
Senegal	12	20	..	2003	5.1	4.1	2003	1.3	..	..
Serbia	31	41	29	2003	45.0	35.4	2010	14.0	..	..
Sierra Leone	..	..	..	2004	5.5	3.8	..	..	..	..
Singapore	10	17	..	2008	61.7	45.3	..	..	..	..
Slovak Republic	28	27	..	2003	78.9	55.3	2007	9.3[e]	2005	44.7
Slovenia	14	13	..	2008	87.4	63.2	2007	12.7	2005	44.3
Somalia	..	..	..	..	..	..	..	..	..	..
South Africa	45	53	..	2007	6.5	3.7	2006	1.2	..	..
Spain	39	36	..	2005	69.4	48.7	2005	8.1[e]	2006	58.6
Sri Lanka	17	28	..	2006	24.1	14.9	2007	2.0	..	..
Sudan	..	..	19	..	..	..	..	..	..	..
Swaziland	..	..	48	..	..	..	..	..	..	..
Sweden	26	24	..	2005	88.8	72.2	2005	7.7[e]	..	..
Switzerland	8	9	..	2005	95.4	78.7	2005	6.8[e]	2000	40.0
Syrian Arab Republic	13	49	..	2008	26.8	13.8	2004	1.3	..	..
Tajikistan	..	..	..	..	..	..	..	..	2003	25.7
Tanzania	7	10	..	2006	4.3	4.0	2006	0.9	..	..
Thailand	4	5	30	2008	23.0	18.6	..	..	..	..
Timor-Leste	..	..	..	..	..	..	..	..	..	..
Togo	..	..	..	..	..	..	..	..	..	..
Trinidad and Tobago	9	13	..	2008	76.4	54.2	..	..	..	..
Tunisia	..	..	..	2004	48.6	25.5	2003	4.3	..	..
Turkey	25	25	..	2007	60.3	31.0	2008	6.2	2007	61.3
Turkmenistan	..	..	..	..	..	..	..	..	..	..
Uganda	..	..	30	2004	10.3	9.2	2003	0.3	..	..
Ukraine	..	..	49	2010	65.3	52.3	2010	17.8	2007	48.3
United Arab Emirates	8	22	..	..	..	..	..	..	..	..
United Kingdom	22	16	..	2005	93.2	71.5	2005	5.7	..	..
United States	20[b]	15[b]	..	2005	92.2	71.5	2005	6.0[e]	2006	29.2
Uruguay	16	25	..	2007	72.7	56.9	2007	10.0[e]	..	..
Uzbekistan	..	..	..	2005	86.1	57.5	2005	6.5	2005	40.0
Venezuela, RB	12	16	..	2008	32.1	22.7	2001	2.7	..	..
Vietnam	..	..	..	2008	19.3	15.2	..	..	..	..
West Bank and Gaza	39	47	..	2009	18.5	8.0	2009	4.0	..	..
Yemen, Rep.	..	..	..	2006	10.4	5.0	..	..	..	..
Zambia	..	..	24	2006	10.9	8.0	2008	1.0	..	..
Zimbabwe	..	..	38	..	..	..	2002	2.3	..	..
World	.. w	.. w								
Low income	..	..								
Middle income	..	..								
Lower middle income	..	..								
Upper middle income	19	23								
Low & middle income	..	..								
East Asia & Pacific	..	..								
Europe & Central Asia	17	18								
Latin America & Carib.	12	18								
Middle East & N. Africa	18	37								
South Asia	..	..								
Sub-Saharan Africa	..	..								
High income	19	16								
Euro area	21	21								

a. Data are for the most recent year available. b. Limited coverage. c. Includes only expenditure on social pensions. d. Includes old-age, survivors, disability, military, work accident or disease pensions. e. Includes only expenditures on old-age and survivors' benefits.

About the data

As traditionally measured, poverty is a static concept, and vulnerability a dynamic one. Vulnerability reflects a household's resilience in the face of shocks and the likelihood that a shock will lead to a decline in well-being. Thus, it depends primarily on the household's assets and insurance mechanisms. Because poor people have fewer assets and less diversified sources of income than do the better-off, fluctuations in income affect them more.

Enhancing security for poor people means reducing their vulnerability to such risks as ill health, providing them the means to manage risk themselves, and strengthening market or public institutions for managing risk. Tools include microfinance programs, public provision of education and basic health care, and old age assistance (see tables 2.11 and 2.16).

Poor households face many risks, and vulnerability is thus multidimensional. The indicators in the table focus on individual risks—youth unemployment, female-headed households, income insecurity in old age—and the extent to which publicly provided services may be capable of mitigating some of these risks. Poor people face labor market risks, often having to take up precarious, low-quality jobs and to increase their household's labor market participation by sending their children to work (see tables 2.4 and 2.6). Income security is a prime concern for the elderly.

Youth unemployment is an important policy issue for many economies. Experiencing unemployment may permanently impair a young person's productive potential and future employment opportunities. The table presents unemployment among youth ages 15–24, but the lower age limit for young people in a country could be determined by the minimum age for leaving school, so age groups could differ across countries. Also, since this age group is likely to include school leavers, the level of youth unemployment varies considerably over the year as a result of different school opening and closing dates. The youth unemployment rate shares similar limitations on comparability as the general unemployment rate. For further information, see *About the data* for table 2.5 and the original source.

The definition of female-headed household differs greatly across countries, making cross-country comparison difficult. In some cases it is assumed that a woman cannot be the head of any household with an adult male, because of sex-biased stereotype. Caution should be used in interpreting the data.

Pension scheme coverage may be broad or even universal where eligibility is determined by citizenship, residency, or income status. In contribution-related schemes, however, eligibility is usually restricted to individuals who have contributed for a minimum number of years. Definitional issues—relating to the labor force, for example—may arise in comparing coverage by contribution-related schemes over time and across countries (for country-specific information, see Hinz and others 2011). The share of the labor force covered by a pension scheme may be overstated in countries that do not try to count informal sector workers as part of the labor force.

Public interventions and institutions can provide services directly to poor people, although whether these interventions and institutions work well for the poor is debated. State action is often ineffective, in part because governments can influence only a few of the many sources of well-being and in part because of difficulties in delivering goods and services. The effectiveness of public provision is further constrained by the fiscal resources at governments' disposal and the fact that state institutions may not be responsive to the needs of poor people.

The data on public pension spending cover the pension programs of the social insurance schemes for which contributions had previously been made. In many cases noncontributory pensions or social assistance targeted to the elderly and disabled are also included. A country's pattern of spending is correlated with its demographic structure—spending increases as the population ages.

Definitions

• **Youth unemployment** is the share of the labor force ages 15–24 without work but available for and seeking employment. • **Female-headed households** are the percentage of households with a female head. • **Pension contributors** are the share of the labor force or working-age population (here defined as ages 15 and older) covered by a pension scheme. • **Public expenditure on pensions** is all government expenditures on cash transfers to the elderly, the disabled, and survivors and the administrative costs of these programs. • **Average pension** is the average pension payment of all pensioners of the main pension schemes (including old-age, survivors, disability, military, and work accident or disease pensions) divided by the average wage of all formal sector workers.

Data sources

Data on youth unemployment are from the ILO's Key Indicators of the Labour Market, 6th edition, database. Data on female-headed households are from Macro International Demographic and Health Surveys. Data on pension contributors and pension spending are from Hinz and others' *International Patterns of Pension Provision II: Facts and Figures of the 2000s* (2011).

	Public expenditure per student						Public expenditure on education		Trained teachers in primary education	Primary school pupil–teacher ratio
			% of GDP per capita				% of GDP	% of total government expenditure	% of total	pupils per teacher
	Primary		Secondary		Tertiary					
	1999	2009ª	1999	2009ª	1999	2009ª	2009ª	2009ª	2009ª	2009ª
Afghanistan	..	..	..	..	..	..	..	..	..	43
Albania	..	..	..	..	..	..	..	..	..	20
Algeria	12.0	..	..	..	..	..	4.3	20.3	..	23
Angola	..	..	..	..	..	..	..	..	..	..
Argentina	12.9	14.7	18.2	21.9	17.7	15.6	4.9	13.5	..	16
Armenia	..	11.0	..	18.8	..	6.8	3.0	15.0	..	19
Australia	16.4	16.4	15.0	14.5	26.6	20.2	4.5	..	..	..
Austria	25.1	23.3	30.2	26.7	52.1	47.6	5.4	11.1	..	12
Azerbaijan	6.9	..	17.0	..	19.1	15.6	2.8	9.1	99.9	11
Bangladesh	..	10.7	12.5	14.9	50.7	39.8	2.4	14.0	58.4	44
Belarus	..	..	..	..	..	15.0	4.5	10.6	99.9	15
Belgium	18.2	20.5	23.8	33.3	38.3	35.3	6.0	12.4	..	11
Benin	12.1	..	24.6	..	212.7	..	3.5	15.9	40.4	45
Bolivia	14.2	..	11.7	..	44.1	..	..	..	..	24
Bosnia and Herzegovina	..	..	..	..	..	..	..	..	..	..
Botswana	..	12.4	..	37.6	..	251.5	8.9	22.0	97.4	25
Brazil	10.8	17.3	9.5	18.0	57.1	29.6	5.1	16.1	..	23
Bulgaria	15.5	23.5	18.8	22.3	17.9	20.1	4.1	10.0	..	16
Burkina Faso	..	29.0	..	30.2	..	307.1	4.6	21.8	86.1	49
Burundi	14.7	21.1	..	59.4	1,051.5	520.4	8.3	23.4	91.2	51
Cambodia	5.9	..	11.5	..	43.6	..	2.1	12.4	99.5	49
Cameroon	..	7.4	..	30.7	..	35.8	3.7	19.2	..	46
Canada	..	..	..	..	44.0	..	4.9	..	..	..
Central African Republic	..	4.5	..	16.1	..	124.1	1.3	11.7	..	95
Chad	..	12.7	..	24.1	..	217.8	3.2	12.6	34.6	61
Chile	14.4	14.7	14.8	16.0	19.4	12.1	4.0	18.2	..	25
China	..	..	11.5	..	90.0	..	..	..	..	18
Hong Kong SAR, China	12.4	13.8	17.7	16.7	..	56.2	4.5	24.1	95.1	16
Colombia	15.2	15.9	16.1	15.4	37.7	27.4	4.8	14.9	100.0	29
Congo, Dem. Rep.	..	..	..	..	..	..	..	..	93.4	37
Congo, Rep.	..	..	..	..	..	..	..	..	..	64
Costa Rica	15.5	14.6	21.4	14.4	..	..	6.3	37.7	87.6	18
Côte d'Ivoire	14.8	..	42.8	..	146.3	119.1	4.6	24.6	100.0	42
Croatia	..	21.8	..	25.2	35.8	26.2	4.6	10.4	100.0	11
Cuba	27.8	44.7	41.2	51.9	86.2	58.8	13.6	17.5	100.0	9
Czech Republic	11.2	13.0	21.7	22.0	33.7	30.5	4.2	9.9	..	18
Denmark	24.6	24.5	38.1	32.2	65.9	53.8	7.8	15.4	..	..
Dominican Republic	7.2	7.3	..	7.4	..	..	2.3	12.0	83.6	25
Ecuador	4.4	..	9.6	..	..	..	..	..	82.6	17
Egypt, Arab Rep.	..	..	..	..	..	..	3.8	11.9	..	27
El Salvador	8.6	8.5	7.5	9.1	8.9	13.7	3.6	13.1	93.2	31
Eritrea	15.0	..	37.3	..	429.6	..	..	..	92.2	38
Estonia	20.9	20.0	27.2	23.9	31.8	20.8	4.8	13.9	..	12
Ethiopia	..	12.4	..	8.9	..	642.9	5.5	23.3	84.6	58
Finland	17.4	17.5	25.8	30.8	40.4	31.7	5.9	12.5	..	14
France	17.3	17.7	28.5	26.4	29.7	34.8	5.6	10.7	..	19
Gabon	..	..	..	..	..	..	..	..	..	..
Gambia, The	..	..	..	..	..	..	..	..	..	34
Georgia	..	14.5	..	15.2	..	11.2	3.2	7.7	94.6	9
Germany	..	15.7	..	21.8	..	..	4.5	10.3	..	13
Ghana	..	..	..	..	..	..	..	..	47.6	33
Greece	11.7	..	15.5	..	26.2	..	..	..	..	10
Guatemala	6.7	10.5	4.3	6.2	..	19.0	3.2	..	..	29
Guinea	..	7.1	..	6.3	..	102.3	2.4	19.2	73.1	44
Guinea-Bissau	..	..	..	..	..	..	..	..	..	..
Haiti	..	..	..	..	..	..	..	..	..	..
Honduras	..	..	..	..	..	..	..	..	36.4	33

Education inputs

	Public expenditure per student						Public expenditure on education		Trained teachers in primary education	Primary school pupil–teacher ratio
	% of GDP per capita						% of GDP	% of total government expenditure	% of total	pupils per teacher
	Primary		Secondary		Tertiary					
	1999	2009a	1999	2009a	1999	2009a	2009a	2009a	2009a	2009a
Hungary	18.0	24.9	19.1	23.1	34.2	23.8	5.2	10.4	..	10
India	11.9	..	24.7	..	95.0	..	..	..	..	..
Indonesia	..	11.0	..	12.5	..	16.2	2.8	17.9	..	17
Iran, Islamic Rep.	9.1	15.1	9.9	21.0	34.8	22.2	4.7	20.9	98.4	20
Iraq	..	..	..	..	..	..	..	..	..	17
Ireland	11.0	15.7	16.8	23.2	28.6	26.2	4.9	13.8	..	16
Israel	20.5	19.4	21.9	19.0	30.9	22.7	5.9	13.1	..	13
Italy	24.0	22.6	27.7	25.2	27.6	22.1	4.3	9.0	..	10
Jamaica	13.4	15.8	21.0	26.8	70.4	42.4	5.8	..	..	18
Japan	21.1	21.7	20.9	22.4	15.1	20.1	3.5	9.4	..	..
Jordan	13.7	12.7	15.8	16.3	..	..	2.8	..	..	16
Kazakhstan	..	..	..	..	..	7.9	2.8	..	96.8	47
Kenya	21.5	..	14.5	..	209.0	..	..	..	..	..
Korea, Dem. Rep.	..	..	..	..	..	..	..	..	..	24
Korea, Rep.	18.4	17.0	15.7	22.2	8.4	9.0	4.2	14.8	..	..
Kosovo	..	..	..	..	..	..	4.3	17.4	..	..
Kuwait	19.2	10.9	..	14.9	..	..	..	..	100.0	9
Kyrgyz Republic	..	..	..	..	24.3	17.3	5.9	19.0	65.7	24
Lao PDR	2.3	..	4.5	..	68.6	..	2.3	12.2	96.9	29
Latvia	19.5	23.3	23.7	24.1	27.9	16.3	5.0	13.9	..	11
Lebanon	..	..	..	..	13.9	10.2	1.8	7.2	..	14
Lesotho	34.5	22.6	76.7	50.8	875.4	..	12.4	23.7	57.6	37
Liberia	..	5.7	..	8.4	..	..	2.8	12.1	40.2	24
Libya	..	..	..	..	23.9	..	..	..	..	..
Lithuania	..	15.8	..	20.1	34.2	17.1	4.7	13.4	..	13
Macedonia, FYR	..	..	..	..	..	..	..	..	..	17
Madagascar	5.7	7.1	..	10.5	..	132.4	3.0	13.4	..	48
Malawi	14.0	..	10.0	..	2,613.3	..	..	..	..	..
Malaysia	12.5	14.3	21.7	12.4	81.1	34.0	4.1	17.2	..	15
Mali	14.3	13.0	56.1	32.6	241.3	117.7	4.4	22.3	50.0	50
Mauritania	11.4	..	35.9	..	79.0	..	..	..	100.0	39
Mauritius	9.3	9.3	14.2	15.1	25.4	16.7	3.2	11.4	100.0	22
Mexico	11.7	13.3	14.2	13.4	47.8	37.0	4.8	..	95.4	28
Moldova	..	42.4	..	40.3	..	46.1	9.6	21.0	..	16
Mongolia	..	16.2	..	..	..	..	5.6	14.6	100.0	30
Morocco	17.2	16.1	45.1	38.7	96.2	71.1	5.6	25.7	100.0	27
Mozambique	..	..	..	..	1,412.2	..	..	..	71.2	61
Myanmar	..	..	6.9	..	28.0	..	..	..	98.9	29
Namibia	21.4	15.6	35.2	15.8	152.2	..	6.4	22.4	95.6	30
Nepal	9.1	17.6	13.1	11.3	141.6	55.5	4.6	19.5	66.4	33
Netherlands	15.2	16.9	22.2	24.5	47.4	40.2	5.3	11.7	..	..
New Zealand	20.2	17.6	24.1	19.6	40.1	28.6	6.1	..	..	15
Nicaragua	..	..	..	..	..	..	..	..	72.7	29
Niger	..	28.3	..	56.6	..	429.3	4.5	19.3	98.0	39
Nigeria	..	..	..	..	..	..	..	..	..	46
Norway	21.8	18.5	30.4	26.5	45.8	47.3	6.8	16.5	..	..
Oman	11.2	..	21.8	..	..	..	..	..	100.0	12
Pakistan	..	..	..	..	..	..	2.7	11.2	85.2	40
Panama	13.7	7.5	19.1	9.9	33.6	21.6	3.8	..	91.5	24
Papua New Guinea	..	..	..	..	..	..	..	..	..	26
Paraguay	13.6	10.8	18.5	16.3	58.9	26.0	4.0	11.9	..	21
Peru	7.6	8.1	10.8	9.9	21.2	..	2.7	20.7	..	34
Philippines	12.8	9.0	11.0	9.1	15.4	9.6	2.8	16.9	..	10
Poland	..	24.3	10.9	22.0	21.1	16.6	4.9	11.7	..	11
Portugal	19.5	..	27.5	..	28.1	..	..	..	..	12
Puerto Rico	..	..	..	..	..	..	..	..	6.6	12
Qatar	..	9.2	..	9.8	..	337.7	..	..	48.9	11

	Public expenditure per student % of GDP per capita						Public expenditure on education		Trained teachers in primary education	Primary school pupil–teacher ratio
	Primary		Secondary		Tertiary		% of GDP	% of total government expenditure	% of total	pupils per teacher
	1999	2009[a]	1999	2009[a]	1999	2009[a]	2009[a]	2009[a]	2009[a]	2009[a]
Romania	..	20.0	..	16.6	32.6	26.2	4.3	11.8	..	16
Russian Federation	..	..	..	..	10.9	..	..	..	..	17
Rwanda	11.0	8.2	41.9	34.3	1,206.8	222.8	4.1	20.4	93.9	68
Saudi Arabia	..	18.4	..	18.3	..	..	5.6	19.3	91.5	11
Senegal	14.1	20.9	..	25.7	..	191.5	5.8	19.0	..	35
Serbia	..	56.9	..	13.6	..	40.1	4.7	9.3	94.2	16
Sierra Leone	..	7.1	..	18.0	..	..	4.3	18.1	49.4	44
Singapore	..	10.5	..	15.7	..	27.3	3.0	11.6	94.3	19
Slovak Republic	10.2	15.6	18.4	14.7	32.9	19.5	3.6	10.5	..	17
Slovenia	26.3	..	25.7	..	27.9	..	..	..	..	17
Somalia	..	..	..	..	..	..	..	..	..	36
South Africa	14.2	15.1	20.0	17.7	..	..	5.4	16.9	87.4	31
Spain	18.0	19.4	24.4	24.1	19.6	25.1	4.3	11.1	..	12
Sri Lanka	..	..	..	..	..	..	..	..	..	23
Sudan	..	..	..	..	..	..	..	..	59.7	38
Swaziland	8.5	13.0	23.7	36.2	444.5	..	7.8	21.6	94.0	32
Sweden	22.5	25.0	26.2	30.6	52.1	38.3	6.6	12.7	..	10
Switzerland	22.7	22.5	27.3	25.2	53.8	46.7	5.2	16.1	..	..
Syrian Arab Republic	11.2	18.3	21.7	15.5	..	..	4.9	16.7	..	18
Tajikistan	..	..	..	..	..	21.8	3.5	18.7	88.3	23
Tanzania	..	22.1	..	18.8	..	..	6.8	27.5	100.0	54
Thailand	17.8	24.0	15.9	9.1	36.0	22.3	4.1	20.3	..	16
Timor-Leste	..	27.6	..	..	..	92.7	16.8	15.5	..	29
Togo	8.5	13.0	30.3	19.1	..	155.2	4.6	17.6	14.6	41
Trinidad and Tobago	11.5	9.0	12.2	9.9	148.7	..	..	..	88.0	17
Tunisia	15.6	..	27.1	..	89.4	54.5	7.1	22.4	..	17
Turkey	9.8	..	9.6	..	33.5	..	..	..	..	..
Turkmenistan	..	..	..	..	..	..	..	..	..	..
Uganda	..	7.3	..	21.2	..	105.4	3.2	15.0	89.4	49
Ukraine	..	..	..	..	36.5	25.1	5.3	20.2	99.9	16
United Arab Emirates	8.7	4.9	11.6	6.7	41.4	15.5	1.2	23.4	100.0	16
United Kingdom	13.9	23.0	23.8	28.2	25.6	24.4	5.5	11.7	..	18
United States	17.9	22.0	22.5	24.2	27.0	21.7	5.5	14.1	..	14
Uruguay	7.2	..	9.9	..	..	..	..	..	..	15
Uzbekistan	..	..	..	..	..	..	..	..	100.0	17
Venezuela, RB	..	9.2	..	8.2	..	..	3.7	..	86.3	16
Vietnam	..	19.7	..	17.3	..	61.7	5.3	19.8	99.6	20
West Bank and Gaza	..	..	..	..	..	..	..	..	100.0	28
Yemen, Rep.	..	..	..	..	..	..	5.2	16.0	..	..
Zambia	7.2	..	19.4	..	164.6	..	1.3	..	..	61
Zimbabwe	12.7	..	19.3	..	193.0	..	..	..	..	..
World	.. m	.. m	.. m	.. m	.. m	.. m	4.5 m	.. m	.. m	24 w
Low income	..	..	..	..	..	..	3.7	..	80.4	46
Middle income	..	..	..	..	..	..	4.1	..	..	23
Lower middle income	..	..	..	..	..	..	..	..	..	23
Upper middle income	12.0	13.8	16.4	17.0	..	..	4.5	13.5	..	21
Low & middle income	..	..	..	..	..	..	..	..	..	26
East Asia & Pacific	..	..	..	..	38.2	..	3.5	15.9	..	18
Europe & Central Asia	..	..	..	..	..	..	4.2	13.4	..	17
Latin America & Carib.	12.7	12.2	13.7	13.4	..	..	4.0	..	..	24
Middle East & N. Africa	..	..	..	..	..	..	4.6	18.0	..	23
South Asia	..	..	13.6	..	90.8	..	2.9	..	..	..
Sub-Saharan Africa	..	..	..	..	..	..	3.8	..	..	45
High income	18.0	19.4	22.5	23.9	31.4	25.2	5.1	12.5	..	15
Euro area	17.4	17.6	25.1	24.8	29.1	28.9	5.2	11.1	..	15

a. Provisional data.

Data on education are collected by the United Nations Educational, Scientific, and Cultural Organization (UNESCO) Institute for Statistics from official responses to its annual education survey. The data are used for monitoring, policymaking, and resource allocation. While international standards ensure comparable datasets, data collection methods may vary by country and within countries over time.

For most countries the data on education spending in the table refer to public spending—total government spending on education at all levels plus subsidies provided to households and other private entities—and generally exclude the part of foreign aid for education that is not included in the government budget. The data may also exclude spending by religious schools, which play a significant role in many developing countries. Data are gathered from ministries of education and from other ministries or agencies involved in education spending.

The share of public expenditure devoted to education allows an assessment of the priority a government assigns to education relative to other public investments, as well as a government's commitment to investing in human capital development. However, returns on investment to education, especially primary and lower secondary education, cannot be understood simply by comparing current education indicators with national income. It takes a long time before currently enrolled children can productively contribute to the national economy (Hanushek 2002).

High-quality data on education finance are scarce. Improving the quality of education finance data is a priority of the UNESCO Institute for Statistics. Additional resources are being allocated for technical assistance to countries in need, especially those in Sub-Saharan Africa. Interagency partnerships and collaborations with national ministries in charge of education finance data are improving, and actual expenditure data are increasingly being collected. Tracking private educational spending is still a challenge for all countries.

The share of trained teachers in primary education reveals a country's commitment to invest in the development of its human capital engaged in teaching, but it does not take into account differences in teachers' experiences and status, teaching methods, teaching materials, and classroom conditions—all factors that affect the quality of teaching and learning. Some teachers without this formal training may have acquired equivalent pedagogical skills through professional experience.

The primary school pupil–teacher ratio reflects the average number of pupils per teacher at the specified level of education. It differs from the average class size because of the different practices countries employ, such as part-time teachers, school shifts, and multigrade classes. The comparability of pupil–teacher ratios across countries is affected by the definition of teachers and by differences in class size by grade and in the number of hours taught, as well as the different practices mentioned above. Moreover, the underlying enrollment levels are subject to a variety of reporting errors (for further discussion of enrollment data, see *About the data* for table 2.12). While the pupil–teacher ratio is often used to compare the quality of schooling across countries, it is often weakly related to student learning and quality of education.

All education data published by the UNESCO Institute for Statistics are mapped to the *International Standard Classification of Education 1997* (ISCED 1997). This classification system ensures the comparability of education programs at the international level. UNESCO developed the ISCED to facilitate comparisons of education statistics and indicators of different countries on the basis of uniform and internationally agreed definitions. First developed in the 1970s, the current version was formally adopted in November 1997.

The reference years shown in the table reflect the school year for which the data are presented. In some countries the school year spans two calendar years (for example, from September 2009 to June 2010); in these cases the reference year refers to the year in which the school year ended (2010 in the previous example).

• **Public expenditure per student** is public current and capital spending on education divided by the number of students by level as a percentage of gross domestic product (GDP) per capita. • **Public expenditure on education** is current and capital expenditures on education by local, regional, and national governments, including municipalities. • **Trained teachers in primary education** are the percentage of primary school teachers who have received the minimum organized teacher training (pre-service or in-service) required for teaching at the specified level of education in their country. • **Primary school pupil–teacher ratio** is the number of pupils enrolled in primary school divided by the number of primary school teachers (regardless of their teaching assignment).

Data sources

Data on education inputs are from the UNESCO Institute for Statistics (www.uis.unesco.org).

	Gross enrollment ratio				Net enrollment rate				Adjusted net enrollment rate, primary		Children out of school	
	Preprimary	% of relevant age group Primary	Secondary	Tertiary	% of relevant age group Primary		Secondary		% of primary-school-age children Male	Female	thousand primary-school-age children Male	Female
	2009[a]	2009[a]	2009[a]	2009[a]	1991	2009[a]	1999	2009[a]	2009[a]	2009[a]	2009[a]	2009[a]
Afghanistan	..	104	44	4	28	..	..	27	..	..	..	..
Albania	58	119	72	..	..	85	70	..	86	84	15	16
Algeria	23	108	..	31	89	94	..	..	96	94	59	82
Angola	40	128	..	..	..	..	..	..	..	..	..	..
Argentina	69	116	85	68	..	..	76	79	..	..	..	..
Armenia	33	99	93	50	..	84	86	87	92	94	5	3
Australia	82	106	149	77	98	97	90	88	97	98	33	22
Austria	95	100	100	55	90	..	..	..	..	..	..	..
Azerbaijan	24	95	99	19	89	85	75	93	86	85	38	37
Bangladesh	10	95	42	8	64	86	40	41	86	93	1,234	575
Belarus	102	99	95	77	..	94	82	87	94	96	12	7
Belgium	122	103	108	63	96	98	..	..	98	99	6	4
Benin	14	122	..	..	51	95	18	..	99	86	7	91
Bolivia	47	107	81	38	..	91	68	69	92	92	58	53
Bosnia and Herzegovina	15	109	91	37	..	87	..	..	86	88	11	9
Botswana	17	109	82	..	89	87	54	60	86	88	21	18
Brazil	65	120	90	38	..	95	66	52	96	94	289	393
Bulgaria	81	101	89	51	..	96	85	83	97	98	4	3
Burkina Faso	3	78	20	3	27	63	9	15	68	60	392	473
Burundi	10	147	21	3	50	99	..	9	98	100	9	1
Cambodia	19	116	40	10	..	95	15	34	90	87	99	131
Cameroon	26	114	41	9	69	92	..	..	97	86	38	210
Canada	71	98	..	..	98	..	95	..	..	..	..	..
Central African Republic	5	89	14	2	53	67	..	10	77	57	78	149
Chad	1	90	24	2	..	..	7	..	..	..	..	..
Chile	55	106	90	55	..	95	..	85	96	95	35	41
China	47	113	78	25	97	..	..	..	..	..	..	..
Hong Kong SAR, China	121	104	82	57	..	94	74	75	97	100	6	0[b]
Colombia	51	120	95	37	71	90	56	74	93	93	155	152
Congo, Dem. Rep.	4	90	37	6	56	..	..	..	..	..	..	..
Congo, Rep.	13	120	..	6	..	..	..	..	..	..	..	..
Costa Rica	70	110	96	..	87	..	..	..	..	..	..	..
Côte d'Ivoire	4	74	..	8	46	57	19	..	62	52	609	774
Croatia	60	94	90	51	..	91	81	..	91	92	8	8
Cuba	105	104	90	118	94	99	73	83	100	99	2	2
Czech Republic	111	103	95	58	..	..	81	..	..	..	..	..
Denmark	96	98	119	78	98	95	88	90	94	97	12	7
Dominican Republic	37	106	77	..	..	87	38	61	96	89	23	70
Ecuador	131	117	81	42	..	97	46	59	..	..	..	..
Egypt, Arab Rep.	16	100	..	28	..	94	71	..	97	93	137	324
El Salvador	60	115	64	25	..	94	47	55	95	96	23	15
Eritrea	13	48	32	2	20	36	17	27	39	34	190	202
Estonia	95	100	99	64	..	94	84	89	96	97	1	1
Ethiopia	4	102	34	4	30	83	12	..	86	81	929	1,255
Finland	65	97	110	94	99	96	95	96	96	96	7	7
France	110	110	113	55	100	98	94	98	99	99	18	15
Gabon	..	..	..	..	..	..	..	..	..	..	..	..
Gambia, The	22	86	51	5	50	69	26	42	69	74	40	33
Georgia	63	108	108	25	..	100	76	81	96	93	6	10
Germany	109	105	102	..	84	98	..	..	..	..	..	..
Ghana	70	105	57	9	..	76	33	46	76	77	430	398
Greece	69	101	102	91	95	99	82	91	99	100	2	0[b]
Guatemala	29	114	57	18	..	95	24	40	98	95	23	55
Guinea	12	90	37	9	27	73	12	29	78	68	174	244
Guinea-Bissau	..	..	..	..	..	10	..	..	..	..	..	..
Haiti	..	..	..	..	21	..	..	..	..	..	..	..
Honduras	40	116	65	19	88	97	..	..	96	96	22	9

Participation in education

	Gross enrollment ratio				Net enrollment rate				Adjusted net enrollment rate, primary		Children out of school	
		% of relevant age group				% of relevant age group			% of primary-school-age children		thousand primary-school-age children	
	Preprimary	Primary	Secondary	Tertiary	Primary		Secondary		Male	Female	Male	Female
	2009[a]	2009[a]	2009[a]	2009[a]	1991	2009[a]	1999	2009[a]	2009[a]	2009[a]	2009[a]	2009[a]
Hungary	87	99	97	65	..	90	82	91	95	95	9	9
India	54	117	60	13	..	91	..	..	91	88	5,543	7,112
Indonesia	50	121	79	24	95	95	50	69	..	..	..	..
Iran, Islamic Rep.	40	103	83	36	97	99	..	..	..	..	..	..
Iraq	6	103	51	..	76	88	30	43	93	82	176	415
Ireland	..	105	115	58	90	97	84	88	96	98	9	5
Israel	97	111	90	60	..	97	86	86	97	98	13	9
Italy	100	103	101	67	..	98	88	95	100	99	5	15
Jamaica	86	93	91	24	97	80	83	77	82	79	31	35
Japan	89	102	101	58	100	100	99	98	..	..	..	..
Jordan	36	97	88	41	..	89	79	82	93	94	30	23
Kazakhstan	52	108	99	41	..	89	87	89	89	90	52	42
Kenya	51	113	59	4	..	83	33	50	83	84	532	497
Korea, Dem. Rep.	..	..	..	..	..	..	..	..	..	..	..	..
Korea, Rep.	111	105	97	98	99	99	97	95	100	98	4	31
Kosovo	..	..	..	..	..	..	..	..	..	..	..	..
Kuwait	76	95	90	29	47	88	89	80	94	93	6	8
Kyrgyz Republic	18	95	84	51	..	84	..	79	91	91	19	18
Lao PDR	22	121	44	13	59	93[c]	26	36	84	81	65	76
Latvia	89	98	98	69	..	..	..	..	..	..	..	..
Lebanon	77	103	82	53	..	90	..	75	92	90	19	21
Lesotho	..	104	45	..	72	73	17	29	71	76	54	45
Liberia	145	91	..	..	..	..	20	..	..	..	..	..
Libya	..	..	..	..	..	..	..	..	..	..	..	..
Lithuania	72	96	99	77	..	92	90	92	96	96	3	3
Macedonia, FYR	23	88	84	40	..	86	79	..	91	92	6	5
Madagascar	10	160	32	4	72	98	..	26	99	100	16	3
Malawi	..	119	30	0	..	91	29	25	89	94	152	85
Malaysia	71	95	69	36	..	94	65	68	94	94	97	95
Mali	4	95	38	6	..	73	..	30	84	70	165	304
Mauritania	..	104	24	4	..	76	14	16	74	79	66	51
Mauritius	98	100	87	26	93	94	67	..	93	95	4	3
Mexico	114	114	90	27	98	98	56	72	99	100	39	23
Moldova	74	94	88	38	..	88	79	80	91	90	8	8
Mongolia	59	110	92	53	..	90	58	82	99	99	1	1
Morocco	57	107	56	13	56	90	30	..	92	88	154	203
Mozambique	..	114	23	..	42	91	3	15	93	88	149	264
Myanmar	7	116	53	11	..	..	31	50	..	..	..	..
Namibia	..	112	66	9	82	89	39	54	88	92	22	14
Nepal	..	..	..	..	..	..	..	..	..	..	..	..
Netherlands	100	107	121	61	95	99	91	88	99	99	4	9
New Zealand	94	101	119	78	100	99	90	..	99	100	1	0[b]
Nicaragua	56	117	68	..	70	92	35	45	93	94	29	24
Niger	3	62	12	1	23	54	6	9	60	48	511	637
Nigeria	16	93	30	..	..	61	..	26	66	60	4,023	4,626
Norway	95	99	112	73	100	99	96	96	99	99	3	3
Oman	38	84	91	26	69	77	65	82	82	81	33	34
Pakistan	..	85	33	6	..	66	..	33	72	60	3,108	4,191
Panama	66	109	73	45	92	97	59	66	98	97	4	6
Papua New Guinea	..	..	..	..	65	..	..	..	..	..	..	..
Paraguay	109	102	67	29	94	87	46	59	88	88	52	50
Peru	72	109	89	..	86	94	62	71	97	98	54	43
Philippines	49	110	82	29	96	92	50	61	91	93	555	407
Poland	62	97	100	69	..	95	90	94	95	95	62	55
Portugal	81	115	104	60	98	99	82	88	99	99	2	4
Puerto Rico	154	91	84	78	..	..	..	..	..	..	..	..
Qatar	53	106	85	10	89	93	74	77	98	98	1	1

	Gross enrollment ratio				Net enrollment rate				Adjusted net enrollment rate, primary		Children out of school	
		% of relevant age group				% of relevant age group			% of primary-school-age children		thousand primary-school-age children	
	Preprimary	Primary	Secondary	Tertiary	Primary		Secondary		Male	Female	Male	Female
	2009[a]	2009[a]	2009[a]	2009[a]	1991	2009[a]	1999	2009[a]	2009[a]	2009[a]	2009[a]	2009[a]
Romania	73	100	92	66	73	90	75	73	96	97	16	14
Russian Federation	90	97	85	77	..	..	..	..	..	..	..	..
Rwanda	17	151	27	5	..	96	..	..	95	97	38	22
Saudi Arabia	11	99	97	37	..	86	..	72	88	85	205	244
Senegal	12	84	30	8	45	73	..	..	74	76	262	232
Serbia	51	98	91	50	..	94	..	90	96	96	5	6
Sierra Leone	5	158	35	..	..	..	..	25	..	..	..	..
Singapore	..	..	..	..	..	..	..	..	..	..	..	..
Slovak Republic	94	103	92	54	..	..	..	..	..	..	..	..
Slovenia	83	97	97	87	..	97	90	91	98	97	1	1
Somalia	..	33	8	..	..	..	..	..	..	..	..	..
South Africa	64	101	94	..	90	85	63	72	89	91	385	331
Spain	126	107	120	71	100	100	88	95	100	100	1	3
Sri Lanka	..	97	..	..	..	95	..	..	95	96	45	36
Sudan	28	74	38	..	..	..	..	..	..	..	..	..
Swaziland	..	108	53	..	74	83	32	29	82	84	19	18
Sweden	102	95	103	71	100	95	96	99	95	94	16	17
Switzerland	102	103	96	49	84	94	84	85	99	99	3	1
Syrian Arab Republic	9	122	75	..	91	..	36	69	..	..	..	..
Tajikistan	9	102	84	20	..	97	63	83	99	96	2	15
Tanzania	33	105	27	..	51	96	5	..	96	97	160	107
Thailand	92	91	76	45	..	90	..	71	91	89	281	305
Timor-Leste	..	113	51	15	..	82	23	..	84	82	15	17
Togo	7	115	41	5	65	94	20	..	98	89	10	56
Trinidad and Tobago	81	104	89	..	90	93	70	74	97	94	2	4
Tunisia	..	107	92	34	94	98	63	71	99	100	6	0[b]
Turkey	18	99	82	38	89	95	62	74	96	94	147	214
Turkmenistan	..	..	..	..	..	..	..	..	..	..	..	..
Uganda	12	122	27	4	..	92	8	22	91	94	310	213
Ukraine	101	98	94	79	..	89	91	85	89	90	89	81
United Arab Emirates	94	105	95	30	97	90	69	83	98	97	2	4
United Kingdom	81	106	99	57	97	100	95	93	100	100	5	1
United States	58	99	94	83	97	92	88	88	93	94	944	770
Uruguay	86	114	88	65	91	99	..	70	99	99	1	2
Uzbekistan	26	92	104	10	..	87	..	92	91	89	101	119
Venezuela, RB	77	103	82	79	..	92	47	71	94	94	108	96
Vietnam	..	..	..	..	..	..	59	..	..	..	..	..
West Bank and Gaza	34	79	87	46	..	75	77	85	78	77	57	55
Yemen, Rep.	..	85	..	10	..	73	32	..	80	66	395	641
Zambia	..	113	49	..	..	91	17	46	91	94	112	78
Zimbabwe	..	..	..	3	..	..	40	..	..	..	..	..
World	**44 w**	**107 w**	**67 w**	**26 w**	**.. w**	**88 w**	**52 w**	**59 w**	**91 w**	**89 w**		
Low income	15	104	38	6	..	80	..	..	83	79		
Middle income	46	109	68	24	..	88	..	..	92	90		
Lower middle income	42	107	63	19	..	87	..	..	91	88		
Upper middle income	63	111	88	42	..	93	67	75	94	94		
Low & middle income	40	107	63	21	..	87	..	55	90	88		
East Asia & Pacific	44	111	74	..	96	..	..	..	..	..		
Europe & Central Asia	55	99	89	55	90	92	79	81	94	94		
Latin America & Carib.	68	116	89	35	..	94	59	73	95	95		
Middle East & N. Africa	20	105	73	27	..	89	60	64	92	89		
South Asia	..	108	52	11	68	86	..	..	92	88		
Sub-Saharan Africa	17	100	34	6	..	75	..	..	78	75		
High income	77	101	100	67	95	95	88	90	95	96		
Euro area	110	..	..	..	..	..	..	..	..	..		

a. Provisional data. b. Less than 0.5. c. Data are for 2010.

About the data

School enrollment data are reported to the United Nations Educational, Scientific, and Cultural Organization (UNESCO) Institute for Statistics by national education authorities and statistical offices. Enrollment indicators help monitor whether a country is on track to achieve the Millennium Development Goal of universal primary education by 2015, and whether an education system has the capacity to meet the needs of universal primary education.

Enrollment indicators are based on annual school surveys but do not necessarily reflect actual attendance or dropout rates during the year. Also, the length of primary education differs across countries and can influence enrollment rates and ratios, although the International Standard Classification of Education (ISCED) tries to minimize the difference. A shorter duration for primary education tends to increase the ratio; a longer one to decrease it (in part because older children are more at risk of dropping out).

Over- or under-age enrollments are frequent, particularly when parents prefer children to start school at other than the official age. Age at enrollment may be inaccurately estimated or misstated, especially in communities where registration of births is not strictly enforced.

Population data used to calculate population-based indicators are drawn from the United Nations Population Division. Using a single source for population data standardizes definitions, estimations, and interpolation methods, ensuring a consistent methodology across countries and minimizing potential enumeration problems in national censuses.

Gross enrollment ratios indicate the capacity of each level of the education system, but a high ratio may reflect a substantial number of over-age children enrolled in each grade because of repetition or late entry, rather than a successful education system. The net enrollment rate excludes over- and under-age students and more accurately captures the system's coverage and internal efficiency. Differences between the gross enrollment ratio and net enrollment rate show the incidence of over- and under-age enrollments.

The adjusted net enrollment rate in primary education captures primary-school-age children who have progressed to secondary education faster than their peers and who would not be counted in the traditional net enrollment rate.

Data on children out of school (primary-school-age children not enrolled in primary or secondary school—dropouts, children never enrolled, and children of primary age enrolled in preprimary education) are compiled from administrative data. Large numbers of children out of school create pressure to enroll children and provide classrooms, teachers, and educational materials, a task made difficult in many countries by limited education budgets. However, getting children into school is a high priority for countries and crucial for achieving the Millennium Development Goal of universal primary education.

In 2006 the UNESCO Institute for Statistics changed its convention for citing the reference year. For more information, see *About the data* for table 2.11.

Definitions

• **Gross enrollment ratio** is the ratio of total enrollment, regardless of age, to the population of the age group that officially corresponds to the level of education shown. • **Preprimary education** (ISCED 0) refers to programs at the initial stage of organized instruction, designed primarily to introduce very young children, usually from age 3, to a school-type environment and to provide a bridge between the home and school. On completing these programs, children continue their education at the primary level. • **Primary education** (ISCED 1) refers to programs normally designed to give students a sound basic education in reading, writing, and mathematics along with an elementary understanding of other subjects such as history, geography, natural science, social science, art, and music. Religious instruction may also be featured. It is sometimes called elementary education. • **Secondary education** refers to programs of lower (ISCED 2) and upper (ISCED 3) secondary education. Lower secondary education continues the basic programs of the primary level, but the teaching is typically more subject focused, requiring more specialized teachers for each subject area. In upper secondary education, instruction is often organized even more along subject lines, and teachers typically need a higher or more subject-specific qualification. • **Tertiary education** refers to a wide range of programs with more advanced educational content. The first stage of tertiary education (ISECD 5) refers to theoretically based programs intended to provide sufficient qualifications to enter advanced research programs or professions with high-skill requirements and programs that are practical, technical, or occupationally specific. The second stage of tertiary education (ISCED 6) refers to programs devoted to advanced study and original research and leading to the award of an advanced research qualification. • **Net enrollment rate** is the ratio of total enrollment of children of official school age to the population of the age group that officially corresponds to the level of education shown. • **Adjusted net enrollment rate, primary,** is the ratio of total enrollment of children of official school age for primary education who are enrolled in primary or secondary education to the total primary school-age population. • **Children out of school** are the number of primary-school-age children not enrolled in primary or secondary school.

Data sources

Data on participation in education are from the UNESCO Institute for Statistics, www.uis.unesco.org.

	Gross intake ratio in first grade of primary education		Cohort survival rate						Repeaters in primary education		Transition rate to secondary education	
	% of relevant age group		% of grade 1 students						% of enrollment		%	
			Reaching grade 5				Reaching last grade of primary education					
	Male	Female	Male		Female		Male	Female	Male	Female	Male	Female
	2009[a]	2009[a]	1991	2008[a]	1991	2008[a]	2008[a]	2008[a]	2009[a]	2009[a]	2008[a]	2008[a]
Afghanistan	129	93	89	..	89	..	..	..	..	..	..	..
Albania	89	82	..	..	..	..	..	..	2	1	..	..
Algeria	101	99	82	94	79	95	91	95	13	8	90	92
Angola	..	..	..	..	..	..	..	..	..	..	..	..
Argentina	111	111	..	95	..	98	93	97	7	5	93	96
Armenia	86	89	..	..	..	..	98	97	0[b]	0[b]	100	98
Australia	..	..	98	..	99	..	..	..	..	..	..	..
Austria	104	100	..	..	..	..	96	99	0	0	100	99
Azerbaijan	95	94	..	..	..	..	100	97	0[b]	0[b]	100	98
Bangladesh	101	105	..	67	..	66	67	66	14	13	..	..
Belarus	97	102	..	..	..	..	99	99	0[b]	0[b]	100	100
Belgium	97	98	87	90	90	92	86	88	4	3	100	99
Benin	161	152	30	..	31	..	..	..	14	14	..	..
Bolivia	114	113	57	86	51	85	85	82	1	1	96	94
Bosnia and Herzegovina	89	92	..	..	..	..	..	..	0[b]	0[b]	..	..
Botswana	114	112	73	..	81	..	..	..	6	4	98	97
Brazil	..	..	..	..	..	..	..	..	..	..	..	..
Bulgaria	107	108	..	..	..	..	93	94	2	1	95	95
Burkina Faso	90	83	61	73[c]	58	78[c]	61[c]	67[c]	11	11	56[c]	51[c]
Burundi	152	146	66	62	61	68	56	64	32	32	48	23
Cambodia	158	157	..	68	..	71	60	63	10	8	80	81
Cameroon	134	117	67	76	66	79	68	69	15	14	42	45
Canada	..	..	..	..	..	..	..	..	..	..	..	..
Central African Republic	110	86	52	58	39	48	51	41	24	24	45	45
Chad	131	98	43	..	22	..	..	..	22	24	64	65
Chile	101	98	..	96	..	97	..	..	3	2	86	100
China	94	98	..	..	..	..	..	..	0[b]	0[b]	..	..
Hong Kong SAR, China	117	124	..	100	..	100	100	100	1	1	100	100
Colombia	118	114	53	82	59	89	82	89	2	2	100	100
Congo, Dem. Rep.	119	106	66	78	55	77	78	73	15	16	83	76
Congo, Rep.	115	112	66	75	68	79	71	71	21	19	65	62
Costa Rica	98	96	70	95	73	97	93	96	6	4	97	91
Côte d'Ivoire	77	67	68	66	61	66	62	59	19	19	47	45
Croatia	95	94	..	..	..	..	97	99	0[b]	0[b]	100	99
Cuba	100	102	..	96	..	96	96	95	1	0[b]	99	98
Czech Republic	109	107	..	99	..	99	99	99	1	1	99	99
Denmark	98	99	98	100	99	99	99	99	0	0	95	98
Dominican Republic	109	90	..	..	..	..	..	..	9	5	88	92
Ecuador	119	124	..	80	..	83	79	82	6	5	81	77
Egypt, Arab Rep.	98	96	..	..	..	..	..	..	4	2	..	..
El Salvador	123	119	54	78	57	82	74	78	7	5	92	92
Eritrea	45	39	..	74	..	72	74	72	14	13	85	81
Estonia	102	102	..	99	..	98	99	98	1	0[b]	97	99
Ethiopia	158	141	..	43	..	49	35	41	6	5	84	87
Finland	100	98	96	99	97	100	99	100	1	0[b]	100	100
France	..	..	..	..	..	..	..	..	..	..	..	..
Gabon	..	..	47	..	46	..	..	..	..	..	..	..
Gambia, The	91	96	59	71	53	72	68	72	6	5	83	83
Georgia	107	112	..	96	..	95	95	94	0[b]	0[b]	99	99
Germany	100	99	..	..	..	..	95	96	1	1	99	99
Ghana	109	111	72	80	65	78	75	71	7	6	91	92
Greece	102	103	..	98	..	97	98	97	1	1	..	..
Guatemala	123	121	..	71	..	70	65	64	13	11	93	90
Guinea	106	96	43	72	35	64	68	57	15	16	50	40
Guinea-Bissau	..	..	..	..	..	..	..	..	..	..	..	..
Haiti	..	..	47	..	46	..	..	..	..	..	..	..
Honduras	126	122	50	75	43	80	74	79	6	5	82	86

	Gross intake ratio in first grade of primary education		Cohort survival rate						Repeaters in primary education		Transition rate to secondary education	
	% of relevant age group		% of grade 1 students						% of enrollment		%	
			Reaching grade 5				Reaching last grade of primary education					
	Male	Female	Male		Female		Male	Female	Male	Female	Male	Female
	2009[a]	2009[a]	1991	2008[a]	1991	2008[a]	2008[a]	2008[a]	2009[a]	2009[a]	2008[a]	2008[a]
Hungary	103	103	..	..	..	..	99	99	2	1	99	99
India	132	124	..	67	..	70	67	70	3	3	81	81
Indonesia	125	122	..	83	..	89	77	83	4	3	91	93
Iran, Islamic Rep.	100	100	75	94	67	94	94	95	2	2	96	97
Iraq	105	103	75	..	70	..	..	..	19	14	..	..
Ireland	99	101	..	98	..	100	..	..	1	1	..	..
Israel	96	98	..	100	..	98	99	98	2	1	71	70
Italy	102	101	..	99	..	100	99	100	0[b]	0[b]	100	100
Jamaica	90	86	92	..	94	..	..	..	3	3	..	..
Japan	102	102	100	100	100	100	100	100	0	0	..	..
Jordan	99	99	93	..	89	..	..	..	1	1	99	98
Kazakhstan	105	106	..	..	..	..	98[c]	99[c]	0[b]	0[b]	100[c]	100[c]
Kenya	..	..	..	..	..	..	..	..	..	..	..	..
Korea, Dem. Rep.	..	..	..	..	..	..	..	..	..	..	..	..
Korea, Rep.	106	104	92	98	92	99	98	99	0[b]	0[b]	100	100
Kosovo	..	..	..	..	..	..	..	..	..	..	..	..
Kuwait	95	93	..	95	..	96	95	96	1	1	99	100
Kyrgyz Republic	97	97	..	..	..	..	96	97	0[b]	0[b]	99	100
Lao PDR	124	115	34	66	32	68	66	68	15[d]	13[d]	80	77
Latvia	104	105	..	98	..	94	97	94	5	2	92	97
Lebanon	100	105	..	94	..	96	90	93	11	7	84	89
Lesotho	106	98	53	56	77	69	38	56	23	16	68	66
Liberia	117	107	..	64	..	56	49	43	6	7	64	60
Libya	..	..	..	..	..	..	..	..	..	..	..	..
Lithuania	97	94	..	..	..	..	98	98	1	1	99	99
Macedonia, FYR	92	93	..	..	..	..	98	97	0[b]	0[b]	99	100
Madagascar	198	196	31	48	31	50	48	50	21	20	57	55
Malawi	136	144	37	51	33	50	42	42	19	18	75	74
Malaysia	89	89	86	96	87	97	96	96	..	..	100	99
Mali	102	89	48	88	42	85	81	77	13	14	72	68
Mauritania	112	119	52	48	47	51	40	42	2	2	38	31
Mauritius	99	99	..	96	..	99	94	98	4	3	64	75
Mexico	122	122	81	93	82	95	90	93	4	3	94	93
Moldova	94	93	..	..	..	..	95	96	0[b]	0[b]	99	98
Mongolia	147	142	..	94	..	95	94	95	0[b]	0[b]	96	99
Morocco	107	106	70	84	64	85	78	78	13	9	80	78
Mozambique	163	156	42	56[c]	34	51[c]	37[c]	34[c]	7	7	52[c]	55[c]
Myanmar	140	135	..	70	..	69	70	69	0[b]	0[b]	74	73
Namibia	98	99	52	90	57	93	80	85	18	14	80	83
Nepal	..	..	44	60	32	64	60	64	17	17	81	81
Netherlands	101	101	..	99	..	100	..	..	..	..	..	..
New Zealand	..	..	96	..	95	..	..	..	..	..	..	..
Nicaragua	158	148	39	48	48	55	45	52	13	9	..	..
Niger	97	83	68	66[c]	65	62[c]	63[c]	60[c]	5	5	56[c]	62[c]
Nigeria	102	83	..	..	..	..	..	..	..	..	44	44
Norway	97	99	99	99	100	100	99	99	..	..	100	100
Oman	88	86	77	..	78	..	..	..	1	2	..	..
Pakistan	111	96	..	61	..	60	61	60	3	3	73	72
Panama	105	103	..	88	..	91	86	88	6	4	96	97
Papua New Guinea	..	..	55	..	52	..	..	..	..	..	..	..
Paraguay	101	97	58	82	60	85	77	81	5	3	88	89
Peru	100	100	..	87	..	88	82	84	7	7	94	93
Philippines	139	130	..	75	..	82	71	80	3	2	100	98
Poland	..	..	..	..	..	..	..	..	2	1	..	..
Portugal	107	103	..	..	..	..	..	..	..	..	..	..
Puerto Rico	97	94	..	..	..	..	..	..	..	..	..	..
Qatar	103	108	98	92	99	99	91	97	0[b]	0[b]	100	100

	Gross intake ratio in first grade of primary education		Cohort survival rate						Repeaters in primary education		Transition rate to secondary education	
	% of relevant age group		% of grade 1 students						% of enrollment		%	
			Reaching grade 5				Reaching last grade of primary education					
	Male	Female	Male		Female		Male	Female	Male	Female	Male	Female
	2009a	2009a	1991	2008a	1991	2008a	2008a	2008a	2009a	2009a	2008a	2008a
Romania	101	99	..	..	..	..	93	94	2	1	97	97
Russian Federation	..	..	..	..	..	..	..	..	..	..	..	..
Rwanda	194	189	49	46	51	51	..	..	15	14	..	..
Saudi Arabia	102	101	80	99	76	93	98	91	4	4	93	100
Senegal	96	102	78	69	68	71	56	59	8	7	62	57
Serbia	95	94	..	..	..	..	99	97	1	1	100	99
Sierra Leone	201	182	..	..	..	..	..	..	10	10	..	..
Singapore	..	..	..	99	..	99	99	99	0b	0b	86	92
Slovak Republic	100	99	..	..	..	..	97	98	3	3	97	97
Slovenia	97	97	..	..	..	..	..	..	1	0b	..	..
Somalia	..	..	..	..	..	..	..	..	..	..	..	..
South Africa	92	87	61	..	67	..	..	..	8	8	90	91
Spain	105	106	..	99	..	100	99	100	3	2	..	..
Sri Lanka	92	93	97	88	98	89	88	89	1	1	95	97
Sudan	86	76	..	89	..	100	86	98	4	4	90	98
Swaziland	105	101	58	75	64	86	70	74	21	15	..	..
Sweden	104	103	99	100	99	100	100	100	0	0	100	100
Switzerland	93	96	72	..	72	..	..	..	2	1	99	100
Syrian Arab Republic	117	113	87	..	85	..	93	94	9	7	94	96
Tajikistan	106	101	..	..	..	..	..	..	0b	0b	98	98
Tanzania	99	100	69	79	71	83	71	77	2	2	40	32
Thailand	..	..	..	..	..	..	..	..	12	6	85	89
Timor-Leste	142	134	..	72	..	80	68	78	21	18	86	88
Togo	105	102	55	80	38	71	76	62	23	22	66	58
Trinidad and Tobago	102	100	98	97	99	95	93	93	7	5	86	92
Tunisia	106	107	76	96	70	96	94	95	10	6	79	86
Turkey	101	98	93	94	92	94	94	94	2	2	..	..
Turkmenistan	..	..	..	..	..	..	..	..	..	..	..	..
Uganda	140	143	..	57	..	58	54	53	14	14	58	55
Ukraine	100	100	..	..	..	..	96	98	0b	0b	100	100
United Arab Emirates	113	113	78	97	80	97	97	97	2	2	98	99
United Kingdom	..	..	..	..	..	..	..	..	0	0	..	..
United States	103	109	..	..	..	..	..	..	0	0	..	..
Uruguay	101	111	98	93	100	96	93	96	8	5	81	93
Uzbekistan	94	91	..	..	..	..	98	99	0b	0b	100	99
Venezuela, RB	101	98	69	92	80	96	89	95	4	3	97	97
Vietnam	..	..	..	..	..	..	..	..	..	..	..	..
West Bank and Gaza	77	77	..	..	..	..	99	97	0	0	97	97
Yemen, Rep.	110	98	..	..	..	..	..	..	6	5	..	..
Zambia	116	119	..	71	..	70	55	52	6	6	66	67
Zimbabwe	..	..	70	..	72	..	..	..	..	..	..	..
World	**114** w	**110** w	.. w	.. w	.. w	.. w	.. w	.. w	**5** w	**4** w	.. w	.. w
Low income	133	126	..	..	..	..	..	..	11	11	..	..
Middle income	114	110	..	..	..	..	..	..	4	3	..	..
Lower middle income	115	110	..	..	..	..	..	..	4	3	..	..
Upper middle income	..	..	..	..	..	..	..	..	..	..	..	..
Low & middle income	115	111	..	..	..	..	..	..	5	4	..	..
East Asia & Pacific	105	107	..	..	..	..	..	..	1	1	..	..
Europe & Central Asia	..	..	..	..	..	..	..	..	..	..	..	..
Latin America & Carib.	..	..	..	..	..	..	..	..	..	..	..	..
Middle East & N. Africa	104	101	..	..	..	..	..	..	9	5	..	..
South Asia	126	117	..	68	..	70	68	70	4	4	80	80
Sub-Saharan Africa	121	113	..	..	..	..	..	..	10	10	66	65
High income	102	104	..	..	..	..	..	..	1	1	..	..
Euro area	102	101	..	..	..	..	98	99	2	1	..	..

a. Provisional data. b. Less than 0.5. c. Data are for 2009. d. Data are for 2010.

About the data

The United Nations Educational, Scientific, and Cultural Organization (UNESCO) Institute for Statistics calculates indicators of students' progress through school. These indicators measure an education system's success in reaching students, efficiently moving students from one grade to the next, and transmitting knowledge at a particular level of education.

The gross intake ratio to the first grade of primary education indicates the level of access to primary education and the education system's capacity to provide access to primary education. A low gross intake ratio in grade 1 reflects the fact that many children do not enter primary school even though school attendance, at least through the primary level, is mandatory in most countries. Because the gross intake ratio includes all new entrants regardless of age, it can exceed 100 percent in some situations, such as immediately after fees have been abolished or when the number of reenrolled children is large. The indicator is not calculated when new entrants and repeaters are not correctly distinguished in grade 1.

The survival rate to grade 5 and to the last grade of primary education shows the percentage of students entering primary school who are expected to reach the specified grade. It measures an education system's holding power and internal efficiency. Survival rates are calculated based on the reconstructed cohort method, which uses data on enrollment by grade for the two most recent consecutive years and

data on repeaters by grade for the most recent of those two years to reflect current patterns of grade transition. Rates approaching 100 percent indicate high retention and low dropout levels.

Data on repeaters are often used to indicate an education system's internal efficiency. Repeaters not only increase the cost of education for the family and the school system, but also use limited school resources. Country policies on repetition and promotion differ. In some cases the number of repeaters is controlled because of limited capacity. In other cases the number of repeaters is almost 0 because of automatic promotion—suggesting a system that is highly efficient but that may not be endowing students with enough cognitive skills.

The transition rate from primary to secondary school conveys the degree of access or transition between the two levels. As completing primary education is a prerequisite for participating in lower secondary school, growing numbers of primary completers will inevitably create pressure for more available places at the secondary level. A low transition rate can signal such problems as an inadequate examination and promotion system or insufficient secondary school capacity. The quality of data on the transition rate is affected when new entrants and repeaters are not correctly distinguished in the first grade of secondary school. Students who interrupt their studies after completing primary school could also affect data quality.

In 2006 the UNESCO Institute for Statistics changed its convention for citing the reference year. For more information, see *About the data* for table 2.11.

Definitions

• **Gross intake ratio in first grade of primary education** is the number of new entrants in grade 1, regardless of age, expressed as a percentage of the population of the official school age. • **Cohort survival rate** is the percentage of children enrolled in the first grade of primary education who eventually reach grade 5 or the last grade of primary education. The estimate is based on the reconstructed cohort method (*see About the data*). • **Repeaters in primary education** are the number of students enrolled in the same grade as in the previous year as a percentage of all students enrolled in primary school. • **Transition rate to secondary education** is the number of new entrants to the first grade of secondary education (general programs only) in a given year as a percentage of the number of pupils enrolled in the final grade of primary education in the previous year.

There are more overage children among the poor in primary school in Zambia　　**2.13a**

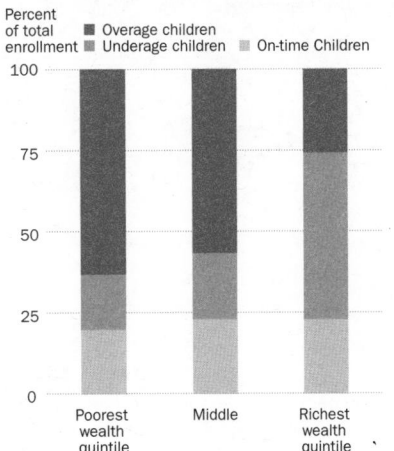

Percent of total enrollment
■ Overage children
■ Underage children
■ On-time Children

Source: World Bank, EdStats.

Data sources

Data on education efficiency are from the UNESCO Institute for Statistics, www.uis.unesco.org.

	Primary completion rate						Youth literacy rate				Adult literacy rate	PISA mathematics literacy
	% of relevant age group						% ages 15–24				% ages 15 and older	Mean score
	Total		Male		Female		Male		Female		Total	
	1991	2009[a]	1991	2009[a]	1991	2009[a]	1990	2005–09[b]	1990	2005–09[b]	2005–09[b]	2009
Afghanistan	28	..	41	..	14	..	..	..	..	..	..	..
Albania	..	90	..	90	..	89	..	99	..	99	96	377
Algeria	80	91	86	90	73	91	86	94	62	89	73	..
Angola	33	..	..	..	..	..	..	81	..	66	70	..
Argentina	100	102	..	100	..	104	..	99	..	99	98	388
Armenia	105	98	..	96	..	100	100	100	100	100	100	..
Australia	..	..	..	..	..	..	..	..	..	..	..	514
Austria	..	99	..	99	..	98	..	..	..	..	..	496
Azerbaijan	95	92	96	92	94	91	..	100	..	100	100	431
Bangladesh	41	61	..	58	..	63	..	74	..	77	56	..
Belarus	94	96	95	93	95	92	100	100	100	100	100	..
Belgium	79	86	76	84	82	88	..	..	..	..	..	515
Benin	22	62	30	71	14	53	..	65	..	43	42	..
Bolivia	71	99	78	99	64	98	..	99	..	99	91	..
Bosnia and Herzegovina	..	..	..	..	..	..	..	100	..	100	98	..
Botswana	90	95	83	93	98	97	..	94	..	97	84	..
Brazil	93						..	97	..	99	90	386
Bulgaria	90	90	88	91	92	89	..	98	..	97	98	428
Burkina Faso	20	43	25	46	15	40	..	47	..	33	29	..
Burundi	46	52	49	54	43	51	59	77	48	76	67	..
Cambodia	45	83	..	83	..	84	..	89	..	86	78	..
Cameroon	53	73	57	80	49	67	..	89	..	77	71	..
Canada	..	..	..	..	..	..	..	..	..	..	..	527
Central African Republic	28	38	37	47	20	29	63	72	35	57	55	..
Chad	18	33	29	42	7	24	26	54	9	39	34	..
Chile	..	95	..	101	..	88	..	99	..	99	99	421
China	107	..	..	..	..	..	97	99	91	99	94	..
Hong Kong SAR, China	102	93	..	92	..	93	..	..	..	..	..	555
Colombia	73	115	70	113	76	117	..	97	..	98	93	381
Congo, Dem. Rep.	48	56	61	66	36	46	..	73	..	62	67	..
Congo, Rep.	54	74	59	77	49	72	..	87	..	78	..	..
Costa Rica	79	96	77	95	81	97	..	98	..	99	96	..
Côte d'Ivoire	42	46	53	54	32	39	60	72	38	61	55	..
Croatia	85	100	..	99	..	100	..	100	..	100	99	460
Cuba	99	98	..	98	..	98	..	100	..	100	100	..
Czech Republic	92	95	91	95	93	95	..	..	..	..	..	493
Denmark	98	101	98	100	98	101	..	..	..	..	..	503
Dominican Republic	61	90	..	90	..	89	..	95	..	97	88	..
Ecuador	91	103	91	101	92	104	97	97	96	97	84	..
Egypt, Arab Rep.	..	95	..	97	..	93	71	88	54	82	66	..
El Salvador	65	89	64	88	66	91	..	95	..	95	84	..
Eritrea	18	48	21	52	15	43	..	92	..	86	67	..
Estonia	..	100	..	100	..	101	100	100	100	100	100	512
Ethiopia	23	55	28	57	18	53	..	56	..	33	30	..
Finland	97	98	98	99	97	97	..	..	..	..	..	541
France	106	..	..	..	..	..	..	..	..	..	..	497
Gabon	62	..	59	..	65	..	..	99	..	97	88	..
Gambia, The	45	79	56	76	34	83	..	71	..	60	46	..
Georgia	..	107	..	110	..	104	..	100	..	100	100	..
Germany	100	104	99	103	100	104	..	..	..	..	..	513
Ghana	64	83	71	85	56	81	..	81	..	79	67	..
Greece	99	101	99	102	98	101	..	99	..	99	97	466
Guatemala	..	80	..	83	..	77	..	89	..	84	74	..
Guinea	17	62	24	71	9	53	..	68	..	54	39	..
Guinea-Bissau	5	..	7	..	3	..	..	78	..	64	52	..
Haiti	27	..	29	..	26	..	..	..	..	..	49	..
Honduras	64	90	67	87	61	93	..	93	..	95	84	..

	Primary completion rate						Youth literacy rate				Adult literacy rate	PISA mathematics literacy
	% of relevant age group						% ages 15–24				% ages 15 and older	Mean score
	Total		Male		Female		Male		Female		Total	
	1991	2009[a]	1991	2009[a]	1991	2009[a]	1990	2005–09[b]	1990	2005–09[b]	2005–09[b]	2009
Hungary	82	95	89	97	90	94	..	99	..	99	99	490
India	64	95	76	95	52	94	..	88	..	74	63	..
Indonesia	93	109	..	109	..	110	97	100	95	99	92	371
Iran, Islamic Rep.	88	101	93	101	82	101	85	99	66	99	85	..
Iraq	58	64	63	73	52	54	..	85	..	80	78	..
Ireland	103	99	103	99	103	99	..	..	..	..	..	487
Israel	..	99	..	99	..	100	..	..	..	..	..	447
Italy	98	104	98	104	97	104	..	100	..	100	99	483
Jamaica	94	89	90	88	98	90	..	92	..	98	86	..
Japan	102	101	102	100	102	101	..	..	..	..	..	529
Jordan	101	100	101	99	101	100	..	99	..	99	92	387
Kazakhstan	103	106	103	106	103	106	100	100	100	100	100	405
Kenya	..	..	..	..	..	..	..	92	..	94	87	..
Korea, Dem. Rep.	..	..	..	..	..	..	..	100	..	100	100	..
Korea, Rep.	99	99	99	100	100	97	..	..	..	..	..	546
Kosovo	..	..	..	..	..	..	..	..	..	..	..	..
Kuwait	57	93	58	94	56	93	91	99	84	99	94	..
Kyrgyz Republic	..	94	..	94	..	95	..	100	..	100	99	331
Lao PDR	41	75	46	78	36	71	..	89	..	79	73	..
Latvia	..	95	..	97	..	93	100	100	100	100	100	482
Lebanon	..	85	..	83	..	87	..	98	..	99	90	..
Lesotho	59	70	42	60	76	81	..	86	..	98	90	..
Liberia	..	58	..	63	..	53	..	70	..	81	59	..
Libya	..	..	..	..	..	..	..	100	..	100	89	..
Lithuania	..	92	..	92	..	92	100	100	100	100	100	477
Macedonia, FYR	98	92	..	91	..	93	..	99	..	99	97	..
Madagascar	36	79	35	79	37	79	..	66	..	64	64	..
Malawi	31	59	35	58	27	60	70	87	49	86	74	..
Malaysia	91	97	91	97	91	97	..	98	..	99	92	..
Mali	9	59	12	67	7	52	..	47	..	31	26	..
Mauritania	33	64	39	63	26	66	..	71	..	64	57	..
Mauritius	115	89	115	89	115	90	91	96	92	98	88	..
Mexico	88	104	91	104	92	105	96	99	95	98	93	419
Moldova	..	93	..	94	..	91	100	99	100	100	98	..
Mongolia	..	93	..	94	..	92	..	95	..	97	97	..
Morocco	48	80	57	84	39	77	..	87	..	72	56	..
Mozambique	26	57	32	63	21	51	..	78	..	64	55	..
Myanmar	..	99	..	98	..	100	..	96	..	95	92	..
Namibia	74	87	67	83	81	91	..	91	..	95	89	..
Nepal	51	..	70	..	41	..	..	87	..	77	59	..
Netherlands	..	..	..	..	..	..	..	..	..	..	..	526
New Zealand	..	..	..	..	..	..	..	..	..	..	..	519
Nicaragua	42	75	43	71	53	78	..	85	..	89	78	..
Niger	17	40	21	47	13	34	..	52	..	23	29	..
Nigeria	..	79	..	84	..	74	..	78	..	65	61	..
Norway	100	98	100	98	100	97	..	..	..	..	..	498
Oman	74	80	78	80	70	79	..	98	..	98	87	..
Pakistan	..	61	..	68	..	54	..	79	..	61	56	..
Panama	86	102	86	102	86	101	95	97	95	96	94	360
Papua New Guinea	46	..	51	..	42	..	..	65	..	70	60	..
Paraguay	68	94	68	93	69	95	..	99	..	99	95	..
Peru	..	101	..	101	..	101	..	98	..	97	90	365
Philippines	88	94	85	91	86	97	96	97	97	98	95	..
Poland	96	96	..	..	..	..	..	100	..	100	100	495
Portugal	..	..	..	..	..	..	..	100	..	100	95	487
Puerto Rico	..	..	..	..	..	..	92	87	94	88	90	..
Qatar	71	108	71	109	72	106	89	98	91	98	95	368

	Primary completion rate						Youth literacy rate				Adult literacy rate	PISA mathematics literacy
	% of relevant age group						% ages 15–24				% ages 15 and older	
	Total		Male		Female		Male		Female		Total	Mean score
	1991	2009a	1991	2009a	1991	2009a	1990	2005–09b	1990	2005–09b	2005–09b	2009
Romania	96	96	96	96	96	96	..	97	..	98	98	427
Russian Federation	92	95	92	..	93	..	100	100	100	100	100	468
Rwanda	50	54	51	52	50	56	..	77	..	77	71	..
Saudi Arabia	..	93	..	95	..	90	..	99	..	97	86	..
Senegal	39	57	48	56	31	57	49	74	28	56	50	..
Serbia	..	96	..	97	..	96	..	..	..	..	..	442
Sierra Leone	..	88	..	101	..	75	..	68	..	48	41	..
Singapore	..	..	..	..	..	..	99	100	99	100	95	562
Slovak Republic	95	96	95	96	96	96	..	..	..	..	..	497
Slovenia	95	96	..	97	..	96	..	100	..	100	100	501
Somalia	..	..	..	..	..	..	..	..	..	..	..	..
South Africa	76	93	72	93	80	94	..	97	..	98	89	..
Spain	104	100	104	100	103	100	..	100	..	100	98	483
Sri Lanka	101	97	101	97	101	98	..	97	..	99	91	..
Sudan	..	57	..	53	..	47	..	89	..	83	70	..
Swaziland	61	72	57	75	64	69	83	92	84	95	87	..
Sweden	96	94	96	95	96	94	..	..	..	..	..	494
Switzerland	53	94	53	93	54	95	..	..	..	..	..	534
Syrian Arab Republic	89	112	94	113	84	111	..	96	..	93	84	..
Tajikistan	..	98	..	97	..	93	100	100	100	100	100	..
Tanzania	55	102	56	102	55	102	86	78	78	76	73	..
Thailand	..	..	..	..	..	..	..	98	..	98	94	419
Timor-Leste	..	80	..	80	..	79	..	..	..	..	51	..
Togo	35	61	48	71	22	52	..	85	..	68	57	..
Trinidad and Tobago	102	93	99	93	105	93	99	100	99	100	99	414
Tunisia	74	93	79	93	70	93	..	98	..	96	78	371
Turkey	90	93	93	95	86	92	97	99	88	97	91	445
Turkmenistan	..	..	..	..	..	..	..	100	..	100	100	..
Uganda	..	72	..	72	..	73	..	90c	..	85c	73c	..
Ukraine	92	95	99	98	99	99	..	100	..	100	100	..
United Arab Emirates	103	99	104	100	103	98	81	94	85	97	90	..
United Kingdom	..	..	..	..	..	..	..	..	..	..	..	492
United States	..	95	..	94	..	97	..	..	..	..	..	487
Uruguay	94	106	91	104	96	108	98	98	99	100	98	427
Uzbekistan	80	92	..	93	..	91	..	100	..	100	99	..
Venezuela, RB	81	95	76	94	86	96	95	98	96	99	95	..
Vietnam	..	..	..	..	..	..	94	97	93	96	93	..
West Bank and Gaza	..	82	..	82	..	81	..	99	..	99	95	..
Yemen, Rep.	..	61	..	72	..	49	..	96	..	72	62	..
Zambia	..	87	..	92	..	82	67	82	66	67	71	..
Zimbabwe	97	..	99	..	96	..	..	98	..	99	92	..
World	**79 w**	**88 w**	**86 w**	**90 w**	**75 w**	**87 w**	**87 w**	**92 w**	**78 w**	**87 w**	**84 w**	
Low income	44	63	..	66	..	60	66	76	52	69	62	
Middle income	83	92	89	93	77	91	88	94	78	88	83	
Lower middle income	82	90	89	92	74	89	87	93	74	86	80	
Upper middle income	88	100	89	100	88	100	94	98	92	97	92	
Low & middle income	78	87	85	89	73	85	86	91	75	85	80	
East Asia & Pacific	101	99	105	98	97	100	96	99	91	99	94	
Europe & Central Asia	92	96	93	97	92	95	99	99	98	99	98	
Latin America & Carib.	84	101	84	100	85	102	91	97	92	97	91	
Middle East & N. Africa	..	95	..	97	..	92	84	93	67	87	74	
South Asia	62	79	75	82	52	76	71	85	47	72	61	
Sub-Saharan Africa	51	64	57	69	47	60	73	77	58	67	62	
High income	..	98	..	98	..	98	99	99	99	99	98	
Euro area	101	..	100	..	100	..	..	..	..	..	..	

a. Provisional data. b. Data are for the most recent year available. c. Data are for 2010.

About the data

Many governments publish statistics that indicate how their education systems are working and developing—statistics on enrollment and such efficiency indicators as repetition rates, pupil–teacher ratios, and cohort progression. The World Bank and the United Nations Educational, Scientific, and Cultural Organization (UNESCO) Institute for Statistics jointly developed the primary completion rate indicator. Increasingly used as a core indicator of an education system's performance, it reflects an education system's coverage and the educational attainment of students. The indicator is a key measure of education outcome at the primary level and of progress toward the Millennium Development Goals and the Education for All initiative. However, a high primary completion rate does not necessarily mean high levels of student learning.

The primary completion rate reflects the primary cycle as defined by the *International Standard Classification of Education (ISCED 97),* ranging from three or four years of primary education (in a very small number of countries) to five or six years (in most countries) and seven (in a small number of countries).

The table shows the primary completion rate, also called the gross intake ratio to last grade of primary education. It is the total number of new entrants in the last grade of primary education, regardless of age, expressed as a percentage of the population at the entrance age to the last grade of primary education. Data limitations preclude adjusting for students who drop out during the final year of primary education. Thus, this rate is a proxy that should be taken as an upper estimate of the actual primary completion rate.

There are many reasons why the primary completion rate can exceed 100 percent. The numerator may include late entrants and overage children who have repeated one or more grades of primary education as well as children who entered school early, while the denominator is the number of children at the entrance age to the last grade of primary education.

Basic student outcomes include achievements in reading and mathematics judged against established standards. The UNESCO Institute for Statistics has established literacy as an outcome indicator based on an internationally agreed definition. The literacy rate is the percentage of the population who can, with understanding, both read and write a short, simple statement about their everyday life. In practice, literacy is difficult to measure. To estimate literacy using such a definition requires census or survey measurements under controlled conditions.

Many countries estimate the number of literate people from self-reported data. Some use educational attainment data as a proxy but apply different lengths of school attendance or levels of completion. Because definitions and methodologies of data collection differ across countries, data should be used cautiously.

The reported literacy data are compiled by the UNESCO Institute for Statistics based on national censuses and household surveys during 1985–2009. For countries without recent literacy data, the UNESCO Institute for Statistics estimates literacy rates with the Global Age-specific Literacy Projections Model (GALP). For detailed information on sources, definitions, and methodology, consult www.uis.unesco.org.

Literacy statistics for most countries cover the population ages 15 and older, but some include younger ages or are confined to age ranges that tend to inflate literacy rates. The youth literacy rate for ages 15–24 reflects recent progress in education: it measures the accumulated outcomes of primary education over the previous 10 years or so by indicating the proportion of people who have passed through the primary education system and acquired basic literacy and numeracy skills. Generally, literacy also encompasses numeracy, the ability to make simple arithmetic calculations.

In many countries national assessments enable ministries of education to monitor progress in learning outcomes. Of the handful of internationally or regionally comparable assessments, one of the largest is the Programme for International Student Assessment (PISA). Coordinated by the Organisation for Economic Co-operation and Development (OECD), it measures the knowledge and skills of 15-year-olds, the age at which students in most countries are nearing the end of their compulsory time in school. The assessment tests reading, mathematical, and scientific literacy in terms of general competencies—that is, how well students can apply the knowledge and skills they have learned at school to real-life challenges. It does not test how well a student has mastered a school's specific curriculum.

The table presents the mean PISA mathematical literacy score, as demonstrated through students' ability to analyze, reason, and communicate effectively while posing, solving, and interpreting mathematical problems that involve quantitative, spatial, probabilistic, or other mathematical concepts. The average score in 2009 was 496. Because the figures are derived from samples, the scores reflect a small measure of statistical uncertainty.

Definitions

• **Primary completion rate** is approximated by the gross intake ratio to last grade of primary education, which is the total number of new entrants in the last grade of primary education, regardless of age, expressed as a percentage of the population at the entrance age to the last grade of primary. • **Youth literacy rate** is the percentage of the population ages 15–24 that can, with understanding, both read and write a short simple statement on their everyday life. • **Adult literacy rate** is the percentage of the population ages 15 and older that can, with understanding, both read and write a short simple statement on their everyday life. • **PISA mathematics literacy** is the country's mean mathematics score from the Programme for International Student Assessment (PISA).

Data sources

Data on education completion and outcomes are from the UNESCO Institute for Statistics. Data on PISA mathematics literacy are from the OECD.

Education gaps by income and gender

	Survey year	Gross intake rate in grade 1		Gross primary participation rate		Average years of schooling		Primary completion rate				Children out of school	
		% of relevant age group		% of relevant age group		Ages 15–19			% of relevant age group			% of relevant age group	
		Poorest quintile	Richest quintile	Poorest quintile	Richest quintile	Poorest quintile	Richest quintile	Poorest quintile	Richest quintile	Male	Female	Poorest quintile	Richest quintile
Armenia	2005	93	80	106	102	9	10	119	116	113	112	2	1
Azerbaijan	2006	92	118	100	108	9	11	94	109	103	105	20	11
Bangladesh	2006	144	147	96	105	8	13	65	97	83	86	12	6
Belize	2006	80	89	106	113	8	11	59	130	107	72	5	7
Benin	2006	67	107	61	114	6	8	31	95	67	52	57	12
Bolivia	2003	92	95	108	129	6	9	76	98	90	81	22	5
Burundi	2005	201	191	91	144	4	7	20	70	44	39	5	3
Cambodia	2005	208	151	113	134	5	8	42	121	88	85	37	13
Cameroon	2006	108	75	93	116	6	14	43	111	90	74	3	2
Colombia	2005	161	84	127	99	6	10	94	109	100	103	11	2
Côte d'Ivoire	2006	51	77	57	110	5	8	47	127	88	71	4	3
Dominican Republic	2007	130	112	113	107	7	11	69	109	88	106	12	4
Egypt, Arab Rep.	2005	107	97	95	99	9	12	84	92	92	88	12	1
Ethiopia	2005	86	124	47	112	3	6	14	90	46	33	74	30
Georgia	2006	90	104	101	103	15	14	102	102	106	104	2	1
Ghana	2006	107	121	81	117	5	8	62	88	93	86	22	12
Guatemala	2000	176	124	81	114	4	8	15	80	34	36	7	3
Guinea	2005	55	119	52	121	5	7	32	93	76	48	60	16
Guinea-Bissau	2006	135	184	94	166	4	7	34	125	80	54	12	11
Guyana	2006	74	76	105	101	10	10	109	118	91	112	2	1
Haiti	2005	177	188	87	159	4	7	31	136	73	82	69	24
Kazakhstan	2006	118	101	106	103	9	9	102	115	102	97	0	1
Kenya	2003	134	125	92	106	6	9	40	76	71	72	38	11
Kosovo	2000	104	119	95	104	9	11	82	94	98	83	1	4
Lesotho	2004	169	111	116	124	5	8	36	122	69	85	18	3
Macedonia, FYR	2005	102	190	89	97	8	10	120	119	133	78	0	0
Madagascar	2003/04	250	153	118	145	3	8	42	141	77	77	33	3
Malawi	2004	235	145	98	122	5	8	24	81	47	35	23	4
Malawi	2006	234	207	133	169	5	7	30	80	49	52	0	0
Mali	2006	41	98	46	110	5	8	36	79	55	41	67	20
Mauritania	2007	67	96	62	116	5	9	17	89	48	52	2	2
Moldova	2005	96	84	99	95	9	12	97	100	96	98	2	1
Mozambique	2003	128	143	75	143	3	6	13	100	57	43	46	7
Namibia	2006	112	104	118	109	7	10	81	109	94	90	11	2
Nepal	2001	184	141	109	139	5	8	49	96	69	62	33	6
Nicaragua	2001	149	106	85	105	4	9	34	124	78	83	40	4
Niger	2006	50	90	35	89	4	7	31	71	60	30	74	28
Nigeria	2003	78	101	70	108	7	10	48	71	70	54	52	6
Panama	2003	125	116	108	102	7	11	100	94	105	88	1	1
Peru	2004	121	90	118	96	7	11	106	99	100	97	6	1
Rwanda	2005	274	195	131	151	3	5	31	88	48	42	13	8
Serbia	2005	90	98	98	100	9	10	86	96	94	89	1	0
Somalia	2005	13	44	8	93	8	10	2	58	26	20	87	46
Swaziland	2006	147	117	117	114	6	9	69	110	85	98	17	4
Syrian Arab Republic	2006	110	149	102	107	7	8	92	93	93	92	0	0
Tanzania	2004	123	123	82	119	5	7	32	108	58	60	44	15
Togo	2006	115	148	99	128	6	7	40	82	67	56	1	1
Turkey	2003	108	111	97	97	6	7	95	85	100	81	20	5
Uganda	2006	180	144	107	124	5	8	27	68	50	42	25	7
Vietnam	2006	99	100	108	100	..	..	99	104	96	103	3	2
Yemen, Rep.	2006	66	109	50	101	7	10	25	103	84	31	2	2
Zambia	2007	135	123	105	112	5	9	50	101	88	73	22	3
Zimbabwe	1999	106	111	144	144	7	10	36	80	51	57	22	8

About the data

The data in the table describe basic information on school participation and educational attainment by individuals in different socioeconomic groups within countries. The data are from Demographic and Health Surveys (DHS) conducted by Macro International with the support of the U.S. Agency for International Development, Multiple Indicator Cluster Surveys (MICS) conducted by the United Nations Children's Fund (UNICEF), and Living Standards Measurement Study conducted by the World Bank Development Economics Research Group. These large-scale household sample surveys, conducted periodically in developing countries, collect information on a large number of health, nutrition, and population measures as well as on respondents' social, demographic, and economic characteristics using detailed questionnaires. The data presented here draw on responses to individual and household questionnaires.

Typically, those surveys collect basic information on educational attainment and enrollment levels from every household member ages 5 or 6 and older as part of the household's socioeconomic characteristics. The surveys are not intended for the collection of detailed education data. As a result, the education section of the surveys does not replace education flows, nor are as detailed as, for instance, the health section for the case of the DHS and MICS. Still, the education data are very useful for providing micro-level information on education that cannot be obtained from administrative data, such as information on children not attending school.

Socioeconomic status as displayed in the table is based on a household's assets, including ownership of consumer items, features of the household's dwelling, and other characteristics related to wealth. Each household asset on which information was collected was assigned a weight generated through principal-component analysis which was then used to create break-points defining wealth quintiles, expressed as quintiles of individuals in the population.

The selection of the asset index for defining socioeconomic status was based on pragmatic rather than conceptual considerations: Demographic and Health Surveys do not collect consumption data but do have detailed information on households' ownership of consumer goods and access to a variety of goods and services. Like income or consumption, the asset index defines disparities primarily in economic terms. It therefore excludes other possibilities of disparities among groups, such as those based on gender, education, ethnic background, or other facets of social exclusion. To that extent the index provides only a partial view of the multidimensional concepts of poverty, inequality, and inequity.

Creating one index that includes all asset indicators limits the types of analysis that can be performed. In particular, the use of a unified index does not permit a disaggregated analysis to examine which asset indicators have a more or less important association with education status. In addition, some asset indicators may reflect household wealth better in some countries than in others—or reflect different degrees of wealth in different countries. Taking such information into account and creating country specific asset indexes with country-specific choices of asset indicators might produce a more effective and accurate index for each country. The asset index used in the table does not have this flexibility.

The analysis was carried out for around 80 countries. The table only shows the estimates for the poorest and richest quintiles, gender, and latest data; the full set of estimates for all indicators, other subgroups including urban and rural areas, and older data are available in the country reports (see *Data sources*). The data in the table differ from data for similar indicators in preceding tables either because the indicator refers to a period a few years preceding the survey date or because the indicator definition or methodology is different. Findings should be used with caution because of measurement error inherent in the use of survey data.

Definitions

- **Survey year** is the year in which the underlying data were collected. • **Gross intake rate in grade 1** is the number of students in the first grade of primary education regardless of age as a percentage of the population of the official primary school entrance age. These data may differ from those in table 2.13. • **Gross primary participation rate** is the ratio of total students attending primary school regardless of age to the population of the age group that officially corresponds to primary education. • **Average years of schooling** are the years of formal schooling received, on average, by youths and adults ages 15–19. • **Primary completion rate** is the total number of students regardless of age in the last grade of primary school, minus the number of repeaters in that grade, divided by the total number of children of official graduation age. These data differ from those in table 2.14 because the source is different. • **Children out of school** are the number of children in the official primary school ages who are not attending primary or secondary education, expressed as a percentage of children of the official primary school ages. Children in the official primary school age, who are attending pre-primary education, are considered out-of-school. These data differ from those in table 2.12 because the source is different.

Data sources

Data on education gaps by income and gender are from an analysis of Demographic and Health Surveys by Macro International, Multiple Indicators Cluster surveys by UNICEF, and Living Standards Measurement Study by World Bank, and these sources are analyzed by the EdStats team of the World Bank Human Development Network Education using ADePT Education. Country reports, further updates, and ADePT Education software are available at www.worldbank.org/education/edstats/.

	Health expenditure						Health workers		Hospital beds	Outpatient visits
	Total % of GDP	Public % of total	Out of pocket % of total	External resources % of total	Per capita $	Per capita PPP $	per 1,000 people Physicians	Nurses and midwives	per 1,000 people	per capita
	2008	**2008**	**2008**	**2008**	**2008**	**2008**	**2004–09**[a]	**2004–09**[a]	**2004–09**[a]	**2000–09**[a]
Afghanistan	7.4[b]	21.5[b]	77.7[b]	17.3[b]	47[b]	57[b]	0.2	0.5	0.4	
Albania	6.8	39.4	58.6	2.1	281	569	1.1	4.0	2.9	1.5
Algeria	5.4	86.1	13.2	0.0	272	437	1.2	2.0	1.7	..
Angola	3.3[c]	85.0[c]	15.0[c]	3.0[c]	148[c]	183[c]	0.1	1.4	0.8	..
Argentina	8.4	62.6	22.2	0.0	695	1,062	3.2	0.5	4.0	..
Armenia	3.8	44.5	51.8	10.4	143	224	3.7	4.9	4.1	2.8
Australia	8.5[d]	65.4[d]	17.9[d]	0.0[d]	4,180[d]	3,365[d]	3.0	9.6	3.8	6.2
Austria	10.5	73.7	15.1	0.0	5,201	4,150	4.7	7.8	7.7	6.7
Azerbaijan	4.3	19.3	73.3	0.6	240	395	3.8	8.4	7.9	4.6
Bangladesh	3.3	31.4	66.2	5.8	17	44	0.3	0.3	0.4	..
Belarus	5.6	72.2	19.9	0.2	351	688	5.1	12.6	11.2	13.2
Belgium	11.1	66.8	20.5	0.0	5,243	4,096	3.0	0.3	6.6	7.0
Benin	4.1	51.7	44.7	17.7	32	61	0.1	0.8	0.5	..
Bolivia	4.4	63.1	30.1	9.1	75	187	..	..	1.1	..
Bosnia and Herzegovina	10.3	58.2	41.8	1.3	506	937	1.4	4.7	3.0	3.3
Botswana	7.6	78.2	7.2	4.2	530	1,053	0.3	2.8	1.8	..
Brazil	8.4	44.0	31.9	0.0	721	875	1.7	6.5	2.4	..
Bulgaria	7.1	57.8	36.5	0.0	482	974	3.6	4.7	6.5	..
Burkina Faso	5.9	59.1	38.1	29.2	37	82	0.1	0.7	0.9	..
Burundi	13.0[c]	40.0[c]	38.1[c]	34.5[c]	19[c]	50[c]	0.0	0.2	0.7	..
Cambodia	5.7	23.8	64.4	17.1	43	118	0.2	0.8	0.1	..
Cameroon	5.3[c]	22.7[c]	73.5[c]	5.5[c]	65[c]	117[c]	0.2	1.6	1.5	..
Canada	9.8	69.5	15.5	0.0	4,445	3,867	1.9	10.1	3.4	6.3
Central African Republic	4.3	39.3	57.7	31.5	20	32	0.1	0.4	1.2	..
Chad	6.4	50.6	47.8	5.3	49	86	0.0	0.3	0.4	..
Chile	7.5	44.0	36.5	0.0	762	1,088	1.3	..	2.1	..
China	4.3	47.3	43.5	0.2	146	265	1.4	1.4	4.1	..
Hong Kong SAR, China	..	..	..	..	..	..	..	..	..	..
Colombia	5.9	83.9	7.9	0.1	317	517	1.4	..	1.0	..
Congo, Dem. Rep.	7.3	54.2	39.2	18.8	13	23	0.1	0.5	0.8	..
Congo, Rep.	2.7	49.9	50.1	4.7	81	108	0.1	0.8	1.6	..
Costa Rica	9.4	66.9	29.3	0.1	618	1,059	..	..	1.2	..
Côte d'Ivoire	5.4	16.9	75.6	5.9	61	88	0.1	0.5	0.4	..
Croatia	7.8	84.9	14.5	0.0	1,230	1,553	2.7	5.6	5.5	6.4
Cuba	12.0	95.5	4.1	0.2	672	495	6.4	8.6	5.9	..
Czech Republic	7.1	80.1	15.7	0.0	1,469	1,830	3.6	8.6	7.2	15.0
Denmark	9.9	80.1	13.6	0.0	6,133	3,814	3.4	14.5	3.6	4.1
Dominican Republic	5.7	37.1	41.8	1.6	261	465	..	..	1.0	..
Ecuador	5.3	42.3	50.4	1.1	216	466	..	..	1.5	..
Egypt, Arab Rep.	4.8	42.2	56.5	0.6	97	261	2.8	3.5	1.7	..
El Salvador	6.0	59.6	35.8	3.5	217	410	1.6	0.4	1.1	..
Eritrea	3.1[c]	44.9[c]	55.1[c]	60.8[c]	10[c]	18[c]	0.1	0.6	1.2	..
Estonia	6.1	77.8	19.7	1.5	1,074	1,325	3.4	6.8	5.7	6.9
Ethiopia	4.3	51.9	38.5	40.7	14	37	0.0	0.2	0.2	..
Finland	8.8	70.7	18.5	0.0	4,481	3,299	2.7	15.5	6.5	4.3
France	11.2	75.9	7.4	0.0	4,966	3,851	3.5	8.9	7.1	6.9
Gabon	2.6[c]	43.7[c]	56.3[c]	2.3[c]	264[c]	384[c]	0.3	5.0	1.3	..
Gambia, The	5.5	48.1	25.1	38.0	27	75	0.0	0.6	1.1	..
Georgia	8.7	30.9	66.5	10.5	258	433	4.5	3.9	3.3	2.2
Germany	10.5	74.6	11.8	0.0	4,720	3,922	3.5	10.8	8.2	7.0
Ghana	7.8	50.0	39.4	14.0	55	114	0.1	1.1	0.9	..
Greece	10.1	60.9	37.0	0.0	3,110	3,010	6.0	3.7	4.8	..
Guatemala	6.5	35.7	57.4	1.8	184	308	..	..	0.6	..
Guinea	5.5	13.6	85.9	10.1	21	58	0.1	0.0	0.3	..
Guinea-Bissau	6.0[c]	26.0[c]	40.7[c]	77.3[c]	17[c]	32[c]	0.0	0.6	1.0	..
Haiti	6.1	22.1	47.4	34.7	40	69	..	..	1.3	..
Honduras	6.3	58.6	34.5	10.4	121	248	..	..	0.8	..

	Health expenditure						Health workers		Hospital beds	Outpatient visits
			Out of pocket	External resources	Per capita		per 1,000 people		per 1,000	
	Total % of GDP	Public % of total	% of total	% of total	$	PPP $	Physicians	Nurses and midwives	people	per capita
	2008	2008	2008	2008	2008	2008	2004–09[a]	2004–09[a]	2004–09[a]	2000–09[a]
Hungary	7.2	68.9	23.9	0.0	1,119	1,506	3.1	6.3	7.0	12.9
India	4.2	32.4	50.3	1.6	45	122	0.6	1.3	0.9	..
Indonesia	2.3	54.4	32.1	1.7	51	91	0.3	2.0	..	..
Iran, Islamic Rep.	5.5	42.4	55.6	0.0	254	613	0.9	1.6	1.4	..
Iraq	3.2[c,e]	70.2[c,e]	29.8[c,e]	8.2[c,e]	109[c,e]	107[c,e]	0.7	1.4	1.3	..
Ireland	8.7	76.9	14.4	0.0	5,253	3,796	3.2	15.7	5.2	..
Israel	7.6	58.4	30.5	0.0	2,093	2,093	3.6	6.2	5.8	7.1
Italy	8.7	76.3	20.2	0.0	3,343	2,836	4.2	6.5	3.7	6.1
Jamaica	4.8	50.4	35.2	1.5	256	364	..	..	1.7	..
Japan	8.3	80.5	14.5	0.0	3,190	2,817	2.1	4.1	13.8	14.4
Jordan	9.4[f]	62.7[f]	30.8[f]	1.8[f]	325[f]	496[f]	2.5	4.0	1.8	..
Kazakhstan	3.9	58.5	41.0	0.2	333	444	3.8	7.8	7.6	6.7
Kenya	4.2	36.3	49.2	26.8	33	66	0.1	..	1.4	..
Korea, Dem. Rep.	..	..	..	..	..	..	..	..	..	..
Korea, Rep.	6.5	53.9	35.0	0.0	1,245	1,806	2.0	5.3	12.3	..
Kosovo	..	..	..	..	..	..	..	..	..	..
Kuwait	2.0	76.3	21.7	0.0	990	932	1.8	4.6	1.8	..
Kyrgyz Republic	5.7	48.4	45.0	12.6	54	123	2.3	5.7	5.1	3.6
Lao PDR	4.0	17.6	62.6	16.1	34	84	0.3	1.0	1.2	..
Latvia	6.6	60.0	38.7	0.0	979	1,206	3.0	4.8	6.4	5.5
Lebanon	8.5	48.3	40.7	4.8	604	1,009	3.5	2.2	3.5	..
Lesotho	7.6	63.3	25.3	19.3	60	119	..	..	1.3	..
Liberia	11.9	33.0	35.0	47.0	26	46	0.0	0.3	0.7	..
Libya	3.0[c]	70.3[c]	29.7[c]	0.1[c]	458[c]	502[c]	1.9	6.8	3.7	..
Lithuania	6.6	68.3	26.8	1.1	931	1,318	3.7	7.3	6.8	6.6
Macedonia, FYR	6.8	68.2	31.6	1.8	328	738	2.5	4.3	4.6	6.0
Madagascar	4.4	70.2	20.2	16.1	22	46	0.2	0.3	0.3	0.5
Malawi	6.5	59.4	11.6	87.0	18	50	0.0	0.3	1.1	..
Malaysia	4.3	44.1	40.9	0.0	353	621	0.9	2.7	1.8	..
Mali	5.6	47.1	52.6	22.2	39	65	0.0	0.3	0.6	..
Mauritania	2.6[c]	61.4[c]	38.6[c]	27.4[c]	27[c]	54[c]	0.1	0.7	0.4	..
Mauritius	5.5	34.8	57.8	2.0	402	681	1.1	3.7	3.3	..
Mexico	5.9	46.9	49.3	0.0	588	837	2.9	4.0	1.6	2.5
Moldova	10.7[g]	50.6[g]	48.3[g]	4.7[g]	181[g]	320[g]	2.7	6.7	6.1	6.0
Mongolia	3.8	81.4	14.6	7.5	73	131	2.8	3.5	5.9	..
Morocco	5.3	36.3	55.0	0.2	149	231	0.6	0.9	1.1	..
Mozambique	4.7	75.2	7.0	80.8	21	39	0.0	0.3	0.8	..
Myanmar	2.0	8.8	87.1	10.7	10	23	0.5	0.8	0.6	..
Namibia	6.9	54.6	8.1	21.4	284	440	0.4	2.8	2.7	..
Nepal	6.0	37.7	45.1	11.0	24	66	0.2	0.5	5.0	..
Netherlands	9.9	75.3	5.7	0.0	5,243	4,233	3.9	0.2	4.3	5.4
New Zealand	9.7	80.2	14.0	0.0	2,917	2,655	2.4	10.9	..	4.4
Nicaragua	9.4	54.6	41.8	10.3	105	251	..	..	0.9	..
Niger	5.9	57.7	40.7	26.3	21	40	0.0	0.1	0.3	..
Nigeria	5.2[c]	36.7[c]	60.4[c]	4.6[c]	73[c]	113[c]	0.4	1.6	0.5	..
Norway	8.5	78.6	15.5	0.0	8,019	5,207	4.1	14.8	3.5	..
Oman	2.1	76.4	14.4	0.0	454	593	1.9	4.1	1.9	..
Pakistan	2.6	32.3	53.7	4.8	22	62	0.8	0.6	0.6	..
Panama	7.2	69.3	25.7	0.2	493	924	..	..	2.2	..
Papua New Guinea	3.2	80.1	8.2	20.6	39	70	0.1	0.5	..	..
Paraguay	6.0	40.1	52.8	1.6	161	281	..	..	1.3	..
Peru	4.5	59.4	30.6	0.8	200	381	0.9	1.3	1.5	..
Philippines	3.7	34.7	53.9	1.5	68	129	1.2	6.0	0.5	..
Poland	7.0	67.4	22.4	0.0	971	1,271	2.1	5.7	6.6	6.1
Portugal	10.6	67.4	22.1	0.0	2,434	2,578	3.8	5.3	3.4	3.9
Puerto Rico	..	..	..	..	..	..	..	..	..	..
Qatar	2.1	79.8	14.8	0.0	1,775	1,689	2.8	7.4	1.4	..

	Health expenditure						Health workers		Hospital beds	Outpatient visits
	Total % of GDP	Public % of total	Out of pocket % of total	External resources % of total	Per capita $	Per capita PPP $	per 1,000 people Physicians	Nurses and midwives	per 1,000 people	per capita
	2008	2008	2008	2008	2008	2008	2004–09[a]	2004–09[a]	2004–09[a]	2000–09[a]
Romania	5.4	78.9	17.6	0.0	517	840	1.9	4.2	6.5	5.6
Russian Federation	4.8	64.3	29.1	0.0	568	985	4.3	8.5	9.7	9.0
Rwanda	9.4	47.8	23.2	42.6	45	102	0.0	0.5	1.6	..
Saudi Arabia	3.6	68.2	17.0	0.0	676	831	0.9	2.1	2.2	..
Senegal	5.7	55.4	35.0	11.4	62	102	0.1	0.4	0.3	..
Serbia	10.0	62.5	35.5	0.4	499	867	2.0	4.4	5.4	..
Sierra Leone	13.3	6.5	83.7	17.0	47	104	0.0	0.2	0.4	..
Singapore	3.3	34.1	62.1	0.0	1,404	1,833	1.8	5.9	3.1	..
Slovak Republic	8.0	67.1	24.9	0.0	1,395	1,849	3.0	6.6	6.6	12.5
Slovenia	8.3	68.6	12.8	0.0	2,238	2,420	2.5	8.2	4.7	6.6
Somalia	..	..	..	..	..	..	0.0	0.1	..	..
South Africa	8.2	39.7	17.9	1.2	459	843	0.8	4.1	2.8	..
Spain	9.0	69.7	20.7	0.0	3,132	2,941	3.7	5.2	3.2	9.5
Sri Lanka	4.1	43.7	48.8	1.8	83	187	0.5	1.9	3.1	..
Sudan	6.9	33.1	64.1	4.3	97	147	0.3	0.8	0.7	..
Swaziland	5.8	60.8	16.6	11.1	141	287	0.2	6.3	2.1	..
Sweden	9.4	78.1	15.6	0.0	4,858	3,622	3.6	11.6	..	2.8
Switzerland	10.7	59.1	30.8	0.0	6,988	4,815	4.1	16.0	5.3	..
Syrian Arab Republic	3.1	38.8	61.2	0.5	71	123	1.5	1.9	1.5	..
Tajikistan	5.0	27.7	68.8	10.5	37	95	2.0	5.0	5.4	8.3
Tanzania	4.5	71.9	18.3	59.2	22	57	0.0	0.2	1.1	..
Thailand	4.1	74.3	17.5	0.3	164	328	0.3	1.5	..	..
Timor-Leste	13.8	73.4	6.8	21.8	71	126	0.1	2.2	..	..
Togo	5.9	24.5	63.5	14.1	38	70	0.1	0.3	0.9	..
Trinidad and Tobago	4.7	48.9	41.8	0.3	908	1,237	1.2	3.6	2.5	..
Tunisia	6.2	54.1	40.0	0.5	248	501	1.2	3.3	2.1	..
Turkey	6.1	73.1	17.4	0.0	623	845	1.6	1.9	2.4	3.1
Turkmenistan	2.2[c]	49.1[c]	50.9[c]	0.3[c]	82[c]	146[c]	2.4	4.5	4.1	3.7
Uganda	8.4	17.4	54.0	27.9	44	112	0.1	1.3	0.4	..
Ukraine	6.8	55.9	40.9	0.4	268	502	3.1	8.5	8.7	10.8
United Arab Emirates	2.5	67.1	21.7	0.0	1,427	868	1.9	4.1	1.9	..
United Kingdom	8.7	82.6	11.1	0.0	3,771	3,222	2.7	10.3	3.4	4.9
United States	15.2	47.8	12.7	0.0	7,164	7,164	2.7	9.8	3.1	9.0
Uruguay	7.8	63.1	12.1	0.2	725	982	3.7	5.6	2.9	..
Uzbekistan	4.9	50.5	48.5	2.4	51	134	2.6	10.8	4.8	8.7
Venezuela, RB	5.4	44.9	49.3	0.0	597	683	..	..	1.3	..
Vietnam	7.2	38.5	55.5	1.7	76	201	1.2	1.0	2.9	..
West Bank and Gaza	..	..	..	..	..	..	..	..	..	..
Yemen, Rep.	5.3	30.1	68.9	4.6	67	137	0.3	0.7	0.7	..
Zambia	5.9	62.0	28.3	38.4	68	80	0.1	0.7	1.9	..
Zimbabwe	..	..	..	..	..	..	0.2	0.7	3.0	..
World	**9.4 w**	**60.5 w**	**17.9 w**	**0.2 w**	**857 w**	**901 w**	**1.4 w**	**3.0 w**	**2.9 w**	**.. w**
Low income	5.3	41.9	47.9	24.2	25	55	0.2	0.5	..	..
Middle income	5.3	51.4	37.0	0.6	186	314	1.3	2.3	2.4	..
Lower middle income	4.3	45.5	45.0	1.1	95	188	1.0	1.7	1.9	..
Upper middle income	6.3	55.4	31.4	0.2	531	792	2.3	4.8	4.5	..
Low & middle income	5.3	51.2	37.2	1.1	163	277	1.1	2.0	2.3	..
East Asia & Pacific	4.2	48.2	42.2	0.5	125	231	1.2	1.7	4.0	..
Europe & Central Asia	5.4	65.4	28.2	0.3	448	738	3.2	6.8	7.3	7.6
Latin America & Carib.	7.2	50.3	34.3	0.2	542	733	2.2	4.8	..	..
Middle East & N. Africa	5.0	53.0	44.3	1.0	176	350	1.5	2.2	1.6	..
South Asia	4.0	32.6	51.5	2.4	40	106	0.6	1.1	0.9	..
Sub-Saharan Africa	6.1	42.9	36.5	9.3	74	132	0.2	1.0	..	..
High income	11.0	62.2	14.2	0.0	4,455	4,136	2.9	7.9	6.1	8.5
Euro area	10.0	73.7	14.2	0.0	4,132	3,458	3.8	7.5	5.8	6.8

a. Data are for the most recent year available. b. GDP includes measures of illicit activities such as opium production. Government expenditures include external assistance (external budget). c. Derived from incomplete data. d. Excludes expenditure in residential facilities for care of the aged. e. Excludes northern Iraq. f. Includes contributions from the United Nations Relief and Works Agency for Palestine. g. Excludes Transdniestria.

Health systems—the combined arrangements of institutions and actions whose primary purpose is to promote, restore, or maintain health (World Health Organization, *World Health Report* 2000)—are increasingly being recognized as key to combating disease and improving the health status of populations. The World Bank's *Healthy Development: Strategy for Health, Nutrition, and Population Results* emphasizes the need to strengthen health systems, which are weak in many countries, in order to increase the effectiveness of programs aimed at reducing specific diseases and further reduce morbidity and mortality (World Bank 2007). To evaluate health systems, the World Health Organization (WHO) has recommended that key components—such as financing, service delivery, workforce, governance, and information—be monitored using several key indicators (WHO 2008b). The data in the table are a subset of the first four indicators. Monitoring health systems allows the effectiveness, efficiency, and equity of different health system models to be compared. Health system data also help identify weaknesses and strengths and areas that need investment, such as additional health facilities, better health information systems, or better trained human resources.

Health expenditure data are broken down into public and private expenditures. In general, low-income economies have a higher share of private health expenditure than do middle- and high-income countries, and out-of-pocket expenditure (direct payments by households to providers) makes up the largest proportion of private expenditure. High out-of-pocket expenditures may discourage people from accessing preventive or curative care and can impoverish households that cannot afford needed care. Health financing data are collected through national health accounts, which systematically, comprehensively, and consistently monitoring health system resource flows. To establish a national health account, countries must define the boundaries of the health system and classify health expenditure information along several dimensions, including sources of financing, providers of health services, functional use of health expenditures, and beneficiaries of expenditures. The accounting system can then provide an accurate picture of resource envelopes and financial flows and allow analysis of the equity and efficiency of financing to inform policy.

This year's table presents out-of-pocket expenditure as a percentage of total health expenditure; previous editions presented out-of-pocket expenditure as a percentage of private health expenditure. For

this reason, data for this indicator should not be compared across editions.

External resources for health are disbursements to recipient countries as reported by donors, lagged one year to account for the delay between disbursement and expenditure. Disbursement data are not available before 2002, so commitments are used. Except where a reliable full national health account study has been done, most data are from the Organisation for Economic Co-operation and Development Development Assistance Committee's Creditor Reporting System database, which compiles data from government expenditure accounts, government records on external assistance, routine surveys of external financing assistance, and special services. Because of the variety of sources, care should be taken in interpreting the data.

In countries where the fiscal year spans two calendar years, expenditure data have been allocated to the later year (for example, 2008 data cover fiscal year 2007/08). Many low-income countries use Demographic and Health Surveys or Multiple Indicator Cluster Surveys funded by donors to obtain health system data.

Data on health worker (physicians, nurses, and midwives) density show the availability of medical personnel. The WHO estimates that at least 2.5 physicians, nurses, and midwives per 1,000 people are needed to provide adequate coverage with primary care interventions associated with achieving the Millennium Development Goals (WHO, *World Health Report* 2006). The WHO compiles data from household and labor force surveys, censuses, and administrative records. Data comparability is limited by differences in definitions and training of medical personnel varies. In addition, human resources tend to be concentrated in urban areas, so that average densities do not provide a full picture of health personnel available to the entire population.

Availability and use of health services, shown by hospital beds per 1,000 people and outpatient visits per capita, reflect both demand- and supply-side factors. In the absence of a consistent definition these are crude indicators of the extent of physical, financial, and other barriers to health care.

• **Total health expenditure** is the sum of public and private health expenditure. It covers the provision of health services (preventive and curative), family planning and nutrition activities, and emergency aid for health but excludes provision of water and sanitation. • **Public health expenditure** is recurrent and capital spending from central and local governments, external borrowing and grants (including donations from international agencies and nongovernmental organizations), and social (or compulsory) health insurance funds. • **Out-of-pocket health expenditure** is the percentage of total expenditure that is direct household outlays, including gratuities and in-kind payments, for health practitioners and pharmaceutical suppliers, therapeutic appliances, and other goods and services whose primary intent is to restore or enhance health. • **External resources for health** are funds or services in kind that are provided by entities not part of the country in question. The resources may come from international organizations, other countries through bilateral arrangements, or foreign nongovernmental organizations and are part of public and private health expenditure. • **Health expenditure per capita** is total health expenditure divided by population in U.S. dollars and in international dollars converted using 2005 purchasing power parity (PPP) rates from the World Bank's International Comparison Project. • **Physicians** include generalist and specialist medical practitioners. • **Nurses and midwives** include professional nurses and midwives, auxiliary nurses and midwives, enrolled nurses and midwives, and other personnel, such as dental nurses and primary care nurses. • **Hospital beds** are inpatient beds for both acute and chronic care available in public, private, general, and specialized hospitals and rehabilitation centers. • **Outpatient visits per capita** are the number of visits to health care facilities per capita, including repeat visits.

Data sources

Data on health expenditures are from the WHO's National Health Account database (latest updates are available at www.who.int/nha/), supplemented by country data. Data on physicians, and nurses and midwives, are from WHO's *Global Atlas of the Health Workforce*. For the latest updates and metadata, see http://apps.who.int/globalatlas/. Data on hospital beds and outpatient visits are from the WHO, supplemented by country data.

	Year last national health account completed	Number of national health accounts completed	Year of last health survey	Year of last census	Completeness		
					Birth registration	% Infant death reporting	Total death reporting
		1995–2009		2001–11	2004–09ª	2004–09ª	2004–09ª
Afghanistan		0	2003		..	..	..
Albania	2009	3	2008/09	2001	99	28	76
Algeria	2003	3	2006	2008	99	..	90
Angola		0	2006/07		..	..	..
Argentina	1997	1		2010	91	100	100
Armenia	2009	6	2005	2001	96	38	100
Australia	2007	13		2006	..	100	96
Austria	2008	14		2001	..	90	100
Azerbaijan		0	2006	2009	94	24	100
Bangladesh	2008	13	2007	2001	10	..	..
Belarus		0	2005	2009	..	55	96
Belgium	2008	6		2001	..	100	97
Benin	2008	4	2006	2002	60	..	..
Bolivia	2007	13	2008	2001	..	..	30
Bosnia and Herzegovina	2009	6	2006		100	54	92
Botswana	2002	3	2000	2001	72	35	47
Brazil	2006	7	1996	2010	91	48	87
Bulgaria	2007	6		2001	..	79	100
Burkina Faso	2008	6	2006	2006	64	29	88
Burundi	2007	1	2005	2008	60	..	..
Cambodia		0	2005	2008	66	0	100
Cameroon	1995	1	2006	2005	70	..	..
Canada	2009	15		2006	..	100	98
Central African Republic		0	2006	2003	49	..	..
Chad		0	2004	2009	9	..	..
Chile	2008	5		2002	99	100	100
China	2007	13		2010	..	..	99
Hong Kong SAR, China		0		2006	..	66	91
Colombia	2003	9	2005	2006	90	52	71
Congo, Dem. Rep.	2009	7	2010		31	..	..
Congo, Rep.	2005	1	2009	2007	81	..	..
Costa Rica	2003	2	1993	2000	..	90	98
Côte d'Ivoire	2008	2	2006		55	..	..
Croatia		0		2001	..	75	100
Cuba		0	2006	2002	100	99	100
Czech Republic	2008	14	1993	2001	..	84	94
Denmark	2007	13		2001	..	97	97
Dominican Republic	2008	8	2007	2010	78	1	54
Ecuador	2008	7	2004	2010	85	58	86
Egypt, Arab Rep.	2008	3	2008	2006	99	47	97
El Salvador	2009	14	2008	2007	99	36	75
Eritrea		0	2002		..	..	..
Estonia	2008	10		2000	..	68	94
Ethiopia	2008	4	2005	2007	7	..	88
Finland	2008	14		2010	..	84	98
France	2008	14		2006	..	95	100
Gabon		0	2000	2003	..	..	..
Gambia, The	2004	3	2005/06	2003	55	..	..
Georgia	2009	9	2005	2002	92	54	83
Germany	2008	14			..	96	99
Ghana	2002	1	2008	2010	71	95	..
Greece		0		2001	..	78	95
Guatemala	2008	14	2002	2002	..	62	93
Guinea		0	2005		43	..	..
Guinea-Bissau		0	2010	2009	39	..	..
Haiti	2006	1	2005/06	2003	81	..	..
Honduras	2005	3	2005/06	2001	94	100	99

	Year last national health account completed	Number of national health accounts completed	Year of last health survey	Year of last census	Completeness		
						%	
					Birth registration	Infant death reporting	Total death reporting
	1995–2009			2001–11	2004–09[a]	2004–09[a]	2004–09[a]
Hungary	2008	14		2001	..	84	97
India	2004	2	2005/06	2001	41	..	..
Indonesia	2008	8	2007	2010	53	..	..
Iran, Islamic Rep.	2007	4	2000	2006	..	..	99
Iraq		0	2006		95	100	100
Ireland	2008	14		2006	..	75	99
Israel	2006	1		2009	..	90	99
Italy	2008	4		2001	..	99	98
Jamaica	2000	1	2005	2001	89	76	68
Japan	2007	13		2010	..	88	98
Jordan	2008	5	2009	2004	..	..	76
Kazakhstan	2007	1	2006	2009	99	95	82
Kenya	2006	2	2008/09	2009	60	37	39
Korea, Dem. Rep.		0	2010	2008	..	43	91
Korea, Rep.	2008	14		2005	..	80	92
Kosovo		0			..	..	..
Kuwait		0	1996	2010	..	100	100
Kyrgyz Republic	2009	5	2005/06	2009	94	78	95
Lao PDR		0	2006	2005	72	..	..
Latvia	2007	5		2000	..	79	96
Lebanon	2005	4	2000		..	..	72
Lesotho		0	2009/10	2006	26	..	..
Liberia	2008	1	2009	2008	4	..	..
Libya		0	2000	2006	..	..	..
Lithuania	2008	7		2001	..	68	95
Macedonia, FYR		0	2005	2002	94	87	99
Madagascar	2007	2	2008/09		75	..	..
Malawi	2006	5	2006	2008	..	..	75
Malaysia	2006	10		2010	..	62	100
Mali	2004	6	2006	2009	53	..	..
Mauritania		0	2007	2000	56	..	..
Mauritius	2004	2		2000	..	80	97
Mexico	2009	15	1995	2010	..	89	100
Moldova		0	2005	2004	..	62	89
Mongolia	2003	5	2005	2010	98	60	96
Morocco	2006	3	2006	2004	..	..	..
Mozambique	2006	4	2009	2007	31	..	..
Myanmar	2007	10	2000		..	56	55
Namibia	2008	11	2006/07	2001	67	..	100
Nepal	2005	5	2006	2001	35	..	..
Netherlands	2008	14		2001	..	84	97
New Zealand	2008	14		2006	..	100	98
Nicaragua	2008	14	2006/07	2005	..	66	68
Niger	2006	4	2006	2001	32	..	..
Nigeria	2005	8	2008	2006	30	..	1
Norway	2008	12		2001	..	97	100
Oman	1998	1	1995	2010	..	100	97
Pakistan	2006	1	2006/07		27	85	84
Panama	2003	1	2003	2010	..	70	88
Papua New Guinea	2000	3	1996	2000	..	..	..
Paraguay	2008	13	2004	2002	..	34	71
Peru	2005	11	2008	2007	93	41	70
Philippines	2007	13	2008	2010	..	39	100
Poland	2008	14		2002	..	95	100
Portugal	2007	8		2001	..	85	95
Puerto Rico		0	1996	2010	..	100	95
Qatar		0		2010	..	95	77

	Year last national health account completed	Number of national health accounts completed	Year of last health survey	Year of last census	Completeness		
						%	
					Birth registration	Infant death reporting	Total death reporting
		1995–2009		2001–11	2004–09[a]	2004–09[a]	2004–09[a]
Romania	2006	9	1999	2002	..	76	96
Russian Federation	2007	13	1996	2010	..	80	95
Rwanda	2006	5	2007	2002	82	..	..
Saudi Arabia		0	2007	2010	..	94	100
Senegal	2005	2	2008/09	2002	55	..	..
Serbia	2009	7	2005/06	2002	99	38	90
Sierra Leone	2006	3	2008	2004	51	..	..
Singapore		0	2005	2010	..	93	72
Slovak Republic	2008	12		2001	..	93	98
Slovenia	2008	14		2002	..	72	96
Somalia		0	2006		3	..	..
South Africa	1998	3	2003	2001	92	81	81
Spain	2008	14		2001	..	99	100
Sri Lanka	2006	12	2006/07	2001	97	63	91
Sudan	2008	1	2006	2008	33	..	..
Swaziland		0	2006/07	2007	30	..	..
Sweden	2008	8			..	83	99
Switzerland	2009	15		2010	..	100	99
Syrian Arab Republic		0	2006	2004	95	..	100
Tajikistan	2008	2	2005	2010	88	19	69
Tanzania	2006	3	2007/08	2002	22	..	..
Thailand	2007	13	2005/06	2010	99	86	65
Timor-Leste		0	2009	2010	..	..	..
Togo	2002	1	2006	2010	78	..	..
Trinidad and Tobago	2000	1	2006	2000	96	50	94
Tunisia	2005	5	2006	2004	..	..	98
Turkey	2005	8	2003	2000	94	56	100
Turkmenistan		0	2006		96	..	..
Uganda	2006	6	2009/10	2002	21	..	..
Ukraine	2008	6	2007	2001	100	90	100
United Arab Emirates		0		2010	..	75	100
United Kingdom	2008	12		2001	..	100	95
United States	2009	15	2009	2010	..	100	100
Uruguay	2008	13		2004	..	78	100
Uzbekistan		0	2006		100	..	..
Venezuela, RB		0	2000	2001	..	62	84
Vietnam	2007	10	2006	2009	88	72	83
West Bank and Gaza		1	2006	2007	96	31	66
Yemen, Rep.	2007	4	2006	2004	22	..	15
Zambia	2006	11	2007	2000	14	..	..
Zimbabwe	2001	3	2005/06	2002	74	..	..

a. Data are for the most recent year available.

Health information | **2.17** PEOPLE

About the data

According to the World Health Organization (WHO), health information systems are crucial for monitoring and evaluating health systems, which are increasingly recognized as important for combating disease and improving health status. Health information systems underpin decisionmaking through four data functions: generation, compilation, analysis and synthesis, and communication and use. The health information system collects data from the health sector and other relevant sectors; analyzes the data and ensures their overall quality, relevance, and timeliness; and converts data into information for health-related decisionmaking (WHO 2008b).

Numerous indicators have been proposed to assess a country's health information system. They can be grouped into two broad types: indicators related to data generation using core sources and methods (health surveys, civil registration, censuses, facility reporting, health system resource tracking) and indicators related to capacity for data synthesis, analysis, and validation. Indicators related to data generation reflect a country's capacity to collect relevant data at suitable intervals using the most appropriate data sources. Benchmarks include periodicity, timeliness, contents, and availability. Indicators related to capacity for synthesis, analysis, and validation measure the dimensions of

the institutional frameworks needed to ensure data quality, including independence, transparency, and access. Benchmarks include the availability of independent coordination mechanisms and micro- and meta-data (WHO 2008a).

The indicators in the table are all related to data generation, including the years the last national health account, last health survey, and latest population census were completed. Frequency of data collection, a benchmark of data generation, is shown as the number of years for which a national health account was completed between 1995 and 2009. National health account data may be collected using different approaches such as Organisation for Economic Co-operation and Development (OECD) System of Health Accounts, WHO National Health Account producers guide approach, local national health accounting methods, or Pan American Health Organization/WHO satellite health accounts approach.

Indicators related to data generation include completeness of birth registration, infant death reporting, and total death reporting.

Definitions

• **Year last national health account completed** is the latest year for which the health expenditure data are available using the national health account approach. • **Number of national health accounts completed** is the number of national health accounts completed between 1995 and 2008. • **Year of last health survey** is the latest year the national survey that collects health information was conducted. • **Year of last census** is the latest year a census was conducted in the last 10 years. • **Completeness of birth registration** is the percentage of children under age 5 whose births were registered at the time of the survey. The numerator of completeness of birth registration includes children whose birth certificate was seen by the interviewer or whose mother or caretaker says the birth has been registered. • **Completeness of infant death reporting** is the number of infant deaths reported by national statistical authorities to the United Nations Statistics Division's *Demographic Yearbook* divided by the number of infant deaths estimated by the United Nations Population Division. • **Completeness of total death reporting** is the number of total deaths from civil registration system reported by national statistical authorities to the United Nations Statistics Division's Demographic Yearbook divided by the number of total deaths estimated by the United Nations Population Division.

Data sources

Data on year last national health account completed and number of national health accounts completed were compiled by staff in the World Health Organization's Health Financing Department and the World Bank's Health, Nutrition, and Population Unit using data on the health expenditures reported by the WHO and OECD and consultation with colleagues from countries and other international organizations. Data on year of last health survey are from Macro International and the United Nations Children's Fund (UNICEF). Data on year of last census are from United Nations Statistics Division's 2011 World Population and Housing Census Program (http://unstats.un.org/unsd/demographic/sources/census/2010_PHC/default.htm.) Data on completeness of birth registration are compiled by UNICEF in *State of the World's Children 2010* based mostly on household surveys and ministry of health data. Data used to calculate completeness of infant death reporting and total death reporting are from the United Nations Statistics Division's *Population and Vital Statistics Report* and the United Nations Population Division's *World Population Prospects: The 2008 Revision.*

South Asia has the highest number of unregistered births 2.17a

Number of unregistered births, 2007 (millions)

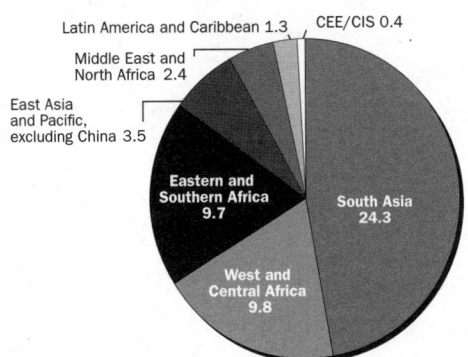

Too many people, especially poor, are never counted. They are born, live, and die uncounted and ignored. Around 50 million, or 40 percent of children born in 2007, have not been registered.

Source: United Nations Children's Fund Childinfo.

Disease prevention coverage and quality

	Access to an improved water source		Access to improved sanitation facilities		Child immunization rate		Children with acute respiratory infection taken to health provider	Children with diarrhea who received oral rehydration and continuous feeding	Children sleeping under treated nets[a]	Children with fever receiving antimalarial drugs	Tuberculosis	
					% of children ages 12–23 months[b]		% of children under age 5 with ARI	% of children under age 5 with diarrhea	% of children under age 5	% of children under age 5 with fever	Treatment success rate	Case detection rate
	% of population		% of population		Measles	DTP3	% of children	% of children	% of children	% of children	% of new registered cases	% of new estimated cases
	1990	2008	1990	2008	2009	2009	2004–09[c]	2004–09[c]	2004–09[c]	2004–09[c]	2008	2009
Afghanistan	..	48	..	37	76	83	..	..	..	..	88	48
Albania	..	97	..	98	97	98	70	63	..	..	91	94
Algeria	94	83	88	95	88	93	53	24	..	..	90	100
Angola	36	50	25	57	77	73	..	..	17.7	29.3	70	75
Argentina	94	97	90	90	99	94	..	..	..	..	44	67
Armenia	..	96	..	90	96	93	36	59	..	..	73	70
Australia	100	100	100	100	94	92	..	..	..	..	80	89
Austria	100	100	100	100	83	83	..	..	..	..	47	48
Azerbaijan	70	80	..	45	67	73	33	31	..	..	56	75
Bangladesh	78	80	39	53	89	94	37	68	..	..	91	44
Belarus	100	100	..	93	99	96	90	54	..	..	71	140
Belgium	100	100	100	100	94	99	..	..	..	..	76	88
Benin	56	75	5	12	72	83	36	42	20.1	54.0	89	47
Bolivia	70	86	19	25	86	85	51	..	..	..	84	64
Bosnia and Herzegovina	..	99	..	95	93	90	91	53	..	..	92	91
Botswana	93	95	36	60	94	96	..	..	..	..	65	62
Brazil	88	97	69	80	99	99	50	..	..	..	71	86
Bulgaria	100	100	99	100	96	94	..	..	..	..	85	86
Burkina Faso	41	76	6	11	75	82	39	42	9.6	48.0	76	14
Burundi	70	72	44	46	91	92	38	23	8.3	30.0	90	25
Cambodia	35	61	9	29	92	94	48	50	4.2	0.2	95	60
Cameroon	50	74	47	47	74	80	35	22	13.1	57.8	76	70
Canada	100	100	100	100	93	80	..	..	..	..	78	93
Central African Republic	58	67	11	34	62	54	32	47	15.1	57.0	71	60
Chad	38	50	6	9	23	23	12	27	..	53.0	54	26
Chile	90	96	84	96	96	97	..	..	..	..	72	130
China	67	89	41	55	94	97	..	..	..	..	94	75
Hong Kong SAR, China	..	..	..	..	..	..	..	..	..	..	68	89
Colombia	88	92	68	74	95	92	62	39	..	..	76	70
Congo, Dem. Rep.	45	46	9	23	76	77	42	42	5.8	29.8	87	46
Congo, Rep.	..	71	..	30	76	91	48	39	6.1	48.0	76	69
Costa Rica	93	97	93	95	81	86	..	..	..	..	89	93
Côte d'Ivoire	76	80	20	23	67	81	35	45	3.0	36.0	76	27
Croatia	..	99	..	99	98	96	..	..	..	..	58	76
Cuba	82	94	80	91	96	96	..	..	..	..	88	120
Czech Republic	100	100	100	98	98	99	..	..	..	..	68	70
Denmark	100	100	100	100	84	89	..	..	..	..	41	79
Dominican Republic	88	86	73	83	79	82	70	55	..	0.6	75	60
Ecuador	72	94	69	92	66	75	..	..	..	..	78	51
Egypt, Arab Rep.	90	99	72	94	95	97	73	19	..	..	89	63
El Salvador	74	87	75	87	95	91	67	..	..	..	91	92
Eritrea	43	61	9	14	95	99	..	..	..	..	76	58
Estonia	98	98	..	95	95	95	..	..	..	..	60	89
Ethiopia	17	38	4	12	75	79	19	15	33.1	9.5	84	50
Finland	100	100	100	100	98	99	..	..	..	..	72	110
France	100	100	100	100	90	99	..	..	..	..	..	77
Gabon	..	87	..	33	55	45	..	..	..	..	53	42
Gambia, The	74	92	..	67	96	98	69	38	49.0	62.6	84	47
Georgia	81	98	96	95	83	88	74	37	..	..	73	100
Germany	100	100	100	100	96	93	..	..	..	..	68	91
Ghana	54	82	7	13	93	94	51	45	28.2	43.0	86	31
Greece	96	100	97	98	99	99	..	..	..	..	..	92
Guatemala	82	94	65	81	92	92	..	..	..	..	83	33
Guinea	52	71	9	19	51	57	42	38	4.5	43.5	78	26
Guinea-Bissau	..	61	..	21	76	68	57	25	39.0	45.7	70	59
Haiti	47	63	26	17	59	59	31	43	..	5.1	82	60
Honduras	72	86	44	71	99	98	56	49	..	0.5	85	68

Disease prevention coverage and quality

	Access to an improved water source		Access to improved sanitation facilities		Child immunization rate		Children with acute respiratory infection taken to health provider	Children with diarrhea who received oral rehydration and continuous feeding	Children sleeping under treated nets[a]	Children with fever receiving antimalarial drugs	Tuberculosis	
					% of children ages 12–23 months[b]						Treatment success rate	Case detection rate
	% of population		% of population				% of children under age 5 with ARI	% of children under age 5 with diarrhea	% of children under age 5	% of children under age 5 with fever	% of new registered cases	% of new estimated cases
	1990	2008	1990	2008	Measles 2009	DTP3 2009	2004–09[c]	2004–09[c]	2004–09[c]	2004–09[c]	2008	2009
Hungary	96	100	100	100	99	99	..	..	..	..	53	82
India	72	88	18	31	71	66	69	33	..	8.2	87	67
Indonesia	71	80	33	52	82	82	66	54	3.3	0.8	91	67
Iran, Islamic Rep.	91	..	83	..	99	99	..	..	..	..	83	74
Iraq	81	79	..	73	69	65	82	64	..	..	88	48
Ireland	100	100	99	99	89	93	..	..	..	..	76	89
Israel	100	100	100	100	96	93	..	..	..	..	81	89
Italy	100	100	..	..	91	96	..	..	..	..	..	66
Jamaica	93	94	83	83	88	90	75	39	..	..	64	78
Japan	100	100	100	100	94	98	..	..	..	..	48	89
Jordan	97	96	..	98	95	98	75	32	..	..	84	100
Kazakhstan	96	95	96	97	99	98	71	48	..	..	64	80
Kenya	43	59	26	31	74	75	56	..	46.1	23.2	85	85
Korea, Dem. Rep.	100	100	..	..	98	93	93	..	..	..	89	93
Korea, Rep.	..	98	100	100	93	94	..	..	..	..	84	89
Kosovo	..	..	..	..	..	..	..	..	..	..	..	..
Kuwait	99	99	100	100	97	98	..	..	..	..	80	89
Kyrgyz Republic	..	90	..	93	99	95	62	22	..	..	84	66
Lao PDR	..	57	..	53	59	57	32	49	40.5	8.2	93	68
Latvia	99	99	..	78	96	95	..	..	..	..	33	94
Lebanon	100	100	..	..	53	74	..	..	..	..	77	78
Lesotho	61	85	32	29	85	83	66	53	..	..	73	93
Liberia	58	68	11	17	64	64	62	47	26.4	67.2	79	52
Libya	54	..	97	97	98	98	..	..	..	..	69	82
Lithuania	..	..	..	..	96	98	..	..	..	..	82	81
Macedonia, FYR	..	100	..	89	96	96	93	45	..	..	89	98
Madagascar	31	41	8	11	64	78	42	47	45.8	19.7	81	44
Malawi	40	80	42	56	92	93	52	27	24.7	24.9	87	49
Malaysia	88	100	84	96	95	95	..	..	..	..	78	76
Mali	29	56	26	36	71	74	38	38	27.1	31.7	82	16
Mauritania	30	49	16	26	59	64	45	32	2.1	20.7	68	24
Mauritius	99	99	91	91	99	99	..	..	..	..	87	41
Mexico	85	94	66	85	95	89	..	..	..	..	85	99
Moldova	..	90	..	79	90	85	60	48	..	..	62	68
Mongolia	58	76	..	50	94	95	63	47	..	..	87	75
Morocco	74	81	53	69	98	99	38	46	..	..	85	93
Mozambique	36	47	11	17	77	76	65	47	22.8	36.7	84	46
Myanmar	57	71	..	81	87	90	..	..	..	..	85	64
Namibia	64	92	25	33	76	83	72	48	10.5	9.8	82	76
Nepal	76	88	11	31	79	82	43	37	..	0.1	89	73
Netherlands	100	100	100	100	96	97	..	..	..	..	85	89
New Zealand	100	100	..	..	89	92	..	..	..	..	73	89
Nicaragua	74	85	43	52	99	98	..	..	..	..	89	90
Niger	35	48	5	9	73	70	47	34	42.8	33.0	81	36
Nigeria	47	58	37	32	41	42	45	25	5.5	33.2	78	19
Norway	100	100	100	100	92	92	..	..	..	..	84	91
Oman	80	88	85	..	97	98	..	..	..	..	98	89
Pakistan	86	90	28	45	80	85	69	37	..	3.3	90	63
Panama	84	93	58	69	85	84	..	..	..	..	79	94
Papua New Guinea	41	40	47	45	58	64	63	..	..	..	64	73
Paraguay	52	86	37	70	91	92	..	..	..	..	81	78
Peru	75	82	54	68	91	93	72	60	..	..	82	97
Philippines	84	91	58	76	88	87	50	60	..	0.0	88	57
Poland	100	100	..	90	98	99	..	..	..	..	74	84
Portugal	96	99	92	100	95	96	..	..	..	..	87	86
Puerto Rico	..	..	..	..	..	..	..	..	..	..	63	89
Qatar	100	100	100	100	99	99	..	..	..	..	73	89

	Access to an improved water source		Access to improved sanitation facilities		Child immunization rate		Children with acute respiratory infection taken to health provider	Children with diarrhea who received oral rehydration and continuous feeding	Children sleeping under treated nets[a]	Children with fever receiving antimalarial drugs	Tuberculosis	
					% of children ages 12–23 months[b]		% of children under age 5 with ARI	% of children under age 5 with diarrhea	% of children under age 5	% of children under age 5 with fever	Treatment success rate	Case detection rate
	% of population		% of population		Measles	DTP3					% of new registered cases	% of new estimated cases
	1990	2008	1990	2008	2009	2009	2004–09[c]	2004–09[c]	2004–09[c]	2004–09[c]	2008	2009
Romania	..	..	71	72	97	97	..	..	..	..	37	79
Russian Federation	93	96	87	87	98	98	..	..	..	..	57	84
Rwanda	68	65	23	54	92	97	28	24	55.7	5.6	87	19
Saudi Arabia	89		..	..	98	98	..	..	..	..	61	89
Senegal	61	69	38	51	79	86	47	43	29.2	9.1	84	31
Serbia	..	99	..	92	95	95	93	71	..	..	86	89
Sierra Leone	..	49	..	13	71	75	46	57	25.8	30.1	86	31
Singapore	100	100	99	100	95	97	..	..	..	..	81	89
Slovak Republic	..	100	100	100	99	99	..	..	..	..	93	89
Slovenia	100	99	100	100	95	96	..	..	..	..	80	80
Somalia	..	30	..	23	24	31	13	7	11.4	7.9	81	42
South Africa	83	91	69	77	62	69	..	..	..	..	76	74
Spain	100	100	100	100	98	96	..	..	..	..	..	89
Sri Lanka	67	90	70	91	96	97	58	67	2.9	0.3	85	70
Sudan	65	57	34	34	82	84	90	56	27.6	54.2	81	52
Swaziland	..	69	..	55	95	95	73	22	0.6	0.6	68	67
Sweden	100	100	100	100	97	98	..	..	..	..	87	89
Switzerland	100	100	100	100	90	95	..	..	..	..	..	89
Syrian Arab Republic	85	89	83	96	81	80	77	34	..	..	86	88
Tajikistan	..	70	..	94	89	93	64	22	1.3	1.9	82	44
Tanzania	55	54	24	24	91	85	59	53	63.8[d]	59.1[d]	88	77
Thailand	91	98	80	96	98	99	84	46	..	..	82	69
Timor-Leste	..	69	..	50	70	72	71	..	..	..	85	84
Togo	49	60	13	12	84	89	23	22	38.4	47.7	79	10
Trinidad and Tobago	88	94	93	92	94	90	74	32	..	..	67	89
Tunisia	81	94	74	85	98	99	59	62	..	..	86	86
Turkey	85	99	84	90	97	96	..	22	..	..	92	77
Turkmenistan	..	..	98	98	99	96	83	25	..	..	83	92
Uganda	43	67	39	48	68	64	73	39	9.7	61.3	70	44
Ukraine	..	98	95	95	94	90	..	..	..	..	62	78
United Arab Emirates	100	100	97	97	92	92	..	..	..	..	68	61
United Kingdom	100	100	100	100	86	93	..	..	..	..	78	94
United States	99	99	100	100	92	95	..	..	..	..	85	89
Uruguay	96	100	94	100	94	95	..	..	..	..	83	96
Uzbekistan	90	87	84	100	95	98	68	28	..	..	81	50
Venezuela, RB	90	..	82	..	83	83	..	..	..	..	83	68
Vietnam	58	94	35	75	97	96	83	65	5.0	2.6	92	54
West Bank and Gaza	..	91	..	89	..	..	..	..	..	..	94	4
Yemen, Rep.	..	62	18	52	58	66	..	48	..	..	85	67
Zambia	49	60	46	49	85	81	68	56	41.1	43.3	88	80
Zimbabwe	78	82	43	44	76	73	25	35	17.3	23.6	74	46
World	**77 w**	**87 w**	**52 w**	**61 w**	**82 w**	**82 w**	**.. w**	**.. w**	**.. w**	**.. w**	**86 w**	**62 w**
Low income	55	64	23	35	78	80	45	39	..	30.6	86	50
Middle income	74	88	45	57	82	81	..	..	..	..	..	..
Lower middle income	70	86	37	50	79	79	..	..	..	..	89	63
Upper middle income	89	95	78	84	93	93	..	..	..	..	72	79
Low & middle income	72	84	43	54	81	81	..	..	..	..	..	..
East Asia & Pacific	69	88	42	59	91	93	..	..	..	..	92	70
Europe & Central Asia	91	95	87	89	96	95	..	..	..	..	67	78
Latin America & Carib.	85	93	69	79	93	92	..	..	..	..	77	73
Middle East & N. Africa	87	87	73	84	87	88	..	..	..	..	86	78
South Asia	74	87	22	36	75	72	67	37	..	7.2	88	64
Sub-Saharan Africa	49	60	27	31	68	70	..	33	20.2	34.4	79	48
High income	99	100	100	99	93	95	..	..	..	..	69	87
Euro area	100	100	100	100	94	96	..	..	..	..	..	..

a. For malaria prevention only. b. Refers to children who were immunized before 12 months or in some cases at any time before the survey (12–23 months). c. Data are for the most recent year available. d. Data are for 2010.

Disease prevention coverage and quality

About the data

People's health is influenced by the environment in which they live. Lack of clean water and basic sanitation is the main reason diseases transmitted by feces are so common in developing countries. Access to drinking water from an improved source and access to improved sanitation do not ensure safety or adequacy, as these characteristics are not tested at the time of the surveys. But improved drinking water technologies and improved sanitation facilities are more likely than those characterized as unimproved to provide safe drinking water and to prevent contact with human excreta. The data are derived by the Joint Monitoring Programme (JMP) of the World Health Organization (WHO) and United Nations Children's Fund (UNICEF) based on national censuses and nationally representative household surveys. The coverage rates for water and sanitation are based on information from service users on the facilities their households actually use rather than on information from service providers, which may include nonfunctioning systems. While the estimates are based on use, the JMP reports use as access, because access is the term used in the Millennium Development Goal target for drinking water and sanitation.

Governments in developing countries usually finance immunization against measles and diphtheria, pertussis (whooping cough), and tetanus (DTP) as part of the basic public health package. In many developing countries lack of precise information on the size of the cohort of one-year-old children makes immunization coverage difficult to estimate from program statistics. The data shown here are based on an assessment of national immunization coverage rates by the WHO and UNICEF. The assessment considered both administrative data from service providers and household survey data on children's immunization histories. Based on the data available, consideration of potential biases, and contributions of local experts, the most likely true level of immunization coverage was determined for each year. Acute respiratory infection continues to be a leading cause of death among young children, killing about 2 million children under age 5 in developing countries each year. Data are drawn mostly from household health surveys in which mothers report on number of episodes and treatment for acute respiratory infection.

Since 1990 diarrhea-related deaths among children have declined tremendously. Most diarrhea-related deaths are due to dehydration, and many of these deaths can be prevented with the use of oral rehydration salts at home. However, recommendations for the use of oral rehydration therapy have changed over time based on scientific progress, so it is difficult to accurately compare use rates across countries. Until the current recommended method for home management of diarrhea is adopted and applied in all countries, the data should be used with caution. Also, the prevalence of diarrhea may vary by season. Since country surveys are administered at different times, data comparability is further affected.

Malaria is endemic to the poorest countries in the world, mainly in tropical and subtropical regions of Africa, Asia, and the Americas. Insecticide-treated nets, properly used and maintained, are one of the most important malaria-preventive strategies to limit human-mosquito contact.

Prompt and effective treatment of malaria is a critical element of malaria control. It is vital that sufferers, especially children under age 5, start treatment within 24 hours of the onset of symptoms, to prevent progression—often rapid—to severe malaria and death.

Data on the success rate of tuberculosis treatment are provided for countries that have submitted data to the WHO. The treatment success rate for tuberculosis provides a useful indicator of the quality of health services. A low rate suggests that infectious patients may not be receiving adequate treatment. An important complement to the tuberculosis treatment success rate is the case detection rate, which indicates whether there is adequate coverage by the recommended case detection and treatment strategy. Uncertainty bounds for the case detection rate, not shown in the table, are available at http://data.worldbank.org or the original source.

Editions before 2010 included the tuberculosis detection rates by DOTS, the internationally recommended strategy for tuberculosis control. This year's edition, like last year's, shows the tuberculosis detection rate for all detection methods, so data on the case detection rate cannot be compared with data in previous editions.

For indicators that are from household surveys, the year in the table refers to the survey year. For more information, consult the original sources.

Definitions

- **Access to an improved water source** refers to people with access to at least 20 liters of water a person a day from an improved source, such as piped water into a dwelling, public tap, tubewell, protected dug well, and rainwater collection, within 1 kilometer of the dwelling. • **Access to improved sanitation facilities** refers to people with at least adequate access to excreta disposal facilities that can effectively prevent human, animal, and insect contact with excreta. Improved facilities range from protected pit latrines to flush toilets. • **Child immunization rate** refers to children ages 12–23 months who, before 12 months or at any time before the survey, had received one dose of measles vaccine and three doses of diphtheria, pertussis (whooping cough), and tetanus (DTP3) vaccine. • **Children with acute respiratory infection (ARI) taken to health provider** are children under age 5 with ARI in the two weeks before the survey who were taken to an appropriate health provider. • **Children with diarrhea who received oral rehydration and continuous feeding** are children under age 5 with diarrhea in the two weeks before the survey who received either oral rehydration therapy or increased fluids, with continuous feeding. • **Children sleeping under treated nets** are children under age 5 who slept under an insecticide-treated net to prevent malaria the night before the survey. • **Children with fever receiving antimalarial drugs** are children under age 5 who were ill with fever in the two weeks before the survey and received any appropriate (locally defined) antimalarial drugs. • **Tuberculosis treatment success rate** is new registered infectious tuberculosis cases that were cured or that completed a full course of treatment as a percentage of smear-positive cases registered for treatment outcome evaluation. • **Tuberculosis case detection rate** is newly identified tuberculosis cases (including relapses) as a percentage of estimated incident cases (case detection, all forms).

Data sources

Data on access to water and sanitation are from the WHO and UNICEF's *Progress on Sanitation and Drinking Water* (2010). Data on immunization are from WHO and UNICEF estimates (www.who.int/immunization_monitoring). Data on children with ARI, with diarrhea, sleeping under treated nets, and receiving antimalarial drugs are from UNICEF's *State of the World's Children 2010*, Childinfo, and Demographic and Health Surveys by Macro International. Data on tuberculosis are from the WHO's *Global Tuberculosis Control: A Short Update to the 2010 Report.*

	Total fertility rate		Adolescent fertility rate	Unmet need for contraception	Contraceptive prevalence rate	Pregnant women receiving prenatal care	Births attended by skilled health staff		Maternal mortality ratio			Lifetime risk of maternal death
	births per woman		births per 1,000 women ages 15–19	% of married women ages 15–49	any method % of married women ages 15–49	%	% of total		per 100,000 live births			Probability 1 woman in:
									National estimates	Modeled estimates		
	1990	2009	2009	2004–09a	2004–09a	2004–09a	1990	2004–09a	2004–09a	1990	2008	2008
Afghanistan	8.0	6.5	117	..	15	36	..	24	..	1,700	1,400	11
Albania	2.9	1.9	14	..	69	97	..	99	21	48	31	1,700
Algeria	4.7	2.3	7	11	61	89	77	95	..	250	120	340
Angola	7.2	5.6	121	..	..	80	..	47	..	1,000	610	29
Argentina	3.0	2.2	56	..	78	99	96	95	40	72	70	600
Armenia	2.5	1.7	35	13	53	93	..	100	27	51	29	1,900
Australia	1.9	1.9	14	..	..	..	100	..	..	10	8	7,400
Austria	1.5	1.4	12	..	..	..	..	..	..	10	5	14,300
Azerbaijan	2.7	2.3	33	23	51	77	..	88	26	64	38	1,200
Bangladesh	4.4	2.3	68	17	53	51	..	24	348	870	340	110
Belarus	1.9	1.5	20	..	73	99	..	100	3	37	15	5,100
Belgium	1.6	1.9	7	..	75	..	..	..	..	7	5	10,900
Benin	6.7	5.4	108	30	17	84	..	74	397	790	410	43
Bolivia	4.9	3.4	76	..	61	86	43	71	310	510	180	150
Bosnia and Herzegovina	1.7	1.2	15	23	36	99	97	100	3	18	9	9,300
Botswana	4.7	2.8	50	..	53	94	77	95	198	83	190	180
Brazil	2.8	1.8	74	..	81	97	72	97	75	120	58	860
Bulgaria	1.8	1.6	40	..	..	..	..	100	6	24	13	5,800
Burkina Faso	6.8	5.8	125	31	17	85	..	54	307	770	560	28
Burundi	6.6	4.5	18	9	9	92	..	34	615	1,200	970	25
Cambodia	5.8	2.9	37	25	51b	83b	..	71b	461	690	290	110
Cameroon	5.9	4.5	122	3	29	82	58	63	669	680	600	35
Canada	1.8	1.6	12	..	..	..	..	100	..	6	12	5,600
Central African Republic	5.8	4.7	96	..	19	69	..	44	543	880	850	27
Chad	6.7	6.1	155	21	3	39	..	14	1,099	1,300	1,200	14
Chile	2.6	1.9	59	..	58	..	..	100	18	56	26	2,000
China	2.3	1.8	10	..	85	91	50	99	34	110	38	1,500
Hong Kong SAR, China	1.3	1.0	6	..	..	..	..	100	..	..	..	..
Colombia	3.1	2.4	72	6	78	94	82	96	76	140	85	460
Congo, Dem. Rep.	7.1	5.9	191	24	21	85	..	74	549	900	670	24
Congo, Rep.	5.4	4.3	106	16	44	86	..	83	781	460	580	39
Costa Rica	3.2	1.9	67	..	80	90	98	99	27	35	44	1,100
Côte d'Ivoire	6.3	4.5	122	29	13	85	..	57	543	690	470	44
Croatia	1.6	1.5	14	..	..	100b	100	100b	13b	8	14	5,200
Cuba	1.8	1.5	46	8	78	100	..	100	47	63	53	1,400
Czech Republic	1.9	1.5	10	..	..	..	..	100	6	15	8	8,500
Denmark	1.7	1.8	6	..	..	..	..	..	..	7	5	10,900
Dominican Republic	3.5	2.6	107	11	73	99	93	98	159	220	100	320
Ecuador	3.7	2.5	82	..	73	84	..	98	60	230	140	270
Egypt, Arab Rep.	4.6	2.8	37	9	60	74	37	79	55	220	82	380
El Salvador	4.0	2.3	81	..	73	94	52	96	59	200	110	350
Eritrea	6.2	4.5	62	..	..	..	..	..	..	930	280	72
Estonia	2.0	1.6	20	..	..	..	..	100	7	48	12	5,300
Ethiopia	7.1	5.2	94	34	15	28	..	6	673	990	470	40
Finland	1.8	1.9	11	..	..	..	..	..	..	7	8	7,600
France	1.8	2.0	6	..	71	..	..	..	..	13	8	6,600
Gabon	5.2	3.2	85	..	..	..	..	..	..	260	260	110
Gambia, The	6.1	5.0	87	..	..	98	44	57	..	750	400	49
Georgia	2.2	1.6	44	..	47	94	..	98	14	58	48	1,300
Germany	1.5	1.4	7	..	..	..	..	100	..	13	7	11,100
Ghana	5.6	3.9	61	35	24	90	40	57	451	630	350	66
Greece	1.4	1.5	8	..	..	..	..	..	..	6	2	31,800
Guatemala	5.6	4.0	104	..	54	..	..	51	133	140	110	210
Guinea	6.7	5.3	147	21	9	88	31	46	980	1,200	680	26
Guinea-Bissau	5.9	5.7	125	25	10	78	..	39	405	1,200	1,000	18
Haiti	5.4	3.4	45	38	32	85	23	26	630	670	300	93
Honduras	5.1	3.2	90	17	65	92	45	67	..	210	110	240

Reproductive health 2.19

	Total fertility rate		Adolescent fertility rate	Unmet need for contraception	Contraceptive prevalence rate	Pregnant women receiving prenatal care	Births attended by skilled health staff		Maternal mortality ratio			Lifetime risk of maternal death
	births per woman		births per 1,000 women ages 15–19	% of married women ages 15–49	any method % of married women ages 15–49	%	% of total		per 100,000 live births National estimates	Modeled estimates		Probability 1 woman in:
	1990	2009	2009	2004–09[a]	2004–09[a]	2004–09[a]	1990	2004–09[a]	2004–09[a]	1990	2008	2008
Hungary	1.8	1.3	19	..	..	..	..	100	17	23	13	5,500
India	4.0	2.7	64	13	54	75	..	53	254	570	230	140
Indonesia	3.1	2.1	37	9	57	93	32	75	228	620	240	190
Iran, Islamic Rep.	4.8	1.8	17	..	79	98	..	97	25	150	30	1,500
Iraq	6.0	3.9	80	..	50	84	54	80	84	93	75	300
Ireland	2.1	2.1	15	..	89	..	..	..	..	6	3	17,800
Israel	2.8	3.0	14	..	..	..	..	..	..	12	7	5,100
Italy	1.3	1.4	5	..	..	..	..	..	..	10	5	15,200
Jamaica	2.9	2.4	75	..	..	91	79	95	..	66	89	450
Japan	1.5	1.4	5	..	54	..	100	100	..	12	6	12,200
Jordan	5.5	3.4	24	11	59	99	87	99	19	110	59	510
Kazakhstan	2.7	2.6	29	..	51	100	..	100	37	78	45	950
Kenya	6.0	4.9	101	..	46	92	50	44	488	380	530	38
Korea, Dem. Rep.	2.4	1.9	0	..	..	..	..	..	77	270	250	230
Korea, Rep.	1.6	1.3	6	..	80	..	98	..	..	18	18	4,700
Kosovo	3.9	2.3	..	..	..	..	..	..	..	..	..	..
Kuwait	3.5	2.2	13	..	..	..	..	..	..	10	9	4,500
Kyrgyz Republic	3.7	2.8	32	1	48	97	..	98	55	77	81	450
Lao PDR	6.0	3.4	34	..	38	35	..	20	405	1,200	580	49
Latvia	2.0	1.3	14	..	..	..	..	100	8	57	20	3,600
Lebanon	3.1	1.8	16	..	58	96	..	98	..	52	26	2,000
Lesotho	4.9	3.3	69	31	47	92	..	62	762	370	530	62
Liberia	6.5	5.8	136	36	11	79	..	46	994	1,100	990	20
Libya	4.8	2.6	3	..	..	..	..	..	..	100	64	540
Lithuania	2.0	1.5	20	..	..	..	..	100	9	34	13	5,800
Macedonia, FYR	2.1	1.4	21	34	14	94	..	100	4	16	9	7,300
Madagascar	6.3	4.6	127	24	40	86	57	44	498	710	440	45
Malawi	7.0	5.5	127	28	41	92	55	54	807	910	510	36
Malaysia	3.7	2.5	12	..	..	79	..	99	29	56	31	1,200
Mali	6.7	6.5	155	31	8	70	..	49	464	1,200	830	22
Mauritania	5.9	4.4	82	25	9	75	40	61	686	780	550	41
Mauritius	2.3	1.5	41	..	..	..	91	99	..	72	36	1,600
Mexico	3.4	2.1	63	..	73	94	..	93	63	93	85	500
Moldova	2.4	1.5	33	7	68	98	..	100	38	62	32	2,000
Mongolia	4.2	2.0	15	14	55	100	..	99	81	130	65	730
Morocco	4.0	2.3	19	10	63	68	31	63	132	270	110	360
Mozambique	6.2	5.0	139	..	16	89	..	55	..	1,000	550	37
Myanmar	3.4	2.3	18	..	41	80	..	64	316	420	240	180
Namibia	5.2	3.3	67	7	55	95	68	81	449	180	180	160
Nepal	5.2	2.8	91	25	48	44	7	19	281	870	380	80
Netherlands	1.6	1.8	4	..	69	..	..	..	..	10	9	7,100
New Zealand	2.2	2.1	21	..	..	..	..	..	..	18	14	3,800
Nicaragua	4.8	2.7	111	8	72	90	..	74	77	190	100	300
Niger	7.9	7.1	152	16	11	46	15	33	648	1,400	820	16
Nigeria	6.6	5.6	118	..	15	58	33	39	545	1,100	840	23
Norway	1.9	2.0	8	..	88	..	100	..	..	9	7	7,600
Oman	6.6	3.0	10	..	..	..	..	99	17	49	20	1,600
Pakistan	6.1	3.9	42	25	30	61	19	39	276	490	260	93
Panama	3.0	2.5	80	..	..	..	..	92	60	86	71	520
Papua New Guinea	4.8	4.0	50	..	32	79	..	53	733	340	250	94
Paraguay	4.5	3.0	69	..	79	96	66	82	118	130	95	310
Peru	3.8	2.5	52	8	73	94	80	83	..	250	98	370
Philippines	4.3	3.0	43	22	51	91	..	62	162	180	94	320
Poland	2.0	1.4	13	..	..	..	..	100	5	17	6	13,300
Portugal	1.4	1.3	15	..	67	..	98	..	..	15	7	9,800
Puerto Rico	2.2	1.7	50	..	..	..	..	100	..	29	18	3,000
Qatar	4.4	2.4	15	..	..	..	..	..	..	15	8	4,400

	Total fertility rate		Adolescent fertility rate	Unmet need for contraception	Contraceptive prevalence rate	Pregnant women receiving prenatal care	Births attended by skilled health staff		Maternal mortality ratio			Lifetime risk of maternal death
					any method					per 100,000 live births		
	births per woman		births per 1,000 women ages 15–19	% of married women ages 15–49	% of married women ages 15–49	%	% of total		National estimates	Modeled estimates		Probability 1 woman in:
	1990	2009	2009	2004–09[a]	2004–09[a]	2004–09[a]	1990	2004–09[a]	2004–09[a]	1990	2008	2008
Romania	1.8	1.4	29	..	70	94	..	99	14	170	27	2,700
Russian Federation	1.9	1.6	24	..	80	..	..	100	32[b]	74	39	1,900
Rwanda	6.8	5.3	35	38	36	96	26	52	750	1,100	540	35
Saudi Arabia	5.8	3.0	25	..	24	..	..	96	14	41	24	1,300
Senegal	6.7	4.7	97	32	12	94	..	52	401	750	410	46
Serbia	1.8	1.4	21	29	41	98	..	99	6	13	8	7,500
Sierra Leone	5.5	5.2	124	..	8	87	..	42	857	1,300	970	21
Singapore	1.9	1.2	4	..	..	..	..	100	..	6	9	10,000
Slovak Republic	2.1	1.4	20	..	..	..	..	100	4	15	6	13,300
Slovenia	1.5	1.5	5	..	..	..	100	100	26	11	18	4,100
Somalia	6.6	6.4	69	26	15	26	..	33	1,044	1,100	1,200	14
South Africa	3.7	2.5	56	..	..	..	..	..	..	230	410	100
Spain	1.3	1.4	12	..	66	..	..	..	..	7	6	11,400
Sri Lanka	2.5	2.3	29	..	68	99	..	99	39	91	39	1,100
Sudan	6.0	4.1	53	6	8	64	69	49	1,107	830	750	32
Swaziland	5.7	3.5	78	24	51	85	..	69	589	260	420	75
Sweden	2.1	1.9	7	..	..	..	..	..	..	7	5	11,400
Switzerland	1.6	1.5	5	..	..	..	..	100	..	8	10	7,600
Syrian Arab Republic	5.5	3.1	55	11	58	84	..	93	..	120	46	610
Tajikistan	5.2	3.4	27	24	37	80	..	88	38	120	64	430
Tanzania	6.2	5.5	128	22	26	76	53	43	578	880	790	23
Thailand	2.1	1.8	36	..	77	98	..	97	12	50	48	1,200
Timor-Leste	5.3	6.4	52	..	22[b]	..	..	..	..	650	370	44
Togo	6.3	4.2	62	41	17	84	31	62	..	650	350	67
Trinidad and Tobago	2.4	1.6	34	27	43	96	..	98	..	86	55	1,100
Tunisia	3.5	2.1	7	..	60	96	69	95	..	130	60	860
Turkey	3.1	2.1	36	18	73	95	..	95	29	68	23	1,900
Turkmenistan	4.3	2.4	18	..	48	99	..	100	15	91	77	500
Uganda	7.1	6.3	142	41	24	94	38	42	435	670	430	35
Ukraine	1.8	1.5	27	10	67	99	..	99	16	49	26	3,000
United Arab Emirates	4.4	1.9	15	..	..	..	..	..	..	28	10	4,200
United Kingdom	1.8	2.0	22	..	..	..	..	..	..	10	12	4,700
United States	2.1	2.1	33	..	..	..	99	..	13	12	24	2,100
Uruguay	2.5	2.0	60	..	78	96	..	99	34	39	27	1,700
Uzbekistan	4.1	2.7	13	8	65	99	..	100	21	53	30	1,400
Venezuela, RB	3.4	2.5	89	..	..	..	..	..	61	84	68	540
Vietnam	3.7	2.0	16	..	80	91	..	88	75	170	56	850
West Bank and Gaza	6.4	4.9	73	..	50	99	..	99	..	..	..	..
Yemen, Rep.	8.1	5.1	64	24	28	47	16	36	..	540	210	91
Zambia	6.5	5.7	133	27	41	94	51	47	591	390	470	38
Zimbabwe	5.2	3.4	61	13	65	93	70	60	555	390	790	42
World	**3.3 w**	**2.5 w**	**50 w**	**.. w**	**61 w**	**82 w**	**50 w**	**65 w**		**400 w**	**260 w**	**140 w**
Low income	5.6	4.2	97	25	33	67	..	41		850	580	39
Middle income	3.3	2.4	46	..	66	85	46	71		350	200	190
Lower middle income	3.4	2.5	45	..	63	83	41	66		400	230	160
Upper middle income	3.0	2.0	49	..	75	95	..	96		120	82	570
Low & middle income	3.6	2.7	54	..	61	82	46	64		440	290	120
East Asia & Pacific	2.6	1.9	17	..	77	91	48	89		200	89	580
Europe & Central Asia	2.3	1.8	27	..	69	..	..	97		69	32	1,700
Latin America & Carib.	3.2	2.2	71	..	75	95	72	89		140	86	480
Middle East & N. Africa	4.9	2.7	34	..	62	83	47	80		210	88	380
South Asia	4.3	2.8	63	15	51	70	32	47		610	290	110
Sub-Saharan Africa	6.3	5.1	112	24	21	71	..	44		870	650	31
High income	1.8	1.7	18	..	..	..	..	..		15	15	3,900
Euro area	1.5	1.6	8	..	..	..	..	..		11	7	10,100

a. Data are for the most recent year available. b. Data are for 2010.

Reproductive health **2.19** |PEOPLE

About the data

Reproductive health is a state of physical and mental well-being in relation to the reproductive system and its functions and processes. Means of achieving reproductive health include education and services during pregnancy and childbirth, safe and effective contraception, and prevention and treatment of sexually transmitted diseases. Complications of pregnancy and childbirth are the leading cause of death and disability among women of reproductive age in developing countries. Total and adolescent fertility rates are based on data on registered live births from vital registration systems or, in the absence of such systems, from censuses or sample surveys. The estimated rates are generally considered reliable measures of fertility in the recent past. Where no empirical information on age-specific fertility rates is available, a model is used to estimate the share of births to adolescents. For countries without vital registration systems fertility rates are generally based on extrapolations from trends observed in censuses or surveys from earlier years.

More couples in developing countries want to limit or postpone childbearing but are not using effective contraception. These couples have an unmet need for contraception. Common reasons are lack of knowledge about contraceptive methods and concerns about possible side effects. This indicator excludes women not exposed to the risk of unintended pregnancy because of menopause, infertility, or postpartum anovulation.

Contraceptive prevalence reflects all methods—ineffective traditional methods as well as highly effective modern methods. Contraceptive prevalence rates are obtained mainly from household surveys, including *Demographic and Health Surveys*, *Multiple Indicator Cluster Surveys*, and contraceptive prevalence surveys (see *Primary data documentation* for the most recent survey and year). Unmarried women are often excluded from such surveys, which may bias the estimates.

Good prenatal and postnatal care improves maternal health and reduces maternal and infant mortality. Indicators on use of antenatal care services, however, provide no information on the content or quality of the services. Data on antenatal care are obtained mostly from household surveys, which ask women who have had a live birth whether and from whom they received antenatal care. The share of births attended by skilled health staff is an indicator of a health system's ability to provide adequate care for pregnant women.

Maternal mortality ratios are generally of unknown reliability, as are many other cause-specific mortality indicators. Household surveys such as *Demographic and Health Surveys* attempt to measure maternal mortality by asking respondents about survivorship of sisters. The main disadvantage of this method is that the

estimates of maternal mortality that it produces pertain to 12 years or so before the survey, making them unsuitable for monitoring recent changes or observing the impact of interventions. In addition, measurement of maternal mortality is subject to many types of errors. Even in high-income countries with vital registration systems, misclassification of maternal deaths has been found to lead to serious underestimation.

The national estimates of maternal mortality ratios in the table are based on national surveys, vital registration records, and surveillance data or are derived from community and hospital records. The modeled estimates are based on an exercise by the World Health Organization (WHO), United Nations Children's Fund (UNICEF), United Nations Population Fund (UNFPA), and World Bank. This year's estimates of maternal mortality include country-level time-series data for the first time. For countries with complete vital registration systems with good attribution of cause of death, the data are used to directly estimate maternal mortality. For countries without complete registration data but with other types of data and for countries with no empirical national data, maternal mortality is estimated with a multilevel regression model using available national-level maternal mortality data and socioeconomic information, including fertility, birth attendants, and GDP. The methodology of this year's interagency estimates differs from previous years', so the data should not be compared with data in previous editions. For further information on methodology, see the original source.

Neither set of ratios can be assumed to provide an exact estimate of maternal mortality for any of the countries in the table.

In countries with a high risk of maternal death, many girls die before reaching reproductive age. Lifetime risk of maternal mortality refers to the probability that a 15-year-old girl will eventually die from a maternal cause.

For the indicators that are from household surveys, the year in the table refers to the survey year. For more information, consult the original sources.

Definitions

• **Total fertility rate** is the number of children that would be born to a woman if she were to live to the end of her childbearing years and bear children in accordance with current age-specific fertility rates. • **Adolescent fertility rate** is the number of births per 1,000 women ages 15–19. • **Unmet need for contraception** is the percentage of fertile, married women of reproductive age who do not want to become pregnant and are not

using contraception. • **Contraceptive prevalence rate** is the percentage of women married or in union ages 15–49 who are practicing, or whose sexual partners are practicing, any form of contraception. • **Pregnant women receiving prenatal care** are the percentage of women attended at least once during pregnancy by skilled health personnel for reasons related to pregnancy. • **Births attended by skilled health staff** are the percentage of deliveries attended by personnel trained to give the necessary care to women during pregnancy, labor, and postpartum; to conduct deliveries on their own; and to care for newborns. • **Maternal mortality ratio** is the number of women who die from pregnancy-related causes during pregnancy and childbirth per 100,000 live births. • **Lifetime risk of maternal death** refers to the probability that a 15-year-old girl will eventually die from a maternal cause if throughout her lifetime she experiences the risks of maternal death and the overall level of fertility and mortality that are observed for a given population. Data are presented as 1 in the number of women who are likely to die from a maternal cause.

Data sources

Data on total fertility are compiled from the United Nations Population Division's *World Population Prospects: The 2008 Revision*, census reports and other statistical publications from national statistical offices, household surveys conducted by national agencies, Macro International, and the U.S. Centers for Disease Control and Prevention, Eurostat's Demographic Statistics, and the U.S. Bureau of the Census International Data Base. Data on adolescent fertility are from *World Population Prospects: The 2008 Revision*, with annual data linearly interpolated by the Development Data Group. Data on women with unmet need for contraception and contraceptive prevalence are from household surveys, including Demographic and Health Surveys by Macro International and Multiple Indicator Cluster Surveys by UNICEF. Data on pregnant women receiving prenatal care, births attended by skilled health staff, and national estimates of maternal mortality ratios are from UNICEF's State of the World's Children 2011 and Childinfo and Demographic and Health Surveys by Macro International. Modeled estimates of maternal mortality ratios and lifetime risk of maternal death are from WHO, UNICEF, UNFPA and the World Bank's Trends in *Maternal Mortality: 1990–2008* (2010).

2011 World Development Indicators **109**

	Prevalence of undernourishment		Prevalence of child malnutrition		Prevalence of overweight children	Low-birthweight babies	Exclusive breast-feeding	Consumption of iodized salt	Vitamin A supplementation	Prevalence of anemia %	
	% of population		% of children under age 5		% of children under age 5	% of births	% of children under 6 months	% of households	% of children 6–59 months	Children under age 5	Pregnant women
	1990–92	2005–09	Underweight 2004–09[a]	Stunting 2004–09[a]	2004–09[a]	2004–09[a]	2004–09[a]	2004–09[a]	2009	2004–09[a]	2004–09[a]
Afghanistan	..	..	32.9	59.3	4.6	..	83	28	95	38	61
Albania	10	<5	6.6	27.0	25.2	7	39	76	..	31	34
Algeria	<5	<5	3.7	15.9	12.9	6	7	61	..	43	43
Angola	67	41	..	..	..	..	..	45	28	..	57
Argentina	<5	<5	2.3	8.2	9.9	7	..	..	..	17	31
Armenia	45	22	4.2	18.2	11.7	7	33	97	..	37	..
Australia	<5	<5	..	..	..	..	..	..	..	8	12
Austria	<5	<5	..	..	..	..	..	..	..	11	15
Azerbaijan	27	<5	8.4	26.8	13.9	10	12	54	79[b]	..	..
Bangladesh	38	27	41.3	43.2	1.1	22	43	84	91	58	39
Belarus	<5	<5	1.3	4.5	9.7	4	9	55	..	27	26
Belgium	<5	<5	..	..	..	..	..	..	..	9	13
Benin	20	12	20.2	44.7	11.4	15	43	67	56	78	75
Bolivia	29	27	4.5	27.2	8.7	6	60	89	45	52	37
Bosnia and Herzegovina	8	<5	1.6	11.8	25.6	5	18	62	..	27	35
Botswana	19	25	..	..	..	13	20	..	89	..	21
Brazil	11	6	2.2	7.1	7.3	8	40	96	..	55	29
Bulgaria	<5	10	1.6	8.8	13.6	9	..	100	..	27	30
Burkina Faso	14	9	26.0	35.1	7.7	16	16	34	100	..	..
Burundi	44	62	..	..	..	11	45	98	90	56	47
Cambodia	38	22	28.8	39.5	2.0	9	66	73	98	62	57
Cameroon	33	21	16.6	36.4	9.6	11	21	49	..	68	51
Canada	<5	<5	..	..	..	..	..	..	..	8	12
Central African Republic	44	40	..	..	..	13	23	62	87	..	..
Chad	60	37	33.9	44.8	4.4	22	2	56	71	71	60
Chile	7	<5	0.5	2.0	9.5	6	85	..	..	24	28
China	18[c]	10[c]	4.5	11.7	5.9	3	28	96	..	..	..
Hong Kong SAR, China	..	..	..	..	..	..	..	..	..	..	..
Colombia	15	10	5.1	16.2	4.2	6	47	..	..	28	31
Congo, Dem. Rep.	26	69	28.2	45.8	6.8	10	36	79	89	71	67
Congo, Rep.	42	15	11.8	31.2	8.5	13	19	82	8	66	55
Costa Rica	<5	<5	..	..	..	7	15	..	..	..	..
Côte d'Ivoire	15	14	16.7	40.1	9.0	17	4	84	88	69	55
Croatia	18	<5	1.0	0.6	8.1	5	98	88	..	23	28
Cuba	6	<5	..	..	..	5	26	88	..	27	39
Czech Republic	<5	<5	..	..	..	..	..	..	..	18	22
Denmark	<5	<5	..	..	..	..	..	..	..	9	12
Dominican Republic	28	24	3.4	10.1	8.3	11	9	19	..	35	40
Ecuador	23	15	6.2	29.0	5.1	10	40	..	..	38	38
Egypt, Arab Rep.	<5	<5	6.8	30.7	20.5	13	53	79	68[b]	49	34
El Salvador	13	9	..	..	..	..	31	..	20	..	..
Eritrea	67	64	..	..	..	..	..	..	44	70	55
Estonia	10	<5	..	..	..	..	..	..	..	23	23
Ethiopia	69	41	34.6	50.7	5.1	20	49	20	84	75	63
Finland	<5	<5	..	..	..	..	..	..	..	11	15
France	<5	<5	..	..	..	..	..	..	..	8	11
Gabon	6	<5	..	..	..	..	..	..	0	44	46
Gambia, The	14	19	15.8	27.6	2.7	20	41	7	28	..	..
Georgia	58	<5	2.3	14.7	21.0	5	11	100	..	41	42
Germany	<5	<5	1.1	1.3	3.5	..	..	..	..	8	12
Ghana	27	5	14.3	28.6	5.9	13	63	32	90	..	..
Greece	<5	<5	..	..	..	..	..	..	..	12	19
Guatemala	15	21	..	..	..	..	50	76	43	..	..
Guinea	20	17	20.8	40.0	5.1	12	48	41	94	76	..
Guinea-Bissau	22	22	17.4	47.7	17.0	24	16	1	80	75	58
Haiti	63	57	18.9	29.7	3.9	25	41	3	..	..	50
Honduras	19	12	8.6	29.9	5.8	10	30	..	..	..	21

	Prevalence of undernourishment		Prevalence of child malnutrition		Prevalence of overweight children	Low-birthweight babies	Exclusive breast-feeding	Consumption of iodized salt	Vitamin A supplementation	Prevalence of anemia %	
	% of population		% of children under age 5		% of children under age 5	% of births	% of children under 6 months	% of households	% of children 6–59 months	Children under age 5	Pregnant women
	1990–92	2005–09	Underweight 2004–09[a]	Stunting 2004–09[a]	2004–09[a]	2004–09[a]	2004–09[a]	2004–09[a]	2009	2004–09[a]	2004–09[a]
Hungary	<5	<5	..	..	..	..	..	..	..	19	21
India	20	21	43.5	47.9	1.9	28	46	51	66	74	50
Indonesia	16	13	17.5[d]	35.6[d]	11.2	11[d]	15[d]	62[d]	84	44	44
Iran, Islamic Rep.	<5	<5	..	..	..	7	23	99	..	35	..
Iraq	..	..	7.1	27.5	15.0	15	25	28	..	56	38
Ireland	<5	<5	..	..	..	..	..	..	..	10	15
Israel	<5	<5	..	..	..	..	..	..	..	12	17
Italy	<5	<5	..	..	..	..	..	..	..	11	15
Jamaica	11	5	2.2	3.7	7.5	14	15	..	..	..	..
Japan	<5	<5	..	..	..	..	..	..	..	11	15
Jordan	<5	5	1.9	8.3	6.6	13	22	..	..	..	..
Kazakhstan	<5	<5	4.9	17.5	14.8	6	17	92	..	..	26
Kenya	33	31	16.4	35.2	5.0	8	32	98	51	..	..
Korea, Dem. Rep.	21	33	20.6	43.1	..	..	65	40	99	..	..
Korea, Rep.	<5	<5	..	..	..	..	..	..	..	..	23
Kosovo	..	..	..	..	..	..	..	..	..	..	31
Kuwait	20	5	1.7	3.8	9.0	..	..	..	..	..	34
Kyrgyz Republic	17	10	2.7	18.1	10.7	5	32	76	99	..	56
Lao PDR	31	23	31.6	47.6	1.3	11	26	84	88	27	25
Latvia	<5	<5	..	..	..	..	..	92	..	..	32
Lebanon	<5	<5	4.2	16.5	16.7	..	..	92	..	..	32
Lesotho	15	14	16.6	45.2	6.8	13	54	91	85	49	25
Liberia	30	33	20.4	39.4	4.2	14	29	..	92	..	..
Libya	<5	<5	5.6	21.0	22.4	..	..	..	..	34	34
Lithuania	<5	<5	..	..	..	..	..	..	..	24	24
Macedonia, FYR	11	<5	1.8	11.5	16.2	6	16	94	..	..	32
Madagascar	21	25	36.8	49.2	6.2	16	51	53	95	68	50
Malawi	43	28	15.5	53.2	11.3	13	57	50	95	73	47
Malaysia	<5	<5	..	..	..	11	..	..	..	32	38
Mali	27	12	27.9	38.5	4.7	19	38	79	100	..	..
Mauritania	12	7	16.7	24.2	2.3	34	35	23	89	68	53
Mauritius	7	5	..	..	..	..	..	..	..	..	..
Mexico	<5	<5	3.4	15.5	7.6	8	..	..	..	24	21
Moldova	5	6	3.2	11.3	9.1	6	46	60	..	41	36
Mongolia	28	26	5.3	27.5	14.2	5	57	83	95	21	37
Morocco	6	<5	9.9	23.1	13.3	..	31	21	..	..	52
Mozambique	59	38	..	..	..	15	37	25	97	63	50
Myanmar	47	16	..	..	..	..	..	93	95	..	..
Namibia	32	19	17.5	29.6	4.6	16	24	..	..	41	31
Nepal	21	16	38.8	49.3	0.6	21	53	..	95	48	42
Netherlands	<5	<5	..	..	..	..	..	..	..	9	13
New Zealand	<5	<5	..	..	..	..	..	..	..	11	18
Nicaragua	50	19	4.3	18.8	5.2	8	31	..	6	17	..
Niger	37	20	39.9	54.8	3.5	27	10	46	95	81	61
Nigeria	16	6	26.7	41.0	10.5	12	13	..	78	..	..
Norway	<5	<5	..	..	..	..	..	..	..	6	9
Oman	..	..	..	..	..	9	..	..	..	42	..
Pakistan	25	26	..	..	..	32	37	..	91	..	..
Panama	18	15	..	..	..	..	..	..	..	..	..
Papua New Guinea	..	..	18.1	43.9	3.4	10	56	92	12	60	55
Paraguay	16	11	..	..	..	9	22	94	..	30	39
Peru	27	15	5.4	29.8	9.1	8	70	91	..	50	43
Philippines	24	15	..	..	..	21	34	45	91	21	43
Poland	<5	<5	..	..	..	..	..	..	..	23	25
Portugal	<5	<5	..	..	..	..	..	..	..	13	17
Puerto Rico	..	..	..	..	..	..	..	..	..	..	..
Qatar	..	..	..	..	..	..	..	..	..	..	29

	Prevalence of undernourishment		Prevalence of child malnutrition		Prevalence of overweight children	Low-birthweight babies	Exclusive breast-feeding	Consumption of iodized salt	Vitamin A supplemen-tation	Prevalence of anemia	
	% of population		% of children under age 5 Underweight	Stunting	% of children under age 5	% of births	% of children under 6 months	% of households	% of children 6–59 months	% Children under age 5	Pregnant women
	1990–92	2005–09	2004–09[a]	2004–09[a]	2004–09[a]	2004–09[a]	2004–09[a]	2004–09[a]	2009	2004–09[a]	2004–09[a]
Romania	<5	<5	..	..	..	8	16	74	..	40	30
Russian Federation	<5	<5	..	..	..	6	..	..	..	27	21
Rwanda	44	34	18.0	51.7	6.7	6	88	88	94	56	..
Saudi Arabia	<5	<5	5.3	9.3	6.1	..	..	..	..	33	32
Senegal	22	17	14.5	20.1	2.4	19	34	41	97	70	58
Serbia	<5[e]	8[e]	1.8	8.1	19.3	6	15	32	..	..	..
Sierra Leone	45	35	21.3	37.4	10.1	14	11	58	99	83	60
Singapore	..	..	..	..	..	..	..	..	..	19	24
Slovak Republic	<5	<5	..	..	..	..	..	..	..	23	25
Slovenia	<5	<5	..	..	..	..	..	..	..	14	19
Somalia	..	..	32.8	42.1	4.7	11	9	1	62	..	..
South Africa	<5	<5	..	..	..	..	..	..	39	..	22
Spain	<5	<5	..	..	..	..	..	..	..	13	18
Sri Lanka	28	19	21.6	19.2	0.8	17	76	92	..	..	..
Sudan	39	22	31.7	37.9	5.3	..	34	11	84	85	58
Swaziland	12	18	6.1	29.5	11.4	9	33	80	27	47	24
Sweden	<5	<5	..	..	..	..	..	..	..	9	13
Switzerland	<5	<5	..	..	..	..	..	..	..	6	..
Syrian Arab Republic	<5	<5	10.0	28.6	18.7	9	29	..	..	41	39
Tajikistan	34	30	14.9	33.1	6.7	10	25	62	87	..	45
Tanzania	28	34	16.7	44.4	4.9	10	50[d]	43	94	72	58
Thailand	26	16	7.0	15.7	8.0	9	5	47	..	..	..
Timor-Leste	39	31	..	..	..	..	52[d]	60	45	..	..
Togo	43	30	22.3	27.8	4.7	12	48	25	100	52	50
Trinidad and Tobago	11	11	..	..	..	19	13	28	..	30	30
Tunisia	<5	<5	3.3	9.0	8.8	5	6	..	..	..	..
Turkey	<5	<5	3.5	15.6	9.1	11	42	69	..	33	40
Turkmenistan	9	6	..	..	..	4	11	87	..	..	30
Uganda	19	21	16.4	38.7	4.9	14	60	96	64	73	64
Ukraine	<5	<5	..	..	..	4	18	18	..	..	27
United Arab Emirates	<5	<5	..	..	..	..	..	..	..	28	28
United Kingdom	<5	<5	..	..	..	..	..	..	..	..	15
United States	<5	<5	1.3	3.9	8.0	..	..	..	..	..	6
Uruguay	5	<5	6.0	13.9	9.4	8	57	..	..	19	27
Uzbekistan	5	11	4.4	19.6	12.8	5	26	53	65	33	40
Venezuela, RB	10	8	3.7	15.6	6.1	8	..	..	..	33	..
Vietnam	31	11	20.2	30.5	3.0	5	17	93	99[b]	..	..
West Bank and Gaza	10	18	2.2	11.8	11.4	7	27	86	..	..	..
Yemen, Rep.	30	31	..	..	..	..	..	..	47[b]	68	58
Zambia	35	43	14.9	45.8	8.4	11	61	..	91	..	..
Zimbabwe	40	30	14.0	35.8	9.1	11	26	91	77	58	47
World	**17 w**	**14 w**	**21.3 w**	**31.7 w**	**6.1 w**	**15 w**	**37 w**	**71 w**	**.. w**	**.. w**	**.. w**
Low income	38	31	27.7	44.0	4.9	15	44	62	86	66	56
Middle income	17	13	20.8	30.0	6.3	15	35	73			
Lower middle income	19	15	24.0	33.1	5.9	17	34	71			
Upper middle income	8	6	..	..	..	8	..	..		36	31
Low & middle income	19	16	22.4	33.3	6.0	15	37	71			
East Asia & Pacific	20	11	8.8	19.0	6.6	6	29	87			
Europe & Central Asia	7	6	..	..	..	7	..	..		30	31
Latin America & Carib.	13	9	3.8	14.1	7.2	8	44	89		38	33
Middle East & N. Africa	7	7	6.8	25.0	16.6	10	31	69		48	..
South Asia	23	22	42.5	47.5	1.9	27	46	55	73	71	49
Sub-Saharan Africa	31	26	24.7	42.0	7.0	14	33	52	81	..	..
High income	5	5	..	..	..	..	..	..	..	..	13
Euro area	5	5	..	..	..	..	..	..	..	10	14

a. Data are for the most recent year available. b. Country's vitamin A supplementation programs do not target children all the way up to 59 months of age. c. Includes Hong Kong SAR, China; Macao SAR, China; and Taiwan, China. d. Data are for 2010. e. Includes Montenegro.

Data on undernourishment are from the Food and Agriculture Organization (FAO) of the United Nations and measure food deprivation based on average food available for human consumption per person, the level of inequality in access to food, and the minimum calories required for an average person.

From a policy and program standpoint, however, this measure has its limits. First, food insecurity exists even where food availability is not a problem because of inadequate access of poor households to food. Second, food insecurity is an individual or household phenomenon, and the average food available to each person, even corrected for possible effects of low income, is not a good predictor of food insecurity among the population. And third, nutrition security is determined not only by food security but also by the quality of care of mothers and children and the quality of the household's health environment (Smith and Haddad 2000).

Estimates of child malnutrition, based on prevalence of underweight and stunting, are from national survey data. The proportion of underweight children is the most common malnutrition indicator. Being even mildly underweight increases the risk of death and inhibits cognitive development in children. And it perpetuates the problem across generations, as malnourished women are more likely to have low-birthweight babies. Stunting, or being below median height for age, is often used as a proxy for multifaceted deprivation and as an indicator of long-term changes in malnutrition. Estimates of overweight children are also from national survey data. Overweight children have become a growing concern in developing countries. Research shows an association between childhood obesity and a high prevalence of diabetes, respiratory disease, high blood pressure, and psychosocial and orthopedic disorders (de Onis and Blössner 2000).

New international growth reference standards for infants and young children were released in 2006 by the World Health Organization (WHO) to monitor children's nutritional status. Differences in growth to age 5 are influenced more by nutrition, feeding practices, environment, and healthcare than by genetics or ethnicity. The previously reported data were based on the U.S. National Center for Health Statistics–WHO growth reference. Because of the change in standards, the data in this edition should not be compared with data in editions prior to 2008.

Low birthweight, which is associated with maternal malnutrition, raises the risk of infant mortality and stunts growth in infancy and childhood. There is also emerging evidence that low-birthweight babies are more prone to noncommunicable diseases such as diabetes and cardiovascular diseases. Estimates of low-birthweight infants are drawn mostly from hospital records and household surveys. Many births in developing countries take place at home and are seldom recorded. A hospital birth may indicate higher income and therefore better nutrition, or it could indicate a higher risk birth. The data should therefore be used with caution.

Improved breastfeeding can save an estimated 1.3 million children a year. Breast milk alone contains all the nutrients, antibodies, hormones, and antioxidants an infant needs to thrive. It protects babies from diarrhea and acute respiratory infections, stimulates their immune systems and response to vaccination, and may confer cognitive benefits. The data on breastfeeding are derived from national surveys.

Iodine deficiency is the single most important cause of preventable mental retardation, and it contributes significantly to the risk of stillbirth and miscarriage. Widely used and inexpensive, iodized salt is the best source of iodine, and a global campaign to iodize edible salt is significantly reducing the risks. The data on iodized salt are derived from household surveys.

Vitamin A is essential for immune system functioning. Vitamin A deficiency, a leading cause of blindness, also causes a greater risk of dying from a range of childhood ailments such as measles, malaria, and diarrhea. Giving vitamin A to new breastfeeding mothers helps protect their children during the first months of life. Food fortification with vitamin A is being introduced in many developing countries.

Data on anemia are compiled by the WHO based mainly on nationally representative surveys, which measured hemoglobin in the blood. WHO's hemoglobin thresholds were then used to determine anemia status based on age, sex, and physiological status. Children under age 5 and pregnant women have the highest risk for anemia. Data should be used with caution because surveys differ in quality, coverage, age group interviewed, and treatment of missing values across countries and over time.

For indicators from household surveys, the year in the table refers to the survey year. For more information, consult the original sources.

• **Prevalence of undernourishment** is the percentage of the population whose dietary energy consumption is continuously below a minimum requirement for maintaining a healthy life and carrying out light physical activity with an acceptable minimum weight for height. • **Prevalence of child malnutrition** is the percentage of children under age 5 whose weight for age (underweight) or height for age (stunting) is more than two standard deviations below the median for the international reference population ages 0–59 months. Height is measured by recumbent length for children up to two years old and by stature while standing for older children. Data are based on the WHO child growth standards released in 2006. • **Prevalence of overweight children** is the percentage of children under age 5 whose weight for height is more than two standard deviations above the median for the international reference population of the corresponding age as established by the WHO child growth standards released in 2006. • **Low-birthweight babies** are the percentage of newborns weighing less than 2.5 kilograms within the first hours of life, before significant postnatal weight loss has occurred. • **Exclusive breastfeeding** is the percentage of children less than six months old who were fed breast milk alone (no other liquids) in the past 24 hours. • **Consumption of iodized salt** is the percentage of households that use edible salt fortified with iodine. • **Vitamin A supplementation** is the percentage of children ages 6–59 months who received at least two doses of vitamin A in the previous year. • **Prevalence of anemia, children under age 5,** is the percentage of children under age 5 whose hemoglobin level is less than 110 grams per liter at sea level. • **Prevalence of anemia, pregnant women,** is the percentage of pregnant women whose hemoglobin level is less than 110 grams per liter at sea level.

Data on undernourishment are from www.fao.org/faostat/foodsecurity/index_en.htm. Data on malnutrition and overweight children are from the WHO's Global Database on Child Growth and Malnutrition (www.who.int/nutgrowthdb). Data on low-birthweight babies, breastfeeding, iodized salt consumption, and vitamin A supplementation are from the United Nations Children's Fund's *State of the World's Children 2011* and Childinfo. Data on anemia are from the WHO's *Worldwide Prevalence of Anemia 1993–2005* (2008c) and Integrated WHO Nutrition Global Databases.

	Prevalence of smoking		Incidence of tuberculosis	Prevalence of diabetes	Prevalence of HIV[a]		Female % of total population with HIV	Youth % of population ages 15–24		Condom use	
	% of adults		per 100,000 people	% of population ages 20–79	Total % of population ages 15–49		population	Male	Female	% of population ages 15–24	
	Male	Female								Male	Female
	2006	2006	2009	2010	1990	2009	2009	2009	2009	2004–09[b]	2004–09[b]
Afghanistan	..	..	189	8.6	..	..	..	..	..	..	..
Albania	43	4	15	4.5	..	..	..	..	..	..	..
Algeria	26	0	59	8.5	<0.1	0.1	30	0.1	<0.1	..	..
Angola	..	..	298	3.5	0.5	2.0	60	0.6	1.6	..	..
Argentina	34	24	28	5.7	0.3	0.5	32	0.3	0.2	..	..
Armenia	61	3	73	7.8	<0.1	0.1	<43	<0.1	<0.1	68	5
Australia	22	19	6	5.7	0.1	0.1	31	0.1	0.1	..	..
Austria	47	41	11	8.9	<0.1	0.3	29	0.3	0.2	..	..
Azerbaijan	..	..	110	7.5	<0.1	0.1	60	<0.1	0.1	25	1
Bangladesh	43	1	225	6.6	<0.1	<0.1	30	<0.1	<0.1	..	..
Belarus	64	22	39	7.6	<0.1	0.3	50	<0.1	0.1	..	..
Belgium	30	24	9	5.3	<0.1	0.2	31	<0.1	<0.1	..	..
Benin	13	1	93	4.6	0.2	1.2	58	0.3	0.7	39	10
Bolivia	34	26	140	6.0	0.1	0.2	32	0.1	0.1	..	..
Bosnia and Herzegovina	49	35	50	7.1	..	..	..	..	..	..	..
Botswana	..	..	694	5.4	3.5	24.8	57	5.2	11.8	..	..
Brazil	19	12	45	6.4	..	..	..	..	..	..	..
Bulgaria	49	38	41	6.5	<0.1	0.1	29	<0.1	<0.1	..	..
Burkina Faso	13	1	215	3.8	3.9	1.2	60	0.5	0.8	..	..
Burundi	..	..	348	1.8	3.9	3.3	60	1.0	2.1	..	..
Cambodia	55[c]	20[c]	442	5.2	0.5	0.5	63	0.1	0.1	31	3
Cameroon	9	1	182	3.9	0.6	5.3	58	1.6	3.9	52	24
Canada	21	18	5	9.2	0.1	0.2	21	0.1	0.1	..	..
Central African Republic	..	..	327	4.5	3.1	4.7	61	1.0	2.2	..	..
Chad	12	1	283	3.7	1.1	3.4	59	1.0	2.5	18	2
Chile	42	31	11	5.7	<0.1	0.4	31	0.2	0.1	..	..
China	59	4	96	4.2	..	0.1[d]	..	..	..	..	..
Hong Kong SAR, China	..	..	82	8.5	..	..	..	..	..	..	..
Colombia	..	..	35	5.2	0.2	0.5	33	0.2	0.1	..	24
Congo, Dem. Rep.	10	1	372	3.2	..	..	..	..	..	16	26
Congo, Rep.	9	0	382	5.1	5.2	3.4	59	1.2	2.6	36	16
Costa Rica	26	7	10	9.3	<0.1	0.3	29	0.2	0.1	..	..
Côte d'Ivoire	11	1	399	4.7	2.4	3.4	58	0.7	1.5	..	..
Croatia	34[e]	27[e]	25	6.9	<0.1	<0.1	<33	<0.1	<0.1	..	..
Cuba	36	28	6	9.5	<0.1	0.1	31	0.1	0.1	..	..
Czech Republic	35	27	9	6.4	<0.1	<0.1	<42	<0.1	<0.1	..	..
Denmark	35	30	7	5.6	<0.1	0.2	27	0.1	0.1	..	..
Dominican Republic	15	11	70	11.2	0.4	0.9	59	0.3	0.7	58	19
Ecuador	23	5	68	5.9	0.3	0.4	31	0.2	0.2	..	..
Egypt, Arab Rep.	24	1	19	11.4	<0.1	<0.1	23	<0.1	<0.1	..	..
El Salvador	..	..	30	9.0	0.1	0.8	34	0.4	0.3	..	..
Eritrea	15	1	99	2.5	0.3	0.8	60	0.2	0.4	..	..
Estonia	48	25	30	7.6	<0.1	1.2	31	0.3	0.2	..	..
Ethiopia	8	1	359	2.5	..	..	..	..	..	18	2
Finland	33	23	9	5.7	<0.1	0.1	<36	0.1	<0.1	..	..
France	36	27	6	6.7	0.3	0.4	32	0.2	0.1	..	..
Gabon	..	..	501	5.0	0.9	5.2	58	1.4	3.5	..	..
Gambia, The	17	1	269	4.3	0.1	2.0	58	0.9	2.4	..	..
Georgia	57	6	107	7.5	<0.1	0.1	43	<0.1	<0.1	..	..
Germany	37	26	5	8.9	0.1	0.1	18	0.1	<0.1	..	..
Ghana	7	1	201	4.3	0.3	1.8	59	0.5	1.3	..	..
Greece	63	39	5	6.0	0.1	0.1	31	0.1	0.1	..	..
Guatemala	24	4	62	8.6	0.1	0.8	33	0.5	0.3	..	..
Guinea	..	..	318	4.3	1.1	1.3	59	0.4	0.9	35	10
Guinea-Bissau	..	..	229	3.9	0.3	2.5	60	0.8	2.0	..	..
Haiti	..	..	238	7.2	1.3	1.9	60	0.6	1.3	42	37
Honduras	..	..	58	9.1	1.1	0.8	32	0.3	0.2	..	7

Health risk factors and future challenges

	Prevalence of smoking		Incidence of tuberculosis	Prevalence of diabetes	Prevalence of HIV[a]					Condom use	
					Total % of population ages 15–49		Female % of total population with HIV	Youth % of population ages 15–24		% of population ages 15–24	
	% of adults		per 100,000 people	% of population ages 20–79				Male	Female	Male	Female
	Male 2006	Female 2006	2009	2010	1990	2009	2009	2009	2009	2004–09[b]	2004–09[b]
Hungary	45	35	16	6.4	0.1	<0.1	<33	<0.1	<0.1	..	..
India	28	1	168	7.8	0.1	0.3	39	0.1	0.1	15	6
Indonesia	66[f]	5[f]	189	4.8	<0.1	0.2	30	0.1	<0.1	..	..
Iran, Islamic Rep.	24	2	19	8.0	<0.1	0.2	29	<0.1	<0.1	..	..
Iraq	29	3	64	10.2	..	..	..	..	..	..	..
Ireland	34	28	9	5.2	<0.1	0.2	29	0.1	0.1	..	..
Israel	31	18	5	6.5	<0.1	0.2	29	0.1	<0.1	..	..
Italy	34	19	6	5.9	0.3	0.3	33	<0.1	<0.1	..	..
Jamaica	18	8	7	10.6	2.1	1.7	33	1.0	0.7	74	66
Japan	42	13	21	5.0	<0.1	<0.1	34	<0.1	<0.1	..	..
Jordan	59	10	6	10.1	..	..	..	..	..	..	..
Kazakhstan	43	9	163	5.8	<0.1	0.1	60	0.1	0.2	..	..
Kenya	23	1	305	3.5	3.9	6.3	59	1.8	4.1	64	40
Korea, Dem. Rep.	58	..	345	5.3	..	..	..	..	..	..	..
Korea, Rep.	53	6	90	7.9	<0.1	<0.1	31	<0.1	<0.1	..	..
Kosovo	..	..	..	..	..	..	..	..	..	..	..
Kuwait	36	4	35	14.6	..	..	..	..	..	..	..
Kyrgyz Republic	46	2	159	5.2	<0.1	0.3	29	0.1	0.1	..	..
Lao PDR	60	13	89	5.6	<0.1	0.2	42	0.1	0.2	..	..
Latvia	53	24	45	7.6	<0.1	0.7	30	0.2	0.1	..	..
Lebanon	31	7	15	7.8	<0.1	0.1	31	0.1	<0.1	..	..
Lesotho	..	..	634	3.9	0.8	23.6	62	5.4	14.2	44	26
Liberia	10	..	288	4.7	0.3	1.5	61	0.3	0.7	19	9
Libya	..	..	40	9.0	..	..	..	..	..	..	..
Lithuania	50	22	71	7.6	<0.1	0.1	<33	<0.1	<0.1	..	..
Macedonia, FYR	..	..	23	6.9	..	..	..	..	..	..	..
Madagascar	..	..	261	3.2	0.2	0.2	31	0.1	0.1	6	3
Malawi	17	2	304	2.3	7.2	11.0	59	3.1	6.8	32	9
Malaysia	49	2	83	11.6	0.1	0.5	11	0.1	<0.1	..	..
Mali	13	1	324	4.2	0.4	1.0	62	0.2	0.5	29	4
Mauritania	24	1	330	4.8	0.2	0.7	31	0.4	0.3	..	..
Mauritius	34	1	22	16.2	<0.1	1.0	29	0.3	0.2	..	..
Mexico	36	12	17	10.8	0.4	0.3	27	0.2	0.1	..	..
Moldova	45	5	178	7.6	<0.1	0.4	42	0.1	0.1	55	22
Mongolia	46	6	224	1.6	<0.1	<0.1	<29	<0.1	<0.1	..	..
Morocco	27	0	92	8.3	<0.1	0.1	32	0.1	0.1	..	..
Mozambique	19	1	409	4.0	1.2	11.5	61	3.1	8.6	..	..
Myanmar	40	13	404	3.2	0.2	0.6	35	0.3	0.3	..	..
Namibia	22	8	727	4.4	1.6	13.1	59	2.3	5.8	78	55
Nepal	30	28	163	3.9	0.2	0.4	33	0.2	0.1	24	8
Netherlands	33	28	8	5.3	0.1	0.2	30	0.1	<0.1	..	..
New Zealand	22	20	8	5.2	0.1	0.1	<37	<0.1	<0.1	..	..
Nicaragua	..	..	44	10.0	<0.1	0.2	31	0.1	0.1	..	..
Niger	..	..	181	3.9	0.1	0.8	53	0.2	0.5	14	1
Nigeria	8	0	295	4.7	1.3	3.6	59	1.2	2.9	50	36
Norway	30	30	6	3.6	<0.1	0.1	30	<0.1	<0.1	..	..
Oman	20	0	13	13.4	<0.1	0.1	<33	<0.1	<0.1	..	..
Pakistan	30	3	231	9.1	<0.1	0.1	29	0.1	<0.1	..	..
Panama	..	..	48	9.6	0.2	0.9	31	0.4	0.3	..	..
Papua New Guinea	..	..	250	3.0	<0.1	0.9	58	0.3	0.8	..	..
Paraguay	33	14	47	4.9	<0.1	0.3	31	0.2	0.1	..	..
Peru	..	..	113	6.2	0.4	0.4	25	0.2	0.1	..	..
Philippines	50	11	280	7.7	<0.1	<0.1	30	<0.1	<0.1	..	..
Poland	30	38	24	7.6	<0.1	0.1	31	<0.1	0.2	..	..
Portugal	34	15	30	9.7	0.1	0.6	31	0.3	0.2	..	..
Puerto Rico	..	..	2	10.6	..	..	..	..	..	..	..
Qatar	..	..	49	15.4	<0.1	0.1	<50	<0.1	<0.1	..	..

	Prevalence of smoking		Incidence of tuberculosis	Prevalence of diabetes	Prevalence of HIV[a]					Condom use	
	% of adults		per 100,000 people	% of population ages 20–79	Total % of population ages 15–49		Female % of total population with HIV	Youth % of population ages 15–24		% of population ages 15–24	
	Male	Female						Male	Female	Male	Female
	2006	2006	2009	2010	1990	2009	2009	2009	2009	2004–09[b]	2004–09[b]
Romania	46	24	125	6.9	<0.1	0.1	30	0.1	<0.1	..	..
Russian Federation	60[g]	22[g]	106	7.6	<0.1	1.0	49	0.2	0.3	..	..
Rwanda	..	..	376	1.6	5.2	2.9	61	1.3	1.9	19	5
Saudi Arabia	22	3	18	16.8	..	..	..	..	..	..	..
Senegal	13	1	282	4.7	0.2	0.9	59	0.3	0.7	48	5
Serbia	40	27	21	6.9	0.1	0.1	24	0.1	0.1	..	..
Sierra Leone	..	..	644	4.4	<0.1	1.6	60	0.6	1.5	20	9
Singapore	34	5	36	10.2	<0.1	0.1	30	<0.1	<0.1	..	..
Slovak Republic	41	20	9	6.4	<0.1	<0.1	<17	<0.1	<0.1	..	..
Slovenia	32	21	12	7.7	<0.1	<0.1	<29	<0.1	<0.1	..	..
Somalia	..	..	285	3.0	0.1	0.7	47	0.4	0.6	..	..
South Africa	27	8	971	4.5	0.7	17.8	62	4.5	13.6	..	..
Spain	37	27	17	6.6	0.4	0.4	24	0.2	0.1	..	..
Sri Lanka	27	0	66	10.9	<0.1	<0.1	<32	<0.1	<0.1	..	..
Sudan	25	2	119	4.2	0.1	1.1	58	0.5	1.3	..	..
Swaziland	21	2	1,257	4.2	2.3	25.9	58	6.5	15.6	66	44
Sweden	17	23	6	5.2	0.1	0.1	31	<0.1	<0.1	..	..
Switzerland	32	23	5	8.9	0.2	0.4	32	0.2	0.1	..	..
Syrian Arab Republic	40	..	21	10.8	..	..	..	..	..	..	..
Tajikistan	..	..	202	5.0	<0.1	0.2	30	<0.1	<0.1	..	..
Tanzania	20	2	183	3.2	4.8	5.6	59	1.7	3.9	36	13
Thailand	40	2	137	7.1	1.0	1.3	40	..	..	..	..
Timor-Leste	..	..	498	3.5	..	..	..	..	..	..	..
Togo	..	..	446	4.3	0.6	3.2	59	0.9	2.2	..	..
Trinidad and Tobago	..	..	23	11.7	0.2	1.5	33	1.0	0.7	..	..
Tunisia	53	6	24	9.3	<0.1	<0.1	<37	<0.1	<0.1	..	..
Turkey	48[e]	15[e]	29	8.0	<0.1	<0.1	30	<0.1	<0.1	..	..
Turkmenistan	..	..	67	5.3	..	..	..	..	..	..	..
Uganda	17	2	293	2.2	10.2	6.5	58	2.3	4.8	36	13
Ukraine	65	24	101	7.6	0.1	1.1	49	0.2	0.3	64	43
United Arab Emirates	24	2	4	18.7	..	..	..	..	..	..	..
United Kingdom	26	24	12	3.6	0.1	0.2	31	0.2	0.1	..	..
United States	25	19	4	10.3	0.5	0.6	25	0.3	0.2	..	..
Uruguay	39	29	22	5.7	0.1	0.5	32	0.3	0.2	..	..
Uzbekistan	23	3	128	5.2	<0.1	0.1	29	<0.1	<0.1	..	..
Venezuela, RB	32	27	33	6.5	..	..	..	..	..	..	..
Vietnam	41	2	200	3.5	<0.1	0.4	30	0.1	0.1	16	8
West Bank and Gaza	..	..	19	8.6	..	..	..	..	..	..	..
Yemen, Rep.	28	6	54	3.0	..	..	..	..	..	..	..
Zambia	17	2	433	4.0	12.7	13.5	57	4.2	8.9	39	17
Zimbabwe	28	2	742	4.1	10.1	14.3	60	3.3	6.9	52	9
World	**39 w**	**8 w**	**137 w**	**6.4 w**	**0.3**	**0.8 w**	**37 w**	**0.4 w**	**0.7 w**	**.. w**	**.. w**
Low income	28	4	294	4.4	2.0	2.7	46	0.9	2.0	..	..
Middle income	42	6	138	6.3	0.2	0.6				..	..
Lower middle income	43	3	147	6.0	0.2	0.4				..	..
Upper middle income	38	16	101	7.5	0.3	1.4	36	0.5	1.2	..	..
Low & middle income	40	6	161	6.1	0.3	0.9	39			..	..
East Asia & Pacific	56	4	136	4.6	0.1	0.2	..	0.1	0.1	..	..
Europe & Central Asia	58	22	89	7.3	0.1	0.6	42	0.1	0.2	..	..
Latin America & Carib.	27	15	45	7.4	0.4	0.5	..	0.2	0.2	..	..
Middle East & N. Africa	28	2	39	9.1	0.1	0.1	28	0.1	0.1	..	..
South Asia	30	2	180	7.8	0.1	0.3	36	0.1	0.1	15	6
Sub-Saharan Africa	14	2	342	3.8	2.4	5.4	58	1.5	3.8	36	19
High income	33	21	14	7.9	0.2	0.3	28	0.2	0.1	..	..
Euro area	37	25	9	7.1	0.2	0.3	27	0.1	0.1	..	..

a. See plausible bounds in the database and original source. b. Data are for the most recent year available. c. Data are for 2010. d. Includes Hong Kong SAR, China. e. Data are for 2008. f. Data are for 2007. g. Data are for 2009.

The limited availability of data on health status is a major constraint in assessing the health situation in developing countries. Surveillance data are lacking for many major public health concerns. Estimates of prevalence and incidence are available for some diseases but are often unreliable and incomplete. National health authorities differ widely in capacity and willingness to collect or report information. To compensate for this and improve reliability and international comparability, the World Health Organization (WHO) prepares estimates in accordance with epidemiological models and statistical standards.

Smoking is the most common form of tobacco use and the prevalence of smoking is therefore a good measure of the tobacco epidemic (Corrao and others 2000). Tobacco use causes heart and other vascular diseases and cancers of the lung and other organs. Given the long delay between starting to smoke and the onset of disease, the health impact of smoking in developing countries will increase rapidly only in the next few decades. Because the data present a one-time estimate, with no information on intensity or duration of smoking, and because the definition of adult varies, the data should be used with caution.

Tuberculosis is one of the main causes of adult deaths from a single infectious agent in developing countries. In developed countries tuberculosis has reemerged largely as a result of cases among immigrants. Since tuberculosis incidence cannot be directly measured, estimates are obtained by eliciting expert opinion or are derived from measurements of prevalence or mortality. These estimates include uncertainty intervals, which are not shown in the table, which are available at http://data.worldbank.org or from the original source.

Diabetes, an important cause of ill health and a risk factor for other diseases in developed countries, is spreading rapidly in developing countries. Highest among the elderly, prevalence rates are rising among younger and productive populations in developing countries. Economic development has led to the spread of Western lifestyles and diet to developing countries, resulting in a substantial increase in diabetes. Without effective prevention and control programs, diabetes will likely continue to increase. Data are estimated based on sample surveys.

Adult HIV prevalence rates reflect the rate of HIV infection in each country's population. Low national prevalence rates can be misleading, however. They often disguise epidemics that are initially concentrated in certain localities or population groups and threaten to spill over into the wider population. In many developing countries most new infections occur in young adults, with young women especially vulnerable.

Data on HIV are from the Joint United Nations Programme on HIV/AIDS (UNAIDS) *Global Report: UNAIDS Report Global AIDS Epidemic 2010*. Changes in procedures and assumptions for estimating the data and better coordination with countries have resulted in improved estimates of HIV and AIDS. For example, improved software was used to model the course of HIV epidemics and their impacts, making full use of information on HIV prevalence trends from surveillance data as well as survey data. The software explicitly includes the effect of antiretroviral therapy (ART) when calculating HIV incidence and models reduced infectivity among people receiving ART, which is having an increasing impact on HIV prevalence, with HIV-positive people living longer lives. The software also allows for changes in urbanization over time—important because prevalence is higher in urban areas and because many countries have seen rapid urbanization over the past two decades.

The estimates include plausible bounds, not shown in the table, which reflect the certainty associated with each of the estimates. The bounds are available at http://data.worldbank.org or from the original source.

Data on condom use are from household surveys and refer to condom use at last intercourse. However, condoms are not as effective at preventing the transmission of HIV unless used consistently. Some surveys have asked directly about consistent use, but the question is subject to recall and other biases. Caution should be used in interpreting the data.

For indicators from household surveys, the year in the table refers to the survey year. For more information, consult the original sources.

• **Prevalence of smoking** is the adjusted and age-standardized prevalence estimate of smoking among adults. The age range varies but in most countries is 18 and older or 15 and older. • **Incidence of tuberculosis** is the number of new and relapse cases of tuberculosis (all types) per 100,000 people. • **Prevalence of diabetes** refers to the percentage of people ages 20–79 who have type 1 or type 2 diabetes. • **Prevalence of HIV** is the percentage of people who are infected with HIV. Total and youth rates are percentages of the relevant age group. Female rate is as a percentage of the total population living with HIV. • **Condom use** is the percentage of the population ages 15–24 who used a condom at last intercourse in the last 12 months.

Data sources

Data on smoking are from the WHO's *Report on the Global Tobacco Epidemic 2009: Implementing Smoke-Free Environments*. Data on tuberculosis are from the WHO's *Global Tuberculosis Control Report 2010*. Data on diabetes are from the International Diabetes Federation's *Diabetes Atlas*, 3rd edition. Data on prevalence of HIV are from UNAIDS's Global Report: UNAIDS *Report on the Global AIDS Epidemic 2010*. Data on condom use are from Demographic and Health Surveys by Macro International.

	Life expectancy at birth		Infant mortality rate		Under-five mortality rate		Child mortality rate		Adult mortality rate		Survival to age 65	
	years		per 1,000 live births		per 1,000		per 1,000 Male Female		per 1,000 Male Female		% of cohort Male Female	
	1990	2009	1990	2009	1990	2009	2004–09[a,b]	2004–09[a,b]	2005–09[a]	2005–09[a]	2009	2009
Afghanistan	41	44	167	134	250	199	..	..	435	409	34	36
Albania	72	77	41	14	51	15	3	1	98	51	82	90
Algeria	67	73	51	29	61	32	..	..	118	98	78	82
Angola	42	48	153	98	258	161	..	..	406	350	37	44
Argentina	72	76	25	13	28	14	..	..	163	75	75	87
Armenia	68	74	48	20	56	22	8	3	162	79	73	85
Australia	77	82	8	4	9	5	..	..	82	47	88	93
Austria	76	80	8	3	9	4	..	..	99	50	85	93
Azerbaijan	65	70	78	30	98	34	9	5	178	108	69	79
Bangladesh	54	67	102	41	148	52	16	20	206	172	66	71
Belarus	71	70	20	11	24	12	..	..	330	115	54	83
Belgium	76	81	9	4	10	5	..	..	108	62	85	92
Benin	54	62	111	75	184	118	64	65	207	170	62	67
Bolivia	59	66	84	40	122	51	18	20	232	172	64	72
Bosnia and Herzegovina	67	75	21	13	23	14	..	..	132	61	79	89
Botswana	64	55	46	43	60	57	..	..	487	505	42	43
Brazil	66	73	46	17	56	21	..	..	226	118	67	81
Bulgaria	72	73	14	8	18	10	..	..	213	91	72	87
Burkina Faso	47	53	110	91	201	166	..	..	331	277	46	52
Burundi	46	51	114	101	189	166	65	65	382	346	42	47
Cambodia	55	62	85	68	117	88	20	20	288	218	56	64
Cameroon	55	51	91	95	148	154	73	72	401	398	43	45
Canada	77	81	7	5	8	6	..	..	92	55	87	92
Central African Republic	49	47	115	112	175	171	74	82	452	426	36	41
Chad	51	49	120	124	201	209	96	101	358	317	42	47
Chile	74	79	18	7	22	9	..	..	129	64	81	90
China	68[c]	73[c]	37	17	46	19	..	..	147	88	76	83
Hong Kong SAR, China	77	83	..	..	..	..	..	..	198	92	72	84
Colombia	68	73	28	16	35	19	4	3	397	348	38	44
Congo, Dem. Rep.	48	48	126	126	199	199	70	64	373	350	46	50
Congo, Rep.	59	54	67	81	104	128	49	43	111	59	82	90
Costa Rica	76	79	16	10	18	11	..	..	305	271	53	59
Côte d'Ivoire	58	58	105	83	152	119	..	..	144	57	77	90
Croatia	72	76	11	5	13	5	1	1	108	68	83	89
Cuba	75	79	10	4	14	6	..	..	143	65	79	90
Czech Republic	71	77	10	3	12	4	..	..	107	67	83	89
Denmark	75	79	8	3	9	4	..	..	206	134	70	79
Dominican Republic	68	73	48	27	62	32	6	4	164	86	76	86
Ecuador	69	75	41	20	53	24	5	5	161	105	72	80
Egypt, Arab Rep.	63	70	66	18	90	21	5	5	285	121	63	81
El Salvador	66	71	48	15	62	17	..	..	374	281	46	58
Eritrea	48	60	92	39	150	55	..	..	283	92	64	87
Estonia	69	75	13	4	17	6	..	..	334	293	49	54
Ethiopia	47	56	124	67	210	104	56	56	129	57	84	93
Finland	75	80	6	3	7	3	..	..	121	55	85	93
France[d]	77	81	7	3	9	4	..	..	317	276	56	61
Gabon	61	61	68	52	93	69	..	..	324	264	48	55
Gambia, The	51	56	104	78	153	103	46	39	195	77	70	84
Georgia	70	72	41	26	47	29	5	4	102	54	85	92
Germany	75	80	7	4	9	4	..	..	323	286	51	56
Ghana	57	57	76	47	120	69	38	28	92	37	86	94
Greece	77	80	9	3	11	3	..	..	232	127	68	80
Guatemala	62	71	57	33	76	40	..	..	252	195	55	63
Guinea	48	58	137	88	231	142	89	86	398	347	39	45
Guinea-Bissau	44	48	142	115	240	193	110	88	284	223	57	64
Haiti	55	61	105	64	152	87	33	36	170	119	73	80
Honduras	66	72	43	25	55	30	8	9	75	33	88	94

	Life expectancy at birth (years)		Infant mortality rate (per 1,000 live births)		Under-five mortality rate (per 1,000)		Child mortality rate (per 1,000) Male 2004–09[a,b]	Female 2004–09[a,b]	Adult mortality rate (per 1,000) Male 2005–09[a]	Female 2005–09[a]	Survival to age 65 (% of cohort) Male 2009	Female 2009
	1990	2009	1990	2009	1990	2009						
Hungary	69	74	15	5	17	6	..	..	250	104	68	86
India	58	64	84	50	118	66	9	12	256	170	59	68
Indonesia	62	71	56	30	86	39	13	12	162	113	72	81
Iran, Islamic Rep.	65	72	55	26	73	31	..	..	142	96	75	82
Iraq	65	68	42	35	53	44	6	7	211	105	66	81
Ireland	75	80	8	4	9	4	..	..	88	56	87	92
Israel	77	82	10	3	11	4	..	..	86	48	87	93
Italy	77	81	8	3	10	4	..	..	82	43	86	94
Jamaica	71	72	28	26	33	31	5	6	221	116	70	81
Japan	79	83	5	2	6	3	..	..	86	43	88	95
Jordan	67	73	32	22	39	25	3	7	159	109	74	82
Kazakhstan	68	68	51	26	60	29	5	4	400	151	47	76
Kenya	60	55	64	55	99	84	27	25	392	403	47	48
Korea, Dem. Rep.	70	67	23	26	45	33	..	..	169	117	67	77
Korea, Rep.	71	80	8	5	9	5	..	..	105	41	83	93
Kosovo	68	70	..	..	..	..	..	..	..	..	..	..
Kuwait	75	78	14	8	17	10	..	..	84	51	85	90
Kyrgyz Republic	68	67	63	32	75	37	8	4	257	122	61	78
Lao PDR	54	65	108	46	157	59	..	..	222	180	63	70
Latvia	69	73	12	7	16	8	..	..	311	114	64	86
Lebanon	69	72	33	11	40	12	..	..	150	98	74	83
Lesotho	59	45	74	61	93	84	22	19	666	633	25	29
Liberia	49	59	165	80	247	112	62	64	251	206	56	63
Libya	68	75	32	17	36	19	..	..	144	89	75	84
Lithuania	71	73	12	5	15	6	..	..	346	116	60	86
Macedonia, FYR	71	74	32	10	36	11	2	1	132	79	77	85
Madagascar	51	61	102	41	167	58	30	31	266	216	57	63
Malawi	49	54	129	69	218	110	52	54	434	395	44	49
Malaysia	70	75	16	6	18	6	..	..	147	84	76	85
Mali	43	49	139	101	250	191	117	114	386	355	39	42
Mauritania	56	57	81	74	129	117	53	44	304	236	50	59
Mauritius	69	73	21	15	24	17	..	..	230	114	67	81
Mexico	71	75	36	15	45	17	..	..	137	76	79	87
Moldova	67	69	30	15	37	17	7	4	279	125	60	78
Mongolia	61	67	73	24	101	29	11	10	284	180	58	71
Morocco	64	72	69	33	89	38	9	11	144	94	74	83
Mozambique	43	48	155	96	232	142	..	..	489	469	36	40
Myanmar	59	62	84	54	118	71	..	..	250	188	58	66
Namibia	62	62	49	34	73	48	24	19	346	334	55	59
Nepal	54	67	99	39	142	48	21	18	196	171	67	71
Netherlands	77	81	7	4	8	4	..	..	81	59	87	92
New Zealand	75	80	9	5	11	6	..	..	87	58	87	91
Nicaragua	64	73	52	22	68	26	..	..	201	113	71	81
Niger	42	52	144	76	305	160	138	135	344	295	44	49
Nigeria	45	48	126	86	212	138	91	93	404	380	40	42
Norway	77	81	7	3	9	3	..	..	82	50	88	92
Oman	70	76	37	9	48	12	..	..	96	71	83	87
Pakistan	61	67	101	71	130	87	14	22	162	131	68	72
Panama	72	76	25	16	31	23	..	..	136	72	79	87
Papua New Guinea	55	61	67	52	91	68	..	..	344	251	50	61
Paraguay	68	72	34	19	42	23	..	..	170	123	73	80
Peru	66	73	62	19	78	21	13	4	162	100	74	83
Philippines	65	72	41	26	59	33	10	9	153	99	74	83
Poland	71	76	15	6	17	7	..	..	209	80	73	89
Portugal	74	79	12	3	15	4	..	..	124	53	83	92
Puerto Rico	75	79	..	..	..	..	..	..	130	52	80	91
Qatar	70	76	17	10	19	11	..	..	109	100	82	83

	Life expectancy at birth (years)		Infant mortality rate (per 1,000 live births)		Under-five mortality rate (per 1,000)		Child mortality rate (per 1,000) Male 2004–09[a,b]	Female 2004–09[a,b]	Adult mortality rate (per 1,000) Male 2005–09[a]	Female 2005–09[a]	Survival to age 65 (% of cohort) Male 2009	Female 2009
	1990	2009	1990	2009	1990	2009						
Romania	70	73	25	10	32	12	..	..	192	82	70	86
Russian Federation	69	69	23	11	27	12	..	..	396	147	47	78
Rwanda	33	51	103	70	171	111	69	55	397	351	40	47
Saudi Arabia	68	73	35	18	43	21	3	4	137	88	76	85
Senegal	52	56	73	51	151	93	43	39	325	266	48	55
Serbia	71	74	25	6	29	7	4	3	153[e]	82[e]	75	86
Sierra Leone	40	48	166	123	285	192	67	61	498	464	30	34
Singapore	74	81	6	2	8	3	..	..	80	41	86	93
Slovak Republic	71	75	13	6	15	7	..	..	195	73	72	88
Slovenia	73	79	9	2	10	3	..	..	149	57	81	92
Somalia	45	50	109	109	180	180	53	54	368	315	42	47
South Africa	61	52	48	43	62	62	..	..	575	517	32	41
Spain	77	82	8	4	9	4	..	..	106	44	86	94
Sri Lanka	70	74	23	13	28	15	..	..	192	76	71	86
Sudan	53	58	78	69	124	108	38	30	302	257	53	59
Swaziland	60	46	67	52	92	73	32	30	605	638	30	29
Sweden	78	81	6	2	7	3	..	..	78	48	88	93
Switzerland	77	82	7	4	8	4	..	..	78	46	88	93
Syrian Arab Republic	68	74	30	14	36	16	5	3	120	81	79	86
Tajikistan	63	67	91	52	117	61	18	13	208	137	64	74
Tanzania	51	56	99	68	162	108	56	52	369	355	49	52
Thailand	69	69	27	12	32	14	..	..	291	170	63	77
Timor-Leste	46	62	138	48	184	56	..	..	259	224	58	63
Togo	58	63	89	64	150	98	55	43	238	197	61	68
Trinidad and Tobago	69	70	30	31	34	35	5	8	236	139	63	78
Tunisia	70	74	40	18	50	21	..	..	122	70	78	87
Turkey	65	72	69	19	84	20	6	6	149	83	74	84
Turkmenistan	63	65	81	42	99	45	..	..	298	151	55	73
Uganda	48	53	111	79	184	128	75	62	401	399	44	47
Ukraine	70	69	18	13	21	15	4	1	385	142	53	80
United Arab Emirates	73	78	15	7	17	7	..	..	76	63	86	89
United Kingdom	76	80	8	5	10	6	..	..	100	61	86	91
United States	75	79	9	7	11	8	..	..	141	81	84	89
Uruguay	73	76	21	11	24	13	..	..	139	63	77	89
Uzbekistan	67	68	61	32	74	36	11	7	237	135	62	75
Venezuela, RB	71	74	27	15	32	18	..	..	175	91	74	84
Vietnam	65	75	39	20	55	24	5	4	134	88	78	85
West Bank and Gaza	68	74	35	25	43	30	3	3	125	90	78	84
Yemen, Rep.	54	63	88	51	125	66	10	11	247	198	60	67
Zambia	51	46	108	86	179	141	66	55	528	518	33	35
Zimbabwe	61	45	54	56	81	90	21	21	687	664	24	27
World	**65 w**	**69 w**	**64 w**	**43 w**	**92 w**	**61 w**	**.. w**	**.. w**	**213 w**	**151 w**	**68 w**	**77 w**
Low income	52	57	108	76	171	118	52	49	312	275	52	58
Middle income	64	69	61	38	85	51	..	..	201	134	67	77
Lower middle income	63	68	66	43	93	57	..	..	201	136	67	75
Upper middle income	68	72	41	19	51	22	..	..	201	122	67	81
Low & middle income	63	67	70	47	100	66	..	..	216	153	65	74
East Asia & Pacific	67	72	41	21	55	26	..	..	158	99	74	82
Europe & Central Asia	68	70	43	19	52	21	..	..	286	123	59	80
Latin America & Carib.	68	74	42	19	52	23	..	..	190	103	72	83
Middle East & N. Africa	64	71	57	27	76	33	..	..	155	104	73	81
South Asia	58	64	89	55	125	71	11	15	242	169	61	69
. Sub-Saharan Africa	50	53	109	81	181	130	68	65	390	358	44	48
High income	75	80	10	6	12	7	..	..	120	63	84	91
Euro area	76	81	8	3	9	4	..	..	107	52	85	93

a. Data are for the most recent year available. b. Refers to a survey year. Values were estimated directly from surveys and cover the 5 or 10 years preceding the survey. c. Includes Taiwan, China. d. Excludes the French overseas departments of French Guiana, Guadeloupe, Martinique, and Réunion. e. Includes Kosovo.

About the data

Mortality rates for different age groups (infants, children, and adults) and overall mortality indicators (life expectancy at birth or survival to a given age) are important indicators of health status in a country. Because data on the incidence and prevalence of diseases are frequently unavailable, mortality rates are often used to identify vulnerable populations. And they are among the indicators most frequently used to compare socioeconomic development across countries.

The main sources of mortality data are vital registration systems and direct or indirect estimates based on sample surveys or censuses. A "complete" vital registration system—covering at least 90 percent of vital events in the population—is the best source of age-specific mortality data. Where reliable age-specific mortality data are available, life expectancy at birth is directly estimated from the life table constructed from age-specific mortality data.

But complete vital registration systems are fairly uncommon in developing countries. Thus estimates must be obtained from sample surveys or derived by applying indirect estimation techniques to registration, census, or survey data (see table 2.17 and *Primary data documentation*). Survey data are subject to recall error, and surveys estimating infant deaths require large samples because households in which a birth has occurred during a given year cannot ordinarily be preselected for sampling. Indirect estimates rely on model life tables that may be inappropriate for the population concerned. Because life expectancy at birth is estimated using infant mortality data and model life tables for many developing countries, similar reliability issues arise for this indicator. Extrapolations based on outdated surveys may not be reliable for monitoring changes in health status or for comparative analytical work.

Estimates of infant and under-five mortality tend to vary by source and method for a given time and place. Years for available estimates also vary by country, making comparison across countries and over time difficult. To make infant and under-five mortality estimates comparable and to ensure consistency across estimates by different agencies, the Inter-agency Group for Child Mortality Estimation, comprising the United Nations Children's Fund (UNICEF), the United Nations Population Division, the World Health Organization (WHO), the World Bank, and other universities and research institutes, developed and adopted a statistical method that uses all available information to reconcile differences. The method uses the weighted least squares method to fit a regression line to the relationship between mortality rates and their reference dates and then extrapolate the trend to the present. (For further discussion of childhood mortality estimates, see UNICEF, WHO, World Bank, and United Nations Population Division 2010; for a graphic presentation and detailed background data, see www.childmortality.org.)

Infant and child mortality rates are higher for boys than for girls in countries in which parental gender preferences are insignificant. Child mortality captures the effect of gender discrimination better than infant mortality does, as malnutrition and medical interventions are more important in this age group. Where female child mortality is higher, as in some countries in South Asia, girls probably have unequal access to resources. Child mortality rates in the table are not compatible with infant mortality and under-five mortality rates because of differences in methodology and reference year. Child mortality data were estimated directly from surveys and cover the 10 years preceding the survey. In addition to estimates from Demographic Health Surveys, estimates derived from Multiple Indicator Cluster Surveys have been added to the table; they cover the 5 years preceding the survey.

Rates for adult mortality and survival to age 65 come from life tables. Adult mortality rates increased notably in a dozen countries in Sub-Saharan Africa between 1995–2000 and 2000–05 and in several countries in Europe and Central Asia during the first half of the 1990s. In Sub-Saharan Africa the increase stems from AIDS-related mortality and affects both sexes, though women are more affected. In Europe and Central Asia the causes are more diverse (high prevalence of smoking, high-fat diet, excessive alcohol use, stressful conditions related to the economic transition) and affect men more.

The percentage of a hypothetical cohort surviving to age 65 reflects both child and adult mortality rates. Like life expectancy, it is a synthetic measure based on current age-specific mortality rates. It shows that even in countries where mortality is high, a certain share of the current birth cohort will live well beyond the life expectancy at birth, while in low-mortality countries close to 90 percent will reach at least age 65.

Annual data series from the United Nations are interpolated based on five-year estimates and thus may not reflect actual events.

Definitions

• **Life expectancy at birth** is the number of years a newborn infant would live if prevailing patterns of mortality at the time of its birth were to stay the same throughout its life. • **Infant mortality rate** is the number of infants dying before reaching one year of age, per 1,000 live births in a given year. • **Under-five mortality rate** is the probability per 1,000 that a newborn baby will die before reaching age 5, if subject to current age-specific mortality rates. • **Child mortality rate** is the probability per 1,000 of dying between ages 1 and 5—that is, the probability of a 1-year-old dying before reaching age 5—if subject to current age-specific mortality rates. • **Adult mortality rate** is the probability per 1,000 of dying between the ages of 15 and 60—that is, the probability of a 15-year-old dying before reaching age 60—if subject to current age-specific mortality rates between those ages. • **Survival to age 65** refers to the percentage of a hypothetical cohort of newborn infants that would survive to age 65, if subject to current age-specific mortality rates.

Data sources

Data on infant and under-five mortality are from *Levels and Trends in Child Mortality, Report 2010* by the Inter-agency Group for Child Mortality Estimation, covered in *About the data*, based mainly on household surveys, censuses, and vital registration data, supplemented by the World Bank's Human Development Network estimates based on vital registration and sample registration data. Data on child mortality are from Demographic and Health Surveys by Macro International and World Bank calculations based on infant and under-five mortality from Multiple Indicator Cluster Surveys by UNICEF. Data on survival to age 65 and most data on adult mortality are linear interpolations of five-year data from *World Population Prospects: The 2008 Revision*. Remaining data on adult mortality are from the Human Mortality Database by the University of California, Berkeley, and the Max Planck Institute for Demographic Research (www.mortality.org). Data on life expectancy at birth are World Bank calculations based on male and female data from *World Population Prospects: The 2008 Revision* (for more than half of countries, most of them developing countries), census reports and other statistical publications from national statistical offices, Eurostat's Demographic Statistics, and the U.S. Bureau of the Census International Data Base.

ENVIRONMENT

Environmental sustainability

The United Nations Conference on the Human Environment, held in Stockholm in 1972, drew worldwide attention to the growing impact of human activity on the environment and to the need for sustainable management of environmental resources. Twenty years later the United Nations Conference on Environment and Development in Rio de Janeiro adopted a comprehensive plan of action for a sustainable future. That plan later became part of the Millennium Declaration, with some of the more important targets included in Millennium Development Goal 7: ensuring environmental sustainability.

Understanding climate change is a central issue for environmental sustainability and for development policy. Public policy should help people cope with new or worsened risks, facilitate investments in clean energy technologies, and adapt land and water management to better protect a threatened natural environment while feeding an expanding and more prosperous population.

The World Bank Group plays a key role in financing climate change adaptation and mitigation. Since 1999 it has led in forming carbon markets, which are now directing funds toward clean low-carbon development. At the UN Climate Change Conference in Copenhagen in 2009, it launched the Carbon Partnership Facility, the latest addition in a family of carbon funds and facilities. The facility assists developing countries in pursuing low-carbon growth and in accelerating reductions of greenhouse gas emissions; it uses carbon finance innovatively to leverage capital for both public and private investment in clean technologies. At the UN Framework Convention on Climate Change conference in Cancun in 2010, the World Bank joined global leaders and policymakers in the Roadmap for Action: Agriculture, Food Security, and Climate Change, which outlines concrete actions linking agricultural investments and policies with the transition to climate-smart growth. It highlights a "triple-win" approach: increasing farm productivity and incomes, making agriculture more resilient to climate change, and making agriculture part of the solution to climate change by sequestering more carbon in the soil and biomass.

Environmental indicators

Monitoring progress toward the environment targets of the Millennium Development Goals and measuring the complexity of environmental phenomena require new measurement frameworks and new data. This year's *Environment* section of *World Development Indicators* includes a new table on natural resource rents that measures human dependence on environmental assets. And in recognition of the mainstreaming of green accounting, the data on adjusted net savings—gross savings adjusted for capital depreciation, resource depletion, pollution damage, and human capital investment—have been moved to the *Economy* section (table 4.11), joining a new table showing corresponding adjustments to national income (table 4.10). Together these tables provide a clearer picture of the impact of the environment on the long-term sustainability of economic growth.

Other indicators in this section describe land use, agriculture and food production, forests and biodiversity, water resources, energy use and efficiency, urbanization, environmental impacts, government commitments, and threatened species. Where possible, the indicators come from international sources to facilitate cross-country comparison. Important to keep in mind is that country coverage may be uneven, ecosystems span national boundaries, and natural resource use may differ locally, regionally, and globally. For example, greenhouse gas emissions and climate change may be measured globally, but their effects are also manifested locally, shaping people's lives and opportunities.

Measuring dependence on environmental assets

Accounting for the contribution of natural resources to economic output is important in building an analytical framework for sustainable development. The extraction or harvesting of natural resources can produce substantial rents—revenues above the cost of extracting them—which are calculated as the difference between the price of a commodity and the average cost of producing it. This is done by estimating the world price of units of specific commodities and subtracting estimates of the average unit costs of extraction or harvesting. These unit rents are then multiplied by the physical quantities countries extract or harvest to determine the rents for each commodity, as a share of gross national income (GNI).

Table 3.16 presents data on rents from oil, gas, coal, and other mineral production and from forests as a share of GNI. In some countries those rents, especially from fossil fuels and minerals, account for 30–50 percent of GNI (figure 3a)—almost 70 percent in Iraq. Rents from nonrenewable resources—fossil fuels and minerals—as well as rents from overharvesting of forests indicate the liquidation of a country's capital stock. When countries use such rents to support current consumption rather than to invest in new capital to replace what is being used up, they are, in effect, borrowing against their future.

For resource-rich countries—where resource rents are at least 5 percent of GNI—transforming nonrenewable natural capital into other forms of wealth is a major development challenge. Figure 3b plots adjusted net savings—net national savings plus education expenditure, minus energy depletion, mineral depletion, net forest depletion, and carbon dioxide and particulate emissions damage—against energy and mineral rents for resource-rich countries. Countries with negative adjusted net savings, such as Angola and Republic of Congo, are depleting natural capital without replacing it and becoming poorer over time. Countries with positive adjusted net savings, such as Botswana and China, are adding to wealth and well-being and reducing natural resource depletion by investing in other types of capital. (See *About the data* for tables 4.10 and 4.11.)

Mainstreaming environmental and wealth accounting in country statistical systems

There has been considerable effort over the past 20 years to develop statistical methods for environmental accounting (a broad framework that includes natural capital accounting) under the aegis of the United Nations Statistical Commission. The commission established the London Group on Environmental Accounting and later a high-level body, the UN Committee of Experts on Environmental and Economic Accounting, to develop methodological guidelines. In 2003 the United Nations and other international organizations produced the *Handbook of National Accounting: Integrated Environmental and Economic Accounting* (UN and others 2003). It is currently under revision and will become part of the statistical standard, like the System of National Accounts, which establishes methodology for national accounts.

Other institutions and individual scholars have also done work on wealth accounting over

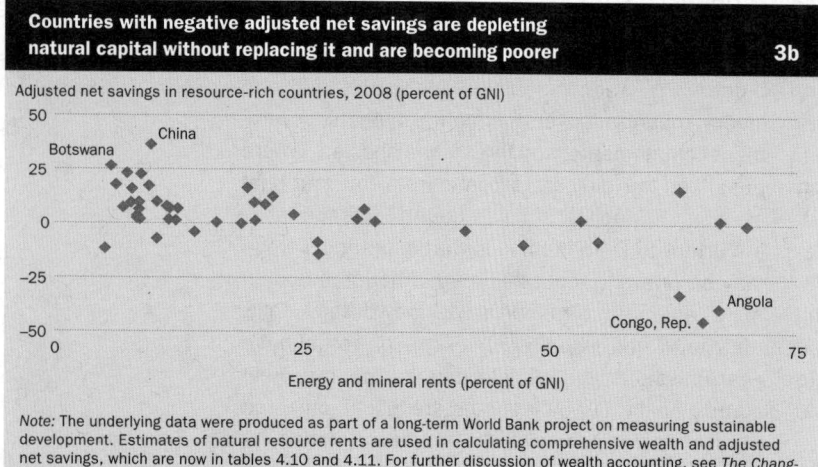

The 10 countries with the highest natural resource rents are primarily oil and gas producers 3a

Natural resource rents, 2009 (percent of GNI)   ■ Forest ■ Minerals ☐ Coal ■ Natural gas ☐ Oil

Source: Table 3.16.

Countries with negative adjusted net savings are depleting natural capital without replacing it and are becoming poorer 3b

Adjusted net savings in resource-rich countries, 2008 (percent of GNI)

Energy and mineral rents (percent of GNI)

Note: The underlying data were produced as part of a long-term World Bank project on measuring sustainable development. Estimates of natural resource rents are used in calculating comprehensive wealth and adjusted net savings, which are now in tables 4.10 and 4.11. For further discussion of wealth accounting, see *The Changing Wealth of Nations* (World Bank 2011).
Source: World Development Indicators data files.

the past 20 years. Official statistical offices in more than 30 countries have institutionalized wealth accounting, and 16 of them regularly compile at least one type of natural resource asset account. The majority of countries focus on mineral and energy assets, but some, notably Australia and Norway, construct more comprehensive accounts for natural capital.

National statistical offices, the academic community, and nongovernmental organizations have produced empirical work on natural capital accounting nationally, regionally, and locally. Together, these studies have deepened our knowledge of wealth accounting, leading to better understanding of the prospects for growth and poverty reduction, especially in resource-rich countries.

Stiglitz, Sen, and Fitoussi (2009) offer further support for the comprehensive wealth approach to sustainable development. They propose ways to modify and extend conventional national accounts to provide a more accurate and useful guide for policy. An important part of the proposed changes, to better reflect the sustainability of economies, is comprehensive wealth. They recommend compiling accounts for all assets (natural, human-made, and human capital) and changes in those assets, which correspond to the components of adjusted net savings.

3.1 | Rural population and land use

	Rural population			Land area	Land use								
	% of total		average annual % growth	thousand sq. km	Forest area		% of land area Permanent cropland		Arable land		Arable land hectares per 100 people			
	1990	2009	1990–2009	2009	1990	2010	1990	2008	1990	2008	1990	2008		
Afghanistan	82	76	2.1	652.2	2.1	2.1	0.2	0.2	12.1	11.9	42.6	26.9		
Albania	64	53	−1.2	27.4	28.8	28.3	4.6	3.2	21.1	22.3	17.6	19.4		
Algeria	48	34	−0.1	2,381.7	0.7	0.6	0.2	0.4	3.0	3.1	28.0	21.8		
Angola	63	42	0.8	1,246.7	48.9	46.9	0.4	0.2	2.3	2.7	27.2	18.9		
Argentina	13	8	−1.6	2,736.7	12.7	10.7	0.4	0.4	9.6	11.7	81.2	80.2		
Armenia	33	36	−0.2	28.5	12.2	9.2	2.1	1.9	14.9	15.8	1.5	14.6		
Australia	15	11	−0.1	7,682.3	20.1	19.4	0.0	0.0	6.2	5.7	280.7	205.4		
Austria	34	33	0.2	82.5	45.8	47.1	1.0	0.8	17.3	16.7	18.5	16.5		
Azerbaijan	46	48	1.3	82.6	11.2	11.3	3.7	2.8	20.5	22.5	0.8	21.4		
Bangladesh	80	72	1.2	130.2	11.5	11.1	2.5	6.1	70.0	60.7	7.9	4.9		
Belarus	34	26	−1.7	202.9	38.4	42.5	0.9	0.6	30.0	27.2	0.5	57.0		
Belgium	4	3	−1.3	30.3	22.4	22.4	0.5[a]	0.8	23.3[a]	27.9	0.2	7.9		
Benin	66	58	2.7	110.6	52.1	41.2	0.9	2.7	14.6	23.1	33.7	29.4		
Bolivia	44	34	0.6	1,083.3	58.0	52.8	0.1	0.2	1.9	3.3	31.5	37.1		
Bosnia and Herzegovina	61	52	−1.5	51.2	43.2	42.7	2.9	1.8	16.6	19.7	3.5	26.7		
Botswana	58	40	−0.1	566.7	24.2	20.0	0.0	0.0	0.7	0.4	31.1	13.0		
Brazil	25	14	−1.7	8,459.4	68.0	61.4	0.8	0.9	6.0	7.2	33.9	31.8		
Bulgaria	34	29	−1.6	108.6	30.1	36.2	2.7	1.7	34.9	28.2	44.2	40.2		
Burkina Faso	86	80	2.7	273.6	25.0	20.6	0.2	0.2	12.9	23.0	39.9	41.4		
Burundi	94	89	1.7	25.7	11.3	6.7	14.0	15.2	36.2	35.0	16.4	11.1		
Cambodia	87	78	1.6	176.5	73.3	57.2	0.6	0.9	20.9	22.1	38.1	26.8		
Cameroon	59	42	0.7	472.7	51.4	42.1	2.6	2.5	12.6	12.6	48.6	31.2		
Canada	23	20	0.1	9,093.5	34.1	34.1	0.7	0.8	5.0	5.0	163.7	135.4		
Central African Republic	63	61	2.0	623.0	37.2	36.3	0.1	0.1	3.1	3.1	65.6	44.5		
Chad	79	73	2.8	1,259.2	10.4	9.2	0.0	0.0	2.6	3.4	53.6	39.4		
Chile	17	11	−0.7	743.5	20.5	21.8	0.3	0.6	3.8	1.7	21.2	7.5		
China	73	56	−0.5	9,327.5	16.8	22.2	0.8	1.5	13.3	11.6	10.9	8.2		
Hong Kong SAR, China	1	0	..	1.0	..	..	..	..	..	..	..	..		
Colombia	32	25	0.5	1,109.5	56.3	54.5	1.5	1.5	3.0	1.6	10.0	4.1		
Congo, Dem. Rep.	72	65	2.5	2,267.1	70.7	68.0	0.5	0.3	2.9	3.0	18.0	10.4		
Congo, Rep.	46	38	1.2	341.5	66.5	65.6	0.1	0.2	1.4	1.4	19.6	13.6		
Costa Rica	49	36	0.5	51.1	50.2	51.0	4.9	5.9	5.1	3.9	8.4	4.4		
Côte d'Ivoire	60	51	1.8	318.0	32.1	32.7	11.0	13.4	7.6	8.8	19.3	13.6		
Croatia	46	43	−0.8	56.0	33.1	34.3	2.0	1.5	21.7	15.4	2.4	19.4		
Cuba	27	24	−0.2	106.4	19.2	27.0	4.2	3.8	31.6	33.5	32.0	31.9		
Czech Republic	25	27	0.4	77.3	34.0	34.4	3.1	3.1	41.1	39.2	32.1	29.0		
Denmark	15	13	−0.4	42.4	10.5	12.8	0.2	0.2	60.4	56.6	49.8	43.7		
Dominican Republic	45	30	−0.4	48.3	40.8	40.8	9.3	10.3	18.6	16.6	12.2	8.0		
Ecuador	45	34	0.0	248.4	49.9	39.7	4.8	5.1	5.8	5.0	15.6	9.2		
Egypt, Arab Rep.	57	57	2.0	995.5	0.0	0.1	0.4	0.8	2.3	2.8	4.0	3.4		
El Salvador	51	39	−0.6	20.7	18.2	13.9	12.5	11.1	26.5	33.1	10.3	11.2		
Eritrea	84	79	2.1	101.0	16.0	15.2	0.0	0.0	4.9	6.6	0.1	13.6		
Estonia	29	31	−0.5	42.4	49.3	52.3	0.3	0.2	26.3	14.1	3.5	44.6		
Ethiopia	87	83	2.5	1,000.0	15.1	12.3	0.5	0.9	10.0	13.6	1.4	16.9		
Finland	39	36	0.1	303.9	71.9	72.9	0.0	0.0	7.4	7.4	45.5	42.4		
France	26	22	−0.2	547.7	26.5	29.1	2.2	2.0	32.9	33.3	31.7	29.3		
Gabon	31	15	−1.5	257.7	85.4	85.4	0.6	0.6	1.1	1.3	31.8	22.4		
Gambia, The	62	43	1.5	10.0	44.2	48.0	0.5	0.5	18.2	39.0	20.3	23.5		
Georgia	45	47	−1.0	69.5	40.0	39.5	4.8	1.7	11.4	6.7	1.0	10.9		
Germany	27	26	0.0	348.6	30.8	31.8	1.3	0.6	34.3	34.2	15.1	14.5		
Ghana	64	49	1.1	227.5	32.7	21.7	6.6	12.5	11.9	19.3	18.0	18.8		
Greece	41	39	0.2	128.9	25.6	30.3	8.3	8.7	22.5	16.3	28.5	18.7		
Guatemala	59	51	1.6	107.2	44.3	34.1	4.5	8.8	12.1	12.4	14.6	9.7		
Guinea	72	65	2.1	245.7	29.6	26.6	2.0	2.8	3.3	9.8	13.1	24.4		
Guinea-Bissau	72	70	2.3	28.1	78.8	71.9	4.2	8.9	8.9	10.7	24.5	19.0		
Haiti	72	52	0.1	27.6	4.2	3.7	11.6	10.9	28.3	36.3	11.0	10.1		
Honduras	60	52	1.5	111.9	72.7	46.4	3.2	3.7	13.1	9.1	29.8	13.9		

Rural population and land use

	Rural population			Land area	Land use								
	% of total		average annual % growth	thousand sq. km	Forest area		Permanent cropland		Arable land		Arable land hectares per 100 people		
					% of land area								
	1990	2009	1990–2009	2009	1990	2010	1990	2008	1990	2008	1990	2008	
Hungary	34	32	−0.5	89.6	20.0	22.6	2.6	2.2	56.2	51.0	48.7	45.6	
India	75	70	1.3	2,973.2	21.5	23.0	2.2	3.8	54.8	53.2	19.2	13.9	
Indonesia	69	47	−0.6	1,811.6	65.4	52.1	6.5	8.3	11.2	12.1	11.4	9.7	
Iran, Islamic Rep.	44	31	−0.3	1,628.6	6.8	6.8	0.8	1.1	9.3	10.5	27.9	23.7	
Iraq	30	34	3.2	437.4	1.8	1.9	0.7	0.6	13.3	11.9	30.7	16.9	
Ireland	43	38	0.7	68.9	6.7	10.7	0.0	0.0	15.1	16.0	29.7	24.9	
Israel	10	8	1.7	21.6	6.1	7.1	4.1	3.6	15.9	13.9	7.4	4.1	
Italy	33	32	0.1	294.1	25.8	31.1	10.1	9.0	30.6	24.2	15.9	11.9	
Jamaica	51	47	0.2	10.8	31.9	31.1	9.2	10.2	11.0	11.5	5.0	4.7	
Japan	37	33	−0.4	364.5	68.4	68.5	1.3	0.9	13.1	11.8	3.9	3.4	
Jordan	28	22	2.1	88.2	1.1	1.1	0.8	0.9	2.0	1.7	5.6	2.6	
Kazakhstan	44	42	−0.4	2,699.7	1.3	1.2	0.1	0.0	13.0	8.4	0.3	144.8	
Kenya	82	78	2.5	569.1	6.5	6.1	0.8	0.9	8.8	9.3	21.3	13.7	
Korea, Dem. Rep.	42	37	0.3	120.4	68.1	47.1	1.5	1.7	19.0	22.4	11.4	11.3	
Korea, Rep.	26	18	−1.2	96.9	64.5	64.2	1.6	1.9	19.8	16.0	4.6	3.2	
Kosovo	..	..	..	10.9[b]	..	..	..	..	..	27.6	..	16.8	
Kuwait	2	2	0.3	17.8	0.2	0.3	0.1	0.2	0.2	0.6	0.2	0.4	
Kyrgyz Republic	62	64	1.1	191.8	4.4	5.0	0.4	0.4	6.9	6.7	1.2	24.2	
Lao PDR	85	68	1.0	230.8	75.0	68.2	0.3	0.4	3.5	5.4	19.0	20.1	
Latvia	31	32	−0.7	62.2	51.1	53.9	0.4	0.1	27.2	18.8	2.0	51.6	
Lebanon	17	13	0.4	10.2	12.8	13.4	11.9	13.9	17.9	14.1	6.2	3.4	
Lesotho	86	74	0.5	30.4	1.3	1.4	0.1	0.1	10.4	11.7	19.8	17.3	
Liberia	55	39	1.4	96.3	51.2	44.9	1.6	2.3	3.6	4.2	16.2	10.5	
Libya	24	22	1.6	1,759.5	0.1	0.1	0.2	0.2	1.0	1.0	41.4	27.8	
Lithuania	32	33	−0.5	62.7	31.0	34.5	0.7	0.4	46.0	29.7	1.5	55.4	
Macedonia, FYR	42	33	−1.0	25.2	35.9	39.6	2.2	1.4	23.8	17.1	3.0	21.2	
Madagascar	76	70	2.5	581.5	23.5	21.6	1.0	1.0	4.7	5.1	24.1	15.4	
Malawi	88	81	2.0	94.1	41.4	34.4	1.4	1.3	23.9	37.2	23.8	23.6	
Malaysia	50	29	−0.7	328.6	68.1	62.3	16.0	17.6	5.2	5.5	9.4	6.7	
Mali	77	67	1.5	1,220.2	11.5	10.2	0.1	0.1	1.7	4.0	23.7	38.2	
Mauritania	60	59	2.5	1,030.7	0.4	0.2	0.0	0.0	0.4	0.4	20.1	12.4	
Mauritius	56	58	1.1	2.0	19.2	17.2	3.0	2.0	49.3	42.9	9.5	6.9	
Mexico	29	23	0.1	1,944.0	36.2	33.3	1.0	1.4	12.5	12.8	29.2	23.3	
Moldova	53	59	−0.5	32.9	9.7	11.7	12.8	9.2	52.8	55.4	61.8	50.1	
Mongolia	43	43	0.9	1,553.6	8.1	7.0	0.0	0.0	0.9	0.5	35.1	32.2	
Morocco	52	44	0.5	446.3	11.3	11.5	1.6	2.1	19.5	18.0	25.5	25.5	
Mozambique	79	62	1.5	786.4	55.2	49.6	0.3	0.3	4.4	5.7	23.4	20.1	
Myanmar	75	67	0.4	653.5	60.0	48.6	0.8	1.7	14.6	16.2	46.6	21.4	
Namibia	72	63	1.5	823.3	10.6	8.9	0.0	0.0	0.8	1.0	46.6	37.6	
Nepal	91	82	1.7	143.4	33.7	25.4	0.5	0.8	16.0	16.4	12.0	8.2	
Netherlands	31	18	−2.5	33.8	10.2	10.8	0.9	1.0	26.0	31.6	5.9	6.5	
New Zealand	15	13	0.5	263.3	29.3	31.4	0.2	0.3	10.0	1.7	76.7	10.6	
Nicaragua	48	43	1.2	120.3	37.5	25.9	1.6	1.9	10.8	15.8	31.4	33.5	
Niger	85	83	3.4	1,266.7	1.5	1.0	0.0	0.0	8.7	11.4	139.6	98.6	
Nigeria	65	51	1.2	910.8	18.9	9.9	2.8	3.3	32.4	41.2	30.3	24.8	
Norway	28	23	−0.5	305.5	30.0	32.9	0.0	0.0	2.8	2.8	20.3	17.7	
Oman	34	28	1.3	309.5	0.0	0.0	0.1	0.1	0.1	0.2	1.9	2.0	
Pakistan	69	63	1.9	770.9	3.3	2.2	0.6	1.1	26.6	26.4	19.0	12.2	
Panama	46	26	−1.1	74.3	51.0	43.7	2.1	2.0	6.7	7.4	20.7	16.1	
Papua New Guinea	85	88	2.7	452.9	69.6	63.4	1.2	1.4	0.4	0.6	4.6	4.1	
Paraguay	51	39	0.7	397.3	53.3	44.3	0.2	0.3	5.3	10.6	49.7	67.3	
Peru	31	29	1.1	1,280.0	54.8	53.1	0.3	0.6	2.7	2.9	16.1	12.7	
Philippines	51	34	−0.1	298.2	22.0	25.7	14.8	16.8	18.4	17.8	8.8	5.9	
Poland	39	39	0.0	304.2	29.2	30.7	1.1	1.3	47.3	41.3	37.7	33.0	
Portugal	52	40	−1.0	91.5	36.4	37.8	8.5	6.4	25.6	11.5	23.7	9.9	
Puerto Rico	28	1	−15.0	8.9	32.4	62.2	5.6	4.2	7.3	6.8	1.8	1.5	
Qatar	8	4	2.7	11.6	0.0	0.0	0.1	0.3	0.9	1.1	2.1	1.0	

	Rural population			Land area	Land use							
	% of total		average annual % growth	thousand sq. km	Forest area		Permanent cropland	% of land area	Arable land		Arable land hectares per 100 people	
	1990	2009	1990–2009	2009	1990	2010	1990	2008	1990	2008	1990	2008
Romania	47	46	−0.5	229.9	27.8	28.6	2.6	1.6	41.2	37.9	40.7	40.5
Russian Federation	27	27	−0.1	16,376.9	49.4	49.4	0.1	0.1	8.1	7.4	0.0	85.7
Rwanda	95	81	1.0	24.7	12.9	17.6	12.4	11.3	35.7	52.3	12.3	13.3
Saudi Arabia	23	18	0.8	2,000.0 c	0.5	0.5	0.0	0.1	1.7	1.7	20.9	13.9
Senegal	61	57	2.4	192.5	48.6	44.0	0.2	0.3	16.1	18.2	41.0	28.7
Serbia	50	48	−0.4	88.4	26.2	30.7	..	3.4	..	37.4	4.5	44.9
Sierra Leone	67	62	1.3	71.6	43.5	38.1	1.9	1.9	6.8	25.1	11.9	32.3
Singapore	0	0	..	0.7	3.0	2.9	1.5	0.3	1.5	0.7	0.0	0.0
Slovak Republic	44	43	0.1	48.1	40.0	40.2	1.0	0.5	32.5	28.7	31.0	25.6
Slovenia	50	52	0.3	20.1	59.0	62.2	1.8	1.3	9.9	9.0	1.8	9.0
Somalia	70	63	1.1	627.3	13.2	10.8	0.0	0.0	1.6	1.6	15.5	11.2
South Africa	48	39	0.7	1,214.5	6.8	4.7	0.7	0.8	11.1	11.9	38.2	29.7
Spain	25	23	0.5	499.1	27.7	36.4	9.7	9.6	30.7	25.0	39.5	27.4
Sri Lanka	83	85	1.0	62.7	37.5	29.7	15.9	15.1	14.4	19.9	5.3	6.2
Sudan	73	56	0.9	2,376.0	32.1	29.4	0.0	0.1	5.4	8.7	47.2	50.1
Swaziland	77	75	1.5	17.2	27.4	32.7	0.7	0.8	10.5	10.3	20.8	15.2
Sweden	17	15	−0.1	410.3	66.5	68.7	0.0	0.0	6.9	6.4	33.2	28.5
Switzerland	27	27	0.7	40.0	28.8	31.0	0.6	0.6	10.3	10.2	6.1	5.3
Syrian Arab Republic	51	45	2.0	183.6	2.0	2.7	4.0	5.3	26.6	25.6	38.4	22.8
Tajikistan	68	74	1.8	140.0	2.9	2.9	0.9	1.0	6.1	5.3	1.0	10.8
Tanzania	81	74	2.4	885.8	46.8	37.7	1.1	1.5	10.2	10.8	35.4	22.6
Thailand	71	66	0.6	510.9	38.3	37.1	6.1	7.1	34.2	29.8	30.9	22.6
Timor-Leste	79	72	1.8	14.9	65.0	49.9	3.9	4.4	7.4	10.8	14.9	14.6
Togo	70	57	1.7	54.4	12.6	5.3	1.7	3.1	38.6	45.2	53.5	38.1
Trinidad and Tobago	92	86	0.2	5.1	47.0	44.1	6.8	4.3	7.0	4.9	3.0	1.9
Tunisia	42	33	0.0	155.4	4.1	6.5	12.5	14.2	18.7	18.2	35.7	27.5
Turkey	41	31	0.0	769.6	12.6	14.7	3.9	3.8	32.0	28.0	43.9	29.2
Turkmenistan	55	51	1.4	469.9	8.8	8.8	0.1	0.1	2.9	3.9	36.7	36.7
Uganda	89	87	3.1	197.1	24.1	15.2	9.4	11.4	25.4	28.7	28.2	17.8
Ukraine	33	32	−0.8	579.3	16.0	16.8	1.9	1.6	57.6	56.1	0.1	70.2
United Arab Emirates	21	22	5.0	83.6	2.9	3.8	0.2	2.4	0.4	0.8	1.9	1.4
United Kingdom	11	10	−0.2	241.9	10.8	11.9	0.3	0.2	27.4	24.8	11.6	9.8
United States	25	18	−0.6	9,147.4	32.4	33.2	0.2	0.3	20.3	18.6	74.4	56.0
Uruguay	11	8	−1.6	175.0	5.3	10.0	0.3	0.2	7.2	9.4	40.6	49.2
Uzbekistan	60	63	1.9	425.4	7.2	7.7	0.9	0.8	10.5	10.1	21.8	15.7
Venezuela, RB	16	6	−2.9	882.1	59.0	52.5	0.9	0.7	3.2	3.1	14.3	9.7
Vietnam	80	72	0.9	310.1	28.8	44.5	3.2	10.0	16.4	20.3	8.1	7.3
West Bank and Gaza	32	28	3.0	6.0	1.5	1.5	19.1	19.5	18.1	16.8	..	2.8
Yemen, Rep.	79	69	2.7	528.0	1.0	1.0	0.2	0.6	2.9	2.4	12.4	5.6
Zambia	61	64	2.9	743.4	71.0	66.5	0.0	0.0	3.1	3.2	29.0	18.7
Zimbabwe	71	62	0.2	386.9	57.3	40.4	0.3	0.3	7.5	9.6	27.6	29.9
World	57 w	50 w	0.6 w	129,561.8 s	32.1 w	31.1 w	1.1 w	1.1 w	9.0 w	10.7 w	22.2 w	20.7 w
Low income	78	71	1.8	17,303.9	31.9	28.2	0.7	0.9	6.4	8.6	20.1	17.9
Middle income	62	52	0.4	78,352.9	33.9	32.8	1.4	1.4	8.4	11.0	17.7	18.2
Lower middle income	70	59	0.5	30,841.8	26.2	25.9	1.8	2.4	14.9	16.0	15.8	13.1
Upper middle income	33	25	−0.3	47,511.0	38.8	37.2	1.0	0.7	4.2	7.8	24.5	37.4
Low & middle income	64	55	0.7	95,656.7	33.5	31.9	1.2	1.3	8.1	10.6	18.0	18.2
East Asia & Pacific	71	55	−0.3	15,853.7	29.0	29.6	2.2	3.1	12.1	11.3	12.0	9.3
Europe & Central Asia	37	36	0.0	22,686.7	38.4	38.6	0.4	0.4	2.1	10.4	12.1	58.8
Latin America & Carib.	29	21	−0.3	20,116.2	51.6	47.0	0.9	1.0	6.6	7.4	30.3	26.4
Middle East & N. Africa	48	42	1.3	8,643.6	2.4	2.4	0.8	1.0	5.9	6.0	22.4	16.0
South Asia	75	70	1.4	4,771.2	16.6	17.1	1.8	2.9	42.6	41.5	18.0	12.8
Sub-Saharan Africa	72	63	1.9	23,585.4	31.3	28.0	0.8	1.0	6.2	8.5	28.4	24.4
High income	27	23	−0.3	33,905.1	28.1	28.9	0.7	0.7	11.8	10.9	41.5	34.0
Euro area	29	27	−0.1	2,552.0	33.6	37.3	4.8	4.2	26.7	24.4	22.1	18.9

a. Includes Luxembourg. b. Data are from national sources. c. Provisional estimate.

About the data

With more than 3 billion people, including 70 percent of the world's poor people, living in rural areas, adequate indicators to monitor progress in rural areas are essential. However, few indicators are disaggregated between rural and urban areas (for some that are, see tables 2.7, 3.5, and 3.11). The table shows indicators of rural population and land use. Rural population is approximated as the midyear nonurban population. While a practical means of identifying the rural population, it is not precise (see box 3.1a for further discussion).

The data in the table show that land use patterns are changing. They also indicate major differences in resource endowments and uses among countries. True comparability of the data is limited, however, by variations in definitions, statistical methods, and quality of data. Countries use different definitions of rural and urban population and land use. The Food and Agriculture Organization of the United Nations (FAO), the primary compiler of the data, occasionally adjusts its definitions of land use categories and revises earlier data. Because the data reflect changes in reporting procedures as well as actual changes in land use, apparent trends should be interpreted cautiously.

Satellite images show land use that differs from that of ground-based measures in area under cultivation and type of land use. Moreover, land use data in some countries (India is an example) are based on reporting systems designed for collecting tax revenue. With land taxes no longer a major source of government revenue, the quality and coverage of land use data have declined. Data on forest area may be particularly unreliable because of irregular surveys and differences in definitions (see *About the data* for table 3.4). The forest area statistics released by FAO between 1948 and 1963 were based mostly on data from country questionnaires. Remote sensing, statistical modeling, and expert analysis of country surveys have been applied since 1980 to improve the forest coverage estimates. FAO's *Global Forest Resources Assessment 2010* covers 233 countries and is the most comprehensive assessment of forests, forestry, and the benefits of forest resources in both scope and number of countries and people involved. It examines status and trends for about 90 variables on the extent, condition, uses, and values of forests and other wooded land.

Definitions

• **Rural population** is calculated as the difference between the total population and the urban population (see *Definitions* for tables 2.1 and 3.11). • **Land area** is a country's total area, excluding area under inland water bodies and national claims to the continental shelf and to exclusive economic zones. In most cases the definition of inland water bodies includes major rivers and lakes. (See table 1.1 for the total surface area of countries.) Variations from year to year may be due to updated or revised data rather than to change in area. • **Land use** is a country's total area, excluding area under inland water bodies and national claims to the continental shelf and to exclusive economic zones. In most cases definitions of inland water bodies includes major rivers and lakes. (See table 1.1 for the total surface area of countries.) Variations from year to year may be due to updated or revised data rather than to change in area. • **Forest area** is land under natural or planted stands of trees of at least 5 meters in situ, whether productive or not, and excludes tree stands in agricultural production systems (for example, in fruit plantations and agroforestry systems) and trees in urban parks and gardens. • **Permanent cropland** is land cultivated with crops that occupy the land for long periods and need not be replanted after each harvest, such as cocoa, coffee, and rubber. Land under flowering shrubs, fruit trees, nut trees, and vines is included, but land under trees grown for wood or timber is not. • **Arable land** is land defined by the FAO as under temporary crops (double-cropped areas are counted once), temporary meadows for mowing or pasture, land under market or kitchen gardens, and land temporarily fallow. Land abandoned as a result of shifting cultivation is excluded.

What is rural? Urban? | 3.1a

The rural population identified in table 3.1 is approximated as the difference between total population and urban population, calculated using the urban share reported by the United Nations Population Division. There is no universal standard for distinguishing rural from urban areas, and any urban-rural dichotomy is an oversimplification (see *About the data* for table 3.11). The two distinct images—isolated farm, thriving metropolis—represent poles on a continuum. Life changes along a variety of dimensions, moving from the most remote forest outpost through fields and pastures, past tiny hamlets, through small towns with weekly farm markets, into intensively cultivated areas near large towns and small cities, eventually reaching the center of a megacity. Along the way access to infrastructure, social services, and nonfarm employment increase, and with them population density and income. Because rurality has many dimensions, for policy purposes the rural-urban dichotomy presented in tables 3.1, 3.5, and 3.11 is inadequate. A 2005 World Bank Policy Research Paper proposes an operational definition of rurality based on population density and distance to large cities (Chomitz, Buys, and Thomas 2005). The report argues that these criteria are important gradients along which economic behavior and appropriate development interventions vary substantially. Where population densities are low, markets of all kinds are thin, and the unit cost of delivering most social services and many types of infrastructure is high. Where large urban areas are distant, farm-gate or factory-gate prices of outputs will be low and input prices will be high, and it will be difficult to recruit skilled people to public service or private enterprises. Thus, low population density and remoteness together define a set of rural areas that face special development challenges.

Using these criteria and the Gridded Population of the World (CIESIN 2005), the authors' estimates of the rural population for Latin America and the Caribbean differ substantially from those in table 3.1. Their estimates range from 13 percent of the population, based on a population density of less than 20 people per square kilometer, to 64 percent, based on a population density of more than 500 people per square kilometer. Taking remoteness into account, the estimated rural population would be 13–52 percent. The estimate for Latin America and the Caribbean in table 3.1 is 21 percent.

Data sources

Data on urban population shares used to estimate rural population are from the United Nations Population Division's *World Urbanization Prospects: The 2009 Revision,* and data on total population are World Bank estimates. Data on land area, permanent cropland, and arable land are from the FAO's electronic files. The FAO gathers these data from national agencies through annual questionnaires and by analyzing the results of national agricultural censuses. Data on forest area are from the FAO's *Global Forest Resources Assessment 2010.*

	Agricultural land[a]			Average annual precipitation	Land under cereal production		Fertilizer consumption		Agricultural employment		Agricultural machinery	
	% of land area		% irrigated	millimeters	thousand hectares		% of fertilizer production	kilograms per hectare of arable land	% of total employment		Tractors per 100 sq. km of arable land	
	1990	2008	2008	2008	1990	2009	2008	2008	1990	2008	1990	2008
Afghanistan	58	58	5.8	327	2,253.0	3,188.0	146.9	3.2	..	..	0.2	1.2
Albania	41	43	10.0	1,485	321.0	146.2	..	38.4	..	58.0	212.4	121.9
Algeria	16	17	2.1	89	2,366.0	3,176.3	226.4	6.8	..	..	129.1	139.6
Angola	46	46	..	1,010	775.1	1,752.1	..	8.3	5.1	..	..	..
Argentina	47	49	..	591	9,015.0	8,031.6	305.9	38.8	0.4	0.8	100.2	..
Armenia	41	61	8.9	562	162.8	169.3	..	18.1	..	46.2	345.5	327.8
Australia	60	54	0.4	534	13,428.8	19,805.6	161.3	33.9	5.6	3.4	..	..
Austria	42	38	1.4	1,110	948.4	838.0	..	109.6	7.9	5.6	2,373.7	2,390.3
Azerbaijan	53	58	30.0	447	627.0	1,113.8	..	20.9	30.9	38.7	194.8	116.1
Bangladesh	77	71	62.0	2,666	11,140.6	12,032.5	141.1	164.5	64.9	48.1	2.4	3.9
Belarus	46	44	0.7	618	2,603.0	2,418.0	22.0	237.4	..	..	206.9	89.8
Belgium	44[b]	45	1.7	847	368.2[b]	345.0	..	..	3.1	1.8	1,523.3[b]	1,127.1
Benin	21	31	..	1,039	643.9	976.1	..	0.0	..	..	1.0	..
Bolivia	33	34	..	1,146	582.5	897.0	..	5.5	1.2	..	24.8	..
Bosnia and Herzegovina	43	42	..	1,028	304.1	295.8	..	11.9	..	..	235.3	..
Botswana	46	46	0.0	416	205.1	85.7	..	..	..	29.9	140.5	134.8
Brazil	29	31	..	1,782	18,512.4	20,220.4	313.5	165.7	22.8	19.3	143.8	129.2
Bulgaria	56	48	1.4	608	2,055.3	1,829.2	68.4	81.8	18.5	7.5	135.8	173.5
Burkina Faso	35	45	..	748	2,528.9	4,178.6	..	3.9	..	..	2.4	..
Burundi	83	85	..	1,274	217.5	222.0	..	2.2	..	..	1.8	..
Cambodia	25	31	..	1,904	1,900.0	2,888.0	..	22.7	..	..	3.3	11.8
Cameroon	19	19	..	1,604	657.6	1,223.3	..	8.6	..	..	0.9	..
Canada	7	7	..	537	21,547.9	14,863.2	25.1	56.9	4.1	2.5	164.8	162.5
Central African Republic	8	8	..	1,343	110.5	264.3	..	..	..	..	..	..
Chad	38	39	..	322	1,075.4	2,486.7	..	..	83.0	..	..	..
Chile	21	21	5.6	1,522	823.5	567.5	102.8	588.8	19.3	12.3	127.6	425.9
China	57	56	10.2	..	93,555.2	88,592.8	99.2	468.0	53.4	..	66.6	277.1
Hong Kong SAR, China	..	..	..	..	..	..	..	..	0.9	0.2	..	..
Colombia	41	38	..	2,612	1,742.8	1,186.0	278.7	492.4	1.4	18.4	96.8	..
Congo, Dem. Rep.	10	10	..	1,543	1,863.6	1,977.3	..	1.0	..	..	..	..
Congo, Rep.	31	31	..	1,646	9.6	27.5	..	1.1	..	..	..	..
Costa Rica	45	35	..	2,926	92.6	74.4	..	707.5	25.9	13.2	25.9	..
Côte d'Ivoire	60	64	..	1,348	1,400.0	853.5	..	18.9	..	..	19.9	..
Croatia	43	23	0.7	1,113	592.7	562.7	70.7	387.6	..	12.8	35.2	..
Cuba	63	62	..	1,335	230.5	419.9	554.4	39.7	24.9	18.7	226.2	203.2
Czech Republic	55	55	0.2	677	1,613.6	1,544.4	117.1	135.1	7.7	3.3	264.6	276.4
Denmark	66	63	9.5	703	1,570.3	1,497.7	..	128.3	5.5	2.7	634.7	486.3
Dominican Republic	53	52	..	1,410	122.2	158.2	..	..	20.3	14.5	25.9	..
Ecuador	28	30	10.2	2,087	802.2	819.1	..	214.1	7.5	8.3	54.2	..
Egypt, Arab Rep.	3	4	..	51	2,283.4	3,129.8	68.5	723.6	39.0	31.2	249.6	372.1
El Salvador	68	75	2.1	1,724	425.4	363.0	..	118.4	10.2	18.9	..	..
Eritrea	73	75	..	384	329.3	492.3	..	0.0	..	..	5.0	..
Estonia	32	19	..	626	453.7	316.4	65.4	100.3	21.0	3.7	455.3	604.7
Ethiopia	31	35	0.5	848	4,040.3	8,748.0	..	7.7	..	8.6	..	..
Finland	8	8	2.8	536	1,212.6	1,133.1	77.4	134.2	8.8	4.5	916.5	784.7
France	56	53	5.4	867	9,060.4	9,388.2	153.8	146.1	5.6	3.0	800.0	635.3
Gabon	20	20	..	1,831	14.4	20.5	..	14.1	41.6	..	..	..
Gambia, The	64	66	..	836	90.0	295.2	..	2.6	64.7	..	..	..
Georgia	46	36	4.0	1,026	248.5	193.8	13.0	37.1	..	53.4	295.6	594.0
Germany	52	49	..	700	6,944.9	6,908.4	55.7	160.4	4.1	2.2	1,309.4	646.0
Ghana	55	69	..	1,187	853.0	1,570.7	..	6.4	62.0	..	7.1	4.5
Greece	72	36	27.4	652	1,470.4	1,174.8	472.4	143.8	23.9	11.4	744.2	1,196.9
Guatemala	40	39	..	1,996	718.5	855.9	..	92.0	12.9	33.2	..	..
Guinea	49	56	..	1,651	729.6	1,863.0	..	1.5	..	..	45.0	..
Guinea-Bissau	51	58	..	1,577	109.3	152.6	..	..	..	..	0.8	..
Haiti	58	65	..	1,440	351.5	437.0	..	..	65.6	..	2.6	..
Honduras	30	28	..	1,976	465.1	382.6	..	107.7	50.1	39.2	30.9	..

	Agricultural land[a]			Average annual precipitation	Land under cereal production		Fertilizer consumption		Agricultural employment		Agricultural machinery	
	% of land area		% irrigated	millimeters	thousand hectares		% of fertilizer production	kilograms per hectare of arable land	% of total employment		Tractors per 100 sq. km of arable land	
	1990	2008	2008	2008	1990	2009	2008	2008	1990	2008	1990	2008
Hungary	72	64	1.4	589	2,778.6	2,883.6	227.2	94.3	18.2	4.5	97.7	261.9
India	61	60	..	1,083	102,536.5	99,880.0	190.6	153.5	..	..	60.7	..
Indonesia	25	27	16.3	2,702	13,660.5	17,044.2	117.6	189.1	55.9	41.2	2.2	..
Iran, Islamic Rep.	38	30	19.0	228	9,468.1	9,095.5	148.1	90.9	..	22.8	141.5	182.8
Iraq	23	22	..	216	3,256.3	2,141.4	132.8	43.8	..	..	65.8	..
Ireland	82	61	..	1,118	298.9	293.5	..	480.3	15.1	5.6	1,623.4	1,476.4
Israel	27	23	..	435	113.8	79.1	2.6	252.6	4.1	1.6	798.8	705.3
Italy	57	46	19.2	832	4,413.4	3,453.8	264.9	156.0	8.8	3.8	1,586.5	..
Jamaica	44	43	..	2,051	2.1	1.5	..	51.3	27.3	18.2	..	..
Japan	16	13	35.1	1,668	2,471.5	1,936.2	135.7	278.2	7.2	4.2	4,492.9	4,382.4
Jordan	12	11	9.5	111	105.8	48.3	3.1	337.4	6.6	..	340.4	366.8
Kazakhstan	82	77	..	250	22,152.4	16,575.0	38.1	3.1	..	..	62.0	17.7
Kenya	47	48	0.1	630	1,785.5	2,329.0	..	33.3	..	..	20.0	..
Korea, Dem. Rep.	21	25	..	1,054	1,605.0	1,265.5	..	..	..	..	..	..
Korea, Rep.	22	19	51.6	1,274	1,441.0	1,018.5	134.0	479.5	17.9	7.4	211.0	1,632.5
Kosovo	..	52	..									
Kuwait	8	8	..	121	0.5	1.4	3.2	1,250.9	1.3	..	220.0	95.6
Kyrgyz Republic	53	56	9.3	533	578.0	612.4	..	19.0	32.7	36.3	189.4	191.1
Lao PDR	7	10	..	1,834	687.0	1,048.9	..	..	..	..	..	..
Latvia	41	29	0.0	641	696.7	540.9	..	124.3	..	7.7	363.7	501.4
Lebanon	59	67	19.9	661	41.2	67.9	8.6	56.2	..	..	174.9	..
Lesotho	76	78	..	788	233.5	179.2	..	..	..	..	57.7	..
Liberia	26	27	..	2,391	175.0	190.0	..	..	..	..	..	..
Libya	9	9	..	56	404.1	342.9	17.2	27.3	..	..	184.3	..
Lithuania	54	43	..	656	1,134.0	1,103.5	13.5	79.1	..	7.7	256.0	631.6
Macedonia, FYR	51	42	2.7	619	235.2	178.9	..	56.2	..	18.2	730.3	1,243.8
Madagascar	62	70	2.2	1,513	1,326.9	1,476.5	..	4.3	..	82.0	4.9	..
Malawi	45	58	..	1,181	1,425.3	1,780.1	3,197.3	1.7	..	..	..	..
Malaysia	22	24	..	2,875	700.7	678.6	242.6	929.9	26.0	14.8	152.9	..
Mali	26	32	..	282	2,438.7	3,988.4	..	9.0	..	..	10.2	2.7
Mauritania	38	38	..	92	118.9	242.9	..	..	..	..	8.4	9.8
Mauritius	56	48	21.4	2,041	0.6	0.1	..	210.1	16.7	9.1	..	..
Mexico	53	53	5.2	752	10,543.1	10,182.4	319.7	44.7	22.6	13.5	123.5	97.2
Moldova	78	76	9.1	450	675.6	881.6	..	12.5	33.8	32.8	310.1	197.5
Mongolia	81	75	..	241	654.1	252.4	..	8.2	39.5	40.6	80.3	38.0
Morocco	68	67	4.4	346	5,603.3	5,316.7	40.0	53.8	3.9	43.3	45.0	..
Mozambique	61	62	..	1,032	1,549.5	1,892.0	..	0.0	..	..	..	..
Myanmar	16	18	24.8	2,091	5,221.4	8,912.0	1,515.4	3.3	69.7	..	13.6	10.9
Namibia	47	47	..	285	214.2	307.2	..	0.3	48.2	..	..	..
Nepal	29	29	27.7	1,500	3,045.2	3,418.0	..	7.7	81.2	..	21.9	122.9
Netherlands	59	57	10.6	778	195.3	220.8	17.9	269.1	4.5	2.7	2,073.1	1,301.5
New Zealand	61	43	..	1,732	172.5	162.7	320.3	1,721.0	10.6	7.2	..	..
Nicaragua	33	43	..	2,391	320.0	438.2	..	32.3	39.3	29.1	20.0	..
Niger	26	34	..	151	6,882.3	9,929.1	..	0.4	..	..	0.2	..
Nigeria	79	86	..	1,150	15,400.0	18,899.0	1,929.1	13.3	..	..	4.7	6.6
Norway	3	3	5.4	1,414	356.4	305.9	24.4	219.0	6.4	2.8	1,779.1	1,539.1
Oman	3	6	..	125	2.4	5.0	2.4	395.0	9.3	..	41.1	..
Pakistan	34	34	73.0	494	11,864.1	13,689.0	115.6	163.3	51.1	43.6	129.7	204.8
Panama	29	30	..	2,692	184.6	144.3	..	35.3	29.1	14.7	102.0	..
Papua New Guinea	2	2	..	3,142	1.7	3.3	..	78.6	..	..	59.4	..
Paraguay	43	51	..	1,130	393.7	1,344.8	..	66.8	1.9	29.5	71.6	61.5
Peru	17	17	..	1,738	683.7	1,286.1	..	81.6	1.2	9.3	36.3	..
Philippines	37	40	..	2,348	7,138.5	7,216.3	973.8	131.2	45.2	36.1	65.2	..
Poland	62	53	0.5	600	8,530.9	8,582.8	100.0	190.4	25.2	14.7	823.6	1,246.0
Portugal	43	38	12.0	854	760.0	305.9	190.1	236.5	17.9	11.5	563.1	1,397.7
Puerto Rico	49	21	8.5	2,054	0.5	0.3	..	..	3.6	1.1	438.5	525.0
Romania	64	59	1.9	637	5,704.1	5,265.5	42.1	45.6	29.1	28.7	140.6	200.4

	Agricultural land[a]			Average annual precipitation	Land under cereal production		Fertilizer consumption		Agricultural employment		Agricultural machinery	
	% of land area		% irrigated	millimeters	thousand hectares		% of fertilizer production	kilograms per hectare of arable land	% of total employment		Tractors per 100 sq. km of arable land	
	1990	2008	2008	2008	1990	2009	2008	2008	1990	2008	1990	2008
Russian Federation	14	13	2.0	460	59,541.3	41,715.7	11.9	15.9	13.9	9.0	97.8	30.0
Rwanda	76	82	..	1,212	254.1	368.2	..	8.3	90.1	..	1.0	..
Qatar	5	6	..	74	1.1	2.0	0.3	276.9	..	3.0	84.0	56.2
Saudi Arabia	..	..	..	59	974.6	466.4	14.5	75.2	..	4.7	19.2	..
Senegal	46	48	0.7	686	1,229.0	1,647.2	53.7	2.4	..	33.7	1.6	..
Serbia	..	57	0.5	..	..	1,919.0	252.9	115.2	..	20.8	..	17.7
Sierra Leone	39	58	..	2,526	468.6	1,111.4	..	..	..	..	4.1	..
Singapore	3	1	..	2,497	..	1,918.9	..	..	0.4	1.1	..	..
Slovak Republic	51	40	1.3	824	836.6	768.7	81.1	130.0	..	4.0	197.5	154.7
Slovenia	28	25	0.8	1,162	112.5	101.9	..	283.6	10.7	10.2	..	..
Somalia	70	70	..	282	732.5	470.2	..	..	..	..	16.0	12.0
South Africa	80	82	..	495	6,162.9	3,318.7	262.4	49.7	..	8.8	107.9	..
Spain	61	56	11.9	636	7,551.4	6,043.3	84.8	106.5	11.5	4.3	483.1	824.4
Sri Lanka	37	42	..	1,712	869.8	1,017.9	2,961.4	284.3	47.8	31.3	..	..
Sudan	52	58	1.3	416	3,734.6	9,453.8	..	3.6	..	..	7.2	12.4
Swaziland	72	71	..	788	85.7	48.7	..	..	..	..	228.9	87.1
Sweden	8	8	..	624	1,285.2	1,032.1	414.7	142.1	3.4	2.2	601.9	592.4
Switzerland	40	39	..	1,537	211.9	153.0	..	226.3	4.2	3.9	2,783.1	2,597.2
Syrian Arab Republic	73	76	9.8	252	4,134.4	2,774.1	184.5	88.0	26.5	..	128.1	233.9
Tajikistan	32	34	15.0	691	266.5	409.5	452.5	0.0	44.7	..	415.4	216.1
Tanzania	38	39	..	1,071	2,629.3	5,087.0	..	6.0	..	74.6	8.2	..
Thailand	42	38	..	1,622	10,536.9	12,282.7	1,462.8	130.9	63.3	41.7	33.0	..
Timor-Leste	21	25	..	..	82.6	103.4	..	..	..	..	8.5	..
Togo	59	67	..	1,168	648.0	826.7	..	4.9	..	..	0.5	0.5
Trinidad and Tobago	15	11	..	2,200	5.9	2.1	17.8	2,337.2	12.3	4.3	..	..
Tunisia	56	64	4.0	207	1,445.7	876.6	8.7	32.1	25.8	..	82.4	142.6
Turkey	52	51	13.3	593	13,640.1	11,955.9	242.3	88.7	46.9	26.2	279.8	488.5
Turkmenistan	69	69	..	161	331.3	970.3	..	..	..	..	464.7	..
Uganda	61	66	..	1,180	1,055.0	1,826.0	..	3.4	..	..	..	..
Ukraine	72	71	5.3	565	12,542.3	15,114.8	40.7	32.8	19.8	16.7	153.3	103.3
United Arab Emirates	3	7	..	78	1.3	0.0	7.6	336.3	..	4.9	51.4	..
United Kingdom	75	73	..	1,220	3,657.3	3,173.0	133.5	208.2	2.1	1.4	760.6	..
United States	47	45	..	715	65,700.0	58,001.4	96.2	103.1	2.9	1.4	238.4	257.6
Uruguay	85	85	1.2	1,265	514.6	1,049.4	1,492.7	118.3	0.0	11.0	260.4	222.4
Uzbekistan	65	63	..	206	1,225.3	1,607.5	..	..	..	..	..	..
Venezuela, RB	25	24	..	1,875	753.9	1,237.1	74.5	232.9	13.4	8.7	..	..
Vietnam	21	32	..	1,821	6,474.6	8,528.5	218.6	286.6	..	..	47.0	..
West Bank and Gaza	62	61	4.6	402	0.0	35.0	..	..	..	15.6	442.2	767.9
Yemen, Rep.	45	45	3.3	167	844.9	672.8	..	14.3	52.6	..	39.0	..
Zambia	27	30	..	1,020	895.2	1,062.5	..	50.1	49.8	..	27.2	..
Zimbabwe	34	41	..	657	1,576.1	2,236.8	164.7	27.9	..	..	60.1	..
World	**37 w**	**38 w**	..	..	**708,090.3 s**	**708,451.8 s**	**94.9 w**	**119.4 w**	.. w	.. w	**186.4 w**	.. w
Low income	35	37	..		63,834.3	92,275.5	221.9	16.7	..	..	15.7	..
Middle income	37	38	..		482,334.4	468,186.3	103.8	139.6	..	..	91.7	..
Lower middle income	49	50	..		307,764.8	321,963.9	115.0	191.8	..	..	66.0	..
Upper middle income	30	30	..		174,569.6	146,222.5	76.9	70.7	20.8	14.9	125.1	..
Low & middle income	37	38	..		546,168.7	560,461.8	104.8	123.1	..	..	85.0	..
East Asia & Pacific	49	48	..		142,232.3	148,824.2	108.5	..	53.6	..	53.2	..
Europe & Central Asia	28	28	..		127,839.3	104,480.3	26.9	33.3	22.9	16.3	132.3	111.0
Latin America & Carib.	34	35	..		47,401.7	50,290.2	279.7	111.8	18.7	15.8	120.9	..
Middle East & N. Africa	24	23	..		29,953.1	27,642.2	57.6	95.3	..	..	114.6	190.2
South Asia	55	55	..		131,803.8	133,310.2	176.9	148.0	..	..	62.2	119.9
Sub-Saharan Africa	42	45	..		66,938.5	95,914.7	578.1	11.6	..	..	20.2	..
High income	39	37	..		161,921.6	147,990.0	73.6	109.3	6.5	3.5	474.9	..
Euro area	51	44	..		34,697.5	31,367.7	95.1	150.5	7.2	3.8	977.3	811.1

a. Includes permanent pastures, arable land, and land under permanent crops. b. Includes Luxembourg.

About the data

Agriculture is still a major sector in many economies, and agricultural activities provide developing countries with food and revenue. But agricultural activities also can degrade natural resources. Poor farming practices can cause soil erosion and loss of soil fertility. Efforts to increase productivity by using chemical fertilizers, pesticides, and intensive irrigation have environmental costs and health impacts. Excessive use of chemical fertilizers can alter the chemistry of soil. Pesticide poisoning is common in developing countries. And salinization of irrigated land diminishes soil fertility. Thus, inappropriate use of inputs for agricultural production has far-reaching effects.

The table provides indicators of major inputs to agricultural production: land, fertilizer, labor, and machinery. There is no single correct mix of inputs: appropriate levels and application rates vary by country and over time and depend on the type of crops, the climate and soils, and the production process used.

The agriculture sector is the most water-intensive sector, and water delivery in agriculture is increasingly important. The table shows irrigated agricultural land as share of total agricultural land area and data on average precipitation to illustrate how countries obtain water for agricultural use.

The data here and in table 3.3 are collected by the Food and Agriculture Organization of the United Nations (FAO) through annual questionnaires. The FAO tries to impose standard definitions and reporting methods, but complete consistency across countries and over time is not possible. Thus, data on agricultural land in different climates may not be comparable. For example, permanent pastures are quite different in nature and intensity in African countries and dry Middle Eastern countries. Data on agricul-tural employment, in particular, should be used with caution. In many countries much agricultural employment is informal and unrecorded, including substantial work performed by women and children. To address some of these concerns, this indicator is heavily footnoted in the database in sources, definition, and coverage.

Fertilizer consumption measures the quantity of plant nutrients. Consumption is calculated as production plus imports minus exports. Because some chemical compounds used for fertilizers have other industrial applications, the consumption data may overstate the quantity available for crops. Fertilizer consumption as a share of production shows the agriculture sector's vulnerability to import and energy price fluctuation. The FAO recently revised the time series for fertilizer consumption and irrigation for 2002 onward, but recent data are not available for all countries. FAO collects fertilizer statistics for production, imports, exports, and consumption through the new FAO fertilizer resources questionnaire. In the previous release, the data were based on total consumption of fertilizers, but the data in the recent release are based on the nutrients in fertilizers. Some countries compile fertilizer data on a calendar year basis, while others do so on a crop year basis

(July–June). Previous editions of *World Development Indicators* reported data on a crop year basis, but this edition uses the calendar year, as adopted by the FAO. Caution should thus be used when comparing data over time.

Definitions

• **Agricultural land** is permanent pastures, arable, and land under permanent crops. Permanent pasture is land used for five or more years for forage, including natural and cultivated crops. Arable land includes land defined by the FAO as land under temporary crops (double-cropped areas are counted once), temporary meadows for mowing or for pasture, land under market or kitchen gardens, and land temporarily fallow. Land abandoned as a result of shifting cultivation is excluded. Land under permanent crops is land cultivated with crops that occupy the land for long periods and need not be replanted after each harvest, such as cocoa, coffee, and rubber. Land under flowering shrubs, fruit trees, nut trees, and vines is included, but land under trees grown for wood or timber is not. • **Irrigated land** refers to areas purposely provided with water, including land irrigated by controlled flooding. • **Average annual precipitation** is the long-term average in depth (over space and time) of annual precipitation in the country. Precipitation is defined as any kind of water that falls from clouds as a liquid or a solid. • **Land under cereal production** refers to harvested areas, although some countries report only sown or cultivated area. • **Fertilizer consumption** is the quantity of plant nutrients applied to arable land. Fertilizer products cover nitrogen, potash, and phosphate fertilizers (including ground rock phosphate). Traditional nutrients—animal and plant manures—are not included. • **Fertilizer production** is fertilizer consumption, exports, and nonfertilizer use of fertilizer products minus fertilizer imports. • **Agricultural employment** is employment in agriculture, forestry, hunting, and fishing (see table 2.3). • **Agricultural machinery** refers to wheel and crawler tractors (excluding garden tractors) in use in agriculture at the end of the calendar year specified or during the first quarter of the following year.

Nearly 40 percent of land globally is devoted to agriculture 3.2a

Total land area in 2008: 130 million sq. km

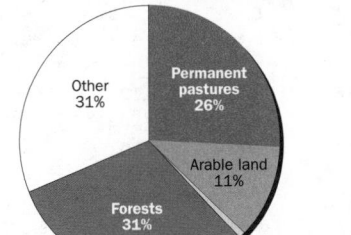

Note: Agricultural land includes permanent pastures, arable land, and land under permanent crops.
Source: Tables 3.1 and 3.2.

Rainfed agriculture plays a significant role in Sub-Saharan agriculture where about 95 percent of cropland depends on precipitation, 2008 3.2b

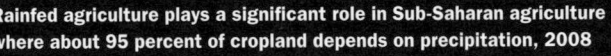
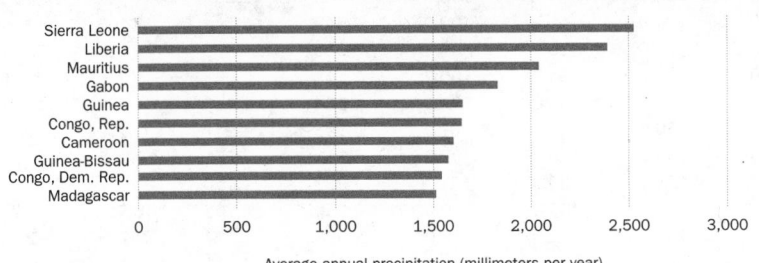

Average annual precipitation (millimeters per year)

Source: Table 3.2.

Data sources

Data on agricultural inputs are from electronic files that the FAO makes available to the World Bank and from the FAO web site (www.fao.org).

3.3 Agricultural output and productivity

	Crop production index		Food production index		Livestock production index		Cereal yield		Agricultural productivity	
	1999–2001 = 100		1999–2001 = 100		1999–2001 = 100		kilograms per hectare		Agriculture value added per worker 2000 $	
	1990	**2009**	**1990**	**2009**	**1990**	**2009**	**1990**	**2009**	**1990**	**2009**
Afghanistan	96.0	176.0	77.0	127.0	63.0	89.0	1,201	1,983	..	..
Albania	107.0	140.0	82.0	115.0	65.0	92.0	2,794	4,315	764	..
Algeria	66.0	196.0	69.0	163.0	80.0	121.0	688	1,654	1,703	2,184
Angola	56.0	250.0	61.0	198.0	72.0	92.0	321	588	200	313
Argentina	64.0	101.0	72.0	106.0	90.0	108.0	2,232	3,167	6,702	9,987
Armenia	106.0	195.0	108.0	191.0	108.0	177.0	1,843	2,230	1,607	5,049
Australia	58.0	88.0	68.0	95.0	82.0	95.0	1,716	1,764	20,150	29,257
Austria	97.0	108.0	89.0	97.0	90.0	94.0	5,577	6,136	13,413	24,715
Azerbaijan	136.0	152.0	107.0	151.0	102.0	152.0	2,113	2,607	1,000	1,342
Bangladesh	74.0	130.0	72.0	132.0	70.0	137.0	2,491	3,890	251	435
Belarus	110.0	161.0	135.0	157.0	146.0	150.0	2,741	3,372	2,042	5,184
Belgium	72.0[a]	113.0	85.0[a]	96.0	88.0[a]	91.0	5,755[a]	9,632	..	42,035
Benin	53.0	110.0	58.0	116.0	88.0	135.0	848	1,330	422	..
Bolivia	62.0	126.0	72.0	133.0	80.0	139.0	1,361	2,089	681	733
Bosnia and Herzegovina	107.0	125.0	119.0	138.0	119.0	167.0	3,553	4,539	..	14,299
Botswana	102.0	120.0	109.0	113.0	110.0	112.0	265	465	770	597
Brazil	74.0	149.0	65.0	148.0	58.0	142.0	1,755	3,526	1,625	3,760
Bulgaria	160.0	103.0	151.0	76.0	165.0	63.0	3,954	3,413	3,983	10,227
Burkina Faso	62.0	144.0	62.0	136.0	65.0	132.0	600	1,035	113	..
Burundi	109.0	108.0	109.0	110.0	131.0	118.0	1,349	1,313	116	..
Cambodia	66.0	202.0	64.0	184.0	59.0	109.0	1,362	2,947	..	411
Cameroon	69.0	117.0	72.0	120.0	83.0	105.0	1,241	1,574	419	730
Canada	90.0	119.0	84.0	119.0	76.0	105.0	2,636	3,301	28,898	44,752
Central African Republic	75.0	110.0	68.0	123.0	64.0	132.0	807	948	321	..
Chad	59.0	118.0	64.0	125.0	82.0	120.0	559	812	168	..
Chile	74.0	113.0	71.0	120.0	66.0	134.0	3,620	5,472	3,453	6,618
China	68.0	130.0	59.0	133.0	45.0	133.0	4,323	5,460	263	525
Hong Kong SAR, China	..	..	..	..	..	..	..	..	..	..
Colombia	91.0	120.0	81.0	128.0	79.0	140.0	2,475	4,017	3,122	2,861
Congo, Dem. Rep.	122.0	97.0	119.0	98.0	102.0	96.0	800	772	209	168
Congo, Rep.	81.0	116.0	79.0	123.0	73.0	157.0	624	776	..	..
Costa Rica	68.0	118.0	68.0	126.0	77.0	126.0	3,097	3,770	2,984	5,232
Côte d'Ivoire	71.0	109.0	73.0	120.0	90.0	132.0	887	1,724	653	926
Croatia	80.0	96.0	100.0	104.0	126.0	129.0	3,975	6,117	5,546	15,137
Cuba	119.0	82.0	127.0	83.0	152.0	109.0	2,342	2,069	4,117	3,647
Czech Republic	..	98.0	..	99.0	..	90.0	..	5,074	..	5,687
Denmark	113.0	113.0	100.0	107.0	86.0	104.0	6,118	6,810	14,588	45,905
Dominican Republic	118.0	111.0	101.0	131.0	74.0	151.0	3,996	4,246	1,925	4,579
Ecuador	75.0	114.0	67.0	126.0	61.0	140.0	1,724	2,974	2,105	1,766
Egypt, Arab Rep.	66.0	136.0	64.0	139.0	62.0	134.0	5,703	7,635	1,737	3,024
El Salvador	95.0	102.0	85.0	116.0	74.0	131.0	1,939	2,727	1,742	2,778
Eritrea	..	154.0	..	126.0	..	101.0	..	938	..	66
Estonia	121.0	127.0	180.0	134.0	192.0	118.0	1,304	2,761	3,288	3,207
Ethiopia	..	153.0	..	151.0	..	140.0	..	1,652	..	215
Finland	116.0	115.0	113.0	104.0	111.0	100.0	3,543	3,760	17,163	43,813
France	96.0	101.0	97.0	98.0	95.0	94.0	6,083	7,460	21,423	58,070
Gabon	81.0	104.0	91.0	103.0	84.0	100.0	1,643	1,663	1,216	1,869
Gambia, The	55.0	114.0	60.0	117.0	95.0	132.0	1,004	1,053	272	275
Georgia	122.0	61.0	99.0	66.0	78.0	67.0	1,998	1,917	2,359	1,872
Germany	86.0	102.0	102.0	103.0	115.0	105.0	5,411	7,201	13,669	31,659
Ghana	43.0	156.0	46.0	155.0	89.0	127.0	989	1,660	..	..
Greece	75.0	76.0	84.0	83.0	105.0	99.0	3,036	4,103	6,707	10,779
Guatemala	73.0	138.0	72.0	141.0	81.0	118.0	1,998	1,624	2,243	2,783
Guinea	71.0	133.0	72.0	133.0	56.0	167.0	1,455	1,711	156	225
Guinea-Bissau	72.0	120.0	73.0	122.0	78.0	128.0	1,531	1,422	..	..
Haiti	111.0	110.0	101.0	112.0	65.0	111.0	1,027	961	..	..
Honduras	100.0	153.0	90.0	145.0	66.0	133.0	1,468	1,752	1,180	1,958

	Crop production index		Food production index		Livestock production index		Cereal yield		Agricultural productivity	
							kilograms per hectare		Agriculture value added per worker 2000 $	
	1999–2001 = 100		1999–2001 = 100		1999–2001 = 100					
	1990	**2009**	**1990**	**2009**	**1990**	**2009**	**1990**	**2009**	**1990**	**2009**
Hungary	119.0	102.0	123.0	100.0	140.0	85.0	4,521	4,713	4,232	10,948
India	78.0	116.0	75.0	119.0	70.0	133.0	1,891	2,471	362	468
Indonesia	80.0	145.0	80.0	146.0	81.0	157.0	3,800	4,813	512	734
Iran, Islamic Rep.	71.0	117.0	69.0	124.0	64.0	142.0	1,445	2,291	1,906	3,061
Iraq	105.0	83.0	111.0	92.0	140.0	128.0	1,061	1,222	..	..
Ireland	91.0	84.0	94.0	90.0	93.0	93.0	6,577	6,798	..	13,573
Israel	112.0	108.0	90.0	122.0	69.0	130.0	3,484	3,250	..	..
Italy	88.0	91.0	90.0	95.0	94.0	103.0	3,945	5,035	10,410	29,498
Jamaica	83.0	95.0	75.0	100.0	64.0	110.0	1,116	1,253	2,224	2,716
Japan	115.0	89.0	109.0	95.0	106.0	101.0	5,846	5,920	20,934	52,062
Jordan	102.0	157.0	81.0	156.0	52.0	139.0	1,220	1,044	2,077	3,030
Kazakhstan	163.0	150.0	163.0	145.0	178.0	141.0	1,338	1,254	1,781	2,033
Kenya	79.0	107.0	83.0	126.0	89.0	147.0	1,562	1,204	400	334
Korea, Dem. Rep.	111.0	107.0	104.0	112.0	124.0	133.0	3,926	3,698	..	..
Korea, Rep.	88.0	96.0	79.0	101.0	62.0	106.0	5,853	7,073	5,338	19,105
Kosovo	..	..	..	..	..	..	..	..	..	..
Kuwait	57.0	122.0	53.0	114.0	63.0	102.0	3,653	2,679	..	..
Kyrgyz Republic	68.0	108.0	78.0	103.0	110.0	105.0	2,772	3,034	684	1,041
Lao PDR	65.0	157.0	60.0	148.0	57.0	126.0	2,268	3,808	387	516
Latvia	129.0	147.0	222.0	138.0	274.0	126.0	1,641	3,075	1,896	3,636
Lebanon	99.0	96.0	92.0	111.0	64.0	149.0	1,878	2,828	..	41,037
Lesotho	101.0	72.0	91.0	72.0	86.0	78.0	1,036	421	260	207
Liberia	71.0	115.0	88.0	131.0	91.0	127.0	1,029	1,553	..	..
Libya	78.0	102.0	77.0	109.0	77.0	116.0	674	623	..	..
Lithuania	79.0	138.0	157.0	138.0	185.0	116.0	1,938	3,450	..	5,369
Macedonia, FYR	108.0	112.0	108.0	115.0	101.0	115.0	2,652	3,387	2,413	5,811
Madagascar	93.0	115.0	91.0	114.0	99.0	111.0	1,945	2,291	214	192
Malawi	54.0	141.0	47.0	129.0	78.0	153.0	992	1,599	89	162
Malaysia	74.0	141.0	67.0	144.0	71.0	133.0	2,740	3,750	3,850	6,529
Mali	68.0	162.0	79.0	183.0	94.0	153.0	726	1,588	406	523
Mauritania	60.0	116.0	86.0	116.0	91.0	115.0	870	873	653	408
Mauritius	108.0	95.0	95.0	106.0	57.0	138.0	4,193	7,895	3,446	5,556
Mexico	81.0	111.0	74.0	117.0	68.0	123.0	2,424	3,111	2,275	3,364
Moldova	135.0	100.0	159.0	105.0	197.0	98.0	2,928	2,417	1,349	1,531
Mongolia	293.0	270.0	101.0	110.0	94.0	101.0	1,098	1,552	1,241	1,888
Morocco	100.0	142.0	93.0	140.0	81.0	128.0	1,120	1,003	1,806	3,306
Mozambique	70.0	130.0	68.0	102.0	47.0	89.0	474	846	132	220
Myanmar	60.0	151.0	61.0	162.0	51.0	248.0	2,762	3,585	..	..
Namibia	77.0	140.0	98.0	101.0	101.0	90.0	457	465	1,267	1,638
Nepal	75.0	135.0	76.0	130.0	78.0	120.0	1,920	2,374	247	238
Netherlands	92.0	100.0	102.0	94.0	101.0	101.0	6,959	9,032	23,593	45,969
New Zealand	78.0	109.0	74.0	115.0	77.0	114.0	5,034	6,922	19,782	25,446
Nicaragua	70.0	117.0	63.0	135.0	59.0	149.0	1,524	1,872	..	2,495
Niger	64.0	210.0	61.0	186.0	56.0	153.0	310	489	235	..
Nigeria	60.0	134.0	60.0	135.0	70.0	121.0	1,148	1,598	..	..
Norway	143.0	90.0	112.0	95.0	101.0	95.0	4,399	3,094	17,454	40,666
Oman	59.0	95.0	57.0	102.0	65.0	122.0	2,160	3,358	1,037	..
Pakistan	77.0	125.0	67.0	132.0	64.0	135.0	1,766	2,803	739	903
Panama	116.0	114.0	91.0	116.0	67.0	116.0	1,867	2,735	2,303	4,185
Papua New Guinea	76.0	112.0	77.0	119.0	79.0	127.0	2,395	3,727	563	672
Paraguay	93.0	122.0	76.0	136.0	81.0	134.0	1,979	2,358	1,657	1,338
Peru	51.0	145.0	55.0	153.0	65.0	158.0	2,601	3,910	907	1,545
Philippines	87.0	131.0	78.0	131.0	57.0	134.0	2,065	3,229	911	1,204
Poland	124.0	99.0	119.0	111.0	123.0	110.0	3,284	3,475	1,605	2,776
Portugal	110.0	86.0	101.0	95.0	82.0	103.0	1,878	3,455	4,495	6,764
Puerto Rico	153.0	105.0	125.0	94.0	119.0	91.0	1,080	1,897	..	..
Qatar	51.0	121.0	64.0	77.0	77.0	46.0	2,897	3,820	..	..

	Crop production index		Food production index		Livestock production index		Cereal yield		Agricultural productivity	
							kilograms per hectare		Agriculture value added per worker 2000 $	
	1999–2001 = 100		1999–2001 = 100		1999–2001 = 100					
	1990	**2009**	**1990**	**2009**	**1990**	**2009**	**1990**	**2009**	**1990**	**2009**
Romania	98.0	100.0	105.0	107.0	124.0	115.0	3,011	2,825	2,351	8,993
Russian Federation	126.0	136.0	129.0	130.0	147.0	118.0	1,743	2,279	1,917	3,031
Rwanda	97.0	132.0	94.0	134.0	79.0	158.0	1,043	1,097	172	..
Saudi Arabia	118.0	124.0	103.0	124.0	64.0	135.0	4,245	5,212	7,863	20,431
Senegal	72.0	130.0	73.0	134.0	80.0	144.0	795	1,135	252	245
Serbia	98.0[b]	..	109.0[b]	..	103.0[b]	..	2,926[b]	4,626	..	..
Sierra Leone	127.0	204.0	121.0	201.0	105.0	144.0	1,202	989	..	..
Singapore	223.0	440.0	335.0	132.0	481.0	105.0	..	..	..	49,867
Slovak Republic	..	102.0	..	97.0	..	80.0	..	4,335	..	9,728
Slovenia	82.0	94.0	76.0	97.0	76.0	97.0	3,279	5,266	13,217	67,838
Somalia	144.0	96.0	101.0	104.0	95.0	105.0	793	417	..	..
South Africa	86.0	111.0	87.0	122.0	93.0	130.0	1,877	4,395	2,290	3,641
Spain	91.0	97.0	88.0	97.0	77.0	103.0	2,485	2,957	8,947	21,831
Sri Lanka	90.0	115.0	91.0	120.0	88.0	123.0	2,965	3,722	678	926
Sudan	49.0	112.0	51.0	119.0	58.0	123.0	456	587	501	922
Swaziland	112.0	101.0	106.0	115.0	108.0	140.0	1,278	560	1,025	1,176
Sweden	126.0	103.0	110.0	100.0	100.0	93.0	4,964	5,086	23,307	51,057
Switzerland	112.0	103.0	104.0	104.0	103.0	106.0	5,984	6,579	20,451	26,726
Syrian Arab Republic	66.0	115.0	71.0	131.0	74.0	143.0	750	1,707	2,613	4,717
Tajikistan	123.0	148.0	134.0	162.0	196.0	168.0	1,020	2,250	370	542
Tanzania	91.0	154.0	86.0	134.0	75.0	104.0	1,506	1,224	220	283
Thailand	76.0	129.0	77.0	126.0	74.0	111.0	2,009	2,954	446	708
Timor-Leste	88.0	105.0	94.0	111.0	89.0	114.0	1,608	1,276	..	..
Togo	71.0	109.0	74.0	132.0	85.0	137.0	747	1,136	351	..
Trinidad and Tobago	120.0	89.0	90.0	125.0	72.0	149.0	2,826	2,659	1,825	1,502
Tunisia	93.0	119.0	81.0	115.0	57.0	110.0	1,143	1,401	2,736	3,602
Turkey	87.0	112.0	88.0	119.0	91.0	125.0	2,214	2,808	2,175	3,491
Turkmenistan	98.0	128.0	60.0	137.0	64.0	129.0	2,210	2,974	1,272	2,930
Uganda	77.0	109.0	78.0	112.0	79.0	120.0	1,498	1,539	177	203
Ukraine	131.0	155.0	147.0	123.0	170.0	101.0	2,834	3,004	1,232	2,461
United Arab Emirates	16.0	52.0	19.0	45.0	54.0	125.0	2,216	2,000	9,042	..
United Kingdom	101.0	96.0	105.0	98.0	105.0	99.0	6,171	7,008	21,400	26,370
United States	86.0	112.0	82.0	115.0	81.0	108.0	4,755	7,238	18,523	49,512
Uruguay	66.0	187.0	74.0	144.0	83.0	127.0	2,182	4,047	6,166	9,064
Uzbekistan	107.0	145.0	93.0	155.0	99.0	137.0	1,777	4,578	1,427	2,584
Venezuela, RB	77.0	116.0	73.0	122.0	73.0	128.0	2,486	3,826	4,443	7,941
Vietnam	57.0	137.0	59.0	138.0	50.0	157.0	3,073	5,075	225	356
West Bank and Gaza	..	104.0	..	102.0	..	93.0	..	1,684	..	..
Yemen, Rep.	75.0	130.0	71.0	144.0	63.0	165.0	908	1,003	428	..
Zambia	81.0	170.0	87.0	135.0	83.0	106.0	1,352	2,068	212	216
Zimbabwe	77.0	55.0	87.0	82.0	79.0	107.0	1,625	313	270	141
World	**81.0[c] w**	**122.2 w**	**80.0[c] w**	**123.0 w**	**82.0[c] w**	**120.3 w**	**2,755[c] w**	**3,514 w**	**803 w**	**998 w**
Low income	76.2	134.1	76.5	134.4	78.3	131.0	1,561	1,966	236	278
Middle income	73.6	128.2	68.8	130.2	62.5	131.5	2,563	3,210	489	777
Lower middle income	71.9	128.6	66.5	130.5	56.5	132.6	2,696	3,446	360	604
Upper middle income	79.2	126.9	75.6	129.3	75.1	129.4	2,103	2,690	2,270	3,683
Low & middle income	73.8	128.7	69.4	130.5	63.3	131.4	2,429	3,005	460	704
East Asia & Pacific	69.9	133.1	62.7	135.1	48.8	135.2	3,795	4,843	313	570
Europe & Central Asia	111.3[b]	129.3	117.7	126.2	136.8	119.1	2,596	2,471	2,188	3,182
Latin America & Carib.	75.8	128.1	71.2	131.2	69.7	132.6	2,089	3,282	2,227	3,436
Middle East & N. Africa	74.7	127.3	72.8	131.6	69.3	134.7	1,471	2,352	1,760	2,896
South Asia	78.0	119.3	74.5	122.7	69.2	132.9	1,926	2,628	372	495
Sub-Saharan Africa	71.1	128.7	72.9	130.0	80.1	125.1	1,033	1,302	304	318
High income	90.7	103.9	90.4	106.3	90.7	104.1	4,138	5,439	14,116	25,066
Euro area	90.9	96.9	95.6	97.7	98.2	100.0	4,490	5,822	11,982	26,730

a. Includes Luxembourg. b. Includes Montenegro. c. FAO estimate.

Agricultural output and productivity | 3.3

About the data

The agricultural production indexes in the table are prepared by the Food and Agriculture Organization of the United Nations (FAO). The FAO obtains data from official and semiofficial reports of crop yields, area under production, and livestock numbers. If data are unavailable, the FAO makes estimates. The indexes are calculated using the Laspeyres formula: production quantities of each commodity are weighted by average international commodity prices in the base period and summed for each year. Because the FAO's indexes are based on the concept of agriculture as a single enterprise, estimates of the amounts retained for seed and feed are subtracted from the production data to avoid double counting. The aggregates represent production available for any use except as seed and feed and presented as "net". The FAO's indexes may differ from those from other sources because of differences in coverage, weights, concepts, time periods, calculation methods, and use of international prices.

To facilitate cross-country comparisons, the FAO uses international commodity prices to value production. These prices, expressed in international dollars (equivalent in purchasing power to the U.S. dollar), are derived using a Geary-Khamis formula applied to agricultural outputs (see Inter-Secretariat Working Group on National Accounts 1993, sections 16.93–96). This method assigns a single price to each commodity so that, for example, one metric ton of wheat has the same price regardless of where it was produced. The use of international prices eliminates fluctuations in the value of output due to transitory movements of nominal exchange rates unrelated to the purchasing power of the domestic currency.

Data on cereal yield may be affected by a variety of reporting and timing differences. Millet and sorghum, which are grown as feed for livestock and poultry in Europe and North America, are used as food in Africa, Asia, and countries of the former Soviet Union. So some cereal crops are excluded from the data for some countries and included elsewhere, depending on their use.

Definitions

- **Crop production index** is agricultural production for each period relative to the average over the base period 1999–2001. It includes all crops except fodder crops. The regional and income group aggregates for the FAO's production indexes are calculated from the underlying values in international dollars, normalized to the average over the base period 1999–2001. • **Food production index** covers food crops that are considered edible and that contain nutrients. Coffee and tea are excluded because, although edible, they have no nutritive value. • **Livestock production index** includes meat and milk from all sources, dairy products such as cheese, and eggs, honey, raw silk, wool, and hides and skins. • **Cereal yield,** measured in kilograms per hectare of harvested land, includes wheat, rice, maize, barley, oats, rye, millet, sorghum, buckwheat, and mixed grains. Production data on cereals refer to crops harvested for dry grain only. Cereal crops harvested for hay or harvested green for food, feed, or silage, and those used for grazing, are excluded. The FAO allocates production data to the calendar year in which the bulk of the harvest took place. But most of a crop harvested near the end of a year will be used in the following year. • **Agricultural productivity** is the ratio of agricultural value added, measured in 2000 U.S. dollars, to the number of workers in agriculture. Agricultural productivity is measured by value added per unit of input. (For further discussion of the calculation of value added in national accounts, see *About the data* for tables 4.1 and 4.2.) Agricultural value added includes that from forestry and fishing. Thus interpretations of land productivity should be made with caution.

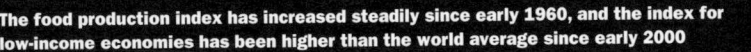

The food production index has increased steadily since early 1960, and the index for low-income economies has been higher than the world average since early 2000 | **3.3a**

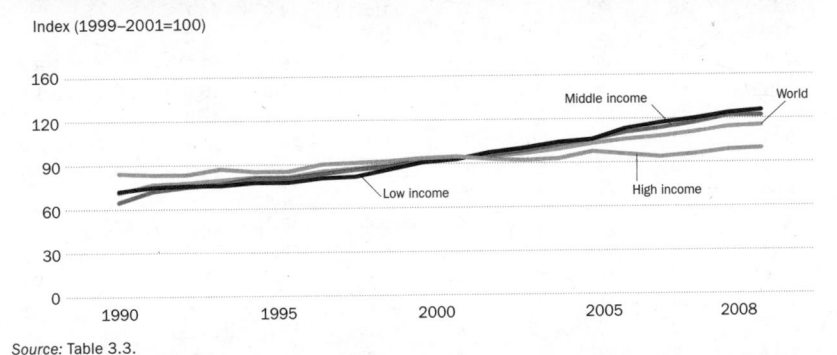

Index (1999–2001=100)

Source: Table 3.3.

Cereal yield in Sub-Saharan Africa increased between 1990 and 2009 but still is the lowest among the regions | **3.3b**

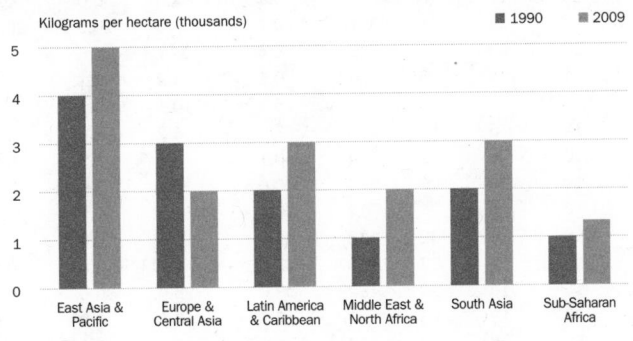

Kilograms per hectare (thousands) ■ 1990 ■ 2009

Source: Table 3.3.

Data sources

Data on agricultural production indexes, cereal yield, and agricultural employment are from electronic files that the FAO makes available to the World Bank. The files may contain more recent information than published versions. Data on agricultural value added are from the World Bank's national accounts files.

	Forest area (thousand sq. km)		Average annual deforestation[a] (%)		Threatened species				GEF benefits index for biodiversity (0–100, no biodiversity to maximum biodiversity)	Terrestrial protected areas (% of total land area)		Marine protected areas (% of territorial waters)	
	1990	2010	1990–2000	2000–10	Mammals 2010	Birds 2010	Fish 2010	Higher plants[b] 2010	2008	1990	2009	1990	2009
Afghanistan	14	14	0.00	0.00	11	13	5	2	3.4	0.4	0.4	..	..
Albania	8	8	0.26	−0.09	3	6	38	0	0.2	4.3	9.8	0.1	1.5
Algeria	17	15	0.54	0.57	14	11	33	15	2.9	6.3	6.3	0.2	0.3
Angola	610	585	0.21	0.21	15	21	37	33	8.3	12.4	12.4	0.1	0.1
Argentina	348	294	0.88	0.80	37	50	36	44	17.7	4.6	5.4	0.8	1.1
Armenia	3	3	1.31	1.48	9	10	3	1	0.2	6.9	8.0	..	..
Australia	1,545	1,493	−0.03	0.37	55	52	100	67	87.7	7.4	10.5	10.9	28.3
Austria	38	39	−0.16	−0.13	3	8	11	4	0.3	20.1	22.9	..	..
Azerbaijan	9	9	0.00	0.00	7	15	10	0	0.8	6.2	7.1	..	..
Bangladesh	15	14	0.18	0.18	34	29	19	16	1.4	1.5	1.6	0.4	0.8
Belarus	78	86	−0.62	−0.42	4	4	2	0	0.0	6.5	7.3	..	..
Belgium	7	7	0.15	−0.16	3	2	10	1	0.0	0.6	0.9	0.0	0.0
Benin	58	46	1.29	1.03	11	5	27	14	0.2	23.8	23.8	0.0	0.0
Bolivia	628	572	0.44	0.49	20	33	0	72	12.5	8.5	18.2	..	..
Bosnia and Herzegovina	22	22	0.11	0.00	4	6	31	1	0.4	0.5	0.6	0.7	0.7
Botswana	137	114	0.90	0.99	7	9	2	0	1.4	30.3	30.9	..	..
Brazil	5,748	5,195	0.51	0.49	80	123	80	387	100.0	10.8	28.0	11.4	20.1
Bulgaria	33	39	−0.14	−1.53	7	12	18	0	0.8	1.9	9.1	0.1	3.0
Burkina Faso	68	56	0.91	1.00	9	6	4	3	0.3	13.3	13.9	..	..
Burundi	3	2	3.71	1.40	10	10	17	2	0.3	3.8	4.8	..	..
Cambodia	129	101	1.14	1.33	37	24	28	30	3.5	0.0	24.0	0.0	0.9
Cameroon	243	199	0.94	1.04	39	16	110	378	12.5	7.0	9.2	0.4	0.4
Canada	3,101	3,101	0.00	0.00	12	15	32	2	21.5	6.0	8.0	0.8	1.2
Central African Republic	232	226	0.13	0.13	8	7	3	17	1.5	14.4	14.7	..	..
Chad	131	115	0.62	0.66	13	9	1	2	2.2	9.4	9.4	..	..
Chile	153	162	−0.37	−0.25	20	34	19	41	15.3	16.0	16.5	3.4	3.7
China	1,571	2,069	−1.20	−1.57	74	85	97	453	66.6	13.5	16.6	0.4	1.4
Hong Kong SAR, China	..	..	..	..	2	17	11	6	..	41.1	41.8	0.0	0.0
Colombia	625	605	0.16	0.17	51	91	50	227	51.5	20.3	20.4	3.7	5.9
Congo, Dem. Rep.	1,604	1,541	0.20	0.20	30	34	81	83	19.9	10.0	10.0	3.7	4.3
Congo, Rep.	227	224	0.08	0.06	11	3	45	37	3.6	5.4	9.4	0.0	2.1
Costa Rica	26	26	0.76	−0.92	9	19	46	116	9.7	18.7	20.9	12.1	12.3
Côte d'Ivoire	102	104	−0.10	−0.07	24	14	43	106	3.4	22.6	22.6	0.1	0.1
Croatia	19	19	−0.19	−0.18	7	10	56	3	0.6	7.1	7.3	1.2	1.2
Cuba	21	29	−1.70	−1.66	14	17	30	166	12.5	4.3	6.2	1.3	2.7
Czech Republic	26	27	−0.03	−0.08	2	6	2	4	0.1	13.7	15.1	..	..
Denmark	4	5	−0.89	−1.13	2	2	14	3	0.2	4.8	5.0	3.7	3.8
Dominican Republic	20	20	0.00	0.00	6	14	17	30	6.0	22.1	22.1	30.4	30.4
Ecuador	138	99	1.53	1.81	43	71	49	1,837	29.3	21.6	25.1	0.1	13.0
Egypt, Arab Rep.	0	1	−2.98	−1.72	17	10	36	2	2.9	1.9	5.9	4.4	9.3
El Salvador	4	3	1.26	1.45	5	5	12	27	0.9	0.6	0.8	3.2	3.2
Eritrea	16	15	0.28	0.28	10	10	18	3	0.8	4.9	5.0	0.0	0.0
Estonia	21	22	−0.71	0.12	1	3	4	0	0.1	19.6	20.0	26.1	26.1
Ethiopia	151	123	0.97	1.08	32	23	14	26	8.4	17.7	18.4	..	..
Finland	219	222	−0.26	0.14	1	4	5	1	0.2	4.2	9.1	3.5	5.0
France	145	160	−0.55	−0.38	9	7	40	15	5.3	10.1	15.1	1.1	3.4
Gabon	220	220	0.00	0.00	14	5	59	120	3.0	4.2	14.9	0.2	7.1
Gambia, The	4	5	−0.42	−0.40	10	6	21	4	0.1	1.5	1.5	0.1	0.1
Georgia	28	27	0.04	0.09	10	10	9	0	0.6	2.8	3.7	0.2	0.4
Germany	107	111	−0.31	0.00	6	6	21	12	0.6	31.8	40.5	35.7	36.3
Ghana	74	49	1.99	2.08	16	9	42	118	1.9	13.9	14.0	0.0	0.0
Greece	33	39	−0.88	−0.81	10	11	73	13	2.8	5.7	13.8	0.6	2.5
Guatemala	47	37	1.20	1.39	16	10	20	82	8.0	26.0	30.6	0.3	12.5
Guinea	73	65	0.51	0.53	22	13	63	22	2.3	6.8	6.8	0.0	0.0
Guinea-Bissau	22	20	0.44	0.47	12	3	30	4	0.6	7.6	16.1	2.7	45.8
Haiti	1	1	0.62	0.76	5	13	17	29	5.2	0.3	0.3	0.0	0.0
Honduras	81	52	2.38	2.06	7	9	22	113	7.2	13.6	18.2	0.0	1.9

Deforestation and biodiversity

	Forest area		Average annual deforestation[a]		Threatened species				GEF benefits index for biodiversity	Terrestrial protected areas		Marine protected areas	
									0–100 (no biodiversity to maximum biodiversity)	% of total land area		% of territorial waters	
	thousand sq. km		%		Mammals	Birds	Fish	Higher plants[b]					
	1990	2010	1990–2000	2000–10	2010	2010	2010	2010	2008	1990	2009	1990	2009
Hungary	18	20	−0.57	−0.62	2	9	8	1	0.2	4.6	5.1	..	..
India	639	684	−0.22	−0.46	94	78	122	255	39.9	5.0	5.3	1.5	1.7
Indonesia	1,185	944	1.75	0.51	183	119	138	393	81.0	10.0	14.1	0.5	1.9
Iran, Islamic Rep.	111	111	0.00	0.00	16	21	29	1	7.3	5.2	7.1	1.3	1.9
Iraq	8	8	−0.17	−0.09	13	18	11	0	1.6	0.1	0.1	0.0	0.0
Ireland	5	7	−3.16	−1.53	5	1	18	1	0.6	0.6	1.0	0.1	0.1
Israel	1	2	−1.49	−0.07	15	13	35	0	0.8	17.2	18.7	1.0	1.0
Italy	76	91	−0.98	−0.90	7	8	42	27	3.8	5.0	9.9	0.5	16.7
Jamaica	3	3	0.12	0.12	5	10	17	209	4.4	10.2	18.9	0.2	4.2
Japan	250	250	0.03	−0.04	28	40	59	15	36.0	13.2	16.3	2.0	5.6
Jordan	1	1	0.00	0.00	13	10	13	1	0.4	8.4	9.4	0.0	20.8
Kazakhstan	34	33	0.17	0.17	16	21	14	16	5.1	2.4	2.5	..	..
Kenya	37	35	0.35	0.33	28	30	66	129	8.8	11.5	11.6	5.1	10.4
Korea, Dem. Rep.	82	57	1.67	2.00	9	22	12	6	0.7	3.9	4.0	0.1	0.1
Korea, Rep.	64	62	0.13	0.11	9	30	17	3	1.7	2.2	2.4	5.0	5.3
Kosovo	..	5[c]	..	..	..	..	..	..	..	..	..	..	..
Kuwait	0	0	−5.24	−1.84	6	9	11	0	0.1	1.6	1.6	0.0	0.0
Kyrgyz Republic	8	10	−0.26	−1.07	6	12	3	14	1.1	6.4	6.9	..	..
Lao PDR	173	158	0.46	0.48	45	22	23	22	5.0	0.8	16.3	..	..
Latvia	32	34	−0.21	−0.34	1	3	5	0	0.0	6.4	17.8	4.6	6.6
Lebanon	1	1	0.00	−0.45	10	7	21	1	0.2	0.5	0.5	0.0	0.1
Lesotho	0	0	−0.49	−0.47	2	7	1	4	0.3	0.5	0.5	..	..
Liberia	49	43	0.63	0.67	19	11	52	47	2.6	18.1	18.1	0.0	0.0
Libya	2	2	0.00	0.00	12	4	21	2	1.6	0.1	0.1	0.0	0.0
Lithuania	19	22	−0.38	−0.67	3	4	5	0	0.0	1.4	4.5	0.8	2.7
Macedonia, FYR	9	10	−0.49	−0.41	5	10	14	0	0.2	4.2	4.8	..	..
Madagascar	137	126	0.42	0.44	63	35	83	280	29.2	2.1	2.9	0.0	0.1
Malawi	39	32	0.88	0.97	7	14	101	14	3.5	15.0	15.0	..	..
Malaysia	224	205	0.36	0.54	70	45	60	692	13.9	16.9	17.9	1.1	1.6
Mali	141	125	0.58	0.61	12	7	3	6	1.5	2.3	2.4	..	..
Mauritania	4	2	2.66	2.66	15	9	30	0	1.3	0.5	0.5	32.1	32.1
Mauritius	0	0	0.00	1.08	6	11	12	88	3.3	1.7	4.5	0.3	0.3
Mexico	703	648	0.52	0.30	99	55	150	255	68.7	2.4	11.1	1.9	16.7
Moldova	3	4	−0.16	−1.77	4	9	9	0	0.0	0.9	1.4	..	..
Mongolia	125	109	0.67	0.72	11	21	1	0	4.2	4.1	13.4	..	..
Morocco	50	51	0.06	−0.22	18	10	45	31	3.5	1.2	1.5	0.7	1.2
Mozambique	434	390	0.52	0.54	12	23	52	52	7.2	14.8	15.8	1.8	3.3
Myanmar	392	318	1.17	0.93	45	41	33	42	10.0	3.1	6.3	0.3	0.3
Namibia	88	73	0.87	0.96	12	24	25	26	5.2	14.4	14.5	0.5	0.5
Nepal	48	36	2.09	0.70	31	33	8	7	2.1	7.7	17.0	..	..
Netherlands	3	4	−0.43	−0.14	4	2	12	0	0.2	11.0	12.4	13.5	21.2
New Zealand	77	83	−0.69	0.00	9	70	21	21	20.2	25.0	25.8	0.4	7.1
Nicaragua	45	31	1.67	2.01	6	11	26	43	3.3	15.4	36.7	0.7	20.1
Niger	19	12	3.74	0.98	12	6	4	2	0.9	6.8	6.8	..	..
Nigeria	172	90	2.68	3.67	27	13	56	172	6.0	11.6	12.8	0.2	0.2
Norway	91	101	−0.19	−0.79	7	2	18	2	1.3	4.7	14.4	1.0	2.3
Oman	0	0	0.00	0.00	9	10	24	6	3.7	0.0	10.7	0.0	1.3
Pakistan	25	17	1.76	2.24	23	26	33	2	4.9	10.3	10.3	1.8	1.8
Panama	38	33	1.18	0.36	15	17	36	202	10.9	17.2	18.7	3.1	4.0
Papua New Guinea	315	287	0.45	0.48	39	37	41	143	25.4	1.9	3.1	0.3	0.3
Paraguay	212	176	0.88	0.96	8	27	0	10	2.8	2.9	5.4	..	..
Peru	702	680	0.14	0.18	54	96	19	274	33.4	4.7	13.6	2.8	2.8
Philippines	66	77	−0.80	−0.74	39	72	65	222	32.3	8.7	10.9	0.2	1.5
Poland	89	93	−0.20	−0.30	5	6	6	4	0.5	15.3	21.8	3.8	4.5
Portugal	33	35	−0.28	−0.10	11	9	47	21	5.5	5.9	5.9	1.8	1.8
Puerto Rico	3	6	−4.92	−1.75	3	8	15	53	4.0	10.1	10.1	1.5	1.6
Qatar	0	0	0.00	0.00	2	5	11	0	0.1	0.0	0.7	0.0	0.3

	Forest area		Average annual deforestation[a]		Threatened species				GEF benefits index for biodiversity	Terrestrial protected areas		Marine protected areas	
									0–100 (no biodiversity to maximum biodiversity)	% of total land area		% of territorial waters	
	thousand sq. km		%		Mammals	Birds	Fish	Higher plants[b]					
	1990	2010	1990–2000	2000–10	2010	2010	2010	2010	2008	1990	2009	1990	2009
Romania	64	66	0.01	−0.32	7	12	18	1	0.7	2.8	7.1	1.5	33.2
Russian Federation	8,090	8,091	0.00	0.00	32	18	35	8	34.1	8.2	9.0	3.1	9.1
Rwanda	3	4	−0.79	−2.37	20	12	9	4	0.9	9.9	10.0	..	..
Saudi Arabia	10	10	0.00	0.00	9	14	22	3	3.2	7.6	31.3	0.6	3.4
Senegal	93	85	0.49	0.49	16	9	41	9	1.0	24.1	24.1	5.8	12.4
Serbia	23	27	−0.62	−0.98	6	11	11	1	0.2	3.0	6.0	..	..
Sierra Leone	31	27	0.65	0.69	17	10	45	48	1.3	5.0	5.0	0.0	0.0
Singapore	0	0	0.00	0.00	11	17	25	57	0.1	5.0	5.4	0.0	1.6
Slovak Republic	19	19	0.01	−0.06	3	7	5	2	0.1	19.5	23.5	..	..
Slovenia	12	13	−0.37	−0.16	4	4	26	0	0.2	7.5	12.1	0.0	0.6
Somalia	83	67	0.97	1.07	15	11	26	21	6.1	0.6	0.6	0.0	0.0
South Africa	82	57	1.67	2.00	24	39	81	97	20.7	6.5	6.9	0.7	6.5
Spain	138	182	−2.09	−0.68	16	15	62	55	6.8	7.7	8.6	0.6	3.4
Sri Lanka	24	19	1.20	1.12	30	14	41	283	7.9	19.6	20.8	0.1	1.1
Sudan	764	699	0.80	0.08	15	14	17	18	5.1	4.7	4.9	0.0	0.0
Swaziland	5	6	−0.93	−0.84	5	9	4	11	0.1	3.0	3.0	..	..
Sweden	273	282	−0.04	−0.29	1	3	11	3	0.3	7.1	11.3	3.7	5.3
Switzerland	12	12	−0.37	−0.38	2	2	9	3	0.2	14.5	22.8	..	..
Syrian Arab Republic	4	5	−1.51	−1.29	16	13	33	3	0.9	0.3	0.6	0.0	0.6
Tajikistan	4	4	−0.05	0.00	8	9	5	14	0.7	1.9	4.1	..	..
Tanzania	415	334	1.02	1.13	35	42	172	298	14.8	26.5	27.7	3.7	10.0
Thailand	195	190	0.28	0.02	57	45	72	91	8.0	14.2	19.6	4.0	4.3
Timor-Leste	10	7	1.22	1.40	4	7	5	0	0.6	0.0	6.0	0.0	6.7
Togo	7	3	3.37	5.13	11	3	24	10	0.3	11.3	11.3	0.0	0.0
Trinidad and Tobago	2	2	0.29	0.35	2	2	19	1	2.2	30.5	31.2	0.2	2.8
Tunisia	6	10	−2.67	−1.86	13	7	31	7	0.5	1.3	1.3	1.1	1.2
Turkey	97	113	−0.47	−1.11	17	15	67	5	6.2	1.7	1.9	2.4	2.4
Turkmenistan	41	41	0.00	0.00	9	15	11	3	1.8	3.0	3.0	..	..
Uganda	48	30	2.03	2.55	22	19	61	41	2.8	7.3	9.7	..	..
Ukraine	93	97	−0.25	−0.20	11	12	21	1	0.5	1.8	3.5	4.1	4.9
United Arab Emirates	2	3	−2.38	−0.22	7	10	13	0	0.2	0.3	5.6	0.3	2.6
United Kingdom	26	29	−0.68	−0.31	5	2	41	14	3.5	21.8	24.4	4.7	5.2
United States	2,963	3,040	−0.13	−0.13	37	74	177	245	94.2	14.8	14.8	18.3	24.7
Uruguay	9	17	−4.38	−2.13	11	23	35	1	1.2	0.3	0.3	0.2	0.2
Uzbekistan	30	33	−0.54	−0.20	10	15	7	15	1.1	2.1	2.3	..	..
Venezuela, RB	520	463	0.57	0.60	32	27	34	70	25.3	39.3	53.7	7.0	15.3
Vietnam	94	138	−2.28	−1.64	54	40	46	146	12.1	4.4	6.2	0.3	2.1
West Bank and Gaza	0	0	0.00	0.00	3	8	0	0	..	..	..	..	..
Yemen, Rep.	5	5	0.00	0.00	9	14	21	159	3.2	0.0	0.5	0.0	1.9
Zambia	528	495	0.32	0.33	9	14	20	9	3.8	36.0	36.0	..	..
Zimbabwe	222	156	1.58	1.88	9	13	3	16	1.9	18.0	28.0	..	..
World	**41,582 s**	**40,204 s**	**0.20 w**	**0.13 w**	**1,131 s**	**1,240 s**	**1,851 s**	**8,724 s**		**9.1 w**	**12.5 w**	**4.8 w**	**9.2 w**
Low income	5,524	4,881	0.63	0.61						10.0	11.2		
Middle income	26,552	25,660	0.24	0.10						8.6	12.4	2.9	6.6
Lower middle income	8,103	7,996	0.26	−0.13						8.8	11.5	0.8	2.0
Upper middle income	18,449	17,664	0.23	0.20						8.4	13.0	4.1	9.4
Low & middle income	32,076	30,541	0.31	0.18						8.9	12.2	3.2	6.6
East Asia & Pacific	4,602	4,698	0.17	−0.38						10.8	14.9	0.5	1.5
Europe & Central Asia	8,703	8,750	−0.02	−0.03						6.6	7.4	3.1	8.8
Latin America & Carib.	10,389	9,460	0.48	0.45						10.5	20.8	6.7	13.1
Middle East & N. Africa	207	211	−0.08	−0.13						3.1	4.0	0.9	2.0
South Asia	795	817	0.01	−0.27						5.5	6.1	1.5	1.7
Sub-Saharan Africa	7,379	6,605	0.58	0.52						11.0	11.7	3.2	4.7
High income	9,506	9,663	−0.13	−0.03						9.9	13.4	8.7	15.1
Euro area	838	930	−0.73	−0.31						11.1	15.4	6.5	10.1

a. Negative values indicate an increase in forest area. b. Flowering plants. c. National sources.

About the data

As threats to biodiversity mount, the international community is increasingly focusing on conserving diversity. Deforestation is a major cause of loss of biodiversity, and habitat conservation is vital for stemming this loss. Conservation efforts have focused on protecting areas of high biodiversity. The Food and Agriculture Organization of the United Nations (FAO) *Global Forest Resources Assessment 2010* provides detailed information on forest cover in 2010 and adjusted estimates of forest cover in 1990 and 2000. The current survey uses a uniform definition of forest. Because of space limitations, the table does not break down forest cover between natural forest and plantation, a breakdown the FAO provides for developing countries. Thus the deforestation data in the table may underestimate the rate at which natural forest is disappearing in some countries.

The number of threatened species is an important measure of the immediate need for conservation in an area. Global analyses of the status of threatened species have been carried out for few groups of organisms. Only for mammals, birds, and amphibians has the status of virtually all known species been assessed. Threatened species are defined using the International Union for Conservation of Nature's (IUCN) classification: *endangered* (in danger of extinction and unlikely to survive if causal factors continue operating) and *vulnerable* (likely to move into the endangered category in the near future if causal factors continue operating).

The Global Environment Facility's (GEF) benefits index for biodiversity is a comprehensive indicator of national biodiversity status and is used to guide its biodiversity priorities. For each country the biodiversity indicator incorporates the best available and comparable information in four relevant dimensions: represented species, threatened species, represented ecoregions, and threatened ecoregions. To combine these dimensions into one measure, the indicator uses dimensional weights that reflect the consensus of conservation scientists at the GEF, IUCN, WWF International, and other nongovernmental organizations.

The World Conservation Monitoring Centre (WCMC) compiles data on protected areas, numbers of certain species, and numbers of those species under threat from various sources. Because of differences in definitions, reporting practices, and reporting periods, cross-country comparability is limited. Nationally protected areas are defined using the six IUCN management categories for areas of at least 1,000 hectares: scientific reserves and strict nature reserves with limited public access; national parks of national or international significance and not materially affected by human activity; natural monuments and natural landscapes with unique aspects; managed nature reserves and wildlife sanctuaries; protected landscapes (which may include cultural landscapes); and areas managed mainly for the sustainable use of natural systems to ensure long-term protection and maintenance of biological diversity. The data in the table cover these six categories as well as terrestrial protected areas that are not assigned to a category by the IUCN. Designating an area as protected does not mean that protection is in force. And for small countries that only have protected areas smaller than 1,000 hectares, the size limit in the definition leads to an underestimate of protected areas.

Due to variations in consistency and methods of collection, data quality is highly variable across countries. Some countries update their information more frequently than others, some have more accurate data on extent of coverage, and many underreport the number or extent of protected areas.

Definitions

• **Forest area** is land spanning more than 0.5 hectares with trees higher than 5 meters and a canopy cover of more than 10 percent or with trees able to reach these thresholds in situ. It does not include land that is predominantly under agricultural or urban land use. • **Average annual deforestation** is the permanent conversion of natural forest area to other uses, including agriculture, ranching, settlements, and infrastructure. Deforested areas do not include areas logged but intended for regeneration or areas degraded by fuelwood gathering, acid precipitation, or forest fires. • **Threatened species** are the number of species classified by the IUCN as endangered, vulnerable, rare, indeterminate, out of danger, or insufficiently known. Mammals exclude whales and porpoises. Birds are listed for the country where their breeding or wintering ranges are located. Plants are native vascular plant species. • **GEF benefits index for biodiversity** is a composite index of relative biodiversity potential based on the species represented in each country and their threat status and diversity of habitat types. The index has been normalized from 0 (no biodiversity potential) to 100 (maximum biodiversity potential). • **Nationally protected areas** are totally or partially protected areas of at least 1,000 hectares that are designated as scientific reserves with limited public access, national parks, natural monuments, nature reserves or wildlife sanctuaries, and protected landscapes. Terrestrial protected areas exclude marine areas, unclassified areas, littoral (intertidal) areas, and sites protected under local or provincial law. Marine protected areas are areas of intertidal or subtidal terrain—and overlying water and associated flora and fauna and historical and cultural features—that have been reserved to protect part or the entire enclosed environment.

At least 33 percent of assessed species are estimated to be threatened   3.4a

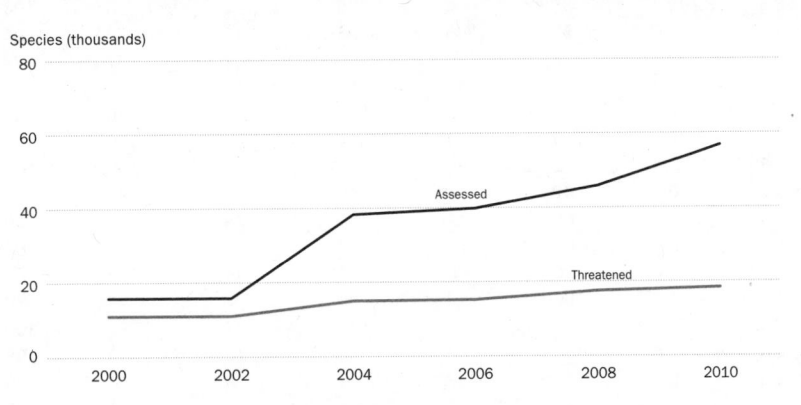

Species (thousands)

Source: International Union for Conservation of Nature.

Data sources

Data on forest area are from the FAO's *Global Forest Resources Assessment 2010* and the FAO's data web site. Data on species are from the electronic files of the United Nations Environment Programme and WCMC, the *2010 IUCN Red List of Threatened Species*, and Froese and Pauly's (2008) FishBase database. The GEF benefits index for biodiversity is from Kiran Dev Pandey, Piet Buys, Ken Chomitz, and David Wheeler's, "Biodiversity Conservation Indicators: New Tools for Priority Setting at the Global Environment Facility" (2006). Data on protected areas are from the United Nations Environment Programme and WCMC, based on data from national authorities and national legislation and international agreements.

3.5 | Freshwater

	Internal renewable freshwater resources[a]		Annual freshwater withdrawals					Water productivity	Access to an improved water source	
	Flows billion cu. m **2007**	Per capita cu. m **2007**	billion cu. m **2007**[b]	% of internal resources **2007**[b]	% for agriculture **2007**[b]	% for industry **2007**[b]	% for domestic **2007**[b]	GDP/water use 2000 $ per cu. m **2007**[b]	% of rural population **2008**	% of urban population **2008**
Afghanistan	55	1,946	23.3	42.3	98	0	2	..	39	78
Albania	27	8,588	1.7	6.4	62	11	27	3	98	96
Algeria	11	332	6.1	54.0	65	13	22	12	79	85
Angola	148	8,431	0.4	0.2	60	17	23	61	38	60
Argentina	276	6,989	29.2	10.6	74	9	17	13	80	98
Armenia	9	2,952	3.0	32.5	66	4	30	1	93	98
Australia	492	23,348	23.9	4.9	75	10	15	22	100	100
Austria	55	6,626	2.1	3.8	1	64	35	105	100	100
Azerbaijan	8	946	12.2	150.5	76	19	4	1	71	88
Bangladesh	105	666	79.4	75.6	96	1	3	1	78	85
Belarus	37	3,834	2.8	7.5	30	47	23	8	99	100
Belgium	12	1,129	0.0	..	..	..	..	..	100	100
Benin	10	1,227	0.1	1.3	45	23	32	23	69	84
Bolivia	304	31,868	1.4	0.5	81	7	13	7	67	96
Bosnia and Herzegovina	36	9,395	0.0	..	..	..	..	..	98	100
Botswana	2	1,268	0.2	8.1	41	18	41	41	90	99
Brazil	5,418	28,498	59.3	1.1	62	18	20	14	84	99
Bulgaria	21	2,742	10.5	50.0	19	78	3	2	100	100
Burkina Faso	13	849	0.8	6.4	86	1	13	5	72	95
Burundi	10	1,283	0.3	2.9	77	6	17	3	71	83
Cambodia	121	8,417	4.1	3.4	98	0	1	2	56	81
Cameroon	273	14,630	1.0	0.4	74	8	18	13	51	92
Canada	2,850	86,426	46.0	1.6	12	69	20	19	99	100
Central African Republic	141	33,119	0.0	0.0	4	16	80	39	51	92
Chad	15	1,412	0.2	1.5	83	0	17	13	44	67
Chile	884	53,137	12.6	1.4	64	25	11	8	75	99
China	2,813	2,134	554.1	22.4	65	23	12	4	82	98
Hong Kong SAR, China	..	..	..	..	..	..	..	..	..	..
Colombia	2,112	47,611	10.7	0.5	46	4	50	13	73	99
Congo, Dem. Rep.	900	14,395	0.4	0.0	31	17	53	16	28	80
Congo, Rep.	222	62,516	0.0	0.0	9	22	70	89	34	95
Costa Rica	112	25,209	2.7	2.4	53	17	29	9	91	100
Côte d'Ivoire	77	3,819	0.9	1.2	65	12	24	11	68	93
Croatia	38	8,499	0.0	..	..	..	..	..	97	100
Cuba	38	3,402	8.2	21.5	69	12	19	6	89	96
Czech Republic	13	1,272	2.6	19.6	2	57	41	30	100	100
Denmark	6	1,099	1.3	21.2	43	25	32	141	100	100
Dominican Republic	21	2,139	3.4	16.1	66	2	32	10	84	87
Ecuador	432	32,379	17.0	3.9	82	5	12	1	88	97
Egypt, Arab Rep.	2	22	68.3	3,794.4	86	6	8	2	98	100
El Salvador	18	2,907	1.3	7.2	59	16	25	13	76	94
Eritrea	3	586	0.6	20.8	95	0	5	1	57	74
Estonia	13	9,475	0.2	1.2	5	38	57	64	97	99
Ethiopia	122	1,551	5.6	4.6	94	0	6	2	26	98
Finland	107	20,232	2.5	2.3	3	84	14	62	100	100
France	200	3,229	31.8	22.4	12	69	18	38	100	100
Gabon	164	115,340	0.1	0.1	42	8	50	49	41	95
Gambia, The	3	1,857	0.0	1.0	65	12	23	19	86	96
Georgia	58	13,339	1.6	2.8	65	13	22	3	96	100
Germany	107	1,301	47.1	44.0	20	68	12	44	100	100
Ghana	30	1,325	1.0	3.2	66	10	24	7	74	90
Greece	58	5,182	7.8	13.4	80	3	16	22	99	100
Guatemala	109	8,177	2.0	1.8	80	13	6	12	90	98
Guinea	226	23,505	1.5	0.7	90	2	8	3	61	89
Guinea-Bissau	16	10,383	0.2	1.1	82	5	13	1	51	83
Haiti	13	1,338	1.0	7.6	94	1	5	4	55	71
Honduras	96	13,372	0.9	0.9	80	12	8	12	77	95

	Internal renewable freshwater resources[a]		Annual freshwater withdrawals					Water productivity	Access to an improved water source	
	Flows billion cu. m 2007	Per capita cu. m 2007	billion cu. m 2007[b]	% of internal resources 2007[b]	% for agriculture 2007[b]	% for industry 2007[b]	% for domestic 2007[b]	GDP/water use 2000 $ per cu. m 2007[b]	% of rural population 2008	% of urban population 2008
Hungary	6	597	7.6	127.3	32	59	9	8	100	100
India	1,276	1,134	40.4	51.2	91	2	7	1	84	96
Indonesia	2,019	8,987	82.8	2.9	82	7	12	1.2	71	89
Iran, Islamic Rep.	129	1,809	93.3	72.6	92	1	7	2	..	98
Iraq	35	1,175	66.0	187.5	79	15	7	0	55	91
Ireland	49	11,246	..	..	..	..	..	125	100	100
Israel	1	104	2.0	260.5	58	6	36	79	100	100
Italy	183	3,074	44.4	24.3	45	37	18	27	100	100
Jamaica	9	3,514	0.4	4.4	49	17	34	25	89	98
Japan	430	3,365	88.4	20.6	62	18	20	59	100	100
Jordan	1	120	0.9	138.0	65	4	31	14	91	98
Kazakhstan	75	4,871	35.0	46.4	82	17	2	1	90	99
Kenya	21	548	2.7	13.2	79	4	17	6	52	83
Korea, Dem. Rep.	67	2,824	9.0	13.5	55	25	20	..	100	100
Korea, Rep.	65	1,338	18.6	28.7	48	16	36	40	88	100
Kosovo	..	..	..	..	..	..	..	..	..	..
Kuwait	0	0	0.5	..	54	2	44	67	99	99
Kyrgyz Republic	46	8,873	10.1	21.7	94	3	3	0	85	99
Lao PDR	190	31,256	3.0	1.6	90	6	4	1	51	72
Latvia	17	7,355	0.3	1.8	13	33	53	48	96	100
Lebanon	5	1,153	1.3	27.3	60	11	29	17	100	100
Lesotho	5	2,574	0.1	1.0	20	40	40	18	81	97
Liberia	200	55,138	0.1	0.1	55	18	27	5	51	79
Libya	1	97	4.3	721.0	83	3	14	11	..	..
Lithuania	16	4,610	0.3	1.7	7	15	78	73	..	..
Macedonia, FYR	5	2,647	0.0	..	..	..	..	..	99	100
Madagascar	337	18,114	15.0	4.4	96	2	3	0	29	71
Malawi	16	1,118	1.0	6.3	80	5	15	2	77	95
Malaysia	580	21,841	9.0	1.6	62	21	17	15	99	100
Mali	60	4,835	6.5	10.9	90	1	9	1	44	81
Mauritania	0[c]	127	1.7	425.0	88	3	9	1	47	52
Mauritius	3	2,182	0.7	26.4	68	3	30	8	99	100
Mexico	409	3,885	78.2	19.1	77	5	17	9	85	96
Moldova	1	273	2.3	231.0	33	58	10	1	49	97
Mongolia	35	13,326	0.4	1.3	52	27	20	4	60	98
Morocco	29	929	12.6	43.4	87	3	10	4	60	98
Mozambique	100	4,586	0.6	0.6	87	2	11	12	29	77
Myanmar	1003	20,415	33.2	3.8	89	1	10	..	69	75
Namibia	6	2,949	0.3	4.9	71	5	24	19	88	99
Nepal	198	7,007	10.2	5.1	96	1	3	1	87	93
Netherlands	11	671	7.9	72.2	34	60	6	55	100	100
New Zealand	327	77,336	2.1	0.6	42	9	48	31	100	100
Nicaragua	190	33,912	1.3	0.7	83	2	15	4	68	98
Niger	4	248	2.2	62.3	95	0	4	1	39	96
Nigeria	221	1,496	8.0	3.6	69	10	21	9	42	75
Norway	382	81,119	2.2	0.6	11	67	23	90	100	100
Oman	1	514	1.3	94.4	88	1	10	20	77	92
Pakistan	55	338	169.4	308.0	96	2	2	1	87	95
Panama	147	44,094	0.8	0.6	28	5	67	21	83	97
Papua New Guinea	801	124,716	0.1	0.0	1	42	56	59	33	87
Paraguay	94	15,343	0.5	0.5	71	8	20	18	66	99
Peru	1,616	56,685	20.1	1.2	82	10	8	4	61	90
Philippines	479	5,399	28.5	6.0	74	9	17	4	87	93
Poland	54	1,406	16.2	30.2	8	79	13	11	100	100
Portugal	38	3,582	11.3	29.6	78	12	10	11	100	99
Puerto Rico	7	1,801	0.0	..	..	..	..	..	..	..
Qatar	0	45	0.4	870.6	59	2	39	90	100	100

3.5 Freshwater

	Internal renewable freshwater resources[a]		Annual freshwater withdrawals					Water productivity	Access to an improved water source	
	Flows billion cu. m 2007	Per capita cu. m 2007	billion cu. m 2007[b]	% of internal resources 2007[b]	% for agriculture 2007[b]	% for industry 2007[b]	% for domestic 2007[b]	GDP/water use 2000 $ per cu. m 2007[b]	% of rural population 2008	% of urban population 2008
Romania	42	1,963	23.2	54.8	57	34	9	2	..	..
Russian Federation	4,313	30,350	76.7	1.8	18	63	19	5	89	98
Rwanda	10	1,005	0.2	1.6	68	8	24	19	62	77
Saudi Arabia	2	99	23.7	986.1	88	3	9	10	..	97
Senegal	26	2,169	2.2	8.6	93	3	4	3	52	92
Serbia	44[c]	5,419[c]	0.0[c]	..	..	..	..	..	98	99
Sierra Leone	160	29,518	0.4	0.2	92	3	5	4	26	86
Singapore	1	131	0.0	..	..	..	..	..	..	100
Slovak Republic	13	2,334	0.0	..	..	..	..	..	100	100
Slovenia	19	9,251	0.0	..	..	..	..	..	99	100
Somalia	6	687	3.3	55.0	99	0	0	..	9	67
South Africa	45	928	12.5	27.9	63	6	31	14	78	99
Spain	111	2,478	35.6	32.0	68	19	13	21	100	100
Sri Lanka	50	2,499	12.6	25.2	95	2	2	2	88	98
Sudan	30	742	37.3	124.4	97	1	3	1	52	64
Swaziland	3	2,293	1.0	39.5	97	1	2	2	61	92
Sweden	171	18,692	3.0	1.7	9	54	37	103	100	100
Switzerland	40	5,350	2.6	6.4	2	74	24	111	100	100
Syrian Arab Republic	7	349	16.7	238.4	88	4	9	2	84	94
Tajikistan	66	9,855	12.0	18.0	92	5	4	0	61	94
Tanzania	84	2,035	5.2	6.2	89	0	10	3	45	80
Thailand	210	3,135	87.1	41.5	95	2	2	2	98	99
Togo	12	1,825	0.2	1.5	45	2	53	9	41	87
Trinidad and Tobago	4	2,891	0.3	8.1	6	26	68	46	93	98
Tunisia	4	410	2.6	62.9	82	4	14	10	84	99
Turkey	227	3,109	40.1	17.7	74	11	15	9	96	100
Turkmenistan	1	273	24.7	1,812.5	98	1	2	0	72	97
Uganda	39	1,273	0.0	..	40	16	43	..	64	91
Ukraine	53	1,142	37.5	70.7	52	35	12	1	97	98
United Arab Emirates	0	34	4.0	2,665.3	83	2	15	28	100	100
United Kingdom	145	2,378	9.5	6.6	3	75	22	185	100	100
United States	2,818	9,344	477.8	17.1	40	46	14	24	94	100
Uruguay	59	17,750	3.2	5.3	96	1	3	8	100	100
Uzbekistan	16	608	58.3	357.0	93	2	5	0	81	98
Venezuela, RB	722	26,287	8.4	1.2	47	7	46	19	75	94
Vietnam	367	4,304	71.4	19.5	68	24	8	1	92	99
West Bank and Gaza	1	212	0.4	..	45	7	48	..	91	91
Yemen, Rep.	2	94	3.4	161.9	90	2	8	4	57	72
Zambia	80	6,513	1.7	2.2	76	7	17	3	46	87
Zimbabwe	12	985	4.2	34.3	79	7	14	1	72	99
World	43,464 s	6,616 w	3,850.0 s	9.0 w	70 w	20 w	10 w	10 w	78 w	96 w
Low income	4,418	5,452	240.9	5.6	93	2	5	1	56	85
Middle income	29,421	6,271	2,672.1	9.1	78	14	9	3	81	95
Lower middle income	11,728	3,155	2,103.9	17.9	81	12	7	2	81	94
Upper middle income	17,694	18,142	568.2	3.2	65	19	15	7	86	98
Low & middle income	33,839	6,150	2,913.0	8.6	79	13	8	3	76	94
East Asia & Pacific	9,454	4,940	959.0	10.2	74	20	7	3	81	96
Europe & Central Asia	5,059	12,911	351.9	7.0	63	27	10	3	89	98
Latin America & Carib.	13,425	24,001	264.9	2.0	71	10	19	10	80	97
Middle East & N. Africa	225	714	275.6	122.3	86	6	8	2	80	95
South Asia	1,819	1,194	941.1	51.7	90	4	6	1	83	95
Sub-Saharan Africa	3,858	4,826	120.5	3.2	87	3	10	4	47	82
High income	9,624	9,017	937.0	10.5	42	43	15	32	98	100
Euro area	955	2,932	200.2	22.0	38	48	15	34	100	100

a. Excludes river flows from other countries because of data unreliability. b. Data are for the most recent year available (see Primary data documentation). c. Includes Kosovo and Montenegro.

About the data

The data on freshwater resources are based on estimates of runoff into rivers and recharge of groundwater. These estimates are based on different sources and refer to different years, so cross-country comparisons should be made with caution. Because the data are collected intermittently, they may hide significant variations in total renewable water resources from year to year. The data also fail to distinguish between seasonal and geographic variations in water availability within countries. Data for small countries and countries in arid and semiarid zones are less reliable than those for larger countries and countries with greater rainfall.

Caution should also be used in comparing data on annual freshwater withdrawals, which are subject to variations in collection and estimation methods. In addition, inflows and outflows are estimated at different times and at different levels of quality and precision, requiring caution in interpreting the data, particularly for water-short countries, notably in the Middle East and North Africa.

Water productivity is an indication only of the efficiency by which each country uses its water resources. Given the different economic structure of each country, these indicators should be used carefully, taking into account the countries' sectoral activities and natural resource endowments.

The data on access to an improved water source measure the percentage of the population with ready access to water for domestic purposes. The data are based on surveys and estimates provided by governments to the Joint Monitoring Programme of the World Health Organization (WHO) and the United Nations Children's Fund (UNICEF). The coverage rates are based on information from service users on actual household use rather than on information from service providers, which may include nonfunctioning systems. Access to drinking water from an improved source does not ensure that the water is safe or adequate, as these characteristics are not tested at the time of survey. While information on access to an improved water source is widely used, it is extremely subjective, and such terms as *safe, improved, adequate,* and *reasonable* may have different meaning in different countries despite official WHO definitions (see *Definitions*). Even in high-income countries treated water may not always be safe to drink. Access to an improved water source is equated with connection to a supply system; it does not take into account variations in the quality and cost (broadly defined) of the service.

Definitions

• **Internal renewable freshwater resources** are the average annual flows of rivers and groundwater from rainfall in the country. Natural incoming flows originating outside a country's borders are excluded. Overlapping water resources between surface runoff and groundwater recharge are also deducted. • **Renewable internal freshwater resources per capita** are calculated using the World Bank's population estimates (see table 2.1). • **Annual freshwater withdrawals** are total water withdrawals, not counting evaporation losses from storage basins. Withdrawals also include water from desalination plants in countries where they are a significant source. Withdrawals can exceed 100 percent of total renewable resources where extraction from nonrenewable aquifers or desalination plants is considerable or where water reuse is significant. Withdrawals for agriculture and industry are total withdrawals for irrigation and livestock production and for direct industrial use (including for cooling thermoelectric plants). Withdrawals for domestic uses include drinking water, municipal use or supply, and use for public services, commercial establishments, and homes. • **Water productivity** is calculated as GDP in constant prices divided by annual total water withdrawal. • **Access to an improved water source** is the percentage of the population with reasonable access to an adequate amount of water from an improved source, such as piped water into a dwelling, plot, or yard; public tap or standpipe; tubewell or borehole; protected dug well or spring; and rainwater collection. Unimproved sources include unprotected dug wells or springs, carts with small tank or drum, bottled water, and tanker trucks. Reasonable access is defined as the availability of at least 20 liters a person a day from a source within 1 kilometer of the dwelling.

Agriculture is still the largest user of water, accounting for some 70 percent of global withdrawals . . . 3.5a

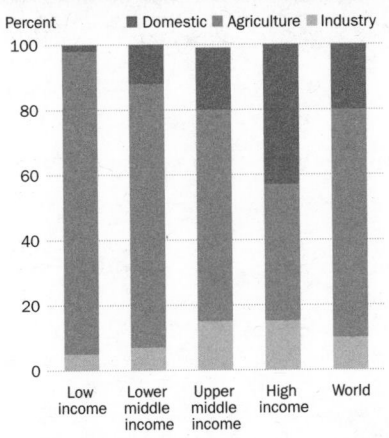

Percent — ■ Domestic ■ Agriculture ▨ Industry

Source: Table 3.5.

. . . and approaching 90 percent in some developing regions 3.5b

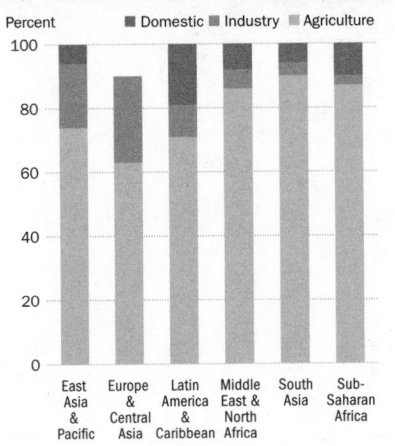

Percent — ■ Domestic ■ Industry ▨ Agriculture

Source: Table 3.5.

Data sources

Data on freshwater resources and withdrawals are from the Food and Agriculture Organization of the United Nations AQUASTAT data. The GDP estimates used to calculate water productivity are from the World Bank national accounts database. Data on access to water are from WHO and UNICEF's *Progress on sanitation and drinking water* (2010).

	Emissions of organic water pollutants				Industry shares of emissions of organic water pollutants							
	thousand kilograms per day		kilograms per day per worker		Primary metals	Paper and pulp	Chemicals	Food and beverages	% of total Stone, ceramics, and glass	Textiles	Wood	Other
	1990	2007[a]	1990	2007[a]	2007[a]	2007[a]	2007[a]	2007[a]	2007[a]	2007[a]	2007[a]	2007[a]
Afghanistan	..	0.2	..	0.21	..	19.7	27.9	14.1	11.7	23.3	..	3.1
Albania	2.4	3.6	0.25	0.25	..	..	..	39.8	..	60.2	..	11.9
Algeria	..	..	..	..	..	..	..	..	..	..	..	..
Angola	..	..	..	..	..	..	..	..	..	..	..	..
Argentina	181.4	155.5	0.21	0.23	3.8	8.4	15.8	30.5	3.5	14.3	2.1	21.6
Armenia	..	..	..	..	..	..	..	..	..	..	..	..
Australia	..	..	..	..	..	..	..	..	..	..	..	..
Austria	90.5	84.4	0.15	0.14	5.7	7.1	9.3	12.2	5.8	4.3	6.0	49.5
Azerbaijan	41.3	20.0	0.15	0.18	8.8	3.0	18.5	19.6	8.4	11.7	1.5	28.6
Bangladesh	250.8	303.0	0.15	0.14	0.7	2.3	3.0	7.6	2.6	79.3	0.5	4.2
Belarus	..	..	..	..	..	..	..	..	..	..	..	..
Belgium	107.8	95.9	0.17	0.17	6.4	7.9	18.6	16.4	3.1	5.5	2.2	40.0
Benin	..	..	..	..	..	..	..	..	..	..	..	..
Bolivia	11.3	11.5	0.24	0.25	0.9	9.8	13.1	35.4	7.7	18.4	5.3	9.5
Bosnia and Herzegovina	..	..	..	..	..	..	..	..	..	..	..	..
Botswana	2.5	3.2	0.30	0.23	..	2.4	..	43.8	0.6	3.9	..	50.0
Brazil	..	..	..	..	..	..	..	..	..	..	..	..
Bulgaria	124.3	102.1	0.17	0.17	3.7	4.3	8.0	17.7	4.8	26.8	3.0	31.7
Burkina Faso	..	..	..	..	..	..	..	..	..	..	..	..
Burundi	..	..	..	..	..	..	..	..	..	..	..	..
Cambodia	3.8	..	0.17		..	..	..	..	..	..	..	..
Cameroon	..	..	..	..	..	..	..	..	..	..	..	..
Canada	300.9	306.6	0.17	0.16	4.3	8.9	10.9	14.0	2.8	7.3	6.5	45.3
Central African Republic	..	..	..	..	..	..	..	..	..	..	..	..
Chad	..	..	..	..	..	..	..	..	..	..	..	..
Chile	..	92.5	..	0.25	7.6	6.3	13.7	35.1	3.6	9.1	6.9	17.7
China	..	9,428.9	..	0.13	7.2	3.9	13.0	7.4	6.3	20.6	1.7	39.9
Hong Kong SAR, China	..	..	..	..	..	..	..	..	..	..	..	..
Colombia	..	87.0	..	0.20	2.3	8.9	17.3	21.3	5.3	24.1	0.9	19.9
Congo, Dem. Rep.	..	..	..	..	..	..	..	..	..	..	..	..
Congo, Rep.	..	..	..	..	..	..	..	..	..	..	..	..
Costa Rica	..	..	..	..	..	..	..	..	..	..	..	..
Côte d'Ivoire	..	..	..	..	..	..	..	..	..	..	..	..
Croatia	48.5	42.9	0.17	0.17	3.1	7.2	9.5	17.6	5.9	14.5	4.9	37.2
Cuba	..	..	..	..	..	..	..	..	..	..	..	..
Czech Republic	177.1	146.5	0.14	0.13	5.4	4.8	10.9	10.9	6.4	7.4	4.4	49.8
Denmark	84.5	61.0	0.18	0.16	1.4	11.5	13.1	16.4	4.8	1.5	4.0	47.3
Dominican Republic	88.6	..	0.18		..	..	..	..	..	..	..	..
Ecuador	28.6	44.7	0.24	0.28	1.8	7.8	12.8	46.4	4.4	12.3	2.2	12.3
Egypt, Arab Rep.	206.5	..	0.19		..	..	..	..	..	..	..	..
El Salvador	..	..	..	..	..	..	..	..	..	..	..	..
Eritrea	2.4	2.5	0.19	0.20	0.2	4.4	9.5	27.3	9.6	29.0	0.1	20.3
Estonia	21.7	16.0	0.15	0.14	0.4	7.3	7.1	14.6	5.5	8.0	16.4	40.8
Ethiopia	18.5	32.2	0.23	0.24	1.4	6.0	10.9	34.7	8.3	27.9	1.5	9.3
Finland	72.5	55.3	0.19	0.14	1.0	15.4	8.7	9.0	4.4	2.8	7.3	51.4
France	326.5	569.4	0.11	0.16	3.2	7.4	15.0	16.6	3.8	4.8	2.4	46.9
Gabon	..	..	..	..	..	..	..	..	..	..	..	..
Gambia, The	0.8	..	0.27		..	..	..	..	..	..	..	..
Georgia	..	..	..	..	..	..	..	..	..	..	..	..
Germany	806.6	936.2	0.13	0.14	3.8	7.1	12.4	11.4	3.4	2.4	1.9	57.6
Ghana	..	16.0	..	0.17	3.0	3.8	15.9	18.6	4.1	10.2	33.3	11.2
Greece	50.9	60.8	0.19	0.20	3.9	9.0	10.1	23.9	7.0	14.4	2.8	28.9
Guatemala	..	..	..	..	..	..	..	..	..	..	..	..
Guinea	..	..	..	..	..	..	..	..	..	..	..	..
Guinea-Bissau	..	..	..	..	..	..	..	..	..	..	..	..
Haiti	5.2	..	0.20		..	..	..	..	..	..	..	..
Honduras	..	..	..	..	..	..	..	..	..	..	..	..

	Emissions of organic water pollutants				Industry shares of emissions of organic water pollutants								
	thousand kilograms per day		kilograms per day per worker		Primary metals	Paper and pulp	Chemicals	Food and beverages	Stone, ceramics, and glass	Textiles	Wood	Other
	1990	2007[a]	1990	2007[a]	2007[a]	2007[a]	2007[a]	2007[a]	2007[a]	2007[a]	2007[a]	2007[a]
Hungary	122.1	110.6	0.18	0.15	2.7	6.4	10.6	15.2	3.7	9.1	3.3	49.0
India	..	..	..	..	..	..	..	..	..	..	..	..
Indonesia	721.8	883.0	0.18	0.19	1.4	4.1	12.0	23.1	4.0	29.2	6.3	19.9
Iran, Islamic Rep.	131.6	160.8	0.16	0.15	7.1	2.8	12.8	16.1	13.8	11.2	0.7	35.5
Iraq	7.7	7.7	0.27	0.27	13.1	25.6	29.9	16.9	5.4	9.1	..	..
Ireland	36.1	28.4	0.19	0.16	1.3	10.2	17.6	14.8	5.9	0.8	3.8	45.5
Israel	54.6	52.7	0.16	0.16	1.6	8.9	13.4	16.4	2.9	7.9	1.2	47.6
Italy	378.3	479.2	0.13	0.13	3.5	5.2	10.3	9.3	5.4	13.6	2.9	49.6
Jamaica	..	..	..	..	..	..	..	..	..	..	..	..
Japan	1,455.0	1,126.9	0.14	0.15	3.3	7.0	11.2	15.0	3.6	5.3	2.0	52.5
Jordan	15.0	29.1	0.18	0.18	2.3	6.1	13.7	20.8	11.5	18.6	2.3	24.5
Kazakhstan	123.5	97.4	0.23	0.24	33.3	2.3	8.9	18.7	9.3	3.9	0.6	23.0
Kenya	..	..	..	..	..	..	..	..	..	..	..	..
Korea, Dem. Rep.	..	..	..	..	..	..	..	..	..	..	..	..
Korea, Rep.	366.9	319.6	0.12	0.11	4.2	5.4	12.1	6.3	3.0	9.3	0.9	58.9
Kosovo	..	..	..	..	..	..	..	..	..	..	..	..
Kuwait	..	..	..	..	..	..	..	..	..	..	..	..
Kyrgyz Republic	28.9	12.2	0.14	0.20	9.8	6.3	8.5	24.2	17.5	9.8	1.6	22.4
Lao PDR	4.3	4.3	0.14	0.14	1.8	2.2	3.8	9.2	7.5	49.2	21.4	4.9
Latvia	39.8	28.4	0.12	0.18	2.7	7.7	5.8	21.1	4.4	11.8	19.1	27.3
Lebanon	14.7	14.7	0.19	0.19	0.5	7.5	6.0	25.5	12.9	16.7	4.5	26.3
Lesotho	..	5.3	..	0.13	0.9	0.5	0.3	2.6	0.8	93.5	..	1.4
Liberia	..	..	..	..	..	..	..	..	..	..	..	..
Libya	..	..	..	..	..	..	..	..	..	..	..	..
Lithuania	54.0	42.2	0.15	0.17	0.9	5.7	8.3	20.5	4.7	17.6	11.4	30.8
Macedonia, FYR	27.0	20.3	0.20	0.18	5.8	4.7	6.3	15.1	3.2	44.7	2.9	17.3
Madagascar	..	92.8	..	0.14	0.3	1.6	12.4	7.6	2.8	58.9	6.3	10.0
Malawi	37.2	32.7	0.40	0.39	..	1.4	3.7	82.1	0.6	7.5	1.1	3.6
Malaysia	..	208.3	..	0.12	2.8	4.9	16.5	9.1	3.8	6.6	7.8	48.5
Mali	..	..	..	..	..	..	..	..	..	..	..	..
Mauritania	..	..	..	..	..	..	..	..	..	..	..	..
Mauritius	16.8	15.4	0.16	0.17	0.4	3.6	5.9	14.7	..	63.9	0.7	10.9
Mexico	425.0	..	0.18	..	..	..	..	..	..	..	..	..
Moldova	29.2	18.8	0.44	0.45	..	3.8	..	95.2	..	..	..	0.9
Mongolia	..	8.8	..	0.22	3.7	5.1	3.3	27.2	9.5	41.6	5.4	4.1
Morocco	..	74.0	..	0.16	1.0	2.9	7.9	16.3	6.5	43.5	2.0	19.9
Mozambique	..	..	..	..	..	..	..	..	..	..	..	..
Myanmar	..	..	..	..	..	..	..	..	..	..	..	..
Namibia	..	..	..	..	..	..	..	..	..	..	..	..
Nepal	26.4	26.8	0.14	0.16	1.6	3.9	7.2	19.2	29.9	29.4	2.0	6.8
Netherlands	142.3	128.2	0.20	0.19	3.1	13.4	14.1	18.2	4.0	2.1	2.6	42.5
New Zealand	46.7	61.6	0.24	0.23	2.0	12.2	8.6	31.1	3.1	5.8	8.0	29.3
Nicaragua	..	..	..	..	..	..	..	..	..	..	..	..
Niger	..	..	..	..	..	..	..	..	..	..	..	..
Nigeria	..	..	..	..	..	..	..	..	..	..	..	..
Norway	51.8	46.9	0.20	0.18	4.9	12.1	7.5	19.1	4.3	2.0	6.0	44.2
Oman	3.8	7.6	0.15	0.16	4.0	4.6	17.8	20.4	20.5	2.4	4.0	26.3
Pakistan	..	153.7	..	0.17	2.2	1.9	9.1	15.1	4.3	55.6	0.4	11.2
Panama	10.3	13.7	0.30	0.32	0.9	11.6	6.9	55.2	4.0	4.7	1.6	15.0
Papua New Guinea	..	..	..	..	..	..	..	..	..	..	..	..
Paraguay	15.3	10.8	0.20	0.28	3.1	9.3	16.7	42.6	5.9	11.0	4.5	6.9
Peru	..	..	..	..	..	..	..	..	..	..	..	..
Philippines	169.0	144.6	0.17	0.15	2.6	4.2	9.5	14.4	2.7	21.6	2.1	42.9
Poland	446.7	359.7	0.16	0.16	3.3	5.1	11.3	18.1	5.5	10.3	4.9	41.5
Portugal	140.6	87.7	0.14	0.17	0.2	8.1	3.4	19.8	5.2	16.3	8.5	38.5
Puerto Rico	..	..	..	..	..	..	..	..	..	..	..	..
Qatar	..	6.4	..	0.12	3.7	6.7	10.5	6.5	18.1	20.7	12.5	21.3

	Emissions of organic water pollutants				Industry shares of emissions of organic water pollutants							
	thousand kilograms per day		kilograms per day per worker		Primary metals	Paper and pulp	Chemicals	Food and beverages	% of total Stone, ceramics, and glass	Textiles	Wood	Other
	1990	**2007**[a]	**1990**	**2007**[a]	**2007**[a]	**2007**[a]	**2007**[a]	**2007**[a]	**2007**[a]	**2007**[a]	**2007**[a]	**2007**[a]
Romania	411.2	222.1	0.12	0.15	4.5	3.5	7.1	13.9	4.0	25.0	5.3	36.8
Russian Federation	1,521.4	1,381.7	0.16	0.17	8.4	4.9	11.6	17.9	8.3	6.3	4.2	38.4
Rwanda	8.1	8.1	0.37	0.37	..	..	9.0	77.1	4.3	1.9	2.9	4.8
Saudi Arabia	..	106.6	..	0.18	3.2	6.9	11.6	20.0	10.7	14.4	3.3	30.0
Senegal	6.1	6.6	0.30	0.29	4.9	6.3	23.8	44.6	3.9	10.5	0.8	5.3
Serbia	..	..	..	..	..	..	..	..	..	..	..	..
Sierra Leone	..	..	..	..	..	..	..	..	..	..	..	..
Singapore	33.1	38.3	0.09	0.09	0.5	5.5	11.9	5.3	1.3	2.3	0.5	72.7
Slovak Republic	72.8	47.9	0.13	0.14	7.9	5.4	9.1	10.7	6.0	5.0	4.2	51.7
Slovenia	28.1	28.8	0.13	0.13	4.6	6.1	12.2	7.7	4.1	10.8	4.9	49.6
Somalia	..	..	..	..	..	..	..	..	..	..	..	..
South Africa	260.5	229.6	0.17	0.17	9.9	6.6	10.6	15.7	5.2	10.4	4.2	37.4
Spain	348.0	378.8	0.16	0.15	3.1	8.0	10.8	15.3	7.9	8.4	3.8	42.7
Sri Lanka	..	266.1	..	0.19	2.6	4.3	9.0	22.4	6.3	43.6	2.5	9.3
Sudan	..	38.6	..	0.29	0.6	1.9	7.0	57.5	14.2	8.0	1.7	9.1
Swaziland	..	..	..	..	..	..	..	..	..	..	..	..
Sweden	116.8	96.9	0.15	0.14	5.3	11.9	9.9	8.6	2.6	1.2	5.6	54.9
Switzerland	..	..	..	..	..	..	..	..	..	..	..	..
Syrian Arab Republic	59.7	80.4	0.16	0.16	1.6	1.9	7.3	19.9	11.3	32.0	5.2	20.9
Tajikistan	29.1	12.8	0.17	0.24	28.2	2.7	2.0	18.0	8.9	38.4	0.3	1.8
Tanzania	..	30.3	..	0.34	2.6	4.8	8.6	61.2	1.9	12.7	2.9	5.3
Thailand	369.4	581.4	0.15	0.15	1.9	4.2	12.4	16.4	4.7	20.5	2.8	37.2
Timor-Leste	..	..	..	..	..	..	..	..	..	..	..	..
Togo	..	..	..	..	..	..	..	..	..	..	..	..
Trinidad and Tobago	7.0	7.6	0.23	0.29	4.8	18.2	21.3	39.3	8.0	7.7	8.5	5.0
Tunisia	..	..	..	..	..	..	..	..	..	..	..	..
Turkey	175.8	346.4	0.18	0.15	3.8	3.8	8.6	12.4	6.6	32.2	1.7	30.9
Turkmenistan	..	..	..	..	..	..	..	..	..	..	..	..
Uganda	3.3	2.1	0.29	0.23	..	7.8	7.3	34.8	13.3	17.2	2.3	19.6
Ukraine	..	498.2	.,	0.19	13.9	4.3	11.2	19.7	6.8	5.6	2.1	36.5
United Arab Emirates	..	..	..	..	..	..	..	..	..	..	..	..
United Kingdom	599.9	521.7	0.16	0.17	2.7	12.5	13.5	14.9	3.6	4.3	2.5	46.1
United States	2,307.0	1,850.8	0.14	0.14	3.5	8.1	13.1	12.0	3.9	4.3	4.1	51.1
Uruguay	..	..	..	..	..	..	..	..	..	..	..	..
Uzbekistan	..	..	..	..	..	..	..	..	..	..	..	..
Venezuela, RB	..	..	..	..	..	..	..	..	..	..	..	..
Vietnam	141.0	544.8	0.16	0.14	1.4	3.5	6.8	12.7	6.4	40.2	3.3	25.8
West Bank and Gaza	..	..	..	..	..	..	..	..	..	..	..	..
Yemen, Rep.	12.6	46.5	0.24	0.21	..	2.1	7.4	35.9	14.6	15.5	5.1	19.4
Zambia	..	..	..	..	..	..	..	..	..	..	..	..
Zimbabwe	29.3	..	0.20	..	..	..	..	..	..	..	..	..

a. Data are derived using the United Nations Industrial Development Organization's (UNIDO) industry database four-digit International Standard Classification (ISIC). Data in italics are for the most recent year available and are derived using UNIDO's industry database at the three-digit ISIC.

About the data

Emissions of organic pollutants from industrial activities are a major cause of degradation of water quality. Water quality and pollution levels are generally measured as concentration or load—the rate of occurrence of a substance in an aqueous solution. Polluting substances include organic matter, metals, minerals, sediment, bacteria, and toxic chemicals. The table focuses on organic water pollution resulting from industrial activities. Because water pollution tends to be sensitive to local conditions, the national-level data in the table may not reflect the quality of water in specific locations.

The data in the table come from an international study of industrial emissions that may have been the first to include data from developing countries (Hettige, Mani, and Wheeler 1998). These data were updated through 2007 by the World Bank's Development Research Group. Unlike estimates from earlier studies based on engineering or economic models, these estimates are based on actual measurements of plant-level water pollution. The focus is on organic water pollution caused by organic waste, measured in terms of biochemical oxygen demand (BOD), because the data for this indicator are the most plentiful and reliable for cross-country comparisons of emissions. BOD measures the strength of an organic waste by the amount of oxygen consumed in breaking it down. A sewage overload in natural waters exhausts the water's dissolved oxygen content. Wastewater treatment, by contrast, reduces BOD.

Data on water pollution are more readily available than are other emissions data because most industrial pollution control programs start by regulating emissions of organic water pollutants. Such data are fairly reliable because sampling techniques for measuring water pollution are more widely understood and much less expensive than those for air pollution.

Hettige, Mani, and Wheeler (1998) used plant- and sector-level information on emissions and employment from 13 national environmental protection agencies and sector-level information on output and employment from the United Nations Industrial Development Organization (UNIDO). Their econometric analysis found that the ratio of BOD to employment in each industrial sector is about the same across countries. This finding allowed the authors to estimate BOD loads across countries and over time. The estimated BOD intensities per unit of employment were multiplied by sectoral employment numbers from UNIDO's industry database for 1980–98. These estimates of sectoral emissions were then used to calculate kilograms of emissions of organic water pollutants per day for each country and year. The data in the table were derived by updating these estimates through 2007.

Definitions

• **Emissions of organic water pollutants** are measured as biochemical oxygen demand, or the amount of oxygen that bacteria in water will consume in breaking down waste, a standard water treatment test for the presence of organic pollutants. Emissions per worker are total emissions divided by the number of industrial workers. • **Industry shares of emissions of organic water pollutants** are emissions from manufacturing activities as defined by two-digit divisions of the International Standard Industrial Classification revision 3.

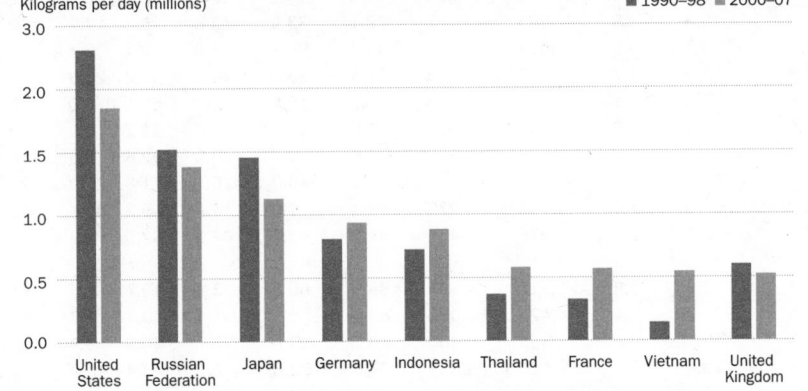

Emissions of organic water pollutants vary among countries from 1990 to 2007 **3.6a**

Kilograms per day (millions)

■ 1990–98 ■ 2000–07

Note: Data are for the most recent year available during the period specified.

Source: Table 3.6.

Data sources

Data on water pollutants are from Hettige, Mani, and Wheeler, "Industrial Pollution in Economic Development: Kuznets Revisited" (1998). The data were updated through 2007 by the World Bank's Development Research Group using the same methodology as the initial study. Data on industrial sectoral employment are from UNIDO's industry database.

	Energy production		Energy use					% of total				Alternative and nuclear energy production	
	Total million metric tons of oil equivalent		Total million metric tons of oil equivalent		average annual % growth	Per capita kilograms of oil equivalent		Fossil fuel		Combustible renewables and waste		% of total energy use	
	1990	2008	1990	2008	1990–2008	1990	2008	1990	2008	1990	2008	1990	2008
Afghanistan	..	..	..	..	..	..	..	..	..	..	..	..	..
Albania	2.4	1.2	2.7	2.1	2.0	809	664	76.5	63.7	13.6	10.3	9.2	15.9
Algeria	100.1	162.0	22.2	37.1	2.8	878	1,078	99.9	99.8	0.1	0.1	0.1	0.1
Angola	28.7	105.8	5.9	11.0	3.6	552	609	25.5	33.5	73.5	63.5	1.1	3.0
Argentina	48.4	82.9	46.1	76.4	2.5	1,418	1,915	88.7	89.8	3.7	3.7	7.5	5.9
Armenia	0.1	0.8	7.7	3.0	−2.8	2,171	974	97.2	73.4	0.1	0.0	1.7	26.6
Australia	157.5	302.1	86.2	130.1	2.3	5,053	6,071	93.9	94.6	4.6	4.2	1.5	1.2
Austria	8.1	11.0	24.8	33.2	1.9	3,214	3,988	79.2	71.6	10.0	16.3	11.0	10.8
Azerbaijan	21.3	58.6	25.8	13.4	−2.7	3,609	1,540	100.0	98.9	0.0	0.0	0.2	1.4
Bangladesh	10.8	23.4	12.7	27.9	4.6	110	175	45.5	68.4	53.9	31.1	0.6	0.5
Belarus	3.3	4.0	45.5	28.1	-1.8	4,470	2,907	95.6	92.1	0.4	5.5	0.0	0.0
Belgium	13.1	14.5	48.3	58.6	1.0	4,844	5,471	76.0	73.8	1.6	4.0	23.1	20.4
Benin	1.8	1.8	1.7	3.0	3.2	346	347	4.8	37.1	94.2	61.0	0.0	0.0
Bolivia	4.9	16.8	2.8	5.7	3.2	416	587	69.1	82.1	27.2	14.4	3.6	3.4
Bosnia and Herzegovina	4.6	4.3	7.0	6.0	2.6	1,627	1,588	93.9	92.8	2.3	3.1	3.8	6.5
Botswana	0.9	1.0	1.3	2.1	2.5	933	1,102	66.1	67.2	33.4	22.3	0.1	0.0
Brazil	104.2	228.1	140.2	248.5	3.1	938	1,295	51.2	52.6	34.1	31.6	13.1	14.3
Bulgaria	9.6	10.2	28.6	19.8	−1.2	3,277	2,595	84.3	76.2	0.6	3.8	13.9	22.3
Burkina Faso	..	..	..	..	..	..	..	..	..	..	..	..	..
Burundi	..	..	..	..	..	..	..	..	..	..	..	..	..
Cambodia	..	3.6	..	5.2	3.5	..	358	..	29.7	..	69.6	..	0.1
Cameroon	11.0	10.1	5.0	7.1	2.2	407	372	18.7	23.9	76.7	71.0	4.6	5.1
Canada	273.8	407.4	208.7	266.8	1.6	7,509	8,008	74.5	74.9	4.0	4.5	21.5	21.6
Central African Republic	..	..	..	..	..	..	..	..	..	..	..	..	..
Chad	..	..	..	..	..	..	..	..	..	..	..	..	..
Chile	7.4	9.0	13.8	31.4	4.8	1,049	1,871	75.1	77.6	19.3	15.5	5.5	6.6
China	886.3	1,993.3	863.0	2,116.4	4.9	760	1,598	75.5	86.9	23.2	9.6	1.3	3.5
Hong Kong SAR, China	0.0	0.1	8.7	14.1	2.5	1,534	2,026	100.0	94.9	0.6	0.4	0.0	0.0
Colombia	48.2	93.6	24.2	30.8	0.7	730	684	67.4	72.7	22.8	14.7	9.8	13.0
Congo, Dem. Rep.	12.0	22.7	11.8	22.3	3.9	319	346	11.2	4.0	84.7	93.4	4.1	2.9
Congo, Rep.	8.7	13.2	0.8	1.4	3.0	326	378	35.0	43.5	59.5	51.3	5.3	2.3
Costa Rica	1.0	2.7	2.0	4.9	5.0	658	1,084	48.3	45.6	36.6	17.3	14.4	37.3
Côte d'Ivoire	3.4	11.4	4.3	10.3	5.1	343	499	23.3	25.0	73.5	74.0	2.6	1.6
Croatia	5.1	3.9	9.0	9.1	1.4	1,884	2,047	86.5	85.1	3.5	3.6	3.6	5.1
Cuba	6.6	5.1	16.5	12.1	−1.1	1,558	1,076	64.3	89.9	35.6	10.0	0.1	0.1
Czech Republic	40.1	32.8	48.8	44.6	0.2	4,705	4,282	93.2	81.2	0.0	4.9	6.9	16.0
Denmark	10.1	26.6	17.3	19.0	0.2	3,374	3,460	89.6	80.4	6.6	15.6	0.3	3.3
Dominican Republic	1.0	1.7	4.1	8.2	3.8	556	820	74.8	79.2	24.4	18.9	0.7	1.8
Ecuador	16.5	28.5	6.0	10.3	3.9	583	767	79.1	83.9	13.8	6.3	7.2	9.4
Egypt, Arab Rep.	54.9	87.5	31.8	70.7	4.8	551	867	94.0	96.1	3.3	2.1	2.7	1.9
El Salvador	1.7	3.0	2.5	4.9	3.7	463	796	31.4	38.4	48.2	31.2	20.3	30.3
Eritrea	0.7	0.5	0.9	0.7	−2.1	276	138	19.3	19.8	80.7	80.0	0.0	0.0
Estonia	5.1	4.2	9.6	5.4	−1.8	6,101	4,026	100.0	88.3	2.0	11.7	0.0	0.2
Ethiopia	14.1	29.6	14.9	31.7	3.5	308	393	5.5	6.7	93.9	92.4	0.6	0.9
Finland	12.1	16.6	28.4	35.3	1.7	5,692	6,635	55.5	48.0	16.1	21.8	20.9	21.2
France	111.9	136.6	223.9	266.5	1.0	3,946	4,279	58.1	51.0	4.9	5.2	38.7	45.3
Gabon	14.6	13.5	1.2	2.1	2.6	1,275	1,431	32.0	43.8	62.9	52.5	5.2	3.7
Gambia, The	..	..	..	..	..	..	..	..	..	..	..	..	..
Georgia	1.8	1.1	12.1	3.0	-6.8	2,217	694	88.6	66.6	3.8	12.7	5.4	21.1
Germany	186.2	134.1	351.4	335.3	-0.1	4,424	4,083	86.8	80.1	1.4	7.0	11.8	13.3
Ghana	4.4	6.9	5.3	9.5	3.4	353	405	18.2	27.8	73.7	66.8	9.3	5.6
Greece	9.2	9.9	21.4	30.4	2.4	2,110	2,707	94.6	92.8	4.2	3.4	1.0	2.2
Guatemala	3.4	5.4	4.4	8.1	3.8	498	590	28.1	42.9	68.5	53.3	3.4	4.0
Guinea	..	..	..	..	..	..	..	..	..	..	..	..	..
Guinea-Bissau	..	..	..	..	..	..	..	..	..	..	..	..	..
Haiti	1.3	2.0	1.6	2.8	3.6	219	281	19.7	28.3	77.8	71.2	2.5	0.6
Honduras	1.7	2.1	2.4	4.6	3.7	486	632	30.0	54.1	62.9	41.7	8.2	4.3

	Energy production		Energy use										Alternative and nuclear energy production	
								% of total						
	Total million metric tons of oil equivalent		Total million metric tons of oil equivalent		average annual % growth	Per capita kilograms of oil equivalent		Fossil fuel		Combustible renewables and waste		% of total energy use	
	1990	2008	1990	2008	1990–2008	1990	2008	1990	2008	1990	2008	1990	2008
Hungary	14.6	10.5	28.7	26.5	0.0	2,762	2,636	81.5	77.8	2.3	5.8	12.8	15.2
India	291.8	468.3	318.9	621.0	3.6	375	545	55.7	71.1	41.9	26.3	2.4	2.4
Indonesia	172.2	347.0	103.9	198.7	3.5	586	874	54.3	65.6	43.3	26.7	2.4	7.7
Iran, Islamic Rep.	179.8	326.9	68.3	202.1	6.1	1,256	2,808	98.2	99.4	1.0	0.5	0.8	0.2
Iraq	104.9	117.7	18.1	34.0	3.8	957	1,107	98.6	99.4	0.1	0.1	1.2	0.1
Ireland	3.5	1.5	10.0	15.0	2.8	2,849	3,385	84.6	90.2	1.1	1.8	0.6	2.0
Israel	0.4	3.3	11.5	22.0	3.5	2,462	3,011	97.2	96.6	0.0	0.0	3.1	4.8
Italy	25.3	26.9	146.6	176.0	1.4	2,584	2,942	93.4	89.9	0.6	3.0	3.9	5.1
Jamaica	0.5	0.5	2.8	4.4	2.7	1,167	1,633	82.6	88.5	17.1	11.1	0.3	0.4
Japan	75.2	88.7	439.3	495.8	0.8	3,556	3,883	84.5	83.0	1.1	1.4	14.4	15.6
Jordan	0.2	0.3	3.3	7.1	4.3	1,028	1,215	98.2	98.0	0.1	0.1	1.8	1.6
Kazakhstan	90.5	148.2	72.7	70.9	-0.8	4,450	4,525	96.9	98.8	0.2	0.2	0.9	0.9
Kenya	9.0	15.1	10.9	18.0	2.8	467	465	17.5	16.2	77.9	76.9	4.5	7.0
Korea, Dem. Rep.	28.9	20.8	33.2	20.3	-2.1	1,649	851	93.1	88.9	2.9	5.1	4.0	6.0
Korea, Rep.	22.6	44.7	93.1	226.9	4.8	2,171	4,669	83.8	81.2	0.8	1.3	15.4	17.5
Kosovo	..	..	..	..	..	..	..	..	..	..	..	..	..
Kuwait	50.4	152.8	7.8	26.3	7.2	3,681	9,637	99.9	100.0	0.1	0.0	0.0	0.0
Kyrgyz Republic	2.5	1.2	7.5	2.9	-3.8	1,693	542	93.5	69.2	0.1	0.1	11.5	32.3
Lao PDR	..	..	..	..	..	..	..	..	..	..	..	..	..
Latvia	1.1	1.8	7.9	4.5	-2.3	2,941	1,979	81.8	64.3	8.4	24.8	4.9	6.1
Lebanon	0.1	0.2	2.2	5.2	3.5	755	1,250	93.5	95.3	4.6	2.7	1.9	1.0
Lesotho	..	..	..	..	..	..	..	..	..	..	..	..	..
Liberia	..	..	..	..	..	..	..	..	..	..	..	..	..
Libya	73.2	103.7	11.3	18.2	2.2	2,596	2,895	98.9	99.1	1.1	0.9	0.0	0.0
Lithuania	4.9	3.9	16.1	9.2	-2.1	4,357	2,733	75.8	60.8	1.8	8.8	28.2	29.1
Macedonia, FYR	1.3	1.7	2.5	3.1	0.9	1,298	1,520	98.0	84.2	0.0	5.6	1.7	2.6
Madagascar	..	..	..	..	..	..	..	..	..	..	..	..	..
Malawi	..	..	..	..	..	..	..	..	..	..	..	..	..
Malaysia	48.8	93.1	22.0	72.7	6.1	1,215	2,693	88.8	95.1	9.7	4.1	1.6	0.9
Mali	..	..	..	..	..	..	..	..	..	..	..	..	..
Mauritania	..	..	..	..	..	..	..	..	..	..	..	..	..
Mauritius	..	..	..	..	..	..	..	..	..	..	..	..	..
Mexico	193.4	233.6	121.3	180.6	2.1	1,457	1,698	88.1	88.8	6.1	4.6	5.9	6.7
Moldova	0.1	0.1	9.9	3.2	-5.2	2,261	867	100.0	89.1	0.4	2.5	0.2	0.2
Mongolia	2.7	3.9	3.4	3.2	-0.9	1,541	1,193	97.0	96.2	2.5	3.3	0.0	0.0
Morocco	0.8	0.6	6.9	15.0	4.0	280	474	93.8	93.7	4.6	3.2	1.5	0.7
Mozambique	5.6	11.5	5.9	9.3	2.8	437	416	5.5	7.3	93.9	81.9	0.4	14.0
Myanmar	10.7	23.1	10.7	15.7	2.4	261	316	14.4	31.0	84.7	66.8	1.0	2.2
Namibia	0.2	0.3	0.7	1.8	5.2	446	823	62.0	71.6	16.0	11.2	17.5	7.0
Nepal	5.5	8.7	5.8	9.8	3.1	303	340	5.1	10.9	93.7	86.4	1.3	2.7
Netherlands	60.5	66.5	65.7	79.7	1.0	4,392	4,845	96.0	92.5	1.4	3.9	1.4	1.9
New Zealand	11.4	14.9	12.7	16.9	1.5	3,682	3,967	67.3	66.7	4.3	6.1	28.1	27.0
Nicaragua	1.5	2.2	2.1	3.5	3.1	506	621	28.3	38.5	53.9	52.3	17.5	9.2
Niger	..	..	..	..	..	..	..	..	..	..	..	..	..
Nigeria	150.5	226.8	70.6	111.2	2.5	725	735	19.3	18.3	80.2	81.2	0.5	0.4
Norway	119.1	219.7	21.0	29.7	1.6	4,952	6,222	51.9	58.6	4.9	4.6	49.6	40.7
Oman	38.3	63.5	3.9	16.4	6.6	2,105	5,903	100.0	100.0	0.0	0.0	0.0	0.0
Pakistan	34.3	63.3	43.0	82.8	3.7	398	499	52.8	61.8	43.7	34.8	3.6	3.4
Panama	0.6	0.7	1.5	2.9	3.4	618	853	58.4	75.7	28.3	12.3	12.7	11.8
Papua New Guinea	..	..	..	..	..	..	..	..	..	..	..	..	..
Paraguay	4.6	7.4	3.1	4.4	1.5	723	699	21.3	28.2	72.5	53.7	76.0	109.4
Peru	10.6	12.3	9.7	14.7	2.3	447	510	63.3	76.1	27.5	12.8	9.2	11.2
Philippines	15.7	23.3	27.5	41.1	2.2	440	455	45.8	56.9	35.2	18.6	19.0	24.5
Poland	103.9	71.4	103.1	97.9	-0.5	2,705	2,567	97.8	93.8	2.2	6.0	0.1	0.3
Portugal	3.4	4.4	16.7	24.2	2.6	1,691	2,274	80.4	78.3	14.8	13.0	4.8	5.4
Puerto Rico	..	..	..	..	..	..	..	..	..	..	..	..	..
Qatar	26.6	124.8	6.9	24.1	7.1	14,732	18,830	99.9	100.0	0.1	0.0	0.0	0.0

	Energy production		Energy use										Alternative and nuclear energy production	
								% of total						
	Total million metric tons of oil equivalent		Total million metric tons of oil equivalent		average annual % growth	Per capita kilograms of oil equivalent		Fossil fuel		Combustible renewables and waste			% of total energy use	
	1990	2008	1990	2008	1990–2008	1990	2008	1990	2008	1990	2008		1990	2008
Romania	40.8	28.8	62.3	39.4	−1.9	2,683	1,830	96.1	79.4	1.0	10.3		1.6	11.2
Russian Federation	1,293.1	1,253.9	879.2	686.8	−1.1	5,929	4,838	93.4	90.9	1.4	0.9		5.2	8.4
Rwanda	..	..	..	..	..	..	..	..	..	..	..		..	..
Saudi Arabia	370.6	579.0	59.0	161.6	4.8	3,631	6,514	100.0	100.0	0.0	0.0		0.0	0.0
Senegal	1.0	1.2	1.7	2.9	3.5	224	234	43.2	57.3	56.8	41.7		0.0	0.7
Serbia	13.4[a]	9.9	19.3[a]	16.0	0.2	2,550[a]	2,181	90.6[a]	89.5	6.0[a]	5.0		4.2[a]	5.4
Sierra Leone	..	..	..	..	..	..	..	..	..	..	..		..	..
Singapore	0.0	0.0	11.5	18.5	1.8	3,760	3,828	100.0	100.0	0.0	0.0		0.0	0.0
Slovak Republic	5.3	6.4	21.3	18.3	−0.1	4,037	3,385	81.6	70.0	0.8	3.7		15.5	26.0
Slovenia	3.1	3.7	5.7	7.7	2.0	2,858	3,827	71.3	69.4	4.7	6.7		25.6	25.6
Somalia	..	..	..	..	..	..	..	..	..	..	..		..	..
South Africa	114.5	163.0	90.9	134.5	2.2	2,581	2,756	86.1	87.2	11.5	10.4		2.5	2.6
Spain	34.6	30.4	90.1	138.8	3.0	2,320	3,047	77.4	81.7	4.5	4.2		18.1	14.6
Sri Lanka	4.2	5.1	5.5	8.9	3.3	322	443	24.1	43.4	71.0	52.6		4.9	4.0
Sudan	8.8	34.9	10.6	15.4	2.6	392	372	17.5	31.2	81.8	68.0		0.8	0.8
Swaziland	..	..	..	..	..	..	..	..	..	..	..		..	..
Sweden	29.7	33.2	47.2	49.6	0.4	5,514	5,379	37.3	33.1	11.7	20.0		50.9	45.9
Switzerland	10.0	12.7	24.0	26.7	0.6	3,581	3,491	59.3	52.7	4.8	8.1		36.7	39.6
Syrian Arab Republic	22.3	23.5	11.4	19.7	2.8	895	957	97.9	98.7	0.0	0.0		2.1	1.3
Tajikistan	2.0	1.5	5.3	2.5	−3.1	1,001	365	71.3	42.3	0.0	0.0		26.7	54.7
Tanzania	9.1	17.5	9.7	19.0	4.1	382	446	6.9	10.6	91.7	88.2		1.4	1.2
Thailand	26.5	63.9	42.0	107.2	5.1	742	1,591	63.9	80.6	34.9	18.7		1.0	0.6
Timor-Leste	..	..	..	..	..	..	..	..	..	..	..		..	..
Togo	1.1	2.1	1.3	2.6	4.3	322	397	15.0	14.3	82.8	83.1		0.6	0.3
Trinidad and Tobago	12.6	40.0	6.0	19.4	7.6	4,899	14,557	99.2	99.9	0.8	0.1		0.0	0.0
Tunisia	5.7	7.5	4.9	9.2	3.7	607	889	87.0	86.3	12.9	13.6		0.1	0.1
Turkey	25.8	29.0	52.8	98.5	3.6	941	1,333	81.8	90.6	13.7	4.9		4.6	4.6
Turkmenistan	74.9	68.6	19.6	18.8	1.5	5,352	3,730	100.0	100.0	0.0	0.0		0.3	0.0
Uganda	..	..	..	..	..	..	..	..	..	..	..		..	..
Ukraine	135.8	81.3	251.8	136.1	−3.0	4,852	2,943	91.8	81.8	0.1	0.7		8.2	17.9
United Arab Emirates	110.2	180.5	19.9	58.4	5.4	10,645	13,030	100.0	100.0	0.0	0.0		0.0	0.0
United Kingdom	208.0	166.7	205.9	208.5	0.1	3,597	3,395	90.7	90.2	0.3	2.2		8.5	7.1
United States	1,652.5	1,706.1	1,915.0	2,283.7	1.1	7,672	7,503	86.4	85.0	3.3	3.7		10.3	11.2
Uruguay	1.1	1.4	2.3	4.2	1.8	725	1,254	58.7	64.9	24.3	23.9		26.8	9.3
Uzbekistan	38.6	62.0	46.4	50.5	0.6	2,261	1,849	99.2	98.1	0.0	0.0		1.2	1.9
Venezuela, RB	148.9	180.7	43.6	64.1	1.6	2,206	2,295	91.5	87.6	1.2	0.8		7.3	11.7
Vietnam	24.7	71.4	24.3	59.4	5.2	367	689	20.4	54.0	77.7	41.8		1.9	3.8
West Bank and Gaza	..	..	..	..	..	..	..	..	..	..	..		..	..
Yemen, Rep.	9.4	15.3	2.5	7.5	6.2	204	326	97.0	99.0	3.1	1.0		0.0	0.0
Zambia	4.9	6.8	5.4	7.4	1.7	683	583	15.6	7.5	74.3	81.0		12.7	11.3
Zimbabwe	8.6	8.5	9.3	9.5	−0.1	889	763	44.8	26.1	50.9	65.3		4.0	3.9
World	**8,840.1 t**	**12,357.7 t**	**8,569.9 t**	**11,899.4 t**	**1.9 w**	**1,669 w**	**1,835 w**	**81.0 w**	**81.1 w**	**10.1 w**	**9.8 w**		**8.7 w**	**9.1 w**
Low income	172.8	264.0	200.3	279.9	2.1	380	357	39.8	29.2	56.0	66.2		4.4	4.4
Middle income	4,796.0	7,284.5	3,864.0	6,002.2	2.5	1,029	1,261	78.9	81.5	16.9	13.3		4.1	5.2
Lower middle income	2,168.7	4,001.4	1,993.4	3,842.7	3.6	679	1,019	70.1	79.0	27.1	16.9		2.9	4.2
Upper middle income	2,627.2	3,284.5	1,871.1	2,161.8	1.0	2,283	2,177	88.2	86.0	6.1	6.8		5.4	7.0
Low & middle income	4,966.5	7,544.8	4,049.8	6,266.2	2.5	966	1,157	77.4	79.7	18.4	15.2		4.1	5.2
East Asia & Pacific	1,226.1	2,658.9	1,139.4	2,655.4	4.6	716	1,380	71.5	83.7	26.6	12.4		1.9	4.0
Europe & Central Asia	1,769.6	1,772.9	1,577.0	1,215.0	−1.1	4,038	3,030	93.0	89.7	1.5	1.7		5.3	8.7
Latin America & Carib.	609.0	922.0	454.0	729.2	2.5	1,044	1,290	71.2	72.4	19.7	16.8		9.2	10.8
Middle East & N. Africa	558.6	856.3	185.5	431.3	4.7	814	1,329	97.2	98.3	1.7	1.1		1.1	0.6
South Asia	349.5	573.6	389.2	756.8	3.6	348	495	53.8	68.9	43.6	28.5		2.5	2.5
Sub-Saharan Africa	475.6	810.3	310.5	497.4	2.6	676	678	41.2	39.8	56.6	57.7		2.3	2.5
High income	3,892.9	4,843.0	4,544.3	5,672.5	1.4	4,649	5,131	84.2	82.6	2.8	3.9		12.8	13.3
Euro area	476.5	463.1	1,059.7	1,226.5	1.0	3,527	3,763	79.8	75.0	3.2	5.9		16.7	18.6

a. Includes Kosovo and Montenegro.

About the data

In developing economies growth in energy use is closely related to growth in the modern sectors—industry, motorized transport, and urban areas—but energy use also reflects climatic, geographic, and economic factors (such as the relative price of energy). Energy use has been growing rapidly in low- and middle-income economies, but high-income economies still use almost five times as much energy on a per capita basis.

Energy data are compiled by the International Energy Agency (IEA). IEA data for economies that are not members of the Organisation for Economic Co-operation and Development (OECD) are based on national energy data adjusted to conform to annual questionnaires completed by OECD member governments.

Total energy use refers to the use of primary energy before transformation to other end-use fuels (such as electricity and refined petroleum products). It includes energy from combustible renewables and waste—solid biomass and animal products, gas and liquid from biomass, and industrial and municipal waste. Biomass is any plant matter used directly as fuel or converted into fuel, heat, or electricity.

Data for combustible renewables and waste are often based on small surveys or other incomplete information and thus give only a broad impression of developments and are not strictly comparable across countries. The IEA reports include country notes that explain some of these differences (see

Data sources). All forms of energy—primary energy and primary electricity—are converted into oil equivalents. A notional thermal efficiency of 33 percent is assumed for converting nuclear electricity into oil equivalents and 100 percent efficiency for converting hydroelectric power.

The IEA makes these estimates in consultation with national statistical offices, oil companies, electric utilities, and national energy experts. The IEA occasionally revises its time series to reflect political changes, and energy statistics undergo continual changes in coverage or methodology as more detailed energy accounts become available. Breaks in series are therefore unavoidable.

Definitions

• **Energy production** refers to forms of primary energy—petroleum (crude oil, natural gas liquids, and oil from nonconventional sources), natural gas, solid fuels (coal, lignite, and other derived fuels), and combustible renewables and waste—and primary electricity, all converted into oil equivalents (see *About the data*). • **Energy use** refers to the use of primary energy before transformation to other end-use fuels, which is equal to indigenous production plus imports and stock changes, minus exports and fuels supplied to ships and aircraft engaged in international transport (see *About the data*). • **Fossil fuel** comprises coal, oil, petroleum, and natural gas products. • **Combustible renewables and waste** comprise solid biomass, liquid biomass, biogas, industrial waste, and municipal waste. • **Alternative and nuclear energy production** is noncarbohydrate energy that does not produce carbon dioxide when generated. It includes hydropower and nuclear, geothermal, and solar power, among others.

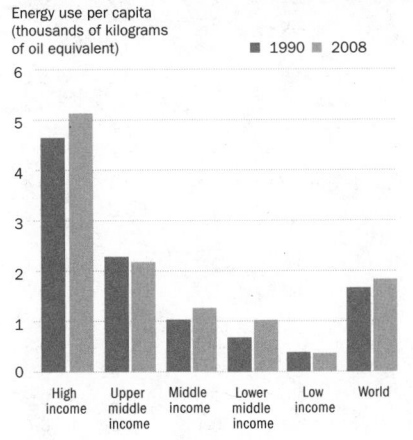

A person in a high-income economy uses more than 14 times as much energy on average as a person in a low-income economy in 2008 3.7a

Energy use per capita (thousands of kilograms of oil equivalent) ▪ 1990 ▪ 2008

Source: Table 3.7.

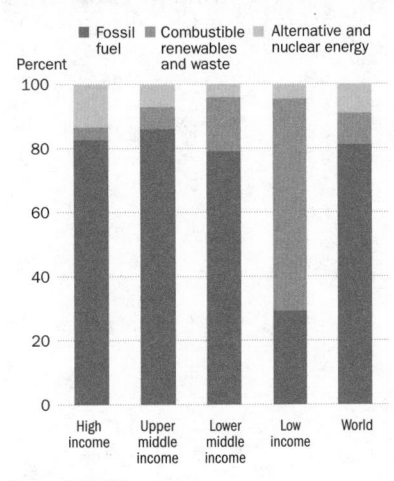

Fossil fuels are still the primary global energy source in 2008 3.7b

▪ Fossil fuel ▪ Combustible renewables and waste ▪ Alternative and nuclear energy

Percent

Source: Table 3.7.

Data sources

Data on energy production and use are from IEA electronic files and are published in IEA's annual publications, *Energy Statistics and Balances of Non-OECD Countries*, *Energy Statistics of OECD Countries*, and *Energy Balances of OECD Countries*.

3.8 Energy dependency and efficiency and carbon dioxide emissions

| | Net energy imports[a] (% of energy use) | | GDP per unit of energy use (2005 PPP $ per kilogram of oil equivalent) | | Carbon dioxide emissions | | | | | | | |
| | | | | | Total (million metric tons) | | Carbon intensity (kilograms per kilogram of oil equivalent energy use) | | Per capita (metric tons) | | kilograms per 2005 PPP $ of GDP | |
	1990	2008	1990	2008	1990	2007	1990	2007	1990	2007	1990	2007
Afghanistan	..	..	..	..	2.7	0.7	..	..	0.1	0.0	..	0.0
Albania	8	45	4.8	11.0	7.5	4.2	2.8	2.0	2.3	1.4	0.6	0.2
Algeria	−351	−337	7.1	6.8	78.8	140.0	3.6	3.8	3.1	4.1	0.5	0.6
Angola	−387	−865	5.8	8.8	4.4	24.7	0.8	2.3	0.4	1.4	0.1	0.3
Argentina	−5	−9	5.3	6.9	112.5	183.6	2.4	2.5	3.5	4.6	0.5	0.4
Armenia	98	73	1.4	5.8	3.7	5.1	0.5	1.8	1.2	1.6	0.4	0.3
Australia	−83	−132	4.7	5.7	292.9	373.7	3.4	3.0	17.2	17.7	0.7	0.5
Austria	67	67	8.0	9.1	60.9	68.7	2.5	2.1	7.9	8.3	0.3	0.2
Azerbaijan	17	−338	1.3	5.3	44.1	31.7	1.9	2.7	7.0	3.7	1.5	0.5
Bangladesh	16	16	6.2	7.1	15.5	43.7	1.2	1.7	0.1	0.3	0.2	0.2
Belarus	93	86	1.5	4.0	98.5	66.7	2.6	2.4	10.9	6.9	1.7	0.7
Belgium	73	75	5.2	6.1	107.5	103.0	2.2	1.8	10.8	9.7	0.4	0.3
Benin	−7	39	3.2	3.9	0.7	3.9	0.4	1.3	0.1	0.5	0.1	0.3
Bolivia	−77	−195	7.0	6.7	5.5	13.2	2.0	2.4	0.8	1.4	0.3	0.4
Bosnia and Herzegovina	34	28	..	4.7	4.7	29.0	1.0	5.2	1.6	7.7	..	1.1
Botswana	28	53	7.6	11.6	2.2	5.0	1.7	2.5	1.6	2.6	0.2	0.2
Brazil	26	8	7.7	7.4	208.7	368.0	1.5	1.6	1.4	1.9	0.2	0.2
Bulgaria	66	48	2.3	4.6	76.6	51.7	2.7	2.6	8.8	6.8	1.2	0.6
Burkina Faso	..	..	..	..	0.6	1.7	..	..	0.1	0.1	0.1	0.1
Burundi	..	..	..	..	0.3	0.2	..	..	0.1	0.0	0.1	0.1
Cambodia	..	30	..	5.0	0.5	4.4	..	0.9	0.0	0.3	..	0.2
Cameroon	−120	−42	5.1	5.4	1.7	6.2	0.3	0.8	0.1	0.3	0.1	0.2
Canada	−31	-53	3.6	4.5	449.7	556.9	2.2	2.1	16.2	16.9	0.6	0.5
Central African Republic	..	..	..	..	0.2	0.3	..	..	0.1	0.1	0.1	0.1
Chad	..	..	..	..	0.1	0.4	..	..	0.0	0.0	0.0	0.0
Chile	46	71	6.3	7.2	34.9	71.6	2.5	2.3	2.6	4.3	0.4	0.3
China	−3	6	1.4	3.6	2,458.7	6,533.0	2.8	3.3	2.2	5.0	2.0	0.9
Hong Kong SAR, China	100	100	15.5	20.0	27.6	39.9	3.1	2.9	4.8	5.8	0.2	0.1
Colombia	−99	−204	8.4	12.0	57.3	63.4	2.4	2.2	1.7	1.4	0.3	0.2
Congo, Dem. Rep.	−2	−2	1.9	0.8	4.1	2.4	0.3	0.1	0.1	0.0	0.2	0.1
Congo, Rep.	−997	-868	10.7	9.6	1.2	1.6	1.5	1.3	0.5	0.4	0.1	0.1
Costa Rica	49	45	9.5	9.6	3.0	8.1	1.5	1.7	1.0	1.8	0.2	0.2
Côte d'Ivoire	22	−11	5.5	3.1	5.8	6.4	1.3	0.6	0.5	0.3	0.2	0.2
Croatia	43	57	7.1	8.5	25.0	24.8	2.8	2.7	5.2	5.6	0.4	0.3
Cuba	60	58	..	..	33.3	27.0	2.0	2.7	3.1	2.4	..	..
Czech Republic	18	26	3.5	5.4	162.6	124.9	3.3	2.7	15.7	12.1	1.0	0.5
Denmark	42	−40	7.5	9.9	50.4	50.0	2.9	2.5	9.8	9.1	0.4	0.3
Dominican Republic	75	79	6.7	9.2	9.6	20.7	2.3	2.6	1.3	2.1	0.3	0.3
Ecuador	−175	−176	9.4	9.9	16.8	30.0	2.8	2.5	1.6	2.2	0.3	0.3
Egypt, Arab Rep.	−72	−24	5.8	5.8	75.9	184.5	2.4	2.7	1.3	2.3	0.4	0.5
El Salvador	31	38	8.0	7.9	2.6	6.7	1.1	1.4	0.5	1.1	0.1	0.2
Eritrea	19	20	1.9	3.8	..	0.6	..	0.8	..	0.1	..	0.2
Estonia	47	22	1.7	4.7	28.2	20.5	2.9	3.6	18.0	15.2	1.8	0.8
Ethiopia	5	7	1.8	2.0	3.0	6.5	0.2	0.3	0.1	0.1	0.1	0.1
Finland	57	53	4.1	5.1	50.9	64.1	1.8	1.8	10.2	12.1	0.4	0.4
France	50	49	6.3	7.4	398.7	371.5	1.8	1.4	7.0	6.0	0.3	0.2
Gabon	−1,139	−552	11.8	9.4	6.1	2.0	5.2	1.1	6.6	1.4	0.4	0.1
Gambia, The	..	..	..	..	0.2	0.4	..	..	0.2	0.2	0.2	0.2
Georgia	85	64	2.4	6.6	15.3	6.0	1.4	1.8	3.2	1.4	0.6	0.3
Germany	47	60	5.8	8.3	960.2	787.3	2.8	2.4	12.0	9.6	0.4	0.3
Ghana	17	27	2.5	3.4	3.9	9.8	0.7	1.0	0.3	0.4	0.3	0.3
Greece	57	68	8.3	10.0	72.7	98.0	3.4	3.0	7.2	8.8	0.4	0.3
Guatemala	24	33	6.7	7.4	5.1	12.9	1.1	1.6	0.6	1.0	0.2	0.2
Guinea	..	..	..	..	1.1	1.4	..	..	0.2	0.1	0.2	0.2
Guinea-Bissau	..	..	..	..	0.3	0.3	..	..	0.2	0.2	0.2	0.2
Haiti	20	28	6.4	3.7	1.0	2.4	0.6	0.9	0.1	0.2	0.1	0.2
Honduras	29	55	5.5	5.7	2.6	8.8	1.1	1.9	0.5	1.2	0.2	0.3

	Net energy imports[a]		GDP per unit of energy use		Carbon dioxide emissions							
			2005 PPP $ per kilogram of oil equivalent		Total million metric tons		Carbon intensity kilograms per kilogram of oil equivalent energy use		Per capita metric tons		kilograms per 2005 PPP $ of GDP	
	% of energy use											
	1990	2008	1990	2008	1990	2007	1990	2007	1990	2007	1990	2007
Hungary	49	60	4.4	6.8	63.4	56.4	2.2	2.1	6.1	5.6	0.5	0.3
India	8	25	3.3	5.1	690.0	1,611.0	2.2	2.7	0.8	1.4	0.7	0.5
Indonesia	−66	−75	3.6	4.2	149.4	396.8	1.5	2.1	0.8	1.8	0.4	0.5
Iran, Islamic Rep.	−163	−62	5.0	3.7	227.0	495.6	3.3	2.7	4.2	7.0	0.7	0.7
Iraq	−480	−246	..	2.9	52.5	100.0	2.9	3.0	2.8	3.3	..	1.1
Ireland	65	90	6.2	11.6	30.3	44.3	3.0	2.9	8.6	10.2	0.5	0.2
Israel	96	85	7.3	8.5	33.5	66.7	2.9	3.0	7.2	9.3	0.4	0.4
Italy	83	85	9.2	9.6	424.7	456.1	2.9	2.6	7.5	7.7	0.3	0.3
Jamaica	83	88	5.1	4.4	8.0	14.0	2.9	2.8	3.3	5.2	0.6	0.7
Japan	83	82	7.3	8.1	1,152.3	1,253.5	2.6	2.4	9.3	9.8	0.4	0.3
Jordan	95	96	3.2	4.2	10.4	21.4	3.2	3.0	3.3	3.8	1.0	0.8
Kazakhstan	−24	−109	1.6	2.3	261.1	227.2	4.0	3.4	18.0	14.7	2.5	1.4
Kenya	18	16	3.0	3.1	5.8	11.2	0.5	0.6	0.2	0.3	0.2	0.2
Korea, Dem. Rep.	13	-3	..	..	244.6	70.7	7.4	3.8	12.1	3.0	..	..
Korea, Rep.	76	80	5.2	5.5	241.5	502.9	2.6	2.3	5.6	10.4	0.5	0.4
Kosovo	..	..	..	..	..	..	..	..	..	..	..	..
Kuwait	−544	−481	2.8	4.8	40.7	86.1	5.2	3.4	19.2	32.3	0.6	0.7
Kyrgyz Republic	67	58	1.5	3.8	11.0	6.1	1.6	2.1	2.8	1.2	1.1	0.6
Lao PDR	..	..	..	..	0.2	1.5	..	..	0.1	0.3	0.1	0.1
Latvia	86	60	3.4	7.9	13.3	7.8	1.9	1.7	5.6	3.4	0.6	0.2
Lebanon	94	96	7.5	8.8	9.1	13.3	4.0	3.3	3.1	3.2	0.5	0.3
Lesotho	..	..	..	..	..	..	..	..	..	..	..	..
Liberia	..	..	..	..	0.5	0.7	..	..	0.2	0.2	0.5	0.5
Libya	−546	−469	..	5.2	40.3	57.3	3.6	3.2	9.2	9.3	..	0.6
Lithuania	69	58	2.9	6.4	22.1	15.3	1.5	1.7	6.8	4.5	0.5	0.3
Macedonia, FYR	49	45	6.4	5.8	10.8	11.3	6.4	3.7	8.3	5.5	1.0	0.7
Madagascar	..	..	..	..	1.0	2.2	..	..	0.1	0.1	0.1	0.1
Malawi	..	..	..	..	0.6	1.1	..	..	0.1	0.1	0.1	0.1
Malaysia	−122	−28	5.5	4.9	56.5	194.3	2.5	2.7	3.1	7.3	0.5	0.6
Mali	..	..	..	..	0.4	0.6	..	..	0.0	0.0	0.1	0.0
Mauritania	..	..	..	..	2.7	1.9	..	..	1.3	0.6	0.9	0.3
Mauritius	..	..	..	..	1.5	3.9	..	..	1.4	3.1	0.2	0.3
Mexico	−60	-29	6.9	7.9	357.2	471.1	2.9	2.6	4.3	4.5	0.4	0.3
Moldova	99	97	1.7	3.1	21.0	4.7	2.4	1.4	5.4	1.3	1.4	0.5
Mongolia	20	−23	1.4	2.8	10.0	10.6	2.9	3.4	4.5	4.0	2.0	1.3
Morocco	89	96	9.7	8.4	23.5	46.4	3.4	3.2	0.9	1.5	0.4	0.4
Mozambique	5	−23	0.9	1.9	1.0	2.6	0.2	0.3	0.1	0.1	0.2	0.2
Myanmar	0	−47	..	..	4.3	13.2	0.4	0.8	0.1	0.3	..	..
Namibia	67	82	9.4	7.3	0.0	3.0	0.0	1.9	0.0	1.5	0.0	0.2
Nepal	5	11	2.3	3.0	0.6	3.4	0.1	0.4	0.0	0.1	0.1	0.1
Netherlands	8	16	6.0	7.9	164.0	173.1	2.5	2.2	11.0	10.6	0.4	0.3
New Zealand	10	12	5.1	6.3	23.9	32.6	1.8	1.9	6.9	7.7	0.4	0.3
Nicaragua	29	39	3.7	4.1	2.6	4.6	1.3	1.3	0.6	0.8	0.3	0.3
Niger	..	..	..	..	1.0	0.9	..	..	0.1	0.1	0.2	0.1
Nigeria	−113	−104	2.0	2.6	45.3	95.2	0.6	0.9	0.5	0.6	0.3	0.3
Norway	−467	−640	6.5	7.9	31.3	42.7	1.5	1.6	7.4	9.1	0.2	0.2
Oman	−888	−286	7.1	4.0	10.3	37.3	2.4	2.4	5.6	13.7	0.4	0.6
Pakistan	20	24	4.2	4.7	68.5	156.3	1.6	1.9	0.6	1.0	0.4	0.4
Panama	59	76	9.8	13.8	3.1	7.2	2.1	2.6	1.3	2.2	0.2	0.2
Papua New Guinea	..	..	..	..	2.1	3.4	..	..	0.5	0.5	0.3	0.3
Paraguay	−49	−69	5.5	6.2	2.3	4.1	0.7	1.0	0.5	0.7	0.1	0.2
Peru	−9	16	10.0	15.4	21.1	43.0	2.2	3.1	1.0	1.5	0.2	0.2
Philippines	43	43	5.4	7.1	44.5	70.9	1.6	1.8	0.7	0.8	0.3	0.3
Poland	−1	27	3.0	6.4	347.6	317.1	3.4	3.3	9.1	8.3	1.1	0.5
Portugal	80	82	9.6	9.7	44.3	58.1	2.6	2.3	4.5	5.5	0.3	0.2
Puerto Rico	..	..	..	..	..	..	..	..	..	..	..	..
Qatar	−286	−418	..	4.5	11.8	63.0	1.7	2.8	25.2	55.4	..	0.7

	Net energy imports[a]		GDP per unit of energy use		Carbon dioxide emissions							
	% of energy use		2005 PPP $ per kilogram of oil equivalent		Total million metric tons		Carbon intensity kilograms per kilogram of oil equivalent energy use		Per capita metric tons		kilograms per 2005 PPP $ of GDP	
	1990	2008	1990	2008	1990	2007	1990	2007	1990	2007	1990	2007
Romania	34	27	2.9	6.4	158.7	94.1	2.5	2.4	6.8	4.4	0.9	0.4
Russian Federation	−47	−83	2.1	3.1	2,073.5	1,536.1	2.7	2.3	15.8	10.8	1.2	0.8
Rwanda	..	..	..	..	0.7	0.7	..	..	0.1	0.1	0.1	0.1
Saudi Arabia	−528	−258	5.3	3.3	214.9	402.1	3.6	2.7	13.2	16.6	0.7	0.8
Senegal	43	57	6.3	7.1	3.2	5.5	1.9	2.0	0.4	0.5	0.3	0.3
Serbia	31	38	4.6	4.7	45.3[b]	53.5[b]	1.5[b]	..	6.4[b]	6.3[b]	..	..
Sierra Leone	..	..	..	..	0.4	1.3	..	..	0.1	0.2	0.1	0.3
Singapore	100	100	6.2	12.5	46.9	54.1	4.1	2.0	15.4	11.8	0.7	0.2
Slovak Republic	75	65	3.1	6.1	44.3	37.0	2.6	2.1	10.4	6.8	0.8	0.4
Slovenia	46	53	5.7	7.1	12.3	15.1	3.2	2.1	9.1	7.5	0.6	0.3
Somalia	..	..	..	..	0.0	0.6	..	..	0.0	0.1	..	..
South Africa	−26	−21	3.1	3.5	333.2	433.2	3.7	3.2	9.5	9.0	1.2	1.0
Spain	62	78	8.5	9.3	227.4	359.0	2.5	2.5	5.9	8.0	0.3	0.3
Sri Lanka	24	43	6.3	9.5	3.8	12.3	0.7	1.3	0.2	0.6	0.1	0.2
Sudan	17	−127	2.5	5.3	5.6	11.5	0.5	0.8	0.2	0.3	0.2	0.2
Swaziland	..	..	..	..	0.4	1.1	..	..	0.5	0.9	0.1	0.2
Sweden	37	33	4.5	6.4	51.7	49.2	1.1	1.0	6.0	5.4	0.2	0.2
Switzerland	59	52	9.3	10.9	42.9	38.0	1.8	1.5	6.4	5.0	0.2	0.1
Syrian Arab Republic	−96	−19	3.3	4.4	37.4	69.8	3.3	3.6	2.9	3.5	1.0	0.8
Tajikistan	62	40	3.1	4.8	21.3	7.2	4.3	1.9	4.5	1.1	1.5	0.6
Tanzania	7	8	2.2	2.6	2.4	6.0	0.2	0.3	0.1	0.1	0.1	0.1
Thailand	37	40	5.3	4.7	95.8	277.3	2.3	2.7	1.7	4.1	0.4	0.6
Timor-Leste	..	..	..	..	..	0.2	..	..	..	0.2	..	0.3
Togo	17	17	2.7	1.9	0.8	1.3	0.6	0.5	0.2	0.2	0.2	0.3
Trinidad and Tobago	−111	−106	2.2	1.7	16.9	37.0	2.8	2.4	13.9	27.9	1.3	1.2
Tunisia	−16	18	6.6	8.3	13.3	23.8	2.7	2.7	1.6	2.3	0.4	0.3
Turkey	51	71	8.3	8.9	150.7	288.4	2.9	2.9	2.7	4.0	0.3	0.3
Turkmenistan	−281	−265	0.7	1.7	28.0	45.8	1.6	2.5	8.6	9.2	2.3	1.6
Uganda	..	..	..	..	0.8	3.2	..	..	0.0	0.1	0.1	0.1
Ukraine	46	40	1.7	2.3	611.0	317.3	2.7	2.3	13.3	6.8	1.6	1.0
United Arab Emirates	−454	−209	4.8	4.2	54.8	135.4	2.8	2.6	29.3	31.0	0.6	0.6
United Kingdom	−1	20	6.6	10.0	569.8	539.2	2.8	2.6	10.0	8.8	0.4	0.3
United States	14	25	4.2	5.8	4,861.0	5,832.2	2.5	2.5	19.5	19.3	0.6	0.4
Uruguay	49	67	10.1	9.3	4.0	6.2	1.8	2.0	1.3	1.9	0.2	0.2
Uzbekistan	17	−23	0.9	1.3	113.9	116.0	2.8	2.4	6.3	4.3	3.1	1.9
Venezuela, RB	−242	−182	4.3	5.1	122.1	165.4	2.8	2.6	6.2	6.0	0.6	0.5
Vietnam	−2	−20	2.5	3.7	21.4	111.3	0.9	2.0	0.3	1.3	0.4	0.5
West Bank and Gaza	..	..	..	..	..	2.3	..	..	..	0.6	..	..
Yemen, Rep.	−273	−104	8.7	6.8	10.1	22.0	3.3	3.0	0.8	1.0	0.5	0.4
Zambia	9	8	1.8	2.1	2.4	2.7	0.5	0.4	0.3	0.2	0.2	0.2
Zimbabwe	8	10	..	..	15.5	9.6	1.7	1.0	1.5	0.8	..	..
World	−3[c] w	−4[c] w	4.2 w	5.5 w	22,529.9[d] t	30,649.4[d] t	2.6[d] w	2.5[d] w	4.3[d] w	4.6[d] w	0.6[d] w	0.5[d] w
Low income	14	6	2.6	3.2	357.6	228.2	2.2	1.0	0.7	0.3	0.8	0.3
Middle income	−24	−21	3.0	4.4	9,758.0	15,574.9	2.6	2.7	2.6	3.3	0.8	0.6
Lower middle income	−9	−4	2.4	4.0	4,772.5	10,391.5	2.4	2.9	1.6	2.8	1.0	0.7
Upper middle income	−40	−52	3.7	5.2	4,984.4	5,175.3	2.7	2.5	6.1	5.3	0.7	0.5
Low & middle income	−23	−20	3.0	4.4	10,115.2	15,802.5	2.5	2.7	2.4	2.9	0.8	0.6
East Asia & Pacific	−8	0	2.0	3.8	3,091.2	7,693.8	2.7	3.1	1.9	4.0	1.4	0.8
Europe & Central Asia	−12	−46	2.2	3.6	4,214.9	2,897.1	2.7	2.3	10.7	7.2	1.2	0.7
Latin America & Carib.	−34	−26	6.9	7.7	1,017.3	1,538.1	2.2	2.2	2.3	2.7	0.3	0.3
Middle East & N. Africa	−201	−99	5.7	4.7	578.7	1,177.0	3.1	2.9	2.5	3.7	0.6	0.6
South Asia	10	24	3.5	5.2	781.4	1,828.9	2.0	2.5	0.7	1.2	0.6	0.5
Sub-Saharan Africa	−54	−63	2.8	3.2	465.1	679.5	1.7	1.6	0.9	0.8	0.6	0.4
High income	15	15	5.3	6.6	11,669.7	13,761.0	2.6	2.4	11.9	12.5	0.5	0.4
Euro area	55	62	6.6	8.2	2,595.7	2,656.8	2.4	2.2	8.6	8.2	0.4	0.3

a. Negative values indicate that a country is a net exporter. b. Includes Kosovo and Montenegro. c. Deviation from zero is due to statistical errors and changes in stock. d. Includes emissions not allocated to specific countries.

Energy dependency and efficiency and carbon dioxide emissions

About the data

Because commercial energy is widely traded, its production and use need to be distinguished. Net energy imports show the extent to which an economy's use exceeds its production. High-income economies are net energy importers; middle-income economies are their main suppliers.

The ratio of gross domestic product (GDP) to energy use indicates energy efficiency. To produce comparable and consistent estimates of real GDP across economies relative to physical inputs to GDP—that is, units of energy use—GDP is converted to 2005 international dollars using purchasing power parity (PPP) rates. Differences in this ratio over time and across economies reflect structural changes in an economy, changes in sectoral energy efficiency, and differences in fuel mixes.

Carbon dioxide emissions, largely by-products of energy production and use (see table 3.7), account for the largest share of greenhouse gases, which are associated with global warming. Anthropogenic carbon dioxide emissions result primarily from fossil fuel combustion and cement manufacturing. In combustion different fossil fuels release different amounts of carbon dioxide for the same level of energy use: oil releases about 50 percent more carbon dioxide than natural gas, and coal releases about twice as much. Cement manufacturing releases about half a metric ton of carbon dioxide for each metric ton of cement produced.

The U.S. Department of Energy's Carbon Dioxide Information Analysis Center (CDIAC) calculates annual anthropogenic emissions from data on fossil fuel consumption (from the United Nations Statistics Division's World Energy Data Set) and world cement manufacturing (from the U.S. Bureau of Mines's Cement Manufacturing Data Set). Carbon dioxide emissions, often calculated and reported as

elemental carbon, were converted to actual carbon dioxide mass by multiplying them by 3.664 (the ratio of the mass of carbon to that of carbon dioxide). Although estimates of global carbon dioxide emissions are probably accurate within 10 percent (as calculated from global average fuel chemistry and use), country estimates may have larger error bounds. Trends estimated from a consistent time series tend to be more accurate than individual values. Each year the CDIAC recalculates the entire time series since 1949, incorporating recent findings and corrections. Estimates exclude fuels supplied to ships and aircraft in international transport because of the difficulty of apportioning the fuels among benefiting countries. The ratio of carbon dioxide per unit of energy shows carbon intensity, which is the amount of carbon dioxide emitted as a result of using one unit of energy in the process of production. The proportion of carbon dioxide per unit of GDP indicates how clean production processes are.

Definitions

- **Net energy imports** are estimated as energy use less production, both measured in oil equivalents.
- **GDP per unit of energy use** is the ratio of gross domestic product (GDP) per kilogram of oil equivalent of energy use, with GDP converted to 2005 international dollars using purchasing power parity (PPP) rates. An international dollar has the same purchasing power over GDP that a U.S. dollar has in the United States. Energy use refers to the use of primary energy before transformation to other end-use fuel, which is equal to indigenous production plus imports and stock changes minus exports and fuel supplied to ships and aircraft engaged in international transport (see *About the data* for table 3.7). • **Carbon dioxide emissions** are emissions from the burning of fossil fuels and the manufacture of cement and include carbon dioxide produced during consumption of solid, liquid, and gas fuels and gas flaring.

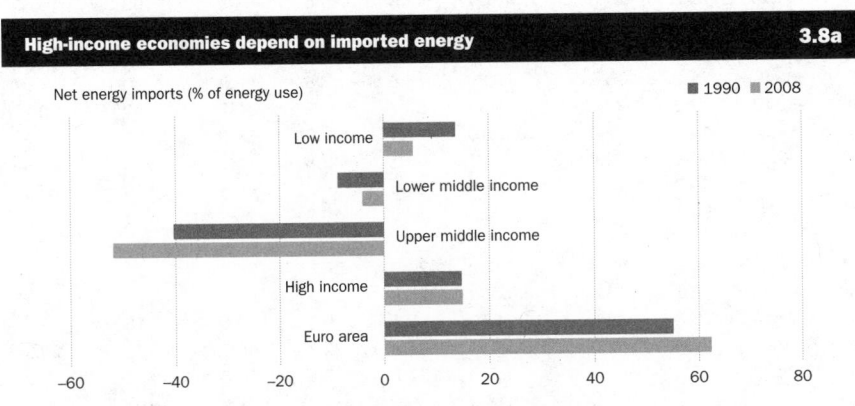

High-income economies depend on imported energy — 3.8a

Net energy imports (% of energy use) ■ 1990 ■ 2008

Note: Negative values indicate that the income group is a net energy exporter.
Source: Table 3.8.

Data sources

Data on energy use are from the electronic files of the International Energy Agency. Data on carbon dioxide emissions are from the CDIAC, Environmental Sciences Division, Oak Ridge National Laboratory, Tennessee, United States.

Trends in greenhouse gas emissions

	Carbon dioxide emissions		Methane emissions				Nitrous oxide emissions				Other greenhouse gas emissions	
	average annual % growth[a] 1990–2007	% change[b] 1990–2007	Total thousand metric tons of carbon dioxide equivalent 2005	% change[b] 1990–2005	From energy processes 2005	Agricultural 2005	Total thousand metric tons of carbon dioxide equivalent 2005	% change[b] 1990–2005	Energy and industry 2005	Agricultural 2005	Total thousand metric tons of carbon dioxide equivalent 2005	% change[b] 1990–2005
					% of total				% of total			
Afghanistan	−7.8	−73.3	..	..	..	..	..	..	..	..	..	..
Albania	2.5	−43.3	2,407	−5.1	20.0	70.8	1,036	−18.7	7.1	78.4	62	..
Algeria	3.7	77.6	54,219	33.1	83.2	8.2	4,898	27.5	22.6	58.6	489	50.0
Angola	10.1	459.0	45,409	−8.3	15.6	27.9	38,881	−6.7	0.4	38.4	20	..
Argentina	2.4	63.1	101,821	−8.3	18.9	70.6	49,821	29.6	3.9	89.2	785	−65.8
Armenia	1.2	21.8	2,962	2.5	50.8	36.7	580	−27.6	1.2	81.6	335	..
Australia	1.4	27.6	126,488	9.7	29.7	55.1	62,966	−0.1	10.3	78.2	6,505	33.5
Austria	1.1	12.7	8,515	−15.0	21.7	48.6	4,448	−13.5	31.0	52.5	2,329	46.2
Azerbaijan	−2.2	−36.2	36,607	110.7	82.0	13.6	2,633	0.4	8.3	77.5	89	−49.5
Bangladesh	6.5	181.7	92,414	6.5	10.0	70.5	21,386	42.1	7.5	83.1	0	..
Belarus	−2.6	−39.9	11,498	−32.8	7.6	70.9	11,680	−28.3	23.1	72.9	467	..
Belgium	−0.3	−4.2	10,063	−21.8	11.6	56.7	6,571	−27.6	38.1	44.3	2,106	583.8
Benin	9.1	442.1	4,080	−15.8	15.6	47.8	2,902	−21.5	4.0	61.5	0	..
Bolivia	4.0	139.6	30,350	30.9	25.6	34.1	15,092	3.2	0.7	36.5	0	..
Bosnia and Herzegovina	14.1	315.2	2,741	−53.5	46.7	42.4	1,196	−40.8	24.7	57.8	571	−7.4
Botswana	4.1	130.2	4,501	−22.6	8.6	84.1	3,081	−44.1	1.4	92.0	0	..
Brazil	3.3	76.3	492,160	56.4	7.6	61.1	235,987	52.6	3.4	67.0	11,816	40.5
Bulgaria	−2.1	−32.5	10,867	−24.8	13.0	18.9	4,227	−55.2	36.0	48.1	383	..
Burkina Faso	5.9	188.8	..	..	..	..	..	..	..	..	..	..
Burundi	−4.7	−41.0	..	..	..	..	..	..	..	..	..	..
Cambodia	16.0	884.6	20,215	35.0	4.9	76.1	5,794	46.9	3.5	66.1	0	..
Cameroon	4.2	254.9	18,518	37.1	39.1	42.4	9,127	−13.3	2.6	75.9	419	−55.0
Canada	1.5	23.8	89,338	30.8	32.2	29.3	40,171	−5.5	23.7	58.9	21,943	69.7
Central African Republic	1.0	27.8	..	..	..	..	..	..	..	..	..	..
Chad	10.5	162.5	..	..	..	..	..	..	..	..	..	..
Chile	4.6	105.4	18,149	49.8	24.4	39.4	8,135	57.5	16.6	73.4	13	−29.5
China	5.2	165.7	1,333,098	28.5	45.8	38.8	467,213	48.5	12.9	74.3	141,394	1,073.0
Hong Kong SAR, China	2.0	44.5	2,820	84.0	26.7	0.0	422	−1.0	38.5	0.0	119	−68.6
Colombia	−0.3	10.6	58,108	13.5	19.9	68.0	21,288	5.2	4.4	86.1	83	98.3
Congo, Dem. Rep.	−3.7	−40.2	56,445	−41.6	10.2	23.1	54,643	−37.3	2.2	31.3	0	..
Congo, Rep.	−0.8	33.6	5,584	−10.4	32.2	31.9	3,566	−17.2	1.0	51.8	5	..
Costa Rica	5.1	174.7	2,580	−31.3	9.5	67.2	1,334	−26.2	4.5	85.4	62	..
Côte d'Ivoire	1.5	10.1	10,997	−2.2	16.9	17.4	7,364	−1.6	2.7	29.3	0	..
Croatia	1.8	−0.8	3,864	−60.5	57.0	33.3	2,851	−24.5	36.6	52.4	59	−93.4
Cuba	−1.3	−18.9	9,455	−21.0	11.2	62.4	6,356	−31.8	15.1	78.7	129	..
Czech Republic	−1.1	−23.2	11,497	−40.3	49.4	33.6	8,878	−10.2	53.0	36.9	1,121	..
Denmark	−1.0	−0.8	7,935	−0.5	16.4	65.2	6,290	−21.5	18.0	73.4	1,422	458.3
Dominican Republic	4.7	116.9	6,081	3.8	7.8	63.7	2,255	11.0	7.8	76.8	0	..
Ecuador	2.9	78.1	17,125	31.2	31.2	57.8	4,571	42.3	3.8	84.9	63	..
Egypt, Arab Rep.	5.2	143.2	46,996	68.8	50.7	31.7	18,996	60.7	8.3	80.0	3,181	54.5
El Salvador	4.7	155.9	3,131	18.0	12.4	53.1	1,377	7.7	8.2	76.2	77	..
Eritrea	7.4	..	2,467	30.9	11.2	73.2	1,189	15.6	3.8	90.9	0	..
Estonia	−2.1	−27.5	2,108	−36.8	42.3	30.5	932	−50.7	21.5	60.5	40	1,790.5
Ethiopia	4.6	115.7	52,243	32.8	14.3	72.5	30,510	19.4	5.2	88.8	10	..
Finland	1.3	26.0	9,742	−2.8	7.4	20.7	7,124	−4.1	42.8	41.7	826	724.4
France	−0.3	−6.8	77,252	−0.3	44.3	47.7	49,058	−30.6	24.2	66.8	15,539	57.1
Gabon	−6.2	−66.6	8,218	1.4	90.4	1.1	482	57.9	10.0	23.3	9	..
Gambia, The	4.2	107.7	..	..	..	..	..	..	..	..	..	..
Georgia	−6.2	−65.1	4,410	−12.4	36.1	50.8	2,019	−26.9	35.5	56.9	12	..
Germany	−1.1	−18.0	67,582	−44.8	32.1	43.8	56,560	−23.9	38.2	52.2	31,543	8.1
Ghana	4.9	149.5	8,990	24.2	23.3	39.5	4,899	−5.5	9.3	70.5	15	−97.5
Greece	2.2	34.9	7,289	2.1	26.3	50.0	5,977	−17.1	22.1	58.2	1,842	−20.9
Guatemala	6.0	154.2	8,306	74.7	12.4	48.8	5,376	121.2	5.5	56.8	481	..
Guinea	1.5	31.6	..	..	..	..	..	..	..	..	..	..
Guinea-Bissau	−0.4	13.0	..	..	..	..	..	..	..	..	..	..
Haiti	7.6	141.3	4,006	34.9	12.1	56.2	1,438	59.6	6.2	84.2	0	..
Honduras	7.4	240.7	5,191	31.5	7.2	78.4	2,865	26.1	3.8	85.9	0	..

Trends in greenhouse gas emissions

	Carbon dioxide emissions		Methane emissions				Nitrous oxide emissions				Other greenhouse gas emissions	
	average annual % growth[a] 1990–2007	% change[b] 1990–2007	Total thousand metric tons of carbon dioxide equivalent 2005	% change[b] 1990–2005	From energy processes 2005 (% of total)	Agricultural 2005 (% of total)	Total thousand metric tons of carbon dioxide equivalent 2005	% change[b] 1990–2005	Energy and industry 2005 (% of total)	Agricultural 2005 (% of total)	Total thousand metric tons of carbon dioxide equivalent 2005	% change[b] 1990–2005
Hungary	−0.6	−11.0	7,767	−22.9	29.1	33.6	6,961	−31.2	30.9	60.1	1,552	121.1
India	4.8	133.5	583,978	10.5	15.9	64.4	212,927	33.3	12.8	73.4	8,433	−11.9
Indonesia	4.6	165.5	208,944	18.4	25.5	46.4	123,275	43.5	3.7	71.5	1,027	−40.6
Iran, Islamic Rep.	4.7	118.3	114,585	32.5	70.6	18.2	26,644	41.1	11.4	75.3	2,569	−2.9
Iraq	3.7	90.5	15,937	−45.8	58.4	18.6	3,440	−9.9	9.7	63.3	86	−66.0
Ireland	2.5	46.1	15,331	14.3	11.9	76.7	7,486	−8.3	4.5	90.5	1,151	3,062.9
Israel	3.6	99.0	3,517	83.8	18.4	31.2	1,793	41.6	15.3	53.0	1,981	88.7
Italy	0.6	7.4	40,790	−13.4	14.7	39.8	28,620	−5.4	39.1	43.7	13,968	211.1
Jamaica	2.4	75.3	1,302	14.4	11.4	50.3	599	29.5	12.1	59.0	51	..
Japan	0.4	8.8	42,771	−36.5	8.1	71.2	29,785	−17.0	41.6	27.9	53,786	81.1
Jordan	4.3	106.2	1,796	111.5	25.0	21.8	667	39.6	8.2	55.4	112	..
Kazakhstan	−2.1	−22.9	47,119	−27.3	66.2	25.3	17,594	−46.2	12.8	62.5	339	..
Kenya	4.6	92.9	22,130	23.3	16.9	65.5	10,542	14.3	5.0	88.8	0	..
Korea, Dem. Rep.	−9.2	−71.1	18,195	−15.0	58.6	23.5	3,422	−60.6	13.2	62.3	2,794	..
Korea, Rep.	4.0	108.2	32,069	2.4	19.9	38.6	13,548	34.7	41.3	35.9	10,221	66.0
Kosovo	..	..	..	..	..	..	650	157.1	27.7	16.9	931	253.9
Kuwait	9.0	111.4	14,380	119.4	93.4	1.1	1,510	−57.7	11.2	72.6	24	..
Kyrgyz Republic	−4.1	−51.2	3,591	−38.1	6.8	72.3	..	..	..	..	..	..
Lao PDR	14.0	554.7	..	..	..	..	1,253	−58.7	11.6	77.4	890	..
Latvia	−4.4	−47.9	3,108	−42.1	53.6	27.7	672	79.1	12.6	58.8	0	..
Lebanon	3.0	46.8	1,003	46.6	9.7	25.5	..	..	..	..	..	..
Lesotho	..	..	..	..	..	..	..	..	..	..	..	..
Liberia	5.3	39.4	..	..	..	..	1,285	9.2	11.2	51.9	280	−0.7
Libya	2.2	42.2	14,682	−34.7	86.3	5.7	2,451	−45.7	5.0	86.0	656	..
Lithuania	−3.1	−38.9	5,516	−34.1	32.0	33.8	599	−33.9	15.9	63.9	120	..
Macedonia, FYR	−0.4	−29.3	1,403	−36.5	32.1	46.6	..	..	..	..	..	..
Madagascar	5.1	128.3	..	..	..	..	..	..	..	..	..	..
Malawi	3.8	72.5	..	..	..	..	15,087	13.5	6.7	64.9	994	66.3
Malaysia	6.4	243.6	46,501	64.7	69.3	12.4	..	..	..	..	..	..
Mali	1.9	37.4	..	..	..	..	..	..	..	..	..	..
Mauritania	−4.6	−26.8	..	..	..	..	..	..	..	..	..	..
Mauritius	6.2	165.7	..	..	..	..	42,514	8.9	10.6	75.2	4,555	53.1
Mexico	1.6	31.9	128,209	26.3	40.2	42.3	849	−51.0	5.5	73.5	8	..
Moldova	−10.5	−80.1	3,372	−17.5	45.2	29.4	3,489	−30.0	2.2	93.2	0	..
Mongolia	−0.7	5.4	6,067	−25.9	2.5	92.1	5,814	12.2	3.0	82.6	0	..
Morocco	3.8	97.1	10,573	15.8	8.0	51.7	9,501	−12.7	3.4	71.4	282	..
Mozambique	5.4	159.7	12,843	18.2	22.7	44.2	30,932	−23.9	2.6	42.9	0	..
Myanmar	6.9	208.5	77,211	−7.4	12.6	69.0	3,797	47.1	1.1	94.3	0	..
Namibia	42.7	..	5,057	47.2	0.3	94.9	4,516	26.0	13.0	76.8	0	..
Nepal	8.1	439.9	22,142	9.7	5.9	82.9	14,596	−10.7	52.5	39.5	3,750	−40.9
Netherlands	0.0	5.6	21,259	−30.4	23.4	43.4	12,930	23.5	3.5	94.2	973	3.4
New Zealand	2.2	36.5	27,635	3.6	3.6	90.2	3,340	10.1	3.3	91.7	0	..
Nicaragua	4.4	73.6	6,018	26.3	6.6	74.8	..	..	..	..	..	..
Niger	−1.2	−4.6	..	..	..	..	21,565	12.6	9.1	77.3	669	176.6
Nigeria	5.9	110.0	130,317	10.9	68.9	19.3	4,737	−3.1	46.5	39.0	5,202	−39.4
Norway	2.9	36.5	16,870	47.2	74.6	12.6	561	82.6	16.0	68.0	175	..
Oman	8.2	260.5	17,849	194.9	94.1	3.0	26,838	46.0	14.5	74.2	819	−18.8
Pakistan	4.8	128.1	137,401	50.7	23.7	63.5	1,204	18.1	4.9	83.7	0	..
Panama	4.4	131.2	3,219	16.5	4.0	79.2	..	..	..	..	..	..
Papua New Guinea	5.3	57.2	..	..	..	..	9,067	0.6	1.7	82.6	0	..
Paraguay	3.0	82.7	15,388	2.0	3.9	84.1	7,560	35.4	2.9	81.9	330	..
Peru	3.6	103.1	17,187	22.7	13.5	61.3	12,950	34.0	9.1	73.1	365	125.6
Philippines	3.1	59.2	51,889	28.6	9.3	63.7	30,198	4.7	33.5	57.7	2,451	360.6
Poland	−1.0	−8.8	70,023	−36.6	62.0	21.9	5,958	24.3	22.0	43.8	783	606.6
Portugal	2.0	31.2	12,173	22.4	13.8	35.4	..	..	..	..	..	..
Puerto Rico	..	..	..	..	..	..	200	105.1	33.9	25.0	0	..
Qatar	5.9	435.5	15,706	387.2	96.5	0.4						

	Carbon dioxide emissions			Methane emissions			Nitrous oxide emissions				Other greenhouse gas emissions	
	average annual % growth[a]	% change[b]	Total thousand metric tons of carbon dioxide equivalent	% change[b]	% of total From energy processes	Agricultural	Total thousand metric tons of carbon dioxide equivalent	% change[b]	% of total Energy and industry	Agricultural	Total thousand metric tons of carbon dioxide equivalent	% change[b]
	1990–2007	1990–2007	2005	1990–2005	2005	2005	2005	1990–2005	2005	2005	2005	1990–2005
Romania	−2.9	−40.7	24,331	−35.1	42.7	36.0	11,537	−44.0	32.4	56.2	746	−62.8
Russian Federation	−2.2	−34.3	562,801	−18.3	79.3	9.1	76,121	−48.7	27.8	44.3	59,673	130.6
Rwanda	0.6	4.8	..	..	..	..	..	..	..	..	..	..
Saudi Arabia	2.6	87.1	48,152	67.4	83.6	4.0	6,501	17.5	14.0	46.1	2,193	−10.6
Senegal	3.0	72.1	7,129	35.1	9.9	68.3	4,083	37.2	2.7	88.5	0	..
Serbia	0.6[c]	−20.1[c]	7,782	−58.7	41.5	43.7	4,581	−8.8	24.2	63.6	4,493	353.7
Sierra Leone	7.4	237.7	..	..	..	..	..	..	..	..	..	..
Singapore	0.3	15.4	2,237	136.6	60.1	1.3	1,068	162.8	77.6	2.8	2,532	396.0
Slovak Republic	−1.6	−32.8	3,911	−39.7	18.2	39.0	3,354	−37.1	52.0	37.7	395	478.0
Slovenia	0.6	−17.3	3,498	0.6	30.7	32.1	1,156	−12.2	13.2	70.4	473	−38.5
Somalia	38.1	..	..	..	..	..	..	..	..	..	..	..
South Africa	1.3	30.0	63,785	24.6	45.4	31.4	24,048	12.9	12.6	59.8	2,552	71.1
Spain	2.9	57.9	36,338	11.9	10.4	56.8	26,529	6.5	18.7	62.6	9,080	47.7
Sri Lanka	7.5	226.3	10,210	−11.2	5.3	65.2	2,056	18.0	12.1	65.1	0	..
Sudan	6.4	107.3	67,441	55.5	7.1	85.2	49,472	34.9	1.3	92.6	0	..
Swaziland	10.0	150.0	..	..	..	..	..	..	..	..	..	..
Sweden	−0.5	−4.8	11,311	1.3	9.9	28.1	5,865	−13.1	26.8	60.2	2,078	133.8
Switzerland	−0.3	−11.6	4,748	−17.1	19.8	67.6	2,415	−15.5	20.8	59.3	2,109	97.4
Syrian Arab Republic	3.6	86.6	12,458	−10.8	53.8	28.1	5,509	33.4	9.0	78.1	0	..
Tajikistan	−6.9	−69.9	3,898	−9.3	12.8	68.6	1,378	0.2	1.4	86.9	383	−86.3
Tanzania	4.9	154.7	32,024	24.0	12.6	63.2	21,647	0.8	2.5	78.8	0	..
Thailand	5.7	189.6	83,257	5.7	16.9	66.0	22,304	15.1	21.7	65.5	1,104	−22.8
Timor-Leste	..	..	..	..	..	..	..	..	..	..	..	..
Togo	3.6	70.1	2,889	5.0	23.5	39.8	1,738	−21.3	5.6	67.5	0	..
Trinidad and Tobago	4.1	118.4	10,070	32.0	83.9	0.7	230	12.4	11.5	60.3	0	..
Tunisia	3.3	79.9	8,160	106.2	55.6	25.5	2,366	18.0	21.4	66.4	0	..
Turkey	3.4	91.4	64,251	46.4	16.0	33.6	32,781	12.8	22.7	66.4	5,066	96.9
Turkmenistan	2.8	44.7	27,984	−5.0	75.2	21.6	4,276	93.8	16.4	78.1	73	..
Uganda	8.3	291.9	..	..	..	..	..	..	..	..	..	..
Ukraine	−4.4	−54.0	70,360	−42.2	62.1	23.3	26,097	−51.4	42.8	45.6	693	209.3
United Arab Emirates	5.5	147.3	23,283	58.0	93.1	2.6	1,169	78.7	18.3	43.6	1,075	27.4
United Kingdom	−0.5	−5.4	65,788	−44.1	24.8	38.2	30,565	−44.7	24.8	60.0	10,403	96.7
United States	1.2	20.0	548,074	−14.4	41.0	34.8	317,153	1.8	30.6	56.4	239,517	158.7
Uruguay	2.0	55.7	19,589	24.1	1.5	94.3	7,017	16.1	1.4	96.9	59	..
Uzbekistan	0.1	−9.7	39,602	24.0	57.3	33.7	10,003	9.4	6.2	84.2	608	..
Venezuela, RB	2.9	35.5	61,183	5.9	47.4	40.0	14,935	23.4	5.0	75.2	2,468	−24.0
Vietnam	11.7	420.3	82,978	40.1	22.7	63.9	23,030	98.3	6.1	83.0	0	..
West Bank and Gaza	19.7	..	..	..	..	..	..	..	..	..	..	..
Yemen, Rep.	4.5	117.4	6,677	73.5	17.0	54.9	3,250	57.4	11.2	72.5	0	..
Zambia	−0.2	10.0	19,294	−28.4	6.7	59.3	25,068	−29.7	2.6	71.7	0	..
Zimbabwe	−3.3	−37.9	9,539	−5.7	11.4	73.3	6,114	−16.1	3.7	85.2	0	..
World	**1.8 w**	**36.0 w**	**7,135,973 s**	**6.2 w**	**37.3 w**	**42.6 w**	**2,852,592 s**	**5.8 w**	**15.4 w**	**66.2 w**	**724,183 s**	**122.4 w**
Low income	−4.1	−36.2	464,616	−4.0	13.6	60.7	239,126	−16.7	4.1	63.6	..	..
Middle income	2.6	59.6	5,128,922	13.9	39.0	42.6	1,799,128	18.3	10.7	70.8	259,893	208.5
Lower middle income	4.3	117.7	3,120,011	18.6	35.1	46.9	1,153,692	30.5	10.8	72.3	159,984	439.4
Upper middle income	0.3	3.8	2,008,911	7.3	45.0	35.8	645,436	1.5	10.6	68.1	99,909	83.1
Low & middle income	2.4	56.2	5,593,538	12.2	36.9	44.1	2,038,253	12.8	10.0	70.0	263,401	200.5
East Asia & Pacific	4.7	148.9	1,928,355	24.5	39.2	43.6	707,496	38.0	10.5	72.2	..	..
Europe & Central Asia	−2.0	−31.3	933,500	−17.2	67.5	17.4	213,150	−38.8	25.4	56.6	74,802	112.0
Latin America & Carib.	2.4	51.2	1,008,557	30.3	17.3	58.6	442,132	32.9	4.6	72.4	20,972	23.5
Middle East & N. Africa	4.2	103.4	287,084	20.0	64.7	20.7	73,539	36.8	10.7	74.5	6,717	20.7
South Asia	4.8	134.1	846,145	14.6	16.1	65.4	267,722	34.9	12.6	74.3	9,253	−12.5
Sub-Saharan Africa	2.2	46.1	589,897	5.4	30.5	44.0	334,216	−7.6	3.7	66.1	..	..
High income	1.0	17.9	1,542,435	−10.8	38.9	37.0	814,339	−8.4	29.1	56.9	460,781	93.7
Euro area	0.2	2.4	315,597	−18.0	25.9	46.9	218,258	−17.8	31.7	55.4	84,190	37.2

a. Calculated using the least squares method, which accounts for ups and downs of all data points in the period (see Statistical methods). b. Calculated as the change in emission since 1990, which is the baseline for Kyoto Protocal requirements. c. Includes Kosovo and Montenegro.

About the data

Greenhouse gases—which include carbon dioxide, methane, nitrous oxide, hydrofluorocarbons, perfluorocarbons, and sulfur hexafluoride—contribute to climate change.

Carbon dioxide emissions, largely a byproduct of energy production and use (see table 3.7), account for the largest share of greenhouse gases. Anthropogenic carbon dioxide emissions result primarily from fossil fuel combustion and cement manufacturing. Burning oil releases more carbon dioxide than burning natural gas, and burning coal releases even more for the same level of energy use. Cement manufacturing releases about half a metric ton of carbon dioxide for each metric ton of cement produced.

Methane emissions result largely from agricultural activities, industrial production landfills and wastewater treatment, and other sources such as tropical forest and other vegetation fires. The emissions are usually expressed in carbon dioxide equivalents using the global warming potential, which allows the effective contributions of different gases to be compared. A kilogram of methane is 21 times as effective at trapping heat in the earth's atmosphere as a kilogram of carbon dioxide within 100 years.

Nitrous oxide emissions are mainly from fossil fuel combustion, fertilizers, rainforest fires, and animal waste. Nitrous oxide is a powerful greenhouse gas, with an estimated atmospheric lifetime of 114 years, compared with 12 years for methane. The per kilogram global warming potential of nitrous oxide is nearly 310 times that of carbon dioxide within 100 years.

Other greenhouse gases covered under the Kyoto Protocol are hydrofluorocarbons, perfluorocarbons, and sulfur hexafluoride. Although emissions of these artificial gases are small, they are more powerful greenhouse gases than carbon dioxide, with much higher atmospheric lifetimes and high global warming potential.

For a discussion of carbon dioxide sources and the methodology behind emissions calculation, see *About the data* for table 3.8.

Definitions

• **Carbon dioxide emissions** are emissions from the burning of fossil fuels and the manufacture of cement and include carbon dioxide produced during consumption of solid, liquid, and gas fuels and gas flaring. • **Methane emissions** are emissions from human activities such as agriculture and from industrial methane production. • **Methane emissions from energy processes** are emissions from the production, handling, transmission, and combustion of fossil fuels and biofuels. • **Agricultural methane emissions** are emissions from animals, animal waste, rice production, agricultural waste burning (nonenergy, on-site), and savannah burning. • **Nitrous oxide emissions** are emissions from agricultural biomass burning, industrial activities, and livestock management. • **Nitrous oxide emissions from energy processes** are emissions produced by the combustion of fossil fuels and biofuels. • **Agricultural nitrous oxide emissions** are emissions produced through fertilizer use (synthetic and animal manure), animal waste management, agricultural waste burning (nonenergy, on-site), and savannah burning. • **Other greenhouse gas emissions** include hydrofluorocarbons, perfluorocarbons, and sulfur hexafluoride, which are to be curbed under the Kyoto Protocol. Hydrofluorocarbons, used as a replacement for chlorofluorocarbons, are used mainly in refrigeration and semiconductor manufacturing. Perfluorocarbons, also used as a replacement for chlorofluorocarbons in manufacturing semiconductors, are a byproduct of aluminum smelting and uranium enrichment. Sulfur hexafluoride is used largely to insulate high-voltage electric power equipment.

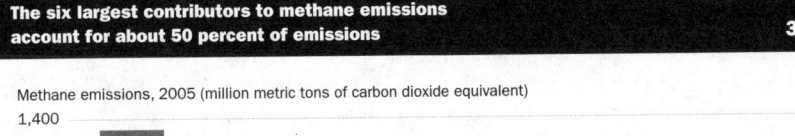

The six largest contributors to methane emissions account for about 50 percent of emissions　3.9a

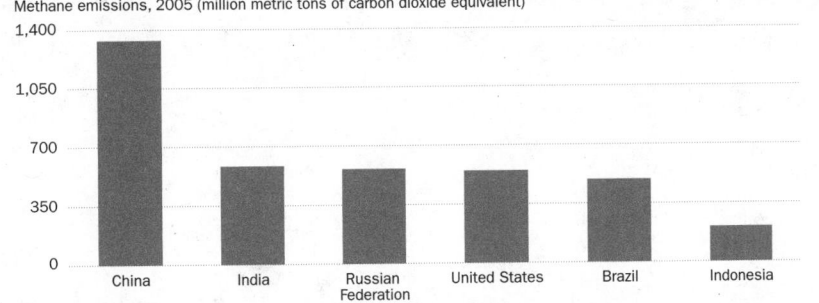

Methane emissions, 2005 (million metric tons of carbon dioxide equivalent)

Source: Table 3.9.

The five largest contributors to nitrous oxide emissions account for about 50 percent of emissions　3.9b

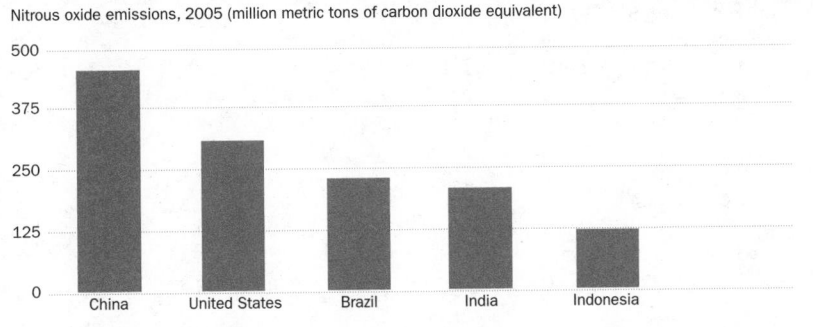

Nitrous oxide emissions, 2005 (million metric tons of carbon dioxide equivalent)

Source: Table 3.9.

Data sources

Data on carbon dioxide emissions are from the Carbon Dioxide Information Analysis Center, Environmental Sciences Division, Oak Ridge National Laboratory, Tennessee, United States. Data on methane, nitrous oxide, and other greenhouse gases emissions are compiled by the International Energy Agency.

| | Electricity production | | Sources of electricity[a] | | | | | | | | | |
| | billion kilowatt hours | | Coal | | Natural Gas | | Oil | | Hydropower | | Nuclear power | |
	1990	2008	1990	2008	1990	2008	1990	2008	1990	2008	1990	2008
Afghanistan	..	..	..	..	..	..	..	..	..	..	..	..
Albania	3.2	3.8	0.0	0.0	0.0	0.0	10.9	0.0	89.1	100.0	0.0	0.0
Algeria	16.1	40.2	0.0	0.0	93.7	97.3	5.4	2.0	0.8	0.7	0.0	0.0
Angola	0.8	4.0	0.0	0.0	0.0	0.0	13.8	3.7	86.2	96.3	0.0	0.0
Argentina	50.7	121.4	1.3	2.3	39.2	53.6	9.8	11.7	35.2	24.9	14.3	6.0
Armenia	10.4	5.8	0.0	0.0	16.4	26.2	68.6	0.0	15.0	31.1	0.0	42.6
Australia	154.3	257.1	78.7	76.9	9.3	15.0	2.3	1.1	9.2	4.6	0.0	0.0
Austria	49.3	64.4	14.2	10.7	15.7	17.4	3.8	1.9	63.9	59.0	0.0	0.0
Azerbaijan	23.2	23.9	0.0	0.0	0.0	84.1	97.0	6.6	3.0	9.3	0.0	0.0
Bangladesh	7.7	35.0	0.0	1.8	84.3	89.0	4.3	5.0	11.4	4.2	0.0	0.0
Belarus	39.5	35.0	0.0	0.0	58.1	96.9	41.8	2.7	0.1	0.1	0.0	0.0
Belgium	70.3	83.6	28.2	8.7	7.7	29.5	1.9	0.5	0.4	0.5	60.8	54.5
Benin	0.0	0.1	0.0	0.0	0.0	0.0	100.0	99.3	0.0	0.7	0.0	0.0
Bolivia	2.1	6.2	0.0	0.0	37.6	46.5	5.3	14.0	55.3	36.6	0.0	0.0
Bosnia and Herzegovina	14.6	13.3	71.8	64.4	0.0	0.0	7.3	1.3	20.9	34.3	0.0	0.0
Botswana	0.9	0.6	88.1	100.0	0.0	0.0	11.9	0.0	0.0	0.0	0.0	0.0
Brazil	222.8	463.4	2.1	2.7	0.3	6.3	2.2	3.8	92.8	79.8	1.0	3.0
Bulgaria	42.1	44.6	50.3	52.1	7.6	5.3	2.9	0.6	4.5	6.3	34.8	35.4
Burkina Faso	..	..	..	..	..	..	..	..	..	..	..	..
Burundi	..	..	..	..	..	..	..	..	..	..	..	..
Cambodia	..	1.5	..	0.0	..	0.0	..	96.5	..	3.1	..	0.0
Cameroon	2.7	5.6	0.0	0.0	0.0	7.7	1.5	15.9	98.5	76.2	0.0	0.0
Canada	482.0	651.2	17.1	17.2	2.0	6.2	3.4	1.5	61.6	58.7	15.1	14.4
Central African Republic	..	..	..	..	..	..	..	..	..	..	..	..
Chad	..	..	..	..	..	..	..	..	..	..	..	..
Chile	18.4	59.7	38.3	23.6	2.1	3.7	9.2	26.9	48.5	40.5	0.0	0.0
China	621.2	3,456.9	71.3	79.1	0.4	0.9	7.9	0.7	20.4	16.9	0.0	2.0
Hong Kong SAR, China	28.9	38.0	98.3	68.2	0.0	31.5	1.7	0.3	0.0	0.0	0.0	0.0
Colombia	36.4	56.0	10.1	5.4	12.4	10.3	1.0	0.3	75.6	82.8	0.0	0.0
Congo, Dem. Rep.	5.7	7.5	0.0	0.0	0.0	0.4	0.4	0.2	99.6	99.4	0.0	0.0
Congo, Rep.	0.5	0.5	0.0	0.0	0.0	18.7	0.6	0.0	99.4	81.3	0.0	0.0
Costa Rica	3.5	9.5	0.0	0.0	0.0	0.0	2.5	7.1	97.5	78.0	0.0	0.0
Côte d'Ivoire	2.0	5.8	0.0	0.0	0.0	65.1	33.3	0.2	66.7	32.7	0.0	0.0
Croatia	9.2	12.2	6.8	20.4	20.2	20.1	31.6	16.2	41.3	42.7	0.0	0.0
Cuba	15.0	17.7	0.0	0.0	0.2	0.0	91.4	97.0	0.8	0.8	0.0	0.0
Czech Republic	62.3	83.2	76.4	59.9	0.6	1.2	0.9	0.2	1.9	2.4	20.2	31.9
Denmark	26.0	36.4	90.7	48.0	2.7	19.0	3.4	3.1	0.1	0.1	0.0	0.0
Dominican Republic	3.7	15.4	1.2	13.8	0.0	12.9	88.6	61.8	9.4	11.2	0.0	0.0
Ecuador	6.3	18.6	0.0	0.0	0.0	7.3	21.5	29.8	78.5	60.7	0.0	0.0
Egypt, Arab Rep.	42.3	131.0	0.0	0.0	39.6	68.4	36.9	19.7	23.5	11.2	0.0	0.0
El Salvador	2.2	6.0	0.0	0.0	0.0	0.0	6.9	38.6	73.5	34.2	0.0	0.0
Eritrea	0.1	0.3	0.0	0.0	0.0	0.0	100.0	99.3	0.0	0.0	0.0	0.0
Estonia	17.4	10.6	85.8	91.0	5.5	4.0	8.3	0.3	0.0	0.3	0.0	0.0
Ethiopia	1.2	3.8	0.0	0.0	0.0	0.0	11.6	12.4	88.4	87.3	0.0	0.0
Finland	54.4	77.4	18.5	11.8	8.6	14.5	3.1	0.5	20.0	22.1	35.3	29.6
France	417.2	570.3	8.5	4.8	0.7	3.8	2.1	1.0	12.9	11.2	75.3	77.1
Gabon	1.0	2.0	0.0	0.0	16.4	24.7	11.2	31.2	72.1	43.8	0.0	0.0
Gambia, The	..	..	..	..	..	..	..	..	..	..	..	..
Georgia	13.7	8.4	0.0	0.0	15.6	15.2	29.2	0.0	55.2	84.8	0.0	0.0
Germany	547.7	631.2	58.7	46.0	7.4	13.9	1.9	1.5	3.2	3.3	27.8	23.5
Ghana	5.7	8.4	0.0	0.0	0.0	0.0	0.0	25.9	100.0	74.1	0.0	0.0
Greece	34.8	62.9	72.4	53.0	0.3	21.9	22.3	15.9	5.1	5.3	0.0	0.0
Guatemala	2.3	8.7	0.0	13.0	0.0	0.0	9.0	26.6	76.0	42.6	0.0	0.0
Guinea	..	..	..	..	..	..	..	..	..	..	..	..
Guinea-Bissau	..	..	..	..	..	..	..	..	..	..	..	..
Haiti	0.6	0.5	0.0	0.0	0.0	0.0	20.6	62.8	76.5	37.2	0.0	0.0
Honduras	2.3	6.5	0.0	0.0	0.0	0.0	1.7	61.9	98.3	35.0	0.0	0.0

	Electricity production		Sources of electricity[a]									
							% of total					
	billion kilowatt hours		Coal		Natural Gas		Oil		Hydropower		Nuclear power	
	1990	**2008**	**1990**	**2008**	**1990**	**2008**	**1990**	**2008**	**1990**	**2008**	**1990**	**2008**
Hungary	28.4	40.0	30.5	18.0	15.7	37.9	4.8	0.9	0.6	0.5	48.3	37.0
India	289.4	830.1	66.2	68.6	3.4	9.9	3.5	4.1	24.8	13.8	2.1	1.8
Indonesia	33.3	149.4	31.5	41.1	2.3	16.9	42.7	28.8	20.2	7.7	0.0	0.0
Iran, Islamic Rep.	59.1	214.5	0.0	0.2	52.5	80.8	37.3	16.6	10.3	2.3	0.0	0.0
Iraq	24.0	36.8	0.0	0.0	0.0	0.0	89.2	98.5	10.8	1.5	0.0	0.0
Ireland	14.2	29.4	41.6	17.8	27.7	54.7	10.0	5.9	4.9	3.3	0.0	0.0
Israel	20.9	56.4	50.1	62.7	0.0	26.2	49.9	10.6	0.0	0.0	0.0	0.0
Italy	213.1	313.5	16.8	15.5	18.6	55.1	48.2	10.0	14.8	13.3	0.0	0.0
Jamaica	2.5	7.8	0.0	0.0	0.0	0.0	92.4	96.0	3.6	2.0	0.0	0.0
Japan	835.5	1,075.0	14.0	26.8	20.0	26.3	18.5	9.7	10.7	7.1	24.2	24.0
Jordan	3.6	13.8	0.0	0.0	11.9	80.6	87.8	18.9	0.3	0.4	0.0	0.0
Kazakhstan	87.4	80.3	71.1	70.3	10.5	10.7	10.0	9.7	8.4	9.3	0.0	0.0
Kenya	3.2	7.1	0.0	0.0	0.0	0.0	7.1	38.4	76.6	40.4	0.0	0.0
Korea, Dem. Rep.	27.7	23.2	40.1	36.0	0.0	0.0	3.6	3.4	56.3	60.6	0.0	0.0
Korea, Rep.	105.4	443.9	16.8	43.2	9.1	18.3	17.9	3.5	6.0	0.7	50.2	34.0
Kosovo	..	..	..	..	..	..	..	..	..	..	..	..
Kuwait	18.5	51.7	0.0	0.0	45.7	30.4	54.3	69.6	0.0	0.0	0.0	0.0
Kyrgyz Republic	15.7	11.9	13.1	3.5	23.5	6.1	0.0	0.0	63.5	90.4	0.0	0.0
Lao PDR	..	..	..	..	..	..	..	..	..	..	..	..
Latvia	6.6	5.3	0.0	0.0	26.1	39.0	5.4	0.0	67.6	58.9	0.0	0.0
Lebanon	1.5	10.6	0.0	0.0	0.0	0.0	66.7	96.5	33.3	3.5	0.0	0.0
Lesotho	..	..	..	..	..	..	..	..	..	..	..	..
Liberia	..	..	..	..	..	..	..	..	..	..	..	..
Libya	10.2	28.7	0.0	0.0	0.0	41.0	100.0	59.0	0.0	0.0	0.0	0.0
Lithuania	28.4	13.3	0.0	0.0	23.8	15.2	14.6	4.2	1.5	3.0	60.0	74.2
Macedonia, FYR	5.8	6.3	89.7	83.8	0.0	0.0	1.8	2.9	8.5	13.3	0.0	0.0
Madagascar	..	..	..	..	..	..	..	..	..	..	..	..
Malawi	..	..	..	..	..	..	..	..	..	..	..	..
Malaysia	23.0	97.4	12.3	26.9	20.4	63.6	50.0	1.9	17.3	7.7	0.0	0.0
Mali	..	..	..	..	..	..	..	..	..	..	..	..
Mauritania	..	..	..	..	..	..	..	..	..	..	..	..
Mauritius	..	..	..	..	..	..	..	..	20.3	15.1	..	..
Mexico	115.8	258.9	6.7	8.3	12.5	50.6	53.6	19.0	20.3	15.1	2.5	3.8
Moldova	16.2	3.6	30.8	0.0	42.3	95.6	25.4	0.4	1.6	2.3	0.0	0.0
Mongolia	3.5	4.1	92.4	96.1	0.0	0.0	7.6	3.9	0.0	0.0	0.0	0.0
Morocco	9.6	20.8	23.0	56.2	0.0	13.8	64.4	24.2	12.7	4.5	0.0	0.0
Mozambique	0.5	15.1	13.9	0.0	0.0	0.1	23.6	0.0	62.6	99.9	0.0	0.0
Myanmar	2.5	6.6	1.6	0.0	39.3	35.7	10.9	3.5	48.1	60.8	0.0	0.0
Namibia	1.4	2.1	1.5	31.1	0.0	0.0	3.3	1.4	95.2	67.5	0.0	0.0
Nepal	0.9	3.1	0.0	0.0	0.0	0.0	0.1	0.4	99.9	99.6	0.0	0.0
Netherlands	71.9	107.6	38.3	24.9	50.9	58.9	4.3	1.9	0.1	0.1	4.9	3.9
New Zealand	32.3	43.8	2.1	11.0	17.7	24.3	0.0	0.3	71.9	51.0	0.0	0.0
Nicaragua	1.4	3.4	0.0	0.0	0.0	0.0	39.8	64.5	28.8	15.9	0.0	0.0
Niger	..	..	..	..	..	..	..	..	..	..	..	..
Nigeria	13.5	21.1	0.1	0.0	53.7	58.2	13.7	14.7	32.6	27.1	0.0	0.0
Norway	121.6	141.7	0.1	0.1	0.0	0.3	0.0	0.0	99.6	98.5	0.0	0.0
Oman	4.5	15.7	0.0	0.0	81.6	82.0	18.4	18.0	0.0	0.0	0.0	0.0
Pakistan	37.7	91.6	0.1	0.1	33.6	32.4	20.6	35.4	44.9	30.3	0.8	1.8
Panama	2.7	6.4	0.0	0.0	0.0	0.0	14.7	37.9	83.2	61.8	0.0	0.0
Papua New Guinea	..	..	..	..	..	..	..	..	..	..	..	..
Paraguay	27.2	55.5	0.0	0.0	0.0	0.0	0.0	0.0	99.9	100.0	0.0	0.0
Peru	13.8	32.4	0.0	2.7	1.7	28.0	21.5	9.0	75.8	58.7	0.0	0.0
Philippines	27.4	60.8	7.0	25.9	0.0	32.2	45.3	8.0	22.1	16.2	0.0	0.0
Poland	134.4	155.6	97.5	92.2	0.1	2.0	1.2	1.5	1.1	1.4	0.0	0.0
Portugal	28.4	45.5	32.1	24.6	0.0	33.4	33.1	9.1	32.3	15.0	0.0	0.0
Puerto Rico	..	..	..	..	..	..	..	..	..	..	..	..
Qatar	4.8	21.6	0.0	0.0	100.0	100.0	0.0	0.0	0.0	0.0	0.0	0.0

	Electricity production		Sources of electricityᵃ									
							% of total					
	billion kilowatt hours		Coal		Natural Gas		Oil		Hydropower		Nuclear power	
	1990	2008	1990	2008	1990	2008	1990	2008	1990	2008	1990	2008
Romania	64.3	65.0	28.8	39.8	35.1	15.3	18.4	1.1	17.7	26.5	0.0	17.3
Russian Federation	1,082.2	1,038.4	14.3	18.9	47.3	47.6	11.5	1.5	15.3	15.9	10.9	15.7
Rwanda	..	..	..	..	..	..	..	..	..	..	..	..
Saudi Arabia	69.2	204.2	0.0	0.0	48.1	43.1	51.9	56.9	0.0	0.0	0.0	0.0
Senegal	0.9	2.4	0.0	0.0	2.3	1.7	93.0	85.8	0.0	9.5	0.0	0.0
Serbia	40.9	36.8	69.1	72.4	3.2	1.1	4.6	0.5	23.1	26.0	0.0	0.0
Sierra Leone	..	..	..	..	..	..	..	..	..	..	..	..
Singapore	15.7	41.7	0.0	0.0	0.0	80.3	100.0	19.7	0.0	0.0	0.0	0.0
Slovak Republic	25.5	28.8	31.9	17.9	7.1	5.6	6.4	2.4	7.4	14.0	47.2	58.1
Slovenia	12.4	16.4	31.3	32.5	0.0	2.9	7.9	0.1	23.7	24.5	37.1	38.3
Somalia	..	..	..	..	..	..	..	..	..	..	..	..
South Africa	165.4	255.5	94.3	94.2	0.0	0.0	0.0	0.1	0.6	0.5	5.1	5.1
Spain	151.2	311.1	40.1	16.1	1.0	39.1	5.7	5.8	16.8	7.6	35.9	19.0
Sri Lanka	3.2	9.2	0.0	0.0	0.0	0.0	0.2	55.1	99.8	44.7	0.0	0.0
Sudan	1.5	4.5	0.0	0.0	0.0	0.0	36.8	67.6	63.2	32.4	0.0	0.0
Swaziland	..	..	..	..	..	..	..	..	..	..	..	..
Sweden	146.0	149.9	1.1	1.1	0.3	0.4	0.9	0.6	49.7	46.1	46.7	42.6
Switzerland	55.0	67.1	0.1	0.1	0.6	1.1	0.7	0.2	54.2	53.7	43.0	41.3
Syrian Arab Republic	11.6	41.0	0.0	0.0	20.5	31.3	56.0	61.7	23.5	7.0	0.0	0.0
Tajikistan	18.1	16.1	0.0	0.0	9.1	1.9	0.0	0.0	90.9	98.1	0.0	0.0
Tanzania	1.6	4.4	0.0	2.7	0.0	36.2	4.9	0.9	95.1	60.1	0.0	0.0
Thailand	44.2	147.4	25.0	21.4	40.2	69.4	23.5	1.1	11.3	4.8	0.0	0.0
Timor-Leste	..	..	..	..	..	..	..	..	..	..	..	..
Togo	0.2	0.1	0.0	0.0	0.0	0.0	39.9	24.4	60.1	74.0	0.0	0.0
Trinidad and Tobago	3.6	7.9	0.0	0.0	99.0	99.6	0.1	0.2	0.0	0.0	0.0	0.0
Tunisia	5.8	15.3	0.0	0.0	63.7	88.7	35.5	10.8	0.8	0.2	0.0	0.0
Turkey	57.5	198.4	35.1	29.1	17.7	49.7	6.9	3.8	40.2	16.8	0.0	0.0
Turkmenistan	14.6	15.0	0.0	0.0	95.2	100.0	0.0	0.0	4.8	0.0	0.0	0.0
Uganda	..	..	..	..	..	..	..	..	..	..	..	..
Ukraine	298.6	192.5	38.2	35.6	16.7	11.4	16.1	0.4	3.5	5.9	25.5	46.7
United Arab Emirates	17.1	86.3	0.0	0.0	96.3	98.3	3.7	1.7	0.0	0.0	0.0	0.0
United Kingdom	317.8	385.3	65.0	32.9	1.6	45.9	10.9	1.6	1.6	1.3	20.7	13.6
United States	3,202.8	4,343.8	53.1	49.1	11.9	21.0	4.1	1.3	8.5	5.9	19.1	19.3
Uruguay	7.4	8.8	0.0	0.0	0.0	0.0	5.1	39.1	94.2	51.4	0.0	0.0
Uzbekistan	56.3	49.4	7.4	4.1	76.4	70.0	4.4	2.9	11.8	23.0	0.0	0.0
Venezuela, RB	59.3	119.3	0.0	0.0	26.2	14.7	11.5	12.5	62.3	72.8	0.0	0.0
Vietnam	8.7	73.0	23.1	20.8	0.1	41.5	15.0	2.1	61.8	35.6	0.0	0.0
West Bank and Gaza	..	..	..	..	..	..	..	..	..	..	..	..
Yemen, Rep.	1.7	6.5	0.0	0.0	0.0	0.0	100.0	100.0	0.0	0.0	0.0	0.0
Zambia	8.0	9.7	0.5	0.0	0.0	0.0	0.3	0.3	99.2	99.7	0.0	0.0
Zimbabwe	9.4	8.0	53.3	46.3	0.0	0.0	0.0	0.3	46.7	53.4	0.0	0.0
World	**11,839.5 t**	**20,201.4 t**	**37.3 w**	**40.8 w**	**14.6 w**	**21.3 w**	**10.2 w**	**5.1 w**	**18.0 w**	**15.8 w**	**17.0 w**	**13.5 w**
Low income	138.9	206.7	13.2	6.4	9.2	17.5	1.7	5.0	53.7	48.9	0.0	0.0
Middle income	3,984.6	8,948.5	32.4	47.4	22.3	19.8	14.6	6.0	23.1	20.4	6.4	4.7
Lower middle income	1,654.0	5,548.8	47.7	63.3	11.7	9.9	14.2	5.0	20.3	16.8	5.0	3.2
Upper middle income	2,330.2	3,402.8	21.6	21.3	29.8	35.8	14.9	7.6	25.1	26.4	7.3	7.2
Low & middle income	4,122.5	9,174.7	31.8	46.4	21.8	19.7	14.1	6.0	24.1	21.0	6.1	4.6
East Asia & Pacific	796.3	4,044.1	61.0	71.6	3.4	6.7	12.6	2.0	21.4	16.4	0.0	1.7
Europe & Central Asia	1,935.8	1,864.6	23.1	25.3	36.7	40.2	13.6	2.0	14.5	16.4	11.7	15.7
Latin America & Carib.	598.1	1,285.3	4.0	4.5	9.4	20.7	17.8	13.5	64.4	55.3	2.1	2.4
Middle East & N. Africa	187.9	566.8	1.2	2.1	36.9	62.5	48.3	29.4	12.4	4.4	0.0	0.0
South Asia	341.7	977.2	56.1	58.3	8.5	14.6	5.3	7.5	27.4	15.4	1.9	1.7
Sub-Saharan Africa	260.2	424.1	62.2	58.0	2.8	4.4	1.9	3.8	15.9	17.2	3.2	3.1
High income	7,736.5	11,079.9	40.2	36.1	10.7	22.5	8.1	4.4	14.7	11.3	22.7	20.8
Euro area	1,694.1	2,352.2	33.7	22.4	8.6	24.0	9.6	3.9	11.1	9.5	35.6	31.6

a. Shares may not sum to 100 percent because some sources of generated electricity (such as wind, solar, and geothermal) are not shown.

About the data

Use of energy is important in improving people's standard of living. But electricity generation also can damage the environment. Whether such damage occurs depends largely on how electricity is generated. For example, burning coal releases twice as much carbon dioxide—a major contributor to global warming—as does burning an equivalent amount of natural gas (see *About the data* for table 3.8). Nuclear energy does not generate carbon dioxide emissions, but it produces other dangerous waste products. The table provides information on electricity production by source.

The International Energy Agency (IEA) compiles data on energy inputs used to generate electricity. IEA data for countries that are not members of the Organisation for Economic Co-operation and Development (OECD) are based on national energy data adjusted to conform to annual questionnaires completed by OECD member governments. In addition, estimates are sometimes made to complete major aggregates from which key data are missing, and adjustments are made to compensate for differences in definitions. The IEA makes these estimates in consultation with national statistical offices, oil companies, electric utilities, and national energy experts. It occasionally revises its time series to reflect political changes. For example, the IEA has constructed historical energy statistics for countries of the former Soviet Union. In addition, energy statistics for other countries have undergone continuous changes in coverage or methodology in recent years as more detailed energy accounts have become available. Breaks in series are therefore unavoidable.

Definitions

• **Electricity production** is measured at the terminals of all alternator sets in a station. In addition to hydropower, coal, oil, gas, and nuclear power generation, it covers generation by geothermal, solar, wind, and tide and wave energy as well as that from combustible renewables and waste. Production includes the output of electric plants designed to produce electricity only, as well as that of combined heat and power plants. • **Sources of electricity** are the inputs used to generate electricity: coal, gas, oil, hydropower, and nuclear power. • **Coal** is all coal and brown coal, both primary (including hard coal and lignite-brown coal) and derived fuels (including patent fuel, coke oven coke, gas coke, coke oven gas, and blast furnace gas). Peat is also included in this category. • **Gas** is natural gas but not natural gas liquids. • **Oil** is crude oil and petroleum products. • **Hydropower** is electricity produced by hydroelectric power plants. • **Nuclear power** is electricity produced by nuclear power plants.

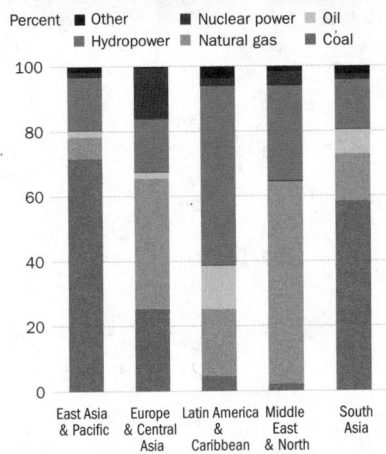

More than 50 percent of electricity in Latin America is produced by hydropower

3.10a

Source: Table 3.10.

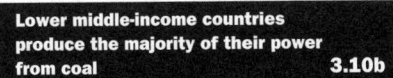
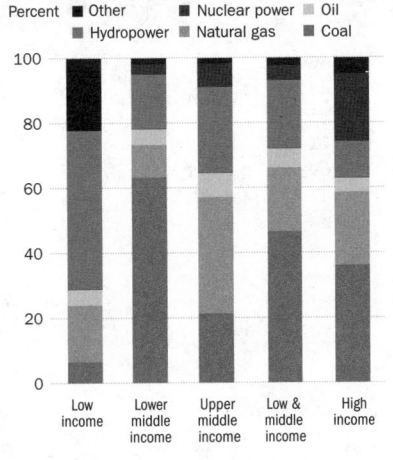

Lower middle-income countries produce the majority of their power from coal

3.10b

Source: Table 3.10.

Data sources

Data on electricity production are from the IEA's electronic files and its annual publications *Energy Statistics and Balances of Non-OECD Countries, Energy Statistics of OECD Countries,* and *Energy Balances of OECD Countries.*

3.11 | Urbanization

	Urban population					Population in urban agglomerations of more than 1 million		Population in largest city		Access to improved sanitation facilities			
	millions		% of total population		average annual % growth	% of total population		% of urban population		% of urban population		% of rural population	
	1990	2009	1990	2009	1990–2009	1990	2009	1990	2009	1990	2008	1990	2008
Afghanistan	·3	7	18	24	4.0	7	12	38	49	..	60	..	30
Albania	1	1	36	47	1.2	..	..	21	29	..	98	..	98
Algeria	13	23	52	66	2.9	7	8	14	12	99	98	77	88
Angola	4	11	37	58	5.2	15	24	40	42	58	86	6	18
Argentina	28	37	87	92	1.4	39	39	37	35	93	91	73	77
Armenia	2	2	68	64	-1.0	33	36	49	56	95	95	..	80
Australia	15	19	85	89	1.5	60	59	25	23	100	100	100	100
Austria	5	6	66	67	0.6	20	20	30	30	100	100	100	100
Azerbaijan	4	5	54	52	0.9	24	22	45	43	..	51	..	39
Bangladesh	23	45	20	28	3.5	8	13	29	32	59	56	34	52
Belarus	7	7	66	74	0.3	16	19	24	26	..	91	..	97
Belgium	10	11	96	97	0.5	17	18	17	18	100	100	100	100
Benin	2	4	35	42	4.3	..	..	30	22	14	24	1	4
Bolivia	4	7	56	66	3.0	25	33	29	25	29	34	6	9
Bosnia and Herzegovina	2	2	39	48	0.4	..	..	24	22	..	99	..	92
Botswana	1	1	42	60	3.8	..	..	22	17	58	74	20	39
Brazil	112	167	75	86	2.1	35	40	13	12	81	87	35	37
Bulgaria	6	5	66	71	-0.3	14	16	21	22	100	100	98	100
Burkina Faso	1	3	14	20	5.0	6	11	44	56	28	33	2	6
Burundi	0	1	6	11	4.8	..	..	66	51	41	49	44	46
Cambodia	1	3	13	22	5.2	6	10	50	46	38	67	5	18
Cameroon	5	11	41	58	4.3	14	19	19	18	65	56	35	35
Canada	21	27	77	81	1.3	40	44	18	20	100	100	99	99
Central African Republic	1	2	37	39	2.4	..	..	43	41	21	43	5	28
Chad	1	3	21	27	4.6	..	..	38	27	20	23	2	4
Chile	11	15	83	89	1.7	35	35	42	39	91	98	48	83
China	311	586	27	44	3.3	9	17	3	3	48	58	38	52
Hong Kong SAR, China	6	7	100	100	1.1	100	100	100	99	..	..	..	..
Colombia	23	34	68	75	2.2	31	37	21	24	80	81	43	55
Congo, Dem. Rep.	10	23	28	35	4.2	13	17	35	37	23	23	4	23
Congo, Rep.	1	2	54	62	2.8	29	35	53	57	..	31	..	29
Costa Rica	2	3	51	64	3.3	24	31	47	48	94	95	91	96
Côte d'Ivoire	5	10	40	49	3.9	17	19	42	38	38	36	8	11
Croatia	3	3	54	58	-0.1	..	..	27	27	..	99	..	98
Cuba	8	8	73	76	0.5	20	19	27	25	86	94	64	81
Czech Republic	8	8	75	74	0.0	12	11	16	15	100	99	98	97
Denmark	4	5	85	87	0.5	20	21	24	24	100	100	100	100
Dominican Republic	4	7	55	70	2.9	21	21	37	30	83	87	61	74
Ecuador	6	9	55	66	2.5	26	33	28	29	86	96	48	84
Egypt, Arab Rep.	25	35	44	43	1.8	21	18	36	31	91	97	57	92
El Salvador	3	4	49	61	1.9	18	25	37	41	88	89	62	83
Eritrea	0	1	16	21	4.0	..	..	72	60	58	52	0	4
Estonia	1	1	71	69	-1.0	..	..	43	43	..	96	..	94
Ethiopia	6	14	13	17	4.5	4	3	29	20	21	29	1	8
Finland	3	3	61	64	0.5	17	21	28	33	100	100	100	100
France	42	49	74	78	0.8	23	23	22	21	100	100	100	100
Gabon	1	1	69	86	3.6	..	..	62	49	..	33	..	30
Gambia, The	0	1	38	57	5.5	..	..	66	45	..	68	..	65
Georgia	3	2	55	53	-1.5	22	26	41	50	97	96	95	93
Germany	58	60	73	74	0.2	8	8	6	6	100	100	100	100
Ghana	5	12	36	51	4.2	13	17	22	19	11	18	4	7
Greece	6	7	59	61	0.8	30	29	51	47	100	99	92	97
Guatemala	4	7	41	49	3.3	9	8	22	16	84	89	51	73
Guinea	2	4	28	35	3.8	15	16	52	45	18	34	6	11
Guinea-Bissau	0	0	28	30	2.7	..	..	53	63	..	49	..	9
Haiti	2	5	29	48	4.6	16	26	56	55	44	24	19	10
Honduras	2	4	40	48	3.2	12	13	29	28	68	80	28	62

	Urban population					Population in urban agglomerations of more than 1 million		Population in largest city		Access to improved sanitation facilities			
	millions		% of total population		average annual % growth	% of total population		% of urban population		% of urban population		% of rural population	
	1990	2009	1990	2009	1990–2009	1990	2009	1990	2009	1990	2008	1990	2008
Hungary	7	7	66	68	0.0	19	17	29	25	100	100	100	100
India	217	345	26	30	2.4	10	13	4	6	49	54	7	21
Indonesia	54	121	31	53	4.2	10	9	15	8	58	67	22	36
Iran, Islamic Rep.	31	50	56	69	2.6	24	24	21	14	86	..	78	..
Iraq	13	21	70	67	2.4	26	23	31	27	..	76	..	66
Ireland	2	3	57	62	1.7	26	24	46	39	100	100	98	98
Israel	4	7	90	92	2.5	56	57	48	47	100	100	100	100
Italy	38	41	67	68	0.4	19	17	9	8	..	..	..	..
Jamaica	1	1	49	54	1.1	..	..	49	40	82	82	83	84
Japan	78	85	63	67	0.5	46	49	42	43	100	100	100	100
Jordan	2	5	72	78	3.9	27	18	37	23	98	98	..	97
Kazakhstan	9	9	56	58	0.0	7	9	12	15	96	97	97	98
Kenya	4	9	18	22	3.8	6	8	32	39	24	27	27	32
Korea, Dem. Rep.	12	15	58	63	1.3	13	12	21	19	..	..	..	..
Korea, Rep.	32	40	74	82	1.2	51	48	33	25	100	100	100	100
Kosovo	..	..	..	..	..	..	..	..	..	..	..	..	..
Kuwait	2	3	98	98	1.5	65	80	67	81	100	100	100	100
Kyrgyz Republic	2	2	38	36	0.8	..	..	38	44	94	94	..	93
Lao PDR	1	2	15	32	6.0	..	..	70	39	..	86	..	38
Latvia	2	2	69	68	-1.0	..	..	49	46	..	82	..	71
Lebanon	2	4	83	87	2.1	43	45	52	52	100	100	..	..
Lesotho	0	1	14	26	4.6	..	..	50	41	29	40	32	25
Liberia	1	2	45	61	4.7	..	29	106	37	21	25	3	4
Libya	3	5	76	78	2.2	20	17	26	22	97	97	96	96
Lithuania	2	2	68	67	-0.6	..	..	23	24	..	..	..	..
Macedonia, FYR	1	1	58	67	1.2	..	..	40	35	..	92	..	82
Madagascar	3	6	24	30	4.2	8	9	36	31	14	15	6	10
Malawi	1	3	12	19	5.2	..	..	24	28	50	51	41	57
Malaysia	9	20	50	71	4.1	8	9	12	8	88	96	81	95
Mali	2	4	23	33	3.9	9	13	37	38	36	45	23	32
Mauritania	1	1	40	41	2.8	..	..	53	52	29	50	8	9
Mauritius	0	1	44	43	0.8	..	..	30	28	93	93	90	90
Mexico	59	83	71	78	1.8	34	36	26	23	80	90	30	68
Moldova	2	1	47	41	-1.6	..	..	32	43	..	85	..	74
Mongolia	1	2	57	57	1.0	..	..	45	62	..	64	..	32
Morocco	12	18	48	56	2.1	18	19	22	18	81	83	27	52
Mozambique	3	9	21	38	5.8	6	7	27	18	36	38	4	4
Myanmar	10	17	25	33	2.6	9	11	29	26	..	86	..	79
Namibia	0	1	28	37	3.8	..	..	35	42	66	60	9	17
Nepal	2	5	9	18	5.9	..	..	23	19	41	51	8	27
Netherlands	10	14	69	82	1.5	13	12	9	8	100	100	100	100
New Zealand	3	4	85	87	1.3	25	32	30	36	..	..	88	..
Nicaragua	2	3	52	57	2.2	18	23	34	29	59	63	26	37
Niger	1	3	15	17	3.9	5	7	35	40	19	34	2	4
Nigeria	34	76	35	49	4.2	12	15	14	13	39	36	36	28
Norway	3	4	72	78	1.1	..	..	22	23	100	100	100	100
Oman	1	2	66	72	2.7	..	..	27	31	97	97	61	..
Pakistan	33	62	31	37	3.3	16	18	22	21	73	72	8	29
Panama	1	3	54	74	3.6	35	39	65	53	73	75	40	51
Papua New Guinea	1	1	15	13	1.6	..	..	32	37	78	71	42	41
Paraguay	2	4	49	61	3.3	26	31	53	51	61	90	15	40
Peru	15	21	69	72	1.7	27	30	39	42	71	81	16	36
Philippines	30	60	49	66	3.6	14	14	26	19	70	80	46	69
Poland	23	23	61	61	0.0	4	4	7	7	96	96	..	80
Portugal	5	6	48	60	1.6	37	39	54	44	97	100	87	100
Puerto Rico	3	4	72	99	2.3	44	69	60	70	..	..	..	..
Qatar	0	1	92	96	6.0	..	..	54	32	100	100	100	100

3.11 | Urbanization

	Urban population					Population in urban agglomerations of more than 1 million		Population in largest city		Access to improved sanitation facilities			
	millions		% of total population		average annual % growth	% of total population		% of urban population		% of urban population		% of rural population	
	1990	2009	1990	2009	1990–2009	1990	2009	1990	2009	1990	2008	1990	2008
Romania	12	12	53	54	-0.3	9	9	17	17	88	88	52	54
Russian Federation	109	103	73	73	-0.3	17	18	8	10	93	93	70	70
Rwanda	0	2	5	19	8.3	..	..	57	49	35	50	22	55
Saudi Arabia	12	21	77	82	2.7	34	41	19	23	100	100	..	..
Senegal	3	5	39	43	3.1	19	22	48	52	62	69	22	38
Serbia	4	4	50	52	0.0	15	15	30	29	..	96	..	88
Sierra Leone	1	2	33	38	2.5	..	..	39	40	..	24	..	6
Singapore	3	5	100	100	2.6	99	95	99	95	99	100	..	..
Slovak Republic	3	3	57	57	0.1	..	..	..	..	100	100	100	99
Slovenia	1	1	50	48	-0.1	..	..	27	26	100	100	100	100
Somalia	2	3	30	37	2.9	16	15	53	40	..	52	..	6
South Africa	18	30	52	61	2.6	28	34	10	12	80	84	58	65
Spain	29	36	75	77	1.0	22	23	15	16	100	100	100	100
Sri Lanka	3	3	17	15	0.2	..	..	21	22	85	88	67	92
Sudan	7	19	27	44	5.0	9	12	33	27	63	55	23	18
Swaziland	0	0	23	25	2.2	..	..	22	25	..	61	..	53
Sweden	7	8	83	85	0.5	12	14	15	16	100	100	100	100
Switzerland	5	6	73	74	0.8	15	15	20	20	100	100	100	100
Syrian Arab Republic	6	12	49	55	3.2	30	32	25	26	94	96	72	95
Tajikistan	2	2	32	26	0.5	..	..	35	38	93	95	..	94
Tanzania	5	11	19	26	4.5	5	7	27	28	27	32	23	21
Thailand	17	23	29	34	1.7	10	10	35	30	93	95	74	96
Timor-Leste	0	0	21	28	3.8	..	..	79	53	..	76	..	40
Togo	1	3	30	43	4.6	16	24	52	56	25	24	8	3
Trinidad and Tobago	0	0	9	14	3.0	..	..	44	32	93	92	93	92
Tunisia	5	7	58	67	2.1	..	..	14	11	95	96	44	64
Turkey	33	52	59	69	2.3	23	28	20	20	96	97	66	75
Turkmenistan	2	3	45	49	2.2	..	..	25	25	99	99	97	97
Uganda	2	4	11	13	4.1	4	5	38	36	35	38	40	49
Ukraine	35	31	67	68	-0.5	12	14	7	9	97	97	91	90
United Arab Emirates	1	4	79	78	4.7	25	33	32	42	98	98	95	95
United Kingdom	51	56	89	90	0.5	26	26	15	15	100	100	100	100
United States	188	252	75	82	1.5	42	45	9	8	100	100	99	99
Uruguay	3	3	89	92	0.6	50	49	56	53	95	100	83	99
Uzbekistan	8	10	40	37	1.1	10	8	26	22	95	100	76	100
Venezuela, RB	17	27	84	94	2.5	34	32	17	11	89	..	45	..
Vietnam	13	25	20	28	3.2	9	12	25	24	61	94	29	67
West Bank and Gaza	1	3	68	72	4.1	..	..	..	..	..	91	..	84
Yemen, Rep.	3	7	21	31	5.5	5	9	25	30	64	94	6	33
Zambia	3	5	39	36	2.0	10	11	24	31	62	59	36	43
Zimbabwe	3	5	29	38	2.3	10	13	35	34	58	56	37	37
World	2,257 s	3,398 s	43 w	50 w	2.2 w	17 w	20 w	17 w	16 w	77 w	76 w	35 w	45 w
Low income	121	243	22	29	3.7	8	11	33	32	39	44	19	32
Middle income	1,437	2,309	38	48	2.5	14	18	14	13	69	71	31	43
Lower middle income	883	1,559	30	41	3.0	11	15	11	11	58	63	28	41
Upper middle income	554	750	68	75	1.6	25	29	19	19	87	90	58	67
Low & middle income	1,558	2,552	36	45	2.6	13	17	16	15	67	69	29	41
East Asia & Pacific	461	875	29	45	3.4	..	..	9	7	54	64	37	54
Europe & Central Asia	246	258	63	64	0.2	16	18	14	16	94	94	75	80
Latin America & Carib.	308	452	71	79	2.0	32	35	24	22	81	86	38	54
Middle East & N. Africa	117	191	52	58	2.6	20	20	26	22	90	92	57	76
South Asia	281	467	25	30	2.7	10	13	9	12	53	57	11	27
Sub-Saharan Africa	145	310	28	37	4.0	11	14	27	26	43	43	21	24
High income	699	845	73	77	1.0	..	..	20	19	100	100	99	98
Euro area	213	241	71	73	0.6	18	18	16	16	100	100	99	100

There is no consistent and universally accepted standard for distinguishing urban from rural areas, in part because of the wide variety of situations across countries (see *About the data* for table 3.1). Most countries use an urban classification related to the size or characteristics of settlements. Some define urban areas based on the presence of certain infrastructure and services. And other countries designate urban areas based on administrative arrangements.

The population of a city or metropolitan area depends on the boundaries chosen. For example, in 1990 Beijing, China, contained 2.3 million people in 87 square kilometers of "inner city" and 5.4 million in 158 square kilometers of "core city." The population of "inner city and inner suburban districts" was 6.3 million and that of "inner city, inner and outer suburban districts, and inner and outer counties" was 10.8 million. (Most countries use the last definition.) For further discussion of urban-rural issues see box 3.1a in *About the data* for table 3.1.

Estimates of the world's urban population would change significantly if China, India, and a few other populous nations were to change their definition of urban centers. According to China's State Statistical Bureau, by the end of 1996 urban residents accounted for about 43 percent of China's population, more than double the 20 percent considered urban in 1994. In addition to the continuous migration of people from rural to urban areas, one of the main reasons for this shift was the rapid growth in the hundreds of towns reclassified as cities in recent years.

Because the estimates in the table are based on national definitions of what constitutes a city or metropolitan area, cross-country comparisons should be made with caution. To estimate urban populations, UN ratios of urban to total population were applied to the World Bank's estimates of total population (see table 2.1).

The table shows access to improved sanitation facilities for both urban and rural populations to allow comparison of access. Definitions of access and urban areas vary, however, so comparisons between countries can be misleading.

• **Urban population** is the midyear population of areas defined as urban in each country and reported to the United Nations (see *About the data*). • **Population in urban agglomerations of more than 1 million** is the percentage of a country's population living in metropolitan areas that in 2005 had a population of more than 1 million. • **Population in largest city** is the percentage of a country's urban population living in that country's largest metropolitan area. • **Access to improved sanitation facilities** is the percentage of the urban or rural population with access to at least adequate excreta disposal facilities (private or shared but not public) that can effectively prevent human, animal, and insect contact with excreta. Improved facilities range from simple but protected pit latrines to flush toilets with a sewerage connection. To be effective, facilities must be correctly constructed and properly maintained.

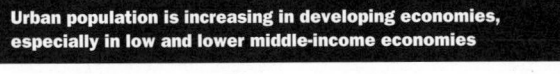

Urban population is increasing in developing economies, especially in low and lower middle-income economies | **3.11a**

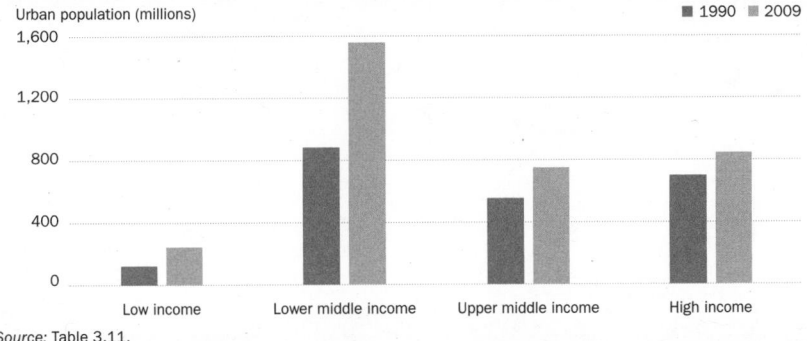

Source: Table 3.11.

Latin America and Caribbean has the greatest share of urban population, even greater than the high-income economies in 2009 | **3.11b**

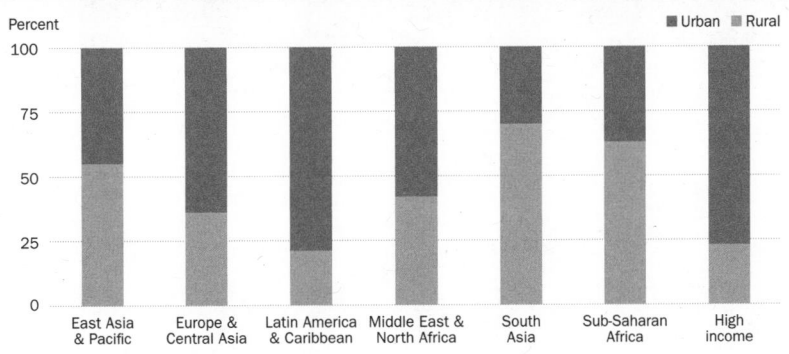

Source: Tables 3.1 and 3.11.

Data on urban population and the population in urban agglomerations and in the largest city are from the United Nations Population Division's *World Urbanization Prospects: The 2009 Revision*. Data on total population are World Bank estimates. Data on access to sanitation are from the World Health Organization and United Nations Children's Fund's *Progress on sanitation and drinking water* (2010).

	Census year	Household size		Overcrowding		Durable dwelling units		Home ownership		Multiunit dwellings		Vacancy rate	
		number of people		Households living in overcrowded dwellings[a] % of total		Buildings with durable structure % of total		Privately owned dwellings % of total		% of total		Unoccupied dwellings % of total	
		National	Urban	National	Urban	National	Urban	National	Urban	National	Urban	National	Urban
Afghanistan		..	..	..	..	..	..	..	..	..	..	..	..
Albania	2001	4.2	3.9	..	..	..	..	65[b]	30[b]	..	..	12	13
Algeria	1998	4.9	..	..	..	..	..	67	..	..	..	19	..
Angola		..	..	..	..	..	..	..	..	..	..	..	..
Argentina	2001	3.6	..	19	..	97	..	..	..	4	..	16[b]	..
Armenia	2001	4.1	4.0	4	6	93	93	95	90	1	1	..	..
Australia	2001	3.8	..	1	..	..	..	..	..	..	..	..	..
Austria	2001	2.4	..	2	..	..	..	48	..	..	..	..	..
Azerbaijan	1999	4.7	4.4	..	..	..	..	74	62	4	5	..	..
Bangladesh	2001	4.8	4.8	..	..	21[b]	42[b]	88[b]	61[b]	..	..	..	..
Belarus	1999	..	..	..	..	..	..	..	..	..	..	..	..
Belgium	2001	2.6	..	0[b]	..	..	..	67	..	32[b]	..	..	..
Benin	1992	5.9	..	..	..	26	..	59	..	..	..	..	..
Bolivia	2001	4.2	4.3	40	..	43	58	70	59	3[b]	5[b]	6	4
Bosnia and Herzegovina		..	..	..	..	..	..	..	..	..	..	..	..
Botswana	2001	4.2	3.9	27	47	88	90[b]	61	47	1	..	..	..
Brazil	2000	3.8	3.7	..	..	..	..	74	75	..	..	..	..
Bulgaria	2001	2.7	2.7	..	..	79	89	98	98	..	..	23	17
Burkina Faso	1996	6.2	5.8	30	53	..	..	..	..	..	..	..	..
Burundi	1990	4.7	..	..	..	..	..	..	..	..	..	..	..
Cambodia	2005	5.0	4.9	35	32	79	88	58	57	27	32	..	..
Cameroon	1987	5.2	5.1	67	77	77	..	73	48	27	42	..	..
Canada	2001	2.6	..	..	..	..	..	64	..	32	..	8	..
Central African Republic	2003	5.2	5.8	32	36[b]	78	92	85	74	..	..	..	..
Chad	1993	5.1	5.1	..	..	..	..	..	..	..	..	..	..
Chile	2002	3.4	3.5	..	..	91	92	66	65	13	15	11	10
China	2000	3.4	3.2	..	..	82	..	88	74	..	..	1	..
Hong Kong SAR, China		..	..	..	..	..	..	..	..	..	..	..	..
Colombia	1993	4.8	..	27[b]	..	83[b]	..	68[b]	..	13	..	10[b]	..
Congo, Dem. Rep.	1984	5.4	..	55	..	..	..	..	..	..	..	..	..
Congo, Rep.	1984	10.5	..	..	..	..	..	76	..	..	..	..	..
Costa Rica	2000	4.0	..	22	..	88	..	72	..	2	3	9	6
Côte d'Ivoire	1998	5.4	..	..	..	..	..	..	..	..	..	..	..
Croatia	2001	3.0	..	..	..	..	..	..	..	..	..	12	..
Cuba	2002	3.1	..	5	..	..	..	..	..	..	..	..	..
Czech Republic	2001	2.4	..	..	..	..	..	52	..	49	..	12	..
Denmark	2001	2.2	..	..	..	..	..	..	..	..	..	..	..
Dominican Republic	2002	3.9	..	..	..	97	..	..	..	8	..	11	..
Ecuador	2001	3.5	3.7	30	..	81	88	68[b]	58[b]	9	14	12	7
Egypt, Arab Rep.	1996	4.7	..	..	..	..	..	75	..	..	..	..	..
El Salvador	1992	..	..	63	..	67	83	70	68	3	6	11	11
Eritrea		..	..	..	..	..	..	..	..	..	..	..	..
Estonia	2000	2.4	2.3	3	..	..	..	..	..	72	..	13	..
Ethiopia	1994	4.8	4.7	..	..	..	23	..	54	..	..	..	..
Finland	2000	2.2	..	..	..	..	..	64	..	44	..	..	..
France	1999	2.5	..	..	..	..	..	55	..	..	..	7	..
Gabon	2003	5.2	..	..	..	..	..	..	..	..	..	..	..
Gambia	1993	8.9	..	..	..	18	..	68	..	..	..	..	..
Georgia	2002	3.5	3.5	..	..	..	..	..	..	..	..	..	..
Germany	2001	2.3	..	..	..	..	..	43	..	..	..	7	..
Ghana	2000	5.1	5.1	..	..	45	..	57	..	53	..	5	..
Greece	2001	3.0	..	1	..	..	..	..	..	..	..	..	..
Guatemala	2002	4.4	4.7	..	..	67[b]	80[b]	81	74	2	4	13	11
Guinea	1996	6.7	..	63	..	..	..	76	..	..	..	..	..
Guinea-Bissau		..	..	..	..	..	..	..	..	..	..	..	..
Haiti	1982	4.2	..	26	..	..	..	92	68	..	..	9	19
Honduras	2001	4.4	..	..	..	69	85	..	..	..	..	14	..

Urban housing conditions

	Census year	Household size		Overcrowding		Durable dwelling units		Home ownership		Multiunit dwellings		Vacancy rate	
		number of people		Households living in overcrowded dwellings[a] % of total		Buildings with durable structure % of total		Privately owned dwellings % of total		% of total		Unoccupied dwellings % of total	
		National	Urban	National	Urban	National	Urban	National	Urban	National	Urban	National	Urban
Hungary	2001	2.6	..	2	..	..	..	..	..	..	..	4	..
India	2001	5.3	5.3	77	71	83	81	87	67	..	..	6	9
Indonesia	2000	4.0	..	..	..	..	..	..	..	..	..	..	..
Iran, Islamic Rep.	1996	4.8	4.6	33[b]	26[b]	72	76	73	67	..	..	..	..
Iraq	1997	7.7	7.2	..	..	88	96	70	66	4	5	13	15
Ireland	2002	3.0	..	..	..	..	..	..	..	8[b]	..	..	..
Israel	1995	3.5	..	..	..	..	..	..	..	..	..	..	..
Italy	2001	2.8	..	..	..	..	..	..	..	..	..	21	..
Jamaica	2001	3.5	..	..	..	98[b]	..	58[b]	..	2[b]	..	..	..
Japan	2000	2.7	..	..	..	..	..	61	..	37	..	..	..
Jordan	2004	5.3	5.1	35	34	..	..	64	60	72	80	..	..
Kazakhstan		..	..	..	..	..	..	..	..	..	..	..	..
Kenya	1999	4.6	3.4	..	..	35	72	72	25	..	..	39	17
Korea, Dem. Rep.	2000	3.8	..	23	..	..	..	50	..	15	..	..	..
Korea, Rep.	1993	4.4	..	..	..	..	..	..	..	..	..	..	..
Kosovo		..	..	..	..	..	..	..	..	..	..	..	..
Kuwait	1995	6.4	..	..	..	..	..	..	..	9[b]	..	11	..
Kyrgyz Republic	1999	4.4	3.6	..	..	..	..	..	..	..	..	..	..
Laos	1995	6.1	6.1	..	..	49	77	96	86	..	..	..	..
Latvia	2000	3.0	2.6	4	..	88	..	58	..	74	..	0	..
Lebanon		..	..	..	..	..	..	..	..	..	..	..	..
Lesotho	2001	5.0	..	10[b]	..	..	..	84	..	0	..	..	..
Liberia	1974	4.8	..	31	..	20	..	1	..	..	..	..	..
Libya		6.4	..	..	..	..	..	..	..	..	..	7	..
Lithuania	2001	2.6	..	7	..	..	..	..	..	..	..	..	..
Macedonia, FYR	2002	3.6	3.6	8[b]	..	95[b]	95[b]	48[b]	..	..	..	7[b]	3[b]
Madagascar	1993	4.9	4.8	64	57	..	..	81	59	..	..	..	..
Malawi	1998	4.4	4.4	30	..	48	84	86	47	..	..	..	..
Malaysia	2000	4.5	4.4	..	..	..	..	..	..	10[b]	16[b]	..	..
Mali	1998	5.6	..	..	..	..	..	..	..	..	..	..	..
Mauritania	1988	..	..	..	..	..	..	..	..	..	..	..	..
Mauritius	2000	3.9	3.8	6	7	91	94	87	81	..	..	7	6
Mexico	2005	4.0	3.9	24	20	..	..	..	..	..	..	3	2
Moldova	2003	..	..	..	..	..	..	..	..	..	..	..	..
Mongolia	2000	4.4	4.5	..	..	..	..	..	..	48	56	..	..
Morocco	1982	5.9	5.3	..	..	..	..	..	..	..	..	..	..
Mozambique	1997	4.4	4.9	37	28	7	20	92	83	1	1	0	..
Myanmar		..	..	..	..	..	..	..	..	..	..	..	..
Namibia	2001	5.3	..	..	..	..	..	..	..	..	..	..	..
Nepal	2001	5.4	4.9	..	..	..	..	88	..	..	..	0	..
Netherlands		..	..	..	..	..	..	..	..	..	..	..	..
New Zealand	2001	2.8	..	1[b]	..	..	..	65	..	17	..	10	..
Nicaragua	1995	5.3	..	..	..	79	87	84	86	0	0	8	..
Niger	2001	6.4	6.0	..	..	..	..	77	40	..	..	..	..
Nigeria	1991	5.0	4.7	..	..	..	..	..	..	..	..	..	..
Norway	1980	2.7	..	1	..	..	..	67	..	38	..	..	..
Oman	2003	7.1	..	..	..	..	..	..	..	..	..	..	..
Pakistan	1998	6.8	6.8	..	..	58	86	81	..	..	..	..	..
Panama	2000	4.1	..	28[b]	..	88	98[b]	80	66[b]	10[b]	10[b]	14	..
Papua New Guinea	1990	4.5[b]	6.5	..	..	..	..	..	44	..	8	..	..
Paraguay	2002	4.6	4.5	38[b]	..[b]	95[b]	98[b]	79	75	1[b]	2[b]	6[b]	6[b]
Peru	2007	3.9	3.9	35	31	..	..	..	..	..	..	..	..
Philippines	2000	4.9	..	..	..	..	..	71	..	12	..	..	..
Poland	1988	3.2	..	..	..	..	..	..	..	..	..	1	..
Portugal	2001	2.8	..	..	..	..	..	76	..	86	..	..	..
Puerto Rico	2005	2.8	.	1	..	..	..	75	..	..	..	..	..
Qatar		..	..	..	..	..	..	..	..	..	..	..	..

	Census year	Household size		Overcrowding		Durable dwelling units		Home ownership		Multiunit dwellings		Vacancy rate	
		number of people		Households living in overcrowded dwellings[a] % of total		Buildings with durable structure % of total		Privately owned dwellings % of total		% of total		Unoccupied dwellings % of total	
		National	Urban	National	Urban	National	Urban	National	Urban	National	Urban	National	Urban
Romania	2002	2.9	2.8	20	20	..	..	84	72	..	..	..	..
Russian Federation	2002	2.8	2.7	7	5	..	..	..	..	73	86	..	..
Rwanda	2002	4.4	3.7	43	36	13	31	79	41	36	60	..	..
Saudi Arabia	2004	5.5	..	..	..	92[b]	..	43	..	..	..	..	..
Senegal	2002	9.2	8.0	72	68	..	..	74	54	..	..	..	..
Serbia	2001	2.9	2.2	..	..	..	..	..	..	..	..	..	..
Sierra Leone	1985	6.8	..	..	..	34	..	68	..	..	..	..	..
Singapore	2000	4.4	..	..	..	..	..	..	..	..	..	..	..
Slovak Republic		..	..	..	..	..	..	..	..	..	..	..	..
Slovenia	2002	2.8	2.7	14	17	..	..	91	87	33	56	..	..
Somalia	1975	..	..	..	..	..	..	..	..	..	..	..	..
South Africa	2007	3.0	2.8	16	15	..	..	43	40	..	..	..	..
Spain	2001	2.9	..	1	..	..	..	82	..	..	..	..	..
Sri Lanka	2001	3.8	..	..	..	93[b]	92[b]	70[b]	58[b]	1	14[b]	13	1[b]
Sudan	1993	5.8	6.0	..	..	..	..	86[b]	58[b]	0[b]	1[b]	..	..
Swaziland	1997	5.4	3.7	..	..	..	..	..	..	..	..	..	..
Sweden	1990	2.0	..	..	..	..	..	..	..	54	..	1	..
Switzerland	2000	2.2	..	1	..	..	..	34	..	77	..	..	..
Syrian Arab Republic	1981	6.3	6.0	..	..	..	..	..	..	..	..	..	..
Tajikistan	2000	..	..	..	..	..	..	..	..	..	..	..	..
Tanzania	2002	4.9	4.5	33[b]	7[b]	..	..	82[b]	43[b]	..	..	..	..
Thailand	2000	3.8	..	..	..	93	93	81	62	3	..	3	..
Timor-Leste		..	..	..	..	..	..	..	..	..	..	..	..
Togo		..	..	..	..	..	..	..	..	..	..	..	..
Trinidad and Tobago	2000	3.7	..	9[b]	..	98[b]	..	74[b]	..	17[b]	..	..	..
Tunisia	1994	8.0	..	..	..	99	..	71	89[b]	6	10[b]	15	12[b]
Turkey	1990	5.0	..	..	..	..	..	70	..	..	..	..	..
Turkmenistan		..	..	..	..	..	..	..	..	..	..	..	..
Uganda	2002	4.7	3.9	..	..	19	61	76	28	37	71	..	..
Ukraine	2003	..	..	..	..	..	..	..	..	..	..	..	..
United Arab Emirates		..	..	..	..	..	..	..	..	..	..	..	..
United Kingdom	2001	..	2.4	..	..	..	..	..	69	..	19	..	..
United States	2005	2.5	..	0	..	..	..	74	..	26	..	..	..
Uruguay	1996	3.3	3.4	22[b]	..	..	..	57[b]	57[b]	..	..	13[b]	13[b]
Uzbekistan		..	..	..	..	..	..	..	..	..	..	..	..
Venezuela. RB	2001	4.4	..	..	..	..	..	78	..	14	..	16	..
Vietnam	1999	4.6	4.5	..	..	77	89	95	86	..	..	..	..
West Bank and Gaza	1997	7.1	..	..	..	..	..	78	..	45	..	..	..
Yemen	1994	6.7	6.8	54[b]	6[b]	..	..	88[b]	68[b]	3[b]	11[b]	..	..
Zambia	2000	5.3	5.9	..	..	..	..	94	30	..	..	..	..
Zimbabwe	1992	4.8	4.2	..	..	..	..	94	30	6	..	..	..

a. More than two people per room. b. Data are from a previous census.

Urban housing conditions | 3.12

About the data

Urbanization can yield important social benefits, improving access to public services and the job market. It also leads to significant demands for services. Inadequate living quarters and demand for housing and shelter are major concerns for policymakers.

The unmet demand for affordable housing, along with urban poverty, has led to the emergence of slums in many poor countries. Improving the shelter situation requires a better understanding of the mechanisms governing housing markets and the processes governing housing availability. That requires good data and adequate policy-oriented analysis so that housing policy can be formulated in a global comparative perspective and drawn from lessons learned in other countries. Housing policies and outcomes affect such broad socioeconomic conditions as the infant mortality rate, performance in school, household saving, productivity levels, capital formation, and government budget deficits. A good understanding of housing conditions thus requires an extensive set of indicators within a reasonable framework.

There is a strong demand for quantitative indicators that can measure housing conditions on a regular basis to monitor progress. However, data deficiencies and lack of rigorous quantitative analysis hamper informed decisionmaking on desirable policies to improve housing conditions. The data in the table are from housing and population censuses, collected using similar definitions. The table will incorporate household survey data in future editions. The table focuses attention on urban areas, where housing conditions are typically most severe. Not all the compiled indicators are presented in the table because of space limitations.

Definitions

• **Census year** is the year in which the underlying data were collected. • **Household size** is the average number of people within a household, calculated by dividing total population by the number of households in the country and in urban areas. • **Overcrowding** refers to the number of households living in dwellings with two or more people per room as a percentage of total households in the country and in urban areas. • **Durable dwelling units** are the number of housing units in structures made of durable building materials (concrete, stone, cement, brick, asbestos, zinc, and stucco) expected to maintain their stability for 20 years or longer under local conditions with normal maintenance and repair, taking into account location and environmental hazards such as floods, mudslides, and earthquakes, as a percentage of total dwellings. • **Home ownership** refers to the number of privately owned dwellings as a percentage of total dwellings. When the number of private dwellings is not available from the census data, the share of households that own their housing unit is used. Privately owned and owner-occupied units are included, depending on the definition used in the census data. State- and community-owned units and rented, squatted, and rent-free units are excluded. • **Multiunit dwellings** are the number of multiunit dwellings, such as apartments, flats, condominiums, barracks, boardinghouses, orphanages, retirement houses, hostels, hotels, and collective dwellings, as a percentage of total dwellings. • **Vacancy rate** is the percentage of completed dwelling units that are currently unoccupied. It includes all vacant units, whether on the market or not (such as second homes).

Selected housing indicators for smaller economies — 3.12a

	Census year	Household size	Overcrowding	Durable dwelling units	Home ownership	Multiunit dwellings	Vacancy rate
		number of people	Households living in overcrowded dwellings[a] % of total	Buildings with durable structure % of total	Privately owned dwellings % of total	% of total	Unoccupied dwellings % of total
Antigua and Barbuda	2001	3.0	..	99[b]	65[b]	3[b]	22
Bahamas	1990	3.8	12	99	55	13	14
Bahrain	2001	5.9	..	94[b]	51	28	6
Barbados	1990	3.5	3	100	76	9	9
Belize	2000	4.6	..	93	63	4	..
Cape Verde	1990	5.1	28	78	72	2	..
Cayman Islands	1999	3.1	..	100	53	38	19
Equatorial Guinea	1993	7.5	14	56[b]	75	14	..
Fiji	1996	5.4	..	60	65	7	..
Guam	2000	4.0	2[b]	93	48	29	19
Isle of Man	2001	2.4	0	..	68	16	..
Maldives	2000	6.6	..	93	..	1	15
Marshall Islands	1999	7.8	..	95	72	12	8
Netherlands Antilles	2001	2.9	24[b]	99	60	16	12
New Caledonia	1989	4.1	..	77	53	9	13
Northern Mariana Islands	1995	4.9	9[b]	99	33	27	17
Palau	2000	5.7	8	76	79	11	3
Seychelles	1997	4.2	15[b]	97	78	..	0
Solomon Islands	1999	6.3	51	23	85	1	..
St. Vincent & Grenadines	1991	3.9	..	98	71	7	..
Turks and Caicos	1990	3.3	4	96	66	11	..
Virgin Islands (UK)	1991	3.0	2	99	40	46	..
Western Samoa	1991	7.3	..	42	90	47	30

a. More than two people per room. b. Data are from a previous census.
Source: National population and housing censuses.

Data sources

Data on urban housing conditions are from national population and housing censuses.

3.13 | Traffic and congestion

	Motor vehicles		Passenger cars	Road density	Road sector energy consumption				Fuel price		Particulate matter concentration	
	per 1,000 people	per kilometer of road	per 1,000 people	km. of road per 100 sq. km. of land area	% of total consumption	kilograms of oil equivalent per capita			$ per liter		Urban-population-weighted PM10 micrograms per cubic meter	
						Total	Diesel fuel	Gasoline fuel	Super grade gasoline	Diesel		
	2008	2008	2008	2008	2008	2008	2008	2008	2010	2010	1990	2008
Afghanistan	27	19	19	6	..	..	..	..	1.15	1.00	68	37
Albania	114	20	84	63	32	213	184	24	1.46	1.40	92	46
Algeria	112	35	72	5	16	173	92	63	0.32	0.19	113	69
Angola	40	..	8	..	11	65	31	30	0.65	0.43	111	55
Argentina	314	..	..	8	18	346	179	102	0.96	1.05	104	68
Armenia	105	42	96	26	10	100	0	64	1.08	0.99	481	69
Australia	687	18	551	11	18	1,091	327	645	1.27	1.23	22	14
Austria	562	42	514	132	22	877	605	199	1.63	1.55	39	29
Azerbaijan	89	13	72	61	12	188	72	108	0.75	0.56	132	33
Bangladesh	2	2	1	166	6	11	5	2	1.09	0.63	237	134
Belarus	282	..	240	46	6	161	89	51	1.08	0.86	23	7
Belgium	543	38	479	503	15	827	659	134	1.87	1.62	30	21
Benin	21	..	17	17	23	79	27	47	1.04	1.21	78	45
Bolivia	68	7	18	6	25	149	72	48	0.70	0.54	113	74
Bosnia and Herzegovina	135	23	119	43	15	242	151	84	1.42	1.42	36	19
Botswana	113	7	56	4	31	340	136	186	0.93	0.97	93	69
Brazil	198	18	158	21	23	298	148	73	1.58	1.14	39	21
Bulgaria	353	67	310	36	13	335	196	78	1.51	1.58	108	51
Burkina Faso	11	2	7	34	..	..	..	..	1.44	1.28	144	64
Burundi	6	..	2	44	..	..	..	..	1.43	1.42	68	31
Cambodia	20	6	18	21	7	26	14	11	1.15	0.98	88	41
Cameroon	..	..	11	11	10	36	17	18	1.20	1.10	122	47
Canada	605	14	399	14	17	1,324	336	889	1.21	1.08	25	15
Central African Republic	0	0	0	..	..	..	..	..	1.71	1.69	60	34
Chad	6	2	..	3	..	..	..	..	1.32	1.31	209	81
Chile	172	36	109	..	18	345	191	137	1.38	1.02	92	62
China	37	13	27	39	5	85	36	45	1.11	1.04	115	66
Hong Kong SAR, China	73	248	55	187	10	204	149	47	1.92	1.32	..	..
Colombia	58	16	41	14	25	171	81	70	1.41	0.95	38	20
Congo, Dem. Rep.	5	..	..	7	1	3	0	3	1.28	1.27	71	40
Congo, Rep.	26	..	15	5	26	98	67	27	1.27	0.84	129	68
Costa Rica	163	19	126	74	30	320	159	144	1.14	0.97	43	32
Côte d'Ivoire	20	5	16	25	4	21	14	6	1.68	1.30	87	32
Croatia	388	59	346	52	21	432	249	153	1.59	1.49	45	27
Cuba	38	7	21	..	3	29	21	5	1.72	1.24	42	23
Czech Republic	513	41	424	166	13	553	330	189	1.75	1.69	67	18
Denmark	477	36	377	170	23	779	442	312	2.00	1.79	29	16
Dominican Republic	123	..	62	..	18	144	48	89	1.23	1.03	43	16
Ecuador	63	19	38	15	38	289	123	151	0.53	0.28	36	20
Egypt, Arab Rep.	43	33	31	10	17	145	79	54	0.48	0.32	212	97
El Salvador	84	..	41	..	16	131	58	67	0.92	0.89	44	28
Eritrea	11	..	6	..	5	7	6	1	2.54	1.07	141	71
Estonia	477	11	412	128	13	542	286	239	1.54	1.57	44	13
Ethiopia	3	4	1	4	4	16	13	2	0.91	0.78	108	59
Finland	534	36	461	23	11	740	419	284	1.94	1.60	22	15
France	598	39	495	173	16	666	483	129	1.98	1.72	18	13
Gabon	..	..	..	3	10	143	106	31	1.14	0.90	9	7
Gambia, The	7	3	5	33	..	..	..	..	0.79	0.75	136	62
Georgia	116	16	95	29	19	135	45	81	1.13	1.13	204	49
Germany	554	71	502	180	15	609	309	243	1.90	1.68	27	16
Ghana	33	13	21	24	12	49	23	23	0.82	0.83	38	24
Greece	560	54	443	88	21	581	192	359	2.05	1.78	64	32
Guatemala	117	..	..	..	23	134	64	63	0.95	0.85	69	60
Guinea	..	..	..	18	..	..	..	..	0.95	0.95	103	53
Guinea-Bissau	33	15	27	12	..	..	..	..	..	..	114	47
Haiti	..	..	..	..	9	25	0	23	1.16	0.89	68	35
Honduras	97	..	69	..	21	135	73	55	1.04	0.92	44	42

	Motor vehicles		Passenger cars	Road density	Road sector energy consumption				Fuel price		Particulate matter concentration	
	per 1,000 people	per kilometer of road	per 1,000 people	km. of road per 100 sq. km. of land area	% of total consumption	kilograms of oil equivalent per capita			$ per liter		Urban-population-weighted PM10 micrograms per cubic meter	
						Total	Diesel fuel	Gasoline fuel	Super grade gasoline	Diesel		
	2008	2008	2008	2008	2008	2008	2008	2008	2010	2010	1990	2008
Hungary	384	20	304	212	16	435	254	149	1.67	1.61	33	16
India	15	4	10	129	7	36	22	10	1.15	0.82	111	59
Indonesia	77	40	43	23	12	103	31	67	0.79	0.51	133	72
Iran, Islamic Rep.	128	53	113	10	19	522	223	249	0.10	0.02	86	55
Iraq	..	..	..	..	30	330	185	129	0.78	0.56	164	138
Ireland	534	24	451	137	29	996	570	385	1.78	1.69	23	13
Israel	313	126	260	82	16	481	155	300	1.85	1.87	66	28
Italy	673	83	596	162	21	626	389	181	1.87	1.69	41	23
Jamaica	188	24	138	202	12	204	0	190	0.98	0.98	55	37
Japan	593	63	319	318	14	541	175	331	1.60	1.37	42	27
Jordan	146	110	102	9	22	264	105	150	1.04	0.73	107	33
Kazakhstan	197	33	164	3	6	277	25	238	0.71	0.51	42	15
Kenya	21	10	15	11	6	26	16	9	1.33	1.27	64	30
Korea, Dem. Rep.	..	..	..	21	2	17	9	7	1.51	1.40	180	59
Korea, Rep.	346	161	257	105	12	559	278	152	1.52	1.35	51	31
Kosovo	..	..	..	..	..	..	..	..	1.63	1.60	..	..
Kuwait	507	233	282	32	14	1,343	401	868	0.23	0.21	77	95
Kyrgyz Republic	59	9	44	17	17	94	0	89	0.85	0.79	76	26
Lao PDR	21	10	2	15	..	..	..	..	1.26	0.97	87	39
Latvia	474	15	412	108	24	481	293	163	1.48	1.49	38	13
Lebanon	..	..	..	67	29	360	3	334	1.13	0.77	64	36
Lesotho	..	..	..	..	..	..	..	..	0.97	1.07	123	46
Liberia	3	..	2	..	..	..	..	..	0.98	0.96	68	31
Libya	291	..	225	..	19	542	325	192	0.17	0.13	101	76
Lithuania	546	23	498	124	18	486	275	122	1.59	1.42	52	17
Macedonia, FYR	144	21	129	54	13	194	106	58	1.52	1.27	45	20
Madagascar	27	10	8	..	..	..	..	..	1.52	1.26	91	33
Malawi	9	..	4	13	..	..	..	..	1.71	1.54	93	35
Malaysia	334	83	298	30	19	523	193	310	0.59	0.56	35	20
Mali	9	..	7	2	..	..	..	..	1.42	1.25	259	112
Mauritania	..	..	..	1	..	..	..	..	1.16	0.99	145	69
Mauritius	159	99	123	99	..	..	..	..	1.55	1.23	21	18
Mexico	264	77	181	19	28	472	128	312	0.81	0.72	67	33
Moldova	139	39	101	38	10	85	53	26	1.21	1.08	109	36
Mongolia	72	4	48	3	13	157	8	139	1.11	1.04	190	111
Morocco	71	38	53	13	24	112	93	15	1.23	0.88	38	27
Mozambique	13	10	9	4	4	18	13	4	1.11	0.86	112	26
Myanmar	7	13	5	4	7	22	11	8	0.80	0.80	113	46
Namibia	109	4	52	..	33	274	77	170	1.06	1.09	73	48
Nepal	5	..	3	12	3	11	7	2	1.18	0.91	67	32
Netherlands	515	62	449	328	15	708	396	252	2.13	1.71	45	31
New Zealand	733	33	616	35	25	1,004	423	529	1.47	0.97	14	12
Nicaragua	57	16	17	16	13	79	44	32	1.09	0.99	44	23
Niger	5	4	4	1	..	..	..	..	1.07	1.16	199	96
Nigeria	31	..	31	21	8	58	8	46	0.44	0.77	195	46
Norway	575	29	461	29	12	733	437	271	2.12	2.01	21	16
Oman	225	12	174	17	11	665	56	567	0.31	0.38	136	94
Pakistan	11	8	9	33	13	63	40	9	0.86	0.92	220	109
Panama	120	30	131	18	17	148	0	138	0.85	0.77	58	34
Papua New Guinea	9	..	6	..	..	..	..	..	0.94	0.90	35	18
Paraguay	82	..	39	..	26	181	140	31	1.28	1.01	106	67
Peru	55	15	35	8	29	148	106	29	1.41	1.10	96	51
Philippines	33	14	11	67	17	76	43	28	1.05	0.84	56	19
Poland	495	49	422	123	15	391	216	105	1.57	1.50	60	35
Portugal	509	70	495	90	25	579	409	140	1.85	1.58	49	21
Puerto Rico	642	..	614	287	..	..	..	..	0.65	0.78	23	21
Qatar	724	..	335	67	12	2,245	1,388	756	0.19	0.19	71	35

3.13 Traffic and congestion

	Motor vehicles		Passenger cars	Road density	Road sector energy consumption				Fuel price		Particulate matter concentration	
				km. of road per 100 sq. km. of land area	% of total consumption	kilograms of oil equivalent per capita	Diesel fuel	Gasoline fuel	$ per liter Super grade gasoline	Diesel	Urban-population-weighted PM10 micrograms per cubic meter	
	per 1,000 people	per kilometer of road	per 1,000 people			Total						
	2008	2008	2008	2008	2008	2008	2008	2008	2010	2010	1990	2008
Romania	219	24	187	83	12	216	136	67	1.46	1.46	36	12
Russian Federation	245	35	206	6	7	318	80	222	0.84	0.72	41	16
Rwanda	4	3	2	53	..	..	..	..	1.63	1.62	60	27
Saudi Arabia	..	20	415	11	20	1,279	568	646	0.16	0.07	157	104
Senegal	23	19	17	8	24	57	45	10	1.57	1.34	92	81
Serbia	227	42	202	45	12	251	182	63	1.50	1.48	33[a]	14[a]
Sierra Leone	5	2	3	..	..	..	..	..	0.94	0.94	87	38
Singapore	150	218	114	475	13	494	305	167	1.42	1.04	107	31
Slovak Republic	319	35	272	89	11	379	230	115	1.70	1.53	46	13
Slovenia	565	29	520	192	26	985	628	316	1.67	1.62	38	29
Somalia	..	..	..	..	..	..	..	..	1.12	1.15	94	31
South Africa	159	..	108	..	11	293	121	161	1.19	1.14	33	22
Spain	606	41	486	132	23	703	539	135	1.56	1.47	41	28
Sri Lanka	61	13	19	148	19	86	56	25	1.19	0.66	94	74
Sudan	28	..	20	..	14	54	36	15	0.62	0.43	282	159
Swaziland	89	25	46	21	..	..	..	..	1.07	1.10	55	35
Sweden	521	8	464	128	16	844	410	365	1.87	1.82	15	11
Switzerland	567	61	522	173	22	754	283	441	1.66	1.77	35	22
Syrian Arab Republic	62	20	27	35	20	189	118	62	0.96	0.45	145	69
Tajikistan	38	..	29	..	4	15	0	12	1.02	0.91	112	43
Tanzania	73	3	4	9	6	26	19	6	1.22	1.19	56	22
Thailand	..	..	54	35	16	262	153	73	1.41	0.95	77	55
Timor-Leste	..	..	..	..	..	..	..	..	1.40	0.90	..	..
Togo	2	..	2	21	11	45	15	27	1.18	1.17	57	29
Trinidad and Tobago	351	..	..	..	4	587	229	327	0.36	0.24	135	105
Tunisia	114	61	76	12	17	151	101	41	0.94	0.82	71	26
Turkey	138	24	92	54	14	181	114	31	2.52	2.03	76	37
Turkmenistan	106	22	80	..	5	191	0	182	0.22	0.20	259	65
Uganda	7	3	3	29	..	..	..	..	1.42	1.11	33	12
Ukraine	152	41	138	28	6	177	55	114	1.01	0.92	71	18
United Arab Emirates	313	..	293	5	14	1,884	964	829	0.47	0.71	281	87
United Kingdom	526	77	462	172	19	641	335	271	1.92	1.98	24	13
United States	809	38	451	68	23	1,703	399	1,148	0.76	0.84	30	19
Uruguay	176	..	151	44	21	259	163	81	1.49	1.44	236	160
Uzbekistan	..	..	..	..	3	63	8	49	0.92	0.83	145	40
Venezuela, RB	147	..	107	..	24	553	81	416	0.02	0.01	21	9
Vietnam	13	7	13	48	13	90	50	38	0.88	0.77	123	53
West Bank and Gaza	39	29	30	85	..	..	..	..	1.71	1.54	..	..
Yemen, Rep.	35	..	..	14	27	90	18	62	0.35	0.23	137	67
Zambia	18	..	11	..	2	10	0	10	1.66	1.52	124	39
Zimbabwe	106	..	91	25	4	27	15	11	1.29	1.15	55	40
World	.. w	.. w	118 w	28 w	14 w	261 w	103 w	135 w	1.21 m	1.07 m	80 w	46 w
Low income	..	..	..	..	5	19	10	7	1.18	1.11	128	60
Middle income	42	..	36	25	10	129	56	61	1.08	0.96	96	53
Lower middle income	23	8	15	50	8	78	37	36	1.05	0.89	121	63
Upper middle income	..	..	129	..	15	320	127	156	1.14	1.03	57	31
Low & middle income	..	..	35	22	10	116	51	55	1.11	0.98	98	54
East Asia & Pacific	47	16	33	36	7	97	42	50	1.08	0.93	112	61
Europe & Central Asia	185	30	152	8	8	228	82	128	1.17	1.11	58	24
Latin America & Carib.	169	..	118	18	23	302	121	136	1.04	0.98	58	32
Middle East & N. Africa	88	..	66	12	19	259	128	111	0.94	0.56	124	71
South Asia	16	4	10	129	7	36	23	9	1.12	0.83	133	72
Sub-Saharan Africa	34	..	25	..	8	57	24	31	1.22	1.15	119	49
High income	622	38	432	43	19	964	356	526	1.63	1.54	38	24
Euro area	592	..	418	140	18	665	422	194	1.78	1.62	33	20

a. Includes Montenegro.

About the data

Traffic congestion in urban areas constrains economic productivity, damages people's health, and degrades the quality of life. In recent years ownership of passenger cars has increased, and the expansion of economic activity has led to more goods and services being transported by road over greater distances (see table 5.10). These developments have increased demand for roads and vehicles, adding to urban congestion, air pollution, health hazards, and traffic accidents and injuries. The data on motor vehicles, passenger cars, and road density in the table are compiled by the International Road Federation (IRF) through questionnaires sent to national organizations. The IRF uses a hierarchy of sources to gather as much information as possible. Primary sources are national road

associations. If they lack data or do not respond, other agencies are contacted, including road directorates, ministries of transport or public works, and central statistical offices. As a result, data quality is uneven. Coverage of each indicator may differ across countries because of different definitions. Comparability is also limited when time series data are reported. The IRF is taking steps to improve the quality of the data in its *World Road Statistics 2010*. Because this effort covers 2003–08 only, time series data may not be comparable. Another reason is coverage. Road density is a rough indicator of accessibility and does not capture road width, type, or condition. Thus comparisons over time and across countries should be made with caution.

Road sector energy consumption includes energy from petroleum products, natural gas, renewable and combustible waste, and electricity. Biodiesel and biogasoline, forms of renewable energy, are biodegradable and emit less sulfur and carbon monoxide than petroleum-derived ones. They can be produced from vegetable oils, such as soybean, corn, palm, peanut, or sunflower oil, and can be used directly only in a modified internal combustion engine. Data are provided by the International Energy Agency.

Data on fuel prices are compiled by the German Agency for International Cooperation (GIZ), from its global network, and other sources, including the Allgemeiner Deutscher Automobile Club (for Europe) and the Latin American Energy Organization for Latin America. Local prices are converted to U.S. dollars using the exchange rate in the *Financial Times* international monetary table on the survey date. When multiple exchange rates exist, the market, parallel, or black market rate is used. Prices were compiled in mid-November 2010, based on the crude oil price of $81 per barrel Brent.

Considerable uncertainty surrounds estimates of particulate matter concentrations, and caution should be used in interpreting them. They allow for cross-country comparisons of the relative risk of particulate matter pollution facing urban residents. Major sources of urban outdoor particulate matter pollution are traffic and industrial emissions, but nonanthropogenic sources such as dust storms may also be a substantial contributor for some cities. Country technology and pollution controls are important determinants of particulate matter. Data on particulate matter for selected cities are in table 3.14.

Data sources

Data on vehicles and road density are from the IRF's electronic files and its annual *World Road Statistics*, except where noted. Data on road sector energy consumption are from the IRF and the International Energy Agency. Data on fuel prices are from the GIZ's electronic files. Data on particulate matter concentrations are from Pandey and others' "Ambient Particulate Matter Concentrations in Residential and Pollution Hotspot Areas of World Cities: New Estimates Based on the Global Model of Ambient Particulates (GMAPS)" (2006b).

Biogasoline consumption as a share of total consumption is highest in Brazil . . .   3.13a

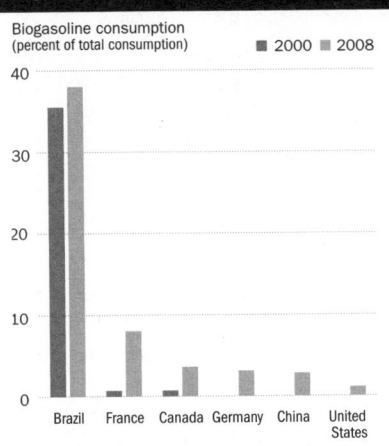

Biogasoline consumption
(percent of total consumption) ■ 2000 ■ 2008

Source: International Energy Agency.

. . . but the United States consumes the most biogasoline   3.13b

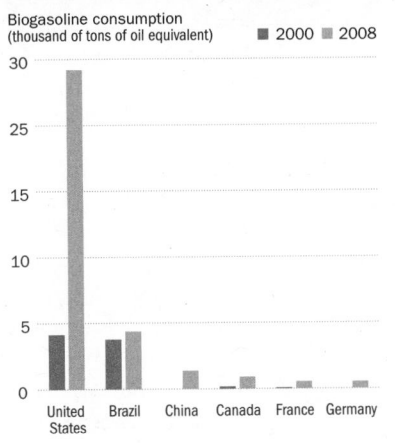

Biogasoline consumption
(thousand of tons of oil equivalent) ■ 2000 ■ 2008

Source: International Energy Agency.

City		City population	Particulate matter concentration		Sulfur dioxide	Nitrogen dioxide
		thousands	Urban-population-weighted PM10 micrograms per cubic meter		micrograms per cubic meter	micrograms per cubic meter
		2009	1990	2008	2001[a]	2001[a]
Argentina	Buenos Aires	12,988	159	104	..	..
	Córdoba	1,479	78	51	..	97
Australia	Melbourne	3,813	17	11	..	30
	Perth	1,578	16	11	5	19
	Sydney	4,395	27	18	28	81
Austria	Vienna	1,693	45	34	14	42
Belgium	Brussels	1,892	33	23	20	48
Brazil	Rio de Janeiro	11,836	49	26	129	..
	São Paulo	19,960	57	30	43	83
Bulgaria	Sofia	1,192	118	55	39	122
Canada	Montréal	3,750	24	15	10	42
	Toronto	5,377[b]	29	17	17	43
	Vancouver	2,197	17	10	14	37
Chile	Santiago	5,883	103	69	29	81
China	Anshan	1,632	132	75	115	88
	Beijing	12,214	141	80	90	122
	Changchun	3,504	117	66	21	64
	Chengdu	4,869	136	77	77	74
	Chongqing	9,348	194	110	340	70
	Dalian	3,252	79	45	61	100
	Guangzhou	8,735	99	56	57	136
	Guiyang	2,125	111	63	424	53
	Harbin	4,224	121	69	23	30
	Jinan	3,186	148	84	132	45
	Kunming	3,062	111	63	19	33
	Lanzhou	2,243	145	82	102	104
	Liupanshui	1,221	94	53	102	..
	Nanchang	2,648	124	70	69	29
	Shanghai	16,344	115	65	53	73
	Shenyang	5,074	160	90	99	73
	Shenzhen	8,847	89	50	..	..
	Tianjin	7,759	198	112	82	50
	Wuhan	7,582	125	71	40	43
	Zhengzhou	2,914	154	87	63	95
	Zibo	2,396	117	66	198	43
	Foshan	4,876	107	61	..	..
	Chengdu	4,869	136	77	..	..
	Xi'an	4,704	221	125	..	..
Colombia	Bogotá	8,262	51	27	..	..
Croatia	Zagreb	779[b]	48	28	31	..
Cuba	Havana	2,140	47	26	1	5
Czech Republic	Prague	1,162	68	19	14	33
Denmark	Copenhagen	1,174	30	17	7	54
Ecuador	Guayaquil	2,634	33	18	15	..
	Quito	1,801	44	24	22	..
Egypt, Arab Rep.	Cairo	10,902	272	124	69	..
Finland	Helsinki	1,107	24	17	4	35
France	Paris	10,410	14	10	14	57
Germany	Berlin	3,438	30	18	18	26
	Frankfurt	680[b]	27	16	11	45
	Munich	1,334	27	16	8	53
Ghana	Accra	2,269	37	24	..	..
Greece	Athens	3,252	69	34	34	64
Hungary	Budapest	1,705	35	16	39	51
Iceland	Reykjavik	319[b]	23	14	5	42
India	Ahmadabad	5,606	127	68	30	21

About the data

Indoor and outdoor air pollution places a major burden on world health. More than half the world's people rely on dung, wood, crop waste, or coal to meet basic energy needs. Cooking and heating with these fuels on open fires or stoves without chimneys lead to indoor air pollution, which is responsible for 1.6 million deaths a year—one every 20 seconds. In many urban areas air pollution exposure is the main environmental threat to health. Long-term exposure to high levels of soot and small particles contributes to a range of health effects, including respiratory diseases, lung cancer, and heart disease. Particulate pollution, alone or with sulfur dioxide, creates an enormous burden of ill health.

Sulfur dioxide and nitrogen dioxide emissions lead to deposition of acid rain and other acidic compounds over long distances, which can lead to the leaching of trace minerals and nutrients critical to trees and plants. Sulfur dioxide emissions can damage human health, particularly that of the young and old. Nitrogen dioxide is emitted by bacteria, motor vehicles, industrial activities, nitrogen fertilizers, fuel and biomass combustion, and aerobic decomposition of organic matter in soils and oceans.

Where coal is the primary fuel for power plants without effective dust controls, steel mills, industrial boilers, and domestic heating, high levels of urban air pollution are common—especially particulates and sulfur dioxide. Elsewhere the worst emissions are from petroleum product combustion.

Sulfur dioxide and nitrogen dioxide concentration data are based on average observed concentrations at urban monitoring sites, which not all cities have.

The data on particulate matter are estimated average annual concentrations in residential areas away from air pollution "hotspots," such as industrial districts and transport corridors. The data are from the World Bank's Development Research Group and Environment Department estimates of annual ambient concentrations of particulate matter in cities with populations exceeding 100,000 (Pandey and others 2006b). A country's technology and pollution controls are important determinants of particulate matter concentrations.

Pollutant concentrations are sensitive to local conditions, and even monitoring sites in the same city may register different levels. Thus these data should be considered only a general indication of air quality, and comparisons should be made with caution. Current World Health Organization (WHO) air quality guidelines are annual mean concentrations of 20 micrograms per cubic meter for particulate matter less than 10 microns in diameter and 40 micrograms for nitrogen dioxide and daily mean concentrations of 20 micrograms per cubic meter for sulfur dioxide.

	City	City population	Particulate matter concentration		Sulfur dioxide	Nitrogen dioxide
			Urban-population-weighted PM10 micrograms per cubic meter		micrograms per cubic meter	micrograms per cubic meter
		thousands 2009	1990	2008	2001[a]	2001[a]
	Bangalore	7,079	69	37	..	..
	Chennai	7,416	57	30	15	17
	Delhi	21,720	229	122	24	41
	Hyderabad	6,627	62	33	12	17
	Kanpur	3,298	166	89	15	14
	Kolkata	15,294	195	104	49	34
	Lucknow	2,815	167	89	26	25
	Mumbai	19,695	96	51	33	39
	Nagpur	2,556	85	45	6	13
	Pune	4,898	71	38	..	..
Indonesia	Jakarta	9,121	138	74	..	..
Iran, Islamic Rep.	Tehran	7,190	86	55	209	..
Ireland	Dublin	1,084	24	13	20	..
Italy	Milan	2,962	46	26	31	248
	Rome	3,357	44	25	..	..
	Turin	1,662	66	38	..	..
Japan	Osaka-Kobe	11,325	48	31	19	63
	Tokyo	36,507	54	35	18	68
	Yokohama	3,654[b]	42	27	100	13
Kenya	Nairobi	3,375	67	32	..	..
Korea, Rep	Pusan	3,439	52	31	60	51
	Seoul	9,778	55	33	44	60
	Taegu	2,458	59	36	81	62
Malaysia	Kuala Lumpur	1,493	36	20	24	..
Mexico	Mexico City	19,319	89	43	74	130
Netherlands	Amsterdam	1,044	45	31	10	58
New Zealand	Auckland	1,360	13	11	3	20
Norway	Oslo	875	27	20	8	43
Philippines	Manila	11,449	78	26	33	..
Poland	Katowice	309[b]	62	36	83	79
	Lódz	742[b]	61	36	21	43
	Warsaw	1,710	67	39	16	32
Portugal	Lisbon	2,808	44	19	8	52
Romania	Bucharest	1,933	40	14	10	71
Russian Federation	Moscow	10,523	42	16	109	..
	Omsk	1,128	44	17	20	34
Singapore	Singapore	4,737	107	31	20	30
Slovak Republic	Bratislava	500[b]	44	13	21	27
South Africa	Cape Town	3,353	20	13	21	72
	Durban	2,837	40	27	31	..
	Johannesburg	3,607	42	28	19	31
Spain	Barcelona	5,029	43	29	11	43
	Madrid	5,762	37	25	24	66
Sweden	Stockholm	1,279	14	10	3	20
Switzerland	Zurich	1,143	33	21	11	39
Thailand	Bangkok	6,902	88	63	11	23
Turkey	Ankara	3,846	74	36	55	46
	Istanbul	10,378	87	42	120	..
Ukraine	Kiev	2,779	91	22	14	51
United Kingdom	Birmingham	2,296	22	11	9	45
	London	8,615	27	17	25	77
	Manchester	2,247	24	12	26	49
United States	Chicago	9,134	33	21	14	57
	Los Angeles	12,675	45	29	9	74
	New York-Newark	19,300	28	18	26	79
Venezuela, RB	Caracas	3,051	32	14	33	57

a. Data are for the most recent year available. b. Data are from national sources.

Definitions

• **City population** is the number of residents of the city or metropolitan area as defined by national authorities and reported to the United Nations.
• **Particulate matter concentration** is fine suspended particulates of less than 10 microns in diameter (PM10) that are capable of penetrating deep into the respiratory tract and causing severe health damage. Data are urban-population-weighted PM10 levels in residential areas of cities with more than 100,000 residents. The estimates represent the average annual exposure level of the average urban resident to outdoor particulate matter. • **Sulfur dioxide** is an air pollutant produced when fossil fuels containing sulfur are burned. • **Nitrogen dioxide** is a poisonous, pungent gas formed when nitric oxide combines with hydrocarbons and sunlight, producing a photochemical reaction. These conditions occur in both natural and anthropogenic activities.

Data sources

Data on city population are from the United Nations Population Division's *World Urbanization Prospects: The 2009 Revision*. Data on particulate matter concentrations are from Kiran D. Pandey, David Wheeler, Bart Ostro, Uwe Deichman, Kirk Hamilton, and Kathrine Bolt's "Ambient Particulate Matter Concentration in Residential and Pollution Hotspot Areas of World Cities: New Estimates Based on the Global Model of Ambient Particulates (GMAPS)" (2006). Data on sulfur dioxide and nitrogen dioxide concentrations are from the WHO's Healthy Cities Air Management Information System and the World Resources Institute.

	Environmental strategies or action plans	Biodiversity assessments, strategies, or action plans	Participation in treaties[a]								
			Climate change[b]	Ozone layer	CFC control	Law of the Sea[c]	Biological diversity[b]	Kyoto Protocol[b]	CITES	CCD	Stockholm Convention
Afghanistan			2002	2004[d]	2004[d]		2002		1985[d]	1996[d]	
Albania	1993		1995	1999[d]	1999[d]	2003[d]	1994[d]	2005	2003[d]	2000[d]	2004
Algeria	2001		1994	1992[d]	1992[d]	1996	1995	2005	1983[d]	1996	2006
Angola			2000	2000[d]	2000[d]	1994	1998	2007		1997	2006[d]
Argentina	1992		1994	1990	1990	1995	1994	2005	1981	1997	2005
Armenia			1994	1999[d]	1999[d]	2002[d]	1993[e]	2005		1997	2003
Australia	1992	1994	1994	1987[d]	1989	1994	1993	2008	1976	2000	2004
Austria			1994	1987	1989	1995	1994	2005	1982[d]	1997[d]	2002
Azerbaijan	1998		1995	1996[d]	1996[d]		2000[f]	2005	1998[d]	1998[d]	2004[d]
Bangladesh	1991	1990	1994	1990[d]	1990[d]	2001	1994	2005	1981	1996	2007
Belarus			2000	1986[e]	1988[e]	2006[d]	1993	2005	1995[d]	2001[d]	2004[d]
Belgium			1996	1988	1988	1998	1996	2005	1983	1997[d]	2006
Benin	1993		1994	1993[d]	1993[d]	1997	1994	2005	1984[d]	1996	2004
Bolivia	1994	1988	1995	1994[d]	1994[d]	1995	1994	2005	1979	1996	2003
Bosnia and Herzegovina			2000	1992[f]	1992[f]	1994[f]	2002[d]	2007	2002	2002[d]	2010
Botswana	1990	1991	1994	1991[d]	1991[d]	1994	1995	2005	1977[d]	1996	2002[d]
Brazil		1988	1994	1990[d]	1990[d]	1994	1994	2005	1975	1997	2004
Bulgaria		1994	1995	1990[d]	1990[d]	1996	1996	2005	1991[d]	2001[d]	2004
Burkina Faso	1993		1994	1989	1989	2005	1993	2005	1989[d]	1996	2004
Burundi	1994	1989	1997	1997[d]	1997[d]		1997	2005	1988[d]	1997	2005
Cambodia	1999		1996	2001[d]	2001[d]		1995[d]	2005	1997	1997	2006
Cameroon		1989	1995	1989[d]	1989[d]	1994	1994	2005	1981[d]	1997	2009
Canada	1990	1994	1994	1986	1988	2003	1992	2005	1975	1996	2001
Central African Republic			1995	1993[d]	1993[d]		1995	2008	1980[d]	1996	2008
Chad	1990		1994	1989[d]	1994		1994	2009	1989[d]	1996	2004
Chile		1993	1995	1990	1990	1997	1994	2005	1975	1998	2005
China	1994	1994	1994	1989[d]	1991[d]	1996	1993	2005	1981[d]	1997	2004
Hong Kong SAR, China											
Colombia	1998	1988	1995	1990[d]	1993[d]		1994	2005	1981	1999	2008
Congo, Dem. Rep.		1990	1995	1994[d]	1994[d]	1995	1996	2005	1976[d]	2004	2005[d]
Congo, Rep.		1990	1997	1994[d]	1994[d]	2008	1994	2007	1983[d]	1997	2007
Costa Rica	1990	1992	1994	1991[d]	1991[d]	1994	1994	2005	1975	1998	2007
Côte d'Ivoire	1994	1991	1995	1993[d]	1993[d]	1994	1994	2007	1994[d]	1997	2004
Croatia	2001	2000	1996	1991[e]	1991[e]	1994[f]	1996	2007	2000[d]	2001[e]	2007
Cuba			1994	1992[d]	1992[d]	1994	1994	2005	1990[d]	1997	2007
Czech Republic	1994		1994	1993[e]	1993[e]	1996	1993[g]	2005	1993[f]	2000[d]	2002
Denmark	1994		1994	1988	1988	2004	1993	2005	1977	1996[d]	2003
Dominican Republic		1995	1999	1993[d]	1993[d]		1996	2005	1986[d]	1997[d]	2007
Ecuador	1993	1995	1994	1990[d]	1990[d]		1993	2005	1975	1996	2004
Egypt, Arab Rep.	1992	1988	1995	1988	1988	1994	1994	2005	1978	1996	2003
El Salvador	1994	1988	1996	1992	1992		1994	2005	1987[d]	1997[d]	2008
Eritrea	1995		1995	2005[d]	2005[d]		1996[d]	2005	1994[d]	1996	2005[d]
Estonia	1998		1994	1996[d]	1996[d]	2005[d]	1994	2005	1992[d]		2008[d]
Ethiopia	1994	1991	1994	1994[d]	1994[d]		1994	2005	1989[d]	1997	2003
Finland	1995		1994	1986	1988	1996	1994[e]	2005	1976[d]	1996[e]	2002[e]
France	1990		1994	1987[g]	1988[g]	1996	1994	2005	1978	1997	2004[g]
Gabon		1990	1998	1994[d]	1994[d]	1998	1997	2007	1989[d]	1996[d]	2007
Gambia, The	1992	1989	1994	1990[d]	1990[d]	1994	1994	2005	1977[d]	1996	2006
Georgia	1998		1994	1996[d]	1996[d]	1996[d]	1994[d]	2005	1996[d]	1999	2006
Germany			1994	1988	1988	1994[d]	1993	2005	1976	1996	2002
Ghana	1992	1988	1995	1989[d]	1989	1994	1994	2005	1975	1997	2003
Greece			1994	1988	1988	1995	1994	2005	1992[d]	1997	2006
Guatemala	1994	1988	1996	1987[d]	1989[d]	1997	1995	2005	1979	1998[d]	2008
Guinea	1994	1988	1994	1992[d]	1992[d]	1994	1993	2005	1981[d]	1997	2007
Guinea-Bissau	1993	1991	1996	2002[d]	2002[d]	1994	1995	2005	1990[d]	1996	2008
Haiti	1999		1996	2000[d]	2000[d]	1996	1996	2005		1996	
Honduras	1993		1996	1993[d]	1993[d]	1994	1995	2005	1985[d]	1997	2005

	Environmental strategies or action plans	Biodiversity assessments, strategies, or action plans	Participation in treaties[a]								
			Climate change[b]	Ozone layer	CFC control	Law of the Sea[c]	Biological diversity[b]	Kyoto Protocol[b]	CITES	CCD	Stockholm Convention
Hungary	1995		1994	1988[d]	1989[d]	2002	1994	2005	1985[d]	1999[d]	2008
India	1993	1994	1994	1991[d]	1992[d]	1995	1994	2005	1976	1997	2006
Indonesia	1993	1993	1994	1992[d]	1992	1994	1994	2005	1978[d]	1998	
Iran, Islamic Rep.			1996	1990[d]	1990[d]		1996	2005	1976	1997	2006
Iraq						1994		2009		2010	
Ireland			1994	1988[d]	1988	1996	1996	2005	2002	1997	2010
Israel			1996	1992[d]	1992		1995	2005	1979	1996	
Italy			1994	1988	1988	1995	1994	2005	1979	1997	
Jamaica	1994		1995	1993[d]	1993[d]	1994	1995	2005	1997[d]	1998[d]	2007
Japan			1994	1988[d]	1988	1996	1993[e]	2005	1980	1998[e]	2002[d]
Jordan	1991		1994	1989[d]	1989[d]	1995[d]	1993	2005	1978[d]	1997	2004
Kazakhstan			1995	1998[d]	1998[d]		1994	2009	2000[d]	1997	2007
Kenya	1994	1992	1994	1988[d]	1988	1994	1994	2005	1978	1997	2004
Korea, Dem. Rep.			1995	1995[d]	1995[d]		1994[g]	2005		2004[d]	2002[d]
Korea, Rep.			1994	1992	1992	1996	1994	2005	1993[d]	1999	2007
Kosovo											
Kuwait			1995	1992[d]	1992[d]	1994	2002	2005	2002	1997	2006
Kyrgyz Republic	1995		2000	2000[d]	2000[d]		1996[g]	2005		1997[d]	2006
Lao PDR	1995		1995	1998[d]	1998[d]	1998	1996[g]	2005	2004[d]	1996[e]	2006
Latvia			1995	1995[d]	1995[d]	2004[d]	1995	2005	1997[d]	2003[d]	2004
Lebanon			1995	1993[d]	1993[d]	1995	1994	2007		1996	2003
Lesotho	1989		1995	1994[d]	1994[d]	2007	1995	2005	2003	1996	2002
Liberia			2003	1996[d]	1996[d]	2008	2000	2006	2005[d]	1998[d]	2002[d]
Libya			1999	1990[d]	1990[d]		2001	2006	2003[d]	1996	2005[d]
Lithuania			1995	1995[d]	1995[d]	2003[d]	1996	2005	2001[d]	2003[d]	2006
Macedonia, FYR			1998	1994[f]	1994[f]	1994[f]	1997[d]	2005	2000[d]	2002[d]	2004
Madagascar	1988	1991	1999	1996[d]	1996[d]	2001	1996	2005	1975	1997	2005
Malawi	1994		1994	1991[d]	1991[d]		1994	2005	1982[d]	1996	2009
Malaysia	1991	1988	1994	1989[d]	1989[d]	1996	1994	2005	1977[d]	1997	
Mali		1989	1995	1994[d]	1994[d]	1994	1995	2005	1994[d]	1996	2003
Mauritania	1988		1994	1994[d]	1994[d]	1996	1996	2005	1998[d]	1996	2005
Mauritius	1990		1994	1992[d]	1992[d]	1994	1992	2005	1975	1996	2004
Mexico		1988	1994	1987	1988	1994	1993	2005	1991[d]	1996	2003
Moldova	2002		1995	1996[d]	1996[d]	2007	1995	2005	2001[d]	1999[d]	2004
Mongolia	1995		1994	1996[d]	1996[d]	1996	1993	2005	1996[d]	1996	2004
Morocco		1988	1996	1995	1995	2007	1995	2005	1975	1997	2004
Mozambique	1994		1995	1994[d]	1994[d]	1997	1995	2005	1981[d]	1997	2005
Myanmar		1989	1995	1993[d]	1993[d]	1996	1995	2005	1997[d]	1997[d]	2004[d]
Namibia	1992		1995	1993[d]	1993[d]	1994	1997	2005	1990[d]	1997	2005[d]
Nepal	1993		1994	1994[d]	1994[d]	1998	1993	2005	1975[d]	1997	2007
Netherlands	1994		1994	1988[d]	1988[e]	1996	1994[e]	2005	1984	1996[e]	2002[e]
New Zealand	1994		1994	1987	1988	1996	1993	2005	1989[d]	2000[d]	2004
Nicaragua	1994		1996	1993[d]	1993[d]	2000	1995	2005	1977[d]	1998	2005
Niger		1991	1995	1992[d]	1992[d]		1995	2005	1975	1996	2006
Nigeria	1990	1992	1994	1988[d]	1988[d]	1994	1994	2005	1974	1997	2004
Norway		1994	1994	1986	1988	1996	1993	2005	1976	1996	2002
Oman			1995	1999[d]	1999[d]	1994	1995	2005		1996	2005
Pakistan	1994	1991	1994	1992[d]	1992[d]	1997	1994	2005	1976[d]	1997	2008
Panama	1990		1995	1989[d]	1989	1996	1995	2005	1978	1996	2003
Papua New Guinea	1992	1993	1994	1992[d]	1992[d]	1997	1993	2005	1975[d]	2001[d]	2003
Paraguay			1994	1992[d]	1992[d]	1994	1994	2005	1976	1997	2004
Peru		1988	1994	1989	1993[d]		1993	2005	1975	1996	2005
Philippines	1989	1989	1994	1991[d]	1991	1994	1993	2005	1981	2000	2004
Poland	1993	1991	1994	1990[d]	1990[d]	1998	1996	2005	1989	2002	2008
Portugal	1995		1994	1988[d]	1988	1997	1993	2005	1980	1996	2004[d]
Puerto Rico											
Qatar								2005		1999	2004[d]

	Environ-mental strategies or action plans	Biodiversity assessments, strategies, or action plans	Participation in treaties[a]								
			Climate change[b]	Ozone layer	CFC control	Law of the Sea[c]	Biological diversity[b]	Kyoto Protocol[b]	CITES	CCD	Stockholm Convention
Romania	1995		1994	1993[d]	1993[d]	1996	1994	2005	1994[d]	1998	2004
Russian Federation	1999	1994	1995	1986[e]	1988[e]	1997	1995	2005	1992	2003	
Rwanda	1991		1998	2001[d]	2001[d]		1996	2005	1980[d]	1999	2002[d]
Saudi Arabia			1995	1993[d]	1993[d]	1996	2001[g]	2005	1996[d]	1997	
Senegal	1984	1991	1995	1993[d]	1993	1994	1994	2005	1977[d]	1996	2003
Serbia								2008		2008	2009
Sierra Leone	1994		1995	2001[d]	2001[d]	1994	1994[g]	2007	1994[d]	1997	2003[d]
Singapore	1993	1995	1997	1989[d]	1989[d]	1994	1995	2006	1986[d]	1999	2005
Slovak Republic			1994	1993[f]	1993[f]	1996	1994[g]	2005	1993	2002	2002
Slovenia	1994		1996	1992[f]	1992[f]	1995[f]	1996	2005	2000[d]	2001	2004
Somalia				2001[d]	2001[d]	1994		2011	1985[d]	2002	2010[d]
South Africa	1993		1997	1990[d]	1990[d]	1997	1995	2005	1975	1997	2002
Spain			1994	1988[d]	1988	1997	1995	2005	1986[d]	1996	2004
Sri Lanka	1994	1991	1994	1989[d]	1989[d]	1994	1994	2005	1979[d]	1999	2005
Sudan			1994	1993[d]	1993[d]	1994	1995	2005	1982	1996	2006
Swaziland			1997	1992[d]	1992[d]		1994	2006	1997[d]	1997	2006
Sweden			1994	1986	1988	1996	1993	2005	1974	1996	2002
Switzerland			1994	1987	1988		1994	2005	1974	1996	2003
Syrian Arab Republic	1999		1996	1989[d]	1989[d]		1996	2006	2003[d]	1997	2005
Tajikistan			1998	1996[d]	1998[d]		1997[g]	2009		1997	2007
Tanzania	1994	1988	1996	1993[d]	1993[d]	1994	1996	2005	1979	1997	2004
Thailand			1995	1989[d]	1989		2004	2005	1983	2001	2005
Togo	1991		1995	1991[d]	1991	1994	1995[e]	2005	1978	1996	2004
Trinidad and Tobago			1994	1989[d]	1989[d]	1994	1996	2005	1984[d]	2000	2002[d]
Tunisia	1994	1988	1994	1989[d]	1989[d]	1994	1993	2005	1974	1996	2004
Turkey	1998		2004	1991[d]	1991[d]		1997	2009	1996[d]	1998	2009
Turkmenistan			1995	1993[d]	1993[d]		1996[g]	2005		1996	
Uganda	1994	1988	1994	1988[d]	1988	1994	1993	2005	1991[d]	1997	2004[d]
Ukraine	1999		1997	1986[e]	1988[e]	1999	1995	2005	1999[d]	2002	
United Arab Emirates			1996	1989[d]	1989[d]		2000	2005	1990[d]	1999	2002
United Kingdom	1995	1994	1994	1987	1988	1997[d]	1994	2005	1976	1997	2005
United States	1995	1995	1994	1986	1988				1974	2001	
Uruguay			1994	1989[d]	1991[d]	1994	1993	2005	1975	1999	2004
Uzbekistan			1994	1993[d]	1993[d]		1995[g]	2005	1997[d]	1996	
Venezuela			1995	1988[d]	1989		1994	2005	1977	1998	2005
Vietnam		1993	1995	1994[d]	1994[d]	2006[d]	1994	2005	1994[d]	1998	2002
West Bank and Gaza											
Yemen, Rep.	1996	1992	1996	1996[d]	1996[d]	1994	1996	2005	1997[d]	1997	2004
Zambia	1994		1994	1990[d]	1990[d]	1994	1993	2006	1980[d]	1996	2006
Zimbabwe	1987		1994	1992[d]	1992[d]	1994	1994	2009	1981[d]	1997	

a. Ratification of the treaty. b. Year the treaty entered into force in the country. c. Convention became effective November 16, 1994. d. Accession. e. Acceptance. f. Succession. g. Approval.

National environmental strategies and participation in international treaties on environmental issues provide some evidence of government commitment to sound environmental management. But the signing of these treaties does not always imply ratification, nor does it guarantee that governments will comply with treaty obligations.

In many countries efforts to halt environmental degradation have failed, primarily because governments have neglected to make this issue a priority, a reflection of competing claims on scarce resources. To address this problem, many countries are preparing national environmental strategies—some focusing narrowly on environmental issues, and others integrating environmental, economic, and social concerns. Among such initiatives are conservation strategies and environmental action plans. Some countries have also prepared country environmental profiles and biodiversity strategies and profiles.

National conservation strategies—promoted by the World Conservation Union (IUCN)—provide a comprehensive, cross-sectoral analysis of conservation and resource management issues to help integrate environmental concerns with the development process. Such strategies discuss current and future needs, institutional capabilities, prevailing technical conditions, and the status of natural resources in a country.

National environmental action plans, supported by the World Bank and other development agencies, describe a country's main environmental concerns, identify the principal causes of environmental problems, and formulate policies and actions to deal with them. These plans are a continuing process in which governments develop comprehensive environmental policies, recommend specific actions, and outline the investment strategies, legislation, and institutional arrangements required to implement them.

Biodiversity profiles—prepared by the World Conservation Monitoring Centre and the IUCN—provide basic background on species diversity, protected areas, major ecosystems and habitat types, and legislative and administrative support. In an effort to establish a scientific baseline for measuring progress in biodiversity conservation, the United Nations Environment Programme (UNEP) coordinates global biodiversity assessments.

To address global issues, many governments have also signed international treaties and agreements launched in the wake of the 1972 United Nations Conference on the Human Environment in Stockholm and the 1992 United Nations Conference on Environment and Development (the Earth Summit) in Rio de Janeiro, which produced Agenda 21—an array of actions to address environmental challenges:

· The Framework Convention on Climate Change aims to stabilize atmospheric concentrations of greenhouse gases at levels that will prevent human activities from interfering dangerously with the global climate.

· The Vienna Convention for the Protection of the Ozone Layer aims to protect human health and the environment by promoting research on the effects of changes in the ozone layer and on alternative substances (such as substitutes for chlorofluorocarbon) and technologies, monitoring the ozone layer, and taking measures to control the activities that produce adverse effects.

· The Montreal Protocol for Chlorofluorocarbon Control requires that countries help protect the earth from excessive ultraviolet radiation by cutting chlorofluorocarbon consumption by 20 percent over their 1986 level by 1994 and by 50 percent over their 1986 level by 1999, with allowances for increases in consumption by developing countries.

· The United Nations Convention on the Law of the Sea, which became effective in November 1994, establishes a comprehensive legal regime for seas and oceans, establishes rules for environmental standards and enforcement provisions, and develops international rules and national legislation to prevent and control marine pollution.

· The Convention on Biological Diversity promotes conservation of biodiversity through scientific and technological cooperation among countries, access to financial and genetic resources, and transfer of ecologically sound technologies.

But 10 years after the Earth Summit in Rio de Janeiro the World Summit on Sustainable Development in Johannesburg recognized that many of the proposed actions had yet to materialize. To help developing countries comply with their obligations under these agreements, the Global Environment Facility (GEF) was created to focus on global improvement in biodiversity, climate change, international waters, and ozone layer depletion. The UNEP, United Nations Development Programme, and World Bank manage the GEF according to the policies of its governing body of country representatives. The World Bank is responsible for the GEF Trust Fund and chairs the GEF.

• **Environmental strategies or action plans** provide a comprehensive analysis of conservation and resource management issues that integrate environmental concerns with development. They include national conservation strategies, environmental action plans, environmental management strategies, and sustainable development strategies. The date is the year a country adopted a strategy or action plan. • **Biodiversity assessments, strategies, or action plans** include biodiversity profiles (see *About the data*). • **Participation in treaties** covers nine international treaties (see *About the data*). • **Climate change** refers to the Framework Convention on Climate Change (signed in 1992). • **Ozone layer** refers to the Vienna Convention for the Protection of the Ozone Layer (signed in 1985). • **CFC control** refers to the Protocol on Substances That Deplete the Ozone Layer (the Montreal Protocol for Chlorofluorocarbon Control) (signed in 1987). • **Law of the Sea** refers to the United Nations Convention on the Law of the Sea (signed in 1982). • **Biological diversity** refers to the Convention on Biological Diversity (signed at the Earth Summit in 1992). • **Kyoto Protocol** refers to the protocol on climate change adopted at the third conference of the parties to the United Nations Framework Convention on Climate Change in December 1997. • **CITES** is the Convention on International Trade in Endangered Species of Wild Fauna and Flora, an agreement among governments to ensure that the survival of wild animals and plants is not threatened by uncontrolled exploitation. Adopted in 1973, it entered into force in 1975. • **CCD** is the United Nations Convention to Combat Desertification, an international convention addressing the problems of land degradation in the world's drylands. Adopted in 1994, it entered into force in 1996. • **Stockholm Convention** is an international legally binding instrument to protect human health and the environment from persistent organic pollutants. Adopted in 2001, it entered into force in 2004.

Data sources

Data on environmental strategies and participation in international environmental treaties are from the Secretariat of the United Nations Framework Convention on Climate Change, the Ozone Secretariat of the UNEP, the World Resources Institute, the UNEP, the Center for International Earth Science Information Network, and the United Nations Treaty Series.

	Total natural resources rents	Oil rents	Natural gas rents	Coal rents, hard and soft	Mineral rents	Forest rents
	% of GDP **2009**	% of GDP **2009**	% of GDP **2009**	% of GDP **2009**	% of GDP **2009**	% of GDP **2009**
Afghanistan	4.0	0.0	0.0	0.0	..	4.0
Albania	1.8	1.7	0.0	0.0	0.0	0.1
Algeria	25.2	15.1	9.7	0.0	0.2	0.1
Angola	39.0	38.6	0.1	0.0	0.0	0.2
Argentina	6.0	3.5	1.9	0.0	0.5	0.1
Armenia	0.8	0.0	0.0	0.0	0.8	0.0
Australia	6.7	0.9	0.8	1.2	4.9	0.1
Austria	0.3	0.1	0.1	0.0	0.0	0.1
Azerbaijan	44.5	39.6	4.9	0.0	0.0	0.0
Bangladesh	3.9	0.0	3.2	0.0	0.0	0.6
Belarus	1.7	1.2	0.1	0.0	0.0	0.5
Belgium	0.0	0.0	0.0	0.0	0.0	0.0
Benin	1.9	0.0	0.0	0.0	0.0	1.9
Bolivia	17.5	4.5	10.3	0.0	2.2	0.4
Bosnia and Herzegovina	2.0	0.0	0.0	1.2	1.5	0.5
Botswana	3.5	0.0	0.0	0.4	3.4	0.2
Brazil	5.0	2.1	0.1	0.0	2.4	0.4
Bulgaria	1.2	0.0	0.0	0.6	1.0	0.2
Burkina Faso	3.7	0.0	0.0	0.0	0.0	3.7
Burundi	11.3	0.0	0.0	0.0	1.2	10.1
Cambodia	1.5	0.0	0.0	0.0	0.0	1.5
Cameroon	9.4	6.8	0.3	0.0	0.1	2.2
Canada	3.7	2.1	0.6	0.1	0.6	0.4
Central African Republic	7.3	0.0	0.0	0.0	0.0	7.3
Chad	36.4	33.7	0.0	0.0	0.0	2.7
Chile	15.6	0.0	0.1	0.0	14.8	0.6
China	2.0	1.4	0.2	2.7	0.3	0.2
Hong Kong SAR, China	0.0	0.0	0.0	0.0	0.0	0.0
Colombia	6.3	5.2	0.5	1.0	0.5	0.1
Congo, Dem. Rep.	28.0	3.9	0.0	0.0	11.6	12.5
Congo, Rep.	56.8	52.8	0.0	0.0	0.0	3.9
Costa Rica	0.4	0.0	0.0	0.0	0.1	0.4
Côte d'Ivoire	5.9	3.6	1.0	0.0	0.0	1.3
Croatia	1.1	0.4	0.5	0.0	0.0	0.2
Cuba	..	..	..	..	..	..
Czech Republic	0.3	0.0	0.0	0.3	0.0	0.2
Denmark	1.8	1.4	0.4	0.0	0.0	0.0
Dominican Republic	0.8	0.0	0.0	0.0	0.8	0.0
Ecuador	15.7	15.3	0.1	0.0	0.0	0.2
Egypt, Arab Rep.	10.7	5.3	5.1	0.0	0.2	0.1
El Salvador	0.5	0.0	0.0	0.0	0.0	0.5
Eritrea	1.4	0.0	0.0	0.0	0.0	1.4
Estonia	0.7	0.0	0.0	1.1	0.0	0.7
Ethiopia	5.0	0.0	0.0	0.0	0.2	4.8
Finland	0.6	0.0	0.0	0.0	0.1	0.5
France	0.1	0.0	0.0	0.0	0.0	0.0
Gabon	45.0	39.9	0.3	0.0	0.1	4.7
Gambia, The	3.2	0.0	0.0	0.0	0.0	3.2
Georgia	0.3	0.2	0.0	0.0	0.0	0.1
Germany	0.1	0.0	0.1	0.1	..	0.0
Ghana	8.6	0.0	0.0	0.0	6.5	2.1
Greece	0.1	0.0	0.0	0.2	0.1	0.0
Guatemala	1.6	0.7	0.0	0.0	0.0	0.9
Guinea	10.5	0.0	0.0	0.0	5.3	5.3
Guinea-Bissau	3.5	0.0	0.0	0.0	0.0	3.5
Haiti	0.7	0.0	0.0	0.0	0.0	0.7
Honduras	1.8	0.0	0.0	0.0	0.6	1.2

	Total natural resources rents	Oil rents	Natural gas rents	Coal rents, hard and soft	Mineral rents	Forest rents
	% of GDP **2009**	% of GDP **2009**	% of GDP **2009**	% of GDP **2009**	% of GDP **2009**	% of GDP **2009**
Hungary	0.5	0.2	0.2	0.1	0.0	0.1
India	4.0	0.8	0.5	2.2	1.7	1.0
Indonesia	5.9	2.4	1.3	2.5	1.6	0.5
Iran, Islamic Rep.	28.4	21.4	6.6	0.0	0.3	0.0
Iraq	68.6	68.1	0.5	0.0	0.0	0.0
Ireland	0.1	0.0	0.0	0.0	0.0	0.0
Israel	0.3	0.0	0.2	0.0	0.1	0.0
Italy	0.1	0.1	0.0	0.0	0.0	0.0
Jamaica	1.2	0.0	0.0	0.0	1.1	0.2
Japan	0.0	0.0	0.0	0.0	..	0.0
Jordan	1.7	0.0	0.1	0.0	1.6	0.0
Kazakhstan	27.3	20.9	4.7	4.3	1.7	0.0
Kenya	1.4	0.0	0.0	0.0	0.0	1.4
Korea, Dem. Rep.	..	..	..	..	..	..
Korea, Rep.	0.0	0.0	0.0	0.0	..	0.0
Kosovo	0.0	0.0	0.0	..	..	..
Kuwait	..	..	..	..	..	..
Kyrgyz Republic	0.5	0.5	0.0	0.3	0.0	0.0
Lao PDR	1.9	0.0	0.0	0.0	0.0	1.9
Latvia	1.1	0.0	0.0	0.0	0.0	1.1
Lebanon	0.0	0.0	0.0	0.0	0.0	0.0
Lesotho	1.8	0.0	0.0	0.0	0.0	1.8
Liberia	15.6	0.0	0.0	0.0	0.7	14.9
Libya	48.4	44.7	3.7	0.0	0.0	0.0
Lithuania	1.4	0.1	0.0	0.0	0.0	1.3
Macedonia, FYR	0.1	0.0	0.0	0.0	0.0	0.1
Madagascar	2.0	0.0	0.0	0.0	0.1	1.9
Malawi	2.5	0.0	0.0	0.0	0.0	2.5
Malaysia	12.3	6.1	5.7	0.0	0.0	0.5
Mali	1.3	0.0	0.0	0.0	0.0	1.3
Mauritania	30.1	0.0	0.0	0.0	29.4	0.6
Mauritius	0.0	0.0	0.0	0.0	0.0	0.0
Mexico	6.8	5.5	0.7	0.1	0.4	0.1
Moldova	0.2	0.1	0.0	0.0	0.0	0.1
Mongolia	12.7	1.4	0.0	3.9	11.0	0.3
Morocco	2.3	0.0	0.0	0.0	2.2	0.1
Mozambique	8.5	0.0	5.1	0.0	0.0	3.4
Myanmar	..	..	..	..	..	..
Namibia	0.5	0.0	0.0	0.0	0.5	0.0
Nepal	5.6	0.0	0.0	0.0	0.0	5.6
Netherlands	1.1	0.1	1.1	0.0	0.0	0.0
New Zealand	2.3	0.7	0.5	0.1	0.4	0.6
Nicaragua	2.9	0.0	0.0	0.0	1.0	1.8
Niger	1.7	0.0	0.0	0.0	..	1.7
Nigeria	23.3	20.3	1.8	0.0	0.0	1.2
Norway	13.2	9.5	3.6	0.0	0.0	0.1
Oman	40.1	32.3	7.7	0.0	0.0	1.0
Pakistan	4.4	0.7	2.7	0.1	0.0	0.1
Panama	0.1	0.0	0.0	0.0	0.0	0.1
Papua New Guinea	32.7	0.0	0.0	0.0	29.7	3.0
Paraguay	1.7	0.0	0.0	0.0	0.0	1.7
Peru	8.2	0.9	0.4	0.0	6.8	0.1
Philippines	1.7	0.0	0.4	0.1	1.1	0.2
Poland	0.8	0.1	0.1	0.9	0.4	0.2
Portugal	0.1	0.0	0.0	0.0	..	0.1
Puerto Rico	..	..	..	..	..	..
Qatar	28.6	14.0	14.6	0.0	0.0	..

	Total natural resources rents	Oil rents	Natural gas rents	Coal rents, hard and soft	Mineral rents	Forest rents
	% of GDP 2009	% of GDP 2009	% of GDP 2009	% of GDP 2009	% of GDP 2009	% of GDP 2009
Romania	2.0	0.9	0.8	0.2	..	0.2
Russian Federation	20.7	13.4	5.8	1.0	1.1	0.3
Rwanda	3.3	0.0	0.0	0.0	0.0	3.3
Saudi Arabia	47.2	43.8	3.4	0.0	0.0	0.0
Senegal	1.8	0.0	0.0	0.0	0.4	1.3
Serbia and Montenegro	..	..	..	..	..	..
Sierra Leone	4.5	0.0	0.0	0.0	0.6	3.8
Singapore	0.0	0.0	0.0	0.0	0.0	0.0
Slovak Republic	0.3	0.0	0.0	0.0	0.0	0.3
Slovenia	0.1	0.0	0.0	0.1	0.0	0.1
Somalia	..	..	..	..	..	..
South Africa	4.7	0.1	0.1	4.2	3.3	1.2
Spain	0.0	0.0	0.0	0.0	..	0.0
Sri Lanka	0.8	0.0	0.0	0.0	0.0	0.8
Sudan	16.9	16.0	0.0	0.0	0.1	0.8
Swaziland	2.3	0.0	0.0	0.0	..	2.3
Sweden	0.8	0.0	0.0	0.0	0.4	0.5
Switzerland	0.0	0.0	0.0	0.0	0.0	0.0
Syrian Arab Republic	14.4	12.4	1.8	0.0	0.2	0.0
Tajikistan	0.2	0.1	0.1	0.1	0.0	0.0
Tanzania	6.3	0.0	0.4	0.0	3.5	2.4
Thailand	3.6	1.6	1.7	0.1	0.0	0.3
Timor-Leste	0.4	0.0	0.0	0.0	0.0	0.4
Togo	4.5	0.0	0.0	0.0	2.1	2.4
Trinidad and Tobago	35.2	10.3	24.9	0.0	0.0	0.0
Tunisia	4.9	3.8	0.9	0.0	..	0.2
Turkey	0.3	0.1	0.0	0.1	0.1	0.1
Turkmenistan	41.0	17.1	24.0	0.0	0.0	..
Uganda	5.2	0.0	0.0	0.0	0.0	5.2
Ukraine	3.6	0.9	2.4	2.4	0.0	0.3
United Arab Emirates	20.9	17.6	3.3	0.0	0.0	..
United Kingdom	1.4	1.0	0.4	0.0	0.0	0.0
United States	0.9	0.5	0.2	0.2	0.1	0.1
Uruguay	0.7	0.0	0.0	0.0	0.0	0.7
Uzbekistan	28.2	2.8	25.4	0.1	0.0	0.0
Venezuela, RB	15.6	13.8	1.2	0.0	0.5	0.0
Vietnam	8.1	6.0	1.3	2.2	0.1	0.7
West Bank and Gaza	..	..	..	..	..	..
Yemen, Rep.	19.7	19.4	0.3	0.0	0.0	0.0
Zambia	18.4	0.0	0.0	0.1	16.4	2.0
Zimbabwe	5.2	0.0	0.0	3.2	1.9	3.3
World	**3.7 w**	**1.9 w**	**0.6 w**	**0.5 w**	**0.5 w**	**0.2 w**
Low income	6.3	0.7	0.9	0.1	2.0	2.6
Middle income	8.7	4.7	1.4	1.4	1.0	0.3
Lower middle income	6.8	2.9	0.8	2.1	0.6	0.4
Upper middle income	11.2	6.8	2.1	0.5	1.5	0.3
Low & middle income	8.7	4.6	1.3	1.3	1.0	0.4
East Asia & Pacific	5.3	1.6	0.6	2.4	0.4	0.2
Europe & Central Asia	13.7	8.2	3.7	0.9	0.7	0.2
Latin America & Carib.	7.0	4.1	0.5	0.1	2.0	0.3
Middle East & N. Africa	22.7	17.6	4.6	0.0	0.4	0.1
South Asia	5.8	0.8	0.8	1.8	1.4	1.1
Sub-Saharan Africa	14.2	8.8	0.5	1.3	1.8	1.7
High income	1.6	0.9	0.3	0.1	0.2	0.1
Euro area	0.2	0.0	0.1	0.0	..	0.0

Note: Components may not sum to 100 percent because of rounding.

Contribution of natural resources to gross domestic product | 3.16

About the data

Accounting for the contribution of natural resources to economic output is important in building an analytical framework for sustainable development. In some countries earnings from natural resources, especially from fossil fuels and minerals, account for a sizable share of GDP, and much of these come in the form of economic rents—revenues above the cost of extracting them. Natural resources give rise to economic rents because they are not produced. For produced goods and services competitive forces expand supply until economic profits are driven to zero, but natural resources in fixed supply often command returns well in excess of their cost of production. Rents from nonrenewable resources—fossil fuels and minerals—as well as rents from overharvesting of forests indicate the liquidation of a country's capital stock. When countries use such rents to support current consumption rather than to invest in new capital to replace what is being used up, they are, in effect, borrowing against their future.

The estimates of natural resources rents shown in the table are calculated as the difference between the price of a commodity and the average cost of producing it. This is done by estimating the world price of units of specific commodities and subtracting estimates of average unit costs of extraction or harvesting costs (including a normal return on capital). These unit rents are then multiplied by the physical quantities countries extract or harvest to determine the rents for each commodity as a share of gross national income.

This definition of economic rent differs from that used in the System of National Accounts, where rents are a form of property income, consisting of payments to landowners by a tenant for the use of the land or payments to the owners of subsoil assets by institutional units permitting them to extract subsoil deposits.

The Environment section of previous editions of the *World Development Indicators* included a table *"Toward a broader measure of savings,"* which showed the derivation of adjusted net savings taking into account consumption of fixed and natural capital and pollution damage and additions to human capital. Adjusted net savings measures the net additions or subtractions from a country's stock of tangible and intangible capital. This table is now included in the *Economy* section as table 4.11 along with the closely related table 4.10 "Toward a broader measure of income."

Definitions

- **Oil rents** are the difference between the value of crude oil production at world prices and total costs of production. • **Natural gas rents** are the difference between the value of natural gas production at world prices and total costs of production. • **Coal rents** are the difference between the value of both hard and soft coal production at world prices and their total costs of production. • **Mineral rents** are the difference between the value of production for a stock of minerals at world prices and their total costs of production. Minerals included in the calculation are tin, gold, lead, zinc, iron, copper, nickel, silver, bauxite, and phosphate. • **Forest rents** are roundwood harvest times the product of average prices and a region-specific rental rate (based on a number of reviews, World Bank 2011). • **Total natural resources rents** are the sum of oil rents, natural gas rents, coal rents (hard and soft), mineral rents, and forest rents.

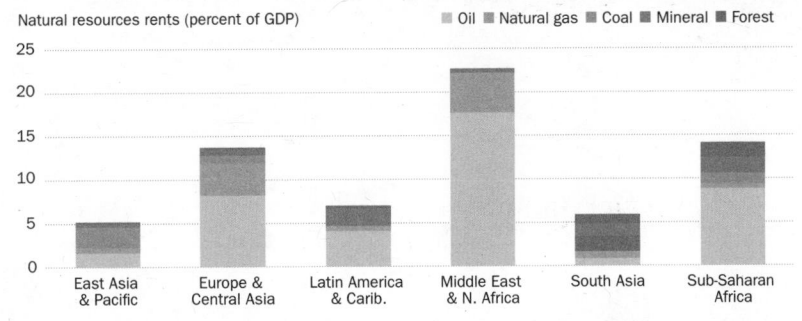

Oil dominates the contribution of natural resources in the Middle East and North Africa — 3.16a

Natural resources rents (percent of GDP) — ■ Oil ■ Natural gas ■ Coal ■ Mineral ■ Forest

Source: Table 3.16.

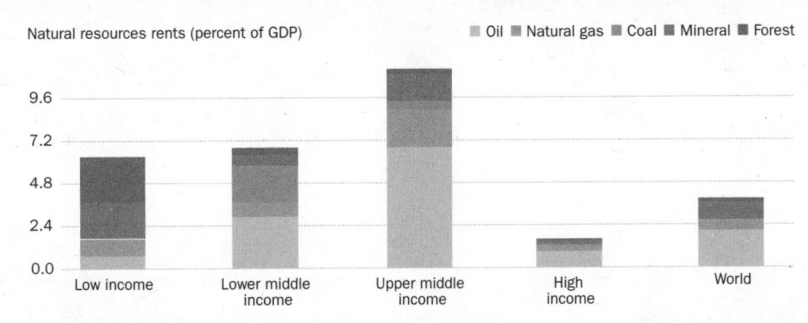

Upper middle-income countries have the highest contribution of natural resources to GDP — 3.16b

Natural resources rents (percent of GDP) — ■ Oil ■ Natural gas ■ Coal ■ Mineral ■ Forest

Source: Table 3.16.

Data sources

Data on contributions of natural resources to GDP are estimates based on sources and methods described in *The Changing Wealth of Nations: Measuring Sustainable Development in the New Millennium* (World Bank 2011a).

ECONOMY

Recently revised data now confirm that in 2009 the world economy experienced the steepest global recession since the Great Depression. World gross domestic product (GDP) contracted 1.9 percent in 2009, with high-income economies contracting 3.3 percent and developing economies expanding just 2.7 percent, down from 8.6 percent in 2008. Among developing country regions, Europe and Central Asia fared the worst, contracting 5.8 percent (figure 4a). Contrast that with East Asia and Pacific, which grew at 7.4 percent, and South Asia, at 7 percent. The global economy rebounded in 2010, with domestic demand in developing countries accounting for 46 percent of global growth. Developing economies' contribution to global growth has been rising since 2000 and was more stable than that of high-income economies during the recent recession (figure 4b). Preliminary estimates, often revised, indicate that the world economy grew 3.9 percent—2.8 percent in high-income economies and 7 percent in developing economies (figure 4c).

Revisions to GDP

Revisions to GDP usually occur one to two months after the initial release, as additional data sources become available. For example, the U.S. Bureau of Economic Analysis releases three versions of quarterly GDP estimates—advance (about a month after the quarter ends), preliminary (two months after), and final (three months after). Other countries follow a similar process, although the reporting lag varies. And some countries compile GDP only annually not quarterly. The differences between GDP estimates decline with each revision, and GDP data become more stable on average (figure 4d).

More significant revisions to GDP involve new methodologies and new or improved data sources and data collection practices. Countries with advanced statistical capacity comprehensively revise GDP estimates every five years. These revisions take into account the latest recommendations of the Intersecretariat Working Group on National Accounts. They may also incorporate a change in the base year used for the constant price data (rebasing). Rebasing adjusts the weights used to compute aggregate measures by selecting a new set of relative component prices in the newly chosen base year.

Comprehensive revisions of GDP estimates are usually higher as improved data sources increase the coverage of the economy and new weights for growing industries more accurately reflect contributions

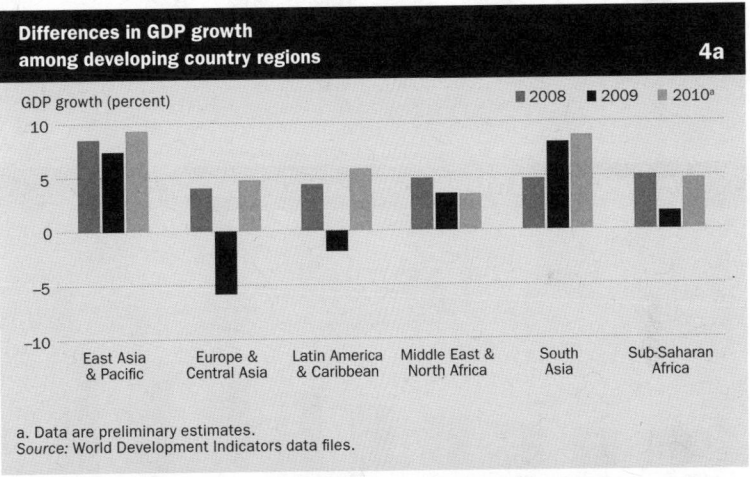

Differences in GDP growth among developing country regions 4a

GDP growth (percent) ■ 2008 ■ 2009 ■ 2010ᵃ

a. Data are preliminary estimates.
Source: World Development Indicators data files.

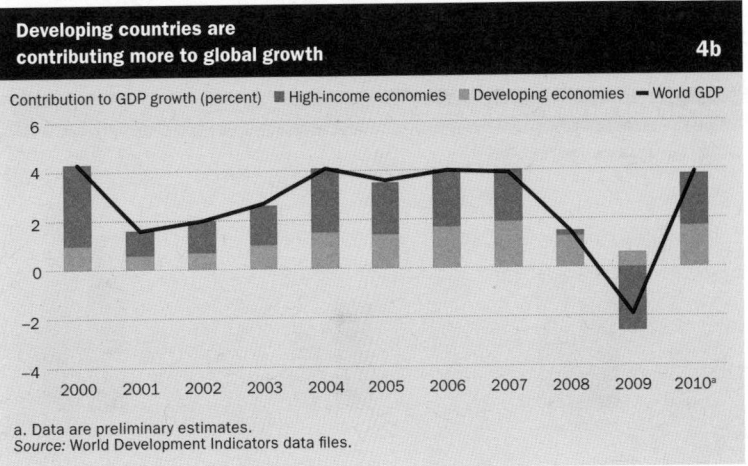

Developing countries are contributing more to global growth 4b

Contribution to GDP growth (percent) ■ High-income economies ■ Developing economies — World GDP

a. Data are preliminary estimates.
Source: World Development Indicators data files.

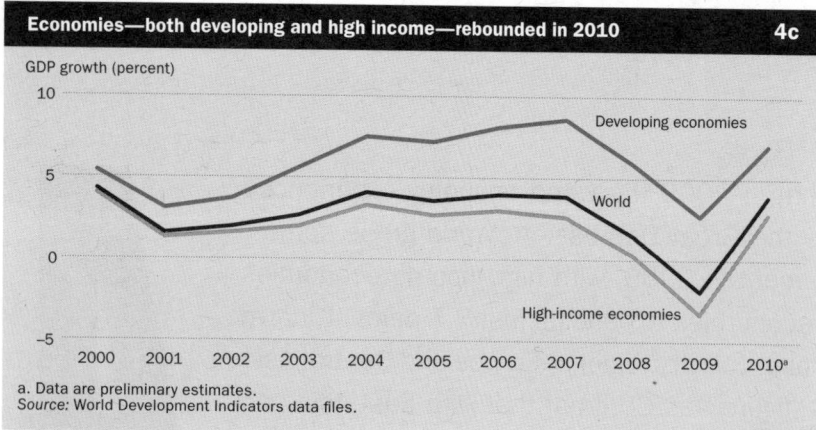

Economies—both developing and high income—rebounded in 2010   **4c**

GDP growth (percent)

Developing economies

World

High-income economies

a. Data are preliminary estimates.
Source: World Development Indicators data files.

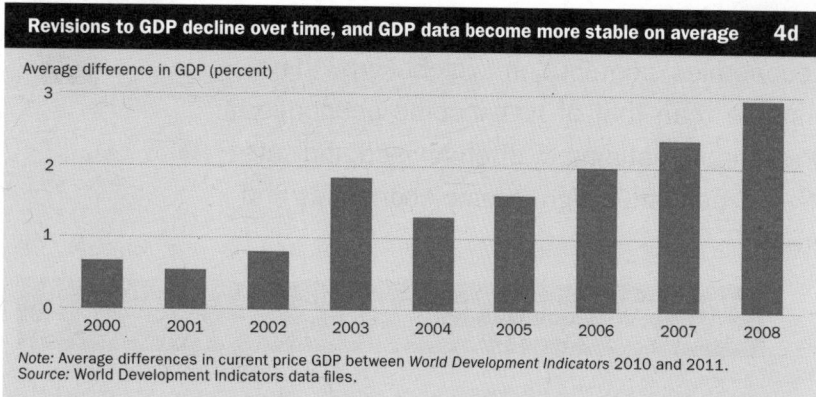

Revisions to GDP decline over time, and GDP data become more stable on average   **4d**

Average difference in GDP (percent)

Note: Average differences in current price GDP between *World Development Indicators* 2010 and 2011.
Source: World Development Indicators data files.

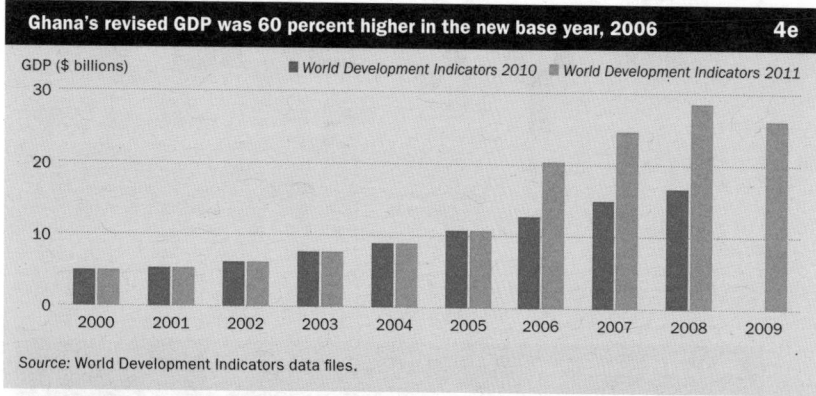

Ghana's revised GDP was 60 percent higher in the new base year, 2006   **4e**

GDP ($ billions)   ■ *World Development Indicators 2010*   ■ *World Development Indicators 2011*

Source: World Development Indicators data files.

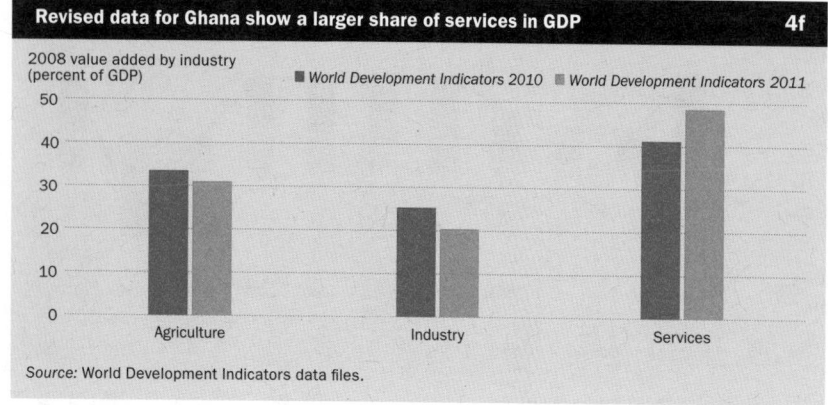

Revised data for Ghana show a larger share of services in GDP   **4f**

2008 value added by industry
(percent of GDP)   ■ *World Development Indicators 2010*   ■ *World Development Indicators 2011*

Agriculture   Industry   Services

Source: World Development Indicators data files.

to the economy. This has been the case for several countries that recently undertook such revisions to their national accounts statistics.

In November 2010 the Ghana Statistical Service revised Ghana's national accounts series, increasing GDP 60 percent in 2006, the new base year (figure 4e). Of the increase, 11 percentage points are in agriculture, 6 in industry, and 44 in services (figure 4f). Other countries have made similar revisions to their national accounts, incorporating improved methodology and data sources. Namibia revised its national accounts in 2008, resulting in 10–30 percent higher GDP estimates for 2000–07. Malawi revised its national accounts in 2007, raising GDP 37 percent. São Tomé and Príncipe revised its national accounts in 2006, resulting in 47.5 percent higher GDP in the new base year 2001. For more information on countries that have recently revised their national accounts data, see *Primary data documentation.*

Many countries do not incorporate new sources of data into national accounts data compilation until they change the base year, which is the base or pricing period for constant price calculations. Such revisions can be substantial because of the long lag between rebasing exercises. The adjustments arising from rebasing can be reduced by incorporating new data sources in a timely manner and ensuring that the accounts are rebased at least every five years.

Data users should be aware that rebasing creates a break in the time series. New data sources and methodologies are usually implemented only for recent years, creating a jump in GDP between the last year of the old data and the first year of the new. For constant price GDP these breaks can be eliminated by linking the old series to the new using historical growth rates. But for nominal GDP data the break in the time series cannot be avoided unless the statistics office revises historical series backward at a detailed level.

Broader measures of income and savings

Two tables have been added to the *Economy* section this year. Table 4.10 contains new measures of adjusted net national income, and table 4.11 contains measures of adjusted net savings, previously included in the *Environment* section. Both tables follow recommendations of the recently published *The Changing Wealth of Nations* (World Bank 2011a).

Adjusted net savings measures the change in a country's national wealth. It begins with gross national savings and then adjusts for consumption of fixed capital, depletion of natural resources, changes in human capital, and damages from carbon dioxide and particulate emissions. If adjusted net savings is negative, capital stocks are declining and future well-being is reduced. The report argues that the key to increasing living standards is building national wealth through investment and national savings to finance the investment.

The table on adjusted net national income presents growth rates of GDP, gross national income (GNI), and adjusted net national income. GNI is more useful than GDP for measuring the economic resources available to residents of an economy because it takes into account inflows of income (profits, wages, and rents) from outside the economy, net of outflows to other economies (box 4g). Adjusted net national income goes one step further by subtracting from GNI a charge for the consumption of fixed capital (or depreciation) and the depletion of natural resources. For some countries, adjusted net national income growth rates tell a story quite different from that of the more widely used GDP growth rates.

Changes to monetary indicators

The monetary indicators in table 4.15 have been revised to reflect the International Monetary Fund's (IMF) new presentation of monetary data for countries reporting in compliance with the *Monetary and Financial Statistics Manual* (IMF 2000) and *Monetary and Financial Statistics Compilation Guide* (IMF 2008). More than 120 countries report their monetary data under

| Commission on the Measurement of Economic and Social Progress | 4g |

Gross domestic product (GDP), the most quoted measure of economic activity, is often used as a measure of welfare. But as the Commission on the Measurement of Economic and Social Progress points out, GDP has many shortcomings as the sole measure of well-being. The commission's report identified problems with the GDP measure itself and recommended including additional measures of the objective and subjective dimensions of well-being and measures of the sustainability of current consumption levels. The commission endorsed the adjusted net savings approach as the "relevant economic counterpart of the notion of sustainability" (Stiglitz, Sen, and Fitoussi 2009, p. 108). But it pointed out that the adjustment for environmental degradation has so far been limited mostly to carbon dioxide emissions. The report also notes the difficulties of pricing natural resources and environmental degradation. Other recommendations for improving GDP measurement include accounting more accurately for improvements in the quality of goods and services produced and the value of government services (usually based on inputs rather than on actual outputs produced).

this new presentation. A majority of these countries transmit the data on standardized report forms for the country's monetary aggregates and for the assets and liabilities of the central bank, other depository corporations, and other financial corporations. This new presentation better classifies financial institution assets and liabilities by financial instrument, sector of the domestic economy, and residency. For many countries the new presentation provides broader institutional coverage of other depository corporations and monetary aggregates.

In the new presentation, the IMF has adopted broad money as the flagship concept. Broad money consists of currency in circulation outside depository corporations, transferable deposits, and other liquid components. Table 4.15 has replaced money and quasi money with broad money. Claims on the private sector have been replaced with other claims on the domestic economy, consisting of the private sector plus state and local governments, public nonfinancial corporations, and other financial corporations. Claims on governments and other public entities have been replaced with net claims on the central government.

	Gross domestic product		Exports of goods and services		Imports of goods and services		GDP deflator		Current account balance		Gross international reserves	
	average annual % growth		average annual % growth		average annual % growth		average annual % growth		% of GDP		$ millions	months of import coverage
	2009	2010[a]	2009	2010[a]	2009	2010[a]	2009	2010[a]	2009	2010[a]	2010[a]	2010[a]
Albania	2.5	3.0	5.9	12.7	−12.0	5.2	2.3	2.0	−15.6	−12.2	2,496	4.5
Algeria	2.1	2.4	−3.0	3.0	16.7	12.5	−9.4	8.6	−10.0	4.6	166,989	42.0
Angola	0.7	3.0	2.4	10.0	6.6	8.5	−5.8	36.1	−10.0	−5.1	..	..
Argentina[b]	0.9	8.0	−6.4	12.8	−19.0	23.1	10.0	9.4	2.8	1.8	52,208	10.2
Armenia	−14.4	4.0	−32.8	8.5	−21.0	4.2	1.4	7.5	−15.7	−12.7	1,859	6.7
Australia	1.3	2.8	2.9	15.0	−9.0	28.7	4.9	5.7	−4.2	−2.2	42,268	1.8
Austria	−3.9	1.5	−16.1	8.2	−14.4	6.8	0.8	0.6	2.9	3.9	22,339	1.4
Azerbaijan	9.3	3.7	2.8	11.0	−5.3	3.5	−16.8	−2.7	23.7	27.2	6,409	7.0
Bangladesh	5.7	5.8	0.0	−9.0	−2.6	−12.5	6.5	10.7	3.7	2.4	11,175	6.4
Belarus	1.4	7.0	−8.2	6.0	−8.6	3.4	3.9	6.4	−13.0	−14.0	5,025	2.0
Belgium	−2.8	2.1	−11.4	9.7	−11.1	8.2	1.1	−2.8	0.7	0.6	26,779	0.9
Bolivia	3.4	4.1	−10.8	11.4	−10.2	12.3	−2.4	6.5	4.7	8.0	..	..
Botswana	−3.7	7.8	−28.0	12.0	−9.3	8.9	−5.7	6.0	−4.4	−2.1	..	..
Brazil	−0.6	7.6	−10.2	26.0	−11.5	35.1	5.7	5.3	−1.5	−2.7	288,575	13.9
Bulgaria	−4.9	0.0	−10.3	11.0	−21.5	3.0	4.1	−0.6	−9.8	−2.4	17,223	7.6
Cambodia	−1.9	4.9	−6.3	8.0	−4.9	12.6	5.1	3.9	−8.8	−8.6	3,787	6.0
Cameroon	2.0	3.0	−4.8	17.0	−5.2	12.0	−3.4	3.4	−5.1	−2.7	..	..
Canada	−2.5	3.0	−14.2	15.5	−13.9	14.6	−2.1	2.7	−2.9	−2.0	57,151	1.4
Chile	−1.5	5.5	−5.6	8.5	−14.3	25.5	4.2	6.6	2.6	0.6	27,827	5.4
China	9.1	10.0	−10.3	33.0	4.1	35.0	−0.6	1.7	6.0	5.5	2,711,162	21.6
Hong Kong SAR, China	−2.8	6.0	−10.1	22.1	−8.8	22.5	0.2	0.3	8.3	22.0	266,055	6.7
Colombia	0.8	4.3	−2.8	17.4	−7.9	21.4	4.9	4.8	−2.1	−2.7	28,076	6.6
Congo, Dem. Rep.	2.7	5.2	5.4	9.3	−11.9	10.8	30.2	21.7	−13.7	−17.2	1,768	7.3
Costa Rica	−1.5	3.6	0.6	6.2	−12.4	13.1	8.9	7.9	−1.8	−3.2	4,630	4.1
Côte d'Ivoire	3.6	3.0	9.3	4.4	11.0	5.0	1.3	1.3	7.2	4.1	3,502	4.8
Croatia	−5.8	−0.8	−16.2	2.5	−20.7	1.5	3.3	1.6	−5.3	−4.4	14,133	7.1
Czech Republic	−4.2	1.7	−10.2	9.4	−10.2	10.4	2.7	1.6	−1.1	−2.7	42,328	3.9
Denmark	−4.9	2.1	−9.7	5.1	−12.5	1.0	0.4	5.3	3.6	5.6	75,077	6.7
Dominican Republic	3.5	4.4	−7.4	8.1	−9.8	11.8	3.0	7.1	−4.6	−5.9	3,501	2.7
Ecuador	0.4	2.3	−6.4	−2.0	−8.0	5.0	4.3	4.4	−0.5	−0.8	2,622	1.1
Egypt, Arab Rep.	4.6	5.1	−14.5	11.8	−17.9	12.0	10.8	11.2	−1.8	−4.1	36,517	5.7
El Salvador	−3.5	1.3	−16.4	9.4	−23.3	15.2	−1.0	3.6	−1.8	−3.1	2,897	3.9
Estonia	−14.1	1.0	−11.2	5.4	−26.8	4.0	−0.6	−1.1	4.7	4.0	2,567	2.3
Ethiopia	8.7	9.0	6.9	11.7	16.4	4.4	24.4	9.9	−7.7	−8.5	..	..
Finland	−8.0	3.0	−20.5	6.8	−18.1	3.5	0.9	−0.4	2.9	3.7	9,547	1.4
France	−2.6	1.6	−12.2	6.6	−10.7	5.2	0.5	1.4	−2.0	−2.1	165,852	2.9
Gabon	−1.0	5.1	−4.9	7.0	−2.8	4.8	−19.0	9.1	..	12.7	..	..
Gambia, The	4.6	5.0	2.5	5.2	3.8	3.1	2.4	4.8	8.6	5.2	..	..
Georgia	−3.9	5.5	−8.4	11.0	−6.4	9.0	−2.0	7.4	−11.3	−12.1	2,264	5.0
Germany	−4.7	3.5	−14.3	10.7	−9.4	9.1	1.4	1.6	5.0	5.9	215,978	2.0
Ghana	4.7	6.6	12.6	8.9	−14.1	10.5	16.7	10.6	−4.6	−3.6	..	..
Greece	−2.0	−4.0	−6.2	0.5	−18.6	−12.1	1.3	4.8	−10.9	−8.5	6,352	0.9
Guatemala	0.6	2.2	−6.2	9.9	−9.4	14.3	2.4	6.4	0.0	−2.5	5,949	5.1
Haiti	2.9	−8.5	9.9	−7.1	5.8	5.9	3.5	12.6	−3.6	−13.6	1,282	5.3
Honduras	−1.9	2.4	−12.6	4.5	−26.0	10.4	4.4	10.5	−3.1	−4.7	..	..
Hungary	−6.3	0.3	−9.1	6.8	−15.4	5.4	4.6	2.7	−0.5	−0.4	44,988	5.5
India	9.1	9.5	−6.7	8.1	−7.3	6.8	7.5	11.5	−1.9	−3.8	300,480	9.7
Indonesia	4.5	5.9	−9.7	24.7	−15.0	32.5	8.4	6.2	2.0	2.6	92,815	7.1
Iran, Islamic Rep.	1.8	1.5	8.5	−3.0	7.8	16.5	0.6	15.0	3.4	6.1	..	..
Ireland	−7.1	−0.6	−4.2	1.7	−9.7	2.1	−3.2	0.6	−2.9	−3.6	2,114	0.2
Israel	0.8	3.8	−11.9	17.8	−17.7	17.5	5.2	4.6	3.9	4.9	70,914	12.0
Italy	−5.0	1.1	−19.1	8.0	−14.5	9.4	2.1	1.6	−3.1	−3.6	158,478	3.5
Jamaica	−3.0	0.6	−10.8	5.7	−11.4	9.3	6.5	16.7	−9.3	−7.9	2,330	4.0
Japan	−5.2	4.4	−24.2	28.7	−16.7	15.6	−0.9	−1.0	2.8	3.8	1,096,069	17.6
Jordan	2.3	4.0	−2.7	5.2	−7.8	6.5	8.1	8.5	−5.0	−4.6	13,388	9.5

Recent economic performance

	Gross domestic product		Exports of goods and services		Imports of goods and services		GDP deflator		Current account balance		Gross international reserves	
	average annual % growth		average annual % growth		average annual % growth		average annual % growth		% of GDP		$ millions	months of import coverage
	2009	2010[a]	2009	2010[a]	2009	2010[a]	2009	2010[a]	2009	2010[a]	2010[a]	2010[a]
Kazakhstan	1.2	5.5	−6.2	13.0	−15.9	6.0	4.7	6.9	−3.7	3.8	28,281	8.4
Kenya	2.6	5.0	−7.0	12.0	−0.2	14.5	6.7	4.8	−5.7	−5.7	4,327	4.1
Korea, Rep.	0.2	6.2	−0.8	28.0	−8.2	28.0	3.4	−0.5	5.1	3.7	292,143	7.0
Kuwait	−4.0	1.9	−11.1	−2.0	−17.0	22.0	−14.7	13.9	25.6	25.1	24,805	8.2
Latvia	−18.0	−2.2	−13.9	4.0	−34.2	1.6	−0.7	−4.9	8.7	1.4	7,604	7.9
Lebanon	9.0	8.0	5.3	20.0	6.5	18.5	5.8	4.5	−21.9	−23.6	44,476	27.3
Lithuania	−15.0	0.4	−14.3	6.5	−29.4	4.2	−2.1	0.0	4.4	2.6	6,836	4.1
Malaysia	−1.7	7.4	−10.4	28.0	−12.3	30.0	−6.7	1.5	16.5	14.7	106,501	6.9
Mauritius	2.1	4.2	−4.8	−4.0	−4.6	3.9	1.5	2.1	−7.9	−9.4	2,619	5.7
Mexico	−6.5	5.2	−14.8	15.5	−18.2	19.4	4.3	4.9	−0.7	−1.0	120,583	4.7
Morocco	4.9	3.5	−13.1	18.4	−6.0	7.6	1.8	2.2	−5.4	−3.2	23,585	7.7
Namibia	−0.8	4.2	−14.0	5.3	5.3	8.3	6.5	4.3	1.3	−1.6	..	..
Nepal	4.7	3.3	38.4	6.4	20.2	6.8	12.1	15.1	−0.1	−3.0	..	..
Netherlands	−4.0	1.7	−7.9	11.7	−8.5	12.7	−0.3	2.9	4.6	5.6	46,147	1.0
New Zealand	−0.4	2.2	0.4	10.5	−14.8	17.5	1.7	4.4	−2.9	−2.5	15,787	4.8
Nigeria	5.6	7.6	1.1	5.9	7.3	8.2	−0.6	17.0	12.5	10.7	..	..
Norway	−1.6	−0.2	−3.9	4.6	−11.4	8.1	−4.0	7.9	13.1	11.8	50,036	5.3
Oman	3.6	4.8	−0.4	8.0	−13.0	18.0	−26.0	21.2	−0.6	8.5	13,025	7.3
Pakistan	3.6	4.4	−3.3	14.1	−15.2	11.2	20.0	13.4	−2.2	−3.1	17,256	5.7
Panama	2.4	5.7	−0.9	5.3	−5.6	13.1	4.1	2.4	−0.2	−6.1	..	..
Paraguay	−3.8	8.5	−12.8	30.1	−13.2	30.3	−0.1	4.8	0.6	−1.8	3,962	5.0
Peru	0.9	8.0	−2.5	−4.1	−11.9	15.3	3.0	3.2	0.2	−1.7	44,215	17.1
Philippines	1.1	6.8	−13.4	23.0	−1.9	23.8	2.6	5.6	5.3	5.3	62,324	12.1
Poland	1.7	3.5	−9.1	6.4	−14.3	7.5	3.7	2.4	−2.2	−3.1	93,472	6.3
Portugal	−2.6	1.4	−11.7	7.4	−10.8	3.6	0.1	1.0	−10.3	−10.6	20,937	2.9
Romania	−8.5	−1.9	−11.8	12.0	−24.6	8.5	6.5	5.5	−4.5	−6.3	48,048	8.0
Russian Federation	−7.9	3.8	−4.7	5.2	−30.4	17.5	2.5	8.0	4.0	5.1	479,222	19.2
Saudi Arabia	0.6	3.7	−2.8	1.5	−8.8	7.5	−21.6	16.7	6.1	7.8	452,391	32.9
Senegal	2.2	4.0	−8.8	6.8	−17.1	4.0	−0.5	0.7	−13.6	−14.3	1,911	3.9
Singapore	−1.3	17.5	−10.1	29.7	−11.7	26.7	−1.8	−2.2	17.9	22.6	..	..
Slovak Republic	−6.2	3.7	8.8	6.9	8.4	6.0	0.0	2.9	−3.2	−0.1	2,156	0.3
Slovenia	−7.8	1.5	−19.3	1.4	−7.9	−4.1	1.9	−0.2	−1.5	−2.2	1,108	0.5
South Africa	−1.8	2.7	−19.5	6.5	−17.4	12.7	7.3	5.6	−4.0	−4.1	43,820	5.8
Spain	−3.6	−0.4	−11.6	7.8	−17.8	7.0	0.2	0.1	−5.5	−6.0	31,872	1.0
Sri Lanka	3.5	7.1	−12.3	2.0	−9.1	11.5	5.7	8.2	−0.5	−3.6	7,240	6.7
Sudan	4.5	5.9	−4.4	7.2	−7.3	7.2	−0.8	13.0	−7.1	−1.9	..	..
Sweden	−5.1	5.2	−13.3	12.2	−13.2	15.0	2.0	0.9	7.7	6.7	48,246	2.9
Switzerland	−1.9	2.7	−8.7	6.7	−5.4	8.3	0.3	0.9	7.9	7.7	269,396	14.5
Syrian Arab Republic	4.0	5.0	5.6	−2.0	6.4	4.5	−7.6	10.2	−4.5	−3.9	..	..
Tanzania	6.0	7.0	15.5	5.3	14.1	6.2	7.4	8.7	−8.5	−8.3	..	..
Thailand	−2.2	7.5	−12.7	21.0	−21.8	32.0	2.0	−1.9	8.3	6.0	172,028	10.4
Trinidad and Tobago	−3.0	2.2	−3.8	3.0	−4.1	4.2	−15.7	4.6	21.8	25.7	..	..
Tunisia	3.1	3.8	−1.6	13.0	6.7	16.1	2.9	3.8	−3.1	−4.8	..	..
Turkey	−4.7	8.1	−5.3	6.5	−14.3	16.0	5.2	7.1	−2.3	−5.9	85,959	5.3
Uganda	7.1	6.3	16.2	3.4	25.2	10.5	16.5	6.1	−2.8	−3.6	..	..
Ukraine	−15.1	4.3	−25.6	9.5	−38.6	5.5	13.4	9.2	−1.5	−2.2	34,571	7.2
United Kingdom	−4.9	1.7	−10.1	7.0	−12.3	9.4	1.4	3.0	−1.7	−2.9	82,365	1.4
United States	−2.6	2.8	−9.5	15.0	−13.8	18.8	0.9	0.6	−2.7	−3.3	488,928	2.3
Uruguay	2.9	7.9	2.5	15.6	−8.6	19.2	5.9	7.1	0.7	−0.6	7,744	9.7
Venezuela, RB	−3.3	−2.3	−12.9	3.2	−19.6	−3.0	8.4	38.5	2.6	5.9	27,700	5.9
Vietnam	5.3	6.7	11.1	25.0	6.7	32.5	6.0	12.5	−7.0	−15.5	..	..
Yemen, Rep.	3.8	8.0	−16.3	43.6	−4.7	14.2	−4.1	13.8	−9.7	−0.6	5,986	10.0
Zambia	6.4	6.4	21.5	20.0	15.6	12.3	12.7	−5.8	−3.2	−4.5	2,094	5.6
Zimbabwe	5.7	5.7	5.2	10.5	36.0	6.2	25.3	4.2	−1.8	−1.3	..	..

a. Data are preliminary estimates based on World Bank staff estimates and National Sources. b. Private analysts estimate that consumer price index inflation was considerably higher for 2007–09 and believe that GDP volume growth has been significantly higher than official reports indicate since the last quarter of 2008.

Source: World Development Indicators data files, the World Bank's *Global Economic Prospects 2011*, and the International Monetary Fund's *International Financial Statistics*.

4.1 Growth of output

	Gross domestic product		Agriculture		Industry		Manufacturing		Services	
	average annual % growth		average annual % growth		average annual % growth		average annual % growth		average annual % growth	
	1990–2000	2000–09	1990–2000	2000–09	1990–2000	2000–09	1990–2000	2000–09	1990–2000	2000–09
Afghanistan	..	10.5	..	4.9	..	14.5	..	8.7	..	13.5
Albania	3.8	5.4	4.3	1.4	−0.5	4.4	..	..	6.9	8.3
Algeria	1.9	4.0	3.6	4.6	1.8	3.3	−2.1	2.6	1.8	5.3
Angola[a]	1.6	13.1	−1.4	14.0	4.4	13.4	−0.3	20.2	−2.2	12.1
Argentina	4.3	5.4[b]	3.5	2.5	3.8	6.1	2.7	5.8	4.5	4.7
Armenia	−1.9	10.5	0.5	6.6	−7.8	11.3	−4.3	4.6	6.4	12.1
Australia	3.7	3.3	3.1	0.0	2.7	2.6	1.8	1.3	4.2	3.7
Austria	2.4	2.0	−0.1	1.3	2.5	2.3	2.5	2.9	2.5	2.1
Azerbaijan	−6.3	17.9	−1.7	5.3	−2.1	23.1	−15.7	10.8	−2.7	10.6
Bangladesh	4.8	5.9	2.9	3.3	7.3	7.8	7.2	7.9	4.5	6.1
Belarus	−1.6	8.4	−4.0	5.2	−1.8	12.3	−0.7	10.8	−0.4	5.9
Belgium	2.2	1.7	2.7	−1.0	1.8	0.7	..	..	2.0	2.0
Benin[a]	4.8	4.0	5.8	4.6	4.1	3.8	5.8	2.7	4.2	3.2
Bolivia	4.0	4.1	2.9	3.1	4.1	5.3	3.8	4.5	4.3	3.1
Bosnia and Herzegovina	..	5.0	..	4.9	..	6.8	..	7.6	..	4.4
Botswana	5.0	4.4	−0.5	1.2	3.7	2.5	4.7	4.8	9.1	5.6
Brazil	2.7	3.6	3.6	3.7	2.4	2.8	2.0	2.6	3.8	3.8
Bulgaria	−1.1	5.4	−3.9	−2.5	−19.5	5.9	..	6.2	..	6.1
Burkina Faso	5.5	5.4	5.9	6.2	5.9	7.3	5.9	6.3	3.9	5.5
Burundi	−2.9	3.0	−1.9	−1.5	−4.3	−6.2	..	..	−2.8	10.4
Cambodia	7.0	9.0	3.7	5.7	14.3	12.0	18.6	11.3	7.1	9.5
Cameroon	1.7	3.3	5.4	3.4	−0.9	−0.4	1.4	..	0.2	6.2
Canada	3.1	2.1	1.1	1.4	3.2	0.1	4.5	−1.6	3.1	3.0
Central African Republic	2.0	0.8	3.8	0.3	0.7	−0.4	−0.2	−0.1	0.2	−2.5
Chad	2.2	10.2	4.9	..	0.6	..	..	..	0.8	..
Chile	6.6	4.1	2.2	5.2	5.6	2.7	4.4	3.2	6.9	4.6
China[a]	10.6	10.9	4.1	4.4	13.7	11.8	12.9	11.4	11.0	11.6
Hong Kong SAR, China	3.6	4.7	..	−3.3	..	−2.6	..	..	..	5.3
Colombia	2.8	4.5	−2.7	2.5	1.4	4.4	−2.5	4.0	4.1	4.7
Congo, Dem. Rep.	−4.9	5.2	1.4	1.7	−8.0	8.7	−8.7	6.3	−13.0	11.2
Congo, Rep.[a]	1.0	4.0	..	..	..	..	..	..	..	..
Costa Rica	5.3	5.1	4.1	3.5	6.2	5.1	6.8	4.7	4.7	5.6
Côte d'Ivoire[a]	3.2	0.8	3.5	1.4	6.3	−0.2	5.5	−1.7	2.0	1.0
Croatia	0.5	3.9	−5.5	2.0	−2.2	4.6	−3.5	3.7	2.2	4.0
Cuba	−0.7	6.7	−3.3	−0.9	−1.0	2.3	0.8	−1.5	−0.7	8.3
Czech Republic	1.1	4.1	0.0	0.1	0.2	5.7	4.3	7.0	1.2	4.3
Denmark	2.7	1.2	4.6	−1.8	2.5	−0.5	2.2	0.4	2.7	1.5
Dominican Republic[a]	6.3	5.5	1.9	3.2	7.1	2.4	7.0	2.7	5.9	7.1
Ecuador	1.9	5.0	−1.7	3.7	2.6	4.2	1.5	5.3	2.4	3.6
Egypt, Arab Rep.	4.4	4.9	3.1	3.3	5.1	5.3	6.3	4.7	4.1	5.4
El Salvador	4.8	2.6	1.2	3.6	5.1	1.7	5.2	2.1	4.0	3.2
Eritrea	5.7	0.2	1.5	2.7	15.0	0.6	10.6	−6.0	5.7	0.5
Estonia	0.4	5.9	−6.2	−2.9	−2.4	8.6	7.3	8.9	3.2	7.1
Ethiopia	3.8	8.5	2.6	7.0	4.1	9.3	3.9	7.2	5.2	10.2
Finland	2.7	2.5	−0.3	2.4	3.8	3.6	6.4	4.1	2.6	1.6
France	1.9	1.5	2.0	0.3	1.1	0.5	..	0.1	2.2	1.9
Gabon[a]	2.3	2.1	2.0	1.4	1.6	0.9	3.0	3.1	3.1	3.2
Gambia, The	3.0	5.2	3.3	3.0	1.0	7.4	0.9	..	3.7	6.1
Georgia	−7.1	7.4	−11.0	0.6	−8.1	10.0	..	10.9	−0.3	8.9
Germany	1.8	1.0	0.1	−0.3	−0.1	0.3	0.1	0.8	2.9	1.5
Ghana	4.3	5.8	..	..	..	..	..	..	..	..
Greece	2.2	3.6	0.5	−1.4	1.0	1.4	..	1.7	2.6	4.7
Guatemala	4.2	3.7	2.8	2.9	4.3	2.8	2.8	2.8	4.7	4.4
Guinea	4.4	3.0	4.3	6.7	4.9	4.4	4.0	3.1	3.6	−2.7
Guinea-Bissau	1.2	1.0	..	..	..	..	..	..	..	..
Haiti	0.5	0.7	..	..	..	..	..	..	..	..
Honduras	3.2	4.9	2.2	3.3	3.6	4.1	4.0	4.6	3.8	6.2

Growth of output | 4.1

	Gross domestic product		Agriculture		Industry		Manufacturing		Services	
	average annual % growth		average annual % growth		average annual % growth		average annual % growth		average annual % growth	
	1990–2000	2000–09	1990–2000	2000–09	1990–2000	2000–09	1990–2000	2000–09	1990–2000	2000–09
Hungary	1.5	2.9	–1.9	5.3	3.5	3.5	7.7	5.0	1.3	3.4
India	5.9	7.9	3.2	2.9	6.1	8.6	6.7	8.7	7.7	9.5
Indonesia[a]	4.2	5.3	2.0	3.4	5.2	4.1	6.7	4.7	4.0	6.2
Iran, Islamic Rep.	3.1	5.4	3.2	5.9	2.6	6.9	5.1	9.9	3.8	5.3
Iraq	..	–0.3	..	..	..	..	..	..	..	..
Ireland	7.4	3.9	0.0	–4.6	11.6	4.0	..	..	8.7	4.4
Israel[a]	5.5	3.6	..	..	..	..	..	..	..	..
Italy	1.5	0.5	2.1	–0.2	1.0	–0.5	1.6	–1.1	1.6	1.0
Jamaica	1.6	1.5	–0.6	–0.7	–0.8	0.2	–1.8	–1.5	3.8	1.9
Japan	1.0	1.1	–1.3	–0.3	–0.3	1.7	0.5	2.8	1.8	1.5
Jordan	5.0	6.9	–3.0	8.3	5.2	8.4	5.6	9.6	5.0	6.1
Kazakhstan	–4.1	8.8	–8.0	4.6	–8.6	9.6	..	6.6	1.1	8.6
Kenya	2.2	4.4	1.9	2.2	1.2	4.8	1.3	4.3	3.2	4.5
Korea, Dem. Rep.	..	..	..	..	..	..	..	..	..	..
Korea, Rep.	5.8	4.2	1.6	2.0	6.0	5.4	7.3	6.3	5.6	3.7
Kosovo	..	4.8	..	..	..	..	..	..	..	..
Kuwait[a]	4.9	8.4	1.0	..	0.3	..	–0.1	..	3.5	..
Kyrgyz Republic	–4.1	4.6	1.5	1.8	–10.3	0.8	–7.5	–1.2	–5.2	7.9
Lao PDR	6.4	6.9	4.8	3.3	11.1	11.9	11.7	–1.9	6.6	7.6
Latvia	–1.5	6.2	–5.2	2.7	–8.3	5.2	–7.3	3.1	2.7	7.0
Lebanon	5.3	4.6	2.9	1.4	–0.2	4.4	1.9	2.2	1.5	4.3
Lesotho	4.0	3.1	2.8	–2.4	5.5	3.6	7.9	5.7	4.5	3.7
Liberia	4.1	0.0	..	..	..	..	..	..	..	..
Libya	..	5.4	..	..	..	..	..	..	..	..
Lithuania	–2.5	6.3	–0.4	1.7	3.3	9.6	6.6	9.0	5.8	7.4
Macedonia, FYR	–0.8	3.1	0.2	2.2	–2.3	3.5	–5.3	2.9	0.5	3.0
Madagascar	2.0	3.6	1.8	2.4	2.4	4.2	2.0	5.1	2.3	3.6
Malawi	3.7	4.8	8.6	2.4	2.0	5.5	0.5	5.0	1.6	6.5
Malaysia[a]	7.0	5.1	0.3	3.5	8.6	3.5	9.5	4.3	8.2	6.4
Mali	4.1	5.3	2.6	4.8	6.4	4.5	–1.4	5.1	3.0	6.5
Mauritania	2.9	4.7	–0.2	0.9	3.4	5.0	5.8	–1.4	4.9	5.5
Mauritius	5.2	3.7	0.0	–0.8	5.4	1.7	5.3	0.4	6.3	5.7
Mexico	3.1	2.2	1.5	2.0	3.8	1.3	4.3	1.1	2.9	2.6
Moldova	–9.6	5.6	–11.2	–0.6	–13.6	–1.7	–7.1	1.3	0.7	10.5
Mongolia	1.0	7.4	2.5	5.9	–2.5	6.5	–9.7	7.1	0.7	8.7
Morocco	2.4	5.0	–0.4	5.8	3.2	4.1	2.6	3.1	3.1	5.0
Mozambique	6.1	7.9	5.2	8.2	12.3	9.1	10.2	7.9	5.0	7.0
Myanmar[a]	..	..	..	..	..	..	..	..	..	..
Namibia	4.0	5.3	3.8	0.5	2.4	6.2	7.4	5.6	4.2	5.5
Nepal	4.9	3.7	2.5	3.1	7.1	2.8	8.9	1.0	6.2	4.1
Netherlands	3.2	1.7	1.8	1.5	1.7	0.9	2.6	1.2	3.6	2.1
New Zealand	3.2	2.5	2.9	1.8	2.5	1.9	..	..	3.6	3.4
Nicaragua	3.7	3.3	4.7	2.7	5.5	3.7	5.3	4.8	5.0	3.7
Niger[a]	2.4	4.3	3.0	..	2.0	..	2.6	..	1.9	..
Nigeria	2.5	6.6	..	..	..	..	..	..	..	..
Norway	3.9	2.1	2.6	2.4	3.8	–0.3	1.5	2.6	3.8	3.0
Oman[a]	4.5	4.5	5.0	..	3.9	..	6.0	..	5.0	..
Pakistan	3.8	5.2	4.4	3.5	4.1	6.8	3.8	8.7	4.4	5.9
Panama	4.7	6.9	3.1	3.5	6.0	5.7	2.7	1.5	4.5	7.4
Papua New Guinea	3.8	3.4	4.5	2.2	5.4	4.1	4.6	3.8	–0.6	3.8
Paraguay[a]	2.2	3.4	3.3	2.3	0.6	1.8	1.4	1.2	2.5	4.3
Peru	4.7	6.0	5.5	4.1	5.4	6.5	3.8	6.2	4.0	6.0
Philippines[a]	3.3	4.9	1.7	3.6	3.5	4.0	3.0	3.9	4.0	6.1
Poland	4.7	4.4	0.5	0.8	7.1	5.8	9.9	8.5	5.1	3.7
Portugal	2.9	0.8	–0.6	–0.3	3.1	–0.8	2.7	–0.6	2.5	1.6
Puerto Rico[a]	4.2	..	..	..	..	..	..	..	..	..
Qatar	..	14.2	..	..	..	..	..	..	..	..

	Gross domestic product		Agriculture		Industry		Manufacturing		Services	
	average annual % growth		average annual % growth		average annual % growth		average annual % growth		average annual % growth	
	1990–2000	2000–09	1990–2000	2000–09	1990–2000	2000–09	1990–2000	2000–09	1990–2000	2000–09
Romania	−0.6	5.6	−1.9	7.3	−1.2	6.0	..	..	0.9	5.2
Russian Federation	−4.7	6.0	−4.9	2.1	−7.1	4.6	..	..	−1.7	7.0
Rwanda[a]	−0.2	7.6	2.5	..	−3.8	..	−5.8	..	−0.9	..
Saudi Arabia[a]	2.1	3.8	1.6	1.4	2.2	3.6	5.6	5.9	2.2	4.2
Senegal	3.0	4.3	2.4	2.0	3.8	3.3	3.1	1.4	3.0	6.3
Serbia	−4.2	5.0	..	..	..	..	..	..	..	..
Sierra Leone	−5.0	9.5	..	..	..	..	..	..	..	..
Singapore	7.6	6.5	..	2.3	7.8	5.4	..	..	7.8	6.2
Slovak Republic	2.2	5.8	0.2	5.0	3.7	10.5	9.3	10.7	5.4	2.4
Slovenia	2.7	3.8	0.4	−0.7	1.6	4.1	1.8	3.7	3.3	4.0
Somalia	..	..	..	..	..	..	..	..	..	..
South Africa	2.1	4.1	1.0	1.5	1.0	2.9	1.6	3.1	3.0	4.1
Spain	2.7	2.8	3.1	−0.2	2.3	1.3	5.2	−0.2	2.7	3.5
Sri Lanka[a]	5.3	5.5	1.8	2.8	6.9	5.5	8.1	4.4	5.7	6.2
Sudan	5.5	7.3	7.4	2.4	8.5	10.2	7.5	4.4	1.9	10.1
Swaziland	3.4	2.6	0.9	1.3	3.2	1.7	2.8	1.8	3.9	3.9
Sweden	2.3	2.4	−0.8	3.5	4.6	2.8	8.9	3.3	1.8	2.2
Switzerland	1.0	1.9	−0.9	0.3	0.3	2.1	1.0	2.5	1.2	1.8
Syrian Arab Republic	5.1	4.4	6.0	3.8	9.2	2.4	..	14.5	1.5	7.7
Tajikistan	−10.4	8.2	−6.8	7.7	−11.4	9.2	−12.6	8.6	−10.8	8.3
Tanzania[c]	3.0	7.1	3.2	4.4	3.1	9.5	2.8	8.7	2.6	7.8
Thailand[a]	4.2	4.6	1.0	2.3	5.7	5.6	6.9	6.6	3.7	4.2
Timor-Leste[a]	..	2.4	..	..	..	..	..	..	..	..
Togo[a]	3.5	2.5	4.0	2.8	1.8	8.1	1.8	7.5	3.9	−0.7
Trinidad and Tobago	3.2	7.4	2.7	−7.2	3.2	10.2	4.9	9.5	3.2	5.3
Tunisia[a]	4.7	4.9	2.3	2.6	4.6	3.6	5.5	3.6	5.3	5.9
Turkey	3.9	4.9	1.3	1.5	4.7	5.4	4.7	5.3	4.0	5.3
Turkmenistan	−4.9	13.9	−4.7	14.3	−2.7	30.3	..	..	−5.8	16.0
Uganda	7.2	7.8	3.9	2.3	12.0	9.5	13.9	6.7	8.3	8.5
Ukraine	−9.3	5.6	−5.6	3.1	−12.6	4.6	−11.2	7.8	−8.1	5.8
United Arab Emirates	4.8	7.0	13.2	3.6	3.0	6.0	11.9	8.1	7.2	9.5
United Kingdom	2.8	2.0	−1.3	0.6	1.3	−0.6	..	..	3.5	2.9
United States	3.6	2.0	3.8	2.1	3.8	0.9	..	2.4	3.6	2.3
Uruguay	3.3	3.4	2.6	2.9	1.1	4.0	−0.1	6.2	1.5	3.4
Uzbekistan	−0.2	6.9	0.5	6.5	−3.4	4.7	0.7	2.3	0.4	8.5
Venezuela, RB	1.6	4.9	1.2	3.6	1.2	3.3	4.5	3.6	−0.1	5.9
Vietnam[a]	7.9	7.6	4.3	3.8	11.9	9.6	11.2	11.3	7.5	7.5
West Bank and Gaza	7.3	−0.9	..	..	..	..	..	..	..	..
Yemen, Rep.[a]	6.0	3.9	5.6	..	8.2	..	5.7	..	5.0	..
Zambia	0.5	5.4	4.2	1.2	−4.2	9.2	0.8	5.0	2.5	5.6
Zimbabwe	2.3	−7.5	4.3	−10.8	0.4	−5.8	0.4	−6.6	3.0	−4.8
World	**2.9 w**	**2.9 w**	**1.9 w**	**2.5 w**	**2.4 w**	**2.8 w**	**.. w**	**4.0 w**	**3.2 w**	**2.9 w**
Low income	3.1	5.4	2.9	3.6	3.4	7.4	3.7	6.4	2.9	5.9
Middle income	3.9	6.4	2.4	3.6	4.5	7.2	6.2	7.6	4.3	6.6
Lower middle income	6.5	8.5	3.1	3.8	8.7	9.6	9.2	9.8	6.8	9.3
Upper middle income	2.1	4.4	0.9	3.0	1.3	3.9	3.3	3.6	3.0	4.5
Low & middle income	3.9	6.4	2.4	3.6	4.5	7.2	6.2	7.6	4.3	6.6
East Asia & Pacific	8.5	9.4	3.4	4.1	11.0	10.2	10.9	10.2	8.6	10.0
Europe & Central Asia	−1.8	5.9	−2.1	3.0	−4.3	6.2	..	..	0.3	6.3
Latin America & Carib.	3.2	3.8	2.0	3.0	3.0	3.2	2.9	2.9	3.5	3.9
Middle East & N. Africa	3.8	4.7	2.9	4.4	4.2	3.6	4.3	6.0	3.3	5.5
South Asia	5.5	7.3	3.3	3.0	6.0	8.2	6.4	8.5	6.9	8.7
Sub-Saharan Africa	2.5	5.1	3.2	3.2	1.9	4.9	2.2	3.4	2.6	4.8
High income	2.7	2.0	1.2	0.9	1.9	1.1	..	2.9	3.0	2.2
Euro area	2.1	1.5	1.5	0.0	1.1	0.7	2.4	0.5	2.5	1.9

a. Components are at producer prices. b. Private analysts estimate that consumer price index inflation was considerably higher for 2007–09 and believe that GDP volume growth has been significantly higher than official reports indicate since the last quarter of 2008. c. Covers mainland Tanzania only.

Growth of output | 4.1

An economy's growth is measured by the change in the volume of its output or in the real incomes of its residents. The 1993 United Nations System of National Accounts (1993 SNA) offers three plausible indicators for calculating growth: the volume of gross domestic product (GDP), real gross domestic income, and real gross national income. The volume of GDP is the sum of value added, measured at constant prices, by households, government, and industries operating in the economy.

Each industry's contribution to growth in the economy's output is measured by growth in the industry's value added. In principle, value added in constant prices can be estimated by measuring the quantity of goods and services produced in a period, valuing them at an agreed set of base year prices, and subtracting the cost of intermediate inputs, also in constant prices. This double-deflation method, recommended by the 1993 SNA and its predecessors, requires detailed information on the structure of prices of inputs and outputs.

In many industries, however, value added is extrapolated from the base year using single volume indexes of outputs or, less commonly, inputs. Particularly in the services industries, including most of government, value added in constant prices is often imputed from labor inputs, such as real wages or number of employees. In the absence of well defined measures of output, measuring the growth of services remains difficult.

Moreover, technical progress can lead to improvements in production processes and in the quality of goods and services that, if not properly accounted for, can distort measures of value added and thus of growth. When inputs are used to estimate output, as for nonmarket services, unmeasured technical progress leads to underestimates of the volume of output. Similarly, unmeasured improvements in quality lead to underestimates of the value of output and value added. The result can be underestimates of growth and productivity improvement and overestimates of inflation.

Informal economic activities pose a particular measurement problem, especially in developing countries, where much economic activity is unrecorded. A complete picture of the economy requires estimating household outputs produced for home use, sales in informal markets, barter exchanges, and illicit or deliberately unreported activities. The consistency and completeness of such estimates depend on the skill and methods of the compiling statisticians.

Rebasing national accounts

When countries rebase their national accounts, they update the weights assigned to various components to better reflect current patterns of production or uses of output. The new base year should represent normal operation of the economy—it should be a year without major shocks or distortions. Some developing countries have not rebased their national accounts for many years. Using an old base year can be misleading because implicit price and volume weights become progressively less relevant and useful.

To obtain comparable series of constant price data, the World Bank rescales GDP and value added by industrial origin to a common reference year. This year's *World Development Indicators* continues to use 2000 as the reference year. Because rescaling changes the implicit weights used in forming regional and income group aggregates, aggregate growth rates in this year's edition are not comparable with those from earlier editions with different base years.

Rescaling may result in a discrepancy between the rescaled GDP and the sum of the rescaled components. Because allocating the discrepancy would cause distortions in the growth rates, the discrepancy is left unallocated. As a result, the weighted average of the growth rates of the components generally will not equal the GDP growth rate.

Computing growth rates

Growth rates of GDP and its components are calculated using the least squares method and constant price data in the local currency. Constant price U.S. dollar series are used to calculate regional and income group growth rates. Local currency series are converted to constant U.S. dollars using an exchange rate in the common reference year. The growth rates in the table are average annual compound growth rates. Methods of computing growth are described in *Statistical methods*.

Changes in the System of National Accounts

World Development Indicators adopted the terminology of the 1993 SNA in 2001. Although many countries continue to compile their national accounts according to the SNA version 3 (referred to as the 1968 SNA), more and more are adopting the 1993 SNA. Some low-income countries still use concepts from the even older 1953 SNA guidelines, including valuations such as factor cost, in describing major economic aggregates. Countries that use the 1993 SNA are identified in *Primary data documentation*.

• **Gross domestic product (GDP)** at purchaser prices is the sum of gross value added by all resident producers in the economy plus any product taxes (less subsidies) not included in the valuation of output. It is calculated without deducting for depreciation of fabricated capital assets or for depletion and degradation of natural resources. Value added is the net output of an industry after adding up all outputs and subtracting intermediate inputs. The industrial origin of value added is determined by the International Standard Industrial Classification (ISIC) revision 3. • **Agriculture** is the sum of gross output less the value of intermediate input used in production for industries classified in ISIC divisions 1–5 and includes forestry and fishing. • **Industry** is the sum of gross output less the value of intermediate input used in production for industries classified in ISIC divisions 10–45, which cover mining, manufacturing (also reported separately), construction, electricity, water, and gas. • **Manufacturing** is the sum of gross output less the value of intermediate input used in production for industries classified in ISIC divisions 15–37. • **Services** correspond to ISIC divisions 50–99. This sector is derived as a residual (from GDP less agriculture and industry) and may not properly reflect the sum of services output, including banking and financial services. For some countries it includes product taxes (minus subsidies) and may also include statistical discrepancies.

Data on national accounts for most developing countries are collected from national statistical organizations and central banks by visiting and resident World Bank missions. Data for high income economies are from Organisation for Economic Co-operation and Development (OECD) data files. The United Nations Statistics Division publishes detailed national accounts for UN member countries in *National Accounts Statistics: Main Aggregates and Detailed Tables* and publishes updates in the *Monthly Bulletin of Statistics*.

	Gross domestic product		Agriculture		Industry		Manufacturing		Services	
	$ millions		% of GDP		% of GDP		% of GDP		% of GDP	
	1995	**2009**	**1995**	**2009**	**1995**	**2009**	**1995**	**2009**	**1995**	**2009**
Afghanistan	..	14,483	..	33	..	22	..	13	..	45
Albania	2,424	12,015	56	21	23	20	14	20	22	60
Algeria	41,764	140,577	11	12	50	55	12	6	39	34
Angola[a]	5,040	75,493	7	10	66	59	4	6	26	31
Argentina	258,032	307,155	6	8	28	32	18	21	66	61
Armenia	1,468	8,714	42	21	32	35	25	16	26	45
Australia	371,091	924,843	3	3	29	29	15	10	68	68
Austria	238,314	381,084	3	2	31	29	20	19	67	69
Azerbaijan	3,052	43,019	27	8	34	60	13	4	39	32
Bangladesh	37,940	89,360	26	19	25	29	15	18	49	53
Belarus	13,973	49,037	17	10	37	42	31	30	46	48
Belgium	284,142	471,161	2	1	28	22	20	14	70	78
Benin[a]	2,009	6,656	34	..	15	..	9	..	51	..
Bolivia	6,715	17,340	17	14	33	36	19	14	50	50
Bosnia and Herzegovina	1,867	17,042	21	8	26	28	11	13	54	64
Botswana	4,774	11,823	4	3	51	40	5	4	45	57
Brazil	768,951	1,594,490	6	6	28	25	19	16	67	69
Bulgaria	13,069	48,722	16	6	28	30	26	15	56	64
Burkina Faso	2,380	8,141	35	..	21	..	15	..	43	..
Burundi	1,000	1,325	48	..	19	..	9	..	33	..
Cambodia	3,441	10,447	50	35	15	23	10	15	36	42
Cameroon	8,733	22,186	24	19	31	31	22	17	45	50
Canada	590,517	1,336,068	3	..	31	..	18	..	66	..
Central African Republic	1,122	2,006	46	56	21	15	10	..	33	30
Chad	1,446	6,839	36	14	14	49	11	7	51	38
Chile	71,349	163,669	9	3	35	42	18	13	55	55
China[a]	728,007	4,985,461	20	10	47	46	34	34	33	43
Hong Kong SAR, China	144,230	210,568	..	..	15	8	8	2	85	92
Colombia	92,507	234,045	15	7	32	34	16	14	53	58
Congo, Dem. Rep.	5,643	10,575	57	43	17	24	9	5	26	33
Congo, Rep.[a]	2,116	9,580	10	5	45	71	8	4	45	24
Costa Rica	11,722	29,240	14	7	30	27	22	19	57	66
Côte d'Ivoire[a]	11,000	23,304	25	24	21	25	15	18	55	50
Croatia	22,046	63,034	7	7	32	27	23	16	61	66
Cuba	30,428	62,705	9	5	23	20	15	10	68	75
Czech Republic	55,257	190,274	5	2	38	37	24	23	57	61
Denmark	181,984	309,596	3	1	25	22	17	13	71	77
Dominican Republic[a]	16,358	46,788	10	6	36	32	26	24	54	61
Ecuador	20,206	57,249	..	6	..	23	..	10	..	71
Egypt, Arab Rep.	60,159	188,413	17	14	32	37	17	16	51	49
El Salvador	9,500	21,101	14	12	30	27	23	21	56	60
Eritrea	578	1,873	21	14	17	22	9	6	62	63
Estonia	4,353	19,084	6	3	33	29	21	17	61	68
Ethiopia	7,606	28,526	57	51	10	11	5	4	33	39
Finland	130,700	237,989	4	3	33	28	25	18	62	69
France	1,569,983	2,649,390	3	2	25	19	..	11	72	79
Gabon[a]	4,959	11,062	8	5	52	54	5	4	40	41
Gambia, The	382	733	30	27	13	15	6	5	57	57
Georgia	2,694	10,744	52	10	16	21	11	12	32	69
Germany	2,522,792	3,330,032	1	1	32	26	23	19	67	73
Ghana	6,457	26,169	43	32	27	19	10	7	31	49
Greece	131,718	329,924	9	3	21	18	..	10	70	79
Guatemala	14,657	37,322	24	12	20	28	14	20	56	59
Guinea	3,694	4,103	19	17	29	53	4	5	52	30
Guinea-Bissau	254	837	55	55	12	13	8	10	33	32
Haiti	2,695	6,479	..	..	..	..	..	..	..	..
Honduras	3,911	14,318	22	12	31	27	18	19	48	60

	Gross domestic product		Agriculture		Industry		Manufacturing		Services	
	$ millions		% of GDP		% of GDP		% of GDP		% of GDP	
	1995	2009	1995	2009	1995	2009	1995	2009	1995	2009
Hungary	44,656	128,964	7	4	32	29	24	22	61	66
India	356,299	1,377,265	26	18	28	27	18	15	46	55
Indonesia[a]	202,132	540,274	17	16	42	49	24	27	41	35
Iran, Islamic Rep.	90,829	331,015	18	10	34	44	12	11	47	45
Iraq	10,114	65,837	9	..	75	..	1	..	16	..
Ireland	67,061	227,193	7	1	38	31	30	24	55	68
Israel[a]	96,065	195,392	..	..	..	..	..	..	..	..
Italy	1,126,041	2,112,780	3	2	30	25	22	16	66	73
Jamaica	5,813	12,070	9	6	37	22	16	9	54	72
Japan	5,264,380	5,068,996	2	1	34	28	23	20	64	71
Jordan	6,727	25,092	4	3	29	32	15	20	67	65
Kazakhstan	20,374	115,306	13	6	31	40	15	11	56	53
Kenya	9,046	29,376	31	23	16	15	10	9	53	62
Korea, Dem. Rep.	..	..	..	..	..	..	..	..	..	..
Korea, Rep.	517,118	832,512	6	3	42	37	28	28	52	61
Kosovo	..	5,387	..	12	..	20	..	17	..	68
Kuwait[a]	27,192	148,024	0	..	55	..	4	..	45	..
Kyrgyz Republic	1,661	4,578	44	29	20	19	9	13	37	51
Lao PDR	1,764	5,939	56	35	19	28	14	9	25	37
Latvia	5,236	26,195	9	3	30	20	21	10	61	77
Lebanon	11,719	34,528	8	5	25	17	14	9	68	78
Lesotho	814	1,579	19	8	43	34	17	17	38	58
Liberia	135	876	82	61	5	17	3	13	13	22
Libya	25,541	62,360	..	2	..	78	..	4	..	20
Lithuania	7,905	37,206	11	4	31	31	19	18	58	64
Macedonia, FYR	4,449	9,221	13	11	30	36	23	23	57	52
Madagascar	3,160	8,590	27	29	9	16	8	14	64	55
Malawi	1,397	4,727	30	31	20	16	16	10	50	53
Malaysia[a]	88,832	193,093	13	10	41	44	26	25	46	46
Mali	2,466	8,996	50	37	19	24	8	3	32	..
Mauritania	1,415	3,024	37	21	25	35	8	4	37	45
Mauritius	4,040	8,589	10	4	32	29	23	19	58	67
Mexico	286,698	874,810	6	4	28	35	21	17	66	61
Moldova	1,753	5,405	33	10	32	13	26	13	35	77
Mongolia	1,227	4,202	41	24	29	33	12	5	30	44
Morocco	32,986	91,375	15	16	34	29	19	16	51	55
Mozambique	2,247	9,790	35	31	15	24	8	14	51	45
Myanmar[a]	..	..	60	..	10	..	7	..	30	..
Namibia	3,503	9,265	12	9	28	33	13	15	60	58
Nepal	4,401	12,531	42	34	23	16	10	7	35	50
Netherlands	418,969	792,128	3	2	27	24	17	13	69	74
New Zealand	62,795	126,679	7	..	27	..	18	..	66	..
Nicaragua	3,191	6,140	23	19	27	30	19	20	49	51
Niger[a]	1,881	5,383	40	..	17	..	6	..	43	..
Nigeria	28,109	173,004	..	33	..	41	..	..	..	27
Norway	148,920	381,766	3	1	34	40	13	10	63	59
Oman[a]	13,803	46,114	3	..	46	..	5	..	51	..
Pakistan	60,636	161,990	26	22	24	24	16	17	50	54
Panama	7,906	24,711	8	6	18	17	9	6	74	77
Papua New Guinea	4,636	7,893	35	36	34	45	8	6	31	20
Paraguay[a]	8,066	14,236	21	19	23	21	16	13	56	59
Peru	53,674	130,325	9	7	31	34	17	14	60	59
Philippines[a]	74,120	161,196	22	15	32	30	23	20	46	55
Poland	139,062	430,076	8	4	35	30	21	16	57	66
Portugal	116,419	232,874	6	2	28	23	19	13	66	75
Puerto Rico[a]	42,647	..	1	..	44	..	42	..	55	..
Qatar	8,138	98,313	..	..	..	..	..	..	..	..

	Gross domestic product		Agriculture		Industry		Manufacturing		Services	
	$ millions		% of GDP		% of GDP		% of GDP		% of GDP	
	1995	**2009**	**1995**	**2009**	**1995**	**2009**	**1995**	**2009**	**1995**	**2009**
Romania	35,477	161,110	21	7	43	26	29	22	36	67
Russian Federation	395,528	1,231,893	7	5	37	33	..	15	56	62
Rwanda[a]	1,293	5,216	44	34	16	15	10	6	40	51
Saudi Arabia[a]	142,458	375,766	6	3	49	51	10	10	45	46
Senegal	4,879	12,822	21	17	24	22	17	13	55	62
Serbia	21,381	42,984	..	13	..	28	..	..	..	59
Sierra Leone	871	1,942	43	51	39	22	9	..	18	27
Singapore	84,291	182,232	..	..	35	26	27	19	65	74
Slovak Republic	25,240	87,642	6	3	38	35	27	19	56	63
Slovenia	20,814	48,477	4	2	35	34	26	22	60	64
Somalia	..	..	..	..	..	..	..	..	..	..
South Africa	151,113	285,366	4	3	35	31	21	15	61	66
Spain	596,751	1,460,250	5	3	29	26	18	13	66	71
Sri Lanka[a]	13,030	41,979	23	13	27	30	16	18	50	58
Sudan	13,830	54,681	39	30	11	26	5	7	51	44
Swaziland	1,699	3,001	12	7	45	49	39	44	43	43
Sweden	253,680	406,072	3	2	30	25	22	16	66	73
Switzerland	315,940	491,924	2	1	30	27	20	19	68	72
Syrian Arab Republic	11,397	52,177	32	21	20	34	15	13	48	45
Tajikistan	1,232	4,978	38	22	39	24	28	11	22	54
Tanzania[b]	5,255	21,368	47	29	15	24	7	10	38	47
Thailand[a]	168,019	263,772	10	12	41	43	30	34	50	45
Timor-Leste[a]	..	558	..	..	..	..	..	..	..	..
Togo[a]	1,309	2,855	38	..	22	..	10	..	40	..
Trinidad and Tobago	5,329	21,204	2	0	47	52	9	6	51	47
Tunisia[a]	18,031	39,561	11	8	29	30	19	17	59	62
Turkey	169,486	614,603	16	9	33	26	23	17	50	65
Turkmenistan	2,482	19,947	17	12	63	54	40	47	20	34
Uganda	5,756	16,043	49	25	14	26	7	8	36	50
Ukraine	48,214	113,545	15	8	43	29	35	18	42	62
United Arab Emirates	42,807	230,252	3	2	52	61	10	12	45	38
United Kingdom	1,157,119	2,174,530	2	1	31	21	21	11	67	78
United States	7,359,300	14,119,000	2	1	26	21	19	13	72	77
Uruguay	19,298	31,511	9	10	29	26	20	16	62	64
Uzbekistan	13,350	32,104	32	20	28	33	12	13	40	47
Venezuela, RB	74,889	326,133	6	..	41	..	15	..	53	..
Vietnam[a]	20,736	97,180	27	21	29	40	15	20	44	39
West Bank and Gaza	3,220	..	..	..	..	..	..	..	..	..
Yemen, Rep.[a]	4,236	26,365	20	..	32	..	14	..	48	..
Zambia	3,478	12,805	18	22	36	34	11	10	46	44
Zimbabwe	7,111	5,625	15	18	29	29	22	17	56	53
World	**29,692,820 t**	**58,259,785 t**	**4 w**	**3 w**	**30 w**	**27 w**	**21 w**	**17 w**	**65 w**	**70 w**
Low income	153,755	432,171	37	26	20	24	11	12	43	50
Middle income	4,811,047	16,213,154	14	10	35	35	23	21	51	55
Lower middle income	1,992,261	8,887,269	21	13	39	39	26	26	40	48
Upper middle income	2,818,895	7,318,398	8	6	32	31	19	17	60	62
Low & middle income	4,965,895	16,657,552	15	10	34	35	22	21	51	55
East Asia & Pacific	1,312,902	6,353,790	19	11	44	45	31	32	36	43
Europe & Central Asia	763,913	2,591,705	14	8	35	30	22	17	51	62
Latin America & Carib.	1,770,557	4,017,912	7	6	29	31	19	17	64	63
Middle East & N. Africa	315,651	1,062,419	16	11	34	43	15	12	50	46
South Asia	476,175	1,700,339	26	18	27	27	17	15	46	55
Sub-Saharan Africa	327,608	945,923	18	13	29	30	16	13	53	57
High income	24,722,778	41,607,730	2	1	30	25	20	16	68	74
Euro area	7,286,803	12,465,331	3	2	29	24	21	15	68	74

a. Components are at producer prices. b. Covers mainland Tanzania only.

About the data

An economy's gross domestic product (GDP) represents the sum of value added by all its producers. Value added is the value of the gross output of producers less the value of intermediate goods and services consumed in production, before accounting for consumption of fixed capital in production. The United Nations System of National Accounts calls for value added to be valued at either basic prices (excluding net taxes on products) or producer prices (including net taxes on products paid by producers but excluding sales or value added taxes). Both valuations exclude transport charges that are invoiced separately by producers. Total GDP shown in the table and elsewhere in this volume is measured at purchaser prices. Value added by industry is normally measured at basic prices. When value added is measured at producer prices, this is noted in *Primary data documentation* and footnoted in the table.

While GDP estimates based on the production approach are generally more reliable than estimates compiled from the income or expenditure side, different countries use different definitions, methods, and reporting standards. World Bank staff review the quality of national accounts data and sometimes make adjustments to improve consistency with international guidelines. Nevertheless, significant discrepancies remain between international standards and actual practice. Many statistical offices, especially those in developing countries, face severe limitations in the resources, time, training, and budgets required to produce reliable and comprehensive series of national accounts statistics.

Data problems in measuring output

Among the difficulties faced by compilers of national accounts is the extent of unreported economic activity in the informal or secondary economy. In developing countries a large share of agricultural output is either not exchanged (because it is consumed within the household) or not exchanged for money.

Agricultural production often must be estimated indirectly, using a combination of methods involving estimates of inputs, yields, and area under cultivation. This approach sometimes leads to crude approximations that can differ from the true values over time and across crops for reasons other than climate conditions or farming techniques. Similarly, agricultural inputs that cannot easily be allocated to specific outputs are frequently "netted out" using equally crude and ad hoc approximations. For further discussion of the measurement of agricultural production, see *About the data* for table 3.3.

Ideally, industrial output should be measured through regular censuses and surveys of firms. But in most developing countries such surveys are infrequent, so earlier survey results must be extrapolated using an appropriate indicator. The choice of sampling unit, which may be the enterprise (where responses may be based on financial records) or the establishment (where production units may be recorded separately), also affects the quality of the data. Moreover, much industrial production is organized in unincorporated or owner-operated ventures that are not captured by surveys aimed at the formal sector. Even in large industries, where regular surveys are more likely, evasion of excise and other taxes and nondisclosure of income lower the estimates of value added. Such problems become more acute as countries move from state control of industry to private enterprise, because new firms and growing numbers of established firms fail to report. In accordance with the System of National Accounts, output should include all such unreported activity as well as the value of illegal activities and other unrecorded, informal, or small-scale operations. Data on these activities need to be collected using techniques other than conventional surveys of firms.

In industries dominated by large organizations and enterprises, such as public utilities, data on output, employment, and wages are usually readily available and reasonably reliable. But in the services industry the many self-employed workers and one-person businesses are sometimes difficult to locate, and they have little incentive to respond to surveys, let alone to report their full earnings. Compounding these problems are the many forms of economic activity that go unrecorded, including the work that women and children do for little or no pay. For further discussion of the problems of using national accounts data, see Srinivasan (1994) and Heston (1994).

Dollar conversion

To produce national accounts aggregates that are measured in the same standard monetary units, the value of output must be converted to a single common currency. The World Bank conventionally uses the U.S. dollar and applies the average official exchange rate reported by the International Monetary Fund for the year shown. An alternative conversion factor is applied if the official exchange rate is judged to diverge by an exceptionally large margin from the rate effectively applied to transactions in foreign currencies and traded products.

Definitions

• **Gross domestic product (GDP)** at purchaser prices is the sum of gross value added by all resident producers in the economy plus any product taxes (less subsidies) not included in the valuation of output. It is calculated without deducting for depreciation of fabricated assets or for depletion and degradation of natural resources. Value added is the net output of an industry after adding up all outputs and subtracting intermediate inputs. The industrial origin of value added is determined by the International Standard Industrial Classification (ISIC) revision 3. • **Agriculture** is the sum of gross output less the value of intermediate input used in production for industries classified in ISIC divisions 1–5 and includes forestry and fishing. • **Industry** is the sum of gross output less the value of intermediate input used in production for industries classified in ISIC divisions 10–45, which cover mining, manufacturing (also reported separately), construction, electricity, water, and gas. • **Manufacturing** is the sum of gross output less the value of intermediate input used in production for industries classified in ISIC divisions 15–37. • **Services** correspond to ISIC divisions 50–99. This sector is derived as a residual (from GDP less agriculture and industry) and may not properly reflect the sum of services output, including banking and financial services. For some countries it includes product taxes (minus subsidies) and may also include statistical discrepancies.

Data sources

Data on national accounts for most developing countries are collected from national statistical organizations and central banks by visiting and resident World Bank missions. Data for high income economies are from Organisation for Economic Co-operation and Development (OECD) data files. The United Nations Statistics Division publishes detailed national accounts for UN member countries in *National Accounts Statistics: Main Aggregates and Detailed Tables* and publishes updates in the *Monthly Bulletin of Statistics*.

	Manufacturing value added		Food, beverages, and tobacco		Textiles and clothing		Machinery and transport equipment		Chemicals		Other manufacturing[a]	
	$ millions		% of total		% of total		% of total		% of total		% of total	
	1998	2009	1998	2007	1998	2007	1998	2007	1998	2007	1998	2007
Afghanistan	..	1,632	..	..	..	..	..	..	..	..	..	..
Albania	268	1,995	20	17	27	22	3	3	5	17	46	41
Algeria	4,372	7,315	33	..	8	..	..	..	11	..	48	..
Angola	407	4,586	..	..	..	..	..	..	..	..	..	..
Argentina	53,326	60,116	26	..	8	..	13	..	15	..	38	..
Armenia	377	1,213	..	..	..	..	..	..	..	..	..	..
Australia	51,505	95,726	..	19	..	3	..	14	..	7	..	58
Austria	37,828	64,124	10	9	5	2	24	28	7	7	54	54
Azerbaijan	370	1,927	..	18	..	1	..	9	..	5	..	66
Bangladesh	6,887	15,472	24	..	40	..	3	..	11	..	21	..
Belarus	4,487	12,638	..	..	..	..	..	..	..	..	..	..
Belgium	45,588	59,032	13	12	6	4	19	19	18	23	44	43
Benin	200	..	..	..	..	..	..	..	..	..	..	..
Bolivia	1,189	2,014	35	..	5	..	0	..	5	..	55	..
Bosnia and Herzegovina	497	1,816	..	..	..	..	..	..	..	..	..	..
Botswana	253	475	23	22	8	5	15	..	5	..	69	73
Brazil	117,276	216,924	20	18	7	6	20	21	13	11	40	44
Bulgaria	2,180	6,424	22	16	13	12	18	14	9	7	39	50
Burkina Faso	387	..	..	..	..	..	..	..	..	..	..	..
Burundi	64	..	..	..	..	..	..	..	..	..	..	..
Cambodia	436	1,403	7	..	87	..	0	..	0	..	7	..
Cameroon	1,843	3,328	35	..	9	..	1	..	6	..	49	..
Canada	104,352	172,050	14	..	4	..	29	..	9	..	44	..
Central African Republic	91	..	..	..	..	..	..	..	..	..	..	..
Chad	188	381	..	..	..	..	..	..	..	..	..	..
Chile	13,540	19,665	32	14	4	2	3	2	10	14	52	69
China	324,603	1,691,153	16	12	12	10	15	24	11	11	46	43
Hong Kong SAR, China	8,868	4,971	12	14	22	12	15	13	3	5	49	55
Colombia	13,770	30,690	32	27	10	9	5	6	17	13	36	45
Congo, Dem. Rep.	370	582	..	..	..	..	..	..	..	..	..	..
Congo, Rep.	136	429	..	..	..	..	..	..	..	..	..	..
Costa Rica	2,972	5,034	46	44	8	5	3	3	11	10	32	39
Côte d'Ivoire	2,499	4,187	42	..	10	..	2	..	12	..	34	..
Croatia	4,163	8,789	..	..	..	..	..	..	..	..	..	..
Cuba	3,103	4,955	..	..	..	..	..	..	..	..	..	..
Czech Republic	14,416	39,662	13	9	6	3	23	29	6	6	52	53
Denmark	24,894	34,971	19	17	3	2	22	19	10	13	46	50
Dominican Republic	5,136	10,577	..	..	..	..	..	..	..	..	..	..
Ecuador	2,912	5,316	22	30	3	4	2	3	3	5	69	58
Egypt, Arab Rep.	14,403	28,712	16	..	16	..	12	..	21	..	35	..
El Salvador	2,569	4,319	29	..	28	..	2	..	16	..	25	..
Eritrea	64	102	49	44	12	19	1	1	6	5	31	31
Estonia	870	2,393	17	12	15	4	10	10	4	4	53	69
Ethiopia	373	1,071	55	41	13	9	1	5	7	5	24	40
Finland	29,158	37,557	8	6	2	2	30	32	6	6	54	54
France	209,123	253,608	13	14	5	3	26	24	12	13	44	45
Gabon	252	479	..	..	..	..	..	..	..	..	..	..
Gambia, The	22	32	..	..	..	..	..	..	..	..	..	..
Georgia	307	1,073	37	34	1	2	12	6	7	8	43	50
Germany	449,216	567,902	8	8	3	2	35	36	10	10	44	45
Ghana	672	1,759	..	..	..	..	..	..	..	..	..	..
Greece	12,338	29,718	24	22	12	8	11	10	10	6	43	54
Guatemala	2,631	6,937	..	..	..	..	..	..	..	..	..	..
Guinea	132	201	..	..	..	..	..	..	..	..	..	..
Guinea-Bissau	19	44	..	..	..	..	..	..	..	..	..	..
Haiti	..	..	..	..	..	..	..	..	..	..	..	..
Honduras	826	2,470	42	..	22	..	1	..	5	..	30	..

	Manufacturing value added		Food, beverages, and tobacco		Textiles and clothing		Machinery and transport equipment		Chemicals		Other manufacturing[a]	
	$ millions		% of total		% of total		% of total		% of total		% of total	
	1998	2009	1998	2007	1998	2007	1998	2007	1998	2007	1998	2007
Hungary	9,959	28,619	15	11	7	3	27	31	11	10	40	44
India	59,562	190,333	13	9	12	9	15	19	24	16	37	47
Indonesia	23,857	142,532	21	26	18	13	14	18	13	11	33	32
Iran, Islamic Rep.	13,607	29,832	13	10	8	4	16	24	13	13	49	50
Iraq	91	..	31	..	15	..	2	..	23	..	29	..
Ireland	26,279	48,709	17	18	2	0	16	16	38	33	28	33
Israel	..	..	12	10	6	3	24	22	12	20	46	44
Italy	236,315	306,459	9	9	13	10	23	23	8	7	47	51
Jamaica	914	973	48	..	7	..	..	..	19	..	27	..
Japan	868,624	970,204	11	11	4	2	33	37	10	11	42	39
Jordan	1,047	4,416	27	23	6	10	4	3	21	17	42	48
Kazakhstan	2,659	12,536	..	..	..	..	..	..	..	..	..	..
Kenya	1,540	2,801	46	30	8	4	4	2	8	4	34	62
Korea, Dem. Rep.	..	..	..	..	..	..	..	..	..	..	..	..
Korea, Rep.	85,569	208,142	9	6	9	5	35	46	11	8	36	35
Kosovo	..	773	..	..	..	..	..	..	..	..	..	..
Kuwait	1,037	..	8	..	5	..	2	..	3	..	83	..
Kyrgyz Republic	233	570	..	..	..	..	..	..	..	..	..	..
Lao PDR	216	478	46	..	22	..	8	..	3	..	22	..
Latvia	965	2,278	26	20	11	7	8	10	3	4	52	60
Lebanon	2,144	2,645	26	..	10	..	3	..	6	..	55	..
Lesotho	140	243	..	..	..	..	..	..	..	..	..	..
Liberia	17	105	..	..	..	..	..	..	..	..	..	..
Libya	..	3,879	..	..	..	..	..	..	..	..	..	..
Lithuania	1,807	7,562	27	23	18	9	12	10	3	9	40	48
Macedonia, FYR	645	1,816	31	18	21	17	9	4	8	6	31	55
Madagascar	399	1,115	31	0	33	30	..	1	6	2	30	67
Malawi	216	447	44	..	8	..	5	..	16	..	28	..
Malaysia	20,774	49,213	10	9	4	2	8	30	11	15	67	44
Mali	101	195	..	..	..	..	..	..	..	..	..	..
Mauritania	100	115	..	..	..	..	..	..	..	..	..	..
Mauritius	877	1,483	22	31	51	31	1	1	4	..	26	37
Mexico	82,015	144,431	24	25	4	3	23	18	15	19	32	35
Moldova	238	568	..	39	..	15	..	4	..	..	..	42
Mongolia	46	176	53	38	33	17	0	1	2	3	12	41
Morocco	6,136	12,909	34	30	18	13	4	5	15	16	28	35
Mozambique	422	1,219	..	..	..	..	..	..	..	..	..	..
Myanmar	..	..	..	..	..	..	..	..	..	..	..	..
Namibia	369	1,247	..	..	..	..	..	..	..	..	..	..
Nepal	436	807	35	..	34	..	0	..	6	..	26	..
Netherlands	58,120	89,029	18	18	2	2	15	19	13	14	51	47
New Zealand	8,495	17,968	30	27	..	2	..	13	..	..	70	58
Nicaragua	538	1,086	..	..	..	..	..	..	..	..	..	..
Niger	128	..	..	..	..	..	..	..	..	..	..	..
Nigeria	..	..	30	..	11	..	7	..	26	..	26	..
Norway	16,863	32,575	16	20	2	1	23	25	8	9	51	45
Oman	654	..	17	8	7	0	2	1	7	12	67	79
Pakistan	9,131	26,290	23	22	26	29	5	8	16	14	30	26
Panama	1,135	1,490	52	..	7	..	..	..	7	..	34	..
Papua New Guinea	351	464	..	..	..	..	..	..	..	..	..	..
Paraguay	1,239	1,850	..	..	..	..	..	..	..	..	..	..
Peru	8,080	16,897	26	30	10	12	4	2	10	12	51	44
Philippines	14,254	32,889	35	24	7	6	21	25	10	8	28	38
Poland	30,022	61,948	25	16	7	4	16	20	7	6	45	52
Portugal	19,959	26,690	12	14	20	12	15	11	6	6	46	63
Puerto Rico	22,994	..	10	9	4	1	5	9	62	62	20	20
Qatar	..	..	4	1	8	2	0	0	21	17	67	80

	Manufacturing value added		Food, beverages, and tobacco		Textiles and clothing		Machinery and transport equipment		Chemicals		Other manufacturing[a]	
	$ millions		% of total		% of total		% of total		% of total		% of total	
	1998	2009	1998	2007	1998	2007	1998	2007	1998	2007	1998	2007
Romania	9,601	31,753	29	15	11	12	14	17	5	5	40	51
Russian Federation	..	161,878	22	15	3	2	18	10	9	8	48	65
Rwanda	223	335	75	..	2	..	..	..	6	..	17	..
Saudi Arabia	15,492	39,128	..	19	..	5	..	6	..	27	..	43
Senegal	723	1,490	44	..	3	..	0	..	29	..	24	..
Serbia	..	..	..	..	..	..	..	..	..	..	..	..
Sierra Leone	26	..	..	..	..	..	..	..	..	..	..	..
Singapore	18,839	33,499	4	2	1	1	52	45	13	32	30	20
Slovak Republic	6,036	15,375	12	7	7	3	21	27	9	4	52	59
Slovenia	4,860	10,566	10	7	10	6	17	20	11	14	51	53
Somalia	..	..	..	..	..	..	..	..	..	..	..	..
South Africa	23,678	39,014	18	17	6	3	14	14	11	7	51	58
Spain	103,971	172,433	15	15	7	4	20	17	10	8	47	55
Sri Lanka	2,343	7,618	39	29	30	29	4	0	7	14	21	27
Sudan	957	3,515	..	..	..	..	..	..	..	..	..	..
Swaziland	519	1,114	..	..	..	..	..	..	..	..	..	..
Sweden	48,915	56,948	8	7	1	1	37	34	9	13	46	46
Switzerland	51,047	88,054	10	..	3	..	15	..	..	..	71	..
Syrian Arab Republic	1,286	6,686	..	..	..	..	..	..	..	..	..	..
Tajikistan	255	479	..	..	..	..	..	..	..	..	..	..
Tanzania[b]	919	1,844	45	62	0	8	2	1	7	2	46	29
Thailand	34,534	89,881	25	16	12	9	27	35	4	6	32	34
Timor-Leste	9	..	..	..	..	..	..	..	..	..	..	..
Togo	110	..	..	..	..	..	..	..	..	..	..	..
Trinidad and Tobago	552	1,334	30	11	1	1	1	0	26	39	42	49
Tunisia	3,660	6,527	17	..	36	..	3	..	11	..	33	..
Turkey	64,408	92,715	15	12	18	19	14	20	8	7	45	42
Turkmenistan	452	9,158	..	..	..	..	..	..	..	..	..	..
Uganda	545	1,190	65	..	5	..	..	..	10	..	20	..
Ukraine	10,578	17,992	..	..	..	..	..	..	..	..	..	..
United Arab Emirates	6,532	24,643	..	..	..	..	..	..	..	..	..	..
United Kingdom	251,809	217,594	13	16	5	3	26	23	10	11	46	47
United States	1,440,500	1,779,474	13	14	4	2	30	25	12	15	41	44
Uruguay	3,598	4,377	36	42	9	7	3	4	8	8	44	39
Uzbekistan	1,346	3,979	..	..	..	..	..	..	..	..	..	..
Venezuela, RB	17,380	..	22	..	2	..	9	..	34	..	41	..
Vietnam	4,666	18,099	30	..	22	..	11	..	7	..	30	..
West Bank and Gaza	..	..	15	27	23	13	2	1	5	4	55	55
Yemen, Rep.	638	..	45	60	5	9	0	0	2	4	48	27
Zambia	372	1,192	..	..	..	..	..	..	..	..	..	..
Zimbabwe	923	826	..	..	..	..	..	..	..	..	..	..
World	**5,516,751 t**	**9,102,310 t**	..	..	..	..	..	..	..	..	..	..
Low income	20,369	44,786	..	..	..	..	..	..	..	..	..	..
Middle income	1,085,340	3,432,566	..	..	..	..	..	..	..	..	..	..
Lower middle income	535,090	2,342,311	..	..	..	..	..	..	..	..	..	..
Upper middle income	563,006	1,036,562	..	..	..	..	..	..	..	..	..	..
Low & middle income	1,105,587	3,479,229	..	..	..	..	..	..	..	..	..	..
East Asia & Pacific	425,997	2,036,104	..	..	..	..	..	..	..	..	..	..
Europe & Central Asia	..	..	..	..	..	..	..	..	..	..	..	..
Latin America & Carib.	334,974	570,166	..	..	..	..	..	..	..	..	..	..
Middle East & N. Africa	49,450	117,926	..	..	..	..	..	..	..	..	..	..
South Asia	78,797	241,774	..	..	..	..	..	..	..	..	..	..
Sub-Saharan Africa	43,316	83,017	..	..	..	..	..	..	..	..	..	..
High income	4,411,013	5,603,504	..	..	..	..	..	..	..	..	..	..
Euro area	1,250,663	1,686,936	..	..	..	..	..	..	..	..	..	..

a. Includes unallocated data. b. Covers mainland Tanzania only.

About the data

The data on the distribution of manufacturing value added by industry are provided by the United Nations Industrial Development Organization (UNIDO). UNIDO obtains the data from a variety of national and international sources, including the United Nations Statistics Division, the World Bank, the Organisation for Economic Co-operation and Development, and the International Monetary Fund. To improve comparability over time and across countries, UNIDO supplements these data with information from industrial censuses, statistics from national and international organizations, unpublished data that it collects in the field, and estimates by the UNIDO Secretariat. Nevertheless, coverage may be incomplete, particularly for the informal sector. When direct information on inputs and outputs is not available, estimates may be used, which may result in errors in industry totals. Moreover, countries use different reference periods (calendar or fiscal year) and valuation methods (basic or producer prices) to estimate value added. (See *About the data* for table 4.2.)

The data on manufacturing value added in U.S. dollars are from the World Bank's national accounts files and may differ from those UNIDO uses to calculate shares of value added by industry, in part because of differences in exchange rates. Thus value added in a particular industry estimated by applying the shares to total manufacturing value added will not match those from UNIDO sources. Classification of manufacturing industries in the table accords with the United Nations International Standard Industrial Classification (ISIC) revision 3. Editions of *World Development Indicators* prior to 2008 used revision 2, first published in 1948. Revision 3 was completed in 1989, and many countries now use it. But revision 2 is still widely used for compiling cross-country data. UNIDO has converted these data to accord with

revision 3. Concordances matching ISIC categories to national classification systems and to related systems such as the Standard International Trade Classification are available.

In establishing classifications systems compilers must define both the types of activities to be described and the units whose activities are to be reported. There are many possibilities, and the choices affect how the statistics can be interpreted and how useful they are in analyzing economic behavior. The ISIC emphasizes commonalities in the production process and is explicitly not intended to measure outputs (for which there is a newly developed Central Product Classification). Nevertheless, the ISIC views an activity as defined by "a process resulting in a homogeneous set of products" (United Nations 1990 [ISIC, series M, no. 4, rev. 3], p. 9).

Firms typically use multiple processes to produce a product. For example, an automobile manufacturer engages in forging, welding, and painting as well as advertising, accounting, and other service activities. Collecting data at such a detailed level is not practical, nor is it useful to record production data at the highest level of a large, multiplant, multiproduct firm. The ISIC has therefore adopted as the definition of an establishment "an enterprise or part of an enterprise which independently engages in one, or predominantly one, kind of economic activity at or from one location . . . for which data are available . . ." (United Nations 1990, p. 25). By design, this definition matches the reporting unit required for the production accounts of the United Nations System of National Accounts. The ISIC system is described in the United Nations' *International Standard Industrial Classification of All Economic Activities, Third Revision* (1990). The discussion of the ISIC draws on Ryten (1998).

Definitions

• **Manufacturing value added** is the sum of gross output less the value of intermediate inputs used in production for industries classified in ISIC major division D. • **Food, beverages, and tobacco** correspond to ISIC divisions 15 and 16. • **Textiles and clothing** correspond to ISIC divisions 17–19. • **Machinery and transport equipment** correspond to ISIC divisions 29, 30, 32, 34, and 35. • **Chemicals** correspond to ISIC division 24. • **Other manufacturing** is calculated as a residual. It covers wood and related products (ISIC division 20), paper and related products (ISIC divisions 21 and 22), petroleum and related products (ISIC division 23), basic metals and mineral products (ISIC division 27), fabricated metal products and professional goods (ISIC division 28), and other industries (ISIC divisions 25, 26, 31, 33, 36, and 37).

Manufacturing continues to show strong growth in East Asia and Pacific through 2009   4.3a

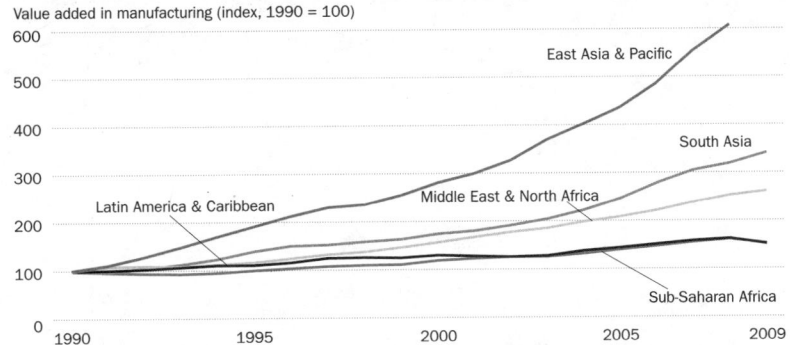

Value added in manufacturing (index, 1990 = 100)

East Asia & Pacific
South Asia
Latin America & Caribbean
Middle East & North Africa
Sub-Saharan Africa

Manufacturing continues to be the dominant sector in East Asia and Pacific, growing an average of about 10.5 percent a year between 1990 and 2009.

Source: World Development Indicators data files.

Data sources

Data on manufacturing value added are from the World Bank's National Accounts files. Data used to calculate shares of industry value added are provided to the World Bank in electronic files by UNIDO. The most recent published source is UNIDO's *International Yearbook of Industrial Statistics 2010.*

	Merchandise exports		Food		Agricultural raw materials		Fuels		Ores and metals		Manufactures	
	$ millions		% of total		% of total		% of total		% of total		% of total	
	1995	2009	1995	2009	1995	2009	1995	2009	1995	2009	1995	2009
Afghanistan	166	560	..	55	..	8	..	..		0	..	18
Albania	202	1,088	11	6	9	3	3	12	12	10	65	70
Algeria	10,258	45,194	1	0	0	0	95	98	1	0	4	2
Angola	3,642	40,080	..	..	..	..	..	..	..	..	..	..
Argentina	20,967	55,668	50	50	4	1	10	10	2	4	34	33
Armenia	271	698	11	20	5	1	1	0	26	47	54	33
Australia	53,111	154,234	22	14	8	2	19	32	18	27	30	19
Austria	57,738	137,672	4	7	3	2	1	3	3	3	88	81
Azerbaijan	635	21,097	4	4	8	0	66	93	1	0	20	3
Bangladesh	3,501	15,084	10	7	3	3	0	2	0	0	85	88
Belarus	4,803	21,283	..	11	..	2	..	37	..	1	..	48
Belgium	178,265[a]	369,854	10[a]	10	1[a]	1	3[a]	7	4[a]	3	77[a]	77
Benin	420	1,000	14	..	75	..	5	..	0	..	6	..
Bolivia	1,100	4,848	21	20	10	1	15	40	35	33	19	6
Bosnia and Herzegovina	152	3,929	..	8	..	6	..	13	..	9	..	61
Botswana	2,142	3,458	..	5	..	0	..	0	..	16	..	78
Brazil	46,506	152,995	29	34	5	4	1	9	10	12	54	39
Bulgaria	5,355	16,455	18	17	3	1	7	13	10	15	60	53
Burkina Faso	276	850	25	27	69	60	0	0	0	1	6	12
Burundi	105	64	91	67	4	5	0	2	1	5	3	21
Cambodia	855	4,200	..	1	..	1	..	0	..	3	..	96
Cameroon	1,651	3,000	27	..	28	..	29	..	8	..	8	..
Canada	192,197	316,713	8	11	9	..	9	25	7	7	63	50
Central African Republic	171	120	4	..	20	..	1	..	30	..	45	..
Chad	243	2,800	..	..	..	..	..	..	..	..	..	..
Chile	16,024	53,735	24	21	12	5	0	1	48	58	13	11
China[†]	148,780	1,201,534	8	3	2	0	4	2	2	1	84	94
Hong Kong SAR, China[b]	173,871	329,422	3	7	0	2	0	4	1	6	94	79
Colombia	10,056	32,853	31	16	5	4	28	51	1	2	35	28
Congo, Dem. Rep.	1,563	3,100	..	..	..	..	..	..	..	..	..	..
Congo, Rep.	1,172	5,600	1	..	8	..	88	..	0	..	3	..
Costa Rica	3,453	8,788	63	25	5	2	1	1	1	1	25	47
Côte d'Ivoire	3,806	8,900	63	48	20	6	10	30	0	0	7	15
Croatia	4,517	10,474	11	13	5	4	9	13	2	4	74	66
Cuba	1,600	3,109	..	..	..	..	..	..	..	..	..	..
Czech Republic	21,335	113,437	6	5	4	1	4	4	3	2	82	87
Denmark	50,906	93,344	24	19	3	2	3	8	1	1	60	65
Dominican Republic	3,780	5,463	19	25	0	1	0	0	0	3	78	70
Ecuador	4,307	13,799	53	36	3	4	36	50	0	0	8	9
Egypt, Arab Rep.	3,450	23,062	10	11	6	2	37	44	6	6	40	37
El Salvador	1,652	3,797	57	23	1	1	0	3	3	1	39	72
Eritrea	86	15	..	..	..	..	..	..	..	..	..	..
Estonia	1,840	9,031	16	10	10	4	6	16	3	2	65	62
Ethiopia	422	1,596	73	77	13	12	3	0	0	1	11	9
Finland	40,490	62,798	2	2	8	4	2	7	3	4	83	77
France	301,162	484,725	14	12	1	1	2	4	3	2	79	79
Gabon	2,713	5,100	0	..	13	..	83	..	2	..	2	..
Gambia, The	16	15	60	53	1	1	0	0	1	7	36	39
Georgia	151	1,135	29	18	3	2	19	3	8	22	41	55
Germany	523,461	1,126,383	5	6	1	1	1	2	3	2	87	82
Ghana	1,724	5,500	58	63	15	9	5	2	9	6	13	19
Greece	11,054	20,093	30	25	4	3	7	9	7	7	50	54
Guatemala	2,155	7,214	65	44	4	3	2	4	0	5	28	43
Guinea	702	1,010	8	2	1	5	0	2	67	59	24	32
Guinea-Bissau	24	115	89	..	11	..	0	..	0	..	0	..
Haiti	110	576	37	..	0	..	0	..	0	..	62	..
Honduras	1,769	5,196	87	54	3	1	0	4	0	4	9	35
[†]Data for Taiwan, China	113,047	203,675	3	1	2	1	1	6	1	2	93	89

	Merchandise exports ($ millions)		Food (% of total)		Agricultural raw materials (% of total)		Fuels (% of total)		Ores and metals (% of total)		Manufactures (% of total)	
	1995	2009	1995	2009	1995	2009	1995	2009	1995	2009	1995	2009
Hungary	12,865	83,778	21	8	2	1	3	2	5	1	68	82
India	30,630	162,613	19	8	1	1	2	13	3	6	74	67
Indonesia	45,417	119,481	11	17	7	5	25	28	6	9	51	41
Iran, Islamic Rep.	18,360	78,113	4	..	1	..	86	..	1	..	9	..
Iraq	496	39,500	..	0	..	0	..	99	..	0	..	0
Ireland	44,705	114,587	19	9	1	0	0	1	1	1	72	86
Israel	19,046	47,935	5	3	2	1	0	0	1	1	89	94
Italy	233,766	405,777	7	8	1	1	1	4	1	2	89	83
Jamaica	1,427	1,316	22	27	0	0	1	17	6	8	71	47
Japan	443,116	580,719	0	1	1	1	1	2	1	3	95	88
Jordan	1,769	6,366	25	17	2	0	0	1	24	9	49	73
Kazakhstan	5,250	43,196	10	4	3	0	25	71	24	11	38	14
Kenya	1,878	4,421	56	44	7	13	6	4	3	2	28	37
Korea, Dem. Rep.	959	1,550	..	..	..	..	..	..	..	..	..	..
Korea, Rep.	125,058	363,534	2	1	1	1	2	6	1	2	93	90
Kosovo	..	..	..	..	..	..	..	..	..	..	..	..
Kuwait	12,785	50,328	0	0	0	0	95	93	0	0	5	6
Kyrgyz Republic	409	1,439	23	24	13	4	11	6	13	3	40	34
Lao PDR	311	940	..	..	..	..	..	..	..	..	..	..
Latvia	1,305	7,688	14	17	23	10	2	5	1	3	58	61
Lebanon	816	4,187	20	16	2	1	0	0	8	8	70	72
Lesotho	160	750	..	..	..	..	..	..	..	..	..	..
Liberia	820	150	..	..	..	..	..	..	..	..	..	..
Libya	8,975	35,600	0	..	0	..	95	..	0	..	5	..
Lithuania	2,705	16,452	18	19	8	2	11	21	5	1	58	55
Macedonia, FYR	1,204	2,692	18	18	5	1	0	1	18	3	58	51
Madagascar	507	1,140	69	29	6	5	1	5	7	3	14	57
Malawi	405	920	90	87	2	4	0	0	0	1	7	9
Malaysia	73,914	157,433	10	11	6	2	7	15	1	2	75	70
Mali	441	2,100	23	28	75	42	0	6	0	1	2	22
Mauritania	488	1,370	57	12	0	0	1	22	42	60	0	0
Mauritius	1,538	1,942	29	32	1	1	0	0	0	1	70	65
Mexico	79,542	229,637	8	7	1	0	10	14	3	3	78	76
Moldova	745	1,288	72	74	2	1	1	0	3	2	23	23
Mongolia	473	1,903	2	2	28	12	0	10	60	70	10	6
Morocco	6,881	13,863	31	22	3	2	2	2	12	9	51	65
Mozambique	168	2,147	66	23	16	3	2	17	2	4	13	12
Myanmar	860	6,710	..	..	..	..	..	..	..	..	..	..
Namibia	1,409	3,553	..	23	..	0	..	0	..	31	..	45
Nepal	345	813	8	25	1	3	0	0	0	5	84	67
Netherlands	203,171	498,330	20	15	4	3	7	8	3	2	63	56
New Zealand	13,645	24,932	45	56	19	10	2	5	5	3	29	23
Nicaragua	466	1,391	75	87	3	1	1	1	1	1	21	10
Niger	288	900	17	18	1	4	0	2	80	69	1	7
Nigeria	12,342	52,500	2	5	2	1	96	90	0	0	1	4
Norway	41,992	120,880	8	6	2	0	47	65	9	5	27	20
Oman	6,068	27,651	5	3	0	0	79	79	2	4	14	10
Pakistan	8,029	17,680	12	17	4	2	1	4	0	1	83	76
Panama	625	948	75	84	0	1	3	1	1	4	20	10
Papua New Guinea	2,654	4,328	13	..	20	..	38	..	25	..	4	..
Paraguay	919	3,167	44	85	36	4	0	0	0	1	19	11
Peru	5,575	26,885	31	23	3	1	5	10	46	49	15	16
Philippines	17,502	38,436	13	8	1	1	2	2	4	4	42	86
Poland	22,895	134,466	10	11	3	1	8	3	7	4	71	80
Portugal	22,783	43,358	7	11	5	2	3	5	2	3	83	72
Puerto Rico	..	..	..	..	..	..	..	..	..	..	..	..
Qatar	3,651	40,500	0	0	0	0	82	94	0	0	17	5

	Merchandise exports ($ millions)		Food (% of total)		Agricultural raw materials (% of total)		Fuels (% of total)		Ores and metals (% of total)		Manufactures (% of total)	
	1995	2009	1995	2009	1995	2009	1995	2009	1995	2009	1995	2009
Romania	7,910	40,633	7	7	3	2	8	6	3	4	78	79
Russian Federation	81,095	303,388	2	3	3	2	43	67	10	6	26	17
Rwanda	54	193	57	42	16	2	0	0	12	32	14	19
Saudi Arabia	50,040	192,296	1	1	0	0	88	88	1	0	10	8
Senegal	993	2,180	9	30	7	1	22	24	12	3	48	41
Serbia	..	8,345	28	19	4	2	2	3	15	10	49	66
Sierra Leone	42	231	..	..	..	..	..	..	..	..	..	..
Singapore[b]	118,268	269,832	4	2	1	0	7	15	2	1	84	74
Slovak Republic	8,580	55,980	6	5	4	1	4	5	4	2	82	87
Slovenia	8,316	26,369	4	4	2	2	1	4	3	3	90	87
Somalia	..	..	..	..	..	..	..	..	..	..	..	..
South Africa	27,853[c]	62,603	8[c]	10	4[c]	2	9[c]	11	8[c]	29	44[c]	47
Spain	97,849	218,511	15	16	2	1	2	4	2	3	78	73
Sri Lanka	3,798	7,345	21	26	4	3	0	0	1	1	73	67
Sudan	555	7,834	44	6	47	1	0	92	0	0	6	0
Swaziland	866	1,500	..	21	..	7	..	1	..	1	..	70
Sweden	80,440	131,243	2	5	6	4	2	6	3	4	79	76
Switzerland	81,641	172,850	3	4	1	0	0	3	3	3	94	90
Syrian Arab Republic	3,563	10,400	12	22	7	1	63	39	1	4	17	33
Tajikistan	750	1,009	..	..	..	..	..	..	..	..	..	..
Tanzania	682	3,096	65	35	23	10	0	1	0	25	10	25
Thailand	56,439	152,498	19	15	5	4	1	5	1	1	73	75
Timor-Leste	..	..	..	..	..	..	..	..	..	..	..	..
Togo	378	800	19	16	42	9	0	0	32	13	7	62
Trinidad and Tobago	2,455	9,126	8	3	0	0	48	79	0	2	43	15
Tunisia	5,475	14,445	10	9	1	0	8	14	2	1	79	75
Turkey	21,637	102,129	20	11	1	0	1	4	3	3	74	80
Turkmenistan	1,880	6,595	1	..	13	..	77	..	1	..	8	..
Uganda	460	2,478	90	63	5	6	0	1	1	2	4	27
Ukraine	13,128	39,703	19	24	1	1	4	5	7	6	68	63
United Arab Emirates	28,364	175,000	8	1	0	0	9	65	55	1	28	4
United Kingdom	237,953	352,491	8	7	1	1	6	11	3	3	81	72
United States	584,743	1,056,043	11	10	4	2	2	6	3	4	77	67
Uruguay	2,106	5,386	44	64	15	8	1	1	1	0	39	26
Uzbekistan	3,430	10,735	..	..	..	..	..	..	..	..	..	..
Venezuela, RB	18,457	57,595	3	0	0	0	77	96	6	1	14	3
Vietnam	5,449	57,096	30	20	3	3	18	20	0	1	44	55
West Bank and Gaza	..	..	..	..	..	..	..	..	..	..	..	..
Yemen, Rep.	1,945	5,594	3	6	1	0	95	92	1	0	1	2
Zambia	1,040	4,312	3	8	1	1	3	1	87	81	7	8
Zimbabwe	2,118	2,269	43	19	7	23	1	1	12	22	37	34
World	**5,172,552 t**	**12,492,190 t**	**9 w**	**8 w**	**3 w**	**2 w**	**7 w**	**12 w**	**3 w**	**4 w**	**76 w**	**70 w**
Low income	24,093	76,170	31	25	10	8	2	3	11	14	44	50
Middle income	894,340	3,720,635	14	11	3	2	12	22	5	5	63	59
Lower middle income	400,844	2,099,993	14	9	3	2	8	14	3	5	69	71
Upper middle income	493,582	1,619,211	15	12	4	2	15	29	6	7	58	48
Low & middle income	918,419	3,796,791	15	11	3	2	11	22	5	5	63	59
East Asia & Pacific	354,784	1,747,540	11	8	4	2	6	8	2	2	74	80
Europe & Central Asia	154,880	650,244	8	8	3	2	29	45	9	5	42	37
Latin America & Carib.	223,980	677,205	20	18	3	2	15	20	7	8	55	51
Middle East & N. Africa	62,002	276,399	6	..	1	..	73	..	3	..	17	..
South Asia	46,657	204,760	17	11	2	1	1	11	3	5	76	68
Sub-Saharan Africa	76,554	242,566	18	14	7	3	36	37	8	15	28	31
High income	4,253,742	8,697,557	8	8	2	1	6	9	3	3	78	73
Euro area	1,744,036	3,597,614	11	10	2	1	2	4	3	2	80	77

Note: Components may not sum to 100 percent because of unclassified trade. Exports of gold are excluded.
a. Includes Luxembourg. b. Includes re-exports. c. Refers to the South African Customs Union (Botswana, Lesotho, Namibia, South Africa, and Swaziland).

Data on merchandise trade are from customs reports of goods moving into or out of an economy or from reports of financial transactions related to merchandise trade recorded in the balance of payments. Because of differences in timing and definitions, trade flow estimates from customs reports and balance of payments may differ. Several international agencies process trade data, each correcting unreported or misreported data, leading to other differences.

The most detailed source of data on international trade in goods is the United Nations Statistics Division's Commodity Trade (Comtrade) database. The International Monetary Fund (IMF) also collects customs-based data on trade in goods. Exports are recorded as the cost of the goods delivered to the frontier of the exporting country for shipment—the free on board (f.o.b.) value. Many countries report trade data in U.S. dollars. When countries report in local currency, the United Nations Statistics Division applies the average official exchange rate to the U.S. dollar for the period shown.

Countries may report trade according to the general or special system of trade. Under the general system exports comprise outward-moving goods that are (a) goods wholly or partly produced in the country; (b) foreign goods, neither transformed nor declared for domestic consumption in the country, that move outward from customs storage; and (c) goods previously included as imports for domestic consumption but subsequently exported without transformation. Under the special system exports comprise categories a and c. In some compilations categories b and c are classified as re-exports. Because of differences in reporting practices, data on exports may not be fully comparable across economies.

The data on total exports of goods (merchandise) are from the World Trade Organization (WTO), which obtains data from national statistical offices and the IMF's *International Financial Statistics*, supplemented by the Comtrade database and publications or databases of regional organizations, specialized agencies, economic groups, and private sources (such as Eurostat, the Food and Agriculture Organization, and country reports of the Economist Intelligence Unit). Country websites and email contact have improved collection of up-to-date statistics, reducing the proportion of estimates. The WTO database now covers most major traders in Africa, Asia, and Latin America, which together with high-income countries account for nearly 95 percent of world trade. Reliability of data for countries in Europe and Central Asia has also improved.

Export shares by major commodity group are from Comtrade. The values of total exports reported here have not been fully reconciled with the estimates from the national accounts or the balance of payments.

The classification of commodity groups is based on the Standard International Trade Classification (SITC) revision 3. Previous editions contained data based on the SITC revision 1. Data for earlier years in previous editions may differ because of this change in methodology. Concordance tables are available to convert data reported in one system to another.

• **Merchandise exports** are the f.o.b. value of goods provided to the rest of the world. • **Food** corresponds to the commodities in SITC sections 0 (food and live animals), 1 (beverages and tobacco), and 4 (animal and vegetable oils and fats) and SITC division 22 (oil seeds, oil nuts, and oil kernels). • **Agricultural raw materials** correspond to SITC section 2 (crude materials except fuels), excluding divisions 22, 27 (crude fertilizers and minerals excluding coal, petroleum, and precious stones), and 28 (metalliferous ores and scrap). • **Fuels** correspond to SITC section 3 (mineral fuels). • **Ores and metals** correspond to the commodities in SITC divisions 27, 28, and 68 (nonferrous metals). • **Manufactures** correspond to the commodities in SITC sections 5 (chemicals), 6 (basic manufactures), 7 (machinery and transport equipment), and 8 (miscellaneous manufactured goods), excluding division 68.

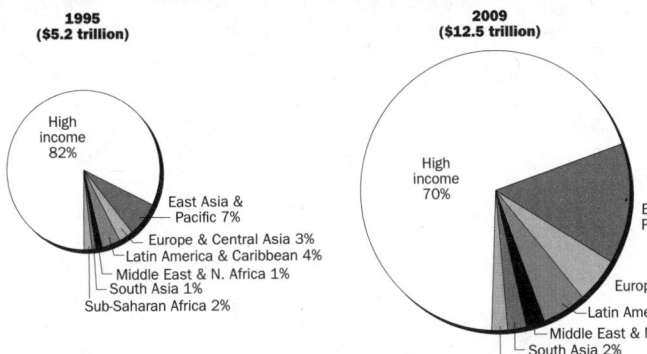

Developing economies' share of world merchandise exports increased 12 percentage points from 1995 to 2009. East Asia and the Pacific was the biggest gainer, capturing an additional 7 percentage points. All other developing country regions also increased their share in world trade.

Source: World Development Indicators data files and World Trade Organization.

Data on merchandise exports are from the WTO. Data on shares of exports by major commodity group are from Comtrade. The WTO publishes data on world trade in its *Annual Report*. The IMF publishes estimates of total exports of goods in its *International Financial Statistics* and *Direction of Trade Statistics*, as does the United Nations Statistics Division in its *Monthly Bulletin of Statistics*. And the United Nations Conference on Trade and Development publishes data on the structure of exports in its *Handbook of Statistics*. Tariff line records of exports are compiled in the United Nations Statistics Division's Comtrade database.

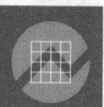

4.5 Structure of merchandise imports

	Merchandise imports $ millions		Food % of total		Agricultural raw materials % of total		Fuels % of total		Ores and metals % of total		Manufactures % of total	
	1995	2009	1995	2009	1995	2009	1995	2009	1995	2009	1995	2009
Afghanistan	387	3,970	..	18	..	0	..	24	..	0	..	17
Albania	714	4,548	34	17	1	1	2	12	1	2	61	68
Algeria	10,100	39,294	29	16	3	1	1	1	2	1	65	80
Angola	1,468	17,000	..	..	..	..	..	..	..	..	..	..
Argentina	20,122	38,780	5	4	2	1	4	6	2	2	86	86
Armenia	674	3,304	31	19	0	1	27	16	0	4	39	59
Australia	61,283	165,471	5	6	2	1	5	13	1	1	86	76
Austria	66,237	143,382	6	8	3	2	4	11	4	4	82	75
Azerbaijan	668	6,514	39	16	1	1	4	1	2	1	53	79
Bangladesh	6,694	21,833	17	22	3	8	8	11	2	3	69	54
Belarus	5,564	28,563	..	8	..	1	..	40	..	3	..	45
Belgium	164,934ᵃ	351,945	11ᵃ	9	2ᵃ	1	6ᵃ	12	5ᵃ	3	71ᵃ	73
Benin	746	2,040	27	..	3	..	9	..	1	..	59	..
Bolivia	1,424	4,410	10	9	2	1	5	11	3	1	82	78
Bosnia and Herzegovina	1,082	8,773	..	19	..	1	..	15	..	2	..	62
Botswana	1,911	4,728	..	13	..	1	..	13	..	2	..	70
Brazil	54,137	133,669	11	5	3	1	12	15	3	3	71	76
Bulgaria	5,660	23,330	8	10	3	1	34	20	4	7	48	59
Burkina Faso	455	2,083	21	16	2	1	14	24	1	1	62	59
Burundi	234	402	21	13	2	1	11	2	1	1	64	81
Cambodia	1,187	6,200	..	7	..	1	..	8	..	2	..	82
Cameroon	1,199	4,250	17	..	3	..	3	..	2	..	76	..
Canada	168,426	329,904	6	8	2	1	4	10	3	2	83	77
Central African Republic	175	300	16	..	10	..	9	..	2	..	64	..
Chad	365	1,950	24	..	1	..	18	..	1	..	56	..
Chile	15,900	42,427	7	7	2	1	9	21	2	2	79	59
Chinaᵗ	132,084	1,005,688	7	5	5	3	4	13	4	14	79	64
Hong Kong SAR, China	196,072	352,241	5	4	2	1	2	3	2	2	88	89
Colombia	13,853	32,898	9	10	3	1	3	4	2	2	78	82
Congo, Dem. Rep.	871	3,600	..	..	..	..	..	..	..	..	..	..
Congo, Rep.	670	2,900	21	..	1	..	20	..	1	..	58	..
Costa Rica	4,036	11,395	10	7	1	1	9	9	2	1	78	60
Côte d'Ivoire	2,931	6,050	21	23	1	1	19	25	1	1	57	49
Croatia	7,352	21,203	12	10	2	1	12	17	3	2	67	70
Cuba	2,825	9,623	..	..	..	..	..	..	..	..	..	..
Czech Republic	25,085	105,179	7	6	3	1	8	9	4	3	77	78
Denmark	45,939	82,947	12	13	3	2	3	6	2	2	73	74
Dominican Republic	5,170	12,283	..	14	..	1	..	21	..	1	..	63
Ecuador	4,152	15,093	8	9	3	1	6	12	2	1	82	76
Egypt, Arab Rep.	11,760	44,946	28	17	7	3	1	11	3	8	61	60
El Salvador	3,329	7,255	15	19	2	2	9	15	2	1	72	63
Eritrea	454	540	..	..	..	..	..	..	..	..	..	..
Estonia	2,546	10,122	14	12	3	2	11	19	1	1	71	60
Ethiopia	1,145	7,963	14	11	2	1	11	16	1	1	72	72
Finland	29,470	60,753	6	7	4	2	9	15	6	5	74	64
France	289,391	559,817	11	9	3	1	7	13	4	2	76	74
Gabon	882	2,200	19	..	1	..	4	..	1	..	75	..
Gambia, The	182	304	36	34	1	1	14	16	0	1	46	48
Georgia	392	4,378	36	15	0	1	39	18	0	2	24	64
Germany	463,872	938,295	10	8	3	1	6	11	4	3	73	67
Ghana	1,906	8,140	8	15	1	1	6	14	0	1	77	69
Greece	25,898	59,858	16	13	2	1	7	15	3	2	71	69
Guatemala	3,292	11,531	12	14	2	1	12	19	1	1	73	64
Guinea	819	1,400	31	13	1	0	19	33	1	0	47	53
Guinea-Bissau	133	230	44	..	0	..	16	..	0	..	40	..
Haiti	653	2,050	..	..	..	..	..	..	..	..	..	..
Honduras	1,879	7,788	13	19	1	1	12	19	1	1	74	60
ᵗData for Taiwan, China	103,558	174,371	6	5	4	1	7	21	6	7	75	65

	Merchandise imports ($ millions)		Food (% of total)		Agricultural raw materials (% of total)		Fuels (% of total)		Ores and metals (% of total)		Manufactures (% of total)	
	1995	2009	1995	2009	1995	2009	1995	2009	1995	2009	1995	2009
Hungary	15,465	78,175	6	5	3	1	12	8	4	2	75	72
India	34,707	249,590	4	4	4	2	24	34	7	6	54	52
Indonesia	40,630	91,749	9	9	6	3	8	20	4	3	73	65
Iran, Islamic Rep.	13,882	50,375	21	..	2	..	2	..	3	..	71	..
Iraq	665	37,000	..	..	..	..	..	..	..	..	..	..
Ireland	32,340	62,507	8	12	1	1	3	10	2	1	76	68
Israel	29,578	49,278	7	8	2	1	6	17	2	2	82	72
Italy	205,990	412,721	12	10	6	2	7	18	5	3	68	65
Jamaica	2,818	5,064	14	18	2	1	13	28	1	0	68	51
Japan	335,882	551,960	16	10	6	1	16	28	7	6	54	52
Jordan	3,697	14,075	21	17	2	1	13	18	3	2	61	60
Kazakhstan	3,807	28,409	10	9	2	1	25	10	5	1	59	80
Kenya	2,991	10,207	10	15	2	1	15	21	2	2	71	60
Korea, Dem. Rep.	1,380	2,080	..	..	..	..	..	..	..	..	..	..
Korea, Rep.	135,119	323,085	6	5	6	2	14	28	6	7	68	58
Kosovo	..	..	..	..	..	..	..	..	..	..	..	..
Kuwait	7,790	17,920	16	15	1	1	1	1	2	3	81	81
Kyrgyz Republic	522	3,037	18	17	3	1	36	4	3	1	40	50
Lao PDR	589	1,260	..	..	..	..	..	..	..	..	..	..
Latvia	1,815	9,765	10	17	2	1	21	16	1	2	66	56
Lebanon	7,278	16,574	21	15	2	1	9	21	2	2	66	61
Lesotho	1,107	1,950	..	..	..	..	..	..	..	..	..	..
Liberia	510	552	..	..	..	..	..	..	..	..	..	..
Libya	5,392	10,150	23	..	1	..	0	..	1	..	75	..
Lithuania	3,650	18,234	13	14	4	2	19	28	4	2	58	53
Macedonia, FYR	1,719	5,043	17	13	3	1	12	5	3	1	64	62
Madagascar	628	3,250	16	11	2	1	14	10	1	0	65	78
Malawi	475	1,700	14	13	1	1	11	10	1	1	73	74
Malaysia	77,691	123,832	5	8	1	2	2	8	3	4	86	76
Mali	772	2,644	20	12	1	0	16	21	1	1	62	65
Mauritania	431	1,430	24	28	1	1	22	35	0	0	53	36
Mauritius	1,976	3,728	17	22	3	2	7	16	1	1	72	59
Mexico	74,427	241,515	6	7	2	1	2	7	2	2	80	80
Moldova	840	3,278	8	15	3	1	46	22	2	1	42	61
Mongolia	415	2,131	14	12	1	0	19	27	1	1	65	60
Morocco	10,023	32,892	20	11	6	2	14	21	4	2	56	63
Mozambique	704	3,764	22	15	3	1	10	15	1	0	62	55
Myanmar	1,348	4,316	..	..	..	..	..	..	..	..	..	..
Namibia	1,616	5,120	..	14	..	1	..	14	..	1	..	70
Nepal	1,333	4,392	12	15	3	2	12	17	3	3	46	62
Netherlands	185,232	445,496	14	11	2	1	8	13	3	2	72	58
New Zealand	13,957	25,545	7	11	1	1	5	15	3	1	83	72
Nicaragua	975	3,477	18	18	1	1	18	22	1	0	63	59
Niger	374	1,500	32	25	1	5	13	17	3	2	51	52
Nigeria	8,222	39,000	18	12	1	1	1	1	2	2	77	84
Norway	32,968	69,292	7	8	3	1	3	5	6	5	81	79
Oman	4,379	18,020	20	11	1	1	2	5	2	3	70	77
Pakistan	11,515	31,710	18	11	6	4	16	28	3	4	57	52
Panama	2,510	7,801	11	12	1	0	14	17	1	1	73	70
Papua New Guinea	1,452	3,200	..	..	..	..	..	..	..	..	..	..
Paraguay	3,144	6,940	19	8	0	1	7	15	1	1	74	76
Peru	7,584	21,706	14	11	2	1	9	14	1	1	75	72
Philippines	28,341	45,878	8	12	2	1	9	17	3	4	58	67
Poland	29,050	146,626	10	8	3	2	9	13	3	3	74	62
Portugal	32,610	69,844	14	13	4	1	8	13	2	2	72	62
Puerto Rico	..	..	..	..	..	..	..	..	..	..	..	..
Qatar	3,398	23,000	9	6	1	0	1	1	2	3	87	90

4.5 Structure of merchandise imports

	Merchandise imports		Food		Agricultural raw materials		Fuels		Ores and metals		Manufactures	
	$ millions		% of total		% of total		% of total		% of total		% of total	
	1995	2009	1995	2009	1995	2009	1995	2009	1995	2009	1995	2009
Romania	10,278	54,247	8	9	2	1	21	9	4	2	63	75
Russian Federation	60,945	191,803	18	17	1	1	3	2	2	2	45	76
Rwanda	236	1,227	19	12	3	1	12	8	3	2	64	76
Saudi Arabia	28,091	95,567	17	11	1	0	0	0	4	3	76	36
Senegal	1,412	4,713	25	24	2	2	30	23	1	1	42	50
Serbia	..	15,582	14	6	4	2	14	17	7	6	60	69
Sierra Leone	133	520	..	..	..	..	..	..	..	..	..	..
Singapore	124,507	245,785	5	3	1	0	8	24	2	2	83	67
Slovak Republic	8,770	55,301	9	7	3	1	13	12	6	2	70	78
Slovenia	9,492	26,464	8	9	5	3	7	11	4	4	74	72
Somalia	..	..	..	..	..	..	..	..	..	..	..	..
South Africa	30,546[b]	73,172	7[b]	7	2[b]	1	8[b]	21	2[b]	1	78[b]	64
Spain	113,537	287,567	14	11	3	1	8	16	4	3	71	68
Sri Lanka	5,306	10,207	16	16	2	1	6	19	1	1	75	62
Sudan	1,218	9,691	24	15	2	1	14	4	0	1	59	78
Swaziland	1,008	1,600	..	21	..	1	..	14	..	1	..	63
Sweden	65,036	119,839	7	10	2	1	6	12	4	3	80	70
Switzerland	80,152	155,706	6	6	2	1	3	7	3	4	85	81
Syrian Arab Republic	4,709	16,300	17	14	3	3	1	31	1	4	76	47
Tajikistan	810	2,569	..	..	..	..	..	..	..	..	..	..
Tanzania	1,675	6,347	10	9	1	1	1	23	4	1	84	66
Thailand	70,786	133,801	4	6	4	2	7	19	3	4	81	69
Timor-Leste	..	..	..	..	..	..	..	..	..	..	..	..
Togo	594	1,500	18	15	2	1	30	27	1	2	49	55
Trinidad and Tobago	1,714	6,955	16	10	1	1	1	33	6	3	76	53
Tunisia	7,902	19,096	13	9	4	2	7	11	3	3	73	75
Turkey	35,709	140,921	7	4	6	2	13	14	6	7	68	64
Turkmenistan	1,365	6,750	24	..	0	..	3	..	2	..	71	..
Uganda	1,056	4,310	16	13	3	1	2	19	2	1	78	66
Ukraine	15,484	45,436	8	11	2	1	48	32	3	3	38	52
United Arab Emirates	23,778	140,000	15	7	0	0	4	1	6	5	75	73
United Kingdom	267,250	481,707	10	11	2	1	4	10	3	3	80	69
United States	770,852	1,605,296	5	5	2	1	8	17	3	2	79	70
Uruguay	2,867	6,907	10	10	4	2	10	24	1	1	74	62
Uzbekistan	2,750	9,023	..	..	..	..	..	..	..	..	..	..
Venezuela, RB	12,649	40,597	14	16	4	1	1	1	4	1	77	79
Vietnam	8,155	69,949	5	7	2	3	10	16	2	4	76	70
West Bank and Gaza	..	..	..	..	..	..	..	..	..	..	..	..
Yemen, Rep.	1,582	8,500	29	28	2	1	8	21	1	1	59	50
Zambia	700	3,793	10	6	2	1	13	14	2	13	72	65
Zimbabwe	2,660	2,900	6	22	2	0	9	13	2	5	78	58
World	**5,228,194 t**	**12,595,548 t**	**9 w**	**8 w**	**3 w**	**1 w**	**7 w**	**15 w**	**4 w**	**3 w**	**75 w**	**69 w**
Low income	36,735	127,386	16	16	3	3	12	16	2	2	66	60
Middle income	947,153	3,519,888	8	8	4	2	7	14	3	5	75	69
Lower middle income	434,758	2,038,080	9	7	5	2	8	18	4	8	72	64
Upper middle income	512,441	1,475,992	8	9	3	1	6	11	3	3	77	74
Low & middle income	983,905	3,647,212	8	8	4	2	7	14	3	5	75	69
East Asia & Pacific	366,062	1,493,538	6	7	4	3	5	14	4	9	78	68
Europe & Central Asia	163,415	626,665	12	10	3	2	15	14	4	4	57	66
Latin America & Carib.	240,278	668,496	8	8	2	1	5	10	2	2	78	77
Middle East & N. Africa	77,167	289,612	22	..	4	..	6	..	3	..	66	..
South Asia	60,322	323,199	8	7	4	2	21	31	6	5	56	53
Sub-Saharan Africa	78,377	253,161	12	11	2	1	10	17	2	2	73	66
High income	4,244,063	8,955,148	9	8	3	1	7	15	4	3	75	69
Euro area	1,647,277	3,519,840	11	10	3	1	7	13	4	3	73	68

Note: Components may not sum to 100 percent because of unclassified trade.
a. Includes Luxembourg. b. Refers to the South African Customs Union (Botswana, Lesotho, Namibia, South Africa, and Swaziland).

Structure of merchandise imports

Data on imports of goods are derived from the same sources as data on exports. In principle, world exports and imports should be identical. Similarly, exports from an economy should equal the sum of imports by the rest of the world from that economy. But differences in timing and definitions result in discrepancies in reported values at all levels. For further discussion of indicators of merchandise trade, see *About the data* for tables 4.4 and 6.2.

The value of imports is generally recorded as the cost of the goods when purchased by the importer plus the cost of transport and insurance to the frontier of the importing country—the cost, insurance, and freight (c.i.f.) value, corresponding to the landed cost at the point of entry of foreign goods into the country. A few countries, including Australia, Canada, and the United States, collect import data on a free on board (f.o.b.) basis and adjust them for freight and insurance costs. Many countries report trade data in U.S. dollars. When countries report in local currency, the United Nations Statistics Division applies the average official exchange rate to the U.S. dollar for the period shown.

Countries may report trade according to the general or special system of trade. Under the general system imports include goods imported for domestic consumption and imports into bonded warehouses and free trade zones. Under the special system imports comprise goods imported for domestic consumption (including transformation and repair) and withdrawals for domestic consumption from bonded warehouses

and free trade zones. Goods transported through a country en route to another are excluded.

The data on total imports of goods (merchandise) in the table come from the World Trade Organization (WTO). For further discussion of the WTO's sources and methodology, see *About the data* for table 4.4. The import shares by major commodity group are from the United Nations Statistics Division's Commodity Trade (Comtrade) database. The values of total imports reported here have not been fully reconciled with the estimates of imports of goods and services from the national accounts (shown in table 4.8) or those from the balance of payments (table 4.17).

The classification of commodity groups is based on the Standard International Trade Classification (SITC) revision 3. Previous editions contained data based on the SITC revision 1. Data for earlier years in previous editions may differ because of this change in methodology. Concordance tables are available to convert data reported in one system to another.

• **Merchandise imports** are the c.i.f. value of goods purchased from the rest of the world valued in U.S. dollars. • **Food** corresponds to the commodities in SITC sections 0 (food and live animals), 1 (beverages and tobacco), and 4 (animal and vegetable oils and fats) and SITC division 22 (oil seeds, oil nuts, and oil kernels). • **Agricultural raw materials** correspond to SITC section 2 (crude materials except fuels), excluding divisions 22, 27 (crude fertilizers and minerals excluding coal, petroleum, and precious stones), and 28 (metalliferous ores and scrap). • **Fuels** correspond to SITC section 3 (mineral fuels). • **Ores and metals** correspond to the commodities in SITC divisions 27, 28, and 68 (nonferrous metals). • **Manufactures** correspond to the commodities in SITC sections 5 (chemicals), 6 (basic manufactures), 7 (machinery and transport equipment), and 8 (miscellaneous manufactured goods), excluding division 68.

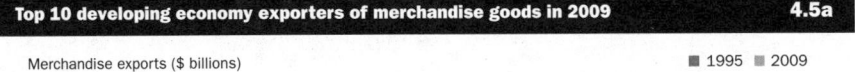

Top 10 developing economy exporters of merchandise goods in 2009   4.5a

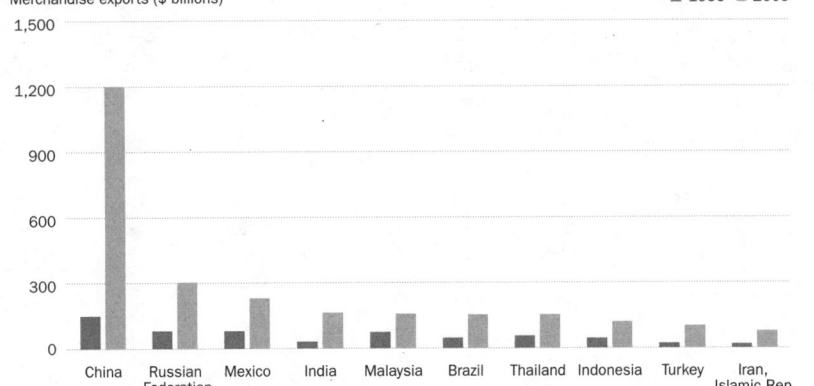

Merchandise exports ($ billions)   ■ 1995   ■ 2009

China continues to dominate merchandise exports among developing economies. Even when developed economies are included, China ranks as the second leading merchandise exporter.

Source: World Development Indicators data files and World Trade Organization.

Data on merchandise imports are from the WTO. Data on shares of imports by major commodity group are from Comtrade. The WTO publishes data on world trade in its *Annual Report*. The International Monetary Fund publishes estimates of total imports of goods in its *International Financial Statistics* and *Direction of Trade Statistics,* as does the United Nations Statistics Division in its *Monthly Bulletin of Statistics.* And the United Nations Conference on Trade and Development publishes data on the structure of imports in its *Handbook of Statistics.* Tariff line records of imports are compiled in the United Nations Statistics Division's Comtrade database.

	Commercial service exports		Transport		Travel		Insurance and financial services		Computer, information, communications, and other commercial services	
	$ millions		% of total		% of total		% of total		% of total	
	1995	2009	1995	2009	1995	2009	1995	2009	1995	2009
Afghanistan	..	..	..	..	..	..	..	..	..	..
Albania	94	2,348	19	11	69	78	1	0	10	11
Algeria	..	..	..	..	..	..	..	..	..	..
Angola	113	623	32	5	1	86	9	0	59	9
Argentina	3,676	10,758	27	15	60	37	0	0	12	48
Armenia	27	580	53	19	5	58	7	3	41	21
Australia	16,076	44,513	29	18	51	56	5	3	15	22
Austria	31,692	54,080	12	22	42	35	4	4	42	38
Azerbaijan	166	1,670	46	40	42	21	0	0	12	39
Bangladesh	469	935	15	15	5	7	0	6	80	72
Belarus	466	3,453	65	66	5	11	0	0	30	23
Belgium	35,466[a]	79,815[a]	..[a]	27[a]	..[a]	12[a]	..[a]	5[a]	..[a]	55[a]
Benin	159	328	26	4	53	72	7	2	14	22
Bolivia	174	498	45	13	32	56	10	14	14	17
Bosnia and Herzegovina	457	1,396	4	20	54	49	3	1	39	30
Botswana	236	842	16	10	68	54	8	4	7	33
Brazil	6,005	26,245	43	15	16	20	17	7	24	57
Bulgaria	1,431	6,889	35	21	33	55	0	3	32	22
Burkina Faso	38	109	17	19	48	57	0	2	35	21
Burundi	4	2	46	22	32	62	0	14	21	2
Cambodia	103	1,592	31	12	52	74	0	0	18	13
Cameroon	242	1,158	48	41	15	19	7	2	30	38
Canada	25,425	57,476	21	15	31	24	11	11	37	50
Central African Republic	0	..	34	..	34	..	20	..	12	..
Chad	23	..	5	..	50	..	2	..	44	..
Chile	3,249	8,401	37	56	28	19	7	4	28	22
China	18,430	128,600	18	18	47	31	10	2	24	49
Hong Kong SAR, China	33,790	86,306	33	31	17	17	9	13	41	39
Colombia	1,641	4,109	34	28	40	49	6	1	19	23
Congo, Dem. Rep.	..	..	..	..	..	..	..	..	..	..
Congo, Rep.	61	303	52	4	22	18	0	31	25	47
Costa Rica	957	3,694	14	8	71	49	0	0	15	43
Côte d'Ivoire	426	816	29	29	21	14	12	0	38	57
Croatia	2,223	11,889	32	9	61	76	1	1	6	15
Cuba	..	..	..	..	..	..	..	..	..	..
Czech Republic	6,638	20,278	22	27	43	32	1	1	34	40
Denmark	15,171	55,346	45	..	24	..	..	..	31	..
Dominican Republic	1,894	4,864	2	9	83	83	0	1	15	7
Ecuador	687	1,130	47	31	37	59	0	0	16	10
Egypt, Arab Rep.	8,262	21,302	39	31	32	50	1	1	28	17
El Salvador	342	806	28	34	25	40	8	4	39	23
Eritrea	49	..	70	..	3	..	1	..	27	..
Estonia	868	4,368	43	37	41	25	0	2	16	36
Ethiopia	310	1,676	77	59	5	20	2	1	16	20
Finland	7,334	27,536	28	10	22	10	2	2	48	78
France	83,108	142,487	25	23	33	35	5	2	37	41
Gabon	191	..	46	..	9	..	3	..	41	..
Gambia, The	38	104	22	19	73	60	0	0	5	21
Georgia	188	1,225	48	51	25	39	0	2	27	8
Germany	73,576	226,638	27	23	25	15	5	7	44	54
Ghana	139	1,722	59	19	8	56	3	1	30	24
Greece	9,528	37,690	4	50	43	39	0	2	52	9
Guatemala	628	1,818	9	14	34	65	4	2	54	20
Guinea	17	67	75	22	5	4	1	9	18	65
Guinea-Bissau	2	44	18	0	14	87	0	1	82	12
Haiti	98	327	5	..	92	96	1	0	2	4
Honduras	221	933	26	5	36	66	2	2	36	28

	Commercial service exports		Transport		Travel		Insurance and financial services		Computer, information, communications, and other commercial services	
	$ millions		% of total		% of total		% of total		% of total	
	1995	2009	1995	2009	1995	2009	1995	2009	1995	2009
Hungary	5,086	18,419	8	19	58	31	3	1	31	49
India	6,763	90,193	28	12	38	12	3	5	31	70
Indonesia	5,342	13,238	1	18	98	48	0	2	2	32
Iran, Islamic Rep.	533	..	26	..	13	..	9	..	53	..
Iraq	..	1,721	..	22	..	0	..	0	..	78
Ireland	4,799	92,964	22	4	46	5	0	20	32	70
Israel	7,906	21,961	25	14	38	17	0	0	36	68
Italy	61,173	101,237	18	13	47	40	7	9	29	38
Jamaica	1,568	2,616	16	13	68	74	1	2	15	11
Japan	63,966	125,918	35	25	5	8	1	4	59	62
Jordan	1,689	4,192	25	19	39	69	0	0	36	12
Kazakhstan	535	3,813	66	57	23	25	0	4	12	14
Kenya	1,183	2,198	59	48	36	31	1	1	3	20
Korea, Dem. Rep.	..	..	..	..	..	..	..	..	..	..
Korea, Rep.	22,133	57,304	42	51	23	16	0	5	34	28
Kosovo	..	..	..	..	..	..	..	..	..	..
Kuwait	1,124	10,425	84	30	11	2	6	1	0	66
Kyrgyz Republic	39	850	40	16	12	54	0	2	48	28
Lao PDR	68	368	23	8	76	73	1	3	1	16
Latvia	718	3,812	92	51	3	19	2	7	3	23
Lebanon	..	16,869	..	2	..	40	..	2	..	56
Lesotho	30	63	7	1	91	64	1	1	1	34
Liberia	..	142	..	10	..	87	..	..	..	3
Libya	20	385	63	68	12	13	..	16	25	3
Lithuania	482	3,769	60	56	16	30	1	1	23	14
Macedonia, FYR	151	845	32	30	14	26	4	2	51	43
Madagascar	219	..	30	..	26	..	2	..	42	..
Malawi	24	..	28	..	72	..	0	..	0	..
Malaysia	11,438	28,727	22	15	35	55	0	2	44	28
Mali	68	442	32	7	37	62	5	1	25	30
Mauritania	19	..	9	..	58	..	0	..	33	..
Mauritius	773	2,225	26	15	56	50	0	4	19	30
Mexico	9,585	15,420	12	10	64	73	7	10	17	6
Moldova	143	647	30	39	40	26	12	1	19	34
Mongolia	47	412	32	33	44	57	5	1	19	9
Morocco	2,020	11,892	20	18	64	56	1	2	14	25
Mozambique	242	544	25	28	..	36	..	1	75	35
Myanmar	353	256	6	51	43	18	0	..	51	31
Namibia	301	505	..	23	92	72	1	1	6	4
Nepal	592	548	9	7	30	68	0	0	61	25
Netherlands	44,646	90,853	40	27	15	14	1	2	44	57
New Zealand	4,401	7,760	35	19	53	59	0	1	13	21
Nicaragua	94	429	18	10	52	81	2	1	27	8
Niger	12	126	3	9	58	62	0	7	39	21
Nigeria	608	1,769	16	62	3	34	1	1	80	3
Norway	13,458	38,537	63	41	17	11	4	5	16	44
Oman	13	1,792	100	32	81	39	0	1	0	28
Pakistan	1,432	2,463	58	44	8	11	1	6	33	39
Panama	1,298	5,463	60	56	24	27	6	7	10	9
Papua New Guinea	321	162	11	9	8	1	1	7	80	84
Paraguay	566	1,288	13	13	24	16	5	2	57	69
Peru	1,042	3,517	32	21	41	58	7	9	19	12
Philippines	9,323	10,101	3	11	12	23	1	1	84	65
Poland	10,637	28,856	29	30	22	31	8	2	41	37
Portugal	8,161	22,539	19	26	59	43	5	2	18	30
Puerto Rico	..	..	..	..	..	..	..	..	..	..
Qatar	..	..	..	..	..	..	..	..	..	..

Structure of service exports

	Commercial service exports		Transport		Travel		Insurance and financial services		Computer, information, communications, and other commercial services	
	$ millions		% of total		% of total		% of total		% of total	
	1995	2009	1995	2009	1995	2009	1995	2009	1995	2009
Romania	1,476	9,737	32	30	40	13	5	2	23	56
Russian Federation	10,567	41,068	36	30	41	23	1	4	23	44
Rwanda	11	249	61	22	22	70	0	1	18	8
Saudi Arabia	3,475	9,335	..	20	..	64	..	13	..	3
Senegal	364	1,177	15	12	46	46	1	1	38	40
Serbia	..	3,478	..	21	..	25	..	1	..	53
Sierra Leone	71	53	14	35	80	48	0	1	6	15
Singapore	27,234	90,690	30	34	28	10	15	12	27	44
Slovak Republic	2,378	6,259	26	30	26	37	5	6	43	26
Slovenia	2,016	5,999	25	25	54	42	1	2	21	31
Somalia	..	..	..	..	..	..	..	..	..	..
South Africa	4,414	11,656	24	12	48	65	10	8	18	15
Spain	40,019	122,101	16	15	63	44	4	5	17	36
Sri Lanka	800	1,874	42	46	28	19	3	4	27	31
Sudan	82	392	1	4	10	76	4	15	86	24
Swaziland	150	191	18	4	32	21	0	11	50	64
Sweden	15,336	59,073	32	16	23	17	2	4	43	62
Switzerland	25,179	72,309	15	8	38	19	28	30	20	43
Syrian Arab Republic	1,632	3,770	15	5	77	84	0	4	8	7
Tajikistan	..	142	..	50	..	2	..	5	..	44
Tanzania	566	1,795	0	19	89	65	0	1	11	16
Thailand	14,652	29,677	17	19	55	53	1	1	28	27
Timor-Leste	..	..	..	..	..	..	..	..	..	..
Togo	64	253	34	43	20	16	2	5	44	36
Trinidad and Tobago	331	918	59	24	23	43	9	25	9	8
Tunisia	2,401	5,241	25	26	64	53	2	2	10	18
Turkey	14,475	32,758	12	23	34	65	2	3	52	9
Turkmenistan	79	..	80	..	9	..	1	..	10	..
Uganda	104	854	18	4	75	78	0	4	7	14
Ukraine	2,846	13,324	76	47	7	27	3	3	15	23
United Arab Emirates	..	..	..	..	..	..	..	..	..	..
United Kingdom	77,549	236,254	21	13	26	13	18	28	35	46
United States	198,501	475,979	23	13	38	25	4	15	35	47
Uruguay	1,309	2,132	31	16	47	62	1	4	21	18
Uzbekistan	..	..	..	..	..	..	..	..	..	..
Venezuela, RB	1,529	1,805	38	39	56	44	0	0	6	18
Vietnam	2,243	5,656	..	..	..	..	..	..	..	..
West Bank and Gaza	265	407	0	4	96	66	0	0	4	30
Yemen, Rep.	141	1,085	22	4	35	83	0	0	43	13
Zambia	112	241	64	48	26	41	0	2	10	9
Zimbabwe	353	..	26	..	51	..	0	..	23	..
World	**1,228,960 t**	**3,417,725 t**	**27 w**	**21 w**	**33 w**	**26 w**	**5 w**	**8 w**	**36 w**	**45 w**
Low income	6,429	21,036	28	20	28	37	1	3	44	41
Middle income	174,925	641,508	25	21	45	42	5	4	27	33
Lower middle income	87,678	377,784	21	21	46	36	5	2	30	42
Upper middle income	87,180	264,293	27	22	43	47	5	5	25	25
Low & middle income	180,841	660,929	25	21	44	42	5	4	28	33
East Asia & Pacific	62,745	220,270	17	17	49	40	5	1	31	41
Europe & Central Asia	35,079	131,431	38	33	34	29	1	3	27	34
Latin America & Carib.	38,013	98,855	24	18	51	54	7	7	18	21
Middle East & N. Africa	..	..	..	..	..	..	..	..	..	..
South Asia	10,333	97,113	32	20	30	13	2	5	36	62
Sub-Saharan Africa	12,144	35,613	26	28	31	53	6	4	40	16
High income	1,047,874	2,755,581	27	21	30	22	6	9	38	48
Euro area	425,302	1,087,280	25	21	33	24	4	6	37	49

a. Includes Luxembourg.

About the data

Balance of payments statistics, the main source of information on international trade in services, have many weaknesses. Disaggregation of important components may be limited and varies considerably across countries. There are inconsistencies in the methods used to report items. And the recording of major flows as net items is common (for example, insurance transactions are often recorded as premiums less claims). These factors contribute to a downward bias in the value of the service trade reported in the balance of payments.

Efforts are being made to improve the coverage, quality, and consistency of these data. Eurostat and the Organisation for Economic Co-operation and Development, for example, are working together to improve the collection of statistics on trade in services in member countries. In addition, the International Monetary Fund (IMF) has implemented the new classification of trade in services introduced in the fifth edition of its *Balance of Payments Manual* (1993).

Still, difficulties in capturing all the dimensions of international trade in services mean that the record is likely to remain incomplete. Cross-border intrafirm service transactions, which are usually not captured in the balance of payments, have increased in recent years. An example is transnational corporations' use of mainframe computers around the clock for data processing, exploiting time zone differences between their home country and the host countries of their affiliates. Another important dimension of service trade not captured by conventional balance of payments statistics is establishment trade—sales in the host country by foreign affiliates. By contrast, cross-border intrafirm transactions in merchandise may be reported as exports or imports in the balance of payments.

The data on exports of services in the table and on imports of services in table 4.7, unlike those in editions before 2000, include only commercial services and exclude the category "government services not included elsewhere." The data are compiled by the IMF based on returns from national sources. Data on total trade in goods and services from the IMF's Balance of Payments database are shown in table 4.17.

International transactions in services are defined by the IMF's *Balance of Payments Manual* (1993) as the economic output of intangible commodities that may be produced, transferred, and consumed at the same time. Definitions may vary among reporting economies. Travel services include the goods and services consumed by travelers, such as meals, lodging, and transport (within the economy visited), including car rental.

Definitions

• **Commercial service exports** are total service exports minus exports of government services not included elsewhere. • **Transport** covers all transport services (sea, air, land, internal waterway, space, and pipeline) performed by residents of one economy for those of another and involving the carriage of passengers, movement of goods (freight), rental of carriers with crew, and related support and auxiliary services. Excluded are freight insurance, which is included in insurance services; goods procured in ports by nonresident carriers and repairs of transport equipment, which are included in goods; repairs of harbors, railway facilities, and airfield facilities, which are included in construction services; and rental of carriers without crew, which is included in other services. • **Travel** covers goods and services acquired from an economy by travelers in that economy for their own use during visits of less than one year for business or personal purposes. • **Insurance and financial services** cover freight insurance on goods exported and other direct insurance such as life insurance; financial intermediation services such as commissions, foreign exchange transactions, and brokerage services; and auxiliary services such as financial market operational and regulatory services. • **Computer, information, communications, and other commercial services** cover such activities as international telecommunications and postal and courier services; computer data; news-related service transactions between residents and nonresidents; construction services; royalties and license fees; miscellaneous business, professional, and technical services; and personal, cultural, and recreational services.

Top 10 developing economy exporters of commercial services in 2009   **4.6a**

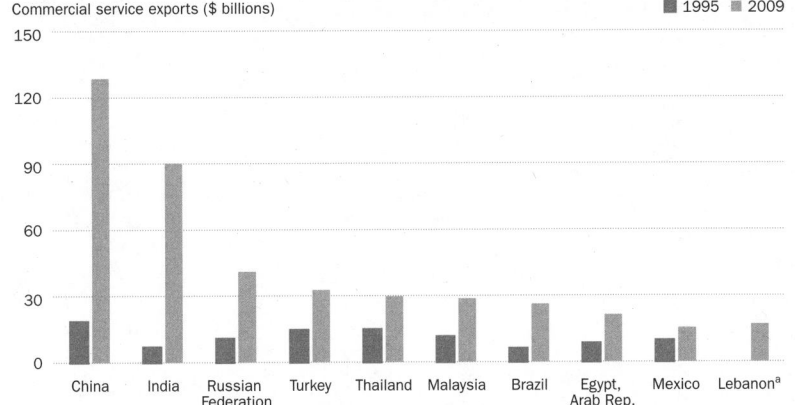

Commercial service exports ($ billions)
■ 1995 ■ 2009

The top 10 developing country exporters of commercial services accounted for almost 68 percent of developing country commercial service exports and 13 percent of world commercial service exports.

a. Data are unavailable for 1995.
Source: International Monetary Fund balance of payments data files.

Data sources

Data on exports of commercial services are from the IMF, which publishes balance of payments data in its *International Financial Statistics* and *Balance of Payments Statistics Yearbook*.

	Commercial service imports		Transport		Travel		Insurance and financial services		Computer, information, communications, and other commercial services	
	$ millions		% of total		% of total		% of total		% of total	
	1995	**2009**	**1995**	**2009**	**1995**	**2009**	**1995**	**2009**	**1995**	**2009**
Afghanistan	..	..	..	..	..	..	..	..	..	..
Albania	98	2,215	61	15	7	72	22	5	10	9
Algeria	..	..	..	..	..	..	..	..	..	..
Angola	1,665	18,210	18	23	5	1	3	4	75	72
Argentina	6,992	11,445	30	23	47	39	7	5	16	33
Armenia	52	839	83	46	6	39	10	7	1	8
Australia	16,979	47,613	37	31	30	39	7	3	26	27
Austria	27,552	36,894	12	29	40	29	6	4	43	38
Azerbaijan	297	3,297	31	24	49	11	1	3	19	62
Bangladesh	1,192	3,202	65	83	20	8	6	2	10	8
Belarus	276	2,031	36	40	32	29	4	4	29	28
Belgium	33,134[a]	73,008	24[a]	25	28[a]	25	10[a]	4	38[a]	47
Benin	235	500	59	62	15	13	10	5	16	20
Bolivia	321	993	66	38	15	29	9	13	10	19
Bosnia and Herzegovina	262	625	51	32	31	38	10	4	8	25
Botswana	440	1,040	43	40	33	22	8	4	16	34
Brazil	13,161	44,074	44	18	26	25	10	8	21	49
Bulgaria	1,278	5,037	42	22	15	35	0	8	43	35
Burkina Faso	116	564	56	59	20	11	5	17	20	13
Burundi	62	160	49	53	41	39	6	3	4	6
Cambodia	181	939	46	58	5	11	4	5	45	27
Cameroon	485	2,081	35	33	22	17	7	4	36	45
Canada	32,985	77,579	24	22	31	31	11	12	34	35
Central African Republic	114	..	44	..	38	..	8	..	10	..
Chad	174	..	55	..	15	..	2	..	29	..
Chile	3,524	9,351	54	52	20	17	4	10	22	20
China	24,635	158,107	39	29	15	28	17	8	29	35
Hong Kong SAR, China	24,962	44,379	22	34	54	34	6	8	18	24
Colombia	2,813	6,860	42	34	31	26	12	8	15	32
Congo, Dem. Rep.	..	..	..	..	..	..	..	..	..	..
Congo, Rep.	690	3,523	19	15	8	5	7	5	67	75
Costa Rica	895	1,407	41	36	36	26	5	9	18	29
Côte d'Ivoire	1,235	2,324	50	58	15	15	11	0	23	27
Croatia	1,373	3,812	28	18	31	27	3	5	38	51
Cuba	..	..	..	..	..	..	..	..	..	..
Czech Republic	4,860	18,887	16	21	34	22	5	3	45	54
Denmark	13,945	50,912	45	..	31	..	..	..	24	..
Dominican Republic	957	1,733	61	58	18	20	10	9	11	13
Ecuador	1,141	2,556	42	54	21	21	6	6	31	18
Egypt, Arab Rep.	4,511	12,765	35	45	28	20	5	11	32	24
El Salvador	488	1,231	55	57	15	15	11	15	19	13
Eritrea	45	..	2	..	7	..	0	..	93	..
Estonia	420	2,496	53	33	22	24	5	2	21	41
Ethiopia	337	2,190	63	67	8	6	7	4	22	22
Finland	9,418	25,687	23	19	24	17	5	2	48	62
France	64,523	126,425	33	26	25	31	6	3	36	41
Gabon	832	..	18	..	17	..	9	..	57	..
Gambia, The	47	83	60	46	30	11	6	8	4	36
Georgia	249	910	27	54	63	20	8	14	2	12
Germany	128,865	253,467	18	21	47	32	2	4	33	43
Ghana	331	2,166	61	41	6	27	6	4	26	28
Greece	4,003	19,525	30	51	33	17	5	8	33	24
Guatemala	672	2,058	41	46	21	35	9	10	29	9
Guinea	252	288	58	37	8	5	7	9	26	50
Guinea-Bissau	27	85	53	38	14	54	5	5	28	4
Haiti	236	736	78	72	15	9	2	1	6	19
Honduras	326	1,077	60	42	18	27	2	6	20	25

	Commercial service imports		Transport		Travel		Insurance and financial services		Computer, information, communications, and other commercial services	
	$ millions		% of total		% of total		% of total		% of total	
	1995	2009	1995	2009	1995	2009	1995	2009	1995	2009
Hungary	3,765	16,407	13	17	40	22	5	3	43	57
India	10,062	80,274	57	44	10	12	6	10	28	35
Indonesia	13,230	27,625	37	44	16	19	3	5	43	32
Iran, Islamic Rep.	2,192	..	43	..	11	..	10	..	36	..
Iraq	..	7,565	..	53	..	10	..	27	..	10
Ireland	11,252	104,551	16	2	18	8	1	14	65	76
Israel	8,131	16,865	45	32	26	17	3	2	26	48
Italy	54,613	114,581	24	20	27	24	10	5	39	50
Jamaica	1,073	1,824	46	43	14	12	9	11	31	34
Japan	121,547	146,965	30	28	30	17	2	6	38	50
Jordan	1,385	3,657	52	53	31	29	6	8	11	10
Kazakhstan	776	9,881	38	19	36	11	0	6	25	64
Kenya	900	1,634	46	51	21	14	10	8	22	26
Korea, Dem. Rep.	..	..	..	..	..	..	..	..	..	..
Korea, Rep.	25,394	74,978	38	31	25	18	2	2	36	49
Kosovo	..	..	..	..	..	..	..	..	..	..
Kuwait	3,826	11,297	39	31	59	66	2	1	0	2
Kyrgyz Republic	193	858	27	48	3	31	4	2	65	19
Lao PDR	119	114	43	12	25	72	4	−4	28	20
Latvia	225	2,260	68	26	11	35	7	5	14	34
Lebanon	..	14,301	..	15	..	28	..	2	..	55
Lesotho	58	91	75	79	23	15	0	0	2	6
Liberia	..	141	..	60	..	20	..	2	..	17
Libya	510	4,323	60	48	15	37	..	14	25	2
Lithuania	457	2,883	64	38	23	41	1	2	12	19
Macedonia, FYR	300	789	50	39	9	13	21	4	21	45
Madagascar	277	..	56	..	21	..	4	..	20	..
Malawi	151	..	67	..	26	..	0	..	7	..
Malaysia	14,821	27,257	38	34	16	24	0	4	47	38
Mali	412	1,022	60	63	12	14	1	5	27	18
Mauritania	197	..	62	..	12	..	1	..	25	..
Mauritius	630	1,586	40	32	25	22	5	5	30	40
Mexico	9,021	21,402	38	13	35	33	12	52	14	2
Moldova	193	678	52	38	29	36	9	3	10	24
Mongolia	87	545	70	37	22	39	0	3	8	21
Morocco	1,350	5,302	48	44	22	21	4	5	26	30
Mozambique	350	1,004	33	35	..	21	2	2	65	42
Myanmar	233	547	11	46	8	7	1	..	81	47
Namibia	538	602	37	37	17	18	9	4	37	41
Nepal	305	771	36	28	45	56	3	4	16	12
Netherlands	43,618	84,625	29	21	27	25	3	3	41	51
New Zealand	4,571	7,825	41	29	28	33	5	4	26	34
Nicaragua	207	517	39	48	19	28	3	11	38	13
Niger	120	599	74	67	11	11	3	4	12	18
Nigeria	4,398	16,127	22	38	21	25	3	3	54	34
Norway	13,052	36,504	38	26	32	34	6	4	24	37
Oman	985	5,555	42	38	5	16	5	10	49	36
Pakistan	2,431	5,844	67	54	18	12	4	4	10	30
Panama	1,049	2,118	71	58	12	16	9	15	9	11
Papua New Guinea	642	1,915	25	23	9	2	3	12	63	63
Paraguay	676	511	66	61	20	25	12	11	1	3
Peru	1,781	4,619	51	37	17	24	10	11	22	28
Philippines	6,906	8,344	30	44	6	29	2	4	63	23
Poland	7,008	23,789	25	22	6	31	14	6	55	41
Portugal	6,339	14,186	27	30	33	27	9	4	31	40
Puerto Rico	..	..	..	..	..	..	..	..	..	..
Qatar	..	..	..	..	..	..	..	..	..	..

	Commercial service imports		Transport		Travel		Insurance and financial services		Computer, information, communications, and other commercial services	
	$ millions		% of total		% of total		% of total		% of total	
	1995	2009	1995	2009	1995	2009	1995	2009	1995	2009
Romania	1,801	10,154	34	28	39	15	5	7	22	51
Russian Federation	20,205	59,241	16	16	57	35	0	4	26	45
Rwanda	58	503	73	63	17	14	0	1	10	22
Saudi Arabia	8,670	45,540	25	25	..	41	3	6	72	28
Senegal	405	1,384	57	55	18	13	7	11	18	21
Serbia	..	3,406	..	27	..	28	..	4	..	40
Sierra Leone	79	107	17	57	63	12	4	9	16	22
Singapore	21,111	82,189	44	32	22	19	10	6	24	42
Slovak Republic	1,800	7,933	17	22	18	26	5	14	60	37
Slovenia	1,429	4,330	31	20	40	31	2	4	27	45
Somalia	..	..	..	..	..	..	..	..	..	..
South Africa	5,756	14,390	40	41	32	29	14	4	14	26
Spain	22,354	86,988	31	20	20	19	7	8	41	52
Sri Lanka	1,169	2,487	58	62	16	17	5	6	21	15
Sudan	150	2,684	27	51	29	32	0	1	44	68
Swaziland	206	539	16	33	21	13	4	6	59	48
Sweden	17,112	44,373	28	16	32	27	1	1	38	56
Switzerland	14,899	38,867	35	19	50	27	1	8	14	46
Syrian Arab Republic	1,358	3,127	57	58	37	26	6	9	6	7
Tajikistan	..	289	..	49	..	2	..	10	..	38
Tanzania	729	1,685	30	36	49	45	3	4	18	15
Thailand	18,629	37,541	42	45	23	12	5	5	30	38
Timor-Leste	..	..	..	..	..	..	..	..	..	..
Togo	148	358	71	71	12	5	4	10	12	14
Trinidad and Tobago	223	271	42	47	31	28	8	3	19	22
Tunisia	1,245	2,812	45	53	20	15	6	10	28	23
Turkey	4,654	15,607	30	42	20	27	8	13	42	19
Turkmenistan	403	..	40	..	18	..	7	..	35	..
Uganda	563	1,408	38	61	14	13	4	10	43	16
Ukraine	1,334	11,070	34	32	16	30	7	13	43	25
United Arab Emirates	..	..	..	..	..	..	..	..	..	..
United Kingdom	62,524	160,036	27	18	40	32	4	7	29	44
United States	129,227	334,311	32	20	36	24	6	21	26	35
Uruguay	814	1,072	46	42	29	31	5	6	20	21
Uzbekistan	..	..	..	..	..	..	..	..	..	..
Venezuela, RB	4,654	9,223	31	44	37	17	3	6	30	33
Vietnam	2,304	7,044	..	..	..	..	..	..	..	..
West Bank and Gaza	349	786	28	8	46	68	3	1	25	23
Yemen, Rep.	604	2,038	36	46	12	11	7	9	45	35
Zambia	282	674	79	57	9	6	0	11	12	26
Zimbabwe	645	..	56	..	19	..	3	..	23	..
World	**1,221,691 t**	**3,144,723 t**	**31 w**	**25 w**	**31 w**	**25 w**	**6 w**	**10 w**	**32 w**	**40 w**
Low income	9,833	29,059	51	58	18	18	5	4	27	19
Middle income	218,955	749,008	39	32	24	26	9	14	28	28
Lower middle income	109,579	443,081	42	38	16	22	10	7	32	32
Upper middle income	109,232	304,268	38	27	30	28	8	20	25	25
Low & middle income	228,417	777,282	40	33	23	25	9	14	28	28
East Asia & Pacific	82,593	272,307	38	35	16	24	10	6	37	35
Europe & Central Asia	35,575	139,286	30	30	33	29	5	8	33	33
Latin America & Carib.	52,313	127,915	41	24	31	29	10	30	17	17
Middle East & N. Africa	19,571	62,588	45	47	21	19	..	11	28	23
South Asia	15,377	93,734	59	51	13	13	5	8	23	29
Sub-Saharan Africa	24,587	88,519	40	42	24	23	9	4	28	31
High income	992,976	2,368,417	29	22	33	25	5	9	33	43
Euro area	422,763	995,810	25	23	32	27	5	4	38	46

a. Includes Luxembourg.

About the data

Trade in services differs from trade in goods because services are produced and consumed at the same time. Thus services to a traveler may be consumed in the producing country (for example, use of a hotel room) but are classified as imports of the traveler's country. In other cases services may be supplied from a remote location; for example, insurance services may be supplied from one location and consumed in another. For further discussion of the problems of measuring trade in services, see *About the data* for table 4.6.

The data on imports of services in the table and on exports of services in table 4.6, unlike those in editions before 2000, include only commercial services and exclude the category "government services not included elsewhere." The data are compiled by the International Monetary Fund (IMF) based on returns from national sources.

International transactions in services are defined by the IMF's *Balance of Payments Manual* (1993) as the economic output of intangible commodities that may be produced, transferred, and consumed at the same time. Definitions may vary among reporting economies.

Travel services include the goods and services consumed by travelers, such as meals, lodging, and transport (within the economy visited), including car rental.

Definitions

• **Commercial service imports** are total service imports minus imports of government services not included elsewhere. • **Transport** covers all transport services (sea, air, land, internal waterway, space, and pipeline) performed by residents of one economy for those of another and involving the carriage of passengers, movement of goods (freight), rental of carriers with crew, and related support and auxiliary services. Excluded are freight insurance, which is included in insurance services; goods procured in ports by nonresident carriers and repairs of transport equipment, which are included in goods; repairs of harbors, railway facilities, and airfield facilities, which are included in construction services; and rental of carriers without crew, which is included in other services. • **Travel** covers goods and services acquired from an economy by travelers in that economy for their own use during visits of less than one year for business or personal purposes. • **Insurance and financial services** cover freight insurance on goods imported and other direct insurance such as life insurance; financial intermediation services such as commissions, foreign exchange transactions, and brokerage services; and auxiliary services such as financial market operational and regulatory services. • **Computer, information, communications, and other commercial services** cover such activities as international telecommunications, and postal and courier services; computer data; news-related service transactions between residents and nonresidents; construction services; royalties and license fees; miscellaneous business, professional, and technical services; and personal, cultural, and recreational services.

The mix of commercial service imports by developing economies is changing | 4.7a

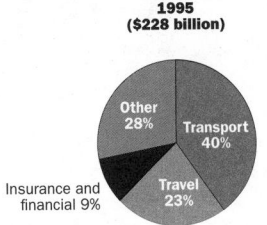

1995
($228 billion)

Other 28%
Transport 40%
Insurance and financial 9%
Travel 23%

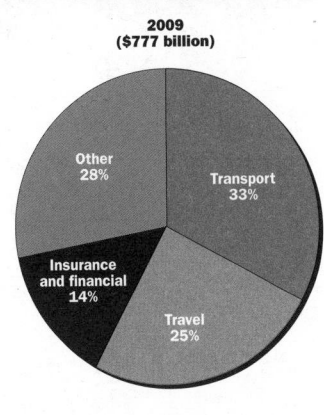

2009
($777 billion)

Other 28%
Transport 33%
Insurance and financial 14%
Travel 25%

Between 1995 and 2009 developing economies' commercial service imports more than tripled. Insurance and financial services and travel services are displacing transport as the most important services imported.

Source: International Monetary Fund balance of payments data files.

Data sources

Data on imports of commercial services are from the IMF, which publishes balance of payments data in its *International Financial Statistics* and *Balance of Payments Statistics Yearbook*.

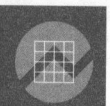
	Household final consumption expenditure		General government final consumption expenditure		Gross capital formation		Exports of goods and services		Imports of goods and services		Gross savings	
	% of GDP		% of GDP		% of GDP		% of GDP		% of GDP		% of GDP	
	1995	2009	1995	2009	1995	2009	1995	2009	1995	2009	1995	2009
Afghanistan	..	88	..	9	..	25	..	16	..	48	..	..
Albania	87	87	14	10	21	29	12	29	35	54	20	17
Algeria	55	41	17	14	31	41	26	40	29	36	..	..
Angola	34	..	40	..	35	15	82	52	68	46	78	10
Argentina	69	59	13	15	18	21	10	21	10	16	16	23
Armenia	109	82	11	11	18	31	24	12	62	36	–9	20
Australia	60	57	18	17	24	28	18	20	20	22	18	21
Austria	56	54	20	20	25	21	35	51	36	46	22	24
Azerbaijan	77	37	13	14	24	22	28	52	42	25	13	45
Bangladesh	83	77	5	5	19	24	11	19	17	27	22	39
Belarus	59	56	21	17	25	38	50	51	54	62	21	25
Belgium	54	52	21	25	21	20	65	73	62	70	29	22
Benin	82	..	11	..	20	25	20	14	33	28	11	11
Bolivia	76	66	14	15	15	17	23	36	27	33	11	23
Bosnia and Herzegovina	..	63	..	23	20	22	20	33	71	58	..	13
Botswana	34	63	29	24	25	24	51	34	38	45	36	16
Brazil	62	62	21	22	18	17	7	11	9	11	16	15
Bulgaria	66	66	17	16	16	26	52	48	50	56	15	16
Burkina Faso	63	..	25	..	24	..	14	..	27	..	29	..
Burundi	89	..	19	..	6	..	13	..	27	..	6	..
Cambodia	95	74	6	8	15	21	31	60	47	63	6	19
Cameroon	72	72	9	9	13	18	24	27	18	31	14	20
Canada	57	59	21	22	19	21	37	29	34	30	18	18
Central African Republic	79	93	15	4	14	11	20	14	28	22	11	..
Chad	91	79	7	16	13	34	22	42	34	70	12	..
Chile	61	60	10	13	26	19	29	38	27	30	25	22
China	43	35	14	13	42	48	20	27	19	22	42	54
Hong Kong SAR, China	62	62	8	9	34	23	143	194	148	187	..	31
Colombia	65	64	15	16	26	23	15	16	21	18	19	18
Congo, Dem. Rep.	81	74	5	8	9	30	28	10	24	22	..	..
Congo, Rep.	49	42	13	12	37	25	65	72	64	51	–2	18
Costa Rica	71	62	14	17	18	20	38	43	40	42	15	20
Côte d'Ivoire	66	72	11	9	16	11	42	42	34	34	12	15
Croatia	67	57	26	20	16	27	33	36	42	39	11	22
Cuba	71	54	24	33	7	11	13	20	16	18	..	..
Czech Republic	51	51	21	22	33	22	51	70	55	64	29	20
Denmark	51	49	25	30	20	17	38	48	33	44	22	22
Dominican Republic	81	85	5	8	18	15	36	22	39	30	16	10
Ecuador	68	69	13	10	22	32	26	37	28	48	17	24
Egypt, Arab Rep.	74	76	11	11	20	19	23	25	28	32	22	17
El Salvador	87	92	9	10	20	13	22	22	38	38	18	11
Eritrea	94	86	44	31	23	11	22	4	83	20	19	..
Estonia	54	53	26	22	28	19	68	71	76	65	24	24
Ethiopia	80	88	8	8	18	22	10	11	16	29	21	16
Finland	52	54	23	25	18	18	37	37	29	35	22	20
France	57	58	24	25	19	19	23	23	22	25	19	16
Gabon	41	41	12	12	23	28	59	52	36	33	33	..
Gambia, The	90	78	14	16	20	26	49	30	73	50	8	19
Georgia	102	83	11	24	4	12	26	30	42	49	1	0
Germany	58	59	20	20	22	16	24	41	23	36	20	21
Ghana	76	82	12	10	20	20	24	31	33	41	18	16
Greece	76	75	15	19	18	16	17	19	27	29	18	3
Guatemala	86	86	6	10	15	13	19	23	25	33	11	12
Guinea	74	75	8	8	21	22	21	41	25	45	21	8
Guinea-Bissau	95	83	6	14	22	23	12	26	35	47	10	..
Haiti	86	..	7	..	26	27	9	14	29	44	..	..
Honduras	64	80	9	19	32	20	44	42	48	61	27	16

	Household final consumption expenditure		General government final consumption expenditure		Gross capital formation		Exports of goods and services		Imports of goods and services		Gross savings	
	% of GDP		% of GDP		% of GDP		% of GDP		% of GDP		% of GDP	
	1995	2009	1995	2009	1995	2009	1995	2009	1995	2009	1995	2009
Hungary	68	67	11	9	21	22	46	81	46	80	17	15
India	64	56	11	12	27	36	11	20	12	24	27	35
Indonesia	62	57	8	10	32	31	26	24	28	21	28	23
Iran, Islamic Rep.	46	45	16	11	29	33	22	32	13	22	37	..
Iraq	..	..	..	..	..	..	..	..	..	..	..	..
Ireland	54	52	16	19	18	14	76	89	65	74	23	9
Israel	56	57	28	24	25	16	29	35	37	32	13	20
Italy	58	60	18	22	20	19	26	24	22	24	22	16
Jamaica	70	81	11	16	29	21	51	35	61	53	25	13
Japan	55	60	15	20	28	20	9	13	8	12	30	24
Jordan	65	83	24	24	33	15	52	43	73	65	29	10
Kazakhstan	71	50	14	12	20	30	39	42	44	34	15	28
Kenya	70	76	15	16	22	21	33	25	39	38	23	15
Korea, Dem. Rep.	..	..	..	..	..	..	..	..	..	..	..	..
Korea, Rep.	52	54	11	16	38	26	29	50	30	46	36	30
Kosovo	..	..	..	18	..	28	..	14	..	54	..	..
Kuwait	43	28	32	13	15	19	52	66	42	26	38	59
Kyrgyz Republic	75	86	20	23	18	22	29	50	42	81	8	14
Lao PDR	..	66	..	8	..	37	23	33	37	44	..	25
Latvia	63	61	24	21	14	19	43	42	45	43	14	29
Lebanon	103	79	12	16	36	30	11	22	62	47	..	13
Lesotho	93	79	35	50	76	31	24	51	128	112	39	28
Liberia	..	202	..	19	..	20	9	31	72	173	..	−2
Libya	59	23	22	9	12	28	29	67	22	27	..	67
Lithuania	68	65	21	19	21	27	47	60	58	72	12	15
Macedonia, FYR	70	81	19	18	21	24	33	44	43	67	13	18
Madagascar	90	80	7	11	11	33	24	28	32	52	2	..
Malawi	79	62	21	21	17	25	30	30	48	38	8	..
Malaysia	48	50	12	14	44	14	94	96	98	75	34	31
Mali	83	77	10	10	23	22	21	26	36	36	15	19
Mauritania	77	72	11	21	20	25	37	50	45	68	14	..
Mauritius	63	75	14	15	26	21	59	48	61	59	25	17
Mexico	67	67	10	12	20	22	30	28	28	29	19	22
Moldova	57	87	27	22	25	27	49	37	58	73	18	19
Mongolia	56	55	13	1	32	50	48	56	49	63	35	42
Morocco	68	57	17	18	21	36	27	29	34	39	17	31
Mozambique	90	84	8	13	27	21	16	25	41	44	9	9
Myanmar	..	..	..	..	14	..	1	..	2	..	..	..
Namibia	54	62	30	24	22	27	49	47	56	60	32	27
Nepal	75	81	9	11	25	30	25	16	35	37	21	38
Netherlands	49	46	24	29	21	18	59	69	54	62	27	22
New Zealand	59	60	17	20	23	18	29	28	28	27	18	16
Nicaragua	83	91	11	12	22	23	19	35	35	61	−1	10
Niger	86	..	14	..	7	..	17	..	24	..	−1	..
Nigeria	..	..	..	..	..	..	44	36	42	27	..	..
Norway	50	43	22	22	22	20	38	42	32	27	26	32
Oman	51	34	25	15	15	30	44	59	36	38	10	39
Pakistan	72	80	12	8	19	19	17	13	19	20	21	22
Panama	52	49	15	10	30	25	101	77	98	61	30	35
Papua New Guinea	44	69	17	11	22	20	61	58	44	57	35	20
Paraguay	76	78	10	12	26	16	59	47	71	52	18	12
Peru	71	64	10	10	25	22	13	24	18	20	16	23
Philippines	74	74	11	11	22	15	36	32	44	31	19	40
Poland	60	61	20	19	19	20	23	39	21	39	20	19
Portugal	65	67	17	21	24	20	27	28	34	36	24	10
Puerto Rico	..	..	..	..	..	..	72	..	97	..	..	..
Qatar	32	21	32	25	35	39	44	47	43	31	..	..

	Household final consumption expenditure		General government final consumption expenditure		Gross capital formation		Exports of goods and services		Imports of goods and services		Gross savings	
	% of GDP		% of GDP		% of GDP		% of GDP		% of GDP		% of GDP	
	1995	2009	1995	2009	1995	2009	1995	2009	1995	2009	1995	2009
Romania	68	61	14	15	24	31	28	33	33	40	19	29
Russian Federation	52	54	19	20	25	19	29	28	26	20	28	23
Rwanda	97	81	10	15	13	22	5	12	26	29	20	15
Saudi Arabia	47	38	24	25	20	26	38	54	28	43	20	32
Senegal	80	83	13	9	14	28	31	24	37	44	8	16
Serbia	73	74	23	19	12	24	17	27	24	44	..	17
Sierra Leone	88	84	14	14	6	15	19	16	26	29	–3	8
Singapore	41	43	8	10	34	29	..	221	..	203	53	45
Slovak Republic	52	47	22	20	24	38	58	99	56	104	27	29
Slovenia	60	55	19	20	24	23	50	59	52	57	23	22
Somalia	..	..	..	..	..	..	..	..	..	..	..	..
South Africa	63	60	18	21	18	19	23	27	22	28	17	15
Spain	60	56	18	21	22	24	22	23	22	26	22	20
Sri Lanka	73	64	11	18	26	25	36	21	46	28	20	24
Sudan	85	67	5	14	14	25	5	15	10	21	3	12
Swaziland	82	73	15	27	16	17	60	60	74	76	16	2
Sweden	49	49	27	28	17	17	40	49	33	42	20	24
Switzerland	60	58	12	11	23	20	36	52	31	41	30	32
Syrian Arab Republic	66	72	13	14	27	16	31	34	38	36	27	14
Tajikistan	62	93	16	28	29	22	66	13	72	56	..	12
Tanzania[a]	86	62	12	20	20	30	24	23	42	35	7	21
Thailand	55	54	10	13	42	22	42	68	49	58	34	30
Timor-Leste	..	..	..	..	..	..	..	..	..	..	..	..
Togo	77	..	12	9	16	..	32	42	37	62	17	..
Trinidad and Tobago	53	49	12	10	21	12	54	68	39	39	27	31
Tunisia	63	63	16	13	25	27	45	52	49	55	20	23
Turkey	68	72	11	15	25	15	20	23	24	24	22	13
Turkmenistan	44	49	12	10	49	11	84	76	84	46	50	..
Uganda	85	76	11	11	12	24	12	23	21	35	13	18
Ukraine	55	65	21	19	27	17	47	46	50	48	23	16
United Arab Emirates	48	46	16	10	30	20	69	87	63	64	..	..
United Kingdom	63	65	20	23	17	14	28	28	28	30	15	12
United States	68	71	15	17	18	14	11	11	12	14	16	10
Uruguay	73	68	12	13	15	18	19	26	19	26	14	17
Uzbekistan	51	56	22	18	27	26	28	36	28	36	..	..
Venezuela, RB	69	64	7	13	18	25	27	18	22	20	21	22
Vietnam	74	66	8	6	27	38	33	68	42	79	20	29
West Bank and Gaza	98	..	18	..	35	..	16	..	68	..	12	..
Yemen, Rep.	71	..	14	..	22	..	51	..	58	..	26	..
Zambia	72	61	15	13	16	22	36	36	40	32	9	19
Zimbabwe	65	113	18	14	20	2	38	36	41	65	18	..
World	**61 w**	**62 w**	**17 w**	**19 w**	**22 w**	**19 w**	**21 w**	**24 w**	**21 w**	**24 w**	**22 w**	**19 w**
Low income	81	78	9	10	18	24	18	23	26	36	17	24
Middle income	60	56	14	15	27	28	23	27	24	26	26	29
Lower middle income	55	50	12	13	34	37	23	29	24	28	33	40
Upper middle income	63	62	15	16	22	20	23	25	23	24	20	19
Low & middle income	60	57	14	15	27	28	23	27	24	26	26	29
East Asia & Pacific	48	42	13	13	40	40	27	35	28	30	38	47
Europe & Central Asia	61	62	16	17	25	19	29	30	31	29	23	19
Latin America & Carib.	66	64	15	16	20	20	18	21	19	21	18	19
Middle East & N. Africa	63	55	15	13	25	28	26	38	29	33	..	..
South Asia	67	61	10	11	25	33	12	19	15	24	25	34
Sub-Saharan Africa	69	67	16	18	18	21	28	30	30	34	16	15
High income	61	63	17	20	21	17	21	24	20	24	21	16
Euro area	57	58	20	22	21	19	29	36	28	35	21	19

a. Covers mainland Tanzania only.

Structure of demand | 4.8

About the data

Gross domestic product (GDP) from the expenditure side is made up of household final consumption expenditure, general government final consumption expenditure, gross capital formation (private and public investment in fixed assets, changes in inventories, and net acquisitions of valuables), and net exports (exports minus imports) of goods and services. Such expenditures are recorded in purchaser prices and include net taxes on products.

Because policymakers have tended to focus on fostering the growth of output, and because data on production are easier to collect than data on spending, many countries generate their primary estimate of GDP using the production approach. Moreover, many countries do not estimate all the components of national expenditures but instead derive some of the main aggregates indirectly using GDP (based on the production approach) as the control total. Household final consumption expenditure (private consumption in the 1968 United Nations System of National Accounts, or SNA) is often estimated as a residual, by subtracting all other known expenditures from GDP. The resulting aggregate may incorporate fairly large discrepancies. When household consumption is calculated separately, many of the estimates are based on household surveys, which tend to be one-year studies with limited coverage. Thus the estimates quickly become outdated and must be supplemented by estimates using price- and quantity-based statistical procedures. Complicating the issue, in many developing countries the distinction between cash outlays for personal business and those for household use may be blurred. *World Development Indicators* includes in household consumption the expenditures of nonprofit institutions serving households.

General government final consumption expenditure (general government consumption in the 1968 SNA) includes expenditures on goods and services for individual consumption as well as those on services for collective consumption. Defense expenditures, including those on capital outlays (with certain exceptions), are treated as current spending.

Gross capital formation (gross domestic investment in the 1968 SNA) consists of outlays on additions to the economy's fixed assets plus net changes in the level of inventories. It is generally obtained from industry reports of acquisitions and distinguishes only the broad categories of capital formation. The 1993 SNA recognizes a third category of capital formation: net acquisitions of valuables. Included in gross capital formation under the

1993 SNA guidelines are capital outlays on defense establishments that may be used by the general public, such as schools, airfields, and hospitals, and intangibles such as computer software and mineral exploration outlays. Data on capital formation may be estimated from direct surveys of enterprises and administrative records or based on the commodity flow method using data from production, trade, and construction activities. The quality of data on government fixed capital formation depends on the quality of government accounting systems (which tend to be weak in developing countries). Measures of fixed capital formation by households and corporations—particularly capital outlays by small, unincorporated enterprises—are usually unreliable.

Estimates of changes in inventories are rarely complete but usually include the most important activities or commodities. In some countries these estimates are derived as a composite residual along with household final consumption expenditure. According to national accounts conventions, adjustments should be made for appreciation of the value of inventory holdings due to price changes, but this is not always done. In highly inflationary economies this element can be substantial.

Data on exports and imports are compiled from customs reports and balance of payments data. Although the data from the payments side provide reasonably reliable records of cross-border transactions, they may not adhere strictly to the appropriate definitions of valuation and timing used in the balance of payments or correspond to the change-of-ownership criterion. This issue has assumed greater significance with the increasing globalization of international business. Neither customs nor balance of payments data usually capture the illegal transactions that occur in many countries. Goods carried by travelers across borders in legal but unreported shuttle trade may further distort trade statistics.

Gross savings represent the difference between disposable income and consumption and replace gross domestic savings, a concept used by the World Bank and included in *World Development Indicators* editions before 2006. The change was made to conform to SNA concepts and definitions. For further discussion of the problems in compiling national accounts, see Srinivasan (1994), Heston (1994), and Ruggles (1994). For an analysis of the reliability of foreign trade and national income statistics, see Morgenstern (1963).

Definitions

• **Household final consumption expenditure** is the market value of all goods and services, including durable products (such as cars and computers), purchased by households. It excludes purchases of dwellings but includes imputed rent for owner-occupied dwellings. It also includes government fees for permits and licenses. Expenditures of nonprofit institutions serving households are included, even when reported separately. Household consumption expenditure may include any statistical discrepancy in the use of resources relative to the supply of resources. • **General government final consumption expenditure** is all government current expenditures for purchases of goods and services (including compensation of employees). It also includes most expenditures on national defense and security but excludes military expenditures with potentially wider public use that are part of government capital formation. • **Gross capital formation** is outlays on additions to fixed assets of the economy, net changes in inventories, and net acquisitions of valuables. Fixed assets include land improvements (fences, ditches, drains); plant, machinery, and equipment purchases; and construction (roads, railways, schools, buildings, and so on). Inventories are goods held to meet temporary or unexpected fluctuations in production or sales, and "work in progress." • **Exports** and **imports of goods and services** are the value of all goods and other market services provided to or received from the rest of the world. They include the value of merchandise, freight, insurance, transport, travel, royalties, license fees, and other services (communication, construction, financial, information, business, personal, government services, and so on). They exclude compensation of employees and investment income (factor services in the 1968 SNA) and transfer payments. • **Gross savings** are gross national income less total consumption, plus net transfers.

Data sources

Data on national accounts indicators for most developing countries are collected from national statistical organizations and central banks by visiting and resident World Bank missions. Data for high-income economies are from Organisation for Economic Co-operation and Development (OECD) data files.

4.9 Growth of consumption and investment

	Household final consumption expenditure				General government final consumption expenditure		Gross capital formation		Goods and services			
	average annual % growth				average annual % growth		average annual % growth		average annual % growth			
	Total		Per capita						Exports		Imports	
	1990–2000	2000–09	1990–2000	2000–09	1990–2000	2000–09	1990–2000	2000–09	1990–2000	2000–09	1990–2000	2000–09
Afghanistan	..	..	..	..	..	..	..	..	..	..	..	..
Albania	1.3	5.3	2.2	4.9	14.5	7.9	25.8	6.1	18.9	9.8	15.7	13.7
Algeria	−0.1	3.6	−1.9	2.1	3.6	9.0	−0.6	8.8	3.2	2.3	−1.0	7.8
Angola	..	..	..	..	..	..	..	..	..	..	..	..
Argentina	2.8	4.7	1.5	3.7	2.2	3.6	7.4	11.1	8.7	6.3	15.6	9.2
Armenia	−0.5	8.8	1.1	8.7	−1.5	10.9	−1.9	18.3	−18.4	5.0	−12.7	8.6
Australia	3.2	3.9	2.0	2.4	2.9	3.2	5.1	7.6	7.7	2.2	7.6	9.2
Austria	1.7	1.4	1.4	0.9	2.7	1.6	2.3	1.2	5.8	4.7	4.8	3.9
Azerbaijan	2.0	14.0	1.0	12.9	−4.8	23.0	41.6	19.3	5.7	23.0	14.1	19.7
Bangladesh	2.6	4.5	0.6	2.8	4.7	8.8	9.2	7.8	13.1	11.5	9.7	8.8
Belarus	−0.5	11.2	−0.3	11.7	−1.9	0.0	−7.5	18.8	−4.8	5.7	−8.7	10.9
Belgium	1.8	1.2	1.6	0.6	1.6	1.6	2.4	3.0	5.3	2.8	5.0	2.9
Benin	2.6	2.3	−0.7	−1.1	4.4	8.3	12.2	7.7	1.8	2.7	2.1	1.8
Bolivia	3.6	3.4	1.4	1.5	3.6	3.5	8.5	3.9	4.5	7.7	6.0	5.6
Bosnia and Herzegovina	..	..	..	..	..	5.3	..	9.0	..	..	..	2.6
Botswana	3.9	6.7	1.4	5.2	6.9	4.9	5.3	3.0	4.9	2.8	4.9	4.8
Brazil	3.7	3.6	2.2	2.4	1.0	3.2	4.2	4.0	5.9	7.1	11.6	7.5
Bulgaria	−2.6	6.3	−2.0	6.9	−8.0	2.0	−5.3	13.5	4.3	7.9	2.9	10.5
Burkina Faso	5.7	4.5	2.8	1.1	2.9	8.7	3.1	9.0	4.4	10.9	1.9	7.2
Burundi	..	..	..	..	..	..	..	..	..	..	..	..
Cambodia	6.0	8.2	3.4	6.4	7.2	11.4	10.3	14.2	21.7	15.2	14.8	14.8
Cameroon	3.1	4.5	0.5	2.1	0.7	2.8	0.4	4.4	3.2	−0.4	5.1	3.8
Canada	2.6	3.4	1.6	2.3	0.3	2.7	4.6	4.7	8.7	−0.4	7.1	3.3
Central African Republic	..	−0.9	..	−2.7	..	−1.3	..	−0.1	..	−3.6	..	−3.9
Chad	1.5	2.7	−1.7	−0.8	−8.3	2.7	4.0	−2.4	2.3	33.6	−1.8	−3.7
Chile	7.3	5.5	5.6	4.4	3.7	4.8	9.3	7.7	9.4	5.6	11.7	10.5
China	8.9	7.7	7.7	7.1	9.6	8.8	10.8	13.9	15.5	20.2	16.7	16.9
Hong Kong SAR, China	3.8	3.7	2.0	3.1	3.7	1.6	4.8	2.2	7.8	9.7	8.4	7.8
Colombia	2.4	4.0	0.6	2.4	10.9	4.0	2.1	9.8	5.0	5.7	9.3	9.7
Congo, Dem. Rep.	−1.1	..	−3.8	..	−20.4	..	2.6	..	−0.5	6.5	−2.4	16.3
Congo, Rep.	..	..	..	..	..	..	..	..	..	..	..	..
Costa Rica	5.1	4.2	2.5	2.4	2.0	2.7	5.1	5.8	10.9	6.9	9.2	5.4
Côte d'Ivoire	4.1	..	0.9	..	0.8	3.1	8.1	2.5	1.9	2.4	8.2	3.9
Croatia	2.3	3.5	3.0	3.5	1.7	2.9	7.2	9.2	6.3	3.8	4.9	5.7
Cuba	4.0	5.0	3.5	4.9	−2.9	7.6	0.7	8.8	−9.0	12.2	−2.9	10.1
Czech Republic	3.0	3.6	3.0	3.3	−0.9	2.2	4.6	2.9	8.7	10.5	12.0	9.1
Denmark	2.2	2.1	1.8	1.7	2.4	1.8	5.7	1.3	5.0	3.4	6.0	5.3
Dominican Republic	6.1	6.7	4.2	5.1	7.0	4.9	11.7	1.7	8.3	1.1	9.9	2.4
Ecuador	2.1	5.4	0.3	4.3	−1.5	4.2	−0.6	7.8	5.3	6.1	2.8	8.7
Egypt, Arab Rep.	3.7	4.4	1.7	2.5	4.4	2.7	5.8	7.3	3.5	16.8	3.0	14.4
El Salvador	5.3	3.3	4.1	2.9	2.8	1.5	7.1	0.7	13.4	2.9	11.6	3.3
Eritrea	−5.0	1.6	−6.6	−2.2	22.6	1.2	19.1	−1.0	−2.5	−6.3	7.5	−3.7
Estonia	0.6	6.8	2.1	7.1	5.7	2.2	0.5	14.6	11.0	6.7	12.0	7.4
Ethiopia	3.6	10.7	0.4	7.9	9.0	0.7	6.5	11.3	7.1	10.1	5.8	16.5
Finland	1.8	3.1	1.4	2.7	0.9	1.6	3.2	2.0	10.3	4.5	6.7	5.1
France	1.6	2.1	1.2	1.4	1.4	1.7	1.8	1.8	6.9	1.4	5.7	3.3
Gabon	−0.3	4.5	−3.1	2.5	3.7	2.1	3.0	5.6	2.1	−2.0	0.1	3.8
Gambia, The	3.6	..	−0.2	..	−2.2	..	1.9	..	0.1	1.1	0.1	1.3
Georgia	..	..	..	..	..	..	..	..	..	..	..	..
Germany	1.9	0.3	1.6	0.4	1.9	0.9	1.1	−0.1	6.0	5.9	5.8	4.7
Ghana	..	..	..	..	..	..	..	..	..	..	..	..
Greece	2.2	3.8	1.4	3.4	2.1	3.1	4.1	1.9	7.6	2.9	7.4	2.7
Guatemala	4.2	3.8	1.8	1.3	5.1	3.0	6.1	0.5	6.1	2.1	9.2	2.1
Guinea	5.2	4.1	2.0	2.1	−0.5	0.3	0.1	−0.5	0.3	2.3	−1.1	0.5
Guinea-Bissau	..	..	..	..	..	..	..	..	..	..	..	..
Haiti	..	..	..	..	..	..	9.0	1.5	10.1	4.4	19.4	2.1
Honduras	3.0	5.2	0.6	3.1	2.0	6.6	6.9	3.9	1.6	5.1	3.8	5.4

Growth of consumption and investment | 4.9

	Household final consumption expenditure				General government final consumption expenditure		Gross capital formation		Goods and services			
	average annual % growth				average annual % growth		average annual % growth		average annual % growth			
	Total		Per capita						Exports		Imports	
	1990–2000	2000–09	1990–2000	2000–09	1990–2000	2000–09	1990–2000	2000–09	1990–2000	2000–09	1990–2000	2000–09
Hungary	−0.1	3.8	0.1	4.1	0.9	1.3	9.6	1.3	9.9	11.2	11.4	10.0
India	4.8	6.9	2.9	5.4	6.6	5.7	6.9	13.4	12.3	16.0	14.4	16.5
Indonesia	6.6	4.3	5.0	2.9	0.1	8.2	−0.6	5.9	5.9	7.8	5.7	8.6
Iran, Islamic Rep.	3.2	7.4	1.6	5.8	1.6	3.6	−0.1	8.3	1.2	5.0	−6.8	13.2
Iraq	..	..	..	..	..	..	..	..	..	..	..	..
Ireland	5.6	3.7	4.7	1.8	4.1	4.3	9.9	1.5	15.7	4.2	14.5	3.9
Israel	5.0	3.4	2.5	1.5	2.7	1.4	2.0	2.3	10.9	5.9	7.6	3.8
Italy	1.6	0.6	1.5	−0.1	−0.2	1.6	1.6	0.3	5.9	0.4	4.4	1.2
Jamaica	..	..	..	..	..	..	..	..	..	..	..	..
Japan	1.4	1.0	1.1	0.9	2.9	1.6	−0.8	−0.9	4.3	5.5	4.3	2.5
Jordan	4.9	7.5	1.1	5.0	4.7	6.7	0.3	6.7	2.6	5.7	1.5	6.9
Kazakhstan	−7.5	9.3	−6.4	8.5	−7.1	7.8	−19.0	17.2	−1.9	5.9	−12.7	5.6
Kenya	3.6	4.0	0.6	1.3	6.9	2.3	6.1	9.0	1.0	6.6	9.4	8.3
Korea, Dem. Rep.	..	..	..	..	..	..	..	..	..	..	..	..
Korea, Rep.	4.9	3.0	3.9	2.6	4.7	4.9	3.4	3.1	16.0	10.6	10.0	8.3
Kosovo	..	..	..	..	..	..	..	..	..	..	..	..
Kuwait	4.5	..	0.6	..	−2.4	..	1.0	..	−1.6	..	0.8	..
Kyrgyz Republic	−4.8	9.9	−5.8	9.0	−7.2	4.2	−1.1	3.8	−1.6	5.1	−8.2	16.0
Lao PDR	..	−7.8	..	−9.4	..	9.7	..	15.2	..	−7.6	..	−7.2
Latvia	−3.9	8.0	−2.7	8.6	1.8	2.1	−3.7	16.4	4.3	7.1	7.6	8.0
Lebanon	−0.2	..	−1.9	..	10.9	..	−5.8	6.3	18.6	10.2	−1.1	6.3
Lesotho	1.8	9.5	0.1	8.4	8.1	6.4	0.2	−0.5	10.3	10.0	2.7	12.2
Liberia	..	..	..	..	..	..	..	..	..	..	..	..
Libya	..	..	..	..	..	..	..	..	..	..	..	..
Lithuania	5.3	9.7	6.1	10.3	1.9	4.3	11.1	13.6	4.9	11.2	7.5	14.0
Macedonia, FYR	2.2	4.8	1.7	4.6	−0.4	0.0	3.6	4.7	4.2	2.4	7.5	4.0
Madagascar	2.2	2.2	−0.8	−0.7	0.0	5.5	3.3	14.1	3.8	6.7	4.1	9.3
Malawi	5.4	..	3.2	..	−4.4	..	−8.4	..	4.0	..	−1.1	..
Malaysia	5.3	7.5	2.6	5.6	4.8	7.9	5.3	2.1	12.0	5.3	10.3	6.1
Mali	3.0	0.9	1.0	−1.5	3.2	..	0.4	6.2	9.9	6.3	3.5	3.9
Mauritania	..	7.4	..	4.5	..	3.1	..	23.8	−1.3	−2.1	0.6	14.1
Mauritius	5.1	5.6	3.9	4.7	3.6	3.8	4.8	5.3	5.6	2.0	5.1	2.3
Mexico	3.9	3.2	2.2	2.1	1.8	0.8	4.7	0.4	14.6	4.3	12.3	4.7
Moldova	9.9	7.9	10.0	8.2	−12.4	5.9	−15.5	9.8	0.7	9.1	5.6	11.1
Mongolia	..	..	..	..	..	..	..	..	..	..	..	..
Morocco	1.8	4.7	0.3	3.5	3.9	3.8	2.5	8.9	5.9	6.4	5.1	8.3
Mozambique	5.8	6.2	2.6	3.6	3.2	−4.6	8.6	5.9	13.1	16.0	7.6	6.2
Myanmar	..	..	..	..	..	..	..	..	..	..	..	..
Namibia	4.8	5.7	2.3	3.7	3.3	4.5	7.3	9.4	3.8	6.0	5.4	9.5
Nepal	..	..	..	..	..	..	..	..	..	..	..	..
Netherlands	3.1	0.6	2.5	0.3	2.0	3.2	4.4	1.1	7.3	4.1	7.6	3.8
New Zealand	3.2	3.4	2.0	2.0	2.4	4.1	6.1	3.7	5.2	2.2	6.2	4.5
Nicaragua	6.1	3.7	3.9	2.3	−1.5	2.7	11.3	2.1	9.3	8.3	12.2	5.1
Niger	..	..	..	..	..	..	..	..	..	..	..	..
Nigeria	..	..	..	..	..	..	..	..	..	..	..	..
Norway	3.5	3.7	3.0	2.9	2.7	2.4	6.0	5.0	5.5	0.7	5.8	5.0
Oman	5.4	..	2.6	..	2.4	..	4.0	..	6.2	..	5.9	..
Pakistan	4.9	4.6	2.3	2.2	0.7	8.3	1.8	6.3	1.7	7.1	2.5	7.3
Panama	6.4	7.2	4.2	5.4	1.7	3.6	10.4	10.2	−0.4	7.8	1.2	6.9
Papua New Guinea	2.5	..	−0.2	..	2.5	..	1.9	..	5.1	..	3.4	..
Paraguay	2.6	3.0	0.3	1.1	2.5	3.3	0.7	3.0	3.1	7.0	2.9	6.0
Peru	4.0	5.2	2.2	3.9	5.2	5.2	7.4	10.5	8.5	7.8	9.0	9.5
Philippines	3.7	5.1	1.5	3.1	3.8	3.1	4.1	1.3	7.8	5.2	7.8	2.9
Poland	5.2	3.7	5.1	3.7	3.7	4.2	10.6	5.9	11.3	9.0	16.7	8.0
Portugal	3.0	1.5	2.7	1.1	2.9	1.5	5.9	−1.8	5.7	3.3	7.6	2.7
Puerto Rico	..	..	..	..	..	..	..	..	1.6	..	4.5	..
Qatar	..	..	..	..	..	..	..	..	..	..	..	..

	Household final consumption expenditure				General government final consumption expenditure		Gross capital formation		Goods and services			
	average annual % growth				average annual % growth		average annual % growth		average annual % growth			
	Total		Per capita						Exports		Imports	
	1990–2000	2000–09	1990–2000	2000–09	1990–2000	2000–09	1990–2000	2000–09	1990–2000	2000–09	1990–2000	2000–09
Romania	1.3	6.2	1.7	6.7	0.8	4.3	−5.1	11.5	8.1	9.6	6.0	13.5
Russian Federation	−0.9	9.9	−0.7	10.3	−2.2	2.1	−19.1	9.0	0.8	7.1	−6.1	15.9
Rwanda	..	..	..	..	..	..	..	..	..	..	..	..
Saudi Arabia	..	5.3	..	2.9	..	7.6	..	11.4	..	6.9	..	16.9
Senegal	2.6	5.3	−0.2	2.5	0.9	−0.6	3.5	9.6	4.1	4.0	2.0	7.8
Serbia	..	3.3	..	3.6	..	4.5	..	18.3	..	10.5	..	10.7
Sierra Leone	..	..	..	..	..	..	..	..	..	..	..	..
Singapore	..	..	..	..	..	..	..	..	..	..	..	..
Slovak Republic	6.0	5.3	5.8	5.2	1.8	3.3	7.7	7.8	9.6	11.0	12.4	9.6
Slovenia	3.9	3.2	4.0	3.0	2.2	3.2	10.4	7.5	1.7	9.1	5.2	8.9
Somalia	..	..	..	..	..	..	..	..	..	..	..	..
South Africa	2.9	4.6	0.6	3.4	0.3	5.0	4.7	9.1	5.8	2.7	7.1	8.1
Spain	2.4	2.8	2.0	1.2	2.7	5.1	3.2	3.3	10.5	2.9	9.4	4.7
Sri Lanka	..	..	..	..	10.5	..	6.9	..	7.5	..	8.6	..
Sudan	3.7	5.9	1.1	3.7	5.5	8.4	22.0	11.2	11.6	14.3	8.4	12.0
Swaziland	7.3	2.0	4.9	1.0	7.1	6.0	−4.7	−0.3	6.4	5.2	6.2	4.7
Sweden	1.5	2.2	1.1	1.7	0.7	0.9	2.0	3.3	8.6	4.6	6.4	4.2
Switzerland	1.1	1.4	0.5	0.6	0.5	1.2	0.7	0.4	4.1	4.7	4.3	3.6
Syrian Arab Republic	3.0	7.5	0.3	4.6	2.0	8.4	3.3	−0.4	12.0	6.5	4.4	11.3
Tajikistan	−11.8	6.1	−13.1	4.8	−15.7	1.6	−17.6	7.3	−5.3	9.5	−6.0	10.6
Tanzania[a]	5.1	6.2	2.0	3.3	−8.8	13.5	−1.1	12.8	11.7	11.6	4.7	15.9
Thailand	3.7	4.0	2.7	3.1	5.1	5.3	−4.0	4.8	9.5	5.8	4.5	5.7
Timor-Leste	..	..	..	..	..	..	..	..	..	..	..	..
Togo	5.0	0.5	2.0	−2.1	0.0	1.3	−0.1	5.9	1.2	6.0	1.1	3.1
Trinidad and Tobago	0.7	13.3	0.1	12.9	0.3	4.3	12.5	4.2	6.9	5.8	9.9	9.5
Tunisia	4.3	5.3	2.6	4.3	4.1	4.4	3.6	2.9	5.1	4.1	3.8	3.6
Turkey	3.8	5.3	2.1	3.9	4.6	4.0	4.7	6.9	11.1	6.4	10.8	8.8
Turkmenistan	..	..	..	..	..	..	..	1.6	−2.4	22.4	7.2	15.2
Uganda	6.7	1.9	3.3	−1.3	7.7	4.0	9.2	12.0	15.4	19.5	9.7	11.2
Ukraine	−6.9	12.1	−6.4	12.9	−4.1	2.6	−18.5	5.1	−3.6	1.1	−6.6	5.2
United Arab Emirates	7.1	..	1.2	..	6.8	..	5.5	..	5.5	..	6.4	..
United Kingdom	3.0	2.1	2.8	1.5	1.0	2.2	4.7	1.6	6.5	3.1	6.8	3.4
United States	3.7	2.4	2.5	1.4	0.7	2.1	7.6	0.0	7.3	4.5	9.8	3.3
Uruguay	5.0	2.9	4.3	2.8	2.3	1.3	6.1	6.6	6.0	7.8	9.9	6.4
Uzbekistan	..	..	..	..	..	..	−2.5	4.7	2.5	4.9	−0.4	4.2
Venezuela, RB	0.6	8.7	−1.5	6.8	3.7	7.0	11.0	11.2	1.0	−2.0	8.2	13.8
Vietnam	5.4	7.8	3.9	6.4	3.2	7.7	19.8	12.3	19.2	11.4	19.5	13.6
West Bank and Gaza	5.3	−1.5	1.1	−4.9	12.7	1.3	9.2	−3.0	8.7	−3.1	7.5	−2.3
Yemen, Rep.	3.2	..	−0.7	..	1.7	..	11.4	..	16.6	..	8.3	..
Zambia	2.4	0.1	−0.5	−2.1	−8.1	24.9	3.9	6.6	6.7	21.9	15.5	15.6
Zimbabwe	..	..	..	..	..	..	..	..	3.9	−10.7	3.1	−5.8
World	**3.0 w**	**2.7 w**	**1.6 w**	**1.5 w**	**1.7 w**	**2.6 w**	**3.3 w**	**3.1 w**	**7.0 w**	**5.9 w**	**7.0 w**	**5.7 w**
Low income	2.9	4.5	0.5	2.2	−1.3	6.8	5.5	8.7	5.5	9.7	5.3	9.4
Middle income	4.1	5.7	2.6	4.5	3.3	5.4	2.6	9.9	7.5	10.4	6.4	10.7
Lower middle income	5.7	6.6	4.1	5.3	6.6	7.4	6.3	12.2	9.3	14.7	8.3	12.9
Upper middle income	3.0	5.0	1.8	4.1	1.4	3.7	−0.5	6.3	6.3	5.5	5.1	8.5
Low & middle income	4.0	5.7	2.4	4.3	3.3	5.5	2.7	9.9	7.4	10.4	6.4	10.7
East Asia & Pacific	7.4	6.9	6.1	6.0	8.0	8.4	7.8	12.4	11.8	14.5	10.9	12.6
Europe & Central Asia	0.5	7.6	0.4	7.5	−0.8	3.3	−11.2	9.1	1.8	7.2	−2.3	11.9
Latin America & Carib.	3.6	4.1	2.0	2.9	1.9	3.3	5.4	5.0	8.1	5.0	10.4	6.7
Middle East & N. Africa	2.8	5.3	0.6	3.3	3.5	3.6	1.2	7.4	4.0	7.7	0.0	9.9
South Asia	4.6	6.4	2.6	4.8	5.9	6.1	6.5	12.4	10.0	14.6	11.2	14.8
Sub-Saharan Africa	3.3	4.9	0.6	2.4	0.3	5.1	4.6	8.5	..	..	5.7	8.8
High income	2.8	2.0	2.1	1.3	1.5	2.1	3.4	0.8	6.9	4.6	7.2	4.3
Euro area	2.0	1.4	1.6	0.8	1.5	1.9	2.2	1.2	6.8	3.8	6.3	3.8

a. Covers mainland Tanzania only.

Growth of consumption and investment 4.9

Measures of growth in consumption and capital formation are subject to two kinds of inaccuracy. The first stems from the difficulty of measuring expenditures at current price levels, as described in *About the data* for table 4.8. The second arises in deflating current price data to measure volume growth, where results depend on the relevance and reliability of the price indexes and weights used. Measuring price changes is more difficult for investment goods than for consumption goods because of the one-time nature of many investments and because the rate of technological progress in capital goods makes capturing change in quality difficult. (An example is computers—prices have fallen as quality has improved.) Several countries estimate capital formation from the supply side, identifying capital goods entering an economy directly from detailed production and international trade statistics. This means that the price indexes used in deflating production and international trade, reflecting delivered or offered prices, will determine the deflator for capital formation expenditures on the demand side.

Growth rates of household final consumption expenditure, household final consumption expenditure per capita, general government final consumption expenditure, gross capital formation, and exports and imports of goods and services are estimated using constant price data. (Consumption, capital formation, and exports and imports of goods and services as shares of GDP are shown in table 4.8.)

To obtain government consumption in constant prices, countries may deflate current values by applying a wage (price) index or extrapolate from

the change in government employment. Neither technique captures improvements in productivity or changes in the quality of government services. Deflators for household consumption are usually calculated on the basis of the consumer price index. Many countries estimate household consumption as a residual that includes statistical discrepancies associated with the estimation of other expenditure items, including changes in inventories; thus these estimates lack detailed breakdowns of household consumption expenditures.

• **Household final consumption expenditure** is the market value of all goods and services, including durable products (such as cars and computers), purchased by households. It excludes purchases of dwellings but includes imputed rent for owner-occupied dwellings. It also includes government fees for permits and licenses. Expenditures of nonprofit institutions serving households are included, even when reported separately. Household consumption expenditure may include any statistical discrepancy in the use of resources relative to the supply of resources. • **Household final consumption expenditure per capita** is household final consumption expenditure divided by midyear population. • **General government final consumption expenditure** is all government current expenditures for goods and services (including compensation of employees). It also includes most expenditures on national defense and security but excludes military expenditures with potentially wider public use that are part of government capital formation. • **Gross capital formation** is outlays on additions to fixed assets of the economy, net changes in inventories, and net acquisitions of valuables. Fixed assets include land improvements (fences, ditches, drains); plant, machinery, and equipment purchases; and construction (roads, railways, schools, buildings, and so on). Inventories are goods held to meet temporary or unexpected fluctuations in production or sales, and "work in progress." • **Exports** and **imports of goods and services** are the value of all goods and other market services provided to or received from the rest of the world. They include the value of merchandise, freight, insurance, transport, travel, royalties, license fees, and other services (communication, construction, financial, information, business, personal, government services, and so on). They exclude compensation of employees and investment income (factor services in the 1968 System of National Accounts) and transfer payments.

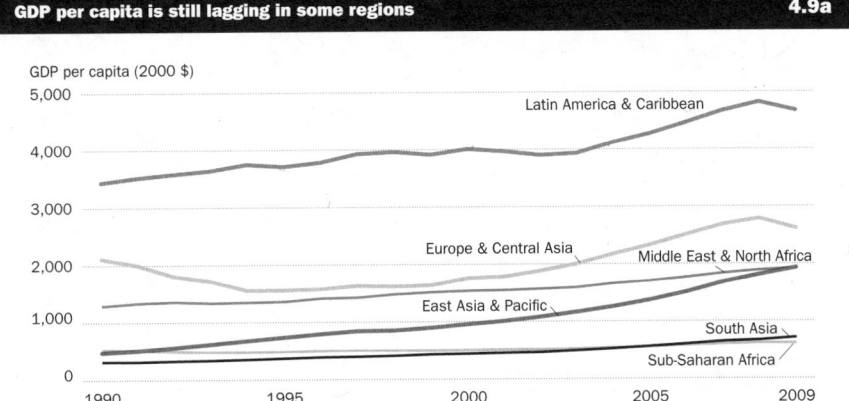

GDP per capita is still lagging in some regions 4.9a

GDP per capita (2000 $)

Although GDP per capita has more than tripled in East Asia and Pacific between 1990 and 2009, it is still less than GDP per capita in Latin America and Carribean and in Europe and Central Asia.

Source: World Development Indicators data files.

Data on national accounts indicators for most developing countries are collected from national statistical organizations and central banks by visiting and resident World Bank missions. Data for high-income economies are from Organisation for Economic Co-operation and Development (OECD) data files.

4.10 Toward a broader measure of national income

	Gross domestic product	Gross national income	Adjustments		Adjusted net national income	Gross domestic product	Gross national income	Adjusted net national income
			Consumption of fixed capital % of GNI	Natural resource depletion % of GNI				
	$ billions 2009	$ billions 2009	2009	2009	$ billions 2009	% growth 2000–2009	% growth 2000–2009	% growth 2000–2009
Afghanistan	14.5	10.6	7.7	3.4	9.5	..	..	..
Albania	12.0	11.9	10.5	1.3	10.5	5.4	5.8	7.3
Algeria	140.6	139.6	10.5	16.9	101.2	4.0	3.7	4.9
Angola	75.5	67.5	11.7	29.1	40.0	13.1	..	..
Argentina	307.2	297.7	11.8	4.9	248.2	5.4	5.1	5.4
Armenia	8.7	8.9	9.7	0.5	8.0	10.5	10.5	11.4
Australia	924.8	900.7	14.4	5.1	725.2	3.3	3.6	3.3
Austria	381.1	377.1	14.3	0.1	322.8	2.0	1.9	2.0
Azerbaijan	43.0	40.3	11.5	32.7	22.5	17.9	19.4	19.8
Bangladesh	89.4	97.5	6.8	2.6	88.3	5.9	5.3	5.9
Belarus	49.0	47.9	11.1	0.9	42.2	8.4	8.6	10.6
Belgium	471.2	475.0	14.0	0.0	408.7	1.7	1.9	1.3
Benin	6.7	6.6	7.9	1.2	6.0	4.0	3.9	3.6
Bolivia	17.3	16.7	9.5	11.2	13.2	4.1	4.3	3.0
Bosnia and Herzegovina	17.0	17.4	10.4	..	..	5.0	5.9	..
Botswana	11.8	11.3	11.5	2.8	9.7	4.4	4.2	3.0
Brazil	1,594.5	1,562.4	11.8	3.1	1,330.0	3.6	3.4	3.6
Bulgaria	48.7	46.6	11.7	1.1	40.7	5.4	6.1	4.9
Burkina Faso	8.1	8.0	7.4	1.6	7.3	5.4	6.0	5.5
Burundi	1.3	1.3	5.5	10.6	1.1	3.0	..	..
Cambodia	9.9	9.4	8.1	0.2	8.6	9.0	9.3	10.2
Cameroon	22.2	22.1	8.6	4.8	19.1	3.3	2.7	4.4
Canada	1,336.1	1,317.3	14.2	2.3	1,100.4	2.1	1.9	2.9
Central African Republic	2.0	2.0	7.2	0.0	1.8	0.8	−0.9	−1.2
Chad	6.8	6.1	9.9	25.2	4.1	10.2	20.2	−5.5
Chile	163.7	153.4	12.6	10.0	118.8	4.1	5.0	4.9
China	4,985.5	5,028.8	10.2	3.1	4,355.8	10.9	10.6	9.9
Hong Kong SAR, China	210.6	216.9	13.6	0.0	188.5	4.7	4.4	4.2
Colombia	234.0	224.5	11.3	6.2	185.3	4.5	4.7	4.3
Congo, Dem. Rep.	10.6	9.8	5.9	10.7	8.2	5.2	5.5	7.5
Congo, Rep.	9.6	6.9	13.6	50.6	2.5	4.0	..	..
Costa Rica	29.2	28.8	11.3	0.2	25.5	5.1	4.6	4.0
Côte d'Ivoire	23.3	22.4	8.8	3.1	19.7	0.8	0.6	0.6
Croatia	63.0	60.5	12.9	0.8	52.2	3.9	4.0	5.2
Cuba	62.7	61.8	..	3.3	52.8	6.7	6.6	6.7
Czech Republic	190.3	178.1	13.6	0.3	153.3	4.1	4.6	4.6
Denmark	309.6	318.3	16.5	1.5	261.1	1.2	0.7	2.0
Dominican Republic	46.8	45.0	11.1	0.5	39.8	5.5	5.4	5.1
Ecuador	57.2	56.1	10.7	9.9	44.5	5.0	4.5	5.2
Egypt, Arab Rep.	188.4	188.6	9.6	7.3	156.9	4.9	5.0	2.8
El Salvador	21.1	20.4	10.5	0.5	18.2	2.6	2.7	2.3
Eritrea	1.9	1.9	6.8	0.8	1.7	0.2	1.4	4.0
Estonia	19.1	18.5	12.8	0.7	16.0	5.9	6.1	6.7
Ethiopia	28.5	28.5	6.7	4.5	25.3	8.5	8.4	10.3
Finland	238.0	238.1	17.0	0.1	197.6	2.5	2.4	1.7
France	2,649.4	2,671.2	14.2	0.0	2,292.1	1.5	1.5	1.4
Gabon	11.1	9.5	13.2	29.2	5.5	2.1	2.6	3.3
Gambia, The	0.7	0.7	7.5	1.0	0.6	5.2	5.4	3.6
Georgia	10.7	10.6	8.8	0.1	9.6	7.4	..	..
Germany	3,330.0	3,377.0	13.8	0.1	2,908.2	1.0	0.6	1.4
Ghana	26.2	25.9	8.6	6.9	19.7	5.8	..	..
Greece	329.9	320.8	13.9	0.2	275.8	3.6	4.1	3.0
Guatemala	37.3	36.1	10.1	1.2	32.0	3.7	3.8	3.2
Guinea	4.1	3.7	7.7	6.6	3.2	3.0	4.1	0.9
Guinea-Bissau	0.8	0.8	7.4	0.0	0.8	1.0	..	..
Haiti	6.5	..	..	..	..	0.7	..	..
Honduras	14.3	13.8	9.6	0.4	12.4	4.9	4.8	3.0

Toward a broader measure of national income

	Gross domestic product	Gross national income	Adjustments		Adjusted net national income	Gross domestic product	Gross national income	Adjusted net national income
			Consumption of fixed capital % of GNI	Natural resource depletion % of GNI				
	$ billions 2009	$ billions 2009	2009	2009	$ billions 2009	% growth 2000–2009	% growth 2000–2009	% growth 2000–2009
Hungary	129.0	121.2	13.0	0.2	105.2	2.9	4.0	3.1
India	1,377.3	1,369.3	8.6	4.2	1,194.1	7.9	7.8	7.5
Indonesia	540.3	478.4	10.9	6.5	395.3	5.3	5.1	3.0
Iran, Islamic Rep.	331.0	328.6	10.7	17.9	234.7	5.4	6.2	6.7
Iraq	65.8	61.8	10.1	45.7	27.4	–0.3	..	..
Ireland	227.2	184.4	17.7	0.1	151.8	3.9	3.8	2.4
Israel	195.4	190.8	13.6	0.2	164.4	3.6	2.6	4.4
Italy	2,112.8	2,076.3	14.0	0.1	1,784.1	0.5	0.6	0.4
Jamaica	12.1	11.4	11.2	0.7	10.1	1.5	..	..
Japan	5,069.0	5,228.3	13.5	0.0	4,521.8	1.1	0.8	1.5
Jordan	25.1	25.7	10.3	1.1	22.8	6.9	6.7	6.9
Kazakhstan	115.3	103.4	12.7	22.0	67.6	8.8	9.9	9.1
Kenya	29.4	29.3	7.4	1.2	26.8	4.4	4.2	5.1
Korea, Dem. Rep.	..	..	..	..	..	..	..	..
Korea, Rep.	832.5	836.9	13.3	0.0	725.3	4.2	4.1	3.3
Kosovo	5.4	5.6	..	..	..	4.8	..	..
Kuwait	148.0	158.1	5.2	37.0	91.3	8.4	..	..
Kyrgyz Republic	4.6	4.4	8.4	0.5	4.0	4.6	4.3	4.8
Lao PDR	5.9	5.8	8.4	0.0	5.3	6.9	6.6	1.0
Latvia	26.2	28.1	11.3	0.3	24.8	6.2	6.0	8.2
Lebanon	34.5	35.4	11.2	0.0	31.4	4.6	3.9	4.7
Lesotho	1.6	1.9	6.4	1.4	1.8	3.1	0.8	8.9
Liberia	0.9	0.6	8.2	11.0	0.5	0.0	..	..
Libya	62.4	62.0	11.9	30.5	35.8	5.4	..	..
Lithuania	37.2	37.2	12.0	0.2	32.7	6.3	8.1	9.3
Macedonia, FYR	9.2	9.0	10.9	0.1	8.0	3.1	3.2	2.9
Madagascar	8.6	8.5	7.3	0.2	7.9	3.6	3.5	2.3
Malawi	4.7	4.7	7.4	0.9	4.3	4.8	..	..
Malaysia	193.1	188.9	11.6	7.9	152.3	5.1	4.5	7.2
Mali	9.0	9.0	7.7	0.0	8.3	5.3	5.9	5.7
Mauritania	3.0	3.0	8.1	18.8	2.2	4.7	3.2	5.1
Mauritius	8.6	8.9	10.9	0.0	7.9	3.7	3.3	2.2
Mexico	874.8	860.2	11.7	5.4	713.2	2.2	2.1	1.5
Moldova	5.4	5.7	8.5	0.2	5.2	5.6	5.0	6.1
Mongolia	4.2	4.0	9.5	11.1	3.1	7.4	..	..
Morocco	91.4	89.5	10.1	1.4	79.2	5.0	4.8	4.4
Mozambique	9.8	9.7	7.1	3.8	8.6	7.9	7.7	6.3
Myanmar	..	..	..	..	..	..	..	..
Namibia	9.3	9.2	10.6	0.3	8.2	5.3	5.7	6.1
Nepal	12.5	12.8	6.8	4.2	11.4	3.7	..	..
Netherlands	792.1	773.9	14.6	0.8	654.9	1.7	2.1	1.3
New Zealand	126.7	121.4	14.1	0.9	103.3	2.5	2.6	2.8
Nicaragua	6.1	5.9	8.8	0.8	5.3	3.3	3.0	2.5
Niger	5.4	5.3	2.9	1.2	5.1	4.3	..	..
Nigeria	173.0	162.9	9.0	15.0	123.8	6.6	..	..
Norway	381.8	376.4	15.2	10.6	279.2	2.1	2.2	3.7
Oman	46.1	58.1	13.5	37.8	28.3	4.5	..	..
Pakistan	162.0	166.4	8.0	3.1	147.8	5.2	4.8	4.7
Panama	24.7	23.1	12.1	0.0	20.3	6.9	7.2	6.7
Papua New Guinea	7.9	7.8	8.6	19.9	5.6	3.4	..	..
Paraguay	14.2	14.0	9.7	0.0	12.6	3.4	3.7	3.3
Peru	130.3	122.6	11.3	5.9	101.6	6.0	6.7	5.2
Philippines	161.2	161.1	8.0	1.0	168.2	4.9	4.1	4.3
Poland	430.1	416.1	12.4	1.0	360.4	4.4	4.7	4.2
Portugal	232.9	225.1	17.2	0.1	186.1	0.8	1.0	0.5
Puerto Rico	..	..	..	..	..	..	..	..
Qatar	98.3	..	..	..	..	14.2	..	..

	Gross domestic product	Gross national income	Adjustments		Adjusted net national income	Gross domestic product	Gross national income	Adjusted net national income
			Consumption of fixed capital	Natural resource depletion				
	$ billions	$ billions	% of GNI	% of GNI	$ billions	% growth	% growth	% growth
	2009	**2009**	**2009**	**2009**	**2009**	**2000–2009**	**2000–2009**	**2000–2009**
Romania	161.1	164.1	11.2	1.3	143.5	5.6	5.4	7.2
Russian Federation	1,231.9	1,192.4	12.0	14.5	876.2	6.0	6.1	8.4
Rwanda	5.2	5.2	7.4	2.4	4.7	7.6	..	..
Saudi Arabia	375.8	384.4	12.6	28.9	226.8	3.8	3.4	6.2
Senegal	12.8	12.8	8.4	0.3	11.7	4.3	4.1	..
Serbia	43.0	42.3	..	..	..	5.0	5.3	..
Sierra Leone	1.9	1.9	6.8	2.1	1.7	9.5	..	..
Singapore	182.2	179.2	14.1	0.0	154.0	6.5	..	..
Slovak Republic	87.6	84.7	13.0	0.3	73.4	5.8	6.1	5.6
Slovenia	48.5	47.3	13.5	0.2	40.8	3.8	4.7	4.4
Somalia	..	..	..	..	..	..	..	..
South Africa	285.4	279.0	14.1	5.4	224.6	4.1	4.1	3.8
Spain	1,460.3	1,430.2	13.9	0.0	1,231.5	2.8	2.9	2.7
Sri Lanka	42.0	41.5	9.5	0.5	37.3	5.5	..	..
Sudan	54.7	49.3	9.7	11.1	39.0	7.3	7.5	5.7
Swaziland	3.0	2.9	10.2	0.1	2.6	2.6	3.2	1.7
Sweden	406.1	413.4	13.3	0.2	357.4	2.4	2.0	2.5
Switzerland	491.9	512.3	14.1	0.0	440.2	1.9	2.6	1.5
Syrian Arab Republic	52.2	50.9	9.9	10.2	40.7	4.4	4.0	6.3
Tajikistan	5.0	4.9	7.9	0.2	4.5	8.2	7.8	5.5
Tanzania[a]	21.4	21.4	7.3	2.5	19.3	7.1	6.9	6.4
Thailand	263.8	252.0	10.9	3.2	216.6	4.6	4.8	4.4
Timor-Leste	0.6	2.9	1.2	..	..	2.4	..	..
Togo	2.9	2.8	7.0	3.6	2.5	2.5	2.3	3.0
Trinidad and Tobago	21.2	20.7	12.9	28.2	12.2	7.4	8.3	5.7
Tunisia	39.6	37.3	11.0	4.6	31.5	4.9	5.0	3.7
Turkey	614.6	606.9	11.7	0.2	534.7	4.9	4.8	4.0
Turkmenistan	19.9	19.2	10.8	..	..	13.9	14.0	..
Uganda	16.0	15.7	7.4	4.7	13.8	7.8	7.8	7.5
Ukraine	113.5	111.1	9.9	3.8	95.9	5.6	5.6	8.1
United Arab Emirates	230.3	..	..	..	..	7.0	..	..
United Kingdom	2,174.5	2,218.1	13.5	1.2	1,892.3	2.0	1.8	2.1
United States	14,119.0	14,011.0	14.3	0.7	11,909.0	2.0	2.2	1.4
Uruguay	31.5	30.8	12.0	0.4	27.0	3.4	3.7	2.8
Uzbekistan	32.1	32.5	8.4	17.8	24.0	6.9	5.0	–6.4
Venezuela, RB	326.1	323.5	12.2	9.8	252.4	4.9	4.6	8.6
Vietnam	90.1	85.2	8.8	7.2	71.5	7.6	8.0	7.0
West Bank and Gaza	..	..	..	..	..	–0.9	0.2	..
Yemen, Rep.	26.4	24.9	9.0	13.2	19.4	3.9	..	..
Zambia	12.8	11.4	9.3	11.5	9.1	5.4	7.4	5.3
Zimbabwe	5.6	5.2	..	3.5	4.6	–7.5	–7.2	–9.0
World	**58,252.1 w**	**57,867.2 w**	**13.1 w**	**2.4 w**	**48,996.8 w**	**2.9 w**	**2.8 w**	**2.6 w**
Low income	431.5	433.8	7.2	3.8	383.4	5.4	5.6	5.6
Middle income	16,206.0	16,112.0	10.7	5.8	13,495.7	6.4	6.4	6.2
Lower middle income	8,880.2	8,952.6	9.9	4.5	7,727.3	8.5	8.4	7.8
Upper middle income	7,318.4	7,173.2	11.8	7.5	5,782.6	4.4	4.3	4.7
Low & middle income	16,649.8	16,558.2	10.7	5.8	13,887.1	6.4	6.3	6.2
East Asia & Pacific	6,346.0	6,307.5	10.3	3.6	5,456.9	9.4	9.2	8.6
Europe & Central Asia	2,591.7	2,521.8	11.7	9.2	1,977.5	5.9	5.9	6.8
Latin America & Carib.	4,017.9	3,921.9	11.7	4.8	3,277.5	3.8	3.7	3.8
Middle East & N. Africa	1,062.4	1,192.9	10.4	14.8	945.9	4.7	4.9	5.0
South Asia	1,700.3	1,702.0	8.4	3.9	1,492.3	7.3	7.3	7.0
Sub-Saharan Africa	945.9	904.2	10.6	9.3	722.6	5.1	4.5	4.2
High income	41,607.7	41,369.3	14.1	1.0	35,134.3	2.0	1.9	1.7
Euro area	12,465.3	12,368.9	14.2	0.1	10,599.8	1.5	1.4	1.4

a. Covers mainland Tanzania only.

About the data

An economy's growth is typically measured by the change in the volume of its output, as shown in table 4.1. However the widely tracked gross domestic product (GDP) may not always be the most relevant summary of aggregated economic performance for all economies, such as when production occurs at the expense of consuming capital stock. For countries with significant exhaustible natural resources and important foreign-investor presence, adjusted net national income complements GDP in assessing economic progress (Hamilton and Ley 2010).

The table presents three measures of economic progress: GDP, gross national income (GNI), and adjusted net national income. GDP accounts for all domestic production, regardless of whether the income accrues to domestic or foreign institutions. GNI accounts for the operation of foreign investors, who may be repatriating some of the income produced domestically. GNI comprises GDP plus net receipts of primary income from nonresident sources. Adjusted net national income goes a step further by subtracting from GNI a charge for the consumption of fixed capital (a calculation that yields net national income) and for the depletion of natural resources. The deduction for the depletion of natural resources, which covers net forest depletion, energy depletion, and mineral depletion, reflects the decline in asset values associated with the extraction and harvest of natural resources. For more discussion of the estimates and methodology of produced capital consumption and natural capital depletion, see *About the data* in table 4.11.

The United Nations System of National Accounts (SNA) includes nonproduced natural assets (such as land, mineral resources, and forests) within the asset boundary when they are under the effective control of institutional units. The calculation of adjusted net national income, which accounts for net forest, energy, and mineral depletion, thus remains within the SNA boundaries. This point is critical because it allows for comparisons across GDP, GNI, and adjusted net national income; such comparisons reveal the impact of natural resource depletion, which is otherwise ignored by the popular economic indicators.

Adjusted net national income is particularly useful in monitoring low-income, resource-rich economies, like many countries in Sub-Saharan Africa, because such economies often see large natural resources depletion as well as substantial exports of resource rents to foreign mining companies. For recent years adjusted net national income gives a picture of economic growth that is strikingly different from the one provided by GDP.

The key to increasing future consumption and thus the standard of living lies in increasing national wealth—including not only the traditional measures of capital (such as produced and human capital), but also natural capital. Natural capital comprises such assets as land, forests, and subsoil resources. All three types of capital are key to sustaining economic growth. By accounting for the consumption of fixed and natural capital depletion, adjusted net national income better measures the income available for consumption or for investment to increase a country's future consumption. For a measure of how comprehensive wealth is changing over time, see table 4.11.

Methods of computing growth are described in Statistical methods. For a detailed note on methodology, see data.worldbank.org/.

GDP and adjusted net national income in Sub-Saharan Africa, 2000–09 (2000 $ billions)

4.10a

Source: World Development Indicators data files.

Toward a broader measure of saving

	Gross savings	Consumption of fixed capital	Education expenditure	Net forest depletion	Energy depletion	Mineral depletion	Carbon dioxide damage	Local pollution damage	Adjusted net savings
	% of GNI 2009	% of GNI 2009	% of GNI 2009	% of GNI 2009	% of GNI 2009	% of GNI 2009	% of GNI 2009	% of GNI 2009	% of GNI 2009
Afghanistan	..	7.7	..	3.4	0.0	0.0	0.1	0.7	..
Albania	17.6	10.5	2.8	0.0	1.3	0.0	0.3	0.2	8.2
Algeria	..	10.5	4.5	0.1	16.7	0.1	0.8	0.2	..
Angola	10.9	11.7	2.3	0.0	29.1	0.0	0.3	1.2	−29.2
Argentina	23.9	11.8	4.9	0.0	4.5	0.3	0.5	1.1	10.6
Armenia	19.5	9.7	2.2	0.0	0.0	0.5	0.5	1.6	9.6
Australia	22.4	14.4	4.5	0.0	1.9	3.1	0.3	0.0	1.7
Austria	24.4	14.3	5.2	0.0	0.1	0.0	0.1	0.1	15.0
Azerbaijan	48.0	11.5	2.9	0.0	32.7	0.0	1.0	0.3	5.4
Bangladesh	35.3	6.8	2.0	0.6	2.1	0.0	0.4	0.4	27.1
Belarus	25.7	11.1	4.4	0.0	0.9	0.0	1.3	0.0	16.9
Belgium	21.7	14.0	5.8	0.0	0.0	0.0	0.2	0.1	13.2
Benin	10.6	7.9	3.3	1.2	0.0	0.0	0.4	0.3	4.1
Bolivia	23.8	9.5	4.7	0.0	9.7	1.5	0.6	1.0	6.2
Bosnia and Herzegovina	12.9	10.4	..	..	0.7	0.9	1.3	0.1	..
Botswana	17.1	11.5	7.4	0.0	0.3	2.5	0.3	0.2	9.6
Brazil	15.0	11.8	4.8	0.0	1.6	1.5	0.2	0.1	4.6
Bulgaria	16.7	11.7	3.8	0.0	0.4	0.7	0.9	0.8	6.1
Burkina Faso	..	7.4	4.3	1.6	0.0	0.0	0.1	0.6	..
Burundi	..	5.5	7.1	9.8	0.0	0.8	0.1	0.1	..
Cambodia	20.3	8.1	1.6	0.2	0.0	0.0	0.4	0.3	13.0
Cameroon	20.4	8.6	3.1	0.0	4.7	0.1	0.2	0.4	6.8
Canada	18.0	14.2	4.7	0.0	1.9	0.4	0.3	0.0	5.8
Central African Republic	..	7.2	1.3	0.0	0.0	0.0	0.1	0.2	..
Chad	..	9.9	2.3	0.0	25.2	0.0	0.0	1.0	..
Chile	23.0	12.6	3.6	0.0	0.1	9.9	0.4	0.5	3.2
China	53.2	10.2	1.8	0.0	2.9	0.2	1.1	0.8	39.7
Hong Kong SAR, China	30.3	13.6	3.0	0.0	0.0	0.0	0.1	..	..
Colombia	19.2	11.3	4.0	0.0	5.9	0.3	0.2	0.1	5.4
Congo, Dem. Rep.	..	5.9	0.9	0.0	2.9	7.9	0.2	0.5	..
Congo, Rep.	26.2	13.6	2.5	0.0	50.6	0.0	0.2	0.7	−44.7
Costa Rica	20.8	11.3	6.2	0.1	0.0	0.1	0.2	0.1	15.2
Côte d'Ivoire	15.4	8.8	4.3	0.0	3.1	0.0	0.2	0.3	7.3
Croatia	22.6	12.9	3.9	0.2	0.7	0.0	0.3	0.2	12.3
Cuba	..	..	13.6	0.0	2.4	1.0	0.3	0.1	..
Czech Republic	21.8	13.6	4.0	0.0	0.3	0.0	0.6	0.0	11.3
Denmark	21.4	16.5	7.4	0.0	1.5	0.0	0.1	0.0	10.7
Dominican Republic	10.5	11.1	1.9	0.0	0.0	0.5	0.4	0.0	0.4
Ecuador	24.1	10.7	1.4	0.0	9.8	0.0	0.4	0.0	4.4
Egypt, Arab Rep.	16.7	9.6	4.4	0.1	7.0	0.1	0.8	0.5	3.1
El Salvador	11.7	10.5	3.3	0.5	0.0	0.0	0.3	0.1	3.7
Eritrea	..	6.8	1.6	0.8	0.0	0.0	0.2	0.3	..
Estonia	24.2	12.8	4.4	0.0	0.7	0.0	0.8	0.0	14.4
Ethiopia	16.2	6.7	3.7	4.4	0.0	0.1	0.2	0.2	8.3
Finland	19.8	17.0	5.5	0.0	0.0	0.1	0.2	0.0	8.1
France	16.3	14.2	5.0	0.0	0.0	0.0	0.1	0.0	7.0
Gabon	..	13.2	3.1	0.0	29.1	0.1	0.2	0.0	..
Gambia, The	20.0	7.5	2.1	1.0	0.0	0.0	0.4	0.4	12.9
Georgia	0.2	8.8	2.8	0.0	0.1	0.0	0.4	0.7	−7.1
Germany	21.2	13.8	4.3	0.0	0.1	0.0	0.2	0.0	11.4
Ghana	15.7	8.6	4.7	2.1	0.0	4.8	0.3	0.0	−4.7
Greece	3.4	13.9	3.3	0.0	0.1	0.0	0.2	0.3	−7.9
Guatemala	12.9	10.1	2.9	0.8	0.4	0.0	0.3	0.1	4.0
Guinea	8.5	7.7	2.3	2.9	0.0	3.7	0.3	0.5	−4.2
Guinea-Bissau	..	7.4	2.3	0.0	0.0	0.0	0.3	0.6	..
Haiti	..	..	1.5	..	..	..	..	0.4	..
Honduras	16.6	9.6	3.5	0.0	0.0	0.4	0.5	0.2	9.5

	Gross savings	Consumption of fixed capital	Education expenditure	Net forest depletion	Energy depletion	Mineral depletion	Carbon dioxide damage	Local pollution damage	Adjusted net savings
	% of GNI **2009**	% of GNI **2009**	% of GNI **2009**	% of GNI **2009**	% of GNI **2009**	% of GNI **2009**	% of GNI **2009**	% of GNI **2009**	% of GNI **2009**
Hungary	*16.0*	13.0	5.3	0.0	0.2	0.0	0.4	0.0	4.5
India	35.2	8.6	3.1	0.9	2.2	1.1	0.9	0.5	24.1
Indonesia	26.2	10.9	3.3	0.0	5.3	1.2	0.6	0.5	11.0
Iran, Islamic Rep.	..	10.7	4.0	0.0	17.7	0.2	1.1	0.5	..
Iraq	..	10.1	..	0.0	45.7	0.0	1.3	2.6	..
Ireland	11.5	17.7	5.2	0.0	0.0	0.0	0.2	0.0	−1.1
Israel	20.8	13.6	5.7	0.0	0.1	0.1	0.3	0.1	12.2
Italy	16.3	14.0	4.1	0.0	0.1	0.0	0.2	0.1	6.1
Jamaica	13.5	11.2	6.2	0.0	0.0	0.7	0.8	0.2	6.9
Japan	22.9	13.5	3.2	0.0	0.0	0.0	0.2	0.2	12.1
Jordan	9.6	10.3	5.6	0.0	0.1	1.0	0.7	0.2	3.0
Kazakhstan	30.8	12.7	4.4	0.0	20.8	1.2	1.6	0.1	−1.2
Kenya	15.4	7.4	6.6	1.2	0.0	0.0	0.3	0.1	13.1
Korea, Dem. Rep.	..	..	..	..	..	..	..	0.8	..
Korea, Rep.	30.1	13.3	3.9	0.0	0.0	0.0	0.5	0.3	20.0
Kosovo	..	..	..	..	..	..	0.0	..	..
Kuwait	55.5	5.2	3.2	0.0	37.0	0.0	0.4	0.3	*15.7*
Kyrgyz Republic	14.4	8.4	5.2	0.0	0.5	0.0	1.1	0.2	9.4
Lao PDR	25.7	8.4	1.1	0.0	0.0	0.0	0.2	0.4	*17.8*
Latvia	26.6	11.3	5.6	0.3	0.0	0.0	0.2	0.0	20.4
Lebanon	12.9	11.2	1.6	0.0	0.0	0.0	0.4	0.2	2.7
Lesotho	22.9	6.4	9.4	1.4	0.0	0.0	0.0	0.1	24.4
Liberia	−2.7	8.2	3.1	10.4	0.0	0.7	1.0	0.3	*−18.3*
Libya	66.8	11.9	..	0.0	30.4	0.0	0.8	1.0	..
Lithuania	*15.1*	12.0	4.4	0.1	0.1	0.0	0.3	0.1	6.0
Macedonia, FYR	18.8	10.9	4.9	0.1	0.0	0.0	1.0	0.1	11.6
Madagascar	..	7.3	2.6	0.2	0.0	0.0	0.2	0.1	..
Malawi	..	7.4	3.5	0.9	0.0	0.0	0.2	0.1	..
Malaysia	31.7	11.6	4.0	0.0	7.9	0.0	0.8	0.0	15.4
Mali	*18.6*	7.7	3.3	0.0	0.0	0.0	0.1	1.1	13.5
Mauritania	..	8.1	3.1	0.5	0.0	18.3	0.5	0.4	..
Mauritius	16.2	10.9	3.1	0.0	0.0	0.0	0.3	0.0	8.0
Mexico	22.1	11.7	4.8	0.0	5.1	0.3	0.4	0.2	9.1
Moldova	17.8	8.5	8.4	0.1	0.1	0.0	0.7	0.6	16.2
Mongolia	44.7	9.5	4.6	0.0	3.8	7.3	2.1	1.6	24.9
Morocco	31.8	10.1	5.2	0.0	0.0	1.4	0.4	0.1	25.0
Mozambique	9.2	7.1	4.0	0.5	3.2	0.0	0.2	0.1	2.0
Myanmar	..	..	0.8	..	..	..	..	0.4	..
Namibia	26.8	10.6	6.4	0.0	0.0	0.3	0.2	0.2	21.9
Nepal	36.8	6.8	3.5	4.2	0.0	0.0	0.2	0.0	29.1
Netherlands	22.7	14.6	4.7	0.0	0.8	0.0	0.2	0.2	11.6
New Zealand	16.6	14.1	6.6	0.0	0.6	0.3	0.2	0.0	8.0
Nicaragua	10.6	8.8	3.0	0.1	0.0	0.7	0.6	0.0	3.4
Niger	..	2.9	3.6	1.2	0.0	0.0	0.1	1.1	..
Nigeria	..	9.0	0.9	0.3	14.7	0.0	0.5	0.5	..
Norway	32.6	15.2	6.2	0.0	10.6	0.0	0.1	0.0	12.8
Oman	*40.3*	13.5	3.7	0.0	37.8	0.0	0.5	0.0	−7.9
Pakistan	21.5	8.0	1.9	1.0	2.2	0.0	0.7	0.8	10.7
Panama	37.4	12.1	3.5	0.0	0.0	0.0	0.3	0.1	28.4
Papua New Guinea	19.7	8.6	..	0.0	0.0	19.9	0.5	0.0	..
Paraguay	12.3	9.7	3.6	0.0	0.0	0.0	0.2	0.8	5.2
Peru	24.0	11.3	2.4	0.0	0.7	5.2	0.3	0.4	8.6
Philippines	35.0	8.0	2.5	0.1	0.3	0.7	0.3	0.1	28.0
Poland	19.2	12.4	4.8	0.1	0.7	0.2	0.6	0.2	9.7
Portugal	10.4	17.2	5.3	0.0	0.0	0.1	0.2	0.0	−1.8
Puerto Rico	..	..	..	..	..	..	..	..	..
Qatar	..	..	..	..	..	..	..	0.1	..

	Gross savings	Consumption of fixed capital	Education expenditure	Net forest depletion	Energy depletion	Mineral depletion	Carbon dioxide damage	Local pollution damage	Adjusted net savings
	% of GNI 2009	% of GNI 2009	% of GNI 2009	% of GNI 2009	% of GNI 2009	% of GNI 2009	% of GNI 2009	% of GNI 2009	% of GNI 2009
Romania	28.4	11.2	3.4	0.0	1.4	0.0	0.5	0.0	18.8
Russian Federation	23.4	12.0	3.5	0.0	13.8	0.7	1.1	0.1	−0.8
Rwanda	15.2	7.4	3.6	2.4	0.0	0.0	0.1	0.1	8.8
Saudi Arabia	31.5	12.6	7.2	0.0	28.9	0.0	0.8	0.7	−3.9
Senegal	16.1	8.4	5.4	0.0	0.0	0.3	0.3	0.5	7.8
Serbia	17.5	..	4.7	..	0.4	0.0	0.0	..	..
Sierra Leone	8.0	6.8	3.4	1.7	0.0	0.4	0.5	0.8	1.2
Singapore	45.2	14.1	2.8	0.0	0.0	0.0	0.3	0.4	33.0
Slovak Republic	29.9	13.0	3.6	0.3	0.0	0.0	0.4	0.0	19.8
Slovenia	22.7	13.5	4.9	0.1	0.1	0.0	0.3	0.1	13.6
Somalia	..	..	..	..	..	..	..	0.4	..
South Africa	15.8	14.1	5.4	0.3	2.8	2.2	1.2	0.1	0.4
Spain	19.9	13.9	4.0	0.0	0.0	0.0	0.2	0.2	9.7
Sri Lanka	24.3	9.5	2.6	0.5	0.0	0.0	0.2	0.2	16.4
Sudan	13.5	9.7	0.9	0.0	11.1	0.0	0.2	0.5	−7.1
Swaziland	2.5	10.2	7.2	0.1	0.0	0.0	0.3	0.0	−0.9
Sweden	23.6	13.3	6.1	0.0	0.0	0.2	0.1	0.0	16.0
Switzerland	31.0	14.1	4.8	0.0	0.0	0.0	0.1	0.1	21.6
Syrian Arab Republic	13.9	9.9	2.6	0.0	10.0	0.1	1.1	0.7	−14.1
Tajikistan	12.4	7.9	3.2	0.0	0.2	0.0	1.1	0.3	6.2
Tanzaniaa	21.1	7.3	2.4	0.0	0.2	2.3	0.2	0.1	13.5
Thailand	31.0	10.9	4.6	0.2	3.0	0.0	0.9	0.2	20.5
Timor-Leste	..	1.2	1.6	..	0.0	0.0	0.0	..	..
Togo	..	7.0	4.5	2.3	0.0	1.3	0.4	0.1	..
Trinidad and Tobago	34.3	12.9	4.0	0.0	28.2	0.0	1.4	0.2	−32.4
Tunisia	24.1	11.0	6.7	0.1	3.5	1.0	0.5	0.1	14.6
Turkey	13.0	11.7	2.6	0.0	0.2	0.0	0.3	0.6	2.9
Turkmenistan	..	10.8	..	..	30.4	0.0	2.1	0.9	..
Uganda	17.9	7.4	3.0	4.7	0.0	0.0	0.1	0.0	8.6
Ukraine	15.9	9.9	5.9	0.0	3.8	0.0	2.4	0.1	5.6
United Arab Emirates	..	..	..	..	..	..	..	0.5	..
United Kingdom	11.9	13.5	5.1	0.0	1.2	0.0	0.2	0.0	2.2
United States	9.8	14.3	4.8	0.0	0.7	0.1	0.3	0.1	−0.8
Uruguay	17.5	12.0	2.3	0.4	0.0	0.0	0.2	1.1	6.1
Uzbekistan	..	8.4	9.4	0.0	17.8	0.0	3.2	0.3	..
Venezuela, RB	21.8	12.2	3.6	0.0	9.5	0.3	0.4	0.0	2.9
Vietnam	31.2	8.8	2.8	0.2	7.0	0.0	1.1	0.3	16.6
West Bank and Gaza	..	..	..	..	..	..	..	..	..
Yemen, Rep.	..	9.0	4.2	0.0	13.2	0.0	0.7	..	..
Zambia	21.3	9.3	1.3	0.0	0.0	11.5	0.2	0.2	1.4
Zimbabwe	..	..	6.9	0.0	2.2	1.3	1.1	0.2	..
World	**21.1 w**	**13.1 w**	**4.2 w**	**0.0 w**	**2.0 w**	**0.3 w**	**0.4 w**	**0.2 w**	**6.4 w**
Low income	23.9	7.2	3.2	1.4	1.2	1.3	0.3	0.3	..
Middle income	33.2	10.7	3.2	0.1	5.1	0.7	0.8	0.5	14.5
Lower middle income	43.3	9.9	2.4	0.2	4.0	0.4	1.0	0.7	26.2
Upper middle income	20.0	11.8	4.1	0.0	6.4	1.0	0.6	0.2	3.9
Low & middle income	33.0	10.7	3.2	0.1	5.0	0.7	0.8	0.5	14.6
East Asia & Pacific	48.7	10.3	2.1	0.0	3.3	0.3	1.0	0.7	33.1
Europe & Central Asia	21.1	11.7	3.6	0.0	8.7	0.4	0.9	0.2	1.4
Latin America & Carib.	18.9	11.7	4.4	0.0	3.5	1.3	0.3	0.3	6.8
Middle East & N. Africa	..	10.4	4.3	0.0	14.5	0.3	0.9	0.6	..
South Asia	33.6	8.4	2.9	0.9	2.1	0.9	0.9	0.5	21.6
Sub-Saharan Africa	15.4	10.6	3.6	0.6	7.5	1.2	0.6	0.3	−1.8
High income	16.5	14.1	4.6	0.0	0.9	0.1	0.2	0.1	5.2
Euro area	18.6	14.2	4.5	0.0	0.1	0.0	0.2	0.1	8.7

a. Covers mainland Tanzania only.

About the data

Adjusted net savings measures the change in value of a specified set of assets, excluding capital gains. If a country's net savings are positive and the accounting includes a sufficiently broad range of assets, economic theory suggests that the present value of social welfare is increasing. Conversely, persistently negative adjusted net savings indicate that an economy is on an unsustainable path.

The table shows the extent to which today's rents from natural resources and changes in human capital are balanced by net savings—that is, this generation's bequest to future generations.

Adjusted net savings is derived from standard national accounting measures of gross savings by making four adjustments. First, estimates of fixed capital consumption of produced assets are deducted to obtain net savings. Second, current public expenditures on education are added to net savings (in standard national accounting these expenditures are treated as consumption). Third, estimates of the depletion of a variety of natural resources are deducted to reflect the decline in asset values associated with their extraction and harvest. And fourth, deductions are made for damages from carbon dioxide and particulate emissions.

The exercise treats public education expenditures as an addition to savings. However, because of the wide variability in the effectiveness of public education expenditures, these figures cannot be construed as the value of investments in human capital. A current expenditure of $1 on education does not necessarily yield $1 of human capital. The calculation should also consider private education expenditure, but data are not available for a large number of countries.

While extensive, the accounting of natural resources depletion and pollution costs still has some gaps. Key estimates missing on the resource side include the value of fossil water extracted from aquifers, net depletion of fish stocks, and depletion and degradation of soils. Important pollutants affecting human health and economic assets are excluded because no internationally comparable data are widely available on damage from ground-level ozone or sulfur oxides.

Estimates of resource depletion are based on the "change in real wealth" method described in Hamilton and Ruta (2008), which estimates depletion as the ratio between the total value of the resource and the remaining reserve lifetime. The total value of the resource is the present value of current and future rents from resource extractions. An economic rent represents an excess return to a given factor of production. Natural resources give rise to rents because they are not produced; in contrast, for produced goods and services competitive forces will expand supply until economic profits are driven to zero. For each type of resource and each country, unit resource rents are derived by taking the difference between world prices (to reflect the social opportunity cost of resource extraction) and the average unit extraction or harvest costs (including a "normal" return on capital). Unit rents are then multiplied by the physical quantity extracted or harvested to arrive at total rent. To estimate the value of the resource, rents are assumed to be constant over the life of the resource (the El Serafy approach), and the present value of the rent flow is calculated using a 4 percent social discount rate. For details on the estimation of natural wealth see World Bank (2011a).

A positive net depletion figure for forest resources implies that the harvest rate exceeds the rate of natural growth; this is not the same as deforestation, which represents a change in land use (see Definitions for table 3.4). In principle, there should be an addition to savings in countries where growth exceeds harvest, but empirical estimates suggest that most of this net growth is in forested areas that cannot currently be exploited economically. Because the depletion estimates reflect only timber values, they ignore all the external and nontimber benefits associated with standing forests.

Pollution damage from emissions of carbon dioxide is calculated as the marginal social cost per unit multiplied by the increase in the stock of carbon dioxide. The unit damage figure represents the present value of global damage to economic assets and to human welfare over the time the unit of pollution remains in the atmosphere.

Pollution damage from particulate emissions is estimated by valuing the human health effects from exposure to particulate matter pollution in urban areas. The estimates are calculated as willingness to pay to avoid illness and death, from cardiopulmonary disease and lung cancer in adults and acute respiratory infections in children, that are attributable to particulate emissions.

Adjusted net savings aims to be as comprehensive a measure as possible to provide a better understanding of the rate of country wealth creation or depletion. To do so, it treats education as investment and accounts for pollution damages to assets and human welfare, which goes outside the boundaries of the United Nations System of National Accounts.

For a detailed note on methodology, see data. worldbank.org/.

Definitions

• **Gross savings** is the difference between gross national income and public and private consumption, plus net current transfers. • Consumption of fixed capital is the replacement value of capital used up in production. • **Education expenditure** is public current operating expenditures in education, including wages and salaries and excluding capital investments in buildings and equipment. • **Net forest depletion** is unit resource rents times the excess of roundwood harvest over natural growth. • **Energy depletion** is the ratio of the value of the stock of energy resources to the remaining reserve lifetime (capped at 25 years). It covers coal, crude oil, and natural gas. • Mineral depletion is the ratio of the value of the stock of mineral resources to the remaining reserve lifetime (capped at 25 years). It covers tin, gold, lead, zinc, iron, copper, nickel, silver, bauxite, and phosphate. • **Carbon dioxide damage** is estimated at $20 per ton of carbon (the unit damage in 1995 U.S. dollars) times tons of carbon emitted. • **Particulate emissions damage** is the willingness to pay to avoid illness and death attributable to particulate emissions. • **Adjusted net savings** is net savings plus education expenditure minus energy depletion, mineral depletion, net forest depletion, and carbon dioxide and particulate emissions damage.

Data sources

Data on gross savings are from World Bank national accounts data files (see table 4.8). Data on consumption of fixed capital are from the United Nations Statistics Division's *National Accounts Statistics: Main Aggregates and Detailed Tables*, extrapolated to 2009. Data on education expenditure are from the United Nations Educational, Scientific, and Cultural Organization Institute for Statistics online database; missing data are estimated by World Bank staff. Data on energy, mineral, and forest depletion are estimates based on sources and methods in World Bank (2011a). Data on carbon dioxide damage are from Fankhauser's *Valuing Climate Change: The Economics of the Greenhouse* (1995). Data on particulate emissions damage are from Pandey and others' "The Human Cost of Air Pollution: New Estimates for Developing Countries" (2006). The conceptual underpinnings of the savings measure appear in Hamilton and Clemens' "Genuine Savings Rates in Developing Countries" (1999).

4.12 Central government finances

	Revenue[a]		Expense		Cash surplus or deficit		Net incurrence of liabilities				Debt and interest payments	
	% of GDP		% of GDP		% of GDP		Domestic		Foreign		Total debt % of GDP	Interest % of revenue
	1995	2009	1995	2009	1995	2009	1995	2009	1995	2009	2009	2009
Afghanistan[b]	..	9.1	..	38.0	..	0.2	..	0.1	..	0.8	..	0.0
Albania[b]	21.2	..	25.6	..	−8.9	..	7.4	..	2.1	..	..	..
Algeria	..	36.6	..	25.0	..	−4.4	..	5.9	..	0.0	..	1.0
Angola	..	..	..	..	..	..	..	..	..	..	..	..
Argentina	..	..	..	..	..	..	..	..	..	..	..	..
Armenia[b]	..	22.1	..	23.7	..	−7.5	..	1.3	..	12.3	..	2.3
Australia	..	24.6	..	26.6	..	−2.4	..	..	..	..	24.1	3.7
Austria	36.6	36.6	42.5	39.6	−5.5	−2.6	..	..	..	..	70.7	7.0
Azerbaijan[b]	..	27.3	..	15.5	..	0.4	..	0.0	..	0.2	..	0.3
Bangladesh[b]	..	11.1	..	11.3	..	−1.7	..	3.1	..	0.4	..	21.7
Belarus[b]	30.0	35.4	28.7	33.0	−2.7	0.2	2.2	−2.5	0.4	8.4	18.1	2.1
Belgium	41.5	40.3	45.7	45.3	−3.9	−5.1	..	1.0	−0.5	6.5	92.4	8.5
Benin[b]	..	17.6	..	15.0	..	−4.5	..	2.2	..	2.1	..	2.5
Bolivia	..	23.3	..	21.8	..	1.2	..	−0.2	..	−0.1	..	8.0
Bosnia and Herzegovina	..	38.6	..	41.2	..	−4.3	..	3.7	..	3.2	..	1.2
Botswana[b]	40.5	..	30.3	..	4.9	..	0.2	..	−0.4	..	..	..
Brazil[b]	26.9	23.1	32.9	25.6	−2.7	−3.5	..	8.3	..	−0.1	61.0	20.7
Bulgaria[b]	35.6	32.3	39.5	31.6	−5.1	−0.1	7.5	−0.4	−0.8	0.5	..	2.2
Burkina Faso	..	14.0	..	13.0	..	−4.8	..	4.5	..	2.9	..	2.2
Burundi[b]	19.3	..	23.6	..	−4.7	..	3.1	..	4.0	..	..	..
Cambodia	..	11.0	..	11.0	..	−2.3	..	−2.0	..	2.3	..	1.3
Cameroon[b]	11.8	..	10.6	..	0.2	..	−0.3	..	0.3	..	..	..
Canada[b]	19.8	17.4	23.8	19.2	−4.0	−1.9	..	..	..	..	53.2	10.1
Central African Republic[b]	..	..	..	..	..	..	..	..	..	..	..	..
Chad	..	..	..	..	..	..	..	..	..	..	..	..
Chile	..	20.1	..	22.6	..	−4.5	..	0.8	..	−0.4	..	2.8
China[b]	5.4	11.1	..	..	..	..	1.6	0.4	..	0.0	..	..
Hong Kong SAR, China	..	19.7	..	18.9	..	0.6	..	1.0	..	−0.1	30.5	0.3
Colombia	..	17.0	..	19.5	..	−4.0	..	5.8	..	0.9	59.3	18.9
Congo, Dem. Rep.[b]	5.3	..	8.2	..	0.0	..	0.0	..	0.2	..	..	..
Congo, Rep.[b]	23.6	..	29.8	..	−8.2	..	..	..	..	..	..	..
Costa Rica	..	24.7	..	26.0	..	−3.4	..	..	..	..	..	8.8
Côte d'Ivoire	..	18.7	..	17.6	..	0.9	..	..	..	..	..	7.1
Croatia[b]	36.8	34.1	36.2	36.2	−1.1	−3.0	−2.3	3.0	0.7	2.2	..	4.8
Cuba	..	..	..	..	..	..	..	..	..	..	..	..
Czech Republic[b]	33.2	29.1	32.6	37.3	−0.9	−6.1	−0.5	2.9	−0.4	1.9	31.9	4.1
Denmark	37.6	40.0	41.5	42.4	−3.7	−2.1	..	..	..	..	41.0	4.9
Dominican Republic	..	16.4	..	16.2	..	−3.8	..	2.4	..	1.5	..	9.7
Ecuador[b]	30.9	..	26.3	..	0.1	..	..	..	..	..	..	..
Egypt, Arab Rep.[b]	34.8	27.0	28.1	30.2	3.4	−6.6	..	9.9	..	−0.2	79.5	15.2
El Salvador	..	17.5	..	21.6	..	−5.0	..	2.0	..	5.9	48.5	12.3
Eritrea	..	..	..	..	..	..	..	..	..	..	..	..
Estonia	36.2	37.1	32.8	36.8	1.6	−1.3	..	..	..	..	9.1	0.6
Ethiopia[b]	12.2	..	12.0	..	−3.1	..	1.8	..	2.6	..	..	..
Finland	40.4	39.0	49.7	35.0	−7.5	4.6	8.9	−0.2	0.2	−0.6	36.2	3.2
France	43.3	40.5	47.6	47.6	−4.1	−7.3	..	..	..	..	82.8	5.4
Gabon	..	..	..	..	..	..	..	..	..	..	..	..
Gambia, The[b]	..	..	..	..	..	..	..	..	..	..	..	..
Georgia[b]	12.2	25.2	15.4	31.0	−4.3	−7.8	2.2	1.3	2.4	3.7	34.7	3.4
Germany	29.9	29.4	38.6	31.7	−8.3	−2.2	..	3.1	..	−0.2	47.2	5.5
Ghana[b]	17.0	15.3	..	17.9	..	−5.6	..	2.8	..	2.6	..	15.2
Greece	35.3	36.2	44.3	50.7	−9.1	−15.2	..	..	..	..	138.5	14.3
Guatemala[b]	8.4	11.0	7.6	12.6	−0.5	−3.2	..	1.4	0.4	1.4	23.3	12.6
Guinea[b]	11.2	..	12.1	..	−4.3	..	−0.1	..	4.5	..	..	..
Guinea-Bissau	..	..	..	..	..	..	..	..	..	..	..	..
Haiti	..	..	..	..	..	..	..	..	..	..	..	..
Honduras	..	20.8	..	24.1	..	−4.5	..	5.0	..	1.0	..	2.9

Central government finances | 4.12

	Revenue[a]		Expense		Cash surplus or deficit		Net incurrence of liabilities % of GDP				Debt and interest payments	
	% of GDP		% of GDP		% of GDP		Domestic		Foreign		Total debt % of GDP	Interest % of revenue
	1995	2009	1995	2009	1995	2009	1995	2009	1995	2009	2009	2009
Hungary	43.0	40.5	53.2	45.3	−9.1	−4.0	17.0	−1.9	0.2	5.8	81.7	10.6
India[b]	12.3	11.9	14.4	16.2	−2.2	−4.9	5.1	5.6	0.0	0.2	53.0	28.5
Indonesia[b]	15.6	15.4	9.5	15.7	1.7	−1.7	..	0.9	−0.4	0.4	28.3	10.9
Iran, Islamic Rep.[b]	24.2	31.9	15.8	24.7	1.1	0.6	..	1.4	0.1	0.0	..	0.6
Iraq	..	..	..	..	..	..	..	..	..	..	..	..
Ireland	35.5	30.4	37.5	43.4	−2.2	−13.9	..	..	..	..	69.2	6.9
Israel	..	34.6	..	40.6	..	−4.3	..	..	..	..	..	9.7
Italy	40.4	38.5	48.0	44.0	−7.5	−4.9	..	..	..	..	118.9	11.1
Jamaica	..	27.0	..	41.5	..	−15.9	..	7.4	..	4.7	115.8	64.5
Japan	..	..	..	..	..	..	..	..	..	..	157.7	..
Jordan[b]	28.2	23.5	26.1	28.6	0.9	−8.5	−2.5	7.6	6.1	1.2	57.9	8.7
Kazakhstan[b]	14.0	9.2	18.7	16.9	−1.8	−2.0	0.8	2.8	2.8	0.5	9.5	2.5
Kenya[b]	21.6	20.5	25.8	21.7	−5.1	−5.5	3.9	3.0	−1.3	0.1	..	10.4
Korea, Dem. Rep.	..	..	..	..	..	..	..	..	..	..	..	..
Korea, Rep.[b]	17.8	23.1	14.3	21.9	2.4	0.0	−0.3	5.4	−0.1	−0.1	..	4.7
Kosovo	..	..	..	..	..	..	..	..	..	..	..	..
Kuwait[b]	36.8	47.1	44.0	21.9	−9.9	20.0	..	..	..	..	..	0.0
Kyrgyz Republic[b]	16.7	19.2	25.6	19.3	−10.8	−1.4	..	0.5	..	7.7	..	3.3
Lao PDR	..	13.9	..	11.3	..	−1.6	..	−0.3	..	2.1	..	3.2
Latvia[b]	25.8	24.9	28.3	34.8	−2.7	−6.4	2.4	−2.7	1.5	15.1	41.8	3.8
Lebanon	..	22.5	..	29.5	..	−8.3	..	11.8	..	0.3	..	48.7
Lesotho[b]	57.1	66.4	39.4	52.1	5.8	5.8	0.0	−0.4	7.2	1.6	..	1.3
Liberia[b]	..	0.4	..	0.3	..	0.0	..	0.0	..	0.0	..	2.1
Libya	..	..	..	..	..	..	..	..	..	..	..	..
Lithuania	..	28.3	..	38.8	..	−9.0	..	1.9	..	9.1	33.3	4.0
Macedonia, FYR[b]	..	34.0	..	31.3	..	−0.8	..	−0.6	..	0.2	..	1.9
Madagascar	..	14.1	..	11.7	..	−1.9	..	0.6	..	3.0	..	3.9
Malawi	..	..	..	..	..	..	..	..	..	..	..	..
Malaysia[b]	23.3	23.3	18.7	22.7	1.5	−6.4	..	6.5	..	0.9	53.3	9.0
Mali	..	17.1	..	14.6	..	−2.1	..	−4.4	..	2.6	..	1.7
Mauritania	..	..	..	..	..	..	..	..	..	..	..	..
Mauritius	..	23.5	..	21.6	..	0.6	..	3.1	..	1.3	38.9	12.0
Mexico[b]	15.3	..	15.0	..	−0.6	..	..	..	5.5	..	..	..
Moldova[b]	28.4	33.1	38.4	38.3	−6.3	−5.7	3.0	2.7	2.7	3.3	24.4	4.0
Mongolia[b]	19.0	29.2	13.8	28.8	2.9	−4.5	1.6	8.6	1.3	5.2	64.8	1.6
Morocco[b]	..	33.1	..	27.9	..	1.0	..	0.1	..	1.7	46.9	3.1
Mozambique	..	..	..	..	..	..	..	..	..	..	..	..
Myanmar[b]	6.4	..	..	..	..	..	..	..	..	..	..	..
Namibia[b]	31.7	29.2	35.7	24.1	−5.0	2.0	..	−0.8	..	−0.1	..	6.3
Nepal[b]	10.5	14.5	..	..	..	..	0.6	3.2	2.5	0.0	43.7	4.9
Netherlands	41.5	41.0	50.8	45.6	−9.2	−4.8	..	..	..	..	58.3	4.6
New Zealand	..	36.1	..	32.1	..	3.1	..	..	..	..	37.9	3.4
Nicaragua[b]	12.8	19.1	14.2	20.9	0.6	−2.3	..	..	3.4	..	..	6.4
Niger	..	13.6	..	11.8	..	−0.9	..	−1.9	..	2.4	..	1.8
Nigeria[b]	..	9.7	..	7.2	..	−1.7	..	0.1	..	..	3.0	6.6
Norway	..	47.2	..	35.9	..	10.7	..	6.3	..	−15.3	36.3	2.1
Oman[b]	27.8	..	32.4	..	−8.9	..	−0.1	..	0.0	..	..	..
Pakistan[b]	17.2	14.0	19.1	16.8	−5.3	−4.8	..	..	..	..	..	41.7
Panama[b]	26.1	..	22.0	..	1.5	..	..	..	..	..	..	..
Papua New Guinea[b]	22.7	..	24.5	..	−0.5	..	1.5	..	−0.7	..	..	..
Paraguay[b]	17.2	19.0	14.5	17.1	0.2	0.1	0.0	1.3	−0.8	0.1	..	3.1
Peru[b]	17.4	17.2	17.4	17.1	−1.3	−1.5	..	0.2	3.9	1.1	23.6	7.2
Philippines[b]	17.7	14.6	15.9	18.6	−0.8	−3.9	−0.5	1.2	−0.7	2.0	48.1	25.7
Poland	..	30.1	..	35.8	..	−6.1	..	1.6	..	3.6	..	8.1
Portugal	33.2	34.7	37.1	43.2	−5.1	−8.7	−1.2	3.4	4.2	5.9	84.4	7.7
Puerto Rico	..	..	..	..	..	..	..	..	..	..	..	..
Qatar[b]	..	47.2	..	19.3	..	15.2	..	..	..	..	..	2.1

	Revenue[a] (% of GDP)		Expense (% of GDP)		Cash surplus or deficit (% of GDP)		Net incurrence of liabilities (% of GDP)				Debt and interest payments	
							Domestic		Foreign		Total debt % of GDP	Interest % of revenue
	1995	2009	1995	2009	1995	2009	1995	2009	1995	2009	2009	2009
Romania	..	30.9	..	33.8	..	-4.6	..	2.4	..	0.9	..	2.0
Russian Federation	..	35.4	..	30.9	..	5.3	..	0.8	..	-0.2	8.6	1.3
Rwanda[b]	10.6	..	15.0	..	-5.6	..	2.9	..	..	..	..	..
Saudi Arabia	..	..	..	..	..	..	..	..	..	..	..	..
Senegal[b]	15.2	..	..	..	..	..	..	..	..	..	..	..
Serbia[b]	..	36.3	..	37.7	..	-2.6	..	2.8	..	1.2	..	2.0
Sierra Leone[b]	9.4	11.6	..	22.5	..	-3.1	0.3	..	..	..	..	8.3
Singapore[b]	26.7	18.2	12.4	15.2	19.8	1.7	10.3	13.7	0.0	..	113.3	0.1
Slovak Republic	..	28.5	..	37.6	..	-7.3	..	2.9	..	3.0	38.1	4.7
Slovenia[b]	35.8	37.5	34.3	42.7	-0.1	-5.5	-0.4	12.4	0.3	-1.2	..	2.9
Somalia	..	..	..	..	..	..	..	..	..	..	..	..
South Africa	..	28.2	..	33.0	..	-4.9	..	7.0	..	1.0	..	8.4
Spain	32.0	22.4	37.1	30.7	-5.8	-8.6	..	6.4	..	4.8	46.5	6.1
Sri Lanka[b]	20.4	14.9	26.0	19.2	-7.6	-6.6	5.2	6.9	3.2	-0.1	85.0	31.0
Sudan[b]	7.2	..	6.8	..	-0.4	..	0.3	..	..	..	..	..
Swaziland[b]	..	..	..	..	..	..	..	..	..	..	..	..
Sweden	38.6	34.7	..	..	..	..	..	..	..	..	44.0	..
Switzerland[b]	22.6	18.4	25.7	17.0	-0.6	1.3	-0.5	2.0	..	..	28.9	3.5
Syrian Arab Republic[b]	22.9	..	..	..	..	..	..	..	..	..	..	..
Tajikistan[b]	9.3	..	11.4	..	-3.3	..	0.1	..	2.3	..	..	..
Tanzania	..	..	..	..	..	..	..	..	..	..	..	..
Thailand	..	18.6	..	19.6	..	-3.0	..	5.3	..	0.0	28.6	5.8
Timor-Leste	..	..	..	..	..	..	..	..	..	..	..	..
Togo	..	18.8	..	17.4	..	-0.6	..	2.7	..	-0.5	..	4.0
Trinidad and Tobago[b]	27.2	36.1	25.3	28.4	-0.1	2.3	2.8	-0.6	2.6	0.5	14.1	5.0
Tunisia[b]	30.0	31.4	28.4	29.9	-2.4	-1.7	0.9	0.3	2.9	0.0	47.1	7.0
Turkey[b]	..	21.8	..	27.3	..	-5.5	..	6.1	..	0.6	51.4	24.1
Turkmenistan	..	..	..	..	..	..	..	..	..	..	..	..
Uganda[b]	10.6	12.4	..	13.7	..	-0.9	..	1.5	..	1.8	32.7	7.7
Ukraine[b]	..	34.5	..	40.6	..	-5.6	..	6.7	..	4.9	..	3.1
United Arab Emirates[b]	10.1	..	11.0	..	0.5	..	..	..	..	..	..	..
United Kingdom	35.2	35.9	40.4	46.4	-5.5	-10.9	..	..	..	..	73.2	5.3
United States	..	15.9	..	26.3	..	-10.4	..	6.5	..	4.7	67.1	11.4
Uruguay[b]	27.6	29.4	27.1	29.3	-1.2	-1.5	7.9	3.8	1.1	2.4	49.5	9.3
Uzbekistan	..	..	..	..	..	..	..	..	..	..	..	..
Venezuela, RB[b]	16.9	..	18.5	..	-2.3	..	1.1	..	0.1	..	..	..
Vietnam	..	..	..	..	..	..	..	..	..	..	..	..
West Bank and Gaza	..	..	..	..	..	..	..	..	..	..	..	1.1
Yemen, Rep.[b]	17.3	..	19.1	..	-3.9	..	..	..	..	..	..	..
Zambia[b]	20.0	17.6	21.4	22.9	-3.1	-0.8	28.0	..	16.2	..	..	7.2
Zimbabwe[b]	26.7	..	32.1	..	-5.4	..	-1.4	..	1.6	..	..	..
World	.. w	24.3 w	.. w	31.1 w	.. w	-7.1 w	.. m	.. m	.. m	.. m	.. m	5.4 m
Low income	..	..	..	..	..	..	..	..	..	..	..	..
Middle income	14.6	20.0	..	..	..	..	..	0.9	..	0.2	..	7.0
Lower middle income	10.7	14.7	..	..	..	..	..	0.5	..	..	..	6.0
Upper middle income	..	..	..	..	..	..	..	3.7	..	0.9	..	7.2
Low & middle income	14.6	19.8	..	..	..	..	..	0.6	..	..	..	4.5
East Asia & Pacific	7.2	13.4	..	..	..	..	..	1.2	..	2.0	..	5.8
Europe & Central Asia	..	29.3	..	30.1	..	-0.4	..	1.9	..	3.3	..	2.5
Latin America & Carib.	21.2	..	23.3	..	-1.4	..	..	0.1	..	-0.2	..	9.1
Middle East & N. Africa	..	30.6	..	27.3	..	-3.0	..	6.7	..	0.1	..	7.0
South Asia	13.1	12.1	15.3	16.0	-2.7	-4.6	3.8	3.2	1.1	0.3	56.5	21.7
Sub-Saharan Africa	..	24.5	..	24.2	..	-1.0	..	..	..	..	..	..
High income	..	24.7	..	32.2	..	-7.7	..	..	..	..	55.7	5.3
Euro area	34.9	34.5	42.3	39.8	-7.4	-5.2	..	0.8	..	0.4	69.9	6.1

a. Excludes grants. b. Data were reported on a cash basis and have been adjusted to the accrual framework.

4.12

About the data

Tables 4.12–4.14 present an overview of the size and role of central governments relative to national economies. The tables are based on the concepts and recommendations of the second edition of the International Monetary Fund's (IMF) *Government Finance Statistics Manual 2001*. Before 2005 *World Development Indicators* reported data derived on the basis of the 1986 manual's cash-based method. The 2001 manual, harmonized with the 1993 United Nations System of National Accounts, recommends an accrual accounting method, focusing on all economic events affecting assets, liabilities, revenues, and expenses, not only those represented by cash transactions. It takes all stocks into account, so that stock data at the end of an accounting period equal stock data at the beginning of the period plus flows over the period. The 1986 manual considered only the debt stock data. Further, the new manual no longer distinguishes between current and capital revenue or expenditures, and it introduces the concepts of nonfinancial and financial assets. Most countries still follow the 1986 manual, however. The IMF has reclassified historical *Government Finance Statistics Yearbook* data to conform to the 2001 manual's format. Because of reporting differences, the reclassified data understate both revenue and expense.

The 2001 manual describes government's economic functions as the provision of goods and services on a nonmarket basis for collective or individual consumption, and the redistribution of income and wealth through transfer payments. Government activities are financed mainly by taxation and other income transfers, though other financing such as

borrowing for temporary periods can also be used. *Government* excludes public corporations and quasi corporations (such as the central bank).

Units of government at many levels meet this definition, from local administrative units to the national government, but inadequate statistical coverage precludes presenting subnational data. Although data for general government under the 2001 manual are available for a few countries, only data for the central government are shown to minimize disparities. Still, different accounting concepts of central government make cross-country comparisons potentially misleading.

Central government can refer to consolidated or budgetary accounting. For most countries central government finance data have been consolidated into one account, but for others only budgetary central government accounts are available. Countries reporting budgetary data are noted in *Primary data documentation*. Because budgetary accounts may not include all central government units (such as social security funds), they usually provide an incomplete picture.

Data on government revenue and expense are collected by the IMF through questionnaires to member countries and by the Organisation for Economic Cooperation and Development. Despite IMF efforts to standardize data collection, statistics are often incomplete, untimely, and not comparable across countries.

Government finance statistics are reported in local currency. The indicators here are shown as percentages of GDP. Many countries report government finance data by fiscal year; see *Primary data documentation* for information on fiscal year end by country.

Definitions

• **Revenue** is cash receipts from taxes, social contributions, and other revenues such as fines, fees, rent, and income from property or sales. Grants, usually considered revenue, are excluded. • **Expense** is cash payments for government operating activities in providing goods and services. It includes compensation of employees, interest and subsidies, grants, social benefits, and other expenses such as rent and dividends. • **Cash surplus or deficit** is revenue (including grants) minus expense, minus net acquisition of nonfinancial assets. In editions before 2005 nonfinancial assets were included under revenue and expenditure in gross terms. This cash surplus or deficit is close to the earlier overall budget balance (still missing is lending minus repayments, which are included as a financing item under net acquisition of financial assets). • **Net incurrence of liabilities** is domestic financing (obtained from residents) and foreign financing (obtained from nonresidents), or the means by which a government provides financial resources to cover a budget deficit or allocates financial resources arising from a budget surplus. The net incurrence of liabilities should be offset by the net acquisition of financial assets (a third financing item). The difference between the cash surplus or deficit and the three financing items is the net change in the stock of cash. • **Total debt** is the entire stock of direct government fixed-term contractual obligations to others outstanding on a particular date. It includes domestic and foreign liabilities such as currency and money deposits, securities other than shares, and loans. It is the gross amount of government liabilities reduced by the amount of equity and financial derivatives held by the government. Because debt is a stock rather than a flow, it is measured as of a given date, usually the last day of the fiscal year. • **Interest payments** are interest payments on government debt—including long-term bonds, long-term loans, and other debt instruments—to domestic and foreign residents.

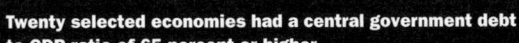

Twenty selected economies had a central government debt to GDP ratio of 65 percent or higher

4.12a

Central government debt, 2009 (percent of GDP)

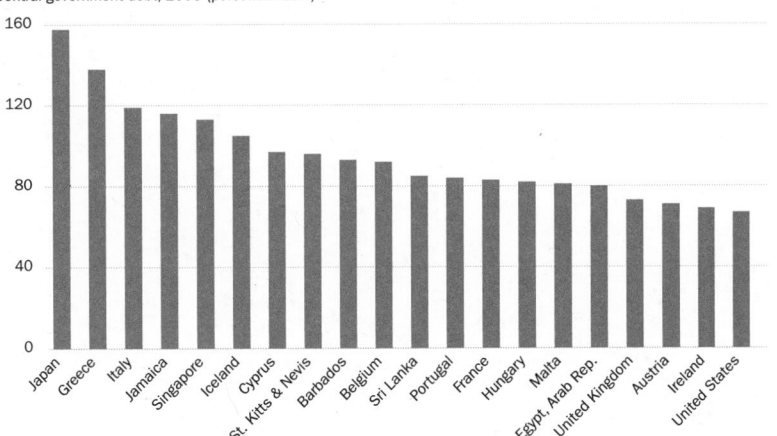

Note: Data are for the most recent year for 2005–2009.
Source: International Monetary Fund, Government Finance Statistics data files, and World Development Indicators data files.

	Goods and services		Compensation of employees		Interest payments		Subsidies and other transfers		Other expense	
	% of expense		% of expense		% of expense		% of expense		% of expense	
	1995	2009	1995	2009	1995	2009	1995	2009	1995	2009
Afghanistan[a]	..	72	..	23	..	0	..	4	..	0
Albania[a]	18	..	14	..	9	..	59	..	0	..
Algeria	..	11	..	34	..	1	..	45	..	8
Angola	..	..	..	..	..	..	..	..	..	..
Argentina	..	..	..	..	..	..	..	..	..	..
Armenia[a]	..	13	..	25	..	2	..	37	..	23
Australia	..	10	..	10	..	3	..	73	..	6
Austria	5	6	14	14	9	7	68	71	6	5
Azerbaijan[a]	..	9	..	12	..	1	..	18	..	61
Bangladesh[a]	..	12	..	19	..	22	..	35	..	12
Belarus[a]	39	12	5	11	1	2	55	70	0	6
Belgium	3	3	7	7	18	8	71	53	2	0
Benin[a]	..	18	..	47	..	3	..	30	..	2
Bolivia	..	14	..	22	..	10	..	47	..	7
Bosnia and Herzegovina	..	23	..	28	..	1	..	44	..	4
Botswana[a]	32	..	30	..	2	..	36	..	2	..
Brazil[a]	5	13	8	19	45	19	45	49	1	0
Bulgaria[a]	18	9	7	19	37	2	38	64	2	6
Burkina Faso	..	19	..	46	..	3	..	11	..	21
Burundi[a]	20	..	30	..	6	..	14	..	10	..
Cambodia	..	32	..	43	..	2	..	21	..	2
Cameroon[a]	17	..	40	..	26	..	14	..	..	..
Canada[a]	8	8	10	12	24	9	57	69	3	3
Central African Republic[a]	..	..	..	..	..	..	..	..	..	..
Chad	..	..	..	..	..	..	..	..	..	..
Chile	..	10	..	20	..	2	..	51	..	19
China[a]	..	..	..	..	..	..	..	..	..	..
Hong Kong SAR, China	..	26	..	22	..	0	..	17	..	38
Colombia	..	6	..	16	..	17	..	47	..	15
Congo, Dem. Rep.[a]	37	..	58	..	1	..	2	..	..	..
Congo, Rep.[a]	7	..	35	..	47	..	10	..	..	..
Costa Rica	..	11	..	46	..	8	..	21	..	14
Côte d'Ivoire	..	29	..	38	..	9	..	16	..	7
Croatia[a]	35	8	27	26	3	5	32	56	3	5
Cuba	..	..	..	..	..	..	..	..	..	..
Czech Republic[a]	7	6	9	8	3	3	75	72	5	11
Denmark	8	9	12	13	14	5	59	17	10	2
Dominican Republic	..	15	..	31	..	10	..	39	..	5
Ecuador[a]	6	..	49	..	26	..	..	..	..	..
Egypt, Arab Rep.[a]	18	8	22	25	26	14	6	45	..	9
El Salvador	..	15	..	36	..	10	..	22	..	18
Eritrea	..	..	..	..	..	..	..	..	..	..
Estonia	21	13	23	21	1	1	39	48	4	4
Ethiopia[a]	35	..	40	..	15	..	18	..	0	..
Finland	8	10	9	10	8	4	68	71	11	8
France	8	6	23	21	6	5	59	54	6	2
Gabon	..	..	..	..	..	..	..	..	..	..
Gambia, The[a]	..	..	..	..	..	..	..	..	..	..
Georgia[a]	52	19	11	17	10	3	26	49	..	12
Germany	4	5	5	5	6	5	67	81	20	4
Ghana[a]	..	16	..	40	..	16	..	28	..	12
Greece	10	12	21	24	25	10	38	50	8	7
Guatemala[a]	15	15	50	29	12	11	18	33	6	12
Guinea[a]	17	..	34	..	28	..	9	..	1	..
Guinea-Bissau	..	..	..	..	..	..	..	..	..	..
Haiti	..	..	..	..	..	..	..	..	..	..
Honduras	..	17	..	54	..	3	..	7	..	19

Central government expenses

	Goods and services		Compensation of employees		Interest payments		Subsidies and other transfers		Other expense	
	% of expense		% of expense		% of expense		% of expense		% of expense	
	1995	2009	1995	2009	1995	2009	1995	2009	1995	2009
Hungary	8	10	10	13	17	10	56	63	13	8
India[a]	14	11	10	10	27	21	33	51	0	7
Indonesia[a]	22	9	20	14	17	11	40	54	2	12
Iran, Islamic Rep.[a]	21	11	56	40	0	1	..	34	..	14
Iraq	..	..	..	..	..	..	..	..	..	..
Ireland	5	10	15	23	14	5	33	40	1	1
Israel	..	27	..	25	..	9	..	32	..	9
Italy	4	4	14	15	24	10	54	66	6	6
Jamaica	..	6	..	14	..	43	..	6	..	31
Japan	..	..	..	..	..	..	..	..	..	..
Jordan[a]	7	11	67	50	11	8	12	30	4	2
Kazakhstan[a]	..	19	..	8	3	2	58	69	..	2
Kenya[a]	15	20	28	37	46	10	..	31	2	1
Korea, Dem. Rep.	..	..	..	..	..	..	..	..	..	..
Korea, Rep.[a]	16	11	15	10	3	5	63	57	3	17
Kosovo	..	..	..	..	..	..	..	..	..	..
Kuwait[a]	34	10	33	16	5	0	21	58	7	15
Kyrgyz Republic[a]	32	30	36	29	5	4	27	34	..	3
Lao PDR	..	27	..	49	..	5	..	10	..	10
Latvia[a]	20	8	20	15	3	3	56	70	0	4
Lebanon	..	3	..	21	..	38	..	36	..	2
Lesotho[a]	32	42	45	35	5	2	8	14	3	6
Liberia[a]	..	37	..	36	..	2	..	24	..	..
Libya	..	..	..	..	..	..	..	..	..	..
Lithuania	..	10	..	16	..	3	..	68	..	6
Macedonia, FYR[a]	..	28	..	17	..	2	..	49	..	4
Madagascar	..	15	..	40	..	7	..	25	..	14
Malawi	..	..	..	..	..	..	..	..	..	..
Malaysia[a]	14	17	34	28	14	9	36	46	1	0
Mali	..	31	..	34	..	2	..	15	..	17
Mauritania	..	..	..	..	..	..	..	..	..	..
Mauritius	..	12	..	34	..	14	..	31	..	10
Mexico[a]	9	..	19	..	19	..	..	..	..	..
Moldova[a]	10	19	8	15	11	4	71	56	1	6
Mongolia[a]	30	20	12	33	2	2	56	45	0	1
Morocco[a]	..	9	..	48	..	4	..	27	..	13
Mozambique	..	..	..	..	..	..	..	..	..	..
Myanmar[a]	..	..	..	..	..	..	..	..	..	..
Namibia[a]	28	20	53	45	1	8	..	13	4	14
Nepal[a]	..	..	..	..	..	..	..	..	..	..
Netherlands	5	8	8	7	9	4	77	79	3	4
New Zealand	..	30	..	25	..	4	..	38	..	7
Nicaragua[a]	14	13	25	39	17	7	29	36	14	5
Niger	..	30	..	30	..	3	..	9	..	28
Nigeria[a]	..	15	..	24	..	9	..	53	..	..
Norway	..	11	..	16	..	3	..	67	..	5
Oman[a]	55	..	30	..	7	..	8	..	0	..
Pakistan[a]	..	22	..	4	28	35	2	21	..	18
Panama[a]	16	..	45	..	8	..	30	..	1	..
Papua New Guinea[a]	19	..	36	..	20	..	26	..	1	..
Paraguay[a]	12	9	51	50	5	4	31	29	0	9
Peru[a]	20	20	19	18	19	7	33	47	8	7
Philippines[a]	15	28	34	30	33	20	15	20	..	2
Poland	..	5	..	12	..	7	..	71	..	7
Portugal	9	7	30	24	15	6	43	51	7	1
Puerto Rico	..	..	..	..	..	..	..	..	..	..
Qatar[a]	..	25	..	32	..	5	..	21	..	16

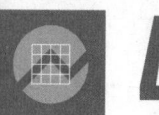
	Goods and services		Compensation of employees		Interest payments		Subsidies and other transfers		Other expense	
	% of expense		% of expense		% of expense		% of expense		% of expense	
	1995	2009	1995	2009	1995	2009	1995	2009	1995	2009
Romania	..	13	..	19	..	2	..	60	..	8
Russian Federation	..	12	..	16	..	1	..	68	..	10
Rwanda[a]	52	..	36	..	12	..	5	..	..	..
Saudi Arabia	..	..	..	..	..	..	..	..	..	..
Senegal[a]	..	..	..	..	..	..	..	..	..	..
Serbia[a]	..	13	..	26	..	2	..	58	..	1
Sierra Leone[a]	..	24	..	28	..	7	..	23	..	18
Singapore[a]	38	36	39	27	8	0	15	0	..	..
Slovak Republic	..	7	..	12	..	4	..	68	..	14
Slovenia[a]	19	13	21	20	3	3	55	62	3	3
Somalia	..	..	..	..	..	..	..	..	..	..
South Africa	..	13	..	13	..	7	..	63	..	4
Spain	5	4	14	8	11	5	42	80	2	5
Sri Lanka[a]	23	14	20	28	22	25	24	23	10	10
Sudan[a]	44	..	38	..	8	..	10	..	..	..
Swaziland[a]	..	..	..	..	..	..	..	..	..	..
Sweden	..	..	..	..	..	..	..	..	..	..
Switzerland[a]	24	6	6	6	4	4	66	83	0	3
Syrian Arab Republic[a]	..	..	..	..	..	..	..	..	..	..
Tajikistan[a]	47	..	8	..	12	..	33	..	..	..
Tanzania	..	..	..	..	..	..	..	..	..	..
Thailand	..	31	..	36	..	5	..	28	..	3
Timor-Leste	..	..	..	..	..	..	..	..	..	..
Togo	..	24	..	40	..	5	..	18	..	13
Trinidad and Tobago[a]	20	14	36	21	20	6	24	38	1	21
Tunisia[a]	7	7	37	36	13	7	36	38	7	13
Turkey[a]	..	10	..	23	..	20	..	44	..	5
Turkmenistan	..	..	..	..	..	..	..	..	..	..
Uganda[a]	..	31	..	14	..	9	..	45	..	1
Ukraine[a]	..	12	..	13	..	3	..	70	..	2
United Arab Emirates[a]	48	..	33	..	..	..	..	..	..	..
United Kingdom	14	18	15	14	9	4	57	53	8	12
United States	..	15	..	12	..	7	..	62	..	6
Uruguay[a]	13	12	17	25	6	9	64	47	0	7
Uzbekistan	..	..	..	..	..	..	..	..	..	..
Venezuela, RB[a]	6	..	22	..	27	..	61	..	2	..
Vietnam	..	..	..	..	..	..	..	..	..	..
West Bank and Gaza	..	12	..	67	..	1	..	18	..	1
Yemen, Rep.[a]	8	..	67	..	16	..	8	..	0	..
Zambia[a]	32	32	35	30	16	7	19	24	0	7
Zimbabwe[a]	16	..	34	..	31	..	19	..	..	..
World	.. m	12 m	.. m	21 m	.. m	5 m	.. m	46 m	.. m	6 m
Low income	..	..	..	..	..	..	..	..	..	..
Middle income	..	12	..	25	..	7	..	45	..	7
Lower middle income	..	15	..	31	..	7	..	36	..	8
Upper middle income	..	12	..	20	..	7	..	47	..	6
Low & middle income	..	15	..	27	..	6	..	37	..	7
East Asia & Pacific	..	27	..	33	..	5	..	28	..	2
Europe & Central Asia	..	13	..	17	..	2	..	58	..	6
Latin America & Carib.	..	13	..	27	..	9	..	35	..	13
Middle East & N. Africa	..	9	..	36	..	7	..	36	..	9
South Asia	..	17	..	14	27	21	24	28	..	10
Sub-Saharan Africa	..	..	..	..	..	..	..	..	..	..
High income	10	9	15	14	9	5	56	62	4	5
Euro area	5	7	14	15	10	5	55	62	5	4

Note: Components may not sum to 100 percent because of rounding or missing data.
a. Data were reported on a cash basis and have been adjusted to the accrual framework.

About the data

The term *expense* has replaced expenditure in the table since the 2005 edition of *World Development Indicators* in accordance with use in the International Monetary Fund's (IMF) *Government Finance Statistics Manual 2001*. Government expenses include all nonrepayable payments, whether current or capital, requited or unrequited. The concept of total central government expense as presented in the IMF's *Government Finance Statistics Yearbook* is comparable to the concept used in the 1993 United Nations System of National Accounts.

Expenses can be measured either by function (health, defense, education) or by economic type (interest payments, wages and salaries, purchases of goods and services). Functional data are often incomplete, and coverage varies by country because functional responsibilities stretch across levels of government for which no data are available. Defense expenses, usually the central government's responsibility, are shown in table 5.7. For more information on education expenses, see table 2.11; for more on health expenses, see table 2.16.

The classification of expenses by economic type in the table shows whether the government produces goods and services and distributes them, purchases the goods and services from a third party and distributes them, or transfers cash to households to make the purchases directly. When the government produces and provides goods and services, the cost is reflected in compensation of employees, use of goods and services, and consumption of fixed capital. Purchases from a third party and cash transfers

to households are shown as subsidies and other transfers, and other expenses. The economic classification can be problematic. For example, subsidies to public corporations or banks may be disguised as capital financing or hidden in special contractual pricing for goods and services. For further discussion of government finance statistics, see *About the data* for tables 4.12 and 4.14.

Definitions

• **Goods and services** are all government payments in exchange for goods and services used for the production of market and nonmarket goods and services. Own-account capital formation is excluded. • **Compensation of employees** is all payments in cash, as well as in kind (such as food and housing), to employees in return for services rendered, and government contributions to social insurance schemes such as social security and pensions that provide benefits to employees. • **Interest payments** are payments made to nonresidents, to residents, and to other general government units for the use of borrowed money. (Repayment of principal is shown as a financing item, and commission charges are shown as purchases of services.) • **Subsidies and other transfers** include all unrequited, nonrepayable transfers on current account to private and public enterprises; grants to foreign governments, international organizations, and other government units; and social security, social assistance benefits, and employer social benefits in cash and in kind. • **Other expense** is spending on dividends, rent, and other miscellaneous expenses, including provision for consumption of fixed capital.

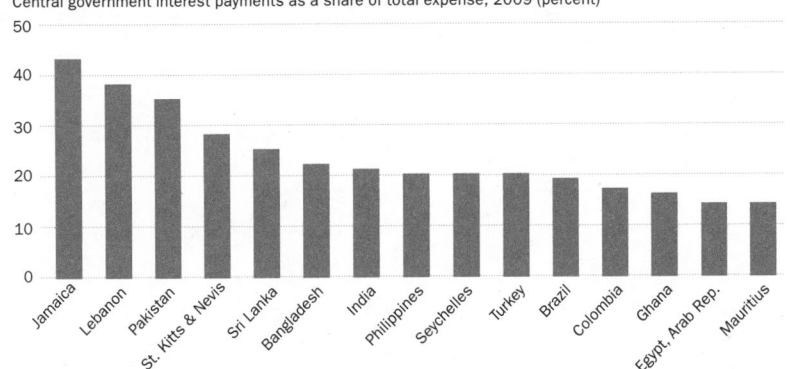

Interest payments are a large part of government expenses for some developing economies   4.13a

Central government interest payments as a share of total expense, 2009 (percent)

Interest payments accounted for more than 14 percent of total expenses in 2009 for 15 countries.

Source: International Monetary Fund, Government Finance Statistics data files.

Data sources

Data on central government expenses are from the IMF's Government Finance Statistics database. Each country's accounts are reported using the system of common definitions and classifications in the IMF's *Government Finance Statistics Manual 2001*. See these sources for complete and authoritative explanations of concepts, definitions, and data sources.

	Taxes on income, profits, and capital gains		Taxes on goods and services		Taxes on International trade		Other taxes		Social contributions		Grants and other revenue	
	% of revenue		% of revenue		% of revenue		% of revenue		% of revenue		% of revenue	
	1995	2009	1995	2009	1995	2009	1995	2009	1995	2009	1995	2009
Afghanistan[a]	..	4	..	3	..	5	..	0	..	0	..	88
Albania[a]	8	..	39	..	14	..	1	..	15	..	22	..
Algeria	..	60	..	28	..	4	..	1	..	..	..	6
Angola	..	..	..	..	..	..	..	..	..	..	..	..
Argentina	..	..	..	..	..	..	..	..	..	..	..	..
Armenia[a]	..	20	..	41	..	3	..	8	..	14	..	14
Australia	..	65	..	23	..	2	..	0	..	..	..	10
Austria	21	23	22	23	0	0	5	5	43	42	9	7
Azerbaijan[a]	..	33	..	23	..	4	..	1	..	..	..	39
Bangladesh[a]	..	19	..	29	..	24	..	3	..	..	..	24
Belarus[a]	16	6	33	29	6	16	11	3	31	33	3	13
Belgium	36	34	23	24	..	..	2	0	36	37	3	3
Benin[a]	..	17	..	39	..	18	..	6	..	2	..	18
Bolivia	..	10	..	43	..	3	..	9	..	7	..	28
Bosnia and Herzegovina	..	5	..	43	..	0	..	2	..	39	..	11
Botswana[a]	21	..	4	..	15	..	0	..	..	..	59	..
Brazil[a]	14	30	24	33	2	2	4	2	31	26	26	6
Bulgaria[a]	17	16	28	45	8	1	3	0	21	23	23	16
Burkina Faso	..	14	..	37	..	12	..	2	..	..	..	36
Burundi[a]	14	..	30	..	20	..	1	..	5	..	30	..
Cambodia	..	11	..	36	..	16	..	0	..	..	..	37
Cameroon[a]	17	..	25	..	28	..	3	..	2	..	25	..
Canada[a]	48	55	18	15	3	1	..	..	21	24	10	8
Central African Republic[a]	..	..	..	..	..	..	..	..	..	..	..	..
Chad	..	..	..	..	..	..	..	..	..	..	..	..
Chile	..	28	..	46	..	1	..	2	..	7	..	16
China[a]	9	26	61	55	7	5	0	3	..	..	22	12
Hong Kong SAR, China	..	44	..	9	..	0	..	13	..	0	..	34
Colombia	..	26	..	32	..	5	..	5	..	6	..	25
Congo, Dem. Rep.[a]	21	..	12	..	21	..	5	..	1	..	41	..
Congo, Rep.[a]	6	..	21	..	18	..	1	..	..	..	54	..
Costa Rica	..	17	..	32	..	4	..	3	..	34	..	10
Côte d'Ivoire	..	15	..	20	..	33	..	8	..	6	..	18
Croatia[a]	11	10	42	43	9	2	1	2	33	35	4	9
Cuba	..	..	..	..	..	..	..	..	..	..	..	..
Czech Republic[a]	15	15	32	27	4	0	1	1	40	45	8	12
Denmark	37	45	40	36	..	..	8	5	4	3	11	..
Dominican Republic	..	22	..	54	..	10	..	5	..	2	..	8
Ecuador[a]	50	..	26	..	11	..	1	..	..	..	12	..
Egypt, Arab Rep.[a]	17	28	13	22	10	5	10	2	10	..	41	43
El Salvador	..	27	..	39	..	5	..	0	..	12	..	17
Eritrea	..	..	..	..	..	..	..	..	..	..	..	..
Estonia	18	8	35	39	0	..	0	..	34	36	..	..
Ethiopia[a]	19	..	13	..	27	..	3	..	1	..	36	..
Finland	16	20	31	32	0	..	1	2	34	31	17	15
France	17	22	25	23	0	0	3	4	47	45	8	6
Gabon	..	..	..	..	..	..	..	..	..	..	..	..
Gambia, The[a]	..	..	..	..	..	..	..	..	..	..	..	..
Georgia[a]	7	32	48	51	10	1	..	1	13	17	22	15
Germany	16	16	20	24	..	..	0	..	58	55	6	4
Ghana[a]	15	23	31	29	24	16	..	..	..	..	9	32
Greece	17	21	32	29	0	0	3	3	31	36	16	12
Guatemala[a]	19	29	46	56	23	7	3	2	2	3	6	4
Guinea[a]	8	..	4	..	62	..	2	..	1	..	23	..
Guinea-Bissau	..	..	..	..	..	..	..	..	..	..	..	..
Haiti	..	..	..	..	..	..	..	..	..	..	..	..
Honduras	..	20	..	39	..	3	..	1	..	13	..	23

Central government revenues

	Taxes on income, profits, and capital gains (% of revenue)		Taxes on goods and services (% of revenue)		Taxes on International trade (% of revenue)		Other taxes (% of revenue)		Social contributions (% of revenue)		Grants and other revenue (% of revenue)	
	1995	2009	1995	2009	1995	2009	1995	2009	1995	2009	1995	2009
Hungary	16	23	28	32	10	0	1	1	35	32	9	12
India[a]	23	47	28	23	24	13	0	0	0	0	25	18
Indonesia[a]	52	37	32	31	5	2	1	4	..	..	10	26
Iran, Islamic Rep.[a]	12	19	5	3	9	6	1	1	6	19	66	52
Iraq	..	..	..	..	..	..	..	..	..	..	..	..
Ireland	37	33	..	..	0	0	2	2	17	22	..	..
Israel	..	26	..	31	..	1	..	5	..	17	..	19
Italy	32	32	21	20	..	..	5	7	35	36	6	5
Jamaica	..	25	..	37	..	7	..	10	..	3	..	18
Japan	..	..	..	..	..	..	..	..	..	..	..	..
Jordan[a]	10	17	23	38	22	6	9	3	..	0	36	36
Kazakhstan[a]	11	24	28	20	3	6	5	0	48	..	6	51
Kenya[a]	35	40	40	41	14	10	1	1	0	..	10	8
Korea, Dem. Rep.	..	..	..	..	..	..	..	..	..	..	..	..
Korea, Rep.[a]	31	28	32	26	7	4	10	9	8	16	12	17
Kosovo	..	..	..	..	..	..	..	..	..	..	..	..
Kuwait[a]	1	1	0	..	2	1	0	0	..	..	97	98
Kyrgyz Republic[a]	26	12	56	42	5	9	1	..	..	..	11	37
Lao PDR	..	21	..	46	..	9	..	1	..	..	..	22
Latvia[a]	7	8	41	35	3	0	0	0	35	31	13	26
Lebanon	..	15	..	44	..	6	..	10	..	1	..	23
Lesotho[a]	15	17	12	12	49	57	1	3	..	..	24	11
Liberia[a]	..	28	..	15	..	39	..	1	..	..	..	18
Libya	..	..	..	..	..	..	..	..	..	..	..	..
Lithuania	..	10	..	36	..	..	..	0	..	42	..	13
Macedonia, FYR[a]	..	13	..	40	..	5	..	0	..	29	..	13
Madagascar	..	12	..	15	..	31	..	6	..	4	..	32
Malawi	..	..	..	..	..	..	..	..	..	..	..	..
Malaysia[a]	38	46	27	16	12	2	6	3	..	..	17	33
Mali	..	19	..	29	..	10	..	10	..	..	..	31
Mauritania	..	..	..	..	..	..	..	..	..	..	..	..
Mauritius	..	23	..	46	..	2	..	7	..	4	..	17
Mexico[a]	27	..	54	..	4	..	2	..	14	..	16	..
Moldova[a]	6	1	38	46	5	4	1	0	38	33	2	16
Mongolia[a]	31	21	18	30	9	6	0	0	15	17	27	26
Morocco[a]	..	28	..	31	..	6	..	5	..	12	..	17
Mozambique	..	..	..	..	..	..	..	..	..	..	..	..
Myanmar[a]	20	..	26	..	12	..	..	..	..	..	42	..
Namibia[a]	27	28	32	19	28	44	2	1	..	0	11	7
Nepal[a]	10	14	33	35	26	16	4	5	..	..	27	29
Netherlands	26	26	24	27	..	..	2	2	40	35	8	10
New Zealand	..	57	..	26	..	3	..	0	..	0	..	15
Nicaragua[a]	9	29	52	49	7	4	0	0	..	..	31	18
Niger	..	12	..	18	..	26	..	3	..	..	..	41
Nigeria[a]	..	1	..	2	..	..	..	..	..	..	..	97
Norway	..	28	..	24	..	0	..	1	..	21	..	26
Oman[a]	21	..	1	..	3	..	2	..	..	..	74	..
Pakistan[a]	18	25	27	32	24	8	7	0	..	..	24	35
Panama[a]	20	..	17	..	11	..	3	..	16	..	34	..
Papua New Guinea[a]	40	..	8	..	27	..	2	..	0	..	23	..
Paraguay[a]	15	16	36	43	18	7	4	1	6	7	22	26
Peru[a]	15	30	46	39	10	2	8	6	10	10	11	13
Philippines[a]	33	39	26	29	29	20	4	..	..	..	8	13
Poland	..	14	..	37	..	0	..	1	..	37	..	10
Portugal	23	23	33	31	0	0	2	2	30	33	..	..
Puerto Rico	..	..	..	..	..	..	..	..	..	..	..	..
Qatar[a]	..	40	..	..	..	2	..	..	..	..	..	58

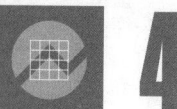

4.14 Central government revenues

	Taxes on income, profits, and capital gains		Taxes on goods and services		Taxes on International trade		Other taxes		Social contributions		Grants and other revenue	
	% of revenue		% of revenue		% of revenue		% of revenue		% of revenue		% of revenue	
	1995	2009	1995	2009	1995	2009	1995	2009	1995	2009	1995	2009
Romania	..	22	..	35	..	0	..	0	..	33	..	10
Russian Federation	..	1	..	16	..	18	..	0	..	17	..	48
Rwanda[a]	11	..	25	..	23	..	3	..	2	..	36	..
Saudi Arabia	..	..	..	..	..	..	..	..	..	..	..	..
Senegal[a]	17	..	19	..	36	..	2	..	..	..	26	..
Serbia[a]	..	9	..	43	..	5	..	0	..	35	..	7
Sierra Leone[a]	15	17	34	25	39	14	0	..	..	..	12	44
Singapore[a]	26	36	20	26	1	0	15	14	..	..	38	24
Slovak Republic	..	9	..	33	..	0	..	0	..	43	..	15
Slovenia[a]	13	13	33	33	9	0	0	0	42	41	3	12
Somalia	..	..	..	..	..	..	..	..	..	..	..	..
South Africa	..	53	..	32	..	3	..	2	..	2	..	8
Spain	28	24	21	13	0	..	0	0	40	58	..	4
Sri Lanka[a]	12	18	49	45	17	14	4	8	1	1	18	14
Sudan[a]	17	..	41	..	27	..	1	..	..	..	14	..
Swaziland[a]	..	..	..	..	..	..	..	..	..	..	..	..
Sweden	13	11	33	37	..	..	4	13	32	25	..	..
Switzerland[a]	11	24	21	26	1	6	2	3	49	36	17	5
Syrian Arab Republic[a]	23	..	37	..	13	..	8	..	0	..	19	..
Tajikistan[a]	6	..	63	..	12	..	0	..	13	..	5	..
Tanzania	..	..	..	..	..	..	..	..	..	..	..	..
Thailand	..	38	..	38	..	5	..	1	..	5	..	14
Timor-Leste	..	..	..	..	..	..	..	..	..	..	..	..
Togo	..	17	..	34	..	18	..	3	..	..	..	28
Trinidad and Tobago[a]	50	63	26	13	6	4	1	8	2	4	15	9
Tunisia[a]	16	27	20	31	28	6	4	4	15	19	17	12
Turkey[a]	..	26	..	51	..	1	..	5	..	..	..	16
Turkmenistan	..	..	..	..	..	..	..	..	..	..	..	..
Uganda[a]	10	22	45	47	7	10	2	0	..	..	37	22
Ukraine[a]	..	10	..	34	..	2	..	0	..	37	..	17
United Arab Emirates[a]	..	15	..	..	..	..	..	..	1	..	84	..
United Kingdom	37	36	32	28	..	..	6	7	20	23	5	6
United States	..	47	..	3	..	1	..	1	..	43	..	6
Uruguay[a]	10	18	32	41	4	3	10	2	31	30	8	6
Uzbekistan	..	..	..	..	..	..	..	..	..	..	..	..
Venezuela, RB[a]	38	..	33	..	9	..	0	..	4	..	19	..
Vietnam	..	..	..	..	..	..	..	..	..	..	..	..
West Bank and Gaza	..	2	..	21	..	11	..	0	..	0	..	66
Yemen, Rep.[a]	17	..	10	..	18	..	3	..	..	..	51	..
Zambia[a]	27	33	22	36	36	8	0	0	0	..	15	23
Zimbabwe[a]	36	..	22	..	17	..	3	..	2	..	19	..
World	.. m	23 m	.. m	32 m	.. m	5 m	.. m	2 m	.. m	.. m	.. m	17 m
Low income	..	..	..	..	..	..	..	..	..	..	..	..
Middle income	..	25	..	36	..	5	..	2	..	..	..	17
Lower middle income	17	26	27	33	16	6	2	1	..	..	23	17
Upper middle income	..	23	..	36	..	4	..	2	..	22	..	16
Low & middle income	..	21	..	36	..	7	..	2	..	..	..	18
East Asia & Pacific	32	37	26	31	10	6	2	1	..	..	23	26
Europe & Central Asia	..	10	..	42	..	4	..	0	..	29	..	16
Latin America & Carib.	..	27	..	39	..	4	..	2	..	10	..	17
Middle East & N. Africa	16	27	16	31	16	6	6	3	..	6	38	23
South Asia	15	19	31	29	24	13	4	0	..	0	25	29
Sub-Saharan Africa	..	..	..	..	..	..	..	..	..	..	..	..
High income	21	24	28	27	..	0	2	2	34	36	10	12
Euro area	22	23	24	27	0	0	2	2	36	37	7	8

Note: Components may not sum to 100 percent because of missing data or adjustment to tax revenue.
a. Data were reported on a cash basis and have been adjusted to the accrual framework.

The International Monetary Fund (IMF) classifies government revenues as taxes, grants, and property income. Taxes are classified by the base on which the tax is levied, grants by the source, and property income by type (for example, interest, dividends, or rent). The most important source of revenue is taxes. Grants are unrequited, nonrepayable, noncompulsory receipts from other government units and foreign governments or from international organizations. Transactions are generally recorded on an accrual basis.

The IMF's Government Finance Statistics Manual 2001 describes taxes as compulsory, unrequited payments made to governments by individuals, businesses, or institutions. Taxes are classified in six major groups by the base on which the tax is levied: income, profits, and capital gains; payroll and workforce; property; goods and services; international trade and transactions; and other. However, the distinctions are not always clear. Taxes levied on the income and profits of individuals and corporations are classified as direct taxes, and taxes and duties levied on goods and services are classified as indirect taxes. This distinction may be a useful simplification, but it has no particular analytical significance except with respect to the capacity to fix tax rates.

Direct taxes tend to be progressive, whereas indirect taxes are proportional.

Social security taxes do not reflect compulsory payments made by employers to provident funds or other agencies with a like purpose. Similarly, expenditures from such funds are not reflected in government expenses (see table 4.13). For further discussion of taxes and tax policies, see *About the data* for table 5.6. For further discussion of government revenues and expenditures, see *About the data* for tables 4.12 and 4.13.

• **Taxes on income, profits, and capital gains** are levied on the actual or presumptive net income of individuals, on the profits of corporations and enterprises, and on capital gains, whether realized or not, on land, securities, and other assets. Intra-governmental payments are eliminated in consolidation. • **Taxes on goods and services** include general sales and turnover or value added taxes, selective excises on goods, selective taxes on services, taxes on the use of goods or property, taxes on extraction and production of minerals, and profits of fiscal monopolies. • **Taxes on international trade** include import duties, export duties, profits of export or import monopolies, exchange profits, and exchange taxes. • **Other taxes** include employer payroll or labor taxes, taxes on property, and taxes not allocable to other categories, such as penalties for late payment or nonpayment of taxes. • **Social contributions** include social security contributions by employees, employers, and self-employed individuals, and other contributions whose source cannot be determined. They also include actual or imputed contributions to social insurance schemes operated by governments. • **Grants and other revenue** include grants from other foreign governments, international organizations, and other government units; interest; dividends; rent; requited, nonrepayable receipts for public purposes (such as fines, administrative fees, and entrepreneurial income from government ownership of property); and voluntary, unrequited, nonrepayable receipts other than grants.

Taxes on income and capital gains as a share of central government revenue, 2009 (percent)

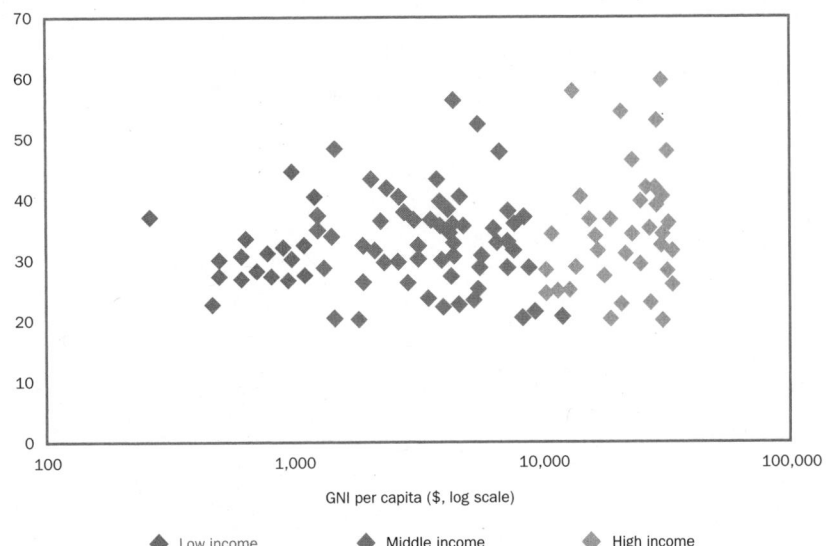

GNI per capita ($, log scale)

◆ Low income ◆ Middle income ◆ High income

High-income economies tend to tax income and property, whereas low-income economies tend to rely on indirect taxes on international trade and goods and services. But there are exceptions in all groups.

Note: Data are for the most recent year for 2005–09.
Source: International Monetary Fund, Government Finance Statistics data files, and World Development Indicators data files.

4.15 | Monetary indicators

	Broad money		Claims on domestic economy		Claims on central government		Interest rate					
									%			
	annual % growth		Annual growth % of broad money		Annual growth % of broad money		Deposit		Lending		Real	
	2000	2009	2000	2009	2000	2009	2000	2009	2000	2009	2000	2009
Afghanistan	..	33.0	..	8.0	..	−9.5	..	..	..	15.0	..	36.1
Albania	12.0	6.8	0.9	5.4	4.8	2.4	8.3	6.8	22.1	12.7	17.0	10.1
Algeria ·	14.1	1.6	8.4	7.7	−11.6	0.2	7.5	1.8	10.0	8.0	−11.7	19.2
Angola[a]	303.7	62.6	35.8	33.3	−413.7	48.1	39.6	7.6 ·	103.2	15.7	−60.8	22.8
Argentina[a]	1.5	17.0	−2.9	5.1	−0.8	18.9	8.3	11.6	11.1	15.7	9.9	5.2
Armenia	38.6	16.4	0.3	15.0	−5.7	−11.8	18.1	8.7	31.6	18.8	33.4	17.1
Australia[a]	3.7	0.5	13.3	8.7	−1.8	−2.7	4.2	2.8	9.3	6.0	6.5	1.0
Austria[b]	..	..	..	..	..	..	2.2	..	5.6	..	5.2	..
Azerbaijan	73.4	−0.3	−23.9	13.2	15.4	4.3	12.9	12.2	19.7	20.0	6.4	44.2
Bangladesh	19.3	20.3	10.7	13.3	5.6	1.3	8.6	8.2	15.5	14.6	13.4	7.6
Belarus	219.3	25.9	59.9	64.6	22.2	−40.9	37.6	10.7	67.7	11.7	−41.2	7.5
Belgium[b]	..	..	..	..	..	..	3.6	..	8.0	9.2	5.9	7.1
Benin[a]	26.0	8.0	8.5	6.7	0.9	7.5	3.5	3.5	..	..	..	..
Bolivia	1.6	11.8	−1.3	6.0	3.1	−3.0	11.0	3.4	34.6	12.4	27.9	15.1
Bosnia and Herzegovina[a]	11.3	−0.1	10.3	−3.8	−0.4	−0.1	14.7	3.6	30.5	7.9	1.3	7.9
Botswana	1.4	−1.3	10.3	5.3	−56.2	18.7	9.4	7.5	15.5	13.8	15.4	20.6
Brazil	19.7	15.8	8.3	6.7	13.5	1.2	17.2	9.3	56.8	44.7	47.7	36.8
Bulgaria	30.8	4.2	6.5	4.2	8.5	2.5	3.1	6.2	11.3	11.3	4.4	7.0
Burkina Faso[a]	6.2	22.3	8.3	1.0	5.3	2.7	3.5	3.5	..	..	..	..
Burundi	15.5	14.5	15.0	8.3	−22.6	13.0	..	..	15.8	14.1	2.3	0.4
Cambodia	26.9	35.6	5.4	6.3	−6.9	5.7	6.8	1.7	..	..	..	..
Cameroon[a]	19.1	6.3	7.4	4.5	−12.3	0.9	5.0	3.3	22.0	15.0	18.6	12.7
Canada	6.6	15.1	3.6	23.3	2.4	4.7	3.5	0.1	7.3	2.4	3.0	4.6
Central African Republic[a]	2.4	13.3	2.9	2.8	6.8	−0.3	5.0	3.3	22.0	15.0	18.3	12.2
Chad[a]	19.4	1.1	0.4	5.7	15.1	72.5	5.0	3.3	22.0	15.0	15.9	9.4
Chile	9.1	1.3	4.1	−0.6	4.0	0.6	9.2	2.0	14.8	7.3	9.8	2.9
China[a]	12.3	28.4	9.5	22.7	0.0	0.6	2.3	2.3	5.9	5.3	3.7	6.0
Hong Kong SAR, China[a]	9.3	5.2	1.7	3.6	0.4	8.8	4.8	0.0	9.5	5.0	13.6	4.8
Colombia	3.6	8.1	8.9	2.7	6.0	7.2	12.1	6.1	18.8	13.0	−10.3	7.7
Congo, Dem. Rep.[a]	40.0	50.4	3.8	19.2	−34.0	−14.5	..	15.9	..	65.4	..	27.0
Congo, Rep.[a]	58.5	5.0	−23.0	5.2	−11.7	12.0	5.0	3.3	22.0	15.0	−17.0	14.4
Costa Rica	24.0	8.0	14.1	4.9	−0.2	2.8	13.4	7.0	24.9	19.7	16.7	9.9
Côte d'Ivoire[a]	−1.9	17.2	2.9	6.0	−7.6	7.4	3.5	3.5	..	..	..	..
Croatia	29.1	−0.6	21.3	−0.6	2.0	0.2	3.7	3.2	12.1	11.6	7.1	8.0
Cuba	..	..	..	..	..	..	..	..	..	..	..	..
Czech Republic	16.0	0.2	−11.0	0.7	2.6	3.9	3.4	1.3	7.2	6.0	5.6	3.2
Denmark	−12.1	7.0	26.1	−4.4	3.0	6.3	3.2	..	8.1	..	4.9	..
Dominican Republic	16.8	13.4	13.2	5.3	2.8	8.0	17.7	7.8	26.8	18.1	18.6	14.7
Ecuador	47.0	10.1	−10.8	5.5	−28.1	8.8	8.8	4.8	17.1	12.1	26.0	6.3
Egypt, Arab Rep.	11.6	9.5	4.1	0.5	7.7	10.5	9.5	6.5	13.2	12.0	7.9	1.0
El Salvador	1.6	2.1	2.6	−4.1	2.3	−1.3	9.3	..	14.0	..	10.5	..
Eritrea	17.3	15.7	3.7	0.2	25.7	11.9	..	..	..	..	..	..
Estonia	25.7	−0.1	..	−9.0	−3.2	−3.6	3.8	4.8	7.4	9.4	2.4	10.0
Ethiopia[a]	13.1	23.4	3.0	17.7	19.8	2.5	6.0	4.7	10.9	8.0	3.8	−17.2
Finland[b]	..	..	..	..	..	..	1.6	..	5.6	..	2.9	..
France[b]	..	..	..	..	..	..	2.6	1.9	6.7	..	5.2	..
Gabon[a]	18.3	2.1	6.2	−2.6	−42.2	4.0	5.0	3.3	22.0	15.0	−4.8	9.3
Gambia, The[a]	34.8	19.4	4.2	5.4	2.7	5.2	12.5	15.5	24.0	27.0	19.6	24.1
Georgia	39.2	8.2	18.7	−18.1	19.8	11.0	10.2	10.3	32.8	25.5	26.8	28.1
Germany[b]	..	..	..	..	..	..	3.4	..	9.6	..	10.4	..
Ghana	54.2	39.2	7.5	30.4	32.9	22.1	28.6	17.1	..	..	..	..
Greece[b]	..	..	..	..	..	..	6.1	..	12.3	..	8.6	..
Guatemala	21.4	11.3	4.2	−2.4	10.2	6.8	10.2	5.6	20.9	13.8	13.2	11.2
Guinea[a]	12.9	..	2.3	..	7.9	..	7.5	..	19.4	..	7.4	..
Guinea-Bissau[a]	60.8	6.9	5.5	3.9	16.2	−13.3	3.5	3.5	..	..	..	..
Haiti	20.3	10.3	12.3	6.2	13.8	−12.4	12.1	1.1	19.1	17.3	7.3	13.3
Honduras	15.4	0.6	7.9	7.1	−2.6	4.8	15.9	10.8	26.8	19.4	−3.1	14.4

	Broad money		Claims on domestic economy		Claims on central government		Interest rate					
	annual % growth		Annual growth % of broad money		Annual growth % of broad money		Deposit		Lending		Real	
	2000	2009	2000	2009	2000	2009	2000	2009	2000	2009	2000	2009
Hungary	12.6	3.3	14.5	−4.2	−2.0	0.1	9.5	5.8	12.6	11.0	0.9	6.1
India[a]	15.2	18.0	9.9	7.8	4.7	9.4	..	..	12.3	12.2	8.5	4.3
Indonesia	16.6	13.0	7.2	6.9	17.2	2.5	12.5	9.3	18.5	14.5	−1.7	5.6
Iran, Islamic Rep.[a]	22.4	27.7	15.8	10.2	−7.9	2.0	11.7	13.1	..	12.0	..	11.3
Iraq	..	26.7	..	2.0	..	33.6	..	7.8	..	15.6	..	61.5
Ireland[b]	..	..	..	..	..	..	0.1	..	4.8	..	−1.1	..
Israel[a]	8.0	6.1	10.7	−0.5	−4.8	1.1	8.6	1.1	12.9	3.7	11.1	−1.4
Italy[b]	..	..	..	..	..	..	1.8	..	7.0	4.8	5.0	2.6
Jamaica	−7.0	5.4	9.1	2.6	−2.3	9.4	11.6	7.0	23.3	16.4	11.5	9.3
Japan	1.3	2.1	−5.4	−2.9	2.6	4.4	0.1	0.4	2.1	1.7	3.9	2.7
Jordan[a]	7.6	24.3	3.2	0.8	−1.2	2.5	7.0	4.9	11.8	9.2	12.2	1.1
Kazakhstan	45.0	19.5	32.2	14.1	−3.2	−4.7	..	..	..	..	..	..
Kenya	4.9	16.5	4.7	11.5	−2.1	8.2	8.1	6.0	22.3	14.8	15.3	7.6
Korea, Dem. Rep.	..	..	..	..	..	..	..	..	..	..	..	..
Korea, Rep.[a]	25.4	12.2	21.9	3.9	−1.4	2.2	7.9	3.5	8.5	5.6	3.4	2.2
Kosovo	−12.2	11.2	12.1	7.6	−37.7	1.8	..	4.0	..	14.1	..	18.1
Kuwait	6.3	13.4	8.5	7.1	−7.4	−1.0	5.9	2.8	8.9	6.2	−9.7	2.5
Kyrgyz Republic[a]	11.7	33.2	3.5	29.2	7.8	−8.8	18.4	3.9	51.9	23.0	19.5	20.5
Lao PDR[a]	46.0	18.3	22.4	19.4	−17.6	−3.4	12.0	4.7	32.0	24.0	5.5	14.4
Latvia	27.0	−2.7	31.2	−25.9	7.8	−9.6	4.4	8.0	11.9	16.2	7.4	17.1
Lebanon[a]	9.8	19.6	2.9	4.8	10.5	4.5	11.2	7.3	18.2	9.6	20.7	3.5
Lesotho	1.4	17.7	6.6	7.2	14.9	−0.5	4.9	4.9	17.1	13.0	14.4	9.2
Liberia[a]	18.3	43.4	−10.0	17.1	197.0	47.7	6.2	4.1	20.5	14.2	22.1	6.3
Libya[a]	3.1	17.4	0.2	2.0	−10.4	1.8	3.0	2.5	7.0	6.0	−9.6	57.8
Lithuania	16.5	0.6	14.4	−12.9	0.5	−4.1	3.9	4.8	12.1	8.4	11.1	10.8
Macedonia, FYR	22.2	5.5	2.7	3.1	−15.9	1.3	11.2	7.0	18.9	10.1	9.9	7.1
Madagascar[a]	17.2	11.3	7.9	3.7	0.1	8.9	15.0	11.5	26.5	45.0	18.0	33.8
Malawi[a]	45.5	24.6	16.5	19.3	7.7	21.2	33.3	3.5	53.1	25.3	17.3	15.6
Malaysia	10.0	7.7	5.5	5.5	2.1	3.3	3.4	2.1	7.7	5.1	−1.1	12.6
Mali[a]	12.2	14.6	−1.5	7.0	−5.0	−13.3	3.5	3.5	..	..	..	..
Mauritania[a]	16.1	..	41.1	..	−64.3	..	9.4	8.0	25.6	23.5	23.9	15.1
Mauritius	9.2	8.1	5.8	0.8	−4.7	1.1	9.6	8.4	20.8	19.3	18.3	17.5
Mexico	−4.5	11.5	10.1	8.1	3.5	4.1	8.3	2.0	16.9	7.1	4.3	2.7
Moldova	41.7	3.2	24.4	−4.0	−5.7	4.0	24.9	14.9	33.8	20.5	5.1	18.1
Mongolia	17.6	26.9	29.6	1.2	−7.1	−6.4	16.8	13.3	37.0	21.7	8.6	21.3
Morocco	8.4	5.8	3.6	9.0	3.6	−1.1	5.2	3.8	13.3	..	14.0	..
Mozambique	38.3	32.6	11.9	32.7	6.9	0.2	9.7	9.5	19.0	15.7	6.3	12.0
Myanmar[a]	42.5	30.6	13.9	5.2	25.0	29.9	9.8	12.0	15.3	17.0	12.5	..
Namibia	13.2	5.9	19.4	11.3	−4.0	−4.1	7.4	6.2	15.3	11.1	−9.0	4.4
Nepal	18.8	29.4	−4.6	26.4	2.6	−1.6	6.0	2.5	9.5	8.0	4.8	−3.6
Netherlands[b]	..	..	..	..	..	..	2.9	2.6	4.8	2.0	0.6	2.3
New Zealand[a]	1.5	−0.6	8.0	1.3	−0.9	2.7	6.4	4.0	9.3	10.4	5.9	8.6
Nicaragua	9.4	14.3	7.0	−7.4	10.0	7.0	10.8	6.0	18.1	14.0	8.8	−2.0
Niger[a]	12.4	18.7	14.8	12.1	−14.1	28.9	3.5	3.5	..	..	..	..
Nigeria	48.1	14.4	5.8	17.5	−43.0	12.7	11.7	13.3	21.3	18.4	−12.2	19.1
Norway[a]	8.7	..	18.0	..	−4.8	..	6.7	2.3	8.9	4.3	−5.8	8.7
Oman	6.0	4.7	1.1	7.3	9.5	1.4	7.6	4.1	10.1	7.4	−8.3	−16.0
Pakistan	12.1	14.8	2.0	8.0	2.6	7.4	..	8.7	..	14.5	..	−4.6
Panama	9.3	10.3	−8.4	2.5	0.2	−0.6	7.1	3.5	10.5	8.2	11.9	4.0
Papua New Guinea	5.0	21.9	1.2	8.4	−4.6	10.1	8.5	2.3	17.5	10.1	3.9	14.2
Paraguay	2.8	22.2	1.7	14.8	4.7	−3.5	15.7	1.5	26.8	28.3	13.1	28.4
Peru[a]	−0.4	2.6	−2.7	0.8	2.3	0.3	9.8	2.8	30.0	21.0	25.4	17.5
Philippines	8.1	10.0	2.2	5.4	1.5	2.5	8.3	2.7	10.9	8.6	4.3	5.9
Poland	11.6	8.1	..	7.9	−5.8	1.7	14.2	2.2	20.0	5.5	12.0	3.9
Portugal[b]	..	..	..	..	..	..	2.4	..	5.2	..	1.8	..
Puerto Rico	..	..	..	..	..	..	..	..	..	..	..	..
Qatar	10.7	16.9	−1.7	2.9	−23.1	26.7	0.0	4.2	..	7.0	..	31.0

	Broad money		Claims on domestic economy		Claims on central government		Interest rate					
									%			
							Deposit		Lending		Real	
	annual % growth		Annual growth % of broad money		Annual growth % of broad money							
	2000	2009	2000	2009	2000	2009	2000	2009	2000	2009	2000	2009
Romania	40.8	9.0	20.0	1.9	−1.1	10.7	33.1	12.0	53.9	17.3	6.7	10.1
Russian Federation	57.9	16.4	33.2	2.1	−18.1	14.0	6.5	8.6	24.4	15.3	−9.6	12.5
Rwanda[a]	15.6	..	10.3	..	−11.4	..	10.1	6.7	17.0	16.5	20.6	3.3
Saudi Arabia[a]	4.5	10.8	3.3	0.0	−3.5	8.9	..	..	..	..	..	..
Senegal[a]	10.7	11.4	19.1	2.6	−3.9	4.3	3.5	3.5	..	..	..	..
Serbia	160.8	21.3	−71.0	18.1	22.5	4.9	78.7	11.8	6.3	11.8	−40.1	1.6
Sierra Leone[a]	12.1	27.5	1.6	14.2	54.6	4.0	9.2	9.7	26.3	24.5	19.0	12.0
Singapore[a]	−2.0	11.3	5.1	1.6	−1.6	8.9	1.7	0.3	5.8	5.4	2.0	7.4
Slovak Republic[b]	..	..	..	..	..	..	8.5	3.7	14.9	5.8	5.0	2.8
Slovenia[b]	..	..	..	..	..	..	10.0	1.4	15.8	5.9	9.9	4.0
Somalia	..		..		..		..		..		..	
South Africa	7.2	1.8	−11.8	0.1	0.2	5.5	9.2	8.5	14.5	11.7	5.2	4.1
Spain[b]	..	..	..	..	..	..	3.0	..	5.2	..	1.7	..
Sri Lanka[a]	12.9	18.7	9.1	−4.6	12.5	4.4	9.2	10.6	16.2	15.7	8.3	9.5
Sudan	36.9	23.7	16.9	13.6	33.9	13.0	..	..	..	..	..	..
Swaziland	−6.6	26.8	16.9	12.5	1.7	17.4	6.5	5.4	14.0	11.4	13.8	5.6
Sweden	1.9	2.5	8.5	3.8	2.4	1.6	2.2	..	5.8	..	4.3	..
Switzerland[a]	−16.9	7.6	−1.2	5.1	2.1	0.6	3.0	0.1	4.3	2.8	3.1	2.5
Syrian Arab Republic	19.0	8.6	−4.1	8.6	−6.1	1.4	4.0	6.4	9.0	10.0	−0.6	19.0
Tajikistan[a]	63.3	−3.6	8.2	145.1	36.6	−9.8	1.3	5.8	25.6	22.9	2.4	8.5
Tanzania	14.8	17.7	12.2	5.8	0.7	6.2	7.4	8.0	21.6	15.0	13.0	7.1
Thailand	4.9	6.8	6.2	3.6	0.5	0.9	3.3	1.0	7.8	6.0	6.4	3.9
Timor-Leste	41.1	39.3	45.7	0.6	−36.8	12.1	0.8	0.8	16.7	11.2	11.4	1.1
Togo[a]	15.2	16.0	0.5	9.7	−0.5	6.3	3.5	3.5	..	..	..	..
Trinidad and Tobago[a]	11.7	30.6	8.8	−3.1	−13.2	25.3	8.2	3.4	16.5	11.9	3.2	32.8
Tunisia[a]	14.1	12.5	23.7	9.7	5.6	1.4	..	..	..	..	..	..
Turkey	40.7	12.7	16.2	9.4	26.8	12.4	47.2	17.6	..	..	..	..
Turkmenistan[a]	83.3	..	10.8	..	−53.4		..	..	..	..	..	..
Uganda	18.1	17.5	8.2	10.1	29.4	0.4	9.8	9.8	22.9	21.0	10.6	3.8
Ukraine	44.5	−5.5	30.9	−3.4	−1.7	9.4	13.7	13.8	41.5	20.9	15.0	6.6
United Arab Emirates[a]	15.3	9.8	8.7	1.4	−9.6	13.3	6.2	..	9.7	..	−9.9	..
United Kingdom[a]	11.1	0.0	17.4	−2.6	−2.4	7.9	4.5	..	6.0	0.6	4.7	−0.7
United States	8.1	−0.6	5.0	−1.3	0.5	4.5	..	..	9.2	3.3	6.9	2.3
Uruguay	9.5	−2.6	45.1	−10.3	−1.8	3.0	18.3	4.4	46.1	15.3	41.1	8.9
Uzbekistan	..	..	..	..	..	..	..	..	..	..	..	..
Venezuela, RB[a]	33.7	26.1	14.3	18.6	−6.4	−1.9	16.3	16.4	25.2	19.9	−3.3	10.6
Vietnam[a]	35.4	26.2	29.6	35.0	−2.4	7.0	3.7	12.7	10.6	10.1	6.9	3.8
West Bank and Gaza	..	..	..	..	..	..	..	..	..	..	..	..
Yemen, Rep.[a]	25.3	12.8	3.6	−1.2	−45.6	26.2	14.0	10.7	19.5	18.0	−4.9	23.1
Zambia	73.8	7.7	−11.4	−3.4	162.0	16.2	20.2	7.1	38.8	22.1	6.7	8.3
Zimbabwe[a]	45.7	111.3	27.2	56.4	29.5	−28.7	50.2	121.5	68.2	579.0	67.8	..

a. For these countries data reported under Claims on domestic economy include claims on private sector only. b. As members of the European Monetary Union, these countries share a single currency, the euro.

About the data

Money and the financial accounts that record the supply of money lie at the heart of a country's financial system. There are several commonly used definitions of the money supply. The narrowest, M1, encompasses currency held by the public and demand deposits with banks. M2 includes M1 plus time and savings deposits with banks that require prior notice for withdrawal. M3 includes M2 as well as various money market instruments, such as certificates of deposit issued by banks, bank deposits denominated in foreign currency, and deposits with financial institutions other than banks. However defined, money is a liability of the banking system, distinguished from other bank liabilities by the special role it plays as a medium of exchange, a unit of account, and a store of value.

The banking system's assets include its net foreign assets and net domestic credit. Net domestic credit includes credit extended to the private sector and general government and credit extended to the nonfinancial public sector in the form of investments in short- and long-term government securities and loans to state enterprises; liabilities to the public and private sectors in the form of deposits with the banking system are netted out. Net domestic credit also includes credit to banking and nonbank financial institutions.

Domestic credit is the main vehicle through which changes in the money supply are regulated, with central bank lending to the government often playing the most important role. The central bank can regulate lending to the private sector in several ways—for example, by adjusting the cost of the refinancing facilities it provides to banks, by changing market interest rates through open market operations, or by controlling the availability of credit through changes in the reserve requirements imposed on banks and ceilings on the credit provided by banks to the private sector.

Monetary accounts are derived from the balance sheets of financial institutions—the central bank, commercial banks, and nonbank financial intermediaries. Although these balance sheets are usually reliable, they are subject to errors of classification, valuation, and timing and to differences in accounting practices. For example, whether interest income is recorded on an accrual or a cash basis can make a substantial difference, as can the treatment of non-performing assets. Valuation errors typically arise for foreign exchange transactions, particularly in countries with flexible exchange rates or in countries that have undergone currency devaluation during the reporting period. The valuation of financial derivatives and the net liabilities of the banking system can also be difficult. The quality of commercial bank reporting also may be adversely affected by delays in reports from bank branches, especially in countries where branch accounts are not computerized. Thus the data in the balance sheets of commercial banks may be based on preliminary estimates subject to constant revision. This problem is likely to be even more serious for nonbank financial intermediaries.

Many interest rates coexist in an economy, reflecting competitive conditions, the terms governing loans and deposits, and differences in the position and status of creditors and debtors. In some economies interest rates are set by regulation or administrative fiat. In economies with imperfect markets, or where reported nominal rates are not indicative of effective rates, it may be difficult to obtain data on interest rates that reflect actual market transactions. Deposit and lending rates are collected by the International Monetary Fund (IMF) as representative interest rates offered by banks to resident customers. The terms and conditions attached to these rates differ by country, however, limiting their comparability. Real interest rates are calculated by adjusting nominal rates by an estimate of the inflation rate in the economy. A negative real interest rate indicates a loss in the purchasing power of the principal. The real interest rates in the table are calculated as $(i - P) / (1 + P)$, where i is the nominal lending interest rate and P is the inflation rate (as measured by the GDP deflator).

In 2009 the IMF began publishing a new presentation of monetary statistics for countries that report data in accordance with the IMF's *Monetary and Financial Statistics Manual 2000*. The presentation for countries that report data in accordance with the IMF's *International Financial Statistics* (IFS) remains the same.

Definitions

• **Broad money** (IFS line 35L..ZK) is the sum of currency outside banks; demand deposits other than those of the central government; the time, savings, and foreign currency deposits of resident sectors other than the central government; bank and traveler's checks; and other securities such as certificates of deposit and commercial paper. Change in broad money is measured as the difference in end-of-year totals relative to the preceding year. For countries reporting under the old presentation of monetary statistics and for all countries prior to 2001, data are based on money plus quasi money. • **Claims on domestic economy** (IFS line 32S..ZK) include gross credit from the financial system to households, nonprofit institutions serving households, nonfinancial corporations, state and local governments, and social security funds. For countries where claims on domestic economy are not available, data are claims on private sector (IFS line 32D..ZK or 32D..ZF) • **Claims on central government** (IFS line 32AN..ZK) include loans to central government institutions net of deposits. • **Deposit interest rate** is the rate paid by commercial or similar banks for demand, time, or savings deposits. • **Lending interest rate** is the rate charged by banks on loans to prime customers. • **Real interest rate** is the lending interest rate adjusted for inflation as measured by the GDP deflator.

Data sources

Data on monetary and financial statistics are published by the IMF in its monthly *International Financial Statistics* and annual *International Financial Statistics Yearbook*. The IMF collects data on the financial systems of its member countries. The World Bank receives data from the IMF in electronic files that may contain more recent revisions than the published sources. The discussion of monetary indicators draws from an IMF publication by Marcello Caiola, *A Manual for Country Economists* (1995). Also see the IMF's *Monetary and Financial Statistics Manual* (2000) for guidelines for the presentation of monetary and financial statistics. Data on real interest rates are derived from World Bank data on the GDP deflator.

	Official exchange rate		Purchasing power parity (PPP) conversion factor		Ratio of PPP conversion factor to market exchange rate	Real effective exchange rate	GDP implicit deflator		Consumer price index		Wholesale price index	
	local currency units to $		local currency units to international $			Index 2000 = 100	average annual % growth		average annual % growth		average annual % growth	
	2009	2010a	1995	2009	2009	2009	1990–2000	2000–09	1990–2000	2000–09	1990–2000	2000–09
Afghanistan	50.23	45.21	..	18.1	0.4	..	..	9.0	..	9.5	..	..
Albania	94.98	104.95	24.4	41.5	0.4	..	37.7	3.5	27.8	2.8	..	4.5
Algeria	72.65	74.25	15.3	35.8	0.5	102.1	18.5	8.6	17.3	3.0	..	4.0
Angola	79.33	92.35	0.0	55.7	0.7	..	739.4	41.1	711.0	41.1	..	..
Argentina	3.71	3.96	1.0	2.0	0.5	..	5.2	12.9b	8.9	10.0	0.1	15.7
Armenia	363.28	360.50	116.6	194.5	0.5	124.4	212.5	4.5	70.5	4.0	..	1.3
Australia	1.28	1.01	1.3	1.5	1.1	100.8	1.4	4.1	2.1	3.0	1.1	3.6
Austriac	0.72	0.76	0.9	0.8	1.2	101.5	1.6	1.7	2.2	2.0	0.3	2.4
Azerbaijan	0.80	0.80	0.2	0.4	0.5	..	203.0	9.9	179.7	8.3	..	..
Bangladesh	69.04	70.63	19.2	26.8	0.4	..	4.1	5.2	5.5	6.8	..	..
Belarus	2,789.49	3,010.98	3.4	1,085.6	0.4	..	355.1	23.1	271.3	18.7	267.8	22.5
Belgiumc	0.72	0.76	0.9	0.9	1.2	104.3	1.8	2.1	1.9	2.1	1.2	2.9
Benin	472.19	496.24	187.4	233.3	0.5	..	8.7	3.4	8.7	3.2	..	..
Bolivia	7.02	7.02	1.7	2.8	0.4	127.6	8.6	6.9	8.7	5.3	..	..
Bosnia and Herzegovina	1.41	1.48	0.6	0.7	0.5	..	4.1	3.9	..	..	..	..
Botswana	7.16	6.58	1.4	3.2	0.5	..	9.7	9.0	10.4	8.9	..	..
Brazil	2.00	1.70	0.7	1.6	0.8	..	211.8	8.3	199.5	6.9	204.9	10.0
Bulgaria	1.41	1.48	0.0	0.7	0.5	126.0	102.1	6.0	117.5	6.4	85.7	6.2
Burkina Faso	472.19	496.24	189.5	205.5	0.4	..	3.7	2.5	5.5	3.1	..	..
Burundi	1,230.18	1,230.91	126.6	500.6	0.4	109.4	13.4	10.4	16.1	9.2	..	..
Cambodia	4,139.33	4,096.00	1,142.3	1,526.8	0.4	..	4.4	5.0	6.3	6.0	..	..
Cameroon	472.19	496.24	241.1	243.3	0.5	108.0	6.3	2.1	6.5	2.5	..	..
Canada	1.14	1.01	1.2	1.2	1.1	96.8	1.5	2.6	1.7	2.1	2.7	1.4
Central African Republic	472.19	496.24	271.9	282.8	0.6	115.8	4.5	2.7	5.3	3.2	6.0	4.4
Chad	472.19	496.24	163.1	221.6	0.5	..	7.1	5.6	6.9	2.7	..	..
Chile	560.86	474.78	264.1	377.1	0.7	100.3	7.9	6.3	..	..	7.0	6.5
China	6.83	6.65	3.4	3.8	0.6	119.8	7.9	4.3	8.6	2.3	..	..
Hong Kong, SAR China	7.75	7.77	7.9	5.4	0.7	..	4.5	–1.3	5.9	0.3	0.6	–0.2
Colombia	2,166.79	1,925.90	417.8	1,233.7	0.6	113.1	22.6	6.1	20.2	5.8	16.4	4.9
Congo, Dem. Rep.	809.79	907.62	0.0	414.3	0.5	597.2	964.9	27.2	930.2	26.9	..	..
Congo, Rep.	472.19	496.24	149.2	289.8	0.6	..	9.0	7.4	9.3	3.4	..	..
Costa Rica	573.29	512.34	103.0	329.5	0.6	108.4	15.9	10.2	15.6	11.2	14.1	13.0
Côte d'Ivoire	472.19	496.24	261.8	306.9	0.7	105.7	9.2	3.5	7.2	3.0	..	..
Croatia	5.28	5.59	3.1	3.8	0.7	108.6	90.0	3.9	86.3	2.9	69.8	3.0
Cuba	..	..	..	..	..	..	6.4	3.3	..	..	..	..
Czech Republic	19.06	19.03	11.1	13.5	0.7	120.4	12.8	2.2	7.8	2.5	8.2	2.3
Denmark	5.36	5.64	8.5	8.0	1.5	105.6	1.6	2.3	2.1	2.0	1.1	2.4
Dominican Republic	36.03	37.41	7.3	19.7	0.6	96.2	9.8	13.7	8.7	14.6	..	..
Ecuador	..	..	0.4	0.5	0.5	98.8	4.4	9.1	37.1	6.6	..	7.9
Egypt, Arab Rep.	5.54	5.74	1.2	2.2	0.4	..	8.7	8.3	8.8	8.0	6.1	9.6
El Salvador	8.75	8.75	0.4	0.5	0.5	..	6.2	3.6	8.5	3.9	..	4.7
Eritrea	15.38	15.38	1.9	9.8	0.6	..	7.9	18.6	..	..	..	..
Estonia	11.26	11.82	4.8	8.1	0.7	..	53.7	5.3	21.6	4.4	8.1	3.4
Ethiopia	11.78	..	2.1	4.3	0.4	..	6.5	10.8	5.5	12.3	..	..
Finlandc	0.72	0.76	1.0	0.9	1.3	103.8	1.9	1.1	1.5	1.5	0.9	2.1
Francec	0.72	0.76	1.0	0.9	1.2	101.8	1.3	2.1	1.6	1.8	..	1.8
Gabon	472.19	496.24	187.9	245.7	0.5	105.3	7.0	5.0	4.6	2.1	..	..
Gambia, The	26.64	28.12	3.9	8.1	0.3	104.4	4.2	9.8	4.0	7.6	..	..
Georgia	1.67	1.76	0.4	0.9	0.5	124.3	356.7	7.0	24.7	7.0	..	6.7
Germanyc	0.72	0.76	1.0	0.8	1.1	102.3	1.7	1.1	2.1	1.7	0.4	2.5
Ghana	1.41	1.49	0.1	1.0	0.7	91.9	26.7	27.2	28.4	16.2	..	..
Greecec	0.72	0.76	0.6	0.7	1.0	106.9	9.2	3.1	9.0	3.2	3.6	4.3
Guatemala	8.16	7.98	2.9	4.6	0.6	..	10.4	5.4	10.1	7.3	..	..
Guinea	..	..	747.4	2,066.8	0.4	..	5.5	16.1	..	..	..	..
Guinea-Bissau	472.19	496.24	58.6	229.0	0.5	..	32.5	11.8	34.0	2.4	..	..
Haiti	41.20	39.90	5.8	23.1	0.6	..	18.1	15.3	21.9	16.5	..	..
Honduras	18.90	18.90	3.0	9.4	0.5	..	19.9	6.4	18.8	7.9	..	..

	Official exchange rate		Purchasing power parity (PPP) conversion factor		Ratio of PPP conversion factor to market exchange rate	Real effective exchange rate	GDP implicit deflator		Consumer price index		Wholesale price index	
	local currency units to $		local currency units to international $			Index 2000 = 100	average annual % growth		average annual % growth		average annual % growth	
	2009	2010a	1995	2009	2009	2009	1990–2000	2000–09	1990–2000	2000–09	1990–2000	2000–09
Hungary	202.34	209.67	61.7	128.2	0.6	103.8	19.6	4.9	20.3	5.5	16.8	3.5
India	48.41	45.16	10.8	17.2	0.4	..	8.1	5.6	9.1	5.3	7.4	5.1
Indonesia	10,389.94	8,948.00	1,031.3	5,813.6	0.6	..	15.8	11.1	13.7	9.1	15.4	11.2
Iran, Islamic Rep.	9,864.30	10,364.64	567.2	3,875.0	0.4	142.1	27.7	16.4	26.0	15.4	28.4	10.8
Iraq	1,170.00	1,170.00	252.5	689.4	0.6	..	..	11.6	..	..	..	..
Ireland^c	0.72	0.76	0.8	0.9	1.3	107.4	3.6	2.1	2.3	3.2	1.6	–0.1
Israel	3.93	3.60	2.8	3.7	1.0	110.2	11.0	1.3	9.7	1.8	8.1	4.5
Italy^c	0.72	0.76	0.8	0.8	1.1	103.2	3.8	2.6	3.7	2.3	2.9	2.7
Jamaica	87.89	85.67	14.6	52.0	0.6	..	24.8	11.2	23.5	11.7	..	..
Japan	93.57	83.43	175.0	114.7	1.2	101.4	0.0	–1.1	0.8	–0.1	–1.0	0.7
Jordan	0.71	0.71	0.4	0.5	0.8	..	3.2	6.1	3.5	4.4	..	9.1
Kazakhstan	147.50	147.41	17.5	93.0	0.6	..	204.7	14.9	67.8	8.6	16.3	13.3
Kenya	77.35	80.57	15.8	36.3	0.5	..	16.6	6.0	15.6	11.3	..	..
Korea, Dem. Rep.	..	..	..	..	..	..	..	..	..	..	..	..
Korea, Rep.	1,276.93	1,146.23	709.6	804.7	0.6	..	5.9	2.2	5.1	3.1	3.7	2.5
Kosovo	0.72	0.76	..	..	..	..	..	0.8	..	1.5	..	..
Kuwait	0.29	0.28	0.2	0.3	0.9	..	1.5	9.8	2.0	3.4	1.4	2.5
Kyrgyz Republic	42.90	47.00	3.5	16.2	0.4	..	110.6	8.3	23.3	6.9	35.6	10.2
Lao PDR	8,516.05	8,245.42	327.6	3,548.2	0.4	..	27.2	8.9	28.3	8.3	..	..
Latvia	0.51	0.53	0.2	0.4	0.7	..	48.0	8.8	29.2	6.5	12.0	7.3
Lebanon	1,507.50	1,507.50	774.7	942.9	0.6	..	19.0	2.6	..	..	..	..
Lesotho	8.47	6.84	2.1	4.5	0.5	93.2	9.7	8.1	5.9	7.8	..	..
Liberia	68.29	71.85	0.6	38.2	0.6	..	51.8	10.3	..	..	..	..
Libya	1.25	1.23	..	0.7	0.6	..	..	17.9	5.6	0.4	..	..
Lithuania	2.48	2.61	1.2	1.6	0.6	..	75.0	4.1	32.6	3.1	24.8	4.8
Macedonia, FYR	44.10	46.55	18.0	17.8	0.4	104.2	79.3	3.8	10.6	2.4	8.5	2.5
Madagascar	1,956.21	2,117.83	287.5	852.8	0.4	..	19.1	11.2	18.7	10.7	..	..
Malawi	141.17	150.80	4.2	55.1	0.4	107.5	33.6	17.0	33.8	12.2	..	..
Malaysia	3.52	3.13	1.4	1.8	0.5	103.3	4.1	4.0	3.6	2.4	3.4	4.8
Mali	472.19	496.24	226.7	275.4	0.6	..	7.0	4.5	5.2	2.5	..	..
Mauritania	262.37	..	62.4	125.0	0.5	..	8.7	10.8	6.1	7.3	..	..
Mauritius	31.96	30.54	10.5	16.8	0.5	..	6.3	6.0	6.9	6.3	..	..
Mexico	13.51	12.40	2.9	7.7	0.6	..	19.0	7.8	19.5	4.5	18.4	6.1
Moldova	11.11	12.15	1.2	5.9	0.5	135.3	119.6	11.0	21.4	10.8	..	..
Mongolia	1,437.80	1,256.47	158.6	643.7	0.5	..	57.8	14.6	35.7	8.7	..	..
Morocco	8.06	8.43	4.9	5.0	0.6	102.4	4.0	2.0	3.9	2.0	2.9	..
Mozambique	27.52	35.64	4.0	13.0	0.5	..	34.1	8.0	31.8	10.9	..	..
Myanmar	5.52	5.42	..	..	..	..	25.3	..	25.9	22.4	..	..
Namibia	8.47	6.84	2.2	5.6	0.7	..	11.1	7.1	..	5.9	..	..
Nepal	77.55	72.38	15.4	28.4	0.4	..	8.0	6.6	8.7	6.2	..	..
Netherlands^c	0.72	0.76	0.9	0.9	1.2	102.7	2.1	2.1	2.4	1.9	1.3	2.7
New Zealand	1.60	1.29	1.5	1.5	1.0	86.4	1.7	3.1	1.8	2.7	1.5	3.3
Nicaragua	20.34	21.84	3.5	8.2	0.4	107.8	42.4	7.7	..	8.8	..	..
Niger	472.19	496.24	203.1	241.0	0.5	..	6.0	3.1	6.1	2.8	..	..
Nigeria	148.90	148.57	15.5	75.6	0.5	109.4	29.5	15.3	32.5	12.5	..	..
Norway	6.29	5.98	9.2	8.9	1.4	97.8	2.7	4.6	2.2	1.8	1.6	7.9
Oman	0.38	0.38	0.2	0.3	0.9	..	0.1	9.8	..	2.9	..	..
Pakistan	81.71	85.77	10.1	28.8	0.4	98.6	11.1	8.5	9.7	8.0	10.4	8.9
Panama	1.00	1.00	0.5	0.6	0.6	..	3.6	2.4	1.1	2.5	1.0	3.8
Papua New Guinea	2.76	2.64	0.7	1.4	0.5	116.1	7.6	6.5	9.3	5.9	..	..
Paraguay	4,965.39	4,667.57	948.9	2,462.5	0.5	135.7	11.5	10.2	13.1	8.4	..	10.3
Peru	3.01	2.82	1.2	1.6	0.5	..	26.7	3.5	27.3	2.4	23.7	2.8
Philippines	47.68	43.95	14.1	23.6	0.5	121.3	8.4	5.1	7.7	5.5	6.3	7.0
Poland	3.12	3.02	1.2	1.9	0.6	98.5	24.7	2.7	25.3	2.5	19.8	2.7
Portugal^c	0.72	0.76	0.7	0.6	0.9	102.1	5.2	2.6	4.5	2.7	..	2.6
Puerto Rico	..	..	..	..	..	..	3.0	..	..	..	..	..
Qatar	3.64	3.64	..	2.8	0.8	..	..	10.6	2.8	7.2	..	..

	Official exchange rate		Purchasing power parity (PPP) conversion factor		Ratio of PPP conversion factor to market exchange rate	Real effective exchange rate	GDP implicit deflator		Consumer price index		Wholesale price index	
	local currency units to $		local currency units to international $			Index 2000 = 100	average annual % growth		average annual % growth		average annual % growth	
	2009	2010a	1995	2009	2009	2009	1990–2000	2000–09	1990–2000	2000–09	1990–2000	2000–09
Romania	3.05	3.24	0.1	1.6	0.5	102.2	98.0	15.9	100.5	11.5	93.8	15.3
Russian Federation	31.74	30.85	1.7	14.6	0.5	115.3	161.5	15.8	99.1	12.5	99.8	15.7
Rwanda	568.28	594.45	126.3	261.0	0.5	..	14.3	10.5	16.2	8.9	..	..
Saudi Arabia	3.75	3.75	1.8	2.4	0.6	103.8	1.6	7.6	1.0	2.2	1.3	2.5
Senegal	472.19	496.24	251.9	265.2	0.6	..	6.0	2.8	5.4	2.2	..	..
Serbia	67.58	80.39	2.9	33.4	0.5	..	..	16.5	50.2	15.4	..	..
Sierra Leone	3,385.65	..	379.5	1,399.7	0.4	104.5	31.9	9.5	..	..	..	..
Singapore	1.45	1.31	1.3	1.1	0.7	107.9	1.3	1.2	1.7	1.5	–1.0	2.8
Slovak Republicc	0.72	0.76	0.4	0.5	0.7	137.2	11.1	3.4	8.4	4.8	9.5	4.7
Sloveniac	0.72	0.76	0.4	0.6	0.9		29.3	4.0	12.0	4.2	9.1	3.9
Somalia	..	..	..	..	..	..	..	..	..	..	..	..
South Africa	8.47	6.84	2.3	4.8	0.6	87.8	9.9	7.2	8.7	5.7	7.7	6.7
Spainc	0.72	0.76	0.7	0.7	1.0	106.2	3.9	3.7	3.8	3.1	2.4	3.2
Sri Lanka	114.94	111.11	18.2	49.8	0.4	..	9.1	10.7	9.9	11.1	8.1	12.4
Sudan	2.30	..	0.3	1.4	0.6	..	65.5	10.0	72.0	8.6	..	..
Swaziland	8.47	6.84	2.2	4.2	0.5	..	10.5	7.9	9.5	7.3	..	..
Sweden	7.65	6.85	9.4	8.9	1.2	89.5	2.2	1.7	1.9	1.5	2.5	2.9
Switzerland	1.09	0.97	2.0	1.5	1.4	101.6	1.1	1.2	1.6	1.0	–0.4	1.1
Syrian Arab Republic	11.23	11.23	12.8	24.4	0.5	..	7.9	8.0	6.4	6.2	4.7	3.2
Tajikistan	4.14	4.40	0.0	1.5	0.4	..	235.0	20.9	..	12.7	..	..
Tanzania	1,320.31	1,462.88	159.4	487.3	0.4	..	23.0	7.3	20.9	6.5	..	..
Thailand	34.29	30.12	15.1	16.7	0.5	..	4.2	3.2	4.9	2.9	3.8	5.5
Timor-Leste	..	..	..	0.6	0.6	..	..	4.5	..	5.1	..	..
Togo	472.19	496.24	238.5	239.5	0.5	104.8	7.0	1.4	8.5	2.8	..	..
Trinidad and Tobago	6.32	6.37	2.8	3.9	0.6	123.7	5.4	6.5	5.7	6.5	2.8	3.8
Tunisia	1.35	1.45	0.5	0.6	0.5	94.2	4.4	3.2	4.4	3.3	3.6	4.5
Turkey	1.55	1.52	0.0	0.9	0.6	..	81.7	15.3	79.9	16.9	75.2	16.9
Turkmenistan	..	..	0.0	1.5	0.5	..	408.2	13.0	..	..	..	..
Uganda	2,030.31	..	500.3	767.5	0.4	103.2	11.6	5.6	8.3	6.7	..	..
Ukraine	7.79	7.96	0.3	3.2	0.4	96.8	271.0	16.4	155.7	10.9	161.6	14.6
United Arab Emirates	3.67	3.67	1.7	3.2	0.9	..	2.2	10.2	..	..	..	..
United Kingdom	0.64	0.64	0.6	0.6	1.0	80.8	2.8	2.6	2.9	2.9	2.4	1.8
United States	1.00	1.00	1.0	1.0	1.0	95.2	2.0	2.6	2.7	2.7	1.2	4.2
Uruguay	22.57	19.99	5.5	16.1	0.7	120.9	32.6	8.4	33.9	9.1	27.2	13.6
Uzbekistan	..	..	11.2	602.5	0.4	..	245.8	24.7	..	..	..	..
Venezuela, RB	2.15	2.59	0.1	2.0	0.9	191.2	45.3	25.0	49.0	21.2	44.1	26.0
Vietnam	17,065.08	18,932.00	3,168.8	6,434.3	0.4	..	15.2	8.3	4.1	7.8	..	..
West Bank and Gaza	..	..	..	..	..	..	5.7	3.4	..	..	..	..
Yemen, Rep.	202.85	214.40	22.1	91.8	0.5	..	22.4	13.0	26.3	11.4	..	..
Zambia	5,046.11	4,735.74	404.0	3,492.7	0.7	119.5	52.1	16.4	57.0	15.9	101.4	..
Zimbabwe	..	..	..	..	..	..	–3.9	4.1	29.0	497.7	25.9	..

Note: The differences in the growth rates of the GDP deflator and the consumer and wholesale price indexes are due mainly to differences in data availability for each of the indexes during the period.

a. Average for December or latest monthly data available. b. Private analysts estimate that consumer price index inflation was considerably higher for 2007–09 and that GDP volume growth has been significantly lower than official reports indicate since the last quarter of 2008. c. As members of the euro area, these countries share a single currency, the euro.

About the data

In a market-based economy, household, producer, and government choices about resource allocation are influenced by relative prices, including the real exchange rate, real wages, real interest rates, and other prices in the economy. Relative prices also largely reflect these agents' choices. Thus relative prices convey vital information about the interaction of economic agents in an economy and with the rest of the world.

The exchange rate is the price of one currency in terms of another. Official exchange rates and exchange rate arrangements are established by governments. Other exchange rates recognized by governments include market rates, which are determined largely by legal market forces, and for countries with multiple exchange arrangements, principal rates, secondary rates, and tertiary rates.

Official or market exchange rates are often used to convert economic statistics in local currencies to a common currency in order to make comparisons across countries. Since market rates reflect at best the relative prices of tradable goods, the volume of goods and services that a U.S. dollar buys in the United States may not correspond to what a U.S. dollar converted to another country's currency at the official exchange rate would buy in that country, particularly when nontradable goods and services account for a significant share of a country's output. An alternative exchange rate—the purchasing power parity (PPP) conversion factor—is preferred because it reflects differences in price levels for both tradable and nontradable goods and services and therefore provides a more meaningful comparison of real output. See table 1.1 for further discussion.

The ratio of the PPP conversion factor to the official exchange rate—the national price level or comparative price level—measures differences in the price level at the gross domestic product (GDP) level. The price level index tends to be lower in poorer countries and to rise with income. The real effective exchange rate is a nominal effective exchange rate index adjusted for relative movements in national price or cost indicators of the home country, selected countries, and the euro area. A nominal effective exchange rate index is the ratio (expressed on the base 2000 = 100) of an index of a currency's period-average exchange rate to a weighted geometric average of exchange rates for currencies of selected countries and the euro area. For most high-income countries weights are derived from industrial country trade in manufactured goods. Data are compiled from the nominal effective exchange rate index and a

cost indicator of relative normalized unit labor costs in manufacturing. For selected other countries the nominal effective exchange rate index is based on manufactured goods and primary products trade with partner or competitor countries. For these countries the real effective exchange rate index is the nominal index adjusted for relative changes in consumer prices; an increase represents an appreciation of the local currency. Because of conceptual and data limitations, changes in real effective exchange rates should be interpreted with caution.

Inflation is measured by the rate of increase in a price index, but actual price change can be negative. The index used depends on the prices being examined. The GDP deflator reflects price changes for total GDP. The most general measure of the overall price level, it accounts for changes in government consumption, capital formation (including inventory appreciation), international trade, and the main component, household final consumption expenditure. The GDP deflator is usually derived implicitly as the ratio of current to constant price GDP—or a Paasche index. It is defective as a general measure of inflation for policy use because of long lags in deriving estimates and because it is often an annual measure.

Consumer price indexes are produced more frequently and so are more current. They are also constructed explicitly, based on surveys of the cost of a defined basket of consumer goods and services. Nevertheless, consumer price indexes should be interpreted with caution. The definition of a household, the basket of goods, and the geographic (urban or rural) and income group coverage of consumer price surveys can vary widely by country. In addition, weights are derived from household expenditure surveys, which, for budgetary reasons, tend to be conducted infrequently in developing countries, impairing comparability over time. Although useful for measuring consumer price inflation within a country, consumer price indexes are of less value in comparing countries.

Wholesale price indexes are based on the prices at the first commercial transaction of commodities that are important in a country's output or consumption. Prices are farm-gate for agricultural commodities and ex-factory for industrial goods. Preference is given to indexes with the broadest coverage of the economy. The least squares method is used to calculate growth rates of the GDP implicit deflator, consumer price index, and wholesale price index.

Definitions

• **Official exchange rate** is the exchange rate determined by national authorities or the rate determined in the legally sanctioned exchange market. It is calculated as an annual average based on monthly averages (local currency units relative to the U.S. dollar).
• **Purchasing power parity (PPP) conversion factor** is the number of units of a country's currency required to buy the same amount of goods and services in the domestic market that a U.S. dollar would buy in the United States. • **Ratio of PPP conversion factor to market exchange rate** is the result obtained by dividing the PPP conversion factor by the market exchange rate. • **Real effective exchange rate** is the nominal effective exchange rate (a measure of the value of a currency against a weighted average of several foreign currencies) divided by a price deflator or index of costs. • **GDP implicit deflator** measures the average annual rate of price change in the economy as a whole for the periods shown. • **Consumer price index** reflects changes in the cost to the average consumer of acquiring a basket of goods and services that may be fixed or may change at specified intervals, such as yearly. The Laspeyres formula is generally used.
• **Wholesale price index** refers to a mix of agricultural and industrial goods at various stages of production and distribution, including import duties. The Laspeyres formula is generally used.

Data sources

Data on official and real effective exchange rates and consumer and wholesale price indexes are from the International Monetary Fund's International Financial Statistics. PPP conversion factors and GDP deflators are from the World Bank's data files.

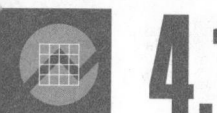

	Goods and services				Net income		Net current transfers		Current account balance		Total reserves[a]	
	$ millions				$ millions		$ millions		$ millions		$ millions	
	Exports		Imports									
	1995	2009	1995	2009	1995	2009	1995	2009	1995	2009	1995	2009
Afghanistan	..	..	..	..	..	..	..	..	..	..	..	..
Albania	304	3,458	836	6,495	44	−145	477	1,307	−12	−1,875	265	2,369
Algeria	..	..	..	..	..	..	..	..	..	..	4,164	155,112
Angola	3,836	41,451	3,519	41,829	−767	−6,823	156	−370	−295	−7,572	213	13,664
Argentina	24,987	66,563	26,066	48,951	−4,636	−9,013	597	34	−5,118	8,632	15,979	48,007
Armenia	300	1,338	726	3,688	40	166	168	814	−218	−1,369	111	2,004
Australia	69,710	234,298	74,841	242,311	−14,036	−39,399	−109	−374	−19,277	−47,786	14,952	41,742
Austria	89,906	189,999	92,055	175,559	−1,597	−1,148	−1,702	−2,296	−5,448	10,995	23,369	17,904
Azerbaijan	785	22,847	1,290	9,872	−6	−3,519	111	722	−401	10,178	121	5,364
Bangladesh	4,431	17,011	7,589	23,165	68	−1,376	2,265	10,875	−824	3,345	2,376	10,342
Belarus	5,269	24,843	5,752	30,360	−51	−1,114	76	242	−458	−6,389	377	5,640
Belgium	190,686[b]	334,175[b]	178,798[b]	328,387[b]	..[b]	6,641[b]	7,822[b]	−8,907[b]	..[b]	3,522[b]	24,120[b]	23,862[b]
Benin	614	1,630	895	2,400	−8	−11	121	245	−167	−536	198	1,230
Bolivia	1,234	5,433	1,574	5,159	−207	−674	244	1,213	−303	813	1,005	8,575
Bosnia and Herzegovina	..	5,480	..	9,464	..	535	..	2,275	..	−1,175	80	3,245
Botswana	2,421	4,179	2,050	5,131	−32	−452	−39	878	300	−526	4,695	8,704
Brazil	52,641	180,723	63,293	174,679	−11,105	−33,684	3,621	3,338	−18,136	−24,302	51,477	238,539
Bulgaria	6,776	23,270	6,502	27,196	−432	−2,116	132	1,291	−26	−4,751	1,635	18,522
Burkina Faso	272	744	483	2,858	−29	−4	255	409	15	−1,709	347	1,296
Burundi	129	116	259	520	−13	−17	153	257	10	−164	216	323
Cambodia	969	5,927	1,375	6,898	−57	−468	277	574	−186	−866	192	3,286
Cameroon	2,040	5,313	1,608	6,540	−412	−303	69	393	90	−1,137	15	3,676
Canada	219,501	383,759	200,991	407,655	−22,721	−12,591	−117	−1,892	−4,328	−38,380	16,369	54,356
Central African Republic	179	..	244	..	−23	..	63	..	−25	..	238	211
Chad	190	..	411	..	−7	..	191	..	−38	..	147	617
Chile	19,358	62,242	18,301	49,335	−2,714	−10,306	307	1,616	−1,350	4,217	14,860	25,292
China†	147,240	1,333,346	135,282	1,113,234	−11,774	43,282	1,435	33,748	1,618	297,142	80,288	2,452,899
Hong Kong SAR, China	..	408,142	..	393,077	..	5,530	..	−3,177	..	17,418	55,424	255,841
Colombia	12,294	38,222	16,012	38,404	−1,596	−9,432	799	4,614	−4,516	−5,001	8,452	24,987
Congo, Dem. Rep.	..	..	..	..	..	..	..	..	..	..	157	1,615
Congo, Rep.	1,374	6,127	1,346	6,386	−695	−1,885	42	−38	−625	−2,181	64	3,806
Costa Rica	4,451	12,566	4,717	12,286	−226	−1,176	134	359	−358	−537	1,060	4,068
Côte d'Ivoire	4,337	11,478	3,806	8,803	−787	−890	−237	−115	−492	1,670	529	3,267
Croatia	6,972	22,626	9,152	24,900	−53	−2,491	802	1,450	−1,431	−3,314	1,896	14,895
Cuba	..	..	..	..	..	..	..	..	..	..	..	..
Czech Republic	28,202	132,920	30,044	122,069	−104	−12,194	572	−805	−1,374	−2,147	14,613	41,608
Denmark	65,655	147,276	57,860	134,738	−4,549	3,933	−1,391	−5,248	1,855	11,222	11,652	76,618
Dominican Republic	5,731	10,465	6,137	14,160	−769	−1,769	992	3,305	−183	−2,159	373	2,905
Ecuador	5,196	15,574	5,708	16,876	−930	−1,463	442	2,497	−1,000	−268	1,788	3,792
Egypt, Arab Rep.	13,260	44,609	17,140	53,842	−405	−2,076	4,031	7,960	−254	−3,349	17,122	34,897
El Salvador	2,040	4,696	3,623	7,966	−67	−664	1,389	3,561	−262	−373	940	3,122
Eritrea	135	..	498	..	8	..	324	..	−31	..	40	58
Estonia	2,573	13,539	2,860	12,435	3	−529	126	318	−158	893	583	3,981
Ethiopia	768	3,433	1,446	9,046	−19	−37	736	3,459	39	−2,191	815	1,781
Finland	47,973	90,571	37,705	83,807	−4,440	2,394	−597	−2,344	5,231	6,814	10,657	11,429
France	362,717	617,335	333,746	663,242	−8,964	31,844	−9,167	−37,796	10,840	−51,857	58,510	131,786
Gabon	2,945	..	1,723	..	−665	..	−42	..	515	..	153	1,993
Gambia, The	175	278	230	343	−5	−8	52	135	−8	63	106	224
Georgia	575	3,207	1,413	5,266	127	−118	197	967	−514	−1,210	199	2,110
Germany	600,347	1,376,861	586,662	1,212,133	−2,814	47,352	−38,768	−46,610	−27,897	165,471	121,816	179,040
Ghana	1,582	7,809	2,120	10,789	−129	−296	523	2,078	−144	−1,198	804	..
Greece	15,523	59,150	24,711	84,204	−1,684	−12,516	8,008	1,657	−2,864	−35,913	16,119	5,486
Guatemala	2,823	9,220	3,728	12,726	−159	−1,111	491	4,626	−572	8	783	5,205
Guinea	700	1,122	1,011	1,391	−85	−168	179	34	−216	−403	87	..
Guinea-Bissau	30	172	89	284	−21	−15	46	98	−35	−29	20	169
Haiti	192	933	802	2,813	−31	13	553	1,635	−87	−232	199	790
Honduras	1,635	6,028	1,852	8,641	−226	−487	243	2,652	−201	−449	270	2,492
†Data for Taiwan, China	128,369	235,091	124,171	202,629	4,188	12,512	−2,912	..	5,474	42,911	95,559	363,010

Balance of payments current account

	Goods and services				Net income		Net current transfers		Current account balance		Total reserves[a]	
	Exports		Imports		$ millions		$ millions		$ millions		$ millions	
	$ millions											
	1995	2009	1995	2009	1995	2009	1995	2009	1995	2009	1995	2009
Hungary	19,765	100,098	19,916	93,412	−1,701	−7,890	203	505	−1,650	−699	12,017	44,181
India	38,013	258,822	48,225	328,036	−3,734	−6,514	8,382	49,102	−5,563	−26,626	22,865	284,683
Indonesia	52,923	133,255	54,461	112,233	−5,874	−15,140	981	4,861	−6,431	10,743	14,908	66,119
Iran, Islamic Rep.	18,953	..	15,113	..	−478	..	−4	..	3,358	..	..	..
Iraq	..	65,695	..	37,731	..	2,106	..	−2,936	..	27,133	8,347	46,461
Ireland	49,439	199,942	42,169	166,569	−7,325	−38,752	1,776	−1,109	1,721	−6,488	8,770	2,151
Israel	27,478	67,877	35,287	63,129	−2,654	−4,558	5,673	7,402	−4,790	7,592	8,123	60,611
Italy	295,618	509,797	250,319	520,563	−15,644	−38,480	−4,579	−16,952	25,076	−66,199	60,690	131,497
Jamaica	3,394	4,038	3,729	6,356	−371	−668	607	1,860	−99	−1,126	681	2,076
Japan	493,991	673,615	419,556	650,364	44,285	131,339	−7,676	−12,397	111,044	142,194	192,620	1,048,991
Jordan	3,479	10,915	4,903	16,300	−279	612	1,444	3,523	−259	−1,251	2,279	12,135
Kazakhstan	5,975	48,258	6,102	38,877	−146	−12,729	59	−900	−213	−4,248	1,660	23,183
Kenya	3,526	7,414	5,922	11,314	−219	−58	1,037	2,297	−1,578	−1,661	384	3,850
Korea, Dem. Rep.	..	..	..	..	..	..	..	..	..	..	..	..
Korea, Rep.	147,761	432,097	155,104	393,172	−1,303	4,554	−19	−811	−8,665	42,668	32,804	270,437
Kosovo	..	..	..	..	..	..	..	..	..	..	..	830
Kuwait	14,215	61,692	12,615	30,679	4,881	7,726	−1,465	−10,133	5,016	28,605	4,543	23,028
Kyrgyz Republic	448	2,560	726	3,680	−35	−190	79	1,208	−235	−102	134	1,584
Lao PDR	408	1,444	748	1,581	−6	−47	110	193	−237	9	99	1,010
Latvia	2,088	11,231	2,193	11,486	19	1,655	71	883	−16	2,284	602	6,902
Lebanon	..	21,600	..	30,215	..	−767	..	1,827	..	−7,555	8,100	39,132
Lesotho	199	789	1,046	1,792	314	424	210	547	−323	−32	457	..
Liberia	..	454	..	1,704	..	−128	..	1,101	..	−277	28	372
Libya	7,513	37,440	5,755	27,065	133	578	−220	−1,572	1,672	9,381	7,415	103,754
Lithuania	3,191	20,309	3,902	20,605	−13	318	109	1,625	−614	1,646	829	6,657
Macedonia, FYR	1,302	3,548	1,773	5,665	−30	−128	213	1,599	−288	−646	275	2,288
Madagascar	749	..	987	..	−167	..	129	..	−276	..	109	1,135
Malawi	470	..	660	..	−44	..	157	..	−78	..	115	163
Malaysia	83,369	186,424	86,851	144,873	−4,144	−4,170	−1,017	−5,580	−8,644	31,801	24,699	96,704
Mali	529	2,551	991	3,760	−41	−313	219	455	−284	−1,066	323	1,604
Mauritania	504	..	510	..	−48	..	76	..	22	..	90	238
Mauritius	2,349	4,181	2,454	5,106	−19	27	101	224	−22	−675	887	2,316
Mexico	89,321	245,206	82,168	257,976	−12,689	−14,925	3,960	21,468	−1,576	−6,228	17,046	99,889
Moldova	884	2,000	1,006	3,989	−18	303	56	1,221	−85	−465	257	1,480
Mongolia	508	2,300	521	2,632	−25	−195	77	186	39	−342	158	1,327
Morocco	9,044	26,381	11,243	37,307	−1,318	−1,495	2,330	7,451	−1,186	−4,971	3,874	23,568
Mozambique	411	2,464	1,055	4,305	−140	−95	339	764	−445	−1,171	195	2,181
Myanmar	1,307	..	2,020	..	−110	..	562	..	−261	..	651	..
Namibia	1,734	4,057	2,100	5,128	139	−70	403	1,261	176	120	221	2,051
Nepal	1,029	1,493	1,624	5,086	9	158	230	3,426	−356	−10	646	..
Netherlands	241,517	518,122	216,558	459,194	7,247	−12,001	−6,434	−10,345	25,773	36,581	47,162	39,284
New Zealand	17,883	33,210	17,248	31,953	−3,955	−5,148	255	267	−3,065	−3,624	4,410	15,594
Nicaragua	662	2,857	1,150	4,482	−372	−235	138	1,018	−722	−841	142	1,573
Niger	321	1,043	457	1,951	−47	26	31	230	−152	−651	95	656
Nigeria	12,342	61,545	12,841	47,843	−2,878	−10,020	799	17,977	−2,578	21,659	1,709	45,510
Norway	56,058	160,687	46,848	104,496	−1,919	−1,660	−2,059	−4,408	5,233	50,122	22,976	48,859
Oman	6,078	29,443	5,035	21,607	−374	−2,810	−1,469	−5,313	−801	−287	1,943	12,204
Pakistan	10,214	22,220	14,185	35,008	−1,939	−3,619	2,562	12,824	−3,349	−3,583	2,528	13,606
Panama	7,610	16,652	7,768	15,446	−466	−1,460	153	210	−471	−44	781	3,028
Papua New Guinea	2,992	4,579	1,905	4,802	−488	−625	75	176	674	−672	267	2,629
Paraguay	4,802	7,253	5,200	7,374	110	−312	195	519	−92	86	1,106	3,862
Peru	6,622	30,538	9,597	25,777	−2,482	−7,371	832	2,856	−4,625	247	8,653	33,225
Philippines	26,795	47,611	33,317	54,950	3,662	−69	880	15,960	−1,980	8,552	7,781	44,206
Poland	35,716	171,071	33,825	170,631	−1,995	−16,575	958	6,537	854	−9,598	14,957	79,522
Portugal	32,260	67,268	39,545	83,259	21	−10,952	7,132	2,992	−132	−23,952	22,063	15,829
Puerto Rico	..	..	..	..	..	..	..	..	..	..	..	..
Qatar	..	..	..	..	..	..	..	..	..	..	848	18,804

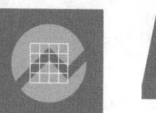

4.17 Balance of payments current account

	Goods and services				Net income		Net current transfers		Current account balance		Total reserves[a]	
	$ millions				$ millions		$ millions		$ millions		$ millions	
	Exports		Imports									
	1995	2009	1995	2009	1995	2009	1995	2009	1995	2009	1995	2009
Romania	9,404	50,491	11,306	60,470	−241	−2,968	369	5,649	−1,774	−7,298	2,624	44,383
Russian Federation	92,987	344,934	82,809	253,233	−3,372	−39,474	157	−2,862	6,963	49,365	18,024	439,342
Rwanda	75	534	374	1,479	7	−37	350	604	57	−379	99	743
Saudi Arabia	53,450	201,964	44,874	160,639	2,800	8,613	−16,694	−27,172	−5,318	22,765	10,399	420,984
Senegal	1,506	3,500	1,821	7,020	−124	−48	195	1,685	−244	−1,884	272	2,123
Serbia	..	11,858	..	18,486	..	−710	..	4,925	..	−2,412	..	15,228
Sierra Leone	128	323	260	628	−30	−36	43	148	−118	−193	35	405
Singapore	159,488	364,332	144,904	325,605	541	−3,061	−894	−3,037	14,230	32,628	68,816	187,803
Slovak Republic	10,969	61,792	10,658	61,806	−14	−1,837	93	−959	390	−2,810	3,863	1,804
Slovenia	10,377	28,542	10,749	27,980	201	−1,081	95	−202	−75	−720	1,821	1,078
Somalia	..	..	..	..	..	..	..	..	..	..	..	..
South Africa	34,402	78,563	33,375	80,816	−2,875	−6,389	−645	−2,684	−2,493	−11,327	4,464	39,603
Spain	133,910	346,893	135,000	374,259	−5,402	−42,120	4,525	−10,889	−1,967	−80,375	40,531	28,051
Sri Lanka	4,617	8,977	5,982	11,708	−137	−488	732	3,005	−770	−215	2,112	5,354
Sudan	681	8,226	1,238	11,212	−3	−2,402	60	1,480	−500	−3,908	163	1,094
Swaziland	1,020	1,860	1,274	2,344	81	−123	144	192	−30	−414	298	959
Sweden	95,525	194,516	81,142	165,275	−6,473	7,303	−2,970	−5,083	4,940	31,460	25,870	47,255
Switzerland	123,320	280,162	108,916	243,800	10,708	14,922	−4,409	−12,312	20,703	38,972	68,620	134,566
Syrian Arab Republic	5,757	19,374	5,541	19,309	−560	−1,149	607	1,150	263	66	448	18,300
Tajikistan	..	1,218	..	3,062	..	−71	..	1,735	..	−180	39	..
Tanzania	1,265	5,219	2,139	7,543	−110	−175	395	683	−590	−1,816	270	3,470
Thailand	70,292	180,653	82,246	155,777	−2,114	−7,499	487	4,484	−13,582	21,861	36,939	138,419
Timor-Leste	..	..	..	..	..	..	..	..	..	..	..	250
Togo	465	1,136	671	1,666	−34	−15	118	324	−122	−222	130	703
Trinidad and Tobago	2,799	19,622	2,110	9,948	−390	−1,202	−4	47	294	8,519	379	9,245
Tunisia	7,979	19,917	8,811	21,091	−716	−2,011	774	1,951	−774	−1,234	1,689	11,294
Turkey	36,581	142,865	40,113	151,453	−3,204	−8,121	4,398	2,299	−2,338	−14,410	13,891	74,933
Turkmenistan	1,774	..	1,796	..	17	..	5	..	0	..	1,168	..
Uganda	664	3,954	1,490	5,210	−96	−329	639	1,133	−281	−451	459	2,994
Ukraine	17,090	54,253	18,280	56,206	−434	−2,440	472	2,661	−1,152	−1,732	1,069	26,501
United Arab Emirates	..	..	..	..	..	..	..	..	..	..	7,778	36,104
United Kingdom	322,114	595,914	327,000	650,834	3,393	40,655	−11,943	−22,786	−13,436	−37,050	49,144	66,550
United States	794,397	1,570,797	890,784	1,945,705	20,899	121,418	−38,073	−124,944	−113,561	−378,435	175,996	404,099
Uruguay	3,507	8,557	3,568	7,794	−227	−689	76	140	−213	215	1,813	8,038
Uzbekistan	..	..	..	..	..	..	..	..	..	..	..	..
Venezuela, RB	20,753	59,600	16,905	48,064	−1,943	−2,652	109	−323	2,014	8,561	10,715	34,318
Vietnam	9,498	62,752	12,334	72,446	−384	−3,028	1,200	6,448	−2,020	−6,274	1,324	16,447
West Bank and Gaza	764	1,168	2,789	4,962	607	911	435	3,418	−984	535	..	..
Yemen, Rep.	2,160	7,092	2,471	10,001	−561	−1,171	1,056	1,515	184	−2,565	638	6,990
Zambia	1,222	4,560	1,338	4,119	−249	−1,363	182	516	−182	−406	223	1,892
Zimbabwe	2,344	..	2,515	..	−294	..	40	..	−425	..	888	..
World	6,395,661 t	15,641,184 t	6,248,111 t	15,144,783 t	..	..	..	..	..	..	..	..
Low income	29,028	104,191	46,738	149,627	..	..	..	..	..	..	..	..
Middle income	1,087,422	4,483,392	1,137,135	4,125,043	..	..	..	..	..	..	..	..
Lower middle income	492,428	2,563,013	532,363	2,390,741	..	..	..	..	..	..	..	..
Upper middle income	594,996	1,906,819	604,453	1,722,447	..	..	..	..	..	..	..	..
Low & middle income	1,115,105	4,583,161	1,182,581	4,271,461	..	..	..	..	..	..	..	..
East Asia & Pacific	397,583	1,969,911	413,806	1,684,481	..	..	..	..	..	..	..	..
Europe & Central Asia	193,610	795,858	205,686	759,347	..	..	..	..	..	..	..	..
Latin America & Carib.	273,265	796,196	288,584	781,728	..	..	..	..	..	..	..	..
Middle East & N. Africa	..	..	106,423	334,137	..	..	..	..	..	..	..	..
South Asia	58,893	310,779	78,652	407,949	..	..	..	..	..	..	..	..
Sub-Saharan Africa	89,266	296,829	99,774	327,513	..	..	..	..	..	..	..	..
High income	5,304,481	11,224,885	5,072,079	11,020,075	..	..	..	..	..	..	..	..
Euro area	2,100,300	4,450,297	1,977,018	4,275,187	..	..	..	..	..	..	..	..

a. International reserves including gold valued at London gold price. b. Includes Luxembourg.

The balance of payments records an economy's transactions with the rest of the world. Balance of payments accounts are divided into two groups: the current account, which records transactions in goods, services, income, and current transfers, and the capital and financial account, which records capital transfers, acquisition or disposal of nonproduced, nonfinancial assets, and transactions in financial assets and liabilities. The table presents data from the current account plus gross international reserves.

The balance of payments is a double-entry accounting system that shows all flows of goods and services into and out of an economy; all transfers that are the counterpart of real resources or financial claims provided to or by the rest of the world without a quid pro quo, such as donations and grants; and all changes in residents' claims on and liabilities to nonresidents that arise from economic transactions. All transactions are recorded twice—once as a credit and once as a debit. In principle the net balance should be zero, but in practice the accounts often do not balance, requiring inclusion of a balancing item, net errors and omissions.

Discrepancies may arise in the balance of payments because there is no single source for balance of payments data and therefore no way to ensure that the data are fully consistent. Sources include customs data, monetary accounts of the banking system, external debt records, information provided by enterprises, surveys to estimate service transactions, and foreign exchange records. Differences in collection methods—such as in timing, definitions of residence and ownership, and the exchange rate used to value transactions—contribute to net errors and omissions. In addition, smuggling and other illegal or quasi-legal transactions may be unrecorded or misrecorded. For further discussion of issues relating to the recording of data on trade in goods and services, see *About the data* for tables 4.4–4.7.

The concepts and definitions underlying the data in the table are based on the fifth edition of the International Monetary Fund's (IMF) *Balance of Payments Manual* (1993). That edition redefined as capital transfers some transactions previously included in the current account, such as debt forgiveness, migrants' capital transfers, and foreign aid to acquire capital goods. Thus the current account balance now reflects more accurately net current transfer receipts in addition to transactions in goods, services (previously nonfactor services), and income (previously factor income). Many countries maintain their data collection systems according to the fourth edition of the *Balance of Payments Manual* (1977). Where necessary, the IMF converts such reported data to conform to the fifth edition (see *Primary data documentation*). Values are in U.S. dollars converted at market exchange rates.

• **Exports** and **imports of goods and services** are all transactions between residents of an economy and the rest of the world involving a change in ownership of general merchandise, goods sent for processing and repairs, nonmonetary gold, and services. • **Net income** is receipts and payments of employee compensation for nonresident workers, and investment income (receipts and payments on direct investment, portfolio investment, and other investments and receipts on reserve assets). Income derived from the use of intangible assets is recorded under business services. • **Net current transfers** are recorded in the balance of payments whenever an economy provides or receives goods, services, income, or financial items without a quid pro quo. All transfers not considered to be capital are current. • **Current account balance** is the sum of net exports of goods and services, net income, and net current transfers. • **Total reserves** are holdings of monetary gold, special drawing rights, reserves of IMF members held by the IMF, and holdings of foreign exchange under the control of monetary authorities. The gold component of these reserves is valued at year-end (December 31) London prices ($386.75 an ounce in 1995 and $1,087.50 an ounce in 2009).

Top 15 economies with the largest reserves in 2009 — 4.17a

	Total reserves ($ billions)		Share of world total (%)	Annual change (%)	Months of imports
	2008	2009	2009	2008–09	2009
China	1,966	2,453	26.1	24.8	25.0
Japan	1,031	1,049	11.2	1.8	18.1
Russian Federation	426	439	4.7	3.0	16.1
Saudi Arabia	451	421	4.5	−6.7	29.4
United States	294	404	4.3	37.4	2.0
Taiwan, China	304	363	3.9	19.6	20.7
India	257	285	3.0	10.6	9.8
Korea, Rep.	202	270	2.9	34.2	8.0
Hong Kong SAR, China	183	256	2.7	40.2	6.3
Brazil	194	239	2.5	23.1	13.2
Singapore	174	188	2.0	7.8	5.9
Germany	139	179	1.9	29.1	1.5
Algeria	148	155	1.7	4.7	..
Thailand	111	138	1.5	24.7	9.8
Switzerland	74	135	1.4	81.6	5.0

Source: International Monetary Fund, International Financial Statistics data files.

Data on the balance of payments are published in the IMF's *Balance of Payments Statistics Yearbook* and *International Financial Statistics*. The World Bank exchanges data with the IMF through electronic files that in most cases are more timely and cover a longer period than the published sources. More information about the design and compilation of the balance of payments can be found in the IMF's *Balance of Payments Manual*, fifth edition (1993), *Balance of Payments Textbook* (1996), and *Balance of Payments Compilation Guide* (1995).

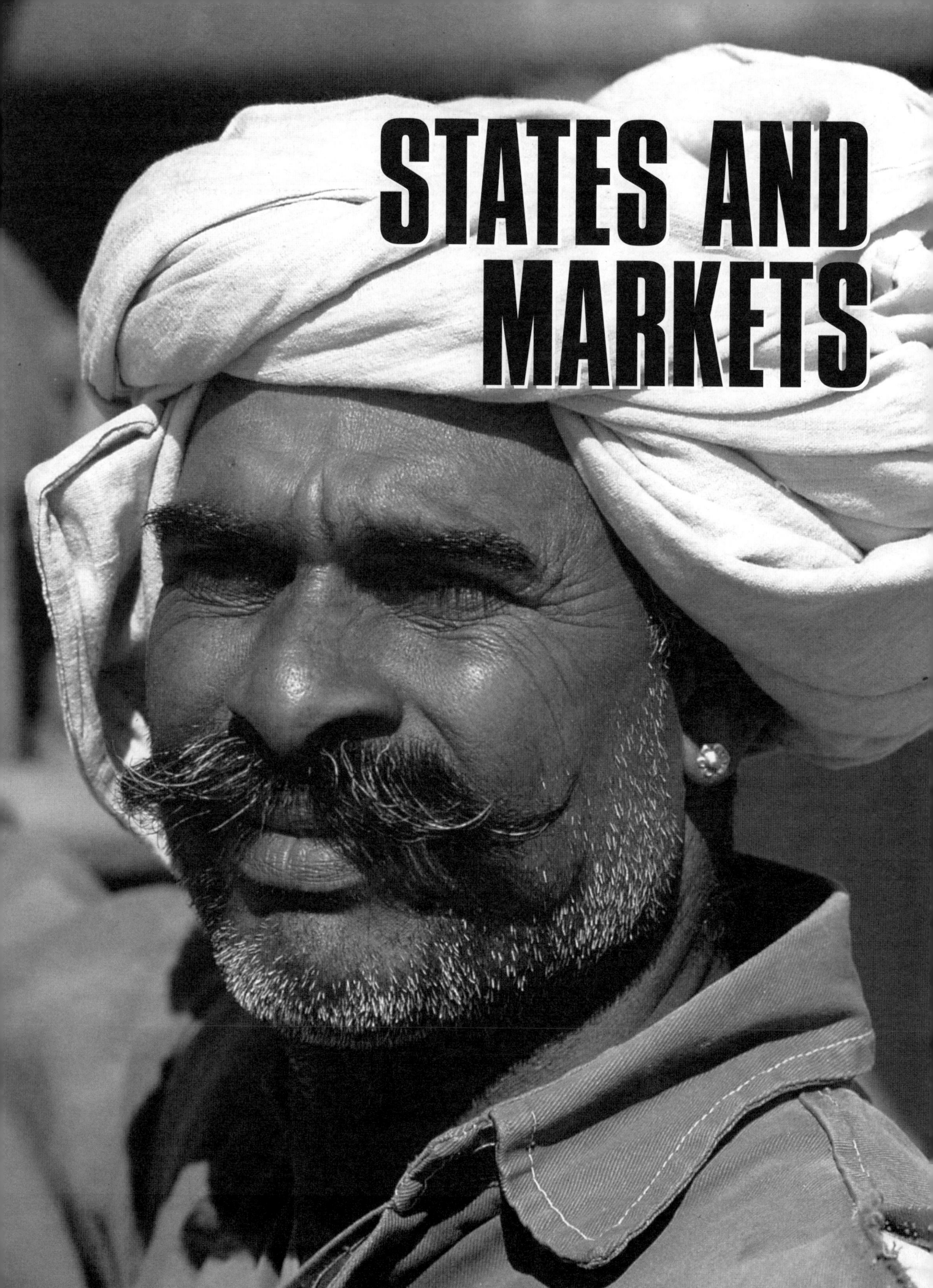

STATES AND MARKETS

N ew firm creation recently declined sharply in most countries, according to the 2010 World Bank Group Entrepreneurial Snapshots. The economic and financial crisis that began in 2008 increased unemployment in many countries, and the fight against poverty could be hampered as spending for human and productive capital is strained. Governments around the world face fiscal deficits and pressure to improve public spending and accelerate business reforms. Partnership between the private sector, which employs people and makes investments, and a capable public sector, which creates a stable regulatory environment, is a key ingredient to successful development.

This section includes a range of indicators showing how effective and accountable government, together with a vibrant private sector, produces employment opportunities and services that empower poor people. Its 13 tables cover cross-cutting themes: private sector development, public sector policies, infrastructure, information, communications, telecommunications, and science and technology. New data show that business reforms are making it easier to do business and create new firms and that more-inclusive financial systems are removing barriers to economic growth and development.

Businesses are created faster in a good business environment

The World Bank Group Entrepreneurship Snapshots (www.enterprisesurveys.org), which cover 112 countries, show that new businesses are created faster in countries with good governance, low corporate taxes, minimal red tape, and a strong legal and regulatory environment. Countries with well developed financial markets also have higher new firm creation than countries with less developed financial markets. The downside is that countries with well developed financial markets also had steeper declines in new firm creation during the recent financial and economic crisis, probably due to the credit crunch. High-income countries created more new limited liability firms—more than 4 per 1,000 working-age people, compared with only about 0.3 in low-income countries. Data on business entry and density are in table 5.1.

The Doing Business database (www.doing business.org) shows that between June 2009 and May 2010, 117 countries adopted 216 business regulation reforms, making it easier to start and operate businesses, strengthening property rights, and improving commercial dispute resolution and bankruptcy procedures. Using data from the Enterprise Snapshots and Doing Business to analyze whether some reforms are more important than others, Klapper and Love (2010a) find that small reforms that reduce costs, time, or number of procedures to register a business by less than 40 percent do not have a significant impact on new firm registration. This suggests that "token" reforms do not boost private sector activity and that countries with weak business environments require larger reforms to increase new firm registration. They find that two reforms occurring simultaneously tend to have more impact than two reforms occuring sequentially over a longer period.

Forty countries made it easier to pay taxes between 2009 and 2010

The World Bank's Doing Business project collects information for 183 countries on tax payments, time spent paying taxes, and the total tax rate borne by a standard firm. In cooperation with Pricewaterhouse-Coopers, the project collects information on business tax systems around the world, allowing governments to benchmark their tax system with others to identify good practices, and researchers to analyze the impact of higher corporate tax rates on business start-ups and investments.

Over June 2009–May 2010, 40 countries made tax compliance easier, reducing costs for firms and encouraging job creation. Higher tax compliance costs are associated with larger informal sectors and more corruption, ultimately limiting employment, investment, and growth. Keeping rules simple

and clear improves compliance and reduces tax evasion. And better compliance keeps the system working and supports government programs and services.

In the past six years more than 60 percent of the countries covered by the Doing Business project made paying taxes easier or lowered the tax burden for local enterprises. Countries that make paying taxes easy for domestic firms usually offer electronic systems for tax filing and payment, have one tax per tax base, and use a filing system based on self-assessment. In high-income countries the average business spends about 180 hours a year preparing, filing, and paying taxes; in Latin America and the Caribbean, more than 400 hours a year (figure 5a).

Previous editions of *World Development Indicators* included data on the highest marginal corporate tax rate (the statutory rate of corporate income tax). It is not a comprehensive indicator of the amount of tax a company pays, however, because it is only one of the many taxes businesses pay. Generous tax allowances in some countries significantly reduce the corporate income tax paid, while disallowances in others can increase the effective rate.

In this year's edition table 5.6 on tax policies includes the total business tax rate as a percent of commercial profit, with details on corporate taxes, labor taxes paid by the employer, social contributions, and other taxes. The total tax rate is a comprehensive measure of the cost of all the taxes a business bears. It differs from the statutory tax rate, which merely provides the factor to be applied to the tax base. In computing the total tax rate, tax payable is divided by commercial profit. The total tax rate is lowest in East Asia and Pacific and is highest in Sub-Saharan Africa (figure 5b). Note that these tax rates are "de jure" tax rates based on case studies of a "standardized business" as defined by the Doing Business project.

Benchmarking the quality of the business environment— Doing Business and Enterprise Surveys are complementary

The World Bank's Enterprise Surveys are based on firm-level surveys of a representative sample of the nonagricultural private sector in a country. The surveys cover a broad range of business environment topics including corruption, infrastructure, crime, competition, performance measures, and access to finance. Data from Enterprise Surveys are presented in table 5.2.

The Doing Business project uses indicator sets and rankings to measure business regulations and quantify the ease of doing business across countries. The indicators cover common transactions such as starting a business or registering property based on standardized case studies. Data are collected through surveys of local experts on business transactions and reflect the country's laws and regulations. Data on Doing Business indicators are in tables 5.3 and 5.6.

Box 5c compares the data sources, coverage, and information collected by Enterprise Surveys and the Doing Business project.

About half the world's households do not have deposit accounts in formal financial institutions

Financial exclusion is a barrier to economic development. Evidence from household surveys indicates that access to basic financial

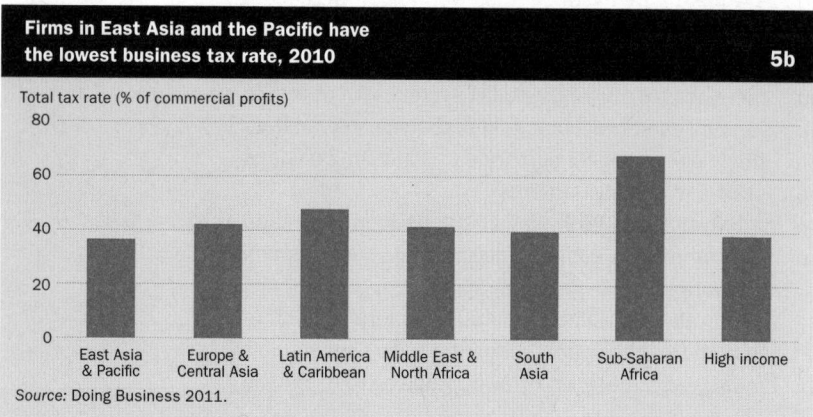

The average business in Latin America and the Caribbean spends about 400 hours a year in preparing, filing, and paying business taxes, 2009 — **5a**

Time to prepare, file, and pay taxes (hours a year)

Source: Doing Business 2011.

Firms in East Asia and the Pacific have the lowest business tax rate, 2010 — **5b**

Total tax rate (% of commercial profits)

Source: Doing Business 2011.

services such as savings, payments, and credit can make an important difference in poor people's lives. For firms, lack of access to finance is often the main obstacle to growth. In an increasingly digitized and globalized world many countries are promoting access to financial services—from establishing a credit facility for indigenous farmers in rural areas to introducing broad consumer protection legislation.

Although financial inclusion mandates, from consumer protection to rural finance promotion, are on the agenda of many financial regulators, insufficient authority and resources to provide broad financial access limit implementation capacity in many developing countries. Nevertheless, more than 70 percent of financial regulators in developing countries have programs to protect consumers, and almost 60 percent promote financial literacy.

Five new financial indicators from *Financial Access 2010* (www.cgap.org/financialindicators) are included in table 5.5 this year: commercial bank deposits, commercial bank loans, commercial bank branches, automated teller machines (ATMs), and point-of-sale terminals.

Although many nonbank institutions (cooperatives, specialized state financial institutions, and microfinance institutions) provide financial services, the most complete information available to central banks and financial regulators is on commercial banks, which account for 85 percent of deposits and 96 percent of accounts. Although financial inclusion, measured as people with commercial bank accounts, is high in some developing country regions such as East Asia and Pacific, it remains low in Sub-Saharan Africa (figure 5d).

Access to deposit and credit services varies by region. Access is greater in countries with higher incomes, better infrastructure, and a well functioning legal environment. People without access to bank accounts and credit from regulated institutions have to rely on informal nonregulated financial services, often more costly and less reliable. Low- and middle-income countries lag behind high-income countries in the number of bank branches, ATMs, and point-of-sale terminals, but the number of ATMs exceeds the number of bank branches in low-income countries. And new technology, including the expansion of electronic payments through mobile and Internet banking, offer hope for bringing financial services to the unbanked.

Two approaches to collecting business environment data: Doing Business and Enterprise Surveys 5c

Topic	Enterprise Surveys	Doing Business
Global coverage	125 countries	183 countries
Data source	Collects firm-level data; face-to-face interview with owner or top manager. Businesses surveyed include manufacturing, retail, construction, transport, communications, and other services	Collects information through surveys administered by local experts (lawyers, accountants, and architects). The information is confirmed through the underlying laws and regulations
Number of observations	150–360 observations in smaller countries; 1,200–1,800 interviews in larger countries	Underlying laws and regulations in addition to an average of 39 surveys per country
Geographical coverage within a country	Main cities or regions of economic activity	Main (most populous) business city and subnational studies in other cities
Information gathered	Objective data on the business environment as experienced by firms, performance measures, firm characteristics, and perceptions regarding obstacles to growth	Time and cost to complete common business transactions based on standardized case studies; underlying laws and regulations
	Business characteristics; approximately 20 Investment climate topics	Standardized business; 10 business regulation topics
Examples of data	Hard data: number of days to obtain a construction permit. Soft data: opinion on whether access to land is an obstacle faced by the establishment	Hard data: laws and regulations, number of procedures, and costs to build a warehouse. Soft data: experts' estimates on the number of days required for each procedure
Inference from the data	Stratified random sampling design of the surveys, which ensures that data are representative of the universe of formal firms (with five or more employees)	Standardized case studies that relate to a common business situation, which makes comparisons and benchmarks valid across countries
	Measures what happens to existing firms—their actual experiences with investment climate issues such as payment of taxes. Also surveys obstacles to business growth	Expectations of a standardized firm following official legal requirements and costs. For instance, "paying taxes" measures the number of payments, time to file, and tax rates
	Measures what happens in practice in the normal course of business; for instance, whether a firm pays a bribe when obtaining an import license and the actual time it takes to obtain the license	Assumes that firms comply with all formal regulations and minimize information gathering time and that all regulations are enforced. Measures what would happen if the firm complied with all regulatory requirements in a lawful manner.
	Can be used to identify potential areas of reform in the business environment as well as assess the impact of reforms on businesses.	Can be used to identify areas for reform based on bottlenecks or weaknesses in specific areas of private sector regulation and learn from practices in other countries.

Source: Summary of www.enterprisesurveys.org/Methodology/Compare.aspx.

People living in developing countries of East Asia and Pacific have more commercial bank accounts than those in other developing country regions, 2009 5d

Deposit accounts in commercial banks (median per 1,000 adults)

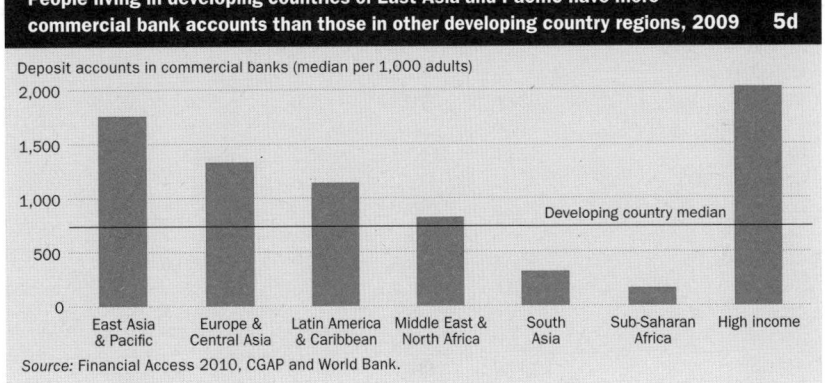

Source: Financial Access 2010, CGAP and World Bank.

	Investment commitments in infrastructure projects with private participation[a] $ millions								Domestic credit to private sector	Businesses registered	
	Telecommunications		Energy		Transport		Water and sanitation		% of GDP	New	Entry density
	2000–05	2006–09	2000–05	2006–09	2000–05	2006–09	2000–05	2006–09	2009	2009	2009
Afghanistan	466.1	1,040.4	1.6	..	..	..	..	..	9.1	..	..
Albania	569.2	670.0	790.6	664.0	308.0	..	8.0	0.0	37.0	2,045	0.84
Algeria	3,422.5	1,925.0	962.0	2,320.0	120.9	269.0	510.0	1,572.0	16.2	10,544	0.44
Angola	278.7	1,129.0	45.0	9.4	..	53.0	..	..	21.2	..	..
Argentina	5,836.8	5,033.6	3,826.9	3,479.0	203.6	1,402.6	791.6	..	13.5	11,924	0.46
Armenia	317.1	488.8	74.0	127.0	63.0	715.0	0.0	0.0	23.1	2,698	1.28
Australia	..	..	..	..	..	..	..	..	127.8	89,960	6.38
Austria	..	..	..	..	..	..	..	..	126.9	3,228	0.58
Azerbaijan	355.6	1,283.5	375.2	..	..	..	0.0	..	19.6	5,314	0.93
Bangladesh	1,294.3	3,729.8	501.5	243.5	0.0	0.0	..	..	41.5	..	..
Belarus	735.4	2,219.2	..	1,875.0	..	4.0	..	..	37.3	5,508	0.80
Belgium	..	..	..	..	..	..	..	..	97.9	29,548	4.28
Benin	116.9	399.7	590.0	..	..	..	..	..	22.2	..	..
Bolivia	520.5	284.7	884.4	137.3	16.6	..	..	..	37.0	2,504	0.43
Bosnia and Herzegovina	0.0	1,086.6	..	800.0	..	..	..	..	57.3	1,896	0.58
Botswana	104.0	183.9	..	..	..	..	..	..	25.5	..	..
Brazil	41,053.8	31,121.4	26,171.6	46,690.5	3,398.4	22,086.9	1,234.4	1,365.4	54.0	315,645	2.38
Bulgaria	2,179.1	1,866.5	3,253.5	2,246.7	2.1	536.2	152.0	..	75.6	35,545	7.20
Burkina Faso	41.9	680.6	..	..	..	..	..	..	17.5	610	0.08
Burundi	53.6	0.0	..	..	..	..	..	..	21.7	..	..
Cambodia	136.1	436.9	82.1	695.8	125.3	40.1	..	..	24.5	2,003	0.22
Cameroon	394.4	701.4	91.8	440.0	0.0	..	..	0.0	11.3	..	..
Canada	..	..	..	..	..	..	..	..	128.6	174,000	7.56
Central African Republic	0.0	20.8	..	..	..	..	..	..	7.0	..	..
Chad	11.0	246.4	0.0	..	..	..	..	..	5.2	..	..
Chile	3,561.6	4,167.6	1,590.5	2,397.7	4,821.2	1,311.1	1,495.2	3.1	97.5	23,541	2.12
China	8,548.0	0.0	10,970.9	7,170.5	15,350.1	15,795.0	3,505.2	3,992.2	127.3	..	..
Hong Kong SAR, China	..	..	..	..	..	..	..	..	158.0	101,023	19.19
Colombia	1,570.9	5,294.7	351.6	944.6	1,005.4	2,344.4	314.3	305.0	29.9	31,132	1.07
Congo, Dem. Rep.	473.4	880.0	..	..	..	..	..	..	7.5	..	..
Congo, Rep.	61.8	330.7	..	..	..	735.0	0.0	..	4.8	..	..
Costa Rica	..	..	80.0	190.0	465.2	373.0	..	..	49.4	26,765	8.78
Côte d'Ivoire	134.9	885.4	0.0	0.0	176.4	..	..	0.0	17.1	..	..
Croatia	1,205.7	3,035.0	7.1	85.0	451.0	492.0	298.7	..	66.3	7,800	2.57
Cuba	60.0	0.0	116.0	60.0	0.0	..	600.0	..	..	..	..
Czech Republic	..	..	..	..	..	..	..	..	55.3	21,717	3.00
Denmark	..	..	..	..	..	..	..	..	231.6	16,519	4.57
Dominican Republic	393.0	220.1	1,306.6	0.0	898.9	879.9	..	..	21.3	12,881	2.13
Ecuador	357.8	1,764.7	302.0	129.0	685.0	766.0	510.0	..	25.3	..	..
Egypt, Arab Rep.	3,471.9	8,864.0	678.0	469.0	821.5	1,370.0	..	..	36.2	6,291	0.13
El Salvador	1,110.6	901.9	85.0	0.0	..	..	..	..	41.3	4,400	1.19
Eritrea	40.0	0.0	..	..	..	..	..	..	16.6	..	..
Estonia	..	..	..	..	..	..	..	..	110.2	7,199	8.10
Ethiopia	..	..	..	4.0	..	..	..	..	17.8	1,327	0.03
Finland	..	..	..	..	..	..	..	..	94.4	11,820	3.37
France	..	..	..	..	..	..	..	..	110.3	128,906	3.08
Gabon	26.6	278.8	0.0	0.0	177.4	3.9	..	..	10.1	3,490	4.27
Gambia, The	6.6	35.0	..	0.0	..	..	..	..	18.9	..	..
Georgia	173.8	612.2	40.0	634.2	..	573.0	..	435.0	31.2	7,226	2.32
Germany	..	..	..	..	..	..	..	..	112.3	64,840	1.19
Ghana	156.5	2,916.0	590.0	100.0	10.0	..	0.0	..	15.9	9,606	0.72
Greece	..	..	..	..	..	..	..	..	91.7	8,426	1.18
Guatemala	560.1	1,511.4	110.0	263.8	..	..	..	6.7	25.4	5,133	0.68
Guinea	50.6	242.2	..	..	..	159.0	..	..	..	..	..
Guinea-Bissau	21.9	96.4	..	..	..	..	..	..	5.6	..	..
Haiti	18.0	306.0	5.5	..	..	..	..	0.0	14.5	..	..
Honduras	135.0	930.5	358.8	..	120.0	..	207.9	..	52.6	..	..

Private sector in the economy

	Investment commitments in infrastructure projects with private participation[a]								Domestic credit to private sector	Businesses registered	
	$ millions						Water and sanitation		% of GDP	New	Entry density
	Telecommunications		Energy		Transport						
	2000–05	2006–09	2000–05	2006–09	2000–05	2006–09	2000–05	2006–09	2009	2009	2009
Hungary	5,172.8	1,523.3	851.6	1,707.0	3,297.5	1,588.0	0.0	0.0	71.3	42,951	6.26
India	20,030.5	33,682.4	8,369.2	50,754.4	4,172.2	23,012.8	112.9	241.7	46.8	84,800	0.12
Indonesia	6,557.2	9,748.1	1,860.5	3,779.3	159.2	1,731.5	44.8	20.2	27.6	28,998	0.18
Iran, Islamic Rep.	695.0	1,506.0	650.0	..	..	..	..	..	36.7	..	..
Iraq	984.0	4,521.0	..	590.0	..	..	..	..	6.4	..	..
Ireland	..	..	..	..	..	..	..	..	230.3	13,188	4.67
Israel	..	..	..	..	..	..	..	..	84.5	19,758	4.46
Italy	..	..	..	..	..	..	..	..	110.8	68,508	1.78
Jamaica	700.3	301.6	201.0	78.0	565.0	..	..	..	28.5	2,003	1.16
Japan	..	..	..	..	..	..	..	..	171.0	105,698	1.28
Jordan	1,589.0	648.6	..	989.0	0.0	1,380.0	169.0	951.0	71.7	2,737	0.74
Kazakhstan	1,153.7	3,170.2	300.0	0.0	231.0	31.0	..	..	50.3	27,978	2.59
Kenya	1,434.0	2,973.8	..	332.7	..	404.0	..	..	31.5	17,896	0.85
Korea, Dem. Rep.	..	400.0	..	..	..	..	..	..	..	..	..
Korea, Rep.	..	..	..	..	..	..	..	..	107.6	60,039	1.72
Kosovo	..	..	..	..	..	..	..	..	36.1	141	0.12
Kuwait	..	..	..	..	..	..	..	..	63.3	..	..
Kyrgyz Republic	11.5	115.9	..	..	..	..	0.0	..	15.1	4,412	1.26
Lao PDR	87.7	135.0	1,250.0	1,425.0	0.0	..	..	..	9.5	..	..
Latvia	700.0	468.1	158.1	184.0	..	135.0	..	..	107.8	7,175	4.62
Lebanon	138.1	0.0	..	..	153.0	..	0.0	..	73.9	..	..
Lesotho	88.4	30.6	0.0	..	..	..	..	..	13.5	..	..
Liberia	70.3	73.8	..	..	..	..	..	..	16.1	..	..
Libya	..	..	..	..	..	..	..	..	10.9	..	..
Lithuania	993.0	490.2	514.3	417.6	..	..	..	..	70.9	5,399	2.18
Macedonia, FYR	706.6	489.6	..	655.0	..	295.0	..	..	44.3	8,074	5.63
Madagascar	12.6	304.8	0.0	..	61.0	17.5	..	..	11.5	724	0.07
Malawi	36.3	197.7	0.0	..	..	..	..	..	14.2	619	0.08
Malaysia	3,777.0	1,700.0	6,637.6	384.5	4,263.0	1,379.0	6,502.2	0.0	117.1	41,638	2.55
Mali	82.6	583.0	365.9	..	55.4	..	..	..	17.4	..	..
Mauritania	92.1	133.1	..	..	..	..	..	..	..	..	..
Mauritius	413.0	102.1	0.0	..	..	..	..	0.0	85.1	6,626	7.33
Mexico	18,758.0	12,622.6	6,749.3	1,483.0	2,970.4	11,434.1	523.7	303.8	23.3	44,084	0.61
Moldova	46.1	392.3	227.2	68.0	0.0	60.0	..	..	36.2	4,180	1.32
Mongolia	22.1	0.0	..	..	..	..	..	..	43.9	..	..
Morocco	6,139.5	2,549.6	1,049.0	..	200.0	200.0	..	..	64.4	26,166	1.28
Mozambique	123.0	156.2	1,205.8	..	334.6	0.0	..	..	25.1	..	..
Myanmar	..	..	..	556.1	..	..	..	..	..	..	..
Namibia	35.0	8.5	1.0	..	..	..	0.0	..	46.8	..	..
Nepal	109.3	26.0	15.1	..	..	..	..	..	59.4	..	..
Netherlands	..	..	..	..	..	..	..	..	215.3	35,100	3.10
New Zealand	..	..	..	..	..	..	..	..	147.0	47,897	17.08
Nicaragua	218.5	380.1	126.3	95.0	104.0	..	..	..	34.4	..	..
Niger	85.5	251.7	..	..	..	..	3.4	..	12.2	24	0.00
Nigeria	6,949.7	11,348.1	1,920.0	280.0	2,355.4	644.1	..	..	37.6	65,089	0.79
Norway	..	..	..	..	..	..	..	..	..	13,805	4.49
Oman	..	..	..	..	..	..	..	..	49.0	3,165	1.67
Pakistan	6,594.9	8,706.5	375.4	4,058.2	112.8	923.7	..	..	23.5	2,759	0.03
Panama	211.4	1,224.0	449.3	576.7	51.4	0.0	..	..	85.7	548	0.26
Papua New Guinea	..	150.0	..	..	..	..	..	..	32.1	..	..
Paraguay	199.0	591.4	..	..	..	..	..	..	29.1	..	..
Peru	2,241.4	2,485.0	2,498.9	1,142.9	522.5	3,157.6	152.0	..	24.1	51,151	2.65
Philippines	4,616.4	4,177.0	3,428.4	9,463.3	943.5	678.9	0.0	530.5	30.3	11,435	0.19
Poland	16,800.1	7,750.0	2,620.5	2,475.4	1,672.0	3,642.3	64.3	0.8	52.9	14,434	0.52
Portugal	..	..	..	..	..	..	..	..	187.8	27,759	3.92
Puerto Rico	..	..	..	..	..	..	..	..	..	..	..
Qatar	..	..	..	..	..	..	..	..	51.5	..	..

	Investment commitments in infrastructure projects with private participation[a]								Domestic credit to private sector	Businesses registered	
	$ millions										
	Telecommunications		Energy		Transport		Water and sanitation		% of GDP	New	Entry density
	2000–05	2006–09	2000–05	2006–09	2000–05	2006–09	2000–05	2006–09	2009	2009	2009
Romania	3,906.9	4,188.9	1,240.8	6,288.7	..	116.8	116.0	41.0	47.1	56,698	3.66
Russian Federation	22,049.4	24,525.8	1,726.0	27,214.2	109.4	191.0	904.7	1,241.7	45.3	261,633	2.61
Rwanda	72.3	351.0	1.6	..	..	..	..	..	..	3,028	0.51
Saudi Arabia	..	..	..	..	..	..	..	..	52.1	..	..
Senegal	593.1	1,333.0	93.3	..	55.4	398.0	0.0	0.0	24.7	1,636	0.22
Serbia	563.5	3,297.4	..	..	..	..	..	0.0	42.2	9,715	1.94
Sierra Leone	48.8	111.2	..	1.2	..	..	..	..	9.3	..	..
Singapore	..	..	..	..	..	..	..	..	103.2	26,416	7.40
Slovak Republic	..	..	..	..	..	..	..	..	44.7	15,825	4.04
Slovenia	..	..	..	..	..	..	..	..	94.0	5,836	4.16
Somalia	13.4	0.0	..	..	..	..	..	..	..	..	..
South Africa	10,519.5	7,714.0	1,251.3	9.9	504.7	3,483.0	31.3	0.0	147.1	24,700	0.77
Spain	..	..	..	..	..	..	..	..	211.5	79,757	2.92
Sri Lanka	766.1	1,444.5	270.8	..	..	..	..	..	24.8	4,223	0.29
Sudan	747.7	1,748.3	..	..	..	30.0	..	120.7	12.3	..	..
Swaziland	27.7	48.3	..	..	..	..	..	..	25.0	..	..
Sweden	..	..	..	..	..	..	..	..	139.3	24,228	4.09
Switzerland	..	..	..	..	..	..	..	..	174.8	25,250	4.88
Syrian Arab Republic	583.0	307.7	..	..	..	82.0	..	..	20.3	..	..
Tajikistan	8.5	125.0	16.0	..	..	..	..	..	29.0	2,171	0.48
Tanzania	515.3	1,484.5	348.0	28.4	27.7	134.0	8.5	..	15.3	..	..
Thailand	5,602.7	3,106.0	4,693.3	2,341.0	939.0	..	522.7	18.8	116.3	27,520	0.59
Timor-Leste	0.0	0.0	..	..	..	..	..	..	18.6	..	..
Togo	0.0	44.0	657.7	190.0	..	..	..	..	21.9	125	0.04
Trinidad and Tobago	..	..	..	..	..	..	..	..	31.5	..	..
Tunisia	751.0	2,805.0	30.0	..	..	840.0	..	..	68.4	9,079	1.23
Turkey	12,788.6	12,068.7	6,754.8	8,862.7	3,118.6	4,138.5	..	..	36.5	44,472	0.87
Turkmenistan	20.0	158.1	..	..	..	..	..	..	..	..	..
Uganda	387.6	1,463.0	113.9	1,000.6	..	404.0	0.0	..	13.1	11,152	0.72
Ukraine	3,162.9	4,508.8	160.0	54.0	..	130.0	100.0	102.0	73.3	19,300	0.60
United Arab Emirates	..	..	..	..	..	..	..	..	93.0	..	..
United Kingdom	..	..	..	..	..	..	..	..	213.5	330,100	8.05
United States	..	..	..	..	..	..	..	..	202.9	..	..
Uruguay	114.2	158.5	330.0	..	251.1	..	368.0	..	20.6	4,664	2.08
Uzbekistan	285.6	942.1	..	..	..	25.0	0.0	..	..	14,428	0.78
Venezuela, RB	3,337.0	2,619.8	39.5	..	34.0	..	15.0	..	21.7	..	..
Vietnam	430.0	1,593.7	2,360.6	297.0	20.0	965.0	266.0	..	112.7	..	..
West Bank and Gaza	279.8	47.0	150.0	..	..	..	..	..	..	..	..
Yemen, Rep.	376.8	392.2	..	15.8	..	220.0	..	..	7.4	..	..
Zambia	208.3	624.0	3.0	..	15.6	..	0.0	..	12.0	5,509	0.88
Zimbabwe	72.0	343.0	..	..	..	..	..	..	..	..	..
World	.. s	.. s	.. s	.. s	.. s	.. s	.. s	.. s	**138.2 w**		
Low income	6,362.3	20,932.3	..	..	..	..	..	..	26.4		
Middle income	227,575.0	248,323.5	107,077.9	191,687.3	50,686.8	105,160.9	16,175.1	6,654.9	72.8		
Lower middle income	84,109.2	27,585.0	38,840.9	82,564.1	26,511.7	51,724.0	3,704.9	5,271.6	92.9		
Upper middle income	143,465.8	134,452.2	49,324.0	109,123.2	5,696.9	41,208.8	407.0	..	47.8		
Low & middle income	233,937.3	269,255.8	87,324.8	196,264.6	5,403.2	86,781.7	..	..	72.0		
East Asia & Pacific	29,862.2	4,662.0	31,290.4	26,112.4	21,800.1	20,589.5	10,840.9	4,561.7	117.1		
Europe & Central Asia	50,274.6	62,911.8	5,316.0	47,981.4	..	..	..	..	45.0		
Latin America & Carib.	81,401.1	72,021.9	45,682.0	57,940.1	16,150.3	43,755.5	2,516.1	..	40.8		
Middle East & N. Africa	13,435.4	23,566.1	..	..	..	..	..	..	34.5		
South Asia	29,314.5	48,647.1	9,533.6	55,257.1	4,285.0	23,936.5	112.9	241.7	43.5		
Sub-Saharan Africa	24,654.4	40,481.6	..	..	..	..	..	..	65.1		
High income	..	..	..	..	..	..	..	..	165.1		
Euro area	..	..	..	..	..	..	..	..	133.0		

a. Data refer to total for the period shown. Includes infrastructure projects with private sector participation that reached financial closure in 1990–2009.

About the data

Private sector development and investment—tapping private sector initiative and investment for socially useful purposes—are critical for poverty reduction. In parallel with public sector efforts, private investment, especially in competitive markets, has tremendous potential to contribute to growth. Private markets are the engine of productivity growth, creating productive jobs and higher incomes. And with government playing a complementary role of regulation, funding, and service provision, private initiative and investment can help provide the basic services and conditions that empower poor people—by improving health, education, and infrastructure.

Investment in infrastructure projects with private participation has made important contributions to easing fiscal constraints, improving the efficiency of infrastructure services, and extending delivery to poor people. Developing countries have been in the forefront, pioneering better approaches to infrastructure services and reaping the benefits of greater competition and customer focus.

The data on investment in infrastructure projects with private participation refer to all investment (public and private) in projects in which a private company assumes operating risk during the operating period or development and operating risk during the contract period. Investment refers to commitments not disbursements. Foreign state-owned companies are considered private entities for the purposes of this measure.

Investments are classified into two types: investments in physical assets—the resources a company commits to invest in expanding and modernizing facilities—and payments to the government to acquire state-owned enterprises or rights to provide services in a specific area or to use part of the radio spectrum.

The data are from the World Bank's Private Participation in Infrastructure (PPI) Project database, which tracks infrastructure projects with private participation in developing countries. It provides information on more than 4,600 infrastructure projects in 137 developing economies from 1984 to 2009. The database contains more than 30 fields per project record, including country, financial closure year, infrastructure services provided, type of private participation, investment, technology, capacity, project location, contract duration, private sponsors, bidding process, and development bank support. Data on the projects are compiled from publicly available information. The database aims to be as comprehensive as possible, but some projects—particularly those

involving local and small-scale operators—may be omitted because they are not publicly reported. The database is a joint product of the World Bank's Finance, Economics, and Urban Development Department and the Public-Private Infrastructure Advisory Facility. Geographic and income aggregates are calculated by the World Bank's Development Data Group. For more information, see http://ppi.worldbank.org/.

Credit is an important link in money transmission; it finances production, consumption, and capital formation, which in turn affect economic activity. The data on domestic credit to the private sector are taken from the banking survey of the International Monetary Fund's (IMF) *International Financial Statistics* or, when unavailable, from its monetary survey. The monetary survey includes monetary authorities (the central bank), deposit money banks, and other banking institutions, such as finance companies, development banks, and savings and loan institutions. Credit to the private sector may sometimes include credit to state-owned or partially state-owned enterprises.

Entrepreneurship is essential to the dynamism of the modern market economy, and a greater entry rate of new businesses can foster competition and economic growth. The table includes data on business registrations from the 2008 World Bank Group Entrepreneurship Survey, which includes entrepreneurial activity in more than 100 countries for 2000–08. Survey data are used to analyze firm creation, its relationship to economic growth and poverty reduction, and the impact of regulatory and institutional reforms. The 2008 survey improves on earlier surveys' methodology and country coverage for better cross-country comparability. Data on total and newly registered businesses were collected directly from national registrars of companies. For cross-country comparability, only limited liability corporations that operate in the formal sector are included. For additional information on sources, methodology, calculation of entrepreneurship rates, and data limitations see http://econ.worldbank.org/research/entrepreneurship.

Definitions

• **Investment commitments in infrastructure projects with private participation** refers to infrastructure projects in telecommunications, energy (electricity and natural gas transmission and distribution), transport, and water and sanitation that have reached financial closure and directly or indirectly serve the public. Incinerators, movable assets, standalone solid waste projects, and small projects such as windmills are excluded. Included are operation and management contracts, concessions (operation and management contracts with major capital expenditure), greenfield projects (new facilities built and operated by a private entity or a public-private joint venture), and divestitures. Investment commitments are the sum of investments in physical assets and payments to the government. Investments in physical assets are resources the project company commits to invest during the contract period in new facilities or in expansion and modernization of existing facilities. Payments to the government are the resources the project company spends on acquiring government assets such as state-owned enterprises, rights to provide services in a specific area, or use of specific radio spectrums. • **Domestic credit to private sector** is financial resources provided to the private sector—such as through loans, purchases of nonequity securities, and trade credits and other accounts receivable—that establish a claim for repayment. For some countries these claims include credit to public enterprises. • **New businesses registered** are the number of limited liability corporations registered in the calendar year. • **Entry density** is the number of newly registered limited liability corporations per 1,000 people ages 15–64.

Data sources

Data on investment commitments in infrastructure projects with private participation are from the World Bank's PPI Project database (http://ppi.worldbank.org). Data on domestic credit are from the IMF's *International Financial Statistics.* Data on business registration are from the World Bank's Entrepreneurship Survey and database (http://econ.worldbank.org/research/entrepreneurship).

	Survey year	Regulations and tax		Permits and licenses	Corruption	Crime	Informality	Gender	Finance	Infrastructure	Innovation	Trade	Workforce
		Time dealing with officials % of management time	Average number of times meeting with tax officials	Time required to obtain operating license days	Informal payments to public officials % of firms	Losses due to theft, robbery, vandalism, and arson % of sales	Firms formally registered when operations started % of firms	Firms with female participation in ownership % of firms	Firms using banks to finance investment % of firms	Value lost due to electrical outages % of sales	Internationally recognized quality certification ownership % of firms	Average time to clear direct exports through customs days	Firms offering formal training[a] % of firms
Afghanistan	2008	6.8	1.2	13.8	41.5	1.5	88.0	2.8	1.4	6.5	8.5	14.6	14.6
Albania	2007	18.7	3.9	21.2	57.7	0.5	89.4	10.8	12.4	13.7	24.6	1.9	19.9
Algeria	2007	25.1	2.3	19.3	64.7	0.9	98.3	15.0	8.9	4.0	5.0	14.1	17.3
Angola	2006	7.1	3.3	24.1	46.8	0.4	..	23.4	2.1	3.7	5.1	16.5	19.4
Argentina	2006	13.8	2.2	78.3	18.7	1.5	93.8	30.3	6.9	1.6	26.9	5.5	52.2
Armenia	2009	10.3	2.1	20.0	11.6	0.6	96.2	31.8	31.9	1.8	26.9	3.3	30.4
Australia		..	..	..	..	..	..	..	..	..	..	..	..
Austria		..	..	..	..	..	..	..	..	..	..	..	..
Azerbaijan	2009	3.0	2.1	15.8	32.0	0.3	85.1	10.8	19.0	1.8	18.2	1.9	10.5
Bangladesh	2007	3.2	1.3	6.0	85.1	0.1	..	16.1	24.7	10.6	7.8	8.4	16.2
Belarus	2008	13.6	1.1	38.2	13.5	0.4	98.5	52.9	35.8	0.8	13.9	2.6	44.4
Belgium		..	..	..	..	..	..	..	..	..	..	..	..
Benin	2009	20.7	1.2	64.3	54.5	1.9	87.9	43.9	4.2	7.5	7.3	9.6	32.4
Bolivia	2006	13.5	1.7	26.0	32.4	0.9	90.5	41.1	22.2	4.4	13.8	15.3	53.9
Bosnia and Herzegovina	2009	11.2	1.0	21.4	8.1	0.2	98.6	32.8	59.7	1.9	30.1	1.4	66.5
Botswana	2006	5.0	0.9	13.7	27.6	1.3	..	40.9	11.3	1.4	12.7	1.4	37.7
Brazil	2009	18.7	1.2	83.5	9.7	1.7	95.8	59.3	48.4	3.0	25.7	15.9	52.9
Bulgaria	2009	10.6	2.2	20.8	8.5	0.5	98.5	33.9	34.7	1.6	19.9	4.2	30.7
Burkina Faso	2009	22.2	1.5	35.8	8.5	0.3	77.7	19.2	25.6	5.8	14.4	7.4	24.8
Burundi	2006	5.7	1.8	27.3	56.5	1.1	..	34.8	12.3	10.7	7.1	..	22.1
Cambodia	2007	5.6	1.0	..	61.2	0.0	87.5	..	11.3	2.4	2.8	1.5	48.4
Cameroon	2009	7.0	4.4	30.0	50.8	1.7	82.1	15.7	31.4	4.9	20.4	15.1	25.5
Canada		..	..	..	..	..	..	..	..	..	..	..	..
Central African Republic		..	..	..	..	..	..	..	..	..	..	..	..
Chad	2009	20.8	3.4	24.3	41.8	2.5	77.1	40.1	4.2	3.3	43.3	11.9	43.4
Chile	2006	9.0	3.0	67.7	8.2	0.6	97.8	27.8	29.1	1.8	22.0	5.8	46.9
China	2003	18.3	14.4	11.6	72.6	0.1	..	..	28.8	1.3	35.9	6.6	84.8
Hong Kong SAR, China		..	..	..	..	..	..	..	..	..	..	..	..
Colombia	2006	14.3	0.6	28.2	8.2	0.7	85.6	43.0	30.6	2.3	5.9	7.0	39.5
Congo, Dem. Rep.	2010	29.4	8.0	40.0	65.7	1.8	61.9	38.9	6.7	22.7	8.5	18.0	24.1
Congo, Rep.	2009	6.0	2.7	..	49.2	3.3	84.3	31.8	7.7	16.4	19.6	..	37.5
Costa Rica	2005	9.6	0.5	..	33.8	0.4	..	65.3	14.9	1.9	10.5	3.5	46.4
Côte d'Ivoire	2009	1.8	3.6	14.5	30.6	3.4	56.4	61.9	13.9	5.0	4.3	16.6	19.1
Croatia	2007	10.9	0.7	26.5	14.5	0.2	98.1	33.5	60.0	0.8	16.5	1.3	28.0
Cuba		..	..	..	..	..	..	..	..	..	..	..	..
Czech Republic	2009	10.4	1.5	19.9	8.7	0.4	98.0	25.0	33.4	0.6	43.5	5.7	70.7
Denmark		..	..	..	..	..	..	..	..	..	..	..	..
Dominican Republic	2005	8.8	0.5	..	26.3	0.7	..	..	12.5	15.2	9.6	11.4	53.3
Ecuador	2006	17.3	0.6	19.9	21.5	0.9	91.1	32.7	24.0	2.7	18.2	7.0	61.6
Egypt, Arab Rep.	2008	8.8	3.4	90.6	15.2	3.0	14.3	34.0	5.6	3.4	21.1	6.2	21.7
El Salvador	2006	9.2	2.7	35.4	34.3	2.6	79.5	39.6	17.3	2.9	11.0	2.5	49.6
Eritrea	2009	0.5	0.2	..	0.0	0.0	100.0	4.2	11.9	0.2	15.1	9.6	26.1
Estonia	2009	5.5	0.4	8.3	1.6	0.9	97.4	36.3	41.5	0.5	21.2	1.8	69.3
Ethiopia	2006	3.8	1.1	11.4	12.4	1.4	..	30.9	11.0	0.9	4.2	4.3	38.2
Finland		..	..	..	..	..	..	..	..	..	..	..	..
France		..	..	..	..	..	..	..	..	..	..	..	..
Gabon	2009	2.8	15.2	12.1	26.1	0.4	63.7	33.1	6.3	1.7	18.6	3.8	30.9
Gambia, The	2006	7.3	2.5	8.4	52.4	2.7	..	21.3	7.6	11.8	22.2	5.0	25.6
Georgia	2008	2.1	0.6	11.8	4.1	0.7	99.6	40.8	38.2	1.4	16.0	3.8	14.5
Germany	2005	1.2	1.3	..	..	0.5	..	20.3	45.0	..	..	4.7	35.4
Ghana	2007	4.0	4.1	6.4	38.8	0.9	66.4	44.0	16.0	6.0	6.8	7.8	33.0
Greece	2005	1.8	1.7	..	21.6	0.0	..	24.4	25.9	..	11.7	5.5	20.0
Guatemala	2006	9.2	2.1	75.4	15.7	1.5	91.3	28.4	12.8	4.5	8.0	4.5	28.1
Guinea	2006	2.7	2.8	13.0	84.8	2.0	..	25.4	0.9	14.0	5.2	4.3	21.1
Guinea-Bissau	2006	2.9	3.4	30.4	62.7	1.1	..	19.9	0.7	5.3	8.4	5.6	12.4
Haiti		..	..	..	..	..	..	..	..	..	..	..	..
Honduras	2006	4.6	1.5	31.6	16.7	2.2	89.4	39.9	8.5	3.8	16.5	6.0	33.3

	Survey year	Regulations and tax		Permits and licenses	Corruption	Crime	Informality	Gender	Finance	Infrastructure	Innovation	Trade	Workforce
		Time dealing with officials % of management time	Average number of times meeting with tax officials	Time required to obtain operating license days	Informal payments to public officials % of firms	Losses due to theft, robbery, vandalism, and arson % of sales	Firms formally registered when operations started % of firms	Firms with female participation in ownership % of firms	Firms using banks to finance investment % of firms	Value lost due to electrical outages % of sales	Internationally recognized quality certification ownership % of firms	Average time to clear direct exports through customs days	Firms offering formal training[a] % of firms
Hungary	2009	13.5	0.8	35.6	4.0	0.1	100.0	42.4	48.7	0.9	39.4	4.3	14.8
India	2006	6.7	2.6	..	47.5	0.1	..	9.1	46.7	6.6	22.5	15.1	15.9
Indonesia	2009	1.9	0.2	21.1	14.6	0.3	29.1	42.8	11.7	2.4	2.9	2.4	4.7
Iran, Islamic Rep.		..	..	..	..	..	..	..	..	..	..	..	..
Iraq		..	..	..	..	..	..	..	..	..	..	..	..
Ireland	2005	2.3	1.3	..	8.3	0.3	..	41.6	37.4	1.5	17.2	2.6	73.2
Israel		..	..	..	..	..	..	..	..	..	..	..	..
Italy		..	..	..	..	..	..	..	..	..	..	..	..
Jamaica	2005	6.3	1.8	..	17.7	1.1	..	32.2	37.0	11.8	16.4	4.3	53.5
Japan		..	..	..	..	..	..	..	..	..	..	..	..
Jordan	2006	6.7	1.7	6.4	18.1	0.1	..	13.1	8.6	1.7	15.5	3.8	23.9
Kazakhstan	2009	4.7	2.6	30.8	23.3	1.0	97.4	34.4	31.0	3.7	10.8	8.5	40.9
Kenya	2007	5.1	6.7	23.4	79.2	3.9	..	37.1	22.9	6.4	9.8	5.6	40.7
Korea, Dem. Rep.		..	..	..	..	..	..	..	..	..	..	..	..
Korea, Rep.	2005	0.1	2.2	..	14.1	0.0	..	19.1	39.9	..	17.6	7.2	39.5
Kosovo	2009	9.8	4.5	18.8	2.2	0.3	89.2	10.9	25.3	17.1	7.9	1.7	24.6
Kuwait		..	..	..	..	..	..	..	..	..	..	..	..
Kyrgyz Republic	2009	4.9	2.1	18.0	37.5	0.3	95.9	60.4	17.9	10.5	16.2	15.8	29.7
Lao PDR	2009	1.6	4.4	13.6	39.8	0.3	93.5	39.4	0.0	4.3	7.2	7.5	11.1
Latvia	2009	9.7	1.5	11.5	11.3	0.3	98.5	46.3	37.3	1.1	18.2	1.9	43.4
Lebanon	2009	8.9	2.2	81.0	23.0	0.0	97.6	33.5	23.8	9.4	17.9	7.6	52.4
Lesotho	2009	5.6	1.8	16.4	14.0	2.9	86.8	18.4	32.7	6.7	24.7	5.4	42.5
Liberia	2009	7.5	6.5	16.0	55.2	2.8	73.8	53.0	10.1	2.9	2.4	..	17.0
Libya		..	..	..	..	..	..	..	..	..	..	..	..
Lithuania	2009	9.3	0.8	65.5	8.5	0.4	97.1	38.7	47.4	0.7	15.6	2.4	46.0
Macedonia, FYR	2009	14.5	3.0	33.8	11.5	0.7	99.2	36.4	47.0	5.9	21.5	2.5	19.0
Madagascar	2009	17.1	0.9	41.3	19.2	1.2	97.5	50.0	12.2	7.7	8.7	14.2	27.0
Malawi	2009	3.5	2.7	15.0	10.8	5.7	78.6	23.9	20.6	17.0	17.9	4.9	48.4
Malaysia	2007	7.8	2.6	22.4	..	1.0	53.0	13.1	48.6	3.0	54.1	2.7	50.1
Mali	2007	2.4	1.6	41.0	28.9	0.6	85.4	18.4	7.0	1.8	8.6	4.8	22.5
Mauritania	2006	5.8	1.8	10.7	82.1	0.6	..	17.3	3.2	1.6	5.9	3.9	25.5
Mauritius	2009	9.4	0.5	19.1	1.6	1.4	84.2	16.9	37.5	2.2	11.1	10.3	25.6
Mexico	2006	20.5	0.6	11.2	22.6	0.7	94.1	24.8	2.6	2.4	20.3	5.2	24.6
Moldova	2009	7.0	1.9	13.9	25.4	0.4	97.9	53.1	30.8	2.0	9.1	2.4	33.1
Mongolia	2009	12.1	2.0	43.5	30.4	0.6	90.1	52.0	26.5	0.8	16.7	18.6	61.2
Morocco	2007	11.4	0.9	3.4	13.4	0.0	86.0	13.1	12.3	1.3	17.3	1.8	24.7
Mozambique	2007	3.3	1.9	35.2	14.8	1.8	85.9	24.4	10.5	2.4	18.7	10.1	22.1
Myanmar		..	..	..	..	..	..	..	..	..	..	..	..
Namibia	2006	2.9	0.3	9.6	11.4	1.3	..	33.4	8.1	0.7	17.6	1.4	44.5
Nepal	2009	6.5	1.3	14.5	15.2	0.9	94.0	27.4	17.5	27.0	3.1	5.6	8.8
Netherlands		..	..	..	..	..	..	..	..	..	..	..	..
New Zealand		..	..	..	..	..	..	..	..	..	..	..	..
Nicaragua	2006	9.3	1.3	19.7	17.2	0.9	85.4	41.4	13.0	8.7	18.7	5.0	28.9
Niger	2009	21.1	1.6	39.7	35.2	0.9	90.5	17.6	9.3	1.9	4.6	2.6	32.1
Nigeria	2007	6.1	3.0	12.1	40.9	4.1	..	20.0	2.7	8.9	8.5	7.5	25.7
Norway		..	..	..	..	..	..	..	..	..	..	..	..
Oman	2003	..	4.4	11.8	33.2	..	..	..	31.0	4.2	10.8	3.4	20.9
Pakistan	2007	2.2	1.6	16.4	27.2	0.5	..	6.7	9.7	9.9	9.6	4.8	6.7
Panama	2006	10.3	1.4	41.2	25.4	0.5	98.0	37.1	19.2	2.4	14.7	5.7	43.9
Papua New Guinea		..	..	..	..	..	..	..	..	..	..	..	..
Paraguay	2006	7.9	0.7	37.8	84.8	0.9	94.0	44.8	8.2	2.5	7.1	5.5	46.9
Peru	2006	13.5	1.4	81.1	11.3	0.4	99.2	32.8	30.9	3.2	14.6	5.4	57.7
Philippines	2009	9.1	1.6	10.6	18.6	1.1	97.5	69.4	22.0	3.4	15.7	8.1	31.1
Poland	2009	12.8	0.6	14.6	5.0	0.5	99.3	47.9	40.7	1.9	17.3	6.0	60.9
Portugal	2005	1.1	1.6	..	14.5	0.2	..	50.8	24.4	..	12.7	7.2	31.9
Puerto Rico		..	..	..	..	..	..	..	..	..	..	..	..
Qatar		..	..	..	..	..	..	..	..	..	..	..	..

5.2 Business environment: Enterprise Surveys

	Survey year	Regulations and tax		Permits and licenses	Corruption	Crime	Informality	Gender	Finance	Infrastructure	Innovation	Trade	Workforce
		Time dealing with officials % of management time	Average number of times meeting with tax officials	Time required to obtain operating license days	Informal payments to public officials % of firms	Losses due to theft, robbery, vandalism, and arson % of sales	Firms formally registered when operations started % of firms	Firms with female participation in ownership % of firms	Firms using banks to finance investment % of firms	Value lost due to electrical outages % of sales	Internationally recognized quality certification ownership % of firms	Average time to clear direct exports through customs days	Firms offering formal training[a] % of firms
Romania	2009	9.2	2.3	23.7	9.8	0.3	98.7	47.9	37.3	2.2	26.1	2.0	24.9
Russian Federation	2009	19.9	1.6	57.4	29.4	0.8	94.7	33.1	30.6	1.2	11.7	4.6	52.2
Rwanda	2006	5.9	3.3	6.5	20.0	1.3	..	41.0	15.9	8.7	10.8	6.7	27.6
Saudi Arabia		..	..	..	..	..	..	..	..	..	..	..	..
Senegal	2007	2.9	1.3	21.4	18.1	0.5	78.9	26.3	19.8	5.0	6.1	7.4	16.3
Serbia	2009	12.2	1.4	28.0	18.0	0.6	95.0	28.8	42.8	1.3	21.8	1.6	36.5
Sierra Leone	2009	7.4	1.9	12.6	18.8	0.8	89.2	7.9	6.9	6.6	13.8	..	18.6
Singapore		..	..	..	..	..	..	..	..	..	..	..	..
Slovak Republic	2009	6.7	0.9	32.1	9.1	0.7	100.0	29.6	33.5	0.3	28.6	2.4	33.1
Slovenia	2009	7.3	0.3	56.1	5.4	0.4	99.9	42.2	52.2	0.5	28.0	2.2	47.5
Somalia		..	..	..	..	..	..	..	..	..	..	..	..
South Africa	2007	6.0	0.8	36.2	15.1	1.0	91.0	22.6	34.8	1.6	26.4	4.5	36.8
Spain	2005	0.8	1.5	..	4.4	0.2	..	34.1	32.6	3.0	21.3	4.9	51.3
Sri Lanka	2004	3.5	4.9	49.5	16.3	0.5	..	..	26.2	..	..	7.6	32.6
Sudan		..	..	..	..	..	..	..	..	..	..	..	..
Swaziland	2006	4.4	1.4	24.0	40.6	1.3	..	28.6	7.7	2.5	22.1	2.1	51.0
Sweden		..	..	..	..	..	..	..	..	..	..	..	..
Switzerland		..	..	..	..	..	..	..	..	..	..	..	..
Syrian Arab Republic	2009	12.2	2.3	169.2	83.8	0.8	..	14.4	20.7	8.6	7.4	5.1	38.3
Tajikistan	2008	11.7	1.4	22.6	40.5	0.3	92.7	34.4	21.4	15.1	16.7	20.4	21.1
Tanzania	2006	4.0	2.7	15.9	49.5	1.2	..	30.9	6.8	9.6	14.7	5.7	36.5
Thailand	2006	0.4	1.0	32.1	..	0.1	..	..	74.4	1.5	39.0	1.3	75.3
Timor-Leste	2009	4.1	0.9	16.6	19.4	1.5	91.8	42.9	1.6	7.6	2.2	..	49.7
Togo	2009	2.7	1.2	56.4	16.7	2.4	75.8	31.8	16.9	10.5	6.6	6.7	31.0
Trinidad and Tobago		..	..	..	..	..	..	..	..	..	..	..	..
Tunisia		..	..	..	..	..	..	..	..	..	..	..	..
Turkey	2008	27.1	1.3	36.0	17.7	0.4	94.1	40.7	51.9	2.8	30.0	5.2	28.8
Turkmenistan		..	..	..	..	..	..	..	..	..	..	..	..
Uganda	2006	5.2	2.4	9.3	51.7	1.0	..	34.7	7.7	10.2	15.5	3.2	35.0
Ukraine	2008	11.3	2.1	31.0	22.9	0.6	95.8	47.1	32.1	4.4	13.0	3.4	24.8
United Arab Emirates		..	..	..	..	..	..	..	..	..	..	..	..
United Kingdom		..	..	..	..	..	..	..	..	..	..	..	..
United States		..	..	..	..	..	..	..	..	..	..	..	..
Uruguay	2006	7.0	0.7	133.8	7.3	0.7	97.8	41.6	6.9	0.9	6.8	2.5	24.6
Uzbekistan	2008	11.1	0.7	9.1	56.2	0.7	100.0	39.8	8.2	5.4	1.3	5.1	9.6
Venezuela, RB	2006	33.6	2.9	41.6	..	1.4	97.3	..	35.7	4.4	12.5	14.1	42.3
Vietnam	2009	4.9	1.1	15.9	52.1	0.3	87.5	59.2	21.5	3.7	16.7	4.5	43.6
West Bank and Gaza	2006	5.7	1.7	21.3	13.3	1.2	..	18.0	4.2	4.6	18.2	6.0	26.5
Yemen, Rep.	2010	11.8	7.3	6.5	68.2	0.6	81.7	6.4	4.2	13.2	4.4	6.2	12.9
Zambia	2007	4.6	1.9	48.3	14.3	1.0	96.2	37.2	10.2	3.7	17.2	2.3	26.0
Zimbabwe		..	..	..	..	..	..	..	..	..	..	..	..

Note: Enterprise surveys are updated several times a year; see www.enterprisesurveys.org for the most recent updates.

a. For survey data collected in 2006 and 2007, data refer to the manufacturing module only.

About the data

The World Bank Group's Enterprise Survey gathers firm-level data on the business environment to assess constraints to private sector growth and enterprise performance. Standardized surveys are conducted all over the world, and data are available on more than 120,000 firms in 125 countries. The survey covers 11 dimensions of the business environment, including regulation, corruption, crime, informality, finance, infrastructure, trade. For some countries, firm-level panel data are available, making it possible to track changes in the business environment over time.

Firms evaluating investment options, governments interested in improving business conditions, and economists seeking to explain economic performance have all grappled with defining and measuring the business environment. The firm-level data from Enterprise Surveys provide a useful tool for benchmarking economies across a large number of indicators measured at the firm level.

Most countries can improve regulation and taxation without compromising broader social interests. Excessive regulation may harm business performance and growth. For example, time spent with tax officials is a burden firms may face in paying taxes. The business environment suffers when governments increase uncertainty and risks or impose unnecessary costs and unsound regulation and taxation. Time to obtain licenses and permits and the associated red tape constrain firm operations.

In some countries doing business requires informal payments to "get things done" in customs, taxes, licenses, regulations, services, and the like. Such corruption harms the business environment by distorting policymaking, undermining government credibility, and diverting public resources. Crime, theft, and disorder also impose costs on businesses and society.

In many developing countries informal businesses operate without formal registration. These firms have less access to financial and public services and can engage in fewer types of contracts and investments, constraining growth.

Equal opportunities for men and women contribute to development. Female participation in firm ownership is a measure of women's integration as decision makers.

Financial markets connect firms to lenders and investors, allowing firms to grow their businesses: creditworthy firms can obtain credit from financial intermediaries at competitive prices. But too often market imperfections and government-induced distortions limit access to credit and thus restrain growth.

The reliability and availability of infrastructure benefit households and support development. Firms with access to modern and efficient infrastructure—telecommunications, electricity, and transport—can be more productive. Firm-level innovation and use of modern technology may help firms compete.

Delays in clearing customs can be costly, deterring firms from engaging in trade or making them uncompetitive globally. Ill-considered labor regulations discourage firms from creating jobs, and while employed workers may benefit, unemployed, low-skilled, and informally employed workers will not. A trained labor force enables firms to thrive, compete, innovate, and adopt new technology.

The data in the table are from Enterprise Surveys implemented by the World Bank's Financial and Private Sector Development Enterprise Analysis Unit. All economies in East Asia and Pacific, Europe and Central Asia, Latin America and the Caribbean, Middle East and North Africa, and Sub-Saharan Africa (for 2009) and Afghanistan, Bangladesh, and India draw a sample of registered nonagricultural businesses, excluding those in the financial and public sectors. Samples for other economies are drawn only from the manufacturing sector and are footnoted in the table. Typical Enterprise Survey sample sizes range from 150 to 1,800, depending on the size of the economy. In each country samples are selected by stratified random sampling, unless otherwise noted. Stratified random sampling allows indicators to be computed by sector, firm size, and region and increases the precision of economywide indicators compared with alternative simple random sampling. Stratification by sector of activity divides the economy into manufacturing and retail and other services sectors. For medium-size and large economies the manufacturing sector is further stratified by industry. Firm size is stratified into small (5–19 employees), medium-size (20–99 employees), and large (more than 99 employees). Geographic stratification divides the national economy into the main centers of economic activity.

Definitions

• **Survey year** is the year in which the underlying data were collected. • **Time dealing with officials** is the average percentage of senior management's time that is spent in a typical week dealing with requirements imposed by government regulations. • **Average number of times meeting with tax officials** is the average number of visits or required meetings with tax officials. • **Time required to obtain operating license** is the average wait to obtain an operating license from the day applied for to the day granted. • **Informal payments to public officials** are the percentage of firms that answered positively to the question "Was a gift or informal payment expected or requested during a meeting with tax officials?" • **Losses due to theft, robbery, vandalism, and arson** are the estimated losses from those causes that occurred on establishments' premises as a percentage of annual sales. • **Firms formally registered when operations started** are the percentage of firms formally registered when they started operations in the country. Firms not formally registered (the residual) are in the informal sector of the economy. • **Firms with female participation in ownership** are the percentage of firms with a woman among the owners. • **Firms using banks to finance investment** are the percentage of firms that invested in fixed assets during the last fiscal year that used banks to finance fixed assets. • **Value lost due to electrical outages** is losses that resulted from power outages as a percentage of annual sales. • **Internationally recognized quality certification ownership** is the percentage of firms that have an internationally recognized quality certification, such as International Organization for Standardization 9000, 9001, 9002, or 14000 or Hazard Analysis and Critical Control Points. • **Average time to clear direct exports through customs** is the average number of days to clear direct exports through customs. • **Firms offering formal training** are the percentage of firms offering formal training programs for their permanent, full-time employees.

Data sources

Data on the business environment are from the World Bank Group's Enterprise Surveys website (www.enterprisesurveys.org).

	Starting a business			Registering property		Dealing with construction permits		Enforcing contracts		Protecting investors	Closing a business
	Number of procedures June 2010	Time required days June 2010	Cost % of per capita income June 2010	Number of procedures June 2010	Time required days June 2010	Number of procedures to build a warehouse June 2010	Time required to build a warehouse days June 2010	Number of procedures June 2010	Time required days June 2010	Disclosure index 0–10 (least to most disclosure) June 2010	Time to resolve insolvency years June 2010
Afghanistan	4	7	26.7	9	250	13	340	47	1,642	1	..
Albania	5	5	16.8	6	42	24	331	39	390	8	..
Algeria	14	24	12.9	11	47	22	240	46	630	6	2.5
Angola	8	68	163.0	7	184	12	328	46	1,011	5	6.2
Argentina	14	26	14.2	6	52	28	338	36	590	6	2.8
Armenia	6	15	3.1	3	7	20	137	49	285	5	1.9
Australia	2	2	0.7	5	5	16	221	28	395	8	1.0
Austria	8	28	5.2	3	21	14	194	25	397	3	1.1
Azerbaijan	6	8	3.1	4	11	31	207	39	237	7	2.7
Bangladesh	7	19	33.3	8	245	14	231	41	1,442	6	4.0
Belarus	5	5	1.6	3	15	16	151	28	225	5	5.8
Belgium	3	4	5.4	8	79	14	169	26	505	8	0.9
Benin	7	31	152.6	4	120	15	320	42	825	6	4.0
Bolivia	15	50	100.8	7	92	17	249	40	591	1	1.8
Bosnia and Herzegovina	12	55	17.7	7	33	16	255	37	595	3	3.3
Botswana	10	61	2.2	5	16	24	167	29	625	7	1.7
Brazil	15	120	7.3	14	42	18	411	45	616	6	4.0
Bulgaria	4	18	1.6	8	15	24	139	39	564	10	3.3
Burkina Faso	4	14	49.8	4	59	15	122	37	446	6	4.0
Burundi	11	32	129.3	5	94	25	212	44	832	4	..
Cambodia	9	85	128.3	7	56	23	709	44	401	5	..
Cameroon	6	19	51.2	5	93	14	213	43	800	6	3.2
Canada	1	5	0.4	6	17	14	75	36	570	8	0.8
Central African Republic	8	22	228.4	5	75	21	239	43	660	6	4.8
Chad	13	75	226.9	6	44	14	164	41	743	6	..
Chile	8	22	6.8	6	31	18	155	36	480	8	4.5
China	14	38	4.5	4	29	37	336	34	406	10	1.7
Hong Kong SAR, China	3	6	2.0	5	36	7	67	24	280	10	1.1
Colombia	9	14	14.7	7	20	10	50	34	1,346	8	3.0
Congo, Dem. Rep.	10	84	735.1	6	54	14	128	43	625	3	5.2
Congo, Rep.	10	160	111.4	6	55	17	169	44	560	6	3.3
Costa Rica	12	60	10.5	6	21	23	191	40	852	2	3.5
Côte d'Ivoire	10	40	133.0	6	62	21	592	33	770	6	2.2
Croatia	6	7	8.6	5	104	13	315	38	561	1	3.1
Cuba	..	..	..	..	..	..	..	..	..	..	..
Czech Republic	9	20	9.3	4	43	36	150	27	611	2	3.2
Denmark	4	6	0.0	3	42	6	69	35	410	7	1.1
Dominican Republic	8	19	19.2	7	60	17	214	34	460	5	3.5
Ecuador	13	56	32.6	9	16	19	155	39	588	1	5.3
Egypt, Arab Rep.	6	7	6.3	7	72	25	218	41	1,010	8	4.2
El Salvador	8	17	45.0	5	31	34	155	30	786	5	4.0
Eritrea	13	84	69.2	11	78	..	..	39	405	4	..
Estonia	5	7	1.9	3	18	14	134	36	425	8	3.0
Ethiopia	5	9	14.1	10	41	12	128	37	620	4	3.0
Finland	3	14	1.1	3	14	18	66	32	375	6	0.9
France	5	7	0.9	8	59	13	137	29	331	10	1.9
Gabon	9	58	21.9	7	39	16	210	38	1,070	6	5.0
Gambia, The	8	27	199.6	5	66	17	146	32	434	2	3.0
Georgia	3	3	5.0	1	2	10	98	36	285	8	3.3
Germany	9	15	4.8	5	40	12	100	30	394	5	1.2
Ghana	7	12	20.3	5	34	18	220	36	487	7	1.9
Greece	15	19	20.7	11	22	15	169	39	819	1	2.0
Guatemala	12	37	49.1	4	23	22	178	31	1,459	3	3.0
Guinea	13	41	146.6	6	104	32	255	50	276	6	3.8
Guinea-Bissau	17	216	183.3	9	211	15	167	40	1,140	6	..
Haiti	13	105	212.0	5	405	11	1,179	35	508	2	5.7
Honduras	13	14	47.2	7	23	17	106	45	900	0	3.8

	Starting a business			Registering property		Dealing with construction permits		Enforcing contracts		Protecting investors	Closing a business
	Number of procedures	Time required days	Cost % of per capita income	Number of procedures	Time required days	Number of procedures to build a warehouse	Time required to build a warehouse days	Number of procedures	Time required days	Disclosure index 0–10 (least to most disclosure)	Time to resolve insolvency years
	June 2010	June 2010	June 2010	June 2010	June 2010	June 2010	June 2010	June 2010	June 2010	June 2010	June 2010
Hungary	4	4	8.2	4	17	31	189	35	395	2	2.0
India	12	29	56.5	5	44	37	195	46	1,420	7	7.0
Indonesia	9	47	22.3	6	22	14	160	40	570	10	5.5
Iran, Islamic Rep.	6	8	4.0	9	36	17	322	39	505	5	4.5
Iraq	11	77	107.8	5	51	14	215	51	520	4	..
Ireland	4	13	0.4	5	38	11	192	20	515	10	0.4
Israel	5	34	4.3	7	144	20	235	35	890	7	4.0
Italy	6	6	18.5	8	27	14	257	41	1,210	7	1.8
Jamaica	6	8	5.2	6	37	10	156	35	655	4	1.1
Japan	8	23	7.5	6	14	15	187	30	360	7	0.6
Jordan	8	13	44.6	7	21	19	87	38	689	5	4.3
Kazakhstan	6	19	1.0	4	40	34	219	38	390	8	1.5
Kenya	11	33	38.3	8	64	11	120	40	465	3	4.5
Korea, Dem. Rep.	..	..	..	..	..	..	..	..	..	..	..
Korea, Rep.	8	14	14.7	7	11	13	34	35	230	7	1.5
Kosovo	10	58	28.7	8	33	21	320	53	420	3	2.0
Kuwait	13	35	1.3	8	55	25	104	50	566	7	4.2
Kyrgyz Republic	2	10	3.7	4	5	13	143	39	260	8	4.0
Lao PDR	7	100	11.3	9	135	24	172	42	443	2	..
Latvia	5	16	1.5	6	42	24	186	27	309	5	3.0
Lebanon	5	9	75.0	8	25	21	218	37	721	9	4.0
Lesotho	7	40	26.0	6	101	15	601	41	785	2	2.6
Liberia	5	20	54.6	10	50	24	77	41	1,280	4	3.0
Libya	..	..	..	..	..	..	..	..	..	..	..
Lithuania	6	22	2.8	3	3	17	162	30	275	5	1.5
Macedonia, FYR	3	3	2.5	5	58	21	146	37	370	9	2.9
Madagascar	2	7	12.9	7	74	16	178	38	871	5	..
Malawi	10	39	108.4	6	49	21	268	42	312	4	2.6
Malaysia	9	17	17.5	5	56	25	261	30	585	10	2.3
Mali	6	8	79.7	5	29	15	168	36	620	6	3.6
Mauritania	9	19	33.6	4	49	25	201	46	370	5	8.0
Mauritius	5	6	3.8	4	26	18	107	36	645	6	1.7
Mexico	6	9	12.3	5	74	11	105	38	415	8	1.8
Moldova	8	10	10.9	5	5	30	292	31	365	7	2.8
Mongolia	7	13	3.2	5	11	21	215	32	314	5	4.0
Morocco	6	12	15.8	8	47	19	163	40	615	7	1.8
Mozambique	9	13	13.9	8	42	17	381	30	730	5	5.0
Myanmar	..	..	..	..	..	..	..	..	..	..	..
Namibia	10	66	18.5	9	23	12	139	33	270	5	1.5
Nepal	7	31	46.6	3	5	15	424	39	735	6	5.0
Netherlands	6	8	5.7	5	7	18	230	26	514	4	1.1
New Zealand	1	1	0.4	2	2	7	65	30	216	10	1.3
Nicaragua	6	39	117.9	8	124	17	219	35	540	4	2.2
Niger	9	17	118.6	4	35	17	265	39	545	6	5.0
Nigeria	8	31	78.9	13	82	18	350	40	457	5	2.0
Norway	5	7	1.8	1	3	14	252	33	280	7	0.9
Oman	5	12	3.3	2	16	15	186	51	598	8	4.0
Pakistan	10	21	10.7	6	50	12	223	47	976	6	2.8
Panama	6	9	10.3	8	32	20	116	31	686	1	2.5
Papua New Guinea	6	51	17.7	4	72	24	217	42	591	5	3.0
Paraguay	7	35	55.1	6	46	13	179	38	591	6	3.9
Peru	6	27	13.6	4	7	19	188	41	428	8	3.1
Philippines	15	38	29.7	8	33	26	169	37	842	2	5.7
Poland	6	32	17.5	6	152	32	311	38	830	7	3.0
Portugal	6	6	6.5	1	1	19	272	31	547	6	2.0
Puerto Rico	7	7	0.7	8	194	22	209	39	620	7	3.8
Qatar	8	12	9.7	10	16	19	76	43	570	5	2.8

	Starting a business			Registering property		Dealing with construction permits		Enforcing contracts		Protecting investors	Closing a business
	Number of procedures June 2010	Time required days June 2010	Cost % of per capita income June 2010	Number of procedures June 2010	Time required days June 2010	Number of procedures to build a warehouse June 2010	Time required to build a warehouse days June 2010	Number of procedures June 2010	Time required days June 2010	Disclosure index 0–10 (least to most disclosure) June 2010	Time to resolve insolvency years June 2010
Romania	6	10	2.6	8	48	17	228	31	512	9	3.3
Russian Federation	9	30	3.6	6	43	53	540	37	281	6	3.8
Rwanda	2	3	8.8	4	55	14	195	24	230	7	..
Saudi Arabia	4	5	7.0	2	2	12	89	43	635	9	1.5
Senegal	4	8	63.1	6	122	16	210	44	780	6	3.0
Serbia	7	13	7.9	6	91	20	279	36	635	7	2.7
Sierra Leone	6	12	110.7	7	86	25	252	40	515	6	2.6
Singapore	3	3	0.7	3	5	11	25	21	150	10	0.8
Slovak Republic	6	16	1.9	3	17	13	287	31	565	3	4.0
Slovenia	2	6	0.0	6	113	14	199	32	1,290	3	2.0
Somalia	..	..	..	..	..	..	..	..	..	..	..
South Africa	6	22	6.0	6	24	17	174	30	600	8	2.0
Spain	10	47	15.1	4	18	11	233	39	515	5	1.0
Sri Lanka	4	35	5.4	8	83	22	214	40	1,318	4	1.7
Sudan	10	36	33.6	6	9	19	271	53	810	0	..
Swaziland	12	56	33.0	9	44	14	116	40	972	2	2.0
Sweden	3	15	0.6	1	7	8	116	30	508	8	2.0
Switzerland	6	20	2.1	4	16	14	154	31	417	0	3.0
Syrian Arab Republic	7	13	38.1	4	19	26	128	55	872	7	4.1
Tajikistan	8	27	36.9	6	37	30	228	34	430	8	1.7
Tanzania	12	29	30.9	9	73	22	328	38	462	3	3.0
Thailand	7	32	5.6	2	2	11	156	36	479	10	2.7
Timor-Leste	10	83	18.4	..	..	22	208	51	1,285	3	..
Togo	7	75	178.1	5	295	15	277	41	588	6	3.0
Trinidad and Tobago	9	43	0.8	8	162	20	261	42	1,340	4	..
Tunisia	10	11	5.0	4	39	20	97	39	565	5	1.3
Turkey	6	6	17.2	6	6	25	188	35	420	9	3.3
Turkmenistan	..	..	..	..	..	..	..	..	..	..	..
Uganda	18	25	94.4	13	77	18	171	38	490	2	2.2
Ukraine	10	27	6.1	10	117	22	374	30	345	5	2.9
United Arab Emirates	8	15	6.4	1	2	17	64	49	537	4	5.1
United Kingdom	6	13	0.7	2	8	11	95	28	399	10	1.0
United States	6	6	1.4	4	12	19	40	32	300	7	1.5
Uruguay	11	65	42.1	8	66	30	234	41	720	3	2.1
Uzbekistan	7	15	11.9	12	78	28	274	42	195	4	4.0
Venezuela, RB	17	141	30.2	8	47	11	395	29	510	4	4.0
Vietnam	9	44	12.1	4	57	13	194	34	295	6	5.0
West Bank and Gaza	11	49	93.7	7	47	21	199	44	540	6	..
Yemen, Rep.	6	12	82.1	6	19	15	107	36	520	6	3.0
Zambia	6	18	27.9	5	40	17	254	35	471	3	2.7
Zimbabwe	9	90	182.8	5	31	17	1,012	38	410	8	3.3
World	**8 u**	**34 u**	**40.7 u**	**6 u**	**58 u**	**18 u**	**207 u**	**38 u**	**605 u**	**5 u**	**2.9 u**
Low income	8	41	107.9	7	94	18	275	39	613	5	3.7
Middle income	8	39	31.7	6	54	19	201	39	638	5	3.1
Lower middle income	8	35	44.4	6	65	18	197	40	679	5	3.3
Upper middle income	8	43	16.1	6	41	19	206	38	588	6	2.9
Low & middle income	8	39	52.6	6	65	19	221	39	631	5	3.3
East Asia & Pacific	8	40	31.5	5	99	19	181	37	564	5	3.1
Europe & Central Asia	6	18	8.9	6	36	23	235	38	382	7	2.9
Latin America & Carib.	9	60	39.6	7	62	16	220	39	698	4	3.2
Middle East & N. Africa	8	23	54.6	7	39	20	181	42	701	6	3.5
South Asia	7	25	24.5	6	100	18	241	44	1,053	4	4.5
Sub-Saharan Africa	9	43	95.2	7	69	18	240	39	641	5	3.4
High income	6	18	7.3	5	38	17	169	35	532	6	2.1
Euro area	6	14	6.7	5	35	14	227	31	602	5	1.6

Note: Regional aggregates are for developing countries only.

Business environment: Doing Business indicators

5.3

About the data

The economic health of a country is measured not only in macroeconomic terms but also by other factors that shape daily economic activity such as laws, regulations, and institutional arrangements. The Doing Business indicators measure business regulation, gauge regulatory outcomes, and measure the extent of legal protection of property, the flexibility of employment regulation, and the tax burden on businesses.

The table presents a subset of Doing Business indicators covering 6 of the 10 sets of indicators: starting a business, registering property, dealing with construction permits, enforcing contracts, protecting investors, and closing a business. Table 5.5 includes Doing Business measures of getting credit, and table 5.6 presents data on paying taxes.

The fundamental premise of the Doing Business project is that economic activity requires good rules and regulations that are efficient, accessible to all who need to use them, and simple to implement. Thus some Doing Business indicators give a higher score for more regulation, such as stricter disclosure requirements in related-party transactions, and others give a higher score for simplified regulations, such as a one-stop shop for completing business startup formalities.

In constructing the indicators, it is assumed that entrepreneurs know about all regulations and comply with them; in practice, entrepreneurs may not be aware of all required procedures or may avoid legally required procedures altogether. But where regulation is particularly onerous, levels of informality are higher, which comes at a cost: firms in the informal sector usually grow more slowly, have less access to credit, and employ fewer workers—and those workers remain outside the protections of labor law. The indicators in the table can help policymakers understand the business environment in a country and—along with information from other sources such as the World Bank's Enterprise Surveys—provide insights into potential areas of reform.

Doing Business data are collected with a standardized survey that uses a simple business case to ensure comparability across economies and over time—with assumptions about the legal form of the business, its size, its location, and nature of its operation. Surveys in 183 countries are administered through more than 8,200 local experts, including lawyers, business consultants, accountants, freight forwarders, government officials, and other professionals who routinely administer or advise on legal and regulatory requirements.

The Doing Business project encompasses two types of data: data from readings of laws and regulations and data on time and motion indicators that measure efficiency in achieving a regulatory goal. Within the time and motion indicators cost estimates are recorded from official fee schedules where applicable. The data from surveys are subjected to numerous tests for robustness, which lead to revision or expansion of the information collected.

The Doing Business methodology has limitations that should be considered when interpreting the data. First, the data collected refer to businesses in the economy's largest city and may not represent regulations in other locations of the economy. To address this limitation, subnational indicators are being collected for selected economies. These subnational studies point to significant differences in the speed of reform and the ease of doing business across cities in the same economy. Second, the data often focus on a specific business form—generally a limited liability company of a specified size—and may not represent regulation for other types of businesses such as sole proprietorships. Third, transactions described in a standardized business case refer to a specific set of issues and may not represent the full set of issues a business encounters. Fourth, the time measures involve an element of judgment by the expert respondents. When sources indicate different estimates, the Doing Business time indicators represent the median values of several responses given under the assumptions of the standardized case. Fifth, the methodology assumes that a business has full information on what is required and does not waste time when completing procedures.

Definitions

• **Number of procedures for starting a business** is the number of procedures required to start a business, including interactions to obtain necessary permits and licenses and to complete all inscriptions, verifications, and notifications to start operations for businesses with specific characteristics of ownership, size, and type of production. • **Time required for starting a business** is the number of calendar days to complete the procedures for legally operating a business using the fastest procedure, independent of cost. • **Cost for starting a business** is normalized as a percentage of gross national income (GNI) per capita. It includes all official fees and fees for legal or professional services if such services are required by law. • **Number of procedures for registering property** is the number of procedures required for a business to legally transfer property. • **Time required for registering property** is the number of calendar days for a business to legally transfer property. • **Number of procedures for dealing with licenses to build a warehouse** is the number of interactions of a company's employees or managers with external parties, including government staff, public inspectors, notaries, land registry and cadastre staff, and technical experts apart from architects and engineers. • **Time required for dealing with construction permits to build a warehouse** is the number of calendar days to complete the required procedures for building a warehouse using the fastest procedure, independent of cost. • **Number of procedures for enforcing contracts** is the number of independent actions, mandated by law or court regulation, that demand interaction between the parties to a contract or between them and the judge or court officer. • **Time required for enforcing contracts** is the number of calendar days from the time of the filing of a lawsuit in court to the final determination and payment. • **Extent of disclosure index** measures the degree to which investors are protected through disclosure of ownership and financial information. Higher values indicate more disclosure. • **Time to resolve insolvency** is the number of years from time of filing for insolvency in court until resolution of distressed assets and payment of creditors.

Data sources

Data on the business environment are from the World Bank's Doing Business project (www.doingbusiness.org).

	Market capitalization				Market liquidity		Turnover ratio		Listed domestic companies		S&P/Global Equity Indices	
	$ millions		% of GDP		Value of shares traded % of GDP		Value of shares traded % of market capitalization		number		% change	
	2000	2010	2000	2009	2000	2009	2000	2010	2000	2010	2009	2010
Afghanistan	..	..	..	..	..	..	..	..	..	..	..	..
Albania	..	..	..	..	..	..	..	..	..	..	..	..
Algeria	..	..	..	..	..	..	..	..	..	..	..	..
Angola	..	..	..	..	..	..	..	..	..	..	..	..
Argentina	166,068	63,910	58.4	15.9	2.1	0.9	4.8	4.6	127	101	97.8[a]	55.3[a]
Armenia	2	28	0.1	1.6	0.0	0.0	11.9	0.2	105	2	..	..
Australia	372,794	1,454,547	89.4	136.1	54.3	82.4	56.5	90.1	1,330	1,913	72.4	12.5
Austria	29,935	67,683	15.7	14.1	4.9	6.7	29.8	79.4	97	72	57.0	10.9
Azerbaijan	3	..	0.1	..	..	..	..	..	2	..	..	..
Bangladesh	1,186	47,000	2.5	7.9	1.6	16.3	74.8	54.4	221	302	38.6[a]	37.6[a]
Belarus	..	..	..	..	..	..	..	..	..	..	..	..
Belgium	182,481	269,342	78.5	55.5	16.4	27.1	20.7	42.0	174	161	54.5	0.5
Benin	..	..	..	..	..	..	..	..	..	..	..	..
Bolivia	1,742	3,388	20.7	16.1	0.8	0.1	5.7	0.4	26	38	..	..
Bosnia and Herzegovina	..	..	..	..	..	..	..	..	..	..	..	..
Botswana	978	4,076	17.4	33.8	0.8	0.9	4.7	3.5	16	21	24.3[a]	−6.8[a]
Brazil	226,152	1,545,566	35.1	73.2	15.7	40.7	44.6	66.4	459	373	125.1	6.5
Bulgaria	617	7,276	4.8	14.6	0.4	0.8	8.7	2.8	503	390	17.2[a]	−15.2[a]
Burkina Faso	..	..	..	..	..	..	..	..	..	..	..	..
Burundi	..	..	..	..	..	..	..	..	..	..	..	..
Cambodia	..	..	..	..	..	..	..	..	..	..	..	..
Cameroon	..	..	..	..	..	..	..	..	..	..	..	..
Canada	841,385	2,160,229	116.1	125.8	87.6	92.8	77.3	71.1	1,418	3,805	57.5	22.0
Central African Republic	..	..	..	..	..	..	..	..	..	..	..	..
Chad	..	..	..	..	..	..	..	..	..	..	..	..
Chile	60,401	341,584	80.3	128.0	8.1	23.0	9.5	19.7	258	227	84.0	47.2
China	580,991	4,762,837	48.5	100.4	60.2	179.6	158.3	164.4	1,086	2,063	66.3	6.9
Hong Kong SAR, China	623,398	2,711,334	368.6	1,088.3	223.4	707.4	61.3	63.9	779	1,396	67.1	21.3
Colombia	9,560	208,502	9.5	57.0	0.4	5.5	3.8	13.4	126	84	75.7[a]	44.1[a]
Congo, Dem. Rep.	..	..	..	..	..	..	..	..	..	..	..	..
Congo, Rep.	..	..	..	..	..	..	..	..	..	..	..	..
Costa Rica	2,924	1,445	18.3	5.0	0.7	0.1	4.0	2.8	21	9	..	..
Côte d'Ivoire	1,185	7,099	11.4	26.4	0.3	0.6	2.5	2.0	41	38	−10.7[a]	19.3[a]
Croatia	2,742	24,912	12.8	40.7	0.9	2.3	7.1	4.1	64	221	31.1[a]	−0.4[a]
Cuba	..	..	..	..	..	..	..	..	..	..	..	..
Czech Republic	11,002	43,056	19.4	27.7	11.6	10.8	57.7	29.4	131	16	23.0	0.2
Denmark	107,666	231,746	67.3	60.4	57.2	47.9	86.0	69.1	225	196	40.6	25.1
Dominican Republic	..	..	..	..	..	..	..	..	..	..	..	..
Ecuador	704	5,263	4.4	7.4	0.1	2.4	2.0	3.8	30	40	−13.1[a]	9.7[a]
Egypt, Arab Rep.	28,741	82,495	28.8	47.7	11.1	28.0	36.1	43.0	1,076	211	35.6	11.5
El Salvador	2,041	4,227	15.5	21.0	0.2	..	1.2	..	40	61	..	..
Eritrea	..	..	..	..	..	..	..	..	..	..	..	..
Estonia	1,846	2,260	32.5	13.9	5.7	2.0	18.0	13.1	23	15	32.9[a]	56.0[a]
Ethiopia	..	..	..	..	..	..	..	..	..	..	..	..
Finland	293,635	118,160	241.2	38.2	169.8	38.3	64.3	97.4	154	123	17.5	10.7
France	1,446,634	1,926,488	108.9	74.4	81.6	51.6	74.1	42.5	808	901	25.6[b]	−9.9[b]
Gabon	..	..	..	..	..	..	..	..	..	..	..	..
Gambia, The	..	..	..	..	..	..	..	..	..	..	..	..
Georgia	24	1,060	0.8	6.8	0.1	0.0	11.3	0.3	269	143	..	..
Germany	1,270,243	1,429,707	66.8	39.0	56.3	38.7	79.1	103.0	1,022	571	25.8[c]	7.4[c]
Ghana	502	3,531	10.1	9.6	0.2	0.2	1.4	3.4	22	35	−42.7[a]	94.1[a]
Greece	110,839	72,639	88.3	16.6	75.7	15.7	60.4	67.7	329	287	22.1	−43.8
Guatemala	172	..	0.9	..	0.1	..	6.4	..	7	..	..	..
Guinea	..	..	..	..	..	..	..	..	..	..	..	..
Guinea-Bissau	..	..	..	..	..	..	..	..	..	..	..	..
Haiti	..	..	..	..	..	..	..	..	..	..	..	..
Honduras	458	..	8.8	..	..	..	..	..	94	..	..	..

	Market capitalization				Market liquidity		Turnover ratio		Listed domestic companies		S&P/Global Equity Indices	
	$ millions		% of GDP		Value of shares traded % of GDP		Value of shares traded % of market capitalization		number		% change	
	2000	**2010**	**2000**	**2009**	**2000**	**2009**	**2000**	**2010**	**2000**	**2010**	**2009**	**2010**
Hungary	12,021	27,708	25.1	21.9	25.4	20.1	85.8	94.5	60	48	73.0	–10.8
India	148,064	1,615,860	32.2	85.6	110.8	79.1	306.5	75.6	5,937	4,987	94.1	18.7
Indonesia	26,834	360,388	16.3	33.0	8.7	21.3	31.5	48.1	290	420	130.1	37.9
Iran, Islamic Rep.	7,350	86,616	7.3	19.1	1.1	5.2	7.4	22.9	304	341	..	..
Iraq	..	..	..	..	..	..	..	..	..	..	..	..
Ireland	81,882	33,722	84.8	13.2	14.9	8.1	19.2	52.9	76	50	44.7	–7.7
Israel	64,081	218,055	51.4	93.2	18.8	45.2	36.6	66.7	654	596	56.8	7.4
Italy	768,364	318,140	70.0	15.0	70.9	21.8	104.0	169.7	291	291	23.1	–17.4
Jamaica	3,582	6,626	39.8	51.4	0.8	1.0	2.5	3.3	46	39	–15.8[a]	22.4[a]
Japan	3,157,222	4,099,591	67.6	66.6	57.7	82.7	69.9	114.5	2,561	3,553	16.4[d]	9.6[d]
Jordan	4,943	30,864	58.4	127.0	4.9	54.4	7.7	30.1	163	277	–13.9[a]	–8.6[a]
Kazakhstan	1,342	60,742	7.3	50.0	0.5	3.5	4.9	3.9	23	60	1.5[a]	–1.0[a]
Kenya	1,283	14,461	10.1	36.6	0.4	1.7	3.5	8.6	57	53	0.6[a]	33.8[a]
Korea, Dem. Rep.	..	..	..	..	..	..	..	..	..	..	..	..
Korea, Rep.	171,587	1,089,217	32.2	100.5	200.2	190.0	376.6	168.9	1,308	1,781	67.2	25.3
Kosovo	..	..	..	..	..	..	..	..	..	..	..	..
Kuwait	20,772	119,621	55.1	72.4	11.2	82.9	21.3	38.8	77	215	–10.4[a]	29.1[a]
Kyrgyz Republic	4	79	0.3	1.6	1.7	1.5	580.6	11.9	80	11	..	..
Lao PDR	..	..	..	..	..	..	..	..	..	..	..	..
Latvia	563	1,252	7.2	7.0	2.9	0.1	47.8	1.8	64	33	2.2[a]	39.4[a]
Lebanon	1,583	12,586	9.2	37.3	0.7	3.0	6.7	14.7	12	10	43.4[a]	–8.7[a]
Lesotho	..	..	..	..	..	..	..	..	..	..	..	..
Liberia	..	..	..	..	..	..	..	..	..	..	..	..
Libya	..	..	..	..	..	..	..	..	..	..	..	..
Lithuania	1,588	5,661	13.9	12.0	1.8	0.8	14.8	5.8	54	39	36.7[a]	44.0[a]
Macedonia, FYR	7	2,647	0.2	10.0	3.3	0.7	1,612.9	2.0	1	34	..	..
Madagascar	..	..	..	..	..	..	..	..	..	..	..	..
Malawi	..	1,363	..	29.3	..	0.4	..	1.5	..	14	..	..
Malaysia	116,935	410,534	124.7	132.6	62.4	37.8	44.6	27.1	795	957	46.7	35.1
Mali	..	..	..	..	..	..	..	..	..	..	..	..
Mauritania	..	..	..	..	..	..	..	..	..	..	..	..
Mauritius	1,331	6,506	29.0	55.2	1.6	3.8	5.1	6.4	40	86	44.2[a]	8.2[a]
Mexico	125,204	454,345	21.5	38.9	7.8	8.8	32.5	27.3	179	130	55.8	26.6
Moldova	38		3.2		1.9	0.2	80.2		34		..	..
Mongolia	37	1,093	3.4	10.2	0.7	0.4	23.2	6.4	410	336	..	..
Morocco	10,899	69,153	29.4	68.8	3.0	32.2	8.9	16.3	53	73	–1.7	13.1
Mozambique	..	..	..	..	..	..	..	..	..	..	..	..
Myanmar	..	..	..	..	..	..	..	..	..	..	..	..
Namibia	311	1,176	8.0	9.1	0.6	0.2	4.4	1.8	13	7	22.6[a]	24.2[a]
Nepal	790	4,843	14.4	43.8	0.6	1.8	5.4	1.9	110	190	..	..
Netherlands	640,456	661,204	166.3	68.5	175.9	76.3	101.4	98.4	234	113	41.7	1.2
New Zealand	18,866	36,295	36.7	52.9	21.0	29.4	45.9	20.8	142	102	40.4	5.2
Nicaragua	..	..	..	..	..	..	..	..	..	..	..	..
Niger	..	..	..	..	..	..	..	..	..	..	..	..
Nigeria	4,237	50,883	9.2	19.3	0.6	2.6	7.3	12.5	195	215	–35.4[a]	20.3[a]
Norway	65,034	250,922	38.6	59.5	35.7	64.9	93.4	90.8	191	195	91.4	13.7
Oman	3,463	20,267	17.4	37.5	2.8	12.6	14.2	18.2	131	120	22.0[a]	12.2[a]
Pakistan	6,581	38,169	8.9	20.5	44.6	14.5	486.8	36.2	762	644	56.7[a]	15.3[a]
Panama	2,794	10,917	24.0	32.6	1.3	0.2	4.7	2.0	29	34	15.4[a]	12.8[a]
Papua New Guinea	1,520	9,742	49.3	116.1	0.0	0.2	0.1	..	7	10	..	..
Paraguay	224	42	3.5	0.3	0.1	0.1	3.5	..	56	50	..	..
Peru	10,562	99,831	19.8	53.5	2.9	2.4	12.7	4.7	230	199	79.3	51.3
Philippines	25,957	157,321	34.2	49.7	10.8	10.7	24.1	22.6	228	251	71.5	56.7
Poland	31,279	190,235	18.3	31.5	8.5	13.0	48.1	47.6	225	569	41.9	11.3
Portugal	60,681	81,996	51.9	42.4	46.5	19.7	85.5	34.6	109	47	35.0	–16.6
Puerto Rico	..	..	..	..	..	..	..	..	..	..	..	..
Qatar	5,152	123,592	29.0	89.4	1.3	25.9	4.5	17.3	22	43	5.1[a]	27.7[a]

	Market capitalization				Market liquidity		Turnover ratio		Listed domestic companies		S&P/Global Equity Indices	
	$ millions		% of GDP		Value of shares traded % of GDP		Value of shares traded % of market capitalization		number		% change	
	2000	2010	2000	2009	2000	2009	2000	2010	2000	2010	2009	2010
Romania	1,069	32,385	2.9	18.8	0.6	1.2	24.3	5.4	5,555	1,383	26.1[a]	−6.6[a]
Russian Federation	38,922	1,004,525	15.0	69.9	7.8	55.4	36.6	85.7	249	345	106.6	21.7
Rwanda	..	..	..	..	..	..	..	..	..	..	..	..
Saudi Arabia	67,171	353,414	35.6	84.8	9.2	89.7	27.1	60.5	75	146	28.5[e]	9.0[e]
Senegal	..	..	..	..	..	..	..	..	..	..	..	..
Serbia	734	9,690	4.9	26.8	0.1	1.3	..	2.2	6	7	..	..
Sierra Leone	..	..	..	..	..	..	..	..	..	..	..	..
Singapore	152,827	370,091	164.8	170.5	98.7	138.4	52.1	82.9	418	461	76.7	18.4
Slovak Republic	1,217	4,150	4.2	5.3	3.1	0.2	78.7	3.9	493	90	−23.1[a]	5.4[a]
Slovenia	2,547	9,428	12.8	24.3	2.3	2.1	19.7	2.6	38	71	16.1[a]	−20.3[a]
Somalia	..	..	..	..	..	..	..	..	..	..	..	..
South Africa	204,952	1,012,538	154.2	247.0	58.3	120.0	33.2	39.6	616	360	53.7	32.1
Spain	504,219	1,171,615	86.8	88.8	169.8	109.5	210.7	76.0	1,019	3,310	29.0	−24.5
Sri Lanka	1,074	19,924	6.6	19.4	0.9	2.1	10.8	23.6	239	241	118.0[a]	84.6[a]
Sudan	..	..	..	..	..	..	..	..	..	..	..	..
Swaziland	73	..	4.9	6.9	0.0	..	..	0.3	6	5	..	..
Sweden	328,339	581,174	132.8	106.5	157.7	96.1	111.2	86.8	292	331	66.0	32.6
Switzerland	792,316	1,229,357	317.0	217.7	243.7	161.7	82.0	75.6	252	246	24.5	11.0
Syrian Arab Republic	..	..	..	..	..	..	..	..	..	..	..	..
Tajikistan	..	..	..	..	..	..	..	..	..	..	..	..
Tanzania	233	1,264	2.3	5.4	0.4	0.1	19.4	..	4	11	..	..
Thailand	29,489	277,732	24.0	52.4	19.0	51.2	52.9	104.8	381	541	72.8	52.1
Timor-Leste	..	..	..	..	..	..	..	..	..	..	..	..
Togo	..	..	..	..	..	..	..	..	..	..	..	..
Trinidad and Tobago	4,330	12,158	53.1	52.6	1.7	1.1	3.1	1.2	27	37	−10.2[a]	0.8[a]
Tunisia	2,828	10,682	14.5	23.1	3.2	3.2	22.6	17.2	44	54	40.6[a]	11.7[a]
Turkey	69,659	306,662	26.1	36.7	67.2	39.6	196.5	158.4	315	337	99.6	21.4
Turkmenistan	..	..	..	..	..	..	..	..	..	..	..	..
Uganda	35	..	0.6	..	0.0	..	1.7	..	2	8	..	..
Ukraine	1,881	39,457	6.0	14.8	0.9	0.5	19.2	7.5	139	183	31.1[a]	53.8[a]
United Arab Emirates	5,727	104,669	8.1	47.6	0.2	28.5	1.8	25.6	54	101	24.6[a]	−6.8[a]
United Kingdom	2,576,992	3,107,038	174.4	128.6	124.2	156.5	66.6	101.9	1,904	2,056	35.2[f]	5.2[f]
United States	15,104,037	17,138,978	152.6	106.8	321.9	331.0	200.8	189.1	7,524	4,279	23.5[g]	12.8[g]
Uruguay	161	157	0.7	0.4	0.0	0.0	0.9	..	16	6	..	..
Uzbekistan	32	..	0.2	..	0.1	0.0	25.7	..	5	..	..	..
Venezuela, RB	8,128	3,991	6.9	2.7	0.6	0.0	8.8	0.8	85	55	..	..
Vietnam	..	20,385	..	21.8	..	6.8	..	141.4	..	164	46.9[a]	0.5[a]
West Bank and Gaza	765	2,450	18.6	..	4.6	..	23.4	18.7	24	41	..	..
Yemen, Rep.	..	..	..	..	..	..	..	..	..	..	..	..
Zambia	236	2,817	7.3	17.4	0.2	0.8	3.1	..	9	19	16.7[a]	17.4[a]
Zimbabwe	2,432	11,476	36.8	161.4	4.2	16.1	11.3	..	69	76	−83.8	..
World	**32,187,124 s**	**56,172,634 s**	**101.7 w**	**85.2 w**	**151.4 w**	**142.5 w**	**140.2 w**	**122.0 w**	**47,751 s**	**47,071 s**		
Low income	..	86,835	..	37.7	..	7.9	18.3	32.5	..	719		
Middle income	1,941,548	13,277,006	36.5	73.2	34.5	82.7	93.8	101.1	21,522	16,778		
Lower middle income	879,123	7,570,880	36.2	82.2	54.6	124.3	162.2	132.4	11,444	11,088		
Upper middle income	1,062,425	5,706,126	36.8	62.1	17.5	31.5	44.2	55.7	10,078	5,690		
Low & middle income	1,948,214	13,363,841	36.1	72.6	34.0	81.9	93.5	100.8	22,094	17,497		
East Asia & Pacific	780,487	6,001,435	47.1	91.0	49.8	149.0	116.2	146.0	3,190	4,758		
Europe & Central Asia	115,145	1,473,816	17.5	50.8	30.1	38.3	131.0	91.2	7,199	2,963		
Latin America & Carib.	620,023	2,750,758	31.7	52.9	8.4	20.9	27.1	46.1	1,672	1,457		
Middle East & N. Africa	57,110	294,845	19.9	38.0	5.1	16.2	21.4	27.7	1,676	1,007		
South Asia	157,695	1,725,795	26.1	73.3	90.2	67.0	308.8	73.5	7,269	6,364		
Sub-Saharan Africa	217,754	1,117,191	89.8	154.1	32.3	48.1	31.7	37.1	1,088	948		
High income	30,238,910	42,808,793	115.2	89.9	175.5	165.3	143.0	128.5	25,657	29,574		
Euro area	5,435,393	6,276,893	86.8	49.3	80.2	45.6	90.1	75.0	5,051	6,278		

a. Refers to the S&P Frontier BMI index. b. Refers to the CAC 40 index. c. Refers to the DAX index. d. Refers to the Nikkei 225 index. e. Refers to Saudi Arabia country index. f. Refers to the FTSE 100. g. Refers to the S&P 500 index.

About the data

The development of an economy's financial markets is closely related to its overall development. Well functioning financial systems provide good and easily accessible information. That lowers transaction costs, which in turn improves resource allocation and boosts economic growth. Both banking systems and stock markets enhance growth, the main factor in poverty reduction. At low levels of economic development commercial banks tend to dominate the financial system, while at higher levels domestic stock markets tend to become more active and efficient relative to domestic banks.

Open economies with sound macroeconomic policies, good legal systems, and shareholder protection attract capital and therefore have larger financial markets. Recent research on stock market development shows that modern communications technology and increased financial integration have resulted in more cross-border capital flows, a stronger presence of financial firms around the world, and the migration of stock exchange activities to international exchanges. Many firms in emerging markets now cross-list on international exchanges, which provides them with lower cost capital and more liquidity-traded shares. However, this also means that exchanges in emerging markets may not have enough financial activity to sustain them, putting pressure on them to rethink their operations.

The indicators in the table are from Standard & Poor's Emerging Markets Data Base. They include measures of size (market capitalization, number of listed domestic companies) and liquidity (value of shares traded as a percentage of gross domestic product, value of shares traded as a percentage of market capitalization). The comparability of such indicators across countries may be limited by conceptual and statistical weaknesses, such as inaccurate reporting and differences in accounting standards. The percentage change in stock market prices in U.S. dollars for developing economies is from Standard & Poor's Global Equity Indices (S&P IFCI) and Standard & Poor's Frontier Broad Market Index (BMI). The percentage change for France, Germany, Japan, the United Kingdom, and the United States is from local stock market prices. The indicator is an important measure of overall performance. Regulatory and institutional factors that can affect investor confidence, such as entry and exit restrictions, the existence of a securities and exchange commission, and the quality of laws to protect investors, may influence the functioning of stock markets but are not included in the table.

Stock market size can be measured in various ways, and each may produce a different ranking of countries. Market capitalization shows the overall size of the stock market in U.S. dollars and as a percentage of GDP. The number of listed domestic companies is another measure of market size. Market size is positively correlated with the ability to mobilize capital and diversify risk.

Market liquidity, the ability to easily buy and sell securities, is measured by dividing the total value of shares traded by GDP. The turnover ratio—the value of shares traded as a percentage of market capitalization—is also a measure of liquidity as well as of transaction costs. (High turnover indicates low transaction costs.) The turnover ratio complements the ratio of value traded to GDP, because the turnover ratio is related to the size of the market and the value traded ratio to the size of the economy. A small, liquid market will have a high turnover ratio but a low value of shares traded ratio. Liquidity is an important attribute of stock markets because, in theory, liquid markets improve the allocation of capital and enhance prospects for long-term economic growth. A more comprehensive measure of liquidity would include trading costs and the time and uncertainty in finding a counterpart in settling trades.

Standard & Poor's Index Services, the source for all the data in the table, provides regular updates on 21 emerging stock markets and 36 frontier markets. Standard & Poor's maintains a series of indexes for investors interested in investing in stock markets in developing countries. The S&P/IFCI index, Standard & Poor's leading emerging markets index, is designed to be sufficiently investable to support index tracking portfolios in emerging market stocks that are legally and practically open to foreign portfolio investment. The S&P/Frontier BMI measures the performance of 36 smaller and less liquid markets. The individual country indexes include all publicly listed equities representing an aggregate of at least 80 percent or more of market capitalization in each market. These indexes are widely used benchmarks for international portfolio management. See www.standardandpoors.com for further information on the indexes.

Because markets included in Standard & Poor's emerging markets category vary widely in level of development, it is best to look at the entire category to identify the most significant market trends. And it is useful to remember that stock market trends may be distorted by currency conversions, especially when a currency has registered a significant devaluation.

About the data is based on Demirgüç-Kunt and Levine (1996), Beck and Levine (2001), and Claessens, Klingebiel, and Schmukler (2002).

Definitions

• **Market capitalization** (also known as market value) is the share price times the number of shares outstanding. • **Market liquidity** is the total value of shares traded during the period divided by gross domestic product (GDP). This indicator complements the market capitalization ratio by showing whether market size is matched by trading. • **Turnover ratio** is the total value of shares traded during the period divided by the average market capitalization for the period. Average market capitalization is calculated as the average of the end-of-period values for the current period and the previous period. • **Listed domestic companies** are the domestically incorporated companies listed on the country's stock exchanges at the end of the year. This indicator does not include investment companies, mutual funds, or other collective investment vehicles. • **S&P/Global Equity Indices** measure the U.S. dollar price change in the stock markets.

Data sources

Data on stock markets are from Standard & Poor's *Global Stock Markets Factbook 2010,* which draws on the Emerging Markets Data Base, supplemented by other data from Standard & Poor's. The firm collects data through an annual survey of the world's stock exchanges, supplemented by information provided by its network of correspondents and by Reuters. Data on GDP are from the World Bank's national accounts data files.

5.5 Financial access, stability, and efficiency

	Getting credit		Financial access and outreach					Bank capital to asset ratio	Ratio of bank non-performing loans to total gross loans	Domestic credit provided by banking sector	Interest rate spread	Risk premium on lending
	Strength of legal rights index 0–10 (weak to strong)	Depth of credit information index 0–6 (low to high)	Deposit accounts at commercial banks per 1,000 adults	Loan accounts at commercial banks per 1,000 adults	Commercial bank branches per 100,000 adults	Automated teller machines per 100,000 adults	Point-of-sale terminals per 100,000 adults				Lending rate minus deposit rate percentage points	Prime lending rate minus treasury bill rate percentage points
								%	%	% of GDP		
	June 2010	June 2010	2009	2009	2009	2009	2009	2009	2009	2009	2009	2009
Afghanistan	6	0	..	4	1.1	0.18	..	..	..	1.5	..	..
Albania	9	4	451	102	21.4	26.87	123	8.7	10.5	68.5	5.9	6.4
Algeria	3	2	683	..	5.3	4.13	8	..	..	-8.9	6.3	7.3
Angola	4	3	..	..	5.5	7.82	25	..	..	29.2	8.1	..
Argentina	4	6	875	503	13.3	33.04	..	13.3	3.0	28.0	4.1	..
Armenia	6	5	572	192	15.7	22.22	94	21.0	4.8	19.9	10.1	9.3
Australia	9	5	..	..	31.8	159.30	3,939	5.0	1.2	143.6	3.2	2.9
Austria	7	6	2,442	..	..	118.37	4,890	7.0	2.3	141.1	..	..
Azerbaijan	6	5	702	..	8.6	23.05	112	..	..	23.1	7.8	16.7
Bangladesh	7	2	319	42	5.2	..	..	6.5	*11.2*	60.4	6.4	..
Belarus	3	5	..	..	44.9	29.71	165	16.6	4.2	34.6	1.0	..
Belgium	7	4	3,725	..	50.0	85.96	1,086	4.5	2.7	119.3	..	5.6
Benin	3	1	..	..	..	..	..	..	..	19.1	..	..
Bolivia	1	6	274	72	6.3	15.11	33	8.7	3.5	49.5	8.9	9.5
Bosnia and Herzegovina	5	5	380	344	25.0	27.14	502	15.2	5.9	58.3	4.3	..
Botswana	7	4	481	80	6.9	29.26	..	..	..	-1.0	6.3	..
Brazil	3	5	..	390	12.2	110.19	1,471	9.5	4.2	97.5	35.4	34.9
Bulgaria	8	6	1,987	456	88.1	78.22	683	10.8	6.4	69.4	5.2	6.2
Burkina Faso	3	1	..	..	..	..	..	..	..	15.2	..	..
Burundi	2	1	21	1	1.7	0.04	0	..	..	36.5	..	..
Cambodia	8	0	76	25	3.7	..	36	..	..	19.0	..	..
Cameroon	3	2	..	..	..	..	..	..	..	6.9	*10.8*	..
Canada	6	6	..	..	23.7	202.78	2,202	5.7	1.3	*178.1*	2.3	2.0
Central African Republic	3	2	..	..	..	..	..	..	..	17.2	*10.8*	..
Chad	3	1	..	..	..	..	..	..	..	8.3	*10.8*	..
Chile	4	5	746	629	15.0	55.56	450	7.4	3.0	98.8	5.2	..
China	6	4	..	..	..	..	..	5.6	1.6	145.2	3.1	..
Hong Kong SAR, China	10	5	..	..	24.4	..	..	12.7	1.1	166.8	5.0	4.9
Colombia	5	5	1,151	..	13.7	26.31	..	13.6	4.1	37.2	6.9	..
Congo, Dem. Rep.	3	0	6	..	0.3	..	..	..	..	7.6	49.5	..
Congo, Rep.	3	2	..	..	..	..	..	..	..	-15.9	*10.8*	..
Costa Rica	5	5	..	..	..	53.35	0	13.9	2.0	54.3	12.8	..
Côte d'Ivoire	3	1	..	..	..	..	..	..	..	22.8	..	..
Croatia	6	4	..	..	33.2	88.62	2,121	13.9	7.8	76.9	8.4	..
Cuba	..	..	..	..	..	..	..	..	..	..	..	..
Czech Republic	6	5	1,680	..	22.4	38.40	651	6.1	4.6	62.4	4.7	4.7
Denmark	9	4	..	..	46.7	70.42	2,023	5.7	0.3	223.0	..	..
Dominican Republic	3	6	..	310	10.0	27.21	..	9.1	4.0	40.6	10.3	..
Ecuador	3	5	494	..	1.6	26.01	..	7.7	2.9	18.9	*7.1*	..
Egypt, Arab Rep.	3	6	..	..	..	..	..	6.4	13.4	75.4	5.5	2.1
El Salvador	5	6	737	..	8.2	22.86	250	13.2	3.6	44.5	..	..
Eritrea	2	0	..	..	..	..	..	..	..	112.1	..	..
Estonia	7	5	2,752	1,022	22.2	89.09	1,417	8.5	5.2	106.2	4.6	..
Ethiopia	4	2	82	1	1.2	..	..	..	..	*37.1*	3.3	7.3
Finland	7	5	..	..	18.5	38.74	66	6.4	0.7	98.7	..	..
France	7	4	..	..	23.0	102.55	2,153	4.5	3.6	128.4	..	..
Gabon	3	2	..	..	..	..	..	16.2	9.8	7.5	*10.8*	..
Gambia, The	5	0	269	44	5.5	1.48	5	..	..	38.7	11.5	..
Georgia	7	6	661	349	18.6	28.77	169	18.3	6.3	33.2	15.2	19.5
Germany	7	6	..	..	16.3	79.74	799	4.8	3.3	131.8	..	..
Ghana	8	3	270	..	4.4	4.16	4	17.0	16.2	27.9	..	..
Greece	3	5	3,219	1,297	38.8	76.06	3,827	6.1	7.7	112.7	..	..
Guatemala	8	6	1,050	374	33.1	22.18	486	10.5	2.7	37.7	8.3	..
Guinea	3	0	..	..	..	..	..	..	..	..	..	..
Guinea-Bissau	3	1	..	..	..	..	..	..	..	4.9	..	..
Haiti	3	2	330	11	..	0.58	..	..	..	25.8	16.2	..
Honduras	6	6	744	..	1.5	21.89	..	..	..	54.1	8.6	..

	Getting credit		Financial access and outreach					Bank capital to asset ratio	Ratio of bank non-performing loans to total gross loans	Domestic credit provided by banking sector	Interest rate spread	Risk premium on lending
	Strength of legal rights index 0–10 (weak to strong)	Depth of credit information index 0–6 (low to high)	Deposit accounts at commercial banks per 1,000 adults	Loan accounts at commercial banks per 1,000 adults	Commercial bank branches per 100,000 adults	Automated teller machines per 100,000 adults	Point-of-sale terminals per 100,000 adults	%	%	% of GDP	Lending rate minus deposit rate percentage points	Prime lending rate minus treasury bill rate percentage points
	June 2010	June 2010	2009	2009	2009	2009	2009	2009	2009	2009	2009	2009
Hungary	7	5	1,571	..	17.1	54.24	585	8.5	6.7	79.9	5.2	2.6
India	8	4	680	124	9.3	3.55	..	6.4	2.3	69.4	..	..
Indonesia	3	4	484	181	6.7	13.44	120	10.3	3.3	36.9	5.2	..
Iran, Islamic Rep.	4	4	..	..	28.8	23.97	1,353	..	..	37.2	-1.1	..
Iraq	3	0	..	..	..	..	..	..	..	-16.3	7.8	1.8
Ireland	8	5	..	..	34.1	..	..	5.6	9.0	219.8	..	..
Israel	9	5	2,254	1,055	19.8	47.38	..	6.0	1.5	78.1	2.6	2.3
Italy	3	5	763	597	53.0	93.93	2,386	8.0	7.0	141.6	..	3.8
Jamaica	8	0	1,172	215	7.2	21.89	674	..	..	59.8	9.5	-3.5
Japan	7	6	..	..	12.5	..	..	4.7	1.7	320.5	1.3	1.6
Jordan	4	2	814	160	16.2	..	..	11.0	6.7	99.3	4.3	..
Kazakhstan	4	5	..	..	21.6	52.83	173	-9.3	21.2	54.6	..	..
Kenya	10	4	296	70	4.0	6.67	..	12.7	7.9	44.8	8.8	7.4
Korea, Dem. Rep.	..	..	..	..	..	..	..	..	..	..	..	..
Korea, Rep.	7	6	..	..	12.6	..	..	10.9	1.2	112.4	2.2	..
Kosovo	8	4	..	..	..	..	..	..	4.4	14.3	10.1	..
Kuwait	4	4	..	..	15.1	50.05	904	12.1	9.7	65.1	3.3	5.2
Kyrgyz Republic	10	3	115	25	6.3	..	..	..	..	14.0	19.2	12.5
Lao PDR	4	0	..	..	1.7	3.06	..	..	..	10.5	19.3	11.5
Latvia	9	5	1,219	687	12.0	..	..	7.4	16.4	93.2	8.2	5.8
Lebanon	3	5	1,310	..	29.1	38.55	1,293	7.0	6.0	165.0	2.3	4.7
Lesotho	6	0	199	18	1.9	7.13	..	7.9	4.0	-15.5	8.2	5.2
Liberia	4	1	..	..	..	..	..	..	..	149.5	10.1	..
Libya	..	..	..	..	..	..	..	..	..	-65.9	3.5	..
Lithuania	5	6	2,142	381	28.8	51.69	1,413	7.9	19.3	69.3	3.6	-0.1
Macedonia, FYR	7	4	1,302	962	22.1	45.98	1,297	11.4	8.9	44.0	3.0	..
Madagascar	2	0	34	21	1.0	0.96	2	..	..	11.6	33.5	37.4
Malawi	7	0	124	17	1.8	1.48	2	..	..	32.0	21.8	15.1
Malaysia	10	6	2,227	973	11.6	43.25	941	9.0	3.7	137.4	3.0	3.0
Mali	3	1	..	..	..	..	..	..	..	10.7	..	..
Mauritania	3	1	37	..	3.8	0.74	..	..	..	..	15.5	13.1
Mauritius	5	3	2,110	417	19.4	37.71	647	..	..	109.7	10.8	..
Mexico	5	6	1,014	..	14.0	40.15	..	9.7	3.1	44.1	5.1	1.6
Moldova	8	0	..	..	9.7	..	..	16.0	16.3	41.6	5.6	9.2
Mongolia	6	3	1,935	272	56.7	18.18	448	..	..	32.2	8.4	15.0
Morocco	3	5	277	..	11.6	16.65	46	7.6	5.5	100.5	..	..
Mozambique	2	4	112	20	2.9	4.32	34	7.7	1.8	22.8	6.2	5.1
Myanmar	..	..	..	..	..	..	..	..	..	..	5.0	..
Namibia	8	5	466	356	7.3	27.31	217	7.9	2.7	43.5	4.9	2.9
Nepal	6	2	165	38	3.2	1.13	..	..	..	69.6	5.5	1.7
Netherlands	6	5	1,772	..	26.1	63.78	2,286	4.3	..	224.4	-0.6	..
New Zealand	10	5	..	..	31.7	72.34	3,916	..	..	154.2	6.3	7.6
Nicaragua	3	5	198	185	6.8	..	..	..	..	67.5	8.0	..
Niger	3	1	..	..	..	..	..	..	..	12.2	..	..
Nigeria	8	0	..	..	..	..	..	18.4	6.6	35.9	5.1	14.6
Norway	7	4	..	..	35.0	59.73	2,827	6.0	1.5	..	2.0	..
Oman	4	2	..	..	22.1	..	..	13.5	3.5	41.9	3.3	..
Pakistan	6	4	226	47	7.5	3.39	47	10.1	12.2	48.4	5.9	2.0
Panama	6	6	757	435	18.9	36.94	427	11.7	1.4	81.6	4.8	..
Papua New Guinea	5	3	..	..	2.8	..	..	..	..	39.1	7.8	3.0
Paraguay	3	6	80	89	6.2	..	..	8.7	1.6	25.5	26.8	..
Peru	7	6	716	367	7.5	17.67	40	9.9	2.7	18.1	18.2	..
Philippines	3	3	517	..	10.5	13.33	..	11.1	4.1	49.4	5.8	5.3
Poland	9	4	1,527	..	32.6	42.16	253	9.0	7.6	61.5	..	..
Portugal	3	5	..	..	55.9	189.60	2,548	6.5	3.2	196.1	..	..
Puerto Rico	7	5	1,026	..	16.6	43.33	1,398	..	..	..	..	..
Qatar	3	2	..	..	..	..	..	..	..	75.7	2.8	..

	Getting credit		Financial access and outreach					Bank capital to asset ratio	Ratio of bank non-performing loans to total gross loans	Domestic credit provided by banking sector	Interest rate spread	Risk premium on lending
	Strength of legal rights index 0–10 (weak to strong)	Depth of credit information index 0–6 (low to high)	Deposit accounts at commercial banks per 1,000 adults	Loan accounts at commercial banks per 1,000 adults	Commercial bank branches per 100,000 adults	Automated teller machines per 100,000 adults	Point-of-sale terminals per 100,000 adults	%	%	% of GDP	Lending rate minus deposit rate percentage points	Prime lending rate minus treasury bill rate percentage points
	June 2010	June 2010	2009	2009	2009	2009	2009	2009	2009	2009	2009	2009
Romania	8	5	..	431	27.6	50.63	460	7.6	15.3	52.7	5.3	6.4
Russian Federation	3	5	..	..	2.9	65.60	275	15.7	9.7	33.8	6.7	..
Rwanda	8	4	202	2	3.1	0.38	1	13.0	13.1	..	9.8	8.9
Saudi Arabia	5	6	..	..	..	..	..	11.9	3.3	0.6	..	..
Senegal	3	1	..	..	..	..	..	9.3	18.7	26.6	..	..
Serbia	8	5	..	..	44.9	41.31	959	21.0	15.5	44.8	0.0	1.4
Sierra Leone	6	0	..	..	..	..	..	18.9	16.5	10.7	14.8	9.0
Singapore	10	4	2,305	899	11.0	50.64	1,887	10.5	2.3	91.2	5.1	5.0
Slovak Republic	9	4	..	..	25.7	47.76	611	9.6	5.3	53.8	4.3	..
Slovenia	5	2	1,394	..	15.7	99.47	1,925	8.3	2.3	94.5	4.5	4.8
Somalia	..	..	..	..	..	..	..	..	..	..	..	..
South Africa	9	6	788	297	8.0	54.85	..	6.7	5.9	183.5	3.2	3.9
Spain	6	5	741	310	40.5	157.10	3,523	6.8	5.1	228.4	..	..
Sri Lanka	4	5	1,652	487	9.1	10.46	..	..	..	39.6	5.1	2.7
Sudan	5	0	..	..	..	..	..	..	..	20.0	..	..
Swaziland	6	5	270	98	2.9	15.96	52	16.9	8.1	9.1	6.0	3.4
Sweden	5	4	..	..	22.8	36.94	..	5.0	2.0	143.8	..	..
Switzerland	8	5	..	..	..	93.70	2,004	5.5	0.4	191.0	2.7	2.8
Syrian Arab Republic	1	2	157	23	2.2	0.95	..	..	..	45.1	3.7	..
Tajikistan	3	0	..	..	3.9	2.97	2	..	..	27.5	17.1	..
Tanzania	8	0	..	..	1.8	2.63	11	..	..	18.1	7.1	7.9
Thailand	4	5	1,498	276	10.9	65.48	..	9.8	5.3	136.9	4.9	4.7
Timor-Leste	1	0	..	..	..	..	..	..	..	-18.4	10.3	..
Togo	3	1	..	..	..	..	..	..	..	30.2	..	..
Trinidad and Tobago	8	4	..	..	..	..	..	..	..	26.5	8.5	9.2
Tunisia	3	5	672	176	13.6	14.26	172	..	13.2	75.2	..	..
Turkey	4	5	1,851	315	17.3	40.99	3,046	13.3	5.6	63.0	..	..
Turkmenistan	..	..	..	..	..	..	..	..	..	..	..	..
Uganda	7	4	154	21	1.9	2.24	3	13.4	4.2	11.2	11.2	13.9
Ukraine	9	3	3,755	..	3.3	70.09	293	13.1	40.2	88.5	7.1	..
United Arab Emirates	4	5	..	..	..	..	..	16.0	4.8	114.5	..	..
United Kingdom	9	6	..	..	..	127.07	2,177	5.4	3.5	228.9	..	0.1
United States	8	6	1,761	..	35.4	169.23	2,156	11.0	5.4	230.5	..	3.1
Uruguay	5	6	507	439	13.9	30.57	275	8.9	1.0	27.9	10.9	3.4
Uzbekistan	2	3	..	..	..	..	..	..	..	..	..	..
Venezuela, RB	2	0	518	484	18.5	27.99	..	9.4	3.0	20.5	3.5	..
Vietnam	8	5	..	..	3.3	..	..	..	..	123.0	3.1	2.0
West Bank and Gaza	0	3	..	..	..	..	..	..	..	..	..	..
Yemen, Rep.	2	2	106	6	1.8	2.44	17	..	..	19.3	7.3	4.5
Zambia	9	5	293	19	3.5	4.54	11	..	..	18.5	15.0	6.7
Zimbabwe	6	0	139	..	2.8	..	..	..	..	..	457.5	330.2
World	**5.5 u**	**3.0 u**						**9.4 m**	**4.2 m**	**169.0 w**	**6.2 m**	
Low income	4.9	1.3								35.1	11.5	
Middle income	5.1	3.1						10.1	4.8	89.4	6.3	
Lower middle income	4.6	2.6						10.0	5.1	110.3	7.3	
Upper middle income	5.7	3.6						9.7	4.2	63.3	5.5	
Low & middle income	5.0	2.6							5.3	88.4	6.8	
East Asia & Pacific	5.8	1.9								134.2	7.1	
Europe & Central Asia	6.3	4.1						13.3	9.3	47.1	5.7	
Latin America & Carib.	5.2	3.4						9.6	3.0	67.1	7.7	
Middle East & N. Africa	2.5	3.1								40.9	4.3	
South Asia	5.4	2.1						6.4	10.5	65.6	5.9	
Sub-Saharan Africa	4.6	1.6								78.5	8.5	
High income	6.7	4.3						6.8	3.4	201.8	..	
Euro area	6.3	4.1						6.5	3.6	152.0	..	

Financial access, stability, and efficiency

About the data

Access to finance can expand opportunities for all with higher levels of access and use of banking services associated with lower financing obstacles for people and businesses. A stable financial system that promotes efficient savings and investment is also crucial for a thriving democracy and market economy.

There are several aspects of access to financial services: availability, cost, and quality of services. The development and growth of credit markets depend on access to timely, reliable, and accurate data on borrowers' credit experiences. Access to credit can be improved by making it easy to create and enforce collateral agreements and increasing information about potential borrowers' creditworthiness. Lenders look at a borrower's credit history and collateral. Where credit registries and effective collateral laws are absent—as in many developing countries—banks make fewer loans. Indicators that cover getting credit include the strength of legal rights index and the depth of credit information index.

The "unbanked" have to resort to informal services to manage their money—saving under the mattress, borrowing from family and friends, or money lenders—that are usually less reliable and more costly than formal banking institutions. The table presents data on financial access covering deposits and loans, and outreach indicators such as the number of branches, automatic teller machines, and point-of-sale terminals.

Data on financial access cover 142 countries and present indicators on savings, credit, and payment services in banks and regulated nonbank financial institutions. Data were collected for commercial banks and regulated nonbank financial institutions such as cooperatives, credit unions, specialized state financial institutions, and microfinance institutions.

The size and mobility of international capital flows make it increasingly important to monitor the strength of financial systems. Robust financial systems can increase economic activity and welfare, but instability in the financial system can disrupt financial activity and impose widespread costs on the economy. The ratio of bank capital to assets, a measure of bank solvency and resiliency, shows the extent to which banks can deal with unexpected losses. Capital includes tier 1 capital (paid-up shares and common stock), a common feature in all countries' banking systems, and total regulatory capital, which includes several types of subordinated debt instruments that need not be repaid if the funds are required to maintain minimum capital levels (tier 2 and tier 3 capital). Total assets include

all nonfinancial and financial assets. Data are from internally consistent financial statements.

The ratio of bank nonperforming loans to total gross loans, a measure of bank health and efficiency, helps identify problems with asset quality in the loan portfolio. A high ratio may signal deterioration of the credit portfolio. International guidelines recommend that loans be classified as nonperforming when payments of principal and interest are 90 days or more past due or when future payments are not expected to be received in full. Domestic credit provided by the banking sector as a share of GDP is a measure of banking sector depth and financial sector development in terms of size. In a few countries governments may hold international reserves as deposits in the banking system rather than in the central bank. Since the claims on the central government are a net item (claims on the central government minus central government deposits), this net figure may be negative, resulting in a negative figure of domestic credit provided by the banking sector.

The interest rate spread—the margin between the cost of mobilizing liabilities and the earnings on assets—is a measure of financial sector efficiency in intermediation. A narrow interest rate spread means low transaction costs, which reduces the cost of funds for investment, crucial to economic growth.

The risk premium on lending is the spread between the lending rate to the private sector and the "risk-free" government rate. Spreads are expressed as annual averages. A small spread indicates that the market considers its best corporate customers to be low risk. A negative rate indicates that the market considers its best corporate clients to be lower risk than the government.

Definitions

• **Strength of legal rights index** measures the degree to which collateral and bankruptcy laws protect the rights of borrowers and lenders and thus facilitate lending. Higher values indicate that the laws are better designed to expand access to credit. • **Depth of credit information index** measures rules affecting the scope, accessibility, and quality of information available through public or private credit registries. Higher values indicate the availability of more credit information. • **Deposit accounts** are accounts at commercial banks that allow money to be deposited and withdrawn by the account holder. The major types of deposits are checking accounts, savings accounts, and time deposits. • **Loan accounts at commercial banks** include loans from banks to individuals, businesses, and others, including home mortgages,

consumer loans, business loans, trade loans, student loans, emergency loans, agricultural loans, and the like. • **Commercial banks branches** are retail locations offering a wide array of face-to-face and automated financial services. • **Automated teller machines** are computerized telecommunications devices that provide clients of a financial institution with access to financial transactions in a public place. • **Point-of-sale terminals** are the equipment used to manage the selling process by a salesperson-accessible interface in the location where a transaction takes place. • **Bank capital to asset ratio** is the ratio of bank capital and reserves to total assets. Capital and reserves include funds contributed by owners, retained earnings, general and special reserves, provisions, and valuation adjustments. • **Ratio of bank nonperforming loans to total gross loans** is the value of nonperforming loans divided by the total value of the loan portfolio (including nonperforming loans before the deduction of loan loss provisions). The amount recorded as nonperforming should be the gross value of the loan as recorded on the balance sheet, not just the amount overdue. • **Domestic credit provided by banking sector** is all credit to various sectors on a gross basis, except to the central government, which is net. The banking sector includes monetary authorities, deposit money banks, and other banking institutions for which data are available. • **Interest rate spread** is the interest rate charged by banks on loans to prime customers minus the interest rate paid by commercial or similar banks for demand, time, or savings deposits. • **Risk premium on lending** is the interest rate charged by banks on loans to prime private sector customers minus the "risk-free" treasury bill interest rate at which short-term government securities are issued or traded in the market.

Data sources

Data on getting credit are from the World Bank's Doing Business project (www.doingbusiness.org). Data on financial access and outreach are from the Consultative Group to Assist the Poor and the World Bank Group's *Financial Access 2010*. Data on bank capital and nonperforming loans are from the IMF's *Global Financial Stability Report*. Data on credit and interest rates are from the IMF's *International Financial Statistics*.

	Tax revenue collected by central government		Taxes payable by businesses					
	% of GDP		Number of payments	Time to prepare, file, and pay taxes hours	Profit tax % of commercial profits	Labor tax and contributions % of commercial profits	Other taxes % of commercial profits	Total tax rate % of commercial profits
	2000	2009	June 2010	June 2010	June 2010	June 2010	June 2010	June 2010
Afghanistan	..	7.3	8	275	0.0	0.0	36.4	36.4
Albania	16.1	..	44	360	8.5	27.3	4.9	40.6
Algeria	..	34.3[a]	34	451	6.6	29.7	35.7	72.0
Angola	..	..	31	282	24.6	9.0	19.5	53.2
Argentina	9.8[a]	..	9	453	2.8	29.4	76.0	108.2
Armenia	..	16.4	50	581	16.6	23.0	1.1	40.7
Australia	23.0[a]	22.1[a]	11	109	25.9	20.7	1.3	47.9
Austria	19.9[a]	18.7[a]	22	170	15.7	34.6	5.1	55.5
Azerbaijan	..	16.7	18	306	13.8	24.8	2.2	40.9
Bangladesh	7.6	8.6	21	302	25.7	0.0	9.2	35.0.
Belarus	16.6	19.4	82	798	22.0	39.3	19.2	80.4
Belgium	27.4[a]	24.0[a]	11	156	4.8	50.4	1.8	57.0
Benin	15.5[a]	16.1[a]	55	270	14.8	27.3	23.9	66.0
Bolivia	13.2[a]	17.0[a]	42	1,080	0.0	15.5	64.6	80.0
Bosnia and Herzegovina	..	19.6[a]	51	422	5.3	12.6	5.0	23.0
Botswana	..	..	19	152	15.9	0.0	3.6	19.5
Brazil	14.0	15.6	10	2,600	21.4	40.9	6.6	69.0
Bulgaria	17.9	20.9	17	616	4.6	20.4	3.9	29.0
Burkina Faso	10.5[a]	12.9[a]	46	270	16.1	22.6	6.2	44.9
Burundi	13.6	..	32	211	19.4	7.8	126.2	153.4
Cambodia	8.2[a]	9.6[a]	39	173	18.9	0.1	3.5	22.5
Cameroon	11.2	..	44	654	29.9	18.3	0.9	49.1
Canada	15.3[a]	11.8[a]	8	131	9.8	12.6	6.9	29.2.
Central African Republic	..	..	54	504	176.8	8.1	18.9	203.8
Chad	..	..	54	732	31.3	28.4	5.7	65.4
Chile	16.7[a]	15.3[a]	9	316	18.0	3.8	3.2	25.0
China	6.8	10.3	7	398	6.0	49.6	7.9	63.5
Hong Kong SAR, China	9.1[a]	13.0[a]	3	80	18.7	5.3	0.1	24.1
Colombia	11.0[a]	11.9[a]	20	208	17.7	33.9	27.1	78.7
Congo, Dem. Rep.	3.5	..	32	336	58.9	7.9	272.8	339.7
Congo, Rep.	5.9	..	61	606	0.0	32.9	32.6	65.5
Costa Rica	..	13.9[a]	42	272	18.9	29.5	6.6	55.0
Côte d'Ivoire	..	16.4[a]	64	270	8.8	20.1	15.5	44.4
Croatia	22.4	19.1	17	196	11.4	19.4	1.6	32.5
Cuba	..	..	..	..	..	..	..	..
Czech Republic	15.4	13.5	12	557	7.4	38.4	3.0	48.8
Denmark	30.8[a]	34.5[a]	9	135	21.9	3.6	3.7	29.2
Dominican Republic	..	14.9[a]	9	324	20.5	18.3	1.8	40.7
Ecuador	..	..	8	654	18.4	13.7	3.2	35.3
Egypt, Arab Rep.	13.4	15.7	29	433	13.2	25.8	3.6	42.6
El Salvador	10.7[a]	12.5[a]	53	320	17.0	17.2	0.8	35.0
Eritrea	..	..	18	216	8.8	0.0	75.8	84.5
Estonia	15.8[a]	17.6[a]	7	81	8.0	39.2	2.4	49.6
Ethiopia	8.1	..	19	198	26.8	0.0	4.3	31.1
Finland	24.7[a]	21.3[a]	8	243	15.9	27.7	1.0	44.6
France	23.2[a]	19.6[a]	7	132	8.2	51.7	5.9	65.8
Gabon	..	..	26	488	18.4	22.7	2.3	43.5
Gambia, The	..	..	50	376	41.4	12.9	238.0	292.3
Georgia	7.7	23.2	18	387	13.3	0.0	2.0	15.3
Germany	11.9[a]	12.0[a]	16	215	23.0	22.0	3.3	48.2
Ghana	17.2	12.5	33	224	18.1	14.1	0.5	32.7
Greece	23.3[a]	19.1[a]	10	224	13.9	31.7	1.6	47.2
Guatemala	10.1	10.4	24	344	25.9	14.3	0.7	40.9
Guinea	11.1	..	56	416	19.4	24.5	10.8	54.6
Guinea-Bissau	..	..	46	208	14.9	24.8	6.1	45.9
Haiti	..	..	42	160	23.3	12.4	4.3	40.1
Honduras	..	14.4[a]	47	224	26.7	10.7	10.9	48.3

	Tax revenue collected by central government		Taxes payable by businesses					
	% of GDP		Number of payments	Time to prepare, file, and pay taxes hours	Profit tax % of commercial profits	Labor tax and contributions % of commercial profits	Other taxes % of commercial profits	Total tax rate % of commercial profits
	2000	2009	June 2010	June 2010	June 2010	June 2010	June 2010	June 2010
Hungary	21.9[a]	23.5[a]	14	277	16.7	34.4	2.2	53.3
India	9.0	9.8	56	258	24.0	18.2	21.1	63.3
Indonesia	11.6	11.4	51	266	26.6	10.6	0.1	37.3
Iran, Islamic Rep.	6.3	9.3	20	344	17.8	25.9	0.4	44.1
Iraq	..		13	312	14.9	13.5	0.0	28.4
Ireland	26.0[a]	20.8[a]	9	76	11.9	11.6	3.0	26.5
Israel	28.7[a]	23.0[a]	33	235	23.8	5.3	2.6	31.7
Italy	23.2[a]	23.0[a]	15	285	22.8	43.4	2.4	68.6
Jamaica	..	21.9[a]	72	414	28.6	13.0	8.5	50.1
Japan	..	9.2[a]	14	355	27.9	14.7	6.0	48.6
Jordan	19.0	16.2	26	101	15.2	12.4	3.6	31.2
Kazakhstan	10.2	8.1	9	271	16.3	11.5	1.9	29.6
Kenya	16.8	19.6	41	393	33.1	6.8	9.9	49.7
Korea, Dem. Rep.	..	..	..	..	..	..	..	..
Korea, Rep.	15.4	15.5	14	250	15.3	12.9	1.6	29.8
Kosovo	..	21.1	33	163	10.2	5.6	0.6	16.5
Kuwait	1.3	0.9	15	118	4.7	10.7	0.0	15.5
Kyrgyz Republic	11.7	15.4	48	202	8.9	21.5	26.7	57.2
Lao PDR	..	12.5	34	362	25.2	5.6	2.9	33.7
Latvia	14.2	12.6	7	293	6.5	27.2	4.8	38.5
Lebanon	11.9[a]	17.3[a]	19	180	6.1	24.1	0.0	30.2
Lesotho	37.4	60.0	21	324	16.4	0.0	3.2	19.6
Liberia	..	0.3	32	158	0.0	5.4	38.3	43.7
Libya	..	..	..	..	..	..	..	..
Lithuania	14.6[a]	13.8[a]	11	175	0.0	35.1	3.6	38.7
Macedonia, FYR	..	19.7	40	119	6.3	0.6	3.8	10.6
Madagascar	11.3[a]	13.0[a]	23	201	15.8	20.3	1.6	37.7
Malawi	..	..	19	157	23.3	1.1	0.7	25.1
Malaysia	13.7	15.7	12	145	16.7	15.6	1.4	33.7
Mali	13.2[a]	14.7[a]	59	270	12.9	32.6	6.7	52.2
Mauritania	..	..	38	696	44.2	17.6	6.6	68.4
Mauritius	..	19.2[a]	7	161	11.8	5.0	7.3	24.1
Mexico	11.7	..	6	404	23.1	26.1	1.3	50.5
Moldova	14.7	17.8	48	228	0.0	30.2	0.7	30.9
Mongolia	14.5	18.0	43	192	9.5	12.4	1.0	23.0
Morocco	19.9[a]	23.8[a]	28	358	18.1	22.2	1.4	41.7
Mozambique	..	..	37	230	27.7	4.5	2.1	34.3
Myanmar	3.0	..	..	..	..	..	..	..
Namibia	27.5	27.3	37	375	4.0	1.0	4.6	9.6
Nepal	8.7	12.2	34	338	16.2	11.3	10.7	38.2
Netherlands	22.3[a]	22.7[a]	9	134	20.9	17.9	1.7	40.5
New Zealand	29.2[a]	30.8[a]	8	192	30.4	3.0	0.9	34.3
Nicaragua	13.8	17.8	64	222	24.8	19.2	19.2	63.2
Niger	..	11.5[a]	41	270	20.1	19.6	6.8	46.5
Nigeria	..	0.3	35	938	21.8	9.7	0.7	32.2
Norway	27.4[a]	25.4[a]	4	87	24.4	15.9	1.3	41.6
Oman	7.2	..	14	62	9.7	11.8	0.1	21.6
Pakistan	10.1	9.3	47	560	14.3	15.0	2.3	31.6
Panama	10.2	..	62	482	17.0	22.6	10.5	50.1
Papua New Guinea	19.0	..	33	194	22.0	11.7	8.6	42.3
Paraguay	10.9	13.0	35	311	9.6	18.6	6.7	35.0
Peru	12.2	13.4	9	380	26.0	11.0	3.2	40.2
Philippines	13.7	12.8	47	195	21.3	10.3	14.2	45.8
Poland	16.0[a]	16.4[a]	29	325	17.7	22.1	2.5	42.3
Portugal	20.6[a]	19.7[a]	8	298	14.9	26.8	1.6	43.3
Puerto Rico	..	..	16	218	26.3	14.4	27.0	67.7
Qatar	..	19.8	3	36	0.0	11.3	0.0	11.3

5.6 Tax policies

	Tax revenue collected by central government		Taxes payable by businesses					
	% of GDP		Number of payments	Time to prepare, file, and pay taxes hours	Profit tax % of commercial profits	Labor tax and contributions % of commercial profits	Other taxes % of commercial profits	Total tax rate % of commercial profits
	2000	2009	June 2010	June 2010	June 2010	June 2010	June 2010	June 2010
Romania	11.7[a]	17.9[a]	113	222	10.4	32.3	2.2	44.9
Russian Federation	13.6[a]	12.9[a]	11	320	9.0	31.8	5.7	46.5
Rwanda	..	..	26	148	21.2	5.7	4.4	31.3
Saudi Arabia	..	..	14	79	2.1	12.4	0.0	14.5
Senegal	16.1	..	59	666	14.8	24.1	7.0	46.0
Serbia	..	21.0	66	279	11.6	20.2	2.2	34.0
Sierra Leone	10.2	10.8	29	357	0.0	11.3	224.3	235.6
Singapore	15.4	13.8	5	84	7.4	14.9	3.1	25.4
Slovak Republic	..	12.4[a]	31	257	7.0	39.6	2.1	48.7
Slovenia	20.6	18.3	22	260	14.8	18.2	2.4	35.4
Somalia	..	..	..	..	..	..	..	..
South Africa	24.0[a]	25.4[a]	9	200	24.4	2.5	3.7	30.5
Spain	16.2[a]	8.5[a]	8	197	20.9	35.0	0.7	56.5
Sri Lanka	14.5	13.3	62	256	27.4	16.9	20.3	64.7
Sudan	6.4	..	42	180	13.8	19.2	3.1	36.1
Swaziland	24.9		33	104	28.1	4.0	4.7	36.8
Sweden	23.6[a]	21.5[a]	2	122	16.4	36.6	1.6	54.6
Switzerland	11.1	10.9	19	63	8.9	17.5	3.6	30.1
Syrian Arab Republic	..	..	20	336	23.2	19.3	0.5	42.9
Tajikistan	7.7	..	54	224	17.7	28.5	39.9	86.0
Tanzania	..	..	48	172	19.9	18.0	7.3	45.2
Thailand	..	15.1[a]	23	264	28.9	5.7	2.8	37.4
Timor-Leste	..	..	6	276	0.0	0.0	0.2	0.2
Togo	..	17.0[a]	53	270	8.8	28.3	13.7	50.8
Trinidad and Tobago	22.1	31.6	40	210	21.6	5.8	5.8	33.1
Tunisia	21.3	21.9	8	144	15.0	25.2	22.5	62.8
Turkey	..	18.9[a]	15	223	17.0	23.1	4.4	44.5
Turkmenistan	..	..	..	..	..	..	..	..
Uganda	10.4	12.0	32	161	23.3	11.3	1.1	35.7
Ukraine	14.1	16.4	135	657	10.4	43.3	1.8	55.5
United Arab Emirates	1.7	..	14	12	0.0	14.1	0.0	14.1
United Kingdom	28.4[a]	26.0[a]	8	110	23.1	10.8	3.3	37.3
United States	12.5[a]	8.2[a]	11	187	27.6	10.0	9.2	46.8
Uruguay	14.7	18.8	53	336	23.6	15.6	2.9	42.0
Uzbekistan	..	..	44	205	1.6	27.1	66.9	95.6
Venezuela, RB	13.3	..	70	864	10.0	18.0	24.6	52.6
Vietnam	..	..	32	941	12.5	20.3	0.3	33.1
West Bank and Gaza	..	..	27	154	16.2	0.0	0.6	16.8
Yemen, Rep.	9.4	..	44	248	35.1	11.3	1.4	47.8
Zambia	18.6	17.1	37	132	1.7	10.4	4.0	16.1
Zimbabwe	..	..	49	242	24.0	6.2	10.1	40.3
World	**15.5 w**	**14.2 w**	**30 u**	**282 u**	**17.9 u**	**16.3 u**	**13.7 u**	**47.8 u**
Low income	10.4	11.6	38	271	24.8	12.6	39.2	76.5
Middle income	10.9	14.1	34	337	17.1	15.8	8.6	41.5
Lower middle income	8.2	11.3	36	326	16.3	14.3	9.6	40.2
Upper middle income	..	15.8	32	351	18.0	17.5	7.5	43.0
Low & middle income	10.9	14.0	35	319	19.2	14.9	17.0	51.1
East Asia & Pacific	7.7	11.1	27	233	18.4	10.3	7.8	36.5
Europe & Central Asia	..	15.0	47	340	10.0	22.7	9.6	42.2
Latin America & Carib.	13.0	..	34	408	21.4	15.3	11.2	47.9
Middle East & N. Africa	12.0	17.5	25	263	16.6	18.9	6.1	41.6
South Asia	9.3	9.7	31	283	17.8	7.8	14.2	39.9
Sub-Saharan Africa	..	17.9	37	311	23.3	13.2	31.7	68.2
High income	16.4	14.2	15	179	14.3	20.1	4.2	38.6
Euro area	19.1	17.1	15	190	13.9	29.2	2.4	45.5

Note: Regional aggregates for Taxes payable by businesses are for developing countries only.
a. Data were reported on a cash basis and have been adjusted to the accrual framework of the International Monetary Fund's Government Finance Statistics Manual 2001.

About the data

Taxes are the main source of revenue for most governments. The sources of tax revenue and their relative contributions are determined by government policy choices about where and how to impose taxes and by changes in the structure of the economy. Tax policy may reflect concerns about distributional effects, economic efficiency (including corrections for externalities), and the practical problems of administering a tax system. There is no ideal level of taxation. But taxes influence incentives and thus the behavior of economic actors and the economy's competitiveness.

The level of taxation is typically measured by tax revenue as a share of gross domestic product (GDP). Comparing levels of taxation across countries provides a quick overview of the fiscal obligations and incentives facing the private sector. The table shows only central government data, which may significantly understate the total tax burden, particularly in countries where provincial and municipal governments are large or have considerable tax authority.

Low ratios of tax revenue to GDP may reflect weak administration and large-scale tax avoidance or evasion. Low ratios may also reflect a sizable parallel economy with unrecorded and undisclosed incomes. Tax revenue ratios tend to rise with income, with higher income countries relying on taxes to finance a much broader range of social services and social security than lower income countries are able to.

The total tax rate payable by businesses provides a comprehensive measure of the cost of all the taxes a business bears. It differs from the statutory tax rate, which is the factor applied to the tax base. In computing business tax rates, actual tax payable is divided by commercial profit. The indicators covering taxes payable by businesses measure all taxes and contributions that are government mandated (at any level—federal, state, or local), apply to standardized businesses, and have an impact in their income statements. The taxes covered go beyond the definition of a tax for government national accounts (compulsory, unrequited payments to general government) and also measure any imposts that affect business accounts. The main differences are in labor contributions and value-added taxes. The indicators account for government-mandated contributions paid by the employer to a requited private pension fund or workers insurance fund but exclude value-added taxes because they do not affect the accounting profits of the business—that is, they are not reflected in the income statement.

To make the data comparable across countries, several assumptions are made about businesses. The main assumptions are that they are limited liability companies, they operate in the country's most populous city, they are domestically owned, they perform general industrial or commercial activities, and they have certain levels of start-up capital, employees, and turnover. For details about the assumptions, see the World Bank's *Doing Business 2011*.

The Doing Business methodology on business taxes is consistent with the Total Tax Contribution framework developed by PricewaterhouseCoopers, which measures the taxes that are borne by companies and affect their income statements. However, PricewaterhouseCoopers bases its calculation on data from the largest companies in the economy, while Doing Business focuses on a standardized medium-sized company.

Definitions

• **Tax revenue collected by central government** is compulsory transfers to the central government for public purposes. Certain compulsory transfers such as fines, penalties, and most social security contributions are excluded. Refunds and corrections of erroneously collected tax revenue are treated as negative revenue. The analytic framework of the International Monetary Fund's (IMF) *Government Finance Statistics Manual 2001* (GFSM 2001) is based on accrual accounting and balance sheets. For countries still reporting government finance data on a cash basis, the IMF adjusts reported data to the GFSM 2001 accrual framework. These countries are footnoted in the table. • **Number of tax payments by businesses** is the total number of taxes paid by businesses during one year. When electronic filing is available, the tax is counted as paid once a year even if payments are more frequent. • **Time to prepare, file, and pay taxes** is the time, in hours per year, it takes to prepare, file, and pay (or withhold) three major types of taxes: the corporate income tax, the value-added or sales tax, and labor taxes, including payroll taxes and social security contributions. • **Profit tax** is the amount of taxes on profits paid by the business. • **Labor tax and contributions** is the amount of taxes and mandatory contributions on labor paid by the business. • **Other taxes** includes the amounts paid for property taxes, turnover taxes, and other small taxes such as municipal fees and vehicle and fuel taxes. • **Total tax rate** measures the amount of taxes and mandatory contributions payable by the business in the second year of operation, expressed as a share of commercial profits. *Doing Business 2011* reports the total tax rate for fiscal 2009. Taxes withheld (such as sales or value added tax or personal income tax) but not paid by the company are excluded. For further details on the method used for assessing the total tax payable, see the World Bank's *Doing Business 2011*.

Data sources

Data on central government tax revenue are from print and electronic editions of the IMF's *Government Finance Statistics Yearbook*. Data on taxes payable by businesses are from *Doing Business 2011* (www.doingbusiness.org).

	Military expenditures				Armed forces personnel				Arms transfers			
	% of GDP		% of central government expenditure		thousands		% of labor force		Trend indicator values 1990 $ millions Exports		Imports	
	2000	2009	2000	2009	2000	2009	2000	2009	2000	2009	2000	2009
Afghanistan	..	1.8	..	4.6	400	256	5.4	2.7	..	..	33	344
Albania	1.2	2.1	5.4	..	68	15	5.2	1.0	..	..	..	25
Algeria	3.4	3.8	..	15.0	305	334	2.7	2.3	..	..	418	942
Angola	6.4	4.2	..	..	118	117	1.9	1.4	2	..	200	11
Argentina	1.1	0.8	5.5	..	102	104	0.6	0.5	2	..	209	11
Armenia	3.6	4.0	..	17.1	42	56	2.9	3.4	..	..	2	1
Australia	1.9	1.9	7.8	7.3	52	57	0.5	0.5	43	51	364	757
Austria	1.0	0.9	2.5	2.3	41	26	1.0	0.6	21	33	25	330
Azerbaijan	2.3	3.5	..	22.9	87	82	2.5	2.0	..	..	3	49
Bangladesh	1.4	1.1	14.9	10.0	137	221	0.2	0.3	..	..	205	12
Belarus	1.3	1.8	5.3	5.5	91	183	1.9	3.7	295	292	41	..
Belgium	1.4	1.1	3.2	2.5	39	39	0.9	0.8	24	217	39	84
Benin	0.6	1.0	4.7	6.8	7	7	0.3	0.2	..	..	6	2
Bolivia	1.9	1.6	7.6	7.9	70	83	2.0	1.8	..	..	19	5
Bosnia and Herzegovina	3.6	1.5	..	3.8	76	11	4.1	0.5	4	..	25	..
Botswana	3.3	3.1	..	..	10	11	1.3	1.1	..	..	52	10
Brazil	1.8	1.6	8.1	6.4	673	713	0.8	0.7	26	49	124	210
Bulgaria	2.7	2.3	8.6	7.2	114	65	3.2	1.8	2	7	7	153
Burkina Faso	1.2	1.3	9.8	10.4	11	11	0.2	0.2	..	..	..	1
Burundi	6.0	3.8	30.3	..	46	51	1.4	1.1	..	..	1	..
Cambodia	2.2	1.2	16.8	13.9	360	191	6.1	2.4	1	..	..	4
Cameroon	1.3	1.5	12.4	..	22	23	0.4	0.3	..	..	1	1
Canada	1.1	1.4	6.0	7.5	69	66	0.4	0.3	110	177	550	80
Central African Republic	1.0	1.8	..	..	5	3	0.3	0.2	..	..	..	..
Chad	1.9	6.4	..	..	35	35	1.1	0.8	..	..	15	23
Chile	3.7	3.1	17.7	13.6	117	104	1.9	1.4	1	133	179	231
China	1.8a	2.0a	19.8a	16.1a	3,910	2,945	0.5	0.4	272	870	2,015	595
Hong Kong SAR, China	..	..	..	..	..	..	..	..	..	..	..	..
Colombia	2.8	4.1	15.6	20.9	247	442	1.6	2.3	..	..	62	250
Congo, Dem. Rep.	1.0	1.1	11.4	..	93	159	0.5	0.6	..	..	74	..
Congo, Rep.	1.4	1.2	5.9	..	15	12	1.2	0.8	..	..	0	0
Costa Rica	..	..	..	..	15	10	1.0	0.5	..	0	..	..
Côte d'Ivoire	..	1.6	..	8.8	15	19	0.2	0.2	..	..	33	..
Croatia	3.1	1.8	7.8	5.0	101	22	5.1	1.1	2	..	70	3
Cuba	..	3.2	..	..	85	76	1.8	1.5	..	..	..	..
Czech Republic	2.0	1.5	6.1	4.1	63	27	1.2	0.5	78	19	16	5
Denmark	1.5	1.4	4.3	3.3	22	19	0.8	0.6	20	12	64	47
Dominican Republic	0.7	0.6	..	3.8	40	40	1.1	0.9	..	..	13	6
Ecuador	1.7	3.3	..	..	58	59	1.2	1.0	..	..	12	46
Egypt, Arab Rep.	3.2	2.1	12.3	7.1	679	866	3.1	3.2	..	..	788	217
El Salvador	0.9	0.6	4.3	3.0	29	33	1.3	1.3	..	..	16	4
Eritrea	36.4	..	..	..	200	202	14.5	9.4	0	..	17	4
Estonia	1.4	2.3	4.7	6.2	8	5	1.2	0.8	..	..	27	56
Ethiopia	7.6	1.3	29.7	..	353	138	1.2	0.3	..	..	124	..
Finland	1.3	1.5	3.7	3.8	35	25	1.3	0.9	9	40	516	70
France	2.5	2.4	5.7	5.1	389	342	1.5	1.2	1,055	1,851	106	149
Gabon	1.8	1.1	..	..	7	7	1.2	0.9	..	..	..	21
Gambia, The	0.8	0.7	..	..	1	1	0.1	0.1	..	..	..	..
Georgia	0.6	5.6	5.3	18.1	33	32	1.4	1.4	54	..	6	81
Germany	1.5	1.4	4.7	4.3	221	251	0.5	0.6	1,603	2,473	135	137
Ghana	1.0	0.4	3.3	2.4	8	16	0.1	0.1	..	..	1	13
Greece	4.3	4.0	9.8	7.9	163	143	3.3	2.8	2	..	710	1,269
Guatemala	0.8	0.4	7.5	3.5	53	34	1.3	0.6	..	..	1	0
Guinea	1.5	..	11.8	..	19	19	0.5	0.4	..	..	19	0
Guinea-Bissau	4.4	..	..	..	9	6	1.7	1.0	..	..	..	..
Haiti	..	..	..	..	5	0	0.1	0.0	..	..	..	1
Honduras	0.5	0.8	..	3.2	14	20	0.6	0.7	..	..	..	0

Military expenditures and arms transfers

	Military expenditures				Armed forces personnel				Arms transfers			
	% of GDP		% of central government expenditure		thousands		% of labor force		Trend indicator values 1990 $ millions			
									Exports		Imports	
	2000	2009	2000	2009	2000	2009	2000	2009	2000	2009	2000	2009
Hungary	1.7	1.3	4.1	2.9	58	42	1.4	1.0	34	6	14	2
India	3.1	2.7	19.5	16.6	2,372	2,626	0.6	0.6	16	22	911	2,116
Indonesia	1.0	0.9	5.8	5.6	492	582	0.5	0.5	16	..	171	452
Iran, Islamic Rep.	3.8	2.7	22.5	12.2	753	563	3.4	1.9	0	5	415	91
Iraq	..	6.3	..	..	479	659	8.0	8.6	..	..	..	365
Ireland	0.7	0.6	2.6	1.5	12	10	0.7	0.5	..	4	0	1
Israel	7.8	6.9	17.6	17.0	181	185	7.2	6.0	354	760	357	158
Italy	2.0	1.7	5.2	3.9	503	327	2.2	1.3	189	588	37	112
Jamaica	0.5	0.6	..	1.6	3	3	0.3	0.2	..	..	5	2
Japan	1.0	1.0	..	..	249	260	0.4	0.4	..	..	431	391
Jordan	6.2	5.5	23.1	19.3	149	111	10.4	5.7	..	44	130	195
Kazakhstan	0.8	1.2	5.7	6.9	99	81	1.3	0.9	19	..	147	49
Kenya	1.3	1.9	7.8	8.7	27	29	0.2	0.2	..	..	9	35
Korea, Dem. Rep.	..	..	..	..	1,244	1,379	11.2	11.2	13	..	18	5
Korea, Rep.	2.6	2.9	15.6	13.2	688	660	3.0	2.7	8	163	1,262	1,172
Kosovo	..	..	..	..	..	..	..	..	..	..	..	..
Kuwait	7.1	3.2	24.9	7.5	20	23	1.8	1.5	99	..	238	17
Kyrgyz Republic	2.9	3.6	18.0	21.4	14	20	0.7	0.8	..	16	..	..
Lao PDR	0.8	0.4	..	3.6	129	129	5.2	4.2	..	..	7	7
Latvia	0.9	2.6	3.2	7.5	9	6	0.8	0.5	..	..	3	0
Lebanon	5.4	4.1	17.7	14.0	77	79	6.5	5.4	45	..	4	47
Lesotho	4.1	2.8	7.8	3.1	2	2	0.2	0.2	..	..	6	..
Liberia	..	0.8	..	..	15	2	1.3	0.1	..	..	8	..
Libya	3.2	1.2	..	..	77	76	4.2	3.2	11	12	145	11
Lithuania	1.7	1.7	6.5	4.4	17	25	1.0	1.6	3	..	5	26
Macedonia, FYR	1.9	2.1	..	5.8	24	8	2.8	0.9	..	..	11	..
Madagascar	1.2	1.1	11.5	9.3	29	22	0.4	0.2	..	..	..	..
Malawi	0.7	1.2	..	..	6	5	0.1	0.1	1	..	..	..
Malaysia	1.6	2.0	9.9	8.9	116	134	1.2	1.1	8	..	30	1,494
Mali	2.4	2.0	20.7	13.4	15	12	0.5	0.3	..	..	7	7
Mauritania	3.5	3.8	..	..	21	21	2.0	1.5	..	..	31	..
Mauritius	0.2	0.2	..	..	2	2	0.3	0.4	..	..	..	..
Mexico	0.6	0.5	3.7	..	208	332	0.5	0.7	..	..	227	57
Moldova	0.4	0.5	1.4	1.2	13	8	0.7	0.5	6	11	..	..
Mongolia	2.2	1.4	9.5	5.8	16	17	1.4	1.2	..	..	..	12
Morocco	2.3	3.3	12.0	12.0	241	246	2.4	2.1	..	..	123	49
Mozambique	1.3	0.9	..	..	6	11	0.1	0.1	..	..	0	..
Myanmar	2.3	..	..	..	429	513	1.7	1.9	..	..	3	3
Namibia	2.4	3.3	8.3	10.7	9	15	1.5	1.9	..	..	18	10
Nepal	1.0	1.6	..	..	90	158	0.9	1.2	..	..	11	..
Netherlands	1.6	1.5	4.0	3.4	57	43	0.7	0.5	280	608	141	243
New Zealand	1.2	1.1	3.5	3.1	9	10	0.5	0.4	1	..	45	48
Nicaragua	0.8	0.7	4.7	3.2	16	12	0.9	0.5	..	..	..	..
Niger	1.1	..	..	..	11	11	0.3	0.2	..	..	..	0
Nigeria	0.8	0.9	..	10.8	107	162	0.3	0.3	..	..	38	73
Norway	1.7	1.5	5.3	4.1	27	26	1.1	1.0	3	17	263	576
Oman	10.6	8.7	40.4	..	48	47	5.4	4.3	..	..	120	93
Pakistan	4.0	3.0	23.4	18.0	900	921	2.2	1.6	3	..	158	1,146
Panama	1.0	..	4.6	..	12	12	0.9	0.8	..	..	0	..
Papua New Guinea	0.9	0.5	2.9	..	4	3	0.2	0.1	..	..	..	..
Paraguay	1.1	0.9	6.4	5.2	35	25	1.5	0.8	..	..	6	..
Peru	2.0	1.2	10.9	6.7	193	192	1.7	1.4	10	..	24	33
Philippines	1.1	0.8	6.2	4.6	149	166	0.5	0.4	..	4	9	4
Poland	1.8	2.0	5.4	5.7	239	121	1.4	0.7	45	93	159	94
Portugal	1.9	2.0	5.1	4.6	91	91	1.7	1.6	..	40	2	431
Puerto Rico	..	..	..	..	..	..	..	..	..	..	..	..
Qatar	4.7	2.2	..	13.7	12	12	3.6	1.2	9	..	11	285

	Military expenditures				Armed forces personnel				Arms transfers			
	% of GDP		% of central government expenditure		thousands		% of labor force		Trend indicator values 1990 $ millions Exports		Imports	
	2000	2009	2000	2009	2000	2009	2000	2009	2000	2009	2000	2009
Romania	2.5	1.4	8.9	4.4	283	152	2.4	1.6	3	3	23	56
Russian Federation	3.7	4.3	19.3	14.0	1,427	1,495	2.0	2.0	3,985	4,469	..	1
Rwanda	3.5	1.4	..	..	76	35	2.0	0.7	..	..	14	6
Saudi Arabia	10.6	11.0	..	..	217	249	3.4	2.9	..	..	80	626
Senegal	1.3	1.6	10.4	..	15	19	0.4	0.3	..	..	..	3
Serbia	5.5	2.2	..	5.9	136	29	..	..	..	..	..	..
Sierra Leone	3.7	2.3	12.8	11.2	4	11	0.2	0.5	..	..	13	..
Singapore	4.7	4.3	28.7	27.9	169	148	8.2	5.5	10	124	622	1,729
Slovak Republic	1.7	1.5	..	4.0	41	17	1.6	0.6	92	8	2	1
Slovenia	1.1	1.8	2.9	4.1	14	12	1.4	1.2	..	..	1	6
Somalia	..	..	..	..	50	2	1.7	0.1	..	..	1	..
South Africa	1.6	1.4	5.6	4.4	72	77	0.5	0.4	18	154	16	139
Spain	1.2	1.3	3.9	4.1	242	222	1.3	1.0	46	925	332	430
Sri Lanka	5.0	3.5	21.9	18.5	204	223	2.6	2.7	..	..	274	64
Sudan	4.7	..	53.0	..	120	127	1.1	0.9	..	..	107	39
Swaziland	1.6	2.1	7.3	..	3	..	0.8	..	..	..	1	..
Sweden	2.0	1.3	..	..	88	22	2.0	0.4	306	353	210	46
Switzerland	1.1	0.8	4.2	4.7	28	26	0.7	0.6	176	270	14	31
Syrian Arab Republic	5.3	4.2	..	..	425	403	8.6	5.8	..	..	19	175
Tajikistan	1.2	..	13.4	..	7	16	0.4	0.6	..	..	..	7
Tanzania	1.3	1.0	..	..	35	28	0.2	0.1	..	..	..	0
Thailand	1.4	1.8	..	9.1	417	420	1.2	1.1	..	..	90	34
Timor-Leste	..	11.8	..	..	..	1	..	0.3	..	..	..	..
Togo	..	2.0	..	13.0	8	9	0.4	0.3	..	..	..	..
Trinidad and Tobago	..	..	..	..	8	4	1.3	0.6	..	..	10	6
Tunisia	1.7	1.4	6.2	4.6	47	48	1.5	1.2	..	..	11	8
Turkey	3.7	2.8	..	10.1	828	613	3.6	2.4	15	36	1,170	675
Turkmenistan	2.9	..	..	..	15	22	0.8	0.9	..	..	..	47
Uganda	2.5	2.2	16.0	15.9	51	47	0.5	0.3	..	..	6	1
Ukraine	3.6	2.9	13.5	7.0	420	215	1.8	0.9	288	214	..	..
United Arab Emirates	9.4	5.6	..	..	66	51	3.5	1.8	..	3	243	604
United Kingdom	2.4	2.7	6.6	5.8	213	178	0.7	0.6	1,484	1,024	829	288
United States	3.0	4.7	15.6	17.8	1,455	1,564	1.0	1.0	7,220	6,795	301	831
Uruguay	1.3	1.6	5.0	5.3	25	25	1.6	1.5	1	..	4	37
Uzbekistan	1.2	..	..	..	79	87	0.9	0.7	..	90	6	..
Venezuela, RB	1.5	1.3	7.1	..	79	115	0.8	0.9	..	17	108	172
Vietnam	..	2.2	..	..	524	495	1.4	1.1	..	..	5	44
West Bank and Gaza	..	..	..	..	..	56	..	5.9	..	..	..	14
Yemen, Rep.	5.0	4.4	23.9	..	136	138	3.2	2.2	..	..	158	45
Zambia	1.8	1.7	10.3	5.7	23	17	0.6	0.3	..	..	27	3
Zimbabwe	5.2	2.8	..	..	62	51	1.2	1.0	3	..	2	..
World	**2.3 w**	**2.6 w**	**10.2 w**	**10.0 w**	**29,353 s**	**27,924 s**	**1.1 w**	**0.9 w**	**.. s**	**.. s**	**18,088 s**	**22,223 s**
Low income	2.2	1.5	..	..	4,040	3,845	1.3	1.0	..	..	572	329
Middle income	2.1	2.2	15.0	12.2	18,924	18,350	1.0	0.8	..	..	8,353	10,467
Lower middle income	2.2	2.1	18.0	14.3	12,446	12,108	0.8	0.7	983	1,251	5,109	5,682
Upper middle income	2.0	2.2	..	9.8	6,478	6,242	1.6	1.4	..	..	3,244	4,785
Low & middle income	2.1	2.1	15.0	12.2	22,965	22,195	1.0	0.8	..	..	8,925	10,889
East Asia & Pacific	1.7	1.9	18.7	14.6	7,794	6,978	0.8	0.6	389	870	2,339	2,644
Europe & Central Asia	3.4	3.3	..	12.0	3,871	3,227	2.1	1.7	4,667	4,830	..	1,162
Latin America & Carib.	1.4	1.5	7.2	..	2,084	2,439	0.9	0.9	..	..	970	1,058
Middle East & N. Africa	3.5	3.5	12.7	12.3	3,379	3,591	3.8	3.1	..	..	2,056	2,065
South Asia	3.1	2.6	19.9	16.5	4,114	4,404	0.8	0.7	19	22	1,548	3,606
Sub-Saharan Africa	2.0	1.7	..	..	1,724	1,554	0.7	0.5	..	..	647	354
High income	2.3	2.8	10.1	9.9	6,388	5,729	1.2	1.0	13,136	16,637	9,163	11,334
Euro area	1.8	1.7	4.8	4.2	1,869	1,569	1.3	1.0	3,319	6,779	2,075	3,322

Note: For some countries data are partial or uncertain or based on rough estimates. See SIPRI (2010).

a. Estimates differ from statistics of the government of China, which has published the following estimates: military expenditure as 1.2 percent of GDP in 2000 and 1.4 percent in 2008 and 7.6 percent of national government expenditure in 2000 and 6.7 percent in 2008 (see National Bureau of Statistics of China, www.stats.gov.cn).

About the data

Although national defense is an important function of government and security from external threats that contributes to economic development, high levels of military expenditures for defense or civil conflicts burden the economy and may impede growth. Data on military expenditures as a share of gross domestic product (GDP) are a rough indicator of the portion of national resources used for military activities and of the burden on the national economy. As an "input" measure military expenditures are not directly related to the "output" of military activities, capabilities, or security. Comparisons of military spending between countries should take into account the many factors that influence perceptions of vulnerability and risk, including historical and cultural traditions, the length of borders that need defending, the quality of relations with neighbors, and the role of the armed forces in the body politic.

Data on military spending reported by governments are not compiled using standard definitions. They are often incomplete and unreliable. Even in countries where the parliament vigilantly reviews budgets and spending, military expenditures and arms transfers rarely receive close scrutiny or full, public disclosure (see Ball 1984 and Happe and Wakeman-Linn 1994). Therefore, the Stockholm International Peace Research Institute (SIPRI) has adopted a definition of military expenditure derived from the North Atlantic Treaty Organization (NATO) definition (see *Definitions*). The data on military expenditures as a share of GDP and as a share of central government expenditure are estimated by SIPRI. Central government expenditures are from the International Monetary Fund (IMF). Therefore the data in the table may differ from comparable data published by national governments.

SIPRI's primary source of military expenditure data is official data provided by national governments. These data are derived from national budget documents, defense white papers, and other public documents from official government agencies, including governments' responses to questionnaires sent by SIPRI, the United Nations, or the Organization for Security and Co-operation in Europe. Secondary sources include international statistics, such as those of NATO and the IMF's *Government Finance Statistics Yearbook.* Other secondary sources include country reports of the Economist Intelligence Unit, country reports by IMF staff, and specialist journals and newspapers.

In the many cases where SIPRI cannot make independent estimates, it uses the national data provided. Because of the differences in definitions and the difficulty in verifying the accuracy and completeness of data, data on military expenditures are not always strictly comparable across countries. However, SIPRI puts a high priority on ensuring that the data series for each country is comparable over time. More information on SIPRI's military expenditure project can be found at www.sipri.org/contents/milap/.

Data on armed forces refer to military personnel on active duty, including paramilitary forces. Because data exclude personnel not on active duty, they underestimate the share of the labor force working for the defense establishment. Governments rarely report the size of their armed forces, so such data typically come from intelligence sources.

SIPRI's Arms Transfers Programme collects data on arms transfers from open sources. Since publicly available information is inadequate for tracking all weapons and other military equipment, SIPRI covers only what it terms *major conventional weapons.* Data cover the supply of weapons through sales, aid, gifts, and manufacturing licenses; therefore the term *arms transfers* rather than *arms trade* is used. SIPRI data also cover weapons supplied to or from rebel forces in an armed conflict as well as arms deliveries for which neither the supplier nor the recipient can be identified with acceptable certainty; these data are available in SIPRI's database.

SIPRI's estimates of arms transfers are designed as a trend-measuring device in which similar weapons have similar values, reflecting both the quantity and quality of weapons transferred. SIPRI cautions that the estimated values do not reflect financial value (payments for weapons transferred) because reliable data on the value of the transfer are not available, and even when values are known, the transfer usually includes more than the actual conventional weapons, such as spares, support systems, and training, and details of the financial arrangements (such as credit and loan conditions and discounts) are usually not known.

Given these measurement issues, SIPRI's method of estimating the transfer of military resources includes an evaluation of the technical parameters of the weapons. Weapons for which a price is not known are compared with the same weapons for which actual acquisition prices are available (core weapons) or for the closest match. These weapons are assigned a value in an index that reflects their military resource value in relation to the core weapons. These matches are based on such characteristics as size, performance, and type of electronics, and adjustments are made for secondhand weapons. More information on SIPRI's Arms Transfers Programme is available at www.sipri.org/research/armaments/transfers.

Definitions

• **Military expenditures** are SIPRI data derived from the NATO definition, which includes all current and capital expenditures on the armed forces, including peacekeeping forces; defense ministries and other government agencies engaged in defense projects; paramilitary forces, if judged to be trained and equipped for military operations; and military space activities. Such expenditures include military and civil personnel, including retirement pensions and social services for military personnel; operation and maintenance; procurement; military research and development; and military aid (in the military expenditures of the donor country). Excluded are civil defense and current expenditures for previous military activities, such as for veterans benefits, demobilization, and weapons conversion and destruction. This definition cannot be applied for all countries, however, since that would require more detailed information than is available about military budgets and off-budget military expenditures (for example, whether military budgets cover civil defense, reserves and auxiliary forces, police and paramilitary forces, and military pensions). • **Armed forces personnel** are active duty military personnel, including paramilitary forces if the training, organization, equipment, and control suggest they may be used to support or replace regular military forces. Reserve forces, which are not fully staffed or operational in peace time, are not included. The data also exclude civilians in the defense establishment and so are not consistent with the data on military expenditures on personnel. • **Arms transfers** cover the supply of military weapons through sales, aid, gifts, and manufacturing licenses. Weapons must be transferred voluntarily by the supplier, have a military purpose, and be destined for the armed forces, paramilitary forces, or intelligence agencies of another country. The trends shown in the table are based on actual deliveries only. Data cover major conventional weapons such as aircraft, armored vehicles, artillery, radar systems and other sensors, missiles, and ships designed for military use, as well as some major components such as turrets for armored vehicles and engines. Excluded are transfers of other military equipment such as most small arms and light weapons, trucks, small artillery, ammunition, support equipment, technology transfers, and other services.

Data sources

Data on military expenditures are from SIPRI's *Yearbook 2010: Armaments, Disarmament, and International Security.* Data on armed forces personnel are from the International Institute for Strategic Studies' *The Military Balance 2011.* Data on arms transfers are from SIPRI's Arms Transfers Programme (www.sipri.org/research/armaments/transfers).

	International Development Association Resource Allocation Index 1–6 (low to high) 2009	Peacebuilding and peacekeeping Operation name[a] December 2010	Peacebuilding and peacekeeping Troops, police, and military observers number December 2010	Battle-related deaths number 2000–08[b]	Intentional homicides per 100,000 people Public health sources 2004	Intentional homicides per 100,000 people Law enforcement and criminal justice sources 2004–08[c]	Military expenditures % of GDP 2009	Business environment Survey year	Business environment Losses due to theft, robbery, vandalism, and arson % of sales	Business environment Firms formally registered when operations started % of firms
Afghanistan	2.8	UNAMA	16	26,589	3.4	..	1.8	2008	1.5	88.0
Angola	2.8		..	3,534	38.6	5.0	4.2	2006	0.4	..
Bosnia and Herzegovina	3.7		..	0	1.9	1.9	1.5	2009	0.2	98.6
Burundi	3.1	BINUB	4	4,937	37.4	..	3.8	2006	1.1	..
Central African Republic	2.6	MINURCAT[e]	3	350	29.8	..	1.8		..	..
Chad	2.5	MINURCAT	..	4,328	19.2	..	6.4	2009	2.5	77.1
Comoros	2.5		..	0	11.9	..	..		..	..
Congo, Dem. Rep.	2.7	MONUC	19,105	75,118	35.0	..	1.1	2010	1.8	61.9
Congo, Rep.	2.8		..	116	19.9	..	1.2	2009	3.3	84.3
Côte d'Ivoire	2.8	UNOCI	9,071	1,265	50.8	0.4	1.6	2009	3.4	56.4
Eritrea	2.2		..	57	16.1	..	..	2009	0.0	100.0
Georgia	4.4		..	648	3.7	7.6	5.6	2008	0.7	99.6
Guinea	2.8		..	1,174	16.9	0.4	..	2006	2.0	..
Guinea-Bissau	2.6		..	0	17.6	..	..	2006	1.1	..
Haiti	2.9	MINUSTAH	11,984	244	21.8	..	0.0		..	..
Iraq	..	UNAMI	235	124,002	7.3	..	6.3		..	..
Kiribati	3.1		..	0	6.6	..	..		..	..
Kosovo	3.4	UNMIK	16	0	..	..	..	2009	0.3	89.2
Liberia	2.8	UNMIL	9,392	2,487	17.4	..	0.8	2009	2.8	73.8
Myanmar	..		..	2,833	15.6	..	..		..	..
Nepal	3.3	UNMIN	72	11,520	13.6	2.2	1.6	2009	0.9	94.0
São Tomé and Príncipe	2.9		..	0	5.3	..	..		..	..
Sierra Leone	3.2		..	212	37.2	2.6	2.3	2009	0.8	89.2
Solomon Islands	2.8	RAMSI	580	0	1.5	..	..		..	..
Somalia	..		..	3,983	3.2	..	..		..	..
Sudan	2.5	UNMIS[g]	10,416	12,363	27.2	..	..		..	..
Tajikistan	3.2		..	0	1.9[h]	2.3	..	2008	0.3	92.7
Timor-Leste	2.9	UNMIT	1,517	0	12.5	..	11.8	2009	1.5	91.8
Togo	2.8		..	0	14.3	..	2.0	2009	2.4	75.8
West Bank and Gaza	..		..	0	..	3.9	..	2006	1.2	..
Western Sahara[j]	..	MINURSO	242	..	..	..	..		..	..
Yemen, Rep.	3.2		..	0	2.5	4.0	4.4	2010	0.6	81.7
Zimbabwe	1.9		..	0	34.3	8.7	2.8		..	..
Fragile situations				275,761 s	21.1 w	..	3.2 w			
Low income				146,844	17.6	..	1.4			

Note: The countries with fragile situations in the table are primarily International Development Association–eligible countries and nonmember or inactive countries and territories with a 3.2 or lower harmonized average of the World Bank's Country Policy and Institutional Assessment rating and the corresponding rating by a regional development bank, or that have had a UN or regional peacebuilding and political mission (for example, by the African Union, European Union, or Organization of American States) or peacekeeping mission (for example, by the African Union, European Union, North Atlantic Treaty Organization, or Organization of American States) during the last three years. This definition is pursuant to an agreement between the World Bank and other multilateral development banks at the start of the International Development Association 15 round in 2007. The list of countries and territories with fragile situations is an interim one, and the World Bank will continue to improve and refine its understanding of fragility.

a. UNAMA is United Nations Assistance Mission in Afghanistan, BINUB is Bureau Intégré des Nations Unies au Burundi (United Nations Integrated Office in Burundi), MINURCAT is United Nations Mission in the Central African Republic and Chad, MONUC is United Nations Organization Mission in DR Congo, UNOCI is United Nations Operation in Côte d'Ivoire, MINUSTAH is United Nations Stabilization Mission in Haiti, UNAMI is United Nations Assistance Mission for Iraq, UNMIK is Interim Administration Mission in Kosovo, UNMIL is United Nations Mission in Liberia, UNMIN is United Nations Mission in Nepal, RAMSI is Regional Assistance Mission to Solomon Islands, UNMIS is United Nations Missions in Sudan, UNMIT is United Nations Integrated Mission in Timor-Leste, and MINURSO is United Nations Mission for the Referendum in Western Sahara. b. Total over the period. c. Data are for the most recent year available. d. Average over the period. e. Includes peacekeepers in Chad. The mission ended in 2010. f. The Internal Displacement Monitoring Centre's (IDMC) high estimate; the low estimate is 50,000. g. Does not include 22,444 troops, police, and military observers from the African Union–UN Hybrid Operation in Darfur. h. Data are for 2005. i. Includes Palestinian refugees under the mandate of the United Nations Relief and Works Agency for Palestine Refugees in the Near East, who are not included in data from the UN High Commissioner for Refugees. j. The designation Western Sahara is used instead of Former Spanish Sahara (the designation used on the maps on the front and back cover flaps) because it is the designation used by the UN operation established there by Security Council resolution 690/1991. Neither designation expresses any World Bank view on the status of the territory so-identified. k. IDMC's high estimate; the low estimate is 570,000.

	Children in employment		Refugees		Internally displaced persons	Access to an improved water source	Access to improved sanitation facilities	Maternal mortality ratio		Under-five mortality rate	Depth of hunger	Primary gross enrollment ratio
								per 100,000 live births			kilocalories per person per day	% of relevant age group
	Survey year	% of children ages 7–14	By country of origin	By country of asylum	number	% of population	% of population	National estimates	Modeled estimates	per 1,000		
			2009	2009	2009	2008	2008	2004–09c	2008	2009	2005–07d	2009
Afghanistan	..		2,887,123	37	297,000	48	37	..	1,400	199	..	104
Angola	2001	30.1	141,021	14,734	20,000	50	57	..	610	161	320	128
Bosnia and Herzegovina	2006	10.6	70,018	7,132	114,000	99	95	3	9	14	140	109
Burundi	2005	11.7	94,239	24,967	100,000	72	46	615	970	166	380	147
Central African Republic	2000	67.0	159,554	27,047	162,000	67	34	543	850	171	300	89
Chad	2004	60.4	55,014	338,495	168,000	50	9	1,099	1,200	209	310	90
Comoros		..	268	..	..	95	36	..	340	104	300	119
Congo, Dem. Rep.	2000	39.8	455,852	185,809	1,900,000	46	23	549	670	199	410	90
Congo, Rep.	2005	30.1	20,544	111,411	7,800	71	30	781	580	128	230	120
Côte d'Ivoire	2006	45.7	23,153	24,604	621,000	80	23	543	470	119	230	74
Eritrea		..	209,168	4,751	10,000	61	14	..	280	55	350	48
Georgia	2006	31.8	15,020	870	230,000	98	95	14	48	29	150	108
Guinea	1994	48.3	10,920	15,325	..	71	19	980	680	142	260	90
Guinea-Bissau	2006	50.5	1,109	7,898	..	61	21	405	1,000	193	250	120
Haiti	2005	33.4	24,116	3	..	63	17	630	300	87	430	..
Iraq	2006	14.7	1,785,212	35,218	2,764,000	79	73	84	75	44	..	103
Kiribati		..	33	..	..	61	31	..	..	46	180	116
Kosovo		..	..	..	19,700	..	..	..	..	..	..	..
Liberia	2007	37.4	71,599	6,952	..	68	17	994	990	112	340	91
Myanmar		..	406,669	..	470,000	71	81	316	240	71	230	116
Nepal	1999	47.2	5,108	108,461	70,000f	88	31	281	380	48	220	..
São Tomé and Príncipe		..	33	..	..	89	26	148	..	78	160	131
Sierra Leone	2007	14.9	15,417	9,051	..	49	13	857	970	192	340	158
Solomon Islands		..	66	..	..	69	29	..	100	36	180	107
Somalia	2006	43.5	678,309	1,815	1,500,000	30	23	1,044	1,200	180	..	33
Sudan	2000	19.1	368,195	186,292	4,900,000	57	34	1,107	750	108	240	74
Tajikistan	2005	8.9	562	2,679	..	70	94	38	64	61	240	102
Timor-Leste		..	7	1	400	69	50	..	370	56	260	113
Togo	2006	38.7	18,378	8,531	1,500	60	12	..	350	98	280	115
West Bank and Gaza		..	95,201	1,885,188i	..	91	89	..	..	30	190	79
Western Saharaj		..	..	..	160,000	..	..	..	..	..	..	..
Yemen, Rep.	2006	18.3	1,934	170,854	175,000	62	52	..	210	66	270	85
Zimbabwe	1999	14.3	22,449	3,995	1,000,000k	82	44	555	790	90	300	..
Fragile situations			7,636,291 s	3,182,120 s	14,047,900 s	64 w	43 w	..	640 w	132 w	290 w	94 w
Low income			5,427,548	1,893,823	..	64	35	..	580	118	285	104

About the data

The table focuses on countries with fragile situations and highlights the links among weak institutions, poor development outcomes, fragility, and risk of conflict. These countries and territories often have weak institutions that are ill-equipped to handle economic shocks, natural disasters, and illegal trade or to resist conflict, which increasingly spills across borders. Organized violence, including violent crime, interrupts economic and social development through lost human and social capital, disrupted services, displaced populations and reduced confidence for future investment. As a result, countries with fragile situations achieve lower development outcomes and make slower progress toward the Millennium Development Goals.

According to the Geneva Declaration on Armed Violence and Development, more than 740,000 people die each year because of the violence associated with armed conflict and large- and small-scale criminality. Recovery and rebuilding can take years, and the challenges are numerous: infrastructure to be rebuilt, persistently high crime, widespread health problems, education systems in disrepair, and landmines to be cleared. Most countries emerging from conflict lack the capacity to rebuild the economy. Thus, capacity building is one of the first tasks for restoring growth and is linked to building peace and creating the conditions that lead to sustained poverty reduction. The World Bank and other international development agencies can help, but countries with fragile situations

have to build their own institutions tailored to their own needs. Peacekeeping operations in post-conflict situations have been effective in reducing the risks of reversion to conflict.

The countries with fragile situations in the table are primarily International Development Association– eligible countries and nonmember or inactive countries or territories of the World Bank with a 3.2 or lower harmonized average of the World Bank's Country Policy and Institutional Assessment rating and the corresponding rating by a regional development bank or that have had a UN or regional peacebuilding mission (for example, by the African Union, European Union, or Organization of American States) or peacekeeping mission (for example, by the African Union, European

5.8 | Fragile situations

Union, North Atlantic Treaty Organization (NATO), or Organization of American States) during the last three years. Peacebuilding and peacekeeping involve many elements—military, police, and civilian—working together to lay the foundations for sustainable peace. The list of countries and territories with fragile situations is an interim one, and the World Bank will continue to improve and refine its understanding of fragility.

An armed conflict is a contested incompatibility that concerns a government or territory where the use of armed force between two parties (one of them the government) results in at least 25 battle-related deaths in a calendar year. There were 35 active armed conflicts in 26 locations in 2009. Separate measures are presented for intentional homicides—unlawful deaths purposefully inflicted on a person by another person—which exclude deaths arising from armed conflict. One measure draws from international public health data sources, while the other draws from estimates by the United Nations Office on Drugs and Crime, which obtains data from national and international law enforcement and criminal justice sources. Data from these two sources measure different phenomena and are therefore unlikely to provide identical numbers.

Data on military expenditures reported by governments are not compiled using standard definitions and are often incomplete and unreliable. Even in countries where the parliament vigilantly reviews budgets and spending, military expenditures and arms transfers rarely receive close scrutiny or full public disclosure. Data are from the Stockholm International Peace Research Institute (SIPRI), which uses NATO's pre-2004 definition of military expenditure (see *Definitions*). Therefore, the data in the table may differ from comparable data published by national governments. For a more detailed discussion of military expenditures, see *About the data* for table 5.7.

Along with public sector efforts, private sector development and investment, especially in competitive markets, has tremendous potential to contribute to growth and poverty reduction. The World Bank's Enterprise Surveys review the business environment, assessing constraints to private sector growth and enterprise performance. In some countries doing business requires informal payments to "get things done" in customs, taxes, licenses, regulations, services, and the like. Crime, theft, and disorder also impose costs on businesses and society. And in many developing countries informal businesses operate without licenses. These firms have less access to financial and public services and can engage in

fewer types of contracts and investments, constraining growth. The table presents data on the loss of sales due to theft, robbery, vandalism, and arson and on the percentage of firms operating informally. For further information on enterprise surveys, see *About the data* for table 5.2.

As the table shows, the human toll of armed violence across various contexts is severe. Additionally, in countries with fragile situations weak institutional capacity often results in poor performance and failure to meet expectations of effective service delivery. Failure to deliver water, health, and education services can weaken struggling governments. The table includes several indicators related to living conditions in fragile situations: children in employment, refugees, internally displaced persons, access to water and sanitation, maternal and under-five mortality, depth of hunger, and primary school enrollment. For more detailed information on these indicators, see *About the data* for table 2.6 (children in employment), table 6.18 (refugees), table 2.18 (access to improved water and sanitation), table 2.19 (maternal mortality), table 2.22 (under-five mortality), and table 2.12 (primary school enrollment).

Definitions

• **International Development Association Resource Allocation Index** is from the Country Policy and Institutional Assessment rating, which is the average score of four clusters of indicators designed to measure macroeconomic, governance, social, and structural dimensions of development: economic management, structural policies, policies for social inclusion and equity, and public sector management and institutions (see table 5.9). Countries are rated on a scale of 1 (low) to 6 (high). • **Peacebuilding and peacekeeping** refer to operations that engage in peacebuilding (reducing the risk of lapsing or relapsing into conflict by strengthening national capacities for conflict management and laying the foundation for sustainable peace and development) or peacekeeping (providing essential security to preserve the peace where fighting has been halted and to assist in implementing agreements achieved by the peacemakers). UN peacekeeping operations are authorized by the UN Secretary-General and planned, managed, directed, and supported by the United Nations Department of Peacekeeping Operations and the Department of Field Support. The UN Charter gives the Security Council primary responsibility for maintaining international peace and security, including the establishment of a UN peacekeeping operation.

• **Troops, police, and military observers** in peacebuilding and peacekeeping refer to people active in peacebuilding and peacekeeping as part of an official operation. Peacekeepers deploy to war-torn regions where no one else is willing or able to go to prevent conflict from returning or escalating. • **Battle-related deaths** are deaths of members of warring parties in battle-related conflicts. Typically, battle-related deaths occur in warfare involving the armed forces of the warring parties (battlefield fighting, guerrilla activities, and all kinds of bombardments of military units, cities, and villages). The targets are usually the military and its installations or state institutions and state representatives, but there is often substantial collateral damage of civilians killed in crossfire, indiscriminate bombings, and other military activities. All deaths—civilian as well as military—incurred in such situations are counted as battle-related deaths. • **Intentional homicides** are estimates of unlawful homicides purposely inflicted as a result of domestic disputes, interpersonal violence, violent conflicts over land resources, intergang violence over turf or control, and predatory violence and killing by armed groups. Intentional homicide does not include all intentional killing; the difference is usually in the organization of the killing. Individuals or small groups usually commit homicide, whereas killing in armed conflict is usually committed by fairly cohesive groups of up to several hundred members and is thus usually excluded. Data are from international public health organizations such as the World Health Organization (WHO) and the Pan American Health Organization and from the United Nations Survey of Crime Trends and Operations of Criminal Justice Systems (CTS), which draws from national and international law enforcement and criminal justice sources. • **Military expenditures** are SIPRI data derived from NATO's pre-2004 definition, which includes all current and capital expenditures on the armed forces, including peacekeeping forces; defense ministries and other government agencies engaged in defense projects; paramilitary forces, if judged to be trained and equipped for military operations; and military space activities. Such expenditures include military and civil personnel, including retirement pensions and social services for military personnel; operation and maintenance; procurement; military research and development; and military aid (in the military expenditures of the donor country). Excluded are civil defense and current expenditures for previous military activities, such as for veterans benefits, demobilization, and weapons conversion and destruction. This definition cannot be applied to all countries, however, since the necessary detailed information is missing in some cases for military budgets and off-budget military expenditures (for example, whether military budgets cover civil defense, reserves and auxiliary forces, police and paramilitary forces, and military pensions). • **Survey year** is the year in which the underlying data were collected. • **Losses due to theft, robbery, vandalism, and arson** are the estimated losses from those causes that occurred on business establishment premises calculated as a percentage of annual sales. • **Firms formally registered when operations started** are the percentage of firms formally registered when they started operations in the country. • **Children in employment** are children involved in any economic activity for at least one hour in the reference week of the survey. • **Refugees** are people who are recognized as refugees under the 1951 Convention Relating to the Status of Refugees or its 1967 Protocol, the 1969 Organization of African Unity Convention Governing the Specific Aspects of Refugee Problems in Africa, people recognized as refugees in accordance with the UN Refugee Agency (UNHCR) statute, people granted refugee-like humanitarian status, and people provided temporary protection. Asylum seekers—people who have applied for asylum or refugee status and who have not yet received a decision, or who are registered as asylum seekers—are excluded. Palestinian refugees are people (and their descendants) whose residence was Palestine between June 1946 and May 1948 and who lost their homes and means of livelihood as a result of the 1948 Arab-Israeli conflict. • **Country of origin** refers to the nationality or country of citizenship of a claimant. • **Country of asylum** is the country where an asylum claim was filed and granted. • **Internally displaced persons** are people or groups of people who have been forced or obliged to flee or to leave their homes or places of habitual residence, in particular as a result of armed conflict, or to avoid the effects of armed conflict, situations of generalized violence, violations of human rights, or natural or human-made disasters and who have not crossed an international border. • **Access to an improved water source** refers to people with reasonable access to water from an improved source, such as piped water into a dwelling, public tap, tubewell, protected dug well, and rainwater collection. Reasonable access is the availability of at least 20 liters a person a day from a source within 1 kilometer of the dwelling. • **Access to improved sanitation facilities** refers to people with at least adequate access to excreta

disposal facilities that can effectively prevent human, animal, and insect contact with excreta. Improved facilities range from protected pit latrines to flush toilets. • **Maternal mortality ratio** is the number of women who die from pregnancy-related causes during pregnancy and childbirth per 100,000 live births. National estimates are based on national surveys, vital registration records, and surveillance data or are derived from community and hospital records. Modeled estimates are based on an exercise by the WHO, United Nations Children's Fund (UNICEF), United Nations Population Fund (UNFPA), and the World Bank. See *About the data* for table 2.19 for further details. • **Under-five mortality rate** is the probability per 1,000 that a newborn baby will die before reaching age 5, if subject to current age-specific mortality rates. • **Depth of hunger**, or the intensity of food deprivation, indicates how much people who are food-deprived fall short of minimum food needs in terms of dietary energy. It is measured by comparing the average amount of dietary energy that undernourished people get from the foods they eat with the minimum amount of dietary energy they need to maintain body weight and undertake light activity. Depth of hunger is low when it is less than 200 kilocalories per person per day and high when it is above 300. • **Primary gross enrollment ratio** is the ratio of total enrollment, regardless of age, to the population of the age group that officially corresponds to the primary level of education. Primary education provides children with basic reading, writing, and mathematics skills along with an elementary understanding of such subjects as history, geography, natural science, social science, art, and music.

Data sources

Data on the International Development Association Resource Allocation Index are from the World Bank Group's International Development Association database (www.worldbank. org/ida). Data on peacebuilding and peacekeeping operations are from the UN Department of Peacekeeping Operations. Data on battle-related deaths are primarily from the Peace Research Institute Oslo/Uppsala Conflict Data Program (UCDP) Armed Conflict Dataset (v.4-2010) 1946-2009 (www.pcr.uu.se/research/ucdp/datasets), supplemented with data from the UCDP Battle-Related Deaths Dataset (v.5-2010). Data

on intentional homicides are from the UN Office on Drugs and Crime's International Homicide Statistics database. Data on military expenditures are from SIPRI's *Yearbook 2010: Armaments, Disarmament, and International Security* and database (www.sipri.org/databases/milex). Data on the business environment are from the World Bank's Enterprise Surveys (www.enterprisesurveys. org). Data on children in employment are estimates produced by the Understanding Children's Work project based on household survey data sets made available by the International Labour Organization's International Programme on the Elimination of Child Labour under its Statistical Monitoring Programme on Child Labour, UNICEF under its Multiple Indicator Cluster Survey program, the World Bank under its Living Standards Measurement Study program, and national statistical offices (see table 2.6). Data on refugees are from the UNHCR's *Statistical Yearbook 2009*, complemented by statistics on Palestinian refugees under the mandate of the United Nations Relief and Works Agency for Palestine Refugees in the Near East as published on its website (www. unrwa.org). Data on internally displaced persons are from the Internal Displacement Monitoring Centre. Data on access to water and sanitation are from the WHO and UNICEF's *Progress on Sanitation and Drinking Water* (2010). National estimates of maternal mortality are from UNICEF's *The State of the World's Children 2009* and Childinfo and Demographic and Health Surveys by Macro International. Modeled estimates for maternal mortality are from WHO, UNICEF, UNFPA, and the World Bank's *Trends in Maternal Mortality in 1990–2008* (2010). Data on under-five mortality estimates by the Inter-agency Group for Child Mortality Estimation (which comprises UNICEF, WHO, the World Bank, United Nations Population Division, and other universities and research institutes) and are based mainly on household surveys, censuses, and vital registration data, supplemented by the World Bank's Human Development Network estimates based on vital registration and sample registration data (see table 2.22). Data on depth of hunger are from the Food and Agriculture Organization's Food Security Statistics (www.fao. org/economic/ess/food-security-statistics/en/). Data on primary gross enrollment are from the United Nations Educational, Scientific, and Cultural Organization's Institute for Statistics.

	International Development Association Resource Allocation Index 1–6 (low to high) 2009	Economic management 1–6 (low to high)				Structural policies 1–6 (low to high)			
		Macroeconomic management 2009	Fiscal policy 2009	Debt policy 2009	Average 2009	Trade 2009	Financial sector 2009	Business regulatory environment 2009	Average 2009
Afghanistan	2.8	3.5	3.0	3.5	3.3	3.0	2.5	2.5	2.7
Angola	2.8	3.0	3.0	3.0	3.0	4.0	2.5	2.0	2.8
Armenia	4.2	5.0	5.0	5.0	5.0	4.5	4.0	4.0	4.2
Azerbaijan	3.8	4.0	4.5	5.0	4.5	4.0	3.5	4.0	3.8
Bangladesh	3.5	4.0	4.0	4.0	4.0	3.5	3.5	3.5	3.5
Benin	3.5	4.0	3.5	3.5	3.7	4.0	3.5	3.5	3.7
Bhutan	3.9	4.5	4.5	4.5	4.5	3.0	3.0	3.5	3.2
Bolivia	3.8	4.0	4.0	4.5	4.2	5.0	4.0	2.5	3.8
Bosnia and Herzegovina	3.7	4.0	3.5	4.0	3.8	4.0	4.0	4.0	4.0
Burkina Faso	3.8	4.5	4.5	4.0	4.3	4.0	3.0	3.5	3.5
Burundi	3.1	3.5	3.5	3.0	3.3	4.0	2.5	2.5	3.0
Cambodia	3.3	4.5	3.5	3.5	3.8	4.0	2.5	3.5	3.3
Cameroon	3.2	4.0	4.0	3.0	3.7	3.5	3.0	3.0	3.2
Cape Verde	4.2	4.5	4.5	4.5	4.5	4.0	4.0	3.5	3.8
Central African Republic	2.6	3.5	3.0	2.5	3.0	3.5	2.5	2.0	2.7
Chad	2.5	2.5	2.5	2.5	2.5	3.0	3.0	2.5	2.8
Comoros	2.5	3.0	2.0	2.0	2.3	3.0	2.5	2.5	2.7
Congo, Dem. Rep.	2.7	3.5	3.5	2.5	3.2	3.5	2.0	2.0	2.5
Congo, Rep.	2.8	3.5	3.0	2.5	3.0	3.5	3.0	2.5	3.0
Côte d'Ivoire	2.8	3.5	2.5	2.5	2.8	4.0	3.0	3.0	3.3
Djibouti	3.2	3.5	3.0	2.5	3.0	4.0	3.5	3.5	3.7
Dominica	3.8	4.0	4.5	3.0	3.8	4.0	3.5	4.5	4.0
Eritrea	2.2	2.0	2.0	1.5	1.8	1.5	1.0	2.0	1.5
Ethiopia	3.4	3.5	4.0	3.5	3.7	3.0	3.0	3.5	3.2
Gambia, The	3.3	4.0	3.5	3.0	3.5	3.5	3.0	3.5	3.3
Georgia	4.4	4.5	4.5	5.0	4.7	6.0	3.5	5.5	5.0
Ghana	3.8	3.5	3.5	4.0	3.7	4.0	4.0	4.0	4.0
Grenada	3.7	3.5	2.5	3.0	3.0	4.5	4.0	4.0	4.2
Guinea	2.8	2.5	2.5	2.0	2.3	4.0	3.0	3.0	3.3
Guinea-Bissau	2.6	2.5	2.5	1.5	2.2	4.0	3.0	2.5	3.2
Guyana	3.4	3.5	3.0	4.0	3.5	4.0	3.5	3.0	3.5
Haiti	2.9	4.0	3.5	2.5	3.3	4.0	3.0	2.5	3.2
Honduras	3.5	3.0	3.5	4.0	3.5	4.5	3.0	3.5	3.7
India	3.8	4.5	3.5	4.0	4.0	3.5	4.0	3.5	3.7
Kenya	3.7	4.5	4.0	4.0	4.2	4.0	4.0	4.0	4.0
Kiribati	3.1	2.5	3.0	5.0	3.5	3.0	3.0	3.0	3.0
Kosovo	3.4	3.5	3.0	3.5	3.3	5.0	3.5	3.5	4.0
Kyrgyz Republic	3.7	4.5	4.0	4.0	4.2	5.0	3.0	3.5	3.8

About the data

The International Development Association (IDA) is the part of the World Bank Group that helps the poorest countries reduce poverty by providing concessional loans and grants for programs aimed at boosting economic growth and improving living conditions. IDA funding helps these countries deal with the complex challenges they face in meeting the Millennium Development Goals.

The World Bank's IDA Resource Allocation Index (IRAI), presented in the table, is based on the results of the annual Country Policy and Institutional Assessment (CPIA) exercise, which covers the IDA-eligible countries. The table does not include Myanmar and Somalia because they were not rated in the 2009 exercise even though they are IDA eligible. Country

assessments have been carried out annually since the mid-1970s by World Bank staff. Over time the criteria have been revised from a largely macroeconomic focus to include governance aspects and a broader coverage of social and structural dimensions. Country performance is assessed against a set of 16 criteria grouped into four clusters: economic management, structural policies, policies for social inclusion and equity, and public sector management and institutions. IDA resources are allocated to a country on per capita terms based on its IDA country performance rating and, to a limited extent, based on its per capita gross national income. This ensures that good performers receive a higher IDA allocation in per capita

terms. The IRAI is a key element in the country performance rating.

The CPIA exercise is intended to capture the quality of a country's policies and institutional arrangements, focusing on key elements that are within the country's control, rather than on outcomes (such as economic growth rates) that are influenced by events beyond the country's control. More specifically, the CPIA measures the extent to which a country's policy and institutional framework supports sustainable growth and poverty reduction and, consequently, the effective use of development assistance.

All criteria within each cluster receive equal weight, and each cluster has a 25 percent weight in the overall

	International Development Association Resource Allocation Index 1–6 (low to high)	Economic management 1–6 (low to high)				Structural policies 1–6 (low to high)			
		Macroeconomic management	Fiscal policy	Debt policy	Average	Trade	Financial sector	Business regulatory environment	Average
	2009	**2009**	**2009**	**2009**	**2009**	**2009**	**2009**	**2009**	**2009**
Lao PDR	3.2	4.0	4.0	3.0	3.7	3.5	2.0	3.0	2.8
Lesotho	3.5	4.0	4.0	4.0	4.0	3.5	3.5	3.0	3.3
Liberia	2.8	3.5	3.5	2.5	3.2	3.0	2.5	3.0	2.8
Madagascar	3.5	4.0	3.0	4.0	3.7	4.0	3.0	3.5	3.5
Malawi	3.4	3.0	3.5	3.0	3.2	4.0	3.0	3.5	3.5
Maldives	3.4	2.5	2.0	3.0	2.5	4.0	3.0	4.0	3.7
Mali	3.7	4.5	4.0	4.5	4.3	4.0	3.0	3.5	3.5
Mauritania	3.2	3.5	2.5	3.5	3.2	4.0	2.5	3.5	3.3
Moldova	3.7	3.5	3.5	4.0	3.7	4.5	3.5	3.5	3.8
Mongolia	3.4	3.5	3.0	3.0	3.2	4.5	2.0	3.5	3.3
Mozambique	3.7	4.5	4.5	4.5	4.5	4.5	3.5	3.0	3.7
Nepal	3.3	3.5	3.5	3.0	3.3	3.5	3.0	3.0	3.2
Nicaragua	3.7	4.0	4.0	4.5	4.2	4.5	3.0	3.5	3.7
Niger	3.3	4.0	3.5	4.0	3.8	4.0	3.0	3.0	3.3
Nigeria	3.5	4.0	4.5	4.5	4.3	3.5	3.5	3.5	3.5
Pakistan	3.2	3.0	3.0	3.5	3.2	3.5	3.5	4.0	3.7
Papua New Guinea	3.3	4.0	3.5	4.5	4.0	4.5	3.0	3.0	3.5
Rwanda	3.8	4.0	4.0	3.5	3.8	4.0	3.5	4.0	3.8
Samoa	4.1	4.0	4.0	5.0	4.3	5.0	4.0	3.5	4.2
São Tomé and Príncipe	2.9	3.0	3.0	2.5	2.8	4.0	2.5	2.5	3.0
Senegal	3.7	4.0	4.0	4.0	4.0	4.0	3.5	4.0	3.8
Sierra Leone	3.2	4.0	3.5	3.5	3.7	3.5	3.0	3.0	3.2
Solomon Islands	2.8	3.5	2.5	3.0	3.0	3.0	3.0	2.5	2.8
Sri Lanka	3.5	3.0	3.0	3.5	3.2	3.5	3.5	4.0	3.7
St. Lucia	3.8	4.0	3.5	3.5	3.7	4.0	3.5	4.5	4.0
St. Vincent & Grenadines	3.8	4.0	3.5	3.5	3.7	4.0	3.5	4.5	4.0
Sudan	2.5	3.5	3.0	1.5	2.7	2.5	2.5	3.0	2.7
Tajikistan	3.2	3.5	3.5	3.5	3.5	4.0	2.5	3.0	3.2
Tanzania	3.8	4.5	4.5	4.0	4.3	4.0	4.0	3.5	3.8
Timor-Leste	2.9	3.0	3.5	3.5	3.3	4.5	2.5	1.5	2.8
Togo	2.8	3.0	3.0	2.5	2.8	4.0	2.5	3.0	3.2
Tonga	3.5	3.0	3.0	3.0	3.0	5.0	3.5	3.0	3.8
Uganda	3.9	4.5	4.5	4.5	4.5	4.0	3.5	4.0	3.8
Uzbekistan	3.3	4.0	4.0	4.0	4.0	2.5	3.0	3.0	2.8
Vanuatu	3.4	4.0	3.5	4.5	4.0	3.5	3.0	3.5	3.3
Vietnam	3.8	4.5	4.5	4.0	4.3	3.5	3.0	3.5	3.3
Yemen, Rep.	3.2	3.5	2.5	3.5	3.2	4.5	2.0	3.5	3.3
Zambia	3.4	4.0	3.0	3.5	3.5	4.0	3.5	3.0	3.5
Zimbabwe	1.9	2.0	2.0	1.0	1.7	3.0	1.5	2.0	2.2

score, which is obtained by averaging the average scores of the four clusters. For each of the 16 criteria countries are rated on a scale of 1 (low) to 6 (high). The scores depend on the level of performance in a given year assessed against the criteria, rather than on changes in performance compared with the previous year. All 16 CPIA criteria contain a detailed description of each rating level. In assessing country performance, World Bank staff evaluate the country's performance on each of the criteria and assign a rating. The ratings reflect a variety of indicators, observations, and judgments based on country knowledge and on relevant publicly available indicators. In interpreting the assessment scores, it should be noted that the

criteria are designed in a developmentally neutral manner. Accordingly, higher scores can be attained by a country that, given its stage of development, has a policy and institutional framework that more strongly fosters growth and poverty reduction.

The country teams that prepare the ratings are very familiar with the country, and their assessments are based on country diagnostic studies prepared by the World Bank or other development organizations and on their own professional judgment. An early consultation is conducted with country authorities to make sure that the assessments are informed by up-to-date information. To ensure that scores are consistent across countries, the process involves

two key phases. In the benchmarking phase a small representative sample of countries drawn from all regions is rated. Country teams prepare proposals that are reviewed first at the regional level and then in a Bankwide review process. A similar process is followed to assess the performance of the remaining countries, using the benchmark countries' scores as guideposts. The final ratings are determined following a Bankwide review. The overall numerical IRAI score and the separate criteria scores were first publicly disclosed in June 2006.

See IDA's website at www.worldbank.org/ida for more information.

	Policies for social inclusion and equity 1–6 (low to high)						Public sector management and institutions 1–6 (low to high)					
	Gender equality	Equity of public resource use	Building human resources	Social protection and labor	Policies and institutions for environmental sustainability	Average	Property rights and rule-based governance	Quality of budgetary and financial management	Efficiency of revenue mobilization	Quality of public administration	Transparency, accountability, and corruption in the public sector	Average
	2009	2009	2009	2009	2009	2009	2009	2009	2009	2009	2009	2009
Afghanistan	2.0	3.0	3.0	2.5	2.5	2.6	1.5	3.5	3.0	2.0	2.0	2.4
Angola	3.5	2.5	2.5	3.0	3.0	2.9	2.0	2.5	2.5	2.5	2.5	2.4
Armenia	4.5	4.5	4.0	4.5	3.0	4.1	3.5	4.5	3.5	4.0	3.0	3.7
Azerbaijan	4.0	4.0	4.0	4.0	3.0	3.8	3.0	4.0	3.5	3.0	2.5	3.2
Bangladesh	4.0	3.5	4.0	3.5	3.0	3.6	3.0	3.0	3.0	3.0	3.0	3.0
Benin	3.5	3.0	3.5	3.0	3.5	3.3	3.0	3.5	3.5	3.0	3.5	3.3
Bhutan	4.0	4.0	4.0	3.5	4.5	4.0	3.5	3.5	4.0	4.0	4.5	3.9
Bolivia	4.0	4.0	4.0	3.5	3.5	3.8	2.5	3.5	4.0	3.0	3.5	3.3
Bosnia and Herzegovina	4.5	3.5	3.5	3.5	3.5	3.7	3.0	3.5	4.0	3.0	3.0	3.3
Burkina Faso	3.5	4.0	3.5	3.5	3.5	3.6	3.5	4.5	3.5	3.5	3.5	3.7
Burundi	4.0	3.5	3.0	3.0	3.0	3.3	2.5	3.0	3.0	2.5	2.0	2.6
Cambodia	4.0	3.0	3.5	3.0	3.0	3.3	2.5	3.5	3.0	2.5	2.0	2.7
Cameroon	3.0	3.0	3.5	3.0	3.0	3.1	2.5	3.0	3.5	3.0	2.5	2.9
Cape Verde	4.5	4.5	4.5	4.5	3.5	4.3	4.0	4.0	3.5	4.0	4.5	4.0
Central African Republic	2.5	2.5	2.5	2.0	3.0	2.5	2.0	2.5	2.5	2.5	2.5	2.4
Chad	2.5	2.5	2.5	2.5	2.0	2.4	2.0	2.0	2.5	2.5	2.0	2.2
Comoros	3.0	2.5	3.0	2.5	2.0	2.6	2.5	2.0	2.5	2.5	2.5	2.4
Congo, Dem. Rep.	2.5	3.0	3.0	3.0	2.5	2.8	2.0	2.5	2.5	2.0	2.0	2.2
Congo, Rep.	3.0	2.5	3.0	2.5	2.5	2.7	2.5	2.5	3.0	2.5	2.5	2.6
Côte d'Ivoire	2.5	2.0	2.5	2.5	2.5	2.4	2.0	2.5	4.0	2.0	2.5	2.6
Djibouti	3.0	3.0	3.5	3.0	3.5	3.2	2.5	3.0	3.5	2.5	2.5	2.8
Dominica	3.5	3.5	4.0	3.5	3.5	3.6	4.0	3.5	4.0	3.5	4.0	3.8
Eritrea	3.5	2.5	3.5	2.5	2.0	2.8	2.5	2.5	3.5	3.0	2.0	2.7
Ethiopia	3.0	4.5	4.0	3.5	3.0	3.6	3.0	3.5	3.5	3.5	2.5	3.2
Gambia, The	3.5	3.5	3.5	2.5	3.5	3.3	3.0	3.0	3.5	3.0	2.0	2.9
Georgia	4.5	4.5	4.5	4.5	3.0	4.2	3.5	4.0	4.5	4.0	3.0	3.8
Ghana	4.0	4.0	4.5	3.5	3.5	3.9	3.5	3.5	4.5	3.5	4.0	3.8
Grenada	4.5	3.5	4.0	3.5	4.0	3.9	3.5	4.0	3.5	3.5	4.0	3.7
Guinea	3.5	3.0	3.0	3.0	2.5	3.0	2.0	3.0	3.0	3.0	2.0	2.6
Guinea-Bissau	2.5	3.0	2.0	2.5	2.5	2.5	2.5	2.5	3.0	2.5	2.5	2.6
Guyana	4.0	3.5	4.0	3.0	3.0	3.5	3.0	3.5	3.5	2.5	3.0	3.1
Haiti	3.0	3.0	2.5	2.5	2.5	2.7	2.0	3.0	2.5	2.5	2.5	2.5
Honduras	4.0	4.0	3.5	3.5	3.5	3.7	3.0	4.0	4.0	2.5	3.0	3.3
India	3.5	4.0	4.0	3.5	3.5	3.7	3.5	4.0	4.0	3.5	3.5	3.7
Kenya	3.0	3.5	4.0	3.5	3.5	3.5	2.5	3.5	4.0	3.5	3.0	3.3
Kiribati	2.5	3.5	2.5	3.0	3.0	2.9	3.5	3.0	3.0	3.0	3.0	3.1
Kosovo	3.5	3.5	2.5	3.5	3.0	3.2	3.0	3.0	4.0	3.5	2.5	3.2
Kyrgyz Republic	4.5	3.5	3.5	3.5	3.0	3.6	2.5	3.5	3.5	3.0	2.5	3.0

Definitions

• **International Development Association Resource Allocation Index** is obtained by calculating the average score for each cluster and then by averaging those scores. For each of 16 criteria countries are rated on a scale of 1 (low) to 6 (high) • **Economic management** cluster: **Macroeconomic management** assesses the monetary, exchange rate, and aggregate demand policy framework. • **Fiscal policy** assesses the short- and medium-term sustainability of fiscal policy (taking into account monetary and exchange rate policy and the sustainability of the public debt) and its impact on growth. • **Debt policy** assesses whether the debt management strategy is conducive to minimizing budgetary risks and ensuring

long-term debt sustainability. • **Structural policies** cluster: **Trade** assesses how the policy framework fosters trade in goods. • **Financial sector** assesses the structure of the financial sector and the policies and regulations that affect it. • **Business regulatory environment** assesses the extent to which the legal, regulatory, and policy environments help or hinder private businesses in investing, creating jobs, and becoming more productive. • **Policies for social inclusion and equity** cluster: **Gender equality** assesses the extent to which the country has installed institutions and programs to enforce laws and policies that promote equal access for men and women in education, health, the economy, and

protection under law. • **Equity of public resource use** assesses the extent to which the pattern of public expenditures and revenue collection affects the poor and is consistent with national poverty reduction priorities. • **Building human resources** assesses the national policies and public and private sector service delivery that affect the access to and quality of health and education services, including prevention and treatment of HIV/AIDS, tuberculosis, and malaria. • **Social protection and labor** assess government policies in social protection and labor market regulations that reduce the risk of becoming poor, assist those who are poor to better manage further risks, and ensure a minimal level of welfare

	Policies for social inclusion and equity 1–6 (low to high)						Public sector management and institutions 1–6 (low to high)					
	Gender equality	Equity of public resource use	Building human resources	Social protection and labor	Policies and institutions for environmental sustainability	Average	Property rights and rule-based governance	Quality of budgetary and financial management	Efficiency of revenue mobilization	Quality of public administration	Transparency, accountability, and corruption in the public sector	Average
	2009	2009	2009	2009	2009	2009	2009	2009	2009	2009	2009	2009
Lao PDR	3.5	4.0	3.0	2.5	4.0	3.4	3.0	3.5	3.0	3.0	2.0	2.9
Lesotho	4.0	3.0	3.5	3.0	3.0	3.3	3.5	3.0	4.0	3.0	3.5	3.4
Liberia	2.5	3.0	2.5	2.5	2.0	2.5	2.5	2.5	3.5	2.5	3.0	2.8
Madagascar	3.5	4.0	3.5	3.5	3.5	3.6	3.5	3.0	4.0	3.5	2.5	3.3
Malawi	3.5	3.5	3.5	3.5	3.5	3.5	3.5	3.0	4.0	3.5	3.0	3.4
Maldives	4.0	4.0	3.5	3.5	4.0	3.8	4.0	3.0	4.0	3.5	3.0	3.5
Mali	3.5	3.5	3.5	3.5	3.0	3.4	3.5	3.5	3.5	3.0	3.5	3.4
Mauritania	4.0	3.5	3.5	3.0	3.0	3.4	3.0	3.0	3.5	3.0	2.5	3.0
Moldova	5.0	3.5	4.0	3.5	3.5	3.9	3.5	4.0	3.5	3.0	3.0	3.4
Mongolia	3.5	3.5	4.0	3.5	3.0	3.5	3.0	4.0	3.5	3.5	3.0	3.4
Mozambique	3.5	3.5	3.5	3.0	3.0	3.3	3.0	4.0	4.0	3.0	3.0	3.4
Nepal	4.0	4.0	4.0	3.0	3.5	3.7	2.5	3.0	3.5	3.0	3.0	3.0
Nicaragua	3.5	3.5	3.5	3.5	3.5	3.5	3.0	4.0	4.0	3.0	3.0	3.4
Niger	2.5	3.5	3.5	3.0	3.0	3.1	3.0	3.5	3.5	3.0	2.5	3.1
Nigeria	3.0	3.5	3.0	3.5	3.0	3.2	2.5	3.0	3.5	3.0	2.5	3.0
Pakistan	2.0	3.5	3.0	3.0	3.0	2.9	2.5	3.0	3.5	2.5	3.0	2.8
Papua New Guinea	2.5	3.5	2.5	3.0	2.0	2.7	2.0	3.0	3.5	2.5	3.0	2.8
Rwanda	3.5	4.5	4.5	3.5	3.5	3.9	3.0	4.0	3.5	3.5	3.5	3.5
Samoa	3.5	4.5	4.0	3.5	4.0	3.9	4.0	3.5	4.5	4.0	4.0	4.0
São Tomé and Príncipe	3.0	3.0	3.0	2.5	2.5	2.8	2.5	3.0	3.5	3.0	3.5	3.1
Senegal	3.5	3.5	3.5	3.0	3.5	3.4	3.5	3.0	4.0	3.5	3.0	3.4
Sierra Leone	3.0	3.0	3.5	3.5	2.5	3.1	2.5	3.5	2.5	3.0	3.0	2.9
Solomon Islands	3.0	2.5	3.0	2.5	2.0	2.6	3.0	2.5	2.5	2.0	3.0	2.6
Sri Lanka	4.0	3.5	4.5	3.5	3.5	3.8	3.5	4.0	3.5	3.0	3.0	3.4
St. Lucia	3.5	4.0	4.0	3.5	3.5	3.7	4.0	3.5	4.5	3.5	4.5	4.0
St. Vincent & Grenadines	4.0	3.5	4.0	3.5	3.5	3.7	4.0	3.5	4.0	3.5	4.0	3.8
Sudan	2.0	2.5	2.5	2.5	2.0	2.3	2.0	2.0	3.0	2.5	1.5	2.2
Tajikistan	4.0	3.5	3.0	3.5	3.0	3.4	2.5	3.0	3.0	3.0	2.0	2.7
Tanzania	3.5	4.0	4.0	3.5	3.5	3.7	3.5	3.5	4.0	3.5	3.0	3.5
Timor-Leste	3.5	3.0	2.5	2.5	2.5	2.8	2.0	3.0	3.0	2.5	3.0	2.7
Togo	3.0	2.0	3.0	3.0	2.5	2.7	2.5	2.5	3.0	2.0	2.0	2.4
Tonga	3.0	4.0	4.0	3.0	3.0	3.4	3.5	3.5	4.0	3.5	3.5	3.6
Uganda	3.5	4.0	4.0	3.5	4.0	3.8	3.5	4.0	3.5	3.0	2.5	3.3
Uzbekistan	4.0	3.5	4.0	3.5	3.5	3.7	2.5	3.5	3.5	3.0	1.5	2.8
Vanuatu	3.5	3.5	2.5	2.0	3.0	2.9	3.5	3.5	4.0	3.5	3.0	3.6
Vietnam	4.5	4.5	4.0	3.5	3.5	4.0	3.5	3.5	4.0	3.5	3.0	3.6
Yemen, Rep.	2.0	3.5	3.0	3.5	3.5	3.1	2.5	3.5	3.0	3.0	3.0	3.0
Zambia	3.5	3.5	4.0	3.5	3.5	3.5	3.0	3.5	3.5	3.0	3.0	3.2
Zimbabwe	2.5	1.5	1.0	1.0	2.0	1.6	1.5	2.0	3.5	1.5	1.5	2.0

to all people. • **Policies and institutions for environmental sustainability** assess the extent to which environmental policies foster the protection and sustainable use of natural resources and the management of pollution. • **Public sector management and institutions** cluster: **Property rights and rule-based governance** assess the extent to which private economic activity is facilitated by an effective legal system and rule-based governance structure in which property and contract rights are reliably respected and enforced. • **Quality of budgetary and financial management** assesses the extent to which there is a comprehensive and credible budget linked to policy priorities, effective financial management systems,

and timely and accurate accounting and fiscal reporting, including timely and audited public accounts. • **Efficiency of revenue mobilization** assesses the overall pattern of revenue mobilization—not only the de facto tax structure, but also revenue from all sources as actually collected. • **Quality of public administration** assesses the extent to which civilian central government staff is structured to design and implement government policy and deliver services effectively. • **Transparency, accountability, and corruption in the public sector** assess the extent to which the executive can be held accountable for its use of funds and for the results of its actions by the electorate, the legislature, and the judiciary and the

extent to which public employees within the executive are required to account for administrative decisions, use of resources, and results obtained. The three main dimensions assessed are the accountability of the executive to oversight institutions and of public employees for their performance, access of civil society to information on public affairs, and state capture by narrow vested interests.

Data sources

Data on public policies and institutions are from the World Bank Group's CPIA database available at www.worldbank.org/ida.

	Roads				Railways			Ports	Air		
	Total road network km	Paved roads %	Passengers carried million passenger-km	Goods hauled million ton-km	Rail lines total route-km	Passengers carried million passenger-km	Goods hauled million ton-km	Port container traffic thousand TEU	Registered carrier departures worldwide thousands	Passengers carried thousands	Air freight million ton-km
	2000–08[a]	2000–08[a]	2000–08[a]	2000–08[a]	2000–09[a]	2000–09[a]	2000–09[a]	2009	2009	2009	2009
Afghanistan	42,150	29.3	..	..	..	..	..	..	..	..	..
Albania	18,000	39.0	197	2,200	423	32	46	..	5	231	0
Algeria	111,261	73.5	..	..	4,723	1,141	1,184	..	53	4,371	4
Angola	51,429	10.4	166,045	4,709				..	3	275	64
Argentina	231,374	30.0	..	..	25,023	6,979	12,025	1,555	75	5,695	112
Armenia	7,704	90.5	2,742	179	845	27	354	..	8	653	6
Australia	818,356	..	302,369	189,847	9,674	1,546	62,083	6,197	403	50,027	2,769
Austria	110,778	100.0	69,000	26,411	5,784	10,210	20,202	..	139	8,521	342
Azerbaijan	52,942	50.6	14,041	9,947	2,079	1,025	7,592	..	10	840	7
Bangladesh	239,226	9.5	..	..	2,835	5,609	870	1,182	16	1,409	0
Belarus	94,797	88.6	8,184	22,767	5,510	7,401	42,742	..	6	333	1
Belgium	153,595	78.2	132,404	46,891	3,578	10,493	6,542	9,701	250	4,859	1,427
Benin	19,000	9.5	..	..	758	..	36	..	..	..	..
Bolivia	62,479	7.0	..	..	2,866	313	1,060	..	19	1,537	7
Bosnia and Herzegovina	21,846	52.3	..	300	1,016	61	988	..	1	80	0
Botswana	25,798	32.6	..	..	888	94	674	..	6	234	0
Brazil	1,751,868	5.5	..	..	29,817	..	267,700	6,246	752	67,946	1,782
Bulgaria	40,231	98.4	13,688	11,843	4,150	2,144	3,152	..	11	798	2
Burkina Faso	92,495	4.2	..	..	622	..	..	..	1	79	0
Burundi	12,322	10.4	..	..	..	..	..	..	..	..	..
Cambodia	38,257	6.3	201	..	650	45	92	..	3	184	1
Cameroon	51,346	8.4	..	..	977	377	978	..	10	466	23
Canada	1,409,000	39.9	493,814	129,600	58,345	2,901	258,280	4,175	1,198	52,584	1,347
Central African Republic	24,307	..	..	..	..	..	..	..	..	..	..
Chad	40,000	0.8	..	..	..	..	..	..	..	..	..
Chile	79,814	20.2	..	..	5,352	840	4,032	2,814	97	8,097	1,179
China	3,730,164	53.5	1,247,611	3,286,819	65,491	787,890	2,523,917	105,977	2,140	229,062	11,976
Hong Kong SAR, China	2,040	100.0	..	..	..	..	..	21,040	150	23,973	13,293
Colombia	164,183	..	157	39,726	1,672	..	11,884	2,042	196	12,115	2,420
Congo, Dem. Rep.	153,497	1.8	..	..	3,641	35	182	..	..	..	..
Congo, Rep.	17,000	7.1	..	..	795	211	234	..	..	..	..
Costa Rica	38,049	25.3	27	1	..	..	..	876	33	933	9
Côte d'Ivoire	81,996	7.9	..	..	639	10	675	..	..	..	..
Croatia	29,248	86.9	4,093	11,042	2,723	1,835	2,641	..	25	1,679	2
Cuba	..	49.0	6,551	2,222	5,076	1,285	1,351	..	11	780	27
Czech Republic	130,573	100.0	88,468	50,877	9,539	6,462	11,249	..	78	5,048	22
Denmark	73,257	100.0	70,173	10,717	2,131	7,312	2,030	..	86	6,773	14
Dominican Republic	12,600	49.4	..	..	..	..	..	1,263	..	..	..
Ecuador	43,670	14.8	11,819	1,193	..	..	..	1,001	46	2,897	3
Egypt, Arab Rep.	104,918	86.9	12,793	..	5,195	40,837	3,840	6,250	56	6,216	180
El Salvador	10,029	19.8	..	..	..	..	..	..	19	1,997	15
Eritrea	4,010	21.8	..	..	..	..	..	..	..	..	..
Estonia	58,034	28.8	3,190	7,641	929	274	5,780	..	9	396	1
Ethiopia	44,359	13.7	219,113	2,456	..	..	..	..	44	2,914	424
Finland	78,860	65.5	71,800	28,500	5,919	3,876	8,872	1,064	105	7,423	484
France	951,200	100.0	769,000	313,000	33,778	87,667	26,482	4,491	772	58,318	6,625
Gabon	9,170	10.2	..	..	810	95	2,485	..	5	525	62
Gambia, The	3,742	19.3	16	..	..	..	..	..	..	..	..
Georgia	20,329	94.1	5,269	586	1,566	626	5,417	..	5	294	2
Germany	644,288	100.0	949,306	472,700	33,706	76,772	93,946	12,765	1,081	103,397	10,188
Ghana	57,614	14.9	..	..	953	85	181	..	..	..	..
Greece	116,711	91.8	..	18,360	1,552	1,413	538	935	113	8,795	31
Guatemala	14,095	34.5	..	..	..	..	..	906	..	..	..
Guinea	44,348	9.8	..	..	..	..	..	..	..	..	..
Guinea-Bissau	3,455	27.9	..	..	..	..	..	..	..	..	..
Haiti	4,160	24.3	..	..	..	..	..	..	..	..	..
Honduras	13,600	20.4	..	..	..	..	..	..	..	..	..

	Roads				Railways			Ports	Air		
	Total road network km 2000–08[a]	Paved roads % 2000–08[a]	Passengers carried million passenger-km 2000–08[a]	Goods hauled million ton-km 2000–08[a]	Rail lines total route-km 2000–09[a]	Passengers carried million passenger-km 2000–09[a]	Goods hauled million ton-km 2000–09[a]	Port container traffic thousand TEU 2009	Registered carrier departures worldwide thousands 2009	Passengers carried thousands 2009	Air freight million ton-km 2009
Hungary	197,534	37.7	20,449	35,743	7,793	5,708	447	..	46	2,953	10
India	4,236,429	49.3	..	..	63,273	838,032	551,448	7,889	602	54,446	1,235
Indonesia	437,759	59.1	..	..	3,370	14,344	4,390	6,394	330	27,421	277
Iran, Islamic Rep.	174,301	73.3	..	..	7,555	15,312	20,540	2,206	134	13,053	96
Iraq	45,550	84.3	..	..	2,025	54	121	..	..	..	..
Ireland	96,424	100.0	..	15,900	1,919	1,683	79	817	528	77,747	121
Israel	18,096	100.0	..	..	1,005	1,968	1,055	2,033	48	4,605	985
Italy	487,700	100.0	97,560	192,700	16,959	45,590	13,569	9,532	383	33,195	400
Jamaica	22,210	73.3	..	..	..	..	..	1,690	17	1,380	10
Japan	1,200,858	79.6	947,562	327,632	20,036	253,555	22,100	16,286	642	86,897	10,486
Jordan	7,816	100.0	..	..	294	..	353	2,033	32	2,324	163
Kazakhstan	93,612	89.9	106,878	63,481	14,205	14,860	197,302	..	19	1,193	15
Kenya	63,265	14.1	..	22	1,917	226	1,399	..	34	2,949	272
Korea, Dem. Rep.	25,554	2.8	..	..	..	..	..	..	2	101	2
Korea, Rep.	104,237	78.5	97,854	12,545	3,378	31,298	9,273	16,054	256	34,169	15,163
Kosovo	..	..	..	..	..	..	..	..	..	..	..
Kuwait	5,749	85.0	..	..	..	..	..	..	18	2,597	281
Kyrgyz Republic	34,000	91.1	6,468	903	417	106	745	..	5	309	2
Lao PDR	34,994	13.5	2,113	287	..	..	..	..	10	303	2
Latvia	69,684	100.0	17,966	12,344	1,885	75	18,693	..	27	1,302	18
Lebanon	6,970	..	..	..	..	..	..	995	14	1,308	94
Lesotho	5,940	18.3	..	..	..	..	..	..	..	..	..
Liberia	10,600	6.2	..	..	..	..	..	..	..	..	..
Libya	83,200	57.2	..	..	..	..	..	..	10	1,147	0
Lithuania	81,030	28.6	42,739	20,419	1,767	357	11,888	..	12	617	7
Macedonia, FYR	13,922	56.5	1,239	3,978	699	154	497	..	1	87	0
Madagascar	49,827	11.6	..	..	854	10	12	..	10	500	14
Malawi	15,451	45.0	..	..	797	44	33	..	4	157	1
Malaysia	98,722	82.8	..	..	1,665	1,527	1,384	15,843	182	23,766	2,853
Mali	18,912	19.0	..	..	733	196	189	..	1	142	0
Mauritania	11,066	26.8	..	..	728	47	7,566	..	11	1,093	153
Mauritius	2,028	98.0	..	..	..	..	..	2,869	222	15,728	714
Mexico	366,096	35.3	463,865	227,290	26,704	449	71,136	2,869	5	402	1
Moldova	12,778	85.8	1,640	1,577	1,157	423	1,017	..	5	257	3
Mongolia	49,250	3.5	1,215	782	1,814	1,009	7,852	..	62	4,931	63
Morocco	58,256	67.8	..	794	2,110	4,190	4,111	1,222	11	490	6
Mozambique	30,331	20.8	..	..	3,116	114	695	..	28	1,527	3
Myanmar	27,000	11.9	..	..	..	4,163	885	..	5	455	0
Namibia	66,467	12.8	47	591	..	..	..	..	7	484	6
Nepal	17,782	55.9	..	..	..	..	..	..	292	29,109	4,520
Netherlands	136,135	90.0	..	77,100	2,886	15,400	4,331	10,066	217	12,104	799
New Zealand	93,911	65.9	..	..	..	..	4,078	2,955	..	..	..
Nicaragua	20,333	12.0	123	..	..	..	..	..	..	..	..
Niger	18,948	20.7	..	..	..	..	..	..	17	1,365	8
Nigeria	193,200	15.0	..	..	3,528	174	77	..	110	8,786	14
Norway	93,247	80.5	63,362	17,564	4,114	2,877	2,092	..	26	2,361	39
Oman	53,430	43.5	..	..	..	..	..	3,768	51	5,303	304
Pakistan	260,420	65.4	263,788	129,249	7,791	24,731	6,187	2,058	66	6,348	0
Panama	13,727	38.1	..	..	..	..	..	4,597	21	847	19
Papua New Guinea	19,600	3.5	..	..	..	..	..	..	10	428	0
Paraguay	29,500	50.8	..	..	..	..	..	..	66	5,843	257
Peru	102,887	13.9	..	..	2,020	78	900	1,335	87	10,481	227
Philippines	200,037	9.9	..	..	479	83	1	4,116	83	4,279	55
Poland	383,313	68.2	26,791	174,223	19,764	16,454	29,940	859	124	9,904	314
Portugal	82,900	86.0	..	46,406	2,842	3,766	872	1,042	..	..	..
Puerto Rico	25,645	95.0	..	10	..	..	..	1,674	77	10,211	2,276
Qatar	7,790	90.0	..	..	..	..	..	..	77	10,211	2,276

	Roads				Railways			Ports	Air		
	Total road network km	Paved roads %	Passengers carried million passenger-km	Goods hauled million ton-km	Rail lines total route-km	Passengers carried million passenger-km	Goods hauled million ton-km	Port container traffic thousand TEU	Registered carrier departures worldwide thousands	Passengers carried thousands	Air freight million ton-km
	2000–08[a]	2000–08[a]	2000–08[a]	2000–08[a]	2000–09[a]	2000–09[a]	2000–09[a]	2009	2009	2009	2009
Romania	198,817	30.2	20,194	56,377	10,776	5,975	8,902	1,381	58	3,268	4
Russian Federation	963,000	80.1	78,000	206,000	85,194	153,500	1,865,305	2,178	475	34,403	2,306
Rwanda	14,008	19.0	..	..	..	..	..	..	..	..	..
Saudi Arabia	221,372	21.5	..	..	1,020	337	1,748	4,431	157	17,508	1,838
Senegal	14,805	29.3	..	..	906	129	384	..	0	573	0
Serbia	40,130	47.7	4,719	1,112	4,058	683	3,013	..	17	927	2
Sierra Leone	11,300	8.0	..	..	..	..	..	..	0	22	8
Singapore	3,325	100.0	5,964	..	..	..	..	25,866	84	18,427	7,391
Slovak Republic	43,848	87.0	32,214	22,114	3,623	2,247	6,465	..	32	3,441	0
Slovenia	38,872	100.0	815	16,261	1,228	840	2,668	..	25	953	3
Somalia	22,100	11.8	..	..	..	..	..	..	..	..	..
South Africa	362,099	17.3	..	434	22,051	13,865	113,342	3,726	151	12,504	676
Spain	667,064	99.0	397,117	132,868	15,043	22,959	7,348	10,193	548	49,289	1,080
Sri Lanka	97,286	81.0	21,067	..	1,463	4,767	135	3,464	17	2,418	279
Sudan	11,900	36.3	..	..	4,508	34	766	..	7	607	42
Swaziland	3,594	30.0	..	..	300	..	..	..	..	..	..
Sweden	574,741	23.6	108,100	42,400	9,946	7,038	11,500	1,251	62	5,824	16
Switzerland	71,355	100.0	93,675	16,226	3,544	17,417	12,460	..	168	14,701	1,058
Syrian Arab Republic	64,983	91.0	589	..	1,801	1,120	2,370	685	19	1,343	11
Tajikistan	27,767	..	150	14,572	616	45	1,282	..	10	765	6
Tanzania	87,524	7.4	..	..	2,600[b]	475[b]	728[b]	..	21	684	1
Thailand	180,053	98.5	..	..	4,429	8,037	3,161	5,898	124	19,619	2,133
Timor-Leste	..	..	..	..	..	..	..	..	..	..	..
Togo	11,652	21.0	..	..	..	..	..	..	..	..	..
Trinidad and Tobago	8,320	51.1	..	..	..	..	..	..	14	1,014	70
Tunisia	19,371	75.2	..	16,611	1,991	1,493	2,073	..	24	2,279	14
Turkey	426,951	..	206,098	181,935	8,686	5,374	9,681	4,522	272	31,339	856
Turkmenistan	24,000	81.2	..	..	3,095	1,685	11,547	..	15	1,706	9
Uganda	70,746	23.0	..	..	259	..	218	..	0	64	27
Ukraine	169,502	97.8	60,671	36,866	21,678	48,327	196,188	1,112	59	3,428	63
United Arab Emirates	4,080	100.0	..	..	..	..	..	14,425	171	31,762	8,960
United Kingdom	419,634	100.0	736,000	173,077	16,173	51,467	12,512	5,987	1,004	102,465	6,615
United States	6,506,221	67.4	7,980,611	1,889,923	226,205	9,476	2,431,181[c]	34,300	9,182[d]	679,423[d]	61,684[d]
Uruguay	77,732	..	2,032	..	2,993	15	284	..	9	564	4
Uzbekistan	81,600	87.3	56,674	21,038	4,230	2,832	24,238	..	23	1,850	76
Venezuela, RB	96,155	33.6	..	..	336	..	81	1,168	124	5,121	2
Vietnam	160,089	47.6	49,372	24,647	2,347	4,129	3,807	4,751	84	11,074	312
West Bank and Gaza	5,147	100.0	..	..	..	..	..	..	..	..	..
Yemen, Rep.	71,300	8.7	..	..	..	..	..	..	15	1,050	26
Zambia	66,781	22.0	..	..	1,273	183	..	..	4	62	..
Zimbabwe	97,267	19.0	..	..	2,583	..	1,580	..	6	261	7
World	**49.0 m**	**.. m**	**.. m**	**.. s**	**2,264 m**	**5,321 m**	**443,740 s**	**26,379 s**	**2,270,901 s**	**202,136 s**	
Low income	12.0	..	..	..	..	..	..	..	228	13,439	783
Middle income	35.4	..	..	..	1,343	4,072	206,537	7,169	664,804	31,329	
Lower middle income	36.3	..	..	..	1,917	4,049	150,612	3,954	398,922	17,548	
Upper middle income	36.8	..	..	..	1,083	5,812	55,926	3,215	265,882	13,781	
Low & middle income	24.3	..	..	..	..	3,910	207,719	7,398	678,243	32,112	
East Asia & Pacific	11.4	..	..	..	4,248	3,483	142,980	3,093	326,294	17,878	
Europe & Central Asia	..	27,816	21,038	171,322	1,025	7,592	11,018	1,018	83,523	3,365	
Latin America & Carib.	22.0	..	..	..	..	..	28,362	1,794	138,460	6,576	
Middle East & N. Africa	81.0	..	..	..	1,493	2,222	..	419	38,022	653	
South Asia	51.8	..	..	..	24,731	3,529	14,593	700	64,196	1,825	
Sub-Saharan Africa	12.1	..	..	..	..	..	..	373	27,749	1,815	
High income	93.4	..	29,505	..	7,038	8,872	236,021	18,981	1,592,658	170,024	
Euro area	100.0	69,000	45,032	130,021	10,210	6,542	62,931	4,488	399,964	33,950	

a. Data are for the latest year available in the period shown. b. Includes Tazara railway. c. Refers to class 1 railways only. d. Covers only carriers designated by the U.S. Department of Transportation as major and national air carriers.

Transport infrastructure—highways, railways, ports and waterways, and airports and air traffic control systems—and the services that flow from it are crucial to the activities of households, producers, and governments. Because performance indicators vary widely by transport mode and focus (whether physical infrastructure or the services flowing from that infrastructure), highly specialized and carefully specified indicators are required. The table provides selected indicators of the size, extent, and productivity of roads, railways, and air transport systems and of the volume of traffic in these modes as well as in ports.

Data for transport sectors are not always internationally comparable. Unlike for demographic statistics, national income accounts, and international trade data, the collection of infrastructure data has not been "internationalized." But data on roads are collected by the International Road Federation (IRF) and data on air transport by the International Civil Aviation Organization (ICAO).

National road associations are the primary source of IRF data. In countries where a national road association is lacking or does not respond, other agencies are contacted, such as road directorates, ministries of transport or public works, or central statistical offices. As a result, definitions and data collection methods and quality differ, and the compiled data are of uneven quality. Moreover, the quality of transport service (reliability, transit time, and condition of goods delivered) is rarely measured, though it may be as important as quantity in assessing an economy's transport system.

Unlike the road sector, where numerous qualified motor vehicle operators can operate anywhere on the road network, railways are a restricted transport system with vehicles confined to a fixed guideway. Considering the cost and service characteristics, railways generally are best suited to carry—and can effectively compete for—bulk commodities and containerized freight for distances of 500–5,000 kilometers, and passengers for distances of 50–1,000 kilometers. Below these limits road transport tends to be more competitive, while above these limits air transport for passengers and freight and sea transport for freight tend to be more competitive. The railways indicators in the table focus on scale and output measures: total route-kilometers, passenger-kilometers, and goods (freight) hauled in ton-kilometers.

Measures of port container traffic, much of it commodities of medium to high value added, give some indication of economic growth in a country.

But when traffic is merely transshipment, much of the economic benefit goes to the terminal operator and ancillary services for ships and containers rather than to the country more broadly. In transshipment centers empty containers may account for as much as 40 percent of traffic.

The air transport data represent the total (international and domestic) scheduled traffic carried by the air carriers registered in a country. Countries submit air transport data to ICAO on the basis of standard instructions and definitions issued by ICAO. In many cases, however, the data include estimates by ICAO for nonreporting carriers. Where possible, these estimates are based on previous submissions supplemented by information published by the air carriers, such as flight schedules.

The data cover the air traffic carried on scheduled services, but changes in air transport regulations in Europe have made it more difficult to classify traffic as scheduled or nonscheduled. Thus recent increases shown for some European countries may be due to changes in the classification of air traffic rather than actual growth. For countries with few air carriers or only one, the addition or discontinuation of a home-based air carrier may cause significant changes in air traffic.

• **Total road network** covers motorways, highways, main or national roads, secondary or regional roads, and all other roads in a country. • **Paved roads** are roads surfaced with crushed stone (macadam) and hydrocarbon binder or bituminized agents, with concrete, or with cobblestones. • **Passengers carried by road** are the number of passengers transported by road times kilometers traveled. • **Goods hauled by road** are the volume of goods transported by road vehicles, measured in millions of metric tons times kilometers traveled. • **Rail lines** are the length of railway route available for train service, irrespective of the number of parallel tracks. • **Passengers carried by railway** are the number of passengers transported by rail times kilometers traveled. • **Goods hauled by railway** are the volume of goods transported by railway, measured in metric tons times kilometers traveled. • **Port container traffic** measures the flow of containers from land to sea transport modes and vice versa in twenty-foot-equivalent units (TEUs), a standard-size container. Data cover coastal shipping as well as international journeys. Transshipment traffic is counted as two lifts at the intermediate port (once to off-load and again as an outbound lift) and includes empty units. • **Registered carrier departures worldwide** are domestic takeoffs and takeoffs abroad of air carriers registered in the country. • **Passengers carried by air** include both domestic and international passengers of air carriers registered in the country. • **Air freight** is the volume of freight, express, and diplomatic bags carried on each flight stage (operation of an aircraft from takeoff to its next landing), measured in metric tons times kilometers traveled.

Data sources

Data on roads are from the IRF's *World Road Statistics*, supplemented by World Bank staff estimates. Data on railways are from a database maintained by the World Bank's Transport, Water, and Information and Communication Technologies Department, Transport Division, based on data from the International Union of Railways. Data on port container traffic are from Containerisation International's *Containerisation International Yearbook*. Data on air transport are from the ICAO's *Civil Aviation Statistics of the World* and ICAO staff estimates.

	Electric power		Telephones[a]								
			Access and use				Quality	Affordability and efficiency			
			per 100 people		International voice traffic minutes per person		Population covered by mobile cellular network %	$ per month			Mobile cellular and fixed-line subscribers per employee
	Consumption per capita kWh	Transmission and distribution losses % of output	Fixed lines	Mobile cellular subscriptions	Fixed lines	Total		Residential fixed-line tariff	Mobile cellular prepaid tariff	Telecommunications revenue % of GDP	
	2008	**2008**	**2009**	**2009**	**2008**	**2008**	**2008**	**2009**	**2009**	**2008**	**2008**
Afghanistan	..	..	0	40	1	7	75	..	..	0.0	58
Albania	1,372	50	12	132	127	263	99	6.0	13.4	6.0	871
Algeria	957	18	7	94	15	34	82	4.2	6.3	2.5	285
Angola	189	15	2	44	..	..	40	16.6	11.0	..	..
Argentina	2,789	13	24	129	42	..	94	3.9	13.7	3.1	1,929
Armenia	1,578	15	20	85	..	..	88	4.1	5.8	4.5	..
Australia	11,217	7	41	111	..	..	99	26.0	34.9	3.4	346
Austria	8,218	5	39	141	..	..	99	27.3	6.8	1.7	843
Azerbaijan	2,317	13	16	88	..	77	99	2.5	4.4	2.4	484
Bangladesh	208	5	1	31	6	..	90	1.6	1.3	..	..
Belarus	3,427	11	41	100	..	..	99	1.0	3.4	2.1	..
Belgium	8,523	5	39	115	..	..	100	33.6	20.8	2.8	732
Benin	76	..	1	56	12	309	80	10.0	14.8	1.0	1,652
Bolivia	561	13	8	72	80	..	46	23.5	7.3	6.8	376
Bosnia and Herzegovina	2,467	17	27	86	109	..	99	8.8	9.4	5.5	567
Botswana	1,503	52	7	96	115	..	99	18.0	8.1	2.9	1,018
Brazil	2,232	17	21	90	..	..	91	13.4	34.6	4.5	358
Bulgaria	4,594	10	29	140	27	105	100	13.8	17.6	5.1	565
Burkina Faso	..	..	1	21	11	..	61	11.5	14.4	4.0	..
Burundi	..	..	0	10	..	..	80	..	..	3.1	492
Cambodia	113	13	0	38	..	..	87	7.8	5.0	..	1,712
Cameroon	263	10	2	38	4	..	58	14.1	14.0	3.1	1,050
Canada	17,061	8	54	68	..	..	98	18.3	17.7	2.5	..
Central African Republic	..	..	0	4	..	..	19	10.1	12.9	..	293
Chad	..	..	0	24	..	..	24	..	..	..	..
Chile	3,319	9	21	97	35	43	100	23.6	10.2	..	592
China	2,455	6	24	56	9	..	97	2.3	3.7	2.5[b]	1,310
Hong Kong SAR, China	5,866	13	60	174	1,435	1,435	100	7.1	0.8	3.6	980
Colombia	974	19	16	92	142	..	83	5.7	9.5	3.7	..
Congo, Dem. Rep.	95	11	0	15	..	6	50	..	..	7.4	3,628
Congo, Rep.	150	77	1	59	..	..	53	..	..	..	..
Costa Rica	1,866	10	33	43	120	132	69	4.1	2.3	1.8	497
Côte d'Ivoire	186	24	1	63	..	..	59	21.7	11.5	5.5	3,274
Croatia	3,878	14	42	136	229	302	100	19.2	18.4	4.6	892
Cuba	1,327	16	10	4	..	..	77	13.2	22.7	..	..
Czech Republic	6,464	6	20	136	136	197	100	29.3	17.7	3.8	812
Denmark	6,460	6	37	134	210	357	..	24.5	6.5	2.4	543
Dominican Republic	1,377	11	10	86	..	..	..	12.3	8.5	..	..
Ecuador	1,137	20	15	100	3	..	84	1.3	9.4	4.1	513
Egypt, Arab Rep.	1,425	11	12	67	27	44	95	3.0	4.1	3.7	855
El Salvador	953	2	18	123	578	510	95	11.5	7.1	4.8	2,275
Eritrea	..	..	1	3	17	29	80	..	..	3.0	117
Estonia	6,348	11	37	203	..	..	100	13.2	12.3	4.5	742
Ethiopia	42	9	1	5	2	5	10	0.9	2.4	1.3	233
Finland	16,350	4	27	144	..	..	100	18.5	13.4	2.3	708
France	7,931	6	57	95	242	301	99	29.3	35.2	2.0	695
Gabon	1,158	18	2	93	..	..	79	..	..	2.0	..
Gambia, The	..	..	3	84	..	..	85	2.4	6.3	..	466
Georgia	1,678	13	15	67	44	268	98	3.5	7.6	6.9	355
Germany	7,149	5	59	128	..	..	99	32.7	9.5	2.5	787
Ghana	268	22	1	63	6	61	73	3.8	4.3	..	1,780
Greece	5,723	8	53	118	..	..	100	25.4	23.6	3.7	813
Guatemala	543	14	10	123	..	206	76	7.8	7.3	..	..
Guinea	..	..	0	56	..	..	80	3.0	3.1	..	..
Guinea-Bissau	..	..	0	35	..	..	65	..	..	..	..
Haiti	23	53	1	36	..	..	..	..	..	..	..
Honduras	708	21	11	103	39	224	90	..	..	7.2	391

Power and communications

| | Electric power | | Telephones[a] | | | | Quality | Affordability and efficiency | | | |
	Consumption per capita kWh	Transmission and distribution losses % of output	per 100 people Fixed lines	per 100 people Mobile cellular subscriptions	International voice traffic minutes per person Fixed lines	International voice traffic minutes per person Total	Population covered by mobile cellular network %	$ per month Residential fixed-line tariff	$ per month Mobile cellular prepaid tariff	Telecommunications revenue % of GDP	Mobile cellular and fixed-line subscribers per employee
	2008	2008	2009	2009	2008	2008	2008	2009	2009	2008	2008
Hungary	3,989	10	31	118	120	159	99	24.0	15.4	3.8	1,127
India	566	23	3	45	..	..	61	3.1	1.4	1.9	..
Indonesia	591	10	15	69	..	..	90	5.6	2.8	..	..
Iran, Islamic Rep.	2,423	18	35	72	..	..	95	0.2	3.6	..	913
Iraq	1,164	7	4	63	0	..	72	..	..	..	1,098
Ireland	6,301	8	47	109	..	..	99	43.8	20.9	2.5	..
Israel	7,054	2	44	121	413	..	100	17.0	13.8	4.0	..
Italy	5,661	7	35	150	..	..	100	28.2	18.4	2.9	1,657
Jamaica	2,552	12	11	110	39	224	95	9.6	5.6	1.4	..
Japan	8,071	5	35	90	..	..	100	22.8	44.3	3.1	12
Jordan	2,087	14	8	101	67	258	99	9.4	5.7	6.3	1,132[b]
Kazakhstan	4,689	9	24	94	47	52	94	1.9	8.8	2.9	253
Kenya	155	15	2	49	3	6	83	10.1	7.5	6.4	2,354
Korea, Dem. Rep.	820	16	5	0	..	..	0	..	..	..	..
Korea, Rep.	8,853	4	40	98	33	64	94	5.2	12.2	4.7	657
Kosovo	..	..	..	..	..	..	..	..	..	..	..
Kuwait	16,747	12	20	107	..	..	100	8.6	7.8	..	..
Kyrgyz Republic	1,449	31	9	84	..	..	24	1.3	2.9	4.8	311
Lao PDR	..	..	2	51	..	..	..	3.8	3.5	..	748
Latvia	3,087	15	29	99	..	..	99	11.2	7.3	4.0	697
Lebanon	2,267	16	18	36	..	190	100	10.3	15.8	..	..
Lesotho	..	..	2	32	..	..	55	12.8	12.9	..	..
Liberia	..	..	0	21	..	..	..	..	..	8.2	..
Libya	3,909	14	17	78	65	..	71	..	..	..	1,717
Lithuania	3,557	8	22	149	57	132	100	14.3	8.6	2.8	402
Macedonia, FYR	3,723	23	22	95	159	256	100	13.4	13.4	6.3	1,065
Madagascar	..	..	1	31	1	8	23	12.2	10.5	3.9	2,427
Malawi	..	..	1	16	..	..	93	3.3	10.8	3.6	..
Malaysia	3,490	3	16	111	..	..	92	4.8	4.9	..	..
Mali	..	..	1	29	2	13	22	9.4	10.0	4.3	2,059
Mauritania	..	..	2	66	4	57	62	11.9	9.9	6.9	2,842
Mauritius	..	..	30	85	100	215	99	5.6	4.5	3.6	..
Mexico	2,020	17	18	78	174	..	100	17.3	8.6	2.7	838
Moldova	1,287	53	32	77	155	457	98	2.9	8.2	10.1	294
Mongolia	1,473	11	7	84	5	..	82[b]	0.7	3.6	6.7[b]	341[b]
Morocco	736	11	11	79	21	87	98	23.5	22.2	5.1	..
Mozambique	461	9	0	26	..	..	44	13.1	8.0	1.2	..
Myanmar	97	27	2	1	..	3	10	0.9	12.8	..	90
Namibia	1,797	18	7	56	..	..	95	13.0	12.8	..	..
Nepal	89	19	3	26	..	..	60[b]	3.0	1.2	1.0	565
Netherlands	7,226	4	44	128	..	..	98	27.8	29.7	0.7	..
New Zealand	9,492	7	43	109	310	..	97	33.1	27.9	2.9	605
Nicaragua	457	24	4	56	39	..	..	4.7	14.0	..	..
Niger	..	..	0	17	..	..	45	12.9	15.3	..	..
Nigeria	126	9	1	47	1	26	83	5.7	10.4	3.4	..
Norway	24,867	7	39	111	..	..	..	29.4	8.7	1.2	..
Oman	4,894	13	11	140	30	431	96	12.8	6.2	2.5	967
Pakistan	436	21	2	61	..	..	90	2.9	1.0	2.7	50
Panama	1,646	14	16	164	61	118	83	12.0	5.0	3.2	380
Papua New Guinea	..	..	1	13	..	..	..	4.0	17.8	..	..
Paraguay	1,002	5	6	88	35	..	..	6.6	5.3	4.8	799
Peru	1,032	8	10	85	..	113	95	14.3	8.9	3.1	624
Philippines	588	13	4	81	..	..	99	15.9	6.2	..	..
Poland	3,732	8	25	117	..	32	99	17.4	9.6	3.9	396
Portugal	4,822	9	38	143	..	..	99	27.5	9.2	4.5	1,534
Puerto Rico	..	..	22	68	..	..	..	..	..	..	..
Qatar	15,682	7	20	175	..	..	100	9.1	8.6	1.7	597

	Electric power		Telephones[a]								
			Access and use				Quality	Affordability and efficiency			
			per 100 people		International voice traffic minutes per person		Population covered by mobile cellular network	$ per month			Mobile cellular and fixed-line subscribers
	Consumption per capita kWh	Transmission and distribution losses % of output	Fixed lines	Mobile cellular subscriptions	Fixed lines	Total	%	Residential fixed-line tariff	Mobile cellular prepaid tariff	Telecommunications revenue % of GDP	per employee
	2008	2008	2009	2009	2008	2008	2008	2009	2009	2008	2008
Romania	2,488	11	25	118	*41*	*124*	98	19.3	10.6	*3.4*	*564*
Russian Federation	6,435	11	32	162	..	..	95	5.4	5.8	2.6	..
Rwanda	..	..	0	24	*11*	8	92	8.1	6.6	3.0	1,952
Saudi Arabia	7,527	9	16	177	..	..	98	9.2	7.4	2.7	1,618
Senegal	158	20	2	55	*27*	*101*	85	24.0	8.3	9.8	*1,859*
Serbia	4,284	16	42	135	136[b]	203[b]	94[b]	3.9	5.2	4.9[b]	883[b]
Sierra Leone	..	..	1	20	..	..	70	..	..	..	..
Singapore	8,185	5	37	133	*1,531*	..	100	7.7	3.9	2.6	..
Slovak Republic	5,268	3	19	101	123	228	100	22.7	24.9	3.3	665
Slovenia	6,920	5	51	103	96	220	100	19.6	15.8	3.3	644
Somalia	..	..	1	7	..	..	..	..	..	..	..
South Africa	4,759	9	9	94	..	..	100	21.6	12.6	7.3	..
Spain	6,315	5	44	111	..	..	99	28.5	31.6	4.1	855
Sri Lanka	409	11	17	69	*34*	..	95	4.7	0.9	..	919
Sudan	96	12	1	36	6	13	66	3.9	3.4	3.2	2,168
Swaziland	..	..	4	55	..	41	91	4.9	12.8	4.5	1,118
Sweden	14,869	7	55	123	..	..	98	26.2	14.8	2.7	894
Switzerland	8,307	6	60	120	..	..	100	31.5	33.7	3.3	601
Syrian Arab Republic	1,521	24	18	46	78	..	96	1.3	7.6	*3.0*	409
Tajikistan	2,072	18	4	70	..	..	..	0.9	2.9	..	..
Tanzania	84	19	0	40	*0*	*1*	65	12.2	10.2	..	..
Thailand	2,079	6	10	123	..	..	38	8.3	2.4	4.0	1,957
Timor-Leste	..	..	..	..	..	..	..	..	..	7.9	..
Togo	99	..	3	33	6	*28*	85	12.8	12.4	7.4	*1,059*
Trinidad and Tobago	5,789	2	24	147	..	443	100	19.5	6.5	2.6	..
Tunisia	1,298	12	12	93	79	..	100[b]	2.8	7.2	4.3	1,004
Turkey	2,308	14	22	84	39	60	100	13.8	23.9	2.3	2,145
Turkmenistan	2,273	14	9	29	..	..	*14*	..	..	..	..
Uganda	..	..	1	29	*7*	..	100	9.9	7.9	..	..
Ukraine	3,534	12	28	120	0	..	100	2.8	4.3	*5.7*	..
United Arab Emirates	16,891	12	34	232	..	..	100	4.1	4.1	3.1	924
United Kingdom	6,061	7	54	130	..	..	100	24.1	16.5	4.3	..
United States	13,654	6	50	97	..	*216*	100	12.8	15.3	2.8	416
Uruguay	2,393	20	29	114	..	125	100	12.5	12.7	3.2	692
Uzbekistan	1,646	9	7	59	..	..	93	1.1	1.1	2.5	739
Venezuela, RB	3,074	28	24	99	..	79	90	9.0	28.6	3.5	*1,500*
Vietnam	799	10	35	101	..	..	70	2.1	3.2	..	..
West Bank and Gaza	..	..	9	30	..	..	95	..	..	..	880
Yemen, Rep.	220	23	5	16	..	..	68	0.7	4.8	..	..
Zambia	602	23	1	34	..	..	50	24.6	12.7	2.6	..
Zimbabwe	1,022	6	3	24	22	19	75	..	..	..	711
World	**2,875 w**	**8 w**	**18 w**	**69 w**	**.. w**	**.. w**	**80 w**	**10.1 m**	**8.7 m**	**3.1 w**	**755 m**
Low income	231	15	1	27	..	..	53	8.8	8.0	..	..
Middle income	1,670	11	15	67	..	..	80	5.7	7.6	3.2	665
Lower middle income	1,318	10	13	58	..	..	77	4.7	7.1	3.0	..
Upper middle income	3,001	13	22	101	..	..	94	10.0	8.8	3.3	576
Low & middle income	1,505	11	13	61	..	..	76	6.6	7.9	3.2	624
East Asia & Pacific	1,972	6	20	62	9	..	93	4.0	3.7	2.6	..
Europe & Central Asia	4,052	12	25	119	..	..	91	3.9	7.6	2.8	462
Latin America & Carib.	1,907	16	18	90	..	..	92	10.6	8.8	3.8	586
Middle East & N. Africa	1,494	15	16	67	27	..	93	3.0	6.3	..	880
South Asia	503	22	3	45	..	..	61	3.0	1.2	2.0	565
Sub-Saharan Africa	531	11	1	37	..	..	56	11.5	10.4	..	..
High income	9,518	6	45	111	..	..	99	22.8	14.8	3.0	765
Euro area	6,970	5	48	123	..	..	99	27.6	19.6	2.6	765

a. Data are from the International Telecommunication Union's (ITU) World Telecommunication Report database. Please cite ITU for third-party use of these data. b. Data are for 2009.

About the data

The quality of an economy's infrastructure, including power and communications, is an important element in investment decisions for both domestic and foreign investors. Government effort alone is not enough to meet the need for investments in modern infrastructure; public-private partnerships, especially those involving local providers and financiers, are critical for lowering costs and delivering value for money. In telecommunications, competition in the marketplace, along with sound regulation, is lowering costs, improving quality, and easing access to services around the globe.

An economy's production and consumption of electricity are basic indicators of its size and level of development. Although a few countries export electric power, most production is for domestic consumption. Expanding the supply of electricity to meet the growing demand of increasingly urbanized and industrialized economies without incurring unacceptable social, economic, and environmental costs is one of the great challenges facing developing countries.

Data on electric power production and consumption are collected from national energy agencies by the International Energy Agency (IEA) and adjusted by the IEA to meet international definitions (for data on electricity production, see table 3.10). Electricity consumption is equivalent to production less power plants' own use and transmission, distribution, and transformation losses less exports plus imports. It includes consumption by auxiliary stations, losses in transformers that are considered integral parts of those stations, and electricity produced by pumping installations. Where data are available, it covers electricity generated by primary sources of energy—coal, oil, gas, nuclear, hydro, geothermal, wind, tide and wave, and combustible renewables. Neither production nor consumption data capture the reliability of supplies, including breakdowns, load factors, and frequency of outages.

Over the past decade new financing and technology, along with privatization and liberalization, have spurred dramatic growth in telecommunications in many countries. With the rapid development of mobile telephony and the global expansion of the Internet, information and communication technologies are increasingly recognized as essential tools of development, contributing to global integration and enhancing public sector effectiveness, efficiency, and transparency. The table presents telecommunications indicators covering access and use, quality, and affordability and efficiency.

Access to telephone services rose on an unprecedented scale over the past 15 years. This growth was driven primarily by wireless technologies and liberalization of telecommunications markets, which have enabled faster and less costly network rollout. In 2002 the number of mobile phones in the world surpassed the number of fixed telephones. The International Telecommunication Union (ITU) estimates that there were 5 billion mobile subscriptions globally in 2010. No technology has ever spread faster around the world. Mobile communications have a particularly important impact in rural areas. The mobility, ease of use, flexible deployment, and relatively low and declining rollout costs of wireless technologies enable them to reach rural populations with low levels of income and literacy. The next billion mobile subscribers will consist mainly of the rural poor.

Access is the key to delivering telecommunications services to people. If the service is not affordable to most people, then goals of universal usage will not be met. Two indicators of telecommunications affordability are presented in the table: fixed-line telephone service tariff and prepaid mobile cellular service tariff. Telecommunications efficiency is measured by total telecommunications revenue divided by GDP and by mobile cellular and fixed-line telephone subscribers per employee.

Operators have traditionally been the main source of telecommunications data, so information on subscribers has been widely available for most countries. This gives a general idea of access, but a more precise measure is the penetration rate—the share of households with access to telecommunications. During the past few years more information on information and communication technology use has become available from household and business surveys. Also important are data on actual use of telecommunications equipment. Ideally, statistics on telecommunications (and other information and communications technologies) should be compiled for all three measures: subscription and possession, access, and use. The quality of data varies among reporting countries as a result of differences in regulations covering data provision and availability.

Definitions

• **Electric power consumption per capita** measures the production of power plants and combined heat and power plants less transmission, distribution, and transformation losses and own use by heat and power plants divided by midyear population. • **Electric power transmission and distribution losses** are losses in transmission between sources of supply and points of distribution and in distribution to consumers, including pilferage. • **Fixed telephone lines** are telephone lines connecting a subscriber to the telephone exchange equipment. • **Mobile cellular telephone subscriptions** are subscriptions to a public mobile telephone service using cellular technology, which provide access to the public switched telephone network. Post-paid and prepaid subscriptions are included. • **International voice traffic** is the sum of international incoming and outgoing telephone traffic (in minutes) divided by total population. • **Population covered by mobile cellular network** is the percentage of people that live in areas served by a mobile cellular signal regardless of whether they use it. • **Residential fixed-line tariff** is the monthly subscription charge plus the cost of 30 three-minute local calls (15 peak and 15 off-peak). • **Mobile cellular prepaid tariff** is based on the Organisation for Economic Co-operation and Development's low-user definition, which includes the cost of monthly mobile use for 25 outgoing calls per month spread over the same mobile network, other mobile networks, and mobile to fixed-line calls and during peak, off-peak, and weekend times as well as 30 text messages per month. • **Telecommunications revenue** is the revenue from the provision of telecommunications services such as fixed-line, mobile, and data divided by GDP. • **Mobile cellular and fixed-line subscribers per employee** are telephone subscribers (fixed-line plus mobile) divided by the total number of telecommunications employees.

Data sources

Data on electricity consumption and losses are from the IEA's *Energy Statistics and Balances of Non-OECD Countries 2010,* the IEA's *Energy Statistics of OECD Countries 2010,* and the United Nations Statistics Division's *Energy Statistics Yearbook.* Data on telecommunications are from the ITU's World Telecommunication Development Report database and TeleGeography.

	Daily newspapers	Households with television[a]	Personal computers and the Internet						Information and communications technology trade		
			Access and use		Quality		Affordability	Application	Goods		Services
			per 100 people		Fixed broadband Internet subscribers[a] per 100 people	International Internet bandwidth[a] bits per second per capita	Fixed broadband Internet access tariff[a] $ per month	Secure Internet servers per million people	Exports % of total goods exports	Imports % of total goods imports	Exports % of total service exports
	per 1,000 people	%	Personal computers[a]	Internet users[a]							
	2000–05[b]	2008	2008	2009	2009	2009	2009	December 2010	2009	2009	2009
Afghanistan	..	..	0.4	3.4	0.00	550	..	1	..	0.4	..
Albania	24	..	4.6	41.2	2.85	1,902	22	9	1.1	5.4	5.7
Algeria	..	..	..	13.5	2.34	..	15	1	0.0	4.9	
Angola	2	36	0.6	3.3	0.11	17	157	3	..	..	5.4
Argentina	36	..	..	30.4	8.80	2,320	31	26	0.4	11.2	12.2
Armenia	8	97	..	6.8	0.19	..	31	17	1.5	5.0	16.1
Australia	155	..	..	72.0	24.69	5,457	26	1,761	1.4	11.4	4.9
Austria	311	97	..	73.5	22.45	20,323	36	857	5.5	7.0	6.5
Azerbaijan	16	99	8.0	42.0	1.14	1,399	49	5	0.0	8.5	4.7
Bangladesh	..	30	2.3	0.4	0.03	4	50	0	0.6	5.7	11.5
Belarus	81	95	..	45.9	11.30	2,277	7	9	0.7	2.4	9.0
Belgium	165	99	..	75.2	29.05	24,945	29	490	2.8	4.3	9.8
Benin	0	25	0.7	2.2	0.02	35	118	0	..	..	0.7
Bolivia	..	69	..	11.2	2.86	225	35	8	0.0	4.6	12.6
Bosnia and Herzegovina	..	97	6.4	37.7	7.76	1,195	19	16	0.6	3.7	9.2
Botswana	41	..	6.2	6.2	0.77	220	62	9	0.4	5.5	3.3
Brazil	36	97	..	39.2	7.51	2,108	28	41	1.8	11.4	2.0
Bulgaria	79	98	11.0	44.8	12.91	37,657	15	73	3.6	6.4	5.6
Burkina Faso	..	18	0.6	1.1	0.04	15	91	0	0.0	2.0	11.6
Burundi	..	..	0.9	0.8	0.00	2	..	0	1.9	10.9	0.0
Cambodia	..	..	0.4	0.5	0.20	19	89	2	0.1	4.0	6.5
Cameroon	..	32	..	3.8	0.00	23	89	1	..	..	6.6
Canada	175	99	94.3	77.7	29.55	16,193	25	1,237	4.4	9.6	11.2
Central African Republic	..	..	..	0.5	0.00	..	1,329	0	..	..	..
Chad	..	..	..	1.7	0.00	1	..	..	..	..	..
Chile	51	100	..	34.0	9.81	4,076	48	53	0.2	6.8	2.8
China	74	..	5.7	28.8	7.78	651	18	2	29.5	24.0	6.0
Hong Kong SAR, China	222	99	69.3	61.4	29.42	560,989	13	455	44.6	43.6	1.7
Colombia	23	88	11.2	45.5	4.64	2,940	35	14	0.3	9.9	7.4
Congo, Dem. Rep.	..	14	..	0.6	0.00	1	..	0	..	..	..
Congo, Rep.	..	..	..	6.7	0.00	0	..	1	..	..	..
Costa Rica	65	96	..	34.5	6.01	4,333	6	108	18.7	17.9	21.9
Côte d'Ivoire	..	..	..	4.6	0.05	40	44	1	0.4	4.5	0.0
Croatia	..	97	..	50.4	15.45	15,892	21	168	5.1	6.3	3.6
Cuba	65	88	5.6	14.3	0.02	27	1,630	0	..	..	..
Czech Republic	183	..	..	63.7	19.26	7,075	43	318	15.6	16.7	8.9
Denmark	353	98	54.9	85.9	37.46	34,506	29	1,866	4.8	8.9	..
Dominican Republic	39	77	..	26.8	3.93	1,387	26	15	3.6	5.4	4.1
Ecuador	99	83	13.0	15.1	1.77	484	40	15	0.2	7.5	4.9
Egypt, Arab Rep.	..	97	3.9	20.0	1.30	1,172	8	2	1.8	4.4	4.7
El Salvador	38	83	..	14.4	2.42	243	20	13	2.9	5.5	16.9
Eritrea	..	..	1.0	4.9	0.00	6	..	..	..	..	..
Estonia	191	98	25.5	72.3	25.25	12,680	28	434	5.8	6.5	8.6
Ethiopia	5	..	0.7	0.5	0.00	3	487	0	0.7	9.5	5.3
Finland	431	93	..	83.9	29.33	17,221	39	1,246	12.6	11.3	25.4
France	164	97	65.2	71.3	30.98	29,356	36	306	5.6	7.8	4.3
Gabon	..	..	3.4	6.7	0.20	141	..	8	..	..	..
Gambia, The	..	..	3.5	7.6	0.02	38	307	3	0.4	4.0	17.8
Georgia	4	..	5.5	30.5	3.52	752	42	13	0.4	7.8	2.6
Germany	267	95	65.6	79.5	30.53	25,654	43	874	6.8	9.3	8.4
Ghana	..	43	1.1	5.4	0.11	97	44	2	0.1	7.3	0.0
Greece	..	100	9.4	44.1	16.99	4,537	24	124	3.0	5.9	2.2
Guatemala	..	69	..	16.3	0.78	186	34	10	0.7	6.3	14.1
Guinea	..	..	..	0.9	0.00	0	503	0	0.0	5.8	21.6
Guinea-Bissau	..	..	..	2.3	0.00	1	..	1	..	..	0.2
Haiti	..	25	5.1	10.0	0.00	16	..	1	..	..	2.5
Honduras	..	68	2.5	9.8	0.00	241	..	8	0.2	6.6	26.8

	Daily newspapers per 1,000 people 2000–05[b]	Households with television[a] % 2008	Personal computers and the Internet — Access and use (per 100 people) Personal computers[a] 2008	Internet users[a] 2009	Quality — Fixed broadband Internet subscribers[a] per 100 people 2009	International Internet bandwidth[a] bits per second per capita 2009	Affordability — Fixed broadband Internet access tariff[a] $ per month 2009	Application — Secure Internet servers per million people December 2010	ICT trade — Goods Exports % of total goods exports 2009	Goods Imports % of total goods imports 2009	Services Exports % of total service exports 2009
Hungary	217	99	25.6	61.6	18.76	5,987	30	166	24.6	18.8	8.8
India	71	55	3.3	5.3	0.67	32	5	2	3.8	8.8	53.1
Indonesia	..	69	2.0	8.7	0.74	. 110	21	2	5.7	9.7	8.4
Iran, Islamic Rep.	..	..	10.6	38.3	0.55	151	30	1	..	..	..
Iraq	..	..	..	1.0	0.00	3	..	0	..	..	0.6
Ireland	182	98	58.2	68.4	21.94	15,261	36	1,005	11.5	14.0	37.1
Israel	..	90	..	49.7	24.86	2,003	7	399	19.2	11.0	36.1
Italy	137	94	..	48.5	19.59	12,989	29	154	3.0	6.7	2.4
Jamaica	..	..	..	58.6	4.16	741	22	39	0.8	3.9	7.1
Japan	551	99	..	77.7	24.86	5,770	37	650	14.7	12.0	1.2
Jordan	..	97	7.6	29.3	3.42	1,811	30	20	3.1	5.4	..
Kazakhstan	..	..	..	33.4	8.61	1,342	17	5	0.1	4.3	3.0
Kenya	..	..	..	10.0	0.02	477	40	3	1.3	6.2	14.5
Korea, Dem. Rep.	..	..	..	0.0	0.00	0	..	0	..	..	..
Korea, Rep.	..	..	57.6	80.9	33.54	6,065	25	1,167	22.6	14.6	1.5
Kosovo	..	..	..	..	..	..	..	..	..	..	..
Kuwait	..	..	..	39.4	1.61	871	19	133	0.4	7.2	60.9
Kyrgyz Republic	1	99	..	41.2	0.10	112	48	1	0.3	2.6	1.2
Lao PDR	3	..	..	4.7	0.13	142	194	1	..	..	8.5
Latvia	154	99	32.7	66.7	11.48	3,537	25	173	6.1	6.2	5.9
Lebanon	54	..	10.2	23.7	5.26	223	23	28	3.0	3.5	2.9
Lesotho	..	..	..	3.7	0.02	5	50	0	..	..	..
Liberia	..	9	..	0.5	..	..	..	1	..	..	..
Libya	..	..	..	5.5	0.16	50	..	1	..	..	2.6
Lithuania	108	98	24.2	58.8	18.98	14,300	15	176	2.9	4.3	3.8
Macedonia, FYR	89	99	36.8	51.8	10.59	17	14	24	0.5	5.5	14.3
Madagascar	..	..	..	1.6	0.02	12	102	0	1.6	3.9	..
Malawi	..	9	..	4.7	0.02	5	493	0	0.3	5.3	..
Malaysia	109	97	23.1	57.6	6.09	5,097	19	42	38.1	32.0	7.0
Mali	..	22	0.8	1.9	0.07	51	55	1	0.2	3.6	23.2
Mauritania	..	..	4.5	2.3	0.27	76	58	2	..	1.6	..
Mauritius	77	96	17.6	22.7	7.25	364	17	87	0.6	4.2	3.7
Mexico	93	93	14.4	26.5	9.24	312	16	22	22.9	20.9	1.3
Moldova	..	..	11.4	35.9	5.19	6,660	13	13	7.5	5.1	20.2
Mongolia	20	88	24.6	13.1	0.91	2,920	8	11	0.1	5.1	3.0
Morocco	12	..	5.7	32.2	1.49	1,600	17	3	4.6	6.0	7.5
Mozambique	3	..	..	2.7	0.05	56	80	1	0.4	3.9	5.8
Myanmar	..	..	0.9	0.2	0.03	20	28	0	..	..	..
Namibia	28	37	23.9	5.9	0.02	27	47	14	0.6	4.9	2.4
Nepal	..	33	..	2.1	0.26	5	22	2	0.2	5.6	..
Netherlands	307	98	91.2	90.0	35.70	78,156	36	2,276	12.6	13.5	11.3
New Zealand	182	99	52.6	83.4	22.73	4,544	29	1,489	1.8	9.4	4.8
Nicaragua	..	67	..	3.5	0.82	144	34	8	0.4	4.4	7.2
Niger	0	10	..	0.8	0.01	11	266	0	0.7	3.6	11.6
Nigeria	..	39	..	28.4	0.05	5	105	1	0.0	7.2	1.6
Norway	516	95	62.9	91.8	37.19	26,904	51	1,653	2.4	8.8	8.6
Oman	..	88	16.9	43.5	1.44	1,365	31	27	1.5	3.2	..
Pakistan	50	58	..	12.0	0.37	43	15	1	0.3	3.7	12.0
Panama	65	83	6.3	27.8	5.82	15,964	17	127	0.0	7.3	4.8
Papua New Guinea	9	..	..	1.9	0.00	2	142	3	..	..	1.2
Paraguay	..	85	..	15.8	2.22	662	22	7	0.2	21.6	1.4
Peru	..	73	..	27.7	2.79	2,646	36	14	0.1	8.3	3.5
Philippines	79	71	7.2	6.5	1.87	113	22	7	54.2	34.5	16.2
Poland	114	98	16.9	58.8	13.54	2,748	14	211	7.5	8.9	5.3
Portugal	..	99	18.2	48.6	17.54	4,790	29	174	4.6	6.6	4.5
Puerto Rico	..	..	..	25.2	10.78	1,764	..	84	..	..	..
Qatar	..	..	15.7	28.3	9.22	2,044	55	99	0.0	8.2	..

	Daily newspapers	Households with television[a]	Personal computers and the Internet						Information and communications technology trade		
			Access and use		Quality		Affordability	Application	Goods		Services
			per 100 people		Fixed broadband Internet subscribers[a] per 100 people	International Internet bandwidth[a] bits per second per capita	Fixed broadband Internet access tariff[a] $ per month	Secure Internet servers per million people	Exports % of total goods exports	Imports % of total goods imports	Exports % of total service exports
	per 1,000 people	%	Personal computers[a]	Internet users[a]							
	2000–05[b]	2008	2008	2009	2009	2009	2009	December 2010	2009	2009	2009
Romania	70	97	19.2	36.2	13.05	18,271	7	40	8.4	9.3	18.9
Russian Federation	92	..	13.3	42.1	9.09	573	13	20	0.6	8.4	6.3
Rwanda	..	3	0.3	4.5	0.08	35	88	1	1.4	12.3	0.1
Saudi Arabia	..	..	69.3	38.6	5.66	1,731	27	18	0.3	4.6	..
Senegal	9	46	..	7.4	0.47	372	40	1	0.4	4.5	15.6
Serbia	..	..	25.8	56.1	8.07	12,660	14	20	2.2	5.4	8.0
Sierra Leone	..	10	..	0.3	0.00	..	..	0	..	..	2.2
Singapore	361	..	74.3	73.3	22.52	22,783	17	523	35.4	28.2	2.9
Slovak Republic	126	99	58.1	75.0	14.36	7,567	29	128	17.5	14.7	8.0
Slovenia	173	99	42.5	63.6	22.79	6,720	22	301	3.8	5.6	7.2
Somalia	..	..	..	1.2	0.00	..	..	0	..	..	..
South Africa	30	69	..	9.0	0.98	70	27	63	2.0	9.8	3.9
Spain	144	100	39.3	61.2	21.05	11,008	29	233	3.0	8.4	6.6
Sri Lanka	26	76	..	8.7	0.84	190	4	4	1.0	3.6	17.2
Sudan	..	..	10.7	9.9	0.11	322	23	0	0.0	4.7	1.2
Swaziland	24	35	3.7	7.6	0.13	35	858	10	0.1	3.6	11.3
Sweden	481	94	88.1	90.3	40.85	49,828	35	1,266	10.0	11.5	14.8
Switzerland	420	92	96.2	70.9	33.91	29,413	33	1,876	3.3	6.6	..
Syrian Arab Republic	..	..	9.0	18.7	0.16	261	31	0	0.2	1.4	4.4
Tajikistan	..	..	..	10.1	0.05	37	364	0	..	..	19.6
Tanzania	2	9	..	1.5	0.02	2	64	0	0.6	6.9	2.7
Thailand	..	92	..	25.8	1.47	818	19	13	19.8	18.1	..
Timor-Leste	..	..	..	..	..	..	..	1	..	..	..
Togo	2	..	..	5.4	0.04	23	186	2	0.1	4.2	18.6
Trinidad and Tobago	149	..	13.2	36.2	7.84	7,916	13	72	0.2	4.0	..
Tunisia	23	..	9.7	33.5	3.57	2,699	12	14	6.0	7.5	4.9
Turkey	..	98	6.1	35.3	8.54	4,323	18	95	2.3	5.9	1.9
Turkmenistan	9	..	..	1.6	0.05	48	..	0	..	..	..
Uganda	..	7	1.7	9.8	0.02	36	194	1	4.9	9.3	6.1
Ukraine	131	97	4.5	33.3	4.15	206	7	13	1.3	2.6	5.6
United Arab Emirates	..	94	33.1	82.2	15.01	13,233	41	243	2.0	5.3	..
United Kingdom	290	99	80.2	83.2	29.68	39,664	24	1,396	8.6	10.5	7.9
United States	193	..	80.5	78.1	27.78	11,279	20	1,443	13.0	15.1	4.6
Uruguay	..	91	..	55.5	7.33	903	18	45	0.1	7.0	9.5
Uzbekistan	..	..	3.1	16.9	0.32	46	199	0	..	..	..
Venezuela, RB	93	95	..	31.2	6.56	628	31	7	0.1	9.3	7.4
Vietnam	..	..	9.6	27.5	3.04	581	15	3	3.8	7.1	..
West Bank and Gaza	10	95	..	8.8	5.76	313	..	4	..	..	5.4
Yemen, Rep.	4	..	2.8	1.8	0.00	28	220	0	0.1	2.5	8.5
Zambia	5	24	..	6.3	0.06	8	51	1	0.1	3.7	8.0
Zimbabwe	..	31	7.6	11.4	0.14	17	..	1	0.6	4.8	..
World	105 w	.. m	15.3 w	27.1 w	7.30 w	3,526 w	30 m	156 w	13.0 w	13.9 w	9.1 w
Low income	..	..	..	2.7	0.04	7	90	1	0.6	..	6.5
Middle income	68	..	5.5	20.9	4.07	348	22	9	16.3	16.6	13.3
Lower middle income	71	..	4.5	17.2	3.37	151	30	3	21.3	18.4	19.9
Upper middle income	..	93	..	34.6	6.69	1,120	19	32	12.2	15.1	5.4
Low & middle income	59	..	5.1	18.1	3.53	299	31	8	16.2	16.4	13.1
East Asia & Pacific	74	..	5.6	24.1	5.81	742	21	3	28.9	24.4	6.8
Europe & Central Asia	..	..	9.8	36.4	7.66	1,087	17	33	1.5	6.6	6.1
Latin America & Carib.	64	85	..	31.5	6.62	1,408	30	27	11.6	15.2	5.5
Middle East & N. Africa	..	..	5.7	21.5	1.25	323	23	2	..	..	..
South Asia	68	55	3.3	5.5	0.55	31	15	2	3.0	7.4	49.9
Sub-Saharan Africa	..	..	..	8.8	0.13	31	88	5	1.0	7.8	4.5
High income	255	98	65.4	72.3	25.78	19,521	29	906	12.2	13.3	8.1
Euro area	201	98	56.0	67.3	25.90	32,455	29	545	6.6	8.6	9.8

a. Data are from the International Telecommunicaton Union's (ITU) World Telecommunication Development Report database. Please cite the ITU for third party use of these data. b. Data are for the most recent year available.

About the data

The digital and information revolution has changed the way the world learns, communicates, does business, and treats illnesses. New information and communications technologies (ICT) offer vast opportunities for progress in all walks of life in all countries—opportunities for economic growth, improved health, better service delivery, learning through distance education, and social and cultural advances.

Comparable statistics on access, use, quality, and affordability of ICT are needed to formulate growth-enabling policies for the sector and to monitor and evaluate the sector's impact on development. Although basic access data are available for many countries, in most developing countries little is known about who uses ICT; what they are used for (school, work, business, research, government); and how they affect people and businesses. The global Partnership on Measuring ICT for Development is helping to set standards, harmonize information and communications technology statistics, and build statistical capacity in developing countries. For more information see www.itu.int/ITU-D/ict/partnership/.

Data on daily newspapers in circulation are from United Nations Educational, Scientific, and Cultural Organization (UNESCO) Institute for Statistics surveys on circulation, online newspapers, journalists, community newspapers, and news agencies.

Estimates of households with television are derived from household surveys. Some countries report only the number of households with a color television set, and so the true number may be higher than reported.

Estimates of personal computers are from an annual International Telecommunication Union (ITU) questionnaire sent to member states, supplemented by other sources. Many governments lack the capacity to survey all places where personal computers are used (homes, schools, businesses, government offices, libraries, Internet cafes) so most estimates are derived from the number of personal computers sold each year. Annual shipment data can also be multiplied by an estimated average useful lifespan before replacement to approximate the number of personal computers. There is no precise method for determining replacement rates, but in general personal computers are replaced every three to five years.

Data on Internet users and related indicators (broadband and bandwidth) are based on nationally reported data to the ITU. Some countries derive these data from surveys, but since survey questions and definitions differ, the estimates may not be strictly comparable. Countries without surveys generally derive their estimates by multiplying subscriber counts reported by Internet service providers by a multiplier. This method may undercount actual users, particularly in developing countries, where many commercial subscribers rent out computers connected to the Internet or prepaid cards are used to access the Internet.

Broadband refers to technologies that provide Internet speeds of at least 256 kilobits a second of upstream and downstream capacity and includes digital subscriber lines, cable modems, satellite broadband Internet, fiber-to-home Internet access, ethernet local access networks, and wireless area networks. Bandwidth refers to the range of frequencies available for signals. The higher the bandwidth, the more information that can be transmitted at one time. Reporting countries may have different definitions of broadband, so data are not strictly comparable.

The number of secure Internet servers, from the Netcraft Secure Server Survey, indicates how many companies conduct encrypted transactions over the Internet. The survey examines the use of encrypted transactions through extensive automated exploration, tallying the number of Web sites using a secure socket layer (SSL). The country of origin of more than a third of the 1.5 million distinct valid third-party certificates is unknown. Some countries, such as the Republic of Korea, use application layers to establish the encryption channel, which is SSL equivalent; these data are reported in the table.

Information and communication technology goods exports and imports are defined by the Working Party on Indicators for the Information Society and are reported in the Organisation for Economic Co-operation and Development's *Guide to Measuring the Information Society* (2005). Information and communication technology service exports data are based on the International Monetary Fund's (IMF) *Balance of Payments Statistics Yearbook* classification.

Definitions

• **Daily newspapers** are newspapers issued at least four times a week that report mainly on events in the 24-hour period before going to press. The indicator is average circulation (or copies printed) per 1,000 people. • **Households with television** are the percentage of households with a television set. • **Personal computers** are self-contained computers designed for use by a single individual, including laptops and notebooks and excluding terminals connected to mainframe and minicomputers intended primarily for shared use and devices such as smart phones and personal digital assistants. • **Internet users** are people with access to the worldwide network. • **Fixed broadband Internet subscribers** are the number of broadband subscribers with a digital subscriber line, cable modem, or other high-speed technology. • **International Internet bandwidth** is the contracted capacity of international connections between countries for transmitting Internet traffic. • **Fixed broadband Internet access tariff** is the lowest sampled cost per 100 kilobits a second per month and are calculated from low- and high-speed monthly service charges. Monthly charges do not include installation fees or modem rentals. • **Secure Internet servers** are servers using encryption technology in Internet transactions. • **Information and communication technology goods exports** and **imports** include telecommunications, audio and video, computer and related equipment; electronic components; and other information and communication technology goods. Software is excluded. • **Information and communication technology service exports** include computer and communications services (telecommunications and postal and courier services) and information services (computer data and news-related service transactions).

Data sources

Data on newspapers are compiled by the UNESCO Institute for Statistics. Data on televisions, personal computers, Internet users, Internet broadband users and cost, and Internet bandwidth are from the ITU's World Telecommunication Development Report database and TeleGeography. Data on secure Internet servers are from Netcraft (www.netcraft.com/) and official government sources. Data on information and communication technology goods trade are from the United Nations Statistics Division's Commodity Trade (Comtrade) database. Data on information and communication technology service exports are from the IMF's Balance of Payments Statistics database.

	Researchers in R&D per million people 2000–08[d]	Technicians in R&D per million people 2000–08[d]	Scientific and technical journal articles 2007	Expenditures for R&D % of GDP 2000–08[d]	High-technology exports $ millions 2009	High-technology exports % of manufactured exports 2009	Royalty and license fees Receipts $ millions 2009	Royalty and license fees Payments $ millions 2009	Patent applications filed[a,b] Residents 2009	Patent applications filed[a,b] Non-residents 2009	Trademark applications filed[a,c] Total 2009
Afghanistan	..	..	4	..	..	..	..	..	..	..	..
Albania	..	..	12	..	10	1	6	14	..	..	3,072
Algeria	170	35	481	0.07	4	1	..	..	84	765	2,144
Angola	..	..	3	..	..	..	0	0	..	..	..
Argentina	980	196	3,362	0.51	1,548	9	106	1,331	..	..	73,717
Armenia	..	..	175	0.21	7	4	0	0	116	11	4,398
Australia	4,224	..	17,831	2.06	3,550	13	703	3,026	2,821	23,525	8,611
Austria	4,123	1,960	4,825	2.66	12,097	11	752	1,280	2,263	292	11,699
Azerbaijan	..	..	97	0.17	6	1	2	19	222	5	3,221
Bangladesh	..	..	235	..	97	1	0	11	29	270	8,232
Belarus	..	..	412	0.96	315	3	9	73	1,510	220	5,403
Belgium	3,435	1,407	7,071	1.92	29,676	10	2,376	2,144	669	148	25,566[e]
Benin	..	..	43	..	0	0	0	3	..	..	..
Bolivia	120	..	51	0.28	15	5	3	19	..	..	6,081
Bosnia and Herzegovina	197	71	54	0.03	76	3	12	6	59	12	3,786
Botswana	..	..	62	0.50	24	1	1	12	..	..	712
Brazil	694	..	11,885	1.10	8,316	14	434	2,512	4,023	17,802	119,841
Bulgaria	1,499	476	801	0.49	714	8	9	117	242	24	7,904
Burkina Faso	..	..	43	0.11	0	1	0	0	..	..	..
Burundi	..	..	3	..	2	12	0	0	..	..	..
Cambodia	17	13	26	0.05	4	0	0	8	..	..	2,866
Cameroon	..	..	154	..	3	3	0	0	..	..	..
Canada	4,260	1,690	27,800	1.84	25,080	18	3,221	7,716	5,067	32,410	40,956
Central African Republic	..	..	4	..	..	..	..	..	..	..	..
Chad	..	..	3	..	..	..	..	..	..	..	..
Chile	833	302	1,740	0.68	266	4	59	461	531	3,421	33,026
China	1,071	..	56,806	1.44	348,295	31	429	11,065	229,096	85,477	808,546
Hong Kong SAR, China	2,650	459	..	0.81	1,849	31	380	1,610	149	11,708	24,754
Colombia	126	..	489	0.16	466	5	48	258	121	1,860	23,952
Congo, Dem. Rep.	..	..	7	0.48	..	..	..	..	..	..	..
Congo, Rep.	34	37	21	..	..	..	..	..	..	..	..
Costa Rica	122	..	100	0.32	1,682	41	1	65	..	..	11,754
Côte d'Ivoire	66	..	37	..	187	12	0	0	..	..	..
Croatia	1,514	605	1,102	0.90	756	11	32	213	250	68	5,990
Cuba	..	..	244	0.49	248	35	..	..	69	189	1,450
Czech Republic	2,886	1,466	3,689	1.47	15,200	16	96	726	789	92	11,047
Denmark	5,670	2,166	5,236	2.72	10,743	18	..	..	1,518	131	8,329
Dominican Republic	..	..	8	..	177	5	0	53	..	..	5,208
Ecuador	69	20	66	0.15	51	4	0	47	..	794	12,605
Egypt, Arab Rep.	617	378	1,934	0.23	95	1	0	285	490	1,452	2,828
El Salvador	49	..	5	0.09	136	5	0	26	..	..	..
Eritrea	..	..	8	..	..	..	..	..	..	..	..
Estonia	2,966	617	502	1.29	656	10	24	46	76	20	3,230
Ethiopia	21	12	149	0.17	7	4	2	3	12	25	719
Finland	7,707	..	4,989	3.46	8,599	18	1,738	1,282	1,806	127	5,564
France	3,496	1,880	30,740	2.02	83,827	23	9,397	5,274	14,295	1,809	84,213
Gabon	..	..	16	..	71	32	..	..	..	..	..
Gambia, The	..	..	17	..	0	1	0	0	..	..	327
Georgia	..	..	129	0.18	21	3	7	9	250	218	4,382
Germany	3,532	1,301	44,408	2.54	142,449	16	13,785	14,104	47,859	11,724	74,676
Ghana	..	..	109	..	6	1	0	0	..	..	677
Greece	1,873	764	4,980	0.57	1,212	11	48	654	698	22	2,458
Guatemala	29	37	22	0.06	141	5	13	86	7	322	11,003
Guinea	..	..	4	..	0	0	0	0	..	..	..
Guinea-Bissau	..	..	10	..	..	..	..	0	..	..	6
Haiti	..	..	4	..	..	..	3	0	..	..	..
Honduras	..	..	6	0.04	7	1	0	18	..	..	7,403

	Researchers in R&D	Technicians in R&D	Scientific and technical journal articles	Expenditures for R&D	High-technology exports		Royalty and license fees		Patent applications filed[a,b]		Trademark applications filed[a,c]
	per million people 2000–08[d]	per million people 2000–08[d]	2007	% of GDP 2000–08[d]	$ millions 2009	% of manufactured exports 2009	$ millions Receipts 2009	Payments 2009	Residents 2009	Non-residents 2009	Total 2009
Hungary	1,733	512	2,452	0.96	17,444	26	862	1,369	757	30	6,671
India	137	94	18,194	0.80	10,143	9	193	1,860	5,314	23,626	130,172
Indonesia	205	..	198	0.05	5,940	13	38	1,530	282	4,324	52,649
Iran, Islamic Rep.	706	..	4,366	0.67	375	6	..	..	5,970	557	3,013
Iraq	..	..	73	..	0	0	1,312	396	..	..	..
Ireland	3,090	684	2,487	1.42	24,738	25	1,697	34,873	908	53	4,091
Israel	..	..	6,623	4.86	10,268	23	761	897	1,387	5,387	10,742
Italy	1,616	..	26,544	1.18	25,988	8	1,115	1,899	8,814	903	40,702
Jamaica	..	..	49	0.06	4	1	9	45	21	132	1,708
Japan	5,573	589	52,896	3.44	99,210	20	21,698	16,835	295,315	53,281	110,622
Jordan	..	..	344	0.34	49	1	0	0	59	507	9,145
Kazakhstan	..	..	106	0.22	1,802	30	0	64	11	162	3,500
Kenya	..	..	262	..	78	5	19	21	38	33	1,430
Korea, Dem. Rep.	..	..	10	..	..	..	..	..	7,956	55	1,351
Korea, Rep.	4,627	720	18,467	3.21	103,400	32	3,185	7,049	127,316	36,207	134,211
Kosovo	..	..	..	..	..	..	..	..	..	..	..
Kuwait	166	33	242	0.09	6	0	0	0	..	..	..
Kyrgyz Republic	..	..	16	0.23	11	5	4	12	135	3	2,580
Lao PDR	16	..	12	0.04	..	..	0	0	..	..	..
Latvia	1,935	543	147	0.61	363	8	7	26	114	37	3,566
Lebanon	..	..	238	..	138	7	0	1	..	..	..
Lesotho	10	11	3	0.06	..	..	18	..	..	..	634
Liberia	..	..	0	..	..	..	..	..	..	..	489
Libya	..	..	30	..	..	..	0	0	..	..	..
Lithuania	2,547	553	456	0.80	931	10	0	29	91	16	4,465
Macedonia, FYR	521	75	58	0.21	42	3	6	20	34	406	3,788
Madagascar	50	15	48	0.14	10	2	..	..	1	43	1,605
Malawi	..	..	63	..	3	3	..	..	..	..	804
Malaysia	372	44	808	0.64	51,560	47	266	1,133	818	4,485	24,070
Mali	42	13	19	..	3	3	0	2	..	..	..
Mauritania	..	..	3	..	..	..	..	..	..	..	..
Mauritius	..	..	18	0.37	13	1	0	5	2	22	24
Mexico	353	186	4,223	0.37	37,354	22	656	0	822	13,459	75,250
Moldova	726	117	70	0.55	10	5	4	11	134	5	5,046
Mongolia	..	..	21	0.23	7	8	0	1	103	110	1,399
Morocco	647	48	378	0.64	646	7	2	49	177	834	3,774
Mozambique	16	35	24	0.53	24	10	0	4	18	22	870
Myanmar	18	137	13	0.16	..	..	..	..	..	..	..
Namibia	..	..	14	..	21	1	0	6	..	..	858
Nepal	59	137	72	..	2	0	..	..	..	..	1,132
Netherlands	3,089	1,764	14,210	1.63	58,450	24	5,473	4,073	2,575	279	..
New Zealand	4,365	894	3,173	1.21	504	10	159	529	1,555	4,803	16,190
Nicaragua	..	..	11	0.05	7	6	0	0	..	..	5,975
Niger	8	10	22	..	2	8	0	0	..	..	..
Nigeria	..	..	427	..	46	3	0	208	..	..	..
Norway	5,468	..	4,079	1.62	4,694	20	637	553	1,140	4,280	13,607
Oman	..	..	129	..	7	0	..	..	..	..	2,103
Pakistan	152	64	741	0.67	227	2	6	90	170	1,375	14,872
Panama	144	106	78	0.21	0	0	0	25	..	371	8,553
Papua New Guinea	..	..	21	..	..	..	..	..	1	45	612
Paraguay	71	..	12	0.09	38	11	295	2	..	..	..
Peru	..	..	153	0.15	87	3	2	147	37	657	24,825
Philippines	81	10	195	0.12	21,531	66	2	421	216	3,095	14,912
Poland	1,623	191	7,136	0.61	7,172	5	103	1,542	2,899	241	17,877
Portugal	3,799	403	3,424	1.51	1,288	4	148	507	381	24	2,681
Puerto Rico	..	..	..	..	..	..	..	..	..	..	..
Qatar	..	..	48	..	..	..	0	0	..	..	..

5.13 Science and technology

	Researchers in R&D	Technicians in R&D	Scientific and technical journal articles	Expenditures for R&D	High-technology exports		Royalty and license fees		Patent applications filed[a,b]		Trademark applications filed[a,c]
	per million people 2000–08[d]	per million people 2000–08[d]	2007	% of GDP 2000–08[d]	$ millions 2009	% of manu-factured exports 2009	Receipts 2009	Payments 2009	Residents 2009	Non-residents 2009	Total 2009
Romania	908	216	1,252	0.59	3,230	10	193	339	1,054	37	12,977
Russian Federation	3,191	493	13,953	1.03	4,576	9	494	4,107	25,598	12,966	49,189
Rwanda	..	..	12	..	11	31	0	1	..	..	238
Saudi Arabia	..	..	589	0.05	40	0	..	..	128	642	..
Senegal	276	..	68	0.09	104	14	0	9	..	..	..
Serbia	1,196	299	1,057	0.35	..	..	63	144	319	40	7,237
Sierra Leone	..	..	3	..	..	..	1	1	..	..	750
Singapore	6,088	529	3,792	2.52	97,207	49	1,340	11,686	750	7,986	15,332
Slovak Republic	2,331	392	971	0.47	3,171	5	92	155	176	63	5,534
Slovenia	3,490	1,696	1,280	1.66	1,264	7	36	290	373	12	4,073
Somalia	..	..	0	..	..	..	..	..	..	..	..
South Africa	393	123	2,805	0.93	1,418	6	48	1,658	..	10,753	26,621
Spain	2,944	1,143	20,981	1.34	10,841	5	1,041	3,449	3,596	207	46,711
Sri Lanka	93	65	125	0.17	44	1	0	0	201	264	5,916
Sudan	..	..	36	0.29	11	34	0	0	3	13	743
Swaziland	..	..	4	..	0	0	0	116	..	..	680
Sweden	5,239	1,871	9,914	3.75	17,059	17	4,709	1,832	2,549	306	12,706
Switzerland	3,436	2,317	9,190	2.90	38,556	25	..	..	1,684	394	28,945
Syrian Arab Republic	..	..	80	..	83	2	0	30	124	133	2,432
Tajikistan	..	..	22	0.06	..	..	1	0	11	1	2,496
Tanzania	..	..	123	..	24	4	0	0	..	..	556
Thailand	311	160	1,728	0.25	28,655	26	145	2,250	802	5,939	36,087
Timor-Leste	..	..	..	..	..	..	..	..	..	..	..
Togo	34	17	12	..	0	0	0	5	..	..	..
Trinidad and Tobago	..	..	67	0.06	3	0	..	..	..	551	..
Tunisia	1,588	43	757	1.02	663	6	25	14	..	..	..
Turkey	680	102	8,638	0.72	1,463	2	..	648	2,555	177	71,466
Turkmenistan	..	..	2	..	..	..	..	..	..	..	2,337
Uganda	..	..	164	0.39	5	1	3	3	6	1	..
Ukraine	1,458	325	1,847	0.85	1,519	3	112	644	2,434	2,380	8,568
United Arab Emirates	..	..	214	..	29	3	..	..	..	..	..
United Kingdom	4,269	893	47,121	1.88	57,178	23	12,928	9,498	15,985	6,480	33,542
United States	4,663	..	209,695	2.82	141,519	23	89,791	25,230	224,912	231,194	266,845
Uruguay	346	..	215	0.64	73	5	0	17	33	706	11,501
Uzbekistan	..	..	166	..	..	..	..	..	238	174	4,541
Venezuela, RB	187	..	497	..	66	4	0	352	..	..	..
Vietnam	115	..	283	0.19	1,685	5	..	..	..	..	4,187
West Bank and Gaza	..	..	..	..	..	..	0	1	..	..	..
Yemen, Rep.	..	..	18	..	0	0	33	−5	11	24	4,518
Zambia	..	..	36	0.03	6	2	0	0	..	..	795
Zimbabwe	..	..	80	..	7	1	..	..	..	..	..
World	**1,281 w**	**.. w**	**758,132 s**	**2.07 w**	**1,858,138 s**	**20 w**	**181,636 s**	**188,861 s**	**994,324 s**	**634,131 s**	**2,884,372 s**
Low income	..	..	1,690	..	..	3	34	67	..	..	..
Middle income	596	..	144,072	0.98	576,048	20	3,767	32,422	179,049	198,050	1,559,267
Lower middle income	479	..	85,227	1.19	414,058	25	1,336	18,747	134,475	131,207	955,629
Upper middle income	1,112	..	58,845	0.79	117,380	14	2,431	13,675	36,842	55,416	603,638
Low & middle income	579	..	145,762	0.98	540,234	20	3,800	32,489	185,505	198,493	1,575,589
East Asia & Pacific	1,071	..	60,164	1.44	..	32	881	16,411	237,052	85,532	890,552
Europe & Central Asia	2,064	351	29,335	0.88	16,275	9	923	6,257	33,042	16,049	214,396
Latin America & Carib.	487	..	23,240	0.68	50,434	13	1,629	5,477	5,287	41,517	313,022
Middle East & N. Africa	..	..	8,700	..	1,571	2	60	343	..	..	14,191
South Asia	129	87	19,375	0.79	..	8	208	1,962	5,580	25,831	151,906
Sub-Saharan Africa	..	..	4,946	..	3,260	6	99	2,039	..	..	..
High income	3,945	..	612,370	2.29	1,116,596	19	177,835	156,372	764,583	406,316	1,104,532
Euro area	2,977	1,376	167,647	1.68	392,305	16	38,296	70,574	84,182	15,710	313,484

a. Original information was provided by the World Intellectual Property Organization (WIPO). The International Bureau of WIPO assumes no responsibility with respect to the transformation of these data. b. Excludes applications filed under the auspices of the African Intellectual Property Organization (448 by nonresidents), European Patent Office (134,580 by nonresidents), and the Eurasian Patent Organization (2,801 by nonresidents). c. Excludes applications filed under the auspices of the Office for Harmonization in the Internal Market (88,086). d. Data are for the most recent year available. e. Includes Luxembourg and the Netherlands.

The United Nations Educational, Scientific, and Cultural Organization (UNESCO) Institute for Statistics collects data on researchers, technicians, and expenditure on R&D through surveys and from other international sources. R&D covers basic research, applied research, and experimental development. Data on researchers and technicians are calculated as full-time equivalents.

Scientific and technical article counts are from journals classified by the Institute for Scientific Information's Science Citation Index (SCI) and Social Sciences Citation Index (SSCI). Counts are based on fractional assignments; articles with authors from different countries are allocated proportionately to each country (see Definitions for fields covered). The SCI and SSCI databases cover the core set of scientific journals but may exclude some of local importance and may reflect some bias toward English-language journals.

R&D expenditures include all expenditures for R&D performed within a country, including capital costs and current costs (wages and associated costs of researchers, technicians, and supporting staff and other current costs, including noncapital purchases of materials, supplies, and R&D equipment such as utilities, reference materials, subscriptions to libraries and scientific societies, and lab materials).

The method for determining high-technology exports was developed by the Organisation for Economic Co-operation and Development in collaboration with Eurostat. It takes a "product approach" (as distinguished from a "sectoral approach") based on R&D intensity (expenditure divided by total sales) for groups of products from Germany, Italy, Japan, the Netherlands, Sweden, and the United States. Because industrial sectors specializing in a few high-technology products may also produce low-technology products, the product approach is more appropriate for international trade. The method takes only R&D intensity into account, but other characteristics of high technology are also important, such as know-how, scientific personnel, and technology embodied in patents. Considering these characteristics would yield a different list (see Hatzichronoglou 1997).

A patent is an exclusive right granted for a specified period (generally 20 years) for a new way of doing something or a new technical solution to a problem—an invention. The invention must be of practical use and display a characteristic unknown in the existing body of knowledge in its field.

Most countries have systems to protect patentable inventions. The international Patent Cooperation Treaty (PCT) provides a two-phase system for filing patent applications. An applicant files an international application for which the 142 eligible countries in 2009 are automatically designated. The application is searched and published, and, optionally, a supplementary international search or preliminary examination can be conducted. In the national or regional phase the applicant requests national processing of the application and initiates the national search and granting procedure in the countries where protection is sought. International applications under the treaty provide for a national patent grant only—there is no international patent. The national filing represents the applicant's seeking of patent protection for a given territory, whereas international filings, while representing a legal right, do not accurately reflect where patent protection is sought. Resident filings are those from residents of the country concerned. Nonresident filings are from applicants abroad. For regional offices such as the European Patent Office, applications from residents of any member state of the regional patent convention are considered nonresident filings. Some offices (notably the U.S. Patent and Trademark Office) use the residence of the inventor rather than the applicant to classify filings. For further information on the PCT, see the PCT Yearly Review at http://www.wipo.int/export/sites/www/ipstats/en/statistics/pct/pdf/901e_2009.pdf.

A trademark is a distinctive sign identifying goods or services as produced or provided by a specific person or enterprise. A trademark protects the owner of the mark by ensuring the exclusive right to use it to identify goods or services or to authorize another to use it. Period of protection varies, but a trademark can be renewed indefinitely for an additional fee. Detailed components of trademark filings, available on the *World Development Indicators* CD-ROM and WDI Online, include applications filed by direct residents (domestic applicants filing directly at a given national or regional intellectual property [IP] office); direct nonresident (applicants from abroad filing directly at a given national or regional IP office); aggregate direct (applicants not identified as direct resident or direct nonresident by the national or regional office); and Madrid (designations received by the national or regional IP office based on international applications filed via the World Intellectual Property Organization (WIPO)–administered Madrid System). Data are based on information supplied to WIPO by IP offices in annual surveys supplemented by data in national IP office reports. Data may be missing for some offices or periods.

• **Researchers in R&D** are professionals engaged in conceiving of or creating new knowledge, products, processes, methods, and systems and in managing the projects concerned. Postgraduate doctoral students (*ISCED97* level 6) engaged in R&D are considered researchers. • **Technicians in R&D and equivalent staff** are people whose main tasks require technical knowledge and experience in engineering, physical and life sciences (technicians), and social sciences and humanities (equivalent staff). They engage in R&D by performing scientific and technical tasks involving the application of concepts and operational methods, normally under researcher supervision. • **Scientific and technical journal articles** are published articles in physics, biology, chemistry, mathematics, clinical medicine, biomedical research, engineering and technology, and earth and space sciences. • **Expenditures for R&D** are current and capital expenditures on creative work undertaken to increase the stock of knowledge, including on humanity, culture, and society, and the use of knowledge to devise new applications. • **High-technology exports** are products with high R&D intensity, such as in aerospace, computers, pharmaceuticals, scientific instruments, and electrical machinery. • **Royalty and license fees** are payments and receipts between residents and nonresidents for authorized use of intangible, nonproduced, nonfinancial assets and proprietary rights (such as patents, copyrights, trademarks, and industrial processes) and for the use, through licensing, of produced originals of prototypes (such as films and manuscripts). • **Patent applications filed** are patent applications filed at a national or regional office; an international patent application (or PCT filing) is in the international phase of the PCT. • **Trademark applications filed** are applications to register a trademark with a national or regional IP office.

Data on R&D are provided by the UNESCO Institute for Statistics. Data on scientific and technical journal articles are from the U.S. National Science Board's *Science and Engineering Indicators 2010*. Data on high-technology exports are from the United Nations Statistics Division's Commodity Trade (Comtrade) database. Data on royalty and license fees are from the International Monetary Fund's *Balance of Payments Statistics Yearbook*. Data on patents and trademarks are from the World Intellectual Property Organization's *World Intellectual Property Indicators* (2010) and www.wipo.int/econ_stat.

GLOBAL LINKS

T he past three years show dramatically how events in one part of the world can affect people in the rest of the world, though sometimes with a lag. The financial crisis that struck high-income economies in 2008 reached low- and middle-income economies in 2009. World exports of goods and services fell 20 percent, from $19.6 trillion in 2008 to $15.6 trillion in 2009, more in high-income economies and somewhat less in low- and middle-income economies. Developing economies' share of world exports increased by 1 percentage point over 2008, continuing a rising trend from 19 percent in 2000 to 27 percent in 2009. Imports of goods and services by high-income economies fell 22 percent, from $14.0 trillion in 2008 to $10.9 trillion in 2009; imports by low and middle income economies fell 19 percent.

The financial crisis also reduced the external financing available to developing economies from private sources, which dropped to $521 billion in 2009 from the record high of $932 billion in 2007. Net inflows of foreign direct investment dropped to $359 billion in 2009 from a high of $597 billion in 2008. In contrast, net inflows of portfolio equity investments rose to $108 billion following net outflows of $53 billion in 2008. Bond issuances, which dropped from $88 billion in 2007 to $24 billion in 2008, recovered in 2009 to reach $51 billion. But commercial and trade-related lending, which declined from $195 billion in 2007 to $172 billion in 2008, dried up in 2009, dropping to $1.7 billion. Total debt flows from private creditors fell 70 percent in 2009, to $59 billion. But net flows from official creditors reached $171 billion in 2009, a 50 percent increase over 2008, driven by such multilateral institutions as the International Monetary Fund (IMF) and the World Bank.

Global food prices soared again in 2010 and 2011, with some commodities exceeding their record high in 2008. The World Bank food price index (table 6.6) averaged 311 in February 2011, exceeding the June 2008 record of 293. Food price inflation has accelerated in several low- and middle-income economies, where consumers often spend more than half their income on food. During the 12 months ending in August 2010, food prices rose 13.2 percent a year in Indonesia, 10.4 percent a year in India, and 9.6 percent a year in Bangladesh.

The financial crisis has also demonstrated the need for more data and more frequently updated data to monitor global transactions. The World Development Indicators database contains more than 400 indicators for monitoring exchanges between economies on an annual basis, and the topics covered have expanded each year. Many others are not included in the database because of their structure or limited country coverage, but they are necessary for understanding global links. Most high-income economies and some low- and middle-income economies now produce economic statistics on a quarterly or monthly basis. This introduction highlights some of these data.

Data sources for bilateral trade flows

World Development Indicators publishes data on merchandise trade values by commodity groups (tables 4.4 and 4.5), values of trade in services (tables 4.6 and 4.7), intra- and extra-regional trade (table 6.5), merchandise trade indices (table 6.2), tariff rates (table 6.8), and indicators for measuring trade facilitation (table 6.9). Demand is rising for more detailed data, such as trade flows by partner economies and by commodities and sectors. Table 6a summarizes the main sources of data on bilateral trade flows. Some of these databases are accessible through the World Integrated Trade Solutions platform (http://wits.worldbank.org).

Barriers to trade in services

Trade in services makes up 22 percent of world trade, up from 20 percent in 2000. In developing economies the nominal value of trade in services grew 16 percent a year over 2000–09, doubling the rate of growth over 1990–2000 and surpassing that of high-income economies, which grew at 11 percent a year over 2000–09. Despite this growing

Source of data for bilateral trade flows

Compiling organization	Name of publication and database	Country coverage	Data coverage	Periodicity	Links
International Monetary Fund	Direction of Trade Statistics database	Most developing and developed economies	Merchandise trade data, no breakdowns of sectors and partners. Available through subscription	Quarterly and annual	http://www2.imfstatistics.org/DOT/ This is a link to a 5-day trial
United Nations Conference on Trade and Development	UNCTADstat Merchandise Trade Matrix	Most developing and developed economies	Merchandise trade by partner economies and by product groups	Annual	http://unctadstat.unctad.org/
United Nations Statistics Division	Commodity Trade Statistics (Comtrade)	Most developing and developed economies	Merchandise trade by partner economies and by commodity classifications	Annual	http://wits.worldbank.org/wits/
Organisation for Economic Co-operation and Development (OECD)	Monthly Statistics of International Trade	OECD member economies	Total merchandise trade by partners	Monthly	http://stats.oecd.org/ Extract databases are available under "International Trade and balance of Payments" theme Full databases are subscription based
	International Trade by Commodity Statistics	OECD member economies plus EU	Merchandise trade by partners and by products	Annual	
	Trade in services	OECD member economies plus EU and a few more economies	Trade in services by partners and by service category	Annual	
Eurostat	External Trade database	27 EU members	Merchandise trade by partners and by products	Monthly, quarterly, and annual	http://epp.eurostat.ec.europa.eu/portal/page/portal/external_trade/data/database

importance, little is known about policies affecting services trade, a major impediment to the analysis of trade policy and trade flows.

To address this gap, the World Bank has built the Services Policy Restrictiveness Database, with information on 102 countries for five major service sectors disaggregated by subsectors and relevant modes of supply in each subsector. So far, the information focuses mainly on discriminatory policy measures affecting foreign service providers. The full database will be released in the second quarter of 2011 at http://econ.worldbank.org/programs/trade/services.

Restrictiveness is assessed by the newly created Services Trade Restrictiveness Index score. The index reveals patterns of restrictiveness by major service sector and across low- and middle-income and high-income economies (figure 6b). In both high-income and low- and middle-income economies, professional services (including the movement of individuals) face the highest trade barriers, followed by transportation services. High-income economies exhibit more open financial, telecommunications, and retail distribution sectors than do low- and middle-income economies (Borchert, Gootiiz, and Mattoo forthcoming).

Foreign direct investment

Countries are increasingly compiling more data on foreign direct investment (FDI) transactions and stocks. Despite recent improvements, however, deficiencies in coverage remain. For example, if recording of FDI transactions were complete and comparable, the total outflows of FDI from investing economies would equal the total inflows recorded by the recipient economies. But in 2009 the divergence between outflows and inflows of FDI at the global level was about $82 billion (7 percent of global outflows; figure 6c). The discrepancies arise from differences in reporting practices. For example, some countries include reinvested earnings in their outflow statistics while others do not include them in their inflow statistics. Furthermore, corporate accounting practices and valuation methods may differ by reporters.

Discrepancies exist among FDI statistics published by various international agencies,

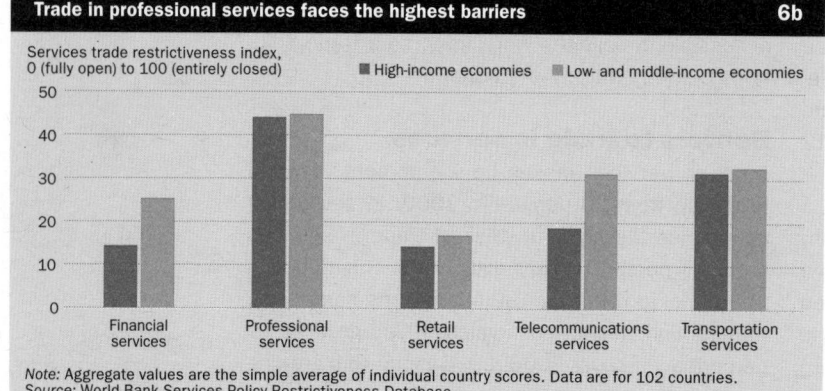

Trade in professional services faces the highest barriers 6b

Services trade restrictiveness index, 0 (fully open) to 100 (entirely closed)

■ High-income economies   ■ Low- and middle-income economies

Note: Aggregate values are the simple average of individual country scores. Data are for 102 countries.
Source: World Bank Services Policy Restrictiveness Database.

even when the agencies adopt common methodological standards. Such discrepancies may reflect differences in comparability and timing of FDI data reported by different countries, discrepancies in sector coverage, and lags in reporting revisions. Recognizing these issues, the IMF is leading a worldwide statistical data collection effort to improve the quality of FDI data (the Coordinated Direct Investment Survey; http://cdis.imf.org). Preliminary results were released in December 2010.

Data on FDI are published in table 6.12. These data cover FDI net inflows received by the reporting economy from foreign residents, and FDI net outflows by the reporting economy residents. Breakdowns of FDI transactions and investment positions by sector and partner, increasingly sought by users, are not published in *World Development Indicators* but are available from other sources. Table 6d summarizes the availability of FDI statistics for some of the main data compilers.

Bilateral remittance flows

World Development Indicators publishes data on total workers' remittances and compensation of employees received and sent by the reporting economies (table 6.18). Data coverage and quality have been improving, but inconsistencies and lack of reporting remain. For example, if all economies reported completely and consistently, the sum of remittances flows recorded by receiving economies would equal the sum of remittance flows recorded by sending economies. But as of 2009 there was a discrepancy of $127 billion (30 percent of total inflows; figure 6e). Large amounts of remittance flows are sent through private and informal channels that are not officially recorded.

No comprehensive dataset is available on the bilateral flow of remittances. Bilateral remittance flows estimated through approximation and allocation methods using the proportions of migrant stocks in destination and sending countries or the incomes of destination and sending countries are available at www.worldbank.org/prospects/migrationandremittances (Ratha and Shaw 2007). The data shed light on patterns of remittance flows, but the estimates are sensitive to the assumptions and allocation method chosen.

Bilateral migration stocks

Because migration data come mostly from destination countries, the quality of global migration

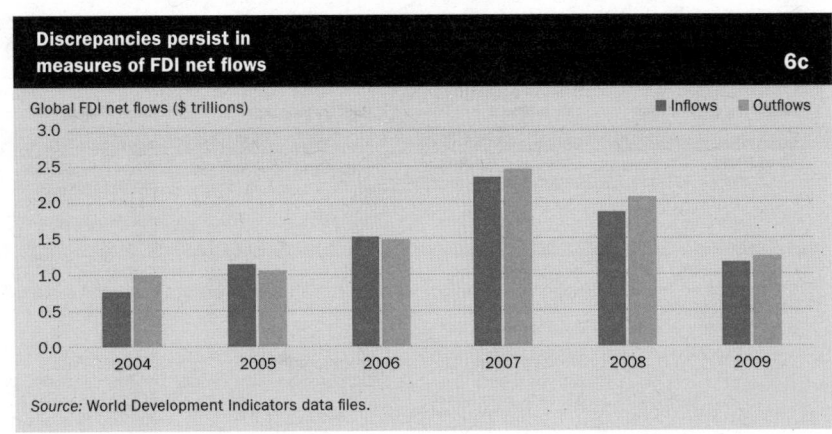

Discrepancies persist in measures of FDI net flows 6c

Global FDI net flows ($ trillions)   ■ Inflows ■ Outflows

Source: World Development Indicators data files.

data depends on how well the destination countries survey migrants within their borders. Systematic recording of migrants is difficult, especially for countries with weak statistical capacity and for those affected by civil disorder and natural disasters. Moreover, ensuring the comparability of migration data is a long-standing challenge, in part because destination countries classify migrants using various criteria. Many countries compile migration data based on immigrants' nationality, while others collect data based on the immigrants' place of birth.

World Development Indicators publishes aggregate data on international migrant stocks and net migration estimated by the United Nations Population Division based on population censuses supplemented by border statistics, administrative records, surveys, and refugee registrations (tables 6.1 and 6.18).

Efforts to produce complete data on bilateral migration have been rare. A 2008 database on immigrants in OECD countries contains data on bilateral migrant stock for OECD members (http://stats.oecd.org/). The dataset includes sociodemographic information such as age, gender, education, and occupation. A series of studies have published data on OECD immigrants by educational attainment (Docquier and Marfouk 2006), gender and educational attainment (Docquier, Lowell, and Marfouk 2009), and age of entry and educational attainment (Beine, Docquier, and Marfouk 2006). Global bilateral databases have been constructed for the 2000 census round (Parsons and others 2007) and for bilateral migration and remittance flows (Ratha and Shaw 2007).

The United Nations Population Division in cooperation with the World Bank, the United Nations Statistics Division, and the Universities of Nottingham and Sussex created the Global

Compiling organization	Name of publication and database	Country coverage	Data coverage	Periodicity	Links
International Monetary Fund (IMF)	Balance of Payments Statistics Yearbook and database	Most developing and developed economies	Aggregate FDI flows and stock by reporting economy. By-partner, by-sector breakdowns are not available. Available through subscription	Quarterly and annual	http://www2.imfstatistics.org/BOP This is a link to 5-day trial
United Nations Conference on Trade and Development (UNCTAD)	World Investment Report and Foreign Direct Investment database	Most developing and developed economies	Aggregate FDI flows and stock by reporting economy	Annual	http://unctadstat.unctad.org
	Transnational Corporations Statistics database	Transnational Corporations Worldwide	Detailed data on transactions of transnational corporations and mergers and acquisitions, by partner and by sector; available through data extract service	Annual	www.unctad.org/Templates/Page.asp?intItemID=3159&lang=1
Organisation for Economic Co-operation and Development (OECD)	International Direct Investment database	32 OECD member economies	FDI stock (annual) and flows (annual and quarterly) by partner economies and by sectors. Full dataset is available to subscribers	Quarterly and annual	http://stats.oecd.org/ Extract databases are available under Globalisation theme
Eurostat	European Union Foreign Direct Investment Yearbook and database	27 EU members	Aggregate and bilateral FDI flows and stock, by partner and by sector	Annual	http://epp.eurostat.ec.europa.eu/portal/page/portal/balance_of_payments/data/database
Association of Southeast Asian Nations	Foreign Direct Investment Statistics	10 ASEAN member economies	Bilateral FDI inflows and outflows	Annual	www.aseansec.org/18144.htm
Centre d'Etudes Prospectives et d'Informations Internationales	Foreign Direct Investment database	96 countries of the GTAP 6.2 database for stocks and 70 countries for flows	Harmonized bilateral flows and stocks of FDI for 26 sectors. Data are gap filled using gravity-based regressions and raw data from IMF, UNCTAD, OECD, and Eurostat.	Annual for 2004 only	www.cepii.fr/anglaisgraph/bdd/fdi.htm
Financial Times	FDI database FDI Intelligence	All countries with greenfield FDI projects;	Greenfield FDI projects since 2003; subscription based. Methodology differs significantly from balance of payments and international investment position standards. The data are based on press reports.	Daily	www.fdimarkets.com
Dealogic	M&A Analytics	Mergers and acquisitions activity worldwide covering an array of transactions	Information for mergers and acquisitions activity, including information on target and acquiror, deal value, and financials.	Monthly	www.dealogic.com

Migration database (www.unmigration.org) in 2008. It contains all publicly available data from more than 230 destination countries and territories over the last five decades on international migrants, classified by age, gender, place of birth, and country of citizenship. However, it still does not include all raw data points needed for a global migration matrix.

These raw data were assembled to construct a global bilateral migration matrix using empirical methods to fill holes in the data (Özden and others forthcoming). The resulting database covers 226 origin and 226 destination countries (forthcoming at www.data.worldbank.org/data-catalog). Construction of such a matrix entails formidable challenges, including selecting the most relevant sources, allocating migrants who "originated" in aggregate geographic regions and migrants of unknown origins to specific countries, and accounting for varying survey dates and definitions. Of all cell-level values in the final matrix, about 12–14 percent are from raw census data, 40–60 percent are based primarily on raw data scaled to United Nations Population Division estimates of migrant stocks or augmented by the disaggregation of aggregate categories, and the remaining 26–48 percent are estimated through interpolation and extrapolation.

This new dataset reveals that the total stock of migrants increased from 92 million in 1960 to 165 million in 2000. The number of migrants from high-income economies remained stable, while the number from low- and middle-income economies rose from 14 million in 1960 to 60 million in 2000 (figure 6f). The increase was driven largely by an increase in migrants residing in the United States (up 24 million) and Western Europe (up 22 million).

Public sector debt

World Development Indicators publishes data on public and publicly guaranteed external debt (tables 6.10, 6.11, and 6.13). But these data present only a portion of total public sector debt, much of which is held by domestic creditors. Domestic debt data are important for economic policymaking because of the implications for local financial markets. To fill the gap, the World Bank and the IMF launched an online Quarterly Public Sector Debt database in 2009 (http://data.worldbank.org/data-catalog). The database provides data on clearly defined tiers of debt for central, state, and local government in developing or emerging market economies as well as on extrabudgetary agencies and funds. It also includes debt data by instruments, valuation methods, maturity types, and creditors.

The level and composition of public sector debt are affected by many external and domestic economic factors. The recent global financial crisis limited the private sector's ability to borrow. The public sector, usually more creditworthy, increased external borrowing to stimulate sluggish domestic economies. Most external financing for developing economies in 2009 was provided by official multilateral institutions such as the IMF and the World Bank. After the Asian financial crises in the late 1990s many governments switched from external to domestic borrowing to reduce their exposure to exchange rate fluctuations, dramatically increasing the size of domestic debt in emerging market economies. Today, domestic debt represents about 78 percent of the total general government debt in developing economies with data. Comparison with earlier period is not possible due to lack of data.

Emerging market economies have also issued local currency–denominated debt to correct currency and maturity mismatches. In September 2010 the estimated local currency

debt among developing economies averaged 67 percent of total government debt (excluding Brazil and China, with upwards of 96 percent).

Financing needed to support fiscal deficits led to a significant increase in the ratio of sovereign debt to GDP. Among developing economies, central government debt for 2009 averaged 46 percent of GDP, up from 42 percent in 2009. Brazil, which undertook aggressive countercyclical spending and tax cuts to stimulate the economy, had the highest share of gross debt in gross domestic product (about 70 percent; figure 6g).

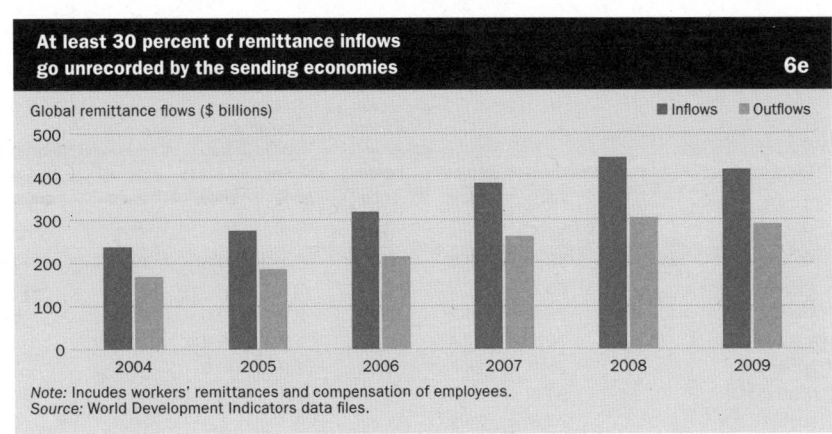

At least 30 percent of remittance inflows go unrecorded by the sending economies 6e

Global remittance flows ($ billions) ■ Inflows ■ Outflows

Note: Incudes workers' remittances and compensation of employees.
Source: World Development Indicators data files.

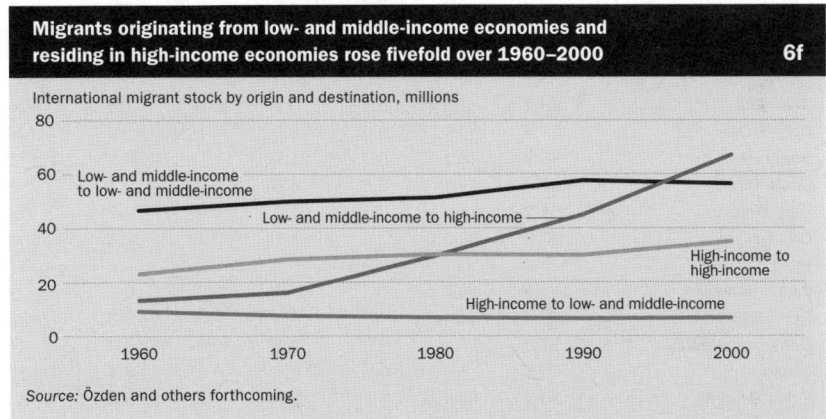

Migrants originating from low- and middle-income economies and residing in high-income economies rose fivefold over 1960–2000 6f

International migrant stock by origin and destination, millions

Low- and middle-income to low- and middle-income

Low- and middle-income to high-income

High-income to high-income

High-income to low- and middle-income

Source: Özden and others forthcoming.

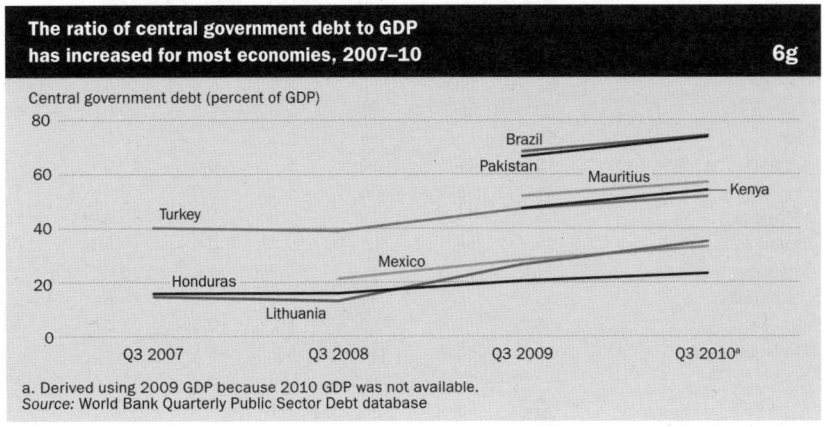

The ratio of central government debt to GDP has increased for most economies, 2007–10 6g

Central government debt (percent of GDP)

Brazil
Pakistan
Mauritius
Kenya
Turkey
Mexico
Honduras
Lithuania

a. Derived using 2009 GDP because 2010 GDP was not available.
Source: World Bank Quarterly Public Sector Debt database

	Trade % of GDP		International finance % of GDP				Movement of people			Communication	
			Financing through international capital markets Gross inflows	Foreign direct investment Net inflows	Net outflows	Workers' remittances and compensation of employees received	Net migration thousands	International migrant stock % of total population	Emigration of people with tertiary education to OECD countries % of population age 25 and older with tertiary education	International voice traffic[a] minutes per person	International Internet bandwidth[a] bits per second per capita
	Merchandise 2009	Services 2009	2009	2009	2009	2009	2005–10	2010	2000	2008	2009
Afghanistan	31.3	..	0.0	1.3	..	..	1,000	0.3	22.6	7	550
Albania	46.9	38.6	0.0	8.1	0.3	11.0	−75	2.8	17.5	263	1,902
Algeria	60.1	..	0.0	2.0	..	1.5[b]	−140	0.7	9.5	34	..
Angola	75.6	26.2	2.2	2.9	0.0	0.1	80	0.3	3.7	..	17
Argentina	30.7	7.4	0.2	1.3	0.2	0.2	30	3.6	2.8	..	2,320
Armenia	45.9	16.6	0.0	8.9	0.6	8.8	−75	10.5	8.9	..	..
Australia	34.6	9.0	..	2.4	3.7	0.4[b]	500	21.1	2.7	..	5,457
Austria	73.8	24.1	..	2.3	1.4	0.9	160	15.6	13.5	..	20,323
Azerbaijan	64.2	11.9	0.1	1.1	0.8	3.0	−50	3.0	1.8	77	1,399
Bangladesh	41.3	6.0	0.2	0.8	0.0	11.8	−570	0.7	4.4	..	4
Belarus	101.6	11.3	0.5	3.8	0.2	0.7	0	11.3	3.2	..	2,277
Belgium	153.2	33.0	..	−8.2	−16.7	2.2	200	9.0	5.5	..	24,945
Benin	45.7	12.8	0.0	1.4	−0.1	3.6[b]	50	2.5	8.7	309	35
Bolivia	53.4	8.8	0.0	2.4	0.0	6.2	−100	1.5	5.8	..	225
Bosnia and Herzegovina	74.5	11.9	0.0	1.4	−0.1	12.2	−10	0.7	20.3	..	1,195
Botswana	69.2	15.9	0.0	2.1	0.0	0.7	15	5.8	5.1	..	220
Brazil	18.0	4.7	3.9	1.6	−0.6	0.3	−229	0.4	2.0	..	2,108
Bulgaria	81.7	24.5	0.0	9.4	−0.3	3.2	−50	1.4	9.6	105	37,657
Burkina Faso	36.0	8.7	0.0	2.1	0.6	1.2[b]	−65	6.4	2.6	..	15
Burundi	35.2	17.1	0.0	0.0	0.0	2.1	323	0.7	9.3	..	2
Cambodia	105.3	26.8	0.0	5.4	0.2	3.4	−5	2.2	21.5	..	19
Cameroon	32.7	15.2	0.6	1.5	1.8	0.7	−19	1.0	17.3	..	23
Canada	48.4	10.3	..	1.5	3.0	..	1,050	21.1	4.7	..	16,193
Central African Republic	20.9	..	0.0	2.1	..	..	5	1.8	7.3	..	..
Chad	69.5	..	0.0	6.8	..	..	−75	3.4	9.1	..	1
Chile	58.8	11.1	3.2	7.8	4.9	0.0	30	1.9	6.0	43	4,076
China	44.3	5.8	1.0	1.6	0.9	1.0[b]	−1,731[c]	0.1[c]	3.8	..	651
Hong Kong SAR, China	323.7	62.1	..	24.9	30.4	0.2	113	38.9	29.6	1,435	560,989
Colombia	28.1	4.8	3.4	3.1	1.3	1.8	−120	0.2	10.4	..	2,940
Congo, Dem. Rep.	63.4	..	0.0	9.0	..	..	−100	0.7	14.9	6	1
Congo, Rep.	88.7	46.1	0.0	21.7	..	0.1[b]	−50	3.8	28.2	..	0
Costa Rica	69.0	17.5	0.0	4.6	0.0	1.8	30	10.5	7.1	132	4,333
Côte d'Ivoire	64.2	14.8	0.0	1.6	0.0	0.8	−145	11.2	6.2	..	40
Croatia	50.3	25.0	..	4.7	2.1	2.3	10	15.8	24.6	302	15,892
Cuba	30.9	..	0.0	..	..	..	−194	0.1	28.8	..	27
Czech Republic	114.9	20.7	..	1.4	0.7	0.6	226	4.3	8.5	197	7,075
Denmark	56.9	34.3	..	0.9	2.1	0.3	30	8.7	7.8	357	34,506
Dominican Republic	37.9	14.6	0.0	4.4	0.0	7.4	−140	4.2	22.4	..	1,387
Ecuador	50.5	6.7	0.0	0.6	0.0	4.4	−350	2.9	9.5	..	484
Egypt, Arab Rep.	36.1	18.8	1.4	3.6	0.3	3.8	−340	0.3	4.7	44	1,172
El Salvador	52.4	9.9	0.0	2.0	−0.6	16.5	−280	0.7	31.7	510	243
Eritrea	29.6	..	0.0	0.0	..	..	55	0.3	35.2	29	6
Estonia	100.4	36.4	..	9.2	8.2	1.7	0	13.6	9.9	..	12,680
Ethiopia	33.5	14.4	0.0	0.8	0.0	0.9	−300	0.6	9.8	5	3
Finland	51.9	22.4	..	0.0	1.6	0.4	55	4.2	7.2	..	17,221
France	39.4	10.2	..	2.3	5.6	0.6	500	10.6	3.5	301	29,356
Gabon	66.0	..	0.4	0.3	..	0.1[b]	5	18.9	14.6	..	141
Gambia, The	43.5	25.5	0.0	5.4	0.0	10.9	15	16.6	67.8	..	38
Georgia	51.3	21.3	0.0	6.1	0.0	6.6	−250	4.0	2.8	268	752
Germany	62.0	14.6	..	1.2	1.8	0.3	550	13.2	5.8	..	25,654
Ghana	52.1	18.0	4.7	6.4	0.0	0.4	−51	7.6	44.7	61	97
Greece	24.2	17.5	..	0.7	0.6	0.6	150	10.0	12.2	..	4,537
Guatemala	50.2	10.7	0.0	1.6	0.1	10.8	−200	0.4	23.9	206	186
Guinea	58.7	9.8	0.0	1.2	0.0	1.6	−300	3.8	4.7	..	0
Guinea-Bissau	41.2	15.2	0.0	1.7	−0.1	5.6	−12	1.2	27.7	..	1
Haiti	40.5	17.9	0.0	0.6	0.0	21.2	−140	0.4	83.4	..	16
Honduras	90.7	14.1	0.2	3.5	0.0	17.6	−100	0.3	24.8	224	241

	Trade		International finance				Movement of people			Communication	
				% of GDP					Emigration of people with tertiary education to OECD countries		International Internet bandwidth[a]
			Financing through international capital markets Gross inflows	Foreign direct investment		Workers' remittances and compensation of employees received		International migrant stock % of total population	% of population age 25 and older with tertiary education	International voice traffic[a] minutes per person	bits per second per capita
	% of GDP			Net inflows	Net outflows		Net migration thousands				
	Merchandise	Services									
	2009	**2009**	**2009**	**2009**	**2009**	**2009**	**2005–10**	**2010**	**2000**	**2008**	**2009**
Hungary	125.6	27.3	..	2.2	2.1	1.7	75	3.7	12.8	159	5,987
India	29.9	12.5	1.6	2.5	1.1	3.6	−1,000	0.5	4.3	..	32
Indonesia	39.1	7.7	2.3	0.9	0.5	1.3	−730	0.1	2.9	..	110
Iran, Islamic Rep.	38.8	..	0.0	0.9	..	0.3[b]	−500	2.9	14.3	..	151
Iraq	116.2	11.5	0.0	1.6	0.0	0.1	−577	0.3	10.9	..	3
Ireland	77.9	86.9	..	11.1	10.6	0.3	200	20.2	33.7	..	15,261
Israel	49.8	20.0	..	2.0	0.6	0.6	85	38.8	7.8	..	2,003
Italy	38.7	10.4	..	1.4	2.1	0.1	1,650	7.4	9.7	..	12,989
Jamaica	52.9	37.5	9.0	4.5	0.5	15.8	−100	1.1	84.7	224	741
Japan	22.3	5.5	..	0.2	1.5	0.0	150	1.7	1.2	..	5,770
Jordan	81.5	33.3	0.0	9.5	0.3	14.3	250	48.8	7.4	258	1,811
Kazakhstan	62.1	12.4	2.1	11.8	2.7	0.1	−100	19.1	1.2	52	1,342
Kenya	49.8	16.1	0.2	0.5	0.2	5.7[b]	−189	2.0	38.5	6	477
Korea, Dem. Rep.	..	..	..	..	..	..	0	0.2	..	..	0
Korea, Rep.	82.5	16.1	..	0.2	1.3	0.3	−30	1.1	7.5	64	6,065
Kosovo	..	..	0.0	7.5	..	..	..	..	..	..	..
Kuwait	75.9	18.0	..	0.0	6.1	..	120	73.3	7.1	..	871
Kyrgyz Republic	97.8	37.7	0.0	4.1	0.0	21.7[b]	−75	4.2	0.9	..	112
Lao PDR	37.0	8.6	0.0	5.4	0.0	0.6	−75	0.3	37.2	..	142
Latvia	66.6	23.4	0.0	0.4	−0.2	2.3	−10	14.9	8.5	..	3,537
Lebanon	60.1	90.4	2.7	13.9	3.3	21.9	−13	17.8	43.9	190	223
Lesotho	171.0	12.5	0.0	4.0	0.0	26.2	−36	0.3	4.1	..	5
Liberia	80.1	162.0	0.0	24.9	0.0	6.2[b]	248	2.3	44.3	..	..
Libya	73.4	8.7	0.0	2.7	1.9	0.0[b]	20	10.4	4.3	..	50
Lithuania	93.2	18.4	6.4	0.6	0.5	3.1	−100	3.9	8.4	132	14,300
Macedonia, FYR	83.9	18.3	2.6	2.7	0.1	4.1	−10	6.3	29.4	256	17
Madagascar	51.1	..	0.0	6.3	..	0.1[b]	−5	0.2	7.7	8	12
Malawi	55.4	..	0.0	1.3	..	0.0[b]	−20	1.8	20.9	..	5
Malaysia	145.7	29.1	5.8	0.7	4.2	0.6	130	8.4	10.5	..	5,097
Mali	52.7	17.0	0.0	1.2	0.0	4.5[b]	−202	1.2	14.8	13	51
Mauritania	92.6	..	0.0	−1.3	..	0.1[b]	10	2.9	8.6	57	76
Mauritius	66.0	44.8	0.0	3.0	0.4	2.5[b]	0	3.3	56.0	215	364
Mexico	53.9	4.5	3.1	1.7	0.9	2.5	−2,430	0.7	15.5	..	312
Moldova	84.5	25.6	0.0	2.4	0.1	22.4	−172	11.4	4.1	457	6,660
Mongolia	96.0	23.1	0.1	14.8	1.3	4.8	−10	0.4	7.4	..	2,920
Morocco	51.2	21.1	0.0	2.2	0.5	6.9	−425	0.2	18.6	87	1,600
Mozambique	60.4	17.1	0.6	9.0	0.0	1.1	−20	1.9	22.6	..	56
Myanmar	..	..	..	..	..	..	−500	0.2	3.9	3	20
Namibia	93.6	12.2	0.0	5.3	0.0	0.1	−1	6.3	3.4	..	27
Nepal	41.5	11.5	0.0	0.3	..	23.8	−100	3.2	4.0	..	5
Netherlands	119.2	22.6	..	4.2	3.5	0.5	100	10.5	9.6	..	78,156
New Zealand	39.8	12.5	..	−1.0	−0.5	0.5	50	22.0	21.8	..	4,544
Nicaragua	79.3	16.7	0.0	7.1	0.0	12.5	−200	0.7	30.2	..	144
Niger	44.6	13.7	0.0	13.7	0.5	1.7	−28	1.3	5.5	..	11
Nigeria	52.9	11.4	0.7	3.3	0.1	5.5[b]	−300	0.7	10.5	26	5
Norway	49.8	19.8	..	3.0	7.1	0.2	135	9.9	6.2	..	26,904
Oman	99.0	15.9	..	4.8	0.9	0.1	20	28.4	0.4	431	1,365
Pakistan	30.5	6.4	0.2	1.5	0.0	5.4	−1,416	2.4	12.7	..	43
Panama	35.4	31.2	8.8	7.2	0.0	0.7	11	3.4	16.7	118	15,964
Papua New Guinea	95.4	26.9	58.3	5.4	0.1	0.2	0	0.4	27.8	..	2
Paraguay	71.0	13.9	0.0	1.4	0.1	4.3	−40	2.5	3.8	..	662
Peru	37.3	6.5	2.6	3.7	0.3	1.8	−625	0.1	5.8	113	2,646
Philippines	52.3	11.6	4.5	1.2	0.2	12.3	−900	0.5	13.6	..	113
Poland	65.4	12.4	3.8	3.2	1.2	1.9	−120	2.2	14.3	32	2,748
Portugal	48.6	15.9	..	1.2	0.5	1.5	200	8.6	19.0	..	4,790
Puerto Rico	..	..	..	..	..	..	−21	8.1	..	..	1,764
Qatar	64.6	..	..	..	..	..	562	86.5	2.1	..	2,044

	Trade		International finance % of GDP				Movement of people			Communication	
	Merchandise % of GDP	Services % of GDP	Financing through international capital markets Gross inflows	Foreign direct investment Net inflows	Foreign direct investment Net outflows	Workers' remittances and compensation of employees received	Net migration thousands	International migrant stock % of total population	Emigration of people with tertiary education to OECD countries % of population age 25 and older with tertiary education	International voice traffic[a] minutes per person	International Internet bandwidth[a] bits per second per capita
	2009	2009	2009	2009	2009	2009	2005–10	2010	2000	2008	2009
Romania	58.9	12.4	0.1	3.9	0.1	3.1	−200	0.6	11.3	124	18,271
Russian Federation	40.2	8.4	2.4	3.0	3.6	0.4	250	8.7	1.4	..	573
Rwanda	27.2	16.5	0.0	2.3	0.0	1.8	15	4.5	31.7	8	35
Saudi Arabia	76.6	22.1	..	2.8	0.6	0.1	150	28.0	0.9	..	1,731
Senegal	53.8	20.6	2.8	1.6	1.0	10.6	−100	1.6	17.2	101	372
Serbia	55.7	16.2	0.0	4.5	0.1	12.6[b,d]	0	7.2	..	203	12,660
Sierra Leone	38.7	8.7	0.0	3.8	0.0	2.4	60	1.8	49.2	..	..
Singapore	282.9	95.1	..	9.2	3.3	..	500	38.3	14.5	..	22,783
Slovak Republic	127.0	16.3	..	0.0	0.5	1.9	20	2.4	14.3	228	7,567
Slovenia	109.0	21.6	−1.2	0.3	0.6	..	22	7.9	11.0	220	6,720
Somalia	..	..	..	..	..	..	−250	0.2	34.5	..	..
South Africa	47.6	9.4	2.7	1.9	0.5	0.3	700	3.7	7.4	..	70
Spain	34.7	14.4	0.4	0.5	0.7	1,750	13.8	4.2	..	11,008
Sri Lanka	41.8	10.5	1.3	1.0	0.0	8.0	−300	1.7	28.2	..	190
Sudan	32.1	5.6	0.0	4.9	0.0	5.5[b]	135	1.7	6.8	13	322
Swaziland	103.3	25.4	0.0	2.2	0.2	3.1	−6	3.4	5.4	41	35
Sweden	61.8	25.6	..	2.8	7.9	0.2	150	13.9	4.5	..	49,828
Switzerland	66.8	23.0	..	5.6	6.8	0.5	100	22.6	9.6	..	29,413
Syrian Arab Republic	51.2	13.3	0.1	2.7	0.0	2.6[b]	800	10.2	6.2	..	261
Tajikistan	71.9	9.5	0.0	0.3	0.0	35.1	−200	4.0	0.6	..	37
Tanzania	44.2	16.7	0.0	1.9	0.0	0.1	−300	1.5	12.1	1	2
Thailand	108.5	25.7	0.3	1.9	1.6	0.6	300	1.7	2.2	..	818
Timor-Leste	..	..	0.0	..	..	..	10	1.2	16.5	..	..
Togo	80.6	22.2	19.9	1.8	−0.5	10.7[b]	−5	2.7	16.5	28	23
Trinidad and Tobago	75.8	4.9	..	3.3	2.7	0.5[b]	−20	2.6	78.9	443	7,916
Tunisia	84.8	21.4	0.1	4.0	0.2	5.0	−20	0.3	12.6	..	2,699
Turkey	39.5	8.2	1.7	1.4	0.3	0.2	−44	1.9	5.8	60	4,323
Turkmenistan	66.9	..	0.0	6.8	..	..	−25	4.0	0.4	..	48
Uganda	42.3	14.9	0.0	3.8	0.0	4.7	−135	1.9	36.0	..	36
Ukraine	75.0	22.3	0.9	4.2	0.1	4.5	−80	11.5	4.3	..	206
United Arab Emirates	136.8	..	..	..	..	..	343	70.0	0.7	..	13,233
United Kingdom	38.4	18.6	..	3.4	2.0	0.3	948	10.4	17.1	..	39,664
United States	18.8	6.1	..	1.0	1.9	0.0	5,052	13.8	0.5	216	11,279
Uruguay	39.0	10.5	1.6	4.0	0.0	0.3	−50	2.4	9.0	125	903
Uzbekistan	61.5	..	0.0	2.3	..	..	−400	4.2	0.8	..	46
Venezuela, RB	30.1	3.6	1.5	−1.0	0.6	0.0	40	3.5	3.8	79	628
Vietnam	141.0	14.1	1.5	8.4	0.8	7.4[b]	−200	0.1	27.0	..	581
West Bank and Gaza	..	..	..	..	..	..	−10	46.3	12.0	..	313
Yemen, Rep.	53.5	12.8	0.0	0.5	0.0	4.4	−135	2.1	6.0	..	28
Zambia	63.3	7.4	0.5	5.5	0.0	0.3	−85	1.8	16.4	..	8
Zimbabwe	91.9	..	0.0	1.1	..	..	−700	2.9	13.1	19	17
World	**42.8 w**	**11.2 w**	**.. w**	**1.8 w**	**2.1 w**	**0.8 w**	**..[e] s**	**3.1 w**	**5.4 w**	**..**	**3,526 w**
Low income	48.9	13.3	0.6	2.7	0.0	6.6	−2,737	1.5	13.1	..	7
Middle income	44.7	8.9	1.8	2.2	0.9	1.8	−13,203	1.4	6.8	..	348
Lower middle income	46.7	9.2	1.2	2.0	0.8	2.4	−9,231	0.9	6.6	..	151
Upper middle income	42.3	8.5	2.5	2.4	1.1	1.1	−3,972	3.3	7.0	..	1,120
Low & middle income	44.8	9.0	1.8	2.2	0.9	1.9	−15,941	1.4	7.1	..	299
East Asia & Pacific	51.5	7.9	1.4	1.6	1.0	1.4	−3,781	0.3	7.0	..	742
Europe & Central Asia	48.3	10.5	1.8	3.3	2.0	1.4	−1,671	6.8	3.4	..	1,087
Latin America & Carib.	33.6	5.9	2.9	1.9	0.3	1.4	−5,214	1.1	10.6	..	1,408
Middle East & N. Africa	53.5	..	0.3	2.6	..	3.2	−1,089	3.6	10.5	..	323
South Asia	31.0	11.5	1.3	2.3	0.9	4.5	−2,376	0.8	5.3	..	31
Sub-Saharan Africa	52.7	13.4	1.4	3.1	0.2	2.5	−1,810	2.1	12.6	..	31
High income	42.0	12.5	..	2.0	2.8	0.3	15,894	12.0	4.1	..	19,521
Euro area	57.1	16.9	..	3.0	3.8	0.5	5,607	11.0	7.1	..	32,455

a. Data are from the International Telecommunication Union's (ITU) World Telecommunication Development Report database. Please cite the ITU for third-party use of these data. b. World Bank estimate. c. Includes Taiwan, China. d. Includes Montenegro. e. World totals computed by the United Nations sum to zero, but because the aggregates shown here refer to World Bank definitions, regional and income group totals do not equal zero.

About the data

Globalization—the integration of the world economy— has been a persistent theme of the past 25 years. Growth of cross-border economic activity has changed countries' economic structure and political and social organization. Not all effects of globalization can be measured directly. But the scope and pace of change can be monitored along four key dimensions: trade in goods and services, financial flows, movement of people, and communication.

Trade data are based on gross flows that capture the two-way flow of goods and services. In conventional balance of payments accounting, exports are recorded as a credit and imports as a debit. The data on merchandise trade are from the World Trade Organization (WTO), which obtains data from national statistical offices and the International Monetary Fund's (IMF) International Financial Statistics, supplemented by the Comtrade database and publications or databases of regional organizations, specialized agencies, economic groups, and private sources. Because of differences in timing and definitions, trade flow estimates from customs reports and balance of payments may differ. See tables 4.4 and 4.5 for data on the main trade components of merchandise trade and tables 4.6 and 4.7 for the same data on services trade.

Financing through international capital markets includes gross bond issuance, bank lending, and new equity placement as reported by Dealogic, a company specializing in the investment banking industry. In financial accounting inward investment is a credit and outward investment a debit. Gross flow is a better measure of integration than net flow because gross flow shows the total value of financial transactions over a period, while net flow is the sum of credits and debits and represents a balance in which many transactions are canceled out. Components of financing through international capital markets are reported in U.S. dollars by market sources.

Foreign direct investment (FDI) includes equity investment, reinvested earnings, and short- and long-term loans between parent firms and foreign affiliates. Distinguished from other kinds of international investment, FDI establishes a lasting interest in or effective management control over an enterprise in another country. FDI may be understated in developing countries because some fail to report reinvested earnings and because the definition of long-term loans differs by country. However, data quality and coverage are improving as a result of continuous efforts by international and national

statistics agencies (see *About the data* for table 6.12). FDI data are recorded on a directional basis, as an inward flow to the economy of the direct investment enterprise, and as an outward flow from the economy of the direct investor. Net flows refer to new investments during the reporting period netted against disinvestments.

The data on workers' remittances and compensation of employees are the sum of three items defined in the IMF's Balance of Payments Manual, 5th edition: workers' remittances, compensation of employees, and migrants' transfers. The distinction among these three items is not always consistent in the data reported by countries to the IMF. In some cases countries compile data on the basis of the citizenship of migrant workers rather than their residency status. Some countries also report remittances entirely as worker's remittances or compensation of employees. Following the fifth edition of the Balance of Payments Manual in 1993, migrants' transfers are considered a capital transaction, but previous editions regarded them as current transfers. For these reasons the figures presented in the table take all three items into account. See *About the data* for table 6.18 for more information.

Migration has increased in importance, accounting for a substantial part of global integration. Data on net migration are estimated by the United Nations Population Division, based on data on immigrant stock and on fertility and mortality assumptions, taking into account the migration history of a country or area, the migration policy of a country, and the influx of refugees in recent periods. The estimates of the international migrant stock are derived from data on people who reside in one country but were born in another, mainly from population censuses (see *About the data* and Definitions for table 6.18).

One negative effect of migration is "brain drain"— emigration of highly educated people. The table shows data on emigration of people with tertiary education, drawn from Docquier, Lowell, and Marfouk (2009), who analyzed skilled migration using data from censuses and registers of Organisation for Economic Development and Co-operation (OECD) countries and provide data disaggregated by gender for 1990 and 2000.

Well developed communications infrastructure attracts investments and allows investors to capitalize on benefits of the digital age. See *About the data* for tables 5.11 and 5.12 for more information.

Definitions

• **Trade in merchandise** is the sum of merchandise exports and imports. • **Trade in services** is the sum of services exports and imports. • **Financing through international capital markets** is the sum of the absolute values of new bond issuance, syndicated bank lending, and new equity placements. • **Foreign direct investment net inflows** and **outflows** are net inflows and outflows of FDI (equity capital, reinvestment of earnings, and other short- and long-term capital). • **Workers' remittances and compensation of employees received** are current transfers by migrant workers and wages and salaries of nonresident workers. • **Net migration** is the number of immigrants minus the number of emigrants, including citizens and noncitizens, for the five-year period. • **International migrant stock** is the number of people born in a country other than that in which they live, including refugees. • **Emigration of people with tertiary education to OECD countries** is adults ages 25 and older, residing in an OECD country other than that in which they were born, with at least one year of tertiary education. • **International voice traffic** is the sum of international incoming and outgoing telephone traffic (in minutes) divided by total population. • **International Internet bandwidth** is the contracted capacity of international connections between countries for transmitting Internet traffic.

Data sources

Data on merchandise trade are from the WTO's *Annual Report*. Data on trade in services are from the International Monetary Fund's (IMF) Balance of Payments database. Data on international capital market financing are based on data from Dealogic. Data on FDI are based on balance of payments data from the IMF, supplemented by staff estimates using data from the United Nations Conference on Trade and Development and official national sources. Data on workers' remittances are World Bank staff estimates based on IMF balance of payments data. Data on net migration are from the United Nations Population Division's *World Population Prospects: The 2008 Revision*. Data on international migrant stock are from the United Nations Population Division's Trends in Total Migrant Stock: The 2008 Revision. Data on emigration of people with tertiary education are from Docquier, Lowell, and Marfouk's *"A Gendered Assessment of Highly Skilled Emigration"* (2009). Data on international voice traffic and international Internet bandwidth are from the International Telecommunication Union's World Telecomunication Development Report database.

Growth of merchandise trade

	Export volume		Import volume		Export value		Import value		Net barter terms of trade index	
	average annual % growth		average annual % growth		average annual % growth		average annual % growth		2000 = 100	
	1990–2000	2000–09	1990–2000	2000–09	1990–2000	2000–09	1990–2000	2000–09	1995	2009
Afghanistan[a]	..	15.2	..	3.9	−0.2	24.0	20.6	9.4	..	107.6
Albania	..	..	..	..	..	..	..	..	.	.
Algeria	2.8	−0.1	−0.8	12.7	2.0	16.3	−1.3	18.8	57.9	161.0
Angola	6.2	12.9	7.1	20.1	6.2	30.7	7.8	24.6	80.8	170.8
Argentina	8.4	5.9	17.7	11.3	10.1	12.2	17.0	14.4	91.6	126.0
Armenia	..	..	..	..	..	..	..	..	..	..
Australia[a]	7.3	7.6	9.2	7.5	5.7	20.0	8.7	12.3	99.4	163.0
Austria[a]	6.2	4.9	5.6	4.2	..	..	..	..	..	..
Azerbaijan	..	..	..	..	..	..	..	..	..	..
Bangladesh	12.9	11.0	5.9	4.6	15.8	12.5	10.4	13.0	111.8	64.5
Belarus[b]	..	6.0	..	10.1	..	18.4	..	19.4		121.0
Belgium[a]	6.0	2.9	5.7	3.5	4.8	10.9	5.3	11.4	104.3	103.1
Benin	1.0	5.9	8.2	6.8	3.3	14.0	9.7	16.1	106.6	83.1
Bolivia	2.8	9.9	9.1	7.8	4.3	21.9	9.7	13.3	89.4	136.9
Bosnia and Herzegovina	..	..	..	..	..	..	..	..	..	..
Botswana	4.8	2.9	4.0	5.1	4.8	7.4	4.2	11.5	89.3	79.1
Brazil	5.1	7.6	16.7	7.2	5.9	16.2	12.6	14.3	110.4	107.8
Bulgaria	..	..	..	..	..	..	..	..	..	..
Burkina Faso	13.2	11.7	3.6	7.3	12.9	17.1	3.6	15.6	131.0	78.6
Burundi	8.6	−4.2	4.0	10.4	−4.3	6.2	−6.9	15.9	163.6	137.9
Cambodia	..	12.8	..	9.4	26.9	15.2	25.2	15.1	..	85.0
Cameroon	0.3	−1.8	5.0	3.7	−3.6	11.2	2.1	13.1	90.4	121.6
Canada[a]	9.1	−0.7	9.0	3.3	9.4	5.6	8.9	7.3	103.2	114.8
Central African Republic	20.0	−3.7	4.3	5.7	3.5	−0.5	0.2	12.7	193.0	78.5
Chad[a]	−0.9	31.7	2.0	6.5	−3.5	49.6	0.5	12.2	92.6	136.0
Chile	11.1	5.1	10.7	11.3	9.4	18.3	10.3	15.3	135.6	166.7
China[†]	13.8	21.9	12.8	15.4	14.5	23.7	13.0	21.6	101.9	79.7
Hong Kong SAR, China	8.4	7.1	8.9	6.9	8.3	7.9	8.8	8.2	99.1	97.6
Colombia	4.5	6.6	8.5	11.4	7.3	14.9	9.7	15.8	86.8	114.4
Congo, Dem. Rep.	−1.8	8.3	4.6	14.6	−7.2	18.8	−0.5	21.5	79.8	112.0
Congo, Rep.	6.6	1.2	4.9	17.7	7.5	16.9	8.7	24.4	52.0	147.5
Costa Rica	14.0	7.6	14.9	7.6	17.0	7.5	13.9	9.9	104.6	87.2
Côte d'Ivoire	5.0	0.9	−0.3	6.6	6.1	12.4	3.0	15.7	122.0	140.4
Croatia	..	..	..	..	..	..	..	..	..	..
Cuba	..	1.5	..	8.2	−1.7	11.9	2.5	13.7	..	111.1
Czech Republic	..	..	..	..	..	..	..	..	..	..
Denmark[a]	5.4	2.7	5.8	3.7	4.1	9.8	4.9	10.7	102.1	102.9
Dominican Republic	3.9	−0.7	11.6	2.7	4.2	2.3	12.0	6.4	98.2	96.8
Ecuador	6.3	8.2	5.9	12.3	6.8	17.3	7.8	17.8	80.6	109.7
Egypt, Arab Rep.	−0.2	10.2	1.8	8.8	0.7	24.6	4.7	17.2	116.3	128.1
El Salvador	2.9	2.4	7.6	4.2	9.0	4.7	10.9	7.3	121.1	99.1
Eritrea	−28.3	−8.7	−3.2	−5.2	−31.0	−5.1	−0.2	1.7	101.7	73.3
Estonia	..	..	..	..	..	..	..	..	..	..
Ethiopia	10.5	7.8	7.3	17.5	10.7	17.8	7.3	25.1	151.0	121.1
Finland[a]	..	..	..	..	..	..	..	..	110.6	83.1
France[a]	8.3	4.9	6.6	6.4	4.9	10.5	3.7	12.2	106.4	99.8
Gabon	5.2	−1.2	2.5	7.2	0.8	13.8	2.2	12.4	125.4	155.3
Gambia, The	−11.6	−3.0	0.1	2.2	−12.3	2.1	0.2	9.8	100.0	85.5
Georgia	..	..	..	..	..	..	..	..	..	..
Germany[a]	6.5	5.6	4.9	5.1	3.7	11.6	2.9	10.9	107.5	105.9
Ghana	7.7	4.8	8.6	10.0	9.0	16.6	8.3	16.5	106.7	178.4
Greece[a]	8.9	..	9.3	..	8.2	..	8.2	..	89.6	90.8
Guatemala	8.5	8.8	10.0	5.8	10.1	13.1	10.4	11.5	117.9	91.4
Guinea	5.0	−7.4	−1.4	3.4	0.6	6.6	−2.6	10.5	89.6	143.3
Guinea-Bissau[a]	12.2	3.6	−16.0	7.2	18.6	9.1	−15.7	17.5	102.7	66.0
Haiti	12.6	5.9	13.3	2.3	12.2	8.6	14.4	9.8	113.2	70.6
Honduras	2.5	3.5	12.7	4.3	5.3	5.8	12.8	9.3	96.3	81.9
[†]Data for Taiwan, China	3.1	7.6	4.8	2.3	7.2	8.0	8.5	7.8	89.9	69.2

	Export volume		Import volume		Export value		Import value		Net barter terms of trade index	
	average annual % growth		average annual % growth		average annual % growth		average annual % growth		2000 = 100	
	1990–2000	2000–09	1990–2000	2000–09	1990–2000	2000–09	1990–2000	2000–09	1995	2009
Hungary[a]	10.1	10.7	11.6	8.0	10.1	16.2	11.8	14.3	104.3	95.6
India	6.9	12.3	9.0	18.4	5.3	20.3	7.9	25.3	108.0	99.4
Indonesia	9.1	8.7	2.9	5.7	8.1	10.9	2.7	15.6	90.4	63.2
Iran, Islamic Rep.	..	2.4	..	10.8	1.2	18.0	–4.8	18.4	..	132.4
Iraq[a]	..	1.0	..	6.8	118.9	17.2	70.3	13.7	..	140.8
Ireland[a]	15.2	1.9	11.3	0.9	13.8	5.4	10.9	5.4	103.9	96.6
Israel[a]	9.7	3.7	8.9	1.8	10.0	8.7	8.2	7.1	92.1	102.7
Italy[a]	4.8	0.3	4.2	0.6	4.6	9.3	3.2	10.2	96.6	103.3
Jamaica	2.2	0.3	..	1.2	2.2	6.0	6.9	9.2	..	77.1
Japan[a]	2.6	2.4	5.3	1.7	2.1	3.2	5.2	8.0	114.9	74.4
Jordan	4.7	4.2	3.8	6.8	6.6	16.3	5.1	17.2	115.6	120.4
Kazakhstan[a]	..	..	..	..	..	..	..	..	..	..
Kenya	3.9	5.1	7.4	8.6	6.3	12.6	6.0	17.7	103.9	94.7
Korea, Dem. Rep.[a]	..	4.3	..	–3.1	–8.5	10.9	1.0	6.3	..	83.9
Korea, Rep.	15.8	12.4	10.0	7.2	10.1	12.7	7.1	13.0	138.5	68.6
Kosovo	..	..	..	..	..	..	..	..	..	..
Kuwait	..	4.6	..	9.8	16.5	20.5	5.5	14.4	..	156.1
Kyrgyz Republic	..	..	..	..	..	..	..	..	..	..
Lao PDR	..	9.9	..	7.7	15.4	18.3	12.7	14.5	..	103.9
Latvia[a]	7.2	..	..	..	11.8	..	..	..	..	..
Lebanon	..	12.9	..	4.0	4.6	21.7	8.7	11.9	..	109.1
Lesotho	13.3	14.7	3.1	7.7	12.4	15.0	2.0	12.4	100.0	78.3
Liberia[a]	..	–6.3	..	5.4	–14.5	–0.4	2.6	9.9	..	111.4
Libya	..	4.5	0.0	16.6	–2.6	21.2	–1.4	23.9	..	140.4
Lithuania	..	..	..	..	..	..	..	..	..	..
Macedonia, FYR	..	..	..	..	..	..	..	..	..	..
Madagascar	4.1	2.8	4.5	10.6	8.5	6.0	6.4	17.6	79.6	75.5
Malawi	2.7	5.7	–2.4	8.0	0.9	10.9	–0.6	15.4	105.7	94.2
Malaysia	13.6	5.8	10.6	5.2	12.2	9.6	9.5	8.7	108.6	99.7
Mali	10.3	2.0	6.4	8.7	6.3	15.4	4.7	17.1	109.6	165.4
Mauritania	1.9	10.4	4.2	11.9	–1.9	24.0	–1.6	18.7	102.2	150.9
Mauritius	2.7	3.2	3.4	6.6	2.2	3.1	3.3	9.5	88.5	81.3
Mexico	15.5	2.7	13.2	3.5	16.1	7.0	14.2	6.8	92.5	104.0
Moldova	..	..	..	..	..	..	..	..	..	..
Mongolia	..	4.5	..	12.0	0.7	21.3	0.5	20.6	..	170.2
Morocco	7.5	0.1	7.2	8.6	7.2	10.3	5.5	16.3	89.1	137.4
Mozambique	15.2	12.5	1.0	8.7	10.2	22.4	1.1	16.3	151.1	98.2
Myanmar	15.5	6.7	13.8	–1.0	14.4	17.2	22.6	6.5	214.3	117.1
Namibia	2.4	7.3	7.7	11.0	0.9	14.9	3.9	15.5	82.6	113.5
Nepal	..	–1.5	..	2.9	11.0	4.0	9.3	12.4	..	80.7
Netherlands[a]	8.0	4.6	8.4	4.5	5.7	11.5	5.5	11.1	97.6	102.5
New Zealand[a]	4.7	3.0	6.0	5.8	4.3	9.6	5.9	10.5	99.0	111.0
Nicaragua	10.4	9.1	9.3	5.7	10.3	12.2	11.6	11.0	128.9	83.9
Niger	3.1	–2.6	–2.1	10.0	0.0	15.9	0.8	18.6	121.4	185.2
Nigeria	3.3	3.2	2.5	14.6	2.9	19.7	3.1	21.7	55.6	145.3
Norway[a]	6.6	0.2	7.8	5.7	5.7	12.8	4.4	12.5	60.3	128.6
Oman	4.0	–1.3	..	11.8	5.7	14.7	6.1	18.1	..	150.1
Pakistan	2.5	7.0	2.4	8.0	4.3	10.0	3.1	18.3	119.2	63.4
Panama	6.0	1.5	7.8	9.7	9.4	3.4	8.7	13.6	100.0	92.4
Papua New Guinea	–7.7	–3.5	..	7.0	3.7	13.8	–0.8	15.8	..	164.1
Paraguay	–0.2	14.5	5.4	15.5	1.7	19.0	6.7	19.4	118.3	104.9
Peru	9.4	8.1	10.6	9.7	8.9	21.6	12.7	17.3	123.4	129.1
Philippines	16.0	2.6	11.3	0.6	18.8	3.0	12.5	5.6	80.2	72.0
Poland[a]	9.8	11.8	19.0	9.4	9.5	21.8	17.0	18.4	102.4	107.1
Portugal[a]	0.3	–2.0	0.5	–1.4	–3.0	4.0	–2.5	4.5	104.7	107.6
Puerto Rico	..	..	..	..	..	..	..	..	..	..
Qatar	..	4.8	..	25.6	10.1	21.4	7.4	30.9	..	173.1

	Export volume		Import volume		Export value		Import value		Net barter terms of trade index	
	average annual % growth		average annual % growth		average annual % growth		average annual % growth		2000 = 100	
	1990–2000	2000–09	1990–2000	2000–09	1990–2000	2000–09	1990–2000	2000–09	1995	2009
Romania	..	..	..	..	..	..	..	..	..	..
Russian Federation	..	..	..	..	..	..	..	..	..	..
Rwanda	–8.0	3.6	0.8	15.2	–4.0	17.8	–1.7	22.7	110.1	155.3
Saudi Arabia	2.9	0.5	..	11.4	3.1	17.6	0.8	17.0	..	175.6
Senegal	10.6	0.8	4.9	7.1	4.0	9.4	3.6	16.5	156.3	99.2
Serbia	..	..	..	..	..	..	..	..	..	..
Sierra Leone[a]	..	28.7	..	3.1	..	35.2	..	14.3	..	64.6
Singapore	11.7	10.9	8.3	8.0	9.9	12.6	7.8	12.0	104.4	82.6
Slovak Republic	..	..	..	..	..	..	..	..	..	..
Slovenia	..	..	..	..	..	..	..	..	..	..
Somalia[a]	..	0.4	..	5.4	2.3	8.3	4.5	13.0	..	101.3
South Africa	4.5	0.5	7.6	6.6	2.5	12.8	5.9	15.7	106.0	135.0
Spain[a]	11.4	3.1	9.3	4.7	8.6	10.6	6.2	11.8	104.3	107.2
Sri Lanka	7.4	3.1	8.0	1.7	11.3	6.3	8.9	9.1	99.0	78.5
Sudan	12.6	8.3	8.4	17.9	14.0	24.7	9.8	23.5	100.0	152.5
Swaziland	4.0	2.5	3.1	4.3	5.9	8.9	5.0	10.2	100.0	112.8
Sweden[a]	8.9	3.5	6.4	4.4	7.4	9.7	5.4	12.1	110.2	89.6
Switzerland[a]	3.7	3.7	4.2	2.5	4.4	5.7	3.6	4.4	96.4	106.6
Syrian Arab Republic	2.2	0.4	..	12.5	0.9	14.1	3.6	20.5	..	148.3
Tajikistan	..	..	..	..	..	..	..	..	..	..
Tanzania	6.0	6.4	–2.0	11.8	6.4	17.0	0.1	20.5	98.0	121.1
Thailand	9.6	7.4	2.6	7.8	10.5	12.6	5.0	13.0	116.0	97.1
Timor-Leste	..	..	..	..	..	..	..	..	..	..
Togo	9.1	3.2	6.0	–1.7	6.6	9.9	5.5	14.8	99.1	28.6
Trinidad and Tobago	..	2.8	..	2.8	6.8	17.9	12.1	12.1	..	131.0
Tunisia	5.7	7.7	4.3	5.0	6.0	13.4	5.2	11.7	95.8	94.3
Turkey	10.7	11.5	11.1	9.8	9.1	19.3	10.3	18.4	105.7	95.0
Turkmenistan	..	..	..	..	..	..	..	..	..	..
Uganda	17.8	15.7	22.4	8.8	15.6	25.9	21.0	16.0	197.2	120.4
Ukraine	..	..	..	..	..	..	..	..	..	..
United Arab Emirates	..	7.8	..	15.9	6.6	20.9	10.7	21.6	..	134.7
United Kingdom[a]	6.3	1.1	6.5	3.2	6.2	6.2	6.5	7.9	100.1	104.0
United States[a]	6.6	4.0	9.1	2.9	7.2	6.6	9.5	6.5	103.3	99.0
Uruguay	6.1	8.1	10.5	5.9	5.2	14.3	10.1	13.3	116.2	98.5
Uzbekistan	..	..	..	..	..	..	..	..	..	..
Venezuela, RB	5.2	–1.9	4.8	12.3	5.4	13.9	5.2	15.7	63.4	187.1
Vietnam	..	11.8	..	12.8	22.7	19.7	22.7	21.2	..	97.4
West Bank and Gaza	..	..	..	..	..	..	..	..	..	..
Yemen, Rep.	..	–4.7	4.4	9.5	20.6	9.9	0.6	18.4	..	126.6
Zambia	6.1	8.9	2.9	15.1	–4.6	25.7	1.3	21.8	189.7	155.9
Zimbabwe	8.8	–5.1	8.0	–2.1	3.4	2.8	1.9	7.4	96.8	90.9

a. Data are from the International Monetary Fund's International Financial Statistics database. b. Data are from national sources.

About the data

Data on international trade in goods are available from each country's balance of payments and customs records. While the balance of payments focuses on the financial transactions that accompany trade, customs data record the direction of trade and the physical quantities and value of goods entering or leaving the customs area. Customs data may differ from data recorded in the balance of payments because of differences in valuation and time of recording. The 1993 United Nations System of National Accounts and the fifth edition of the International Monetary Fund's (IMF) *Balance of Payments Manual* (1993) attempted to reconcile definitions and reporting standards for international trade statistics, but differences in sources, timing, and national practices limit comparability. Real growth rates derived from trade volume indexes and terms of trade based on unit price indexes may therefore differ from those derived from national accounts aggregates.

Trade in goods, or merchandise trade, includes all goods that add to or subtract from an economy's material resources. Trade data are collected on the basis of a country's customs area, which in most cases is the same as its geographic area. Goods provided as part of foreign aid are included, but goods destined for extraterritorial agencies (such as embassies) are not.

Collecting and tabulating trade statistics are difficult. Some developing countries lack the capacity to report timely data, especially landlocked countries and countries whose territorial boundaries are porous. Their trade has to be estimated from the data reported by their partners. (For further discussion of the use of partner country reports, see *About the data* for table 6.3.) Countries that belong to common customs unions may need to collect data through direct inquiry of companies. Economic or political concerns may lead some national authorities to suppress or misrepresent data on certain trade flows, such as oil, military equipment, or the exports of a dominant producer. In other cases reported trade data may be distorted by deliberate under- or overinvoicing to affect capital transfers or avoid taxes. And in some regions smuggling and black market trading result in unreported trade flows.

By international agreement customs data are reported to the United Nations Statistics Division, which maintains the Commodity Trade (Comtrade) and Monthly Bulletin of Statistics databases. The United Nations Conference on Trade and Development (UNCTAD) compiles international trade statistics, including price, value, and volume indexes, from national and international sources such as the IMF's International Financial Statistics database, the United Nations Economic Commission for Latin America and the Caribbean, the U.S. Bureau of Labor Statistics, Japan Customs and Bank of Japan, and UNCTAD's Commodity Price Statistics. The IMF also compiles data on trade prices and volumes in its International Financial Statistics (IFS) database.

Unless otherwise noted, the growth rates and terms of trade in the table were calculated from index numbers compiled by UNCTAD. The growth rates and terms of trade for selected economies were calculated from index numbers compiled in the IMF's *International Financial Statistics*. In some cases price and volume indexes from different sources vary significantly as a result of differences in estimation procedures. Because the IMF does not publish trade value indexes, for selected economies the trade value indexes were derived from the volume and price indexes. All indexes are rescaled to a 2000 base year.

The terms of trade measures the relative prices of a country's exports and imports. There are several ways to calculate it. The most common is the net barter (or commodity) terms of trade index, or the ratio of the export price index to the import price index. When a country's net barter terms of trade index increases, its exports become more valuable or its imports cheaper.

Definitions

• **Export** and **import volumes** are indexes of the quantity of goods traded. They are derived from UNCTAD's volume index series and are the ratio of the export or import value indexes to the corresponding unit value indexes. Unit value indexes are based on data reported by countries that demonstrate consistency under UNCTAD quality controls, supplemented by UNCTAD's estimates using the previous year's trade values at the Standard International Trade Classification three-digit level as weights. To improve data coverage, especially for the latest periods, UNCTAD constructs a set of average prices indexes at the three-digit product classification of the Standard International Trade Classification revision 3 using UNCTAD's Commodity Price Statistics, international and national sources, and UNCTAD secretariat estimates and calculates unit value indexes at the country level using the current year's trade values as weights. For economies for which UNCTAD does not publish data, the export and import volume indexes (lines 72 and 73) in the IMF's *International Financial Statistics* are used to calculate the average annual growth rates. • **Export** and **import values** are the current value of exports (free on board, f.o.b.) or imports (cost, insurance, and freight, c.i.f.), converted to U.S. dollars and expressed as a percentage of the average for the base period (2000). UNCTAD's export or import value indexes are reported for most economies. For selected economies for which UNCTAD does not publish data, the value indexes are derived from export or import volume indexes (lines 72 and 73) and corresponding unit value indexes of exports or imports (lines 74 and 75) in the IMF's *International Financial Statistics*. • **Net barter terms of trade index** is calculated as the percentage ratio of the export unit value indexes to the import unit value indexes, measured relative to the base year 2000.

Data sources

Data on trade indexes are from UNCTAD's annual *Handbook of Statistics* for most economies and from the IMF's *International Financial Statistics* for selected economies.

Direction of trade

High-income importers

% of world trade, 2009

Source of exports	European Union	Japan	United States	Other high-income	Total
High-income economies	28.5	2.3	6.5	13.1	50.4
European Union	21.9	0.4	2.3	4.6	29.2
Japan	0.6	..	0.8	1.5	2.8
United States	1.8	0.4	..	3.1	5.3
Other high-income economies	4.2	1.5	3.4	3.8	13.0
Low- and middle-income economies	6.5	1.6	5.4	6.2	19.7
East Asia & Pacific	2.3	1.3	2.3	4.2	10.2
China	1.8	0.8	1.8	2.9	7.3
Europe & Central Asia	1.9	0.1	0.1	0.6	2.7
Russian Federation	0.9	0.1	0.1	0.3	1.3
Latin America & Caribbean	0.7	0.1	2.2	0.5	3.5
Brazil	0.3	0.0	0.1	0.2	0.6
Middle East & N. Africa	0.8	0.1	0.2	0.2	1.3
Algeria	0.2	0.0	0.1	0.0	0.3
South Asia	0.4	0.0	0.2	0.5	1.1
India	0.3	0.0	0.1	0.4	0.9
Sub-Saharan Africa	0.4	0.1	0.3	0.2	1.0
South Africa	0.1	0.0	0.0	0.1	0.3
World	35.0	4.0	11.8	19.3	70.1

Low- and middle-income importers

% of world trade, 2009

Source of exports	East Asia & Pacific	Europe & Central Asia	Latin America & Caribbean	Middle East & N. Africa	South Asia	Sub-Saharan Africa	Total
High-income economies	8.2	2.6	3.3	1.4	1.5	1.0	18.2
European Union	1.2	2.0	0.7	0.9	0.4	0.6	5.7
Japan	1.4	0.0	0.2	0.0	0.1	0.1	1.8
United States	0.8	0.1	1.8	0.1	0.2	0.1	3.2
Other high-income economies	4.8	0.4	0.5	0.4	0.9	0.3	7.5
Low- and middle-income economies	2.7	1.6	1.7	0.9	1.1	0.8	9.2
East Asia & Pacific	1.7	0.5	0.5	0.3	0.5	0.3	3.9
China	0.6	0.4	0.4	0.2	0.3	0.3	2.4
Europe & Central Asia	0.2	1.0	0.0	0.3	0.1	0.0	1.6
Russian Federation	0.2	0.3	0.0	0.1	0.0	0.0	0.6
Latin America & Caribbean	0.4	0.1	1.0	0.1	0.1	0.1	1.8
Brazil	0.2	0.0	0.3	0.0	0.0	0.0	0.6
Middle East & N. Africa	0.2	0.1	0.0	0.2	0.2	0.0	0.7
Algeria	0.0	0.0	0.0	0.0	0.0	0.0	0.1
South Asia	0.2	0.0	0.0	0.1	0.1	0.1	0.5
India	0.2	0.0	0.0	0.1	0.1	0.1	0.4
Sub-Saharan Africa	0.1	0.0	0.1	0.0	0.1	0.2	0.7
South Africa	0.1	0.0	0.0	0.0	0.0	0.1	0.2
World	11.7	4.3	5.2	2.3	2.5	1.8	27.5

High-income importers

average annual % growth, 1999–2009

Source of exports	European Union	Japan	United States	Other high-income	Total
High-income economies	9.1	6.6	3.8	9.1	8.1
European Union	9.3	4.5	5.8	10.8	9.1
Japan	2.8	..	−0.6	6.9	3.4
United States	5.4	0.1	..	5.5	5.0
Other high-income economies	11.3	9.9	3.9	11.8	8.6
Low- and middle-income economies	16.7	11.3	11.0	17.4	14.6
East Asia & Pacific	18.9	10.7	15.2	17.3	16.1
China	26.4	13.3	21.8	22.7	21.9
Europe & Central Asia	19.8	17.1	7.8	18.5	18.6
Russian Federation	20.3	16.9	4.6	17.5	18.3
Latin America & Caribbean	12.5	11.5	7.1	15.7	9.0
Brazil	12.6	10.5	7.3	19.8	12.0
Middle East & N. Africa	13.3	14.0	19.9	17.1	14.9
Algeria	13.8	22.9	26.4	25.1	17.5
South Asia	14.5	6.7	8.6	20.5	14.6
India	16.5	8.1	10.8	22.9	17.2
Sub-Saharan Africa	11.7	19.5	18.2	14.3	14.6
South Africa[a]	10.4	22.0	14.8	14.3	13.3
World	10.2	8.3	6.4	11.1	9.6

Low- and middle-income importers

average annual % growth, 1999–2009

Source of exports	East Asia & Pacific	Europe & Central Asia	Latin America & Caribbean	Middle East & N. Africa	South Asia	Sub-Saharan Africa	Total
High-income economies	15.4	19.4	8.0	13.6	19.6	13.0	14.2
European Union	15.8	19.0	8.8	11.8	15.9	12.0	14.7
Japan	12.6	27.1	8.9	11.9	12.1	10.8	12.4
United States	12.0	13.5	6.5	12.1	20.3	13.1	8.8
Other high-income economies	17.0	22.7	12.6	19.2	22.5	15.6	17.5
Low- and middle-income economies	22.6	22.9	17.6	23.2	25.2	21.7	22.1
East Asia & Pacific	21.4	37.9	26.6	25.5	27.2	26.9	25.2
China	27.4	40.9	31.3	30.5	35.3	31.7	32.2
Europe & Central Asia	18.7	20.1	20.4	22.9	23.2	22.1	20.7
Russian Federation	19.0	19.3	21.0	21.5	19.8	14.6	19.6
Latin America & Caribbean	30.9	20.3	14.5	17.4	25.1	24.1	17.9
Brazil	32.2	21.9	16.6	20.8	20.3	26.8	20.6
Middle East & N. Africa	25.0	17.8	15.2	24.9	34.1	25.0	24.7
Algeria	42.4	12.5	8.4	21.6	60.7	10.1	17.2
South Asia	26.1	15.9	21.8	23.7	19.9	24.6	22.7
India	27.9	14.2	24.2	26.8	20.1	25.8	24.2
Sub-Saharan Africa	20.5	24.7	21.8	13.8	15.8	15.7	21.0
South Africa[a]	28.0	18.7	12.0	20.4	20.7	12.9	17.0
World	17.3	20.8	10.7	16.4	21.2	16.0	16.3

a. Data for 1999 are based on imports from South Africa reported by other economies because data on exports for South Africa were not available.

The table provides estimates of the flow of trade in goods between groups of economies. The data are from the International Monetary Fund's (IMF) Direction of Trade database. All high-income economies and major developing economies report trade on a timely basis, covering about 85 percent of trade for recent years. Trade by less timely reporters and by countries that do not report is estimated using reports of trading partner countries. Because the largest exporting and importing countries are reliable reporters, a large portion of the missing trade flows can be estimated from partner reports. Partner country data may introduce discrepancies due to smuggling, confidentiality, different exchange rates, overreporting of transit trade, inclusion or exclusion of freight rates, and different points of valuation and times of recording.

In addition, estimates of trade within the European Union (EU) have been significantly affected by changes in reporting methods following the creation of a customs union. The current system for collecting data on trade between EU members—Intrastat, introduced in 1993—has less exhaustive coverage than the previous customs–based system and has resulted in some problems of asymmetry (estimated imports are about 5 percent less than exports). Despite these issues, only a small portion of world trade is estimated to be omitted from the IMF's *Direction of Trade Statistics Yearbook* and Direction of Trade database.

Most countries report their trade data in national currencies, which are converted into U.S. dollars using the IMF's published period average exchange rate (series rf or rh, monthly averages of the market or official rates) for the reporting country or, if unavailable, monthly average rates in New York. Because imports are reported at cost, insurance, and freight (c.i.f.) valuations, and exports at free on board (f.o.b.) valuations, the IMF adjusts country reports of import values by dividing them by 1.10 to estimate equivalent export values. The accuracy of this approximation depends on the set of partners and the items traded. Other factors affecting the accuracy of trade data include lags in reporting, recording differences across countries, and whether the country reports trade according to the general or special system of trade. (For further discussion of the measurement of exports and imports, see *About the data* for tables 4.4 and 4.5.)

The regional trade flows in the table are calculated from current price values. The growth rates are in nominal terms; that is, they include the effects of changes in both volumes and prices.

• **Merchandise trade** includes all trade in goods; trade in services is excluded. • **High-income economies** are those classified as such by the World Bank (see front cover flap). • **European Union** is defined as all high-income EU members: Austria, Belgium, Cyprus, Czech Republic, Denmark, Estonia, Finland, France, Germany, Greece, Hungary, Ireland, Italy, Luxembourg, Malta, the Netherlands, Portugal, Slovak Republic, Slovenia, Spain, Sweden, and the United Kingdom. • **Other high-income economies** include all high-income economies (both Organisation for Economic Co-operation and Development members and others) except the high-income European Union, Japan, and the United States. • **Low- and middle-income regional groupings** are based on World Bank classifications (see back cover flap for regional groupings) and may differ from those used by other organizations.

More than half of the world's merchandise trade takes place between high-income economies. But low- and middle-income economies' participation in the global trade has increased in the past 15 years

6.3a

1996

Low- and middle-income to low- and middle-income 4.5%
Unspecified 3.0%
Low- and middle-income to high-income 14.1%
High-income to low- and middle-income 16.0%
High-income to high-income 62.4%

2009

Low- and middle-income to low- and middle-income 9.2%
Unspecified 2.5%
Low- and middle-income to high-income 19.7%
High-income to low- and middle-income 18.2%
High-income to high-income 50.4%

Trade among low- and middle-income economies accounted for about 9.2 percent of the world's merchandise trade in 2009, compared with 4.5 percent in 1996. The share of trade from low- and middle-income economies to high-income economies increased 9.8 percentage points between 1996 and 2009.

Source: World Bank staff calculations based on data from the International Monetary Fund's Direction of Trade database.

Data on the direction and growth of merchandise trade were calculated using the IMF's Direction of Trade database. Regional and income group classifications are according to the World Bank classification of economies as of July 1, 2010, and are as shown on the cover flaps of this report.

High-income economy trade with low- and middle-income economies

Exports to low-income economies

	High-income economies		European Union		Japan		United States	
	1999	2009	1999	2009	1999	2009	1999	2009
Total ($ billions)	**32.0**	**86.9**	**15.7**	**40.2**	**3.5**	**6.1**	**3.4**	**12.0**
% of total exports								
Food	12.5	10.5	14.2	9.8	0.4	0.3	25.2	17.2
Cereals	4.0	4.1	3.2	3.0	0.2	0.2	17.4	12.6
Agricultural raw materials	2.5	2.1	1.8	1.5	1.2	2.3	4.8	4.6
Ores and nonferrous metals	1.0	1.4	0.9	1.3	0.6	0.7	0.6	1.5
Fuels	4.9	11.5	3.1	15.6	0.3	0.3	1.8	5.9
Crude petroleum	0.1	0.4	0.1	0.0	0.0	0.0	0.0	0.0
Petroleum products	4.4	10.7	2.7	15.3	0.3	0.1	1.2	5.1
Manufactured goods	77.1	67.3	78.4	68.0	96.4	94.4	62.0	58.7
Chemical products	12.3	11.0	15.2	12.0	3.4	3.1	10.6	7.3
Iron and steel	2.6	2.9	2.3	2.2	6.9	8.1	0.8	1.2
Machinery and transport equipment	44.2	42.0	43.6	40.4	74.2	74.5	37.9	41.9
Furniture	0.4	0.3	0.6	0.4	0.1	0.1	0.3	0.2
Textiles	5.9	2.2	2.5	1.7	3.0	1.2	5.2	1.0
Footwear	0.2	0.1	0.2	0.2	0.0	0.0	0.2	0.2
Other	11.6	9.0	14.0	11.1	8.8	7.4	6.8	6.9
Miscellaneous goods	2.0	7.2	1.5	3.8	1.2	2.1	5.5	12.2

Imports from low-income economies

	High-income economies		European Union		Japan		United States	
	1999	2009	1999	2009	1999	2009	1999	2009
Total ($ billions)	**40.2**	**100.4**	**20.1**	**47.7**	**2.1**	**2.9**	**11.8**	**34.5**
% of total imports								
Food	23.0	15.1	31.9	22.0	37.1	23.7	7.5	4.3
Cereals	0.7	0.7	0.3	0.3	0.0	0.0	0.1	0.1
Agricultural raw materials	5.5	2.4	6.8	3.6	9.9	2.7	1.1	0.6
Ores and nonferrous metals	5.1	5.1	5.6	5.0	17.1	23.3	2.1	0.6
Fuels	23.3	39.5	13.3	29.6	8.9	23.0	41.4	64.3
Crude petroleum	21.2	34.1	12.5	23.5	7.6	5.3	36.3	61.2
Petroleum products	1.7	1.6	0.5	0.2	0.1	5.0	4.6	2.8
Manufactured goods	41.5	33.2	41.2	38.9	24.0	26.4	47.6	29.5
Chemical products	0.6	0.8	0.9	1.2	0.3	0.6	0.1	0.2
Iron and steel	0.5	0.1	0.4	0.1	2.3	0.8	0.4	0.0
Machinery and transport equipment	1.9	1.6	2.4	2.9	1.6	0.8	0.3	0.1
Furniture	0.2	0.2	0.2	0.1	0.1	0.1	0.2	0.3
Textiles	30.1	27.4	25.5	31.0	15.0	14.3	42.3	28.0
Footwear	0.4	0.7	0.5	0.9	1.7	7.6	0.0	0.1
Other	7.9	2.4	11.3	2.7	2.9	2.1	4.4	1.0
Miscellaneous goods	1.7	4.8	1.2	0.9	3.0	1.0	0.4	0.7

Simple applied tariff rates on imports from low-income economies (%)[a]

	High-income economies		European Union		Japan		United States	
	1999	2009	1999	2009	1999	2009	1999	2009
Average	**4.3**	**2.7**	**1.3**	**0.8**	**3.0**	**1.3**	**5.2**	**3.5**
Food	6.8	3.0	3.1	0.7	9.1	2.6	3.8	2.3
Cereals	16.9	5.8	24.0	0.1	2.6	5.3	2.7	0.4
Agricultural raw materials	3.3	1.6	0.1	0.1	0.7	0.1	0.4	0.2
Ores and nonferrous metals	1.2	1.1	0.2	0.2	1.3	0.0	0.1	0.1
Fuels	3.1	1.2	0.2	0.0	2.0	0.5	0.4	0.2
Crude petroleum	1.3	0.5	0.0	0.0	1.2	0.0	0.3	0.0
Petroleum products	4.5	1.6	0.4	0.0	6.3	1.1	0.9	0.4
Manufactured goods	4.1	2.8	1.1	0.9	2.1	1.3	5.9	4.0
Chemical products	2.7	2.1	1.2	0.3	1.1	0.2	0.3	0.1
Iron and steel	4.2	2.4	0.8	0.2	0.2	0.0	0.4	0.0
Machinery and transport equipment	1.7	1.3	0.4	0.2	0.1	0.0	0.2	0.1
Furniture	3.2	2.2	0.1	0.1	0.0	0.0	0.6	0.9
Textiles	7.5	4.5	2.5	2.4	3.6	1.6	10.7	7.3
Footwear	7.2	4.4	2.9	1.7	6.4	4.4	12.5	8.7
Other	2.1	1.6	0.6	0.2	0.7	1.1	1.0	0.7
Miscellaneous goods	0.7	0.8	0.2	0.2	0.0	0.0	0.4	0.0

Exports to middle-income economies

	High-income economies		European Union		Japan		United States	
	1999	2009	1999	2009	1999	2009	1999	2009
Total ($ billions)	**646.4**	**1845.4**	**224.9**	**700.5**	**89.0**	**222.8**	**184.4**	**346.7**
% of total exports								
Food	6.7	6.5	8.1	6.1	0.4	0.4	8.2	12.8
Cereals	1.7	1.4	1.5	1.1	0.1	0.0	3.0	2.8
Agricultural raw materials	1.8	1.9	1.3	1.5	1.0	1.1	2.1	3.6
Ores and nonferrous metals	2.0	4.5	1.5	2.7	1.9	3.8	1.5	3.9
Fuels	3.1	6.2	1.7	3.2	0.5	1.6	2.1	7.1
Crude petroleum	0.5	0.5	0.2	0.1	0.0	0.0	0.0	0.0
Petroleum products	1.9	4.4	1.3	2.7	0.4	1.4	1.5	5.4
Manufactured goods	83.8	75.2	85.7	82.5	93.3	88.2	81.6	63.4
Chemical products	11.7	14.0	13.7	14.6	8.2	9.9	10.5	14.4
Iron and steel	2.5	3.4	2.4	3.3	5.9	6.8	1.0	1.5
Machinery and transport equipment	48.8	41.8	46.3	45.4	63.9	58.0	50.0	33.2
Furniture	0.5	0.4	0.9	0.7	0.1	0.3	0.7	0.3
Textiles	6.2	2.6	5.4	3.3	3.6	1.7	5.7	1.9
Footwear	0.1	0.2	0.3	0.4	0.0	0.0	0.1	0.0
Other	14.1	13.3	16.7	14.8	11.6	11.6	13.7	12.1
Miscellaneous goods	2.6	5.7	1.6	4.0	2.9	4.8	4.4	9.3

Imports from middle-income economies

Total ($ billions)	**1,010.3**	**2,816.6**	**285.1**	**998.3**	**106.5**	**243.4**	**364.4**	**796.0**
% of total imports								
Food	10.0	7.6	14.2	9.4	15.6	9.2	6.5	5.9
Cereals	0.4	0.5	0.3	0.4	0.4	0.3	0.2	0.3
Agricultural raw materials	2.3	1.1	3.4	1.3	4.3	2.0	1.2	0.7
Ores and nonferrous metals	4.8	3.7	6.3	3.3	8.8	8.7	2.7	1.8
Fuels	13.3	19.8	18.8	25.6	13.8	16.6	11.3	19.1
Crude petroleum	9.0	12.7	13.0	16.2	6.6	7.0	8.9	15.8
Petroleum products	1.9	3.6	2.5	3.8	1.1	1.8	2.1	2.9
Manufactured goods	67.8	64.0	56.4	56.9	56.2	62.0	75.5	69.6
Chemical products	2.9	3.6	3.7	3.7	2.7	4.1	2.0	2.9
Iron and steel	1.9	1.7	2.1	1.8	1.0	1.0	1.6	1.0
Machinery and transport equipment	29.2	31.8	18.6	24.6	21.6	27.8	36.9	36.2
Furniture	1.7	1.8	1.4	1.6	1.5	1.7	2.4	2.7
Textiles	13.9	9.5	15.3	11.0	14.9	12.0	12.6	9.4
Footwear	2.6	1.7	2.1	2.0	1.7	1.4	3.2	2.1
Other	15.7	14.2	13.3	12.3	12.7	14.0	16.8	15.3
Miscellaneous goods	1.8	3.8	0.9	3.4	1.3	1.6	2.8	2.8

Simple applied tariff rates on imports from middle-income economies (%)[a]

Average	**5.6**	**3.2**	**3.9**	**1.1**	**2.9**	**2.2**	**3.4**	**2.5**
Food	10.3	4.3	9.7	2.9	13.5	6.9	3.6	2.9
Cereals	15.2	6.7	22.1	0.7	10.0	10.5	2.3	1.1
Agricultural raw materials	2.5	1.9	1.0	0.4	0.9	0.5	0.5	0.4
Ores and nonferrous metals	1.9	1.3	1.4	0.5	0.1	0.0	0.3	0.4
Fuels	2.8	1.5	0.9	0.1	1.3	0.2	0.6	1.3
Crude petroleum	1.5	0.4	0.0	0.0	1.2	0.0	0.5	0.0
Petroleum products	5.5	2.1	2.9	0.1	4.2	0.6	1.7	3.0
Manufactured goods	5.2	3.1	3.4	1.0	1.6	1.8	3.6	2.5
Chemical products	3.6	2.0	3.3	0.6	0.6	0.3	1.2	1.1
Iron and steel	3.6	1.6	2.3	0.1	0.1	0.2	2.0	0.3
Machinery and transport equipment	3.0	1.9	1.6	0.2	0.0	0.0	0.4	0.5
Furniture	5.0	3.2	0.7	0.0	0.0	0.1	0.3	0.4
Textiles	9.7	6.0	7.6	3.3	4.2	4.9	10.3	6.8
Footwear	11.6	6.4	8.6	3.4	19.7	16.9	13.3	8.0
Other	3.8	2.3	2.3	0.3	0.4	0.7	0.9	0.8
Miscellaneous goods	1.7	0.9	1.2	0.5	0.0	0.0	0.5	0.3

a. Includes ad valorem equivalents of specific rates.

About the data

Developing economies are becoming increasingly important in the global trading system. Since the early 1990s trade between high-income economies and low- and middle-income economies has grown faster than trade among high-income economies. The increased trade benefits consumers and producers. But as was apparent at the World Trade Organization's (WTO) Ministerial Conferences in Doha, Qatar, in October 2001; Cancun, Mexico, in September 2003; and Hong Kong SAR, China, in December 2005, achieving a more pro-development outcome from trade remains a challenge. Doing so will require strengthening international consultation. After the Doha meetings negotiations were launched on services, agriculture, manufactures, WTO rules, the environment, dispute settlement, intellectual property rights protection, and disciplines on regional integration. At the most recent negotiations in Hong Kong SAR, China, trade ministers agreed to eliminate subsidies of agricultural exports by 2013; to abolish cotton export subsidies and grant unlimited export access to selected cotton-growing countries in Sub-Saharan Africa; to cut more domestic farm supports in the European Union, Japan, and the United States; and to offer more aid to developing countries to help them compete in global trade.

Trade flows between high-income and low- and middle-income economies reflect the changing mix of exports to and imports from developing economies. While food and primary commodities have continued to fall as a share of high-income economies' imports, manufactures as a share of goods imports from both low- and middle-income economies have grown. And trade between developing economies has grown substantially over the past decade, a result of their increasing share of world output and liberalization of trade, among other influences.

Yet trade barriers remain high. The table includes information about tariff rates by selected product groups. Applied tariff rates are the tariffs in effect for partners in preferential trade agreements such as the North American Free Trade Agreement. When these rates are unavailable, most favored nation rates are used. The difference between most favored nation and applied rates can be substantial. Simple averages of applied rates are shown because they are generally a better indicator of tariff protection than weighted average rates are.

The data on trade flows are from the United Nations Statistics Division's Commodity Trade (Comtrade) database. Partner country reports by high-income economies were used for both exports and imports. Because of differences in sources of data, timing, and treatment of missing data, the numbers in the table may not be fully comparable with those used to calculate the direction of trade statistics in tables 6.3 and 6.5 or the aggregate flows in tables 4.4, 4.5, and 6.2. Tariff data are from United Nations Conference on Trade and Development (UNCTAD)'s Trade Analysis and Information System (TRAINS) database. Tariff line data were matched to Standard International Trade Classification (SITC) revision 2 codes to define commodity groups. For further discussion of merchandise trade statistics, see *About the data* for tables 4.4, 4.5, 6.2, 6.3, and 6.5, and for information about tariff barriers, see table 6.8.

Definitions

The product groups in the table are defined in accordance with SITC revision 2: **food** (0, 1, 22, and 4) and **cereals** (04); **agricultural raw materials** (2 excluding 22, 27, and 28); **ores and nonferrous metals** (27, 28, and 68); **fuels** (3), **crude petroleum** (crude petroleum oils and oils obtained from bituminous minerals; 333), and **petroleum products** (noncrude petroleum and preparations; 334); **manufactured goods** (5–8 excluding 68), **chemical products** (5), **iron and steel** (67), **machinery and transport equipment** (7), **furniture** (82), **textiles** (65 and 84), **footwear** (85), and **other manufactured goods** (6 and 8 excluding 65, 67, 68, 82, 84, and 85); and **miscellaneous goods** (9). • **Exports** are all merchandise exports by high-income economies to low-income and middle-income economies as recorded in the United Nations Statistics Division's Comtrade database. Exports are recorded free on board (f.o.b.). • **Imports** are all merchandise imports by high-income economies from low–income and middle-income economies as recorded in the United Nations Statistics Division's Commodity Trade (Comtrade) database. Imports include insurance and freight charges (c.i.f.). • **High-, middle-, and low-income economies** are those classified as such by the World Bank as of July 1, 2010 (see front cover flap). • **European Union** is defined as all high-income EU members: Austria, Belgium, Cyprus, Czech Republic, Denmark, Estonia, Finland, France, Germany, Greece, Hungary, Ireland, Italy, Luxembourg, Malta, the Netherlands, Portugal, Slovak Republic, Slovenia, Spain, Sweden, and the United Kingdom.

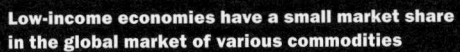

Low-income economies have a small market share in the global market of various commodities **6.4a**

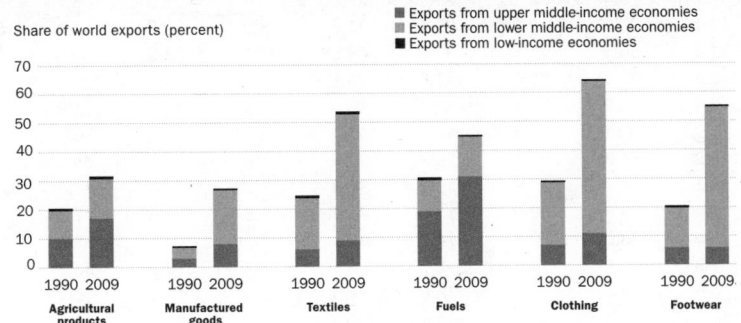

Low-income economies specialize in labor-intensive sectors, but their share in the global market of labor intensive products is very small. Lower middle-income economies provided most of the textiles, clothing, and footwear traded globally in 2009. High-income economies accounted for the majority of trade in agricultural products and manufactured goods.
Source: World Bank staff estimates, based on data from United Nations Statistics Division's Comtrade database.

Data sources

Data on trade values are from United Nations Statistics Division's Comtrade database. Data on tariffs are from UNCTAD's TRAINS database and are calculated by World Bank staff using the World Integrated Trade Solution system, available at http://wits.worldbank.org.

	Exports						Imports					
	% of total merchandise exports						% of total merchandise imports					
	To developing economies				To high-income economies		From developing economies				From high-income economies	
	Within region		Outside region				Within region		Outside region			
	1999	2009	1999	2009	1999	2009	1999	2009	1999	2009	1999	2009
East Asia & Pacific	8.1 w	11.9 w	7.2 w	15.5 w	83.9 w	73.7 w	11.0 w	15.9 w	8.9 w	18.0 w	80.5 w	64.1 w
Cambodia	7.4	3.6	0.3	1.4	60.5	96.5	38.0	54.6	1.8	2.7	60.0	44.0
China	4.2	6.6	8.6	17.7	87.2	77.9	6.8	9.1	8.0	17.1	82.8	65.4
Fiji	8.9	19.6	0.1	1.5	80.6	51.2	8.0	18.7	2.2	3.4	89.1	76.0
Indonesia	11.1	22.4	8.1	14.1	80.8	64.0	14.6	26.4	7.9	10.0	76.8	63.4
Korea, Dem. Rep.	7.5	50.8	42.0	35.7	50.5	13.7	34.8	43.2	25.4	50.3	39.8	6.5
Lao PDR	..	..	0.6	0.2	32.1	18.0	81.8	83.5	1.0	1.7	16.0	13.5
Malaysia	9.9	23.8	6.6	10.9	83.5	65.5	12.7	28.1	3.1	6.6	82.8	64.7
Mongolia	..	..	14.5	4.1	28.4	34.3	19.1	27.0	37.1	41.1	53.8	32.0
Myanmar	20.1	57.6	13.4	22.1	53.2	14.3	49.2	66.7	1.7	4.8	49.0	28.4
Papua New Guinea	8.0	10.1	0.1	1.3	63.3	50.4	11.6	24.3	1.7	1.2	85.8	73.3
Philippines	8.7	16.2	1.8	2.5	88.2	79.7	12.4	26.2	4.2	5.1	82.2	68.7
Thailand	13.2	27.0	6.0	11.9	79.2	60.7	14.7	27.0	7.3	7.1	76.0	64.3
Vietnam	20.7	20.2	6.2	6.7	72.0	69.1	17.8	37.2	4.9	7.8	77.0	53.5
Europe & Central Asia	22.5 w	19.9 w	11.3 w	14.2 w	64.0 w	55.7 w	27.9 w	26.1 w	12.9 w	14.7 w	61.1 w	54.6 w
Albania	3.3	5.1	0.1	6.9	96.6	87.7	12.3	16.8	1.1	8.3	86.5	72.9
Armenia	24.8	35.7	10.5	7.0	56.6	56.3	32.4	43.1	13.6	19.2	50.4	37.7
Azerbaijan	31.0	12.4	5.3	12.6	62.3	77.3	46.3	46.2	7.6	14.7	45.7	39.5
Belarus	65.6	46.5	11.3	10.6	22.8	42.9	66.5	65.5	3.4	6.3	30.1	26.8
Bosnia and Herzegovina	5.6	5.9	..	..	91.7	92.4	4.0	9.9	..	..	95.8	89.2
Bulgaria	25.8	27.4	5.7	6.9	66.5	64.7	28.4	33.1	7.1	7.8	64.0	59.1
Georgia	58.3	66.3	5.8	4.4	35.6	29.4	55.7	53.8	3.4	9.1	40.9	37.8
Kazakhstan	29.0	26.1	14.6	18.1	49.5	43.2	46.9	41.7	6.6	27.7	46.4	30.7
Kyrgyz Republic	42.7	80.0	..	..	47.8	9.5	46.6	22.6	10.1	71.5	41.7	6.0
Lithuania	19.5	24.5	1.3	3.6	79.1	72.8	25.3	33.9	4.0	4.4	69.1	62.4
Macedonia, FYR	29.0	31.5	1.6	1.8	68.8	55.2	31.2	33.3	4.3	11.2	64.5	55.6
Moldova	66.4	62.3	1.7	1.9	32.0	34.9	59.6	51.5	1.6	11.0	38.9	37.6
Romania	11.7	16.0	8.1	6.6	79.7	77.9	12.9	15.5	5.4	8.7	80.3	77.1
Russian Federation	20.0	14.5	11.5	12.2	67.2	55.9	29.7	12.8	13.8	23.4	56.1	62.2
Serbia	..	32.3	..	1.9	..	57.4	..	20.6	..	4.7	..	64.6
Tajikistan	46.1	36.7	..	..	50.7	15.1	78.9	62.2	..	..	18.6	15.8
Turkey	8.7	13.3	11.6	24.1	74.9	59.1	11.2	21.0	12.2	23.1	72.9	55.6
Turkmenistan	52.1	45.2	..	..	25.2	36.3	51.9	42.8	..	..	35.0	35.4
Ukraine	38.5	42.9	21.8	26.0	39.6	29.8	60.0	48.1	5.3	12.0	34.5	40.3
Uzbekistan	51.4	69.3	..	..	40.2	13.1	33.9	41.9	..	..	63.4	36.9
Latin America & Carib.	14.4 w	18.8 w	4.0 w	13.9 w	77.6 w	66.0 w	14.3 w	19.2 w	3.5 w	12.8 w	78.0 w	62.1 w
Argentina	45.1	42.3	15.3	23.6	39.5	32.6	30.4	40.1	9.4	17.5	58.4	38.1
Bolivia	38.4	64.4	0.6	3.7	59.4	31.5	41.8	67.2	2.3	4.6	55.7	28.0
Brazil	23.0	22.4	10.9	28.2	64.3	48.0	19.0	17.1	9.9	26.8	71.0	56.1
Chile	20.3	16.3	5.3	28.7	67.9	51.4	28.1	29.5	8.6	14.9	49.9	45.0
Colombia	24.1	29.3	1.1	6.7	73.4	63.1	25.9	25.9	4.4	15.8	68.7	55.0
Costa Rica	12.4	26.2	0.7	12.1	26.9	61.3	20.1	22.5	3.3	9.6	41.1	63.5
Cuba	8.8	24.9	36.0	31.6	55.3	43.5	17.0	43.5	17.5	23.2	65.5	33.4
Dominican Republic	2.8	17.4	0.5	2.6	96.5	71.1	17.5	25.1	1.7	7.6	80.7	63.6
Ecuador	21.6	42.3	5.5	6.4	72.2	50.7	32.7	39.9	4.4	11.7	61.9	47.3
El Salvador	60.9	44.0	1.5	1.2	37.1	58.3	40.0	41.4	2.1	6.2	56.3	61.4
Guatemala	22.2	37.7	1.0	2.2	74.2	56.7	29.3	34.6	3.9	8.9	65.7	55.0
Haiti	2.5	9.7	0.8	2.1	96.9	87.9	15.2	34.8	3.9	11.4	80.5	53.7
Honduras	7.7	29.0	0.1	3.0	82.6	68.0	15.1	44.4	2.8	7.8	72.2	47.8
Jamaica	2.9	5.0	7.1	3.9	89.5	89.9	11.7	24.5	3.7	7.3	81.4	66.2
Mexico	3.2	6.3	0.3	1.9	96.1	94.5	2.3	4.3	3.4	18.5	93.7	80.7
Nicaragua	31.9	47.7	0.1	0.6	62.4	50.9	48.6	53.5	0.4	12.1	45.4	35.5
Panama	23.6	45.9	0.8	10.7	73.6	43.0	24.4	9.2	1.2	15.7	60.7	68.5
Paraguay	62.0	69.6	0.6	14.4	30.3	14.1	54.9	48.5	3.2	32.7	41.7	18.4
Peru	16.2	15.5	8.6	17.9	75.1	81.2	30.4	33.5	3.3	23.2	66.2	48.1
Uruguay	53.0	44.1	9.2	22.2	36.8	33.5	47.8	52.6	8.9	20.6	42.8	28.3
Venezuela, RB	15.2	12.0	..	10.5	63.2	56.0	18.2	38.4	0.2	10.9	69.4	47.3

Direction of trade of developing economies

	Exports % of total merchandise exports						Imports % of total merchandise imports					
	To developing economies				To high-income economies		From developing economies				From high-income economies	
	Within region		Outside region				Within region		Outside region			
	1999	2009	1999	2009	1999	2009	1999	2009	1999	2009	1999	2009
Middle East & N. Africa	**3.2 w**	**8.0 w**	**13.0 w**	**25.8 w**	**78.2 w**	**61.1 w**	**3.5 w**	**7.4 w**	**12.3 w**	**22.1 w**	**72.7 w**	**59.9 w**
Algeria	1.8	3.0	15.1	15.6	83.1	81.4	1.5	3.2	17.2	32.9	81.4	64.5
Egypt, Arab Rep.	7.2	21.1	11.9	22.8	65.6	52.9	1.1	2.9	21.7	34.7	69.3	60.9
Iran, Islamic Rep.	..	2.1	13.7	42.1	73.4	39.8	..	0.6	22.3	38.8	65.6	59.5
Iraq	4.1	2.4	5.9	29.0	90.0	68.6	12.8	22.9	37.1	42.5	50.1	34.7
Jordan	20.8	31.2	35.4	22.2	40.8	44.6	15.3	10.7	17.1	28.2	65.4	60.9
Lebanon	17.6	40.5	12.2	10.5	69.4	48.3	6.0	14.2	18.5	26.1	73.9	58.6
Libya	4.1	3.7	8.5	14.1	87.4	82.1	11.4	11.9	9.9	27.9	78.6	60.1
Morocco	2.4	3.3	10.4	22.3	80.7	73.1	1.7	6.2	9.0	18.3	79.0	75.8
Syrian Arab Republic	8.5	52.5	11.9	5.7	76.2	41.8	4.8	17.4	26.8	36.2	45.9	46.5
Tunisia	5.7	11.8	5.9	7.5	84.1	77.9	4.4	8.6	7.8	16.0	85.9	74.8
Yemen, Rep.	0.9	2.7	62.0	73.5	35.8	22.8	4.0	3.9	20.7	43.9	72.8	51.3
South Asia	**4.3 w**	**5.4 w**	**14.7 w**	**25.1 w**	**78.8 w**	**67.4 w**	**3.8 w**	**3.6 w**	**10.7 w**	**15.5 w**	**66.8 w**	**58.1 w**
Afghanistan	46.6	48.3	17.6	19.3	35.8	32.4	24.8	30.1	35.2	24.5	40.0	45.5
Bangladesh	1.9	2.6	4.4	6.8	78.7	76.8	13.5	14.3	16.4	36.1	52.5	43.5
India	4.2	4.5	17.5	27.4	78.2	65.3	0.9	0.6	29.6	39.7	69.5	59.4
Nepal	29.6	64.6	..	..	60.2	29.6	14.0	52.9	..	..	45.1	15.8
Pakistan	4.5	12.4	12.0	23.8	81.2	61.9	2.3	4.2	23.3	31.8	72.8	63.1
Sri Lanka	3.1	5.7	10.4	16.0	82.4	115.8	10.1	19.9	14.3	35.5	61.4	61.2
Sub-Saharan Africa	**13.3 w**	**13.7 w**	**13.8 w**	**27.9 w**	**66.4 w**	**57.9 w**	**12.0 w**	**11.8 w**	**12.7 w**	**22.7 w**	**70.3 w**	**52.3 w**
Angola	1.0	3.9	8.9	47.1	90.1	49.0	11.5	5.1	12.7	32.7	75.8	62.7
Benin	5.9	30.8	68.7	54.7	25.1	14.5	24.3	7.2	16.9	58.4	58.5	34.5
Burkina Faso	10.2	15.5	31.6	37.9	55.8	43.1	39.5	37.2	5.1	13.8	51.1	44.5
Burundi	2.1	8.8	..	12.5	72.3	66.7	23.8	24.2	8.1	18.9	57.8	46.9
Cameroon	6.9	12.8	8.4	18.1	84.1	68.4	20.0	18.6	10.7	26.5	68.1	55.1
Central African Republic	1.4	9.2	14.6	32.8	84.0	58.0	18.0	14.9	7.9	14.3	57.9	43.8
Chad	5.5	0.4	..	..	81.3	96.0	31.6	19.1	..	..	62.4	55.9
Comoros	..	..	..	..	93.4	66.5	..	..	..	..	51.4	46.4
Congo, Dem. Rep.	1.1	21.0	0.6	46.9	98.0	31.9	50.6	48.1	5.6	15.2	41.5	36.7
Congo, Rep.	1.6	1.3	8.1	33.2	88.0	65.3	12.9	4.7	9.0	30.0	64.3	63.9
Cote d'Ivoire	24.8	27.6	16.5	7.7	58.7	84.4	16.8	26.8	14.3	26.3	63.0	53.3
Ethiopia	1.7	5.1	18.4	24.9	70.5	55.1	2.3	2.7	19.1	35.1	70.5	33.8
Gabon	0.9	3.2	10.1	24.9	83.3	56.0	5.7	9.7	2.6	16.8	90.9	72.3
Gambia, The	18.1	5.9	4.7	61.7	77.2	32.4	8.4	16.3	24.2	53.4	67.4	30.4
Ghana	7.8	10.3	12.1	24.6	74.0	53.2	23.9	24.5	15.0	33.0	60.4	41.8
Guinea	4.7	2.6	1.1	24.1	90.0	51.8	11.1	5.8	16.3	17.3	72.5	33.6
Guinea-Bissau	1.6	26.8	..	..	16.8	2.4	15.4	18.7	..	..	44.1	36.6
Kenya	30.7	34.3	16.2	14.8	51.9	42.9	9.5	12.2	15.2	33.6	74.6	53.4
Liberia	2.4	18.3	9.3	8.9	88.3	72.9	4.6	0.9	1.8	19.0	93.5	80.1
Madagascar	5.8	4.8	8.5	11.0	74.6	76.2	8.7	8.4	22.1	46.7	59.5	37.2
Malawi	19.4	19.7	9.0	32.6	71.2	47.3	67.5	56.4	6.3	16.1	25.1	27.7
Mali	5.7	9.2	32.3	50.9	60.1	28.3	23.7	27.2	5.8	10.9	38.6	32.9
Mauritania	11.3	14.1	9.0	46.9	78.6	37.8	6.3	5.4	17.2	35.6	68.3	49.8
Mauritius	6.7	14.2	0.9	3.5	92.4	82.4	13.9	11.4	24.1	46.0	62.0	42.6
Mozambique	45.1	16.5	13.2	8.3	40.6	63.2	29.9	36.6	7.1	18.8	20.2	32.1
Niger	39.1	26.9	0.3	0.5	60.6	72.8	31.0	17.6	21.1	31.7	46.2	51.0
Nigeria	10.6	10.9	27.6	24.8	61.2	63.1	3.8	4.7	24.6	27.2	71.3	52.0
Rwanda	4.8	56.5	14.7	19.8	43.3	23.0	27.8	42.0	6.2	12.4	47.3	44.7
Senegal	25.5	44.3	18.8	11.7	49.1	37.9	12.3	15.9	19.6	32.8	66.5	74.0
Sierra Leone	..	9.3	..	11.0	66.9	75.7	11.4	24.5	11.9	32.9	72.0	38.2
Somalia	0.7	4.2	30.9	21.4	68.4	74.4	12.9	8.5	61.1	65.0	15.0	14.1
South Africa	16.3	18.7	8.5	21.8	60.1	60.3	3.7	7.0	14.4	35.3	81.7	58.0
Sudan	10.4	1.6	24.2	77.0	65.2	21.3	4.0	6.5	37.1	48.7	58.8	41.3
Tanzania	16.7	18.1	24.1	28.4	57.3	44.6	18.8	16.2	23.4	39.5	57.7	40.7
Togo	24.0	58.8	30.5	32.5	41.1	8.1	21.4	16.0	9.7	31.6	65.2	50.5
Uganda	3.1	46.8	5.0	7.3	92.0	43.2	49.4	25.2	10.3	23.1	39.7	51.8
Zambia	35.6	22.8	12.2	16.0	32.0	63.8	55.8	60.2	4.5	9.7	35.3	30.2
Zimbabwe	29.1	49.1	14.5	20.6	54.8	30.4	46.0	73.3	6.6	8.7	39.1	14.0

Note: Bilateral trade data are not available for Timor-Leste, Kosovo, West Bank and Gaza, Botswana, Eritrea, Lesotho, Namibia, and Swaziland. Components may not sum to 100 percent because of trade with unspecified partners or with economies not covered by World Bank classification.

About the data

Developing economies are an increasingly important part of the global trading system. Their share of world trade rose from 15 percent in 1990 to 30 percent in 2009. And trade between high-income economies and low- and middle-income economies has grown faster than trade between high-income economies. This increased trade benefits both producers and consumers in developing and high-income economies.

The table shows trade in goods between developing economies in the same region and other regions and between developing economies and high-income economies. Data on exports and imports are from the International Monetary Fund's (IMF) Direction of Trade database and should be broadly consistent with data from other sources, such as the United Nations Statistics Division's Commodity Trade (Comtrade) database. All high-income economies and major developing economies report trade to the IMF on a timely basis, covering about 85 percent of trade for recent years. Trade by less timely reporters and by countries that do not report is estimated using reports of trading partner countries. Therefore, data on trade between developing and high-income economies shown in the table should be generally complete. But trade flows between many developing economies—particularly those in Sub-Saharan Africa—are not well recorded, and the value of trade among developing economies may be understated. The table does not include some developing economies because data on their bilateral trade flows are not available. Data on the direction of trade between selected high-income economies are presented and discussed in tables 6.3 and 6.4.

At the regional level most exports from developing economies are to high-income economies, but the share of intraregional trade is increasing. Geographic patterns of trade vary widely by country and commodity. Larger shares of exports from oil- and resource-rich economies are to high-income economies.

The relative importance of intraregional trade is higher for both landlocked countries and small countries with close trade links to the largest regional economy. For most developing economies—especially smaller ones—there is a "geographic bias" favoring intraregional trade. Despite the broad trend toward globalization and the reduction of trade barriers, the relative share of intraregional trade increased for most economies between 1999 and 2009. This is due partly to trade-related advantages, such as proximity, lower transport costs, increased knowledge from repeated interaction, and cultural and historical affinity. The direction of trade is also influenced by preferential trade agreements that a country has made with other economies. Though formal agreements on trade liberalization do not automatically increase trade, they nevertheless affect the direction of trade between the participating economies. Table 6.7 illustrates the size of existing regional trade blocs that have formal preferential trade agreements.

Although global integration has increased, developing economies still face trade barriers when accessing other markets (see table 6.8).

Definitions

• **Exports to developing economies within region** are the sum of merchandise exports from the reporting economy to other developing economies in the same World Bank region as a percentage of total merchandise exports by the economy. • **Exports to developing economies outside region** are the sum of merchandise exports from the reporting economy to other developing economies in other World Bank regions as a percentage of total merchandise exports by the economy. • **Exports to high-income economies** are the sum of merchandise exports from the reporting economy to high-income economies as a percentage of total merchandise exports by the economy. • **Imports from developing economies within region** are the sum of merchandise imports by the reporting economy from other developing economies in the same World Bank region as a percentage of total merchandise imports by the economy. • **Imports from developing economies outside region** are the sum of merchandise imports by the reporting economy from other developing economies in other World Bank regions as a percentage of total merchandise imports by the economy. • **Imports from high-income economies** are the sum of merchandise imports by the reporting economy from high-income economies as a percentage of total merchandise imports by the economy.

Developing economies are trading more with other developing economies ⟶ 6.5a

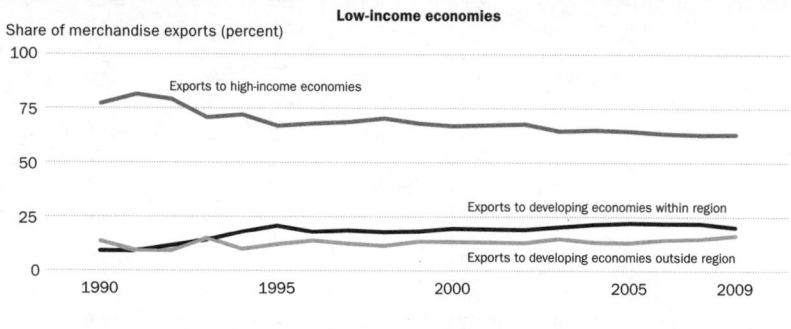

Low-income economies

Share of merchandise exports (percent)

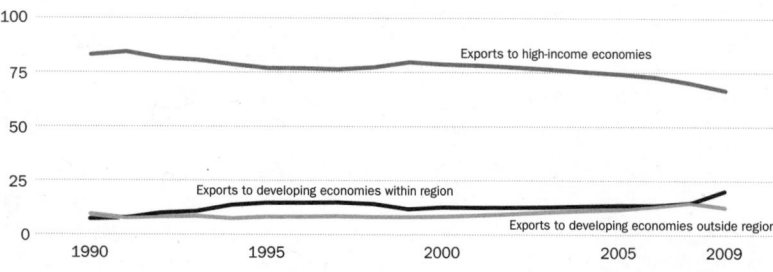

Middle-income economies

Share of merchandise exports to high-income economies have been declining for both low- and middle-income economies. On the other hand, their exports to other developing economies have increased, especially exports to developing economies within the same region.

Source: World Bank staff calculations based on data from International Monetary Fund's Direction of Trade database.

Data sources

Data on merchandise trade flows are published in the IMF's *Direction of Trade Statistics Yearbook* and *Direction of Trade Statistics Quarterly;* the data in the table were calculated using the IMF's Direction of Trade database. Regional and income group classifications are according to the World Bank classification of economies as of July 1, 2010, and are as shown on the cover flaps of this report.

	1970	1980	1990	1995	2000	2004	2005	2006	2007	2008	2009	2010
World Bank commodity price index												
(2000= 100)												
Energy	19	153	79	53	100	123	171	197	209	274	179	225
Nonenergy commodities	183	177	115	117	100	121	135	172	192	218	178	224
Agriculture	188	195	113	122	100	118	121	134	154	184	165	192
Beverages	230	273	117	136	100	109	125	130	145	168	184	210
Food	201	199	116	117	100	123	121	131	158	198	171	186
Fats and oils	237	196	105	126	100	134	120	123	178	222	181	203
Grains	204	199	121	124	100	115	115	134	161	225	179	179
Other food	151	205	124	101	100	117	129	140	127	142	152	170
Raw materials	136	143	105	125	100	109	119	143	149	157	141	197
Timber	97	92	88	105	100	90	100	113	117	120	116	119
Other raw materials	179	198	124	146	100	129	140	177	185	196	168	282
Fertilizers	82	177	98	110	100	125	148	151	205	453	245	232
Metals and minerals	185	141	122	106	100	126	162	251	268	261	197	288
Base metals	200	145	124	112	100	127	152	253	272	230	174	247
Steel products[a]	..	134	131	118	100	153	170	162	155	231	190	190
Commodity prices												
(2000 prices)												
Energy												
Coal, Australian ($/mt)	..	49	39	33	26	48	43	44	56	102	60	82
Natural gas, Europe ($/mmBtu)	..	5.21	2.48	2.26	3.86	3.88	5.74	7.57	7.30	10.72	7.27	6.87
Natural gas, U.S. ($/mmBtu)	0.57	1.91	1.65	1.43	4.31	5.35	8.09	6.01	5.96	7.09	3.30	3.64
Natural gas, liquefied, Japan ($mmBtu)	..	7.02	3.54	2.86	4.71	4.66	5.44	6.32	6.56	10.04	7.46	9.00
Petroleum, avg., spot ($/bbl)	4	45	22	14	28	34	48	57	61	78	52	66
Beverages (cents/kg)												
Cocoa	233	321	123	119	91	141	140	142	167	206	241	260
Coffee, Arabica	397	427	192	277	192	161	230	225	232	247	265	358
Coffee, robusta	316	400	115	230	91	72	101	133	163	186	137	144
Tea, avg., 3 auctions	289	205	200	124	188	153	150	168	174	194	227	239
Tea, Colombo auctions	217	137	182	118	179	162	167	171	215	223	262	273
Tea, Kolkata auctions	343	253	273	145	181	156	147	157	164	180	210	233
Tea, Mombasa auctions	307	224	144	108	203	141	134	175	142	177	210	212
Food												
Fats and oils ($/mt)												
Coconut oil	1,376	831	327	556	450	600	560	542	784	979	606	932
Copra[a]	779	558	224	364	305	409	376	360	518	653	401	622
Groundnut oil	1,312	1,059	937	823	714	1,054	963	867	1,154	1,705	988	1,164
Palm oil	901	719	282	521	310	428	383	427	666	759	570	747
Palmkernell oil[a]	..	..	..	..	444	588	569	519	758	904	585	982
Soybeans	405	365	240	215	212	278	249	240	328	418	365	373
Soybean meal	355	324	195	164	189	219	195	187	263	340	340	314
Soybean oil	992	737	435	519	338	559	495	535	752	1,007	709	833
Grains ($/mt)												
Barley	..	96	78	86	77	90	86	104	147	160	107	131
Maize	202	154	106	103	89	102	90	109	140	178	138	154
Rice, Thailand, 5%	438	506	263	266	202	216	260	272	279	520	463	405
Rice, Thailand, 25%[a]	..	..	254	247	173	205	241	248	262	425	382	366
Rice, Thailand, A1[a]	..	..	152	218	143	186	198	196	232	386	273	318
Sorghum[a]	179	159	101	99	88	100	87	110	139	166	126	137
Wheat, Canada[a]	218	235	152	172	147	169	179	194	256	364	251	259
Wheat, U.S., hard red winter	190	213	132	147	114	142	138	172	218	261	187	185
Wheat, U.S., soft red winter[a]	197	208	125	139	99	131	123	142	204	217	155	190

	1970	1980	1990	1995	2000	2004	2005	2006	2007	2008	2009	2010
Commodity prices (continued)												
(2000 prices)												
Food (continued)												
Other food												
Bananas, U.S. ($/mt)	573	467	526	369	424	476	547	605	577	675	707	720
Beef (cents/kg)	452	340	249	158	193	228	238	228	222	251	220	278
Chicken meat (cents/kg)	..	85	96	92	119	138	135	124	134	136	143	143
Fishmeal ($/mt)[a]	682	621	401	411	413	589	664	1,040	1,005	906	1,027	1,399
Oranges ($/mt)	582	482	516	441	363	780	794	741	817	886	759	857
Shrimp. Mexico (cents/kg)	..	1,420	1,039	1,253	1,515	928	939	915	862	855	789	1,033
Sugar, EU domestic (cents/kg)	39	60	57	57	56	61	60	58	58	56	44	37
Sugar, U.S. domestic (cents/kg)	57	82	50	42	43	41	43	44	39	37	46	66
Sugar, world (cents/kg)	29	78	27	24	18	14	20	29	19	23	33	39
Agricultural raw materials												
Cotton A index (cents/kg)	219	252	177	177	130	124	110	113	119	126	115	189
Logs, Cameroon ($/cu. m)[a]	149	310	334	282	275	301	304	285	325	421	352	355
Logs, Malaysia ($/cu. m)	149	241	172	212	190	179	184	214	229	234	240	231
Rubber, Singapore.(cents/kg)	141	176	84	131	67	116	135	186	193	207	160	303
Rubber, TSR 20 (cents/kg)[a]	..	..	..	..	63	110	126	174	184	202	150	280
Plywood (cents/sheet)[a]	357	338	345	485	448	422	462	532	547	516	471	472
Sawnwood, Malaysia ($/cu. m)	608	489	518	614	595	528	599	670	688	711	673	703
Tobacco ($/mt)[a]	3,727	2,806	3,297	2,194	2,976	2,488	2,533	2,653	2,830	2,871	3,541	3,570
Woodpulp ($/mt)[a]	615	661	792	708	664	582	577	624	655	656	513	719
Fertilizers ($/mt)												
Diammonium phosphate	187	274	167	180	154	201	224	233	369	774	270	415
Phosphate rock	38	58	39	29	44	37	38	40	61	276	102	102
Potassium chloride	109	143	95	98	123	113	144	156	171	456	526	275
Triple superphosphate	147	222	128	124	138	169	183	180	289	703	215	317
Urea	63	237	116	155	101	159	199	199	264	394	208	239
Metals and minerals												
Aluminum ($/mt)	1,926	1,795	1,593	1,499	1,549	1,558	1,724	2,297	2,252	2,058	1,390	1,802
Copper ($/mt)	4,904	2,690	2,586	2,437	1,813	2,602	3,340	6,007	6,076	5,564	4,300	6,248
Gold ($/toz)[a]	125	750	373	319	279	372	404	540	595	697	812	1,016
Iron ore (cents/dmtu)	34	35	32	24	29	34	59	69	72	112	84	134
Iron ore, spot, cfr China ($/dmtu)	..	..	..	..	..	..	..	..	108	125	69	126
Lead (cents/kg)	105	112	79	52	45	80	89	115	220	167	144	178
Nickel ($/mt)	9,860	8,037	8,614	6,830	8,638	12,551	13,387	21,675	31,778	16,888	12,237	18,084
Silver (cents/toz)[a]	614	2,544	475	431	500	607	666	1,034	1,145	1,200	1,227	1,675
Tin (cents/kg)	1,273	2,068	591	516	544	773	670	785	1,241	1,481	1,133	1,692
Zinc (cents/kg)	102	94	147	86	113	95	125	293	277	150	138	179
MUV G-5 index	29	81	103	120	100	110	110	112	117	125	120	121

Note: bbl = barrel, cu. m = cubic meter, dmtu = dry metric ton unit, kg = kilogram, mmBtu = million British thermal unit, mt = metric ton, toz = troy ounce.
a. Series not included in the nonenergy index.

About the data

Primary commodities—raw or partially processed materials that will be transformed into finished goods—are often developing countries' most important exports, and commodity revenues can affect living standards. Price data are collected from various sources, including international commodity study groups, government agencies, industry trade journals, and Bloomberg and Datastream. Prices are compiled in U.S. dollars or converted to U.S. dollars when quoted in local currencies.

The table is based on frequently updated price reports. Prices are those received by exporters when available, or the prices paid by importers or trade unit values. Annual price series are generally simple averages based on higher frequency data. The constant price series in the table are deflated by the manufactures unit value (MUV) index for the Group of Five (G-5) countries (see below).

Commodity price indexes are calculated as Laspeyres index numbers; the fixed weights are the 2002–04 average export values for low- and middle-income economies (based on 2001 gross national income) rebased to 2000. Data for exports are from the United Nations Statistics Division's Commodity Trade Statistics (Comtrade) database Standard International Trade Classification (SITC) revision 3, the Food and Agriculture Organization's FAOSTAT database, the International Energy Agency database, BP's *Statistical Review of World Energy*, the World Bureau of Metal Statistics, and World Bank staff estimates.

Each index in the table represents a fixed basket of primary commodity exports over time. The nonenergy commodity price index contains 41 price series for 34 nonenergy commodities.

Separate indexes are compiled for energy and steel products, which are not included in the nonenergy commodity price index.

The MUV index is a composite index of prices for manufactured exports from the five major (G-5) industrial economies (France, Germany, Japan, the United Kingdom, and the United States) to low- and middle-income economies, valued in U.S. dollars. The index covers products in groups 5–8 of SITC revision 1. For the MUV G-5 index, unit value indexes in local currency for each country are converted to U.S. dollars using market exchange rates and are combined using weights determined by each country's export share in the base year (1995). The export shares were 8.2 percent for France, 17.4 percent for Germany, 35.6 percent for Japan, 6.6 percent for the United Kingdom, and 32.2 percent for the United States.

Definitions

• **Energy price index** is the composite price index for coal, petroleum, and natural gas, weighted by exports of each commodity from low- and middle-income countries. • **Nonenergy commodity price index** covers the 34 nonenergy primary commodities that make up the agriculture, fertilizer, and metals and minerals indexes. • **Agriculture** includes beverages, food, and agricultural raw materials. • **Beverages** include cocoa, coffee, and tea. • **Food** includes fats and oils, grains, and other food items. Fats and oils include coconut oil, groundnut oil, palm oil, soybeans, soybean oil, and soybean meal. Grains include barley, maize, rice, and wheat. Other food items include bananas, beef, chicken meat, oranges, shrimp, and sugar. • **Agricultural raw materials** include timber and other raw materials. Timber includes tropical hard logs and sawnwood. Other raw materials include cotton, natural rubber, and tobacco. • **Fertilizers** include phosphate, phosphate rock, potassium, and nitrogenous products. • **Metals and minerals** include base metals and iron ore. • **Base metals** include aluminum, copper, lead, nickel, tin, and zinc. • **Steel products price index** is the composite price index for eight steel products based on quotations free on board (f.o.b.) Japan excluding shipments to the United States for all years and to China prior to 2001, weighted by product shares of apparent combined consumption (volume of deliveries) for Germany, Japan, and the United States. • **Commodity prices**—for definitions and sources, see "Commodity price data" (also known as the "Pink Sheet") at the World Bank Prospects for Development website (www.worldbank.org/prospects, click on Products). • **MUV G-5 index** is the manufactures unit value index for G-5 country exports to low- and middle-income economies.

Primary commodity prices soared again in 2010 — 6.6a

World Bank commodity price index, current prices (2000 = 100)

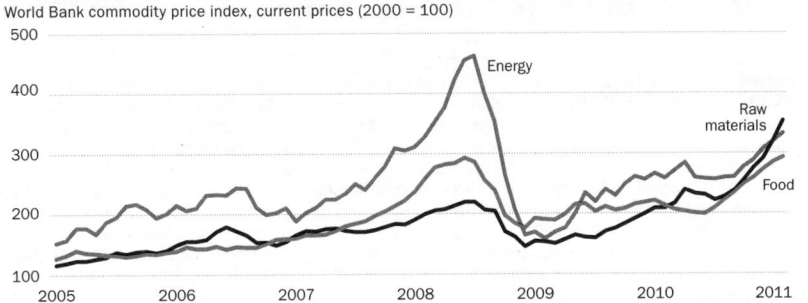

The food commodity price index started rising again in the beginning of 2009, and by the end of February 2011 exceeded the record high in June 2008. The price index for raw materials reached new highs, and the energy price index also rose throughout 2009 and 2010.

Source: World Bank commodity price data.

Data sources

Data on commodity prices and the MUV G-5 index are compiled by the World Bank's Development Prospects Group. Monthly updates of commodity prices are available at www.worldbank.org/prospects and http://data.worldbank.org/data-catalog.

Merchandise exports within bloc

	Year of creation	Year of entry into force of the most recent agreement	Type of most recent agreement[a]	$ millions 1990	1995	2000	2005	2007	2008	2009
High-income and low- and middle-income economies										
APEC[b]	1989		None	901,560	1,688,708	2,261,791	3,318,699	4,192,784	4,606,339	3,738,989
EEA	1994	1994	EIA	1,079,711	1,463,232	1,714,018	3,037,759	4,025,418	4,446,686	3,392,597
EFTA	1960	2002	EIA	782	925	831	1,252	2,196	2,910	2,006
European Union	1957	1958	EIA, CU	1,032,397	1,404,255	1,641,609	2,905,551	3,846,547	4,233,112	3,237,024
NAFTA	1994	1994	FTA	226,273	394,472	676,141	824,359	951,258	1,013,245	768,820
SPARTECA	1981	1981	PTA	5,299	9,135	8,579	15,201	18,617	20,263	17,079
Trans-Pacific SEP	2006	2006	EIA, FTA	1,110	2,614	1,438	2,345	3,290	4,262	3,548
East Asia and Pacific and South Asia										
APTA	1975	1976	PTA	2,429	21,728	37,895	127,340	193,951	233,617	204,745
ASEAN	1967	1992	FTA	27,365	79,544	98,060	165,458	216,727	251,285	198,915
MSG	1993	1994	PTA	5	18	22	51	78	89	78
PICTA	2001	2003	FTA	4	4	8	22	34	38	34
SAARC	1985	2006	FTA	945	2,081	2,894	8,619	12,747	13,177	11,095
Europe, Central Asia, and Middle East										
Agadir Agreement	2004		NNA	156	226	294	635	1,046	1,913	2,075
CEFTA	1992	1994	FTA	..	619	1,187	2,847	6,160	7,543	5,083
CEZ	2003	2004	FTA	..	10,154	13,283	23,469	43,003	47,731	19,094
CIS	1991	1994	FTA	..	31,277	28,422	58,113	98,050	123,052	60,389
EAEC	1997	2000	CU	..	10,919	13,936	24,818	45,714	51,186	21,872
ECO	1985	2003	PTA	1,243	4,746	4,518	12,579	22,064	26,739	18,412
GCC	1981	2003[c]	CU	6,906	6,832	8,029	15,408	24,372	31,514	21,849
PAFTA (GAFTA)	1997	1998	FTA	13,204	12,948	16,188	41,659	61,100	82,267	61,881
UMA	1989	1994[c]	NNA	958	1,109	1,041	1,885	2,695	4,570	3,422
Latin America and the Caribbean										
Andean Community	1969	1988	CU	544	1,788	2,046	4,572	5,926	7,029	5,785
CACM	1961	1961	CU	667	1,594	2,655	4,311	5,637	6,475	5,287
CARICOM	1973	1997	EIA	456	877	1,078	2,235	3,112	3,808	2,716
LAIA (ALADI)	1980	1981	PTA	13,350	35,986	44,253	71,711	110,006	143,283	98,510
MERCOSUR	1991	2005	EIA	4,127	14,199	17,829	21,128	32,421	46,657	32,689
OECS	1981	1981[c]	NNA	29	39	38	68	104	118	104
Sub-Saharan Africa										
CEMAC	1994	1999	CU	139	120	96	201	305	355	300
CEPGL	1976		NNA	7	8	10	20	29	73	64
COMESA	1994	1994	FTA	1,146	1,367	1,443	2,695	4,021	6,676	6,114
EAC	1996	2000	CU	335	628	689	1,075	1,385	1,797	1,572
ECCAS	1983	2004[c]	NNA	160	157	182	255	385	449	378
ECOWAS	1975	1993	PTA	1,532	1,875	2,715	5,497	6,717	9,355	7,312
Indian Ocean Commission	1984	2005[c]	NNA	63	113	106	162	214	217	183
SADC	1992	2000	FTA	1,655	3,615	4,427	7,799	12,051	16,011	11,697
UEMOA	1994	2000	CU	621	560	741	1,390	1,735	2,281	1,927

Note: Regional bloc memberships are as follows: **Agadir Agreement,** the Arab Republic of Egypt, Jordan, Morocco, and Tunisia; **Andean Community,** Bolivia, Colombia, Ecuador, and Peru; **Arab Maghreb Union (UMA),** Algeria, Libyan Arab Republic, Mauritania, Morocco, and Tunisia; **Asia Pacific Economic Cooperation (APEC),** Australia, Brunei Darussalam, Canada, Chile, China, Hong Kong SAR, China, Indonesia, Japan, the Republic of Korea, Malaysia, Mexico, New Zealand, Papua New Guinea, Peru, the Philippines, the Russian Federation, Singapore, Taiwan (China), Thailand, the United States, and Vietnam; **Asia-Pacific Trade Agreement (APTA; formerly Bangkok Agreement),** Bangladesh, China, India, the Republic of Korea, the Lao People's Democratic Republic, and Sri Lanka; **Association of South East Asian Nations (ASEAN),** Brunei Darussalam, Cambodia, Indonesia, the Lao People's Democratic Republic, Malaysia, Myanmar, the Philippines, Singapore, Thailand, and Vietnam; **Caribbean Community and Common Market (CARICOM),** Antigua and Barbuda, the Bahamas, Barbados, Belize, Dominica, Grenada, Guyana, Haiti, Jamaica, Montserrat, St. Kitts and Nevis, St. Lucia, St. Vincent and the Grenadines, Suriname, and Trinidad and Tobago; **Central American Common Market (CACM),** Costa Rica, El Salvador, Guatemala, Honduras, and Nicaragua; **Central European Free Trade Area (CEFTA),** Albania, Bosnia and Herzegovina, Croatia, Kosovo, Macedonia, Moldova, Montenegro, and Serbia; **Common Economic Zone (CEZ),** Belarus, Kazakhstan, and the Russian Federation; **Common Market for Eastern and Southern Africa (COMESA),** Burundi, Comoros, the Democratic Republic of Congo, Djibouti, the Arab Republic of Egypt, Eritrea, Ethiopia, Kenya, Libyan Arab Republic, Madagascar, Malawi, Mauritius, Rwanda, Seychelles, Sudan, Swaziland, Uganda, Zambia, and Zimbabwe; **Commonwealth of Independent States (CIS),** Armenia, Azerbaijan, Belarus, Georgia, Kazakhstan, Kyrgyz Republic, Moldova, the Russian Federation, Tajikistan, Turkmenistan, Ukraine, and Uzbekistan; **East African Community (EAC),** Burundi, Kenya, Rwanda, Tanzania, and Uganda; **Economic and Monetary Community of Central Africa (CEMAC; formerly Central African Customs and Economic Union [UDEAC]),** Cameroon, the Central African Republic, Chad, the Republic of Congo, Equatorial Guinea, and Gabon; **Economic Community of Central African States (ECCAS),** Angola, Burundi, Cameroon, the Central African Republic, Chad, the Democratic Republic of Congo, the Republic of Congo, Equatorial Guinea, Gabon, and São Tomé and Príncipe; **Economic Community of the Great Lakes Countries (CEPGL),** Burundi, the Democratic Republic of Congo, and Rwanda; **Economic Community of West African States (ECOWAS),** Benin, Burkina Faso, Cape Verde, Côte d'Ivoire, the Gambia, Ghana, Guinea, Guinea-Bissau, Liberia, Mali, Niger, Nigeria, Senegal, Sierra Leone, and Togo; **Economic Cooperation Organization (ECO),** Afghanistan, Azerbaijan, the Islamic Republic of Iran, Kazakhstan, the Kyrgyz Republic, Pakistan, Tajikistan, Turkey, Turkmenistan, and

Merchandise exports within bloc

	Year of creation	Year of entry into force of the most recent agreement	Type of most recent agreement[a]	% of total bloc exports						
				1990	1995	2000	2005	2007	2008	2009
High-income and low- and middle-income economies										
APEC[b]	1989		None	68.3	71.7	73.0	70.8	67.3	65.2	66.3
EEA	1994	1994	EIA	68.8	67.9	69.0	73.0	73.3	72.8	71.9
EFTA	1960	2002	EIA	0.8	0.7	0.6	0.5	0.7	0.8	0.7
European Union	1957	1958	EIA, CU	67.3	66.5	67.7	71.6	71.9	71.4	70.4
NAFTA	1994	1994	FTA	41.4	46.2	55.7	55.7	51.3	49.5	48.0
SPARTECA	1981	1981	PTA	10.5	12.9	10.7	11.4	10.5	8.9	9.1
Trans-Pacific SEP	2006	2006	EIA, FTA	1.5	1.7	0.8	0.8	0.8	1.0	1.0
East Asia and Pacific and South Asia										
APTA	1975	1976	PTA	1.6	6.8	8.0	11.0	11.0	11.4	11.6
ASEAN	1967	1992	FTA	18.9	24.4	23.0	25.3	25.2	25.5	24.5
MSG	1993	1994	PTA	0.3	0.4	0.6	0.8	0.8	0.8	0.8
PICTA	2001	2003	FTA	0.3	0.1	0.3	0.4	0.4	0.4	0.4
SAARC	1985	2006	FTA	3.5	4.5	4.6	6.6	6.6	5.9	5.4
Europe, Central Asia, and Middle East										
Agadir Agreement	2004		NNA	1.3	1.4	1.4	1.8	2.0	2.7	3.8
CEFTA	1992	1994	FTA	..	9.0	14.5	16.3	21.2	22.4	20.2
CEZ	2003	2004	FTA	..	11.6	11.0	8.4	10.4	8.8	5.6
CIS	1991	1994	FTA	..	28.4	19.8	17.7	20.1	18.0	14.8
EAEC	1997	2000	CU	..	12.3	11.5	8.9	10.9	9.3	6.3
ECO	1985	2003	PTA	3.2	7.9	5.6	6.9	8.0	6.8	7.2
GCC	1981	2003[c]	CU	8.0	6.8	4.9	4.4	5.0	4.5	5.1
PAFTA (GAFTA)	1997	1998	FTA	10.2	9.8	7.2	9.2	9.4	8.9	10.6
UMA	1989	1994[c]	NNA	2.9	3.8	2.2	1.9	2.0	2.5	3.1
Latin America and the Caribbean										
Andean Community	1969	1988	CU	4.0	8.6	7.7	9.0	7.8	7.5	7.5
CACM	1961	1961	CU	15.3	21.8	19.6	23.2	23.5	24.8	22.3
CARICOM	1973	1997	EIA	8.0	12.0	14.4	12.1	13.1	12.9	13.7
LAIA (ALADI)	1980	1981	PTA	11.6	17.3	13.2	13.6	15.3	16.5	15.5
MERCOSUR	1991	2005	EIA	8.9	20.3	20.0	12.9	14.7	14.7	15.2
OECS	1981	1981[c]	NNA	8.1	12.6	10.0	11.5	12.1	12.0	13.0
Sub-Saharan Africa										
CEMAC	1994	1999	CU	2.3	2.1	1.0	0.9	1.1	0.8	1.2
CEPGL	1976		NNA	0.5	0.5	0.8	1.2	1.4	1.9	2.2
COMESA	1994	1994	FTA	4.7	6.1	4.6	4.6	4.5	5.3	7.2
EAC	1996	2000	CU	17.7	19.5	22.6	18.0	17.8	19.2	18.9
ECCAS	1983	2004[c]	NNA	1.4	1.5	1.0	0.6	0.6	0.4	0.6
ECOWAS	1975	1993	PTA	8.0	9.0	7.6	9.3	7.8	8.5	9.9
Indian Ocean Commission	1984	2005[c]	NNA	3.9	5.9	4.4	4.9	5.8	5.7	5.8
SADC	1992	2000	FTA	6.6	10.2	9.5	9.3	10.2	10.3	11.0
UEMOA	1994	2000	CU	13.0	10.3	13.1	13.4	14.9	15.9	13.2

Uzbekistan; **Eurasian Economic Community (EAEC)**, Belarus, Kazakhstan, Kyrgyz Republic, the Russian Federation, Tajikistan, and Uzbekistan; **European Economic Area (EEA)**, European Union plus Iceland, Liechtenstein, and Norway; **European Free Trade Association (EFTA)**, Iceland, Liechtenstein, Norway, and Switzerland; **European Union (EU; formerly European Economic Community and European Community)**, Austria, Belgium, Bulgaria, Cyprus, Czech Republic, Denmark, Estonia, Finland, France, Germany, Greece, Hungary, Ireland, Italy, Latvia, Lithuania, Luxembourg, Malta, the Netherlands, Poland, Portugal, Romania, Slovak Republic, Slovenia, Spain, Sweden, and the United Kingdom; **Gulf Cooperation Council (GCC)**, Bahrain, Kuwait, Oman, Qatar, Saudi Arabia, and the United Arab Emirates; **Indian Ocean Commission**, Comoros, Madagascar, Mauritius, Réunion, and Seychelles; **Latin American Integration Association (LAIA; formerly Latin American Free Trade Area)**, Argentina, Bolivia, Brazil, Chile, Colombia, Cuba, Ecuador, Mexico, Paraguay, Peru, Uruguay, and Bolivarian Republic of Venezuela; **Melanesian Spearhead Group (MSG)**, Fiji, Papua New Guinea, Solomon Islands, and Vanuatu; **North American Free Trade Agreement (NAFTA)**, Canada, Mexico, and the United States; **Organization of Eastern Caribbean States (OECS)**, Anguilla, Antigua and Barbuda, British Virgin Islands, Dominica, Grenada, Montserrat, St. Kitts and Nevis, St. Lucia, and St. Vincent and the Grenadines; **Pacific Island Countries Trade Agreement (PICTA)**, Cook Islands, Kiribati, Nauru, Niue, Papua New Guinea, Samoa, Solomon Islands, Tonga, Tuvalu, and Vanuatu; **Pan-Arab Free Trade Area (PAFTA; also known as Greater Arab Trade Area [GAFTA])**, Bahrain, Egypt, Iraq, Jordan, Kuwait, Lebanon, Libya, Morocco, Oman, Qatar, Saudi Arabia, Sudan, Syrian Arab Republic, Tunisia, the United Arab Emirates, and Yemen; **South Asian Association for Regional Cooperation (SAARC)**, Afghanistan, Bangladesh, Bhutan, India, Maldives, Nepal, Pakistan, and Sri Lanka; **South Pacific Regional Trade and Economic Cooperation Agreement (SPARTECA)**, Australia, Cook Islands, Fiji, Kiribati, Marshall Islands, Federated States of Micronesia, Nauru, New Zealand, Niue, Papua New Guinea, Solomon Islands, Tonga, Tuvalu, Vanuatu, and Western Samoa; **Southern African Development Community (SADC)**, Angola, Botswana, the Democratic Republic of Congo, Lesotho, Madagascar, Malawi, Mauritius, Mozambique, Namibia, Seychelles, South Africa, Swaziland, Tanzania, Zambia, and Zimbabwe; **Southern Common Market (MERCOSUR)**, Argentina, Brazil, Paraguay, Uruguay, and Bolivarian Republic of Venezuela; **Trans-Pacific Strategic Economic Partnership (Trans-Pacific SEP)**, Brunei Darussalam, Chile, New Zealand, and Singapore; **West African Economic and Monetary Union (WAEMU or UEMOA)**, Benin, Burkina Faso, Côte d'Ivoire, Guinea-Bissau, Mali, Niger, Senegal, and Togo.

Merchandise exports by bloc

	Year of creation	Year of entry into force of the most recent agreement	Type of most recent agreement[a]	% of world exports						
				1990	1995	2000	2005	2007	2008	2009
High-income and low-										
and middle-income economies										
APEC[b]	1989		None	39.0	46.4	48.5	45.1	44.8	44.1	45.7
EEA	1994	1994	EIA	46.4	42.4	38.9	40.1	39.5	38.1	38.3
EFTA	1960	2002	EIA	2.9	2.4	2.2	2.3	2.3	2.3	2.4
European Union	1957	1958	EIA, CU	45.3	41.5	38.0	39.1	38.5	37.0	37.3
NAFTA	1994	1994	FTA	16.2	16.8	19.0	14.3	13.4	12.8	13.0
SPARTECA	1981	1981	PTA	1.5	1.4	1.3	1.3	1.3	1.4	1.5
Trans-Pacific SEP	2006	2006	EIA, FTA	2.2	3.0	2.7	2.9	2.9	2.8	2.9
East Asia and Pacific and South Asia										
APTA	1975	1976	PTA	4.5	6.3	7.5	11.2	12.7	12.8	14.3
ASEAN	1967	1992	FTA	4.3	6.4	6.7	6.3	6.2	6.1	6.6
MSG	1993	1994	PTA	0.1	0.1	0.1	0.1	0.1	0.1	0.1
PICTA	2001	2003	FTA	0.0	0.1	0.0	0.1	0.1	0.1	0.1
SAARC	1985	2006	FTA	0.8	0.9	1.0	1.3	1.4	1.4	1.7
Europe, Central Asia, and Middle East										
Agadir Agreement	2004		NNA	0.3	0.3	0.3	0.3	0.4	0.4	0.4
CEFTA	1992	1994	FTA	..	0.1	0.1	0.2	0.2	0.2	0.2
CEZ	2003	2004	FTA	..	1.7	1.9	2.7	3.0	3.4	2.8
CIS	1991	1994	FTA	..	2.2	2.2	3.2	3.5	4.3	3.3
EAEC	1997	2000	CU	..	1.7	1.9	2.7	3.0	3.4	2.8
ECO	1985	2003	PTA	1.1	1.2	1.3	1.8	2.0	2.5	2.1
GCC	1981	2003[c]	CU	2.6	2.0	2.6	3.3	3.5	4.3	3.5
PAFTA (GAFTA)	1997	1998	FTA	3.8	2.6	3.5	4.4	4.7	5.8	4.7
UMA	1989	1994[c]	NNA	1.0	0.6	0.8	0.9	1.0	1.1	0.9
Latin America and the Caribbean										
Andean Community	1969	1988	CU	0.4	0.4	0.4	0.5	0.5	0.6	0.6
CACM	1961	1961	CU	0.1	0.1	0.2	0.2	0.2	0.2	0.2
CARICOM	1973	1997	EIA	0.2	0.1	0.1	0.2	0.2	0.2	0.2
LAIA (ALADI)	1980	1981	PTA	3.4	4.1	5.3	5.1	5.2	5.4	5.2
MERCOSUR	1991	2005	EIA	1.4	1.4	1.4	1.6	1.6	2.0	1.7
OECS	1981	1981[c]	NNA	0.0	0.0	0.0	0.0	0.0	0.0	0.0
Sub-Saharan Africa										
CEMAC	1994	1999	CU	0.2	0.1	0.1	0.2	0.2	0.3	0.2
CEPGL	1976		NNA	0.0	0.0	0.0	0.0	0.0	0.0	0.0
COMESA	1994	1994	FTA	0.7	0.4	0.5	0.6	0.6	0.8	0.7
EAC	1996	2000	CU	0.1	0.1	0.0	0.1	0.1	0.1	0.1
ECCAS	1983	2004[c]	NNA	0.3	0.2	0.3	0.4	0.5	0.7	0.5
ECOWAS	1975	1993	PTA	0.6	0.4	0.6	0.6	0.6	0.7	0.6
Indian Ocean Commission	1984	2005[c]	NNA	0.0	0.0	0.0	0.0	0.0	0.0	0.0
SADC	1992	2000	FTA	0.7	0.7	0.7	0.8	0.9	1.0	0.9
UEMOA	1994	2000	CU	0.1	0.1	0.1	0.1	0.1	0.1	0.1

a. CU is customs union; EIA is economic integration agreement; FTA is free trade agreement; PTA is preferential trade agreement; and NNA is not notified agreement, which refers to preferential trade arrangements established among member countries that are not notified to the World Trade Organization (these agreements may be functionally equivalent to any of the other agreements). b. No preferential trade agreement. c. Years of the most recent agreement are collected from the official website of the trade bloc.

About the data

Trade blocs are groups of countries that have established preferential arrangements governing trade between members. Although in some cases the preferences—such as lower tariff duties or exemptions from quantitative restrictions—may be no greater than those available to other trading partners, such arrangements are intended to encourage exports by bloc members to one another—sometimes called intratrade.

Most countries are members of a regional trade bloc, and more than a third of the world's trade takes place within such arrangements. While trade blocs vary in structure, they all have the same objective: to reduce trade barriers between member countries. But effective integration requires more than reducing tariffs and quotas. Economic gains from competition and scale may not be achieved unless other barriers that divide markets and impede the free flow of goods, services, and investments are lifted. For example, many regional trade blocs retain contingent protections on intrabloc trade, including antidumping, countervailing duties, and "emergency protection" to address balance of payments problems or protect an industry from import surges. Other barriers include differing product standards, discrimination in public procurement, and cumbersome border formalities.

Membership in a regional trade bloc may reduce the frictional costs of trade, increase the credibility of reform initiatives, and strengthen security among partners. But making it work effectively is challenging. All economic sectors may be affected, and some may expand while others contract, so it is important to weigh the potential costs and benefits of membership.

The table shows the value of merchandise intratrade (service exports are excluded) for important regional trade blocs and the size of intratrade relative to each bloc's exports of goods and the share of the bloc's exports in world exports. Although the Asia Pacific Economic Cooperation (APEC) has no preferential arrangements, it is included because of the volume of trade between its members.

The data on country exports are from the International Monetary Fund's (IMF) Direction of Trade database and should be broadly consistent with those from sources such as the United Nations Statistics Division's Commodity Trade (Comtrade) database. All high-income economies and major developing economies report trade to the IMF on a timely basis, covering about 85 percent of trade for recent years. Trade by less timely reporters and by countries that do not report is estimated using reports of trading partner countries. Therefore, data on trade between developing and high-income economies shown in the table should be generally complete. But trade flows between many developing countries—particularly those in Sub-Saharan Africa—are not well recorded, and the value of trade among developing countries may be understated.

Membership in the trade blocs shown is based on the most recent information available (see Data sources). Other types of preferential trade agreements may have entered into force earlier than those shown in the table and may still be effective. Unless otherwise indicated in the footnotes, information on the type of agreement and date of enforcement are based on the World Trade Organization's (WTO) list of regional trade agreements. Information on trade agreements not notified to the WTO was collected from the Global Preferential Trade Agreements database (box 6.7a) and from official websites of the trade blocs.

Although bloc exports have been calculated back to 1990 on the basis of current membership, several blocs came into existence after that and membership may have changed over time. For this reason, and because systems of preferences also change over time, intratrade in earlier years may not have been affected by the same preferences as in recent years. In addition, some countries belong to more than one trade bloc, so shares of world exports exceed 100 percent. Exports include all commodity trade, which may include items not specified in trade bloc agreements. Differences from previously published estimates may be due to changes in membership or revisions in underlying data.

Definitions

• **Merchandise exports within bloc** are the sum of merchandise exports by members of a trade bloc to other members of the bloc. They are shown both in U.S. dollars and as a percentage of total merchandise exports by the bloc. • **Merchandise exports by bloc** as a share of world exports are the bloc's total merchandise exports (within the bloc and to the rest of the world) as a share of total merchandise exports by all economies in the world. • **Type of most recent agreement** includes customs union, under which members substantially eliminate all tariff and nontariff barriers among themselves and establish a common external tariff for nonmembers; economic integration agreement, which liberalizes trade in services among members and covers a substantial number of sectors, affects a sufficient volume of trade, includes substantial modes of supply, and is nondiscriminatory (in the sense that similarly situated service suppliers are treated the same); free trade agreement, under which members substantially eliminate all tariff and nontariff barriers but set tariffs on imports from nonmembers; preferential trade agreement, which is an agreement notified to the WTO that is not a free trade agreement, a customs union, or an economic integration agreement; and not notified agreement, which is a preferential trade arrangement established among member countries that is not notified to the World Trade Organization (the agreement may be functionally equivalent to any of the other agreements).

Global Preferential Trade Agreements Database | **6.7a**

The Global Preferential Trade Agreement Database (GPTAD) provides information on preferential trade agreements around the world, including those not notified to the World Trade Organization (WTO). It is designed to help trade policymakers, scholars, and business operators better understand and navigate the world of preferential trade agreements. The GPTAD is updated regularly and currently comprises more than 330 preferential trade agreements in their original language, which have been indexed by WTO criteria and can be downloaded as PDFs. Users can search by provision or keyword, compare provisions across multiple agreements, and sort agreements by membership, date of signature, in-force status, and other key criteria. The database was developed jointly by the World Bank and the Center for International Business at the Tuck School of Business at Dartmouth College. It is supported by the Multidonor Trust Fund for Trade and Development with financing from the governments of Finland, Norway, Sweden, and the United Kingdom. The GPTAD is integrated with the World Integrated Trade Solution database and is part of the World Bank's Open Data initiative (http://wits.worldbank.org/gptad/).

Data sources

Data on merchandise trade flows are published in the IMF's *Direction of Trade Statistics Yearbook* and *Direction of Trade Statistics Quarterly;* the data in the table were calculated using the IMF's Direction of Trade database. Data on trade bloc membership are from the World Bank Policy Research Report *Trade Blocs* (2000), UNCTAD's *Trade and Development Report 2007,* WTO's Regional Trade Agreements Information System, and the World Bank and the Center for International Business at the Tuck School of Business at Dartmouth College's Global Preferential Trade Agreements Database.

6.8 Tariff barriers

	Most recent year	Binding coverage	Simple mean bound rate	All products % Simple mean tariff	Weighted mean tariff	Share of tariff lines with international peaks	Share of tariff lines with specific rates	Primary products % Simple mean tariff	Weighted mean tariff	Manufactured products % Simple mean tariff	Weighted mean tariff
Afghanistan	2008	..	..	6.2	6.4	4.4	0.0	7.0	6.7	6.1	6.3
Albania	2009	100.0	7.1	5.7	5.1	0.0	0.0	6.8	5.4	5.5	4.9
Algeria	2009	..	..	14.2	8.6	53.2	0.0	14.5	7.8	14.0	8.8
Angola	2009	100.0	59.2	7.4	7.4	23.4	0.0	11.6	13.9	6.7	5.9
Antigua and Barbuda	2009	97.9	58.7	13.8	14.6	49.4	0.0	17.2	14.8	13.0	14.5
Argentina	2010	100.0	31.9	11.4	6.2	24.3	0.0	7.5	1.6	11.8	7.0
Armenia	2008	100.0	8.5	3.7	2.3	0.0	0.3	5.6	2.2	3.5	2.4
Australia	2010	97.0	10.0	2.9	1.9	0.0	0.0	1.3	0.4	3.1	2.5
Azerbaijan	2009	..	..	8.3	3.9	46.5	0.0	9.5	3.8	8.0	3.9
Bahamas, The	2006	..	..	28.5	23.9	77.4	0.0	24.4	15.1	29.4	29.7
Bahrain	2009	73.6	34.8	4.3	3.6	0.2	0.0	6.7	6.9	4.0	3.1
Bangladesh	2008	15.9	169.9	13.9	13.0	38.0	0.0	16.3	8.8	13.5	14.0
Barbados	2007	97.8	78.1	15.1	14.8	44.9	0.6	26.3	21.9	13.4	12.2
Belarus	2009	..	..	8.0	2.3	27.2	0.0	6.8	0.6	8.2	4.3
Belize	2009	97.9	58.4	11.2	5.9	30.1	0.0	17.2	4.0	10.1	9.3
Benin	2010	39.5	28.7	13.3	15.4	50.2	0.0	15.5	12.4	12.9	17.0
Bermuda	2009	..	..	18.1	27.8	66.7	0.0	10.0	16.1	19.5	28.8
Bhutan	2007	..	..	18.2	17.8	50.7	0.0	43.5	44.9	15.6	16.0
Bolivia	2010	100.0	40.0	9.6	5.4	11.9	0.0	8.4	5.8	9.6	5.2
Bosnia and Herzegovina	2009	..	..	3.7	2.0	5.7	0.0	1.6	1.3	3.9	2.5
Botswana	2010	96.1	19.0	8.8	5.2	20.2	0.0	6.1	0.5	9.0	6.6
Brazil	2010	100.0	31.4	13.4	7.6	26.4	0.0	8.1	1.5	13.9	9.6
Brunei Darussalam	2010	95.3	24.1	3.8	4.1	20.8	0.0	0.2	0.1	4.4	5.0
Burkina Faso	2010	39.4	42.5	12.4	8.8	44.5	0.0	11.4	8.1	12.5	9.2
Burundi	2010	22.3	67.8	9.8	5.5	29.8	0.0	15.4	9.4	9.1	4.5
Cambodia	2008	100.0	19.1	12.4	9.9	19.7	0.0	13.8	11.8	12.1	9.6
Cameroon	2009	13.7	79.9	18.4	15.0	52.5	0.0	20.5	12.9	18.1	16.0
Canada	2010	99.7	5.2	3.3	1.0	7.2	0.0	2.1	0.3	3.5	1.3
Cape Verde	2010	100.0	15.8	14.7	11.6	44.3	0.0	16.2	12.2	14.3	10.9
Central African Republic	2007	62.5	36.0	17.5	13.6	47.4	0.0	18.9	13.8	17.3	13.3
Chad	2009	13.9	79.9	17.6	14.7	47.4	0.0	22.5	17.2	16.7	13.8
Chile	2010	100.0	25.1	4.9	4.0	0.0	0.0	4.4	2.7	4.9	4.8
China[†]	2009	100.0	10.0	8.2	4.2	13.4	0.0	8.1	1.7	8.1	5.5
Hong Kong SAR, China	2010	45.8	0.0	0.0	0.0	0.0	0.0	0.0	0.0	0.0	0.0
Macao SAR, China	2010	28.2	0.0	0.0	0.0	0.0	0.0	0.0	0.0	0.0	0.0
Colombia	2010	100.0	43.1	11.2	8.9	19.8	0.0	10.9	8.8	11.2	8.8
Comoros	2008	..	..	7.8	7.8	42.8	0.0	4.2	3.8	8.7	10.3
Congo, Dem. Rep.	2009	100.0	96.2	12.9	11.0	42.5	0.0	14.2	10.8	12.6	11.1
Congo, Rep.	2007	16.5	27.4	18.6	14.7	52.6	0.0	21.9	18.6	18.1	14.1
Costa Rica	2009	100.0	43.2	4.8	2.4	0.7	0.0	6.3	3.3	4.6	2.0
Côte d'Ivoire	2010	33.8	11.2	13.1	7.3	47.9	0.0	15.1	5.4	12.8	9.3
Croatia	2010	100.0	6.0	2.4	1.2	4.1	0.0	4.5	1.9	2.1	0.9
Cuba	2010	31.7	21.4	10.5	8.7	11.6	0.0	11.1	6.2	10.4	9.8
Djibouti	2009	100.0	41.2	20.6	15.2	69.4	0.0	15.9	8.7	21.4	18.6
Dominica	2007	94.7	58.7	11.9	7.9	43.3	0.0	19.2	5.7	10.5	9.3
Dominican Republic	2008	100.0	34.9	9.0	4.9	28.8	0.0	11.6	4.5	8.6	5.2
Ecuador	2010	100.0	21.7	9.3	6.0	20.2	0.0	9.0	4.3	9.3	6.7
Egypt, Arab Rep.	2009	99.3	37.3	12.6	8.0	18.3	0.0	37.5	6.2	9.3	9.1
El Salvador	2010	100.0	36.9	5.1	5.5	1.9	0.0	8.4	7.4	4.7	4.2
Equatorial Guinea	2007	..	..	18.3	15.6	52.3	0.0	21.5	21.4	17.7	14.3
Eritrea	2006	..	..	9.6	5.4	22.4	0.0	9.2	3.5	9.5	7.1
Ethiopia	2009	..	..	18.1	9.7	55.4	0.0	19.2	5.6	17.9	12.8
European Union	2010	100.0	4.2	1.8	1.4	1.1	0.0	2.4	0.6	1.6	1.9
Fiji	2009	51.4	40.1	11.9	10.1	20.9	0.0	13.7	7.7	11.6	12.8
French Polynesia	2009	..	..	6.8	4.2	28.1	0.0	4.1	2.7	7.3	5.2
Gabon	2009	100.0	21.4	18.7	14.5	53.1	0.0	21.2	15.1	18.3	14.3
Gambia, The	2009	13.7	101.8	18.7	14.8	91.2	0.0	16.9	12.8	19.1	16.9
Georgia	2009	100.0	7.2	0.5	0.4	0.0	0.0	4.0	1.0	0.1	0.0
Ghana	2009	14.4	92.5	13.0	8.6	40.5	0.0	16.6	8.9	12.4	8.5
[†]Data for Taiwan, China	2010	100.0	6.0	5.3	2.5	6.0	0.0	8.4	2.0	4.7	2.7

	Most recent year	Binding coverage	Simple mean bound rate	All products %				Primary products %		Manufactured products %	
				Simple mean tariff	Weighted mean tariff	Share of tariff lines with international peaks	Share of tariff lines with specific rates	Simple mean tariff	Weighted mean tariff	Simple mean tariff	Weighted mean tariff
Grenada	2008	100.0	56.8	10.6	8.8	43.3	0.0	14.1	9.9	10.0	8.4
Guatemala	2009	100.0	42.3	4.4	2.7	18.1	0.0	4.9	2.1	4.3	3.1
Guinea	2009	38.6	20.3	13.5	11.9	56.1	0.0	15.6	13.9	13.2	10.2
Guinea-Bissau	2010	97.6	48.6	13.3	9.9	51.8	0.0	14.6	10.0	12.9	9.7
Guyana	2008	100.0	56.8	10.7	6.8	41.3	0.0	17.7	5.9	9.7	7.3
Haiti	2009	89.8	17.6	3.0	5.1	5.1	0.0	5.8	4.1	2.5	5.9
Honduras	2009	100.0	32.5	6.4	6.5	0.5	0.0	9.9	8.1	5.9	5.4
Iceland	2009	95.0	13.5	1.9	0.9	5.7	0.0	2.4	1.1	1.8	0.8
India	2009	74.5	50.2	10.2	7.9	6.6	0.0	20.0	7.3	8.7	8.0
Indonesia	2009	96.6	37.5	5.2	3.1	11.4	0.0	5.6	2.0	5.2	3.5
Iran, Islamic Rep.	2008	..	..	24.8	19.6	56.5	0.0	21.7	12.5	24.8	21.1
Iraq		..	..	..	..	..	..	..	..	..	..
Israel	2009	75.2	22.0	5.5	3.2	1.1	0.0	5.5	2.2	5.4	3.6
Jamaica	2007	100.0	49.7	9.2	9.0	36.1	0.0	16.1	8.6	8.3	9.3
Japan	2010	99.7	3.0	2.6	1.6	8.6	0.0	5.1	1.6	2.1	1.6
Jordan	2009	100.0	16.3	9.7	5.2	29.5	0.0	14.2	3.9	8.9	5.9
Kazakhstan	2008	..	..	4.3	2.7	8.8	11.5	7.3	1.3	4.0	3.1
Kenya	2010	15.2	95.3	12.1	9.2	36.6	0.0	16.0	12.6	11.7	6.6
Korea, Dem. Rep.		..	..	..	..	..	..	..	..	..	..
Korea, Rep.	2010	95.1	16.1	10.3	8.7	7.0	0.0	26.3	12.7	7.3	5.0
Kosovo		..	..	..	..	..	..	..	..	..	..
Kuwait	2009	99.9	100.0	4.1	4.2	0.0	0.0	3.2	3.1	4.2	4.4
Kyrgyz Republic	2009	99.9	7.5	3.6	8.4	0.9	0.0	4.4	1.3	3.5	9.4
Lao PDR	2008	..	..	9.3	13.2	20.4	0.0	16.0	14.2	8.4	12.6
Lebanon	2007	..	..	5.6	4.8	11.6	0.0	8.2	5.0	5.2	5.0
Lesotho	2010	100.0	78.9	9.5	10.5	21.6	0.0	9.2	1.6	9.5	10.9
Liberia		..	..	..	..	..	..	..	..	..	..
Libya	2006	..	..	0.0	0.0	0.0	0.0	0.0	0.0	0.0	0.0
Macedonia, FYR	2009	100.0	6.9	4.3	3.2	14.5	0.0	7.6	6.0	3.9	2.4
Madagascar	2008	30.5	27.3	12.1	8.3	41.1	0.0	13.9	4.2	11.9	10.4
Malawi	2009	32.0	75.9	13.0	7.0	47.5	0.0	14.8	8.6	12.7	6.5
Malaysia	2009	83.9	14.6	5.3	3.1	16.3	0.0	2.4	2.1	5.8	3.6
Maldives	2009	97.0	37.2	21.7	20.6	88.1	0.0	17.5	18.4	22.8	22.6
Mali	2010	40.5	28.9	12.8	8.4	47.9	0.0	12.8	7.9	12.8	8.7
Mauritania	2007	39.4	19.6	12.6	10.1	49.0	0.0	11.1	9.2	12.8	11.0
Mauritius	2009	17.7	98.3	2.0	1.0	10.4	0.0	1.2	0.3	2.1	1.6
Mayotte	2009	..	..	5.3	1.8	2.6	0.0	3.8	1.3	5.5	2.1
Mexico	2010	100.0	35.1	7.8	6.1	6.4	0.0	10.7	11.5	7.4	4.6
Moldova	2008	99.9	6.7	4.2	3.0	7.7	3.4	6.6	3.6	3.8	2.7
Mongolia	2009	100.0	17.5	4.9	5.1	0.1	0.0	5.2	5.4	4.9	4.9
Montenegro	2009	..	..	2.2	3.2	5.4	0.0	6.2	5.2	1.6	2.4
Morocco	2009	100.0	41.3	9.1	7.1	23.6	0.0	18.0	8.9	8.2	5.7
Mozambique	2009	14.0	97.4	7.7	4.5	25.4	0.0	8.2	4.4	7.5	4.3
Myanmar	2008	17.6	83.8	4.0	3.2	4.1	0.0	5.1	2.7	3.9	3.4
Namibia	2010	96.1	19.4	6.3	1.8	16.7	0.0	4.1	2.1	6.7	1.6
Nepal	2009	99.4	26.2	12.8	14.3	50.4	0.0	15.6	11.0	12.5	16.5
New Zealand	2010	100.0	10.0	2.5	1.6	0.0	0.0	1.4	0.4	2.6	2.1
Nicaragua	2009	100.0	41.7	4.4	2.6	17.1	0.0	5.9	3.0	4.2	2.2
Niger	2010	96.6	44.9	13.0	9.1	48.9	0.0	14.0	10.7	12.8	7.6
Nigeria	2010	19.5	119.4	10.9	10.6	34.9	0.0	11.8	9.1	10.7	10.8
Norway	2009	100.0	3.0	0.4	0.3	0.5	0.0	1.8	1.0	0.3	0.2
Oman	2009	100.0	13.9	3.6	3.2	0.2	0.0	4.4	3.3	3.5	3.2
Pakistan	2009	98.6	60.0	14.8	9.5	45.3	0.0	14.2	6.4	14.7	12.1
Palau	2006	..	..	2.6	2.2	0.5	0.0	0.5	0.6	3.1	3.2
Panama	2009	99.9	23.5	7.6	7.6	2.8	0.0	11.5	8.4	7.1	7.2
Papua New Guinea	2008	100.0	31.5	4.8	2.6	24.4	0.7	15.2	3.3	3.4	2.2
Paraguay	2010	100.0	33.5	8.1	3.7	18.3	0.0	5.8	0.8	8.2	4.8
Peru	2010	100.0	30.1	4.8	2.5	10.0	0.0	3.8	1.3	4.9	3.0
Philippines	2010	67.2	25.8	5.3	4.8	5.4	0.0	6.8	5.1	5.0	4.6
Puerto Rico		..	..	..	..	..	..	..	..	..	..

	Most recent year	Binding coverage	Simple mean bound rate	All products %		Share of tariff lines with international peaks	Share of tariff lines with specific rates	Primary products %		Manufactured products %	
				Simple mean tariff	Weighted mean tariff			Simple mean tariff	Weighted mean tariff	Simple mean tariff	Weighted mean tariff
Qatar	2009	100.0	16.0	4.2	3.8	0.2	0.0	5.0	4.0	4.1	3.8
Russian Federation	2009	..	..	8.1	5.9	24.6	0.0	7.7	4.4	8.2	6.2
Rwanda	2010	100.0	89.3	9.9	6.0	31.4	0.0	11.5	6.4	9.7	5.9
Saudi Arabia	2009	100.0	10.8	4.0	3.9	0.0	0.0	3.3	2.8	4.1	4.2
Senegal	2010	100.0	30.0	13.4	8.9	50.5	0.0	14.1	7.7	13.2	10.2
Serbia	2005[a]	..	..	8.1	6.0	17.8	0.0	10.9	4.5	7.8	6.8
Seychelles	2007	..	..	6.5	28.3	12.8	0.0	14.0	50.5	4.8	6.4
Sierra Leone	2004	100.0	47.4	..	..	..	..	..	..	..	..
Singapore	2010	69.6	7.0	0.0	0.0	0.0	0.0	0.0	0.0	0.0	0.0
Solomon Islands	2008	100.0	78.7	9.9	17.3	2.6	0.8	14.8	23.3	9.2	8.8
Somalia		..	..	..	..	..	..	..	..	..	..
South Africa	2010	96.1	19.4	7.6	4.4	17.9	0.0	5.4	1.9	7.8	5.6
Sri Lanka	2009	38.1	30.1	10.1	6.4	42.7	0.0	15.3	8.4	9.4	5.2
St. Kitts and Nevis	2009	97.9	75.9	14.3	13.7	43.1	0.0	16.5	13.5	13.7	13.7
St. Lucia	2007	99.6	61.9	9.6	9.0	39.9	0.0	12.7	4.9	9.1	12.2
St. Vincent & Grenadines	2007	99.7	62.5	11.3	8.4	44.4	0.2	15.1	7.8	10.5	8.6
Sudan	2009	..	..	13.4	7.9	25.4	0.0	15.9	7.7	13.0	7.9
Suriname	2010	27.6	18.1	11.6	11.9	36.2	0.0	18.3	15.0	10.4	10.4
Swaziland	2010	96.1	19.4	10.9	10.2	26.2	0.0	9.7	1.3	11.1	15.9
Switzerland	2010	99.8	0.0	0.0	0.0	0.0	0.0	0.0	0.0	0.0	0.0
Syrian Arab Republic	2010	..	..	6.7	6.1	27.6	0.0	6.5	6.1	6.5	5.7
Tajikistan	2006	..	..	4.9	3.8	0.1	0.7	5.4	2.1	4.9	5.3
Tanzania	2010	13.8	120.0	12.9	8.2	39.9	0.0	17.5	8.7	12.4	8.0
Thailand	2009	74.7	26.1	10.8	4.9	19.3	0.0	14.0	2.7	10.2	5.9
Timor-Leste		..	..	..	..	..	..	..	..	..	..
Togo	2010	14.3	80.0	12.8	14.2	47.3	0.0	14.4	12.4	12.6	14.9
Tonga	2009	100.0	17.6	10.8	7.3	64.7	0.0	12.1	5.5	10.5	9.0
Trinidad and Tobago	2008	100.0	55.8	8.7	10.0	43.6	0.4	16.6	3.1	7.6	17.2
Tunisia	2008	58.3	58.0	21.9	16.0	57.8	0.0	26.8	12.0	21.2	17.9
Turkey	2009	50.3	29.2	2.4	2.3	4.6	0.0	13.8	4.3	1.2	1.4
Turkmenistan	2002	..	..	5.4	2.9	14.8	2.8	14.7	12.6	3.8	1.1
Uganda	2010	16.1	73.5	12.1	8.2	37.5	0.0	15.7	8.8	11.6	7.9
Ukraine	2010	100.0	5.8	4.5	2.8	1.1	0.0	5.9	2.5	4.3	3.0
United Arab Emirates	2009	100.0	14.8	4.3	3.7	0.2	0.0	4.5	2.7	4.2	4.2
United States	2010	100.0	3.7	2.9	1.8	3.4	0.0	2.6	1.2	3.0	2.0
Uruguay	2010	100.0	31.6	9.6	3.6	29.3	0.0	5.6	1.1	9.9	5.2
Uzbekistan	2009	..	..	11.8	6.9	20.1	0.0	12.6	3.9	11.7	7.3
Vanuatu	2009			16.8	15.0	65.0	0.0	19.5	16.9	16.1	14.2
Venezuela, RB	2010	100.0	36.5	13.1	10.6	21.9	0.0	12.2	10.0	13.1	10.7
Vietnam	2008	100.0	11.5	8.0	5.2	19.8	0.0	10.7	4.1	7.4	5.7
West Bank and Gaza		..	..	..	..	..	..	..	..	..	..
Yemen, Rep.	2009	..	..	5.5	4.2	1.4	0.0	7.1	3.8	5.2	4.6
Zambia	2009	17.1	106.9	10.8	3.8	51.2	0.0	9.2	3.1	10.9	4.1
Zimbabwe	2007[b]	22.2	91.4	16.7	17.3	38.8	0.0	17.4	20.4	16.1	14.7
World		**77.8 w**	**27.3 w**	**6.2 w**	**2.5 w**	**10.8 w**	**0.0 w**	**6.6 w**	**2.4 w**	**6.1 w**	**2.5 w**
Low income		42.2	57.7	12.1	10.0	40.6	0.0	14.4	9.4	11.8	10.2
Middle income		86.6	30.3	8.9	6.3	16.0	0.0	8.6	5.4	8.9	6.5
Lower middle income		84.7	31.8	8.4	5.8	15.4	0.0	9.7	4.8	8.2	6.2
Upper middle income		88.3	29.0	9.2	6.4	16.3	0.0	7.9	5.6	9.3	6.6
Low & middle income		73.9	35.5	9.5	6.4	18.5	0.0	9.8	5.7	9.4	6.6
East Asia & Pacific		67.2	25.8	5.3	4.8	5.4	0.0	6.8	5.1	5.0	4.6
Europe & Central Asia		100.0	5.8	4.5	2.8	1.1	0.0	5.9	2.5	4.3	3.0
Latin America & Carib.		90.0	32.5	9.2	6.6	15.7	0.0	8.6	6.2	9.2	6.7
Middle East & North Africa		99.9	30.4	6.7	6.1	27.6	0.0	6.5	6.1	6.5	5.7
South Asia		81.5	41.6	13.0	8.2	37.4	0.0	17.1	7.3	12.3	8.4
Sub-Saharan Africa		61.7	41.8	11.1	7.5	33.6	0.0	12.1	5.9	10.9	8.1
High income		87.9	7.9	2.7	1.8	3.5	0.0	4.2	1.9	2.5	1.8
OECD		99.0	10.7	3.6	2.2	4.0	0.0	5.3	2.3	3.3	2.1
Non-OECD		73.1	9.1	1.8	0.6	3.2	0.0	2.5	0.7	1.6	0.6

a. Includes Montenegro. b. Rates are most favored nation rates.

About the data

Poor people in developing countries work primarily in agriculture and labor–intensive manufactures, sectors that confront the greatest trade barriers. Removing barriers to merchandise trade could increase growth in these countries—even more if trade in services.

In general, tariffs in high-income countries on imports from developing countries, though low, are twice those collected from other high-income countries. But protection is also an issue for developing countries, which maintain high tariffs on agricultural commodities, labor-intensive manufactures, and other products and services.

Countries use a combination of tariff and nontariff measures to regulate imports. The most common form of tariff is an ad valorem duty, based on the value of the import, but tariffs may also be levied on a specific, or per unit, basis or may combine ad valorem and specific rates. Tariffs may be used to raise fiscal revenues or to protect domestic industries from foreign competition—or both. Nontariff barriers, which limit the quantity of imports of a particular good, include quotas, prohibitions, licensing schemes, export restraint arrangements, and health and quarantine measures. Because of the difficulty of combining nontariff barriers into an aggregate indicator, they are not included in the table.

Unless specified as most favored nation rates, the tariff rates used in calculating the indicators in the table are effectively applied rates. Effectively applied rates are those in effect for partners in preferential trade arrangements such as the North American Free Trade Agreement. The difference between most favored nation and applied rates can be substantial. Because more countries now report their free trade agreements, suspensions of tariffs, and other special preferences, this year's *World Development Indicators* includes effectively applied rates for most countries. All estimates are calculated using the most recent information, which is not necessarily revised every year. As a result, data for the same year may differ from data in last year's edition.

Three measures of average tariffs are shown: simple bound rates and the simple and the weighted tariffs. Bound rates are based on all products in a country's tariff schedule, while the most favored nation or applied rates are calculated using all traded items. Weighted mean tariffs are weighted by the value of the country's trade with each trading partner. Simple averages are often a better indicator of tariff protection than weighted averages, which are biased downward because higher tariffs discourage

trade and reduce the weights applied to these tariffs. Bound rates result from trade negotiations incorporated into a country's schedule of concessions and are thus enforceable.

Some countries set fairly uniform tariff rates across all imports. Others are selective, setting high tariffs to protect favored domestic industries. The share of tariff lines with international peaks provides an indication of how selectively tariffs are applied. The effective rate of protection—the degree to which the value added in an industry is protected—may exceed the nominal rate if the tariff system systematically differentiates among imports of raw materials, intermediate products, and finished goods.

The share of tariff lines with specific rates shows the extent to which countries use tariffs based on physical quantities or other, non–ad valorem measures. Some countries such as Switzerland apply mainly specific duties. To the extent possible, these specific rates have been converted to their ad valorem equivalent rates and have been included in the calculation of simple and weighted tariffs.

Data are classified using the Harmonized System at the six- or eight-digit level. Tariff data are from the United Nations Conference on Trade and Development's (UNCTAD) Trade Analysis and Information System (TRAINS) database and the World Trade Organization's (WTO) Integrated Data Base (IDB) and Consolidated Tariff Schedules (CTS) database. Tariff line data were matched to Standard International Trade Classification (SITC) revision 2 codes to define commodity groups and import weights. Import weights were calculated using the United Nations Statistics Division's Commodity Trade (Comtrade) database. The table shows tariff rates for three commodity groups: all products, primary products, and manufactured products. Effectively applied rates at the six- and eight-digit product level are averaged for products in each commodity group. When an effectively applied rate is not available, the most favored nation rate is used instead.

Data are shown only for the last year for which complete data are available and for all economies with populations of 1 million or more and for economies with populations of less than 1 million when available. EU member countries apply a common tariff schedule that is listed under European Union and are thus not listed separately.

Definitions

• **Binding coverage** is the percentage of product lines with an agreed bound rate. • **Simple mean bound rate** is the unweighted average of all the lines in the tariff schedule in which bound rates have been set. • **Simple mean tariff** is the unweighted average of effectively applied rates or most favored nation rates for all products subject to tariffs calculated for all traded goods. • **Weighted mean tariff** is the average of effectively applied rates or most favored nation rates weighted by the product import shares corresponding to each partner country. • **Share of tariff lines with international peaks** is the share of lines in the tariff schedule with tariff rates that exceed 15 percent. • **Share of tariff lines with specific rates** is the share of lines in the tariff schedule that are set on a per unit basis or that combine ad valorem and per unit rates. • **Primary products** are commodities classified in SITC revision 2 sections 0–4 plus division 68 (nonferrous metals). • **Manufactured products** are commodities classified in SITC revision 2 sections 5–8 excluding division 68.

Data sources

All indicators in the table were calculated by World Bank staff using the World Integrated Trade Solution system, available at http://wits.worldbank.org. Data on tariffs were provided by UNCTAD's TRAINS database and the WTO's IDB and CTS database. Data on global imports are from the United Nations Statistics Division's Comtrade database.

	Logistics Performance Index	Burden of customs procedures	Lead time		Documents		Liner Shipping Connectivity Index	Quality of port infrastructure	Freight costs to the United States
			days		number				1 kilogram DHL nondocument air package[a] $
	1–5 (worst to best) 2009	1–7 (worst to best) 2009–10[b]	To export 2009	To import 2009	To export June 2010	To import June 2010	0–100 (low to high) 2010	1–7 (worst to best) 2009–10[b]	2011
Afghanistan	2.24	..	2.0	4.0	12	11	..	..	143.10
Albania	2.46	4.0	1.7	2.0	7	9	4.3	3.5	155.85
Algeria	2.36	3.2	4.6	7.1	8	9	31.4	3.2	157.10
Angola	2.25	2.8	6.0	8.0	11	8	10.7	2.1	157.10
Argentina	3.10	2.7	3.7	3.8	9	7	27.6	3.8	90.75
Armenia	2.52	2.6	..	..	3	6	..	2.9[c]	143.10
Australia	3.84	5.0	2.6	2.8	6	5	28.1	4.9	98.00
Austria	3.76	5.3	2.0	3.7	4	5	..	4.8[c]	129.45
Azerbaijan	2.64	3.5	7.0	3.0	9	14	..	4.2[c]	155.85
Bangladesh	2.74	3.4	1.4	1.4	6	8	7.5	3.4	98.00
Belarus	2.53	..	..	..	8	8	..	..	155.85
Belgium	3.94	4.6	1.7	1.6	4	5	84.0	6.4	112.50
Benin	2.79	4.2	3.0	7.0	7	7	11.5	4.0	157.10
Bolivia	2.51	2.7	15.0	28.3	8	7	..	2.9[c]	90.75
Bosnia and Herzegovina	2.66	3.6	2.0	2.0	5	7	..	1.6	155.85
Botswana	2.32	4.7	..	..	6	9	..	3.8[c]	157.10
Brazil	3.20	3.3	2.8	3.9	8	7	31.7	2.9	90.75
Bulgaria	2.83	3.5	2.0	3.9	5	7	5.5	3.8	155.85
Burkina Faso	2.23	4.4	4.0	14.0	10	10	..	3.9[c]	157.10
Burundi	2.29	3.0	..	..	9	10	..	3.0[c]	157.10
Cambodia	2.37	3.5	1.3	4.0	10	10	4.5	3.9	95.70
Cameroon	2.55	3.8	3.4	8.9	11	12	11.3	3.3	157.10
Canada	3.87	4.9	2.8	3.7	3	4	42.4	5.7	72.20
Central African Republic	..	..	..	..	9	17	..	..	157.10
Chad	2.49	2.7	74.0	35.0	6	10	..	2.6[c]	157.10
Chile	3.09	5.7	3.5	3.0	6	7	22.1	5.5	90.75
China	3.49	4.5	2.8	2.6	7	5	143.6	4.3	84.55
Hong Kong SAR, China	3.88	6.5	1.7	1.6	4	4	113.6	6.8	90.45
Colombia	2.77	4.1	7.0	7.0	6	8	26.1	3.5	90.75
Congo, Dem. Rep.	2.68	..	2.0	3.0	8	9	5.2	..	157.10
Congo, Rep.	2.48	..	..	..	11	10	10.5	..	157.10
Costa Rica	2.91	4.0	2.0	2.0	6	7	12.8	2.7	90.75
Côte d'Ivoire	2.53	3.8	1.0	1.0	10	9	17.5	5.0	157.10
Croatia	2.77	4.1	1.0	1.0	7	8	9.0	4.0	155.85
Cuba	2.07	..	..	..	..	..	6.6	..	75.05
Czech Republic	3.51	4.6	2.5	3.5	4	7	0.4	4.6[c]	155.85
Denmark	3.85	5.6	1.0	1.0	4	3	26.8	6.1	129.45
Dominican Republic	2.82	4.7	2.2	3.5	6	7	22.2	4.3	75.05
Ecuador	2.77	3.5	2.1	3.4	9	7	18.7	3.7	90.75
Egypt, Arab Rep.	2.61	4.5	1.3	3.1	6	6	47.5	4.2	143.10
El Salvador	2.67	4.2	2.0	2.0	8	8	9.6	4.1	90.75
Eritrea	1.70	..	3.0	3.0	9	13	0.0	..	157.10
Estonia	3.16	5.3	4.0	4.0	3	4	5.7	5.6	155.85
Ethiopia	2.41	3.6	5.0	6.0	8	8	..	4.4[c]	157.10
Finland	3.89	5.7	1.6	1.8	4	5	8.4	6.4	129.45
France	3.84	4.9	3.2	4.5	2	2	74.9	5.9	112.50
Gabon	2.41	..	4.3	13.0	7	8	8.5	..	157.10
Gambia, The	2.49	5.4	4.6	3.5	6	8	5.4	5.1	157.10
Georgia	2.61	4.7	..	..	4	4	4.0	4.0	155.85
Germany	4.11	5.1	3.6	2.4	4	5	90.9	6.4	112.50
Ghana	2.47	3.8	2.9	6.8	6	7	17.3	4.5	157.10
Greece	2.96	4.1	3.0	3.5	5	6	34.3	4.0	129.45
Guatemala	2.63	4.2	2.6	3.4	10	10	13.3	4.5	90.75
Guinea	2.60	..	3.5	3.9	7	9	6.3	..	157.10
Guinea-Bissau	2.10	..	..	..	6	6	3.5	..	157.10
Haiti	2.59	..	4.2	5.3	8	10	7.6	..	75.05
Honduras	2.78	4.2	2.4	3.2	6	10	9.1	5.3	90.75

	Logistics Performance Index	Burden of customs procedures	Lead time		Documents		Liner Shipping Connectivity Index	Quality of port infrastructure	Freight costs to the United States
			days		number				1 kilogram DHL nondocument air package[a] $
	1–5 (worst to best) 2009	1–7 (worst to best) 2009–10[b]	To export 2009	To import 2009	To export June 2010	To import June 2010	0–100 (low to high) 2010	1–7 (worst to best) 2009–10[b]	2011
Hungary	2.99	4.3	3.5	5.0	5	7	..	4.0[c]	155.85
India	3.12	4.0	2.3	5.3	8	9	41.4	3.9	98.00
Indonesia	2.76	3.9	2.1	5.4	5	6	25.6	3.6	98.00
Iran, Islamic Rep.	2.57	3.5	2.6	28.3	7	8	30.7	3.9	143.10
Iraq	2.11	..	..	..	10	10	4.2	..	143.10
Ireland	3.89	5.2	1.0	1.0	4	4	7.6	4.4	112.00
Israel	3.41	4.3	2.0	2.0	5	4	33.2	4.6	143.10
Italy	3.64	4.2	2.6	3.0	4	4	59.6	3.9	112.50
Jamaica	2.53	3.8	10.0	10.0	6	6	33.1	5.3	75.05
Japan	3.97	4.6	1.0	1.0	4	5	67.4	5.2	120.80
Jordan	2.74	4.5	3.2	4.6	7	7	17.8	4.4	143.10
Kazakhstan	2.83	3.5	2.8	11.5	10	12	..	3.3[c]	155.85
Kenya	2.59	3.3	3.0	5.9	8	7	13.1	3.8	157.10
Korea, Dem. Rep.	..	..	..	..	..	..	..	..	95.70
Korea, Rep.	3.64	4.5	1.6	2.0	3	3	82.6	5.5	98.00
Kosovo	..	..	..	..	8	8	..	..	..
Kuwait	3.28	4.1	2.0	3.0	8	10	8.3	4.4	143.10
Kyrgyz Republic	2.62	3.0	2.0	..	7	7	..	1.4[c]	155.85
Lao PDR	2.46	..	..	..	9	10	..	..	95.70
Latvia	3.25	4.1	1.3	1.6	5	6	6.0	4.7	155.85
Lebanon	3.34	3.5	3.4	2.2	5	7	30.3	4.5	143.10
Lesotho	2.30	3.8	..	..	6	8	..	3.1[c]	157.10
Liberia	2.38	..	4.0	5.0	10	9	5.9	..	157.10
Libya	2.33	3.5	3.2	10.0	..	..	5.4	3.2	157.10
Lithuania	3.13	4.8	2.0	2.3	6	6	9.5	4.7	155.85
Macedonia, FYR	2.77	4.3	..	..	6	6	..	3.7[c]	155.85
Madagascar	2.66	3.9	..	..	4	9	7.4	3.4	157.10
Malawi	2.42	3.9	4.2	3.7	11	10	..	3.6[c]	157.10
Malaysia	3.44	4.8	2.6	2.8	7	7	88.1	5.6	98.00
Mali	2.27	4.1	5.0	4.0	7	10	..	3.7[c]	157.10
Mauritania	2.63	4.5	2.0	3.0	11	11	5.6	3.6	157.10
Mauritius	2.72	4.6	3.0	2.4	5	6	16.7	4.5	157.10
Mexico	3.05	3.9	2.1	2.5	5	4	36.3	3.7	58.80
Moldova	2.57	3.4	..	..	6	7	..	2.9	155.85
Mongolia	2.25	3.3	14.0	12.0	8	8	..	3.3[c]	95.70
Morocco	2.38	4.3	2.0	3.2	7	10	49.4	4.4	157.10
Mozambique	2.29	3.7	..	..	7	10	8.2	3.5	157.10
Myanmar	2.33	..	4.6	8.4	..	..	3.7	..	95.70
Namibia	2.02	4.2	3.0	3.0	11	9	14.4	5.6	157.10
Nepal	2.20	3.4	1.8	6.3	9	10	..	2.9[c]	95.70
Netherlands	4.07	5.2	1.8	1.9	4	5	90.0	6.6	112.50
New Zealand	3.65	5.8	1.3	1.6	7	5	18.4	5.4	98.00
Nicaragua	2.54	3.6	3.2	3.2	5	5	8.7	2.9	90.75
Niger	2.54	..	..	..	8	10	..	..	157.10
Nigeria	2.59	3.1	2.5	4.1	10	9	18.3	3.0	157.10
Norway	3.93	5.2	1.0	2.0	4	4	7.9	5.7	129.45
Oman	2.84	5.2	..	..	9	9	48.5	5.3	143.10
Pakistan	2.53	3.6	2.3	1.6	9	8	29.5	4.0	143.10
Panama	3.02	4.4	1.4	1.4	3	4	41.1	6.0	90.75
Papua New Guinea	2.41	..	..	..	7	9	6.4	..	95.70
Paraguay	2.75	3.8	1.0	4.0	8	10	0.0	3.4[c]	90.75
Peru	2.80	4.5	2.0	3.8	6	8	21.8	3.3	90.75
Philippines	3.14	3.0	1.8	5.0	8	8	15.2	2.8	98.00
Poland	3.44	4.3	3.0	3.6	5	5	26.2	3.3	155.85
Portugal	3.34	4.9	2.5	5.0	4	5	38.1	4.9	129.45
Puerto Rico	..	4.7	..	..	7	10	..	5.4	..
Qatar	2.95	4.9	3.8	2.3	5	7	7.7	5.4	143.10

	Logistics Performance Index	Burden of customs procedures	Lead time		Documents		Liner Shipping Connectivity Index	Quality of port infrastructure	Freight costs to the United States
			days		number				1 kilogram DHL nondocument air package[a] $
	1–5 (worst to best) 2009	1–7 (worst to best) 2009–10[b]	To export 2009	To import 2009	To export June 2010	To import June 2010	0–100 (low to high) 2010	1–7 (worst to best) 2009–10[b]	2011
Romania	2.84	3.9	2.0	2.0	5	6	15.5	3.0	155.85
Russian Federation	2.61	2.9	4.0	2.9	8	13	20.9	3.7	155.85
Rwanda	2.04	4.8	..	..	8	8	..	2.8	157.10
Saudi Arabia	3.22	4.9	2.3	6.3	5	5	50.4	5.2	143.10
Senegal	2.86	4.7	1.4	2.7	6	5	13.0	4.7	157.10
Serbia	2.69[d]	3.6	2.0[d]	3.0[d]	6	6	3.0[d]	2.8	155.85
Sierra Leone	1.97	..	2.0	32.0	7	7	5.8	..	157.10
Singapore	4.09	6.3	2.2	1.8	4	4	103.8	6.8	90.45
Slovak Republic	3.24	4.4	3.0	5.0	6	8	..	4.0[c]	155.85
Slovenia	2.87	5.2	1.0	2.0	6	8	20.6	5.3	155.85
Somalia	1.34	..	..	..	..	..	4.2	..	157.10
South Africa	3.46	4.4	2.3	3.3	8	9	32.5	4.7	157.10
Spain	3.63	4.6	4.0	7.1	6	7	74.3	5.6	129.45
Sri Lanka	2.29	4.2	1.3	2.5	8	6	40.2	4.9	98.00
Sudan	2.21	..	39.0	5.0	6	6	10.1	..	157.10
Swaziland	..	3.5	..	..	9	10	..	4.2	157.10
Sweden	4.08	5.8	1.0	2.6	3	3	30.6	6.2	129.45
Switzerland	3.97	5.1	2.6	2.6	4	5	2.6	5.2[c]	129.45
Syrian Arab Republic	2.74	2.8	2.5	3.2	8	9	15.2	3.1	143.10
Tajikistan	2.35	3.6	7.0	..	10	9	..	1.9[c]	155.85
Tanzania	2.60	3.4	3.2	7.1	5	7	10.6	3.0	157.10
Thailand	3.29	4.1	1.6	2.6	4	3	43.8	5.0	98.00
Timor-Leste	1.71	3.6	..	..	6	7	..	2.5	95.70
Togo	2.60	..	..	..	6	8	14.2	..	157.10
Trinidad and Tobago	..	3.1	..	..	5	6	15.8	4.3	75.05
Tunisia	2.84	4.7	1.7	7.0	4	7	6.5	5.0	157.10
Turkey	3.22	3.8	2.2	3.8	7	8	36.1	4.1	143.10
Turkmenistan	2.49	..	3.0	..	..	..	..	..	155.85
Uganda	2.82	4.1	5.5	14.0	6	8	..	3.5[c]	157.10
Ukraine	2.57	3.0	1.7	7.0	6	8	21.1	3.6	155.85
United Arab Emirates	3.63	5.8	2.5	2.0	4	5	63.4	6.2	143.10
United Kingdom	3.95	4.8	3.3	1.9	4	4	87.5	5.5	112.50
United States	3.86	4.5	2.8	4.0	4	5	83.8	5.5	..
Uruguay	2.75	4.0	3.0	3.0	10	10	24.5	5.2	90.75
Uzbekistan	2.79	..	1.4	2.0	7	9	..	..	155.85
Venezuela, RB	2.68	2.2	9.4	12.1	8	9	18.6	2.4	90.75
Vietnam	2.96	3.6	1.4	1.7	6	8	31.4	3.6	98.00
West Bank and Gaza	..	..	..	..	6	6	..	..	..
Yemen, Rep.	2.58	..	3.1	3.6	6	9	12.5	..	143.10
Zambia	2.28	4.2	9.2	4.0	6	8	..	3.6[c]	157.10
Zimbabwe	2.29	3.6	25.0	18.0	7	9	..	4.4[c]	157.10
World	**2.87[e] u**	**4.2 u**	**3.8[e] u**	**4.6[e] u**	**7 u**	**7 u**		**4.3 u**	**..**
Low income	2.38	3.8	6.8	7.2	8	9		3.5	
Middle income	2.69	3.8	3.8	5.0	7	8		3.8	
Lower middle income	2.62	3.7	4.4	5.1	7	8		3.8	
Upper middle income	2.75	3.9	3.1	4.9	7	8		3.9	
Low & middle income	2.59	3.8	4.6	5.6	7	8		3.7	
East Asia & Pacific	2.73	3.8	3.6	4.9	7	7		3.8	
Europe & Central Asia	2.68	3.7	2.9	3.1	7	8		3.3	
Latin America & Carib.	2.74	3.8	3.9	5.5	7	7		3.9	
Middle East & N. Africa	2.60	3.8	2.7	7.2	7	8		4.0	
South Asia	2.49	3.7	1.9	3.3	9	9		3.8	
Sub-Saharan Africa	2.42	3.9	8.1	7.0	8	9		3.8	
High income	3.54	4.9	2.1	2.7	5	5		5.3	
Euro area	3.57	4.9	2.2	2.9	4	5		5.3	

a. Transportation charges only; excludes fuel, assessorial/surcharges, duties and taxes. b. Average of the 2009 and 2010 survey ratings. c. Landlocked country. d. Includes Montenegro.
e. Aggregates are computed according to the World Bank classification of economies as of July 1, 2010 and may differ from data published in the original source.

About the data

Broadly defined, trade facilitation encompasses customs efficiency and other physical and regulatory environments where trade takes place, harmonization of standards and conformance to international regulations, and the logistics of moving goods and associated documentation through countries and ports. Though collection of trade facilitation data has improved over the last decade, data that allow meaningful evaluation, especially for developing economies, are lacking. Data on trade facilitation are drawn from research by private and international agencies. Most data are perception-based evaluations by business executives and professionals. Because of different backgrounds, values, and personalities, those surveyed may evaluate the same situation quite differently. Caution should thus be used when interpreting perception-based indicators. Nevertheless, they convey much needed information on trade facilitation.

The table presents data from Logistics Performance Surveys conducted by the World Bank in partnership with academic and international institutions and private companies and individuals engaged in international logistics. The Logistics Performance Index assesses logistics performance across six aspects of the logistics environment (see *Definitions),* based on more than 5,000 country assessments by nearly 1,000 international freight forwarders. Respondents evaluate eight markets on six core dimensions on a scale from 1 (worst) to 5 (best). The markets are chosen based on the most important export and import markets of the respondent's country, random selection, and, for landlocked countries, neighboring countries that connect them with international markets. Scores for the six areas are averaged across all respondents and aggregated to a single score. Details of the survey methodology and index construction methodology are in Arvis and others (2010).

Data on the burden of customs procedures are from the World Economic Forum's Executive Opinion Survey. The 2010 round included more than 15,000 respondents from 139 countries. Sampling follows a dual stratification based on company size and the sector of activity. Data are collected online or through in-person interviews. Responses are aggregated using sector-weighted averaging. The data for the latest year are combined with the data for the previous year to create a two-year moving average. Respondents evaluated the efficiency of customs procedures in their country. The lowest value (1) rates the customs procedure as extremely inefficient, and the highest score (7) as extremely efficient.

The direct costs of cross-border trade include freight, customs, and storage fees. Indirect costs include the value of time to import or export and the risk of delay or loss of shipments. Long lead times and burdensome regulatory procedures may lower competitiveness. Data on lead time are from the LPI survey. Respondents provided separate values for the best case (10 percent of shipments) and the median case (50 percent of shipments). The data are exponentiated averages of the logarithm of single value responses and of midpoint values of range responses for the median case.

Data on the number of documents needed to export or import are from the World Bank's Doing Business surveys, which compile procedural requirements for exporting and importing a standardized cargo of goods by ocean transport from local freight forwarders, shipping lines, customs brokers, port officials, and banks. To make the data comparable across economies, several assumptions about the business and the traded goods are used (see www.doingbusiness.org).

Access to global shipping and air freight networks and the quality and accessibility of ports and roads affect logistics performance. The table shows two indicators related to trade and transport service infrastructure: the Liner Shipping Connectivity Index and the quality of port infrastructure rating. The Liner Shipping Connectivity Index captures how well countries are connected to global shipping networks. It is computed by the United Nations Conference on Trade and Development (UNCTAD) based on five components of the maritime transport sector: number of ships, their container-carrying capacity, maximum vessel size, number of services, and number of companies that deploy container ships in a country's ports. For each component a country's value is divided by the maximum value of each component in 2004, the five components are averaged for each country, and the average is divided by the maximum average for 2004 and multiplied by 100. The index generates a value of 100 for the country with the highest average index in 2004.

The quality of port infrastructure measures business executives' perception of their country's port facilities. Values range from 1 (port infrastructure considered extremely underdeveloped) to 7 (port infrastructure considered efficient by international standards). Respondents in landlocked countries were asked: "How accessible are port facilities (1 = extremely inaccessible; 7 = extremely accessible.)"

The costs of transport services are a crucial determinant of export competitiveness. The proxy indicator in the table is the shipping rates to the United States of an international freight moving business.

Definitions

- **Logistics Performance Index** reflects perceptions of a country's logistics based on efficiency of customs clearance process, quality of trade- and transport-related infrastructure, ease of arranging competitively priced shipments, quality of logistics services, ability to track and trace consignments, and frequency with which shipments reach the consignee within the scheduled time. The index ranges from 1 to 5, with a higher score representing better performance. • **Burden of customs procedure** measures business executives' perceptions of their country's efficiency of customs procedures. Values range from 1 to 7, with a higher rating indicating greater efficiency. • **Lead time to export** is the median time (the value for 50 percent of shipments) from shipment point to port of loading. • **Lead time to import** is the median time (the value for 50 percent of shipments) from port of discharge to arrival at the consignee. • **Documents to export** and **documents to import** are all documents required per shipment by government ministries, customs authorities, port and container terminals, health and technical control agencies, and banks to export or import goods. Documents renewed annually and not requiring renewal per shipment are excluded. • **Liner Shipping Connectivity Index** indicates how well countries are connected to global shipping networks based on the status of their maritime transport sector. The highest value in 2004 is 100. • **Quality of port infrastructure** measures business executives' perceptions of their country's port facilities. Values range from 1 to 7, with a higher rating indicating better development of port infrastructure. • **Freight costs to the United States** is the DHL international U.S. inbound worldwide priority express rate for a 1 kilogram nondocument air package. Fuel, assessorial/surcharges, duties, and taxes are excluded.

Data sources

Data on the Logistics Performance Index and lead time to export and import are from Arvis and others' *Connecting to Compete: Trade Logistics in the Global Economy 2010.* Data on the burden of customs procedure and quality of port infrastructure ratings are from the World Economic Forum's *Global Competitiveness Report 2010–2011.* Data on number of documents to export and import are from the World Bank's Doing Business project (www.doingbusiness. org). Data on the Liner Shipping Connectivity Index are from UNCTAD's *Review of Maritime Transport 2010.* Freight costs to the United States are based on DHL's "DHL Express Standard Rate Guideline 2011" (2011).

	Total external debt		Long-term debt						Short-term debt		Use of IMF credit	
					$ millions Public and publicly guaranteed							
				Total	IBRD loans and IDA credits		Private nonguaranteed					
	$ millions								$ millions		$ millions	
	1995	2009	1995	2009	1995	2009	1995	2009	1995	2009	1995	2009
Afghanistan	..	2,328	..	2,203	..	471	..	0	..	20	..	106
Albania	456	4,719	330	2,829	109	874	0	983	62	835	65	71
Algeria	33,053	5,345	31,314	2,871	2,049	10	0	982	261	1,492	1,478	0
Angola	11,500	16,715	9,543	13,722	81	385	0	0	1,958	2,634	0	359
Argentina	98,465	120,183	54,913	72,923	4,913	5,305	16,066	27,723	21,355	19,537	6,131	0
Armenia	371	4,935	298	2,376	96	1,214	0	1,461	2	512	70	587
Australia	..	..	..	..	..	..	..	..	..	..	..	..
Austria	..	..	..	..	..	..	..	..	..	..	..	..
Azerbaijan	321	4,865	206	3,403	30	939	0	590	14	810	101	62
Bangladesh	15,726	23,820	14,905	21,206	5,692	10,746	0	0	199	1,939	622	675
Belarus	1,694	17,158	1,301	4,758	116	256	0	1,504	110	8,024	283	2,871
Belgium	..	..	..	..	..	..	..	..	..	..	..	..
Benin	1,398	1,073	1,267	990	498	309	0	0	47	45	84	39
Bolivia	5,272	5,745	4,459	2,545	865	316	239	2,647	307	554	268	0
Bosnia and Herzegovina	..	9,583	..	3,569	472	1,520	..	4,051	..	1,677	48	286
Botswana	717	1,617	707	1,388	108	5	0	0	10	229	0	0
Brazil	160,469	276,932	98,260	87,317	6,038	10,065	30,830	149,826	31,238	39,789	142	0
Bulgaria	10,379	40,582	8,808	4,772	444	1,509	342	17,232	512	18,578	717	0
Burkina Faso	1,271	1,835	1,140	1,725	608	721	0	0	56	0	75	110
Burundi	1,162	518	1,099	420	591	147	0	0	15	7	48	91
Cambodia	2,284	4,364	2,110	4,099	65	566	0	0	102	265	72	0
Cameroon	10,950	2,941	9,620	2,128	1,082	303	288	615	991	23	51	175
Canada	..	..	..	..	..	..	..	..	..	..	..	..
Central African Republic	946	396	854	250	414	9	0	0	57	67	35	78
Chad	843	1,743	777	1,711	379	896	0	0	17	4	49	29
Chile	22,038	71,646	7,178	9,282	1,383	216	11,429	44,888	3,431	17,476	0	0
China	118,090	428,442	94,674	93,125	14,248	22,226	1,090	94,808	22,325	240,509	0	0
Hong Kong SAR, China	..	..	..	..	..	..	..	..	..	..	..	..
Colombia	25,044	52,223	13,946	35,364	2,559	6,571	5,553	12,749	5,545	4,110	0	0
Congo, Dem. Rep.	13,239	12,183	9,636	10,788	1,413	2,497	0	0	3,118	596	485	800
Congo, Rep.	5,887	5,041	4,867	4,785	279	298	0	0	1,002	213	19	43
Costa Rica	3,766	8,070	3,097	3,190	303	58	214	2,538	430	2,341	24	0
Côte d'Ivoire	18,899	11,701	11,902	10,979	2,386	1,823	2,660	271	3,910	99	427	352
Croatia	..	..	..	..	..	..	..	..	..	..	..	..
Cuba	..	..	..	..	..	..	..	..	..	..	..	..
Czech Republic	..	..	..	..	..	..	..	..	..	..	..	..
Denmark	..	..	..	..	..	..	..	..	..	..	..	..
Dominican Republic	4,447	11,003	3,653	7,714	300	756	19	843	616	1,679	160	767
Ecuador	13,877	12,930	11,951	6,910	1,108	542	440	4,600	1,312	1,419	173	0
Egypt, Arab Rep.	33,475	33,257	30,687	30,622	2,356	3,250	313	74	2,372	2,561	103	0
El Salvador	2,509	11,384	1,979	6,131	327	578	5	3,139	525	2,114	0	0
Eritrea	37	1,019	37	1,013	24	477	0	0	0	6	0	0
Estonia	..	..	..	..	..	..	..	..	..	..	..	..
Ethiopia	10,322	5,025	9,788	4,812	1,470	1,422	0	0	460	45	73	168
Finland	..	..	..	..	..	..	..	..	..	..	..	..
France	..	..	..	..	..	..	..	..	..	..	..	..
Gabon	4,361	2,130	3,977	2,022	110	18	0	0	287	108	97	0
Gambia, The	426	520	385	449	162	64	0	0	15	42	26	29
Georgia	1,240	4,231	1,039	2,596	84	1,253	0	518	85	330	116	786
Germany	..	..	..	..	..	..	..	..	..	..	..	..
Ghana	5,495	5,720	4,200	4,126	2,434	1,581	27	0	620	1,323	648	271
Greece	..	..	..	..	..	..	..	..	..	..	..	..
Guatemala	3,282	13,801	2,328	4,931	158	1,112	142	7,644	811	1,226	0	0
Guinea	3,248	2,926	2,991	2,827	847	1,269	0	0	164	40	94	59
Guinea-Bissau	895	1,111	794	950	210	304	0	0	95	151	6	10
Haiti	821	1,244	766	1,078	389	39	0	0	27	0	29	166
Honduras	4,851	3,675	4,247	2,446	828	502	123	880	382	317	99	32

	Total external debt		Long-term debt						Short-term debt		Use of IMF credit	
			$ millions Public and publicly guaranteed									
			Total		IBRD loans and IDA credits		Private nonguaranteed					
	$ millions								$ millions		$ millions	
	1995	2009	1995	2009	1995	2009	1995	2009	1995	2009	1995	2009
Hungary	..	..	..	..	..	..	..	..	..	..	..	..
India	95,174	237,692	81,091	76,531	27,348	34,028	6,618	118,211	5,049	42,950	2,416	0
Indonesia	124,413	157,517	65,323	86,020	13,259	10,111	33,123	52,834	25,966	18,662	0	0
Iran, Islamic Rep.	21,565	13,435	15,116	7,524	316	836	0	0	6,449	5,911	0	0
Iraq	..	..	..	..	..	..	..	..	..	..	..	..
Ireland	..	..	..	..	..	..	..	..	..	..	..	..
Israel	..	..	..	..	..	..	..	..	..	..	..	..
Italy	..	..	..	..	..	..	..	..	..	..	..	..
Jamaica	4,581	10,959	3,721	6,664	595	398	128	3,241	492	1,054	240	0
Japan	..	..	..	..	..	..	..	..	..	..	..	..
Jordan	7,661	6,615	6,624	5,445	806	1,109	0	0	785	1,158	251	12
Kazakhstan	3,750	109,873	2,834	2,487	295	547	103	98,710	381	8,676	432	0
Kenya	7,309	8,005	5,857	6,543	2,412	3,156	445	0	634	1,011	374	451
Korea, Dem. Rep.	..	..	..	..	..	..	..	..	..	..	..	..
Korea, Rep.	..	..	..	..	..	..	..	..	..	..	..	..
Kosovo	..	359	..	359	..	359	..	0	..	0	..	0
Kuwait	..	..	..	..	..	..	..	..	..	..	..	..
Kyrgyz Republic	609	2,900	472	2,320	141	656	0	332	13	81	124	167
Lao PDR	2,155	5,539	2,091	2,923	285	680	0	2,601	0	0	64	16
Latvia	..	..	..	..	..	..	..	..	..	..	..	..
Lebanon	2,974	24,864	1,559	20,979	113	318	50	670	1,365	3,096	0	119
Lesotho	684	705	642	681	207	313	0	0	4	0	38	24
Liberia	2,466	1,660	1,153	677	269	69	0	0	978	92	336	891
Libya	..	..	..	..	..	..	..	..	..	..	..	..
Lithuania	769	31,717	430	9,059	62	23	29	16,708	49	5,949	262	0
Macedonia, FYR	1,277	5,589	788	1,874	181	653	289	1,816	143	1,900	57	0
Madagascar	4,302	2,213	3,687	1,846	1,121	1,105	0	4	542	262	73	101
Malawi	2,238	1,093	2,078	899	1,306	213	0	0	44	67	116	127
Malaysia	34,343	66,390	16,023	21,364	1,059	39	11,046	21,332	7,274	23,695	0	0
Mali	2,958	2,667	2,739	2,592	863	698	0	0	72	32	147	44
Mauritania	2,396	2,029	2,127	1,851	347	282	0	0	169	163	100	16
Mauritius	1,416	742	1,148	661	157	212	267	81	1	0	0	0
Mexico	165,379	192,008	93,902	99,374	13,823	10,143	18,348	69,299	37,300	23,335	15,828	0
Moldova	695	3,457	450	783	152	443	9	1,203	6	1,318	230	154
Mongolia	531	2,212	472	1,817	59	392	0	141	12	72	47	182
Morocco	23,771	23,752	23,190	19,219	3,999	2,557	331	2,354	198	2,179	52	0
Mozambique	7,458	4,168	5,209	3,354	890	1,356	1,769	0	279	643	202	171
Myanmar	5,771	8,186	5,378	6,320	777	777	0	0	393	1,866	0	0
Namibia	..	..	..	..	..	..	..	..	..	..	..	..
Nepal	2,410	3,683	2,339	3,563	1,023	1,483	0	0	23	44	48	76
Netherlands	..	..	..	..	..	..	..	..	..	..	..	..
New Zealand	..	..	..	..	..	..	..	..	..	..	..	..
Nicaragua	10,396	4,420	8,572	2,461	341	418	0	1,093	1,785	716	39	150
Niger	1,604	991	1,347	909	598	266	133	7	72	18	52	57
Nigeria	34,092	7,846	28,140	4,157	3,489	2,852	301	175	5,651	3,514	0	0
Norway	..	..	..	..	..	..	..	..	..	..	..	..
Oman	..	..	..	..	..	..	..	..	..	..	..	..
Pakistan	30,169	53,710	23,727	41,484	6,403	11,844	1,593	3,265	3,235	1,466	1,613	7,495
Panama	6,098	12,418	3,781	11,282	175	435	0	1,136	2,207	0	111	0
Papua New Guinea	2,506	1,555	1,668	1,037	407	231	711	397	78	121	50	0
Paraguay	2,574	4,323	1,453	2,308	189	296	338	1,263	784	752	0	0
Peru	30,833	29,593	18,931	20,791	1,729	2,846	1,288	4,073	9,659	4,730	955	0
Philippines	39,379	62,911	28,525	41,738	5,185	2,669	4,847	17,171	5,279	4,002	728	0
Poland	..	..	..	..	..	..	..	..	..	..	..	..
Portugal	..	..	..	..	..	..	..	..	..	..	..	..
Puerto Rico	..	..	..	..	..	..	..	..	..	..	..	..
Qatar	..	..	..	..	..	..	..	..	..	..	..	..

	Total external debt		Long-term debt						Short-term debt		Use of IMF credit	
					$ millions Public and publicly guaranteed							
						IBRD loans and IDA credits		Private nonguaranteed				
	$ millions		Total						$ millions		$ millions	
	1995	2009	1995	2009	1995	2009	1995	2009	1995	2009	1995	2009
Romania	6,832	117,511	3,957	17,904	844	2,995	534	69,031	1,303	21,032	1,038	9,544
Russian Federation	121,401	381,339	101,582	99,990	1,524	3,211	0	250,725	10,201	30,624	9,617	0
Rwanda	1,029	747	971	725	512	254	0	0	32	6	26	15
Saudi Arabia	..	..	..	..	..	..	..	..	..	..	..	..
Senegal	3,916	3,503	3,266	2,961	1,160	921	44	357	260	18	347	167
Serbia	10,785[a]	33,402	6,788[a]	8,725	1,252[a]	2,459	1,773[a]	19,076	2,139[a]	4,000	84[a]	1,601
Sierra Leone	1,220	444	1,028	371	234	124	0	0	27	0	165	73
Singapore	..	..	..	..	..	..	..	..	..	..	..	..
Slovak Republic	..	..	..	..	..	..	..	..	..	..	..	..
Slovenia	..	..	..	..	..	..	..	..	..	..	..	..
Somalia	2,678	2,973	1,961	1,987	432	448	0	0	551	810	166	176
South Africa	25,358	42,101	9,837	15,063	0	21	4,935	13,764	9,673	13,274	913	0
Spain	..	..	..	..	..	..	..	..	..	..	..	..
Sri Lanka	8,395	17,208	7,175	13,647	1,512	2,487	90	967	535	1,873	595	721
Sudan	17,603	20,139	9,779	12,998	1,279	1,306	496	0	6,368	6,739	960	403
Swaziland	249	418	238	391	25	10	0	0	11	27	0	0
Sweden	..	..	..	..	..	..	..	..	..	..	..	..
Switzerland	..	..	..	..	..	..	..	..	..	..	..	..
Syrian Arab Republic	21,897	5,236	16,955	4,480	471	16	0	0	4,942	756	0	0
Tajikistan	634	2,514	590	1,603	0	373	0	855	43	15	0	41
Tanzania	7,365	7,325	6,204	4,637	2,269	2,598	0	1,016	964	1,342	197	329
Thailand	100,039	58,755	16,826	11,185	1,906	133	39,117	19,689	44,095	27,881	0	0
Timor-Leste	..	..	..	..	..	..	..	..	..	..	..	..
Togo	1,476	1,640	1,286	1,502	541	586	0	0	85	47	105	91
Trinidad and Tobago	..	..	..	..	..	..	..	..	..	..	..	..
Tunisia	10,818	21,709	9,022	14,837	1,766	1,405	193	2,070	1,310	4,801	293	0
Turkey	73,781	251,372	50,317	84,875	5,069	9,816	7,079	118,814	15,701	39,725	685	7,958
Turkmenistan	402	576	385	463	1	13	0	38	17	75	0	0
Uganda	3,609	2,490	3,089	2,245	1,792	1,379	0	0	103	235	417	9
Ukraine	8,429	93,153	6,581	10,449	491	3,294	84	51,857	223	19,873	1,542	10,974
United Arab Emirates	..	..	..	..	..	..	..	..	..	..	..	..
United Kingdom	..	..	..	..	..	..	..	..	..	..	..	..
United States	..	..	..	..	..	..	..	..	..	..	..	..
Uruguay	5,318	12,159	3,833	10,955	513	1,099	127	80	1,336	1,124	21	0
Uzbekistan	1,799	4,109	1,415	3,238	157	368	15	727	212	144	157	0
Venezuela, RB	35,744	54,503	28,428	35,184	1,639	0	2,013	3,310	3,063	16,009	2,239	0
Vietnam	25,428	28,674	21,778	23,403	231	6,270	0	0	3,272	5,186	377	84
West Bank and Gaza	..	..	..	..	..	..	..	..	..	..	..	..
Yemen, Rep.	6,251	6,356	5,562	5,861	827	2,187	0	0	689	442	0	53
Zambia	6,958	3,049	5,291	1,210	1,434	407	13	1,020	415	474	1,239	345
Zimbabwe	4,989	5,015	3,462	3,742	896	985	381	89	685	1,068	461	116
World	.. s	.. s	.. s	.. s	.. s	.. s	.. s	.. s	.. s	.. s	.. s	.. s
Low income	130,267	135,593	109,551	110,863	33,428	39,578	2,818	5,946	11,139	12,833	6,760	5,951
Middle income	1,729,983	3,409,521	1,151,625	1,296,127	144,453	185,309	205,673	1,346,264	319,724	720,903	52,961	46,227
Lower middle income	841,940	1,417,085	578,607	597,241	97,821	123,481	94,497	394,555	156,647	402,423	12,188	22,866
Upper middle income	888,043	1,992,436	573,018	698,886	46,632	61,827	111,176	951,710	163,077	318,479	40,772	23,361
Low & middle income	1,860,250	3,545,114	1,261,176	1,406,990	177,881	224,887	208,491	1,352,210	330,863	733,736	59,721	52,179
East Asia & Pacific	455,544	825,602	255,399	293,956	37,604	44,253	89,982	208,994	108,826	322,361	1,337	291
Europe & Central Asia	246,178	1,126,252	189,044	269,524	11,522	33,110	10,256	656,239	31,250	165,385	15,628	35,103
Latin America & Carib.	608,666	912,980	371,875	432,115	38,485	41,907	87,303	340,984	122,856	138,637	26,632	1,243
Middle East & N. Africa	161,737	141,321	140,298	112,569	12,751	11,847	887	6,150	18,375	22,402	2,177	200
South Asia	152,282	339,983	129,636	159,965	42,036	61,257	8,301	122,442	9,051	48,495	5,293	9,081
Sub-Saharan Africa	235,842	198,976	174,924	138,861	35,483	32,512	11,760	17,399	40,504	36,456	8,654	6,261
High income	..	..	..	..	..	..	..	..	..	..	..	..
Euro area	..	..	..	..	..	..	..	..	..	..	..	..

a. Includes Montenegro.

About the data

External indebtedness affects a country's creditworthiness and investor perceptions. Data on external debt are gathered through the World Bank's Debtor Reporting System. Indebtedness is calculated using loan-by-loan reports submitted by countries on long-term public and publicly guaranteed borrowing and information on short-term debt collected by the countries or from creditors through the reporting systems of the Bank for International Settlements (BIS). These data are supplemented by information from major multilateral banks and official lending agencies in major creditor countries and by estimates by World Bank and International Monetary Fund (IMF) staff. The table includes data on long-term private nonguaranteed debt reported to the World Bank or estimated by its staff.

Data coverage, quality, and timeliness vary by country. Coverage varies for debt instruments and borrowers. The widening spectrum of debt instruments and investors alongside the expansion of private nonguaranteed borrowing makes comprehensive coverage of external debt more complex. Reporting countries differ in their capacity to monitor debt, especially private nonguaranteed debt. Even data on public and publicly guaranteed debt are affected by coverage and reporting accuracy—because of monitoring capacity and sometimes because of unwillingness to provide information. A key part often underreported is military debt. Currently, 128 developing countries report to the Debtor Reporting System (DRS). Nonreporting countries might have outstanding debt with the World Bank, other international financial institutions, and private creditors.

Debt data, normally reported in the currency of repayment, are converted into U.S. dollars to produce summary tables. Stock figures (amount of debt outstanding) are converted using end-of-period exchange rates, as published in the IMF's *International Financial Statistics* (line ae). Flow figures are converted at annual average exchange rates (line rf). Projected debt service is converted using end-of-period exchange rates. Debt repayable in multiple currencies, goods, or services and debt with a provision for maintenance of the value of the currency of repayment are shown at book value.

Because flow data are converted at annual average exchange rates and stock data at end-of-period exchange rates, year-to-year changes in debt outstanding and disbursed are sometimes not equal to net flows (disbursements less principal repayments); similarly, changes in debt outstanding, including undisbursed debt, differ from commitments less repayments. Discrepancies are particularly notable when exchange rates have moved sharply during the year. Cancellations and reschedulings of other liabilities into long-term public debt also contribute to the differences.

Variations in reporting rescheduled debt also affect cross-country comparability. For example, rescheduling of official Paris Club creditors may be subject to lags between completion of the general rescheduling agreement and completion of the specific bilateral agreements that define the terms of the rescheduled debt. Other areas of inconsistency include country treatment of arrears and of nonresident national deposits denominated in foreign currency.

Aggregate data on long-term private nonguaranteed debt are reported annually. DRS countries recognize the importance of monitoring borrowing by their private sector, particularly when it accounts for a significant share of total external debt, but many find doing so difficult. Detailed data are available only from countries with registration requirements for private nonguaranteed debt, most commonly in connection with exchange controls. Where formal registration of private nonguaranteed debt is not mandatory, compilers must rely on balance of payments data and financial surveys. The data on private nonguaranteed debt in the table are as reported or estimated for countries where this type of external debt is known to be significant. Estimates are based on national data on quarterly external debt statistics.

The DRS encourages debtor countries to voluntarily provide information on their short-term external obligations. By its nature, short-term external debt is difficult to monitor: loan-by-loan registration is normally impractical, and monitoring systems typically rely on information requested periodically by the central bank from the banking sector. The World Bank regards the debtor country as the authoritative source of information on its short-term debt. Where such information is not available from the debtor country, data from creditor sources may be used as an indication of the magnitude of a country's short-term external debt. These data are derived from BIS data on international bank lending based on time remaining to original maturity. The data are reported based on residual maturity, but an estimate of short-term external liabilities by original maturity can be derived by deducting from claims due in one year those that, 12 months earlier, had a maturity of between one and two years. However, not all commercial banks report to the BIS in a way that allows the full maturity distribution to be determined, and the BIS data include liabilities only to banks within the BIS reporting area. The results should thus be interpreted with caution.

Data related to the operations of the IMF are provided by the IMF Treasurer's Department. They are converted from special drawing rights into U.S. dollars using end-of-period exchange rates for stocks and average-over-the-period exchange rates for flows. The IMF's loan instruments have changed over time to address the specific circumstances of its members.

Definitions

• **Total external debt** is debt owed to nonresident creditors and repayable in foreign currencies, goods, or services by public and private entities in the country. It is the sum of long-term external debt, short-term debt, and use of IMF credit. Debt repayable in domestic currency is excluded. • **Long-term debt** is debt that has an original or extended maturity of more than one year. It has three components: public, publicly guaranteed, and private nonguaranteed debt. • **Public and publicly guaranteed debt** comprises the long-term external obligations of public debtors, including the national government and political subdivisions (or an agency of either) and autonomous public bodies, and the external obligations of private debtors that are guaranteed for repayment by a public entity. • **IBRD loans and IDA credits** are extended by the World Bank. The International Bank for Reconstruction and Development (IBRD) lends at market rates. The International Development Association (IDA) provides credits at concessional rates. • **Private nonguaranteed debt** consists of the long-term external obligations of private debtors that are not guaranteed for repayment by a public entity. • **Short-term debt** is debt owed to nonresidents having an original maturity of one year or less and interest in arrears on long-term debt and on the use of IMF credit. • **Use of IMF credit** denotes members' drawings on the IMF other than those drawn against the country's reserve tranche position and includes purchases and drawings under the Extended Credit Facility, Standby Credit Facility, Rapid Credit Facility, Stand-By Arrangements, Flexible Credit Line, and the Extended Fund Facility.

Data sources

Data on external debt are mainly from reports to the World Bank through its Debtor Reporting System from member countries that have received IBRD loans or IDA credits, with additional information from the files of the World Bank, the IMF, the African Development Bank and African Development Fund, the Asian Development Bank and Asian Development Fund, and the Inter-American Development Bank. Summary tables of the external debt of developing countries are published annually in the World Bank's *Global Development Finance, Global Development Finance* CD-ROM, and Global Development Finance database.

Ratios for external debt

	Total external debt		Total debt service		Multilateral debt service		Short-term debt				Present value of debt	
	% of GNI		% of exports of goods and services and income[a]		% of public and publicly guaranteed debt service		% of total debt		% of total reserves		% of GNI[a]	% of exports of goods, services, and income[a]
	1995	2009	1995	2009	1995	2009	1995	2009	1995	2009	2009	2009
Afghanistan	..	..	..	0.4	..	73.4	..	0.9	..	..	5	25
Albania	18.5	40.3	2.8	6.9	11.4	43.1	13.7	17.7	23.5	35.2	31	96
Algeria	83.5	3.8	..	..	17.7	0.4	0.8	27.9	6.3	1.0	3	5
Angola	311.9	28.2	12.0	8.4	0.6	0.3	17.0	15.8	919.7	19.3	24	21
Argentina	38.9	40.1	30.2	17.3	21.6	44.7	21.7	16.3	133.6	40.7	41	156
Armenia	25.3	55.3	3.2	20.9	69.8	55.6	0.6	10.4	1.9	25.5	36	148
Australia	..	..	..	..	..	..	..	..	..	..	..	..
Austria	..	..	..	..	..	..	..	..	..	..	..	..
Azerbaijan	10.6	12.1	1.3	1.7	21.8	28.4	4.4	16.6	11.6	15.1	10	14
Bangladesh	40.2	24.0	16.1	5.6	28.0	70.2	1.3	8.1	8.4	18.8	17	90
Belarus	12.2	35.6	3.4	5.0	55.4	3.1	6.5	46.8	29.2	142.3	30	51
Belgium	..	..	..	..	..	..	..	..	..	..	..	..
Benin	71.2	16.1	7.5	..	54.6	74.5	3.4	4.2	23.7	3.6	12[b]	62[b]
Bolivia	81.2	34.5	29.5	14.4	75.5	84.0	5.8	9.6	30.5	6.5	16[b]	34[b]
Bosnia and Herzegovina	..	54.6	..	10.5	..	72.7	..	17.5	..	51.7	45	106
Botswana	15.1	14.1	3.1	1.2	76.0	59.6	1.4	14.2	0.2	2.6	8	16
Brazil	21.2	17.9	38.5	23.4	18.5	28.3	19.5	14.4	60.7	16.7	17	125
Bulgaria	81.9	90.4	16.5	21.3	10.5	55.1	4.9	45.8	31.3	100.3	85	132
Burkina Faso	53.6	22.9	..	..	76.7	65.0	4.4	0.0	16.1	0.0	17[b]	154[b]
Burundi	117.6	38.9	27.6	..	70.6	95.8	1.3	1.4	6.9	2.3	13[b]	143[b]
Cambodia	67.6	45.0	0.7	0.8	11.9	75.1	4.5	6.1	53.1	8.1	38	60
Cameroon	133.4	13.6	21.0	7.4	61.0	37.3	9.0	0.8	6,444.5	0.6	4[b]	12[b]
Canada	..	..	..	..	..	..	..	..	..	..	..	..
Central African Republic	85.9	20.0	..	..	100.0	65.0	6.0	17.0	24.0	31.9	12[b]	75[b]
Chad	58.5	28.6	..	2.8	86.1	85.3	2.0	0.2	11.6	0.6	22[b]	41[b]
Chile	32.1	46.7	24.5	22.6	76.2	3.7	15.6	24.4	23.1	69.1	43	84
China	16.5	8.7	9.9	2.9	7.6	27.2	18.9	56.1	27.8	9.8	9	25
Hong Kong SAR, China	..	..	..	..	..	..	..	..	..	..	..	..
Colombia	27.5	23.6	33.5	22.4	32.7	36.6	22.1	7.9	65.6	16.4	20	111
Congo, Dem. Rep.	271.4	121.4	..	..	..	35.5	23.6	4.9	1,980.9	36.9	24[b]	71[b]
Congo, Rep.	479.3	83.8	13.5	..	21.1	18.4	17.0	4.2	1,575.1	5.6	20[b]	18[b]
Costa Rica	32.8	28.1	14.2	9.6	50.6	25.4	11.4	29.0	40.5	57.5	27	50
Côte d'Ivoire	188.7	53.0	23.1	9.5	59.3	96.0	20.7	0.8	739.1	3.0	46[b]	88[b]
Croatia	..	..	..	..	..	..	..	..	..	..	..	..
Cuba	..	..	..	..	..	..	..	..	..	..	..	..
Czech Republic	..	..	..	..	..	..	..	..	..	..	..	..
Denmark	..	..	..	..	..	..	..	..	..	..	..	..
Dominican Republic	28.5	24.6	7.0	12.1	39.8	25.2	13.8	15.3	165.3	57.8	22	73
Ecuador	72.0	23.3	26.6	40.8	32.0	12.9	9.5	11.0	73.4	37.4	23	59
Egypt, Arab Rep.	55.8	17.6	16.0	6.5	26.3	30.2	7.1	7.7	13.9	7.3	16	53
El Salvador	26.4	54.3	13.4	25.2	55.1	67.9	20.9	18.6	55.9	67.7	49	162
Eritrea	6.3	..	0.1	..	100.0	56.1	0.0	0.6	0.0	..	34[b]	811[b]
Estonia	..	..	..	..	..	..	..	..	..	..	..	..
Ethiopia	136.8	17.6	18.5	3.1	41.9	45.8	4.5	0.9	56.5	2.5	12[b]	89[b]
Finland	..	..	..	..	..	..	..	..	..	..	..	..
France	..	..	..	..	..	..	..	..	..	..	..	..
Gabon	101.6	22.3	15.3	8.1	17.9	16.9	6.6	5.1	187.8	5.4	19	18
Gambia, The	113.0	75.3	15.5	..	49.1	51.4	3.5	8.1	14.0	18.9	30[b]	81[b]
Georgia	48.2	40.0	..	7.3	0.4	47.4	6.9	7.8	43.0	15.7	28	80
Germany	..	..	..	..	..	..	..	..	..	..	..	..
Ghana	86.9	37.3	24.2	2.9	48.4	18.7	11.3	23.1	77.1	..	27[b]	60[b]
Greece	..	..	..	..	..	..	..	..	..	..	..	..
Guatemala	22.6	38.8	12.5	18.4	47.5	74.9	24.7	8.9	103.6	23.6	33	126
Guinea	90.0	48.3	24.9	..	30.5	62.8	5.0	1.4	188.9	..	44[b]	152[b]
Guinea-Bissau	379.4	253.2	52.4	..	86.3	100.0	10.6	13.6	469.2	89.5	203[b]	647[b]
Haiti	..	..	51.0	4.6	92.2	81.0	3.2	0.0	13.4	0.0	15[b]	113[b]
Honduras	132.9	25.9	34.7	6.8	55.9	44.0	7.9	8.6	141.7	..	13[b]	25[b]

	Total external debt		Total debt service		Multilateral debt service		Short-term debt				Present value of debt	
	% of GNI		% of exports of goods and services and income[a]		% of public and publicly guaranteed debt service		% of total debt		% of total reserves		% of GNI[a]	% of exports of goods, services, and income[a]
	1995	2009	1995	2009	1995	2009	1995	2009	1995	2009	2009	2009
Hungary	..	..	..	..	..	..	..	..	..	..	..	..
India	27.0	18.2	34.4	5.9	24.2	31.9	5.3	18.1	22.1	15.1	17	71
Indonesia	63.4	30.2	30.3	18.4	28.4	25.3	20.9	11.8	174.2	28.2	30	99
Iran, Islamic Rep.	23.9	4.1	29.7	..	1.3	4.2	29.9	44.0	..	..	4	..
Iraq	..	..	..	..	..	..	..	..	..	..	..	..
Ireland	..	..	..	..	..	..	..	..	..	..	..	..
Israel	..	..	..	..	..	..	..	..	..	..	..	..
Italy	..	..	..	..	..	..	..	..	..	..	..	..
Jamaica	82.3	77.8	18.8	33.9	40.6	17.6	10.7	9.6	72.2	50.8	82	178
Japan	..	..	..	..	..	..	..	..	..	..	..	..
Jordan	118.8	28.3	16.7	4.8	33.5	50.7	10.2	17.5	34.4	9.5	27	46
Kazakhstan	18.5	113.0	3.9	80.2	7.8	45.7	10.2	7.9	23.0	37.4	96	157
Kenya	83.8	26.5	25.3	5.0	32.5	40.7	8.7	12.6	164.9	26.3	19	72
Korea, Dem. Rep.	..	..	..	..	..	..	..	..	..	..	..	..
Korea, Rep.	..	..	..	..	..	..	..	..	..	..	..	..
Kosovo	..	6.4	..	20.8	..	100.0	..	0.0	..	0.0	4	25
Kuwait	..	..	..	..	..	..	..	..	..	..	..	..
Kyrgyz Republic	37.5	65.8	13.3	14.0	59.0	78.1	2.1	2.8	9.7	5.1	36[b]	62[b]
Lao PDR	122.6	95.5	6.1	..	37.4	79.7	0.0	0.0	0.0	0.0	78	233
Latvia	..	..	..	..	..	..	..	..	..	..	..	..
Lebanon	24.4	70.7	..	18.0	13.5	5.7	45.9	12.5	16.9	7.9	80	105
Lesotho	55.8	33.2	6.1	3.0	60.3	81.7	0.6	0.0	0.9	..	19	27
Liberia	..	257.5	..	..	..	30.3	39.6	5.5	3,481.0	..	316[b]	347[b]
Libya	..	..	..	..	..	..	..	..	..	..	..	..
Lithuania	9.8	85.3	1.3	31.0	31.8	8.9	6.4	18.8	6.0	89.4	72	120
Macedonia, FYR	29.0	62.2	..	14.8	99.9	63.9	11.2	34.0	51.9	83.0	59	100
Madagascar	143.3	..	7.7	2.3	74.3	61.9	12.6	11.8	497.1	23.0	17[b]	59[b]
Malawi	165.8	24.7	24.9	..	51.4	33.4	1.9	6.1	37.8	41.0	16[b]	65[b]
Malaysia	40.6	35.8	7.0	5.2	15.5	1.9	21.2	35.7	29.5	24.5	31	27
Mali	122.3	29.6	16.1	..	45.5	57.5	2.4	1.2	22.2	2.0	14[b]	51[b]
Mauritania	175.3	66.6	23.1	..	49.6	58.1	7.1	8.0	187.9	68.4	83[b]	153[b]
Mauritius	35.2	8.4	8.7	2.7	34.5	35.6	0.1	0.0	0.1	0.0	7	11
Mexico	60.5	22.3	28.1	16.0	19.5	9.3	22.6	12.2	218.8	23.4	18	61
Moldova	40.3	59.7	7.9	14.9	79.1	43.1	0.9	38.1	2.3	89.0	55	109
Mongolia	44.2	55.8	10.2	4.8	2.8	29.9	2.2	3.3	7.4	5.4	35	57
Morocco	75.1	26.4	40.4	12.5	30.3	49.8	0.8	9.2	5.1	9.2	23	65
Mozambique	360.6	43.0	34.5	1.6	17.4	71.4	3.7	15.4	142.8	..	18[b]	53[b]
Myanmar	..	..	18.9	..	15.0	8.4	6.8	22.8	60.4	..	..	..
Namibia	..	..	..	..	..	..	..	..	..	..	..	..
Nepal	54.7	28.7	7.9	10.4	54.2	77.6	0.9	1.2	3.5	..	23	154
Netherlands	..	..	..	..	..	..	..	..	..	..	..	..
New Zealand	..	..	..	..	..	..	..	..	..	..	..	..
Nicaragua	368.6	76.2	43.1	17.2	30.3	49.8	17.2	16.2	1,256.8	45.5	36[b]	68[b]
Niger	87.6	18.8	17.1	4.5	95.5	92.0	4.5	1.9	75.6	2.8	13[b]	67[b]
Nigeria	131.7	5.1	14.7	0.8	45.4	61.0	16.6	44.8	330.7	7.7	4	8
Norway	..	..	..	..	..	..	..	..	..	..	..	..
Oman	..	..	..	..	..	..	..	..	..	..	..	..
Pakistan	49.4	31.3	30.9	15.0	43.2	50.5	10.7	2.7	128.0	10.8	24	157
Panama	80.9	52.5	3.4	5.5	52.7	22.5	36.2	0.0	282.4	0.0	54	66
Papua New Guinea	57.3	19.9	20.8	11.7	31.7	58.0	3.1	7.8	29.1	4.6	18	21
Paraguay	31.5	29.5	5.8	6.1	48.0	52.6	30.4	17.4	70.8	19.5	26	48
Peru	60.3	24.8	17.3	11.8	49.9	33.2	31.3	16.0	111.6	14.2	23	78
Philippines	51.7	39.2	16.3	18.5	29.2	13.5	13.4	6.4	67.8	9.1	35	90
Poland	..	..	..	..	..	..	..	..	..	..	..	..
Portugal	..	..	..	..	..	..	..	..	..	..	..	..
Puerto Rico	..	..	..	..	..	..	..	..	..	..	..	..
Qatar	..	..	..	..	..	..	..	..	..	..	..	..

	Total external debt		Total debt service		Multilateral debt service		Short-term debt				Present value of debt	
			% of exports of goods and services and income[a]		% of public and publicly guaranteed debt service		% of total debt		% of total reserves		% of GNI[a]	% of exports of goods, services, and income[a]
	% of GNI											
	1995	2009	1995	2009	1995	2009	1995	2009	1995	2009	2009	2009
Romania	19.4	71.6	10.5	31.4	21.3	44.1	19.1	17.9	49.7	47.4	53	166
Russian Federation	31.0	31.9	6.3	17.7	9.7	4.7	8.4	8.0	56.6	7.0	26	74
Rwanda	79.2	14.9	20.5	4.7	99.0	70.4	3.1	0.8	.32.3	0.9	8[b]	64[b]
Saudi Arabia	..	..	..	..	..	..	..	..	..	..	..	..
Senegal	82.9	27.1	17.8	..	62.2	59.1	6.6	0.5	95.6	0.8	20[b]	73[b]
Serbia	..	79.7	..	37.1	100.0[c]	51.9	19.8[c]	12.0	..	26.3	71	223
Sierra Leone	149.0	23.4	63.6	2.2	8.4	62.9	2.2	0.0	77.8	0.0	20[b]	104[b]
Singapore	..	..	..	..	..	..	..	..	..	..	..	..
Slovak Republic	..	..	..	..	..	..	..	..	..	..	..	..
Slovenia	..	..	..	..	..	..	..	..	..	..	..	..
Somalia	..	..	..	..	..	..	20.6	27.2	..	..	..	..
South Africa	17.1	15.1	9.5	9.3	0.0	2.5	38.1	31.5	216.7	33.5	15	44
Spain	..	..	..	..	..	..	..	..	..	..	..	..
Sri Lanka	65.3	41.5	9.3	15.6	14.0	20.0	6.4	10.9	25.3	35.0	35	136
Sudan	136.3	40.5	10.1	5.8	100.0	22.3	36.2	33.5	3,898.2	615.9	73[b]	352[b]
Swaziland	14.0	15.4	1.5	2.1	64.0	82.8	4.5	6.5	3.7	2.8	13	16
Sweden	..	..	..	..	..	..	..	..	..	..	..	..
Switzerland	..	..	..	..	..	..	..	..	..	..	..	..
Syrian Arab Republic	188.9	10.3	4.5	..	55.3	30.2	22.6	14.4	1,102.7	4.1	9	24
Tajikistan	53.6	51.2	..	38.4	..	39.8	6.8	0.6	..	..	39	114
Tanzania	143.5	34.0	17.4	3.5	66.7	69.6	13.1	18.3	356.6	38.7	13[b]	57[b]
Thailand	60.5	23.3	11.6	6.8	20.9	4.8	44.1	47.5	119.4	20.1	22	28
Timor-Leste	..	..	..	..	..	..	..	..	..	..	..	..
Togo	116.7	57.5	6.2	..	75.5	98.3	5.8	2.9	65.1	6.7	50[b]	136[b]
Trinidad and Tobago	..	..	..	..	..	..	..	..	..	..	..	..
Tunisia	63.0	58.2	18.3	10.1	45.2	41.7	12.1	22.1	77.6	42.5	54	80
Turkey	44.4	41.2	30.1	41.6	20.7	13.4	21.3	15.8	113.0	53.0	35	144
Turkmenistan	16.1	3.0	..	..	1.9	2.2	4.3	13.0	1.5	..	3	4
Uganda	63.3	16.2	19.8	2.0	69.7	66.0	2.8	9.4	22.4	7.9	8[b]	34[b]
Ukraine	17.8	83.8	6.6	36.2	13.6	16.9	2.6	21.3	20.9	75.0	62	123
United Arab Emirates	..	..	..	..	..	..	..	..	..	..	..	..
United Kingdom	..	..	..	..	..	..	..	..	..	..	..	..
United States	..	..	..	..	..	..	..	..	..	..	..	..
Uruguay	28.0	34.5	22.1	21.0	27.3	22.3	25.1	9.2	73.7	14.0	37	121
Uzbekistan	13.5	12.5	..	..	1.9	21.6	11.8	3.5	..	..	12	29
Venezuela, RB	49.0	16.7	22.9	6.4	11.6	13.4	8.6	29.4	28.6	46.6	19	66
Vietnam	124.0	32.3	..	1.8	2.9	18.3	12.9	18.1	247.2	31.5	27	34
West Bank and Gaza	..	..	..	..	..	..	..	..	..	..	..	..
Yemen, Rep.	169.9	25.5	4.6	..	78.3	58.7	11.0	7.0	107.9	6.3	17	47
Zambia	215.1	26.8	..	3.8	50.6	48.6	6.0	15.6	186.2	25.1	10[b]	24[b]
Zimbabwe	73.5	..	..	..	33.6	0.0	13.7	21.3	77.2	..	..	335
World	.. w	.. w	.. w	.. w	.. w	.. w	.. w	.. w	.. w	.. w	..	..
Low income	88.4	30.9	..	3.9	40.2	57.1	8.6	9.5	96.0	16.2	..	..
Middle income	36.8	21.8	18.0	11.6	22.5	20.2	18.5	21.1	72.7	14.9	..	..
Lower middle income	40.4	15.6	17.2	6.2	25.5	27.9	18.6	28.4	70.4	12.2	..	..
Upper middle income	33.9	30.3	18.6	19.5	20.0	15.4	18.4	16.0	74.8	21.0	..	..
Low & middle income	38.8	22.1	18.0	11.3	23.0	21.0	17.8	20.7	73.3	15.0	..	..
East Asia & Pacific	35.5	13.2	12.7	4.8	18.2	18.4	23.9	39.0	64.9	11.3	..	..
Europe & Central Asia	32.7	44.7	10.9	26.9	16.6	13.3	12.7	14.7	67.6	24.4	..	..
Latin America & Carib.	35.8	23.7	27.3	17.9	26.2	23.3	20.2	15.2	88.6	25.0	..	..
Middle East & N. Africa	59.2	15.4	21.1	..	19.7	23.3	11.4	15.9	31.1	..	..	..
South Asia	32.2	20.7	29.7	6.8	27.4	38.4	5.9	14.3	29.5	15.4	..	..
Sub-Saharan Africa	76.1	22.9	16.2	5.9	35.0	25.1	17.2	18.3	193.5	21.3	..	..
High income	..	..	..	..	..	..	..	..	..	..	..	..
Euro area	..	..	..	..	..	..	..	..	..	..	..	..

a. The numerator refers to 2009, whereas the denominator is a three-year average of 2007–09 data. b. Data are from debt sustainability analyses for low-income countries. Present value estimates for these countries are for public and publicly guaranteed debt only. c. Includes Montenegro.

About the data

A country's external debt burden, both debt outstanding and debt service, affects its creditworthiness and vulnerability. The table shows total external debt relative to a country's size—gross national income (GNI). Total debt service is contrasted with countries' ability to obtain foreign exchange through exports of goods, services, income, and workers' remittances.

Multilateral debt service (shown as a share of the country's total public and publicly guaranteed debt service) are obligations to international financial institutions, such as the World Bank, the International Monetary Fund (IMF), and regional development banks. Multilateral debt service takes priority over private and bilateral debt service, and borrowers must stay current with multilateral debts to remain creditworthy. While bilateral and private creditors often write off debts, international financial institution bylaws prohibit granting debt relief or canceling debts directly. However, the recent decrease in multilateral debt service ratios for some countries reflects debt relief from special programs, such as the Heavily Indebted Poor Countries (HIPC) Debt Initiative and the Multilateral Debt Relief Initiative (MDRI) (see table 1.4.) Other countries have accelerated repayment of debt outstanding. Indebted countries may also apply to the Paris and London Clubs to renegotiate obligations to public and private creditors.

Because short-term debt poses an immediate burden and is particularly important for monitoring vulnerability, it is compared with the total debt and foreign exchange reserves that are instrumental in providing coverage for such obligations. The present value of external debt provides a measure of future debt service obligations.

The present value of external debt is calculated by discounting the debt service (interest plus amortization) due on long-term external debt over the life of existing loans. Short-term debt is included at face value. The data on debt are in U.S. dollars converted at official exchange rates (see *About the data* for table 6.10). The discount rate on long-term debt depends on the currency of repayment and is based on commercial interest reference rates established by the Organisation for Economic Co-operation and Development. Loans from the International Bank for Reconstruction and Development (IBRD), credits from the International Development Association (IDA), and obligations to the IMF are discounted using a special drawing rights reference rate. When the discount rate is greater than the loan interest rate, the present value is less than the nominal sum of future debt service obligations.

Debt ratios are used to assess the sustainability of a country's debt service obligations, but no absolute rules determine what values are too high. Empirical analysis of developing countries' experience and debt service performance shows that debt service difficulties become increasingly likely when the present value of debt reaches 200 percent of exports. Still, what constitutes a sustainable debt burden varies by country. Countries with fast-growing economies and exports are likely to be able to sustain higher debt levels.

Definitions

• **Total external debt** is debt owed to nonresidents and comprises public, publicly guaranteed, and private nonguaranteed long-term debt, short-term debt, and use of IMF credit. It is presented as a share of GNI. • **Total debt service** is the sum of principal repayments and interest actually paid in foreign currency, goods, or services on long-term debt; interest paid on short-term debt; and repayments (repurchases and charges) to the IMF. • **Exports of goods, services, and income** are the total value of exports of goods and services, receipts of compensation of nonresident workers, and investment income from abroad. • **Multilateral debt service** is the repayment of principal and interest to the World Bank, regional development banks, and other multilateral and intergovernmental agencies. • **Short-term debt** includes all debt having an original maturity of one year or less and interest in arrears on long-term debt. • **Total reserves** comprise holdings of monetary gold, special drawing rights, reserves of IMF members held by the IMF, and holdings of foreign exchange under the control of monetary authorities. • **Present value of debt** is the sum of short-term external debt plus the discounted sum of total debt service payments due on public, publicly guaranteed, and private nonguaranteed long-term external debt over the life of existing loans.

Ratio of debt services to exports for middle-income economies have sharply increased in 2009 as export revenues declined 6.11a

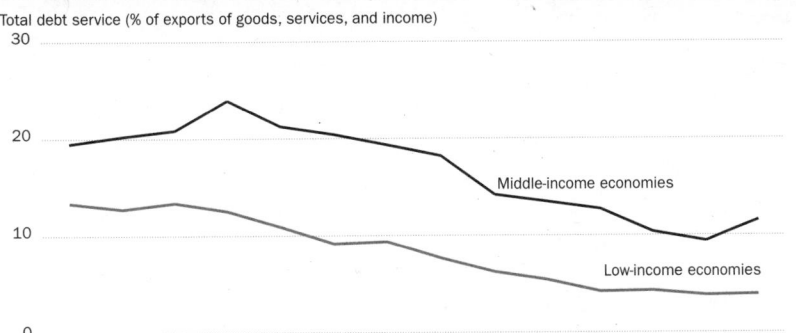

Total debt service (% of exports of goods, services, and income)

Due to global financial crisis, export revenues in 2009 declined by 20 percent for middle-income economies, and by 8 percent for low-income economies. Reduction in export revenues caused sharp raise in the ratio of debt service to exports, which has been declining since 2000 thanks to debt reduction efforts and export growth.

Source: Global Development Finance data files.

Data sources

Data on external debt are mainly from reports to the World Bank through its Debtor Reporting System from member countries that have received IBRD loans or IDA credits, with additional information from the files of the World Bank, the IMF, the African Development Bank and African Development Fund, the Asian Development Bank and Asian Development Fund, and the Inter-American Development Bank. Data on GNI, exports of goods and services, and total reserves are from the World Bank's national accounts files and the IMF's Balance of Payments and International Financial Statistics databases. Summary tables of the external debt of developing countries are published annually in the World Bank's *Global Development Finance, Global Development Finance* CD-ROM, and Global Development Finance database.

Global private financial flows

	Equity flows				Debt flows			
	$ millions				$ millions			
	Foreign direct investment		Portfolio equity		Bonds		Commercial bank and other lending	
	1995	**2009**	**1995**	**2009**	**1995**	**2009**	**1995**	**2009**
Afghanistan	0	185	..	..	..	0	..	0
Albania	70	978	0	4	0	0	0	451
Algeria	..	2,847	..	..	−278	0	788	−607
Angola	472	2,205	0	0	0	0	123	156
Argentina	5,609	3,902	1,552	−212	3,705	−1,114	754	−1,849
Armenia	25	777	..	1	0	0	0	42
Australia	12,026	22,572	2,585	..	..	..	..	..
Austria	1,901	8,714	1,262	498	..	..	..	..
Azerbaijan	330	473	..	0	0	0	0	400
Bangladesh	2	674	−15	−154	0	0	−20	−13
Belarus	15	1,884	..	1	0	0	103	−31
Belgium	10,689[a]	−38,860	6,505[a]	−3,242	..	..	..	..
Benin	13	93	0	..	0	0	0	0
Bolivia	393	423	0	0	0	−10	41	−156
Bosnia and Herzegovina	..	235	..	..	..	0	..	−40
Botswana	70	252	6	18	0	0	−6	−1
Brazil	4,859	25,949	2,775	37,071	2,636	19,111	8,283	4,731
Bulgaria	90	4,595	0	8	−6	−372	−93	304
Burkina Faso	10	171	..	..	0	0	0	−3
Burundi	2	0	0	..	0	0	−1	0
Cambodia	151	530	..	0	0	0	13	0
Cameroon	7	340	0	0	0	0	−65	−12
Canada	9,319	19,898	−3,077	23,349	..	..	..	..
Central African Republic	6	42	..	..	0	0	0	0
Chad	33	462	..	..	0	0	0	0
Chile	2,957	12,702	−249	316	489	1,900	1,773	2,572
China	35,849	78,193	0	28,161	317	−39	4,696	−12,050
Hong Kong SAR, China	..	52,395	..	9,492	..	..	..	..
Colombia	968	7,207	165	67	1,008	6,768	1,250	−1,018
Congo, Dem. Rep.	−22	951	0	..	0	0	0	−61
Congo, Rep.	125	2,083	0	..	0	0	−53	−1
Costa Rica	337	1,347	0	0	−4	−225	−20	538
Côte d'Ivoire	211	381	1	−9	0	0	14	−143
Croatia	108	2,951	4	23	..	..	..	..
Cuba	..	..	..	..	..	..	..	..
Czech Republic	2,568	2,666	1,236	−311	..	..	..	..
Denmark	4,139	2,905	..	8,152	..	..	..	..
Dominican Republic	414	2,067	..	0	0	−125	−31	−213
Ecuador	452	316	13	2	0	−2,987	59	−997
Egypt, Arab Rep.	598	6,712	0	393	0	0	−311	−33
El Salvador	38	431	0	0	0	0	−31	175
Eritrea	..	0	..	..	0	0	0	0
Estonia	201	1,751	10	−131	..	..	..	..
Ethiopia	14	221	..	0	0	0	−48	1,019
Finland	1,044	60	2,027	−273	..	..	..	..
France	23,736	59,989	6,823	68,285	..	..	..	..
Gabon	−315	33	..	..	0	−44	−75	74
Gambia, The	8	39	..	0	0	0	0	0
Georgia	..	658	..	13	0	0	0	135
Germany	11,985	39,153	−1,513	11,806	..	..	..	..
Ghana	107	1,685	0	0	0	0	38	224
Greece	1,053	2,419	0	764	..	..	..	..
Guatemala	75	600	..	0	44	−50	−34	-574
Guinea	1	50	..	0	0	0	−15	4
Guinea-Bissau	0	14	..	..	0	0	0	0
Haiti	7	38	..	0	0	0	0	0
Honduras	50	500	0	0	−13	50	38	222

	Equity flows			Debt flows			
	$ millions			$ millions			
	Foreign direct investment		Portfolio equity		Bonds		Commercial bank and other lending	
	1995	2009	1995	2009	1995	2009	1995	2009
Hungary	4,804	2,783	−62	954	..	..	..	..
India	2,144	34,577	1,590	21,112	285	1,822	955	8,343
Indonesia	4,346	4,877	1,493	787	2,248	5,112	60	5,872
Iran, Islamic Rep.	17	3,016	0	..	0	0	−37	−1,417
Iraq	2	1,070	..	..	..	..	..	..
Ireland	1,447	25,233	0	29,184	..	..	..	..
Israel	1,350	3,894	991	2,122	..	..	..	..
Italy	4,842	28,976	5,358	20,915	..	..	..	..
Jamaica	147	541	0	0	13	740	15	−62
Japan	39	11,834	50,597	12,432	..	..	..	..
Jordan	13	2,382	0	-30	0	-2	−201	−3
Kazakhstan	964	13,619	..	46	0	-2,108	240	6,554
Kenya	42	141	5	3	0	0	−163	24
Korea, Dem. Rep.	..	..	..	..				
Korea, Rep.	1,776	1,506	4,219	25,661	..	..	..	..
Kosovo	..	406	..	0		0	..	0
Kuwait	7	145	0	0	..	..	..	..
Kyrgyz Republic	96	189	..	1	0	0	0	29
Lao PDR	95	319	0	0	0	0	0	387
Latvia	180	94	0	−8	..	..	..	..
Lebanon	..	4,804	..	929	350	789	333	−41
Lesotho	275	63	..	..	0	0	12	−1
Liberia	5	218	..	0	0	0	0	−32
Libya	−88	1,711	..	0	..	..	..	..
Lithuania	73	230	6	−2	0	2,488	55	−1,971
Macedonia, FYR	9	248	..	−14	0	244	0	244
Madagascar	10	543	..	..	0	0	−4	0
Malawi	6	60	..	..	0	0	−23	0
Malaysia	4,178	1,387	0	−449	2,440	143	1,231	−1,592
Mali	111	109	..	..	0	0	0	1
Mauritania	7	−38	0	..	0	0	0	−1
Mauritius	19	257	22	−33	150	0	126	29
Mexico	9,526	14,462	519	4,169	3,758	7,499	1,401	−9,314
Moldova	26	128	−1	2	0	−6	24	−18
Mongolia	10	624	0	4	0	0	−14	46
Morocco	92	1,970	20	−4	0	0	158	−61
Mozambique	45	881	0	0	0	0	24	20
Myanmar	280	323	..	..	0	0	36	0
Namibia	153	490	46	4	..	..	..	..
Nepal	..	38	0	..	0	0	−5	−1
Netherlands	12,206	33,287	−743	19,256	..	..	..	..
New Zealand	3,316	−1,259	..	967	..	..	..	..
Nicaragua	89	434	0	0	0	0	−81	−75
Niger	7	739	..	..	0	0	−24	−7
Nigeria	1,079	5,787	0	522	0	0	−448	−55
Norway	2,393	11,271	636	2,470	..	..	..	..
Oman	46	2,210	0	326	..	..	..	..
Pakistan	723	2,387	10	−37	0	−500	317	26
Panama	223	1,773	0	0	0	1,323	−12	70
Papua New Guinea	455	423	..	..	−32	0	−311	25
Paraguay	103	205	0	0	0	0	−16	425
Peru	2,557	4,760	171	47	0	2,828	43	−258
Philippines	1,478	1,948	0	−1,096	1,110	3,527	−215	−783
Poland	3,659	13,796	219	1,579	..	..	..	..
Portugal	685	2,808	−179	1,616	..	..	..	..
Puerto Rico	..	..	..	..			..	..
Qatar	..	..	..	..			..	..

	Equity flows				Debt flows			
	$ millions					$ millions		
	Foreign direct investment		Portfolio equity		Bonds		Commercial bank and other lending	
	1995	**2009**	**1995**	**2009**	**1995**	**2009**	**1995**	**2009**
Romania	419	6,310	0	7	0	32	413	7,022
Russian Federation	2,065	36,751	47	3,369	−810	−1,968	444	7,328
Rwanda	2	119	0	0	0	0	0	0
Saudi Arabia	−1,875	10,499	0	..	..	..	..	..
Senegal	32	208	4	..	0	200	−25	157
Serbia	45[b]	1,921	..	23	0	0	0	104
Sierra Leone	7	74	0	6	0	0	−28	0
Singapore	11,535	16,809	−159	2,058	..	..	..	..
Slovak Republic	236	−31	−16	182	..	..	..	..
Slovenia	150	−579	..	31	..	..	..	..
Somalia	1	108	..	..	0	0	0	0
South Africa	1,248	5,354	2,914	9,364	731	1,750	748	2,291
Spain	8,086	6,451	4,216	9,378	..	..	..	..
Sri Lanka	56	404	..	−382	0	400	103	238
Sudan	12	2,682	0	0	0	0	0	0
Swaziland	52	66	1	−7	0	0	0	0
Sweden	14,939	11,538	1,853	1,400	..	..	..	..
Switzerland	4,158	27,588	5,851	9,241	..	..	..	..
Syrian Arab Republic	100	1,434	0	..	0	0	−1	0
Tajikistan	10	16	..	0	0	0	0	−54
Tanzania	120	415	0	3	0	0	18	84
Thailand	2,068	4,976	2,253	1,334	2,123	−341	3,702	−1,134
Timor-Leste	..	..	..	..	..	..	..	..
Togo	26	50	0	..	0	0	0	0
Trinidad and Tobago	299	709	17	..	..	..	..	..
Tunisia	264	1,595	12	−89	588	−313	−96	30
Turkey	885	8,403	195	2,827	627	1,152	174	−12,036
Turkmenistan	233	1,355	..	..	0	0	20	−24
Uganda	121	604	0	122	0	0	−9	0
Ukraine	267	4,816	..	105	−200	−1,115	−19	−1,605
United Arab Emirates	..	..	..	..	..	..	..	..
United Kingdom	21,731	72,924	8,070	78,845	..	..	..	..
United States	57,800	134,710	16,523	160,534	..	..	..	..
Uruguay	157	1,262	0	−12	144	−420	39	−19
Uzbekistan	−24	750	..	..	0	0	201	−118
Venezuela, RB	985	−3,105	270	121	−468	4,992	−216	−322
Vietnam	1,780	7,600	..	128	0	−20	356	−1
West Bank and Gaza	123	..	0	..	..	..	..	..
Yemen, Rep.	−218	129	..	0	0	0	−2	−1
Zambia	97	699	..	−13	0	0	−37	−36
Zimbabwe	118	60	..	..	−30	0	140	0
World	**340,573 s**	**1,163,874 s**	**127,074 s**	**744,295 s**	**.. s**	**.. s**	**.. s**	**.. s**
Low income	1,540	10,950	−10	−33	−30	0	−107	1,601
Middle income	93,318	348,451	13,835	108,577	20,954	51,121	26,661	88
Lower middle income	54,045	177,583	5,397	50,913	6,470	8,555	8,991	−2,246
Upper middle income	39,273	170,868	8,438	57,663	14,484	42,566	17,670	2,335
Low & middle income	94,858	359,401	13,824	108,544	20,924	51,121	26,554	1,689
East Asia & Pacific	50,797	101,428	3,746	28,868	8,206	8,383	9,554	−9,217
Europe & Central Asia	5,599	86,067	248	6,386	−389	−1,653	1,563	6,921
Latin America & Carib.	30,212	76,629	5,216	41,570	11,311	40,290	13,240	−6,172
Middle East & N. Africa	907	27,766	32	1,200	660	473	632	−2,132
South Asia	2,931	38,414	1,585	20,539	285	1,722	1,350	8,575
Sub-Saharan Africa	4,411	29,096	2,998	9,981	851	1,906	214	3,715
High income	245,715	804,473	113,249	635,751	..	..	..	..
Euro area	89,322	371,020	23,747	296,975	..	..	..	..

a. Includes Luxembourg. b. Includes Montenegro.

About the data

Private financial flows—equity and debt—account for the bulk of development finance. Equity flows comprise foreign direct investment (FDI) and portfolio equity. Debt flows are financing raised through bond issuance, bank lending, and supplier credits. Data on equity flows are based on balance of payments data reported by the International Monetary Fund (IMF). FDI data are supplemented by staff estimates using data from the United Nations Conference on Trade and Development and official national sources.

The internationally accepted definition of FDI (from the fifth edition of the IMF's Balance of Payments Manual [1993]), includes three components: equity investment, reinvested earnings, and short- and long-term loans between parent firms and foreign affiliates. Distinguished from other kinds of international investment, FDI is made to establish a lasting interest in or effective management control over an enterprise in another country. A lasting interest in investment enterprise typically involves establishing warehouses, manufacturing facilities, and other permanent or long-term organizations abroad. Direct investments may take the form of greenfield investment, where the investor starts a new venture in a foreign country by constructing new operational facilities; joint venture, where the investor enters into a partnership agreement with a company abroad to establish a new enterprise; or merger and acquisition, where the investor acquires an existing enterprise abroad. The IMF suggests that investments should account for at least 10 percent of voting stock to be counted as FDI. In practice many countries set a higher threshold. Many countries fail to report reinvested earnings, and the definition of long-term loans differs among countries.

FDI data do not give a complete picture of international investment in an economy. Balance of payments data on FDI do not include capital raised locally, an important source of investment financing in some developing countries. In addition, FDI data omit nonequity cross-border transactions such as intrafirm flows of goods and services. For a detailed discussion of the data issues, see the World Bank's World Debt Tables 1993–94 (vol. 1, chap. 3).

Statistics on bonds, bank lending, and supplier credits are produced by aggregating transactions of public and publicly guaranteed debt and private nonguaranteed debt. Data on public and publicly guaranteed debt are reported through the Debtor Reporting System by World Bank member economies that have received loans from the International Bank for Reconstruction and Development or credits from the International Development Association. The reports are cross-checked with data from market sources that include transactions data. Information on private nonguaranteed bonds and bank lending is collected from market sources when data are not reported by countries to the Debtor Reporting System.

Data on equity flows are shown for all countries for which data are available. Debt flows are shown only for 128 developing countries that report to the Debtor Reporting System; nonreporting countries may also receive debt flows.

The volume of global private financial flows reported by the World Bank generally differs from that reported by other sources because of differences in sources, classification of economies, and method used to adjust and disaggregate reported information. In addition, particularly for debt financing, differences may also reflect how some installments of the transactions and certain offshore issuances are treated.

Definitions

• **Foreign direct investment** is net inflows of investment to acquire a lasting interest in or management control over an enterprise operating in an economy other than that of the investor. It is the sum of equity capital, reinvested earnings, other long-term capital, and short-term capital, as shown in the balance of payments. Net inflows refer to new investments made during the reporting period netted against disinvestments. • **Portfolio equity** includes net inflows from equity securities other than those recorded as direct investment and including shares, stocks, depository receipts, and direct purchases of shares in local stock markets by foreign investors • **Bonds** are securities issued with a fixed rate of interest for a period of more than one year. They include net flows through cross–border public and publicly guaranteed and private nonguaranteed bond issues. • **Commercial bank and other lending** includes net commercial bank lending (public and publicly guaranteed and private nonguaranteed) and other private credits.

Data sources

Data on equity and debt flows are compiled from a variety of public and private sources, including the World Bank's Debtor Reporting System, the IMF's International Financial Statistics and Balance of Payments databases, and Dealogic. These data are also published annually in the World Bank's *Global Development Finance,* Global Development Finance CD-ROM, and Global Development Finance database.

6.13 Net official financial flows

	Total		International financial institutions							United Nations[b,c]			
	$ millions		World Bank[a]		IMF		Regional development banks[b]			$ millions			
	From bilateral sources	From multilateral sources[a,b,c]	IDA	IBRD	Concessional	Non-concessional	Concessional	Non-concessional	Other institutions	UNICEF	UNRWA	UNTA	Others
	2009	2009	2009	2009	2009	2009	2009	2009	2009	2009	2009	2009	2009
Afghanistan	1.0	194.1	26.7	0.0	17.4	0.0	73.9	0.0	7.4	39.5	0.0	1.0	28.2
Albania	26.3	130.8	25.5	6.9	−12.1	1.9	0.0	21.1	83.0	1.0	0.0	0.4	3.1
Algeria	−84.8	7.2	0.0	−0.5	0.0	0.0	0.0	0.0	−0.8	1.0	0.0	0.9	6.6
Angola	786.6	386.4	13.5	0.0	0.0	353.3	1.6	−0.4	0.8	8.5	0.0	0.8	8.3
Argentina	282.5	1,437.1	0.0	235.6	0.0	0.0	0.0	914.8	282.3	0.8	0.0	1.0	2.6
Armenia	610.9	758.9	128.5	48.6	−23.4	465.7	119.1	1.3	11.4	0.8	0.0	1.6	5.3
Australia													
Austria													
Azerbaijan	−17.5	304.9	36.1	121.6	−15.6	−2.9	15.1	93.8	47.1	1.0	0.0	0.6	8.1
Bangladesh	−146.1	1,004.7	62.8	0.0	−23.4	0.0	149.8	701.9	38.7	22.2	0.0	0.8	51.9
Belarus	975.7	3,040.3	0.0	213.5	0.0	2,825.2	0.0	−2.1	0.0	0.7	0.0	0.5	2.5
Belgium													
Benin	25.3	134.2	51.4	0.0	15.7	0.0	25.5	0.0	22.9	4.9	0.0	0.8	13.0
Bolivia	61.9	168.3	32.3	0.0	0.0	0.0	95.7	−36.1	67.9	1.5	0.0	0.6	6.4
Bosnia and Herzegovina	33.8	483.8	18.0	−24.7	0.0	281.7	0.0	129.5	69.4	0.8	0.0	0.8	8.3
Botswana	−5.1	982.5	−0.5	0.0	0.0	0.0	−3.6	971.7	8.3	1.2	0.0	0.4	5.0
Brazil	2,998.3	441.6	0.0	−597.9	0.0	0.0	0.0	1,018.9	12.1	1.1	0.0	1.5	5.9
Bulgaria	−5.2	259.3	0.0	285.0	0.0	0.0	0.0	−13.6	−12.1	..		..	..
Burkina Faso	13.6	270.6	89.7	0.0	54.2	0.0	78.3	0.0	4.1	17.7	0.0	1.1	25.5
Burundi	0.0	63.5	8.6	0.0	13.4	0.0	4.2	0.0	2.6	9.9	0.0	0.6	24.2
Cambodia	116.0	96.5	16.4	0.0	0.0	0.0	47.6	0.0	4.5	7.3	0.0	0.8	19.9
Cameroon	−38.9	225.1	46.3	−5.4	147.3	0.0	23.6	−21.9	12.1	6.8	0.0	1.0	15.3
Canada													
Central African Republic	−3.4	30.1	2.1	0.0	20.3	0.0	−1.8	0.0	−2.0	4.5	0.0	0.5	6.5
Chad	−1.9	25.3	−14.6	0.0	−12.7	0.0	0.4	0.0	9.4	13.4	0.0	0.5	28.9
Chile	−20.8	58.6	−0.7	14.9	0.0	0.0	0.0	40.7	0.0	0.8	0.0	0.9	2.0
China	−339.4	1,098.7	−329.8	298.5	0.0	0.0	0.0	1,069.1	17.7	10.5	0.0	2.2	30.5
Hong Kong SAR, China	..	..	..	..	..	..	..	..	..	..	..	..	..
Colombia	−113.6	1,633.2	−0.7	1,115.6	0.0	0.0	−2.6	534.9	−23.6	1.3	0.0	0.8	7.5
Congo, Dem. Rep.	−168.9	264.6	78.1	0.0	131.7	0.0	14.3	−43.1	−13.1	55.4	0.0	1.3	40.0
Congo, Rep.	−62.6	2.8	0.8	0.0	3.7	0.0	−0.4	−8.5	−3.6	1.3	0.0	0.2	9.3
Costa Rica	74.8	143.9	−0.2	16.7	0.0	0.0	−9.2	3.8	128.7	0.8	0.0	0.7	2.6
Côte d'Ivoire	−15.4	−289.9	−27.3	−73.3	282.9	−125.4	−4.2	−369.4	−4.3	8.4	0.0	1.1	21.6
Croatia	..	..	0.0	39.8	..	..	..	..	..	0.3	0.0	0.6	2.9
Cuba	..	..	..	..	..	..	..	..	..	1.0	0.0	1.4	3.4
Czech Republic	..	..	0.0	0.0	..	..	..	..	..	..		..	..
Denmark													
Dominican Republic	203.2	977.0	−0.7	298.6	0.0	261.2	−21.3	373.5	62.3	0.8	0.0	0.8	1.8
Ecuador	−175.1	61.4	−1.1	−80.7	0.0	0.0	−26.4	125.6	38.5	0.8	0.0	0.8	3.9
Egypt, Arab Rep.	−907.4	858.9	−50.5	595.4	0.0	0.0	−5.0	145.0	160.8	3.5	0.0	1.4	8.3
El Salvador	−38.8	402.1	−0.8	169.3	0.0	0.0	−22.9	233.3	17.6	1.3	0.0	0.7	3.6
Eritrea	41.6	23.0	0.8	0.0	0.0	0.0	3.4	0.0	0.6	2.7	0.0	1.1	14.4
Estonia	..	..	0.0	−6.7	..	..	..	..	..	..		..	..
Ethiopia	335.1	977.1	549.2	0.0	165.0	0.0	163.0	−6.7	21.6	35.9	0.0	1.1	48.0
Finland													
France													
Gabon	−99.4	20.1	0.0	−2.3	0.0	0.0	−0.2	33.3	−16.0	0.7	0.0	0.4	4.2
Gambia, The	2.9	46.5	2.0	0.0	15.8	0.0	7.4	0.0	12.9	1.4	0.0	0.3	6.7
Georgia	23.8	655.4	155.2	100.0	−27.7	340.6	111.4	−5.9	−27.6	0.8	0.0	0.8	7.8
Germany													
Ghana	99.2	476.8	239.7	0.0	104.3	0.0	99.6	−2.0	2.2	8.2	0.0	0.9	23.9
Greece	..	..	0.0	0.0	..	..	..	..	..	..		..	..
Guatemala	−10.8	554.1	0.0	306.3	0.0	0.0	−6.9	255.5	−5.4	0.8	0.0	0.6	3.2
Guinea	3.9	−29.3	−27.2	0.0	−12.8	0.0	2.9	−5.6	−12.3	7.6	0.0	0.5	17.6
Guinea-Bissau	0.0	9.6	0.0	0.0	−1.6	2.7	−1.2	0.0	0.0	2.7	0.0	0.2	6.8
Haiti	109.1	159.2	−11.0	0.0	57.4	0.0	75.6	0.0	11.8	2.4	0.0	0.8	22.2
Honduras	12.7	87.4	49.4	0.0	0.0	0.0	32.7	−19.8	16.2	0.7	0.0	1.1	7.1

	Total ($ millions)		International financial institutions ($ millions)							United Nations[b,c] ($ millions)			
			World Bank[a]		IMF		Regional development banks[b]						
	From bilateral sources	From multilateral sources[a,b,c]	IDA	IBRD	Concessional	Non-concessional	Concessional	Non-concessional	Other institutions	UNICEF	UNRWA	UNTA	Others
	2009	2009	2009	2009	2009	2009	2009	2009	2009	2009	2009	2009	2009
Hungary	..	−23.1	0.0	−23.1	..	..	..	..	..	..	..	..	..
India	−152.3	2,079.7	455.3	671.5	0.0	0.0	0.0	857.9	12.0	42.0	0.0	0.3	40.7
Indonesia	−1,099.1	1,131.2	212.8	908.6	0.0	0.0	88.6	−99.4	0.0	6.3	0.0	1.1	13.2
Iran, Islamic Rep.	−247.4	81.8	0.0	74.7	0.0	0.0	0.0	0.0	0.0	1.7	0.0	0.6	4.8
Iraq	..	..	..	..	..	..	..	..	..	2.0	0.0	0.4	7.8
Ireland													
Israel	..	..	..	..	..	..	..	..	..	..	..	..	..
Italy													
Jamaica	−61.3	185.4	0.0	71.1	0.0	0.0	−4.6	81.6	34.7	1.1	0.0	0.3	1.2
Japan		..											
Jordan	−65.1	548.3	−2.6	240.0	0.0	−15.9	0.0	0.0	190.1	0.8	133.5	0.9	1.5
Kazakhstan	−13.3	604.2	0.0	83.8	0.0	0.0	−0.2	532.6	−16.1	1.0	0.0	0.3	2.8
Kenya	59.8	385.0	82.9	0.0	191.2	0.0	54.0	−5.0	11.1	11.8	0.0	1.9	37.1
Korea, Dem. Rep.	..	..								5.5	0.0	1.4	7.6
Korea, Rep.													
Kosovo	0.0	−199.4	0.0	−207.7	0.0	0.0	0.0	0.0	0.0	1.5	0.0	0.0	6.8
Kuwait	..	..	..	..	..	..	..	..	..	..	..	..	..
Kyrgyz Republic	332.0	17.8	−4.1	0.0	−0.3	0.0	12.2	−4.6	4.7	1.4	0.0	1.3	7.2
Lao PDR	114.9	44.0	−9.6	0.0	−5.6	0.0	8.1	0.5	33.9	2.7	0.0	0.7	13.3
Latvia	..	..	0.0	273.2	..	..	..	..	..	..	..	..	..
Lebanon	−95.9	106.3	0.0	−49.8	0.0	0.0	0.0	0.0	29.1	0.8	123.0	1.0	2.2
Lesotho	12.8	3.9	5.9	−0.7	−5.9	0.0	−4.6	0.0	0.4	1.4	0.0	0.6	6.8
Liberia	0.0	37.6	−3.3	0.0	17.6	0.0	−1.0	0.0	0.0	5.7	0.0	0.4	18.2
Libya	..	..	..	..	..	..	..	..	..	0.0	0.0	0.4	2.5
Lithuania	−2.3	1,000.6	0.0	−3.1	0.0	0.0	0.0	−8.0	1,011.7	..	..	..	..
Macedonia, FYR	6.4	20.5	−7.0	33.3	0.0	0.0	0.0	−4.9	−5.4	0.9	0.0	1.0	2.6
Madagascar	34.8	92.5	30.4	0.0	0.0	0.0	27.1	0.0	−0.9	12.7	0.0	1.3	21.9
Malawi	12.2	84.8	24.2	0.0	0.0	0.0	18.3	−2.0	7.9	9.3	0.0	1.0	26.1
Malaysia	−912.1	−89.6	0.0	−46.7	0.0	0.0	0.0	−40.3	−7.2	0.7	0.0	0.6	3.3
Mali	84.3	383.8	159.2	0.0	3.1	0.0	58.8	0.0	132.1	14.7	0.0	0.7	15.2
Mauritania	33.3	204.6	37.9	0.0	0.0	0.0	24.8	−8.0	133.0	2.1	0.0	0.7	14.1
Mauritius	−24.8	107.1	−0.6	101.0	0.0	0.0	−0.2	13.6	−10.0	0.0	0.0	0.6	2.7
Mexico	466.6	6,463.4	0.0	4,213.3	0.0	0.0	0.0	2,247.5	0.0	1.0	0.0	1.0	0.6
Moldova	−22.8	11.9	18.0	−17.6	−8.6	−6.4	0.0	−3.5	19.2	0.9	0.0	1.5	8.4
Mongolia	57.2	262.9	51.0	0.0	−6.5	165.5	43.3	0.0	1.6	0.8	0.0	1.2	6.0
Morocco	606.8	1,301.8	−1.4	2.7	0.0	0.0	−1.1	545.2	751.1	1.5	0.0	0.9	2.9
Mozambique	193.6	484.7	197.1	0.0	153.3	0.0	68.8	0.0	20.6	16.3	0.0	0.8	27.8
Myanmar	−7.9	34.7	0.0	0.0	0.0	0.0	0.0	0.0	−0.8	17.0	0.0	1.1	17.4
Namibia	..	..	..	..	..	..	..	..	..	1.1	0.0	0.7	5.3
Nepal	−10.7	35.6	−33.5	0.0	−2.2	0.0	14.9	0.0	16.1	7.4	0.0	1.1	31.8
Netherlands													
New Zealand													
Nicaragua	−11.3	265.8	66.7	0.0	36.7	0.0	106.6	25.8	20.7	1.3	0.0	1.4	6.6
Niger	6.3	110.5	15.8	0.0	5.1	0.0	19.5	0.0	35.2	18.2	0.0	0.7	16.0
Nigeria	−72.1	386.2	475.6	−96.1	0.0	0.0	15.4	−91.3	4.3	48.8	0.0	1.0	28.5
Norway		..											
Oman	..	..	0.0	0.0	..	..	..	..	..	0.0	0.0	0.1	0.4
Pakistan	887.5	4,639.2	988.8	−163.3	−223.3	3,307.1	223.6	419.4	18.1	19.8	0.0	1.9	47.1
Panama	15.2	292.0	0.0	164.3	0.0	0.0	−6.1	131.6	2.0	0.7	0.0	0.5	−1.0
Papua New Guinea	−20.1	6.5	10.5	−9.0	0.0	0.0	−9.2	9.5	−3.9	1.5	0.0	0.5	7.1
Paraguay	−12.9	60.3	−1.5	68.1	0.0	0.0	−15.7	−2.1	7.7	0.8	0.0	0.5	2.5
Peru	−961.9	1,689.9	0.0	134.4	0.0	0.0	−3.5	1,380.8	171.0	0.9	0.0	0.8	5.5
Philippines	−425.8	1,067.9	−7.0	−32.7	0.0	0.0	−38.9	1,116.4	13.0	3.1	0.0	0.8	13.2
Poland	..	..	0.0	2,658.3	..	..	..	..	..	..	..	..	..
Portugal													
Puerto Rico	..	..	..	..	..	..	..	..	..	..	..	..	..
Qatar	..	..	..	..	..	..	..	..	..	..	..	..	..

	Total		International financial institutions							United Nations[b,c]			
	$ millions				$ millions						$ millions		
	From bilateral sources	From multilateral sources[a,b,c]	World Bank[a]		IMF		Regional development banks[b]		Other institutions	UNICEF	UNRWA	UNTA	Others
			IDA	IBRD	Concessional	Non-concessional	Concessional	Non-concessional					
	2009	2009	2009	2009	2009	2009	2009	2009	2009	2009	2009	2009	2009
Romania	−14.4	12,394.0	0.0	441.6	0.0	9,390.6	0.0	−26.0	2,587.8	..	..	..	..
Russian Federation	−296.3	−764.1	0.0	−634.9	0.0	0.0	0.0	−130.5	1.3	..	..	..	..
Rwanda	12.0	115.1	10.5	0.0	3.6	0.0	21.7	0.0	46.4	9.6	0.0	0.8	22.5
Saudi Arabia	..	..	..	..	..	..	..	..	..	..	..	..	..
Senegal	127.2	324.2	134.5	0.0	99.8	0.0	38.5	−12.8	43.1	6.3	0.0	1.3	13.5
Serbia	477.1	1,916.3	16.6	55.7	0.0	1,575.1	0.0	109.1	151.2	0.6	0.0	1.0	7.0
Sierra Leone	−1.5	79.5	15.1	0.0	18.8	0.0	16.8	0.0	2.9	8.4	0.0	1.1	16.4
Singapore	..	..	..	..	..	..	..	..	..	..	..	..	..
Slovak Republic	..	..	0.0	−43.4	..	..	..	..	..	..	..	..	..
Slovenia	..	..	0.0	−6.1	..	..	..	..	..	..	..	..	..
Somalia	0.0	38.9	0.0	0.0	0.0	0.0	0.0	0.0	0.0	10.0	0.0	0.0	28.9
South Africa	0.0	−25.2	0.0	−5.5	0.0	0.0	0.0	−32.1	0.0	4.0	0.0	0.5	7.9
Spain													
Sri Lanka	341.6	827.9	90.8	0.0	−11.8	552.6	60.4	88.5	21.9	3.4	0.0	1.2	20.9
Sudan	551.3	99.2	0.0	0.0	0.0	−10.6	0.0	−2.7	57.6	13.8	0.0	0.8	40.3
Swaziland	9.0	1.9	−0.3	−6.6	0.0	0.0	−1.4	−5.0	9.0	0.9	0.0	0.6	4.7
Sweden													
Switzerland													
Syrian Arab Republic	−324.9	181.8	−1.5	0.0	0.0	0.0	0.0	0.0	108.3	0.8	60.1	1.3	12.8
Tajikistan	88.0	125.3	4.9	0.0	25.1	0.0	62.7	1.8	16.2	3.4	0.0	0.8	10.4
Tanzania	4.8	1,256.8	607.6	0.0	306.8	0.0	222.9	−1.0	41.2	21.4	0.0	1.1	56.8
Thailand	−334.6	−46.6	−3.4	9.3	0.0	0.0	−46.2	−4.4	−11.3	0.9	0.0	1.2	7.3
Timor-Leste	..	..	..	..	..	..	..	..	..	1.1	0.0	0.5	6.0
Togo	22.2	17.4	−21.8	0.0	41.3	0.0	−1.9	0.0	−13.5	4.5	0.0	0.5	8.3
Trinidad and Tobago	..	..	0.0	−7.7	..	..	..	..	..	0.0	0.0	0.1	0.7
Tunisia	40.3	443.7	−2.1	31.7	0.0	0.0	0.0	149.0	260.6	0.9	0.0	0.8	2.8
Turkey	405.0	1,984.6	−5.9	1,619.0	0.0	−706.5	0.0	0.0	1,067.5	1.3	0.0	0.6	8.6
Turkmenistan	−87.2	−0.2	0.0	−1.3	0.0	0.0	0.0	0.0	−1.5	0.9	0.0	0.0	1.7
Uganda	9.8	508.9	363.3	0.0	0.0	0.0	73.5	−0.9	−1.0	22.1	0.0	1.1	50.8
Ukraine	−154.6	6,992.3	0.0	274.5	0.0	6,081.6	0.0	549.7	78.3	0.8	0.0	1.8	5.6
United Arab Emirates	..	..	..	..	..	..	..	..	..	..	..	..	..
United Kingdom													
United States													
Uruguay	−21.2	704.6	0.0	364.7	0.0	0.0	−2.1	318.0	20.2	0.8	0.0	0.6	2.4
Uzbekistan	100.9	157.1	27.6	−27.3	0.0	0.0	18.7	78.0	48.2	3.5	0.0	0.4	8.0
Venezuela, RB	151.3	443.9	0.0	0.0	0.0	0.0	0.0	143.6	292.0	1.4	0.0	0.5	6.4
Vietnam	922.2	2,218.4	1,158.6	0.0	−38.3	0.0	392.4	647.3	26.2	3.7	0.0	1.5	27.0
West Bank and Gaza	..	..	..	..	..	..	..	..	..	4.9	455.3	0.1	8.5
Yemen, Rep.	66.4	121.1	58.8	0.0	−41.0	−2.8	0.0	0.0	68.8	9.2	0.0	0.9	27.2
Zambia	−5.0	312.7	32.5	0.0	243.6	0.0	32.4	−5.4	−15.5	9.0	0.0	1.6	14.5
Zimbabwe	12.9	25.3	0.0	0.0	−0.1	0.0	0.0	0.0	0.0	6.6	0.0	0.5	18.3
World	.. s	.. s	.. s	.. s	.. s	.. s	..	.. s	.. s	1,086.2 s	771.8 s	645.3 s	2,561.1 s
Low income	1,421.6	8,153.0	2,579.9	0.0	1,552.6	1.0	1,469.8	619.9	579.9	456.0	0.0	33.1	860.8
Middle income	4,206.7	65,736.3	3,871.5	11,287.2	198.1	24,750.4	1,257.5	14,527.3	8,079.3	268.3	771.8	111.8	613.1
Lower middle income	114.0	30,161.2	3,782.9	2,998.2	193.2	11,114.1	1,293.0	7,063.5	2,251.4	236.9	648.8	39.3	539.9
Upper middle income	4,092.7	35,590.5	88.5	8,289.0	4.9	13,636.3	−35.6	7,463.8	5,827.9	31.5	123.0	25.0	136.2
Low & middle income	5,628.3	75,594.8	6,451.3	11,287.1	1,750.7	24,751.5	2,727.3	15,147.1	8,659.3	1,085.1	771.8	644.3	2,319.3
East Asia & Pacific	−1,882.0	5,945.1	1,099.7	1,126.6	−41.5	165.5	482.7	2,699.7	70.8	66.8	0.0	98.3	176.5
Europe & Central Asia	2,478.3	29,917.9	417.2	2,357.9	−62.6	20,246.6	338.9	1,315.9	5,162.0	21.7	0.0	13.7	106.6
Latin America & Carib.	2,975.6	16,487.2	136.2	6,489.2	126.7	269.6	251.2	7,784.3	1,174.5	28.4	0.0	67.8	159.3
Middle East & N. Africa	−997.0	4,246.7	6.4	894.2	−42.9	−18.7	10.5	839.2	1,584.6	29.2	771.8	71.9	100.5
South Asia	1,006.3	8,845.7	1,614.0	508.2	−240.2	3,861.3	545.5	2,075.8	110.4	137.5	0.0	6.4	226.8
Sub-Saharan Africa	2,047.0	8,987.7	3,177.8	−88.9	2,011.1	227.1	1,098.5	432.3	557.0	454.7	0.0	156.0	962.1
High income	..	..	..	..	..	..	..	..	..	1.1	0.0	1.0	6.2
Euro area	..	..	..	..	..	..	..	..	..	..	..	..	..

a. Aggregates include amounts for economies that do not report to the World Bank's Debtor Reporting System and may differ from aggregates published in *Global Development Finance 2011*.
b. Aggregates include amounts for economies not specified elsewhere. c. World and income group aggregates include flows not allocated by country or region.

About the data

The table shows concessional and nonconcessional financial flows from official bilateral sources, the major international financial institutions, and UN agencies. The international financial institutions fund nonconcessional lending operations primarily by selling low-interest, highly rated bonds backed by prudent lending and financial policies and the strong financial support of their members. Funds are then on-lent to developing countries at slightly higher interest rates with 15- to 20-year maturities. Lending terms vary with market conditions and institutional policies.

Concessional flows from international financial institutions are credits provided through concessional lending facilities. Subsidies from donors or other resources reduce the cost of these loans. Grants are not included in net flows. The Organisation for Economic Co-operation and Development's (OECD) Development Assistance Committee (DAC) defines concessional flows from bilateral donors as flows with a grant element of at least 25 percent, evaluated assuming a 10 percent nominal discount rate.

World Bank concessional lending is done by the International Development Association (IDA) based on gross national income (GNI) per capita and performance standards assessed by World Bank staff. The cutoff for IDA eligibility, set at the beginning of the World Bank's fiscal year, has been $1,165 since July 1, 2010, measured in 2009 U.S. dollars using the *Atlas* method (see *Users Guide*). In exceptional circumstances IDA extends temporary eligibility to countries above the cutoff that are undertaking major adjustments but are not creditworthy for International Bank for Reconstruction and Development (IBRD) lending. Exceptions are also made for small island economies. The IBRD lends to creditworthy countries at a variable base rate of six-month LIBOR plus a spread, either variable or fixed, for the life of the loan. The lending rate is reset every six months and applies to the interest period beginning on that date. Although some outstanding IBRD loans have a low enough interest rate to be classified as concessional under the DAC definition, all IBRD loans in the table are classified as nonconcessional. Lending by the International Finance Corporation, Multilateral Investment Guarantee Agency, and the International Centre for the Settlement of Investment Disputes is excluded.

The International Monetary Fund (IMF) makes concessional funds available through its Extended Credit Facility (which replaced the Poverty Reduction and Growth Facility in 2010), the Standby Credit Facility, and the Rapid Credit Facility. Eligibility is based principally on a country's per capita income and eligibility under IDA. Nonconcessional lending from the IMF is provided mainly through Stand-by Arrangements, the Flexible Credit Line, and the Extended Fund Facility. The IMF's loan instruments have changed over time to address the specific circumstances of its members.

Regional development banks also maintain concessional windows. Their loans are recorded in the table according to each institution's classification and not according to the DAC definition.

Data for flows from international financial institutions are available for 128 countries that report to the World Bank's Debtor Reporting System. World Bank flows for nonreporting countries were collected from its operational records. Nonreporting countries may have net flows from other international financial institutions.

Official flows from the United Nations are mainly concessional flows classified as official development assistance but may include nonconcessional flows classified as other official flows in OECD DAC databases.

Definitions

• **Total net official financial flows** are disbursements of public or publicly guaranteed loans and credits, less repayments of principal. • **IDA** is the International Development Association, the concessional arm of the World Bank Group. • **IBRD** is the International Bank for Reconstruction and Development, the founding and largest member of the World Bank Group. • **IMF** is the International Monetary Fund, which provides concessional lending through its Extended Credit Facility, Standby Credit Facility, and Rapid Credit Facility and nonconcessional lending through credit to members, mainly for balance of payments needs. • **Regional development banks** are the African Development Bank, which serves Africa, including North Africa; the Asian Development Bank, which serves South and Central Asia and East Asia and Pacific; the European Bank for Reconstruction and Development, which serves Europe and Central Asia; and the Inter-American Development Bank, which serves the Americas. • **Concessional** financial flows are disbursements through concessional lending facilities. • **Nonconcessional** financial flows are all disbursements that are not concessional. • **Other institutions**, a residual category, include such institutions as the Caribbean Development Fund, Council of Europe, European Development Fund, Islamic Development Bank, and Nordic Development Fund. • **United Nations** includes the United Nations Children's Fund (UNICEF), United Nations Relief and Works Agency for Palestine Refugees in the Near East (UNRWA), United Nations Regular Programme for Technical Assistance (UNTA), and other UN agencies, such as the International Atomic Energy Agency, International Fund for Agricultural Development, Joint United Nations Programme on HIV/AIDS, United Nations Development Programme, United Nations Economic Commission for Europe, United Nations Population Fund, United Nations Refugee Agency, World Food Programme, and World Health Organization.

Data sources

Data on net financial flows from international financial institutions are from the World Bank's Debtor Reporting System and published in the World Bank's *Global Development Finance: External Debt of Developing Countries* and electronically in Global Development Finance database. Data on official flows from UN agencies are from the OECD DAC annual *Development Co-operation Report* and are available electronically on the OECD DAC *International Development Statistics* CD-ROM and at www.oecd.org/dac/stats/idsonline.

6.14 Financial flows from Development Assistance Committee members

Net disbursements

$ millions	Total net flows[a] 2009	Official development assistance[a] Total 2009	Bilateral grants 2009	Bilateral loans 2009	Contributions to multilateral institutions 2009	Other official flows[a] 2009	Private flows[a] Total 2009	Foreign direct investment 2009	Bilateral portfolio investment 2009	Multilateral portfolio investment 2009	Private export credits 2009	Net grants by NGOs[a] 2009
Australia	3,188	2,762	2,224	88	450	426	0	0	0	0	0	0
Austria	3,273	1,142	513	−6	635	−44	2,035	2,551	46	0	−562	140
Belgium	3,224	2,610	1,594	−9	1,025	90	147	3	0	0	144	377
Canada	7,340	4,000	3,182	−41	859	−1,138	3,140	6,604	−37	0	−3,427	1,338
Denmark	3,757	2,810	1,914	−8	904	233	599	599	0	0	0	116
Finland	3,185	1,290	765	26	499	137	1,741	791	950	0	0	17
France	38,418	12,600	5,814	1,205	5,581	294	25,524	16,300	9,434	0	−210	0
Germany	26,003	12,079	6,747	350	4,983	187	12,367	9,726	58	1,242	1,341	1,369
Greece	850	607	297	0	310	0	241	241	0	0	0	2
Ireland	4,188	1,006	693	0	313	0	3,000	0	3,000	0	0	182
Italy	5,569	3,297	871	4	2,423	−72	2,181	129	1,590	0	463	162
Japan	49,405	9,469	5,327	674	3,467	8,216	31,187	19,440	10,981	1,987	−1,220	533
Korea, Rep	6,442	816	366	214	235	452	5,018	5,018	0	0	0	156
Luxembourg	428	415	266	0	149	0	0	0	0	0	0	13
Netherlands	6,045	6,426	4,914	−116	1,628	0	−923	540	−2,853	989	401	542
New Zealand	387	309	226	0	83	8	24	24	0	0	0	46
Norway	4,089	4,086	3,125	43	918	4	0	0	0	0	0	0
Portugal	1,209	513	225	52	236	0	692	−2	−63	0	757	4
Spain	12,809	6,584	4,098	375	2,111	0	6,225	6,294	0	0	−70	0
Sweden	7,164	4,548	2,919	90	1,539	68	2,473	885	0	0	1,588	74
Switzerland	9,106	2,310	1,734	16	559	0	6,438	5,570	0	1,462	−593	357
United Kingdom	68,936	11,491	6,994	663	3,834	−13	57,129	55,947	−2,143	0	3,326	329
United States	115,276	28,831	25,992	−819	3,658	988	69,168	28,275	27,223	13,160	510	16,288
Total	380,290	120,000	80,800	2,802	36,398	9,836	228,407	158,934	48,185	18,839	2,449	22,047

Official development assistance

	Commitments[b] $ millions 2000	2009	Gross disbursements[b] $ millions 2000	2009	Net disbursements $ millions[b] 2000	2009	Per capita $[b] 2000	2009	% of GNI[a] 2000	2009	% of general government disbursements[a] 2000	2009
Australia	2,251	2,963	1,939	2,912	1,939	2,912	101	136	0.27	0.29	0.71	0.87
Austria	1,026	1,252	792	1,188	787	1,174	97	141	0.23	0.30	0.44	0.57
Belgium	1,558	3,068	1,558	2,750	1,517	2,670	148	250	0.36	0.55	0.72	1.02
Canada	3,412	4,925	3,023	4,372	2,981	4,328	97	130	0.25	0.30	0.59	0.68
Denmark	2,994	2,938	3,193	2,960	3,159	2,923	592	530	1.06	0.88	1.94	1.54
Finland	618	1,639	661	1,323	649	1,323	125	248	0.31	0.54	0.63	0.97
France	8,699	14,928	9,276	15,933	7,616	12,920	129	207	0.30	0.47	0.60	0.85
Germany	9,825	16,924	9,973	13,693	8,641	12,397	105	151	0.27	0.35	0.59	0.76
Greece	451	618	451	618	451	618	41	55	0.20	0.19	0.39	0.36
Ireland	450	1,083	450	1,083	450	1,083	119	250	0.29	0.54	0.77	0.93
Italy	3,115	3,918	3,082	3,514	2,653	3,334	46	56	0.13	0.16	0.27	0.30
Japan	16,257	16,429	15,485	14,848	12,833	8,545	101	67	0.28	0.18	0.74	0.45
Korea, Rep	399	2,206	282	949	260	910	6	19	0.04	0.10	0.18	0.31
Luxembourg	257	435	257	435	257	435	583	889	0.70	1.04	1.61	1.86
Netherlands	6,580	6,490	6,171	6,841	5,995	6,676	376	405	0.84	0.82	1.84	1.57
New Zealand	229	358	216	333	216	333	56	78	0.25	0.28	0.56	0.61
Norway	2,481	5,902	2,800	4,650	2,787	4,650	621	969	0.76	1.06	1.77	2.32
Portugal	822	633	822	565	535	528	52	51	0.26	0.23	0.56	0.45
Spain	2,940	6,724	2,940	7,213	2,531	6,800	63	147	0.22	0.46	0.53	0.98
Sweden	2,287	5,230	2,861	5,090	2,861	5,085	323	549	0.80	1.12	1.32	2.03
Switzerland	1,536	2,753	1,513	2,286	1,509	2,276	210	296	0.34	0.45	1.01	1.39
United Kingdom	6,723	17,757	6,723	13,400	6,649	13,162	113	216	0.32	0.52	0.83	1.03
United States	15,431	33,018	13,293	29,286	12,182	28,469	44	94	0.10	0.21	0.30	0.48
DAC Countries, Total	90,339	152,192	87,757	136,242	79,456	123,551	89	131	0.22	0.31	0.56	0.69

Note: Components may not sum to totals because of gaps in reporting.
a. At current prices and exchange rates. b. At 2008 prices and exchange rates.

About the data

The flows of official and private financial resources from the members of the Development Assistance Committee (DAC) of the Organisation for Economic Co-operation and Development (OECD) to developing economies are compiled by DAC, based principally on reporting by DAC members using standard questionnaires issued by the DAC Secretariat.

The table shows data reported by DAC member economies and does not include aid provided by the European Union Institutions—a multilateral member of DAC.

DAC exists to help its members coordinate their development assistance and to encourage the expansion and improve the effectiveness of the aggregate resources flowing to recipient economies. In this capacity DAC monitors the flow of all financial resources, but its main concern is official development assistance (ODA). Grants or loans to countries and territories on the DAC list of aid recipients have to meet three criteria to be counted as ODA. They are provided by official agencies, including state and local governments, or by their executive agencies. They promote economic development and welfare as the main objective. And they are provided on concessional financial terms (loans must have a grant element of at least 25 percent, calculated at a discount rate of 10 percent). The DAC Statistical Reporting Directives provide the most detailed explanation of this definition and all ODA-related rules.

This definition excludes nonconcessional flows from official creditors, which are classified as "other official flows," and aid for military and anti-terrorism purposes. Transfer payments to private individuals, such as pensions, reparations, and insurance payouts, are in general not counted. In addition to financial flows, ODA includes technical cooperation, most expenditures for peacekeeping under UN mandates and assistance to refugees, contributions to multilateral institutions such as the United Nations and its specialized agencies, and concessional funding to multilateral development banks.

The DAC list of aid recipients shows all countries and territories eligible to receive ODA. These consist of all low- and middle-income countries, except members of the Group of Eight or the European Union (including countries with a firm date for EU accession). The DAC revises the list every three years. Countries that have exceeded the high-income threshold for three consecutive years at the time of the review are removed. In line with this review process, the DAC last revised the list in September 2008. A further update took place in August 2009 to accommodate changes in respect of Kosovo and the Former Yugoslav Republic of Macedonia. In the past DAC distinguished aid going to Part I and Part II countries. Part I countries, the recipients of ODA, comprised many of the countries classified by the World Bank as low- and middle-income economies. Part II countries, whose assistance was designated official aid, included the more advanced countries of Central and Eastern Europe, countries of the former Soviet Union, and certain advanced developing countries and territories. This distinction has been dropped with the 2005 aid flows.

Flows are transfers of resources, either in cash or in the form of commodities or services measured on a cash basis. Short-term capital transactions (with one year or less maturity) are not counted. Repayments of the principal (but not interest) of ODA loans are recorded as negative flows. Proceeds from official equity investments in a developing country are reported as ODA, while proceeds from their later sale are recorded as negative flows.

The table is based on donor country reports and does not provide a complete picture of the resources received by developing economies for two reasons. First, flows from DAC members are only part of the aggregate resource flows to these economies. Second, the data that record contributions to multilateral institutions measure the flow of resources made available to those institutions by DAC members, not the flow of resources from those institutions to developing economies.

Aid as a share of gross national income (GNI), aid per capita, and ODA as a share of the general government disbursements of the donor are calculated by the OECD. The denominators used in calculating these ratios may differ from corresponding values elsewhere in this book because of differences in timing or definitions.

Definitions

• **Net disbursements** are gross disbursements of grants and loans minus repayments of principal on earlier loans. • **Total net flows** are ODA flows, other official flows, private flows, and net grants by nongovernmental organizations. • **Official development assistance** refers to flows that meet the DAC definition of ODA and are made to countries and territories on the DAC list of aid recipients. • **Bilateral grants** are transfers of money or in kind for which no repayment is required. • **Bilateral loans** are loans extended by governments or official agencies with a grant element of at least 25 percent (at a 10 percent discount rate). • **Contributions to multilateral institutions** are concessional funding received by multilateral institutions from DAC members as grants or capital subscriptions. • **Other official flows** are transactions by the official sector whose main objective is other than development or whose grant element is less than 25 percent. • **Private flows** are flows at market terms financed from private sector resources in donor countries. They include changes in holdings of private long-term assets by reporting country residents. • **Foreign direct investment** is investment by residents of DAC member countries to acquire a lasting management interest (at least 10 percent of voting stock) in an enterprise operating in the recipient country. The data reflect changes in the net worth of subsidiaries in recipient countries whose parent company is in the DAC source country. • **Bilateral portfolio investment** is bank lending and the purchase of bonds, shares, and real estate by residents of DAC member countries in recipient countries. • **Multilateral portfolio investment** is transactions of private banks and nonbanks in DAC member countries in the securities issued by multilateral institutions. • **Private export credits** are loans extended to recipient countries by the private sector in DAC member countries to promote trade; they may be supported by an official guarantee. • **Net grants by nongovernmental organizations (NGOs)** are private grants by NGOs, net of subsidies from the official sector. • **Commitments** are obligations, expressed in writing and backed by funds, undertaken by an official donor to provide specified assistance to a recipient country or multilateral organization. • **Gross disbursements** are the international transfer of financial resources, goods, and services, valued at the cost to the donor.

Data sources

Data on financial flows are compiled by OECD DAC and published in its annual statistical report, *Geographical Distribution of Financial Flows to Developing Countries*, and its annual *Development Co-operation Report*. Data are available electronically on the OECD DAC *International Development Statistics* CD-ROM and at www.oecd.org/dac/stats/idsonline.

6.15 Allocation of bilateral aid from Development Assistance Committee members

6.15a Aid by purpose

	Net disbursements		Share of bilateral ODA net disbursements									
								%				
	$ millions[a]		Development projects, programs, and other resource provisions		Technical cooperation[b]		Debt-related aid		Humanitarian assistance		Administrative costs	
	2000	2009	2000	2009	2000	2009	2000	2009	2000	2009	2000	2009
Australia	758	2,312	27.8	32.7	55.1	49.2	1.1	0.1	9.7	13.3	6.2	4.7
Austria	273	507	28.7	23.6	41.8	49.7	20.4	11.6	2.7	7.2	6.4	7.9
Belgium	477	1,585	33.6	40.9	46.9	39.2	6.6	6.6	5.4	7.4	7.5	6.0
Canada	1,160	3,141	39.6	15.4	43.0	64.2	1.1	1.5	5.0	10.3	11.4	8.6
Denmark	1,024	1,905	65.8	71.9	25.3	11.0	1.0	1.9	0.0	6.8	8.0	8.5
Finland	217	791	40.8	31.1	41.4	45.6	0.0	0.0	10.5	13.1	7.2	10.1
France	2,829	7,019	25.4	10.9	50.6	42.7	17.0	39.5	0.4	0.6	6.7	6.3
Germany	2,687	7,097	16.8	24.6	63.8	65.0	6.6	1.2	4.1	5.2	8.7	4.1
Greece	99	297	69.6	14.8	23.8	72.2	0.0	0.0	6.4	5.1	0.2	7.9
Ireland	154	693	79.1	75.9	0.4	3.6	0.0	0.0	15.5	14.1	5.1	6.5
Italy	377	875	10.2	49.4	8.1	10.9	57.5	19.9	18.3	13.0	5.9	6.8
Japan	9,768	6,001	60.4	59.7	24.9	38.4	4.2	−14.5	0.9	4.4	9.5	12.1
Korea, Rep.	131	581	77.8	66.8	15.7	25.5	0.0	0.0	0.4	2.9	6.1	4.8
Luxembourg	99	266	84.4	74.6	3.2	3.6	0.8	0.0	10.4	14.4	1.2	7.3
Netherlands	2,243	4,798	41.1	71.3	33.7	14.5	6.8	0.9	9.1	6.3	9.4	6.9
New Zealand	85	226	39.7	54.3	48.1	28.3	0.0	0.0	3.4	6.9	8.8	10.6
Norway	934	3,168	57.9	56.2	23.0	27.9	1.0	0.5	11.3	8.6	6.9	6.8
Portugal	179	277	30.4	49.6	50.4	53.4	14.6	−10.0	1.9	0.4	2.7	6.6
Spain	720	4,473	69.3	60.1	17.9	23.5	2.3	2.2	3.7	9.9	6.8	4.2
Sweden	1,242	3,009	60.9	64.1	13.6	15.9	3.1	0.7	14.6	12.0	7.7	7.3
Switzerland	627	1,751	58.6	42.3	19.4	30.1	0.9	9.3	20.2	9.1	0.9	9.3
United Kingdom	2,710	7,657	47.7	75.9	25.5	8.9	5.7	0.6	12.7	9.5	8.4	5.2
United States	7,405	25,174	14.6	70.5	64.4	6.0	1.7	0.7	9.6	17.4	9.7	5.4
Total	**36,195**	**83,602**	**40.6**	**54.6**	**39.3**	**25.2**	**5.3**	**3.5**	**6.1**	**10.3**	**8.6**	**6.3**

a. At current exchange rates and prices. b. Includes aid for promoting development awareness and aid provided to refugees in the donor economy.

About the data

Aid can be used in many ways. The sector to which aid goes, the form it takes, and the procurement restrictions attached to it are important influences on aid effectiveness. The data on allocation of official development assistance (ODA) in the table are based principally on reporting by members of the Organisation for Economic Co-operation and Development (OECD) Development Assistance Committee (DAC). For more detailed explanation of ODA, see *About the data* for table 6.14.

The form in which an ODA contribution reaches the benefiting sector or the economy is important. A distinction is made between resource provision and technical cooperation. Resource provision involves mainly cash or in-kind transfers and financing of capital projects, with the deliverables being financial support and the provision of commodities and supplies. Technical cooperation includes grants to nationals of aid-recipient countries receiving education or training at home or abroad, and payments to consultants, advisers, and similar personnel and to teachers and administrators serving in recipient countries. Technical cooperation is spent mostly in the donor economy.

Two other types of aid are presented because they serve distinctive purposes. Debt-related aid aims to provide debt relief on liabilities that recipient countries have difficulty servicing. Thus, this type of aid may not provide a full value of new resource flows for development, in particular for heavily indebted poor countries. Humanitarian assistance provides relief following sudden disasters and supports food programs in emergency situations. This type of aid does not generally contribute to financing long-term development.

Definitions

• **Net disbursements** are gross disbursements of grants and loans minus repayments of principal on earlier loans • **Development projects, programs, and other resource provisions** are aid provided as cash transfers, aid in kind, development food aid, and the financing of capital projects, intended to increase or improve the recipient's stock of physical capital and to support recipient's development plans and other activities with finance and commodity supply. • **Technical cooperation** is the provision of resources whose main aim is to augment the stock of human intellectual capital, such as the level of knowledge, skills, and technical know-how in the recipient country (including the cost of associated equipment). Contributions take the form mainly of the supply of human resources from donors or action directed to human resources (such as training or advice). Also included are aid for promoting development awareness and aid provided to refugees in the donor economy. Assistance specifically to facilitate a capital project is not included. • **Debt-related aid** groups all actions relating to debt, including forgiveness, swaps, buybacks, rescheduling, and refinancing. • **Humanitarian assistance** is emergency and distress relief (including aid to refugees and assistance for disaster preparedness). • **Administrative costs** are the total current budget outlays of institutions responsible for the formulation and implementation of donor's aid programs and other administrative costs incurred by donors in aid delivery.

Data sources

Data on aid flows are published by OECD DAC in its annual statistical report, *Geographical Distribution of Financial Flows to Developing Countries*, and its annual *Development Co-operation Report*. Data are available electronically on the OECD DAC *International Development Statistics* CD-ROM and at www.oecd.org/dac/stats/idsonline.

6.15b Aid by sector

Share of bilateral ODA commitments (%)	Total sector-allocable aid 2009	Social infrastructure and services						Economic infrastructure, services, and production sector			Multi-sector or cross-cutting 2009	Untied aid[a] 2009
		Total 2009	Education 2009	Health 2009	Population 2009	Water supply and sanitation 2009	Government and civil society 2009	Total 2009	Transport and communication 2009	Agriculture 2009		
Australia	77.7	48.7	11.9	7.5	2.2	1.9	22.6	11.8	5.3	4.6	17.2	90.8
Austria	67.5	45.8	23.8	5.9	0.4	4.3	9.1	15.2	1.8	2.0	6.6	55.2
Belgium	73.2	39.5	13.1	9.2	1.6	3.2	9.7	28.0	4.7	7.7	5.7	95.5
Canada	72.7	52.4	15.4	15.2	2.5	2.0	16.2	12.2	0.4	6.8	8.1	98.3
Denmark	68.8	42.2	5.1	7.6	2.8	8.5	16.3	18.0	3.4	5.8	8.5	96.6
Finland	72.9	32.6	6.7	3.3	0.5	4.3	14.1	28.1	6.2	7.8	12.2	90.3
France	68.8	36.3	19.2	1.5	0.3	8.8	1.6	16.3	6.8	5.3	16.2	89.2
Germany	87.6	49.6	19.1	3.6	1.9	8.7	14.7	27.8	2.6	3.7	10.1	97.1
Greece	74.5	62.8	32.4	4.6	2.6	1.0	16.0	6.1	2.4	1.3	5.6	49.8[b]
Ireland	70.8	58.0	13.0	13.5	4.0	2.5	16.4	9.5	0.1	8.0	3.3	100.0[b]
Italy	64.1	35.6	10.3	9.4	0.9	4.9	6.5	23.9	3.9	16.7	4.6	56.2
Japan	74.5	28.9	5.3	2.0	0.4	18.9	1.2	41.3	26.7	4.9	4.2	94.7
Korea, Rep.	96.2	27.6	9.7	10.4	0.2	4.7	1.7	64.5	52.1	3.5	4.0	48.3
Luxembourg	68.1	47.2	12.5	12.7	4.6	8.4	5.1	10.7	0.2	5.0	10.2	100.0[b]
Netherlands	71.1	26.8	4.2	2.7	2.1	3.7	10.7	12.7	1.0	3.3	31.6	80.8
New Zealand	61.9	45.5	21.0	5.5	2.3	1.1	14.4	14.6	7.2	3.7	1.9	90.1
Norway	64.0	40.6	8.6	6.2	2.0	1.3	19.9	14.3	0.2	6.8	9.2	100.0
Portugal	70.3	56.9	24.1	2.9	0.1	0.1	22.3	10.2	8.3	1.5	3.2	27.9
Spain	70.8	44.6	7.1	6.2	4.3	12.7	9.9	20.4	2.5	3.8	5.8	76.6
Sweden	54.3	33.4	3.1	3.5	1.9	2.5	19.8	12.3	1.2	2.5	8.6	99.9
Switzerland	42.9	21.6	3.1	3.1	0.2	2.4	11.8	11.5	0.8	3.5	9.7	99.2
United Kingdom	72.4	41.7	8.9	7.8	5.0	1.4	14.7	20.1	2.6	1.7	10.6	100.0
United States	73.2	53.5	4.0	3.7	19.0	1.6	18.6	15.1	4.5	5.0	4.6	69.8
Total	**72.8**	**42.7**	**8.8**	**4.6**	**6.7**	**6.2**	**12.5**	**21.3**	**7.4**	**4.7**	**8.8**	**84.5**

a. Excludes technical cooperation and administrative costs. b. Gross disbursements.

About the data

The Development Assistance Committee (DAC) records the sector classification of aid using a three-level hierarchy. The top level is grouped by themes, such as social infrastructure and services; economic infrastructure, services, and production; and multisector or cross-cutting areas. The second level is more specific. Education and health and transport and storage are examples. The third level comprises subsectors such as basic education and basic health. Some contributions are reported as non-sector-allocable aid.

Reporting on the sectoral destination and the form of aid by donors may not be complete. Also, measures of aid allocation may differ from the perspectives of donors and recipients because of difference in classification, available information, and recording time.

The proportion of untied aid is reported because tying arrangements may prevent recipients from obtaining the best value for their money. Tying requires recipients to purchase goods and services from the donor country or from a specified group of countries. Such arrangements prevent a recipient from misappropriating or mismanaging aid receipts, but they may also be motivated by a desire to benefit donor country suppliers.

Definitions

• **Bilateral official development assistance (ODA) commitments** are firm obligations, expressed in writing and backed by the necessary funds, undertaken by official bilateral donors to provide specified assistance to a recipient country or a multilateral organization. Bilateral commitments are recorded in the full amount of expected transfer, irrespective of the time required for completing disbursements. • **Total sector-allocable aid** is the sum of aid that can be assigned to specific sectors or multisector activities. • **Social infrastructure and services** refer to efforts to develop the human resources potential and improve the living conditions of aid recipients. • **Education** refers to general teaching and instruction at all levels, as well as construction to improve or adapt educational establishments. Training in a particular field is reported for the sector concerned. • **Health** refers to assistance to hospitals, clinics, other medical and dental services, public health administration, and medical insurance programs. • **Population** refers to all activities related to family planning and research into population problems. • **Water supply and sanitation** refer to assistance for water supply and use, sanitation, and water resources development (including rivers). • **Government and civil society** refer to assistance to strengthen government

administrative apparatus and planning and activities promoting good governance and civil society. • **Economic infrastructure, services, and production sector** group assistance for networks, utilities, services that facilitate economic activity, and contributions to all directly productive sectors. • **Transport and communication** refer to road, rail, water, and air transport; post and telecommunications; and television and print media. • **Agriculture** refers to sector policy, development, and inputs; crop and livestock production; and agricultural credit, cooperatives, and research. • **Multisector or cross-cutting** refers to support for projects that straddle several sectors. • **Untied aid** is ODA not subject to restrictions by donors on procurement sources.

Data sources

Data on aid flows are published annually by the Organisation for Economic Co-operation and Development (OECD) DAC in *Geographical Distribution of Financial Flows to Developing Countries* and *Development Co-operation Report*. Data are available electronically on the OECD DAC *International Development Statistics* CD-ROM and at www.oecd.org/dac/stats/idsonline.

	Net official development assistance (ODA)				Aid dependency ratios							
	Total $ millions		Per capita $		Net ODA as % of GNI		Net ODA as % of gross capital formation		Net ODA as % of imports of goods, services, and income		Net ODA as % of central government expense	
	2000	2009	2000	2009	2000	2009	2000	2009	2000	2009	2000	2009
Afghanistan	136	6,070	6	204	..	..	..	..	..	..	..	112.5
Albania	317	358	103	113	8.4	3.0	34.8	10.3	21.0	5.1	..	..
Algeria	200	319	7	9	0.4	0.2	1.5	0.6	..	..	..	0.9
Angola	302	239	21	13	4.1	0.4	22.0	2.1	4.1	0.5	..	..
Argentina	52	128	1	3	0.0	0.0	0.1	0.2	0.1	0.2	..	..
Armenia	216	528	70	171	11.0	5.9	60.6	19.3	21.2	12.5	..	25.6
Australia												
Austria												
Azerbaijan	139	232	17	26	2.8	0.6	12.8	2.5	5.8	1.7	..	..
Bangladesh	1,172	1,227	8	8	2.4	1.3	10.8	5.6	11.7	5.0	..	12.2
Belarus	..	98	..	10	..	0.2	..	0.5	..	0.3	..	0.6
Belgium	..	..	..	..	..	..	..	..	..	..	..	..
Benin	243	683	37	76	10.9	10.3	57.0	41.1	32.7	..	..	68.2
Bolivia	482	726	58	74	5.9	4.4	31.6	24.7	19.7	12.0	..	..
Bosnia and Herzegovina	737	415	199	110	12.1	2.4	65.1	11.0	17.4	4.3	..	5.9
Botswana	31	280	18	143	0.6	2.5	1.7	9.8	1.0	4.7	..	..
Brazil	231	338	1	2	0.0	0.0	0.2	0.1	0.2	0.2	0.2	0.1
Bulgaria	..	..	..	..	..	..	..	..	..	..	..	..
Burkina Faso	180	1,084	15	69	6.9	13.5	41.1	..	26.0	..	..	102.5
Burundi	93	549	14	66	12.9	41.2	213.8	..	56.5	102.0	..	..
Cambodia	396	722	31	49	10.9	7.7	60.3	34.3	16.1	9.7	..	62.9
Cameroon	377	649	24	33	4.0	2.9	22.4	..	12.7	9.4	..	..
Canada												
Central African Republic	75	237	20	54	8.0	11.9	82.4	111.2	..	..	..	..
Chad	130	561	15	50	9.5	9.2	40.4	24.2	..	..	..	..
Chile	49	80	3	5	0.1	0.1	0.3	0.3	0.2	0.1	0.3	0.2
China	1,712	1,132	1	1	0.1	0.0	0.4	0.0	0.6	0.1	..	..
Hong Kong SAR, China	..	..	..	..	..	..	..	..	..	..	..	..
Colombia	186	1,060	5	23	0.2	0.5	1.2	2.0	1.0	2.2	..	2.3
Congo, Dem. Rep.	177	2,354	3	36	4.5	23.9	119.1	74.6	..	..	15.2	..
Congo, Rep.	32	283	11	77	1.4	4.1	4.4	12.0	1.6	..	5.0	..
Costa Rica	10	109	2	24	0.1	0.4	0.4	1.9	0.1	0.8	..	1.4
Côte d'Ivoire	351	2,366	20	112	3.6	10.6	31.2	90.4	7.9	23.9	..	57.6
Croatia	66	169	15	38	0.3	0.3	1.6	1.0	0.6	0.6	0.8	0.7
Cuba	44	116	4	10	0.1	..	1.2	..	..	..	..	..
Czech Republic	..	..	..	..	..	..	..	..	..	..	..	..
Denmark												
Dominican Republic	56	120	6	12	0.2	0.3	1.0	1.7	0.5	0.7	..	..
Ecuador	146	209	12	15	1.0	0.4	4.6	1.1	2.3	1.1	..	..
Egypt, Arab Rep.	1,327	925	19	11	1.3	0.5	6.8	2.5	5.6	1.6	..	1.6
El Salvador	180	277	30	45	1.4	1.4	8.1	10.0	3.0	3.1	..	53.2
Eritrea	176	145	48	29	27.7	7.8	116.6	..	34.4	..	..	..
Estonia	..	..	..	..	..	..	..	..	..	..	..	..
Ethiopia	686	3,820	10	46	8.4	13.4	41.4	59.7	41.0	42.0	..	..
Finland												
France												
Gabon	12	78	9	53	0.3	0.8	1.1	2.5	0.5	..	..	..
Gambia, The	50	128	38	75	12.4	18.5	67.8	67.3	..	35.3	..	..
Georgia	169	908	36	213	5.3	8.6	20.8	69.7	13.6	15.6	47.9	27.3
Germany	..	..	..	..	..	..	..	..	..	..	..	..
Ghana	598	1,583	31	66	12.4	6.1	50.0	30.9	17.2	14.1	..	33.8
Greece												
Guatemala	263	376	23	27	1.4	1.0	7.6	7.7	4.4	2.7	12.5	8.0
Guinea	153	215	18	21	5.0	5.8	24.9	24.2	15.7	13.6	..	..
Guinea-Bissau	81	146	62	90	39.9	17.6	333.0	..	..	..	..	..
Haiti	208	1,120	24	112	..	..	20.7	63.1	15.1	39.5	..	..
Honduras	448	457	72	61	6.4	3.3	22.3	16.3	8.9	5.0	..	13.3

	Net official development assistance (ODA)				Aid dependency ratios							
	Total $ millions		Per capita $		Net ODA as % of GNI		Net ODA as % of gross capital formation		Net ODA as % of imports of goods, services, and income		Net ODA as % of central government expense	
	2000	2009	2000	2009	2000	2009	2000	2009	2000	2009	2000	2009
Hungary	..	..	..	..	..	..	..	..	..	..	..	..
India	1,373	2,393	1	2	0.3	0.2	1.2	0.5	1.7	0.7	1.9	1.1
Indonesia	1,651	1,049	8	5	1.1	0.2	4.5	0.6	2.5	0.8	..	1.2
Iran, Islamic Rep.	130	93	2	1	0.1	0.0	0.4	..	0.7	..	0.2	0.1
Iraq	100	2,791	4	89	..	4.5	..	..	..	..	..	..
Ireland												
Israel	..	..	..	..	..	..	..	..	..	..	..	..
Italy												
Jamaica	9	150	3	55	0.1	1.3	..	5.8	0.2	2.1	..	3.0
Japan	..	..	..	..	..	..	..	..	..	..	..	..
Jordan	552	761	115	128	6.5	3.0	29.2	20.5	8.7	4.5	24.1	10.6
Kazakhstan	189	298	13	19	1.1	0.3	5.6	0.8	1.8	0.6	7.5	1.5
Kenya	509	1,778	16	45	4.1	6.1	23.0	29.0	12.9	15.4	23.9	27.9
Korea, Dem. Rep.	73	67	3	3								
Korea, Rep.												
Kosovo	1	788	1	437	..	14.0	..	52.7	..	..	..	..
Kuwait	..	..	..	..	..	..	..	..	..	..	..	..
Kyrgyz Republic	215	315	44	59	16.7	7.1	78.3	31.2	28.5	8.1	99.2	35.7
Lao PDR	281	420	52	66	16.9	7.2	57.2	..	44.0	25.2	..	62.5
Latvia	..	..	..	..	..	..	..	..	..	..	..	..
Lebanon	199	641	53	152	1.1	1.8	5.7	6.2	..	1.9	3.8	6.3
Lesotho	37	123	19	60	3.8	6.4	11.1	24.8	4.4	6.7	..	..
Liberia	67	505	24	128	17.4	78.3	..	..	..	27.3	..	..
Libya	..	39	..	6	..	0.1	..	..	..	0.1	..	..
Lithuania	..	..	..	..	..	..	..	..	..	..	..	..
Macedonia, FYR	250	193	124	95	7.1	2.2	31.3	8.6	10.5	3.2	..	..
Madagascar	320	445	21	23	8.4	5.2	54.9	15.9	20.2	..	77.8	..
Malawi	446	772	38	51	26.1	16.6	188.6	65.6	65.6	..	..	..
Malaysia	45	144	2	5	0.1	0.1	0.2	0.5	0.0	0.1	0.3	0.3
Mali	288	985	27	76	12.0	11.0	48.4	..	27.5	..	102.4	74.9
Mauritania	221	287	85	87	20.2	9.4	105.5	37.7	..	..	..	..
Mauritius	20	156	17	122	0.4	1.8	1.7	8.5	0.7	2.8	..	8.4
Mexico	−58	185	−1	2	0.0	0.0	0.0	0.1	0.0	0.1	−0.1	..
Moldova	123	245	30	68	9.4	4.3	39.7	16.7	11.2	5.7	32.9	11.8
Mongolia	217	372	91	139	20.0	9.4	68.6	17.6	27.4	13.1	85.2	30.7
Morocco	419	912	15	28	1.2	1.0	4.4	2.8	3.1	2.3	..	3.6
Mozambique	906	2,013	50	88	22.6	20.8	68.9	98.2	51.4	44.1	..	..
Myanmar	106	357	2	7	..	..	..	..	..	4.0	..	..
Namibia	152	326	84	150	3.9	3.6	22.8	13.0	8.2	5.9	13.7	..
Nepal	386	855	16	29	7.0	6.7	28.9	23.0	21.1	16.6	..	..
Netherlands												
New Zealand												
Nicaragua	560	774	110	135	15.0	13.1	47.2	53.7	23.5	16.4	86.4	60.2
Niger	208	470	19	31	11.7	8.9	101.4	..	43.0	..	..	..
Nigeria	174	1,659	1	11	0.4	1.0	..	..	1.1	2.8	..	..
Norway												
Oman	45	212	19	75	0.2	..	1.9	..	0.6	0.8	0.9	..
Pakistan	700	2,781	5	16	1.0	1.7	5.5	9.1	4.8	7.1	5.7	10.6
Panama	15	66	5	19	0.1	0.3	0.5	1.1	0.1	0.4	0.6	..
Papua New Guinea	275	414	51	61	8.3	5.3	35.7	26.3	13.7	7.6	26.2	..
Paraguay	82	148	15	23	1.1	1.1	6.1	6.7	2.3	1.8	6.6	6.1
Peru	397	442	15	15	0.8	0.4	3.7	1.5	3.4	1.3	4.2	2.0
Philippines	572	310	7	3	0.8	0.2	3.6	1.3	1.1	0.5	4.3	1.0
Poland	..	..	..	..	..	..	..	..	..	..	..	..
Portugal												
Puerto Rico	..	..	..	..	..	..	..	..	..	..	..	..
Qatar	..	..	..	..	..	..	..	..	..	..	..	..

6.16 Aid dependency

| | Net official development assistance (ODA) | | | | Aid dependency ratios | | | | | | | |
| | Total $ millions | | Per capita $ | | Net ODA as % of GNI | | Net ODA as % of gross capital formation | | Net ODA as % of imports of goods, services, and income | | Net ODA as % of central government expense | |
	2000	2009	2000	2009	2000	2009	2000	2009	2000	2009	2000	2009
Romania	..	..	..	..	..	..	..	..	..	..	..	..
Russian Federation	..	..	..	..	..	..	..	..	..	..	..	..
Rwanda	321	934	40	93	18.7	18.0	101.2	82.3	71.2	61.0	..	..
Saudi Arabia	22	..	1	..	0.0	..	0.1	..	0.0	..	..	..
Senegal	429	1,018	43	81	9.3	8.0	44.7	28.4	22.3	..	71.9	..
Serbia	1,134[a]	608	151[a]	83	18.6[a]	1.4	212.2[a]	5.9	..	3.1	..	3.8
Sierra Leone	181	437	43	77	29.3	23.0	413.2	148.8	68.8	64.8	98.8	101.9
Singapore	..	..	..	..	..	..	..	..	..	..	..	..
Slovak Republic	..	..	..	..	..	..	..	..	..	..	..	..
Slovenia	61	..	31	..	0.3	..	1.1	..	0.5	..	187.8	..
Somalia	101	662	14	72	..	..	..	..	..	..	..	..
South Africa	486	1,075	11	22	0.4	0.4	2.3	1.9	1.3	1.2	1.3	1.1
Spain												
Sri Lanka	275	704	15	35	1.7	1.7	6.0	6.8	3.2	5.7	7.3	..
Sudan	220	2,289	6	54	1.9	4.6	9.7	16.6	8.5	16.8	..	..
Swaziland	13	58	12	49	0.9	2.0	5.1	11.4	0.9	2.1	3.9	..
Sweden												
Switzerland												
Syrian Arab Republic	158	245	10	12	0.9	0.5	4.7	2.9	2.4	..	..	..
Tajikistan	124	409	20	59	15.0	8.3	152.5	37.9	..	13.0	160.3	..
Tanzania	1,063	2,934	31	67	10.6	13.7	62.0	46.1	47.6	37.2	..	..
Thailand	697	−77	11	−1	0.6	0.0	2.5	−0.1	0.9	0.0	..	−0.1
Timor-Leste	231	217	284	191	71.6	..	285.9	..	..	..	..	..
Togo	70	499	13	75	5.4	17.5	29.4	..	10.5	..	..	100.6
Trinidad and Tobago	−2	7	−1	5	0.0	0.0	−0.1	..	0.0	..	..	..
Tunisia	222	474	23	45	1.2	1.3	4.2	4.5	2.1	2.0	4.1	4.0
Turkey	327	1,362	5	18	0.1	0.2	0.6	1.5	0.5	0.8	..	0.8
Turkmenistan	31	40	7	8	1.2	0.2	3.1	1.8	..	..	..	..
Uganda	853	1,786	35	55	14.0	11.4	70.7	46.8	54.2	32.0	96.5	86.9
Ukraine	..	668	..	15	..	0.6	..	3.4	..	1.1	..	1.4
United Arab Emirates	..	..	..	..	..	..	..	..	..	..	..	..
United Kingdom												
United States												
Uruguay	17	51	5	15	0.1	0.2	0.5	0.9	0.3	0.6	0.3	0.5
Uzbekistan	186	190	8	7	1.4	0.6	8.3	2.3	..	..	..	..
Venezuela, RB	76	67	3	2	0.1	0.0	0.3	0.1	0.1	0.1	0.3	..
Vietnam	1,681	3,744	22	43	5.5	4.4	18.2	10.9	9.3	4.9	..	..
West Bank and Gaza	637	3,026	212	748	13.3	..	47.4	..	19.2	..	..	..
Yemen, Rep.	263	500	14	21	3.0	2.0	14.3	..	6.2	4.4	..	..
Zambia	795	1,269	76	98	25.8	11.1	140.8	44.7	53.1	23.1	..	..
Zimbabwe	176	737	14	59	2.8	14.1	19.6	581.9	..	..	..	..
World	**49,527 s**	**127,527 s**	**8 w**	**19 w**	**0.2 w**	**0.2 w**	**0.7 w**	**1.0 w**	**0.5 w**	**0.7 w**	..	..
Low income	12,349	39,834	18	47	7.0	9.2	35.3	38.7	22.8	24.9	..	..
Middle income	25,127	50,840	6	11	0.5	0.3	1.8	1.0	1.5	1.1	..	..
Lower middle income	18,635	39,070	5	10	0.7	0.4	2.5	1.1	2.4	1.5	..	..
Upper middle income	5,777	10,762	6	11	0.2	0.2	0.9	0.7	0.6	0.5	..	..
Low & middle income	49,234	127,093	10	22	0.9	0.8	3.5	2.5	2.8	2.7	..	..
East Asia & Pacific	8,563	10,278	5	5	0.5	0.2	1.6	0.4	1.4	0.6	..	..
Europe & Central Asia	4,462	8,101	11	20	0.6	0.3	3.2	1.6	1.8	0.9	..	..
Latin America & Carib.	4,847	9,104	9	16	0.2	0.2	1.2	1.2	0.9	1.0	..	..
Middle East & N. Africa	4,472	13,589	16	41	1.0	1.1	4.0	..	3.3	3.9	..	..
South Asia	4,114	14,332	3	9	0.7	0.8	2.9	2.5	3.5	3.3	..	..
Sub-Saharan Africa	13,067	44,510	19	53	4.0	4.9	23.0	25.0	10.9	12.0	..	..
High income	294	433	0	0	0.0	0.0	0.0	0.0	0.0	0.0	..	..
Euro area	..	..	..	..	..	..	..	..	..	..	..	..

Note: Regional aggregates include data for economies not listed in the table. World and income group totals include aid not allocated by country or region—including administrative costs, research on development issues, and aid to nongovernmental organizations. Thus regional and income group totals do not sum to the world total.
a. Includes Montenegro.

About the data

The table shows data for official development assistance (ODA; see *About the data* for table 6.14) for aid-receiving countries. The data cover loans and grants from Development Assistance Committee (DAC) member countries, multilateral organizations, and non-DAC donors. They do not reflect aid given by recipient countries to other developing countries. As a result, some countries that are net donors (such as Saudi Arabia) are shown in the table as aid recipients (see table 6.16a).

The table does not distinguish types of aid (program, project, or food aid; emergency assistance; postconflict peacekeeping assistance; or technical cooperation), which may have different effects on the economy. Expenditures on technical cooperation do not always directly benefit the economy to the extent that they defray costs incurred outside the country on salaries and benefits of technical experts and overhead costs of firms supplying technical services.

Ratios of aid to gross national income (GNI), gross capital formation, imports, and government spending provide measures of recipient country dependency on aid. But care must be taken in drawing policy conclusions. For foreign policy reasons some countries have traditionally received large amounts of aid. Thus aid dependency ratios may reveal as much about a donor's interests as about a recipient's needs. Ratios are generally much higher in Sub-Saharan Africa than in other regions, and they increased in the 1980s. High ratios are due only in part to aid flows. Many African countries saw severe erosion in their terms of trade in the 1980s, which, along with weak policies, contributed to falling incomes, imports, and investment. Thus the increase in aid dependency ratios reflects events affecting both the numerator (aid) and the denominator (GNI).

Because the table relies on information from donors, it is not necessarily consistent with information recorded by recipients in the balance of payments, which often excludes all or some technical assistance—particularly payments to expatriates made directly by the donor. Similarly, grant commodity aid may not always be recorded in trade data or in the balance of payments. Moreover, DAC statistics exclude aid for military and antiterrorism purposes.

The nominal values used here may overstate the real value of aid to recipients. Changes in international prices and exchange rates can reduce the purchasing power of aid. Tying aid, still prevalent though declining in importance, also tends to reduce its purchasing power (see *About the data* for table 6.15).

The aggregates refer to World Bank classifications of economies and therefore may differ from those of the Organisation for Economic Co-operation and Development (OECD).

Definitions

- **Net official development assistance** is flows (net of repayment of principal) that meet the Development Assistance Committee (DAC) definition of ODA and are made to countries and territories on the DAC list of aid recipients. See *About the data* for table 6.14. • **Net official development assistance per capita** is net ODA divided by midyear population. • **Aid dependency ratios** are calculated using values in U.S. dollars converted at official exchange rates. Imports of goods, services, and income refer to international transactions involving a change in ownership of general merchandise, goods sent for processing and repairs, nonmonetary gold, services, receipts of employee compensation for nonresident workers, and investment income. For definitions of GNI, gross capital formation, and central government expense, see *Definitions* for tables 1.1, 4.8, and 4.10.

Official development assistance from non-DAC donors, 2005–09 | 6.16a

Net disbursements ($ millions)

	2005	2006	2007	2008	2009
OECD members (non-DAC)					
Czech Republic	135	161	179	249	215
Hungary	100	149	103	107	117
Iceland	27	41	48	48	34
Israel[a]	95	90	111	138	124
Poland	205	297	363	372	375
Slovak Republic	56	55	67	92	75
Slovenia	35	44	54	68	71
Turkey	601	714	602	780	707
Arab countries					
Kuwait	218	158	110	283	221
Saudi Arabia	1,026	2,025	1,551	4,979	3,134
United Arab Emirates	141	219	429	88	834
Other donors					
Taiwan, China	483	513	514	435	411
Thailand	..	74	67	178	40
Others[b]	51	77	134	275	313
Total	3,175	4,617	4,333	8,094	6,672

Note: The table does not reflect aid provided by several major emerging non–Organisation for Economic Co-operation and Development (OECD) donors because information on their aid has not been disclosed.
a. The statistical data for Israel are supplied by and under the responsibility of the relevant Israeli authorities. The use of such data by the OECD is without prejudice to the status of the Golan Heights, East Jerusalem, and Israeli settlements in the West Bank under the terms of international law. The figures include $49.2 million in 2005, $45.5 million in 2006, $42.9 million in 2007, $43.6 million in 2008, and $35.4 million in 2009 for first-year sustenance expenses for people arriving from developing countries (many of which are experiencing civil war or severe unrest) or people who have left their country for humanitarian or political reasons. b. Includes Cyprus, Estonia, Latvia, Liechstenstein, Lithuania, Malta, and Romania.

Source: Organisation for Economic Co-operation and Development.

Data sources

Data on financial flows are compiled by OECD DAC and published in its annual statistical report, *Geographical Distribution of Financial Flows to Developing Countries,* and in its annual *Development Co-operation Report.* Data are available electronically on the OECD DAC *International Development Statistics* CD-ROM and at www.oecd.org/dac/stats/idsonline. Data on population, GNI, gross capital formation, imports of goods and services, and central government expense used in computing the ratios are from World Bank and International Monetary Fund databases.

6.17 Distribution of net aid by Development Assistance Committee members

| | Total $ millions 2009 | Ten major DAC donors $ millions | | | | | | | | | | Other DAC donors $ millions 2009 |
		United States 2009	EU Institutions 2009	United Kingdom 2009	Germany 2009	France 2009	Japan 2009	Netherlands 2009	Spain 2009	Norway 2009	Canada 2009	
Afghanistan	5,319.2	2,979.9	395.4	324.4	337.3	49.8	170.5	147.9	98.9	115.9	232.6	466.5
Albania	314.9	33.0	69.3	2.2	58.8	4.2	-2.0	8.2	14.3	1.0	0.1	125.7
Algeria	282.9	8.1	82.8	3.6	13.1	94.5	1.9	0.0	54.4	0.9	2.8	20.9
Angola	170.4	41.5	38.9	4.4	8.4	4.2	6.8	-3.3	20.3	17.8	0.9	30.4
Argentina	100.2	2.6	21.3	1.0	22.7	12.3	9.0	0.2	24.1	0.1	2.1	4.8
Armenia	273.8	78.5	38.8	1.0	31.0	5.7	98.7	3.0	0.4	3.1	0.7	13.0
Australia												
Austria												
Azerbaijan	136.5	40.4	12.5	1.4	42.7	27.9	-2.0	0.0	0.7	4.0	0.3	8.7
Bangladesh	849.5	63.8	131.9	250.1	67.3	-3.6	14.1	70.4	6.0	14.6	52.5	182.5
Belarus	72.3	12.2	11.1	0.6	21.7	4.5	0.6	0.0	0.8	2.6	0.0	18.3
Belgium												
Benin	472.3	58.9	146.6	0.0	43.1	50.4	25.8	42.0	3.5	0.0	7.0	94.9
Bolivia	562.8	101.6	77.8	0.5	45.7	10.0	31.8	45.6	97.6	6.4	24.3	121.6
Bosnia and Herzegovina	349.0	31.1	72.6	9.6	27.6	4.7	5.0	21.8	36.9	15.9	4.1	120.0
Botswana	255.7	214.4	32.3	0.9	2.1	1.0	-2.6	0.0	0.1	1.8	1.3	4.4
Brazil	328.0	8.1	18.8	13.1	196.1	47.1	-93.2	0.6	64.9	29.5	10.8	32.2
Bulgaria	..	..	..	..	..	..	..	..	..	..	..	..
Burkina Faso	618.3	51.1	165.4	0.2	47.5	77.4	49.8	66.0	10.2	0.5	23.5	126.6
Burundi	391.9	47.6	131.1	14.4	27.9	12.9	20.4	18.3	5.7	25.1	6.1	82.5
Cambodia	516.8	68.6	43.1	32.3	37.9	29.8	127.5	0.1	29.1	3.2	10.9	134.4
Cameroon	326.9	31.4	59.2	2.3	91.0	90.6	8.1	0.1	4.0	0.4	7.1	32.7
Canada												
Central African Republic	153.3	30.5	54.7	2.4	6.6	25.9	6.1	2.8	4.3	0.6	3.8	15.6
Chad	474.5	169.6	119.0	5.6	27.9	41.0	14.0	8.4	13.2	2.2	12.1	61.6
Chile	70.5	1.8	10.8	0.6	11.5	9.6	7.9	0.2	9.6	13.3	2.0	3.2
China	1,199.8	52.9	42.9	116.0	340.9	364.4	142.0	5.3	45.8	21.7	11.1	57.1
Hong Kong SAR, China	..	..	..	..	..	..	..	..	..	..	..	..
Colombia	1,044.4	652.3	45.9	7.8	45.2	22.5	-6.7	32.5	148.6	11.6	25.3	59.4
Congo, Dem. Rep.	1,332.0	238.7	232.8	225.5	79.4	30.3	65.7	43.4	42.7	28.1	44.9	300.7
Congo, Rep.	252.3	9.3	26.2	0.0	25.8	93.2	0.4	0.0	44.4	0.1	7.6	45.4
Costa Rica	105.5	-0.6	6.8	2.6	15.0	4.7	58.3	3.8	9.3	0.7	2.1	2.8
Côte d'Ivoire	1,794.4	230.7	71.9	0.2	15.1	1,200.6	10.4	36.5	50.8	1.6	43.7	133.1
Croatia	160.7	3.7	129.9	1.9	12.6	4.0	-0.7	0.2	0.7	3.6	0.1	4.6
Cuba	103.5	20.0	16.9	1.0	2.5	2.7	3.6	0.1	37.7	0.8	7.7	10.7
Czech Republic	..	..	..	..	..	..	..	..	..	..	..	..
Denmark												
Dominican Republic	118.3	14.1	66.1	0.1	-2.2	3.4	0.2	0.0	29.2	0.3	2.6	4.4
Ecuador	209.9	52.1	62.6	-0.2	24.7	1.2	-11.8	1.6	48.7	1.6	3.2	26.0
Egypt, Arab Rep.	784.7	185.1	204.7	35.6	138.8	111.6	-18.8	17.8	20.6	0.7	17.0	71.7
El Salvador	284.6	82.1	24.9	0.0	18.1	2.4	-3.8	0.4	125.7	0.5	3.2	31.1
Eritrea	86.3	3.6	42.9	6.5	1.4	0.5	8.8	3.7	1.8	9.6	0.6	7.0
Estonia	..	..	..	..	..	..	..	..	..	..	..	..
Ethiopia	2,019.0	726.0	202.5	342.9	79.8	38.3	97.8	85.9	94.0	37.8	87.2	226.9
Finland												
France												
Gabon	61.8	1.2	9.2	0.0	-3.3	54.0	0.1	0.0	0.4	0.0	1.0	-0.8
Gambia, The	37.1	5.0	15.2	3.7	0.3	0.3	11.4	0.7	3.0	0.1	1.2	-3.9
Georgia	603.6	279.1	167.7	7.3	67.0	14.0	12.3	5.1	0.9	11.0	0.8	38.5
Germany												
Ghana	987.2	150.5	166.9	153.9	61.2	49.7	64.8	98.3	24.1	2.5	99.8	115.5
Greece												
Guatemala	369.3	83.9	28.0	0.7	16.1	2.9	26.0	28.4	113.4	7.7	7.1	55.2
Guinea	212.2	34.9	41.2	0.9	19.5	82.1	18.2	0.0	5.0	0.0	5.2	5.4
Guinea-Bissau	110.7	1.1	60.1	0.1	0.4	6.1	9.4	0.0	13.1	0.0	1.2	19.2
Haiti	806.8	319.6	102.7	8.0	16.9	49.0	24.8	0.2	144.9	4.3	119.7	16.8
Honduras	344.5	128.8	39.8	0.1	15.9	1.4	41.7	0.8	58.4	1.4	24.1	32.2

	Total $ millions 2009	Ten major DAC donors $ millions										Other DAC donors $ millions 2009
		United States 2009	EU Institutions 2009	United Kingdom 2009	Germany 2009	France 2009	Japan 2009	Netherlands 2009	Spain 2009	Norway 2009	Canada 2009	
Hungary	..	..	..	..	..	..	..	..	..	..	..	..
India	1,567.6	48.1	98.9	521.1	263.4	−29.0	517.0	7.2	25.3	16.1	11.5	87.8
Indonesia	446.0	121.3	113.1	68.8	-34.8	187.1	-512.8	81.1	3.4	12.9	20.0	385.9
Iran, Islamic Rep.	67.7	0.7	1.9	0.7	46.1	14.6	-17.4	4.5	5.2	0.8	3.3	7.3
Iraq	2,686.0	2,346.3	57.3	48.6	38.2	9.3	28.1	7.3	2.4	11.6	12.1	124.9
Ireland												
Israel	..	..	..	..	..	..	..	..	..	..	..	..
Italy												
Jamaica	112.3	−2.1	105.9	8.3	−6.9	−0.8	−5.3	−4.3	1.2	0.1	5.9	10.2
Japan												
Jordan	571.7	394.6	85.4	1.5	39.8	58.9	−57.4	0.6	10.2	0.8	11.0	26.3
Kazakhstan	185.5	97.3	13.3	7.0	17.5	2.9	37.1	0.6	-0.4	3.1	0.1	7.0
Kenya	1,308.3	590.2	84.3	131.2	85.7	44.8	33.7	25.4	50.7	15.5	31.7	215.1
Korea, Dem. Rep.	49.8	13.5	3.4	0.1	2.7	0.3	0.0	1.2	2.0	4.8	3.6	18.2
Korea, Rep.												
Kosovo	744.6	207.4	315.9	11.8	32.6	1.0	0.2	0.5	0.9	21.2	0.0	153.3
Kuwait	..	..	..	..	..	..	..	..	..	..	..	..
Kyrgyz Republic	168.4	52.5	28.7	8.9	24.0	0.9	17.8	0.1	1.3	3.4	0.1	30.7
Lao PDR	285.9	7.4	25.9	0.3	27.4	19.1	92.4	0.0	1.7	3.2	1.8	106.8
Latvia	..	..	..	..	..	..	..	..	..	..	..	..
Lebanon	463.3	136.9	74.3	5.4	31.6	102.5	3.5	0.7	24.2	9.8	13.9	60.7
Lesotho	86.8	24.7	16.1	8.2	5.4	-1.5	2.6	0.0	9.8	1.0	1.0	19.7
Liberia	400.3	96.9	59.5	33.4	28.1	0.3	14.7	0.0	5.8	15.4	2.2	144.1
Libya	34.4	5.7	2.2	1.9	3.6	19.1	0.1	0.0	0.0	0.0	0.1	1.8
Lithuania	..	..	..	..	..	..	..	..	..	..	..	..
Macedonia, FYR	186.5	29.9	53.2	2.0	18.8	3.0	24.2	18.3	1.8	7.0	0.0	28.6
Madagascar	297.2	76.6	55.6	1.3	17.8	97.5	19.0	0.3	4.1	8.4	2.1	14.5
Malawi	519.3	111.4	84.1	111.7	30.2	0.3	35.8	0.9	9.8	63.6	19.5	52.0
Malaysia	133.0	16.3	0.1	4.2	11.0	−0.1	91.8	0.1	0.1	0.7	0.1	8.8
Mali	676.4	111.3	101.7	0.1	46.9	74.7	35.5	77.3	24.3	12.6	83.5	108.5
Mauritania	157.9	10.2	35.7	0.8	11.6	35.0	9.6	0.0	44.7	0.7	1.3	8.3
Mauritius	156.8	0.1	93.2	20.8	0.5	43.2	−2.1	0.0	0.0	0.4	0.3	0.4
Mexico	164.8	129.4	6.1	11.6	40.8	13.1	−30.7	−0.3	−14.5	0.0	4.4	4.8
Moldova	202.4	32.2	106.2	3.2	9.0	7.0	3.1	2.1	0.4	3.7	0.0	35.5
Mongolia	212.6	34.9	5.4	0.7	25.4	2.1	74.7	9.6	−1.3	1.3	2.7	57.1
Morocco	987.1	31.6	282.4	4.8	81.7	238.1	97.9	1.7	190.7	0.0	8.4	49.9
Mozambique	1,492.3	255.6	204.7	54.9	113.8	14.7	60.7	99.3	68.8	80.4	75.2	464.4
Myanmar	310.8	35.2	76.8	53.1	9.7	2.1	48.3	5.8	1.1	18.9	2.5	57.4
Namibia	279.1	90.3	32.6	0.7	36.7	50.1	39.8	1.9	12.0	−6.7	0.7	21.0
Nepal	548.8	73.5	44.0	103.2	59.6	−3.4	45.3	3.1	49.6	45.3	5.5	123.2
Netherlands												
New Zealand												
Nicaragua	519.0	89.3	46.1	7.1	28.8	1.1	17.4	31.0	142.4	17.5	13.6	124.8
Niger	319.8	37.1	64.4	6.2	22.0	57.4	35.1	0.1	22.2	1.6	9.8	63.9
Nigeria	769.4	354.0	81.9	188.9	26.7	9.1	28.9	4.5	7.0	9.2	17.5	41.8
Norway												
Oman	8.4	5.3	0.0	0.6	0.7	0.7	0.7	0.3	0.0	0.0	0.0	0.1
Pakistan	1,428.3	613.0	97.6	217.5	107.5	8.8	131.4	38.9	13.7	46.6	41.9	111.4
Panama	60.8	16.7	2.2	0.1	1.7	0.1	33.5	0.0	6.3	0.0	0.8	-0.5
Papua New Guinea	354.5	2.8	32.4	1.0	2.5	0.1	−4.2	0.0	0.9	1.7	0.2	317.1
Paraguay	152.9	26.5	31.5	0.0	6.2	0.6	37.3	0.0	38.9	0.9	2.2	8.6
Peru	412.5	104.4	73.8	1.1	79.8	9.0	−36.8	0.3	100.2	−7.3	17.9	70.1
Philippines	294.8	89.5	50.4	4.4	40.1	−7.3	−8.4	2.2	−31.4	1.8	17.0	136.3
Poland	..	..	..	..	..	..	..	..	..	..	..	..
Portugal												
Puerto Rico	..	..	..	..	..	..	..	..	..	..	..	..
Qatar	..	..	..	..	..	..	..	..	..	..	..	..

6.17 Distribution of net aid by Development Assistance Committee members

| | | | | | Ten major DAC donors | | | | | | | |
	Total $ millions 2009	United States 2009	EU Institutions 2009	United Kingdom 2009	Germany 2009	France 2009	Japan 2009	Netherlands 2009	Spain 2009	Norway 2009	Canada 2009	Other DAC donors $ millions 2009
Romania	..	..	..	..	..	..	..	..	..	..	..	..
Russian Federation	..	..	..	..	..	..	..	..	..	..	..	..
Rwanda	624.3	145.9	104.5	89.9	44.0	3.5	21.3	54.2	25.0	3.6	13.7	118.8
Saudi Arabia	..	..	..	..	..	..	..	..	..	..	..	..
Senegal	648.8	67.7	134.5	6.5	22.2	140.9	46.7	45.7	59.3	0.5	54.5	70.5
Serbia	565.4	46.5	292.9	7.7	114.5	12.7	3.7	2.6	4.0	19.9	4.8	56.0
Sierra Leone	305.3	17.0	108.9	80.3	15.8	0.3	37.4	1.5	3.4	3.1	8.9	28.8
Singapore	..	..	..	..	..	..	..	..	..	..	..	..
Slovak Republic	..	..	..	..	..	..	..	..	..	..	..	..
Slovenia	..	..	..	..	..	..	..	..	..	..	..	..
Somalia	607.5	194.9	108.0	43.8	20.9	4.7	22.6	14.8	52.8	33.3	25.7	85.9
South Africa	1,014.6	523.7	153.3	67.3	86.9	−15.6	4.7	48.9	5.3	36.1	13.0	90.9
Spain												
Sri Lanka	433.2	32.3	59.2	18.2	−5.6	12.7	91.6	2.7	18.6	35.3	25.0	143.2
Sudan	2,136.8	954.6	225.8	292.4	47.2	10.4	111.0	97.3	26.0	92.1	105.0	174.9
Swaziland	33.7	15.6	15.1	−3.8	−0.2	0.2	1.2	0.0	1.2	3.2	0.9	0.3
Sweden												
Switzerland												
Syrian Arab Republic	116.0	18.6	54.8	1.1	37.8	25.7	−54.5	0.1	6.3	0.0	0.9	25.3
Tajikistan	177.6	40.5	37.3	4.5	26.1	4.7	26.2	0.3	6.3	3.1	2.5	26.0
Tanzania	1,547.2	283.7	138.4	216.7	87.1	7.9	120.5	62.6	25.1	116.4	94.0	394.9
Thailand	−71.2	23.6	21.3	9.9	1.9	−11.7	−150.3	3.6	4.5	0.7	2.8	22.5
Timor-Leste	193.3	29.1	10.3	0.1	5.6	0.1	11.9	0.0	10.8	8.5	2.0	114.8
Togo	408.2	3.8	46.4	10.4	24.0	40.5	34.1	0.9	3.8	0.1	2.5	241.7
Trinidad and Tobago	6.0	0.5	1.6	0.4	0.2	1.1	0.1	0.0	0.1	0.0	1.8	0.2
Tunisia	457.6	−5.3	108.1	3.8	30.8	170.0	14.4	−0.8	124.1	0.0	2.1	10.3
Turkey	1,345.1	−6.5	787.0	2.2	6.7	154.6	210.8	−0.3	135.3	0.2	−2.3	57.5
Turkmenistan	17.4	10.8	4.0	0.3	1.9	0.2	−1.2	0.0	0.0	0.6	0.0	0.8
Uganda	1,141.3	366.9	128.0	117.4	60.1	14.6	54.1	45.0	5.9	67.3	16.9	265.3
Ukraine	574.0	103.0	177.0	2.4	121.6	19.5	61.9	0.0	3.8	3.1	18.0	63.7
United Arab Emirates	..	..	..	..	..	..	..	..	..	..	..	..
United Kingdom												
United States												
Uruguay	44.2	1.0	11.8	0.0	−0.3	1.4	2.4	0.0	12.2	0.2	1.3	14.1
Uzbekistan	83.6	9.9	6.1	1.8	32.1	2.9	20.4	0.0	0.7	0.3	0.0	9.4
Venezuela, RB	50.2	11.7	3.4	2.2	8.7	7.1	2.1	0.1	12.9	0.0	0.5	1.5
Vietnam	2,127.8	78.1	51.9	93.8	112.5	142.9	1,191.4	45.4	32.7	15.9	35.3	327.9
West Bank and Gaza	2,275.9	844.3	538.3	94.9	98.7	79.2	76.7	46.2	99.4	100.1	41.2	256.9
Yemen, Rep.	276.0	26.2	23.6	35.9	82.9	5.9	37.2	30.9	3.9	0.7	2.5	26.3
Zambia	852.9	231.9	152.4	73.5	55.5	7.4	36.6	64.8	11.8	62.7	13.0	143.4
Zimbabwe	700.1	249.7	79.7	109.9	34.7	4.6	12.4	22.3	8.2	28.9	28.3	121.4
World	**96,623.9 s**	**25,173.7 s**	**13,021.4 s**	**7,657.0 s**	**7,096.7 s**	**7,019.4 s**	**6,001.2 s**	**4,798.0 s**	**4,473.1 s**	**3,168.2 s**	**3,141.0 s**	**15,074.3 s**
Low income	27,536.0	7,955.5	3,842.7	2,622.5	1,702.3	993.6	1,553.4	1,067.9	927.6	836.8	1,152.7	4,881.1
Middle income	39,141.0	10,578.1	6,543.1	2,083.3	3,199.0	4,510.2	2,729.5	899.5	2,240.8	655.9	775.7	4,925.8
Lower middle income	28,607.7	8,235.8	3,859.8	1,852.0	2,103.0	3,157.9	2,329.6	609.1	1,461.4	484.1	610.8	3,904.0
Upper middle income	9,649.3	2,276.5	2,327.5	225.9	965.2	1,254.3	398.9	255.7	738.7	150.8	144.1	911.8
Low & middle income	96,408.4	25,163.7	12,879.0	7,653.4	7,083.1	7,010.9	6,001.0	4,797.4	4,450.5	3,164.6	3,135.4	15,069.4
East Asia & Pacific	7,305.6	823.5	526.8	389.5	604.5	899.2	1,228.5	157.0	100.4	97.1	146.1	2,333.0
Europe & Central Asia	6,418.5	1,340.6	2,240.2	74.4	714.3	273.7	522.3	66.2	209.7	110.5	29.4	837.4
Latin America & Carib.	7,714.7	2,030.9	1,117.6	158.6	917.4	231.7	142.5	262.0	1,501.4	138.1	452.6	761.9
Middle East & N. Africa	9,508.6	4,082.5	1,623.7	247.5	703.5	1,000.9	142.1	108.9	589.7	137.1	125.4	747.3
South Asia	10,370.5	3,906.6	845.4	1,438.0	844.6	35.4	1,013.7	274.8	212.4	280.3	372.5	1,146.7
Sub-Saharan Africa	30,845.3	7,436.4	4,816.7	2,708.4	1,781.1	3,396.9	1,374.3	1,197.6	1,127.2	902.4	1,308.7	4,795.8
High income	215.5	9.9	142.4	3.6	13.5	8.5	0.3	0.5	22.6	3.6	5.6	4.9
Euro area	..	..	..	..	..	..	..	..	..	..	..	..

Note: Regional aggregates include data for economies not specified elsewhere. World and income group totals include aid not allocated by country or region.

About the data

The table shows net bilateral aid to low- and middle-income economies from members of the Development Assistance Committee (DAC) of the Organisation for Economic Co-operation and Development (OECD). DAC has 24 members, of which 23 are economies and 1 is a multilateral institution (the European Union Institutions). Previous editions of the table included only DAC member economies; this year's edition includes data for the European Union Institutions.

The table is based on donor country reports of bilateral programs, which may differ from reports by recipient countries. Recipients may lack access to information on such aid expenditures as development-oriented research, stipends and tuition costs for aid-financed students in donor countries, and payment of experts hired by donor countries. Moreover, a full accounting would include donor country contributions to multilateral institutions, the flow of resources from multilateral institutions to recipient countries, and flows from countries that are not members of DAC.

Data in this table exclude DAC members' multilateral aid (contributions to the regular budgets of the multilateral institutions). These are included in data reported in table 6.14. Projects executed by multilateral institutions or nongovernmental organizations

on behalf of DAC members are classified as bilateral aid (since it is the donor country that effectively controls the use of the funds) and are included in the data reported in this table.

The data include aid to some countries and territories not shown in the table and aid to unspecified economies recorded only at the regional or global level. Aid to countries and territories not shown in the table has been assigned to regional totals based on the World Bank's regional classification system. Aid to unspecified economies is included in regional totals and, when possible, income group totals. Aid not allocated by country or region—including administrative costs, research on development, and aid to nongovernmental organizations—is included in the world total. Thus regional and income group totals do not sum to the world total.

Some of the aid recipients shown in table are also aid donors. Development cooperation activities by non-DAC members have increased in recent years and in some cases surpass those of individual DAC members. Some non-DAC donors report their development cooperation activities to DAC on a voluntary basis. Many others do not yet report their aid flows to DAC. See table 6.16a for a summary of ODA from non-DAC countries.

Definitions

• **Net aid** refers to net bilateral official development assistance that meets the DAC definition of official development assistance and is made to countries and territories on the DAC list of aid recipients. See *About the data* for table 6.14. • **Other DAC donors** are Australia, Austria, Belgium, Denmark, Finland, Greece, Ireland, Italy, the Republic of Korea, Luxembourg, New Zealand, Portugal, Sweden, and Switzerland.

Beyond the DAC: The role of other providers of development assistance · 6.17a

Development assistance flows from non-DAC donor countries ($ millions)

Country	Estimate	Year	Source
20 countries reporting to DAC (see table 6.16a)	8,094	2008	OECD/DAC Statistics
Brazil	437	2007	DAC *Development Co-operation Report*, estimates by Brazilian officials
China	1,800–3,000	2008	*Fiscal Yearbook*, Ministry of Finance, China. Upper estimate: Brautigam 2009
India	610	2008/09	*Annual Reports*, Ministry of Foreign Affairs, India
Russian Federation	200	2008	Russian Federation statement at DAC Senior Level Meeting, April 2010
South Africa	109	2008/09	Estimates of Public Expenditures 2009, Foreign Affairs, National Treasury of South Africa

Many countries that are not members of the OECD DAC have provided development assistance for decades. The past 10 years have seen their numbers rise fast, and in some cases their levels of development assistance now surpass those of individual DAC members. DAC estimates total net development assistance flows from non-DAC donors at $12–$14 billion in 2008, or 9–10 percent of global official development assistance (ODA) flows (assuming that the flows were consistent with the definition of ODA). Estimating overall aid volumes from non-DAC donors is challenging. Twenty countries, mostly emerging donors and Arab donors, voluntarily report aid volumes to DAC annually (see table 6.16a). Many others, including most major providers of aid from developing countries to developing countries (such as Brazil, China, India, and South Africa), do not. Estimates of aid volumes of countries that do not report to DAC must be treated with caution. Official figures often omit important cooperation activities, such as contributions to international organizations focused on development, leading to underestimates, and they often include expenditures that would not qualify as ODA, such as security-related or culturally motivated spending, or insufficiently concessional loans, leading to overestimates.

Source: Smith, Fordelone, and Zimmermann 2010 and OECD 2010.

Data sources

Data on financial flows are compiled by DAC and published in its annual statistical report, *Geographical Distribution of Financial Flows to Aid Recipients*, and its annual *Development Cooperation Report*. Data are available electronically on the OECD DAC *International Development Statistics* CD-ROM and at www.oecd.org/dac/stats/idsonline.

	Net migration		International migrant stock		Refugees				Workers' remittances and compensation of employees			
							thousands			$ millions		
	thousands		thousands		By country of origin		By country of asylum		Received		Paid	
	1990–95	2005–10	1995	2010	1995	2009	1995	2009	1995	2009	1995	2009
Afghanistan	3,266	1,000	70	91	2,679.1	2,887.1	19.6	0.0	..	..	..	..
Albania	–423	–75	71	89	5.8	15.7	4.7	0.1	427	1,317	..	10
Algeria	–50	–140	299	242	1.5	8.2	192.5	94.1	1,120[a]	2,059[a]	..	..
Angola	143	80	38	65	246.7	141.0	10.9	14.7	5	82	210	716
Argentina	120	30	1,588	1,449	0.3	0.6	10.3	3.2	64	658	195	702
Armenia	–500	–75	682	324	201.4	18.0	219.0	3.6	65	769	17	145
Australia	371	500	3,854	4,711	0.0	0.0	62.1	22.5	1,651	4,089[a]	700	3,000[a]
Austria	234	160	989	1,310	0.0	0.0	34.4	38.9	1,012	3,286	346	3,377
Azerbaijan	–116	–50	525	264	200.5	16.9	233.7	1.6	3	1,274	9	652
Bangladesh	–500	–570	1,006	1,085	57.0	10.4	51.1	228.6	1,202	10,523	1	8
Belarus	0	0	1,185	1,090	0.1	5.5	29.0	0.6	29	358	12	112
Belgium	85	200	916	975	0.0	0.1	31.7	15.5	4,937	10,437	3,252	4,136
Benin	105	50	146	232	0.1	0.4	23.8	7.2	100	243[a]	26	88
Bolivia	–100	–100	70	146	..	..	0.7	0.7	7	1,069	9	103
Bosnia and Herzegovina	–1,025	–10	73	28	769.8	70.0	40.0	7.1	..	2,081	..	61
Botswana	14	15	39	115	0.0	0.0	0.3	3.0	59	88	200	102
Brazil	–184	–229	731	688	0.1	1.0	2.1	4.2	3,315	4,234	347	1,003
Bulgaria	–349	–50	47	107	4.2	2.7	1.3	5.4	42	1,558	34	101
Burkina Faso	–128	–65	464	1,043	0.1	1.0	29.8	0.5	78[a]	99[a]	50[a]	100
Burundi	–250	323	295	61	350.6	94.2	173.0	25.0	..	28	5	1
Cambodia	150	–5	116	336	61.2	17.0	0.0	0.1	12	338	52	215
Cameroon	–5	–19	246	197	2.0	14.8	45.8	100.0	11	148	22	94
Canada	643	1,050	5,047	7,202	0.0	0.1	152.1	169.4	..	..	..	..
Central African Republic	37	5	67	80	0.2	159.6	33.9	27.0	0	..	27	..
Chad	–10	–75	78	388	59.7	55.0	0.1	338.5	1	..	15	..
Chile	90	30	136	320	14.3	1.3	0.3	1.5	..	4	13[a]	6
China	–829[b]	–1,731[b]	437[b]	686[b]	124.7[c]	200.6[c]	288.3	301.0	878[a]	48,729[a]	86[a]	4,444
Hong Kong SAR, China	300	113	2,431	2,742	0.2	0.0	1.5	0.1	..	348	..	413
Colombia	–250	–120	109	110	1.9	389.8	0.2	0.2	815	4,180	150	92
Congo, Dem. Rep.	1,208	–100	1,919	445	89.7	455.9	1,433.8	185.8	..	..	..	..
Congo, Rep.	–14	–50	131	143	0.2	20.5	19.4	111.4	4	14[a]	27	102
Costa Rica	62	30	228	489	0.2	0.3	24.2	19.1	123	513	36	239
Côte d'Ivoire	375	–145	1,985	2,407	0.2	23.2	297.9	24.6	151	185	457	756
Croatia	153	10	721	700	245.6	76.5	198.6	1.2	544	1,476	16	99
Cuba	–120	–194	25	15	24.9	7.5	1.8	0.5	..	..	..	..
Czech Republic	8	226	454	453	2.0	1.1	2.7	2.3	191	1,201	101	2,562
Denmark	58	30	297	484	0.0	0.0	64.8	20.4	523	894	209	3,413
Dominican Republic	–129	–140	322	434	0.0	0.2	1.0	..	839	3,467	7	29
Ecuador	–50	–350	88	394	0.2	1.0	0.2	116.6	386	2,502	4	81
Egypt, Arab Rep.	–498	–340	174	245	0.9	7.0	5.4	94.4	3,226	7,150	223	255
El Salvador	–249	–280	28	40	23.5	5.1	0.2	0.0	1,064[a]	3,482	1[a]	21
Eritrea	–359	55	12	16	286.7	209.2	1.1	4.8	..	..	..	..
Estonia	–108	0	309	182	0.4	0.2	..	0.0	1	325	3	81
Ethiopia	768	–300	795	548	101.0	62.9	393.5	121.9	27	262	0	27
Finland	43	55	103	226	0.0	0.0	10.2	7.4	74	859	54	454
France	239	500	6,085	6,685	0.0	0.1	155.2	196.4	4,640	15,551	4,935	5,224
Gabon	20	5	164	284	0.0	0.1	0.8	8.8	4	10[a]	99	186
Gambia, The	45	15	148	290	0.2	2.0	6.6	10.1	19[a]	80	..	8
Georgia	–544	–250	250	167	0.3	15.0	0.1	0.9	284	714	12	32
Germany	2,649	550	8,992	10,758	0.4	0.2	1,267.9	593.8	4,523	10,879	11,348	15,924
Ghana	40	–51	1,038	1,852	13.6	14.9	83.2	13.7	17	114	5	6
Greece	470	150	549	1,133	0.2	0.1	4.4	1.7	3,286	2,020	300	1,843
Guatemala	–360	–200	46	59	42.9	5.8	1.5	0.1	358	4,019	8	22
Guinea	350	–300	814	395	0.4	10.9	672.3	15.3	1	64	10	45
Guinea-Bissau	20	–12	32	19	0.8	1.1	15.4	7.9	2[a]	47	3	17[a]
Haiti	–133	–140	22	35	13.9	24.1	..	0.0	..	1,376	..	135
Honduras	–120	–100	31	24	1.2	1.2	0.1	0.0	124	2,520	8	12

	Net migration		International migrant stock		Refugees				Workers' remittances and compensation of employees			
							thousands				$ millions	
					By country of origin		By country of asylum		Received		Paid	
	thousands		thousands									
	1990–95	2005–10	1995	2010	1995	2009	1995	2009	1995	2009	1995	2009
Hungary	104	75	293	368	2.3	1.5	11.4	6.0	152	2,130	146	1,223
India	−960	−1,000	7,022	5,436	5.0	19.5	227.5	185.3	6,223	49,468	419	2,893
Indonesia	−725	−730	219	123	9.8	18.2	0.0	0.8	651	6,793	..	2,702
Iran, Islamic Rep.	−1,164	−500	3,016	2,129	112.4	72.8	2,072.0	1,070.5	1,600[a]	1,045[a]	..	..
Iraq	−154	−577	134	83	718.7	1,785.2	116.7	35.2	..	71	..	31[a]
Ireland	−1	200	264	899	0.0	0.0	0.4	9.6	347	576	173	1,988
Israel	484	85	1,919	2,940	0.9	1.3	..	17.7	701	1,267	1,407	3,283
Italy	294	1,650	1,723	4,463	0.1	0.0	74.3	55.0	2,364	2,683	1,824	12,986
Jamaica	−113	−100	22	30	0.0	0.9	0.0	0.0	653	1,912	74	314
Japan	474	150	1,363	2,176	0.0	0.2	5.4	2.3	1,151	1,776	1,820	4,069
Jordan	509	250	1,608	2,973	0.5	2.1	1,288.9[d]	2,434.5[d]	1,441	3,597	107	502
Kazakhstan	−1,509	−100	3,295	3,079	0.1	3.7	15.6	4.3	116	124	503	3,138
Kenya	222	−189	528	818	9.3	9.6	234.7	358.9	298[a]	1,686[a]	9	61
Korea, Dem. Rep.	0	0	35	37	0.0	0.9	..	..	..	..	..	..
Korea, Rep.	−627	−30	584	535	0.0	0.6	0.0	0.3	1,080	2,522	635	3,120
Kosovo	..	..	..	..	..	..	..	..	..	..	..	..
Kuwait	−598	120	1,090	2,098	0.8	0.9	3.3	0.2	..	..	1,354	9,912
Kyrgyz Republic	−273	−75	482	223	0.0	2.6	13.4	0.4	1	992[a]	41	188
Lao PDR	−30	−75	23	19	58.2	8.4	..	..	22	38	9	22
Latvia	−134	−10	527	335	0.2	0.8	..	0.0	41	591	1	46
Lebanon	230	−13	656	758	13.5	16.3	348.0[d]	476.1[d]	1,225[a]	7,558	..	5,749
Lesotho	−84	−36	6	6	0.0	0.0	0.1	..	411	414	75	35
Liberia	−523	248	199	96	744.6	71.6	120.1	7.0	..	54[a]	..	1
Libya	10	20	506	682	0.6	2.2	4.0	9.0	..	14[a]	222	1,361
Lithuania	−99	−100	272	129	0.1	0.5	0.0	0.8	1	1,169	1	620
Macedonia, FYR	−27	−10	115	130	12.9	7.9	9.0	1.5	68	381	1	26
Madagascar	−7	−5	44	38	0.1	0.3	0.1	..	14	10[a]	11	21
Malawi	−920	−20	325	276	0.0	0.1	1.0	5.4	1	1[a]	1	0[a]
Malaysia	287	130	1,193	2,358	0.1	0.5	5.3	66.1	116	1,131	1,329	6,529
Mali	−260	−202	174	163	77.2	2.9	17.9	13.5	112	405[a]	42	105
Mauritania	−15	10	118	99	84.3	39.1	34.4	26.8	5	2[a]	14	..
Mauritius	−7	0	18	43	0.0	0.0	..	..	132[a]	211[a]	1	12
Mexico	−1,364	−2,430	458	726	0.4	6.4	38.7	1.2	4,368	21,953	..	..
Moldova	−121	−172	473	408	0.5	5.9	..	0.1	1	1,211	1	104
Mongolia	−173	−10	7	10	0.3	1.5	..	0.0	..	200	..	83
Morocco	−450	−425	55	49	0.3	2.3	0.1	0.8	1,970	6,270	20	61
Mozambique	650	−20	246	450	125.6	0.1	0.1	3.5	59	111	21	63
Myanmar	−126	−500	114	89	152.3	406.7	..	..	81	137[a]	..	32[a]
Namibia	−13	−1	118	139	0.0	0.9	1.7	7.2	16	14	11	16
Nepal	−101	−100	625	946	0.0	5.1	124.8	108.5	57	2,986	9	12
Netherlands	191	100	1,387	1,753	0.1	0.0	80.0	76.0	1,359	3,691	2,802	14,212
New Zealand	143	50	594	962	..	0.0	3.8	3.3	1,652	628	427	977
Nicaragua	−114	−200	27	40	23.9	1.5	0.6	0.1	75	768	..	..
Niger	−3	−28	171	202	10.3	0.8	27.6	0.3	8	89	29	22[a]
Nigeria	−96	−300	582	1,128	1.9	15.6	8.1	9.1	804[a]	9,585[a]	5	66
Norway	42	135	237	485	0.0	0.0	47.6	37.8	239	631	603	4,174
Oman	23	20	582	826	0.0	0.1	..	0.0	39	39	1,537	5,313
Pakistan	−2,611	−1,416	4,077	4,234	5.3	35.1	1,202.5	1,740.7	1,712	8,717	4	8
Panama	8	11	73	121	0.2	0.1	0.9	16.9	112	175	20	229
Papua New Guinea	0	0	31	25	2.0	0.1	9.6	9.7	16	12	16	323
Paraguay	−30	−40	183	161	0.1	0.1	0.1	0.1	287	609	..	..
Peru	−300	−625	51	38	5.9	6.3	0.6	1.1	599	2,378	34	85
Philippines	−900	−900	210	435	0.5	1.0	0.8	0.1	5,360	19,766	151	58
Poland	−77	−120	964	827	19.7	2.1	0.6	15.3	724	8,126	262	1,330
Portugal	0	200	528	919	0.0	0.0	0.2	0.4	3,953	3,585	527	1,460
Puerto Rico	−4	−21	339	324	0.0	..	..	..	..	..	..	..
Qatar	14	562	406	1,305	0.0	0.1	..	0.1	..	..	..	..

Movement of people across borders

	Net migration (thousands)		International migrant stock (thousands)		Refugees (thousands)				Workers' remittances and compensation of employees ($ millions)			
					By country of origin		By country of asylum		Received		Paid	
	1990–95	2005–10	1995	2010	1995	2009	1995	2009	1995	2009	1995	2009
Romania	−529	−200	135	133	17.0	4.4	0.2	1.1	9	4,929	2	310
Russian Federation	2,220	250	11,707	12,270	207.0	109.5	246.7	4.9	2,502	5,359	3,938	18,548
Rwanda	−1,681	15	337	465	1,819.4	129.1	7.8	54.0	21	93	1	71
Saudi Arabia	−500	150	4,611	7,289	0.3	0.6	13.2	0.6	..	217	16,594	25,969
Senegal	−100	−100	291	210	17.6	16.3	66.8	22.2	146	1,365	76	144[a]
Serbia	451	0	874	525	86.1[e]	195.6	650.7[e]	86.4	1,295	5,406[a]	..	91
Sierra Leone	−450	60	101	107	379.5	15.4	4.7	9.1	24	47	0	3
Singapore	250	500	992	1,967	0.0	0.1	0.1	0.0	..	..	..	..
Slovak Republic	−3	20	114	131	0.0	0.3	2.3	0.4	26	1,671	3	134
Slovenia	38	22	200	164	12.9	0.0	22.3	0.3	272	279	31	191
Somalia	−893	−250	19	23	638.7	678.3	0.6	1.8	..	..	..	..
South Africa	900	700	1,098	1,863	0.5	0.4	101.4	48.0	105	902	629	1,158
Spain	324	1,750	1,041	6,378	0.0	0.0	5.9	4.0	3,237	9,904	868	12,646
Sri Lanka	−256	−300	426	340	107.6	145.7	0.0	0.3	809	3,363	16	435
Sudan	−168	135	1,111	753	445.3	368.2	674.1	186.3	346	2,993[a]	1	2[a]
Swaziland	−38	−6	35	40	0.0	0.0	0.7	0.8	83	93	4	11
Sweden	151	150	906	1,306	0.0	0.0	199.2	81.4	288	652	336	787
Switzerland	227	100	1,471	1,763	0.0	0.0	82.9	46.2	1,473	2,524	10,114	19,562
Syrian Arab Republic	−70	800	817	2,206	8.0	17.9	373.5[d]	1,526.6[d]	339	1,332[a]	15	212[a]
Tajikistan	−296	−200	305	284	59.0	0.6	0.6	2.7	..	1,748	..	124
Tanzania	591	−300	1,134	659	0.1	1.2	829.7	118.7	1	23	1	81
Thailand	−39	300	549	1,157	0.2	0.5	106.6	105.3	1,695	1,637	..	..
Timor-Leste	0	10	10	14	..	0.0	..	0.0	..	..	..	..
Togo	−122	−5	169	185	93.2	18.4	10.9	8.5	15	307[a]	5	58[a]
Trinidad and Tobago	−24	−20	46	34	0.0	0.2	..	0.0	32	99[a]	14	..
Tunisia	−43	−20	38	34	0.3	2.3	0.2	0.1	680	1,964	36	13
Turkey	−70	−44	1,212	1,411	44.9	146.4	12.8	10.4	3,327	970	..	141
Turkmenistan	50	−25	260	208	0.0	0.7	23.3	0.1	4	..	7	..
Uganda	120	−135	661	647	24.2	7.6	229.4	127.3	..	750	..	463
Ukraine	100	−80	6,172	5,258	1.7	24.5	5.2	7.3	6	5,073	1	25
United Arab Emirates	340	343	1,716	3,293	0.0	0.4	0.4	0.3	..	..	..	..
United Kingdom	167	948	4,191	6,452	0.1	0.2	90.9	269.4	2,469	7,252	2,581	3,400
United States	6,565	5,052	28,522	42,813	0.2	2.4	623.3	275.5	2,179	2,947	22,181	48,308
Uruguay	−20	−50	93	80	0.3	0.2	0.1	0.2	..	101	..	6
Uzbekistan	−340	−400	1,474	1,176	0.1	6.7	2.6	0.6	..	..	..	..
Venezuela, RB	40	40	1,019	1,007	0.5	6.2	1.6	201.3	2	131	203	581
Vietnam	−840	−200	39	69	543.5	339.3	34.4	2.4	..	6,626[a]	..	..
West Bank and Gaza	1	−10	1,201	1,924	72.8	95.2	1,201.0[d]	1,885.2[d]	582	1,261[a]	19	9[a]
Yemen, Rep.	650	−135	378	518	0.4	1.9	53.5	170.9	1,081	1,160	61	337
Zambia	−11	−85	271	233	0.0	0.2	130.0	56.8	..	41	59	66
Zimbabwe	−192	−700	433	372	0.0	22.4	0.5	4.0	44	..	7	..
World	..[f] s		..[f] s	165,674[g] s	213,450[g] s	18,068.7[s,d] h	15,163.2[s,d] h	18,068.7[d] s	15,163.2[d] s	101,254 s	416,158 s	100,950 s	289,122 s
Low income	287	−2,737	13,555	13,368	7,990.4	5,427.5	4,727.2	1,893.8	2,189	22,706	357	2,047
Middle income	−13,401	−13,203	63,453	67,824	4,260.8	4,558.6	10,086.9	11,285.2	53,012	284,357	10,230	57,377
Lower middle income	−9,961	−9,231	31,848	34,166	2,733.4	3,451.1	6,322.0	9,104.7	31,182	206,323	2,147	15,095
Upper middle income	−3,441	−3,972	31,605	33,657	1,527.3	1,107.4	3,764.8	2,180.5	21,830	78,033	8,084	42,283
Low & middle income	−13,114	−15,941	77,009	81,192	12,251.1	9,986.1	14,814.0	13,179.1	55,202	307,063	10,587	59,425
East Asia & Pacific	−3,285	−3,781	3,048	5,434	952.9	996.7	447.0	485.5	8,925	85,788	1,703	14,459
Europe & Central Asia	−3,386	−1,671	29,607	27,346	1,611.6	655.6	1,221.3	163.8	6,482	35,433	4,507	24,427
Latin America & Carib.	−3,388	−5,214	5,454	6,569	155.5	462.0	93.9	367.4	13,322	56,590	1,138	3,788
Middle East & N. Africa	−1,044	−1,089	8,985	11,957	948.0	2,014.0	5,683.0	7,809.6	13,275	33,442	704	8,536
South Asia	−1,262	−2,376	13,257	12,175	2,958.7	3,192.1	1,625.5	2,263.4	10,005	75,061	476	3,471
Sub-Saharan Africa	−749	−1,810	16,659	17,710	5,624.4	2,665.8	5,743.4	2,089.5	3,193	20,749	2,060	4,743
High income	13,097	15,894	88,665	132,259	287.1	90.8	3,254.7	1,984.1	46,052	109,095	90,363	229,697
Euro area	4,604	5,607	23,080	36,135	13.9	1.0	1,690.4	1,011.4	30,827	67,529	28,741	85,677

a. World Bank estimate. b. Includes Taiwan, China. c. Includes Tibetans, who are listed separately by the UN Refugee Agency (UNHCR). d. Includes Palestinian refugees under the mandate of the United Nations Relief and Works Agency for Palestine Refugees in the Near East (UNRWA), who are not included in data from the UNHCR. e. Includes Montenegro. f. World totals computed by the United Nations sum to zero, but because the aggregates refer to World Bank definitions, regional and income group totals do not. g. World totals are computed by the World Bank and include only economies covered by *World Development Indicators*, so data may differ from what is published by the United Nations Population Division. h. Includes refugees without specified country of origin and Palestinian refugees under the mandate of the UNRWA, so regional and income group totals do not sum to the world total.

About the data

Movement of people, most often through migration, is a significant part of global integration. Migrants contribute to the economies of both their host country and their country of origin. Yet reliable statistics on migration are difficult to collect and are often incomplete, making international comparisons a challenge.

The United Nations Population Division provides data on net migration and migrant stock. Net migration is the total number of immigrants minus the total number of emigrants. However, data on emigrant stock are not collected because it is difficult for countries to gather information on people who are not within their borders. To derive estimates of net migration, the migration history of a country or area, the migration policy of a country, and the influx of refugees in recent periods are taken into account. The data to calculate these official estimates come from a variety of sources, including border statistics, administrative records, surveys, and censuses. When no official estimates can be made because of insufficient data, net migration is derived through the balance equation, which is the difference between overall population growth and the natural increase during the 1990–2000 intercensal period.

The data used to estimate the international migrant stock at a particular time are obtained mainly from population censuses. The estimates are derived from the data on foreign-born population—people who have residence in one country but were born in another country. When data on the foreign-born population are not available, data on foreign population— that is, people who are citizens of a country other than the country in which they reside—are used as estimates.

After the breakup of the Soviet Union in 1991 people living in one of the newly independent countries who were born in another were classified as international migrants. Estimates of migrant stock in the newly independent states from 1990 on are based on the 1989 census of the Soviet Union.

For countries with information on the international migrant stock for at least two points in time, interpolation or extrapolation was used to estimate the international migrant stock on July 1 of the reference years. For countries with only one observation, estimates for the reference years were derived using rates of change in the migrant stock in the years preceding or following the single observation available. A model was used to estimate migrants for countries that had no data.

The table shows data on refugees because they are an important part of migrant stock. Refugee figures shown here refer to people who have crossed an international border to find sanctuary and have been granted refugee or refugee-like status or temporary protection. Asylum seekers and internally displaced people—who are often confused with refugees—are not included. Unlike refugees, internally displaced people remain under the protection of their own government, even if their reason for fleeing was similar to that of refugees.

Registrations, together with other sources—including estimates and surveys—are the main sources of refugee data. But there are difficulties in collecting accurate statistics. Although refugees are often registered individually, the accuracy of registrations varies greatly. Many refugees may not be aware of the need to register or may choose not to do so. And administrative records tend to overestimate the number of refugees because it is easier to register than to de-register. The UN Refugee Agency (UNHCR) collects and maintains data on refugees, except for Palestinian refugees residing in areas under the mandate of the United Nations Relief and Works Agency for Palestine Refugees in the Near East (UNRWA). The UNRWA provides services to Palestinian refugees who live in certain areas and who register with the agency. Registration is voluntary, and estimates by the UNRWA are not an accurate count of the Palestinian refugee population. The table shows estimates of refugees collected by the UNHCR, complemented by estimates of Palestinian refugees under the UNRWA mandate. Thus, the aggregates differ from those published by the UNHCR.

Workers' remittances and compensation of employees are World Bank staff estimates based on data from the International Monetary Fund's (IMF) *Balance of Payments Statistics Yearbook*. The IMF data are supplemented by World Bank staff estimates for missing data for countries where workers' remittances are important. The data reported here are the sum of three items defined in the fifth edition of the IMF's *Balance of Payments Manual*: workers' remittances, compensation of employees, and migrants' transfers.

The distinction among these three items is not always consistent in the data reported by countries to the IMF. In some cases countries compile data on the basis of the citizenship of migrant workers rather than their residency status. Some countries also report remittances entirely as workers' remittances or compensation of employees. Following the fifth edition of the *Balance of Payments Manual* in 1993, migrants' transfers are considered a capital transaction, but previous editions regarded them as current transfers. For these reasons the figures presented in the table take all three items into account.

Definitions

• **Net migration** is the net total of migrants during the period. It is the total number of immigrants less the total number of emigrants, including both citizens and noncitizens. Data are five-year estimates. • **International migrant stock** is the number of people born in a country other than that in which they live. It includes refugees. • **Refugees** are people who are recognized as refugees under the 1951 Convention Relating to the Status of Refugees or its 1967 Protocol, the 1969 Organization of African Unity Convention Governing the Specific Aspects of Refugee Problems in Africa, people recognized as refugees in accordance with the UNHCR statute, people granted refugee-like humanitarian status, and people provided temporary protection. Asylum seekers—people who have applied for asylum or refugee status and who have not yet received a decision or who are registered as asylum seekers—are excluded. Palestinian refugees are people (and their descendants) whose residence was Palestine between June 1946 and May 1948 and who lost their homes and means of livelihood as a result of the 1948 Arab-Israeli conflict. • **Country of origin** refers to the nationality or country of citizenship of a claimant. • **Country of asylum** is the country where an asylum claim was filed and granted. • **Workers' remittances and compensation of employees** received and paid comprise current transfers by migrant workers and wages and salaries earned by nonresident workers. Remittances are classified as current private transfers from migrant workers resident in the host country for more than a year, irrespective of their immigration status, to recipients in their country of origin. Migrants' transfers are defined as the net worth of migrants who are expected to remain in the host country for more than one year that is transferred to another country at the time of migration. Compensation of employees is the income of migrants who have lived in the host country for less than a year.

Data sources

Data on net migration are from the United Nations Population Division's *World Population Prospects: The 2008 Revision*. Data on migration stock are from the United Nations Population Division's *Trends in Total Migrant Stock: The 2008 Revision*. Data on refugees are from the UNHCR's *Statistical Yearbook 2009*, complemented by statistics on Palestinian refugees under the mandate of the UNRWA as published on its website. Data on remittances are World Bank staff estimates based on IMF balance of payments data.

	International tourists				Inbound tourism expenditure				Outbound tourism expenditure			
	thousands				$ millions		% of exports		$ millions		% of imports	
	Inbound		Outbound									
	1995	2009	1995	2009	1995	2009	1995	2009	1995	2009	1995	2009
Afghanistan	..	..	..	..	..	..	..	..	..	..	..	..
Albania	304[a,b]	1,856[a,b]	12	3,404	70	2,012	23.2	58.2	19	1,692	2.3	26.0
Algeria	520[a,c]	1,912[a,c]	1,090	1,677	32[d]	330[d]	..	..	186[d]	470[d]	..	..
Angola	9	366	3	..	27	554	0.7	1.3	113	270	3.2	0.6
Argentina	2,289	4,329	3,815	4,975	2,550	4,478	10.2	6.7	4,013	5,759	15.4	11.8
Armenia	12	575	..	526	14	374	4.7	27.9	12	379	1.7	10.3
Australia	3,726[a]	5,584[a]	2,519	6,285	11,915	27,864	17.1	*11.9*	7,260	21,459	9.7	*10.0*
Austria	17,173[e]	21,355[e]	*3,713*	10,121	14,529	21,239	16.2	11.2	11,686	12,771	12.7	7.3
Azerbaijan	..	*1,409*	*432*	*2,162*	87	516	11.1	2.3	165	456	12.8	4.6
Bangladesh	156	267	830	2,254	25[f]	76[f]	0.6	0.4	234[f]	651	3.1	2.8
Belarus	161	95	626	316	28	562	0.5	2.3	101	702	1.8	2.3
Belgium	5,560[e]	6,815[e]	5,645	11,123	4,548[f]	11,144	2.4	3.3	8,115[f]	19,673	4.5	6.0
Benin	138	190	..	..	85[f]	236	13.8	*14.5*	48	*102*	5.4	*4.3*
Bolivia	284	671	249	628	92	306	7.5	5.6	72	388	4.6	7.5
Bosnia and Herzegovina	*115[e]*	311[e]	..	..	257	761	22.9	13.9	97	284	2.4	3.0
Botswana	521	1,553	..	..	176	454[f]	7.3	10.9	153	231[f]	7.5	4.5
Brazil	1,991	4,802	2,600	4,952	1,085	5,635	2.1	3.1	3,982	12,897	6.3	7.4
Bulgaria	3,466	5,739	3,524	4,993	662	4,273	9.8	18.4	312	1,955	4.8	7.2
Burkina Faso	124[g]	269[g]	..	..	..	82	..	11.0	..	*110*	..	3.8
Burundi	34[c]	*201[c]*	36	..	2	2	1.9	1.5	25[f]	71	9.7	13.7
Cambodia	..	2,046	31	340	71	1,312	7.3	22.1	22	162	1.6	2.3
Cameroon	100[g]	*185[g]*	..	..	75	222	3.7	4.2	140	549	8.7	8.4
Canada	16,932	15,737	18,206	*27,037*	9,176	15,555	4.2	4.1	12,658	30,232	6.3	7.4
Central African Republic	26[b]	52[b]	..	*11*	4[d]	6	..	..	43[d]	61	..	..
Chad	19[g]	*25[g]*	..	..	43[d]	..	..	..	38[d]	..	..	..
Chile	1,540	2,750	1,070	2,895	1,186	2,270	6.1	3.6	934	1,956	5.1	4.0
China	20,034	50,875	4,520	47,656	8,730[f]	42,632	5.9	3.2	3,688[f]	47,108	2.7	4.2
Hong Kong SAR, China	*7,137*	16,926	..	81,958	9,604[d,f]	20,884[d]	3.5	5.1	10,497[d,f]	15,960[d,f]	6.5	4.1
Colombia	1,399[a]	2,147[a]	1,057	2,122	887	2,671	7.2	7.0	1,162	2,302	7.3	6.0
Congo, Dem. Rep.	35[b]	53[b]	50		..	..	..	..	..	..	..	..
Congo, Rep.	37[g]	85[g]	..	..	15	*54*	1.1	0.9	69	*168*	5.1	2.6
Costa Rica	785	1,923	273	579	763	1,985	17.1	15.8	336	463	7.1	3.8
Côte d'Ivoire	188	..	..	..	103	113[f]	2.4	1.0	312	345[f]	8.2	3.9
Croatia	1,485[e]	9,335[e]	..	2,497	1,349[f]	9,224	19.3	40.8	422[f]	1,034	4.6	4.2
Cuba	742[b]	2,405[b]	72	206	1,100[f]	2,106	..	..	..	..	..	..
Czech Republic	3,381[e]	6,032[e]	..	6,618	2,880[f]	7,396	10.2	5.6	1,635[f]	4,157	5.4	3.4
Denmark	2,124[e]	4,503[e]	5,035	6,347	3,691[f]	6,686[f]	5.6	3.6	4,288[f]	9,678[f]	7.4	5.5
Dominican Republic	1,776[b,c]	3,992[b,c]	168	415	1,571[f]	4,051[f]	27.4	38.7	267	514[f]	4.4	3.6
Ecuador	440[a,h]	968[a,h]	271	814	315	674	6.1	4.3	331	806	5.8	4.8
Egypt, Arab Rep.	2,871	11,914	2,683	*4,531*	2,954	11,757	22.3	26.4	1,371	2,941	8.0	5.5
El Salvador	235	1,091	348	*1,012*	152	549	7.5	11.7	99	253	2.7	3.2
Eritrea	315[a,c]	79[a,c]	..	..	58[d]	26	43.1	..	..	..	..	..
Estonia	530	1,900	1,764	752	452	1,444	17.6	10.7	121	697	4.2	5.6
Ethiopia	103[b]	*330[c]*	120	..	177	1,119	23.1	32.6	30	139[f]	2.1	1.5
Finland	*2,644*	3,423	5,147	5,832	2,383	4,141	5.0	4.6	2,853	5,205	7.6	6.2
France	60,033	76,800	18,686	*23,347*	31,295	58,480	8.6	9.5	20,699	45,938	6.2	6.9
Gabon	125[b]	*358*	203	..	94	..	3.2	..	182	..	10.6	..
Gambia, The	45	142	..	307	28[f]	64	16.0	23.0	16	9	7.0	2.6
Georgia	85[a]	1,500[a]	228	1,980	75	531	*13.1*	16.6	*171*	311	*12.1*	5.9
Germany	14,847[e]	24,220[e]	*55,800*	72,300	24,052	47,505	4.0	3.5	66,527	92,738	11.3	7.7
Ghana	286[c]	803[c]	..	..	30	1,049	1.9	13.4	74	848	3.5	7.9
Greece	10,130	14,915	..	..	4,182	14,796	26.9	25.0	1,495	3,401	6.0	4.0
Guatemala	563[a]	1,777[a]	333	1,326	216	820[f]	7.7	8.9	167	680	4.5	5.3
Guinea	12[b]	30[b]	..	..	1	5	0.1	0.4	29	28	2.9	2.0
Guinea-Bissau	..	30	..	..	3	38	5.5	22.2	6	46	6.5	*16.2*
Haiti	145	*304*	..	..	90[f]	315	46.8	33.8	35[f]	443	4.4	15.7
Honduras	271	870	149	395	85	611	5.2	10.1	99	355	5.3	4.1

	International tourists				Inbound tourism expenditure				Outbound tourism expenditure			
	thousands				$ millions		% of exports		$ millions		% of imports	
	Inbound		Outbound									
	1995	2009	1995	2009	1995	2009	1995	2009	1995	2009	1995	2009
Hungary	..	9,058	13,083	16,906	2,938	6,740	14.9	6.7	1,501	4,117	7.5	4.4
India	2,124[h]	5,109[h]	3,056	11,067	2,582[f]	11,509	6.8	4.4	996[f]	11,507	2.1	3.5
Indonesia	4,324	6,324	..	5,053	5,229[f]	6,773	9.9	5.1	2,172[f]	9,579	4.0	8.5
Iran, Islamic Rep.	489	2,034	1,000	..	205	2,196	1.1	..	247	9,482	1.6	..
Iraq	61[a]	..	..	..	18[f]	555	..	1.4	117[f]	705	..	3.3
Ireland	4,818	7,189	2,547	7,047	2,698	8,187	5.5	4.1	2,034[f]	8,887	4.8	5.3
Israel	2,215[h]	2,321[h]	2,259	4,007	3,491	4,332	12.7	6.4	2,626	3,869	7.4	6.1
Italy	31,052	43,239	18,173	29,060	30,426	41,872	10.3	8.2	17,219	34,329	6.9	6.6
Jamaica	1,147[b,c]	1,831[b,c]	..	..	1,199	2,070	35.3	51.3	173	259	4.6	4.1
Japan	3,345[a,h]	6,790[a,h]	15,298	15,446	4,894	12,537	1.0	1.9	46,966	34,788	11.2	5.3
Jordan	1,075[h]	3,789[c]	1,128	2,368	973	3,468	28.0	31.8	719	1,202	14.7	7.4
Kazakhstan	..	3,118	523	5,243	155	1,184	2.6	2.5	296	1,320	4.9	3.4
Kenya	918	1,392	..	..	785	1,095	22.3	14.8	230	234[f]	3.9	2.1
Korea, Dem. Rep.	..	..	..	..	..	..	..	..	..	..	..	..
Korea, Rep.	3,753[a,c]	7,818[a,c]	3,819	9,494	6,670	12,927	4.5	3.0	6,947	14,648	4.5	3.7
Kosovo	..	..	..	..	..	..	..	..	..	..	..	..
Kuwait	72[g]	297[g]	878	2,649	307	553	2.2	0.9	2,514	8,244	19.9	26.9
Kyrgyz Republic	36	2,435	42	1,521	5[f]	506	1.1	19.8	7[f]	391	1.0	10.6
Lao PDR	60	1,239	..	..	52	271[f]	12.8	18.8	34	91[f]	4.5	5.8
Latvia	539	1,323	1,812	3,268	37	1,013	1.8	9.0	62	906	2.8	7.9
Lebanon	450	1,844	..	..	710	7,157	..	33.1	..	4,928	..	16.3
Lesotho	87	320	..	..	29	40[f]	14.6	5.1	17	22	1.6	1.2
Liberia	..	..	..	..	..	123[f]	..	27.1	..	51	..	3.0
Libya	..	34	484	..	4	159	0.1	0.4	493	1,683	8.6	6.2
Lithuania	650	1,341	1,925	1,288	102	1,183	3.2	5.8	107	1,140	2.7	5.5
Macedonia, FYR	147[e]	259[e]	..	..	19[f]	232	2.7	6.5	27[f]	150	1.7	2.6
Madagascar	75[b]	163[b]	39	..	106	518	14.2	..	79	123[f]	8.0	..
Malawi	192	755	..	..	22	48	4.7	..	53	84	8.0	..
Malaysia	7,469	23,646	20,642	..	5,044	17,231	6.1	9.2	2,722	7,196	3.1	5.0
Mali	42[b,g]	160[b,g]	..	..	26	286	4.9	11.2	74	228	7.5	6.1
Mauritania	..	..	..	..	11[f]	..	2.2	..	30	..	5.9	..
Mauritius	422	871	107	196	616	1,390	26.2	33.2	184	384	7.5	7.5
Mexico	20,241[c]	21,454[c]	8,450	13,942	6,847	12,309	7.7	5.0	3,587	8,628	4.4	3.3
Moldova	32	7	71	93	71	235	8.0	11.7	73	307	7.3	7.7
Mongolia	108	411	..	..	33	253[f]	6.5	11.0	22	242	4.2	9.2
Morocco	2,602[c]	8,341[c]	1,317	2,293	1,469	7,978	16.2	30.2	356	1,712	3.2	4.6
Mozambique	..	2,224	..	..	49	217	10.2	8.8	68	249	6.6	5.8
Myanmar	117	243	..	..	169	59	12.9	1.2	18[f]	40	0.9	1.4
Namibia	272	931	..	..	278[f]	469	16.0	11.6	90[f]	109	4.3	2.1
Nepal	363	510	100	589	232	397	22.5	26.6	167	511	10.3	10.0
Netherlands	6,574[e]	9,921[e]	12,313	18,408	10,611	17,876	4.4	3.5	13,151	21,076	6.1	4.6
New Zealand	1,475	2,422	920	1,917	2,318[f]	4,396[f]	13.0	13.2	1,259[f]	2,559[f]	7.3	8.0
Nicaragua	281	932	255	858	51	346[f]	7.7	12.1	56	224	4.9	5.0
Niger	35	73	10	..	7[f]	86	2.2	8.2	26	98	5.7	5.0
Nigeria	656	1,313	..	..	47	791	0.4	1.3	938	5,308	7.3	11.1
Norway	2,880	4,288	590	3,395	2,730	4,444	4.9	2.8	4,481	12,366[f]	9.6	11.8
Oman	279[g]	1,273[g]	..	..	193	1,108	2.5	3.8	349[f]	1,277	6.3	5.9
Pakistan	378	823	..	..	582	903	5.7	4.1	654	1,098	4.6	3.1
Panama	345	1,200	185	336	372	2,279	4.9	13.7	181	503	2.3	3.3
Papua New Guinea	42	114	51	..	25[f]	1	0.8	0.0	58[f]	48	3.0	1.0
Paraguay	438[h]	439[h]	427	280	162	247	3.4	3.4	173	288	3.3	3.9
Peru	479	2,140	508	1,958	521	2,471	7.9	8.1	428	1,379	4.5	5.3
Philippines	1,760[c]	3,017[c]	1,615	3,066	1,141	2,837	4.3	6.0	551	2,989	1.7	5.4
Poland	19,215	11,890	36,387	50,243	6,927	9,853	19.4	5.8	5,865	7,842	17.3	4.6
Portugal	9,511[h]	12,321[c]	..	20,989	5,646	12,329	17.5	18.3	2,539	4,604	6.4	5.5
Puerto Rico	3,131[b]	3,551[b]	1,237	1,319	1,828[d]	3,473[d]	..	..	1,155[d]	1,613[d]	..	..
Qatar	309[g]	1,405[g]	..	..	..	874[d]	..	..	..	3,751[d]	..	..

	International tourists (thousands)				Inbound tourism expenditure				Outbound tourism expenditure			
	Inbound		Outbound		$ millions		% of exports		$ millions		% of imports	
	1995	2009	1995	2009	1995	2009	1995	2009	1995	2009	1995	2009
Romania	5,445[a]	7,575[a]	5,737	11,723	689	1,669	7.3	3.3	749	1,769	6.6	2.9
Russian Federation	10,290[a]	23,676[a]	21,329	36,538	4,312[f]	12,300	4.6	3.6	11,599[f]	23,529	14.0	9.3
Rwanda	..	699	..	..	4	218[f]	5.4	40.8	13	115	3.5	7.8
Saudi Arabia	3,325	10,897	..	6,032	..	6,678[d]	..	3.3	..	20,964[d]	..	13.1
Senegal	..	875	..	..	168	637	11.2	18.2	154	276	8.5	3.9
Serbia	..	645	..	..	..	986	..	8.3	..	1,076	..	5.8
Sierra Leone	38[b]	36[b]	6	73	57[f]	25[f]	44.4	7.7	51	16	19.4	2.5
Singapore	6,070	7,489	2,867	6,961	7,611[f]	9,200[f]	4.8	2.5	4,663[f]	15,808[f]	3.2	4.9
Slovak Republic	903[e]	1,298[e]	218	19,917	630	2,539	5.7	4.1	338	2,249	3.2	3.6
Slovenia	732[e]	1,824[e]	..	2,586	1,128	2,733	10.9	9.6	606	1,533	5.6	5.5
Somalia	..	..	..	..	..	..	..	..	..	..	..	..
South Africa	4,488	9,934	2,520	4,424	2,654	8,683	7.7	11.1	2,414	6,420	7.2	7.9
Spain	34,920	52,231	3,648	12,844	27,369	58,586	20.4	16.9	5,826	21,482	4.3	5.7
Sri Lanka	403[h]	448[h]	504	963	367	754	7.9	8.4	279	735	4.7	6.3
Sudan	29	420	195	..	8[f]	299[f]	1.2	3.6	43[f]	868[f]	3.5	7.7
Swaziland	300[i]	908[g]	..	1,245	54	40	5.3	2.2	45	98	3.5	4.2
Sweden	2,310[e]	4,678[e]	10,127	11,699	4,390	12,114	4.6	6.2	6,816	13,432	8.4	8.1
Switzerland	6,946[g]	8,294[g]	11,148	11,147	11,354	16,335	9.2	5.8	9,478	12,552	8.7	5.1
Syrian Arab Republic	815[e]	6,092[e]	1,746	5,215	1,258[f]	5,152	21.9	16.4	498[f]	910[f]	9.0	4.7
Tajikistan	..	..	..	..	..	20	..	1.6	..	6[f]	..	0.2
Tanzania	285	714	157	..	502[f]	1,192	39.7	22.8	360[f]	806	16.8	10.7
Thailand	6,952[c]	14,150	1,820	4,535	9,257	19,421	13.2	10.8	4,791	5,659	5.8	3.6
Timor-Leste	..	..	..	..	..	..	..	..	..	..	..	..
Togo	53[g]	150[g]	..	..	13[f]	44	2.8	3.9	40	68	6.0	4.1
Trinidad and Tobago	260[b]	413[b]	261	..	232	557	8.3	2.8	91	102	4.3	1.0
Tunisia	4,120[h]	6,901[h]	1,778	2,623	1,838	3,526	23.0	17.7	294	492	3.3	2.3
Turkey	7,083	25,506	3,981	10,493	4,957[f]	24,556	13.6	17.2	911[f]	4,627	2.3	3.1
Turkmenistan	218	8	21	38	13	..	0.7	..	74	..	4.1	..
Uganda	160	817	148	337	78[f]	683	11.7	17.3	80[f]	336	5.4	6.4
Ukraine	3,716	20,798	6,552	15,334	191[f]	4,349	1.1	8.0	210[f]	3,751	1.1	6.7
United Arab Emirates	2,315[c,i]	..	..	..	632	7,162[d]	..	..	..	13,288[d]	..	..
United Kingdom	21,719	28,199	41,345	58,614	27,577	38,545	8.6	6.5	30,749	61,130	9.4	9.4
United States	43,490	54,884	51,285	61,419	93,700	147,554	11.8	9.4	60,924	105,202	6.8	5.4
Uruguay	2,022	2,056	562	826	725	1,408	20.7	16.5	332	436	9.3	5.6
Uzbekistan	92	1,069	246	1,150	15	64[d]	..	..	..	..	..	..
Venezuela, RB	700	615	534	1,651	995	853	4.8	1.4	1,852	2,234	11.0	4.6
Vietnam	1,351[a]	3,747[a]	..	..	..	3,050[d]	..	4.9	..	1,100	..	1.5
West Bank and Gaza	220[g]	396[g]	..	..	255[f]	269[f]	33.4	23.0	162[f]	544[f]	5.8	11.0
Yemen, Rep.	61[g]	434[g]	..	..	50[f]	496[f]	2.3	7.0	76[f]	277	3.1	2.8
Zambia	163	710	..	..	29	98	2.4	2.1	83	83	6.2	2.0
Zimbabwe	1,416[a]	1,956[a]	256	593	145	294[d]	..	..	106[d]	..	..	..
World	537,385 t	894,012 t	555,382 t	961,575 t	487,033 t	1,022,301 t	7.6 w	6.4 w	458,869 t	923,915 t	7.4 w	5.9 w
Low income	6,379	18,801	..	..	3,253	11,845	12.2	12.9	2,591	7,641	5.1	5.0
Middle income	139,405	329,738	129,489	327,671	82,794	270,868	7.7	6.2	60,850	214,809	5.4	5.1
Lower middle income	58,101	160,100	35,678	134,442	40,251	135,230	8.5	5.3	20,926	110,735	4.0	4.5
Upper middle income	82,221	171,751	86,296	..	42,566	135,451	7.1	7.3	39,917	104,850	6.7	5.9
Low & middle income	147,674	352,280	141,222	363,391	85,892	281,994	7.8	6.3	63,336	222,402	5.4	5.1
East Asia & Pacific	43,654	107,674	33,153	..	31,197	94,687	7.8	4.8	14,770	75,780	3.5	4.4
Europe & Central Asia	33,946	106,987	47,292	106,450	12,014	58,244	6.3	7.3	16,380	48,211	8.1	6.2
Latin America & Carib.	39,151	60,093	21,841	41,194	21,838	49,773	7.6	6.0	18,774	41,573	6.5	5.3
Middle East & N. Africa	13,555	44,880	13,407	25,352	9,771	43,050	13.0	20.5	4,844	19,825	5.7	6.7
South Asia	3,819	7,949	5,151	17,100	4,016	14,339	6.8	4.6	2,393	14,787	3.0	3.6
Sub-Saharan Africa	12,978	31,497	..	..	6,928	22,170	7.8	7.5	6,810	25,420	6.8	6.4
High income	384,359	535,465	374,257	564,431	401,084	740,277	7.6	6.4	394,726	703,266	7.9	6.3
Euro area	203,060	280,972	141,785	235,326	164,475	310,544	7.8	6.9	155,113	280,349	7.8	6.5

Note: Aggregates are based on World Bank country classifications and differ from those of the World Tourism Organization. Regional and income group totals include countries not shown in the table for which data are available.
a. Arrivals of nonresident visitors at national borders. b. Excludes nationals residing abroad. c. Includes nationals residing abroad. d. Data are from national sources. e. Arrivals in all types of accommodation establishments. f. Refers to expenditure of travel-related items only; excludes passenger transport items. g. Arrivals in hotels and similar establishments. h. Arrivals in hotels only. i. Arrivals by air only.

About the data

Tourism is defined as the activities of people traveling to and staying in places outside their usual environment for no more than one year for leisure, business, and other purposes not related to an activity remunerated from within the place visited. The social and economic phenomenon of tourism has grown substantially over the past quarter century.

Statistical information on tourism is based mainly on data on arrivals and overnight stays along with balance of payments information. These data do not completely capture the economic phenomenon of tourism or provide the information needed for effective public policies and efficient business operations. Data are needed on the scale and significance of tourism. Information on the role of tourism in national economies is particularly deficient. Although the World Tourism Organization reports progress in harmonizing definitions and measurement, differences in national practices still prevent full comparability.

The usual environment of an individual is a key concept in tourism statistics and is defined as the geographical area within which an individual conducts regular life routines. This concept excludes as visitors travelers who commute regularly between their place of usual residence and place of work or study or who frequently visit places within their current life routine—for instance, homes of friends or relatives; shopping centers, and religious, healthcare, or other facilities a substantial distance away or in a different administrative area that are regularly and frequently visited.

Tourism can be either domestic or international. The table shows data relevant to international tourism, where the traveler's country of residence differs from the visiting country. International tourism consists of inbound and outbound tourism. The data are from the World Tourism Organization, a United Nations agency. The data on inbound and outbound tourists refer to the number of arrivals and departures, not to the number of people traveling. Thus a person who makes several trips to a country during a given period is counted each time as a new arrival. Unless otherwise indicated in the footnotes, the data on inbound tourism show the arrivals of nonresident tourists (overnight visitors) at national borders. When data on international tourists are unavailable or incomplete, the table shows the arrivals of international visitors, which include tourists, same-day visitors, cruise passengers, and crew members.

Sources and collection methods for arrivals differ across countries. In some cases data are from border statistics (police, immigration, and the like) and supplemented by border surveys. In other cases data are from tourism accommodation establishments.

For some countries number of arrivals is limited to arrivals by air and for others to arrivals staying in hotels. Some countries include arrivals of nationals residing abroad while others do not. Caution should thus be used in comparing arrivals across countries.

The World Tourism Organization is improving its coverage of tourism expenditure data, using balance of payments data from the International Monetary Fund (IMF) supplemented by data from individual countries. These data, shown in the table, include travel and passenger transport items as defined in the IMF's (1993) *Balance of Payments Manual*. When the IMF does not report data on passenger transport items, expenditure data for travel items are shown.

Tourism expenditure does not include all types of payments that visitors might make. It excludes payments not for consumption of goods and services, such as taxes and duties that are not part of the purchase prices of the products acquired by the visitor; purchase of financial and nonfinancial assets including land and real estate; purchase of goods for resale; and donations to charities or other individuals. The timing of tourism expenditure is also important because transportation and accommodation are often booked and paid for before being consumed. Payment might also happen after consumption of such services, such as when a visitor pays off a credit card or a special loan drawn for travel purposes. Tourism expenditure should be reported for the period when the services are actually consumed and goods are actually acquired, regardless of when payment was made. Finally, the valuation of tourism expenditure depends on the form of acquisition of the goods and services concerned. In a market transaction expenditure should be valued using the purchaser price—value paid by the visitor. This price should include all taxes and voluntary and compulsory tips prevalent in the accommodation and food services sectors. Discounts and rebates of sales tax or value added tax to nonresidents should be taken into account, even if refunded at the border. However, following these recommendations for tourism statistics may not be easy for countries. Tourism expenditures reported in the table may not be fully comparable, so caution should be used when making cross-country comparisons.

The aggregates are calculated using the World Bank's weighted aggregation methodology (see *Statistical methods*) and differ from the World Tourism Organization's aggregates.

Definitions

• **International inbound tourists** (overnight visitors) are the number of tourists who travel to a country other than that in which they usually reside, and outside their usual environment, for a period not exceeding 12 months and whose main purpose in visiting is other than an activity remunerated from within the country visited. When data on number of tourists are not available, the number of visitors, which includes tourists, same-day visitors, cruise passengers, and crew members, is shown instead. • **International outbound tourists** are the number of departures that people make from their country of usual residence to any other country for any purpose other than an activity remunerated in the country visited. • **Inbound tourism expenditure** is expenditures by international inbound visitors, including payments to national carriers for international transport. These receipts include any other prepayment made for goods or services received in the destination country. They may include receipts from same-day visitors, except when these are important enough to justify separate classification. For some countries they do not include receipts for passenger transport items. Their share in exports is calculated as a ratio to exports of goods and services (all transactions between residents of a country and the rest of the world involving a change of ownership from residents to nonresidents of general merchandise, goods sent for processing and repairs, nonmonetary gold, and services). • **Outbound tourism expenditure** is expenditures of international outbound visitors in other countries, including payments to foreign carriers for international transport. These expenditures may include those by residents traveling abroad as same-day visitors, except when these are important enough to justify separate classification. For some countries they do not include expenditures for passenger transport items. Their share in imports is calculated as a ratio to imports of goods and services (all transactions between residents of a country and the rest of the world involving a change of ownership from nonresidents to residents of general merchandise, goods sent for processing and repairs, nonmonetary gold, and services).

Data sources

Data on visitors and tourism expenditure are from the World Tourism Organization's *Yearbook of Tourism Statistics* and *Compendium of Tourism Statistics 2011*. Data in the table are updated from electronic files provided by the World Tourism Organization. Data on exports and imports are from the IMF's *Balance of Payments Statistics Yearbook* and data files.

PRIMARY DATA DOCUMENTATION

As a major user of socioeconomic data, the World Bank recognizes the importance of data documentation to inform users of differences in the methods and conventions used by primary data collectors—usually national statistical agencies, central banks, and customs services—and by international organizations, which compile the statistics that appear in the World Development Indicators database. These differences may give rise to significant discrepancies over time both within countries and across them. Delays in reporting data and the use of old surveys as the base for current estimates may further compromise the quality of data reported here.

The tables in this section provide information on sources, methods, and reporting standards of the principal demographic, economic, and environmental indicators in *World Development Indicators*. Additional documentation is available from the World Bank's Bulletin Board on Statistical Capacity at http://data.worldbank.org/.

The demand for good-quality statistical data is increasing. Timely and reliable statistics are key to the broad development strategy often referred to as "managing for results." Monitoring and reporting on publicly agreed indicators are central to implementing poverty reduction strategies and lie at the heart of the Millennium Development Goals and the Results Measurement System adopted for the 14th replenishment of the International Development Association.

A global action plan to improve national and international statistics was agreed on during the Second Roundtable on Managing for Development Results in February 2004 in Marrakech, Morocco. The plan, now referred to as the Marrakech Action Plan for Statistics, or MAPS, has been widely endorsed and forms the overarching framework for statistical capacity building. The third roundtable conference, held in February 2007 in Hanoi, Vietnam, reaffirmed MAPS as the guiding strategy for improving the capacity of the national and international statistical systems. See www.mfdr.org/RT3 for reports from the conference.

PRIMARY DATA DOCUMENTATION

	Currency	Base year		Reference year	System of National Accounts	SNA price valuation	Alternative conversion factor	PPP survey year	Balance of Payments Manual in use	External debt	System of trade	Accounting concept	IMF data dissemination standard
Afghanistan	Afghan afghani	2002/03				VAB				Actual	G	C	G
Albania	Albanian lek		a	1996	b	VAB		2005	BPM5	Actual	S	C	G
Algeria	Algerian dinar	1980				VAB			BPM4	Actual	S	B	G
American Samoa	U.S. dollar												
Andorra	Euro												G
Angola	Angolan kwanza	1997				VAP	1991–96	2005	BPM5	Actual			G
Antigua and Barbuda	East Caribbean dollar	1990				VAB			BPM5		G		G
Argentina	Argentine peso	1993			b	VAB	1971–84	2005	BPM5	Actual	S	C	S
Armenia	Armenian dram		a	1996		VAB	1990–95	2005	BPM5	Actual	G	C	S
Aruba	Aruban florin	1995							BPM5		G		
Australia	Australian dollar		a	2007	b	VAB		2005	BPM5		G	C	S
Austria	Euro	2000			b	VAB		2005	BPM5		S	C	S
Azerbaijan	New Azeri manat		a	2003	b	VAB	1992–95	2005	BPM5	Actual	G	B	G
Bahamas, The	Bahamian dollar	2006			b	VAB			BPM5		G	B	G
Bahrain	Bahraini dinar	1985				VAP		2005	BPM5		G	B	G
Bangladesh	Bangladeshi taka	1995/96			b	VAB		2005	BPM5	Actual	G	C	G
Barbados	Barbados dollar	1974				VAB			BPM5		G	B	G
Belarus	Belarusian rubel		a	2000	b	VAB	1990–95	2005	BPM5	Actual	G	C	S
Belgium	Euro	2000			b	VAB		2005	BPM5		S	C	S
Belize	Belize dollar	2000			b	VAB			BPM5	Actual	G	B	
Benin	CFA franc	1985				VAP	1992	2005	BPM5	Actual	G	B	G
Bermuda	Bermuda dollar	1996				VAB			BPM5				
Bhutan	Bhutanese ngultrum	2000			b	VAB		2005		Actual	G	C	G
Bolivia	Bolivian Boliviano	1990			b	VAB	1960–85	2005	BPM5	Actual	S	C	G
Bosnia and Herzegovina	Bosnia and Herzegovina convertible mark		a	1996	b	VAB		2005	BPM5	Actual	S	C	
Botswana	Botswana pula	1993/94			b	VAB		2005	BPM5	Actual	S	B	G
Brazil	Brazilian real	2000			b	VAB		2005	BPM5	Actual	S	C	S
Brunei Darussalam	Brunei dollar	2000				VAP		2005			S		
Bulgaria	Bulgarian lev		a	2002	b	VAB	1978–89, 1991–92	2005	BPM5	Actual	S	C	S
Burkina Faso	CFA franc	1999				VAB	1992–93	2005	BPM4	Estimate	G	B	G
Burundi	Burundi franc	1980				VAB		2005	BPM5	Actual	G	C	
Cambodia	Cambodian riel	2000				VAB		2005	BPM5	Actual	G	C	G
Cameroon	CFA franc	2000			b	VAB		2005	BPM5	Actual	S	B	G
Canada	Canadian dollar	2000			b	VAB		2005	BPM5		G	C	S
Cape Verde	Cape Verde escudo	1980				VAP		2005	BPM5	Actual	S	C	G
Cayman Islands	Cayman Islands dollar												
Central African Republic	CFA franc	2000				VAB		2005	BPM4	Preliminary	S	B	G
Chad	CFA franc	1995			b	VAB		2005	BPM4	Actual			G
Channel Islands	Pound sterling	2003, 2007		2007	b	VAB							
Chile	Chilean peso	2003			b	VAB		2005	BPM5	Actual	S	C	S
China	Chinese yuan	2000			b	VAP	1978–93	2005	BPM5	Preliminary	G	B	G
Hong Kong SAR, China	Hong Kong dollar	2008			b	VAB		2005	BPM5		G	C	S
Macao SAR, China	Macao pataca	2002				VAB		2005	BPM5		G	C	G
Colombia	Colombian peso	2005			b	VAB	1992–94	2005	BPM5	Actual	G	B	S
Comoros	Comorian franc	1990				VAP		2005		Preliminary	G		
Congo, Dem. Rep.	Congolese franc	1987			b	VAB	1999–2001	2005	BPM4	Estimate		C	G
Congo, Rep.	CFA franc	1978				VAP	1993	2005	BPM5	Preliminary		C	G
Costa Rica	Costa Rican colon	1991			b	VAB			BPM5	Actual	S	C	S
Côte d'Ivoire	CFA franc	1996				VAP		2005	BPM5	Actual	S	C	G
Croatia	Croatian kuna		a	2000	b	VAB		2005	BPM5		S	C	S
Cuba	Cuban peso	1990				VAB					S		
Cyprus	Euro		a	2000		VAB		2005	BPM5		G	C	S
Czech Republic	Czech koruna	2000		1995	b	VAB		2005	BPM5		S	C	S
Denmark	Danish krone	2000			b	VAB		2005	BPM5		G	C	S
Djibouti	Djibouti franc	1990				VAB		2005		Actual			

PRIMARY DATA DOCUMENTATION

	Latest population census	Latest demographic, education, or health household survey	Source of most recent income and expenditure data	Vital registration complete	Latest agricultural census	Latest industrial data	Latest trade data	Latest water withdrawal data
Afghanistan	1979	MICS, 2003	IHS, 2008			2009	2009	2000
Albania	2001	DHS, 2008/09	LSMS, 2008	Yes	1998	2009	2008	2000
Algeria	2008	MICS, 2006	IHS, 1995		2001	2009	2008	2000
American Samoa	2010			Yes			2009	
Andorra	c			Yes			2006	
Angola	1970	MICS, 2001; MIS, 2006/07	IHS, 2000		1964–65	2009	1991	2000
Antigua and Barbuda	2001			Yes		2009	2007	1990
Argentina	2010		IHS, 2009	Yes	2002	2009	2009	2000
Armenia	2001	DHS, 2005	IHS, 2009	Yes		2009	2009	2000
Aruba	2010			Yes			2009	
Australia	2006		ES/BS, 1994	Yes	2001	2008	2009	2000
Austria	2001		IS, 2000	Yes	1999–2000	2009	2009	2000
Azerbaijan	2009	DHS, 2006	ES/BS, 2008	Yes		2008	2009	2005
Bahamas, The	2010					2006	2009	
Bahrain	2010			Yes		1995	2007	2003
Bangladesh	2001	DHS, 2007	IHS, 2005		2005	2009	2007	2000
Barbados	2010			Yes		2005	2009	2000
Belarus	2009	MICS, 2005	ES/BS, 2009	Yes	1994	2009	2009	2000
Belgium	2001		IHS, 2000	Yes	1999–2000d	2009	2009	
Belize	2010	MICS, 2006	ES/BS, 1999			2008	2008	2000
Benin	2002	DHS, 2006	CWIQ, 2003		1992	2005	2006	2001
Bermuda	2010			Yes			2009	
Bhutan	2005		IHS, 2003		2000	2009	2009	2000
Bolivia	2001	DHS, 2008	IHS, 2007		1984–88	2009	2009	2000
Bosnia and Herzegovina	1991	MICS, 2006	LSMS, 2007	Yes		2009	2010	
Botswana	2001	MICS, 2000	ES/BS, 2003		1993	2009	2009	2000
Brazil	2010	DHS, 1996	LFS, 2008		1996	2009	2010	2000
Brunei Darussalam	2001			Yes		2006	2006	
Bulgaria	2001		ES/BS, 2007	Yes		2009	2009	2000
Burkina Faso	2006	MICS, 2006	CWIQ, 2003		1993	2006	2009	2000
Burundi	2008	MICS, 2005	CWIQ, 2007			2005	2009	2000
Cambodia	2008	DHS, 2005	IHS, 2007			2009	2008	2000
Cameroon	2005	MICS, 2006	PS, 2007		1984	2007	2006	2000
Canada	2006		LFS, 2000	Yes	1996/2001	2007	2009	2000
Cape Verde	2010	DHS, 2005	ES/BS, 2007	Yes	2004	2009	2009	
Cayman Islands	2010			Yes				
Central African Republic	2003	MICS, 2006	PS, 2008		1985	2006	2005	2000
Chad	2009	DHS, 2004	PS, 2002/03			2008	1995	2000
Channel Islands	2001							
Chile	2002		IHS, 2009	Yes	1997	2009	2009	2000
China	2010	NSS, 2007	IHS, 2005		1997	2009	2009	2000
Hong Kong SAR, China	2006			Yes		2008	2009	
Macao SAR, China	2006			Yes		2007	2009	
Colombia	2006	DHS, 2005	IHS, 2009		2001	2009	2009	2000
Comoros	2003	MICS, 2000	IHS, 2004			2009	2007	
Congo, Dem. Rep.	1984	MICS, 2010	1-2-3, 2005/06		1990	2009	1986	2000
Congo, Rep.	2007	DHS, 2005; AIS, 2009	CWIQ/PS, 2005		1985–86	2009	2005	2002
Costa Rica	2000	RHS, 1993	LFS, 2009	Yes	1973	2009	2009	2000
Côte d'Ivoire	1998	MICS, 2006	IHS, 2008		2001	2009	2009	
Croatia	2001		ES/BS, 2008	Yes	2003	2009	2009	
Cuba	2002	MICS, 2006		Yes		2008	2006	2000
Cyprus	2001			Yes		2008	2009	2000
Czech Republic	2001	RHS, 1993	IS, 1996	Yes	2000	2009	2009	2000
Denmark	2001		ITR, 1997	Yes	1999–2000	2009	2009	2000
Djibouti	2009	MICS, 2006	PS, 2002			2007	2009	2000

	Currency	National accounts						Balance of payments and trade			Government finance	IMF data dissemination standard
		Base year	Reference year	System of National Accounts	SNA price valuation	Alternative conversion factor	PPP survey year	Balance of Payments Manual in use	External debt	System of trade	Accounting concept	
Dominica	East Caribbean dollar	1990		b	VAB			BPM5	Actual	S		G
Dominican Republic	Dominican peso	1991			VAB			BPM5	Actual	G	C	G
Ecuador	U.S. dollar	2000		b	VAB		2005	BPM5	Actual	S	B	S
Egypt, Arab Rep.	Egyptian pound	1991/92			VAB		2005	BPM5	Actual	G	C	S
El Salvador	U.S. dollar	1990			VAB			BPM5	Actual	G	C	S
Equatorial Guinea	CFA franc	2000			VAB	1965–84	2005					
Eritrea	Eritrean nakfa	1992			VAB			BPM4	Actual			
Estonia	Estonian kroon	2000		b	VAB	1987–95	2005	BPM5		G	C	S
Ethiopia	Ethiopian birr	1999/2000		b	VAB		2005	BPM5	Actual	G	B	G
Faeroe Islands	Danish krone				VAB			BPM5		G		
Fiji	Fijian dollar	2005			VAB		2005	BPM5	Actual	G	B	G
Finland	Euro	2000		b	VAB		2005	BPM5		S	C	S
France	Euro	a 2000		b	VAB		2005	BPM5		S	C	S
French Polynesia	CFP franc									S		
Gabon	CFA franc	1991			VAP	1993	2005	BPM5	Preliminary	S		G
Gambia, The	Gambian dalasi	1987			VAB		2005	BPM5	Estimate	G	C	G
Georgia	Georgian lari	a 1996		b	VAB	1990–95	2005	BPM5	Actual	G	C	S
Germany	Euro	2000		b	VAB		2005	BPM5		S	C	S
Ghana	New Ghanaian cedi	2006			VAB	1973–87	2005	BPM5	Actual	G	B	G
Gibraltar	Gibraltar pound											
Greece	Euro	a 2000			VAB		2005	BPM5		S	C	S
Greenland	Danish krone									G		
Grenada	East Caribbean dollar	1990			VAB			BPM5	Actual	S	B	G
Guam	U.S. dollar											
Guatemala	Guatemalan quetzal	2001		b	VAB			BPM5	Actual	G	B	G
Guinea	Guinean franc	1996			VAB		2005	BPM5	Estimate	S	B	G
Guinea-Bissau	CFA franc	2005			VAB		2005	BPM5	Estimate			G
Guyana	Guyana dollar	2006			VAB			BPM5	Actual	S		
Haiti	Haitian gourde	1986/87			VAB	1991		BPM5	Actual			G
Honduras	Honduran lempira	2000		b	VAB	1988–89		BPM5	Actual	S	C	G
Hungary	Hungarian forint	a 2000		b	VAB		2005	BPM5		S	C	S
Iceland	Iceland krona	2000			VAB		2005	BPM5		S	C	S
India	Indian rupee	2004/05		b	VAB		2005	BPM5	Actual	G	C	S
Indonesia	Indonesian rupiah	2000			VAP		2005	BPM5	Actual	G	B	S
Iran, Islamic Rep.	Iranian rial	1997/98			VAB	1980–2002	2005	BPM4	Actual	S	C	
Iraq	Iraqi dinar	1997			VAB	1997, 2004	2005	BPM5				G
Ireland	Euro	2000		b	VAB		2005	BPM5		G	C	S
Isle of Man	Pound sterling	2005	2003									
Israel	Israeli new shekel	2005		b	VAP		2005	BPM5		S	C	S
Italy	Euro	2000		b	VAB		2005	BPM5		S	C	S
Jamaica	Jamaican dollar	2003			VAB			BPM5	Actual	G	C	G
Japan	Japanese yen	2000			VAB		2005	BPM5		G	C	S
Jordan	Jordanian dinar	1994			VAB		2005	BPM5	Actual	S	B	S
Kazakhstan	Kazakh tenge	a 2000		b	VAB	1987–95	2005	BPM5	Actual	G	C	S
Kenya	Kenyan shilling	2001		b	VAB		2005	BPM5	Actual	G	B	G
Kiribati	Australian dollar	2006			VAB					S		G
Korea, Dem. Rep.	Democratic People's Republic of Korean won							BPM4				
Korea, Rep.	Korean won	2000		b	VAB		2005	BPM5		G	C	S
Kosovo	Euro								Actual			
Kuwait	Kuwaiti dinar	1995			VAP		2005	BPM5		S	B	G
Kyrgyz Republic	Kyrgyz som	a 1995		b	VAB	1990–95	2005	BPM5	Actual	G	B	S
Lao PDR	Lao kip	1990			VAB		2005	BPM5	Preliminary		B	
Latvia	Latvian lats	2000		b	VAB	1987–95	2005	BPM5		S	C	S
Lebanon	Lebanese pound	1997			VAB		2005	BPM5	Actual	S	B	G
Lesotho	Lesotho loti	1995		b	VAB		2005	BPM5	Actual	G	C	G

PRIMARY DATA DOCUMENTATION

	Latest population census	Latest demographic, education, or health household survey	Source of most recent income and expenditure data	Vital registration complete	Latest agricultural census	Latest industrial data	Latest trade data	Latest water withdrawal data
Dominica	2001			Yes		2009	2008	
Dominican Republic	2010	DHS, 2007	IHS, 2007		1971	2009	2009	2000
Ecuador	2010	RHS, 2004	LFS, 2009		1999–2000	2009	2009	2000
Egypt, Arab Rep.	2006	DHS, 2008	ES/BS, 2004/05	Yes	1999–2000	2009	2008	2000
El Salvador	2007	RHS, 2008	IHS, 2008	Yes	1970–71	2009	2009	2000
Equatorial Guinea	2002					2009		2000
Eritrea	1984	DHS, 2002				2009	2003	2004
Estonia	2000		ES/BS, 2004	Yes	2001	2009	2009	2000
Ethiopia	2007	DHS, 2005	ES/BS, 2005		2001–02	2009	2009	2002
Faeroe Islands	c			Yes			2009	
Fiji	2007		ES/BS, 2009	Yes		2009	2009	2000
Finland	2010		IS, 2000	Yes	1999–2000	2009	2009	2000
France	2006e		ES/BS, 1994/95	Yes	1999–2000	2009	2009	2000
French Polynesia	2007			Yes			2010	
Gabon	2003	DHS, 2000	CWIQ/IHS, 2005		1974–75	2009	2006	2000
Gambia, The	2003	MICS, 2005/06	IHS, 2003		2001–02	2009	2009	2000
Georgia	2002	MICS, 2005; RHS, 2005	IHS, 2008	Yes	2004	2009	2008	2005
Germany	c		IHS, 2000	Yes	1999–2000	2009	2009	2000
Ghana	2010	DHS, 2008	LSMS, 2006		1984	2009	2008	2000
Gibraltar	2001			Yes				
Greece	2001		IHS, 2000	Yes	1999–2000	2009	2009	2000
Greenland	2010			Yes			2007	
Grenada	2001			Yes		2009	2009	
Guam	2010			Yes				
Guatemala	2002	RHS, 2002	LSMS, 2006	Yes	2003	2009	2009	2000
Guinea	1996	DHS, 2005	CWIQ, 2007		2000–01	2009	2008	2000
Guinea-Bissau	2009	MICS, 2010	CWIQ, 2002		1988	2002	2005	2000
Guyana	2002	MICS, 2006	IHS, 1998			2009	2009	2000
Haiti	2003	DHS, 2005/06	IHS, 2001		1971		1997	2000
Honduras	2001	DHS, 2005/06	IHS, 2007		1993	2009	2009	2000
Hungary	2001		ES/BS, 2007	Yes	2000	2008	2009	2000
Iceland	c			Yes		2008	2009	2000
India	2001	DHS, 2005/06	IHS, 2004/05		1995–96/ 2000–01	2009	2009	2000
Indonesia	2010	DHS, 2007	IHS, 2007		2003	2009	2009	2000
Iran, Islamic Rep.	2006	DHS, 2000	ES/BS, 2005	Yes	2003	2007	2006	2004
Iraq	1997	MICS, 2006	IHS, 2007		1981	2002	2008	2000
Ireland	2006		IHS, 2000	Yes	2000	2009	2009	2000
Isle of Man	2006			Yes				
Israel	2009		ES/BS, 2001	Yes	1981		2009	2004
Italy	2001		ES/BS, 2000	Yes	2000	2009	2009	2000
Jamaica	2001	MICS, 2005	LSMS, 2007	Yes	1996	2009	2009	2000
Japan	2010		IS, 1993	Yes	2000	2008	2009	2000
Jordan	2004	DHS, 2009	ES/BS, 2006		1997	2009	2009	2005
Kazakhstan	2009	MICS, 2006	ES/BS, 2007	Yes		2009	2009	2000
Kenya	2009	SPA, 2004; DHS, 2008/09	IHS, 2005-06		1977–79	2009	2009	2003
Kiribati	2005					2009	2009	
Korea, Dem. Rep.	2009	MICS, 2010						2000
Korea, Rep.	2005		ES/BS, 1998	Yes	2000	2009	2009	2000
Kosovo	1981		IHS, 2006			2009		
Kuwait	2010	FHS, 1996		Yes	1970	2003	2009	2002
Kyrgyz Republic	2009	MICS, 2005/06	ES/BS, 2007	Yes	2002	2008	2009	2000
Lao PDR	2005	MICS, 2006	ES/BS, 2008		1998–99	2008	1975	2000
Latvia	2000		IHS, 2008	Yes	2001	2009	2009	2000
Lebanon	1970	MICS, 2000		Yes	1998–99	2009	2009	2005
Lesotho	2006	DHS, 2009/10	ES/BS, 2002/03		1999–2000	2009	2004	2000

PRIMARY DATA DOCUMENTATION

	Currency	National accounts — Base year	Reference year	System of National Accounts	SNA price valuation	Alternative conversion factor	PPP survey year	Balance of payments and trade — Balance of Payments Manual in use	External debt	System of trade	Government finance — Accounting concept	IMF data dissemination standard
Liberia	Liberian dollar	1992			VAP		2005	BPM5	Estimate		B	G
Libya	Libyan dinar	1999			VAB	1986		BPM5				G
Liechtenstein	Swiss franc				VAB					S		
Lithuania	Lithuanian litas	2000		[b]	VAB	1990–95	2005	BPM5	Actual	S	C	S
Luxembourg	Euro		2000		VAB		2005	BPM5		S	C	S
Macedonia, FYR	Macedonian denar	1997	1995	[b]	VAB		2005	BPM5	Actual	S		G
Madagascar	Malagasy ariary	1984			VAB		2005	BPM5	Actual	G	C	G
Malawi	Malawi kwacha	1994			VAB		2005	BPM5	Actual	G		G
Malaysia	Malaysian ringgit	2000			VAP		2005	BPM5	Estimate	G	B	S
Maldives	Maldivian rufiyaa	1995			VAB		2005	BPM5	Actual	G	C	
Mali	CFA franc	1987			VAB		2005	BPM4	Preliminary	G	B	G
Malta	Euro	2005			VAB		2005	BPM5		G	C	S
Marshall Islands	U.S. dollar	1991			VAB					G		
Mauritania	Mauritanian ouguiya	1998			VAB		2005	BPM4	Actual	G		G
Mauritius	Mauritian rupee	2006			VAB		2005	BPM5	Preliminary	G	C	G
Mayotte	Euro									G		
Mexico	Mexican peso	2003		[b]	VAB		2005	BPM5	Actual	G		S
Micronesia, Fed. Sts.	U.S. dollar	1998			VAB							
Moldova	Moldovan leu		[a] 1996	[b]	VAB	1990–95	2005	BPM5	Actual	G	C	S
Monaco	Euro									S		
Mongolia	Mongolian tugrik	2005		[b]	VAB		2005	BPM5	Actual	G	C	G
Montenegro	Euro	2000		[b]	VAB		2005	BPM5	Actual			
Morocco	Moroccan dirham	1998			VAB		2005	BPM5	Actual	S	C	S
Mozambique	New Mozambican metical	2003			VAB	1992–95	2005	BPM5	Actual	G		G
Myanmar	Myanmar kyat	1985/86			VAP			BPM5	Estimate		C	
Namibia	Namibian dollar	2004/05		[b]	VAB		2005	BPM5		G	B	G
Nepal	Nepalese rupee	2000/01			VAB		2005	BPM5	Actual		C	G
Netherlands Antilles	Netherlands Antilles guilder							BPM5		S		
Netherlands	Euro		[a] 2000	[b]	VAB		2005	BPM5		S	C	S
New Caledonia	CFP franc									S		
New Zealand	New Zealand dollar	2000/01			VAB		2005	BPM5		G	C	
Nicaragua	Nicaraguan gold cordoba	1994		[b]	VAB	1965–95		BPM5	Actual	S	B	G
Niger	CFA franc	1987			VAP	1993	2005	BPM4	Actual	G	B	G
Nigeria	Nigerian naira	2002			VAB	1971–98	2005	BPM5	Actual	G	B	G
Northern Mariana Islands	U.S. dollar											
Norway	Norwegian krone		[a] 2000	[b]	VAB		2005	BPM5		G	C	S
Oman	Rial Omani	1988			VAP		2005	BPM5		G	B	G
Pakistan	Pakistani rupee	1999/2000		[b]	VAB		2005	BPM5	Actual	G	B	G
Palau	U.S. dollar	1995			VAB							
Panama	Panamanian balboa	1996		[b]	VAB			BPM5	Actual	S	C	G
Papua New Guinea	Papua New Guinea kina	1998			VAB	1989		BPM5	Actual	G	B	
Paraguay	Paraguayan guarani	1994			VAP		2005	BPM5	Actual	G	B	G
Peru	Peruvian new sol	1994			VAB	1985–90	2005	BPM5	Actual	S	C	S
Philippines	Philippine peso	1985			VAP		2005	BPM5	Actual	G	B	S
Poland	Polish zloty		[a] 2002	[b]	VAB		2005	BPM5		S	C	S
Portugal	Euro	2000		[b]	VAB		2005	BPM5		S	C	S
Puerto Rico	U.S. dollar	1954			VAP					G		
Qatar	Qatari riyal	2001			VAP		2005			S	B	G
Romania	New Romanian leu		[a] 2005	[b]	VAB	1987–89, 1992	2005	BPM5	Actual	S	C	S
Russian Federation	Russian ruble	2000		[b]	VAB	1987–95	2005	BPM5	Preliminary	G	C	S
Rwanda	Rwandan franc	1995			VAP	1994	2005	BPM5	Estimate	G	C	G
Samoa	Samoan tala	2002			VAB			BPM5	Actual	G		
San Marino	Euro	1995	2000	[b]	VAB						C	G

	Latest population census	Latest demographic, education, or health household survey	Source of most recent income and expenditure data	Vital registration complete	Latest agricultural census	Latest industrial data	Latest trade data	Latest water withdrawal data
Liberia	2008	DHS, 2007; MIS, 2009	CWIQ, 2007			2008	1985	2000
Libya	2006	MICS, 2000			2001	2008	2004	2000
Liechtenstein	2010			Yes				
Lithuania	2001		ES/BS, 2008	Yes	2003	2008	2009	2000
Luxembourg	2001			Yes	1999–2000^d	2009	2009	
Macedonia, FYR	2002	MICS, 2005	ES/BS, 2008	Yes	1994	2009	2009	
Madagascar	1993	DHS, 2008/09	PS, 2005		2004	2009	2009	2000
Malawi	2008	MICS, 2006	LSMS, 2004/05		1993	2009	2010	2000
Malaysia	2010		ES/BS, 2009	Yes		2009	2009	2000
Maldives	2006	DHS, 2009	IHS, 2004	Yes		2009	2008	
Mali	2009	DHS, 2006	IHS, 2006		1984	2007	2008	2000
Malta	2005			Yes	2001	2009	2009	2000
Marshall Islands	1999					1999		
Mauritania	2000	MICS, 2007	IHS, 2000		1984–85	2009	2008	2000
Mauritius	2000			Yes		2009	2009	2003
Mayotte	2007			Yes			2009	
Mexico	2010	ENPF, 1995	LFS, 2008		1991	2009	2009	2000
Micronesia, Fed. Sts.	2000		IHS, 2000					
Moldova	2004	DHS, 2005	ES/BS, 2008	Yes		2009	2009	2000
Monaco	2008			Yes				
Mongolia	2010	MICS, 2005	LSMS, 2007/08	Yes		2009	2007	2000
Montenegro	2003	MICS, 2005/06	ES/BS, 2008	Yes		2009		
Morocco	2004	MICS, 2006	ES/BS, 2007		1996	2009	2009	2000
Mozambique	2007	DHS, 2003; AIS, 2009	ES/BS, 2008		1999–2000	2009	2009	2000
Myanmar	1983	MICS, 2000			2003		2001	2000
Namibia	2001	DHS, 2006/07	ES/BS, 1993/94		1996–97	2009	2008	2000
Nepal	2001	DHS, 2006	LSMS, 2003/04		2002	2009	2009	2000
Netherlands Antilles	2001			Yes			2008	2000
Netherlands	2001		IHS, 1999	Yes	1999–2000^d	2009	2009	
New Caledonia	2009			Yes		1997	2008	
New Zealand	2006		IS, 1997	Yes	2002	2009	2010	2000
Nicaragua	2005	RHS, 2006/07	LSMS, 2005		2001	2009	2009	2000
Niger	2001	DHS, 2006	CWIQ/PS, 2005		1980	2003	2008	2000
Nigeria	2006	DHS, 2008	IHS, 2003/04		1960	2006	2009	2000
Northern Mariana Islands	2010							
Norway	2001		IS, 2000	Yes	1999	2009	2010	2000
Oman	2010	FHS, 1995			1978–79	2004	2009	2003
Pakistan	1998	DHS, 2006/07	IHS, 2006		2000	2009	2009	2000
Palau	2010			Yes		2007		
Panama	2010	LSMS, 2003	LFS, 2009		2001	2009	2009	2000
Papua New Guinea	2000	DHS, 1996	IHS, 1996			2009	2004	2000
Paraguay	2002	RHS, 2004	IHS, 2008		1991	2009	2009	2000
Peru	2007	DHS, 2007/08	IHS, 2009		1994	2009	2009	2000
Philippines	2010	DHS, 2008	ES/BS, 2009	Yes	2002	2009	2009	2000
Poland	2002		ES/BS, 2008	Yes	1996/2002	2009	2009	2000
Portugal	2001		IS, 1997	Yes	1999	2009	2009	2000
Puerto Rico	2010	RHS, 1995/96		Yes	1997/2002	2001		
Qatar	2010			Yes	2000–01		2008	2005
Romania	2002	RHS, 1999	LFS, 2008	Yes	2002	2009	2009	2000
Russian Federation	2010	RHS, 1996	IHS, 2008	Yes	1994–95	2009	2009	2000
Rwanda	2002	DHS, 2007/08	IHS, 2005		1984	2009	2009	2000
Samoa	2006	DHS, 2009			1999	2009	2009	
San Marino	2010			Yes				

PRIMARY DATA DOCUMENTATION

	Currency	National accounts						Balance of payments and trade			Government finance	IMF data dissemination standard
		Base year	Reference year	System of National Accounts	SNA price valuation	Alternative conversion factor	PPP survey year	Balance of Payments Manual in use	External debt	System of trade	Accounting concept	
São Tomé & Príncipe	São Tomé & Príncipe dobra	2001			VAP		2005		Preliminary	S		G
Saudi Arabia	Saudi Arabian riyal	1999			VAP		2005	BPM5		G		G
Senegal	CFA franc	1999	1987	b	VAB		2005	BPM5	Actual	G	B	G
Serbia	Serbian dinar	a	2002	b	VAB		2005	BPM5	Actual	G	C	G
Seychelles	Seychelles rupee	1986			VAP			BPM5	Actual	G	C	G
Sierra Leone	Sierra Leonean leone	1990		b	VAB		2005	BPM5	Preliminary		B	G
Singapore	Singapore dollar	2000		b	VAB		2005	BPM5		G	C	S
Slovak Republic	Euro	2000	1995	b	VAB		2005	BPM5		S	C	S
Slovenia	Euro	a	2000	b	VAB		2005	BPM5		S	C	S
Solomon Islands	Solomon Islands dollar	1990			VAB			BPM5	Actual	S		
Somalia	Somali shilling	1985			VAB	1977–90			Estimate			
South Africa	South African rand	2005		b	VAB		2005	BPM5	Preliminary	G	C	S
Spain	Euro	2000		b	VAB		2005	BPM5		S	C	S
Sri Lanka	Sri Lankan rupee	2002			VAP		2005	BPM5	Actual	G	B	G
St. Kitts and Nevis	East Caribbean dollar	1990		b	VAB			BPM5	Preliminary	S	C	G
St. Lucia	East Caribbean dollar	1990			VAB			BPM5	Actual	G		G
St. Vincent & Grenadines	East Caribbean dollar	1990			VAB			BPM5	Actual	S	B	G
Sudan	Sudanese pound	1981/82f	1996		VAB		2005	BPM5	Actual	G	B	G
Suriname	Suriname dollar	1990		b	VAB			BPM5		G		G
Swaziland	Swaziland lilangeni	2000			VAB		2005	BPM5	Actual	G	B	G
Sweden	Swedish krona	a	2000		VAB		2005	BPM5		S	C	S
Switzerland	Swiss franc	2000			VAB		2005	BPM5		S	C	S
Syrian Arab Republic	Syrian pound	2000			VAB	1970–2008	2005	BPM5	Actual	S	C	G
Tajikistan	Tajik somoni	a	2000	b	VAB	1990–95	2005	BPM4	Actual		C	G
Tanzania	Tanzanian shilling	a	2001		VAB		2005	BPM5	Actual	G		G
Thailand	Thai baht	1988			VAP		2005	BPM5	Actual	S	C	S
Timor-Leste	U.S. dollar	2000			VAP					G		
Togo	CFA franc	1978			VAP		2005	BPM5	Actual	S	B	G
Tonga	Tongan pa'anga	2000/01			VAB			BPM5	Actual	G		G
Trinidad and Tobago	Trinidad and Tobago dollar	2000		b	VAB			BPM5		S	C	G
Tunisia	Tunisian dinar	1990			VAP		2005	BPM5	Actual	G	C	S
Turkey	New Turkish lira	1998			VAB		2005	BPM5	Actual	S	B	S
Turkmenistan	New Turkmen manat	a	2007	b	VAB	1987–95, 1997–2007		BPM4	Estimate			
Turks and Caicos Islands	U.S. dollar									G		
Tuvalu	Australian dollar											
Uganda	Ugandan shilling	2001/02			VAB		2005	BPM5	Actual	G	B	G
Ukraine	Ukrainian hryvnia	a	2003	b	VAB	1987–95	2005	BPM5	Actual	G	C	S
United Arab Emirates	U.A.E. dirham	1995			VAB			BPM4		S	B	G
United Kingdom	Pound sterling	2000		b	VAB		2005	BPM5		G	C	S
United States	U.S. dollar	a	2000		VAB		2005	BPM5		G	C	S
Uruguay	Uruguayan peso	2005			VAB		2005	BPM5		G	C	S
Uzbekistan	Uzbek sum	a	1997	b	VAB	1990–95		BPM4	Actual			
Vanuatu	Vanuatu vatu	2006			VAP			BPM5	Actual	G	C	G
Venezuela, R.B.	Venezuelan bolivar fuerte	1997			VAB		2005	BPM5	Actual	G	C	G
Vietnam	Vietnamese dong	1994		b	VAP	1991	2005	BPM4	Preliminary	S		G
Virgin Islands (U.S.)	U.S. dollar	1982								G		
West Bank and Gaza	Israeli new shekel	1997			VAB			BPM5		S	B	G
Yemen, Rep.	Yemeni rial	1990			VAP	1990–96	2005	BPM5	Actual	S	B	G
Zambia	Zambian kwacha	1994			VAB	1990–92	2005	BPM5	Preliminary	S	B	G
Zimbabwe	U.S. dollar	2009			VAB	1991, 1998	2005	BPM4	Actual	G	C	G

	Latest population census	Latest demographic, education, or health household survey	Source of most recent income and expenditure data	Vital registration complete	Latest agricultural census	Latest industrial data	Latest trade data	Latest water withdrawal data
São Tomé & Príncipe	2001	DHS, 2008/09	PS, 2000/01			2005	2009	
Saudi Arabia	2010	Demographic survey, 2007			1999	2009	2009	2006
Senegal	2002	DHS, 2005; MIS, 2008/09	PS, 2005		1998–99	2009	2009	2002
Serbia	2002	MICS, 2005/06	IHS, 2008	Yes			2008	
Seychelles	2010		IHS, 2007	Yes	1998	2009	2008	2003
Sierra Leone	2004	DHS, 2008	IHS, 2003		1984–85	2003	2002	2000
Singapore	2010	General household, 2005		Yes		2009	2009	
Slovak Republic	2001		IS, 1996	Yes	2001	2009	2009	
Slovenia	2002		ES/BS, 2004	Yes	2000	2008	2009	
Solomon Islands	2009					2009	2007	
Somalia	1987	MICS, 2006			1990	1982		2003
South Africa	2001	DHS, 2003	ES/BS, 2005		2000	2009	2009	2000
Spain	2001		IHS, 2000	Yes	1999	2009	2009	2000
Sri Lanka	2001	DHS, 2006/07	ES/BS, 2007	Yes	2002	2009	2009	2000
St. Kitts and Nevis	2001			Yes		2009	2008	
St. Lucia	2010		IHS, 1995	Yes		2009	2008	
St. Vincent & Grenadines	2001			Yes		2009	2009	
Sudan	2008	MICS/PAPFAM, 2006				2009	2009	2000
Suriname	2004	MICS, 2006	ES/BS, 1999	Yes		2008	2008	2000
Swaziland	2007	DHS, 2006/07	ES/BS, 2000/01		2003	2009	2007	2000
Sweden	c		IS, 2000	Yes	1999–2000	2009	2009	2000
Switzerland	2010		ES/BS, 2000	Yes	2000	2009	2009	2000
Syrian Arab Republic	2004	MICS, 2006	ES/BS, 2004		1981	2009	2008	2003
Tajikistan	2010	MICS, 2005	LSMS, 2004		1994	2009	2000	2000
Tanzania	2002	DHS, 2004/05; AIS, 2007/08	ES/BS, 2007		2002–03	2009	2009	2002
Thailand	2010	MICS, 2005/06	IHS, 2009		2003	2009	2009	2000
Timor-Leste	2010	DHS, 2009	LSMS, 2007			2000	2005	
Togo	2010	MICS, 2006	CWIQ, 2006		1996	2005	2007	2002
Tonga	2006			Yes	2001	2009	2007	
Trinidad and Tobago	2000	MICS, 2006	IHS, 1992	Yes	2004	2009	2009	2000
Tunisia	2004	MICS, 2006	IHS, 2000		2004	2009	2009	2000
Turkey	2000	DHS, 2003	LFS, 2008		2001	2009	2009	2003
Turkmenistan	1995	MICS, 2006	LSMS, 1998	Yes		2009	2000	2000
Turks and Caicos Islands	2001			Yes			2009	
Tuvalu	2002						2008	
Uganda	2002	DHS, 2006; MIS, 2009/10	PS, 2005		1991	2009	2008	
Ukraine	2001	DHS, 2007	ES/BS, 2008	Yes		2009	2009	2000
United Arab Emirates	2010				1998	2007	2009	2005
United Kingdom	2001		IS, 1999	Yes	1999–2000[d]	2009	2009	2000
United States	2010	CPS (monthly)	LFS, 2000	Yes	1997/2002	2009	2009	2000
Uruguay	2004		IHS, 2009	Yes	2000	2009	2009	2000
Uzbekistan	1989	MICS, 2006	ES/BS, 2003	Yes		2009		2000
Vanuatu	2009	MICS, 2007				2008	2007	
Venezuela, R.B.	2001	MICS, 2000	IHS, 2009	Yes	1997	2005	2009	
Vietnam	2009	MICS, 2006	IHS, 2008	Yes	2001	2009	2008	2000
Virgin Islands (U.S.)	2010			Yes				
West Bank and Gaza	2007	PAPFAM, 2006	IHS, 2009		1971		2008	
Yemen, Rep.	2004	MICS, 2006	ES/BS, 2005		2002	2003	2009	2000
Zambia	2000	DHS, 2007	IHS, 2004/05		1990	2009	2009	2000
Zimbabwe	2002	DHS, 2005/06	IHS, 2003		1960	2009	2009	2002

Note: For explanation of the abbreviations used in the table see notes following the table.
a. Original chained constant price data are rescaled. b. Country uses the 1993 System of National Accounts methodology. c. Register based. d. Conducted annually. e. Rolling census.
f. Reporting period switch from fiscal year to calendar year from 1996. Pre-1996 data converted to calendar year.

• **Base year** is the base or pricing period used for constant price calculations in the country's national accounts. Price indexes derived from national accounts aggregates, such as the implicit deflator for gross domestic product (GDP), express the price level relative to base year prices. • **Reference year** is the year in which the local currency, constant price series of a country is valued. The reference year is usually the same as the base year used to report the constant price series. However, when the constant price data are chain linked, the base year is changed annually, so the data are rescaled to a specific reference year to provide a consistent time series. When the country has not rescaled following a change in base year, World Bank staff rescale the data to maintain a longer historical series. To allow for cross-country comparison and data aggregation, constant price data reported in *World Development Indicators* are rescaled to a common reference year (2000) and currency (U.S. dollars). • **System of National Accounts** identifies countries that use the 1993 System of National Accounts (1993 SNA), the terminology applied in *World Development Indicators* since 2001, to compile national accounts. Although more countries are adopting the 1993 SNA, many still follow the 1968 SNA, and some low-income countries use concepts from the 1953 SNA. • **SNA price valuation** shows whether value added in the national accounts is reported at basic prices (VAB) or producer prices (VAP). Producer prices include taxes paid by producers and thus tend to overstate the actual value added in production. However, VAB can be higher than VAP in countries with high agricultural subsidies. See *About the data* for tables 4.1 and 4.2 for further discussion of national accounts valuation. • **Alternative conversion factor** identifies the countries and years for which a World Bank–estimated conversion factor has been used in place of the official exchange rate (line rf in the International Monetary Fund's [IMF] *International Financial Statistics*). See *Statistical methods* for further discussion of alternative conversion factors. • **Purchasing power parity (PPP) survey year** is the latest available survey year for the International Comparison Program's estimates of PPPs. See *About the data* for table 1.1 for a more detailed description of PPPs. • **Balance of Payments Manual** in use refers to the classification system used to compile and report data on balance of payments items in table 4.17. BPM4 refers to the 4th edition of the IMF's *Balance of Payments Manual* (1977), and BPM5 to the 5th edition (1993). • **External debt** shows debt reporting status for 2009 data. *Actual* indicates that data are as reported, *preliminary* that data are based on reported or collected information but include an element of staff estimation, and *estimate* that data are World Bank staff

estimates. • **System of trade** refers to the United Nations general trade system (G) or special trade system (S). Under the general trade system goods entering directly for domestic consumption and goods entered into customs storage are recorded as imports at arrival. Under the special trade system goods are recorded as imports when declared for domestic consumption whether at time of entry or on withdrawal from customs storage. Exports under the general system comprise outward-moving goods: (a) national goods wholly or partly produced in the country; (b) foreign goods, neither transformed nor declared for domestic consumption in the country, that move outward from customs storage; and (c) nationalized goods that have been declared for domestic consumption and move outward without being transformed. Under the special system of trade, exports are categories a and c. In some compilations categories b and c are classified as re-exports. Direct transit trade—goods entering or leaving for transport only—is excluded from both import and export statistics. See *About the data* for tables 4.4, 4.5, and 6.2 for further discussion. • **Government finance accounting concept** is the accounting basis for reporting central government financial data. For most countries government finance data have been consolidated (C) into one set of accounts capturing all central government fiscal activities. Budgetary central government accounts (B) exclude some central government units. See *About the data* for tables 4.12, 4.13, and 4.14 for further details. • **IMF data dissemination standard** shows the countries that subscribe to the IMF's Special Data Dissemination Standard (SDDS) or General Data Dissemination System (GDDS). S refers to countries that subscribe to the SDDS and have posted data on the Dissemination Standards Bulletin Board at http://dsbb.imf.org. G refers to countries that subscribe to the GDDS. The SDDS was established for member countries that have or might seek access to international capital markets to guide them in providing their economic and financial data to the public. The GDDS helps countries disseminate comprehensive, timely, accessible, and reliable economic, financial, and sociodemographic statistics. IMF member countries elect to participate in either the SDDS or the GDDS. Both standards enhance the availability of timely and comprehensive data and therefore contribute to the pursuit of sound macroeconomic policies. The SDDS is also expected to improve the functioning of financial markets. • **Latest population census** shows the most recent year in which a census was conducted and in which at least preliminary results have been released. The preliminary results from the very recent censuses could be reflected in timely revisions if basic data are available, such as population by

age and sex, as well as the detailed definition of counting, coverage, and completeness. Countries that hold register-based censuses produce similar census tables every 5 or 10 years. Germany's 2001 census is a register-based test census using a sample of 1.2 percent of the population. A rare case, France has been conducting a rolling census every year since 2004; the 1999 general population census was the last to cover the entire population simultaneously (www.insee.fr/en/recensement/page_accueil_rp.htm). • **Latest demographic, education, or health household survey** indicates the household surveys used to compile the demographic, education, and health data in section 2. AIS is HIV/AIDS Indicator Survey, CPS is Current Population Survey, DGHS is Demographic and General Health Survey, DHS is Demographic and Health Survey, ENPF is National Family Planning Survey (Encuesta Nacional de Planificacion Familiar), FHS is Family Health Survey, LSMS is Living Standards Measurement Survey, MICS is Multiple Indicator Cluster Survey, MIS is Malaria Indicator Survey, NSS is National Sample Survey on Population Change, PAPFAM is Pan Arab Project for Family Health, RHS is Reproductive Health Survey, and SPA is Service Provision Assessments. Detailed information for AIS, DHS, MIS, and SPA are available at www.measuredhs.com/aboutsurveys; for MICS at www.childinfo.org; and for RHS at www.cdc.gov/reproductivehealth/surveys. • **Source of most recent income and expenditure data** shows household surveys that collect income and expenditure data. Names and detailed information on household surveys can be found on the website of the International Household Survey Network (www.surveynetwork.org). Core Welfare Indicator Questionnaire Surveys (CWIQ), developed by the World Bank, measure changes in key social indicators for different population groups—specifically indicators of access, utilization, and satisfaction with core social and economic services. Expenditure survey/budget surveys (ES/BS) collect detailed information on household consumption as well as on general demographic, social, and economic characteristics. Integrated household surveys (IHS) collect detailed information on a wide variety of topics, including health, education, economic activities, housing, and utilities. Income surveys (IS) collect information on the income and wealth of households as well as various social and economic characteristics. Labor force surveys (LFS) collect information on employment, unemployment, hours of work, income, and wages. Living Standards Measurement Studies (LSMS), developed by the World Bank, provide a comprehensive picture of household welfare and the factors that affect it; they typically incorporate data collection at the individual, household, and community levels. Priority surveys (PS) are a light monitoring survey, designed by the World Bank, for collecting data from a large number of households cost-effectively and quickly. Income tax registers (ITR) provide information on a population's income and allowance, such as gross income, taxable income, and taxes by socioeconomic group. 1-2-3 surveys (1-2-3) are implemented in three phases and collect sociodemographic and employment data, data on the informal sector, and information on living conditions and household consumption. • **Vital registration complete** identifies countries which report to have at least 90 percent complete registries of vital (birth and death) statistics to the United Nations Statistics Division and reported in Population and Vital Statistics Reports. Countries with complete vital statistics registries may have more accurate and more timely demographic indicators than other countries. • **Latest agricultural census** shows the most recent year in which an agricultural census was conducted and reported to the Food and Agriculture Organization of the United Nations. • **Latest industrial data** show the most recent year for which manufacturing value added data at the three-digit level of the International Standard Industrial Classification (ISIC, revision 2 or 3) are available in the United Nations Industrial Development Organization database. • **Latest trade data** show the most recent year for which structure of merchandise trade data from the United Nations Statistics Division's Commodity Trade (Comtrade) database are available. • **Latest water withdrawal data** show the most recent year for which data on freshwater withdrawals have been compiled from a variety of sources. See *About the data* for table 3.5 for more information.

Exceptional reporting periods

In most economies the fiscal year is concurrent with the calendar year. Exceptions are shown in the table at right. The ending date reported here is for the fiscal year of the central government. Fiscal years for other levels of government and reporting years for statistical surveys may differ.

The **reporting period for national accounts data** is designated as either calendar year basis (CY) or fiscal year basis (FY). Most economies report their national accounts and balance of payments data using calendar years, but some use fiscal years. In *World Development Indicators* fiscal year data are assigned to the calendar year that contains the larger share of the fiscal year. If a country's fiscal year ends before June 30, data are shown in the first year of the fiscal period; if the fiscal year ends on or after June 30, data are shown in the second year of the period. Balance of payments data are reported in *World Development Indicators* by calendar year.

Economies with exceptional reporting periods

Economy	Fiscal year end	Reporting period for national accounts data
Afghanistan	Mar. 20	FY
Australia	Jun. 30	FY
Bangladesh	Jun. 30	FY
Botswana	Jun. 30	FY
Canada	Mar. 31	CY
Egypt, Arab Rep.	Jun. 30	FY
Ethiopia	Jul. 7	FY
Gambia, The	Jun. 30	CY
Haiti	Sep. 30	FY
India	Mar. 31	FY
Indonesia	Mar. 31	CY
Iran, Islamic Rep.	Mar. 20	FY
Japan	Mar. 31	CY
Kenya	Jun. 30	CY
Kuwait	Jun. 30	CY
Lesotho	Mar. 31	CY
Malawi	Mar. 31	CY
Myanmar	Mar. 31	FY
Namibia	Mar. 31	CY
Nepal	Jul. 14	FY
New Zealand	Mar. 31	FY
Pakistan	Jun. 30	FY
Puerto Rico	Jun. 30	FY
Sierra Leone	Jun. 30	CY
Singapore	Mar. 31	CY
South Africa	Mar. 31	CY
Swaziland	Mar. 31	CY
Sweden	Jun. 30	CY
Thailand	Sep. 30	CY
Uganda	Jun. 30	FY
United States	Sep. 30	CY
Zimbabwe	Jun. 30	CY

Revisions to national accounts data

National accounts data are revised by national statistical offices when methodologies change or data sources improve. National accounts data in *World Development Indicators* are also revised when data sources change. The following notes, while not comprehensive, provide information on revisions from previous data. • **Bulgaria.** The National Statistical Office has revised national accounts data from 1995 onward. GDP in current prices are about 4 percent higher than previous estimates. • **Colombia.** The base year has been changed from 2000 to 2005, and data from 2000 onward are new. GDP in current prices average 2.8 percent higher than previous estimates. • **Croatia.** The Statistical Bureau revised national accounts for 1995–2007. The new base year is 2000. • **Cuba.** National accounts data for 1970–2008 are revised with data from the United

Nations Statistics Division. The new base year is 1990, and the SNA price valuation has been changed to basic prices. • **Fiji.** The new base year is 2005. Data are revised from 2005 onward based on official government data. • **Ghana.** The Ghana Statistical Service revised Ghana's national accounts series from 1993 to 2006. New GDP data are about 60 percent higher than previously reported and incorporate improved data sources and methodology. • **Guinea-Bissau.** National accounts data for 2003–09 are revised. The new data have broader coverage of all sectors of the economy, and the new base year is 2005. GDP in current prices average 89 percent higher than previous estimates. • **Guyana.** The Bureau of Statistics has introduced a new series of GDP rebased to year 2006. Current price GDP average 63 percent higher than previous estimates. • **India.** The base year has been changed from 1999 to 2004. Data are revised from 2004 onward with official government data. GDP at current prices average 4 percent higher than previous estimates. • **Kazakhstan.** National accounts data have been revised by the National Statistical Office. The new base year is 2000. • **Kiribati.** The base year has been changed from 2005 to 2006. Data are revised from 2000 onward with official government data. • **Namibia.** The Central Bureau of Statistics has revised national accounts data for 2000–07. An expanded data survey has resulted in a substantial upward adjustment to estimates of output, particularly in mining, services, and manufacturing. The constant price series were rebased from 1995 to 2004 prices. GDP in current prices average 14 percent higher than previous estimates. • **South Africa.** The base year has been changed from 2000 to 2005. Data are revised from 2000 onward with official government data. • **Tonga.** Data are revised from 1995 onward with official government data. GDP in current prices average 20 percent higher than previous estimates. • **Vanuatu.** The base year has been changed from 1983 to 2006. Data are revised from 1998 onward with official government data. GDP in current prices average 11 percent higher than previous estimates.

Changes to national currencies

• **Malta.** On January 1, 2008, the euro replaced the Maltese liri as Malta's currency. • **Zimbabwe.** As of January 2009, multiple hard currencies, such as rand, pound sterling, euro and U.S. dollar are in use. Data are reported in U.S. dollars, the most-used currency.

STATISTICAL METHODS

This section describes some of the statistical procedures used in preparing *World Development Indicators*. It covers the methods employed for calculating regional and income group aggregates and for calculating growth rates, and it describes the *World Bank Atlas* method for deriving the conversion factor used to estimate gross national income (GNI) and GNI per capita in U.S. dollars. Other statistical procedures and calculations are described in the *About the data* sections following each table.

Aggregation rules

Aggregates based on the World Bank's regional and income classifications of economies appear at the end of most tables. The countries included in these classifications are shown on the flaps on the front and back covers of the book. Most tables also include the aggregate euro area. This aggregate includes the member states of the Economic and Monetary Union (EMU) of the European Union that have adopted the euro as their currency: Austria, Belgium, Cyprus, Finland, France, Germany, Greece, Ireland, Italy, Luxembourg, Malta, Netherlands, Portugal, Slovak Republic, Slovenia, and Spain. Other classifications, such as the European Union and regional trade blocs, are documented in *About the data* for the tables in which they appear.

Because of missing data, aggregates for groups of economies should be treated as approximations of unknown totals or average values. Regional and income group aggregates are based on the largest available set of data, including values for the 155 economies shown in the main tables, other economies shown in table 1.6, and Taiwan, China. The aggregation rules are intended to yield estimates for a consistent set of economies from one period to the next and for all indicators. Small differences between sums of subgroup aggregates and overall totals and averages may occur because of the approximations used. In addition, compilation errors and data reporting practices may cause discrepancies in theoretically identical aggregates such as world exports and world imports.

Five methods of aggregation are used in *World Development Indicators*:

- For group and world totals denoted in the tables by a *t*, missing data are imputed based on the relationship of the sum of available data to the total in the year of the previous estimate. The imputation process works forward and backward from 2000. Missing values in 2000 are imputed using one of several proxy variables for which complete data are available in that year. The imputed value is calculated so that it (or its proxy) bears the same relationship to the total of available data. Imputed values are usually not calculated if missing data account for more than a third of the total in the benchmark year. The variables used as proxies are GNI in U.S. dollars, total population, exports and imports of goods and services in U.S. dollars, and value added in agriculture, industry, manufacturing, and services in U.S. dollars.

- Aggregates marked by an *s* are sums of available data. Missing values are not imputed. Sums are not computed if more than a third of the observations in the series or a proxy for the series are missing in a given year.

- Aggregates of ratios are denoted by a *w* when calculated as weighted averages of the ratios (using the value of the denominator or, in some cases, another indicator as a weight) and denoted by a *u* when calculated as unweighted averages. The aggregate ratios are based on available data, including data for economies not shown in the main tables. Missing values are assumed to have the same average value as the available data. No aggregate is calculated if missing data account for more than a third of the value of weights in the benchmark year. In a few cases the aggregate ratio may be computed as the ratio of group totals after imputing values for missing data according to the above rules for computing totals.

- Aggregate growth rates are denoted by a *w* when calculated as a weighted average of growth rates. In a few cases growth rates may be computed from time series of group totals. Growth rates are not calculated if more than half the observations in a period are missing. For further discussion of methods of computing growth rates see below.

- Aggregates denoted by an *m* are medians of the values shown in the table. No value is shown if more than half the observations for countries with a population of more than 1 million are missing.

Exceptions to the rules occur throughout the book. Depending on the judgment of World Bank analysts, the aggregates may be based on as little as 50 percent of the available data. In other cases, where missing or excluded values are judged to be small or irrelevant, aggregates are based only on the data shown in the tables.

Growth rates

Growth rates are calculated as annual averages and represented as percentages. Except where noted, growth rates of values are computed from constant price series. Three principal methods are used to calculate growth rates: least squares, exponential endpoint, and geometric endpoint. Rates of change from one period to the next are calculated as proportional changes from the earlier period.

Least squares growth rate. Least squares growth rates are used wherever there is a sufficiently long time series to permit a reliable calculation. No growth rate is calculated if more than half the observations in a period are missing. The least squares growth rate, *r*, is estimated by fitting a linear regression trend line to the logarithmic annual values of the variable in the relevant period. The regression equation takes the form

$$\ln X_t = a + bt$$

which is the logarithmic transformation of the compound growth equation,

$$X_t = X_0 (1 + r)^t.$$

In this equation X is the variable, t is time, and $a = \ln X_0$ and $b = \ln (1 + r)$ are parameters to be estimated. If $b*$ is the least-squares estimate of b, then the average annual growth rate, r, is obtained as $[\exp(b*) - 1]$ and is multiplied by 100 for expression as a percentage. The calculated growth rate is an average rate that is representative of the available observations over the entire period. It does not necessarily match the actual growth rate between any two periods.

Exponential growth rate. The growth rate between two points in time for certain demographic indicators, notably labor force and population, is calculated from the equation

$$r = \ln(p_n/p_0)/n$$

where p_n and p_0 are the last and first observations in the period, n is the number of years in the period, and ln is the natural logarithm operator. This growth rate is based on a model of continuous, exponential growth between two points in time. It does not take into account the intermediate values of the series. Nor does it correspond to the annual rate of change measured at a one-year interval, which is given by $(p_n - p_{n-1})/p_{n-1}$.

Geometric growth rate. The geometric growth rate is applicable to compound growth over discrete periods, such as the payment and reinvestment of interest or dividends. Although continuous growth, as modeled by the exponential growth rate, may be more realistic, most economic phenomena are measured only at intervals, in which case the compound growth model is appropriate. The average growth rate over n periods is calculated as

$$r = \exp[\ln(p_n/p_0)/n] - 1.$$

Like the exponential growth rate, it does not take into account intermediate values of the series.

World Bank Atlas method

In calculating GNI and GNI per capita in U.S. dollars for certain operational purposes, the World Bank uses the *Atlas* conversion factor. The purpose of the *Atlas* conversion factor is to reduce the impact of exchange rate fluctuations in the cross-country comparison of national incomes.

The *Atlas* conversion factor for any year is the average of a country's exchange rate (or alternative conversion factor) for that year and its exchange rates for the two preceding years, adjusted for the difference between the rate of inflation in the country and that in Japan, the United Kingdom, the United States, and the euro area. A country's inflation rate is measured by the change in its GDP deflator.

The inflation rate for Japan, the United Kingdom, the United States, and the euro area, representing international inflation, is measured by the change in the "SDR deflator." (Special drawing rights, or SDRs, are the International Monetary Fund's unit of account.) The SDR deflator is calculated as a weighted average of these countries' GDP deflators in SDR terms, the weights being the amount of each country's currency in one SDR unit. Weights vary over time because both the composition of the SDR and the relative exchange rates for each currency change. The SDR deflator is calculated in SDR terms first and then converted to U.S. dollars using the SDR to dollar *Atlas* conversion factor. The *Atlas* conversion factor is then applied to a country's GNI. The resulting GNI in U.S. dollars is divided by the midyear population to derive GNI per capita.

When official exchange rates are deemed to be unreliable or unrepresentative of the effective exchange rate during a period, an alternative estimate of the exchange rate is used in the *Atlas* formula (see below).

The following formulas describe the calculation of the *Atlas* conversion factor for year t:

$$e_t^* = \frac{1}{3}\left[e_{t-2}\left(\frac{p_t}{p_{t-2}} \Big/ \frac{p_t^{S\$}}{p_{t-2}^{S\$}} \right) + e_{t-1}\left(\frac{p_t}{p_{t-1}} \Big/ \frac{p_t^{S\$}}{p_{t-1}^{S\$}} \right) + e_t \right]$$

and the calculation of GNI per capita in U.S. dollars for year t:

$$Y_t^\$ = (Y_t/N_t)/e_t^*$$

where e_t^* is the *Atlas* conversion factor (national currency to the U.S. dollar) for year t, e_t is the average annual exchange rate (national currency to the U.S. dollar) for year t, p_t is the GDP deflator for year t, $p_t^{S\$}$ is the SDR deflator in U.S. dollar terms for year t, $Y_t^\$$ is the *Atlas* GNI per capita in U.S. dollars in year t, Y_t is current GNI (local currency) for year t, and N_t is the midyear population for year t.

Alternative conversion factors

The World Bank systematically assesses the appropriateness of official exchange rates as conversion factors. An alternative conversion factor is used when the official exchange rate is judged to diverge by an exceptionally large margin from the rate effectively applied to domestic transactions of foreign currencies and traded products. This applies to only a small number of countries, as shown in *Primary data documentation*. Alternative conversion factors are used in the *Atlas* methodology and elsewhere in *World Development Indicators* as single-year conversion factors.

CREDITS

1. World view

Section 1 was prepared by a team led by Eric Swanson. Eric Swanson wrote the introduction with input from Uranbileg Batjargal and Neil Fantom. Bala Bhaskar Naidu Kalimili coordinated tables 1.1 and 1.6. Shota Hatakeyama, Mehdi Akhlaghi, Buyant Khaltarkhuu, and Masako Hiraga prepared tables 1.2, 1.3, and 1.5. Uranbileg Batjargal prepared table 1.4, with input from Azita Amjadi. Signe Zeikate of the World Bank's Economic Policy and Debt Department provided the estimates of debt relief for the Heavily Indebted Poor Countries Debt Initiative and Multilateral Debt Relief Initiative.

2. People

Section 2 was prepared by Masako Hiraga and Shota Hatakeyama, in partnership with the World Bank's Human Developmebnt Network and the Development Research Group in the Development Economics Vice Presidency. The introduction was written by Sulekha Patel and Masako Hiraga, with valuable inputs and comments from Eric Swanson. The poverty estimates at national poverty lines were compiled by the Global Poverty Working Group: a team of poverty experts from the Poverty Reduction and Equality Network, the Development Research Group, and the Development Data Group. The poverty estimates at international poverty lines were prepared by Shaohua Chen and Prem Sangraula of the World Bank's Development Research Group. The data on children at work were prepared by Lorenzo Guarcello and Furio Rosati from the Understanding Children's Work project. Other contributions were provided by Emi Suzuki (population, health, and nutrition); Montserrat Pallares-Miralles and Carolina Romero Robayo (vulnerability and security); Sara Elder of the International Labour Organization (labor force); Amelie Gagnon, Said Ould Voffal, and Weixin Lu of the United Nations Educational, Scientific, and Cultural Organization Institute for Statistics (education and literacy); the World Health Organization's Chandika Indikadahena (health expenditure), Charu Garg (national health account), Monika Bloessner and Mercedes de Onis (malnutrition and overweight), Neeru Gupta and Teena Kunjument (health workers), Jessica Ho (hospital beds), Rifat Hossain (water and sanitation), and Hazim Timimi (tuberculosis); Delice Gan of the International Diabetes Federation (diabetes); and Nyein Nyein Lwin of the United Nations Children's Fund (health). Eric Swanson provided valuable comments and suggestions on the introduction and at all stages of production.

3. Environment

Section 3 was prepared by Mehdi Akhlaghi in partnership with the World Bank's Sustainable Development Network. The introdcution was prepared by Soong Sup Lee and Neil Fantom. The guidance of Glenn-Marie Lange is gratefully acknowledged. Carola Fabi and Edward Gillin of the Food and Agriculture Organization of the United Nations; Ricardo Quercioli and Karen Treanton of the International Energy Agency; Laura Battlebury of the World Conservation Monitoring Centre; and Gerhard Metchies and Armin Wagner of German International Cooperation (GIZ). The World Bank's Environment Department devoted substantial staff resources to the book, for which the team is very grateful. Other contributors were Brian Blankespoor, Lopamudra Chakraborti, Susmita Dasgupta, Olivier Dupriez, Kirk Hamilton, Esther Grace Lee, Craig Meisner, Kiran Pandey, Giovanni Ruta, and Akiko Saesaka.

4. Economy

Section 4 was prepared by Bala Bhaskar Naidu Kalimili, Mahyar Eshragh-Tabary, and Soong Sup Lee in close collaboration with the Sustainable Development and Economic Data Team of the World Bank's Development Data Group. Soong Sup Lee wrote the introduction with valuable suggestions from Eric Swanson and the IMF's Financial Institutions Division, Statistics Department. Contributions to the section were provided by Azita Amjadi, Lopamudra Chakraborti, Kirk Hamilton, Barbro Hexeberg, Esther Grace Lee, Giovanni Ruta, and from Justin Thyme Matz and Yutong Li of the IMF's Statistical Information Management Division, Statistics Department. The national accounts data for low- and middle-income economies were gathered by the World Bank's regional staff through the annual Unified Survey. Maja Bresslauer, Mahyar Eshragh-Tabary, Bala Bhaskar Naidu Kalimili, and Buyant Khaltarkhuu worked on updating, estimating, and validating the databases for national accounts. The team is grateful to Eurostat, the International Monetary Fund, Organisation for Economic Co-operation and Development, United Nations Industrial Development Organization, and World Trade Organization for access to their databases.

5. States and markets

Section 5 was prepared by David Cieslikowski and Buyant Khaltarkhuu, in partnership with the World Bank's Financial and Private Sector Development Network, Poverty Reduction and Economic Management Network, Sustainable Development Network, the International Finance Corporation, and external partners. David Cieslikowski wrote the introduction to the section with input from Eric Swanson. Other contributors include Ada Karina Izaguirre (privatization and infrastructure projects); Leora Klapper and Inessa Love (business registration); Federica Saliola and Joshua Wimpey (Enterprise Surveys); Sylvia Solf and Carolin Geginat (Doing Business); Alka Banerjee and Michael Orzano (Standard & Poor's global stock market indexes); Oya Pinar Ardic Alper (financial access); Satish Mannan (public policies and institutions); Henry Boyd and James Hackett of the International Institute for Strategic Studies (military personnel); Sam Perlo-Freeman and Siemon Wezeman of the Stockholm International Peace Research Institute (military expenditures and arms transfers); Kacem Iaych of the International Road Federation, Narjess Teyssier and Zubair Anwar of the International Civil Aviation Organization, and Hélène Stephan (transport); Jane Degerlund of Containerisation International (ports); Vanessa Grey, Esperanza Magpantay, and Susan Teltscher of the International Telecommunication Union; Georges Boade of the United Nations Educational, Scientific, and Cultural Organization Institute for Statistics (research and development, researchers, and technicians); and Ryan Lamb of the World Intellectual Property Organization (patents and trademarks).

6. Global links

Section 6 was prepared by Uranbileg Batjargal in partnership with the Financial Data Team of the World Bank's Development Data Group, Development Research Group (trade), Development Prospects Group (commodity prices and remittances), International Trade Department (trade facilitation), and external partners. Uranbileg Batjargal wrote the introduction, with substantial input from Ingo Borchert (Services Policy Restrictiveness Database), Caglar Ozden (bilateral migration matrix), and Evis Rucaj (public sector debt). Eric Swanson provided valuable comments. Substantial input for the data and tables came from Azita Amjadi (trade and tariffs) and Yasue Sakuramoto (external debt and financial data). Other contributors include Frederic Docquier (emigration rates); Flavine Creppy and Yumiko Mochizuki of the United Nations Conference on Trade and Development (trade); Betty Dow (commodity prices); Thierry Geiger of the World Economic Forum (trade facilitation); Jeff Reynolds and Joseph Siegel of DHL (freight costs); Yasmin Ahmad and Elena Bernaldo of the Organisation for Economic Co-operation and Development (aid); Hiroko Maeda and Ibrahim Levent (external debt); Henrik Pilgaard of the United Nations Refugee Agency (refugees); Costanza Giovannelli and Bela Hovy of the United Nations Population Division (migration); Sanket Mohapatra and Ani Rudra Silwal (remittances); and Teresa Ciller of the World Tourism Organization (tourism). Ramgopal Erabelly, Shelley Lai Fu, and William Prince provided valuable technical assistance.

Other parts of the book

Jeff Lecksell of the World Bank's Map Design Unit coordinated preparation of the maps on the inside covers. William Prince prepared *Users guide*. Eric Swanson wrote *Statistical methods*. Maja Bresslauer, Buyant Khaltarkhuu, and William Prince prepared *Primary data documentation*. Alison Kwong prepared *Partners* and *Index of indicators*.

Database management

William Prince coordinated management of the World Development Indicators database. Operation of the database management system was made possible by Ramgopal Erabelly, Shelley Fu, and Shahin Outadi in the Data and Information Systems Team under the leadership of Reza Farivari.

Design, production, and editing

Azita Amjadi, Alison Kwong, and Jomo Tariku coordinated all stages of production. Jomo Tariku prepared the cover. Deborah Arroyo, Jomo Tariku, and Elaine Wilson typeset the book. Communications Development Incorporated provided overall design direction and editing, led by Meta de Coquereaumont, Bruce Ross-Larson, and Christopher Trott. Katrina Van Duyn proofread of the book. Staff from External Affairs Office of the Publisher oversaw printing and dissemination of the book.

Client services

The Development Data Group's Client Services and Communications Team (Azita Amjadi, Buyant Erdene Khaltarkhuu, Alison Kwong, Beatriz Prieto-Oramas, Jomo Tariku, and Vera Wen) contributed to the design and planning and helped coordinate work with the Office of the Publisher.

Administrative assistance, office technology, and systems support

Awatif Abuzeid, Elysee Kiti, Premi Ratham Raj and Estela Zamora provided administrative assistance. Jean-Pierre Djomalieu, Gytis Kanchas, and Nacer Megherbi provided information technology support. Ramvel Chandrasekaran, Ugendran Machakkalai, Atsushi Shimo, and Malarvizhi Veerappan provided systems support on the Development Data Platform application.

Publishing and dissemination

The Office of the Publisher, under the direction of Carlos Rossel, provided valuable assistance throughout the production process. Denise Bergeron, Nazim Aziz Gokdemir, Stephen McGroarty, and Nora Ridolfi coordinated printing and supervised marketing and distribution. Merrell Tuck-Primdahl of the Development Economics Vice President's Office managed the communications strategy.

World Development Indicators CD-ROM

Software preparation and testing was managed by Vilas Mandlekar with the assistance of Ramgopal Erabelly, Buyant Erdene Khaltarkhuu, Parastoo Oloumi, and William Prince. Systems development was undertaken by the Data and Information Systems Team led by Reza Farivari. William Prince coordinated user interface design and overall production and provided quality assurance, with assistance from Jomo Tariku. Photo credits belong to the World Bank photo library.

Open Data and Online Access

Coordination of the Open Data website (data.worldbank.org/) was provided by Neil Fantom and Nicole Frost. Design, programming, and testing were carried out by Reza Farivari and his team: Azita Amjadi, Ramvel Chandrasekaran, Shelley Fu, Buyant Erdene Khaltarkhuu, Ugendran Machakkalai, Shanmugam Natarajan, Atsushi Shimo, Lakshmikanthan Subramanian, Jomo Tariku, Malarvizhi Veerappan, and Vera Wen. William Prince coordinated production and provided quality assurance. Support from the Corporate Communications Unit in External Affairs was provided by a team including Livia Barton, George Gongadze and Jeffrey Mccoy. The multilingual web team was led by Valerie Hufbauer.

Client feedback

The team is grateful to the many people who have taken the time to provide feedback and suggestions, which have helped improve this year's edition. Please contact us at data@worldbank.org.

BIBLIOGRAPHY

AbouZahr, Carla, John Cleland, Francesca Coullare, Sarah Macfarlane, Francis Notzon, Philip Setel, and **Simone Szreter**. 2007. "Who Counts? 4. The Way Forward." Lancet 370 (9601): 1791–99.

Amin, Mohammad. 2010. "Necessity vs. Opportunity Entrepreneurs in the Informal Sector." Enterprise Surveys Note 17. World Bank, Washington, D.C.

Aminian, Nathalie, K.C. Fung, and **Francis Ng**. 2008. "Integration of Markets vs. Integration by Agreements." Policy Research Working Paper 4546. World Bank, Development Research Group, Washington, D.C.

Anderson, Kym, Marianne Kurzweil, Will Martin, Damiano Sandri, and **Ernesto Valenzuela**. 2008. "Measuring Distortions to Agricultural Incentives, Revisited." Policy Research Working Paper 4612. World Bank, Development Research Group, Washington, D.C.

Arvis, Jean-François, Monica Alina Mustra, Lauri Ojala, Ben Shepherd, and **Daniel Saslavsky**. 2010. *Connecting to Compete 2010: Trade Logistics in the Global Economy: The Logistics Performance Index and Its Indicators*. Washington, D.C.: World Bank, International Trade Department.

Arvis, Jean-François, Monica Alina Mustra, John Panzer, Lauri Ojala, and **Tapio Naula**. 2007. *Connecting to Compete 2007: Trade Logistics in the Global Economy: The Logistics Performance Index and Its Indicators*. Washington, D.C.: World Bank, International Trade Department.

Asian Development Bank. 2009. "The GMS Program." [www.adb.org/GMS/Program]. Manila.

ASEAN (Association of Southeast Asian Nations). n.d. Foreign Direct Investment Statistics. Online database. [www.aseansec.org/18144.htm]. Jakarta.

Aung, Malar. 2010. "Gender Statistics in Myanmar." Presentation at the Global Forum on Gender Statistics, October 11–13, Manila.

Babinard, Julie, and **Peter Roberts**. 2006. "Maternal and Child Mortality Development Goals: What Can the Transport Sector Do?" Transport Paper 12. World Bank, Transport Sector Board, Washington, D.C.

Ball, Nicole. 1984. "Measuring Third World Security Expenditure: A Research Note." *World Development* 12 (2): 157–64.

Beck, Thorsten, and **Ross Levine**. 2001. "Stock Markets, Banks, and Growth: Correlation or Causality?" Policy Research Working Paper 2670. World Bank, Development Research Group, Washington, D.C.

Behrman, Jere R. 2008. "What Have We Learned and What's Next?" In John Cockburn and Martin Valdivia, eds., *Reaching the MDGs: An International Perspective*. Dakar: Poverty and Economic Policy Research Network.

Berg, Andrew, and **Anne Kruger**. 2003. "Trade, Growth, and Poverty: A Selective Survey." Working Paper 03/30. International Monetary Fund, Washington, D.C.

Boerma, Ties, and **Sally Stansfield**. 2007. "Health Statistics Now: Are We Making the Right Investments?" *Lancet* 369 (9563): 779–86.

Borchert, Ingo, Batshur Gootiiz, and **Aaditya Mattoo**. Forthcoming. "Policy Barriers To International Trade In Services: New Empirical Evidence." World Bank, Washington, D.C.

Bourzac, Katherine. 2010. "Bacteria Make Diesel from Biomass." *Technology Review*, January 28.

Bown, Chad P. 2009. "The Pattern of Antidumping and Other Types of Contingent Protection." *PREMnotes* 144. World Bank, Poverty Reduction and Economic Management Network, Washington, D.C.

Bown, Chad P. 2010. "Taking Stock of Antidumping, Safeguards, and Countervailing Duties, 1990-2009". Policy Research Working Paper 5436. World Bank, Development Research Group, Washington, D.C.

Brautigam, Deborah. 2009. *The Dragon's Gift: The Real Story of China in Africa*, Oxford University Press, New York.

Buys, Piet, Uwe Deichmann, and **David Wheeler**. 2006. "Road Network Upgrading and Overland Trade Expansion in Sub-Saharan Africa." Policy Research Working Paper 4097. World Bank, Development Research Group, Washington, D.C.

Caiola, Marcello. 1995. *A Manual for Country Economists*. Training Series 1, Vol. 1. Washington, D.C.: International Monetary Fund.

CEPII (Centre d'Etudes Prospectives et d'Informations Internationales). n.d. Foreign Direct Investment Database. Online database. [www.cepii.fr/anglaisgraph/bdd/fdi.htm]. Paris.

CGAP (Consultative Group to Assist the Poor) and World Bank. 2010. *Financial Access 2010: The State of Financial Inclusion Through the Crisis*. Washington, D.C.: Consultative Group to Assist the Poor.

Chen, Shaohua, and **Martin Ravallion**. 2008. "The Developing World Is Poorer than We Thought, but No Less Successful in the Fight Against Poverty." Policy Research Working Paper 4703. World Bank, Washington, D.C.

Chomitz, Kenneth M., Piet Buys, and **Timothy S. Thomas**. 2005. "Quantifying the Rural-Urban Gradient in Latin America and the Caribbean." Policy Research Working Paper 3634. World Bank, Development Research Group, Washington, D.C.

CIESIN (Center for International Earth Science Information Network). 2005. Gridded Population of the World. [http://sedac.ciesin.columbia.edu/gpw/]. New York and Cali, Columbia.

CIIFAD (Cornell International Institute for Food, Agriculture and Development). n.d. "The System of Rice Intensification." [http://sri.ciifad.cornell.edu]. Ithaca, N.Y.

Claessens, Stijn, Daniela Klingebiel, and **Sergio L. Schmukler**. 2002. "Explaining the Migration of Stocks from Exchanges in Emerging Economies to International Centers." Policy Research Working Paper 2816. World Bank, Washington, D.C.

Commission on Growth and Development. 2008. *The Growth Report: Strategies for Sustainable Growth and Inclusive Development*. Washington, D.C.: World Bank.

Containerisation International. 2009. *Containerisation International Yearbook 2009*. London: Informa Maritime and Transport.

Cooper, Richard, Babatunde Osotimehin, Jay Kaufman, and **Terrence Forrester**. 1998. "Disease Burden in Sub-Saharan Africa: What Should We Conclude in the Absence of Data?" *Lancet* 351 (9097): 208–10.

Corrao, Marlo Ann, G. Emmanuel Guindon, Namita Sharma, and Dorna Fakhrabadi Shokoohi. 2000. *Tobacco Control Country Profile*. Atlanta, Ga.: American Cancer Society.

Dealogic. n.d. M&A Analytics. Online database. [www.dealogic.com/]. New York.

De Onis, Mercedes, and Monika Blössner. 2003. "The WHO Global Database on Child Growth and Malnutrition: Methodology and Applications." *International Journal of Epidemiology* 32: 518–26.

De Onis, Mercedes, Adelheid W. Onyango, Elaine Borghi, Cutberto Garza, and Hong Yang. 2006. "Comparison of the World Health Organization (WHO) Child Growth Standards and the National Center for Health Statistics/WHO International Growth Reference: Implications for Child Health Programmes." *Public Health Nutrition* 9 (7): 942–47.

Demirgüç-Kunt, Asli, and Ross Levine. 1996. "Stock Market Development and Financial Intermediaries: Stylized Facts." *World Bank Economic Review* 10 (2): 291–321.

DHL. 2011. "DHL Express Standard Rate Guide 2011." Bonn, Germany.

Djankov, Simeon, Caroline L. Freund, and Cong S. Pham. 2010. "Trading on Time." *Review of Economics and Statistics* 92 (1): 166–73.

Docquier, Frédéric, B. Lindsay Lowell, and Abdeslam Marfouk. 2009. "A Gendered Assessment of Highly Skilled Emigration." *Population and Development Review* 35 (2): 297–322.

Docquier, Frédéric, and Abdeslam Marfouk. 2006. "International Migration by Educational Attainment (1990–2000). Release 1.1." In Çaglar Özden and Maurice Schiff, eds., *International Migration, Remittances and Development*. New York: Palgrave Macmillan.

Eurostat (Statistical Office of the European Communities). n.d. Demographic Statistics. [http://epp.eurostat.ec.europa.eu/portal/page/portal/eurostat/home/]. Luxembourg.

———. Various years. *European Union Foreign Direct Investment Yearbook*. Luxembourg

———. Various years. *Statistical Yearbook*. Luxembourg

———. n.d. European Union Foreign Direct Investment Database. Online database. [http://epp.eurostat.ec.europa.eu/portal/page/portal/balance_of_payments/data/database]. Paris.

———. n.d. External Trade Database. Online database. [http://epp.eurostat.ec.europa.eu/portal/page/portal/external_trade/data/database]. Paris.

Fankhauser, Samuel. 1995. *Valuing Climate Change: The Economics of the Greenhouse*. London: Earthscan.

FAO (Food and Agriculture Organization of the United Nations). 2001. "Global Estimates of Gaseous Emissions of NH3, NO and N2O from Agricultural Land, 2001." Food and Agriculture Organization of the United Nations, Rome.

———. 2003. "How the World Is Fed." In *Agriculture, Food and Water*. Rome: Food and Agriculture Organization.

———. 2005. *Global Forest Resources Assessment 2005*. Rome: Food and Agriculture Organization. [Can this be dropped now that the 2010 edition is cited?]

———. 2007. *Coping with Water Scarcity: Challenge of the Twenty-First Century*. Report for World Water Day 2007. Rome: Food and Agriculture Organization.

———. 2008a. "Climate Change Adaptation and Mitigation in the Food and Agriculture Sector." Technical background document from the expert consultation, March 5–7, Rome.

———. 2008b. "Climate Change and Food Security: A Framework Document." Food and Agriculture Organization, Rome.

———. 2009a. "2050: A Third More Mouths to Feed." Press release, September 23. Food and Agriculture Organization, Rome.

———. 2009b. "More People Than Ever Are Victims of Hunger." Press release, June 19. Food and Agriculture Organization, Rome.

———. 2010a. *Global Forest Resources Assessment 2010*. Rome: Food and Agriculture Organization.

———. 2010b. "Water and Poverty: An Issue of Life and Livelihoods." [www.fao.org/nr/water/issues/scarcity.html]. Rome.

———. n.d. FAOSTAT. Online database. [http://faostat.fao.org/default.aspx]. Rome.

———. Various years. *The State of Food Insecurity in the World*. Rome: Food and Agriculture Organization.

Faurès, Jean-Marc, Jippe Hoogeveena, and Jelle Bruinsmab. 2004. "The FAO Irrigated Area Forecast for 2030." Food and Agriculture Organization, Rome.

Filmer, Deon, Amer Hasan, and Lant Pritchett. 2006. "A Minimum Learning Goal: Measuring Real Progress in Education." Working Paper 97. Center for Global Development, Washington, D.C.

Financial Times. n.d. fDi Markets: Crossborder Invesment Monitor. Online database. [www.fdimarkets.com]. London.

Fredricksen, Birger. 1993. *Statistics of Education in Developing Countries: An Introduction to Their Collection and Analysis*. Paris: United Nations Educational, Scientific, and Cultural Organization.

Froese, R., and D. Pauly, eds. n.d. FishBase. Online database. [www.fishbase.org]. Manila.

Geneva Declaration. 2008. *Global Burden of Armed Violence*. Geneva: Geneva Declaration.

Glasier, Anna, A. Metin Gulmezoglu, George P. Schmid, Claudia Garcia Moreno, and Paul F. A. van Look. 2006. "Sexual and Reproductive Health: A Matter of Life and Death." *Lancet* 368 (9547): 1595–1607.

Goss, Sarah, and Ignacio Mas. 2010. "Broadening the Financial Inclusion Cast of Characters." Technology Blog, December 16. [http://technology.cgap.org/2010/12/16/broadening-the-financial-inclusion-cast-of-characters/]. Consultative Group to Assist the Poor, Washington, D.C.

Hamilton, Kirk, and Michael Clemens. 1999. "Genuine Savings Rates in Developing Countries." *World Bank Economic Review* 13 (2): 333–56.

———. 2006. *Where Is the Wealth of Nations? Measuring Capital for the 21st Century*. Washington, D.C.: World Bank.

BIBLIOGRAPHY

Hamilton, Kirk, and Giovanni Ruta. 2008. "Wealth Accounting, Exhaustible Resources and Social Welfare." *Environmental and Resource Economics* 42 (1): 53–64.

Hanushek, A. Eric. 2002. *The Long-Run Importance of School Quality.* NBER Working Paper 9071. Cambridge, Mass.: National Bureau of Economic Research.

Hanushek, A. Eric, and Ludger Wössman. 2007. *Education Quality and Economic Growth.* Washington, D.C.: World Bank.

Happe, Nancy, and John Wakeman-Linn. 1994. "Military Expenditures and Arms Trade: Alternative Data Sources." Working Paper 94/69. International Monetary Fund, Policy Development and Review Department, Washington, D.C.

Hatcher, Jefrrry. 2009 "Securing Tenure Rights and Reducing Emissions from Deforestation and Degradation (REDD): Costs and Lessons Learned." Social Development Paper 120. World Bank, Development Research Group, Washington, D.C.

Hatzichronoglou, Thomas. 1997. "Revision of the High-Technology Sector and Product Classification." STI Working Paper 1997/2. Organisation for Economic Co-operation and Development, Directorate for Science, Technology, and Industry, Paris.

Hausman, Warren H., Hau L. Lee, and Uma Subramanian. 2005. "Global Logistics Indicators, Supply Chain Metrics, and Bilateral Trade Patterns." Policy Research Working Paper 3773. World Bank, Development Research Group, Washington, D.C.

Heston, Alan. 1994. "A Brief Review of Some Problems in Using National Accounts Data in Level of Output Comparisons and Growth Studies." *Journal of Development Economics* 44 (1): 29–52.

Hettige, Hemamala, Muthukumara Mani, and David Wheeler. 1998. "Industrial Pollution in Economic Development: Kuznets Revisited." Policy Research Working Paper 1876. World Bank, Development Research Group, Washington, D.C.

Hill, Kenneth, Kenji Shibuya, and Prabhat Jha. 2007. "Who Counts? 3. Interim Measures for Meeting Needs for Health Sector Data: Births, Deaths, and Cause of Death." *Lancet* 370 (9600) 1726–35.

Hinz. Richard P., Montserrat Pallares-Miralles, Carolina Romero, and Edward Whitehouse. April 2011. "International Patterns of Pension Provision II. Facts and Figures of the 2000s., Social Protection Discussion Paper. World Bank, Washington, D.C.

Hogge, Becky. 2010. "Open Data Study: Commissioned by the Transparency and Accountability Initiative." Accessed on line at http://www.soros.org/initiatives/information/focus/communication/articles_publications/publications/open-data-study-20100519/open-data-study-100519.pdf.

ICAO (International Civil Aviation Organization). 2010. *Civil Aviation Statistics of the World.* Montreal: International Civil Aviation Organization.

IDMC (International Displacement Monitoring Centre). 2010. Internal Displacement: Global Overview of Trends and Development in 2009. Geneva.

IEA (International Energy Agency). 2009. "World Energy Outlook 2009 Fact Sheet: Why Is Our Current Energy Pathway Unsustainable?" International Energy Agency, Paris.

——. Various years. *Energy Balances of OECD Countries.* Paris: International Energy Agency.

——. Various years. *Energy Statistics and Balances of Non-OECD Countries.* Paris: International Energy Agency.

——. Various years. *Energy Statistics of OECD Countries.* Paris: International Energy Agency.

ILO (International Labour Organization). 2009a. *Guide to the New Millennium Development Goals Employment Indicators.* Geneva: International Labour Office.

——. 2009b. Resolution Concerning Statistics of Child Labour. Resolution II, Rpt. ICLS/18/2008/IV/FINAL, 18th International Conference of Labour Statisticians, Geneva.

——. 2010. *Accelerating Action Against Child Labour.* Geneva: International Labour Office.

——. Various years. *Key Indicators of the Labour Market.* Geneva: International Labour Organization.

——. Various years. *Yearbook of Labour Statistics.* Geneva: International Labour Organization.

IMF (International Monetary Fund). 1977. *Balance of Payments Manual.* 4th ed. Washington, D.C.: International Monetary Fund.

——. 1993. *Balance of Payments Manual.* 5th ed. Washington, D.C.: International Monetary Fund.

——. 1995. *Balance of Payments Compilation Guide.* Washington, D.C.: International Monetary Fund.

——. 1996. *Balance of Payments Textbook.* Washington, D.C.: International Monetary Fund.

——. 2000. *Monetary and Financial Statistics Manual.* Washington, D.C.: International Monetary Fund.

——. 2001. *Government Finance Statistics Manual.* Washington, D.C.: International Monetary Fund.

——. 2004. *Compilation Guide on Financial Soundness Indicators.* Washington, D.C.: International Monetary Fund.

——. 2008. *Monetary and Financial Statistics Compilation Guide.* Washington, D.C.: International Monetary Fund.

——. 2009. *World Economic Outlook: Sustaining the Recovery.* Washington, D.C.: International Monetary Fund.

——. 2010. *Global Financial Stability Report.* Washington, D.C.

——. Various issues. *Direction of Trade Statistics Quarterly.* Washington, D.C.: International Monetary Fund.

——. Various issues. *Government Finance Statistics Yearbook.* Washington, D.C.: International Monetary Fund.

——. Various issues. *International Financial Statistics.* Washington, D.C.: International Monetary Fund.

——. Various years. *Balance of Payments Statistics Yearbook.* Parts 1 and 2. Washington, D.C.: International Monetary Fund.

———. Various years. *Direction of Trade Statistics Yearbook*. Washington, D.C.: International Monetary Fund.

———. Various years. *International Financial Statistics* Yearbook. Washington, D.C.: International Monetary Fund.

Inter-agency Group for Child Mortality Estimation. 2010. *Levels and Trends in Child Mortality: 201, Report*. New York: Inter-agency Group for Child Mortality Estimation.

———. n.d. Child Mortality Estimation Info database. [www.childmortality.org]. New York.

International Diabetes Federation. Various years. *Diabetes Atlas*. Brussels: International Diabetes Federation.

International Institute for Strategic Studies. 2011. *The Military Balance 2011*. London: Oxford University Press.

International Trade Centre, UNCTAD (United Nations Conference on Trade and Development), and WTO (World Trade Organization). n.d. The Millennium Development Goals database. Online database. [www.mdg-trade.org]. Geneva.a

International Working Group of External Debt Compilers. 1987. *External Debt Definitions*. Washington, D.C.: International Working Group of External Debt Compilers.

IPCC (Intergovernmental Panel on Climate Change). 2007. *Climate Change 2007: The Physical Science Basis. Contribution of Working Group I to the Fourth Assessment Report of the Intergovernmental Panel on Climate Change*. Cambridge, U.K.: Cambridge University Press.

IRF (International Road Federation).2010. *World Road Statistics 2010*. Geneva.

ITU (International Telecommunication Union). 2010. World Telecommunication Indicators database. Geneva.

IUCN International Union for Conservation of Nature). 2008. *2008 IUCN Red List of Threatened Species*. Gland, Switzerland: International Union for Conservation of Nature.

Kenyan National Coordinating Agency for Population and Developmena, Kenyan Ministry of Health, Kenyan Central Bureau of Statistics, and ORC Macro. 2005. *Kenya Service Provision Assessment Survey 2004*. Nairobi: Kenyan National Coordinating Agency for Population and Development, Kenyan Ministry of Health, Kenyan Central Bureau of Statistics, and ORC Macro.

Khandker, Shahidur, Zaid Bakht, and Gayatri B. Koolwal. 2006. "The Poverty Impact of Rural Roads: Evidence from Bangladesh." Policy Research Working Paper 3875. World Bank, Washington, D.C.

Klapper, Leora, and Inessa Love. 2010a. "The Impact of Business Environment Reforms on New Firm Registration." Policy Research Working Paper 5493. World Bank, Washington, D.C.

———. 2010b. "The Impact of the Financial Crisis on New Firm Registration. Policy Research Working Paper 5444. World Bank, Washington, D.C.

———. 2010c. "New Firm Creation." Viewpoint Note 324. World Bank, Financial and Private Sector Development Vice Presidency, Washington, D.C.

Kundzewicz, Zbigniew W., and Luis José Mata. 2007. "Freshwater Resources and Their Management." In S. Solomon, D. Qin, M. Manning, Z. Chen, M. Marquis, K.B. Averyt, M. Tignor and H. L. Miller, eds., *Climate Change 2007: Climate Change Impacts, Adaptation and Vulnerability. Working Group II Contribution to the Fourth Assessment Report of the Intergovernmental Panel on Climate Change*. Cambridge, U.K.: Cambridge University Press.

Kunte, Arundhati, Kirk Hamilton, John Dixon, and Michael Clemens. 1998. "Estimating National Wealth: Methodology and Results." Environmental Economics Series 57. World Bank, Environment Department, Washington, D.C.

Lin, Justin Yifu. 2010. "Stimulus in a Volatile Financial World." World Bank, Washington, D.C.

Lloyd, Peter J., Johanna L. Croser, and Kym Anderson. 2009. "Global Distortions to Agricultural Markets New Indicators of Trade and Welfare Impacts, 1955 to 2007." Policy Research Working Paper 4865. World Bank, Development Research Group, Washington, D.C.

Luxembourg Income Study. n.d. Online database. [www.lisproject.org]. Luxembourg.

Macro International. Various years. *Demographic and Health Surveys*. [www. measuredhs.com]. Calverton, Md.: Macro International.

Mahapatra, Prasanta, Kenji Shibuya, Alan Lopez, Francesca Coullare, Francis Notzon, Chalapati Rao, and Simon Szreter. 2007. "Who Counts? 2. Civil Registration Systems and Vital Statistics: Successes and Missed Opportunities." *Lancet* 370 (9599): 1656–63.

Manning, Richard. 2009. "Using Indicators to Encourage Development: Lessons from the Millennium Development Goals." Report 2009:01. Danish Institute for International Studies, Copenhagen.

Mishra, Prachi, and David Newhouse. 2007. "Health Aid and Infant Mortality." Working Paper 07/100. International Monetary Fund, Fiscal Affairs and Research Departments, Washington, D.C.

Morgenstern, Oskar. 1963. *On the Accuracy of Economic Observations*. Princeton, N.J.: Princeton University Press.

Murray, Christopher, Julie Knoll Rajaratnam, Jacob Marcus, Thomas Laakso, and Alan Lopez. 2010. "What Can We Conclude from Death Registration? Improved Methods for Evaluating Completeness." *PLoS Medicine* 7 (4).

National Science Board. 2010. *Science and Engineering Indicators 2010*. Arlington, Va.: National Science Foundation.

Netcraft. 2010. "Netcraft Secure Server Survey." [www.netcraft.co/].

OECD (Organisation for Economic Co-operation and Development). 2005. *Guide to Measuring the Information Society*. DSTI/ICCP/ISS (2005)/6. Paris: Organisation for Economic Co-operation and Development.

———. 2008. *A Profile of Immigrant Populations in the 21st Century: Data from OECD Countries*. Paris: Organisation for Economic Co-operation and Development.

———. 2009. *Agricultural Policies in OECD Countries: Monitoring and Evaluation*. Paris: Organisation for Economic Co-operation and Development.

———. 2010a. *OECD Economic Surveys: China 2010*. Paris: Organisation for Economic Co-operation and Development.

BIBLIOGRAPHY

————. 2010b *Restoring Fiscal Sustainability: Lessons for the Public Sector*. Paris: Organisation for Economic Co-operation and Development.

————. n.d. Creditor Reporting System. Online database. [http://stats.oecd.org/index.aspx?datasetcode=crsnew].

————. n.d. Database on Immigrants in OECD Countries. Online database. [http://stats.oecd.ors]. Paris.

————. n.d. International Direct Investment database Online database. [http://stats.oecd.orn]. Paris.

————. n.d. International Trade by Commodity Statistics. Online database. [http://stats.oecd.ors]. Paris.

————. n.d. Monthly Statistics of International Trade. Online database. [http://stats.oecd.ors]. Paris.

————. n.d. Producer and Consumer Support Estimates. Online database. [www.oecd.org/tad/support/psecse]. Paris.

————. n.d. Trade in Services. Online database. [http://stats.oecd.ors]. Paris.

————. Various issues. *Main Economic Indicators*. Paris: Organisation for Economic Co-operation and Development.

————. Various years. *National Accounts*. Vol. 1, Main Aggregates. Paris: Organisation for Economic Co-operation and Development.

————. Various years. *National Accounts*. Vol. 2, Detailed Tables. Paris: Organisation for Economic Co-operation and Development.

————. Various years. *OECD Health Data*. Paris: Organisation for Economic Co-operation and Development.

OECD (Organisation for Economic Co-operation and Development) DAC (Development Assistance Committee). 1996. *Shaping the 21st Century: The Contribution of Development Cooperation*. Paris: Organisation for Economic Co-operation and Development.

————. Various years. *Development Co-operation Report*. Paris: Organisation for Economic Co-operation and Development.

————. Various years. *Geographical Distribution of Financial Flows to Developing Economies*. Paris: Organisation for Economic Co-operation and Development.

————. Various years. *International Development Statistics*. CD-ROM. Paris: Organisation for Economic Co-operation and Development.

Özden, Çaglar, Christopher R. Parsons, Maurice Schiff, and Terrie L. Walmsley. Forthcoming. "Where on Earth is Everybody? The Evolution of Global Bilateral Migration 1960–2000., *World Bank Economic Review*.

Pandey, Kiran D., Piet Buys, Kenneth Chomitz, and David Wheeler. 2006b. "Biodiversity Conservation Indicators: New Tools for Priority Setting at the Global Environmental Facility." World Bank, Development Economics Research Group and Environment Department, Washington, D.C.

Pandey, Kiran D., David Wheeler, Bart Ostro, Uwe Deichmann, Kirk Hamilton, and Katie Bolt. 2006c. "Ambient Particulate Matter Concentrations in Residential and Pollution Hotspots of World Cities: New Estimates Based on the Global Model of Ambient Particulates (GMAPS)." World Bank, Development Economics Research Group and Environment Department, Washington, D.C.

PARIS21 (The Partnership in Statistics for Development in the 21st Century). 2009. "PARIS21 at Ten: Improvements in Statistical Capacity since 1999." The Partnership in Statistics for Development in the 21st Century, Paris.

Parsons, Christopher R., Ronald Skeldon, Terrie L. Walmsley, and L. Alan Winters. 2007, "Quantifying the International Bilateral Movements of Migrants."Çaglar Özden and Maurice Schiff,(ed). *International Migration, Economic Development and Policy*, New York: Palgrave Macmillak.

Partnership on Measuring ICT for Development. 2008. *The Global Information Society: A Statistical View*. Santiago: United Nations.

Patterson, Neil, Marie Montanjees, John Motala, and Colleen Cardillo. 2004, *Foreign Direct Investment: Trends, Data Availability, Concepts, and Recording Practices*, Washington, D.C.: International Monetary FunC.

Pollock, Rufus. 2010. "Welfare Gains from Opening Up Public Sector Information in the UK."Accessed online at http://www.rufuspollock.org/economics/papers/psi_openness_gains.pdf

PricewaterhouseCoopers, International Finance Corporation, and World Bank. 2010. *Paying Taxes 2011: The Global Picture*. London and Washington, D.C

Rahemtulla, Hanif. 2011. "The Open Data Revolution and the Emergence of Linked Data in Higher Education." Processed. School of Geography, University of Nottingham. Processed.

RAMSI (Regional Assistance Mission to Solomon Islands). 2011. [www.ramsi.org]. Honiara, Solomon Islands.

Ratha, Dilip, and William Shaw. 2007. "South-South Migration and Remittances., Working Paper 102, World Bank, Washington, D.C.

Ravallion, Martin, and Shaohua Chen. 1996. "What Can New Survey Data Tell Us about the Recent Changes in Living Standards in Developing and Transitional Economies?" Policy Research Working Paper 16943. World Bank, Development Research Group, Washington, D.C.

Ravallion, Martin, Shaohua Chen, and Prem Sangraula. 2008. "Dollar a Day Revisited." Policy Research Working Paper 4620. World Bank, Development Research Group, Washington, D.C.

Ravallion, Martin, Gaurav Datt, and Dominique van de Walle. 1991. "Quantifying Absolute Poverty in the Developing World." *Review of Income and Wealth* 37(4): 345–61.

Ruggles, Robert. 1994. "Issues Relating to the UN System of National Accounts and Developing Countries." *Journal of Development Economics* 44 (1): 77–85.

Rwandan National Institute of Statistics, Rwanda Ministry of Health, and Macro International Inc. 2008. *Rwanda Service Provision Assessment Survey 2007*. Calverton, Md.: Rwandan National Institute of Statistics, Rwandan Ministry of Health, and Macro International Inc.

Ryten, Jacob. 1998. "Fifty Years of ISIC: Historical Origins and Future Perspectives." ECA/STAT.AC. 63/22. United Nations Statistics Division, New York.

Schwartz, Jordan, Luis Andres, and Georgeta Dragoiu. 2009. "Crisis in Latin America: Infrastructure Investment, Employment and the Expectations of Stimulus." Policy Research Working Paper 5009. World Bank, Washington, D.C.

Setel, Philip, Sarah Macfarlane, Simon Szreter, Lene Mikkelsen, Prabhat Jha, Susan Stout, and Carla AbouZahr. 2007. "Who Counts? 1. A Scandal of Invisibility: Making Everyone Count by Counting Everyone." Lancet 370 (959): 1569–77.

Setel, Philip, Osman Sankoh, Chalapati Rao, Victoria Velkoff, Colin Mathers, Yang Gonghuan, Yusuf Hemed, Prabhat Jha, and Alan Lopez. 2005. "SamplerRegistration of Vital Events with Verbal Autopsy: ArRenewed Commitment to Measurine and Monitoring Vital Statistics." Bulletin of the World Health Organizatio. 83 (8): 611–17.

Shankar, Anuraj, Linda Bartlett, Vincent Fauveau, Monir Islam, and Nancy Terreri. 2008. "Delivery of MDG 5 by Active Management with Data." Lancet 371 (9620): 12–18.

Singh, R.B., P. Kumar, and T. Woodhead. 2002. "Smallholder Farmers in India: Food Security and Agricultural Policy." Food and Agriculture Organization, Regional Office for Asia and the Pacific, Bangkok.

SIPRI (Stockholm International Peace Research Institute). 2010. SIPRI Yearbook 2010: Armaments, Disarmament, and International Security. Oxford, U.K.: Oxford University Press.

Smith Kimberly, Talita Yamashiro Fordelone, and Felix Zimmermann. 2010. "Beyond the DAC: The Welcome Role of Other Providers of Development Co-operation." DCD Issues Brief. Organisation for Economic Co-operation and Development, Development Co-operation Directorate, Paris.

Smith, Lisa, and Laurence Haddad. 2000. "Overcoming Child Malnutrition in Developing Countries: Past Achievements and Future Choices." 2020 Brief 64. International Food Policy Research Institute, Washington, D.C.

SPC (Secretariat of the Pacific Community.). n.d. Online Statistics and Demography. [www.spc.int]. Nouméa.

Srinivasan, T. N. 1994. "Database for Development Analysis: An Overview." Journal of Development Economics 44 (1): 3–28.

Standard & Poor's. 2000. The S&P Emerging Market Indices: Methodology, Definitions, and Practices. New York: Standard & Poor's.

———. 2010. Global Stock Markets Factbook 2010. New York: Standard & Poor's.

Stiglitz, Joseph E., Amartya Sen, and Jean-Paul Fitoussi. 2009. Report by the Commission on the Measurement of Economic Performance and Social Progress. Paris: Commission on the Measurement of Economic Performance and Social Progress.

Takle, Eugene, and Don Hofstrand. 2008. "Global Warming: Agriculture's Impact on Greenhouse Gas Emissions." Ag Decision Maker, April.

Taylor, Benjamin J., and John S. Wilson. 2009. "The Crisis and Beyond: Why Trade Facilitation Matters." Research at the World Bank: A Brief from the Development Research Group. World Bank, Washington, D.C.

UNAIDS (Joint United Nations Programme on HIV/AIDS) and WHO (World Health Organizatio.). Various years. Report on the Global AIDS Epidemic. Geneva: Joint United Nations Programme on HIV/AIDS.

UNCTAD (United Nations Conference on Trade and Development). 2001. Electronic Commerce and Development Report 2001. New York and Geneva: United Nations Conference on Trade and Development.

———. 2007. Trade and Development Report 2007: Regional Cooperation for Development. New York and Geneva: United Nations Conference on Trade and Development.

———. 2008. Trade and Development Report 2008: Commodity Prices, Capital Flows and the Financing of Investment. New York and Geneva: United Nations Conference on Trade and Development.

———. 2009. UNCTAD Training Manual on Statistics for FDI and the Operations of TNCs, Vols I, II, and III. New York and Geneva: United Nations Conference on Trade and Development.

———. 2010. Review of Maritime Transport 2010. New York and Geneva: United Nations Conference on Trade and Development.

———. n.d. UnctadStat. Online database. [http://unctadstat.unctad.org/]. New York and Geneva.

———. Various years. Handbook of Statistics. New York and Geneva: United Nations Conference on Trade and Development.

———. Various years. World Investment Report. New York and Geneva: United Nations Conference on Trade and Development.

UNCTAD (United Nations Conference on Trade and Development) and UNEP (United Nations Environment Programme). 2008. Organic Agriculture and Food Security in Africa. UNCTAD-UNEP Capacity Building Task Force on Trade, Environment and Development. New York: United Nations.

Understanding Children's Work (UC.). n.d. Online database. [www.ucw-project. org]. Rome.

UNDP (United Nations Development Programme). 1990. Human Development Report 1990. New York: Oxford University Press.

UNDPKO (United Nations Department of UN Peacekeeping Opeaations). 2011. "Current Peacekeeping Operations." [www.un.org/en/peacekeeping/operations/current.shtml] New York

UNESCO (United Nations Educational, Scientific, and Cultural Organization). 1997. International Standard Classification of Education. Paris: United Nations Educational, Scientific, and Cultural Organization.

———. 2009. World Water Development Report 3: Water in a Changing World. Paris: United Nations Educational, Scientific, and Cultural Organization.

———. 2010. UNESCO Science Report 2010. Paris: United Nations Educational, Scientific, and Cultural Organization.

———. Various years. EFA Global Monitoring Report. Paris: United Nations Educational, Scientific, and Cultural Organization.

UNESCO (United Nations Educational, Scientific, and Cultural Organization) Institute for Statistics. 2008a. "A Typology of Out-of-School Children to Improve Policies that Address Exclusion." Background document for the 48th Session of the International Conference on Education, November 25–28, Geneva.

———. n.d. Online database. [www.uis.unesco.org]. Montreal.

BIBLIOGRAPHY

——. Various years. *Global Education Digest*. Paris.

UNHCR (The UN Refugee Agency**)**. Various years. *Statistical Yearbook*. Geneva: The UN Refugee Agency.

UNICEF (United Nations Children's Fund). Various years. *Multiple Indicator Cluster Surveys*. [www.childinfo.org]. New York.

——. Various years. *The State of the World's Children*. New York: Oxford University Press.

——. n.d. Online database. [www.childinfo.org].

UNIDO (United Nations Industrial Development Organizatio.). Various years. *International Yearbook of Industrial Statistics*. Vienna: United Nations Industrial Development Organization.

UNIFEM (United Nations Development Fund for Women). 2005. *Progress of the World's Women*. New York: United Nations Development Fund for Women.

United Nations. 1990. *International Standard Industrial Classification of All Economic Activities, Third Revision*. Statistical Papers Series M, No. 4, Rev. 3. New York: United Nations.

——. 1992. "Kyoto Protocol to the United Nations Framework Convention on Climate Change." United Nations, New York.

——. 2001. *UN Secretary-General's Road Map towards the Implementation of the Millennium Declaration*. New York: United Nations.

——. 2009a. "Copenhagen Accord." December 18. United Nations Framework Convention on Climate Change, Copenhagen.

——. 2009b. "Fact Sheet: Stepping Up International Action on Climate Change: The Road to Copenhagen. United Nations Framework Convention on Climate Change, New York.

——. 2009d. *World Economic and Social Survey 2009: Promoting Development, Saving the Planet*. New York: United Nations, Department of Economic and Social Affairs.

United Nations Population Division. 2006. *World Population Prospects: The 2004 Revision*. Vol. III. Analytical Report. New York: United Nations, Department of Economic and Social Affairs.

——. 2009a. *Trends in Total Migrant Stock: 2008 Revision*. New York: United Nations, Department of Economic and Social Affairs.

——. 2009b. *World Population Prospects: The 2008 Revision*. New York: United Nations, Department of Economic and Social Affairs.

——. 2010. "United Nations Climate Change Conference Cancu —COP 16." November 29–December 10, Cancun, Mexico.

——. Various years. *World Urbanization Prospects*. New York: United Nations, Department of Economic and Social Affairs.

United Nations Statistics Division. n.d. Cement Manufacturing Data Set. New York: United Nations.

——. n.d. Comtrade database. New York.

——. n.d. *International Standard Industrial Classification of All Economic Activities, Third Revision*. [http://unstats.un.org/unsd/cr/registry/]. New York.

——. n.d. World Energy Data Set. New York: United Nations.

——. Various issues. *Monthly Bulletin of Statistics*. New York: United Nations.

——. Various issues. *Population and Vital Statistics Report*. New York: United Nations.

——. Various years. *Demographic Yearbook*. New York: United Nations.

——. Various years. *Energy Statistics Yearbook*. New York: United Nations.

——. Various years. *International Trade Statistics Yearbook*. New York: United Nations.

——. Various years. *National Accounts Statistics: Main Aggregates and Detailed Tables. Parts 1 and 2*. New York: United Nations.

——. Various years. *National Income Accounts*. New York: United Nations.

——. Various years. *Statistical Yearbook*. New York: United Nations.

University of California, Berkeley, and Max Planck Institute for Demographic Research. n.d. Human Mortality Database. Online database. [www.mortality.ore] [www.humanmortality.de simply redirects to mortality.org]. Berkley, Calif., and Rostock, Germany.

UNODC (United Nations Office on Drugs and Crime).

——. 2010. *International Homicide Statistics*. Vienna: United Nations Office on Drugs and Crime.

USAID (U.S. Agency for International Development). 2007. "Calculating Tariff Equivalents for Time in Trade." U.S. Agency for International Development, Washington, D.C.

U.S. Census Bureau. n.d. International Data Base). [www.census.gov/ipc/www/idb/]. Washington, D.C.

U.S. Center for Disease Control and Prevention. Various years. International Reproductive Health Surveys. [www.cdc.gov/reproductivehealth/Surveys/]. Atlanta, Ga.

U.S. National Science Board. 2008. *Science and Engineering Indicators 2008*. Arlington, Va.: National Science Foundation.

U.S. President. 2010. *Economic Report of the President*. Washington, D.C.: U.S. Government Printing Office.

Vandermoortele, Jan. 2009. "Taking the MDGs Beyond 2015: Hasten Slowly." European Association for Development Research and Training Institutes, Bonn, Germany.

Watkins, Kevin. 2008. *The Millennium Development Goals: Three Proposals for Renewing the Vision and Reshaping the Future*. Paris: United Nations Educational, Scientific, and Cultural Organization.

WHO (World Health Organization). 2007. "Civil Registration: Why Counting Births and Deaths Is Important." Fact sheet 324. [www.who.int/mediacentre/factsheets/fs324/en]. Geneva.

——. 2008a. *Health Metrics Network Framework and Standards for Country Health Information Systems*. Geneva: World Health Organization.

——. 2008b. "Measuring Health System Strengthening and Trends: A Toolkit for Countries." World Health Organization, Geneva.

————. 2008c. *Worldwide Prevalence of Anemia 1993–2005*. Geneva: World Health Organization.

————. 2009. *WHO Report on the Global Tobacco Epidemic 2009: Implementing Smoke-Free Environments*. Geneva: World Health Organization.

————. n.d. Global Database on Child Growth and Malnutrition. Online database. [www.who.int/nutgrowthdb]. Geneva.

————. n.d. National Health Account database. Online database. [www.who.int/nha/en/]. Geneva.

————. Various years. *Global Tuberculosis Control Report*. Geneva: World Health Organization.

————. Various years. *World Health Report*. Geneva: World Health Organization.

————. Various years. *World Health Statistics*. Geneva: World Health Organization.

WHO (World Health Organization) and UNICEF (United Nations Children's Fund). 2003. *Antenatal Care in Developing Countries: Promises, Achievements, andm-Missed Opportunities*. Geneva: World Health Organization and United Nations Children's Fund.

————. 2010. *Progress on Sanitation and Drinking Water*. Geneva: World Health Organization and United Nations Children's Fund.

————. 2011. *Global Atlas of the Health Workforce*. Geneva: World Health Organization and United Nations Children's Fund.

————. Various years. WHO-UNICEF estimates of national immunization coverage database. Online database. [www.who.int/immunization_monitoring/routine/immunization_coverage/en/index4.html]. Geneva.

WHO (World Health Organization), UNICEF (United Nations Children's Fund), UNFPA (United Nations Population Fund), and **World Bank**. 2010. *Trends in Maternal Mortality: 1990–2008 Estimates Developed by WHO, UNICEF, UNFPA, and the World Bank*. Geneva: World Health Organization.

WIPO (World Intellectual Property Organization). 2010. *WIPO Patent Report: Statistics on Worldwide Patent Activity*. Geneva: World Intellectual Property Organization.

World Bank. 1990. *World Development Report 1990: Poverty*. Washington, D.C.: World Bank.

————. 2000. *Trade Blocs*. New York: Oxford University Press.

————. 2001. *World Development Report 2000/2001: Attacking Poverty*. New York: Oxford University Press.

————. 2002. *Global Economic Prospects 2002: Making Trade Work for the World's Poor*. Washington, D.C.: World Bank.

————. 2007. *Healthy Development: The World Bank Strategy for Health, Nutrition, and Population Results*. Washington, D.C.: World Bank.

————. 2008a. "Brazil Country Partnership Strategy 2008–2011." World Bank, Latin America and the Caribbean Region, Washington, D.C.

————. 2008b. "Improving Trade and Transport for Landlocked Developing Countries: World Bank Contributions to Implementing the Almaty Programme of Action: A Report for the Mid-Term Review October 2008." World Bank, International Trade Department, Washington, D.C.

————. 2009a. *Africa's Development in a Changing Climate: Act Now, Act Together, Act Differently*. Washington, D.C.: World Bank.

————. 2009b. "Air Freight: A Market Study with Implications for Landlocked Countries." Transport Paper 26. World Bank, Washington, D.C.

————. 2010a. *Doing Business 2011*. Washington, D.C.: World Bank.

————. 2010b. "Investment in New Private Infrastructure Projects and Developing Countries Slowed Down in the First Quarter of 2010." PPI Data Update Note 38, World bank, Washington, D.C.

————. 2010c. *The World Bank's Country Policy and Institutional Assessment: An IEG Evaluation*. Washington, D.C.

————. 2011a. *The Changing Wealth of Nations: Measuring Sustainable Development in the New Millennium*. Washington, D.C.: World Bank.

————. 2011b. *Global Economic Prospects Volume 2: January 2011: Navigating Strong Currents*. Washington, D.C.: World Bank.

————. n.d. Enterprise Surveys. [www.enterprisesurveys.org]. Washington, D.C.

————. n.d. Performance Assessments and Allocation of IDA Resources Online database. [www.worldbank.org/ida]. Washington, D.C.

————. n.d. PovcalNet oOnline database. [http://iresearch.worldbank.org/PovcalNet]. Washington, D.C.

————. n.d. Private Participation in Infrastructure Database. Online database. [http://ppi.worldbank.org/]. Washington, D.C.

————.n.d. Quarterly Public Sector Debt. Online database. [http://databank.worldbank.org/ddp/home.do?Step=12&id=4&CNO=3009]. Washington, D.C.

————. n.d. World Trade Indicators. Online database. [www.worldbank.org/wti]. Washington, D.C.

————. Various issues. *Commodity Market Review*. Washington, D.C.: World Bank, Development Prospects Group.

————. Various issues. *Food price watch*. Washington, D.C.: World Bank, Poverty Reduction and equity Group.

————. Various issues. *Commodity Price Data*. Washington, D.C.: World Bank, Development Prospects Group.

————. Various issues. *Migration and Development Briefs*. Washington, D.C.: World Bank, Development Prospects Group.

————. Various years. *Global Development Finance: External Debt of Developing Countries*. Washington, D.C.: World Bank.

————. Various years. *Global Development Finance: Volumes I and II*. Washington, D.C.: World Bank.

————. Various years. *World Debt Tables*. Washington, D.C.: World Bank.

————. Various years. *World Development Indicators*. Washington, D.C.: World Bank.

World Bank and Dartmouth College. n.d. Global Preferential Trade Agreements Database. Online database. [http://wits.worldbank.org/gptad/]. Washington, D.C.

World Bank and IFPRI (International Food Policy Research Institute). 2006. *Agriculture and Achieving the Millennium Development Goals*. Report 32729-GLB. Washington, D.C.: World Bank.

BIBLIOGRAPHY

World Bank and IMF (International Monetary Fund). 2011. *Global Monitoring Report 2011: Improving the Odds of Achieving the MDGs: Heterogeneity, Gaps, and Challenges.* Washington, DC: World Bank.

World Economic Forum. 2010. The Global Competitiveness Report 2010–2011. Geneva: World Economic Forum.

World Tourism Organization. Various years. *Compendium of Tourism Statistics.* Madrid: World Tourism Organization.

———. Various years. *Yearbook of Tourism Statistics.* Vols. 1 and 2. Madrid: World Tourism Organization.

WTO (World Trade Organization). n.d. Regional Trade Agreements Gateway. [www.wto.org/english/tratop_e/region_e/region_e.htm]. Geneva.

———. n.d. Regional Trade Agreements Information System. Online database. [http://rtais.wto.org/]. Geneva.

———. Various years. *Annual Report.* Geneva.

INDEX OF INDICATORS

References are to table numbers.

INDEX OF INDICATORS

D

E

INDEX OF INDICATORS

INDEX OF INDICATORS

H

INDEX OF INDICATORS

INDEX OF INDICATORS

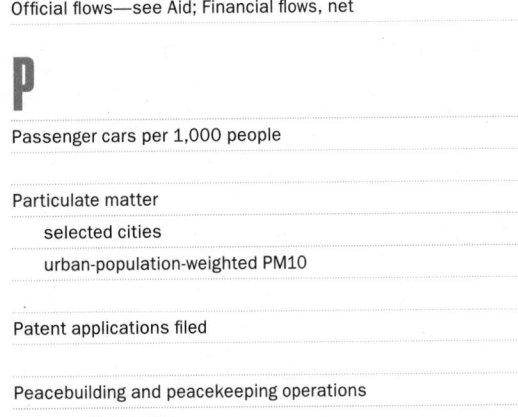

INDEX OF INDICATORS

INDEX OF INDICATORS

INDEX OF INDICATORS

productivity	3.5

Women in development	
female-headed households	2.10
female population, as share of total	1.5
life expectancy at birth	1.5
pregnant women receiving prenatal care	1.5, 2.19
teenage mothers	1.5
unpaid family workers	1.5
vulnerable employment	2.4
women in nonagricultural sector	1.5
women in parliaments	1.5

Workforce, firms offering formal training	5.2

World Bank, net financial flows from	6.13
See also International Bank for Reconstruction and Development; International Development Association	